Fifth Edition

Politics *in* Canada

CULTURE, INSTITUTIONS, BEHAVIOUR AND PUBLIC POLICY

ROBERT J. JACKSON

DOREEN JACKSON

Prentice
Hall

Toronto

Dedicated to Henry B. Mayo, renowned colleague and friend

Canadian Cataloguing in Publication Data

Jackson, Robert J., 1936–
    Politics in Canada : culture, institutions, behaviour and public policy

5th ed.
Includes bibliographical references and index
ISBN 0-13-027315-5

1. Canada – Politics and government. I. Jackson, Doreen, 1939–   . II. Title.

JL65 2001.J32 2001   320.971   C00-930155-0

ISBN 0-13-027315-5

Vice President, Editorial Director: Michael Young
Marketing Manager: Christine Cozens
Acquisitions Editor: Kathleen McGill
Developmental Editor: Lisa Phillips
Production Editor: Joe Zingrone
Copy Editor: Judith Turnbull
Production Coordinator: Peggy Brown
Page Layout: Steve Eby
Art Director: Mary Opper
Interior/Cover Design: Sarah Battersby
Cover Image: John Oresnik

13 14 15 DPC 06 05 04

Printed and bound in Canada.

CONTENTS

Preface   **xvii**

PART I   INTRODUCTION   1

Chapter 1   Governing Canada: Issues and Challenges   2

Challenges in Canadian Politics   5

Key Issues in Canadian Politics   6
  One Country or Two?   6
  Economic Prosperity?   7
  Politics and Government   9
  Approaches within Political Science   10
  States and Nations   15
  The State and Citizens   15
  The Nation   17
  Nationalism and Regionalism   18
  The Development of the Modern State   20

The Basic Premises of Democracy in Canada   22

The Critics of Democracy   27

Summary   28

Discussion Questions   28

Selected Bibliography   28

List of Weblinks   29

Chapter 2   The Canadian Nation and State: Yesterday and Today   31

Pre-Confederation History   32
  Early Settlement   32
  From Colony to Confederation   33
  The American Revolution   34
  Founding Nations: Native Peoples, French and English   34
  Confederation   37

The Land and the People   39
  Territorial Expansion   39
  Population Growth   42
  Immigration Trends   43
  Demographic Trends   44

The Development of the Canadian Nation   45
  Problems of Nation-Building in Canada   46

Contents

      External Impediments   47
      Internal Impediments   48
      Nation-Building and Contemporary Politics   51
   The Development of the Canadian State   52
      External Sovereignty and Its Constraints   53
      Internal State-Building in the Nineteenth Century   54
      The Growth of the State in the Twentieth Century   56
      The Extent of the State in Canada   57
   Summary   59
   Discussion Questions   60
   Selected Bibliography   60
   List of Weblinks   61

PART II   CULTURE 63

Chapter 3   **The Fabric of Canadian Society: Ethno-Linguistic and Regional Cleavages   64**

What Is Political Culture?   65
The Three Strands of Canadian Political Culture   66
Nation-State Political Culture   67
   Ideology and Political Culture   67
   Overarching Values   70
   Overarching Symbols   72
   Political Attitudes   75
   Behaviour: Participation and Efficacy   78
Ethno-Linguistic Cleavages and Political Culture   80
   The French–English Cleavage   80
   English-Speaking Canadians: A Cultural Fruitcake   85
   Native Peoples: Indians, Métis and Inuit   92
Regional Cleavages and Political Culture   98
   Six Regional Profiles   99
   Regional Alienation: Distance and Division   103
   Regional Political Cultures   104
Summary   105
Discussion Questions   106
Selected Bibliography   107
List of Weblinks   108

Chapter 4   **Social and Political Context and Cleavages: Education, Media, Government, Gender and Class   109**

Acquiring Political Orientations   110
   Families and Peer Groups   111
Education and Political Orientations   112
   Organizational Structure   115
The Media and Political Orientations   119

Media Origins and Government Policy   120
Broadcast Media: Television and Radio   122
Print Media: Newspapers   127
Government Information and Political Orientations   130
Early Government Information Services   131
The Issue of Government Advertising   131
Gender, Class and Political Orientations   134
Gender Stratification and Inequality   134
Gender Theory   135
Class Stratification and Inequality   139
Summary   141
Discussion Questions   142
Selected Bibliography   143
List of Weblinks   144
Case Study — Culture   145

PART III   INSTITUTIONS   147

Chapter 5   **The Constitution Today: Legal Foundations, Failed Reforms and the Courts   148**

Law and the Constitution   149
The Rule of Law   150
The Origin and Evolution of the Canadian Constitution   152
The British North America Act   152
The Federal Constitutional Bargain   156
The Federal/Provincial Division of Powers   157
Problems over the Division of Powers   158
Rhetoric and Reality over Constitutional Amendment   161
Patriation of Canada's Constitution   164
Federal/Provincial Constitutional Agreement   165
The New Canadian Constitution   167
The Charter of Rights and Freedoms   169
Impasse with Québec   172
The Failed 1987 Constitutional Accord (Meech Lake and Langevin)   173
A New Constitutional Approach   174
The Failed 1992 Charlottetown Accord   176
Meech Plus or Minus: The Response to Québec   176
The Canada Clause   177
Division of Powers   177
Native Self-Government   178
Social and Economic Union   179
Proposed Institutional Changes   179
Institutional Complexity   180
The Charlottetown Senate: A Fatal Attraction?   181
The 1992 Constitutional Referendum   183

Contents

The Structure and Role of the Courts   183

Charter Cases and the Constitution   187

Summary   194

Discussion Questions   195

Selected Bibliography   195

List of Weblinks   196

Chapter 6 **Contested Federalism: The Division of Powers and Financial Resources   197**

What Is Federalism?   198

  Concepts of Federalism   199

  Evaluations of Federalism and Separatism   200

The Trajectory of Canadian Federalism   201

  The Origins of Federalism   201

  The Evolution of Federalism   202

Federal/Provincial Mechanisms and Conflict Resolution   205

Contested Federalism and Decentralization   207

Financing Federalism   208

  A Brief History of Fiscal Federalism   209

  Basic Concepts of Fiscal Federalism   212

  Key Mechanisms   214

  Fiscal Arrangements in Flux   215

  The New System during Contested Federalism — Post-1996   217

Summary   219

Discussion Questions   220

Selected Bibliography   220

List of Weblinks   221

Chapter 7 **Nationalism and Regionalism: Québec, the West and the Rest   222**

Nationalism   222

  Roots of Nationalism: Early French–English Conflicts   224

  Modern Nationalism in Québec   226

  Separatist Parties in Québec   227

Language Issues   228

  Language Law in Québec   230

  Arguments for and against Bilingualism   233

Québec Referendums on Separation   234

  The Québec Referendum, 1980   234

  The Québec Referendum, 1995   235

1995 Québec Referendum Fallout   244

  Federal Strategy   244

Québec Nationalist Strategy   248

Regionalism   250

  Alienation: Views from the West   251

Summary   253

Discussion Questions   253
Selected Bibliography   253
List of Weblinks 254

Chapter 8   **The Executive: Governor General, Prime Minister and Cabinet   255**

The Formal Executive: Crown, Monarchy and Governor General   256
   Crown and Monarch   256
   Governor General and Lieutenant-Governors   257
The Political Executive   260
The Powers of the Prime Minister   262
Prime Ministers in Practice   265
The Ministry and Cabinet   267
   Cabinet Conventions   270
Policy-Making in Central Government   271
The Central Coordinating Agencies   275
   The Prime Minister's Office   275
   The Privy Council Office   277
   The Treasury Board   279
   The Department of Finance   280
   Conflicts of Interest   281
   Patronage   284
Prime Ministerial Government?   285
Summary   288
Discussion Questions   288
Selected Bibliography   289
List of Weblinks   289

Chapter 9   **Legislative Politics: Symbolism or Power?   290**

What Is a Legislature?   291
The Roles of Legislatures   292
   Legislative Politics   295
The Legislative Process in Parliament   295
   The Parliamentary Life Cycle   296
   Types of Bills   296
   The Stages of Legislation   297
The House of Commons   301
   Conflict and Compromise   303
   The Business of the House   306
MPs in Groups: The Committee System   309
   Committee Recruitment, Composition and Staffing   311
   The Committee System at Work: An Evaluation   312
   Committees: Problems and Reforms   315
MPs in Parties: Government and Opposition   316
   Intra-Party Relations: Rebels and Whips   317
   Inter-Party Relations   319

House of Commons Reform: Symbolism or Power? 321

The Senate 323
  Recruitment and Formal Roles 324
  Organization and Rules 326
  Legislative Politics in the Senate 327
  Senate Reform: Symbolism or Power? 329

Summary 331
Discussion Questions 332
Selected Bibliography 333
List of Weblinks 333

Chapter 10 **Bureaucracy and Democracy: Public Servants, Budgets and Accountability 334**

What Is Bureaucracy? 335
  The Concept of Bureaucracy 335
  Bureaucracy versus Democracy 336

Organization of the Federal Bureaucracy 338
  Federal Government Departments 339
  Crown Agencies 339
  Advisory Bodies 341
  Semi-Independent Agencies 342
  Principles and Linkages: Ministers and Deputy Ministers 342

The Public Service 346
  Basic Principles of the Public Service 346
  Profile of the Public Service 348
  Women and Equity-Designated Groups 350

Bureaucrats and Budgets: Deficits and Debts 354
  The Two Budgetary Processes 357

Democratic Control of the Bureaucracy 359
  Are More Reforms Needed? 363

Summary 363
Discussion Questions 364
Selected Bibliography 364
List of Weblinks 365
Case Study — Institutions 366

PART IV   POLITICAL BEHAVIOUR 367

Chapter 11 **Political Parties: Continuity and Transition 368**

What Are Political Parties? 369
  Party Functions 369
  Classifying Parties and Party Systems 371

The Canadian Party System: Origin and Development 374
  From Origins to Two-Party System 374

Two-and-a-Half-Party System   375
Multi-Party Dominant System   376
Problems in the Canadian Party System: Federalism and Regionalism   377
Ideology: The Ideas behind Canadian Political Parties   381
Liberalism   382
Conservatism   383
Socialism   384
Nationalism and Populism   385
Established Parties: History and Ideas   385
The Progressive Conservative Party   386
The Liberal Party   389
The CCF/NDP   391
New Parties   393
The Reform Party   393
The Bloc Québécois   394
Minor and Historical Fringe Parties   395
Party Structure and Organization   397
Constituency Level   398
National Level   399
Women in Parties   399
Party Conventions   400
Party Program Formulation   401
National Party Leadership Selection   403
Party Leaders   407
The Role of the Leader in the Party   408
Party Finance   410
Summary   412
Discussion Questions   413
Selected Bibliography   413
List of Weblinks   415

Chapter 12   **Elections and Political Behaviour: Voting, Public
Opinion and the Media   416**

Representation and Elections   417
Referendums   417
Referendums in Canada   419
The 1992 Referendum   420
Functions of Elections   421
Types of Electoral Systems   422
Single-Member Plurality   423
Single-Member Majoritarian   423
Multi-Member Proportional Representation   424
Mixed Systems   425
The Effects of Electoral Systems   425
Elections in Canada   431
The Franchise and the Ridings   431
By-elections   432

Electoral Procedure   434
The Candidates   436
The Campaigns   437
Public Opinion Surveys   438
Media and Voters   439
Election Financing   441
Electoral Behaviour   442
Voters and Non-Voters   442
Electoral Choice   443
Long-Term Factors in Election Outcomes   444
Short-Term Factors in Election Outcomes   447
Party Identification and Historical Analysis of Electoral Outcomes   448
General Election Results: 1867–1997   449
Case Study of the 1997 General Election   449
Background: The 1993 General Election   449
The 1997 Campaign   454
Media, Polls and Party Advertising in the Campaign   455
Issues in the Campaign   457
The Outcome   458
Analysis   460
Summary   462
Discussion Questions   463
Selected Bibliography   463
List of Weblinks   464

Chapter 13   **Interest Groups and Political Movements: Influencing Public Policy   465**

What Are Interest Groups?   466
Interest Groups, Policy Communities and Networks   467
Interest Groups in Canada   469
Classifying Interest Groups   470
Canadian Groups: A Catalogue   471
Ingredients for Interest Group Success   473
Lobbying in Canada   474
Legislation to Control Lobbying   476
Common Tactics and Strategies   478
Access Points: Pre-Parliamentary and Parliamentary   480
Primary Interest Group Targets   483
Lobbying in Canada: Casting the Net Wide   487
What Are Social and Political Movements?   489
The Women's Movement: A Case Study   491
Summary   493
Discussion Questions   494
Selected Bibliography   494
List of Weblinks   495
Case Study — Political Behaviour   496

PART V   PUBLIC POLICY 497

Chapter 14   **Public Policy and Government Expenditure: Choice and Restraint 498**

What Is Public Policy? 499

Public Policy and Theories of Policy-Making 500
    Micro-Level Approaches to Public Policy Analysis   502
    Macro-Level Approaches to Public Policy Analysis   504
    The Approaches Compared 510

Policy Instruments and Processes 512
    Exhortation and Symbolic Outputs 512
    Expenditure Instruments 512
    Regulation 514
    Public Ownership 515
    Policy Instruments and the Policy Process 516

The Growth and Size of the Canadian State 517
    Explanations for the Growth and Size of the State 521

Government Restraint, Downsizing and Renewal 523
    Public Policy and Bureaucracy in an Age of Restraint: Mulroney and Chrétien 524
    Public Service 2000 and Public Service Renewal 525

Summary 525

Discussion Questions 526

Selected Bibliography 526

List of Weblinks 527

Chapter 15   **Canada in the Global Economy: Foreign, Trade and Defence Policy   528**

What Is Foreign Policy? 529

Sources of Canadian Foreign Policy 530
    Prime Minister and Cabinet   530
    Department of Foreign Affairs and International Trade   531
    Parliament and Political Parties   534
    Non-Governmental Actors: Interest Groups, the Media and Public Opinion 535
    Provinces and Foreign Policy 536
    Québec Foreign Policy 538

Canadian Trade Policy 540
    Canada and Global Economics 540

International and Multilateral Organization 542
    Canada and the United Nations   542
    The Commonwealth   543
    La Francophonie   544
    Canada and the OAS   545

Contents

Canada's Relations with the United States   545
Free Trade: FTA and NAFTA   547
Canada's Relations with Other Areas   552
    Canada and Western Europe   552
    Canada and the Pacific Rim   552
    Canada, Developing Countries and the Rest of the World   553
Canadian Defence Policy   554
    Canadian Security Policy   555
    Organization of National Defence   555
    The Canadian Forces   556
    Peacekeeping   557
Summary   559
Discussion Questions   560
Selected Bibliography   560
List of Weblinks   561
Case Study — Public Policy   562

Appendix I: **A Consolidation of the Constitution Acts 1867 to 1982**   **563**

Appendix II: **Reference re Secession of Quebec 607**

Glossary   615

Index   623

LIST OF CLOSE-UP BOXES

Power and Students (p. 11)
Age Cohorts and Public Policy (p. 46)
Value Changes (p. 72)
The Status of Comprehensive Claims (1999) (p. 96)
Highlights of the Royal Commission on Aboriginal Peoples (p. 98)
Significant Developments in Aboriginal Affairs, 1996–99 (p. 99)
The Maritimes in Comparative Perspective (p. 100)
Lack of Civic Knowledge in Canada? (p. 115)
Canada's Press Baron, Conrad Black (p. 129)
Some High-Profile TV and Radio Journalists (p. 131)
Promoting Canada (p. 133)
Women and Education: A Pioneer of the Women's Movement (p. 134)
Constitution-Speak: Some Jargon You Need to Know (p. 161)
Canada's Constitutional Highlights (p. 167)
Constitutional Negotiations — A Unique Canadian Style? (p. 169)
The Supreme Court and Sex: Privacy and the Presumption of Innocence (p.189)
Federalism and the Provinces (p. 206)
Québec's Objection to Ottawa's Spending Power (p. 209)
Funding for Colleges and Universities (p. 217)
The Québec Referendum Question, October 30, 1995 (p. 237)
Parliament's Distinct Society Motion (p. 245)
Guy Bertrand's Fight in Québec's Courts (p. 248)
Byng-King and Dissolution (p. 259)
Chrétien versus Black (p. 264)
Morality in Parliament (p. 283)
To Leak or Not to Leak (p. 315)
Formal Conflict-of-Interest Rules for MPs and Senators (p. 327)
Fairness or Scandal in the Senate? (p. 329)
Departmental Names Reflect Values and Biases (p. 343)
Key Financial Terms (p. 354)
The Ideological Shift to the Right in Canada (p. 384)
Joe Clark Victorious with PC's Radical New Leadership Selection Process (p. 407)
How Much Is Your Vote Worth? (p. 433)
Summary of the New Electoral Rules (p. 435)
Polling Restrictions: Are They Justified? (p. 439)
Advertising Agencies and Electoral Campaigns (p. 442)
Are Election Promises Meaningful? The Liberals and the GST (p. 452)
The Ongoing Debate on Cigarette Advertising (p. 481)
Using the System (p. 486)
A Typology of Selected Domestic Policy Activities (p. 501)
Ethical Foreign Policy? (p. 543)
Department of National Defence and Somalia (p. 557)

LIST OF CASE STUDIES

Footnotes on the Future, (p. 145)
Québec: The Referendum, (p. 366)
Conservatives: What Kind of Future? (p. 496)
Budget '96: What's in It for You? (p. 562)

LIST OF WEBLINKS

CHAPTER 1

www.uottawa.ca/
associations/cpsa-acsp

Canadian Political Science Association This site contains useful information about the study of political science in Canada as well as links to other useful political science Web sites.

canada.gc.ca/canadiana/
map_e.html

Map of Canada This site provides a map of Canada and the different provincial boundaries.

CHAPTER 2

www.nlc-bnc.ca/
confed/e-1867.htm

Canadian Confederation This site provides useful information about Canadian history and Confederation.

www-nais.ccm.emr.
ca/wwwnais/select/ethnic/
english/html/ethnic.html

Canadian Ethnic Diversity Map This Web site provides maps of the ethnic composition of Canada.

npc.nunavut.ca/eng

Nunavut Planning Commission The structure and organization of the new territory of Nunavut are presented at this site.

cicnet.ci.gc.ca

Canadian Department of Citizenship and Immigration This is the Web page for the Canadian Department of Citizenship and Immigration.

CHAPTER 3

canada.gc.ca/canadiana/
symb_e.html

Symbols of Canada Canadian political symbols are presented in this Web site.

www.inac.gc.ca

Canadian Department of Indian and Northern Affairs This is the Web page for the Canadian Department of Indian and Northern Affairs.

www.afn.ca

Assembly of First Nations This is the Web page for the Assembly of First Nations.

CHAPTER 4

www.statcan.ca

Statistics Canada This Web site offers a variety of information about the social and economic conditions of Canadians.

www.canpress.ca/
canpress

Canadian Press This site contains links to various Canadian media resources.

CHAPTER 5

Canada.justice.gc.ca/
en/dept/pub/trib/
index.html

Canada's Court System This Web page outlines the structure of the Canadian court system.

www.scc-csc.gc.ca

The Supreme Court of Canada This is the Web page of the Canadian Supreme Court.

www.lexum.umontreal.
ca/csc-scc/

Supreme Court Decisions on the Canadian Charter of Rights and Freedoms This site contains Supreme Court decisions based on the *Canadian Charter of Rights and Freedoms*.

CHAPTER 6

collections.ic.gc.ca/
discourspm/anglais/
jam/jam.html

Sir John A. Macdonald This Web site contains information about Canada's first prime minister, who was a key designer of the Canadian political system.

www.pco-bcp.gc.ca/aia

Intergovernmental Affairs Conference Secretariat The Intergovernmental Affairs Conference Secretariat is the branch of government that organizes First Ministers Conferences.

www.fin.gc.ca/
fedprove/ftpe.html

Federal Financial Transfers to the Provinces This Web site identifies the amount of money that the federal government annually transfers to the provinces.

CHAPTER 7

www.visi.com/~homelands/
canada/canada.html

Canadian Secessionist Movements This Web site contains information about various secessionist movements in Canada.

dsp-psd.pwgsc.gc.ca/
InfoSource/Info_1/COL-e.html

Commissioner of Official Languages The Commissioner of Official Languages is responsible for monitoring bilingualism in Canada.

CHAPTER 8

www.gg.ca/menu_e.html

Governor General This is the official Web page of the Governor General of Canada.

pm.gc.ca

Prime Minister of Canada This is the official Web page of the Prime Minister of Canada.

canada.gc.ca/howgoc/
cab/ministry_e.html

Cabinet Ministers and Portfolios This Web site lists the different members of the federal Cabinet and their portfolios.

CHAPTER 9

www.parl.gc.ca/
36/main-e.htm

Parliament of Canada This is the official Web page for the Parliament of Canada.

www.cpac.ca

Canadian Parliamentary Affairs Channel CPAC Online provides information about the parliamentary channel and links to other government resources.

www.hansard.ca/links.html

Hansard This is the Web site for the record of the daily debates that take place in the House of Commons.

CHAPTER 10

Canada.gc.ca/depts/
major/depind_e.html

Federal Government Departments This Web site lists various federal government departments and organizations.

www.indigenous.bc.ca

Royal Commission on Aboriginal Peoples The final report of the Royal Commission, at the Web site of the Institute of Indigenous Government.

www.aecb-ccea.gc.ca

Atomic Energy Control Board This is the official Web site for Canada's nuclear regulatory authority.

www.oag-bvg.gc.ca

Auditor General This is the Web page for Canada's Auditor General.

CHAPTER 11

www.psr.keele.ac.uk/
thought.htm

Political Ideologies This Web page provides links to sites describing different types of political thought.

Canadian Reform
Conservative Alliance –
www.canadianalliance.ca

Canadian Political Parties These are the Web pages for some of Canada's major political parties.

Liberal Party –
www.liberal.ca

New Democratic Party –
www.ndp.ca

**Progressive Conservative
Party** – www.pcparty.ca

Bloc Québécois –
blocquebecois.org

CHAPTER 12

www.elections.ca **Elections Canada** Elections Canada organizes and monitors national elections in Canada.

www.cbc.ca **Canadian Broadcasting Corporation** The CBC and other news providers play an important role in conveying information during election campaigns.

www.Angusreid.com **Public opinion polls** The following sites link to two of the major political polling companies in Canada, the Angus Reid Group and Pollara.

**www.pollara.ca/
new/POLLARA_NET.html**

CHAPTER 13

www.chamber.ca **Canadian Chamber of Commerce** The Canadian Chamber of Commerce is the largest business association in Canada.

www.ethnocultural.ca **Canadian Ethnocultural Council** The Canadian Ethnocultural Council is an organization set up to represent ethno-cultural interests in Canada.

green.ca **Green Party of Canada** The Green party is a political party with close ties to the environmental movement in Canada.

CHAPTER 14

www.psc-cfp.gc.ca **Canadian Public Service Commission** This is the Web site for the Public Service Commission, which is responsible for overseeing and organizing the Canadian Public Service.

www.crtc.gc.ca **Canadian Radio-television and Telecommunications Commission** This is the Web site for the CRTC, which regulates broadcasting and communications in Canada.

www.mailposte.ca **Canada Post Corporation** This is the official Web site of this national service, which was recently changed from a government department to a Crown corporation.

www.ccra-adrc.gc.ca **Canadian Department of Revenue** This is the Web page for the Canadian Department of Revenue.

CHAPTER 15

www.dfait-maeci.gc.ca **Canada's Department of Foreign Affairs and International Trade** This is the Web page for the Department of Foreign Affairs and International Trade.

www.un.org **The United Nations** This is the United Nations' Web page.

www.oas.org **The Organization of American States** This is the Web page for the Organization of American States; it includes links to other resources in the Americas.

PREFACE

This fifth edition of *Politics in Canada* continues to stress the importance of politics in the study of Canadian government with up-to-date examples, issues and research. As in its earlier editions, *Politics in Canada* provides a general treatment of Canadian federal politics, useful for both introductory and advanced courses. The book purposely avoids the rigidity imposed by the adoption of a single approach or framework for the study of politics, but goes beyond mere description of governmental institutions and processes. It attempts to provide a coherent understanding of Canadian politics, eschewing the simplicities of myths, but reckoning with the resistance to order exerted by the seemingly incoherent events in the day-to-day world. As in earlier editions, the text is clearly and concisely written with little academic jargon.

The fifth edition of *Politics in Canada* offers a novel perspective on politics. Instead of adopting only one approach, the text takes an objective and detached perspective on the relations among culture, institutions, behaviour and public policy. It provides a well-rounded view of the entire political process. The book discusses the historical development and background of Canadian politics, but concentrates on the contemporary, offering the latest information and perspectives on such vital topics as the Constitution, Cabinet, federalism, Québec nationalism and the threat of separatism; interest groups, regionalism, conflict of interest, and the most recent elections and party leaders. It looks at the role of Native peoples in Canadian society; the growing role of women in public affairs; the negative image of politics and politicians in society; how Parliament and the public service can be reformed; and the crushing economic implications of the federal deficit and debt. It relates these and other issues to NAFTA and allows the reader to locate Canadian government in a global framework, examining the interrelationship of domestic, foreign and defence policies.

Politics in Canada retains much of its original structure, but each section has been thoroughly revised and rewritten to make it as clear, concise and up-to-date as possible. We have incorporated the newest social science research, including books, journal articles, government publications and official government inquiries that highlight various aspects of Canadian society at the turn of the century.

New to the Fifth Edition

Content: The chapters have all been revised to bring the book up to the year 2000. Major new sections have been added on the role of the Supreme Court, especially concerning legal and equality rights as well as the fundamental debate over privacy and the presumption of innocence. The success and strategy of the Reform party are fleshed out, and issues about morality in Parliament and foreign policy are carefully explored. All new aspects of federalism are analyzed, including the controversial agreement on the social union, the 1998 Supreme Court judgement on Québec separatism, and the 1999 federal and Québec governments' legislation on this topic.

Close-Up Boxes: New text boxes have been added to highlight topics of current interest and further integrate the four themes of culture, institutions, behaviour and public policy.

Weblinks: This exciting feature has been updated to give students a list of useful Web sites relating to each chapter. They have been researched and tested for quality and relevance.

Appendix 2: A new appendix presents the Supreme Court of Canada's 1998 ruling on the three questions relating to the unilateral secession of Québec from Canada.

Organization

This volume's orientation is comprehensive, drawing upon a wide variety of concepts and theories about Canadian politics. Each chapter is organized around one or two central concepts, which are discussed in general terms before being applied to the Canadian context.

There are five parts. The first is introductory; the remainder correspond to the four elements incorporated in the title: culture, institutions, behaviour and public policy.

Part 1, the **Introduction**, consists of two chapters. Chapter 1 establishes Canada's place in the world and introduces students to the paramount issues of the debt and separatism which are dealt with throughout the book. It analyzes some key concepts in the study of politics — power, state, nation, citizenship, nationalism and democracy — and offers a rationale for the organization of the book. Chapter 2 provides necessary historical, economic and contextual background through an examination of the origins and development of the Canadian people and the Canadian state. It traces the growth and changing nature of the population from the aboriginals who originally inhabited the land to the multicultural society of today. Similarly it traces the development of the Canadian state, both in terms of the physical boundaries of the country and the expansion of the role of government in Canadian society.

The two chapters in Part 2, **Culture**, provide an intimate portrait of Canadian society. Chapter 3 examines Canada's political fabric including the political, ethnic and regional cleavages that define politics in Canada. It focuses on the different background and aspirations of French Canadians, English-speaking Canadians and Native peoples, stressing the importance to the Canadian political community of overarching commonly shared values that help preserve the unity of the country. This chapter provides an examination of current issues such as immigration, multiculturalism, regionalism and aboriginal concerns including self-government, land claims and relative deprivation. Chapter 4 asks how Canadians acquire the political ideas that underlie their political behaviour. Families and peer groups play a role here, as do institutions such as schools, universities, the media and even government. Two very significant cleavages that cut horizontally across Canadian society — gender and class — are also highlighted. The extent to which each of these factors contributes to the political orientation of Canadians and to Canadian unity is described and assessed.

Part 3, **Institutions**, argues that political institutions reflect both the structure and the values of society. It presents six chapters dealing in turn with the constitution, federalism, nationalism, the executive, Parliament and bureaucracy. This section is considerably expanded in the fifth edition, with new material on Québec nationalism and an enhanced discussion of the key concepts and mechanisms of federalism. The growing role of the courts in the political process with respect to the constitutional developments following the defeat of the Québec referendum on separation in 1995, especially the Court decisions on separatism and individual and collective rights, is thoroughly assessed. Chapter 8 considers the executive — the inner circle comprising the prime minister, Jean Chrétien, his 2000 ministry, Cabinet and the central coordinating agencies — which forms the nexus of political power in Canada. Chapter 9 focuses on Parliament and includes revised discussions of the committee system and the issue of Senate reform. Chapter 10 details the changes in government organization and the public service that have been brought about by the Chrétien government. It pays particular attention to measures taken to reduce the deficit to zero and increase Canadian prosperity.

Part 4, **Behaviour**, demonstrates how both culture and institutions structure individual and collective action in the political process. Chapters 11, 12 and 13 discuss respectively political parties, elections and electoral behaviour, and interest groups. The party system has undergone a major realignment; new regional parties have taken the place of the traditional opposition parties and are affecting the traditional functioning of Parliament. Chapter 13 deals with the new rules governing interest groups and lobbying. It also considers the growth of movements that share many of the same functions of interest groups, and examines the women's movement in particular.

Lastly, in Part 5, **Public Policy**, culture, institutions and behaviour are linked together as determinants and components of Canadian public policy and the policy-making process. Chapter 14 deals with domestic public policy, including approaches to the study of public policy, policy instruments and a discussion of current economic problems and policy constraints. Chapter 15 on Canada in a global economy deals with international economics, Canadian foreign and defence policy, including Canadian-American relations, free trade, NAFTA, national security policies, and peacekeeping.

The authors' biases toward Canadian politics and the three vital issues (the Constitution, the debt and international economics) are balanced. We believe that the appropriate strategy for the federal government on constitutional issues should reflect Canadian national interests while being consistent with provincial trends and realities, including those in Québec. Policies toward resolving the national debt should be consistent with the values of most Canadians — namely, based on concern for the weak and disadvantaged, young and old. And thirdly, federal government policy on international economics and regional integration in North America should be as concerned with questions of independence and sovereignty as they are with money. These balanced positions address the issues as we see them.

Politics is an honourable and worthy profession that has been tarnished by misunderstandings and the greed and corruption of a few. This book gives credit where it is due for substantial achievement, but also finds many political reforms desirable. The authors are optimistic but concerned about the fundamental ability of the Canadian political process to meet its major challenges — its ability to transcend regional and cultural cleavages and assure the survival of Canada.

Recently, we wrote another book on Canadian politics to meet the needs of some professors and students who require a relatively short description of Canadian governmental institutions. Entitled *Canadian Government in Transition: Disruption and Continuity*, this slimmer volume is written for one-semester courses. Some chapter contents and points of view are the same as those in *Politics in Canada*. However, despite their superficial similarity, the two books differ in many respects, and are meant for different audiences.

The shorter book does not replace or summarize this comprehensive work. *Politics in Canada* goes much further in both content and approach, linking culture, institutions, behaviour and public policy together in a unified theory to depict and explain the dynamics of politics. Moreover, it adds depth to the discussion of the vital issues of public debt, separatism and free trade. This larger, more comprehensive work sets these topics in the context of government policy-making, both domestic and foreign.

Supplements

- *Instructor's Manual*: Contains Teaching Tips and Activities, Course Outlines, Lecture Notes, Resource Material Guide, Overhead Transparency Masters. ISBN: 0-13-028045-3
- *Pearson Education Canada Video Library* for *Politics in Canada*: This collection of hand-picked video clips is perhaps the most dynamic of all the supplements you can use to enhance your classes. Pearson Education has worked to bring you the best and most comprehensive Canadian video package available in the college market. These tapes have extremely high production quality, substantial content, and are hosted by well-versed, well-known anchors. ISBN: 0-13-029429-2

- *Test Item File*: Nearly a thousand multiple choice and essay questions. ISBN: 0-13-028044-5
- *Computerized Test Bank*: Electronic version of the Test Item File, available in Windows. ISBN: 0-13-028042-9

Acknowledgements

The authors are extremely appreciative of the many students, professors and interested readers who have taken time to comment on aspects of *Politics in Canada* and have given support and encouragement. Many friends and scholars have contributed, directly and indirectly, to the discussion of ideas and issues it contains. The very long list must include Michael Atkinson, Nicolas Baxter-Moore, David Bellamy, Scott Bennett, Alan Cairns, Barbara Caroll, Terry Caroll, Brian Crowley, Abbie Dann, Piotr Dutkiewicz, John Fakouri, Jean-Pierre Gaboury, Brian Galligan, Janice Gross-Stein, Jack Grove, Ken Hart, Carl Hodge, Kal Holsti, Bill Hull, Carl Jacobsen, Christian Jaekl, Tom Joseph, Robert Keaton, Ken Kernaghan, Peyton Lyon, Maureen Mancuso, Roman March, Bill Matheson, Ken McRae, Greg Mahler, Henry Mayo, Allan McDougall, John Meisel, Kim Nossal, Randy Olling, Jeremy Paltiel, K. Z. Paltiel, Anton Pelinka, George Roseme, Donald Rowat, David Siegel, Richard Simeon, Michael Stein, David Stewart, Sharon Sutherland, Stewart Sutley, Elliott Tepper, Hugh Thorburn, Martin Westmacott, Patrick Weller and Glen Williams. Over a decade, several reviewers of the various editions have diligently ferreted out errors of omission and commission in the preliminary manuscripts. We gratefully acknowledge the insight and detailed knowledge that Donald Blake, Fred Englemann, Susan McCorquodale, Mary Beth Montcalm, David E. Smith, Robert Williams, and Nelson Wiseman brought to our manuscript. This fifth edition has been enhanced by the wisdom and perceptive comments of Elizabeth Smythe (Concordia University College of Alberta), Rob Huebert (University of Manitoba), Keith Brownsey (Mount Royal College), Peter McCormick (University of Lethbridge), David Stewart (University of Alberta), Tracy Summerville (University of Northern British Columbia), and Miriam Smith (Carleton University). We thank them for their thoughtful suggestions and corrections. We also thank Joanna Everitt for researching the Weblinks for each chapter.

We are grateful to our friends at Prentice Hall, including Kathleen McGill, Lisa Phillips and Joe Zingrone, for bringing this new edition to fruition. Judith Turnbull edited the manuscript quickly, carefully and professionally. At the University of Redlands, Lynnae Merget provided organization and support in a myriad of ways that enabled time and energy to be focused on this project.

We also wish to express our gratitude to two very special people — Velma, a wonderful mother and friend whose enthusiasm for politics is a delight, and Nicole, our extraordinary daughter whose love of government and politics has taken her abroad to a new world of challenges.

Finally, we dedicate this volume to Henry B. Mayo, renowned scholar, colleague and friend who made much of our careers in political science possible.

Robert J. Jackson and Doreen Jackson
University of Redlands, California,
and Carleton University, Ottawa
2000

Abbreviations Used

AEI–*American Enterprise Institute*
APSR–*American Political Science Review*
BJPS–*British Journal of Political Science*
CIIA–Canadian Institute of International Affairs
CJEPS–*Canadian Journal of Economics and Political Science*
CJPS–*Canadian Journal of Political Science* (replaced the CJEPS as of March 1968)
CPA–*Canadian Public Administration*
DEA–Department of External Affairs
IIR–Institute of Intergovernmental Affairs
IRPP–Institute for Research on Public Policy
PAR–*Public Administration Review*

PART

1

Introduction

· · · · · · · ·

Canadian politics is an exciting and complex field of study. Political issues, leaders and governments in Canada seem to be in a state of constant effervescence and change. Yet beneath the apparent turmoil is a solid framework of laws, procedures, customs and culture that keeps the change within reasonable limits.

The study of politics requires three major tools. First is an understanding of the approaches available to facilitate such study and the strengths and weaknesses of those ideas. Second is an understanding of the complexities of basic concepts such as democracy, power, nation, state and even politics itself. Third is a fundamental knowledge of the unique country of Canada — its land, its people and its historical background.

The study of politics examines how political institutions resolve conflict and work for the betterment of society. For that reason, Part 1 introduces two of the most outstanding issues of our time: government debt, which affects almost every facet of politics, and Québec nationalism, which threatens the very existence of Canada as a united country. These issues at the core of much of the politics in Canada today are discussed in their various aspects throughout this book. A third vital new issue, globalization, is discussed in Part 5.

1

Governing Canada

• • • • • • • •

Issues and Challenges

The Québec referendum of October 1995 was a watershed in Canadian politics. It illustrated that almost half of the population of the second-largest province wanted to create a new country. Led by Jacques Parizeau and Lucien Bouchard, the separatists convinced 60 percent of Québec francophones that the province could, and should, be a member of the United Nations in its own right by the turn of the century. Despite the fact that Jean Chrétien, leader of the federal Liberals and Prime Minister of Canada, was from Québec and possessed a strong majority in the House of Commons, federalists were unable to mount a positive approach to "renewing Canada." Even as begin a new millennium, the division over the future integrity of Canada remains the fundamental issue facing the country.

Understanding Canada in the new millennium with federalism still under attack and a heavily indebted federal government is not easy for politicians, professors or students. Rapid social and economic developments are changing the political culture, behaviour and public policy of the country. To comprehend modern Canada, students must confront themselves: Who are Canadians? Who *could* they be? Who do they want to be?

As a whole, Canadians must reassess who they are as a people, what values they wish to uphold and what languages they want to speak. They must decide how they should organize themselves and what institutions are worthy of their loyalty. These questions can be answered realistically only by maintaining an objective and comparative perspective concerning how Canada works. How does it compare to the rest of the world? In short, it is time to assess Canada's political maturity.

The earliest political science texts on Canada were concerned with the country's march to independence and autonomy. Later volumes have concentrated on understanding Canada in the context of new academic developments in political science — concepts, frameworks and theories that came mostly from the United States. Today, the challenge is to understand how Canadians will confront the new century. The questions concern not whether this new century belongs to Canada but whether there will indeed continue to *be* a Canada in the twenty-first century.

There have been many turning points in Canadian history, but possibly none were more important than 1867, 1931, 1982, 1992 and 1995. These dates mark Canada's march to political maturity. In 1867, the new state was born. In 1931, it received independence from Britain. It took another half century, until 1982, before Canadians had the courage and confidence to patriate the Constitution and break the last link with the mother country. Finally, in 1992 a massive constitutional reform proposal, the Charlottetown accord, which had been fashioned and sold to Canadians by the leaders of Parliament and all 10 provinces and territories, was defeated when the people stood defiantly against it in a referendum. In a 1995 referendum Québeckers came within half a percentage point of dividing the country in two.

These five historical events, and others like them, such as the 1998 Supreme Court decision on separatism, have had a profound effect on the evolution of Canada's culture, institutions and public policy. The 1992 referendum marked the end of the politics of the twentieth century. It indicated a shift to a new politics — one that is more open, less elitist and, perhaps, more threatening to the *status quo* and the institutions of Canada. The 1995 Québec referendum ended the dream that Canada could confront the twenty-first century as a harmonious country ready to compete at the global level.

Today, cleavages of the past continue to divide French and English, aboriginal and settler, Westerner and Easterner, man and woman. But these cleavages have been given new direction and emotion in parties and movements and in novel approaches to old problems. What will their legacy be to Canadians in the coming years? In this and subsequent chapters we shall marshal evidence about what is old and what is new in Canadian politics. We shall, for example, assess arguments about individual versus collective rights, examine movements and parties, and consider issues such as whether Québec will integrate more into Canada or become an independent, sovereign country.

The 1997 election gave an indication of who the main federal political players will be and what directions Canadians will take at the beginning of the new century. Prime Minister Jean Chrétien gained a second term in office, but the country is highly regionalized with the official opposition largely representing the West while the Bloc Québécois holds a large majority of the parliamentary seats from Québec. The Reform party has recast itself as the Canadian Reform Conservative Alliance.

We need to examine contemporary politics in light of the experience of the past as well as the dimmer light of the future. Today, as the last vestiges of a colonial past are disappearing, Canada ranks proudly among the world's states. A brief profile of the country — its political base, people and socioeconomic status — reads impressively when examined in a comparative perspective.

Since Confederation, Canada has enjoyed a stable, liberal-democratic government; it is one of the very few countries in the world never to have experienced a civil war or a military coup. This stability has been achieved despite many factors that complicate political decision-making. Its size alone is a great barrier to progress. Canada has several thousand square kilometres more area to administer than all of Europe combined. A Canadian driving from St. John's, Newfoundland, to Victoria, British Columbia, covers the same distance as a Spaniard driving from Madrid and traversing at least 10 countries almost to Mongolia. Québec, homeland of the French Canadian nation, is almost equal in size to the entire European Community.

This enormous land mass houses over 30 million people at the turn of the century. Yet Canada has a population problem — not in the traditional sense of over-populated countries afflicted by high birth rates, but in a demographic sense. Four-fifths of the territory has never been settled permanently. This results in great regional imbalances in population, from congested urban centres to uninhabited wastelands. Certain areas are being depopulated, while there is an undesirable rate of growth in others. Large tracts of land are being devoured by greedy cities. Today, in this country that was settled originally by farmers, most of the population lives in urban areas that occupy one percent of the land. Only one-eighth of the territory is suitable for agriculture; settlement has therefore been confined to a long thin line along the southern border, linked by the world's longest national highway.

To these problematic demographic and geographic factors must be added the unique ethnic composition of the population. Besides the original Native groups and the two founding French and English nations, at least 100 other ethnic groups make their homes here. The French Canadian nation is centred in Québec but is in no sense limited to that province. Large pockets of French-speaking Canadians live in Manitoba, New Brunswick and Ontario. Of the Native peoples, more than half reside in the Prairies and British Columbia. The many other ethnic groups scattered across the country add a multicultural dimension that has been the source of much division but also much pride for Canadians.

Canada is a land of extremes, in terms not only of territory and population but also of landscape and climate. Fertile rain forests, arctic barrens, mountains and plains — the variety is as large as the country itself. Most Canadians endure harsh winters, but even here there is great diversity. For example, the area near Kitimat holds the record for the highest average snowfall at 1 071 centimetres a year, but there is almost no snow at all in Victoria. At Eureka on Ellesmere Island it snows all year round, yet, at the other extreme, towns such as Midale in Saskatchewan record summer temperatures of 37°C.

Even with these disparities, Canada is one of the elite rich among the world's states. Canadians enjoy clean and abundant water, great resource wealth, a plentiful food supply, modern industries, safe cities, and good health-care and educational facilities. These attributes add up to one of the highest material standards of living in the world.

The facts bear out this conclusion. In 1999, the United Nations once again placed Canada first in the world in terms of a crude index based on a combination of purchasing power, life expectancy, literacy and educational attainment — called the Human Development Index (HDI).[1] (See Table 1.1.) Canada lagged in economic performance but did much better in the fields of health and education. The 1999 report also examined each country's success at reducing deprivation in the same three categories measured by the HDI. If that statistic is used, Canada ranked only ninth among the richest industrialized countries, indicating a possible growing gap between the richest and poorest Canadians.

Trade accounts for a very significant proportion of Canada's wealth. As one of the world's top trading nations, Canada is among the very few countries in the world to enjoy a greater volume of exports than imports. A high percentage of these exports consists of natural resources: fish, lumber and energy.

TABLE 1.1   1999 HUMAN DEVELOPMENT REPORT: INDEX FOR TOP 10 COUNTRIES

Country	Life Expectancy at Birth	Adult Literacy Rate	Real GDP (*per capita* U.S. dollars)
1. Canada	79.0	99.0	22 480
2. Norway	78.1	99.0	24 450
3. U.S.	76.7	99.0	29 010
4. Japan	80.0	99.0	24 070
5. Belgium	77.2	99.0	22 750
6. Sweden	78.5	99.0	19 790
7. Australia	78.2	99.0	20 210
8. Netherlands	77.9	99.0	21 110
9. Iceland	79.0	99.0	22 497
10. United Kingdom	77.2	99.0	20 730

The Human Development Index includes three indexes: life expectancy at birth; a combination of adult literacy rates and mean years educational attainment; and standard of living measured by real purchasing power.

Source: Information adapted from 174-country index in United Nations, *Human Development Report 1999* (New York: Oxford University Press, 1999), p 128.

1. United Nations, *Human Development Report 1999* (New York: Oxford University Press, 1999).

Yet even within the economy problems exist. More than three-quarters of all Canadian merchandise exports go to the United States, a convenience that costs dearly in terms of dependence on American markets. Both lumber and fish stocks are dwindling and will not be as lucrative in the years ahead; many other resources are not renewable. Supplies of oil, gas, coal and electricity, many as yet untapped, have allowed Canadians to become energy gluttons: consumers of more energy *per capita* than any other state. Canadians need to provide better planning and management of these resources and develop a broader industrial base.

CHALLENGES IN CANADIAN POLITICS

A political scientist once commented that "asking a person to say what government is about is like asking for a description of an inkblot. Its form is ambiguous, signifying different things to different people."[2] However, it is clearly the task of government to create some uniform conditions and standards for all citizens within the diversity of Canada. Sharing the wealth and resources of the country and assuring certain minimal national standards in areas such as health, communications and education are primary functions of governing in Canada. Unfortunately, there is no consensus about the degree to which it is desirable for governments to be directly involved in the lives of their citizens by directing the economy or providing social services, let alone agreement about how these things should be accomplished.

Since 1867, the Canadian government has developed into an institution respected around the globe as well as within its own borders. Its significance derives from its size, resources, economic power and moral suasion in many parts of the world. Among other world links, Canada is a member of the Commonwealth, la Francophonie and the North Atlantic Treaty Organization (NATO), contributes to United Nations peacekeeping forces in various parts of the world, and has taken a leading position in developing a dialogue between countries of the North and South in order to ameliorate the conditions of the world's poor.

Internally, the government is paramount in making laws and regulations for its citizens. The battle to control the offices and activities of this mammoth institution should be understood by every inquiring and intelligent citizen. The constant evolution of governmental structures and priorities necessitates an unceasing re-evaluation of the policies and direction of government and even of the institution itself. In many areas, there is room for reform and improvement. It has been suggested, for example, that one test of a good government is how well it provides for the most vulnerable of its citizens: the young, the aged, the sick and the disabled. The Canadian government subsidizes a great range of social services whose primary intent is sharing the resources of the country more equitably. However, despite these efforts, between three and five million Canadians, depending on definitions and statistics, live below the poverty line. The high gross domestic product disguises the fact that the country's wealth is very unevenly distributed among Canadians.

Within Canada, the political struggle is focused on institutions, behaviour and policies. The result is an agenda for the resolution of conflict over the very basics of life. As the new century begins, many fundamental questions need to be addressed. Will the country achieve economic stability? Will the distribution of wealth, education and power remain heavily influenced by membership in privileged groups, or will the government continue to attempt its redistribution among

---

2. Richard Rose, *What Is Governing? Purpose and Policy in Washington* (Englewood Cliffs, N.J.: Prentice Hall, 1978), p. 2.

individuals and regions? Will women assume their rightful place in Canadian society? Will Canadians of Indian, Métis and Inuit origin and new immigrants be successfully harmonized into Canadian society? Will Canada prosper under the North American Free Trade Agreement with the United States and Mexico? Will Canada adopt new foreign and defence policies now that the Soviet Union has disintegrated and the influence of communism has waned?

In the broader context of Canada in the world, there are many more unknowns in the years ahead. A report commissioned by the Canadian government predicts that, as basic resources become scarce in the world, pressures upon Canada to provide them will increase.[3] For instance, in times of famine, Canada may well find itself in the unenviable position of having to decide who eats and who does not. The government must conserve resources and ensure that the exploitation of natural wealth will be dictated not by short-term gains or political expediency but by longer-term national and global interests. It will become increasingly important for Canada to turn outward, pursuing foreign trade and playing a role in the resolution of global issues. *Ad hoc* decision-making must give way to greater government investment in research and development and in planning for the future.

The supreme test of any polity is whether it has the capacity to establish acceptable and enduring solutions from multiple conflicting demands. The crucial challenge to the present Canadian political system concerns its ability to manage the policy conflicts discussed above and others equally critical.

This book is based on the premise that Canadians need to agree on one major issue — how these choices will be made. In a country as diverse as Canada, realists cannot expect agreement on fundamental philosophies about people and their community. What can be expected is a fair, open process of democracy that is responsive to the public will, and consensus about how this process ought to work. Two fundamental issues dominate contemporary debates — Québec and the debt.

KEY ISSUES IN CANADIAN POLITICS

At the centre of Canadian political debates today are two vital topics that impact on most other political issues. These are the massive Canadian government debt and the continuing uncertainty of the future of Québec in the federation. Emotions run high about these central issues. How they are resolved will determine the health and future of the Canadian political system. Both issues must be resolved in order for the Canadian state to remain in its present form. Since they affect so many aspects of politics in Canada, various aspects of the debt and Québec nationalism are addressed throughout this book.

One Country or Two?

On October 30, 1995, the province of Québec held its second referendum in 15 years on the issue of sovereignty. The 1980 vote had produced a clear majority of 60 percent for the federalist side, and federalists initially anticipated a similar result in 1995. In the end, however, only 50.6 percent voted No; 49.4 percent voted Yes. With a massive voter turnout of over 93 percent, this amounted to a division of the Québec population into two almost equal camps. Such a high vote made it clear that, for the first time ever, a majority (slightly less than 60 percent) of French-speakers had voted in favour of sovereignty. Only in areas with significant non-francophone populations — Montréal,

---

3. G.O. Barnes, P.H. Freeman and C.A. Ulinski, *Global 2000: Implications for Canada* (Toronto: Pergamon Press, 1981).

the Outaouais, the Eastern Townships and the far North — did a majority vote No. Elsewhere in the province, where few non-francophones live, the Yes side won, and often by large margins. Of the 125 ridings in Québec, the No side won a majority in only 44, while the Yes side got a majority in 81. The Cree and the Inuit in northern Québec each held their own separate referendums. Both produced massive majorities for staying in Canada if Québec should choose to separate.

The sovereignists lost the referendum, but clearly they had gained considerable support over 15 years. The unhealthy element of ethnic nationalism that had fuelled this rise was revealed by provincial premier Jacques Parizeau the night of the referendum when he blamed "money and the ethnic vote" for dashing the dreams of francophone Québécois.

The issue of Québec nationalism — how to counteract it and accommodate it as much as possible within the Canadian framework — will be a continuing challenge in the coming years. All politicians are bracing for yet another referendum on separation, which could be held early in the new century.

How to accommodate Québec's interests satisfactorily and still maintain a strong, united country has proven to be extremely difficult. Two attempts, the Meech Lake accord and the Charlottetown accord, were dismal failures. Accommodation that requires constitutional amendment is difficult, if not possible, to achieve. When one province demands new powers, it creates a bandwagon effect in which every other province asks for something. Most provincial premiers argue that all provinces ought to be treated exactly the same, while Québec wants to negotiate with the federal government as an "equal." However, the Québec separatist government wants considerably more constitutional powers, and that requires changing the federal "bargain." What powers could the federal government decentralize, or give over to the provinces, without jeopardizing the country by making it too weak to stay together? The issue of how to share power between the provinces and the federal government will dominate politics in Canada in the coming years. The issues concerning the Constitution and federalism are discussed in Chapters 5, 6 and 7. Nationalism and its ramifications are discussed in Chapter 7.

Economic Prosperity?

Canadians, on average, are less well off financially in 1999–2000 than they were a few years earlier. Their disposable income has been shrinking, and that trend may continue. Unemployment has become a massive social and economic problem. When economic resources become scarce, political quarrels about how to share them intensify. Anger and disillusionment with governments and politicians also increase, because despite promises to solve the problems, the situation continues to get worse for many people.

Just how ill is the Canadian economy? To understand the financial situation, one must be clear about two terms: debt and deficit. The **deficit** is the amount by which government spending exceeds revenues in one year. The **debt** is the accumulation of deficits over the years. Every year for about three decades until 1998, the Canadian federal government spent more than it took in. That is, each year it had a deficit. Those deficits added together represent the debt. As of 1999–2000, the debt is about $580 billion. High debts require higher taxes because governments must pay the interest on the debt.

During the past three decades, the need, obviously, was to balance the annual government budget and to start paying off the debt. But this was extremely difficult because the debt was so large that the required yearly interest payments took up a huge percentage of the budget — about 35 percent in 1996–97. This left an ever smaller amount of money each year to cover *other* costs. The federal government was struggling just to balance the books and achieve a zero deficit. It did so to great fanfare in 1998. The economy grew and the government accounts were balanced, so it became possible to pay off the debt — or to use the surplus for other purposes, such as reducing taxes or increasing spending. The political conflict has now moved to which group or groups should benefit from the surplus, or whether it should go toward lowering the debt or reducing taxes.

To compound the debt problem, however, a large percentage of the country's debt — over 40 percent — is held outside Canada. This means that Canada is increasingly vulnerable to foreign influence. For example, if foreign investors become dissatisfied or fearful that their investment may not produce adequate returns, they can simply withdraw their money and force interest rates up in Canada. This was very clear during the 1995 Québec referendum campaign, when there were indications that, in the event of a Yes vote, foreign investors would sell off their holdings in Canada. This would have caused a substantial drop in the value of the Canadian dollar and forced higher interest rates.

Aislin, *The Gazette* (Montréal). Reprinted with permission.

In Canada, the declining economy has brought anger and disappointment. It is clear that the country has been living beyond its means and that changes must be made. Deciding who will take the brunt of the cuts, however, involves difficult choices. So far, business interests have been winning. There has been a movement away from traditional liberal values to more conservative ways of thinking. This pattern is reflected particularly in two right-wing Conservative governments at the provincial level led by Ralph Klein in Alberta and Mike Harris in Ontario. At the federal level, Finance Minister Paul Martin Jr. also moved to a more conservative position in his quest to cut government debt. Social programs that were built up in more prosperous times are being cut. Governments are down-sizing — drastically reducing the number of public servants and government programs. Proponents argue that governments have grown too big, that many of their functions should either be eliminated or given over to private enterprise. Social programs, they maintain, are often superficial responses to underlying problems and do not solve anything. Opponents argue that this approach amounts to solving the debt crisis on the backs of the poor. They argue that social services should be maintained and businesses should share the burden more fairly.

If Canada is so indebted, why do many people around the world persistently conclude that Canada is one of the best countries in which to live — that compared to many other countries it is rich? It is partly because in terms of the market value of all final goods and services produced in a specific period — its **gross domestic product** (GDP) — Canada does very well. However, when we look at the debt as a percentage of the GDP, we see that the debt increased as a percentage of GDP throughout the 1980s, plateaued for a few years, and increased again in the 1990s. In 1999–2000, it was 64 percent.

The issue of government spending is covered in detail in Chapter 10 on public administration, where we consider how the government's current and projected budgets are prepared and discuss the options available to the Minister of Finance and the public service in this task. It is addressed further in Chapter 14, which is concerned with how public policy is made.

While the Canadian government struggles with its debt problems, globalization of the economy in terms of free trade and capital flow has created other problems for Canadians to quarrel over. Proponents of globalization argue that in the long run it will produce higher standards of living in all countries. Opponents argue that globalization exposes industrial countries such as Canada to "downward pressure" in labour and environmental standards. Globalization, they say, causes Canada's high employment rate of approximately 10 percent. This third major issue of Canadian politics is discussed in Chapter 15.

When political scientists study these and other political issues, they employ specific approaches, a specialized precise vocabulary and theories about the polity. The next section provides the tools necessary to study politics in Canada in a systematic and objective manner.

Politics and Government

Politics is as old as human history. It is a fascinating form of behaviour, concerning disputes and decisions about human ideals and interests. Defined by the non-specialist as manipulation or the struggle for advantage, it is omnipresent: in relations between husband and wife, parent and child, employer and employee — in short, in all societal relations. However, political scientists do not study all social relations; they are concerned primarily with organized dispute and its collective resolution.

Two definitions of politics contend in the literature. The most widespread of them, put forth by David Easton, one of the foremost experts of systems analysis, is general and abstract. He defined politics as "the authoritative allocation of values."[4] By values, Easton did not mean moral ideas, but rather the benefits and opportunities that people value or desire. The second, a more restricted definition, was conceived by Harold Lasswell, who pointed out that politics always concerns "who gets what, when and how" in society.[5] In the present volume, we delimit the subject by proffering a definition of politics that combines the insights of both Easton and Lasswell: **Politics** embraces all activity that impinges upon making binding decisions about who gets what, when and how. It is an activity through which contending interests and differences may be reconciled for the supposed advantage of society.

Since valued possessions such as wealth and status are invariably scarce and unevenly distributed, disagreement can be expected to arise among people as they attempt to satisfy their seemingly endless wants. It is such general dispute that gives rise to the organized conflict that pervades society, whether in the election of the president of the National Action Committee on the Status of Women (NAC), in the struggle within the United Church over its policy toward human sexuality or in the election of the Canadian prime minister. Sometimes, political conflict becomes violent, as it did at the Oka Indian reserve in Québec in 1990. It is no wonder that some cynics adapt Henry Adams' definition of politics as "the systematic organization of hatreds."[6]

To reduce this endless conflict over power, mechanisms have evolved to enforce decisions for all members of society. We refer to these mechanisms as government. Politics and governing are both about organized dispute over power, but are often artificially demarcated; politics is concerned

---

4. David Easton, *A Framework for Political Analysis* (Englewood Cliffs, N.J.: Prentice Hall, 1965), pp. 50–56.
5. Harold Lasswell, *Politics: Who Gets What, When and How* (New York: McGraw-Hill, 1936).
6. Cited in Garry Wills, "The Politics of Grievance," *The New York Review of Books*, vol. 37, no. 12 (July 19, 1990), p. 3.

with influencing the governors, while governing consists of the actions of public officials in making decisions. Much of the dynamic character of politics comes from the pervasive conflict between the rulers and the ruled.

Government is thus the organization of people for the resolution of dispute and conflict. Even the simplest societies have some means of settling disputes. In modern societies, government not only provides law and order but also regulates many aspects of private and public affairs. It is one of the most complex and important of institutions.

While anthropologists and sociologists study the rules that regulate all forms of behaviour, political scientists concentrate on describing and analyzing the institutions and behaviour of the political governance of states. Insofar as social processes influence or are influenced by politics or governance, they are also part of the study of political science.

The concept of *power* is central to the study of politics. The word comes from the Latin verb *potere*, which means "to be able." Thus, in the broadest meaning of the word, power is being able to achieve what one wants. Power has been part of the vocabulary of politics since the time of Machiavelli, yet it remains the most perplexing issue within the discipline of political science. Even the fundamental question of whether it can be possessed like gold or is simply the result of social relationships remains unanswered.[7] But where would our understanding of politics be without the notion that some individuals hold power over others? Substituting words such as "influence," "coercion," "compulsion," "control" and "persuasion" for "power" only compounds the difficulties. The essential problem stems from the difficulty of ascertaining whether power is absolute or relative. A person's ability to influence other individuals to act in a certain way often relies more on bargaining than on the application of naked force. Thus **power** must be understood to include the ability to influence (convince) and/or to coerce (force) others to accept certain objectives or behave in a particular manner. (See "Power and Students.")

Approaches within Political Science

Each generation brings to the study of politics its own interests, values and methodologies. The study of politics usually carries over ideas from other disciplines such as history, law, philosophy, sociology, economics or anthropology. In this sense, the study of politics includes multiple approaches and is in reality a multidisciplinary subject. The inconsistencies caused by this diversity in the tools for obtaining political understanding are reduced by the accepted principle that scientists should be self-consciously analytical and comparative, and should avoid basing generalizations on casual observation.

Theories provide explanations of *why* politics takes place the way it does. The concept of theory derives from the Greek word *theoria*, which means contemplation. Casual observation or opinion about facts is not theory. To use **theory** in political science (or in physics) means to make sense of the facts of a situation by explaining how they are interconnected. It means distinguishing the significant from the irrelevant by elucidating the most convincing explanation about the facts. Whether political research is based on experiments, statistics or configurative case studies, it is disciplined by the desire to be explicit in the rules employed to describe and analyze politics. Students must be aware, however, that some authors may use analysis as the proverbial drunk uses a streetlight — more for support than illumination.

---

7. For a discussion of the complex methodological issues, see R.A. Dahl, "Power," *International Encyclopedia of the Social Sciences* (New York: Macmillan, 1968), vol. 12, pp. 405–15; R.A. Dahl, *Modern Political Analysis*, 2nd ed. (Englewood Cliffs, N.J.: Prentice Hall, 1970), pp. 14–34; and H.D. Lasswell and A. Kaplan, *Power and Society: A Framework for Political Inquiry* (New Haven: Yale University Press, 1950).

Some scholars believe that the only way to study politics is to employ a general theory of the polity in an effort to obtain scientific, law-like generalizations about politics.[8] Such general theories purport to identify all the critical structures and processes of society, to explain all the inter-relationships and then to predict a wide variety of outcomes.[9] Few Canadians have adhered to this view of the discipline. Beginning with William Ashley, who gave the first political science lecture in the country over 100 years ago, the discipline has been pluralistic; there has been no commitment to one theory or approach. Early writers such as George Bourinot, Stephen Leacock, Harold Innis, R.A. MacKay, Alexander Brady, H.M. Clokie and J.A. Corry commanded academic and public esteem, but they did not slavishly accept a single theory.[10]

In terms of influence in Canada, MacGregor Dawson's 1946 institutional analysis probably came closest to imposing a single approach on the discipline.

CLOSE-UP ON Definition

POWER AND STUDENTS

Why are you reading this book?

Of course, there will be many answers to this question, but one thing is fairly certain. *Power* was exercised in getting you to spend time reading it rather than enjoying a movie or spending time with friends. Power may have been exercised in various forms. You may have been *forced* to read it in order to pass an exam. In other words, you may have been *influenced* by the rewards or punishments that the instructor holds over you. Or, you may be reading this book because you respect the professor and believe *authority* accords him or her the right to assign readings for students. Or, if you have a very good professor, he or she may have convinced you that this book provides material that is of value to you and thus you were *persuaded* to read the book.

Dawson and some of his students adhered to a strict **legal/formal** description of Canadian government and politics.[11] Critics of this style of analysis founded their arguments on the position that Dawson and much of his generation eschewed the study of culture, behaviour and public policy while concentrating exclusively on formal institutions.

Other general theories of politics have been applied to Canada; the best known among them is **systems analysis.** It has been used as an introduction to many textbooks since about 1965. While it was rarely employed in a methodical fashion, it usually served as a short-hand introduction to the study of politics. The essence of this general theory is that the politics of a country can be depicted by the interaction between the societal environment and an abstract political system that processes its demands and supports into outputs, producing an overall stability or homeostasis.[12]

A related general theory is **functionalism.** In essence, functionalism specifies the activities of a viable political system and explains how they help to maintain stability. If the polity does not perform these functions, it ceases to exist.[13] Though it has influenced writing about politics, functionalism has never found a place as a theory to explain the Canadian polity. Somewhat more in vogue is **structural functionalism.** In this approach researchers attempt to determine which "structures" perform which "functions" — as in these statements: "interest aggregation" is expressed by political parties, or "rule-making" is performed by Parliament.

---

8. An introduction to the basic concepts and theories is found in Robert J. Jackson and Doreen Jackson, *An Introduction to Political Science: Comparative and World Politics,* 3rd ed. (Toronto: Prentice Hall Canada, 2000).

9. For intelligent overview and criticism, see Joseph LaPalombara, *Politics within Nations* (Englewood Cliffs, N.J.: Prentice Hall, 1975), chs. 1, 2.

10. Robert J. Jackson, "The Classics in Canadian Political Science," *Research Tools in Canadian Studies*, vol. 10, no. 4 (1988), pp. 7–18.

11. R. MacGregor Dawson's celebrated *Government of Canada* (Toronto: University of Toronto Press) was first published in 1947.

12. Easton, *A Framework for Political Analysis*, passim.

13. See Gabriel Almond and G. Bingham Powell, *Comparative Politics: A Developmental Approach* (Boston: Little, Brown, 1966).

The **political economy** approach has always had many advocates in Canada and gained popularity among Canadian researchers in the 1990s. Political economy studies are concerned with the relationships between economics and government and in particular with the study of **public policy** — or what governments do. Since different ideologies and political beliefs conflict over what this relationship should be, two opposing views are reflected in contemporary studies of political economy — a relatively new **public choice** school, sometimes referred to as "liberal political economy" because it tends to follow the logic of classical economics, and **neo-Marxism** based on Karl Marx's ideas about the structural relations among society, economy and politics.

All these schools of thought, except the Marxists (and some elite theorists), at least partially accept **pluralism** — the idea that power is widely dispersed and many groups compete for it. As a compromise, a new **state-centred** approach views the state as being able to act without responding to the demands of society. The state is visualized as being at least partially autonomous from the public's interests as expressed in the pluralist model.[14]

The essential problem with systems analysis, as well as with other general theories such as functionalism, public choice and traditional Marxism,[15] is that it is often at such a high level of abstraction that it is remote from empirical research. Such theories describe the polity in such general terms that they neither generate testable propositions nor aid our understanding of concrete political phenomena or problems. Marxist approaches utterly fail to reduce all policy issues to class and capitalist hegemony. Public choice advocates err in trying to remove the "irrational" in policy choice, and state-centred theorists are unconvincing in their efforts to describe a limited role for society in government decision-making. Moreover, such general theories have also failed in their fundamental task of identifying all the critical structures and processes of the political system and explaining the relationships among them.

In Canada, no single general theory of politics has ever been totally accepted. The various theories have been used as heuristic devices to help authors and students collect and analyze fragments of political reality. In Chapter 14, we outline in detail the contemporary determinist, pluralist, public choice and neo-Marxist theories of public policy, but let it be clear that by the year 2000 no single theory or approach has been taken as uniquely valid; few, if any, scholars accept the notion that one approach can exhaust all that is to be known about Canadian politics.

Even if no single theory or approach is, or should be, pre-eminent in the study of Canadian politics, students ought to be aware of the underlying principles governing many of the basic arguments in the field. Gabriel Almond and Stephen Genco point out that two analogies summarize the core of the debate on the status of theory in political science. According to these authors, the discipline is divided over whether the analogy underlying the study of politics should be likened to the shifting formlessness of clouds or to the precise causation involved in a machine such as a watch. They conclude that "the current quandary in political science can, to a large extent, be explained by the fact that, by themselves, clock-model assumptions are inappropriate for dealing with the substance of political phenomena."[16] What this argument suggests, then, is that there is no adequate theory about politics that must not perforce include transient and fleeting phenomena. Politics is not totally

---

14. See Eric Nordlinger, *On the Autonomy of the Democratic State* (Cambridge, Mass.: Harvard University Press, 1981). For use of these theories, see William Coleman and Grace Skogstad, eds., *Policy Communities and Public Policy in Canada* (Mississauga: Copp Clark Pitman, 1991).

15. For an application to the Canadian context, see Leo V. Panitch, ed., *The Canadian State* (Toronto: University of Toronto Press, 1977).

16. Gabriel A. Almond and Stephen J. Genco, "Clouds, Clocks and the Study of Politics," *World Politics*, vol. 29, no. 4 (July 1977), p. 505.

predictable; its study has not uncovered a world of cause and effect. Almond and Genco's article contends that political reality has distinctive properties that make it unamenable to the forms of explanation used in the natural sciences. Thus, the science of politics should not be seen as a set of methods with a predetermined theory, but as a "commitment to explore and attempt to understand a given segment of empirical reality." Such an argument calls for an eclectic approach to Canadian politics and to comparative government.

Entirely eschewing approaches or theories in the discipline is not much help either. What political scientists call "hyperfactualism" or "barefooted empiricism" may simply lead to the collection of facts without purpose. Collecting parts of reality without any reference to hunches and ideas from theories is as misleading as the wholesale adoption of a single theory of the polity. We need guides to the facts to be collected and examined.

In this volume, we adopt a variety of analytic and institutional approaches — what Joseph LaPalombara has called "partial" theories.[17] Our information and conclusions are based on the best available research, but not on the basis that knowledge is obtained uniquely by scientific methods. To adopt a purely scientific approach would be tantamount to declaring that the only knowledge we can have about torture must come from conducting experiments in this field.

If no general theory underlies the framework of this book, what segments of politics have been selected for examination? The choice of the analytical dimensions to be studied is always difficult, but the subject must somehow be delimited. In this volume, we analyze Canadian **culture**, **institutions**, **behaviour** and **public policy**. These four dimensions all impinge on the competing ideas, interests, issues and people that make up the polity. They direct us toward those aspects of the political process that can be observed, compared and evaluated; they are the primary segments of a society concerned with politics and power.

The formal institutions of government are the most visible elements of the political process. **Institutions** are social structures that are organized to achieve goals for society. Such structures as constitutions, parliaments, bureaucracies and executives are well known to students of Canadian politics and government. And formal institutions do explain much about politics. Too often, however, they are treated as epiphenomena — that is, as being caused by self-interested individuals and groups. Institutions are important in their own right as units of analysis — they shape the interests, resources and conduct of political leaders who in turn shape the institutions.[18] The way institutions are structured affects political actors, bureaucrats and citizens — as well as who gets what, when and how.

Whereas traditional Canadian political science focuses on studies of institutions, contemporary political culture and socialization studies focus on **culture**, emphasizing the study of values and beliefs. The latter studies assume that political outcomes are determined by amalgamations of individual preferences. Certainly, the values of members of society influence social and political decisions. However, institutions also affect social outcomes. Institutions, therefore, can be thought of as "congealed tastes" or conventions about values that are condensed into institutions that make rules for society.[19]

It is extremely difficult to assess the relative significance of institutions and culture for the development of government policy. Probably both are necessary. If institutions are constant or stable, we

17. Joseph LaPalombara, "Macro-theories and Micro-applications in Comparative Politics: A Widening Chasm," *Comparative Politics*, vol. 1, no. 1 (October 1968), pp. 52–78.

18. See Robert J. Jackson, "Australian and Canadian Comparative Research," in Malcolm Alexander and Brian Galligan, eds., *Comparative Political Studies* (Sydney: Pitman, 1992).

19. William H. Riker, "Implications from the Disequilibrium of Majority Rule for the Study of Institutions," *APSR*, vol. 74, no. 2 (June 1980), pp. 432–46.

ought to be able to predict outcomes from cultural values or tastes. If tastes are constant, we ought to be able to predict outcomes from institutions. In turbulent times, institutions, and often values, are constantly evolving. As William Riker noted, "one fundamental and unsolved problem of social science is to penetrate the illusion and to learn to take both values and institutions into account."[20]

The distinction between individual behaviour and institutions is also blurred. If, in calling institutions "structures," we are referring to a process of change so slow as to be negligible for the purposes of investigation,[21] then institutions are stable configurations that change only over long periods and so are merely the organized collective behaviour of individuals. The collectivity may be more than the sum of its parts, but there is no doubt that its parts are individuals behaving in some routine manner. The study of **behaviour** and institutions is therefore intertwined at the logical as well as the empirical level of analysis. As Karl R. Popper so aptly put it, "institutions are like fortresses. They must be well designed *and* properly manned."[22]

Public policy is a more recent concept in political science.[23] As government has grown, the vast array of government programs and policies has become more difficult for the average Canadian to comprehend. In response to this complexity, the study of public policy has flourished in the discipline of political science. Usually, policy is defined by its ability to set the parameters of future decisions by developing a long-term perspective on an issue. Policy-making is the activity of arriving at these perspectives. Policies result from the interplay among culture, institutions and behaviour. They feed back into the politics of a country, helping to determine political culture, to structure institutions and to limit political behaviour.

Thus, as we see in Figure 1.1, culture, institutions, behaviour and public policy all interact to form the Canadian variety of politics. There are two basic approaches to the study of these and other

FIGURE 1.1 POLITICS IN CANADA: CULTURE, INSTITUTIONS, BEHAVIOUR AND PUBLIC POLICY

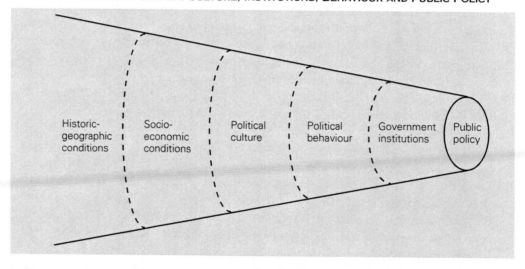

20. Ibid., p. 432.

21. See Karl W. Deutsch, "The Crisis of the State," *Government and Opposition*, vol. 16, no. 3 (Summer 1981), pp. 331–43.

22. Karl R. Popper, *The Poverty of Historicism* (London: Routledge, 1961), p. 157. For neo-institutional approaches in general, see Jeffrey Pfeffer, *Organizations and Organization Theory* (Marshfield, Mass.: Pitman, 1982).

23. For an introduction to this literature, see Stephen Brooks, *Public Policy in Canada,* 2nd ed. (Toronto: McClelland & Stewart, 1993).

factors in Canadian politics. In the **synchronic** approach, specific political factors in Canada are compared with those of other states. In the **diachronic** approach, political factors are examined in one or more countries over historical time. Both approaches are important. Dynamic (over a period of time) and static views of the four dimensions are also useful in formulating generalizations about the Canadian polity.[24]

In this volume we search for significant regularities, similarities and differences in Canadian culture, institutions, behaviour and policies. The approach used is comprehensive, seeking evidence through both dynamic and comparative avenues. Too many volumes on Canada have been parochial and cynical about Canada and its future. Too many texts have attempted to compress the facts into immutable pigeon-holes that create an improper, negative understanding of the country. Canada's system of government is best understood and appreciated when it is compared, even briefly, with those of other countries. Democratic equilibrium is fostered by a comprehensive interplay of culture, institutions, behaviour and policy. Understanding this phenomenon requires sensitivity to the political and administrative environment within which government must operate, as well as an appreciation of both the cohesive and the disruptive forces of our history and society.

States and Nations

A useful starting point in placing Canada within a comparative context is to consider it as a "state." As one of the 188 states currently recognized by the United Nations, Canada may be compared synchronically with a multitude of other more or less similar political entities. Furthermore, a consideration of the origins and development of the Canadian state provides a basis for diachronic comparison and a historical setting for contemporary Canadian politics.

Since the rise of absolutism in the sixteenth and seventeenth centuries, when sovereigns in certain parts of Europe began integrating feudal fiefdoms, petty principalities and conquered territories into unified kingdoms, the state has emerged as the dominant form of political organization. Of course, other types of political systems have existed and continue to exist. Empires have come and gone. Considerable decision-making power may be wielded at subnational levels of government, especially in federal systems; and the number of international actors, such as the United Nations and the European Union, has grown. States, too, are born and disappear over time. For example, the Baltic states of Estonia, Latvia and Lithuania, which were recognized as independent countries after the First World War, were forced into the Soviet Union after the Second World War and then recently became independent again. The Soviet Union itself has fragmented into multiple republics, of which Russia is the largest. The general tendency has been for the number of states to grow almost yearly. Of the 188 members of the United Nations, well over half have become independent since 1945.

The State and Citizens

The **state** is usually defined as a form of political organization in which governmental institutions are capable of maintaining order and implementing rules or laws (through coercion if necessary) over a given population and within a given territory. The usual point of departure for such formulations is German sociologist Max Weber's definition of the state as a human community that "successfully upholds a claim to the monopoly of the legitimate use of physical force in the enforcement of its order ... within a given territorial area."[25] Thus, the state as an organization is defined in terms

---

24. See Jackson and Jackson, *Comparative Government*, chs. 4 and 5.
25. Max Weber, *The Theory of Social and Economic Organization*, edited and translated by A.M. Henderson and Talcott Parsons (New York: Oxford University Press, 1947), p. 154.

of its relation to power.[26] A state is normally admitted to the United Nations, for example, when it has satisfied the members of this international body that, like them, it wields state power and is capable of maintaining order within its territorial boundaries — that is, when it is considered to be **sovereign**. It should be noted, however, that some states recognized as sovereign are not members of the UN — for example, Switzerland and the Vatican.

While many practical problems circumscribe the concept of **sovereignty**, a state usually is recognizable by its internal and external powers: its ability to tax its citizens and its ability to conduct external relations. Or, as Joseph LaPalombara puts it: "As applied to *internal* matters, national sovereignty means that supreme and final authority rests in the national government as opposed to all other private and governmental organizations that may compose the nation-state itself."[27] External sovereignty, on the other hand, represents the recognition by the international community of the right of a people or government to run their own affairs, free from interference by other states or governments.

Within a particular country an individual may also be a **citizen** — a formal member of a state who is eligible to enjoy specified rights and privileges. States normally consider all persons born on their territory, and their children, to be citizens. Other individuals may acquire citizenship through a specified formal process — action such as residing in the country for a certain length of time and going through a formal ceremony such as swearing an oath of allegiance. In Canada an immigrant may apply for citizenship after living for three years in the country. Many non-citizens also live on Canadian soil. They are residents here on an extended or short-term basis.

A state is also characterized by the degree of its citizens' subjective feeling for it. While some states do exist without widespread public identification with their institutions, this is not usually the case. Normally people strongly identify with their state. When citizens accept that a government ought, or has the right, to make decisions for them, political scientists say the system has **legitimacy**. Legitimacy is closely linked to the concept of **authority**, which we define as the government's power to make binding decisions and issue obligatory commands.

According to Weber, authority stems from three main sources. **Traditional authority**, which arises from custom and history, is most frequently gained through inheritance and thus has been enjoyed by royal dynasties throughout the ages. **Charismatic authority** is derived from popular admiration of the personal "heroic" qualities of the individual in whom it is vested — whether prophet, warlord or orator. Lastly, **rational-legal** or **bureaucratic authority**, the most common form in western societies, is vested not in individuals *per se* but in the offices they hold and the mechanisms that placed them there.[28] Thus, the authority of the Canadian prime minister (though charismatic to some) is derived primarily from the fact that he or she is leader of a government placed in power by the routine and legitimate process of popular election. As soon as one leader ceases to be prime minister, the authority currently vested in that person passes to the new incumbent of the office. In Canada and many other modern societies, therefore, legitimacy and authority are vested not in individuals but in the political institutions and offices of the state.

The concept of legitimacy may be applied not only to regimes and governments but also to their individual acts. Thus, a legitimate government may do some things that are perceived to be

---

26. The reader must be wary of all single definitions of the state; as early as 1931 one scholar found 145 different usages of the term "state." See Sabine Cassese, "The Rise and Decline of the Nation or State," *International Political Science Review*, vol. 7, no. 2 (1986), p. 120. For an illuminating essay on the "the state," see Gabriel A. Almond, "The Return to the State," *APSR*, vol. 82, no. 3 (September 1988), pp. 853–75.

27. LaPalombara, *Politics within Nations*, p. 36.

28. Weber, *The Theory of Social and Economic Organization*, ch. 3.

illegitimate. Legitimacy in this sense should not be confused with **legality** — while the former de- notes the degree of subjective authority vested in the government by public opinion, the latter relates to the constitutional or legal propriety of undertaking certain activities. Some events may there- fore be legal (that is, within the letter of the law) without being considered legitimate. The Canadian government's use of the *War Measures Act* to suppress civil liberties during the 1970 Québec crisis was legal, but many Canadians did not think it was legitimate; they did not believe that the federal government ought to have exercised such powers. Or, to cite another example, a majority of the Supreme Court of Canada concluded in 1981 that while an attempt by the federal government to pa- triate the Constitution unilaterally was strictly legal, it was not legitimate because it flouted the con- vention that provincial assent should be obtained. Conversely, certain events can be viewed as legitimate without being legal. Some Canadians, for example, supported the action of the RCMP in burning a barn to prevent a "subversive" meeting, but the action was not legal; in fact, it was a crim- inal offence.

The ability of a state and its political institutions to govern a given population and territory rests on the twin foundations of sovereignty and legitimacy. To resolve conflict, a government requires the consent necessary to allocate values and resources authoritatively. All states attempt to maintain po- litical order and viability, to resolve societal conflicts without tearing the country apart, to defend the territory against external enemies, and to maintain essential services such as the food and water supply, transportation, health facilities and educational institutions. While a balance is maintained be- tween power on the one hand and legitimacy and support on the other, the manner in which these and other policy-making activities are performed is at the core of the study of politics and government.

The Nation

The identification of citizens with their state, and therefore its legitimacy, may be enhanced by the perception that the state and its institutions serve to represent the interests of the population as a whole — in other words, the interests of the *nation.*

In popular usage, and as the title of the United Nations suggests, "nation" is often taken to refer to all people living within a certain territory and under a single government. In this sense, however, the meaning of nation becomes indistinguishable from that of the citizenry of a state. Alternatively, a nation is sometimes identified with respect to certain objective criteria, such as the possession of a common language, racial or physical characteristics, ancestry or cultural heritage. But this usage fails to explain why all peoples who share such characteristics — for example, Argentineans and Chileans — continue to think of themselves as constituting separate nations.

The key to understanding the concept of nation is that, "like any other form of social iden- tity," national identity (and its associated concept, ethnic identity) is "essentially subjective, a sense of social belonging and ultimate loyalty."[29] While objective criteria such as language or race may play a part in reinforcing these identities, the essence of a *nation* is that it is a collectivity of people united by a shared sense of loyalty and a common feeling of belonging together. Thus, immigrants to Canada from eastern Europe or Lebanon may feel themselves to be just as Canadian, as much a part of the Canadian nation, as those who were born in Canada. On the other hand, while some French Canadians are first and foremost *"canadien,"* others, who share the same language and cultural heritage, consider themselves *"québécois."*

---

29. George De Vos and Lola Romanucci-Ross, *Ethnic Identity: Cultural Continuities and Change* (Palo Alto, Cal.: Mayfield Publishing Co., 1975), p. 3; and Anthony D. Smith, *National Identity* (London: Penguin, 1991).

...**entity** is, therefore, a sense of belonging to a particular community, often (but not ...orced by a common language, culture, customs, heritage or shared experience of liv... ...me government. At the same time, national identity consists of a sense of distinc... ...her peoples who may or may not share certain of these characteristics. This dual ...t of the nation is clearly expressed in one satirical definition of a nation as "a soci- ...ommon error as to its origins and a common aversion to its neighbours."[30]

...ectivities that consider themselves culturally or linguistically distinct necessarily ...ate nations. When individuals and minorities do share cultures distinct from those ... , social scientists label them "ethnic groups" or "ethnic minorities." **Ethnicity**, like national identity, is primarily a subjective phenomenon, although it is usually reinforced by the presence of objective traits such as a language or dialect, religion, customs and cultural heritage, and, often, distinct racial or physical characteristics. In many societies, such as the United States or much of Canada, ethnic groups may live side by side and consider themselves, though culturally distinct, to constitute one nation. In others, however, certain ethnic groups may think of themselves as nations in their own right. In the latter case, as in Québec, they may mobilize and pursue political action in order to gain independence. The boundary between ethnic group and nation is therefore tenuous, but it is possible to relate the two if, as in this volume, we define a **nation** as a politically conscious and mobilized ethnic group (usually with a clear sense of territory) that possesses, or aspires to, more autonomy, self-government or independent statehood.

The concepts of "nation" and "ethnicity" are important to the study of politics because, despite the widespread lip-service paid to the principles of national self-determination, only rarely do territorial and ethnic boundaries coincide. For example, the co-existence of several languages is generally taken as one indication of ethnic pluralism. At the same time, in only about half of the world's states do more than 75 percent of the population speak the same language. Few states in the world consist basically of one ethnic group, as do Japan and South Korea. The term **nation-state** is used to represent this conceptual marriage between the cultural principle *nation* and the territorial and governmental principles inherent in the idea of the *state*. Some states, such as Canada and the United Kingdom, contain aspiring nations within them. Other nations are governed by more than one state — for example, Koreans in North and South Korea or Palestinians in a number of Middle Eastern states. The politicization of demands for the reunification of nations, as in Korea or Ireland, or for the division of multinational states into more ethnically homogeneous self-governing communities, as in Cyprus, results in highly emotional and frequently violent conflict; it causes serious problems of accommodation for political authorities. Attempting to account for these strains and find solutions for them is a major concern for politicians and political scientists alike.

Nationalism and Regionalism

Two generations ago, "nation-building" was a dominant theme in political science, especially among those studying the political development of new states in the so-called Third World or developing world, many of which faced the task of integrating fragmented societies into cohesive political units. The prevailing view was that the ongoing processes of economic development, urbanization and industrialization would reduce territorial and cultural tensions, just as they had already apparently enhanced the integration of western advanced industrial societies.[31] In the last decade, however,

---

30. Julian Huxley and Alfred Court Haddon, *We Europeans: A Survey of "Racial" Problems* (London: Jonathan Cape, 1935), p. 16.

31. Critiques of these forecasts are found in M.J. Esman, ed., *Ethnic Conflict in the Western World* (Ithaca, N.Y.: Cornell University Press, 1977), pp. 46–64. For a discussion of the fundamental issues in this field, see Robert J. Jackson and Michael Stein, *Issues in Comparative Politics* (New York: St. Martin's Press, 1971).

Alan King, *The Ottawa Citizen,* June 29, 1996. Reprinted by permission.

many advanced states have been subjected to pressures of a nationalist or regional nature, previously dismissed as threats only to "new" nations.[32]

Nationalism, as it is found in a number of western societies today, is a potentially divisive force. In several cases, territorially concentrated ethnic minorities, previously subjects of a larger state, have demanded increased self-determination and even total independence. The breakdown of

---

32. On the types of nationalism, see Anthony D. Smith, *Nationalism in the Twentieth Century* (Oxford: Martin Robertson, 1979). On Québec, see Robert J. Jackson and Abina Dann, "Quebec Foreign Policy? Canada and Ethno-Regionalism," in Werner J. Feld and Werner Link, eds., *The New Nationalism* (New York: Pergamon, 1979), pp. 89–105.

multiple republics and then the violent fragmentation of two of them, Bosnia and the most visible of these circumstances.

ities in most advanced industrial societies have not been totally assimilated or forces of modernization. Indeed, since the Second World War, they have become nd vocal. However, not all examples of organized ethnic interest should be la- Many ethnic demands, such as those of Italian or Ukrainian minorities in no challenge to the integrity of the existing state and quite easily may be accom- within its confines. Examples are demands for minority-language education or ethnically oriented television programs. Nationalism should therefore be viewed as part of a continuum of ethnic activity: demands that may be accommodated within the existing state structure become demands for political (and usually economic and cultural) autonomy, or even for total separation from the larger state.[33] Thus, in this volume **nationalism** is defined in its contemporary sense as the collective action of a politically conscious ethnic group (or nation) in pursuit of increased territorial autonomy or sovereignty. Examples of contemporary nationalist movements (often labelled "ethno-nationalist" or "neo-nationalist") may be found in many advanced industrial societies, including Canada, where Québec nationalists strive to make that province a separate state.

In many states, territorial tensions have also been manifested by movements espousing *regionalist* demands and protests, even where a separate ethnic or national identity has been absent. In contrast to nationalism, which seeks to alter existing political structures, **regionalism** refers to territorial tensions "brought about by certain groups that ... demand a change in the political, economic and cultural relations between regions and central powers *within* the existing state."[34] Regionalist discontent is most often articulated in economic terms, especially by representatives of poorer, peripheral regions within a country. However, such discontent can also find expression in political terms — as when *"nouveau riche"* regions object to the central government's power to impose constraints on their new-found prosperity. Regionalism is an important dimension of politics in Canada — particularly in the West. Nationalism and regionalism in Canada are the main focus of Chapter 7. Cultural implications of nationalism and regionalism are also discussed in Chapter 3.

The Development of the Modern State

Territorial strains manifested in nationalism and regionalism are one aspect of what some writers have referred to as a "crisis" of the contemporary state.[35] The modern state originally emerged in western Europe before the industrial revolution as a strategic and economic unit. As John Herz has aptly put it, the territorial state provided a "hard shell" against the external environment. Strategically, the hard shell of the state "rendered it to some extent secure from foreign penetration, and thus made it an ultimate unit of protection for those within its boundaries."[36] At the same time, the state became the major locus of economic activity and the guarantor of economic autonomy. In many countries, the state institutions themselves played an active role in promoting economic development, providing transportation networks and other forms of industrial infrastructure, if not actually developing certain industries under state ownership. Less directly, almost all states provided a hard shell for their

---

33. See James Lightbody, "A Note on the Theory of Nationalism as a Function of Ethnic Demands," *CJPS*, vol. 2, no. 3 (September 1969), pp. 327–37.

34. Riccardo Petrella, "Nationalist and Regionalist Movements in Western Europe," in C.R. Foster, ed., *Nations without a State*, p. 10 (emphasis added).

35. For example, Deutsch, "The Crisis of the State"; John H. Herz, *The Nation-State and the Crisis of World Politics* (New York: David McKay Co., 1976), esp. ch. 3.

36. Herz, *The Nation-State and the Crisis of World Politics*, p. 101.

domestic markets through the imposition of tariffs, quotas and other protective measures, and through the management of external trade relations.

As the concept of national self-determination developed, the hard, hollow shell of the territorial state gained substance. The modern state emerged in Europe in the sixteenth and seventeenth centuries and was carried by colonists to the Americas, Australasia and Africa, where new states were formed for self-defence or in emulation of Europe. The idea that the state should govern on behalf of all the people, instead of on behalf of a privileged minority, was first realized by the French Revolution of 1789. With the spread of the principles and institutions of popular sovereignty, often in the form of liberal democracy, the strategic and economic unit also became the primary focus of cultural and political loyalties.

Today, the hard shell of the state has been rendered much less resistant by changes in the world economy, technology and communications and by the development of new instruments of warfare. As strategic units, most western states are no longer able to defend their citizens against realistic external threats. They are forced to rely instead on the protective cloak offered by the United States and NATO. The economic autonomy of states has been challenged by the increasing interdependence of national economies, the growing importance of international finance capital and multinational corporations, dependence on energy supplies and raw materials imported from more assertive developing countries, and the need for economic markets greater than those encompassed by traditional state boundaries. In some cases, these factors have led to the development of new economic and political institutions on a transnational level, perhaps best exemplified by the growth of the European Union. More generally, and particularly in Canada, the result has been dependence on foreign capital investment, especially from the United States. Overall, it has become increasingly difficult for states to control the internal dynamics of their own economies.

It is in this context that one author refers to the economic and strategic "inadequacy" of the contemporary state.[37] The state is no longer able to maintain its hard shell against the outside world. The implied danger for the state and its authorities is that the legitimacy and loyalty owed to the state will be undermined if this inadequacy is widely perceived by the general public. Herein may also be found one factor behind the nationalist demands of ethnic minorities: many of the original economic and strategic advantages of remaining within the larger state no longer exist.

Until the twentieth century, the role of the state was by and large restricted to the maintenance of law and order, the administration of justice, the defence of the realm and the conduct of diplomacy. In order to maintain or enhance their legitimacy or popular support, states have assumed many new tasks. In particular, state authorities have increasingly taken on service functions — such as education, health care, housing, pensions and unemployment insurance — to provide for the welfare of their citizens. This growth of the "welfare state" has been accompanied by a more interventionist role for the state in the economy. Many governments have intervened directly with budgetary policies or by state ownership of particular industries, for example, air and rail transport,

> *The measure of a nation's greatness does not lie in the conquest, or its Gross National Product, or the size of its gold reserves or the height of its skyscrapers. The real measure of a nation is the quality of its national life, what it does for the least fortunate of its citizens and the opportunities it provides for its youth to live useful and meaningful lives.*
>
> **The Ottawa Citizen, October 16, 1993**

37. Smith, "The Crisis of the West European State."

telecommunications, energy development and public utilities. Others have played less overt economic roles, for example, by regulating the private sector (environmental regulations and health and safety standards) or designing tariff policies to protect domestic industries or markets.

The influence of the state in the daily lives of its citizens is therefore immense. As the scope of government activity has enlarged, the machinery of government has grown more complex, and decision-making has become more centralized and bureaucratized. The increased number of state functions, and the personnel to carry them out, must be paid for. The average share of the national income consumed by the public sector in western societies has risen from between 5 and 10 percent in the late nineteenth century to between 35 and 50 percent today. In countries with large and well-developed welfare state programs, such as Sweden or the Netherlands, total government expenditures actually exceed half the national income. Consequently, a large proportion of each wage-earner's income disappears into the hands of the government, either directly in the form of income tax and pension contributions, or indirectly through sales tax and customs duties.

This growth of the state in the twentieth century underlines another dimension of the perceived crisis of the contemporary state. Some political scientists and politicians allege that in addition to being strategically and economically inadequate, as outlined above, the institutions of government are *overloaded*.[38] The "overload" thesis consists of two complementary aspects: first, the state has taken on more functions than it can perform or afford; second, the policy-making process has become too complex and cumbersome to respond effectively to the expectations of the citizens. Particularly in liberal democracies, the state faces a loss of public support and legitimacy if it cannot cope with the demands of its citizens. More generally, in a number of western societies there has also been a backlash against "big government" and high levels of government expenditure and taxation.

Although under fire, the state remains the pre-eminent political actor in both the domestic and the international arenas. International organizations such as the European Union, NATO and, particularly, the United Nations remain the creatures of the states that comprise them. Debates regarding nationalism, regionalism and war are carried to the state capital. Indeed, nationalist movements perpetuate the logic of the nation-state by demanding secession from the larger state in order to form another, smaller one. Although the state, by and large, may not be quite as sovereign as it once was — even questions of sovereignty or foreign ownership of the economy have become national political issues — its institutions, policy-making processes, functions and powers remain at the heart of the study of politics. Thus, an examination of the origins and development of the Canadian state is an essential precursor to the more detailed analysis of politics in Canada. Before turning to this examination in Chapter 2, we shall first discuss the type of state that Canadians have adopted.

THE BASIC PREMISES OF DEMOCRACY IN CANADA

States vary greatly in their governmental forms, politics and policies. Canada is a democracy, and its governmental form is that of a constitutional monarchy with a federal basis. The principles and structures inherent in this description will be fleshed out in detail throughout this volume. Although

---

38. See, for example, Michel J. Crozier, Samuel P. Huntington and Joji Watanuki, *The Crisis of Democracy* (New York: New York University Press, 1975); and Richard Rose, ed., *Challenge to Governance: Studies in Overload Polities* (Beverly Hills, Cal.: Sage Publications, 1980).

these concepts may appear fuzzy and debate over their meaning can be expected, they are extremely important in the daily lives of Canadians.

The type of political system enjoyed by a state is usually encapsulated in the nature and limits of power exercised within it. Aesop's fable of the frogs searching for the right leadership in their pond comes readily to mind. It seems that the frogs longed for a king, so they appealed to the god Zeus to send them one. He sent them King Log. When the log lolled about without exercising any authority, the frogs demanded another king. Zeus sent King Stork, who immediately gobbled them up.

Aesop's fable illustrates the principle that in political systems there is a continuum between total freedom and the government's use of persuasion or coercion. In the real world, an element of power — and so coercion — is always present or implied. The poet Yeats expressed the idea that violence is always available to the state when he wrote in "The Great Day":

> *Hurrah for revolution and more cannon-shot!*
> *A beggar upon horseback lashes a beggar on foot.*
> *Hurrah for revolution and cannon come again!*
> *The beggars have changed places, but the lash goes on.*[39]

States differ remarkably in their openness and types of participation. Certain features of each polity are unique, yet the essentials of political systems are similar because all perform the same basic functions. At the heart of the study of comparative politics lies the question of whether political systems fall into distinguishable categories or classes.

The search for understanding on this subject usually begins with Aristotle's analysis of the Greek city-states in the fourth century before Christ. This Greek philosopher, the godfather of comparative politics, set out the fundamental rules for scientific investigation and developed the first significant classification of types of political systems.

Aristotle's classical division of polities was based on his knowledge of the 158 Greek city-states. While he lived in Athens, with its principle of equal access of citizens to government positions, he studied the constitutions and governments of other city-states to determine the causes of political instability and change. He employed two criteria to classify these states: the number of people who participated in governing; and whether they ruled in their own or in the general interest. A sixfold classification resulted. Aristotle found that only two categories — *aristocracy* and *polity* — were reasonably stable, and concluded that stability depended on active participation, or at least some degree of representation, of all citizens. (See Table 1.2.)

This classification of rule by the one, the few or the many (with its resultant spectrum from tyrannical rule to democracy) has become part of western thought. While considerably simplifying reality, the classification helped introduce some order into the immense variety of political ideas

TABLE 1.2   THE ARISTOTELIAN CLASSIFICATION

Number of Rulers	Rule in the General Interest	Self-Interested Rule
One	Monarchy	Tyranny
Few	Aristocracy	Oligarchy
Many	Polity	Democracy or ochlocracy

---

39. Quoted in Michael Curtis, *Comparative Government and Politics* (New York: Harper & Row, 1968), p. 43.

and systems. It has gradually become clear, however, that there is no right or wrong classification, and that comparison requires agreement on at least principles and definitions.

In the contemporary world, the governors are never in total control, so a classification that forces either/or distinctions can only be a starting point. The next step is to examine political systems on a spectrum. The most standard continuums are those between democratic and authoritarian governments, and between traditional and modern societies. In both cases, the difficulty lies in determining the degree to which a state is democratic or modern. This task of measuring the degree of forms of government is very difficult. In this volume, we use the following basic definitions: a **democratic** system conciliates competing political interests; an **autocratic** system imposes one dominating interest on all others.[40] Thus, in these terms the form of government is determined by its method of reconciling political diversity and conflict. In autocratic regimes, representative institutions are absent or are facades.

Democracy is an ambiguous concept. It is used as a *source* of authority for government, as well as for the *purposes* served by government, and for the *procedures* for constituting government.[41] Originally, the word democracy came from two Greek roots — *demos*, meaning the people, and *kratos*, meaning authority. As we have seen, in ancient Greek culture democracy meant government by the many. In some Greek city-states, all citizens participated in making and implementing laws. Save for rare exceptions (an example occurs in some Swiss communes), such systems no longer exist. Instead, most democracies, Canada among them, consist of a system of elected representatives who make laws for the country. In other words, democracy is a set of procedures for constituting governments.

For Aristotle, "democracy" was characterized by the "poor" ruling in their own favour. When we characterize Canada as a democracy, we tend to place it in the "rule in the general interest" category, under which, to some extent, the people govern themselves. Unfortunately, today practically all states describe themselves as "democratic" in some fashion. Even the former East Germany referred to itself as the German Democratic Republic. The British writer Bernard Crick played lightly but brilliantly with this problem of the meaning of words and their usage in the real world. For him, "democracy" is perhaps the most promiscuous word in the world of public affairs: "She is everybody's mistress and yet somehow retains her magic even when her lover sees that her favours are being, in his light, illicitly shared by many another. Indeed, even amid our pain at being denied her exclusive fidelity, we are proud of her adaptability to all sorts of circumstances."[42]

Yet, if a democracy is defined as a state in which opposition parties have a reasonable chance of winning office, not all members of the UN would be called democratic. Only about a third of the states have established over time that they can change their governments without recourse to revolution, coups d'état or other violent forms of change, and Canada is one of them. The fact is that democracy in the sense just cited is not very widespread in the developing world.

---

40. Classification of the world's states is discussed in Robert J. Jackson and Doreen Jackson, *Comparative Government,* chs. 4 and 5.

41. Samuel P. Huntington, *The Third Wave: Democratization in the Twentieth Century* (Norman: University of Oklahoma Press, 1991). See also Bruce Russett, *Grasping the Democratic Peace* (Princeton, N.J.: Princeton University Press, 1993); G. Sorensen, *Democracy and Democratization* (Boulder, Colo.: Westview Press, 1993); Doh Chull Shin, "On the Third Wave of Democratization: A Synthesis and Evaluation of Recent Theory and Research," *World Politics,* vol. 47 (October 1994), pp. 135–70; David Lake, "Powerful Pacifists: Democratic States and War," *APSR,* vol. 86, no. 1 (1992), pp. 24–37; and Mancur Olson, "Dictatorship, Democracy and Development," *APSR,* vol. 87, no. 3 (September 1993), pp. 567–76.

42. Bernard Crick, *In Defence of Politics* (London: Penguin, 1964), p. 56.

The pure model of democracy encompasses popular assemblies as in the Athenian sense. Readers may recall that, at that time, elections to high office were carried out by lottery because the Athenians believed that if choices between individuals were made then the richer, or better connected, candidates would win. In the modern day, few observers expect democracy to be rule by the people as a whole. The closest to this goal is representative democracy, in which the people choose those who are to make and administer the laws. In principle, all citizens should have equal access to and influence on government policy-making through participation in fair and competitive elections. In this book, we define **representative democracy** as a political system in which the governors who make decisions with the force of law obtain their authority directly or indirectly as a result of free elections in which the bulk of the population may participate.

Thus, democracy in Canada is not equivalent to rule by the people as a whole. Our form of government is, properly speaking, a representative democracy, in which those elected to high office are invested with the legitimacy of power to make decisions having the force of law. The system provides a method of electing and monitoring these representatives. It also allows regular and institutionalized opportunities for changing those responsible for governing the political system.[43] Moreover, the elected representatives do not mirror the views of the people or the various regions they represent. If they did so, formulating coherent policy might well be impossible.

Representative democracy requires complex structures, but its basic attributes may be fairly easily outlined. Its essential characteristic is reconciling the need for political order with a degree of influence for competing political interests. Associated with this basic feature are the values of liberty and equality. The primary premise is that representative democracy is the best means or technique of governing a complex society. It is a political means and not necessarily an end in itself. However, representative democracy is generally thought to be accompanied by other political values that are embedded in the notion of reconciling diverse interests through the majority principle: freedom of press and opinion, contested elections, competing political parties, civil rights, rule of law, limited terms of office and constitutional limits on the power of the elected. The assumption is that political weight and authority can shift from one group to another, and that any group or party seeking power will have to enlist the cooperation of other groups. No single elite or oligarchy will remain in control over time and over all issues. In other words, *pluralism* is assumed.

The values of democracy are often debated. Some authors consider democracy to be essentially equivalent to certain fundamental values such as the protection of individual liberty or equality or other goals. In this volume we shall describe, analyze and assess the Canadian political system as a *means* or *technique* of government. It is the procedures of democracy that will be in question, not the substance of the policies produced. For example, it is possible to have a democratic political system with either a capitalist or a socialist economy.

Since public policies are not scientifically determinable, we are best advised to put our faith in free and fair elections with the concomitant necessary values.[44] Placing such high hopes in the "system" of democracy is best defended by Winston Churchill's well-used maxim that it is the "least worst" system of government. If it were possible to determine scientifically the best government policies, then the obvious connection of intelligent citizens should be to agree with Plato and set up an elite of philosopher kings to rule. However, this contention is difficult to uphold. The ruler of Bahrain, the smallest and least prosperous of the independent Gulf states, personally makes the

---

43. See Seymour Martin Lipset, "Some Social Requisites of Democracy: Economic Development and Political Legitimacy," *APSR*, vol. 53, no. 1 (March 1959), pp. 69–105.

44. Henry B. Mayo, *An Introduction to Democratic Theory* (New York: Oxford, 1960).

rules or laws for his citizens. Citizens merely appear on Friday morning, make a verbal appeal, hand in a written petition and wait for the judgement to come down from on high. While there may be some merit — such as efficiency — in such a process, it is certainly not procedurally democratic. There is no institutionalized way for the citizens to change their ruler. The outstanding worth of democracy is that it allows citizen participation in the orderly succession of rulers. Governments elected by the people will more likely produce government *for* the people. As Aristotle put it, an expert cook knows best how to bake a cake, but the person who eats it is a better judge of how it tastes.

Countries are "more" or "less" democratic. While the level of democracy that a country possesses changes over time, crossnational (diachronic) comparisons indicate that Canada always appears high on a list of states on this criterion. Yet within the subset of developed democracies, Canada has been placed first on an index of democratization by two authors, but ninth and eleventh out of twelve respectively, by two others.[45] Therefore, although Canada is usually complimented when placed in global comparison, Canada's ability to be "as democratic" as some other developed countries has been challenged by a few serious scholars.

In adopting a democratic system, Canada did not shed its ties to the monarchy, as occurred in the United States where a republic was established. The number of monarchies in the world has steadily decreased. Some members of the Commonwealth, such as India, have opted to become republics. Canada, on the other hand, like the United Kingdom, continues as a **constitutional monarchy** — monarchical because Queen Elizabeth II sits on the throne of Britain and presides as the Queen of Canada. The symbols that historically indicated this attachment — "God Save the Queen" as our national anthem and the Union Jack as our flag — have disappeared, but our monarchical origins have had a lasting impact on the system of central government and administration. Symbols such as those on the Great Seal, badges of the Royal Canadian Mounted Police, and the reverse side of coins and some bills illustrate the monarchical ties that remain.

Furthermore, Canada is a **constitutional democracy**, because the Constitution shapes and limits political power. The documents and behaviour that comprise the Constitution limit the powers of the government by specifying the form of involvement of elected representatives and the division of authority among the partners in the federation. The Constitution also defines the power of those chosen to govern us. The choice of a parliamentary system rather than a presidential one followed logically from the adoption of a monarchical form. In the presidential system of the United States, the chief executive and symbolic head is the elected president. In the parliamentary system, the monarch retains the latter honour and the chief political executive officer is relegated to a lower status for purposes of protocol. In other words, in a presidential system the president is both the nominal and political head of state, whereas parliamentary systems usually have a political head and also a separate nominal head of state whose functions are chiefly ceremonial and whose influence is marginal.

Throughout this volume (particularly in Chapters 5 and 6), we shall describe and analyze these constitutional mechanisms. The basic form rests on British parliamentary traditions, but the Constitution also divides power by a federal principle. The essential difference between a unitary and a federal form of government is simply that a **unitary system**, such as that found in France, has a central government that possesses total authoritative power, whereas a **federal system** divides such power among jurisdictions and over geographical areas.

---

45. Compare Lipset, "Some Social Requisites of Democracy"; Phillips Cutright, "National Political Development: Its Measurement and Social Correlates," in N.W. Polsby, R.A. Dentler, P.A. Smith, eds., *Political and Social Life* (Boston: Houghton Mifflin, 1963), pp. 569–82; Deane E. Neubauer, "Some Conditions of Democracy," *APSR*, vol. 61, no. 4 (December 1967), pp. 1002–9; and Robert A. Dahl, *Polyarchy: Participation and Opposition* (New Haven: Yale University Press, 1971).

THE CRITICS OF DEMOCRACY

Democracy is often attacked for its elitism. This is an important but simple and misplaced contention. In all states, a relatively small number of people dominate the political process. As we have seen, Aristotle's sixfold classification was based on the typology that states are ruled by one, few or many people. In his terms, the ruling group, or **political elite**, may therefore be fairly closed, or it may be open to many interests. Two schools of thought dominate the discussion in political science about this issue — elite and pluralist theories.

Elite theories are based on the contention that all states, even democracies, have a maldistribution of power within them. Vilfredo Pareto (1848–1923) and Gaetano Mosca (1858–1941) both argued that all societies possess a small governing elite that obtains its authority because of a set of attributes such as money or prestige. Robert Michels (1876–1936) extended this argument. After studying political parties, especially in Germany, he concluded that "who says organization, says oligarchy." In other words, even supposed democratic institutions such as political parties have an elite.[46]

Many studies of democracy have confirmed the basic thesis that some people have more power than others. The best known of these studies at the level of the U.S. as a whole was *The Power Elite*, by C. Wright Mills, which contended that power in the U.S. was dominated by a military-industrial complex led by top military, corporate and political leaders.[47]

Pluralist theorists, by contrast, contend that power in democracies is not held by a single ruling class or elite. They maintain that while democracies may not allow all the people to govern (or even to take part in the major decisions), power is reasonably diffused in society. In his path-breaking book *Who Governs?* and later in *Polyarchy*, Robert Dahl shows that there is never a cohesive, single ruling elite in the United States. According to Dahl, different minorities rule on different issues over time.[48] J. Schumpeter best articulates the idea that the state is an arena of political struggle in which the people may choose their rulers but may not actually govern. His classic definition is that democracy is a process involving elites that engage in a competitive struggle for people's votes.[49]

This issue cannot be resolved in this book, but even in democracies it is clear that "the people" do not rule and, therefore, this type of political system should not be equated with "good" government. Democratically elected governments may do wicked things. They may interfere in the affairs of other countries, as the United States did in Grenada in 1984. They may not provide a "just" society because of the way money is distributed within the country, as is clearly the case in many countries. But we contend that the people's ability to "throw the rascals out" distinguishes democracies from authoritarian regimes. For that reason, we have deliberately adopted a *procedural* conception of democracy.

46. Geraint Parry, *Political Elites* (New York: Routledge Chapman & Hall, 1969).

47. C. Wright Mills, *The Power Elite* (New York: Oxford University Press, 1956).

48. Robert Dahl, *Who Governs?* (New Haven: Yale University Press, 1961); and Robert Dahl, *Polyarchy* (New Haven: Yale University Press, 1971).

49. J. Schumpeter, *Capitalism, Socialism and Democracy* (New York: Harper & Row, 1943).

SUMMARY

In over 12 decades of independent existence, Canadians have shown the vision required to master the huge desolate spaces of the northern hemisphere, to exploit the riches of the land and to solve the puzzles of a bilingual and multicultural society. The Fathers of Confederation created a structure of government that so far has met the tests of viability and flexibility under stress. In the decades ahead, the tests may be much more difficult, and possibly even violent, but they will nonetheless relate to past Canadian crises and to the way politics is played in Canada.

To describe, analyze and explain contemporary politics in Canada requires an understanding of the origin, territorial expansion and development of the Canadian state. In the next chapter, a brief developmental history will introduce this subject and illustrate the major importance of the growth of the state.

The four parts of the volume that follow examine those dimensions of politics in Canada that the authors regard as the most significant: political culture, institutions, behaviour and public policy. All four have an impact on the Canadian people, directing daily life and shaping the future.

Part 2 (Chapters 3 and 4) describes the Canadian political culture, how it is acquired through such means as gender, class, education and the media, and how it is transferred from generation to generation. Part 3 (Chapters 5, 6, 8, 9, 10) outlines and dissects the institutions, such as the Constitution, federalism, the executive and the legislature, that give structure to the culture and to political options. Chapter 7 addresses the vital issue of nationalism and how it affects Canada's political institutions. Part 4 (Chapters 11, 12, 13) assesses the behaviour of individuals within these formal institutions and other organizations in the political process, including the 1997 general election and its consequences. The last section, Part 5 (Chapters 14 and 15), evaluates the impact of Canadian culture, institutions and behaviour on public policy-making. Woven throughout the discussion is the importance of the development of the Canadian state, and its social divisions over the allocation of the resources of the territory — in brief, politics in the new millennium.

DISCUSSION QUESTIONS

1. In the global context, how does Canada rate as a place to live?
2. What, in your opinion, are the major issues and problems that the Canadian government must cope with in the coming few years?
3. Is Canada a state, a nation or both? Justify your answer.
4. What is democracy? What are the main arguments of its critics?

Selected Bibliography

General and Theoretical

Almond, Gabriel A., *A Discipline Divided: Schools and Sects in Political Science* (Newbury Park, Cal.: Sage, 1990).

Blair, R.S. and J.T. McLeod, eds., *The Canadian Political Tradition* (Scarborough: Nelson, 1993).

Brooks, Stephen, *Canadian Democracy: An Introduction* (Toronto: McClelland & Stewart, 1993).

Cerny, Philip G., *The Changing Architecture of Politics: Structure, Agency and the Future of the State* (London: Sage, 1990).

Coleman, William and Grace Skogstad, *Policy Communities and Public Policy in Canada* (Mississauga: Copp Clark Pitman, 1991).

Dahl, Robert, *Democracy and Its Critics* (New Haven: Yale University Press, 1989).

——————, *On Democracy* (New Haven: Yale University Press, 1999).

Derbyshire, J.D. and I. Derbyshire, *World Political Systems: An Introduction to Comparative Government* (Edinborough: Chambers, 1991).

Di Palma, Giuseppe, *To Craft Democracies* (Berkeley: University of California Press, 1990).

Dogan, Mattei and Ali Kazancigil, eds., *Comparing Nations: Concepts, Strategies, Substance* (Oxford: Blackwell, 1994).

Greenfield, Liah, *Nationalism: Five Roads to Modernity* (Cambridge, Mass.: Harvard University Press, 1992).

Gutmann, Amy and Dennis Thompson, *Democracy and Disagreement* (Cambridge, Mass.: Harvard University Press, 1997).

Huntington, Samuel P., *The Third Wave: Democratization in the Late Twentieth Century* (Norman: University of Oklahoma Press, 1991).

Jackson, Robert J. and Doreen Jackson, *An Introduction to Political Science: Comparative and World Politics* (Toronto: Prentice Hall Canada, 2000).

Jackson, Robert J. and Michael B. Stein, *Issues in Comparative Politics* (New York: St. Martin's Press, 1971).

Lane, Jan-Erik and Svante Ersson, *Comparative Politics* (Cambridge, Mass.: Polity Press, 1994).

Lindblom, C.E., *Inquiry and Change* (New Haven: Yale University Press, 1990).

Macridis, Roy C. and Bernard E. Brown, eds., *Comparative Politics*, 7th ed. (Pacific Grove: Brooks/Cole, 1990).

Minogue, Kenneth, *Politics: A Very Short Introduction* (Oxford: Oxford University Press, 1995).

Needler, M.C., *The Concepts of Comparative Politics* (New York: Praeger, 1991).

Rustow, D.A. and K.P. Erickson, eds., *Comparative Political Dynamics: Global Research Perspectives* (New York: Harper Collins, 1991).

Smith, Anthony D., *National Identity* (Las Vegas: University of Nevada Press, 1991).

Sniderman, Paul M., Joseph F. Fletcher, Peter H. Russell and Philip Tetlock, *The Clash of Rights: Liberty, Equality and Legitimacy in Pluralist Democracy* (New Haven: Yale University Press, 1997).

Wiarda, H.J., *New Directions in Comparative Politics* (Boulder, Colo.: Westview Press, 1991).

Wilson, Jeremy, *Analyzing Politics* (Scarborough: Prentice Hall Canada, 1988).

Also see the periodicals *Canadian Journal of Political Science*, *American Political Science Review* and other national and regional quarterlies.

WEBLINKS

www.uottawa.ca/ associations/cpsa-acsp

Canadian Political Science Association This site contains useful information about the study of political science in Canada as well as links to other useful political science Web sites.

canada.gc.ca/canadiana/ map_e.html

Map of Canada This site provides a map of Canada and the different provincial boundaries.

2

The Canadian Nation and State

Yesterday and Today

How and why have present cultural attitudes, institutions and modes of governing developed in Canada? What has made Canadians who they are? How and when were the territorial boundaries for today's state and nation determined? Answers to these vital questions indicate to what a large extent contemporary politics is circumscribed by the broad constraints of the past. Without some understanding of Canada's economic, social and political history, it is impossible to grasp how Canadians forged a positive and dynamic system of government when the country was vulnerable to dangers on all sides. In this chapter, therefore, a historical framework is developed as a context for an appreciation of contemporary politics.

> *Not to know what happened before one was born is always to remain a child.*
>
> **Cicero, as cited in *Harper's Magazine* (November 1993), p. 10.**

Canada achieved statehood through the *British North America Act (BNA Act)* in 1867. In chronological terms, it is now one of the world's oldest states — 45th oldest of the present 188 members of the United Nations. Canada is one of a very few states that can claim continuous existence as an independent entity for over a century. Yet it is considerably "younger" than the majority of current West European countries.

Canada also postdates most of the countries of South and Central America, which gained their independence from the Spanish Empire largely between 1810 and 1840 and many of which are still considered to be part of the developing, as opposed to the developed, world. Unlike many of these Latin American examples, however, Canada has established a highly stable political system based upon the western European norm of parliamentary democracy, and has become very much a part of the developed world of advanced industrial societies, as evidenced by its membership in the Organization for Economic Cooperation and Development (OECD), the North Atlantic Treaty Organization (NATO) and, especially, the Group of Seven economic summits attended by the leaders of selected major western economies.

Other aspects of contemporary political life in Canada are similar to problems faced by newer states. Until 1982, concerns were voiced over political and constitutional dependence on the United Kingdom. Economic dependence on the United States is an ongoing issue, as is the enormous debt that the state has accumulated. And internal linguistic, nationalist and regional conflicts suggest a lack of political integration typical of many countries in the developing world.

Thus, Canada may justifiably be labelled one of the "first new nations,"[1] inasmuch as it shares with many developing countries the past experience of European colonization and colonial rule before gaining independence as a sovereign state. Furthermore, in spite of its high level of economic development, Canada continues to face many of the problems of state-building and national integration suffered by newer, less affluent states in the developing world. Canada is, therefore, something of a paradox. A stable parliamentary democracy, with over a century of self-government and a highly industrialized economy, it still faces some of the difficulties of much younger states. How Canadians cope with these problems constitutes much of the subject-matter of this book and comprises the source of many challenges and issues in Canadian politics.

In this chapter, we link the past and the present, the history of yesterday with the politics of today. From a historical perspective, we outline Canada's early colonial settlement, and examine the expansion and development of the nation and the state from 1867 to the present. The many obstacles to nation-building in Canada are considered. We conclude with a discussion of how the role of the state has grown and affects the everyday lives of Canadians.

PRE-CONFEDERATION HISTORY

The development of Canada as a modern state began with the act of Confederation that united three British North American colonies — New Brunswick, Nova Scotia and Canada (East and West) — in 1867. But that act of union, and the problems that ensued in Canadian federalism, cannot be understood outside its historical context.

Early Settlement

Archaeologists have discovered traces of human life in Canada dating back as far as 30 000 years, but relatively little is known about this early pre-history. We do know that the Native Indian and Inuit populations (our First Peoples) are descended from Asiatic nomads, who probably crossed on foot from Siberia into Alaska and northern Canada during the last Ice Age. Slowly, they spread over the continent, creating diverse languages, lifestyles, and social and political structures. Most tribes were nomadic, but by 1500 AD Indian population patterns in Canada were fairly well defined. About 45 different tribes had identifiable territories.[2]

Around 1000 AD, the Vikings became the first Europeans to discover and settle briefly on the Canadian east coast, which they called "Vinland." However, not for another five centuries did

---

1. For use of the term "new nation" applied to former colonies that are now mature and affluent states, see Seymour M. Lipset, *The First New Nation: The United States in Comparative Perspective* (New York: Basic Books, 1963).

2. The first comprehensive study of Canadian Indians, Diamond Jenness, *The Indians of Canada* (Toronto: University of Toronto Press, 1932, 1977), identifies seven main groups, each associated with a particular "cultural area" or "physiographic region": Algonkian tribes of the Eastern Woodlands; the Iroquois in the St. Lawrence Valley and lower Great Lakes; the Plains tribes in the western plains; the tribes of the Pacific coast; the tribes of the Cordillera or Mountain Barrier; and the Inuit, a distinct people who migrated from Asia much later than the southern Indians. For recent literature on Native peoples, see Chapter 3.

permanent European settlements tentatively begin and eventually thrive. John Cabot first arrived on the Atlantic shores in 1497, five years after Columbus' historic "discovery," and within seven years St. John's, Newfoundland, was established as an English fishing port. The French, Portuguese and Spanish also began to use East Coast harbours as bases for the exploitation of the rich North Atlantic fisheries.

Thirty years later, in 1534, Jacques Cartier explored the coastal area, describing it contemptuously as "the land God gave to Cain." The following year, however, he discovered the Indian settlements of Hochelaga (Montréal) and Stadacona (Québec) in the St. Lawrence valley and established a French interest in this more promising region. Yet it was not until 1605 that the first French colony was established at Port Royal in Acadia. Three years later, Samuel de Champlain, the first governor of New France, founded Québec City. In the next century and a half, approximately 10 000 French immigrants arrived to settle along the shores of the St. Lawrence.

Early English settlement in North America was restricted primarily to what is now New England and the eastern seaboard of the United States, although the area around Hudson Bay was also claimed by London-based commercial interests. In the early eighteenth century, successive wars in Europe between England and France began to spill over into North America. In 1710, a combined force of British troops and American colonial militia captured Port Royal; the *Treaty of Utrecht* (1713) subsequently recognized British possession of Hudson Bay, Newfoundland and the new colony of Nova Scotia. The French retained the rest of eastern mainland Canada, Île St. Jean (now Prince Edward Island) and Île Royale (Cape Breton), which was defended by the newly constructed fortress of Louisbourg.

In 1754, war broke out again in North America. In rapid succession the British expelled the French-speaking Acadians from Nova Scotia, shipping them off to other British North American colonies, and captured both Louisbourg and the Lake Ontario stronghold of Fort Frontenac (present-day Kingston). In 1759, the forces of Wolfe and Montcalm met on the Plains of Abraham outside Québec City and the capital of New France fell into British hands. A year later, the remnants of the French army surrendered at Montréal, ending military resistance to the British conquest. The French colony was formally ceded to Britain in 1763 as part of the *Treaty of Paris*, which ended the Seven Years War in Europe. The British now controlled all of North America north and east of the Mississippi, except for the tiny islands of St. Pierre and Miquelon, which remain part of France to this day. But British domination was not to endure.

From Colony to Confederation

For over 250 years, between the establishment of the first permanent European settlements on the North American mainland and the time of Confederation, parts of what is now Canada were governed as colonies, primarily by laws made on the other side of the Atlantic Ocean. From the founding of the first French colony at Port Royal in 1605 until the British conquest of Québec in 1759, much of the future Dominion was in French hands. Although many settlers established themselves in the St. Lawrence valley and on the coasts of Nova Scotia and Cape Breton, the primary function of these colonies was to provide raw materials (especially fish and fur) to the economy of mainland France.

In serving this purpose, the colonies of New France and Acadia (now Nova Scotia) were no different from most others. A **colony**, in general terms, is an area of land geographically remote from the metropolis (the centre of the colonial power) and incorporated into the colonial empire either by right of first possession or by conquest. For the British in the mid-eighteenth century, the

French colonies of North America offered substantial natural resources. They also posed a threat to both the British colonies on the eastern seaboard of what is now the United States and the rich fur-bearing interior then owned by the Hudson's Bay Company. As an extension of repeated wars between Britain and France in Europe, Britain gradually procured, through treaty concessions and by conquest, the French colonies in North America. Along with access to the natural resources of the region, the British acquired the problem of how to deal with the French-speaking population that had settled there — a problem that grew in complexity as the number of British merchants and English-speaking immigrants to the colonies increased.

The American Revolution

In 1776, the southern colonies of British North America revolted against the British Crown in order to found the United States of America. Forty thousand Empire Loyalists, American colonists loyal to the Crown, sought refuge in the remaining British colonies, particularly in the Maritimes (where their influx resulted in the creation of the colony of New Brunswick in 1784) and in what was then western Québec (now Ontario).

The boundaries between the newly sovereign United States and the British colonies were gradually settled over the next century. The *Treaty of Paris* had established an approximate southern border for the new British acquisition of Québec between the Atlantic Ocean and the western tip of Lake of the Woods (now the Ontario-Manitoba border). Large parts of this border were subsequently adjusted by *Jay's Treaty* in 1794 and the *Webster-Ashburton Treaty* of 1842. The *Rush-Bagot Treaty* of 1817 clarified the boundary through the Great Lakes. In 1818, the *Treaty of London* fixed the westward border along the 49th parallel to the Rockies and paved the way for western settlement. The final step, to the Pacific Ocean around the southern tip of Vancouver Island, was determined by the *Oregon Treaty* of 1846. This formalized the bulk of the borders well before Confederation, but two remaining treaties settled smaller land disputes: in 1872, the San Juan Islands were ceded to the United States, and the boundary between Alaska and British Columbia was finally agreed upon in 1903. British dominion over the Arctic Islands had passed to Canada in 1880.

These boundary agreements were often preceded by disputes, but were always achieved without violence. The single major hostile outbreak between the United States and Canada was occasioned less by overt dispute over territory than by America's desire to demonstrate the complete nature of its break from Britain. Although some American leaders may have hoped that the colonists to the north would throw off British rule in order to join the United States, the War of 1812–14 was mostly an affirmation of American sovereignty against what was seen as continued British interference. First, the U.S. resented the seizure of neutral American ships on the suspicion that they were trading with the French, with whom Britain was once again at war. Second, British traders were accused of arming and inciting a potential Indian rebellion in the American midwest. Despite incursions by each side into the territory of the other, the *Treaty of Ghent* of 1814 left the pre-war boundaries intact. If the war achieved anything on the Canadian side, it was to lay the basis for a future Canadian nationalism that would come to fruition with Confederation, as well as for the periodic upsurges of anti-Americanism that still manifest themselves within Canadian political culture today.

Founding Nations: Native Peoples, French and English

Relations between the British Crown and the aboriginal population in British North America were, in the early colonial years, straightforward and accommodating. Before 1867, Indians were seen as valuable allies who helped extend the fur trade to the Pacific, and in doing so helped define the boundary between Canada and the United States.[3] Later they were allies in the struggle against threats of American incursion. The *Royal Proclamation of 1763* recognized Native land rights and described a rough "Proclamation Line" that divided hunting grounds from land that could be settled by Europeans. The Crown retained title to the land mass of Canada, but recognized the right of Native peoples to use and occupy the land. The Proclamation did not, however, state the exact eastern or western extent of the reserved lands. It was a vague document that belied the harsh treatment aboriginals would later receive.

As settlements grew and pushed farther westward, the Crown undertook separate treaty negotiations with tribes that occupied different sections of land, striking bargains concerning land use. In 1830, Indian settlement on reserves commenced under government trusteeship, and efforts began to integrate aboriginal peoples into non-aboriginal society. Meanwhile, contact with Europeans was disrupting and radically changing traditional Indian and Inuit ways of life, exposing them to European technology, religion and disease. Before Europeans arrived, there were about one million Native people in what is now Canada. By Confederation, only about 140 000 were left.

Among the Europeans, the cessation of hostilities with the United States allowed the British colonial administrators in Canada to return to the long-term problem of relations between the two European founding nations[4] of British North America. The intention of the British government in 1763 had been to promote immigration by English-speaking Protestant settlers and to assimilate the French-speaking Roman Catholic population as rapidly as possible. However, in the first few years, only about 200 English families, mostly merchants, settled in the new colony. For this reason, neither of the first two British governors was prepared to establish the representative assembly in the new colony as promised in the *Royal Proclamation of 1763*. They both considered that such a body would have represented only the 600 English settlers and not the 90 000 French who, as Roman Catholics, were excluded from the franchise under British law at that time.

With the failure of the assimilation strategy and the growing realization that French Canadian loyalty might prove vital as the southern colonies became increasingly restive, Governor Carleton persuaded the British government to revise its policy toward Québec. The *Québec Act* of 1774 withdrew the provision for an assembly, placing full authority in the hands of the governor and an appointed advisory council consisting of both English and French speakers. The French culture was to be preserved. Neither language was specifically guaranteed, but Roman Catholics were allowed freedom of worship and the right to hold civil office. The Catholic Church was given official sanction, and both French civil law and the seigneurial landholding system were retained to protect the property rights of individuals.

The decision to respect the cultural heritage of French Canada was clear, and the French population warmly approved of the Act. Many English Canadians, on the other hand, resented it. The break in the tradition of representative government in the British colonies arising from the special circumstances of a French-speaking majority was anathema to many English-speaking colonists, who felt unjustly deprived of their right to a representative assembly and British civil law — rights to which they had grown accustomed. The English merchants were slightly mollified by the expansion of the colony's boundaries to encompass the rich fur-trading area between the Ohio and Mississippi Rivers — but most of that gain was lost under the *Treaty of Versailles*, which finally settled the American War of Independence in 1783.

---

3. Randall White, *Voice of Region* (Toronto: Dundurn Press, 1990), p. 16 and ch. 2.

4. These are the people present from early settlement to 1867. It should be noted that the western provinces were later settled largely by immigrants who were not of French, English or aboriginal extraction. In this larger sense, Canada had many founding nations, including Ukrainians, Germans and a host of other ethnic groups, all of which are usually included under the English-speaking umbrella.

Partly in response to demands from the Empire Loyalists who had settled in what is now Ontario, the British next attempted to satisfy both ethnic communities with the *Constitutional Act* of 1791. This act maintained the commitment to the French culture established by the *Québec Act*, but within a new political context. The old colony of Québec was divided in two: Upper Canada, west of the Ottawa River, which was predominantly English-speaking; and Lower Canada, which was predominantly French. The right of representative government was now granted to each group and, whereas French civil law and seigneurial landholding were retained in Lower Canada, English common law and freehold land tenure were established in Upper Canada. Thus, English Canadians outside Montréal were placated and the French Canadians were largely protected from absorption and conflict.

This promising new arrangement deteriorated over the next few years as the representative assemblies grew increasingly frustrated by their lack of control over the executive. The appointed members of the governors' legislative councils often abused their privileged positions in order to enhance their personal wealth and power and paid scant attention to the elected members of the assemblies. Political and social agitation began against Upper Canada's "Family Compact" and Lower Canada's "Château Clique." Finally, open rebellion under the leadership of William Lyon Mackenzie in Upper Canada and Louis-Joseph Papineau in Lower Canada forced Britain to re-evaluate its policies.

In 1838, Lord Durham was dispatched to report on the situation and recommend a course of action. In Lower Canada, he found all the problems of the other British colonies, plus an ethnic war. Britain's approach, he decided, had been wrong; the colony of Canada should have remained united so that the French population gradually would have been assimilated. Consequently, his recommendations included reverting to the pre-1791 union and granting responsible government, which he believed would, given the first condition, function effectively.[5]

The British government did not see fit to accept Durham's philosophy wholeheartedly; instead, it took a middle course. The *Union Act* of 1840 re-established the two Canadas as one political unit (although each was to retain its own version of the law), with English as the sole official language of record. Although Durham had recommended representation by population, the two former colonies were each granted 42 members in the assembly. Canada West (formerly Upper Canada) with its lesser numbers, gladly accepted this equality of representation. Not surprisingly, however, a decade later, after rapid immigration had elevated its population to majority status, Canada West declared the allocation grossly unfair. Durham's other major recommendation, that the government be made responsible to the elected assembly, was not implemented in 1840, though it became effective in practice some eight years later. Also at this date, the English-only language policy was deemed unworkable and the two languages were declared officially equal.

Perhaps because of the half-hearted adoption of Durham's recommendations, or because of the separation of the two Canadas 50 years earlier, relations between the two founding nations did not unfold according to Durham's desires and predictions. Repeated attempts to find a workable solution to the ethnic problem showed the leadership's great determination to satisfy both cultures. From about 1849, Cabinets in the colony included representatives from both ethnic groups. Rather than a single prime minister at the head of government, there were two party leaders, one from each group, as well as separate attorneys-general to mirror the dual legal system. Some legislation applied to one or both; sometimes dual legislation was enacted. For a number of years, even the

5. Gerald M. Craig, ed., *Lord Durham's Report* (Toronto: McClelland & Stewart, 1963).

capital of the colony alternated between Toronto and Québec City until Queen Victoria settled the problem by deciding on the (then) backwoods logging town of Bytown (now Ottawa).[6]

The theory of cooperation was excellent, but the practice impossible. Soon, Montréal merchants in Canada East were openly supporting union with the United States, while George Brown's Reformers in Canada West demanded "Rep by Pop" (representation by population) and, eventually, a federal solution to the colony's governmental problems. Ethnic and religious antagonisms were exacerbated by these circumstances to such an extent that it became impossible for any government to retain the confidence of the assembly. By about 1857 the government had reached a virtual impasse. United in their common search for a solution to this political deadlock, French and English leaders came to embrace the goal of British North American unity.

Confederation

In many ways, the fulfillment of the Canadian dream was a response to events in the United States. In the mid-1860s, Anglo-American relations were at a new low and the Canadian colonies were isolated and vulnerable to attack. The American Civil War was drawing to a close and the army of the northern states would soon be available for an attack on Canada. Westward migration in the United States had become a threat to the political vacuum west of the colony of Canada. Furthermore, Britain had neither the resources nor the desire to protect these colonies from American aggression.

In 1864, therefore, after having discouraged for several years the efforts by those few Canadians who wished to have the issue of a federal union of British North America taken seriously (notably Macdonald, Cartier, Galt, Tupper, Tilley, Brown and McGee), the British government suddenly deemed it propitious to encourage Canadian unity and independence. It was recognized that if British North America were united it would be not only more economically viable and easier to defend, but also, as a self-governing dominion, more responsible for the cost of its own defence. The colonies of New Brunswick and Canada, which shared long boundaries with the United States, supported a union, but Nova Scotia, with no American border, was less easily persuaded.

The 1864 Charlottetown Conference, instigated by Nova Scotia premier Dr. Charles Tupper, was originally called to discuss the prospects for Maritime union. The Canadians invited themselves and had the agenda changed to deal with their proposals for a larger entity. The Québec and Maritime leaders were adamant that the new arrangements should be federal in order to prevent Canada West from dominating the future Dominion by virtue of its population. John A. Macdonald was willing to accept federalism as a second choice rather than delay or thwart the project on this point. Thus, Charlottetown concluded with a basic agreement that the new larger union would be a federal, not a unitary, arrangement and that another meeting would be held to discuss the details.[7]

The Québec Conference that followed in October 1864 was very brief. Within three weeks the leaders had produced the 72 resolutions that were to provide the basis for Confederation. They concluded that "the sanction of the Imperial and Local Parliaments shall be sought for the Union of the Provinces on the principles adopted by the Conference."[8] The future provinces acted in very different ways. The legislature of Canada debated at length and finally adopted the 72 resolutions by

6. David B. Knight, *Choosing Canada's Capital: Jealousy and Friction in the Nineteenth Century* (Toronto: McClelland & Stewart, 1977).

7. See Chapter 6, Figure 6.1, for further explanation of federal government, unitary government and confederation.

8. Quoted in R. MacGregor Dawson, *The Government of Canada*, 5th ed., revised by Norman Ward (Toronto: University of Toronto Press, 1970), p. 32.

a three-to-one majority (with most of the "nays" coming from Canada East). But Canada was the only colony to approve the project formally. The government of New Brunswick called a general election and was soundly defeated. Premier Tupper, afraid of similar unpopularity in Nova Scotia, avoided an assembly vote on the resolutions by introducing a motion to approve a Maritime Union. Prince Edward Island and Newfoundland rejected any association with the Conference or its proposals. Nevertheless, the Canadian group persevered and took the results of the Québec Conference to London where, this time, they received a sympathetic audience.

Although the colonies were by then internally self-governing, Britain retained direct influence over their policies through its colonial governors. Britain refused to consider Nova Scotia's stated preference for the Maritime Union, and the governors of the Maritime colonies were instructed to sway their respective political executives in favour of the proposed wider confederation. By 1866, the legislatures of both Nova Scotia and New Brunswick (the latter now under threat of invasion from the United States by the Fenians)[9] had reconsidered their earlier dismissal of the Québec Resolutions and sought a renewal of consultations toward a union with the Canadas.

In December 1866, delegates from the three participating colonies incorporated the essence of the Québec Resolutions into an act of confederation at the Westminster Palace Conference in London. The *British North America Act* was given Royal Assent on March 29, 1867, and came into effect three months later on July 1, 1867, without the colonies having any further opportunity to discuss or approve the birth of their future state.

The *BNA Act* brought into formal existence the Dominion of Canada. In light of the continuing tensions between English and French Canada, it is somewhat ironic that it was the combined leadership of the United Canadas that provided the direct impetus for Confederation. The French Canadian leaders at that time supported the federal union, although there was some disquiet within the newly created province of Québec among those who feared that the addition of the largely English-speaking Maritimes would further exaggerate the minority status of French Canadians within Canada. However, it was Nova Scotia, not French Canada, that welcomed Dominion Day in 1867 by draping the streets in black!

It should be noted that Confederation was not directly approved by the people. There was no referendum or election to determine public sentiment, nor was the omission deemed significant at the time. Confederation grew out of the gentlemanly agreement of a few men united by a noble ideal regarding the type of political system most appropriate to achieving their common goals. In the final analysis, it was a series of external circumstances that eventually allowed the Fathers of Confederation to combine their ideals with practical necessity and proceed on the path to statehood. Had these men not clung tenaciously to their dream and acted when they did, it is questionable whether the Canadian state ever would have existed. The Canadian colonies almost certainly would have been annexed or absorbed by the United States by the turn of the century. As one historian has observed, "perhaps the most striking thing about Canada is that it is not part of the United States."[10]

The union of 1867 provided immediate solutions for three major problems facing the former colonies and the British government. The reorganization of the internal government of the United Provinces of Canada (by the creation of the separate provinces of Ontario and Québec) provided relief from the political impasse there. The threat of American invasion was allayed once Nova Scotia

---

9. The Fenian Brotherhood, an organization of Irish-Americans, sought to pursue the cause of Irish independence by provoking war between Britain and the United States.

10. J.B. Brebner, *Canada: A Modern History* (Ann Arbor: University of Michigan Press, 1960), p. ix.

and, particularly, New Brunswick joined Canada and arrangements had been made to connect the provinces by rail. Lastly, the provisions made in the Act of Confederation to bring other territories into the union enabled the political vacuum west of Ontario to be filled and laid the basis for a "Dominion from sea to sea."

These tentative steps toward the development of a Canadian state were merely the beginning of a long and sometimes arduous process of territorial consolidation, national integration and state-building that is not complete even today.

THE LAND AND THE PEOPLE

The concept of a country or state embodies four interrelated ideas: a clearly defined area of territory; a set of state (or political) institutions that governs the territory and maintains both internal and external sovereignty; a given population that is subject to the state; and a sense of community or common identity ("nationhood") among that population. The Dominion of Canada founded by the *BNA Act* in 1867 was considerably smaller, in both area and population, than it is today. Consequently, before we examine the problems encountered by the new Dominion in developing a sense of "nationhood" and attaining sovereign status, we need to understand the territorial and population expansion of Canada.

Territorial Expansion

The territorial outline of the state formulated at Confederation was gradually expanded and filled in over the succeeding years. In 1670, England's King Charles II had granted all the lands that drained into Hudson Bay to a company of that name. Proceedings were initiated in 1867 to bring this territory under Canadian control, and eventually the company sold it to the Canadian government for $300 000. In 1870, both Rupert's Land and the North-Western Territory were formally annexed to the Dominion. (See Figure 2.1.) In the same year, the Red River Colony (under the new name of Manitoba) became the first additional province in the union, although it was much smaller then than today. Lured by the promise of permanent railway communications with eastern Canada, British Columbia was admitted by Imperial Order-in-Council in 1871. Two years later, the previously uninterested Prince Edward Island also decided to join.

The next major jurisdictional change occurred in 1905, when Alberta and Saskatchewan were carved out of a large portion of the Northwest Territories and granted provincial status. Seven years later, Manitoba, Ontario and Québec were allowed to annex more land from the Territories to assume more or less their current forms. The tenth and final province, Newfoundland, entered the federation in 1949, over 80 years after the original invitation and even then only after two referendums to decide its future.[11]

The rest of the land within the boundaries of the Canadian state, the Yukon Territory (created out of the Northwest Territories in 1898) and the Northwest Territories, currently remains under federal jurisdiction; however, changes are underway. In 1990, an agreement on the largest land claim in Canadian history gave about 18 000 Inuit ownership of an area about half the size of Alberta.[12]

---

11. See Henry B. Mayo, "Newfoundland's Entry into the Dominion," *CJEPS*, vol. 15, no. 4 (November 1949), pp. 505–22.

12. The Inuit relinquished title to about 80 percent of their ancestral land claim. In return they received the promise of self-government, a cash settlement of more than $1 billion over 14 years and title to 35 000 square kilometres of land in the eastern Arctic.

FIGURE 2.1   CANADA'S BOUNDARY CHANGES

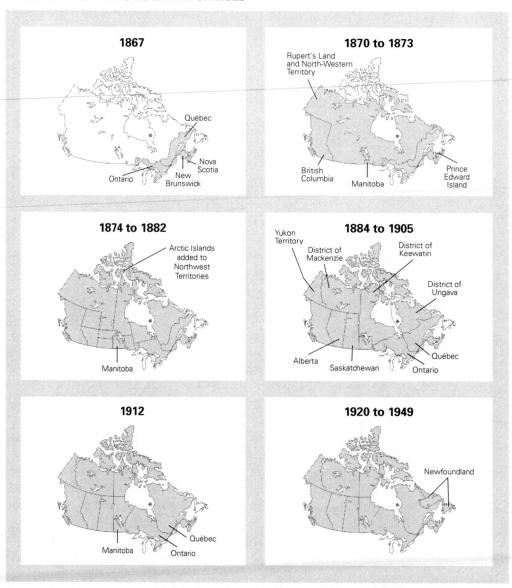

Source: Adapted from Department of the Secretary of State of Canada, *Symbols of Nationhood* (Ottawa: Supply and Services, 1991), p. 16. Reproduced by authority of the Minister responsible for Statistics Canada, 1993.

Shortly after, in 1992, a political accord made provisions to divide the Northwest Territories and create a new territory, Nunavut ("our land" in Inuktitut). This was accomplished in April 1999. (See Figure 2.2.) The territory will employ laws and services inherited from the Northwest Territories government until its own arrangements are complete. It is anticipated that by the year 2008 the Nunavut government will achieve full powers along the lines of the Northwest Territories legislature in Yellowknife. Inuit constitute about 85 percent of the new territory's population, so they will have virtual self-government. However, less than half the population of the Northwest Territories (which previously had a 61 percent Native majority) now consists of Native peoples (Dene, Métis and Inuit).

FIGURE 2.2   MAP OF NUNAVUT

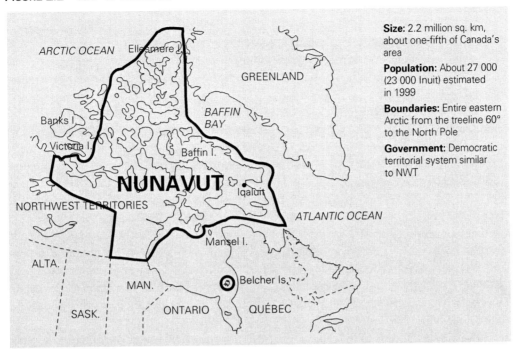

Size: 2.2 million sq. km, about one-fifth of Canada's area

Population: About 27 000 (23 000 Inuit) estimated in 1999

Boundaries: Entire eastern Arctic from the treeline 60° to the North Pole

Government: Democratic territorial system similar to NWT

Nunavut — the new territory carved from the Northwest Territories. The division created three northern territories: Yukon, Northwest Territories and Nunavut. The area of Nunavut is twice the size of British Columbia, but its entire population would not fill half of Toronto's 50 000-seat SkyDome.

Canada's external boundaries have therefore changed very little since shortly after Confederation. Except for the later addition of Newfoundland, all of Canada's current territory was formally part of the Dominion by 1873. Thus, the territorial development of the Canadian state has been primarily a process of internal adjustment: creating or admitting new provinces and territories, or extending the boundaries of existing ones. But, as a number of contemporary political issues would suggest, this process is not necessarily complete. There is, for example, a lingering boundary dispute between Québec and Newfoundland over the status of Labrador. Québec has never accepted the 1927 decision of the Judicial Committee of the (British) Privy Council that gave more than 260 000 square kilometres of Labrador to Newfoundland. As well, maritime boundaries have taken on new importance in recent years, with ownership of potentially huge reserves of offshore oil and natural gas at stake.[13]

In addition, Canada has been, and continues to be, subject to the regionalist and nationalist territorial strains often observed in states with multi-ethnic populations. In particular, recurring secessionist aspirations of dissatisfied groups in Québec impose a certain degree of doubt on the long-term integrity of Canada's external boundaries. If Québec did separate, what would its boundaries be — those in existence at the date of its independence, or those it originally brought to Confederation in 1867? This is discussed further in Chapter 7.

---

13. Some significant changes have occurred regarding maritime boundaries. Following incidents with an American oil tanker in the early 1970s, Canada extended its territorial waters from 3 miles to 12 miles — so that waters within 12 miles now have the legal status of land (except for right of innocent passage for foreign ships). At the same time, the *Arctic Waters Pollution Prevention Act* unilaterally gave Canada the right to create environmental regulations within a 100-mile zone (but did not provide sovereign control). Finally, in 1977, Canada declared a 200-mile Economic Fishing Zone.

Population Growth

At the time of Confederation, the population of the member provinces totalled approximately 3.5 million people. The number of Canadians has steadily increased to over 30 million people. As the size of the population has grown, so too has its ethnic diversity. Today, Canada is regarded by many as a multi-ethnic or multicultural society, a view given formal recognition in the new Constitution of 1982.

This was not always the case. In 1763, when the French colony in North America was officially ceded to Britain by the *Treaty of Paris*, the total European population of what is now Canada was under 100 000. The vast majority were French Canadian descendants of immigrants from the old France to the new. By 1812, partly "as a result of one of the highest birth rates in recorded history,"[14] the French Canadian population of Lower Canada had reached about 330 000; but the number of English-speakers had also increased rapidly, swelled by immigration from Britain and by the large influx of Loyalist settlers from the United States into Upper Canada and the Maritimes. After further immigration from Britain, the United States and Ireland, the English-speaking population reached parity with the French and then surpassed it. In 1867, the new province of Ontario was the most populous of the four founding provinces of Confederation, and the predominantly French-speaking majority in Québec constituted only about one-third of the total population of Canada. New aboriginal populations were gradually absorbed, including Pacific Coast Indians, tribes of the Yukon and Mackenzie basins, and the Inuit.

Even when referring to the time of Confederation, it would be a misleading oversimplification to see Canada's population purely in terms of the two founding European nations or, as John Porter labelled them, "the charter groups."[15] For one thing, the English-speaking segment was by no means homogeneous, consisting as it did of immigrants from England, Scotland and Ireland and their descendants, the descendants of the Empire Loyalists, and many subsequent settlers from the United States who had migrated north in search of farmland or employment offered by the economic expansion of Canada West. Even among those who had migrated directly from the British Isles there were profound differences. For instance, many of the Scots and Irish settlers were Catholic, not Protestant, a distinction that proved a source of conflict in Ontario and the Maritimes. Religious division was reflected in the creation of denominational schools and "a whole network of colleges, newspapers, hospitals and charitable and welfare institutions" that served to separate Catholics of both language groups from Protestants in everyday life.[16] Furthermore, many of the Scots and Irish immigrants originally spoke Gaelic rather than English, and although their descendants have long been assimilated into the English Canadian linguistic majority, small enclaves preserving the Gaelic language and culture have survived, especially in Newfoundland and Cape Breton.

Second, as the census of 1871 illustrates, although members of the two charter groups constituted over 90 percent of Canada's population at that time, representatives of other ethnic groups were already becoming established or had been previously established in the new Dominion. In addition to the Native peoples, both Indian and Inuit (about 0.7 percent of the total population), there were nearly 30 000 Dutch (0.9 percent), over 200 000 Germans (5.8 percent), and a smattering of other

---

14. Ramsay Cook et al., *Canada: A Modern Study* (Toronto: Clarke, Irwin and Co., 1963), p. 21.

15. John Porter, *The Vertical Mosaic: An Analysis of Social Class and Power in Canada* (Toronto: University of Toronto Press, 1965), p. 60 ff.

16. Kenneth D. McRae, "Consociationalism and the Canadian Political System," in McRae, ed., *Consociational Democracy: Political Accommodation in Segmented Societies* (Toronto: McClelland & Stewart, 1974), p. 243.

ethnic minorities, including some American Blacks (chiefly in Nova Scotia and southwestern Ontario) who had arrived around the same time as the Loyalists.

Since Confederation, the population of Canada has grown rapidly through a combination of natural increase (the excess of births over deaths in any given period), a generally high rate of immigration and, to a lesser degree, the incorporation of new territory (for instance, approximately 360 000 people were added to Canada's population by the accession of Newfoundland in 1949).

Immigration Trends

Canada is a settler society. The early colonists were all immigrants: the French settled Québec, the British colonized the Maritimes and what is now Ontario, the Loyalists followed. Each group multiplied; the population of Canada in 1867 consisted largely of their descendants. Although much of Canada's population growth may be ascribed to natural increase, after Confederation the new Dominion sought more immigrants to settle the vast western spaces uninhabited by Europeans. As new immigrants and their descendants helped swell Canada's population after Confederation, the ethnic composition of the Canadian population began to change. Although English-speaking immigrants from the British Isles and the United States continued to form the largest groups, other Europeans arrived in increasing numbers. Significant concentrations of Germans, Dutch and Scandinavians were present by 1900; they were joined in the early decades of the twentieth century by Eastern Europeans, chiefly from Poland and Ukraine. After 1945, large numbers of new Canadians came from countries devastated by the Second World War, especially Germany, Italy, the Netherlands and Eastern Europe.

After 1962, when the regulations were changed to eliminate explicit discrimination on the basis of race or nationality, the preponderance of English-speaking and European immigrants began to decline. Previously, the only significant groups of non-white immigrants were from China and Japan. By the late 1970s, over one-quarter of new immigrants came from Asian countries (Hong Kong, India, the Philippines and China among them), and there were also significant increases in the numbers entering from Africa, South and Central America and the West Indies. Today, over 17 percent of Canada's population are immigrants, nearly half of whom have lived here more than 20 years. (See Figure 2.3.) In 1995, about 212 000 immigrants came to Canada. Immigration is discussed in more detail in Chapter 3.

As a consequence of changes in immigration patterns over the last century, Canada today is a truly multicultural society. In 1871, 61 percent of the population was of British origin, 31 percent French. In the 1996 census, 17 percent of Canadians who claimed a single ethnic heritage said they were of British origin, 14 percent said French. Apart from these two large groups, the census also categorized over 100 smaller ethnic groups. Interestingly, 29 percent claimed their single ethnic origin simply as Canadian.

Furthermore, despite the bicultural image projected by conflict between the two major language groups, Canada is a "nation of many tongues." Although the 1996 census showed that about 62 percent of Canadians had English or French as the language first learned in the home, the remaining 38 percent

Citizenship Oath:

I swear (or affirm) that I will be faithful and bear true allegiance to Her Majesty Queen Elizabeth the Second, Queen of Canada, Her Heirs and Successors, and that I will faithfully observe the laws of Canada and fulfil my duties as a Canadian citizen.

Citizenship Act (6)

FIGURE 2.3   IMMIGRANTS AS A PERCENTAGE OF TOTAL POPULATION

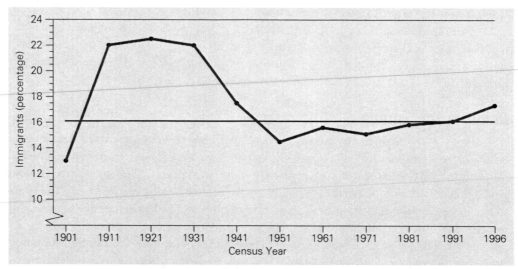

Source: Reproduced from Statistics Canada, *The Daily*, Catalogue 11-001, December 8, 1992.

cited over 70 other languages. The integration of this multicultural and multilingual population into Canadian society and the creation of a common sense of national identity and political community have posed additional challenges for the development of the Canadian state.

Demographic Trends

From Confederation to today, Canada's population grew from 3.5 million to over 30 million. It continues to grow at slightly more than one percent per year; about two-thirds is caused by natural increase and one-third by immigration. The country is projected to have 37 million people by 2016.

As we have noted, the population is extremely concentrated and highly urban. It is concentrated in three ways: 90 percent live in a 320-kilometre strip along the Canada–United States border; about 60 percent live in central Canada in Ontario and Québec; and over three-quarters of Canadians live in metropolitan areas. Thirty-three percent live in the country's three largest cities: Toronto, Montréal and Vancouver. (See Figure 2.4.)

Three basic variables affect demography: fertility, mortality and immigration. As in other developed countries, Canadian fertility rates began to decline in 1961 after the baby boom of the late 1940s and 1950s. The average number of births per woman is 1.64. The highest fertility rates correlate with several different variables: women who marry young; women who remain married the longest; women who live in rural areas; women who are not well educated; and women who work in the home. Given current social patterns, these variables indicate that low fertility rates will continue in the near future.

Mortality rates are also changing. The average life expectancy at Confederation was about 45; in 1997 it was closer to 79. Women live six to seven years longer than men. The lowest life expectancy correlates with several specific groups: unskilled and blue-collar workers; the unmarried; and Native Indians. In 1996, more than three-quarters of a million Canadians were over 80 years old — twice as many as 25 years earlier.

Immigration has played a vital role in Canada's development. Canada has one of the largest proportions of foreign-born residents of any country in the world — double that of the United States.

FIGURE 2.4   POPULATION DISTRIBUTION IN CANADA, 1951 AND 1995

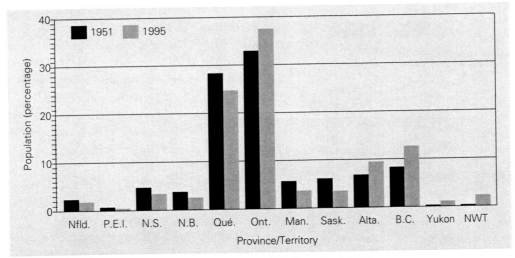

Source: Adapted from Statistics Canada, *The Daily*, Catalogue 11-001, December 8, 1992.

Internal migration, too, has played an important role in Canada's demography. Canada has a very mobile population, enabling swift population changes in response to challenging economic circumstances, although most of the migration is generated by a small minority of the population.

In overall composition, Canada's population is now "middle aged" and aging rapidly. In 1881, the median age was 20; by 2001 it will be over 30. This trend is due mainly to declining fertility and the stabilization of a low birth rate.

For a more complete picture of the Canadian population, these demographic facts must be combined with social stratification data. This is discussed in detail in Chapter 4, but here we should note that social class can be characterized by such variables as economic circumstances, education and occupation. Canadians as a whole have experienced an absolute increase in real wealth in this century and, as we saw in Chapter 1, they are also very well-off compared to citizens of other countries. This rosy picture masks a plethora of problems. (See "Age Cohorts and Public Policy.") Real incomes have declined dramatically in the last decade, and there are significant inequalities of opportunity and distribution of wealth in Canada.

THE DEVELOPMENT OF THE CANADIAN NATION

Most analysts agree that two factors — successful national integration and a clearly defined and legitimate role for the state — are prerequisites for the emergence of stable political systems.[17] In ideal

17. For example, Gabriel Almond and G. Bingham Powell, *Comparative Politics: A Developmental Approach* (Boston: Little, Brown, 1966); Karl Deutsch and William J. Foltz, eds., *Nation Building* (New York: Atheston Press, 1966); Samuel Eisenstadt and Stein Rokkan, eds., *Building States and Nations*, 2 vols. (Beverly Hills and London: Sage Publications, 1973). For studies of older "new nations," see Kenneth D. McRae, "Empire, Language, and Nation: The Canadian Case," in Eisenstadt and Rokkan, eds., *Building States and Nations*, vol. 2, pp. 144–76; Lipset, *The First New Nation*.

CLOSE-UP ON
Demography

AGE COHORTS AND PUBLIC POLICY

In his book *Boom, Bust and Echo*, David Foot illustrates how the birth rate, the number of women in childbearing years and immigration patterns can be used to understand Canadian society. A very large cohort of children — known as baby boomers — were born between 1947 and 1966. This rise was caused by the return of Canadian troops from the Second World War and the large influx of young immigrants. Later, in the period 1967–79, the number of children born declined dramatically due to changing values concerning women, economic hard times and new technology. This cohort is often called the "baby bust." Beginning in 1980, a new rise in the number of births took place as the large number of boomers began to have children, creating a small "baby echo" in recent years.

Many observers are concerned about the ramifications of this "aging" Canada. The first baby boomers turned 50 years of age in 1997 and at the turn of the century many millions of them are approaching retirement. By 2041, almost one in four Canadians will be of pensionable age. Because of the lower number of births in later years, the number of young people working to support the number of old people in retirement (known as the dependency ratio) will decline. Recent changes to the federal government's old age pension programs and dire warnings about future reductions are tied to this situation.

How many people will you have to support when you are in the labour force? How many are you prepared to support? How much of your taxes should go toward supporting seniors?

Source: David K. Foot, *Boom, Bust and Echo* (Toronto: Macfarlane, Walter & Ross, 1996).

terms, the development of a sense of national identity among the inhabitants of a territorial state — otherwise known as **nation-building** — increases the sense of loyalty and legitimacy accruing to that state. The state thus replaces region, church or ethnic group as the primary focus of citizen allegiance, reducing the number and intensity of potential sources of conflict within the population.

The establishment of the second factor — called **state-building** — similarly involves integration and consolidation. Again in ideal terms, the imposition of the supreme authority of state institutions and laws throughout the land integrates the various parts of the state's territory into a single cohesive unit and guarantees its domestic sovereignty — that is, its authority over and above the rival claims of other internal sources of political influence. In addition, the state requires external sovereignty, which frees it to manage its own affairs, independent of constraints imposed by any other country.

We have already referred to the regional, religious and ethnic conflicts, and to the problems of geographic diversity and external influence, that hampered the formation of a sense of national integration and state-building in Canada. The remainder of this chapter examines the impact of these factors on Canada's progress since Confederation toward the "ideal-typical" model of an integrated and sovereign modern state.

Problems of Nation-Building in Canada

The concept of national identity is rather like a coin in that it too bears two sides. The "heads" of the national identity coin consists of a sense of belonging together in a single political community, while the "tails" represents a sense of distinctiveness from all other peoples. In different countries and different periods, one side or the other will predominate. It sometimes seems that in the case of Canada there is a distinct bias in favour of "tails."

On one side of the coin, the emergence of a separate Canadian identity has largely involved a process of differentiation from the United Kingdom and the United States. The need for Canadians to cut the colonial ties that bound them to the United Kingdom in the nineteenth and early twentieth centuries has more recently transformed into the problem of establishing a Canadian identity and culture distinct from that of the United States.

The other side of the coin, the development of a sense of belonging together, has been hindered by several obstacles: the historic conflict between English-speaking and French-speaking Canadians; the definition of a satisfactory relationship with aboriginal peoples; the integration of minority ethnic groups into the community; and the pervasive effects of regionalism, exacerbated by the federal nature of the political system, the uneven distribution of economic activity and the peculiar configuration of settlement in Canada. Many aspects of each of these problems will be examined in greater detail in other parts of the book (notably, Chapters 3, 4, 6 and 7), but an overview linking the various obstacles to nation-building in Canada is provided here.

External Impediments

The American Revolution and the entry of the Empire Loyalists into the northern colonies marked the initial differentiation of Canada from the United States, based on loyalty to the British Crown and Empire. The identification with Britain was further strengthened by the successful defence of Canada in the War of 1812 and by massive immigration from Britain in the next few decades. As Kenneth McRae argues, "the literature of the period suggests that they [the newcomers] did not see migration as involving a change of allegiance. They remained simply British subjects who lived in the colonies."[18]

Canadian Confederation was "largely a response to the American presence; as a defence strategy, as imitation, and as a general alternative."[19] Faced with a potentially expansionist United States, the Fathers of Confederation were motivated by "the fear of slow death by absorption and a quick one by annexation [that] hung over Canadian constitutional debates."[20] The British, for their part, were increasingly unwilling to devote resources to the defence of their North American colonies and were happy to give self-government to a new Dominion whose inhabitants remained loyal to the Crown and the Empire. Indeed, for many Canadians of British stock, there appeared to be little conflict in values between the new Canadian nationality created at Confederation and continued loyalty to the British Empire — a dual allegiance that remained widespread, although dwindling, among English Canadians up to the First World War.

Since 1920, this duality has gradually declined in favour of a more exclusive identification with Canada. Growing national consciousness has been bolstered by the adoption of specifically Canadian national symbols, such as the Maple Leaf flag to replace the Red Ensign, the substitution of "O Canada" for "God Save the Queen" as Canada's national anthem and, most recently, the patriation of the "made in Canada" Constitution. A degree of imperial and monarchical sentiment lives on, partly because of reinforcement by continued immigration from the United Kingdom and by the activities of organizations such as the Imperial Order of the Daughters of the Empire and the Monarchist League, and partly because remnants of the Tory and Empire Loyalist traditions remain as components of Canadian political culture. A movement pressuring to depose the Queen as head of state and to make Canada a republic has never taken hold here as it has in Australia. But these elements aside, the separation of the Canadian national identity from British influence is complete.

In the eyes of many Canadians, a more pressing concern today is the need to emphasize Canada's distinctness from the United States. Although Canadians no longer fear direct military annexation by the Americans, concern is now directed toward economic and cultural penetration of Canada by its much larger neighbour. Economic relations, including Canada's trade dependence on the United States, American ownership of Canadian industry and natural resources, and the impact of economic interdependence promoted by the North American Free Trade Agreement (NAFTA) are among the major foreign policy issues examined in detail in Chapter 15. But, just as important for many Canadians, and more pertinent to the present discussion, is the issue of cultural independence from the United States.

It is, of course, difficult to separate the economic from the cultural dimensions of Canada-U.S. relations, since the concern for cultural independence seems to mirror economic realities. Since

---

18. McRae, "Empire, Language, and Nation: The Canadian Case," p. 149.

19. John H. Redekop "Continentalism: The Key to Canadian Politics," in Redekop, ed., *Approaches to Canadian Politics*, 2nd ed. (Scarborough: Prentice Hall Canada, 1983), p. 35.

20. Janet Morchain, *Sharing a Continent* (Toronto: McGraw-Hill Ryerson, 1973), p. 108.

the Second World War, the United States has been responsible for well over 70 percent of foreign investment and simultaneously has been viewed as a major cultural threat. Concern over assimilation into America, or continental North American culture, waxes and wanes. The proximity of most Canadians to the border with the United States, the existence of a shared language, the relative size of the two populations, and the penetration of Canadian society by American mass media and other culture-bearers are all viewed as potential threats to the emergence or maintenance of a distinct Canadian identity. Some observers suggest that a determination to resist total cultural assimilation remains a fundamental component of the Canadian national identity.

Internal Impediments

There are several *internal* impediments to nation-building in Canada, all of which have been present to different degrees since 1867.

First, a harsh conflict between English and French Canadians has surfaced on numerous occasions since Confederation. The execution of Louis Riel, the conscription crises of 1917 and 1944, the October Crisis of 1970, the exclusion of Québec from the constitutional settlement of 1982, and the failure to resolve the constitutional dilemma with either the Meech Lake or Charlottetown accord are among the low points in relations between the two charter groups. (For details, see Chapters 5, 6 and 7.) No satisfactory long-term *modus vivendi* has ever been apparent between the

Nation-state building requires political co-operation.

Rodewalt illustration, originally published in *Policy Options*.

founding nations. Today, the Parti Québécois and the Bloc Québécois officially espouse separation from the Canadian state and the foundation of an independent, sovereign state of Québec.

Second is the question of integrating non-charter, ethnic groups into Canadian society. To a degree, government policies and popular support for multiculturalism have allowed each ethnic minority to preserve its own cultural identity and heritage while it becomes part of Canada's social tapestry. A few minority groups, such as the Sons of Freedom sect of the Doukhobors, have refused to acknowledge the sovereignty of the Canadian state. However, the general pattern among immigrants has been one of willingness to concur with the norms of their host society. In turn, the host society usually has been willing to accept them. However, examples of both institutionalized (governmental) discrimination and public racism, even racial violence, have surfaced at various periods of Canadian history.

Perhaps the most disruptive impact of minority ethnic groups on nation-building in Canada has occurred with respect to the French–English relationship. The fact that, until recently, the majority of new immigrants have tended to learn English rather than French as their first official language, even in Montréal, has exaggerated the minority status of French-speaking Canadians in Canada and exacerbated relations between the two charter groups.

Third, Canada's Native peoples, for a long time, were deliberately excluded from the nation-building process. The expansion of the Canadian colonies and state in the nineteenth century brought Native and European groups into direct competition for possession of land. Following the conquest of Québec, the British authorities made repeated attempts to accommodate the interests of the French-speaking population but they demonstrated little regard for the rights and customs of Canada's aboriginal peoples. Successive colonial and, later, Dominion administrations deprived the Indians of their land (by fair means or foul) as part of the process of opening up western Canada for settlement and railway construction, herding them onto reserves and subjecting them to the draconian, paternalistic measures of the nineteenth-century Indian acts. (See Chapter 3.)

Although some of the more discriminatory provisions of the legislation pertaining to Native people have since been relaxed — for example, after 1960 Indians on reserves were at last allowed to vote in federal elections — status Indians still occupy a dependent, quasi-colonial position *vis-à-vis* the federal government. Non-status Indians and Métis who attempt integration into mainstream society usually find themselves among the poorer and under-privileged sections of the Canadian population, often being subject to discrimination and racial stereotyping.

Because of their geographical isolation the Inuit were largely bypassed in the process of nation-building and modernization until about four decades ago. Like status Indians, the Inuit, until 1950, were explicitly excluded from the federal franchise. Even then, many Inuit living in the high Arctic could not actually exercise their right to vote until 1963, following the creation of a new parliamentary riding covering the entire Northwest Territories. From 1953 to 1962, there was a constituency of "Mackenzie River," which excluded the territorial districts of Keewatin and Franklin. From 1963 to 1979, the "Northwest Territories" riding covered all three districts. After the 1979 general election, the NWT was represented by two members of Parliament, one for "Western Arctic" and one for "Nunatsiaq." In addition, in 1975 the NWT and Yukon were finally given representation in the Senate, one senator each. Finally, in 1999, when Nunavut and its new government were inaugurated, the new territory was represented in the federal Parliament by one MP (the former Nunatsiaq representative) and one senator (like the other territories).

During the past five decades, the Inuit have been forced into co-existing with an advanced industrial society within the Canadian state. Their traditional lifestyle has been encroached upon by attempts to develop Arctic energy and other mineral resources and by the construction of the Distant Early Warning (DEW) line of radar stations and other military installations. Many Inuit, like the

Indians, are resentful of the disruption of their customary mode of life by modernization and economic development.

For Native organizations such as the Inuit Tapirisat of Canada or the Dene Nation, minority status and the lack of institutionalized channels have made it difficult to compete within the established mechanisms of federal/provincial negotiation. It is perhaps not surprising that some Native groups feel themselves to be non-participants in the Canadian state, and actively oppose further modernization and development.

Fourth in this examination of the impediments to nation-building in Canada comes regionalism. Regionalism is not a new phenomenon in Canada. Even in pre-Confederation days there was little contact between the colonies of British North America. The events leading up to the establishment of the Dominion suggest profound regional differences in attitudes toward the founding of the Canadian state. Today, well into the second century of Confederation, many of those differences and local interests continue to exist.

The persistence of regionalism within the Canadian state can be ascribed to several factors, such as the sheer size of the country, the very different historical backgrounds of the provinces and their populations, and the uneven development of economic activity across Canada. The regions have separate economic interests to advance and protect. Thus, there are several economic bases for regional conflict: oil-producing versus oil-consuming regions, agricultural versus industrial areas, resource-rich versus poorer provinces, among others.

Another factor that promotes regionalism in Canada is the country's peculiar pattern of settlement, with 90 percent of the population clustered within a strip 320 kilometres wide extending along the American border. One result is that, unlike in many other western societies, there is no single centre of population concentration to serve as a cultural and economic core. Nor is there a dominant city in Canada. Rather, Canada has a "polycephalic" city network, with several regional centres (Halifax, Montréal, Toronto, Winnipeg, Calgary, Vancouver, etc.) as the political, economic, social and cultural foci for the populations clustered around them. Instead of possessing a single metropolis dominating and easing the integration of the peripheries of the state (such as Paris and London), Canada consists of a series of core–periphery (or city–hinterland) relationships that divide the country into more or less self-contained regions and communication networks.

Even within central Canada (that is, Ontario and Québec), which is sometimes portrayed as the centre in relation to the peripheries of east and west, no dominant city emerges. Ottawa is the political capital of Canada, but little else; Toronto is the economic and cultural centre of Ontario, as well as a provincial capital; Montréal is the economic core of Québec and the cultural centre for French Canadians; Québec City is increasingly viewed as the political capital by Québec nationalists. Clearly, none of these can claim to dominate central Canada, let alone the whole country.

The federal system of government compounds the effect of this core–periphery network. Regional interests are primarily articulated by provincial governments in competition with each other and with the federal government. It is this factor that is chiefly responsible for the frequent equation of "regions" with "provinces" in Canada. But the representation of regional interests by provincial governments exaggerates differences between regions and understates intra-regional variations. Richard Simeon, for one, has argued that the provincial governments have a "vested interest in maintaining and strengthening the salience of the regional dimension"; each one, therefore, "is motivated to accentuate the degree of internal unity, and to exaggerate the extent of difference with Ottawa."[21] Thus, while Canada's federal system was intended to reflect and take into account the

---

21. Richard Simeon, "Regionalism and Canadian Political Institutions," in J.P. Meekison, ed., *Canadian Federalism: Myth or Reality*, 3rd ed. (Toronto: Methuen, 1977), pp. 301–2.

diversity among the original provinces, it has perpetuated, institutionalized and exacerbated regional differences and conflicts among the members of the Canadian federation.

A final factor contributing to the persistence of regional particularism in Canada is the absence of nationally oriented mass media that, according to many theorists, often serve as an integrative force. Where the media focus is upon local news about political and social issues, there is little opportunity for the consumer to acquire knowledge about other parts of the country or to learn what people elsewhere think about his or her own region. Despite their best efforts, the Canadian mass media have provided little nationally integrative force. (See Chapter 4.)

We conclude that a number of factors combine to ensure the persistence of regionally based attitudes and interests in Canada: the sheer size of the country, historical patterns of ethnic settlement, variations in economic activity and wealth, uneven population distribution and the polycephalic city network, the institutionalization of regional differences by the federal system and the vested interests of provincial governments, and the lack of information and awareness of the regions of Canada about one another and about national affairs. The results are that Canadians often do not share a strong sense of belonging together, and regional or provincial interests frequently take precedence over those of the state.

Nation-Building and Contemporary Politics

Canadians today have, on the whole, accepted that their country is a country of differences. This willingness to accept diversity may well be one of the distinguishing marks of the Canadian national identity — a contrast to the pressures toward conformity that characterize many other national cultures, in particular the United States. However, potential dangers lie in store for the Canadian state when these latent cleavages become politicized.

Some of the most bitter recent debates among Canadian politicians, including the long-drawn-out and bitter wrangling over the Constitution, reflect the persistence of divisions among regions and between the two founding nations. Concern about anglophone oppression, real or reconstructed, fuels the nationalist aspirations of the Parti Québécois in its quest to lead Québec out of Confederation. Although based on a sense of physical and political marginality rather than ethnic discontent, similar resentment against "the Centre" or "the East" underlies potential problems in the West. Furthermore, a combination of regional economic disparities, perceived historical grievances and (in some cases) a sense of physical remoteness often exacerbates tensions among the provinces and between the provinces and the federal government.

Relations between the various levels of government and tensions with Native populations also reflect the impact of what might be called "the unfinished nation-building process" on contemporary politics. The relative isolation of most indigenous groups, whether on reserves or in the far North, is gradually being broken down by the expansion of state activity and by the ongoing process of economic development. Native people have increasingly been drawn into the mainstream of economic and political life. As they have become more politicized, they have introduced new political issues with which governments are inadequately prepared to cope. Consequently, pressures for and conflict over self-government and the settlement of Native land claims are likely to continue in the new millennium.

In a country as large and diverse as Canada, it may be unrealistic to expect the process of nation-building to eradicate all differences or integrate all disparities. As we argue in Chapter 3, certain overarching values and attitudes shared by all Canadians have developed that counterbalance the potentially disintegrative effects of ethnic and regional differences. But the historic rivalries remain and threaten to tear the country apart. In Chapters 6 and 7, we discuss in detail the continued impact of these divisions upon the contemporary politics of Canadian federalism. Perhaps, when all is said and done, one of the fascinations of Canadian politics is the fact that Canada has survived for as long as it has, despite the persistence of strains and conflicts left unresolved in the nation-building process.

THE DEVELOPMENT OF THE CANADIAN STATE

Perhaps the most distinguishing characteristic of a state is its geographical territory. By 1873, Canada's borders were established virtually as they are today, with the exception of the Alaska–British Columbia boundary, drawn in 1903, and the addition of Newfoundland in 1949. But, while the boundaries of the Canadian Dominion were defined early in its history, the acquisition of sovereignty over the territory enclosed by them was a somewhat slower process.

The major task was to establish external sovereignty. This process was naturally linked to Canada's gradual acquisition of independence from Britain. In fact, the goal of external sovereignty existed even before Confederation, as the elected assemblies of the British North American colonies strove for responsible self-government within the context of Britain's colonial administration. Progress was slow. Between 1758 (in the case of Nova Scotia) and 1791 (Lower Canada), each colony was granted what might be called a popularly elected assembly. But the early years of these assemblies saw them dominated by their respective governors and their appointed executive and legislative councils.

By the time Lord Durham recommended the political union of Upper and Lower Canada under "responsible government" in his 1838 *Report*, the governors' power was under strenuous attack. Although the first of Lord Durham's recommendations, the *Act of Union*, was implemented by the British government, the second, responsible government, was initially ignored. But the first governor of the new united colony of Canada, Lord Sydenham, combined his gubernatorial duties with those of prime minister and leader of his own party of adherents, appealing directly to the population to provide his followers a majority in assembly elections. This practice was followed by other colonial governors and eventually proved to be counter-productive, since elections confirmed that power resided, in part at least, in the people, and not solely in the Crown. **Representative** government, thus, arrived with the acceptance that the legislative branch must be representative of the citizenry.

In 1846, a change in the British government produced an administration more sympathetic to responsible government in the colonies, and newly appointed governors of Canada and Nova Scotia were instructed in 1847 to select their councils from the leaders of the majority factions or parties in their respective assemblies. Within a year, non-confidence motions passed in the popular assemblies resulted in changes of ministries in united Canada, Nova Scotia and New Brunswick.

In this fashion, the principle of **responsible government**, whereby the governor retained his advisors only as long as they were collectively able to retain majority support in the assembly, became established in British North America. The next stage in the development of representative and responsible self-government occurred over the next decade with the effective separation of the political executive ("Cabinet") from the formal executive (the governor). Governors increasingly absented themselves from the deliberations of their political advisors, while acting on their recommendations.

Thus, even before Confederation, the Canadian colonies had achieved a moderate degree of self-government by developing responsible government and parliamentary democracy. But their assemblies and governments were not sovereign; there were constraints upon their autonomy and on the supremacy of their parliamentary institutions. When the British North American colonies were each granted assemblies in the eighteenth century, they were given the power to legislate on local matters, subject to two conditions: first, that they did not attempt to enact laws having effect outside their territorial boundaries; and second, that their laws did not contravene the established laws of England.

Obstacles to the outright independence of governmental institutions continued, even after the creation of the new Dominion in 1867. First, legislative competence within Canada was divided between two different levels of government, federal and provincial. This in itself did not directly affect the external sovereignty of the Canadian state, but it did have an indirect impact: neither the federal division of powers nor any other provisions of the *BNA Act* could be amended by any Canadian legislature, only by the British Parliament. Moreover, the creation of separate fields of legislative competence had important and restrictive consequences for internal state-building.

As well, certain matters were withheld from all levels of government in Canada. In particular, legislation having extraterritorial effect (such as laws pertaining to copyright or merchant shipping) was reserved exclusively for the British Parliament. Similarly, the Canadian government was not regarded as an independent actor in the world of international relations. Canada was effectively an appendage of Britain when it came to the conduct of diplomatic affairs, which remained the exclusive preserve of the British government.

Third, even within the legal competence of Canadian federal or provincial legislatures, parliamentary supremacy could be overridden by the powers of reservation given to the Governor General and the Lieutenant-Governors (as representatives of the Crown in Canada) and by the powers of disallowance retained by the British government.

These factors and others (for example, the retention until 1949 of the Judicial Committee of the Privy Council in the United Kingdom as the highest court of appeal, a device that permitted substantial outside meddling in Canada's internal affairs) combined to maintain Canada in quasi-colonial relationship with Britain long after Confederation.

External Sovereignty and Its Constraints

In the present century, however, two major periods of constitutional change, some 50 years apart, have served to secure Canada's *de facto* and *de jure* independence from the United Kingdom.

The first series of events involved the Imperial Conferences of 1926 and 1930, culminating in the 1931 *Statute of Westminster*. At the Imperial Conference of 1930, the disallowance and reservation powers of the British government and the Governor General were declared constitutionally obsolete. They had, in any case, long ceased to be of much practical relevance. The **Statute of Westminster** paved the way for the Dominions to emerge as independent foreign-policy actors by stating that a Dominion Parliament had full power to make laws having extraterritorial operation.[22] A further provision of the Statute laid down that the British Parliament no longer had the right to legislate for any Dominion except at the request of the Dominion concerned — for example, by way of a petition to amend the *BNA Act*.

These changes highlight the role of the *Statute of Westminster* as the watershed between the effective ending of colonial status for Canada and its emergence as a more or less independent state. According to the historian A.R.M. Lower,

---

22. It should be remarked that, a few years earlier, Canada had already negotiated and signed its first treaty with the United States, the *Halibut Treaty* of 1923, after the King gave specific permission to do so.

> *the Statute of Westminster came as close as was practicable without revolutionary scissors to legislating the independence of the 'Dominions'. There is good ground for holding December 11, 1931 as Canada's Independence Day, for on that day she became a sovereign state.*[23]

Further colonial remnants were removed in 1949. That year the Supreme Court replaced the British Judicial Committee of the Privy Council as Canada's highest court of appeal. In addition, the *British North America Act* (No. 2) of 1949 permitted the Parliament of Canada to amend certain portions of the Act without recourse to Westminster. However, in order to achieve fundamental constitutional reforms, it was still necessary for the Canadian government to go cap-in-hand to Westminster to ask for amending legislation from the British Parliament. While Westminster was traditionally willing to accede to any such requests from Canada, the necessity remained a limitation to Canada's self-determination.

Thus, one of the dominant political issues of the 1970s was Prime Minister Pierre Trudeau's crusade to patriate the Canadian Constitution — a quest that finally came to fruition with the passage of the *Canada Act* by the British Parliament in 1982. This Act gave effect to Canada's request for Britain to consent to the *Constitution Act, 1982*. At last, Canada, like other sovereign states, had its own Constitution and was able to determine its internal political structure without reference to external authorities. In formal terms at least, it was the year 1982, over half a century after the *Statute of Westminster* and 115 years from Confederation, that marked the final stage in Canada's evolution from colony to sovereign state.

This final, formal severance of ties with the United Kingdom did not mean, however, that Canadian governments could do just as they please. In the modern era, increasing interdependence among states and their economies has severely constrained the capacity of governments to act independently of all external pressures. This is especially the case for countries that have a high degree of economic integration with a larger, more powerful neighbour.

While Canada is a genuinely sovereign state in international law, the nature of its relationship with the United States imposes limits upon government policy-making. Canada's defence policy is conducted within the context of the NATO alliance, in which the United States is the largest single actor — a position it uses to attempt to sway the policies of its partners. Canadian fiscal and budgetary policies are heavily influenced by American interest rates and by capital flows between the two countries. Energy and industrial policies have to take into account American ownership of Canadian branch-plants and American investment in Canadian resources. The success of Canadian environmental policy depends partly, for example, upon the extent to which American governments can be persuaded to impose their own controls on the emission of industrial pollutants. As well, large international corporations have acquired more economic power than most governments. Thus, contemporary issues of external sovereignty now revolve, not around Canadian–British, but around Canadian–American relations (to be further examined in Chapter 15).

Internal State-Building in the Nineteenth Century

In contrast to the long, drawn-out process of Canada's acquisition of external sovereignty, the initial stages of internal state-building were quite rapid. After the political unification of the original

---

23. Arthur R.M. Lower, *Colony to Nation: A History of Canada*, 4th ed., revised (Don Mills, Ont.: Longmans Canada, 1964), p. 489.

provinces in 1867 and the subsequent expansion of Canada's territory, it was imperative to integrate this vast area into a governable political entity. The three major components in this late-nineteenth-century integration process were the imposition of law and order over the entire territory, the development of means of transportation and communication, and attempts to create a viable national economy.

One of the key characteristics of the modern state is the government's ability to ensure that its laws are obeyed and, where necessary, to utilize its monopoly of the legitimate use of physical force in order to maintain its authority. Since the birth of the Dominion, Canadian governments have not been averse to using large-scale coercion when deemed necessary. On at least four occasions — the Riel Rebellions of 1870–71 and 1885, the Winnipeg General Strike of 1919, and the 1970 October Crisis — large numbers of police and troops were mobilized to crush perceived or actual uprisings against the Canadian state.

One year after Confederation, the federal government created the Dominion Police to enforce laws in central and eastern Canada. The major symbol of central authority in the west of Canada in the late nineteenth century was the red coat of the Mountie. Four years after the annexation of lands from the Hudson's Bay Company in 1869, the North-West Mounted Police force (later combined with the Dominion Police to become the Royal Canadian Mounted Police, or RCMP) was created to impose a uniform code of law on the territories. The Mounties were responsible for keeping the peace in all federally administered lands from the American border to the Arctic and between Hudson Bay and the Rocky Mountains. The RCMP still maintains a federal presence throughout Canada. In addition to its tasks of enforcing federal laws everywhere, acting as the sole police force in the two remaining territories and, until recently, providing Canada's internal security, the force is under contract to perform police functions in every province except Ontario and Québec and in a vast number of municipalities.

The second medium of internal state-building in the new Dominion was the improvement of transportation and communications among its provinces and regions. An efficient system of transportation was necessary for security purposes, for economic reasons, and for the movement of people, mail and other sources of information. In the second half of the nineteenth century, the most efficient form of transport for all such purposes was the railway. Thus, one of the conditions under which New Brunswick and Nova Scotia were willing to join Confederation was that a railway be built to link Halifax and the Saint John valley to the St. Lawrence. The construction of this "Intercolonial Railway" was enshrined in the original *BNA Act* as one of the duties of the Dominion government.[24]

Transportation became even more of a challenge as the Dominion spread from sea to sea. The building of a transcontinental railway consequently became one of the most important political issues and objectives of Canada's first 20 years. Through a mixture of government intervention and private enterprise, Canada's railway system slowly took shape, highlighted by the completion of the transcontinental Canadian Pacific Railway when the famous "last spike" was driven in 1885.[25]

Railway construction was also very much a part of the third aspect of nineteenth-century state-building. The so-called "National Policy," first publicized by John A. Macdonald in the general election campaign of 1878, became the basis for Canada's economic development for the next 50 years. The **National Policy** consisted of three interrelated objectives: the development of a comprehensive

24. *British North America Act*, section 145 — repealed in 1893 after the government had fulfilled its duty.
25. See Pierre Berton's popular histories *The National Dream: The Great Railway 1871–1881* and *The Last Spike: The Great Railway 1871–1885* (Toronto: McClelland & Stewart, 1970 and 1971).

railway system; the opening up of western Canada by encouraging immigration, settlement and agriculture on the prairies; and national economic development by protecting Canadian industries through an external tariff.

In order to realize the dream of a Dominion stretching *a mare usque ad mare*, and also to forestall the danger of United States expansion into western Canada, it was deemed necessary for Canadians to populate the vast open plains between Manitoba (at that time little more than the area around Winnipeg) and British Columbia. The government therefore opened the door to immigrants, largely from Central and Eastern Europe, who were willing to settle and farm on the prairies, and gave them land grants and financial aid to help them become established. The railways were of great importance to such settlement, particularly for the transportation of wheat and other prairie products to consumer markets in the East and to the coasts for export abroad.

At the same time, the Macdonald government attempted to develop other sectors of the Canadian economy. In particular, the high rate of emigration from Canada in the 1870s brought home the realization that Canada required secondary or manufacturing industries to provide jobs for its non-agricultural labour force. But such emerging industries required protection from more advanced foreign competition. Interprovincial tariffs had already been removed to aid the free flow of raw materials and goods within Canada. Now, as the third plank of the National Policy, the government imposed an external tariff designed to reduce the flow of imports (especially certain manufactured products) into the country. The tariff did aid indigenous economic development in certain industries. As well, in combination with the new railways, it increased the volume of east–west trade within Canada at the expense of north–south trade with the United States.

The National Policy was an explicit attempt by Canadian governments of the late nineteenth century to enhance the economic and political integration of the Dominion. To a certain extent, it was as important for its symbolic contribution to nationalism and independence as for its contribution to Canada's economic development; in fact, its economic impact has often come under critical re-evaluation by historians and political scientists.[26] But the National Policy is also noteworthy in that it represented the first major incursion of the state into economic life in Canada.

The Growth of the State in the Twentieth Century

One important trait of the modern state has been its inexorably expanding significance in the lives of its citizens. Whether this phenomenon is referred to as the growth of the state, the growing sphere of government or the enlargement of the public sector, it is common to all countries, particularly the industrial societies of the western world. In the second half of the nineteenth century, when the Canadian state began to take shape, the role of government was everywhere more limited than today. The main functions of central state institutions were to provide for external defence and the maintenance of internal law and order, to conduct foreign policy and trade relations, to manage the currency and the national debt, and to oversee certain services such as the postal system and harbour and navigation facilities. Additional tasks were performed by local or municipal authorities: building and maintaining roads, ensuring a water supply, and employing local law enforcement officers. Municipalities might also provide for some elementary education and minimal health-care and social services, although these were more often the preserve of private, charitable or religious organizations. In brief, in the nineteenth century, there were no major welfare state programs.

---

26. For an overview of the critiques of the National Policy, see Michael Bliss, "'Rich by Nature, Poor by Policy': The State and Economic Life in Canada," in R.K. Carty and W.P. Ward, eds., *Entering the Eighties: Canada in Crisis* (Toronto: Oxford University Press, 1980); and Wallace Clement and Glen Williams, eds., *The New Canadian Political Economy* (Kingston and Montréal: McGill-Queen's University Press, 1989).

By contrast, contemporary states, including Canada, offer free primary and secondary education to all students and subsidize university and college education; provide massive medical care, unemployment and old-age pension programs; and have become involved in a wide variety of other social welfare policies ranging from family allowances to low-cost public housing. In addition, the state has become increasingly important in the economic sphere: as an owner and entrepreneur in resource development, transportation and other nationalized industries; as a regulator of both the public and the private sector; and as a manager of the national economy, through economic and regional planning, intervention in the capital and credit markets, budgetary policy and its own spending decisions. Consequently, in some western societies, total government expenditure per annum near the end of the twentieth century exceeds 50 percent of the total national income.

This last point raises the question of how the growth of the state can be measured in real terms. As the state has expanded its activities, so government expenditure has grown. Of course, even if a government continues to perform exactly the same functions over time, expenditure in money terms will increase as the cost of goods, labour and services purchased by the government also grows. Therefore, when an attempt is made to measure the growth of government (and the growth of the state) in real terms, it is usually expressed as a proportion of the country's gross national product (GNP), its gross domestic product (GDP) or some other indicator of national income, expenditure or product.

As well, the growth of the role of the state can be measured in terms of the increase in governmental activities: the number of new government programs, new laws and regulations, and new statutes establishing new public corporations or nationalized industries. A third way of expressing the growth of the state is in terms of the actual size of government, that is, either the number of governmental organizations or the percentage of the labour force employed by the state. Lastly, these government activities and employees must be paid for; the state must have revenues in order to meet its expenditures. Thus, a final indicator of the growing role of the state is the size of government revenues, especially those accruing from the taxation of individual and corporate citizens.

The Extent of the State in Canada

Internal state-building in Canada since the National Policy has been more complex than in many other states because of the federal nature of the political system. Rather than a simple one-to-one relationship between unitary state and society, Canadian state-building has consisted of a trilateral relationship among society, federal institutions and the set of provincial governments. Competition between the particularistic objectives of province-building and the centralizing bias of federal state-building has aggravated existing regional conflicts and the broader context of federal/provincial relations. Despite these complexities, political institutions have assumed an increasingly activist role in Canadian society and the economy.

The initial thrust of state intervention in Canada was primarily economic. As the example of the National Policy indicates, the role of the state was originally conceived as one of indirect intervention (through taxes, land grants and so on) to provide the infrastructure and other conditions conducive to private sector economic development. In the twentieth century, however, the state has intervened more directly in the economy, especially through public ownership of Crown corporations. The federal government takeover of Canadian National Railways in 1917 was followed in the 1930s by the establishment of the Canadian Radio Broadcasting Commission (now the CBC), the Bank of Canada and Trans-Canada Airlines (later Air Canada); more recent examples include Atomic Energy of Canada Limited (1952), Telesat Canada (1969) and Petro-Canada (1976). Moves by Brian Mulroney's government (1984–93) to reduce the role of the federal government considerably altered this original pattern (see Chapter 14).

Reproduced with permission, Dennis Pritchard.

While Canadian state institutions have a long history of intervention in the economic sector, the development of social policies leading to the current welfare state system occurred relatively late. This tardiness has been attributed to many factors: the delayed nature of Canada's industrial revolution; the weakness and late emergence of the working class as an organized political force; the strength of the business community in restricting the role of the state to promotion and protection of its own interests; and the peculiarly Canadian form of conservatism, which reconciles strong state leadership of the economy with private responsibility (through family or community) for individual social welfare. It is not surprising that many innovations in social policy were initiated by provincial governments in the prairies, where frontier isolation created a somewhat more collectivist culture.

Although some programs had been introduced earlier (for example, workers' compensation in almost every province by 1920 or the federal government's old-age pension legislation of 1927), it was not really until the period between 1930 and 1945 that the Canadian welfare state began to take shape. The combined impact of the Depression and the Second World War created a climate more conducive to social intervention by both federal and provincial governments. A number of factors have been cited as contributing to this change: the growing militancy of western farmers and industrial workers in the Depression; the threat posed to government parties by the electoral successes of the Co-operative Commonwealth Federation (CCF) in the early 1940s; the inability of municipalities and private welfare agencies to cope with the demand for relief during the Depression; the emergence of a more collectivist national spirit induced by the shared tribulations of economic disaster and world war; and reduced opposition from a business community that saw that its interests might be served, rather than hampered, by welfare legislation. At first, the federal government provided a series of temporary relief measures to alleviate poverty in the Depression, but more permanent legislation followed, especially in the fields of unemployment insurance (1940) and family allowances (1944).

Since the Second World War, both federal and provincial governments have introduced many programs into the welfare state system, including health-care plans and hospital insurance, the Canada and Québec Pension Plans, housing policies, grants for higher education and guaranteed income supplements, among others. As a percentage of national income, total government spending at all levels on welfare state policies (health, education and social welfare) approximately tripled from the end of the Second World War until the 1990s. But from a state-building perspective, it may be argued that it was in the decade preceding 1945 that the major shift in perception of the role of the state occurred, allowing Canada to join the ranks of other "welfare societies." At that time, Canadians began to view poverty less as a sign of individual weakness, and more as a social problem whose alleviation could be beneficial to the rest of society and that therefore could be regarded as a responsibility of the Canadian state.

Once governmental responsibility for social welfare functions was accepted, as it had already been for economic development, the last major step in the state-building process was accomplished. Since that time, the role of the state (or "government," or "public sector") in Canadian society has continued to expand, with minor reversals. Whether the size of the state is measured by the proportion of national income spent by governments, the number of laws and regulations, or the number of public servants, twentieth-century Canada differs greatly from the nineteenth-century laissez-faire state.

Summary

Politics is more than the product of historical, social and economic forces. But these forces do influence political life, and the historical development of the Canadian state and its people continues to have a profound impact on Canadian politics.

Many of the major issues and conflicts emerging from the processes of nation-building and state-building in Canada have been only partially resolved. Consequently, some of the most contentious subjects of debate in the political arena today have their origins in the strains and antipathies created by the evolution of the state. Furthermore, these same strains often hamper the reconciliation of other, apparently unrelated disputes among actors in the Canadian political system.

Even the final settlement of Canada's sovereign status *vis-à-vis* the United Kingdom served to exacerbate tensions. The proclamation of Canada's new Constitution on April 17, 1982, was accompanied by political controversy and acrimony in parts of the country. Thousands of Québécois joined René Lévesque at a Montréal demonstration to protest Québec's exclusion from the constitutional accord between the federal government and the nine other provinces. Later, in October 1995, Québec nationalist aspirations were almost fulfilled when an independence referendum came within about half a percentage point of permanently dividing the country. In the same vein, Indian organizations, whose demands for the entrenchment of Native rights in the 1982 Constitution had not been fulfilled, also boycotted the patriation ceremonies in Ottawa and declared that any Indians celebrating the event were committing treason against their nation.

With regard to internal nation-building, conflicts among regions or provinces continue to intrude on the political agenda. Jurisdictional disputes, especially over ownership and control of natural resources, exacerbate federal/provincial relations. Attempts to reduce regional economic disparities are frequently declaimed as unfair by the "have" provinces and inadequate by the "have-nots." The politicization of Native movements adds another new dimension to contemporary regional and ethnic politics in Canada. Despite all these differences, however, the country stays together, united by the almost indefinable sense of "being Canadian."

Lastly, the growth of the Canadian state from the nineteenth-century National Policy to the present day has also provided a subject for political debate. Today, conservatives argue that governments are too large and too interventionist, while socialists condemn them for not being active enough. Meanwhile, provincial governments criticize debts and budgetary deficits, simultaneously protesting cutbacks in federal contributions to provincially managed programs such as health care and higher education.

Many of the major issues in contemporary Canadian politics have their source in the origins, expansion and development of the state over the past 300 years. Furthermore, the attitudes, myths and grievances that evolved from the nation- and state-building experience profoundly affect the approach of contending sides to other, less directly related questions. Those attitudes and myths are examined in more detail in the next two chapters. The purpose of this chapter has been to draw together the various strands of Canadian historical evolution in order to provide a base from which to commence the exploration of politics in Canada.

DISCUSSION QUESTIONS

1. Can you find in pre-Confederation history the roots of political problems that remain unresolved in Canada today?

2. In what ways has the ethnic composition of the Canadian population changed since Confederation?

3. What is sovereignty? What are the main historical steps since Confederation that have made Canada a sovereign country?

4. How and why has the Canadian state grown in the twentieth century?

Selected Bibliography

Brooks, Stephen, *Canadian Democracy: An Introduction* (Toronto: McClelland & Stewart, 1993).

Bumstead, J.M., *The Peoples of Canada*, 2 vols. (London: Oxford University Press, 1993).

Clement, Wallace and Glen Williams, *The New Canadian Political Economy* (Montréal: McGill-Queen's University Press, 1989).

Foot, David, *Boom, Bust and Echo* (Toronto: Macfarlane, Walter & Ross, 1996).

Gibbins, Roger, *Conflict and Unity: An Introduction to Canadian Political Life* (Scarborough: Nelson, 1994).

Howlett, Michael and M. Ramesh, *Political Economy of Canada* (Toronto: McClelland & Stewart, 1992).

Johnson, David, *Public Choice: An Introduction to the New Political Economy* (Toronto: McClelland & Stewart, 1993).

Kaplan, William, ed., *Belonging: The Meaning and Future of Canadian Citizenship* (Montréal: McGill-Queen's University Press, 1993).

Williams, Glen, *Not for Export: Toward a Political Economy of Canada's Arrested Industrialization* (Toronto: McClelland & Stewart, 1993).

LIST OF WEBLINKS

www.nlc-bnc.ca/ confed/e-1867.htm

Canadian Confederation This site provides useful information about Canadian history and Confederation.

www-nais.ccm.emr. ca/wwwnais/select/ethnic/ english/html/ethnic.html

Canadian Ethnic Diversity Map This Web site provides maps of the ethnic composition of Canada.

npc.nunavut.ca/eng

Nunavut Planning Commission The structure and organization of the new territory of Nunavut are presented at this site.

cicnet.ci.gc.ca

Canadian Department of Citizenship and Immigration This is the Web page for the Canadian Department of Citizenship and Immigration.

PART
2

Culture

. . . .

Government and politics exist within the context of culture and society, where they are nourished by ideas, people and events, and shaped by various accidents of history, of geography, and even of climate and natural resources. Governments reflect the political ideas and interests of the people they serve. The internal cleavages and conflicts that exist in society are played out on the public stage of politics and government.

Part 2 focuses on the cultural environment of government and politics. Canadian society is like a tapestry with three primary interwoven strands. One consists of the shared ideas and aspirations that draw Canadians together. Another strand is the major ethno-linguistic groups—French- and English-speaking Canadians and Native peoples. The third comprises the country's major regions. These three strands of society should be viewed in the context of the larger picture. Separating one from the rest and focusing only on it weakens one's understanding of the whole tapestry.

Canadians acquire political ideas from the ethno-linguistic, class and gender groups in which they live. They also learn their political ideas from institutions such as the educational system, the media and even government. Yet, these socialization mechanisms are all limited in their ability to unify the country.

3

The Fabric of Canadian Society

· · · · · · · ·

Ethno-Linguistic and Regional Cleavages

Certain myths about Canada and Canadians are common in foreign countries, some based on reality, some not. These include conceptions of Canadians as a solid, stolid, northern, reliable, prosperous, tough, not sexy people blessed by good government and policies and one of the world's greatest police forces.[1] At home, Canadians often characterize themselves as modest, hard-working, tolerant peace-keepers who distrust personal achievement among their peers. Potential Canadian heroes are regularly cut down to size. The story is told of a Nova Scotia fisherman who observed some lobsters, several of which appeared to be trying to climb out of a pail. "These are definitely Canadian lobsters," he concluded. "One is trying to crawl out so the rest are trying to pull it down."

This chapter looks beyond such impressionistic generalizations in the search to learn in a systematic way who Canadians are and what motivates them to act politically. It examines the attitudes and values that Canadians hold about themselves, their country and their system of government, all of which in turn affect their political behaviour.

Citizens of all countries develop perceptions and expectations of what their political system can and should do for them, and what obligations they have in return. This interaction provides the value structure within which political decisions are made. It delineates the accepted parameters of government and individual political activity, and enables organizations and institutions to function coherently.

The political culture of Canada is like a colourful tapestry. A tapestry is composed of different strands or elements. Only when these basic units are interwoven and viewed together as a whole is the unique design of the tapestry visible. This chapter examines three main strands of Canada's political culture in order to achieve a more meaningful view of the whole. But first, the concept of political culture must be clarified.

---

1. See, for example, "The Maiden Aunt among Nations," *International Herald Tribune*, Paris, November 1, 1979.

WHAT IS POLITICAL CULTURE?

Political culture is one of the most controversial concepts in political science. The term was first coined in the United States in the 1950s and only later applied in Canada.[2] It has been defined in a multitude of ways.

We use the term **political culture** in this book to refer to the broad patterns of individual values and attitudes toward political objects. These may be concrete objects such as government institutions or national symbols such as the flag, but they may also be intangibles such as power. In the latter case, it is important to understand how Canadians perceive the distribution of power between themselves and government, and what institutions or positions they view as the greatest sources of political power. Students of political culture, therefore, attempt to determine the degree of the individual citizen's knowledge and awareness of the political system, as well as the attitudes held about politics and political objects and the perceptions of the personal role in societal affairs.

Political culture, though but a small part of the general culture of a society, serves many purposes: it draws individuals together; supports thought, judgement and action; constitutes the character and personality of a community; differentiates it from other communities; and encourages its members to seek common objectives. What citizens know and feel about their political system affects the number and kinds of demands they make on the system and also their responses to laws and political leadership. Political culture renders the government's decision-making processes acceptable by demarcating the boundaries within which the government can legitimately act.

Understanding the relationship between political culture and the political system assists in identifying and appreciating how political change can be effected. The extent to which values and beliefs are shared greatly affects the degree of national cohesion and stability in a country. Deep cleavages within a state over such issues as language or economic well-being obstruct the sharing of values and beliefs and contribute to political instability. Knowledge about the political attitudes of individual citizens helps to predict their political actions both inside the system, through such means as voting, and outside the electoral process, through demonstrations, strikes and, even, violence.

The study of political culture is a multidisciplinary endeavour to which political science, sociology and psychology all contribute. Citizens' beliefs and values that formerly were ignored by political scientists are now scrutinized to determine their effect on voting behaviour and other forms of political participation or non-participation.

Political culture studies in Canada have been influenced, among others, by the empirical work of Gabriel Almond and Sidney Verba, American pioneers in the field. These political scientists conducted the first statistically based, cross-national study of political beliefs, symbols and values in an attempt to measure and compare national political attitudes.[3]

In the course of their study, these specialists encountered serious difficulties with survey research, not all of which have been resolved. For example, large-scale opinion surveys and interviews are extremely expensive to administer and difficult to interpret. The answers elicited are not always truthful or thoughtful and can be influenced by temporary events or personalities, and so may

---

2. The concept was first introduced by Gabriel Almond in "Comparative Political Systems," *Journal of Politics*, vol. 18, no. 3 (August 1956), pp. 391–409; reprinted in Gabriel Almond, *Political Development* (Boston: Little, Brown, 1970). For a concise history of the term "political culture" and its application to the Canadian situation see David Bell and Lorne Tepperman, *The Roots of Disunity*, 2nd ed. (Toronto: Oxford University Press, 1992), ch. 1.

3. Gabriel A. Almond and Sidney Verba, *The Civic Culture* (Boston: Little, Brown, 1965). See also Gabriel A. Almond and Sidney Verba, eds., *The Civic Culture Revisited* (Boston: Little, Brown, 1980).

not reflect deeply held beliefs on which people will act. As well, an empirical approach to comparing states is limited because it lacks a historical or contextual dimension and therefore fails to recognize the constantly changing nature of political culture. Nevertheless, Almond and Verba effectively demonstrated that national cultures vary considerably with regard to beliefs about government and politics, and that these beliefs affect essential aspects of political behaviour.

As we shall see, social scientists have studied Canadian political culture in quite different ways. Some have employed empirical methodology, using surveys and questionnaires to learn about mass attitudes and behaviour. Others have carried out more qualitative research on the historical development of political ideas. Although they cannot be compared directly, and each has shortcomings, both methods contribute to an understanding of the Canadian political system.

THE THREE STRANDS OF CANADIAN POLITICAL CULTURE

We now return to our analogy of Canadian political culture as a tapestry composed of separate but interwoven parts. We can identify three major strands. For the sake of simplicity, in this chapter, the subject of political culture is divided into three sections that correspond to those three strands.

The first section examines Canadian political culture in terms of the values and attitudes common to *all* citizens of the state, searching out the roots of the Canadian heritage. It attempts to determine whether there is a common ideology behind Canadian political thought and, if so, what its origins may be. This broad level of interpretation also considers what characteristics distinguish Canadians from citizens of other countries. These pan-Canadian attitudes and values reveal one strand of Canadian political culture.

The second section examines the most important subcultures created by *ethnic* and *linguistic* cleavages in the country. The literature dealing with this strand of political culture focuses on three distinct groups: (1) the French Canadian community, whose cultural and linguistic differences are reinforced by historical, geographical and economic circumstances; (2) the broad range of members of ethnic and visible minorities who constitute the "English-speaking" sector, as it is generally called because of the official bilingual status of the country; and (3) the aboriginals who constitute yet another subculture of the Canadian community.

The third section examines *regionalism* in Canada. Regional boundaries may vary from one academic study to another, but they often coincide with political boundaries. The values and beliefs Canadians hold about their political system are conditioned by the distinct geographic and economic characteristics of the region in which they live. People of different origins and interests settled in areas that offered greatly varied resources and potential for industrial development. Canada's federal system of government has helped to reinforce and perpetuate these regions. We consider how distinctive the regions are, and what evidence exists that there are several geographically based political cultures in Canada.

Because political values and beliefs are far from uniform across the state, some scholars argue that there is no such thing as a Canadian political culture, but rather there are several cultures based on ethnic or regional divisions. This chapter argues that regional and ethnic political subcultures do exist, but that they are tied together by the overarching values of a national culture. We examine the three strands of Canadian political culture under three headings: nation-state political culture, ethno-linguistic political culture and regional political culture.

NATION-STATE POLITICAL CULTURE

Nation-state political culture encompasses the values and attitudes that pertain to the entire Canadian political system. These include traditions of personal freedom and civil liberties, respect for the law, and co-existence of heterogeneous communities that underlie the political system. Deep historical roots anchor these political ideas.

Ideology and Political Culture

There are a few classic arguments about what traditional values form the base of Canada's political system. Before we consider them, it is important to clarify the confusion that sometimes arises between the terms "political culture" and "ideology." Both refer to political attitudes, values and beliefs, but ideologies are more coherent and explicit.[4] As used in this book, ideology is narrower in scope than political culture. **Ideology** refers to an explicit doctrinal structure, providing a particular diagnosis of the ills of society, plus an accompanying "action program" for implementing the prescribed solutions. Political culture, on the other hand, refers to vaguer, more implicit orientations whether or not they embrace any explicit, formal ideology.

Within Canadian society, for example, we can identify certain ideologies — socialism, conservatism and liberalism among them. Liberalism and conservatism originated in Europe in the nineteenth century as philosophers and thinkers struggled to create logical and consistent patterns of thought about how to restructure the medieval social and political order that new technological developments were rendering obsolete. **Liberalism** became the ideology of the rising commercial class, while **conservatism** justified the positions of the aristocracy and Church. Both ideologies spawned political parties. Liberal thought became dominant in the western world in the latter part of the nineteenth century, and for that reason some view the nineteenth century as the century of liberalism. **Socialism** developed slightly later, but, again, in response to fundamental changes in society: the technological advances of the industrial revolution had brought the growth of a large urban working class that existed in wretched conditions. Socialists sought to ameliorate the lot of these workers. By the beginning of the twentieth century, the ideological and party battlefield was a three-way contest as the socialist ideology produced socialist, labour and communist parties in Europe.

There are several competing interpretations about the origin of political thought in Canada. Louis Hartz's book *The Liberal Tradition in America* is a source of many ideas concerning the traditional attitudes that underlie Canadian political culture.[5] This volume was published in 1953, before the popularization of the concept of political culture. Consequently, the word "ideology" is used in this and subsequent writing on the topic in a way that differs from the usage here — not as an action-oriented system of ideas, but as a relatively vague set of attitudes that form the foundation of political culture. Had the systematic discussion of political culture begun a decade earlier, Hartz and other authors might have substituted "political culture" for "ideology." As it is, much of the literature that followed Hartz, and that is discussed here, uses the latter term in the loose sense of a set of general principles.

4. See Bell and Tepperman, *The Roots of Disunity*, ch. 1, for a brief examination of the concept of ideology as used by Karl Marx and Karl Mannheim.
5. Louis Hartz, *The Liberal Tradition in America* (New York: Harcourt Brace & World, 1953).

The thesis put forward by Hartz, and later expanded by Kenneth McRae,[6] is that North America, like other societies founded by European settlement, is a "fragment society." According to Hartz, the New World societies based their political cultures on single European ideologies brought as "cultural baggage" during colonization. Immigrants to the new land did not represent all elements of the society that they had left. Institutions and myths set up and passed on by the founding peoples perpetuated those beliefs and values. McRae argues that, because it has two founding nations, Canada is a classic instance of a "two-fragment" society.

The settlers in New France represented one fragment, the feudal strain from France. As a result, a kind of "feudal catholicism" dominated rival ideologies there, and excluded others through expulsion or assimilation. The second fragment, English Canada, was very similar to its liberal American counterpart. English-speaking immigrants were predominantly liberal. In pre-revolutionary United States, the liberalism of the philosopher John Locke became the prevailing ideology. The beliefs of which Locke was the primary spokesman were based on the importance of the individual, free enterprise and the right of the individual to pursue personal interests without government interference. Loyalists who flooded into Canada at the time of the American Revolution brought these liberal values with them — along with strong anti-American, pro-British sentiments.

The differences that developed between English Canada and the United States were subtle and minor, according to Hartz and McRae. In both cases, the liberal ideology had "congealed" before socialism developed in Europe; therefore, socialism did not take hold in North America. Liberal thought, with its belief in maximizing individual freedom and satisfaction of private desires, is widely diffused and dominant in the political culture of English North Americans. However, Hartz, McRae and others argue, Canadian thought is more conservative and collectivist than that of the United States.[7] For instance, Canadians feel strongly that the state is responsible for its citizens and is obligated to provide for their collective well-being. Americans, on the other hand, believe in noninterference by the government and the primacy of individual liberties.

George Grant, writing on this matter, lamented the widespread diffusion of liberal thought in Canada. He warned that the triumph of liberalism over conservatism and socialism in Canadian society represents the defeat of Canadian nationalism because it brings total conformity with the ideological structure of the United States.[8] Others have argued that Canadian anglophones have never been able to accept liberal ideology totally, because it was the natural culture of the Americans. They see the tension between adhering to the British connection and fostering antipathy toward the American culture, which was ideologically very similar to Canada's own, as the origin of a serious identity crisis for Canadians.[9]

Hartz's "fragment" theory of political culture considers the culture of founding groups as a kind of "genetic code," one that does not determine, but rather imposes boundaries on, later cultural developments. This approach offers the advantage of historical depth, since political thought is viewed as a phenomenon that develops over time, rather than being static. A drawback is that it

6. Louis Hartz, ed., *The Founding of New Societies* (New York: Harcourt Brace & World, 1964). See McRae's analysis in "The Structure of Canadian History" in Chapter 7. See also Kenneth D. McRae, "Louis Hartz's Concept of the Fragment Society and Its Applications to Canada," *Canadian Studies/Études canadiennes*, vol. 5 (1978), pp. 17–30.
7. Gad Horowitz, "Conservatism, Liberalism and Socialism in Canada: An Interpretation," *CJEPS*, vol. 32, no. 2 (May 1966), pp. 143–71. See also Horowitz, "Notes on 'Conservatism, Liberalism and Socialism in Canada,'" *CJEPS*, vol. 11, no. 2 (June 1978), pp. 383–99.
8. George Grant, *Lament for a Nation: The Defeat of Canadian Nationalism* (Toronto: McClelland & Stewart, 1965).
9. Bell and Tepperman, *The Roots of Disunity*, ch. 3.

fails to explain how fragment cultures survive, how they are transmitted to new immigrants and new generations. Why, for example, did new immigrant groups not establish new competing cultures? This question is considered in the next chapter.

Part of the Hartz and McRae thesis has been challenged by Gad Horowitz, who maintains that the respective heritages of Canada and the United States indeed are very different because Canadian liberalism had not "congealed" before British and European immigrants arrived in Canada in the late nineteenth and early twentieth centuries, bringing with them newer ideas from the old societies.[10] The fact that a socialist movement grew illustrates that, unlike the United States, Canada has had an enduring, though small, socialist "fragment." Thus, political thought in Canada was not totally buried beneath an unqualified liberalism. Even among the English-speaking group, Horowitz maintains, there is no single dominant ideology.

In another study, Roger Gibbins and Neil Nevitte find that Americans display "far greater attitudinal coherence, and stronger ideological linkages among sets of attitudes," than do English-speaking Canadians. Québec francophones diverge even more from Americans in that they demonstrate the "virtual absence of an ideological right." The authors maintain that their study provides evidence that the political culture of the United States "is more ideologically structured than that found in English Canada, and even more so than that found in francophone Québec."[11]

Other authors, such as Seymour Martin Lipset, conversely stress the conservative inheritance of the Canadian political culture.[12] Using census data and a comparative framework comprising the United States, Britain, Australia and Canada, he concludes that Canadian values are generally conservative, closer to those of Europeans than Americans. He bases this conclusion on evidence that Canadians are more elitist than their American neighbours. For example, he finds that, compared to the United States, Canada has a much lower *per capita* crime rate, and less political corruption — both of which facts, he believes, might be traced to elitist values.[13] Many of Lipset's conclusions about Canadian values are currently being challenged by other scholars, such as Neil Nevitte. (See "Value Changes," page 72)

Lipset credits Canadian–American differences to very different "formative events" in the history of the two countries. He notes that Canada became independent through evolution, the United States through revolution. Canada had a relatively civilized westward expansion, not a "wild west." Religious traditions, too, differed: Canada was settled predominantly by Anglicans and Roman Catholics rather than by Calvinists and fundamentalists.

Colin Campbell and William Christian have added to the debate by rejecting the view that the Canadian ideological system congealed in the way suggested by either McRae or Horowitz.[14] They maintain that the Loyalists introduced strains of Tory thought into English Canada. The Loyalist presence shifted the patterns of settlement in subsequent years so that more liberally inclined immigrants went to the United States, while more conservative individuals chose to remain under the British Crown. Close ties with Britain reinforced this Tory strain. Of course, French Canada was even further

---

10. Horowitz, "Conservatism, Liberalism and Socialism in Canada."

11. Roger Gibbins and Neil Nevitte, "Canadian Political Ideology: A Comparative Analysis," *CJPS*, vol. 18, no. 3 (September 1985), pp. 577–98.

12. Seymour Martin Lipset, "Revolution and Counterrevolution: Canada and the United States," in O. Kruhlak et al., eds., *The Canadian Political Process: A Reader* (Toronto: Holt, Rinehart and Winston, 1970), pp. 13–38.

13. Lipset, "Revolution and Counterrevolution," p. 19.

14. William Christian and Colin Campbell, *Political Parties and Ideologies in Canada: Liberals, Conservatives, Socialists, Nationalists,* 2nd ed. (Toronto: McGraw-Hill Ryerson, 1983).

removed from the liberalism of John Locke. "Many of the immigrants to New France had left France at a time when liberal ideas were virtually nonexistent, and hence they brought with them to the new land an attitude to the state and to the society which was more tory/feudal than liberal."[15] As for Canadian socialism, Campbell and Christian contend that it was indigenous, a natural product of the post–First World War Depression.

In yet another approach to the topic, Gordon Stewart traces the roots of Canada's political culture to the historical circumstances of Canada's colonial political system. Stewart builds on the work of Hartz and McRae by assessing the "workings of politics" during the colonial period. He concludes that the impact of the 1790–1850 formative period was so powerful that "it created a distinctive and enduring pattern of Canadian politics."[16] Stewart argues persuasively that characteristics of the Canadian political culture such as patronage, influence, active government and intense localism were imported and firmly established during the colonial period and "went from strength to strength" after Confederation in 1867.

The various interpretations suggest that Canadian political culture, unlike its American counterpart, was open to both conservative and socialist thought. Canadian political culture has a European flavour, placing a high value on tradition, order, historical continuity and group interests rather than individual interests. But liberalism is, as David Bell and Lorne Tepperman aptly phrase it, "the ideology of the dominant class; it has the full force of the state, Church, media and educational system behind it: it has been trained into all of us."[17] It is our contention that liberal values, based on belief in a capitalist society, a market economy and the right to private property, dominate in Canada, although not to the exclusion of other perspectives.

Overarching Values

The political values of a country form the broad base of its political system. Though generally taken for granted and not articulated, they set the parameters of acceptable behaviour and underlie citizens' attitudes toward specific political objects, providing guidelines to define what is right or wrong, what is or is not valuable or acceptable. In Canada, these include certain democratic rights and, as we have seen, liberal values with strains of socialist and conservative thought. These values are reflected in political symbols such as national emblems or institutions, and are often enshrined in the country's constitution.

In April 1982, the *Canadian Charter of Rights and Freedoms* was proclaimed. It became the first comprehensive statement of the fundamental values of Canadians to be entrenched in the Constitution. The preamble sets out the premise that "Canada is founded upon principles that recognize the supremacy of God and the Rule of Law." The Charter then proceeds to guarantee the fundamental rights of Canada's "free and democratic society." The implicit values of Canadians, as formalized in the Charter, are rooted in the western political tradition and the Judeo-Christian religious tradition.

Democracy, as we discussed in Chapter 1, is such an ambiguous concept that it has become a cliché to claim it as a basic value. It is espoused by *all types* of political systems. However, in Canada,

---

15. Christian and Campbell, *Political Parties and Ideologies in Canada*, pp. 227–28.

16. Gordon T. Stewart, *The Origins of Canadian Politics: A Comparative Approach* (Vancouver: University of British Columbia Press, 1986), p. 92.

17. Bell and Tepperman, *The Roots of Disunity*, 1st ed. (Toronto: McClelland & Stewart, 1979), p. 232. For a discussion of dominant ideologies and counter-ideologies, see M. Patricia Marchak, *Ideological Perspectives on Canada*, 2nd ed. (Toronto: McGraw-Hill Ryerson, 1981).

democratic rights are outlined in the *Charter of Rights and Freedoms*. Embedded in the process of representative democracy are a great many values. One is the individual right to *fundamental freedoms*. These include (1) freedom of conscience and religion; (2) freedom of belief and expression, including freedom of the press and freedom of association; (3) freedom of peaceful assembly; and (4) freedom of association. Another democratic right is *equality* before and under the law, without discrimination. (These and other constitutionally approved values are detailed in Chapter 5.) In the political sphere, equality presumes associated values such as *universal suffrage* and elections contested by competing political parties that give voters alternatives from which to choose. Another associated value is acceptance of the *rule of law*, with civil rights for all citizens. Still another implicit value of representative democracy is *majority rule*. In Canada, governments are based on an ability to retain a majority of votes in the House of Commons, and members of Parliament are elected in a system that gives credence to the majority principle but that, in fact, allows members to be elected by a plurality.

It is deemed necessary to protect *minority rights* in Canada, so a few specific collective rights are also protected in the Constitution. These include French and English minority-language rights in the federal and Québec legislatures and courts and Roman Catholic and Protestant minority education rights. Basic collective rights are generally considered inviolable, beyond even the right of the majority to change.

Comparing Canada to the United States also can help to identify Canadian values. Lipset, for example, finds Canadians are more (1) aware of class, (2) elitist, (3) law abiding, (4) statist, (5) collectivity-oriented, and (6) particularistic than Americans.[18] He traces many of these differences to British values that remained strong in Canada long after they were abruptly curtailed in the United States by the American Revolution.

Canadians, Lipset maintains, tend to be more class-conscious than Americans, who see their social structure as relatively fluid. Canadian society is characterized more by elitism, hierarchy and deference. The educated elite is smaller, creating a more rigid conception of social hierarchy that can be viewed as a part of the feudal and monarchical traditions inherited from Britain and reinforced by the Roman Catholic and Anglican churches. Canadians also show more respect for authority than do Americans — for the law, police, RCMP.

Lipset notes that in politics Canadians prefer to divide their economy relatively evenly between the public and private sectors, whereas Americans promote a much stronger private sector. In Canada, the state is expected to interfere more in the economy, acting as a distributive force to share the benefits of being Canadian. Government expenditure in Canada accounts for more of the gross domestic product (GDP) than in the United States. Compared to the United States, Canada has a relatively comprehensive public health insurance system, many federal and provincial Crown corporations and a more comprehensive social security system. Canadians are much more willing than Americans to pay higher taxes in order to have such benefits. The belief that governments should interfere in the economy when necessary makes Canada a more "caring" society.

Canada also demonstrates more "particularistic" characteristics. This is especially true with respect to the integration of immigrants. Beyond Lipset's reasoning, it can be said that Canada encourages ethnic minorities to preserve their culture, so that Canada can be seen more as a "fruitcake" than the "melting pot" of the United States. Multiculturalism is a reflection of the ideal of tolerance that, though not always lived up to, is highly valued by Canadians. Compromise, too, is highly valued. This is evident in the workings of the federal system of government itself that seeks to accommodate diverse regional interests. It can also be seen in the international reputation Canada

---

18. Seymour Martin Lipset, *Continental Divide* (New York: Routledge, 1990), p. 8.

CLOSE-UP ON
Culture

VALUE CHANGES

A recent study by Neil Nevitte challenges some of Seymour Martin Lipset's contentions about Canadian values. Nevitte found that in recent years there have been significant value changes on a whole range of issues. Canadians, he says, have become less preoccupied with accumulating material goods and more concerned with what has come to be termed "post-materialism." An increasingly large proportion of the Canadian population has been born since the traumas of the Second World War and the Depression. As a consequence, Nevitte maintains, they are less concerned with acquiring material goods and more concerned with "self-actualization."

Politically, Nevitte says, post-materialists tend to think of themselves as "new left," a concept that refers to concern for the environment, tolerance of alternative lifestyles (e.g., gays, lesbians and other groups) and veering away from traditional Church-inspired notions of moral standards. They are also less concerned with traditional notions of authority. As Canadians have become better educated and more cosmopolitan, Nevitte says, they have also become more difficult to govern. While they are politically motivated, their attachment to traditional political parties and to hierarchical institutions has declined. Canadians are, therefore, less deferential than they used to be.

Another new study by two American and two Canadian academics concludes that the difference in values between Americans and Canadians today is not as acute as generally assumed. They find Canadians to be more liberal and left-wing than Americans on gay rights and affirmative action, and also in their belief that governments should ensure jobs and a decent living standard. Apart from these areas, they say, differences are not marked.

Are your observations in accord with these new value studies?

Sources: Neil Nevitte, *The Decline of Deference* (Toronto: Broadview Press, 1996); and Paul M. Sniderman et al., *The Clash of Rights: Liberty, Equality and Legitimacy in Pluralist Democracy* (New Haven: Yale University Press, 1997).

has earned as a peace-keeper under the United Nations' auspices.

A study by Neil Nevitte — *The Decline of Deference* — indicates that Canadian values and characteristics are changing over time, however — often in line with those of other industrialized states. In a larger comparative context, Nevitte concludes that Canadians have a greater sense of material well-being than do Americans. As well, contrary to Lipset, he finds them to be less deferential than Americans — more willing to engage in boycotts and other forms of low-level political protest. In some economic values, such as orientation toward economic competition, free enterprise and workplace participation, Canadians and Americans are, he says, close. However, on levels of political interest, as well as permissiveness, absence of restrictions on euthanasia, homosexuality or abortion, Canadian orientations are more like those in Europe.[19]

These facets of the Canadian identity are rounded out by a picture of Canadians as inhabitants of a huge, diverse country with a harsh northern climate, a federal system of government and a parliamentary system adopted from Britain with some modifications inspired by the United States. Canada has evolved from a country of aboriginal peoples and two European nations to one that includes people of widely diverse origins. The values of that heritage are expressed in official policies of bilingualism and multiculturalism.

Overarching Symbols

The political values of a country are symbolized by such objects as flags, anthems, leaders, national holidays and historical heroes. These symbols help enforce respect for and emotional attachment to political institutions and can be a focal point for national unity. The name Canada itself symbolizes the aboriginal heritage of the country. "Kanata," the Huron-Iroquois word for "village" or "settlement," became "Canada" and by 1547 was used on maps to designate everything north of the St. Lawrence River. The first use of "Canada" as an official name was in 1791 when the Province of Québec was divided into the colonies of Upper and Lower Canada. In 1841, the two Canadas were reunited as the Province of Canada. At Confederation, the new country assumed the official title the Dominion of Canada.[20]

---

19. Neil Nevitte, *The Decline of Deference* (Toronto: Broadview Press, 1996).
20. Department of the Secretary of State, *Symbols of Nationhood* (Ottawa: Supply and Services, 1991), p. 5.

Canada's passage from colony to nation is clearly reflected in the country's changing national symbols. In the early stages, they manifested a dual allegiance to Britain and Canada, but were gradually transformed to reflect national pride and unity without reference to Britain.

The evolution of the Canadian flag is perhaps the best illustration. At Confederation in 1867, Canada was granted permission to fly the Red Ensign, the flag of the British Merchant Navy. Attempts to replace it with a uniquely Canadian flag began as early as 1925 but did not succeed until four decades later. The transition was difficult. There were bitter debates both in and outside Parliament concerning not only the choice of a replacement but also the question of whether Canada should jettison the flag that represented its historical attachment to Britain. In the end, of course, a flag was selected that features a red maple leaf, a distinctively Canadian symbol that had been adopted quite separately by both English and French Canadians well before Confederation, and that has deep historical roots in heraldic arms, regimental colours and literary publications.[21] The present flag was flown for the first time on February 15, 1965, and today many Canadians would not leave the country without a tiny facsimile on their lapels or knapsacks.

A similar evolution occurred in the acquisition of a Canadian coat of arms. Following the First World War, representation was made to the Crown for a coat of arms that was uniquely Canadian. For years a controversy simmered over whether Canada should be symbolized by living green leaves or dead red ones. (Sir Robert Borden, then prime minister, thought green far more appropriate.) The dispute was not settled until 1957, when it was agreed that three red leaves would adorn the base of the shield and a lion would proudly display a fourth.

Another progression to a specifically Canadian symbol occurred in the choice of the national anthem. The English version of "The Maple Leaf Forever" was quite unacceptable to French Canadians for the good reason that it referred to the French defeat at Québec. At the time of Confederation, therefore, "God Save the Queen" became the unofficial anthem. Finally, on July 1, 1980, "O Canada," based on music written by Calixa Lavallée a century earlier, was proclaimed Canada's national anthem. There have been many English versions, and disagreement over the wording has often been intense. Rather than inspiring loyalty and devotion, phrases that include "native land," "sons' command," "true North," and "God" tend to give rise to resentment among immigrants, women, Westerners, Easterners and atheists. And of course, there are also royalists who still prefer "God Save the Queen." The French version of "O Canada," with lyrics that resemble the English only in that they refer to the same country, also contains some questionable wording.

It is important that a symbol of unity cause as little friction as possible, and Canadian efforts to compromise and please were evident at the formal adoption ceremony for the new anthem. There had been hot debate over whether the choir should sing first in English or in French. What was later called a "typically Canadian" solution was found: the choir was divided in two and sang both versions simultaneously.

Other minor conflicts and reminders of the British heritage have emerged from time to time with regard to other symbols. One concerns the country's official name, the Dominion of Canada. For most of our history, the first of July, Canada's national holiday, was known as Dominion Day. Although the word "dominion" had been chosen explicitly by the Fathers of Confederation to mean sovereignty from sea to sea, many Canadians came to feel that it smacked of colonial dependence. With some trepidation because of the controversy the topic engendered, in November 1982, the Canadian Parliament finally changed the title of the holiday to Canada Day — in spite of the country's official name.

---

21. Strome Galloway, "Why the Maple Leaf Is Our National Emblem," *Canadian Geographic* (June 1982). Red and white are the official colours of Canada, appointed by George V in 1921.

In many countries, the constitution provides a concrete focus for pride and unity. This has only recently been the case in Canada. As with the other symbols we have discussed, the process of wrenching away from British ties and establishing a unique, Canadian symbol was not easy. The *British North America Act*, Canada's written Constitution, was passed by the British Parliament. It was increasingly embarrassing to Canadians in the twentieth century as a national symbol, both because it could not be amended without British approval and because it contained no formal guarantee of rights. The remedy finally came in the spring of 1982 when the revised Constitution was patriated. Like the American Constitution, the new document has begun to provide a common focus of pride for Canadians.

Two other predominant political symbols deserving of mention here, although they are discussed extensively in Chapters 5 and 8, are the monarch and her representative, the Governor General. Canada is a constitutional monarchy, and the role of Her Majesty Queen Elizabeth II as Sovereign of Canada and head of state is ceremonial. As sovereign, she personifies the nation and for many is a symbol of allegiance, unity and authority. Federal and provincial legislators, Cabinet ministers, public servants, military and police personnel, and new citizens all swear allegiance to the Queen (not the flag or Constitution). Laws are promulgated and elections are called in the Queen's name. She is custodian of the democratic powers vested in the Crown. Historian W.L. Morton pointed out that allegiance to a monarch alleviates pressures for uniformity: "Anyone ... can be a subject of the Queen and a citizen of Canada without in any way ceasing to be himself."[22] The monarchy, in this sense, is well adapted to the bilingual, multicultural, regional character of Canada.

Yet, the relevance of the English monarchy as an appropriate symbol for French Canadians has often been questioned. An overtly hostile reception for the Queen during a royal visit to Québec in 1964, for example, prompted officials of the Québec government to disassociate themselves and their constituents from the monarchy. It is evident that the ability of this institution to serve as a unifying symbol for Canada's two founding cultural groups is limited.

The role of Governor General has evolved considerably from its British origins. The Queen's representative to Canada was originally selected by Britain. However, since 1936, the Governor General has been appointed only after consultation with the Canadian Cabinet, which means, in effect, that the prime minister makes the choice. The appointment of the first Canadian, Vincent Massey, came in 1952. This final transition to a Canadian Governor General nominated in Canada may have increased the potential of the position as a unifying symbol for Canadians.

Finally, we must allude briefly to historical heroes as symbols of national pride and unity. Gradual evolution to nationhood, as opposed to dramatic revolution, does not produce charismatic hero material. And independence on the installment plan has no glamour as a national event. To compound the difficulties, French and English Canadians each tend to cultivate their own heroes, based on different interpretations of history. In fact, Canadian heroes often gained reputations in their own communities by resisting or defeating their counterparts. The dearth of common national heroes and events to rally around has undoubtedly encouraged substitutions from south of the border, a problem discussed more fully in the following chapter. F.R. Scott aptly described this situation in a satirical poem entitled "National Identity":[23]

---

22. Quoted in ibid.

23. From *The Collected Poems of F.R. Scott*, John Newlove, ed., 1981. Used by permission of the Canadian publishers McClelland & Stewart Ltd., Toronto.

The Canadian Centenary Council
Meeting in Le Reine Elizabeth
To seek those symbols
Which will explain ourselves to ourselves
Evoke unlimited responses
And prove that something called Canada
Really exists in the hearts of all
Handed out to every delegate
At the start of the proceedings
A portfolio of documents
On the cover of which appeared
In gold letters
 not
A Mare Usque Ad Mare
 not
E Pluribus Unum
 not
Dieu et Mon Droit
 but
Courtesy of Coca-Cola Limited.

Political Attitudes

Overarching values set the general parameters of political behaviour in Canada. Specific attitudes toward political objects are more differentiated than basic values and more fleeting, but they may be more immediate determinants of political behaviour. Three types of attitudes can be distinguished: cognitive, affective and evaluative. **Cognitive** attitudes reflect the degree of knowledge, accurate or otherwise, that citizens have about political objects. **Affective** attitudes reflect the degree of citizens' attachment to or rejection of the political objects that surround them: how do Canadians feel about their country, their government or the political symbols we have discussed? **Evaluative** attitudes reflect the moral judgements made by individuals about the "goodness" or "badness" of political objects. The three types of attitudes are interrelated and often difficult to distinguish in practice.

Attitudes toward specific political issues of the day, as opposed to more permanent political objects, are ephemeral. Issues change and so do people, but institutions and symbols remain. Such transient attitudes are sometimes defined as public opinion, and although they can be important in determining short-term behaviour they are less helpful in understanding the overall political culture of a country. An Angus Reid poll published in 1996, for example, indicated what Canadians perceived to be the most important issues facing the country at that time. They were: jobs, national unity, economy, deficit and health care, in that order. (See Figure 3.1.) These perceptions will change over the coming months and years.

With respect to cognitive attitudes, Canadians appear to have the basic information necessary to allow them to operate effectively at both provincial and federal levels of government. They also demonstrate a high degree of feeling for both their country and their province of residence.[24]

---

24. Harold D. Clarke et al., *Political Choice in Canada* (Toronto: McGraw-Hill Ryerson, 1979). For a later study of the *sources* of political knowledge, both factual and conceptual, see Ronald D. Lambert et al., "The Social Sources of Political Knowledge," *CJPS*, vol. 21, no. 2 (June 1988).

FIGURE 3.1   THE ISSUES MOST IMPORTANT TO CANADIANS

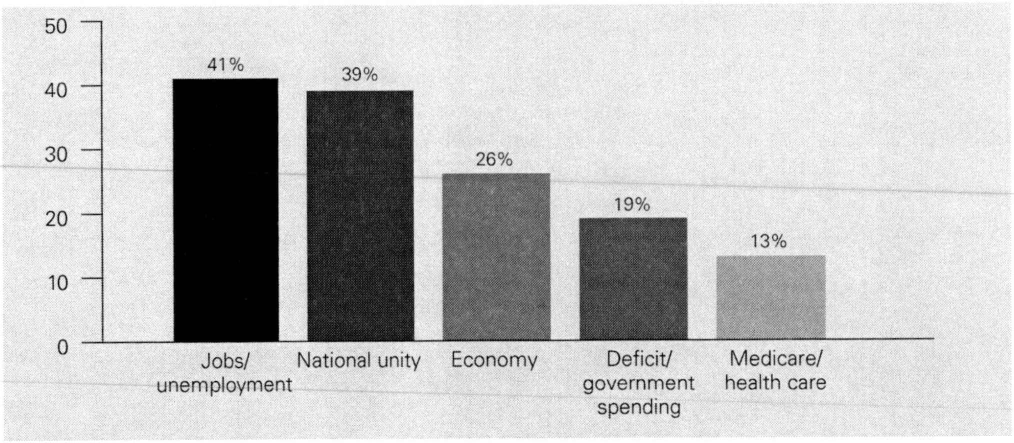

Source: Angus Reid poll reported in *The Ottawa Citizen*, June 29, 1996. The results are accurate within 2.31 percentage points 19 times out of 20.

Despite these positive attitudes, however, there are disquieting findings about the nature of some specific affective attitudes toward objects in the Canadian political system. (See Figure 3.2.) In the 1970s, a study by Clarke et al. found that Canadians lacked faith or trust that politicians and the political system would respond positively to their interests.[25] Public cynicism continued to grow in the 1980s, fuelled by government scandals and mismanagement. A 1992 survey concluded that "Canadian political discontent is at its highest since polling began." Questioned about honesty and ethical standards of MPs in 1989, for example, Canadians ranked MPs 11th of 12 professions, below labour unions and building contractors.[26]

Declining respect and confidence in government institutions and politicians were evident in the fall of 1992 when the Mulroney government called a national referendum on a set of constitutional proposals. The proposals were widely rejected despite massive financial and political support from all provincial governments and the major political parties. As Figure 3.2 shows, none of the major institutions, Parliament, political parties or the federal government, had commanded high respect only two years earlier. Respect for political parties dropped from 30 percent in 1979 to only 9 percent in March 1992. (See Figure 3.3.)

In 1991, André Blais and Elisabeth Gidengil also found political discontent to be at a historically high level in Canada.[27] They discovered that 49 percent of Canadians did not trust the federal government, and that 52 percent even believed that "quite a few of the people running the government are a little bit crooked." Two government commissions in the early 1990s also confirmed a high degree of discontent and considerable lack of confidence in politicians and institutions. The Citizen's Forum on Canada's Future (the Spicer Commission) and the Royal Commission on Electoral Reform and Party Financing both witnessed an outpouring of criticism that Canada lacked

---

25. Clarke et al., *Political Choice*, ch. 3.

26. Peter Dobell and Byron Berry, "Anger at the System: Political Discontent in Canada," *Parliamentary Government*, no. 39 (1992), p. 5.

27. André Blais and Elisabeth Gidengil, "Representative Democracy: The Views of Canadians (1991), Royal Commission on Electoral Reform and Party Financing," *Reforming Electoral Democracy*, vol. 1 (Ottawa: Supply and Services, 1992), p. 225.

FIGURE 3.2   NATIONAL INSTITUTIONS: LEVELS OF PUBLIC RESPECT AND CONFIDENCE, 1990

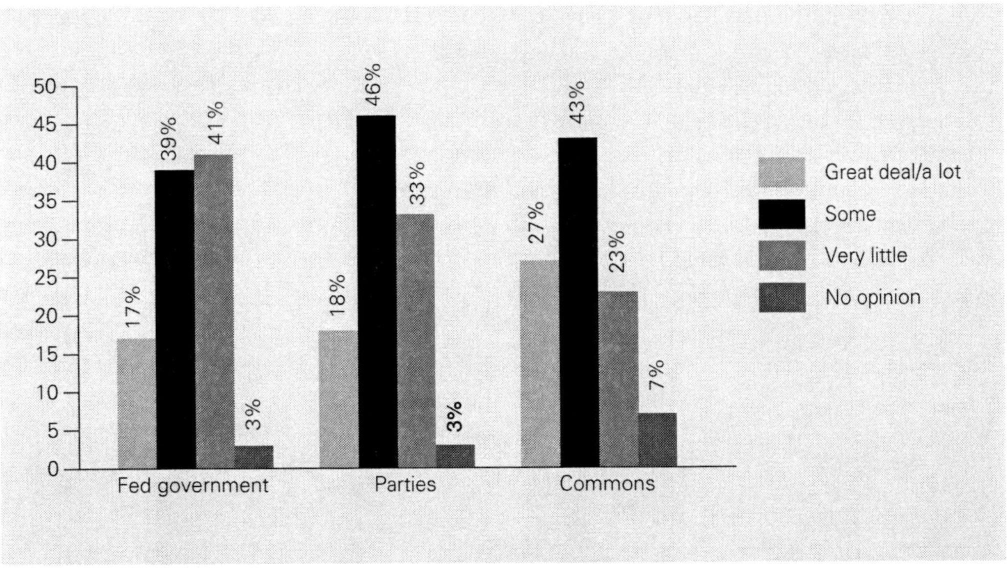

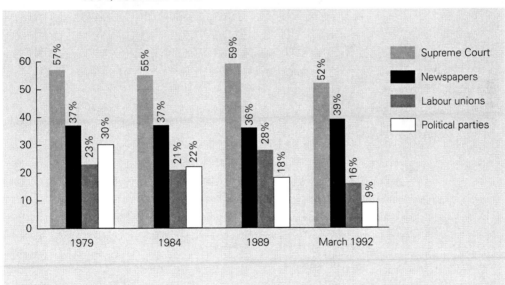

Source: *Gallup Report*s, June 4, 1990, and September 17, 1990.

FIGURE 3.3   NATIONAL INSTITUTIONS: LEVELS OF PUBLIC RESPECT AND CONFIDENCE, 1979, 1984, 1989 AND 1992

Respondents were asked to rate how much respect and confidence they had for the institution listed. Scores are for those who answered "a great deal" or "a lot," as opposed to "some" or "no opinion."

Source: *Gallup Report*, March 16, 1992.

responsible leadership, that current leaders were not trustworthy, that Canada lacked strong leaders, and so on.[28]

---

28. Citizen's Forum on Canada's Future, *Report to the People and Government of Canada* (Ottawa, Supply and Services, 1991); and Royal Commission on Electoral Reform and Party Financing, *Reforming Electoral Democracy*, vol. 1 (Ottawa: Supply and Services, 1992).

Such attitudes can fluctuate over a relatively short period and are not uniform across the population; however, they have been persistent in recent years. Some negative emotion was undoubtedly related to the economic recession and unpopularity of policies such as the free trade deal with the United States and the Goods and Service Tax. Cynical attitudes do not, of course, preclude diffuse support for the government in Canada or hamper political participation at either level of government. Neither do they indicate a rejection of government authority. Individual Canadians are quite willing to comply with basic political laws, and major political groups rarely offer unconditional resistance. Acts of Parliament are automatically considered legitimate and are carried out voluntarily by citizens without the need for coercive security forces. Crimes against the state are rare, even when laws are unpopular.[29]

Reproduced with permission, Gable, *The Globe and Mail.*

Behaviour: Participation and Efficacy

Values and attitudes are often difficult to ascertain. Impressionistic studies and survey research are helpful, but as we have noted both have limitations. Another approach is to deduce from people's behaviour the attitudes and values that make them act in a certain way. One of the best deductive methods is to examine the extent to which people *participate* in the political world around them and

---

29. The empirical data suggest that Canada experiences an incidence of violence comparable to that of most industrialized democracies. Robert J. Jackson, Michael J. Kelly and Thomas H. Mitchell, "Collective Conflict, Violence, and the Media in Canada," in Ontario Royal Commission on Violence in the Communications Industry, Report, *Learning from the Media*, vol. 5 (Toronto: Queen's Printer, 1977).

then to generalize from this behaviour. The individual's self-perception is an important factor here, because self-esteem can affect the degree and intensity of participation.

Relative to most democratic countries, Canadians participate very readily in electoral politics; about 75 percent vote regularly in federal and provincial elections. French Canadians are less active politically at the national level than English Canadians, but more active at the provincial level. Corresponding to this relatively high level of electoral participation, feelings of political efficacy with regard to voting are very high: Canadians feel that their individual vote is important. Their reasons for feeling they should vote are mixed. Some are committed to the principles of democracy and a feeling of civic duty; others feel it important to render judgement on a government or certain politicians, perhaps seeking to punish parties or politicians by voting them out of office.

Apart from the act of voting, however, overall feelings of political efficacy are low. As a result, Canadians are said to have a "quasi-participant" political culture. Canadians are not confident that they can understand and affect the political process. In general, they express feelings of distrust, cynicism and powerlessness in the face of government domination by powerful interests. But Canadians are not alone in harbouring these sentiments. Comparative analysis of responses to similar questions raised in surveys undertaken in Canada and the United States indicates that, on most items, Canadians have as high a sense of efficacy as Americans, and similar levels of trust in government.

Active participation in politics beyond casting a ballot is low in Canada.[30] Only 4 or 5 percent of the electorate participate regularly in political parties or hold elected office at either the federal or provincial level. Unless the level of interest is artificially high because of colourful personalities or issues, Canadians retain only a vague spectator interest in politics and rarely show strong ideological commitment. Political protest, even peaceful demonstration, is engaged in by a very small percentage of Canadians. Moreover, political participation aside from voting is very uneven across different groups in Canadian society. The higher an individual's social status, the more likely he or she is to participate politically. The most active participants tend to be wealthy, well-educated, male, middle-aged Protestant members of the English "charter group." Women participate less than men, and that pattern does not appear to be changing quickly.[31] Lower socioeconomic and less well educated groups participate only infrequently. As we have noted, however, recent research by Nevitte indicates that rates of low-level political participation in Canada may be changing. (See "Value Changes" on page 72.) He found that Canadians are becoming more willing to participate in boycotts and other low-level forms of protest. Participation in parties and elections is discussed further in Chapters 11 and 12.

Although there is a drastic drop in political participation when voting is excluded, it must be noted that only 25 to 30 percent of Canadians confine their participation exclusively to casting a ballot. About 60 percent of the public participate in at least one political activity in addition to voting. Although Canadians are less active in political life than would befit the democratic ideal, they are considerably closer to that goal than citizens of the majority of the world's states. Unfortunately, the least influential in society — the poor, the young and the old, for example — participate the least in the political process, and exhibit the least political efficacy.

30. For a survey of participation in Canada, see William Mishler and Harold D. Clarke, "Political Participation in Canada," in Michael S. Whittington and Glen Williams, eds., *Canadian Politics in the 1990s*, 4th ed. (Scarborough: Nelson, 1995).
31. Barry J. Kay et al., "Gender and Political Activity in Canada, 1965–1984," *CJPS*, vol. 20, no. 4 (Spring 1987), pp. 851–64.

ETHNO-LINGUISTIC CLEAVAGES AND POLITICAL CULTURE

There are many political subcultures that do not share all of the values and attitudes discussed above. Among the most significant of these subcultures are ethnic groups. As we noted in Chapter 1, **ethnicity** is primarily a subjective phenomenon, although it is often reinforced by different customs, language, religion, dialect and cultural heritage, and sometimes distinct racial or physical characteristics. Language can be particularly significant in defining an ethnic group. **Ethnic origin** refers to the ethnic or cultural group(s) to which an individual's ancestors belonged; it pertains to the ancestral roots or origins of the population and not to place of birth, citizenship or nationality. Ethnically, of course, there is no such thing as a Canadian race. If an original decision had been made to engulf minorities in a unitary rather than a federal system of government, cultural diversity might not have been sustained, and perhaps ethnic groups would not have the political significance they do today. In Canada, cultural pluralism has also been encouraged by the size of the country, its sparse population and, particularly, the federal system of government. That pluralism, which is a significant, vibrant and humane cultural characteristic of Canada, also creates serious ethno-linguistic cleavages. By **cleavages** we refer to major and persistent differences among groups — differences that are politically relevant. Ethno-linguistic cleavages are significant in terms of political debate and controversy, and even national unity.

There are three major ethno-linguistic cleavages in Canada that profoundly affect the country's political culture. The first, between the two founding European nations, French and English, is based on the conception of Canada as a bicultural, bilingual state. The second important division pits the interests of these two founding groups against more recent and varied ethnic groups to arrive in Canada, and is based on the conception of Canada as a multicultural country. The third cleavage concerns the country's original inhabitants, the Native peoples, who today are struggling for recognition and self-government. We shall consider each in turn.

Before we begin, however, let us recall the changing ethnic composition of Canadian society. Members of more than 100 ethnic groups live in Canada. In fact, the 1996 census found that for the first time in history less than half of Canada's total population of immigrants come from European countries. The largest ethnic groups are still people with British or French backgrounds, but their percentages are dropping and neither group alone represents a majority of the population. The 1996 census showed that only about 17 percent of Canadians claim British-only ethnic origin and 14 percent French-only. Many others with French or English ancestry claim multiple ethnic or "Canadian" origins and are not included in this single-origin category. More indicative of the size of the French population is mother tongue — see below.

The French–English Cleavage

The primary cleavage in Canadian politics is between the French- and English-speaking populations and is founded on the different histories, cultures and languages of the two groups. As of 1996, 23.5 percent of Canadians claimed French as their mother tongue. Of these, 81 percent were concentrated in the province of Québec. Francophones, particularly in Québec, have distinct characteristics based on their common ethno-linguistic and historical background. English-speaking Canadians, in comparison, encompass multiple linguistic groups with many different ethnic and religious backgrounds. While francophones are relatively culturally homogeneous and united in their cultural goals, English-speaking Canadians are often unable to speak with one voice as a "cultural nation."

The cleavage dividing French and English developed very early in Canadian history. We have discussed Hartz's and McRae's concept of New France as a fragment founded by bearers of a feudal tradition who had left France before the liberal revolution. From 1663, when it came under royal control, the political development of the colony was dominated by French-style absolutism, modified somewhat by circumstances in the New World. When the British conquest ended French rule, most merchants and officials returned to France, and the forces for modernization and change departed with them. Isolated from the turmoil of the French Revolution, the culture of New France was enveloped and preserved by a few remaining institutions: the Catholic Church, the French language and civil law, and the feudal landholding system.

So tightly sealed was French Canadian society in Québec that a great many francophones there today are descendants of the original 10 000 French colonists who arrived before 1760. From this inheritance of political thought, historical events produced a political subculture very different from its English Canadian counterpart. The most visible differences are language, a civil law code unique to Québec, and traditions, myths and heroes based on early Québec history. Less tangible is the fear of assimilation that permeates politics because of the francophone minority status.

In direct contrast to the encapsulated and preserved feudal fragment in New France, Canadian anglophone society was open to outside influences. An extremely high percentage of the early inhabitants of the northern British colonies were Loyalists who fled the American Revolution; indeed, their numbers — 30 000 to 60 000 — submerged the fewer than 15 000 English colonists already in Canada. The Loyalists brought with them attitudes still prevalent in English Canadian society: some aspects of the liberal American tradition, but also anti-American sentiments and a corresponding loyalty to the British Crown. Some authors have termed this bond with Britain a colonial mentality, "an artificial loyalty to the Crown that grew ever more strained as new Canadians without British origins poured into the population."[32] Arguably, the net effect was to delay the development of a unified and coherent nation.

As noted in Chapter 2, one fundamental difference between the French and English in Canada lies in each group's understanding of the term "nation." To French Canadians, the word tends to mean "people" or "society." To English Canadians, it means "nation-state," the combined people of a country. Léon Dion's description of this difference is tripartite: francophones see Canada as two distinct societies or nations, one French-speaking and the other English-speaking; these two societies are qualitatively equal in every way; and the Canadian Constitution should accordingly give special status to francophones within federal political institutions and also to the province of Québec.[33] Thus, while it is thought that many anglophone Canadians view Canada as one nation, with an enclave of French Canadians in Québec, francophones begin with the dualistic conception of a political system composed of "Québec" and "the rest of the country." This conception of Québec as a separate "nation" can be traced throughout the history of the province.

In 1867, the Fathers of Confederation created what has been called a "political nation," giving Canada every power a political nation needed to thrive. George Étienne Cartier negotiated for Québec and gave his strong support to this vision. But he also saw it as the responsibility of the provinces to preserve what he called "cultural nations" — cultures imported from England, Ireland, Scotland and pre-revolutionary France. After Cartier's death, however, his Québec critics claimed that Confederation was really a "compact" between French and English nations. This myth flourished,

---

32. Bell and Tepperman, *The Roots of Disunity*, 1st ed., p. 63.
33. Léon Dion, *Québec: The Unfinished Revolution* (Montréal: McGill-Queen's University Press, 1976), p. 180.

nourishing the notion of "two founding nations" that provided some French Canadians with a collective claim to equality rather than simple minority status within Canada. The word "compact" also implied a right to secede from the bargain. This "compact" myth continues to be expounded by Québec's political leaders.

> *Canada is "not a real country."*
>
> **Lucien Bouchard**
> **Premier of Québec**

Whether Canada is one nation or two is obviously a matter of definition. We agree with constitutional expert Eugene Forsey, who expressed the situation this way: "In the ethnic, cultural, sociological sense, Canada is 'two nations'.... In the political, legal, constitutional sense, Canada is one nation."[34]

It is generally accepted today that the Confederation arrangement was an implicit bargain between the French and the English to create one strong political unit, a country that would protect the rights and assist the advancement of two culturally diverse peoples. English- and French-language communities were to be protected. But it did not work that way in practice. From the outset, English was a legal language in the Québec legislature and courts. In the other provinces, however, the practice until the 1940s was for English-speaking Canadians, wherever they were in the majority, to refuse French-speaking Canadian minorities the use of their language in government institutions and deprive them of public school facilities in their native language.

Several historical crises marked the breakdown of good will between English and French people in Canada, stimulating frustration and eventually separatist movements. Although they are given relatively cursory recognition by Canadians outside Québec, French Canadians dwell upon these events and find in them the emotional justification for the need to defend themselves as a distinct, cultural minority in Canada. They include the Manitoba schools question (1885–96), conscription issues during both world wars (1917, 1942) and the rejection of the Meech Lake constitutional accord (1987). These events and the growth of nationalism in Québec are discussed fully in Chapters 5, 6 and 7.

French Canadians: A Cultural Nation

As of 1996, 23.5 percent of Canadians claim French as their first language. They are concentrated mainly in Québec (81 percent) with other significant groupings residing in Ontario and New Brunswick. Over the years, the French Canadian culture has developed and thrived.

Until the 1960s, the Roman Catholic Church was fairly successful in directing and fostering attitudes of withdrawal and non-participation among French Canadians in Québec. They were concerned mainly with *la survivance*, cultural preservation, that necessitated resistance to change and withdrawal from external influences that would alter the composition of francophone society. French Canadians were content, even within their provincial government, to resist change rather than control it. They neither participated as a group in the political affairs of the country nor even exploited to any degree the control that they, the majority, could have wielded within the provincial jurisdiction.

---

34. Eugene Forsey, "Canada, One Nation or Two?" *Le Canada, expérience ratée ... ou réussie?* (Québec: Congrès des affaires canadiennes, 1962), pp. 55–57.

The situation began to change in the early 1960s, when the election of the Jean Lesage government on a *"maîtres chez nous"* platform revealed a change in the character and aspirations of French Canadian society — the beginning of the "Quiet Revolution." The influence of the Catholic Church declined dramatically. Québec francophones had come to believe that if they were to maintain their identity, they had to take control of their own destiny. The cultural spectrum of Québec politics expanded from defensive, conservative nationalism to ideologies of liberalism, socialism and more radical thought.

The Quiet Revolution soon became a challenge to Canadian federalism (see Chapters 6 and 7). The Royal Commission on Bilingualism and Biculturalism confirmed that the state of affairs established in 1867, and never before seriously questioned, was being rejected by francophone Québeckers. The strategy of *la survivance* had been replaced by *l'épanouissement* — in this case, a desire to develop French Canadian culture to its full extent and participate actively in fulfilling their aspirations.[35] Thus, the relationships between francophones and anglophones and between the federal and Québec governments have changed over time. Until the Quiet Revolution, the needs and aspirations of both communities and governments were relatively congruent; since then they have often diverged or conflicted.

During the 1960s, the federal Liberal government responded to the Quiet Revolution by declaring Canadian federal institutions to be officially bilingual. It increased the number of bilingual civil servants in the government and improved government services in both languages. In 1973, for example, many public service positions were designated bilingual, a process that continues to this day.

The rise in Québec national consciousness directed and channelled economic, social and political change in that province. The provincial government became the focus of political modernization, assuming a much greater role in the economy and society than ever before. Traditional socio-economic patterns gradually shifted as the anglophone business elite left the province in great numbers in the 1970s and francophones began to occupy an ever larger proportion of the economic middle class in Québec. A prolific and dynamic francophone business elite eventually moved beyond Québec into other Canadian and international markets. Francophones today control a greater portion of the province's economic base and hold more senior management positions than ever before.

French-speaking Canadians, particularly in areas where they are more concentrated, do share a distinct history, language and culture. That does not prevent them from being Canadian. Acadian author Antonine Maillet made this clear in an interview when she was awarded the prestigious Prix Goncourt for French literature in 1979. She was asked how she regarded herself — as Acadian, French, French Canadian, French Acadian, Canadian or some other. She replied that she considered herself to be *all* of them in different proportions. Like Antonine Maillet, Canadians have "layered" cultures. Belonging to an ethnic group, whether French or any other, need not detract from being a Canadian.[36]

Nationalist Attitudes of French Canadians

What attitudes do francophones hold about their province, country, and federal and provincial governments? Attitudinal surveys of French Canadians have, for practical reasons, generally been confined to citizens of Québec. In this unique province, where political and ethnic boundaries more or

---

35. For a more detailed discussion of the Quiet Revolution, see Kenneth McRoberts, *Quebec: Social Change and Political Crises*, 3rd ed. (Toronto: McClelland & Stewart, 1988); and, by the same author, *Misconceiving Canada: The Struggle for National Unity* (Toronto: Oxford University Press, 1997).

36. See Antonine Maillet, "Canada: What's That?" *Queen's Quarterly*, vol. 99, no. 3 (Fall 1992), pp. 642–50.

less coincide, Canadians often hold political attitudes that are distinct from those of other regions or provinces.[37]

Public opinion polls in the province of Québec show considerable ambiguity concerning French Canadian desires for federalism, sovereignty and independence. *L'Actualité* polls in 1992, for example, showed beyond a doubt that confusion and indecision reigned on all questions about the future of the province. A CROP poll conducted in April 1992 found that 16 percent of Québec residents were hard-core Québec nationalists, 22 percent were moderate Québec nationalists, 26 percent were hard-core Canadian nationalists, 18 percent were moderate Canadian nationalists and 18 percent were very undecided. A cartoon summarizing the results of the polling showed a puzzled young boy saying essentially, "It's like having to choose between chocolate and ice cream for life ... it's very hard when you like them both!"[38]

Surveys that measure the relative attachment of francophone Québeckers to Canada and Québec indicate an attachment to Québec that is somewhat or much stronger than attachment to Canada. Maurice Pinard examined the system of dual loyalties in Québec in terms of attachment to, perceived importance of, and interest in the two levels of government. He concluded that "in ethnically segmented societies, precisely because of this segmentation, people tend to develop a system of dual loyalties."[39] Pinard concluded that Québec francophones feel the provincial government looks after their interests better than the federal government, and that they are correspondingly more loyal to the former. His surveys show that, in any conflict between the two governments, 40 percent of the francophone population favour the Québec government, compared to 15 percent who support the federal government. Therefore, "if there is a system of dual loyalties, loyalty to Québec nevertheless seems often much stronger than loyalty to Ottawa."[40]

The intensity and forms of loyalty among French Canadians appear to have changed in recent years. Between surveys done in 1970 and 1977, the group's self-identification increased substantially from "French Canadian," in which identification was with all French in Canada, to "Québécois," limited to the francophone population in the province of Québec. This was accompanied by increased support for sovereignty-association. In a 1992 study, however, Pinard concluded that in spite of the growth of support for sovereignty-association in recent years, Québécois prefer federalism:

> *From 1977 to 1991, many studies have measured both support for sovereignty-association and support for some form of renewed federalism, and they have in all instances found greater support for the latter.[41]*

---

37. Research on Québec attitudes is replete with controversy. The results seem to shift because of particular events and the manner and type of questions asked in the surveys. The more questions are posed in terms of the outright separation of Québec from Canada, the fewer positive responses are given. The more the question implies a "renewed" Canada, a "reformed" constitution or the like, the more positive the responses are. In other words, response pattern is determined by the nuances in the questions.

38. "Mon père m'a dit que c'est un peu comme s'il fallait choisir entre le chocolat et la crème glacé pour la vie...c'est très difficile quand on aime les deux!" *L'Actualité*, July 1992, p. 20.

39. See Maurice Pinard, "Ethnic Segmentation, Loyalties, Incentives and Constitutional Options in Quebec," p. 4. Paper presented at twinned workshop organized by the Canadian Political Science Association and the Israel Political Science Association at Sde Boker, Israel, December 11–16, 1978.

40. Ibid., p. 12.

41. Maurice Pinard, "The Dramatic Reemergence of the Quebec Independence Movement," *Journal of International Affairs,* vol. 45 (Winter 1992), pp. 471–97.

A majority of Québec francophones have long demonstrated a preference for remaining in Canada. But polls indicate that they only want to stay if their culture and language can be protected. This implies special powers for Québec, a privilege that raises objections and hostility in other provinces. These results correspond to a rise in support for greater autonomy for Québec. Escalating support for separatism in Québec during the 1980s and 1990s and the language issue are discussed in Chapter 7.

English-Speaking Canadians: A Cultural Fruitcake

While French Canadians enjoy cultural unity, English-speaking Canadians are a cultural mix. In fact, 38 percent of Canadians claimed an ethnic background other than Canadian, French or British in the 1996 census. Established anglophone groups often find their values and interests challenged by the newer groups. And members of the newer groups often feel threatened and discriminated against, resenting what they view as francophone privileges.

As we noted in Chapter 2, the many ethnic groups in Canada are very unevenly mixed throughout the population. Many are first-generation Canadians. According to the 1996 census, about 17.4 percent of Canadians are foreign-born, more than half of whom live in five large cities: Toronto, Montréal, Vancouver, Edmonton and Winnipeg. The top 15 ethnic origins are listed in Table 3.1. Toronto's population, for example, is more than 42 percent foreign-born. And, in Vancouver, English is spoken in fewer than half of the homes. Figure 3.4 indicates the immigration settlement patterns that give rise to this mixed ethnic composition of Canada's major cities.

World history shows that many states can successfully accommodate vast ethnic differences, but they do so in different ways. The United States is often viewed as a "melting pot," because it

TABLE 3.1   TOP 15 ETHNIC ORIGINS, BASED ON TOTAL RESPONSES, 1996 CENSUS*

	Total Responses	Single Responses	Muiltiple Responses
Total population	28 528 125	18 303 625	10 224 495
Canadian	8 806 275	5 326 995	3 479 285
English	6 832 095	2 048 275	4 783 820
French	5 597 845	2 665 250	2 932 595
Scottish	4 260 840	642 970	3 617 870
Irish	3 767 610	504 030	3 263 580
German	2 757 140	726 145	2 030 990
Italian	1 207 475	729 455	478 025
Aboriginal origins	1 101 955	477 630	624 330
Ukrainian	1 026 475	331 680	694 790
Chinese	921 585	800 470	121 115
Dutch (Netherlands)	916 215	313 880	602 335
Polish	786 735	265 930	520 805
South Asian origins	723 345	590 145	133 200
Jewish	351 705	195 810	155 900
Norwegian	346 310	47 805	298 500

*Ethnic origin, as defined in the census, refers to the ethnic or cultural group(s) to which an individual's ancestors belonged.
Source: Statistics Canada, Internet site www.statcan.ca

FIGURE 3.4   IMMIGRATION BY METRO AREA, 1994

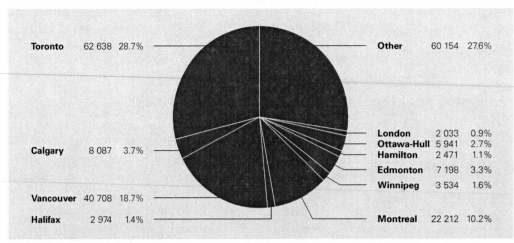

Toronto	62 638	28.7%
Other	60 154	27.6%
London	2 033	0.9%
Ottawa-Hull	5 941	2.7%
Hamilton	2 471	1.1%
Edmonton	7 198	3.3%
Winnipeg	3 534	1.6%
Calgary	8 087	3.7%
Vancouver	40 708	18.7%
Halifax	2 974	1.4%
Montreal	22 212	10.2%

Source: Citizenship and Immigration Canada, *A Broader Vision: 1996 Immigration Plan* (Ottawa: Supply and Services, 1996), p. 26. Reproduced with the permission of the Minister of Public Works and Government Services Canada, 1997.

was built through shared experiences and commitment to similar political ideals and values. Canada, on the other hand, is more of a "fruitcake." The Canadian approach has been to encourage different cultures to exist side by side in harmony and tolerance — not to "boil them down" in one melting pot. In other words, the Canadian model has been *integrative* or *pluralist,* as opposed to *assimilationist.* That approach was established in the Constitution (see Chapter 5) and continued with policies such as official bilingualism, multiculturalism, constitutional guarantees for aboriginal rights and equality provisions in the 1982 *Charter of Rights and Freedoms.* When non-English- or non-French-speaking immigrants choose Canada, they learn to speak English or French, and the process of "cultural layering" that Antonine Maillet spoke of begins. As the flow of immigrants to Canada increases and the ethnic composition of the country changes, the challenge is to maintain the balance between national loyalty and respect for diversity that has been such an important part of the Canadian political culture.[42] The importance of the challenge cannot be overstated.

Immigration: Patterns and Policies

Immigration is the basis of Canada's multi-ethnic population. In Canada, immigration is a shared jurisdiction between federal and provincial governments. Accordingly, the federal and provincial governments consult annually about desired numbers of immigrants and settlement measures. Because of its special concerns, the *Canada–Québec Accord* gives Québec the unique responsibility for the selection of immigrants destined to that province.

Since Confederation, immigrants have come to Canada in several large waves, the first three of which were related to depressed economic and/or postwar conditions in Europe. The first was between 1896 and 1914, and was composed mostly of British labourers, eastern European peasants and American farmers. The second wave was in the mid-1920s, when more hands were needed, particularly in the West, to clear marginal land and increase settlements. The majority of newcomers in the second wave were central and eastern Europeans. Many were refugees and most were

---

42. See Robert J. Jackson and Doreen Jackson, *Stand Up for Canada* (Scarborough: Prentice Hall, 1992), ch. 1.

TABLE 3.2   IMMIGRATION: TOP TEN COUNTRIES OF ORIGIN

Country	Number
Hong Kong	43 689
Philippines	18 720
India	16 655
China	12 283
Taiwan	7 338
Sri Lanka	6 301
Vietnam	6 125
United States	6 085
United Kingdom	5 857
Bosnia-Herzegovina	4 806

Source: Citizenship and Immigration Canada, *A Broader Vision: 1996 Immigration Plan* (Ottawa: Supply and Services, 1996), p. 25. Figures are for 1994. Reproduced with the permission of the Minister of Public Works and Government Services Canada, 1997.

very poor. Immigration ceased almost completely during the Depression in the 1930s. The third wave did not begin until after the Second World War; it lasted until 1960. Predominantly European in origin, it included significantly more well-educated professionals than the earlier waves.

The adoption of the Canadian Bill of Rights in 1960 was a turning point in Canada's immigration policy. For the first time a federal statute in Canada barred discrimination on the grounds of race, national origin, colour, religion or gender. In 1962, changes in federal immigration regulations resulted in a shift in the main source of immigrants to Canada from those with British or French origins to Asians. Immigration levels rose again in the mid-1960s, and despite fluctuations has remained well above 100 000 for most of the period until today. By 1991, the composition of immigrants had changed so that almost 75 percent came from Asia, Africa, Latin America and the Caribbean. (See Table 3.2 and Chapter 2.) In 1992, the pinnacle of the most recent wave, Canada accepted 253 000 immigrants and refugees.

In its 1993 pre-election *Red Book*, the Liberal party pledged to achieve annual immigration levels of about one percent of the national population — about 300 000. Instead, by 1995 it had cut the intake to about 200 000, arguing that the *composition* of immigration must change in order for the country to be able to absorb the higher levels envisioned in its campaign promise. To that end, it unveiled a new 10-year immigration plan, which shifted the balance away from favouring the unification of families. An increasing proportion of independent immigrants is now being selected on the basis of their skills and capacity to "settle in" and contribute quickly to Canadian society and the economy. In 1996, Canada accepted about 235 000 immigrants, including a small percentage of refugees and asylum-seekers. European-born immigrants continued to account for the largest proportion of all immigrants living in Canada in 1996, but their percentage was shrinking. They constituted 47 percent of the total immigrant population, while 31 percent were born in Asia and the Middle East.

Multiculturalism: Solution or Problem?

Over the years, the reception and accommodation of newcomers to Canada have changed considerably. The initial tendency was toward assimilation. Later, however, during the high immigration period of the later 1940s and the 1950s (a period of economic recovery marked by a rising tide of Canadian nationalism), cultural pluralism or, more commonly, multiculturalism gained popularity. **Multiculturalism** postulates that within the context of Canadian citizenship and economic and political integration, ethnic customs and cultures should be valued, preserved and shared. As noted above, it is an *integrative* approach, as opposed to an *assimilationist* approach. The basic assumption of this multicultural policy is that confidence in one's own cultural foundations helps to break down prejudice and discrimination between ethnic groups.

There were many reasons for the growth of liberal views toward ethnic groups, which began as early as the 1950s. Economic prosperity had eased cultural conflicts, and the new wave of immigrants (many of whom were educated or professional Europeans) helped to break down the rigid correlation between class and ethnicity. Britain was declining as a world power and therefore provided a less attractive model; at the same time, rising Canadian nationalism required a new self-image to distinguish Canada from the American melting pot. Perhaps the most immediate reasons for the advance of pluralist ideas at this time were the dramatic changes brought about by the Quiet Revolution in Québec. Many ethnic groups found the dualist image conveyed by the recommendations of the Royal Commission on Bilingualism and Biculturalism offensive and sought official assurance that their own aspirations and interests would not be overlooked. In fact, in response to their pressures, the Royal Commission produced a fourth volume dealing with the role of "other ethnic groups" in Canada.[43]

In the early 1970s, the federal government and the provincial governments of Ontario, Manitoba, Saskatchewan and Alberta formally adopted a policy of multiculturalism. In 1971, the federal government defined Canada as being multicultural within a bilingual English-French framework, and established the Cabinet position of Minister of State for Multiculturalism. Services on which ethnic groups could draw were steadily increased throughout the 1970s. A comprehensive *Multiculturalism Act* was passed in 1988, and a separate department, Multiculturalism and Citizenship Canada, was established in 1991, later to be merged into the portfolio of Canadian Heritage in 1993.

The difficulties of settling and integrating approximately 200 000 immigrants a year has made multiculturalism and immigration very controversial in recent years. The peak immigration years of 1990–92 occurred during a recession. The provinces, therefore, had to accept additional costs of absorbing record numbers of immigrants through language training, welfare and settlement programs. (See Figure 3.5.) Ontario, for example, accepted 52 percent of immigrants and 60 percent of refugees at the same time as the recession cut jobs and increased unemployment and welfare caseloads. Concurrently, the federal government cut the immigration department's budget and also the number of employees. Federal funding to the provinces also declined. The mismatch of strong demand and weak facilities caused considerable frustration and anger.

Apart from these immediate problems, multiculturalism creates a tension between duality and plurality in Canadian society. A commitment to multiculturalism makes it difficult to discriminate between "ethnic" and "official" languages in geographical areas where other-ethnic groups are concentrated and outnumber French-speaking or English-speaking minority populations. In Toronto and western Canada, in particular, where high other-ethnic populations exist under an English-language umbrella, there is pressure to make French no more important than other minority languages.

Since the Second World War, only Israel and Australia have accepted numbers of immigrants in proportion to their populations on a scale comparable to Canada. To date, Canadian society has proven remarkably resilient in accommodating large numbers of newcomers with relatively little social stress. However, it is vital that adequate infrastructures such as language, culture and citizenship

---

43. *Report of the Royal Commission on Bilingualism and Biculturalism*, Book 4 (Ottawa: Queen's Printer, 1970).

FIGURE 3.5   IMMIGRATION BY PROVINCE

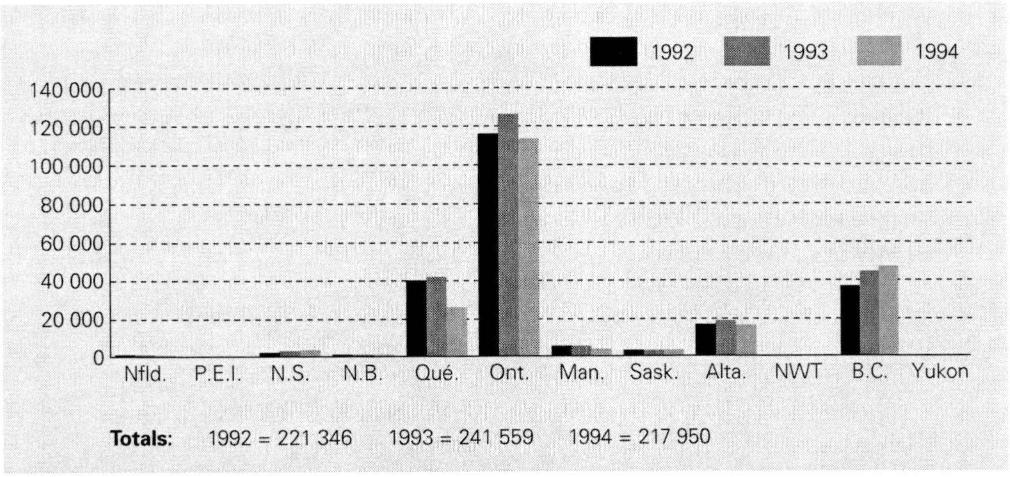

Source: Citizenship and Immigration Canada, *A Broader Vision: Immigration Plan* (Ottawa: Supply and Services, 1996), p. 26. Reproduced with the permission of the Minister of Public Works and Government Services Canada, 1997.

training are available to help immigrants adapt and integrate successfully. This is particularly urgent, since the pattern of immigrant sources has changed dramatically over the last decade, with increasing numbers coming from developing countries.

Racism

Over 3.2 million Canadians are members of visible minority groups as of 1996 — about 11 percent of the total population. More than half live in Ontario, 21 percent in British Columbia, and 14 percent in Québec. In spite of Canada's integrative and pluralist model, ethnic cleavages persist. Ethnic visible minorities tend to integrate less easily into Canadian society than do white European immigrants. In part this is because they struggle against racist attitudes in the population. **Racial discrimination** is the imposition of handicaps, barriers and different treatment on individuals because of their race. It is fed by prejudice and negative stereotypes. It creates a vicious cycle in which mainstream society is fearful and suspicious and the minority group is withdrawn and defensive. Often members of minority groups become concentrated in specific neighbourhoods or geographical areas, and this tends to reinforce their social and ethnic differences.

Unintentional *institutional* discrimination known as **systemic discrimination** creates an additional hurdle for visible minorities. It manifests itself in higher levels of unemployment and exclusion from certain sectors of the economy for certain ethnic groups. Unfortunately, cultural tolerance is a self-congratulatory ideal that Canadians have not always lived up to. Incidents of racial bigotry in Canadian history include the shameful internment of Japanese Canadians during the Second World War and the often shabby treatment of Native peoples. Racist ideologies are condemned, but still persist. Some sociologists even maintain that "racism is a virulent ideology held by Canadians. There is a belief that certain groups (non-whites) are inferior to whites and this justifies invidious distinctions and behaviours directed toward them."[44]

---

44. Alan B. Anderson and James S. Frideres, *Ethnicity in Canada* (Toronto: Butterworths, 1981), p. 229. See also Jean Leonard Elliot and Augie Fleras, *Unequal Relations: An Introduction to Race and Ethnic Dynamics in Canada* (Scarborough: Prentice Hall, 1992).

Evidence of both overt and covert racism in Canadian society led in 1981 to the federal government announcement of a national program to combat racism, and the establishment of a Race Relations Unit within the Multiculturalism Directorate. Shortly after, a Special Committee on the Participation of Visible Minorities in Canadian Society was set up to seek positive ideas for ameliorating relations within Canada between visible minorities and other Canadians. Their report, published in 1984, presented evidence of discriminatory mechanisms in Canadian government and society.[45] Systemic discrimination is being addressed by public policy solutions. The committee report emphasized that attitudinal changes need to be addressed to foster awareness, understanding and tolerance — particularly since contemporary immigration trends indicate that Canadians must anticipate an even greater racial mix in the population.

Cartoon by Steve Nease. Used with permission.

A study by T. John Samuel concludes that the number of Canadians who are members of a visible minority will rise to 5.7 million by 2001 — an increase from 9.6 to 17.7 percent of the total population in just a decade. In large metropolitan areas, the percentage will be higher.[46] He concludes that as a group these visible minorities will be relatively affluent, controlling about 20 percent of the country's GDP. This will represent a significant change in Canada's societal composition. The potential for increased racial tension is high.

Ethnicity and Political Culture

The existence of significant subcultures within a country can be disruptive to the dominant political culture if group ties are stronger than loyalty to the country. Does ethnic diversity in Canada fragment the overall political culture and make the country less cohesive? Certainly, Canada has experienced several ethnic crises in which group loyalties conflicted strongly with larger community loyalty, although these were confined to the two founding groups. In these extreme situations, doubts were raised about the efficacy of the federal system of government to meet the needs of an ethnically diverse country and even about whether the country should stay united. However, it would be pessimistic to regard such crises as the norm.

Optimistic conclusions about the multi-ethnic nature of Canadian society can be drawn from research by David Elkins that reinforces the suggestion of the Bilingualism and Biculturalism Commission

---

45. Special Committee on the Participation of Visible Minorities in Canadian Society, *Equality Now!* (Ottawa: Queen's Printer, 1984).

46. T. John Samuel, "Social Dimensions of Immigration Policy in Canada," paper presented at the International Conference on Race Relations: Policy Practices and Research in 1990. Toronto: York University, June 27–30, 1990; and Pamela M. White and T. John Samuel, "Immigration and Ethnic Diversity in Urban Canada, *International Journal of Canadian Studies,* vol. 3 (Spring 1991), pp. 70–85.

that multiculturalism strengthens Canadian unity. Elkins concluded that ignorance of one's own and other nations is associated with parochial, localist sentiments, while knowledge about and appreciation of other nations is an enriching experience that encourages individuals to feel warmer toward their own country.[47] A partial explanation, he suggested, lies in the fact that most immigrants to Canada are from countries with strong central governments. For example, the largest single group of immigrants comes from Britain, which has a unitary system of government. It is logical that these newcomers would support the familiar idea that the central government should be the strongest and most important voice in the country. Elkins found that native-born Canadians are more provincially oriented than immigrants, and that the longer immigrants are in the country, the more provincially oriented they become.

Another counter-intuitive finding about immigrants to Canada is that they are on average slightly more efficacious in their political attitudes than native-born Canadians. Elkins speculates that individuals who act positively to improve their personal environment by emigrating may demonstrate self-reliant, efficacious behaviour that might explain their high score on political efficacy.[48]

As well as having warmer feelings toward the whole country than do native-born Canadians who remain in one region, immigrants and internal migrants adopt norms and patterns of behaviour characteristic of the province in which they settle. This assimilation to provincial values and attitudes appears to be a function of both length of residence and type of background. Relatively recent or first-generation immigrant minorities tend to be concerned primarily with problems of adjustment to their new circumstances, whereas well-established minorities are less concerned with the persistence of their ethnicity than with increasing their collective economic and political strength.[49] When language, religious affiliation and adherence to custom are used as criteria, ethnic identity is not static, but changes steadily from one generation to the next as individuals adapt to Canadian circumstances. The 1981 census, for example, showed that 10 percent of those with a first language other than English or French were able to speak not one but *both* official languages — 2 percent higher than those whose first language was English.

Today, except in Québec, minority groups are most valued where they are most concentrated. The 1996 census results showed Ontario to be by far the largest centre for nearly all ethnic groups, followed by British Columbia, Alberta and Manitoba. About one-quarter of Ontario's population comprised immigrants. Newfoundland, at the other extreme, counted fewer than 2 percent of its population as immigrants.

Low acceptance of minority groups by Québec respondents reflects the tendency of some French Canadians to regard other cultures and languages as a potential threat. Any acceptance of other ethnic claims, it is argued, undermines the concept of dualism for the country and reduces the French claim to that of the largest of the minority cultures.

Bilingualism and multiculturalism are uniquely Canadian responses that deal with uniquely Canadian circumstances. To date, research supports the positive effect of the cultural mosaic and indicates that multiculturalism is not to be feared, but encouraged. Ethnic cultures erode over time: studies of language, religion and customs as indicators of ethnic strength all support this view. Given this erosion, it is sometimes argued that multiculturalism is a form of assimilation. On the other

47. David Elkins, "The Sense of Place," in David J. Elkins and Richard Simeon, eds., *Small Worlds* (Toronto: Methuen, 1980), pp. 1–30.

48. Ibid., and David Elkins, "The Horizontal Mosaic: Immigrants and Migrants in the Provincial Political Cultures," in Elkins and Simeon, eds., *Small Worlds*, pp. 106–30.

49. Wsevolod Isajiw, "Immigration and Multiculturalism — Old and New Approaches," paper presented at the Conference on Multiculturalism and Third World Immigrants in Canada, University of Alberta, Edmonton, September 3–5, 1975, p. 2.

hand, there is no doubt that to encourage immigrants to remain in a cultural ghetto, emphasizing their difference from mainstream Canadian culture, delays their integration into Canadian society and thereby fragments national cohesiveness.

In many ways, the term "multicultural" is misleading: multi-ethnic describes the Canadian reality more accurately. Whether or not one views multiculturalism as a viable policy depends on how it is defined. Jean Burnet addressed the issue by saying, "multiculturalism within a bilingual framework can work, if it is interpreted as is intended — that is, as encouraging those members of ethnic groups who want to do so to maintain a proud sense of the contribution of their own group to Canadian society."[50] In this way, the policy becomes something very Canadian: a voluntary, marginal differentiation among peoples who are equal participants in society. Cultures cannot be preserved in their entirety; immigrants do adapt to the language and customs of the majority. But in doing so they add a richness, variety and depth to the cultural tapestry. The formal adoption of bilingual and multicultural policies enshrines ethnic tolerance among the other important values of Canadian government but it does not necessarily mean that they are realized in society.

> There cannot be one cultural policy for Canadians of British and French origin, another for the original peoples and yet a third for all others. For although there are two official languages, there is no official culture, nor does any ethnic group take precedence over any other.... A policy of multiculturalism within a bilingual framework commends itself to the government as the most suitable means of assuring the cultural freedom of Canadians.
>
> **Pierre Trudeau, in Parliament, October 8, 1971**

Native Peoples: Indians, Métis and Inuit

A third ethno-linguistic division lies between Canada's Native peoples — a group that consists of status and non-status Indians, Métis and Inuit — and other Canadians. These aboriginal peoples are spread through every province and territory, with the largest population in Ontario. Each group is distinctive. Altogether, Native peoples constitute about 3 percent of the Canadian population.

The term "Indian" was legally defined in the first *Indian Act* in 1876. Since then, anyone whose name appears on the band list of any Indian community in Canada, or on a central registry list, is considered to be Indian. The concept of "status Indian" was adopted in order to determine who had rights to Indian land. Status Indians are either Indians who are registered members of a band that "took treaty" with the Crown, surrendering land rights for specific benefits, or registered Indians who did not. Since they are registered, both types of status Indians receive benefits and privileges from the federal government. There are over 600 Indian bands across Canada and approximately 300 000 Indians living on reserves. However, more than half of all status Indians live in urban centres. The greatest total number is in Metropolitan Toronto, but aboriginal people form a higher percentage of the total population in cities such as Winnipeg, Regina and Saskatoon.

---

50. Jean Burnet, "The Policy of Multiculturalism within a Bilingual Framework: An Interpretation," in A. Wolfgang, *The Education of Immigrant Students: Issues and Answers* (Toronto: Ontario Institute for Studies in Education, 1975). See Stephen Brooks, *Public Policy in Canada: An Introduction* (Toronto: McClelland & Stewart, 1993), ch. 9, for a good summary and comments on federal policy on language and ethnicity.

Non-status Indians are all others of Indian ancestry and cultural affiliation who actively or passively have given up their status rights but not their Indian identity. Métis, for example, are descendants of unions between whites and Indians. They retain their Indian identity but do not enjoy special status under federal policy.[51] Apart from a few settlements in Alberta and Manitoba, Métis and non-status Indians do not have reserves at all. In fact, the exact size of the Métis population is not even known. According to Martin Dunn, a very rough and conservative estimate is that there are three Métis and non-status Indians for every registered Indian.[52] They are thinly scattered across the country and do not benefit from the special provisions for reserves and services under the *Indian Act.* In 1985, Parliament provided a procedure to restore Indian status to those who had lost it.

The Inuit in Canada, scattered throughout the Arctic in eight distinct communities, have never been subject to the *Indian Act* and were largely ignored by government until 1939, when they officially became a federal responsibility. Since that time they have been classified as "Indians" for the purposes of the Constitution. In 1996, about 800 000 people claimed aboriginal ancestry, of whom 70 percent were North American Indians, 25 percent were Métis, and about 5 percent were Inuit.

Today's aboriginal issues are rooted deep in the past. While nineteenth-century British authorities made many efforts to accommodate the French minority, they demonstrated little such concern for the rights of the "First Nations." At Confederation, the federal Parliament was assigned legislative jurisdiction over Indians and the land reserved for them.[53] Shortly thereafter, Parliament passed legislation that represented a clear policy of assimilation of aboriginal peoples. Essentially, Indians on reserves were to be protected temporarily until they learned European methods of farming. They would then be qualified to relinquish their Indian status. Reserve privileges were considered as a kind of probationary period of Canadian citizenship.

The *Indian Act* of 1876 was amended frequently in subsequent years, but always with the aim of suppressing Indian traditions and extending government control over status Indians on reserves. The current Act, passed in 1951, remains an essentially nineteenth-century statute that reflects early biases and intentions. Although it has been widely condemned as paternalistic, the *Indian Act* was intended to protect Native people within Canadian society and to provide a broad range of social programs. All Indians receive the same benefits as other Canadians, such as family allowances and pensions, and status Indians also have a right to a wide variety of other benefits in the field of education, health care and housing. In fact, however, these people have been left dependent on government.

Aboriginal Rights

Court decisions over the years have been unable to define aboriginal rights adequately. Until the *Constitution Act, 1982,* Parliament had the power to pass laws extinguishing any or all such rights. However, Native groups never agreed that Parliament had such sweeping powers. The *Constitution Act, 1982,* clears up the situation to a degree. It recognizes aboriginal and treaty rights and provides a new basis for court challenges. (See Chapter 5.)

Aboriginal rights are based on Native peoples' occupancy and use of North America before Europeans arrived. Traditional aboriginal societies were based primarily on hunting and gathering and, to a minor extent, agriculture. Therefore, their relationship to the land defines aboriginal

51. See *Canada, Aboriginal Peoples, Self-Government, and Constitutional Reform* (Ottawa: Supply and Services, 1991).
52. Martin Dunn, *Access to Survival: A Perspective on Aboriginal Self-Government for the Constituency of the Native Council of Canada* (Kingston: Queen's Institute for Intergovernmental Relations, 1986).
53. *BNA Act,* 91:24. For background, see J.R. Miller, *Skyscrapers Hide the Heavens: A History of Indian-White Relations in Canada* (Toronto: University of Toronto Press, 1989).

culture and economy. They consider that land was put here by the Creator for the use of *all* people and, therefore, in aboriginal culture, belongs to everyone living today and to the unborn to come.

Although aboriginal rights are not defined in detail in Canada's Constitution, it is generally agreed that they include rights to hunt and fish, harvest food, and have access to and occupancy of land to conduct these activities. Where previous treaty or land-claims agreements are not in place surrendering such rights, governments are bound by the Constitution to protect or compensate aboriginals before they can sell the land or grant interest in it to third parties.

Native peoples still occupy a dependent, semi-colonial position in regard to the federal and provincial governments. Proposals to end Indian status and repeal the *Indian Act* have been called for by Natives who want greater recognition of their traditional rights, settlement of land claims and power to manage their own lands and affairs. The Grand Chief of the Assembly of First Nations, Georges Erasmus, put the case this way: "We want to have a relationship with this country that is nation to nation" as expressed in the "two-row wampum" analogy of the Mohawks.

> *The two-row wampum is an agreement whereby two nations co-exist and travel the River of Life in peace and friendship.... Legally, it means that each of the two nations retains its own respective laws and jurisdiction. Neither of the two nations can apply or impose its laws over the other.*[54]

Aboriginal people have different values than do mainstream Canadians because of their unique history in a hunting-and-gathering economy. The values of these diverse groups of people tend to be collectivist, based on an organic concept of community where individuals are only a specialized part of a whole society. Decision-making is generally consensual, not majoritarian. Traditional leadership tends to be diffuse with different leaders in different areas of specialization. Today, these values are being incorporated into new governments in the North, and also in First Nation self-government agreements.

Relative Deprivation

The traditional ways of life of Canada's aboriginal peoples have been eroded over the years and their economic well-being seriously threatened. As a whole, compared with other Canadians, Canada's Native peoples are economically deprived. Many are plagued by alcoholism and depression as they strive to cope with the loss of their traditional lifestyle because of the encroachments of modern society and environmental disasters. Métis and non-status Indians usually find themselves among the underprivileged sections of Canadian society and are subject to similar racial stereotyping and prejudice. The Inuit, because of their location in the Northwest Territories, northern Québec and Labrador, largely have been bypassed in the economic and political modernization of Canada.

> *We cannot escape the fact that we have built a great liberal democracy in part through the dispossession of aboriginal peoples and the imposition of our cultural norms.*
> **The Royal Commission on Aboriginal Peoples, 1996**

Past treatment of Native peoples is a point of shame for Canadians. The condition of status Indians who live on reserves is indicative of the problem. In modern times, this population has grown substantially, largely because of reductions in infant mortality rates and high rates of fertility.

54. As recorded in documents sent to Québec premier Robert Bourassa, August 20, 1990.

Their rate of population growth is well over twice that of the rest of Canadians. Approximately 40 percent of the Indian population are between the ages of 15 and 35, compared to 35 percent of the total Canadian population.

During the post–Second World War period, Indian migration to the cities increased dramatically due to poor conditions on the reserves. There, the migrants suffered from the same type of conditions as they had hoped to escape — high unemployment and economic deprivation.

Despite (some would say because of) government assistance, Indians on reserves live in abysmal social conditions. While all non-Native municipalities in Canada meet basic standards, one in five Indian reserves has water and sewage systems comparable to the worst of the developing countries.[55] As well, the rate of tuberculosis is 43 times higher than among non-aboriginal Canadians who were born in this country.[56]

Further examples of these conditions in the 1980s and 1990s can be summarized as follows:

- High school completion rates are low: 20 percent compared to about 70 percent for non-Natives.

- Only 22 percent of the adult Indian population have training beyond high school, compared to 40 percent of the rest of the Canadian population.

- Participation in the labour force is low: 50 percent compared to 65 percent for non-Natives.

- Unemployment is about twice as high as the national average.

- Employment pay is about two-thirds the national average.

- Life expectancy, infant mortality, rates of suicide and violent death are all worse for Natives than non-Natives.

- Native children are four times as likely to die by the age of 14 as non-Natives.

- The rate of death by fire on reserves is six times that of the Canadian population.

- Environmental hazards threaten traditional ways of life: industrial and resource development have polluted waterways and disrupted fish and game stocks on which many depend for food and livelihood.

- Reserves endure low housing standards, with overcrowding and insufficient access to indoor plumbing, running water and electricity as the norm. One government task force concluded that fewer than 50 percent of Indian houses were fully serviced with sewers and water compared to a national rate of 90 percent.[57]

Further evidence of deprivation is found in studies commissioned by the Department of Indian Affairs and Northern Development on the future of aboriginal life in Canada. These studies of demographic trends, social conditions and the economic future for Canada's Native peoples for the years 1981 to 2001 indicate that while improvements are being made, the gap between them and their fellow Canadians will remain fairly constant unless there are major policy innovations.[58]

---

55. From a draft report by Health Canada and Indian Affairs, in *The Ottawa Citizen*, May 3, 1995.

56. Statistics Canada, reported in *The Globe and Mail*, November 30, 1994.

57. For figures, see Erik Nielsen, *New Management Initiatives* (Ottawa: Government of Canada, 1985). A 1992 study by Health and Welfare Canada found that Natives are more than three times as likely to die a violent death before age 65 as non-Natives and about twice as likely to die of any cause before 65. *The Globe and Mail*, December 30, 1992.

58. Department of Indian Affairs and Northern Development, *Highlights of Aboriginal Conditions 1981–2001: Demographic Trends, Social Conditions, Economic Conditions* (Ottawa: Department of Indian Affairs and Northern Development, 1989).

CLOSE-UP ON
Culture

THE STATUS OF COMPREHENSIVE CLAIMS (1999)

Settled Claims

- James Bay and Northern Québec Agreement (1975)
- The Northeastern Québec Agreement (1978)
- Inuvialuit Final Agreement (1984)
- Gwich'in Agreement — NWT (1992)
- Nunavut Land Claims Agreement (1993)
- Sahtu Dene and Métis Agreement (1994)
- Four Yukon First Nations Final Agreements (1994)
- Treaties 1 to 11

Redressing Grievances: Land Claims and Self-Government

While they are divided on many other issues, Native peoples are united in a quest for settlement of their land claims and recognition of their "inherent right of self-government."

Land Claims

As we noted in Chapter 2, land claims are an urgent problem. In some areas treaties have not been signed; in others they are blatantly unfair or not respected. In recent years, as courts began to make judgements favouring aboriginal claimants, governments have speeded up attempts to negotiate comprehensive and specific land-claims agreements. (See "The Status of Comprehensive Claims [1999]") These are intended by governments to replace undefined aboriginal rights with defined rights in an agreement or treaty. Where treaties exist, courts are forcing governments to live up to former "treaty obligations" and are providing compensation where it is due.

Despite the federal government's authority over Native peoples, *provincial* governments are in control of public lands, so negotiations are complicated. Only in the North, where the federal government is in charge of the land, have claims moved relatively quickly. As of 1993, all of Canada's North above the 60th parallel was covered by final agreements or agreements in principle about land claims. Further south, the reserves are generally inadequate for economic development and the resource needs of the aboriginal communities. In order to become economically self-sufficient, these peoples must be assured of a secure and expanded land base. The alternative is for them to remain dependent on governments, and for increasing numbers of aboriginal groups to seek court settlements over disputes in such matters as logging and mining on Crown lands licensed by provincial governments.

About half the over 600 status Indian bands of Canada have not ceded their traditional territories by treaty with the Canadian government. The Indians of most of British Columbia, Québec and the territories have not entered into such treaties, and claim outstanding aboriginal rights over, and title to, their traditional lands. They have asserted historic rights to roughly half the country. In British Columbia, for example, Native groups claim 110 percent of the provincial land mass because of overlapping claims by bands.[59] In 1998, the Nisga'a claim was initialled by authorities from Ottawa, British Columbia and Native leaders. After considerable controversy, it was approved by the House of Commons a year later. However, 50 other claims are still under negotiation in the province of British Columbia alone. In Québec, Native groups claim about 85 percent of the province. The current comprehensive land-claims process is notoriously complicated and slow; only a few claims across the country can be in negotiation at any one time. All other groups must wait until those negotiations are completed, and each case can take as many as 20 years to settle. At this rate injustices will continue, and claims will still be heard well into the twenty-first century.

---

59. The government has stated that it will cede no more than 5 percent of the total B.C. land mass to settle all claims, and that no privately owned land will be included. Most Crown land will also be protected. This figure was chosen because Indians make up about 5 percent of the B.C. population. *The Globe and Mail*, May 29, 1995.

A further complication of territorial claims is that Québec's Indians do not want to remain part of that province if it decides to separate from Canada. The Assembly of First Nations' report on the Charlottetown constitutional proposal stated: "If Quebec has the right to separate from Canada, First Nations have the right to make their own decisions. And if that means separation from Quebec, so be it." The Cree claim more than a million square kilometres of sparsely populated land, a tract bigger than Ontario and nearly twice the size of France. The claim includes the land on which the James Bay power installations, which generate nearly half of Québec's current electricity, are located, as well as the vast untapped hydro potential of other northern rivers. (See Chapter 7.)

Self-Government

Self-government is another broad, contentious issue concerning Native peoples. Attempts to achieve constitutional recognition failed with the collapse of the Charlottetown accord (see Chapter 5), and the courts have not yet ruled whether there is an aboriginal right to self-government. In fact, there is no agreement about what self-government means. For some it is to be a level of government much like a municipality. For others the "First Nations" would constitute a third order of government. According to some Native leaders, such rights should not even be defined in documents such as the Constitution because they are "inherent rights."

Under self-government, as conceived by the Chrétien government, First Nations would remain subject to almost all federal and provincial laws and their powers would be only slightly greater than those of Canadian villages, towns or cities. However, Native leaders maintain they cannot accept any imposition on the inherent right of their people to govern themselves. They argue that no Canadian government is in a position to grant a right that predates it and that has no source in any imperial, colonial or Dominion authority. They consider that their right to govern themselves is a pre-existing, continuing, natural right given to them by the Great Creator. It cannot be given or taken away by any government. They reason that they have never themselves given up their right to self-government, and it has never been extinguished by any legislation (because such power could not exist). The courts and international law affirm that aboriginal rights may be extinguished only by treaty or conquest, or by an explicit act of the Parliament of Canada.

> *We've made enough mistakes for them. It's time for them to make their own mistakes.*
>
> **Jean Chrétien**

In spite of these differences, however, the federal and several provincial and territorial governments have begun to negotiate agreements with First Nation peoples concerning how they will relate to other governments in Canada within the existing constitutional framework. There already exist many limited self-government arrangements that give bands powers equal to or greater than those of a municipal government, allowing Native reserves to order their land and allocate their resources. Beyond this, plans are in place to dismantle the offices of the Department of Indian and Northern Affairs in some provinces, beginning with Manitoba, which was chosen for the first major self-government project. Public opinion polls indicate strong support for Native self-government, although it appears that neither the Canadian public nor Native groups themselves have a clear idea of what exactly is meant by the term or what it will cost.

In late 1996, the Royal Commission on Aboriginal Peoples delivered a five-volume report with over 400 recommendations, which, in essence, said that the relationship between aboriginal people and non-aboriginal people in Canada should "be restructured fundamentally." Some of those recommendations proposed radical changes such as a new, third level of government. (See "Highlights of the Royal Commission on Aboriginal Peoples.")

The response of the Liberal government was muted. Essentially, it said that the estimated $30 billion cost of the proposals was too great, and that it would have to set priorities. However, there have been several landmark events since 1996. (See "Significant Developments in Aboriginal Affairs, 1996–99.")

CLOSE-UP ON Culture

HIGHLIGHTS OF THE ROYAL COMMISSION ON ABORIGINAL PEOPLES

- An aboriginal parliament should be created, to be known as the House of First Peoples.

- All governments should recognize that the inherent right of aboriginal self-government is a treaty right affirmed in the Constitution.

- An independent lands and treaties tribunal should be created to decide on land claims, and to ensure that treaty negotiations are conducted and financed fairly.

- The Department of Indian and Northern Affairs should be replaced with an aboriginal relations department and an Indian and Inuit services department.

- Governments should negotiate with Métis representatives on self-government and provide them with adequate land bases.

- Government funds should be increased for Native peoples: $1.5 billion a year until 2003 and $2 billion a year for 10 more years.

- Aboriginal women should be assured of full and equal participation in decision-making bodies responsible for physical and emotional security.

REGIONAL CLEAVAGES AND POLITICAL CULTURE

There is widespread acceptance in the theoretical literature of comparative politics of the thesis that strong regional interests are incompatible with mature statehood, that state-building involves a gradual reduction of conflict between regional and national interests. While this contention is not without severe critics, it remains one of the primary hypotheses about the growth and development of states and their legitimacy.[60] In this section, we address the question that links culture and regionalism: How strong is regionalism in Canada and is it increasing or decreasing? Other aspects of regionalism are discussed in Chapters 5, 6 and 7. The strong effect of regionalism on electoral results is discussed in Chapter 12.

Impressive factual data exist about distinct regional forms of social behaviour in Canada. Some researchers have argued that Canada has not merely one or even two "political cultures," but several that are regionally based. In view of the distinctions we made earlier, these are not "cultures" *per se*, but rather important subcultures within the overarching Canadian political culture. The establishment of a federal form of government gave a structural guarantee that some form of regionalism would flourish in Canada; indeed, it was chosen partly because it would allow regional diversity.

Numerous factors promote and sustain this constitutionalized regionalism. People of varying historical, cultural and linguistic backgrounds settled in different parts of the country. (See Table 3.3.) Geographical and economic disparities among the regions fostered distinct viewpoints, loyalties and attitudes toward national political problems. Regional economic disparities based on natural resources, manufacturing centres, climate and proximity to markets create "have" and "have not" provinces. People who live in the various regions feel the impact of these differences in terms of average disposable income, unemployment and poverty levels. Distinct political cultures and ways of life arise based on different circumstances and

60. See Raymond Breton, "Regionalism in Canada," in David Cameron, ed., *Regionalism and Supranationalism* (Montréal: Institute for Research on Public Policy, 1981).

needs. The institutions and policies of the various provincial governments reflect differences in the values and attitudes of their citizens.

The term **regionalism** is particularly obtuse. It implies a sociopsychological dimension in that the population displays an emotional identification with or attachment to a given territory. There is also a political dimension in that specific interests — cultural, economic and political — can be defined and articulated for a particular area. There is thus general agreement that regions are more than purely scientific artifacts, but many different opinions surface about exactly what they are, how many there are or what their boundaries might be.

Some researchers hold that the boundaries of each of the 10 provinces demarcate regions with separate political cultures. Others maintain that there are three, four or five regions. In the following pages, we have adopted a popular conception of Canadian regional boundaries wherein six regions are identified: the Atlantic provinces (Newfoundland, Nova Scotia, New Brunswick and Prince Edward Island); Québec; Ontario; the Prairies (Manitoba, Saskatchewan and Alberta); British Columbia; and the North (Yukon, Northwest Territories and Nunavut). However, the reader should be aware that basing regions on provincial boundaries (or groups of provinces) is largely a convenience, and that significant variations in cultural patterns may well occur within these borders — for example, between northern and southern Ontario.

Six Regional Profiles

Four main categories of regional differences lead researchers to expect cultural diversity: physical factors (such as climate, terrain and land quality); demographic factors (including ethnic and religious composition, and urbanization); economic development (including natural resources and type of economy); and services that affect the quality of life (such as transportation, health and welfare). The following brief profiles of Canada's six regions illustrate some of these important differences.

As Table 3.3 shows, the four *Atlantic provinces* in 1996 possessed 8.1 percent of the population of Canada. The inhabitants are largely of British and Irish ancestry, with pockets of Acadian French, centred in New Brunswick. The majority are Protestant, but Roman Catholics constitute the largest single denomination. Their formal educational level is relatively low, they are relatively poor, and they usually have the highest unemployment levels in Canada. (See "The Maritimes in Comparative Perspective.") Most reside in rural areas and small towns. Economically, the major contribution comes through the fisheries, of which more than half

CLOSE-UP ON Culture

SIGNIFICANT DEVELOPMENTS IN ABORIGINAL AFFAIRS, 1996–99

Since 1996, a combination of events and court rulings have strengthened the hand of aboriginal peoples regarding land claims and other rights. The major developments include:

1996: The report of the Royal Commission on Aboriginal Peoples is released.

1997: The Supreme Court of Canada overturns a decision by a British Columbia court in ruling that aboriginal oral histories are a valid basis for land claims. It also confirms that Native lands cannot be sold, except to the Crown. These lands are communally owned with exclusive right of use by the Native communities concerned.

1998: The federal Minister of Indian Affairs responds to the 1996 Royal Commission with a Statement of Reconciliation, apologizing for the residential school system and allocating $600 million for Native initiatives.

1998: British Columbia, Ottawa and Native leaders initial the Nisga'a land claim giving the Nisga'a $253 million over 15 years and more than 2 000 square kilometres of land, resource rights and powers of self-government. The deal was approved by the House of Commons after an arduous debate in late 1999.

1999: The Supreme Court of Canada rules that a 1760 treaty gives Mi'kmaq year-round fishing rights. The Court later clarifies the decision by claiming that the federal government still has a role to play in issues relating to fishing regulations in the area.

1999: The Federal Court of Appeal rules that the National Energy Board did not adequately deal with Native concerns when it granted a private company rights to build a $1.7 billion Sable Island natural gas pipeline.

1999: Nisga'a land claim was approved by the House of Commons.

TABLE 3.3   PERCENTAGE DISTRIBUTION OF CANADIAN POPULATION BY PROVINCE AND REGION, 1996

Province	%	Region	%
Newfoundland	1.9	Atlantic Provinces	8.1
Prince Edward Island	0.5	Québec	24.7
Nova Scotia	3.2	Ontario	37.6
New Brunswick	2.5	Prairie Provinces	16.5
Québec	24.7	British Columbia	12.9
Ontario	37.6	Northland	0.3
Manitoba	3.8		100.1
Saskatchewan	3.4		
Alberta	9.3		
British Columbia	12.9		
Yukon Territory	0.1		
Northwest Territory	0.2		
	100.1		

Source: Data adapted from *Canada Year Book 1999*, p. 85.

CLOSE-UP ON Culture

THE MARITIMES IN COMPARATIVE PERSPECTIVE

The Atlantic region is commonly regarded by Canadians as a collection of four have-not provinces. This idea should, however, be kept in perspective. Together, Nova Scotia, New Brunswick, Newfoundland and Prince Edward Island may have incomes lower than in other parts of the country but they are not poor by other standards. According to one study comparing the Maritimes data with that of the 1996 United Nations Human Development Index, "Atlantic Canada's performance ... is roughly one percent ahead of the U.S. and Japan, but as much as three to four percent ahead of Italy." As a country, Atlantic Canada would rank as the second-best place in the world to live.

Source: *The Ottawa Citizen*, June 10, 1996.

Canada's total are located here. The region is seriously deficient in secondary industries and contributes less than the other regions to the national wealth in proportion to the population. Federal transfer payments make up 30 to 50 percent of provincial revenues. Both internal and external communications are relatively inadequate. Low immigration and a tendency toward outward migration have often meant a net loss of inhabitants for the region as a percentage of the country's total population. For example, it dropped from 12 percent in 1951 to 8.1 percent in 1996.

Québec is the bastion of French language and culture, and is largely Roman Catholic in composition. Eighty-three percent of Québec residents were French-speaking at the time of the 1991 census. The province's population growth is below the country's average. Québec's percentage of Canada's population in 1996 was down to 24.7 percent from 29 percent about two decades earlier. Economically, Québec and neighbouring Ontario are the most industrialized regions, with major contributions to agriculture, mining, forestries, electric power, manufacturing and construction. Québec has a rapidly growing urban population that is located in a few major cities; 80 percent of its population was classified as urban in 1986. In 1996, Montréal had the highest poverty rate of any city in the country.[61]

---

61. In a list of 25 Canadian cities, Montréal was followed by Trois Rivières, Sherbrooke and Québec City — which were ranked second, fourth and seventh respectively with respect to poverty level. *The Ottawa Citizen*, June 29, 1996.

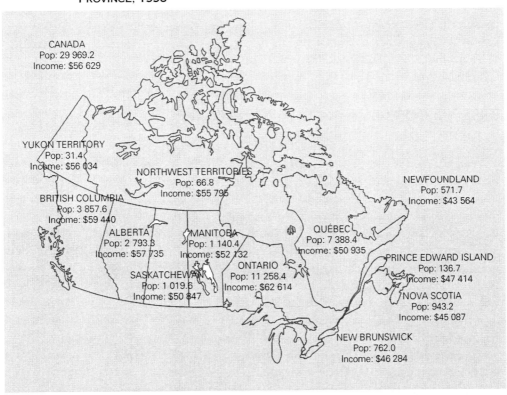

FIGURE 3.6   POPULATION (IN THOUSANDS), 1997, AND FAMILY INCOME IN CANADA BY
PROVINCE, 1996

CANADA
Pop: 29 969.2
Income: $56 629

YUKON TERRITORY
Pop: 31.4
Income: $56 034

NORTHWEST TERRITORIES
Pop: 66.8
Income: $55 795

NEWFOUNDLAND
Pop: 571.7
Income: $43 564

BRITISH COLUMBIA
Pop: 3 857.6
Income: $59 440

ALBERTA
Pop: 2 793.8
Income: $57 735

MANITOBA
Pop: 1 140.4
Income: $52 132

QUÉBEC
Pop: 7 388.4
Income: $50 935

PRINCE EDWARD ISLAND
Pop: 136.7
Income: $47 414

SASKATCHEWAN
Pop: 1 019.6
Income: $50 847

ONTARIO
Pop: 11 258.4
Income: $62 614

NOVA SCOTIA
Pop: 943.2
Income: $45 087

NEW BRUNSWICK
Pop: 762.0
Income: $46 284

Sources: Data from *Canada Year Book 1999*, pp. 85, 209, and 210. Income figures for Yukon Territory and Northwest Territories are from the 1991 Census, *Canada Year Book 1997*, p. 77. For 1999 estimate of population in the new territory of Nunavut, see Chapter 2.

Ontario contains over 37 percent of the Canadian population. Although still predominantly of British stock, Ontarians include large groups of French, Italian and German, in that order, and many other ethnic groups in smaller numbers. In 1996, 49.9 percent of the Canadian population with non-official first languages resided in Ontario and ethnic populations other than French and English represented about 37 percent of the provincial population. Roman Catholic and Protestant denominations dominate, but many other religious groups are also represented. As noted above, Ontario, along with Québec, forms the industrial heartland of Canada. Economic readjustments required in the early 1990s left the Ontario government with a ballooning deficit and a severe decline in its customary economic position. However, urban, well-educated Ontario residents continued to be well serviced medically, and to own more televisions, telephones and automobiles *per capita* than most of their fellow Canadians. The number of Ontario residents regularly increases by well above the national average of about 1.2 percent a year.

The three *Prairie provinces* are ethnically extremely diverse and still reflect the influence of the European peasants who flocked to settle the prairie farmlands in the late nineteenth and early twentieth centuries. The first European settlers in the region were Scottish crofters in the Red River valley in Manitoba. Today, the largest single group in the Prairie region is still of British origin, but there are exceptionally large numbers of German and Ukrainian descent, a large percentage of Native Indians, as well as many citizens of Polish, Dutch and Scandinavian origin. No single religion dominates. Economically dependent on natural resources for their above-average wealth, the Prairie provinces make outstanding contributions in agriculture, particularly wheat, mining, and oil and gas production. Development of the Alberta oil fields has dramatically increased the prosperity and prestige of that province in recent years.

Since the Second World War, the agrarian nature of the Prairie region has been changing and an increasing percentage of the population is urban, although Saskatchewan is still one of the least urbanized Canadian provinces. Alberta, the richest and most urban of the Prairie provinces, and the most attractive for immigrants because of the oil and gas industries, accounts for much of the significant increase in net migration in the Prairie region during the past two decades. It sustained the most rapid population growth of all the provinces and territories between 1971 and 1991 (39.1 percent) but most of that gain was prior to 1982. Manitoba and Saskatchewan grow slower than the national average, Alberta faster.

British Columbia is cut off from the rest of the country by the Rocky Mountains. Immigrants in the early years were primarily British but today the ethnic composition is diverse because of high immigration and internal migration. In 1996, British Columbia had 12.9 percent of the total Canadian population. Over 55 percent of the province's population in the 1996 census responded that their single ethnic origin was other than English, French or Canadian. Religious affiliation is also diverse; however, the United and Anglican churches make up the majority. Economically prosperous, British Columbia makes major contributions through fisheries and forestry and, to some extent, through its manufacturing and construction industries. Despite relying on primary resource industries, the region is relatively urban, with a number of heavily populated centres.

Canada's largest region, the vast *Northland* of the Northwest Territories, the Yukon Territory, and Nunavut, comprises 39 percent of the country's total land mass. However, the thinly scattered population, which includes the Dene Nation, several Inuit peoples and Métis, and a small white population, constitutes only 0.3 percent of the Canadian population, in spite of rapid growth in percentage terms since 1971. Only in Nunavut does the Native population outnumber the non-Native inhabitants.

The economy of the Yukon Territory has grown rapidly over the past decade largely because of demand for certain minerals, but the economy of the Northwest Territories remains precarious. Communications in the entire region are tenuous. For Canada's Native peoples, as we have seen, living conditions are difficult.

In November 1992, the federal government agreed to reshape the political boundaries of the Northwest Territories, creating another territory from its eastern regions so that the inhabitants would not have to rely on a single regional government in Yellowknife. Nunavut became Canada's newest territory on April 1, 1999. It is Canada's largest jurisdiction, with one-fifth of the country's land mass and spanning three time zones. The new territory began acquiring self-government in 1999. It represented the first major self-government agreement to give Native peoples powers equivalent to those of a province.

The differences in historical development, ethnic and demographic make-up and economic structure within Canada are evident in these brief profiles of the six regions. However, since provincial governments provide the only institutional focus through which regions can mobilize, it is questionable whether particular groups of provinces can ever be as effective as individual provinces in political terms. Indeed, it is not even clear that they want to be. A former premier of Prince Edward Island, Alex Campbell, once said publicly that "we in Atlantic Canada have not yet made the decision to develop as a region. We are four separate competitive, jealous and parochial provinces."[62] That remark applies to all Canadian provinces.

Regional Alienation: Distance and Division

At the beginning of the twenty-first century, Canada continues to face persistent demands from alienated regions, especially the western provinces. Western discontent reflects the region's unique history and population mix. A dominant perception of Canada's national needs has been built around the concept of two founding peoples because of the long historical relationships between French and English Canadians. This is not, however, the western vision of Canada. Since the population is ethnically varied and relatively new to the West, the people do not tend to state their interests in terms of the early history of central and eastern Canada.

In the Prairie region, particularly Alberta and Saskatchewan, there is a commonly held belief that their region is exploited by Easterners. This feeling is based on the perceived economic and political domination of the rest of the country, especially by the tiny Golden Horseshoe area of southern Ontario and by Montréal. Former Alberta premier Harry Strom's imagery illustrates it well: "We have always had a sense of economic exploitation. This notion has marked all political parties in the West. The cartoon that has captured these sentiments is one of a large cow standing on a map of Canada munching grass in Alberta and Saskatchewan, with milk pouring from a bulging udder into the large bucket in Ontario."[63] The main thrust of western discontent, however, hinges on a feeling of marginalization and alienation from the centres of economic and political power rather than on a simple desire for separation from those centres, and may "reflect frustration at the lack of national integration as much as it does resistance to integration."[64]

The underlying problem of regional alienation is easily stated, but not easily resolved. The combined population of Ontario and Québec considerably exceeds 50 percent of the entire country. Because of this fact, the outer regions generally perceive that the federal parliamentary system represents only central Canada and, therefore, to an extent, is merely a regional government for citizens in other parts of the country. Many solutions to alienation have been proposed over the years by Westerners: switch political parties, abolish parties, electoral reform, Senate reform, abolish party discipline and so on. The landscape is littered with reform initiatives. Westerners have agreed only on a goal — a more effective voice at the centre — but not how to achieve it.

It is important to note, however, that these regional economic disparities and the manner they are dealt with are distinguishing features of Canadian politics. Since Confederation, the belief that the rich provinces and regions should help the poorer ones has been a fundamental part of the Canadian political culture. Sharing through redistribution is built into the political system and is viewed by Canadians as the "just" way to cope with differences in wealth.

Disputes over formulas and provincial jostling for a fair share of the economic pie take place within this basic redistribution framework. One study commissioned by the Task Force on Canadian Unity in 1978 concluded that attachment to either region or province does not threaten national

---

62. Quoted in Roger Gibbins, *Regionalism: Territorial Politics in Canada and the United States* (Toronto: Butterworths, 1982), p. 178.

63. Quoted in David Elton and Roger Gibbins, "Western Alienation and Political Culture," in R. Schultz et al., eds., *The Canadian Political Process*, 3rd ed. (Toronto: Holt, Rinehart and Winston, 1979), p. 85.

64. Gibbins, *Regionalism*, p. 181. See also J.F. Conway, *The West: The History of a Region in Confederation* (Toronto: Lorimer, 1983).

integration.[65] It has even been suggested that regional discontent may be more a fabrication of elites than a strong feeling of the mass public.[66] It is often to the benefit of the local political elite to exacerbate differences between provinces or regions and the federal government. Provincial premiers play on regional sentiments to gain support in striking tough financial bargains with the federal government.

Regional Political Cultures

Richard Simeon and David Elkins are among those who have argued that Canada embraces several regional political cultures.[67] Basing their argument on survey data, they compared the provinces and examined differences among their populations regarding patterns of political orientations and explanations of these differences. They concluded that "there are indeed differences between the provinces which may be called cultural, which are rooted in the matrix of historical and sociological factors unique to each province."[68]

It is interesting to speculate on the possible sources of the cultural variations among the provinces. Some of the factors outlined in the regional profiles above are undoubtedly significant. Levels of industrialization and economic development are extremely low in the Maritime provinces, high in Ontario and British Columbia. Emigration from the Maritime area is high, immigration low. The extreme weakness of the economy and the consistent historical inability of Maritime governments to solve the problem likely engenders lack of political trust and feelings of inability to change the situation. As well, the peculiar pattern of settlement along the American border and the polycephalic city network discussed in Chapter 2 help perpetuate regionally based interests and attitudes.

Although it has become widely accepted among Canadian political scientists that regionalism is an important facet of Canadian life, the salient spatial boundaries of the regions have not been determined. Nor has the theoretical explanation of their persistence been satisfactorily developed. Some argue that it is premature to conclude that Canadian politics is largely regional, because there has been no thorough study of class structure, or of the socioeconomic issues dividing right and left branches of public opinion. After analyzing a national sample survey, one study, for example, concluded that Canadian politics is regional only if political views are narrowly defined as attitudes toward electoral politics and governmental institutions.[69] Other researchers have shown that regional variations in opinions are neither strong nor consistent on topics that have no readily apparent territorial connotations, and that Canadians over the past 30 years have been becoming more alike in their responses to important public policy issues, regardless of region.[70]

Regional cleavages, like ethnic divisions, are not necessarily detrimental; they can be normal and healthy, and non-threatening to national cohesiveness. One study shows that although regional

---

65. Relevant findings from the Atlantic Provinces Study conducted for the Task Force on Canadian Unity can be found in Gibbins, *Regionalism*, pp. 179–80.

66. See, for example, Richard Simeon and Donald E. Blake in "Regional Preferences: Citizens' Views of Public Policy," in Elkins and Simeon, *Small Worlds*, pp. 77–105.

67. Richard Simeon and David J. Elkins, "Regional Political Cultures in Canada," *CJPS*, vol. 7, no. 3 (September 1974), pp. 397–437. The revised version of this article is "Provincial Political Cultures in Canada," in *Small Worlds*, pp. 31–76.

68. Simeon and Elkins, "Regional Political Cultures in Canada," p. 68.

69. M. Ornstein et al., "Region, Class and Political Culture in Canada," *CJPS*, vol. 8, no. 2 (June 1980), p. 267.

70. R. Gibbins, *Regionalism*, p. 184; and Simeon and Blake, "Regional Preferences," p. 100.

loyalty is often high in Canada, it is not at the expense of national loyalty. In fact, feelings toward province and nation are strongly correlated: positive feelings toward the province are usually accompanied by positive feelings for the country. In addition, the more knowledgeable Canadians are about their country, and the more sensitive they are to regionalism, the more they favour the federal government over their provincial governments. Canadian nationalists not only tend to be well informed about Canada; they are also a cosmopolitan people who feel warmly about other countries.[71]

In conclusion, then, the divisive effect of regional differences should not be exaggerated. Not enough is known about whether territorial identities are compatible with strong national identification. But it is clear that strong regional identities alone do not prove that national identification is weak or threatened. Western regional demands are not inherently nationalistic; they usually do not call for the development of a new state, as is often the case in the province of Québec. Western regional leaders restrict their demands to changes in the economic and political arrangements between the region and the central government.

There is enough evidence to indicate that, in the case of ethnic identities, multiple loyalties alone need not be feared; in fact, they make Canada richer as a country. However, when strong regional loyalties are linked to general perceptions of injustice, regionalism may become a potent political force. The federal government must be sensitive enough to relieve tensions on these occasions. Canadians should not be forced by governments to choose whether they prefer to be Acadians, French Canadians or Canadians first. David Elkins expressed the matter this way: "Multiple loyalties can have ... a civilizing result, since they encourage us to reject absolute choices and teach us to give assent and express dissent in graduated and qualified terms."[72]

SUMMARY

Canadians have a rich variety of perceptions and knowledge about their country, their provinces and their regions. The very nature of the country, with its geographical, historical, economic and demographic differences, dictates that this will be so. Surely it is this very diversity that is at the heart of the distinctive Canadian political culture.

Canadians did not create an ideologically based nation. Ideological diversity resulted naturally from a combination of such factors as strong American influence, a high rate of population turnover and strong regional, economic and ethnic differences. Canadians also suffered a prolonged condition of colonial mentality that delayed the development of national symbols and pride. When the Constitution was brought home from Britain in 1982, Canada finally matured legally. Perhaps political and cultural maturity will follow.

It is difficult to measure something as elusive as a sense of political community. However, while we recognize that regional and ethnic variations do exist, we can also say that the models of governing that Canada inherited from Britain and the United States have fostered certain types of values,

71. David Elkins, "The Sense of Place," in *Small Worlds*, pp. 23 and 25.
72. Ibid., p. 26.

attitudes and behaviour toward the political system and government-related activities. The collective heritage of beliefs, opinions and preferences shared by Canadians is greater than the rhetoric of provincial autonomy and regional cleavages would lead one to believe. The federal structure and the party system, with their apparent inability to bridge regional and linguistic cleavages, exaggerate differences that exist among Canadians. In fact, it is often in the interests of the provincial or federal political elites to frame issues so that their own interests and ambitions are accommodated. In a successful federal system, citizens should feel positively about both federal and provincial levels of government. We know that Canadians do. Those who feel strongly about their province also generally feel strongly about their country. The two are not mutually exclusive; rather, they are strongly correlated.

Three major political developments during the 1980s and 1990s could dramatically affect the direction of the Canadian political culture in the new millennium; the *Charter of Rights and Freedoms* has shifted Canada toward a more individualist focus and away from the country's communitarian, collectivist roots; the Free Trade Agreement with the United States is having a "homogenizing" effect on Canadian culture by opening the borders further between the two countries; and the North American Free Trade Agreement with the United States and Mexico is having similar repercussions along these lines. However, despite these developments, Canadians in all regions are becoming increasingly similar in their expectations and preferences with respect to most areas of public policy. They want provincial or regional equity in government services and programs.

The Earl of Balfour wrote in 1927 in his introduction of Bagehot's book on the British constitution that "our whole political machinery presupposes a people so fundamentally at one that they can safely afford to bicker: and so sure of their own moderation that they are not dangerously disturbed by the never-ending din of political conflict."[73] It is not clear exactly what the British people were "fundamentally at one" about, nor is it clear today for Canadians, but the cohesion in the Canadian political culture has been strong enough to permit division and conflict without the eruption of widespread and continual violence. Politicians and government officials can rely on deep-seated attitudes to maintain the authority of government in Canada.

There is a distinctive Canadian political culture. Within the country, provincial political cultures are strong, and provide an assimilative framework for immigrants and internal migrants. However, this should not be seen as subversive of the whole. The provinces also have many features in common. There is unity in diversity, just as the strength and beauty of a tapestry is determined by the very different strands of which it is composed.

DISCUSSION QUESTIONS

1. What common values do Canadians share and how are they manifested? Why do you think Canadians as a whole are so concerned with the question of Canadian identity?

2. Which concept or concepts do you believe more adequately represent the overall Canadian political culture — "melting pot," "bicultural," "multicultural," "mosaic," or "tapestry"?

3. Can the French and English concepts of "nation" be reconciled? Is Canada one nation or two?

---

73. Introduction by the Earl of Balfour to Walter Bagehot, *The English Constitution* (London: World's Classics Edition, 1955), p. xxiv.

4. Is multiculturalism a disruptive or integrative force in Canadian society?

5. What are the main grievances of Canada's aboriginal peoples and what should be done to redress them? Is the government taking appropriate steps?

Selected Bibliography

Political Culture — General

Beaujot, Roderic, *Population Change in Canada: The Challenges of Policy Adaptation* (Toronto: McClelland & Stewart, 1991).

Bell, David V.J., *The Roots of Disunity: A Study of Canadian Political Culture* (Toronto: Oxford University Press, 1992).

Blair, R.S. and J.T. McLeod, *The Canadian Political Tradition: Basic Readings* (Scarborough: Nelson, 1993).

Dickason, Olive Patricia, *Canada's First Nations* (Toronto: McClelland & Stewart, 1992).

Gibbins, R., *Conflict and Unity* (Scarborough: Nelson, 1990).

Kaplan, William, ed., *Belonging: The Meaning and Future of Canadian Citizenship* (Montréal: McGill-Queen's University Press, 1993).

Lipset, S.M., *Continental Divide* (New York: Routledge, 1990).

Saul, John Ralston, *Reflections of a Siamese Twin: Canada at the End of the Twentieth Century* (Toronto: Penguin, 1997).

Woshinsky, Oliver H., *Culture and Politics: An Introduction to Mass and Elite Behaviour* (Englewood Cliffs, N.J.: Prentice Hall, 1995).

Political Participation

Blais, André and Elisabeth Gidengil, *Making Representative Democracy Work* (Toronto: Dundurn Press, Royal Commission, 1991).

Mishler, William and Harold Clarke, "Political Participation in Canada," in Michael S. Whittington and Glen Williams, eds., *Canadian Politics in the 1990s*, 4th ed. (Scarborough: Nelson, 1995).

Ethnic Relations/Multiculturalism

Bibby, Reginald W., *Mosaic Madness: The Poverty and Potential of Life in Canada* (Toronto: Stoddart, 1990).

Bissoondath, Neil, *Selling Illusions: The Cult of Multiculturalism in Canada* (Toronto: Penguin, 1995).

Driedger, Leo, *Multi-Ethnic Canada: Identities and Inequalities* (Ottawa: Renouf, 1996).

Edwards. John, ed., *Language in Canada* (Cambridge: Cambridge University Press, 1998.)

Elliot, Jean Leonard and Augie Fleras, eds., *Multiculturalism in Canada: The Challenge of Diversity* (Scarborough: Nelson, 1991).

—————, *Unequal Relations: An Introduction to Race and Ethnic Dynamics in Canada* (Scarborough: Prentice Hall, 1992).

Gutman, Amy et al., *Multiculturalism* (Princeton: Princeton University Press, 1994).

Kelly, Ninette and Michael Trebilcock, *The Making of the Mosaic* (Toronto: University of Toronto Press, 1998).

Megyery, K., *Ethnocultural Groups and Visible Minorities in Canadian Politics: The Question of Access* (Toronto: Dundurn Press, 1991).

Taylor, Charles, *Multiculturalism and "The Politics of Recognition"* (Princeton: Princeton University Press, 1991).

Troper, Harold and M. Weinfeld, eds., *Ethnicity, Politics and Public Policy: Case Studies in Canadian Diversity* (Toronto: University of Toronto Press, 1999).

Wsevolod, W. Isajiw, *Understanding Diversity: Ethnicity and Race in the Canadian Context* (Toronto: Thompson, 1999).

Regionalism

Bercuson, David J. and Barry Cooper, *Deconfederation* (Toronto: Key Porter, 1992).

Campbell, Robert and Leslie Pal, *The Real Worlds of Canadian Politics*, 2nd ed. (Peterborough: Broadview Press, 1991).

French Canada (See also Chapter 7)

Beheils, M.D., ed., *Quebec Since 1945: Selected Readings* (Toronto: Copp Clark Pitman, 1987).

Gagnon, Alain G. and Mary Beth Montcalm, *Quebec Beyond the Quiet Revolution* (Scarborough: Nelson, 1990).

Young, Brian and John A. Dickinson, *A Short History of Quebec* (Mississauga: Copp Clark Pitman, 1988).

Native Peoples

Boldt, Menno, *Surviving Indians: The Challenge of Self Government* (Toronto: University of Toronto Press, 1993).

Cassidy, Frank, ed., *Aboriginal Self-Government* (Halifax: Institute for Research on Public Policy, 1991).

Smith, Melvin H., *Our Home or Native Land?* (Victoria: Crown Western, 1995).

Tennant, Paul, *Aboriginal Peoples and Politics* (Vancouver: University of British Columbia Press, 1990).

Trigger, Bruce G. and Wilcomb E. Washburn, eds., *The Cambridge History of the Native Peoples of the Americas* (Cambridge, U.K.: Cambridge University Press, 1996).

Wright, Ronald, *Stolen Continents* (Boston: Houghton Mifflin, 1992).

LIST OF WEBLINKS

canada.gc.ca/ canadiana/symb_e.html
Symbols of Canada Canadian political symbols are presented in this Web site.

www.inac.gc.ca
Canadian Department of Indian and Northern Affairs This is the Web page for the Canadian Department of Indian and Northern Affairs.

www.afn.ca
Assembly of First Nations This is the Web page for the Assembly of First Nations.

4

Social and Political Context and Cleavages

. . . .

Education, Media, Government, Gender and Class

We have seen that an overarching political culture unites the diverse Canadian population, providing a degree of national unity. Since Confederation in 1867, strands of national, ethno-linguistic and regional cultures in Canada have become layered and intertwined, creating the political culture of a relatively prosperous and peaceful country. At the same time, however, differences between these three cultural strands have created tensions in the body politic, contributing to societal cleavages and providing the environment for politics in Canada. How is this political culture maintained over generations of Canadians? What institutions and processes contribute to what Canadians think and feel about their country, their government and politics in general? What other social cleavages have an impact on the political culture?

At the individual level, Canadians are very different from one another in many respects. They do not have equal chances to succeed in life. They have different personal characteristics, abilities and health, and are born into different social and economic circumstances. Factors such as gender, education and socioeconomic class help to shape an individual's ideas and orientation to politics. A woman from a poor family with little education has experiences and self-expectations that are very different from those of a man raised in a wealthy, well-educated, professional family. These two individuals experience unique treatment by parents, peers, teachers and employers. What is expected of them and what kinds of opportunities will be open to them in life differ greatly.

The chance circumstances into which one is born, then, help to shape an individual's general political culture. Gender assignment and socioeconomic class, in particular, provide and also deny opportunities and experiences. Based on these factors, individuals may be inclined to take particular stands on issues, orient themselves on such abstract constructs as a left–right continuum, and decide how and even whether they wish to participate in the political process. It is therefore important to understand how institutions and social groupings help to determine who and what we are as Canadians.

In this chapter, we examine some of the major ways that Canadians acquire political ideas and orientations about their country and its government and politics. We begin by looking briefly at the general process of socialization by which values and attitudes are learned, particularly at how the process occurs in families and peer groups. We then focus on the controversial roles played by three institutions — the educational system, media and government — in transmitting ideas and contributing to political orientations in Canada.

Finally, in the last section, we examine two significant cleavage structures — gender and socio-economic class — that also help to define who and what we are in society, and in doing so condition political orientations. Combined with the ethno-linguistic and regional cleavages we discussed in the last chapter, gender and class round out the picture of how Canadians are divided in their political quest for who gets what, when and how.

ACQUIRING POLITICAL ORIENTATIONS

Acquiring political ideas and orientations is a lifelong process. Political culture is learned and transmitted at both the individual and community levels through **political socialization**. In Canada, children experience casual, informal learning of values and attitudes from family and peers, and more direct learning in schools. As they mature, other more explicit agents of political socialization and such factors as socioeconomic class become influential. While political socialization is a continuous, lifelong process, some stages may be more important than others.

Development of the political self begins early in childhood. By five or six years of age, children in western societies acquire emotional attachments, which are nearly always positive, to the political community to which they belong. Authority figures are seen as benevolent "helpers"; symbols of the political community such as the Queen and the flag generally are regarded positively. Concurrently, children identify with a gender group, social and economic class, and an ethnic or racial group, although again with little or no factual information. Laws are regarded as absolute and unchanging; authority is seen as people such as police officers or teachers, rather than in abstract terms such as law or responsible government. Political attitudes and beliefs learned at this time are less likely to change than those learned later, which involve more information. This is important for the political culture and the political system inasmuch as it allows a high degree of continuity and intergenerational agreement about basic values to be taken for granted by the government, making it relatively easy to predict citizens' reactions and expectations on many topics.

Between the ages of seven and thirteen, children increasingly understand and relate to more abstract political symbols. As they develop the capacity to see political leaders more critically, and as their factual knowledge increases, they gain a better understanding of their political system and its leaders. Ages 11 to 13 may be the most significant in terms of the ability to reason and grasp abstractions. This stage is followed by a gradual and steady increase in political participation and involvement in the remaining adolescent years.[1] Of course, political learning continues during adulthood, but it is less likely that changes in basic political culture will occur. Adults may alter their ideas and orientations toward specific government policies and develop evaluations of political

---

1. The early development of political orientation is discussed more fully in Richard E. Dawson, Kenneth Prewitt and Karen S. Dawson, *Political Socialization*, 2nd ed. (Boston: Little, Brown, 1977), ch. 4.

parties and leaders, but they are less likely to change broad cultural attitudes and beli
ideological goals or conceptions of the legitimate means of selecting political rulers.[2]

Although political attitudes are formed early and tend to persist, they are retained
degrees by individuals as a result of discontinuities in their political socialization. If, for e
cialization is inconsistent, or a long time elapses between socialization and the assump
litical role, then attitudes may be weakly held. The more diverse the agents of political socia....
to which an individual is exposed, the greater the likelihood that contradictory messages will be received and changes or discontinuities in attitudes occur. Experiences at one stage of life can contradict
others later. Some forms of socialization are indirect in that they are not overtly political. Others are
relatively direct in that they transmit explicit political orientations.

Families and Peer Groups

As the basic unit of our society, the family is a primary socializing agent. However, the political
learning that families offer is likely to be sporadic and incomplete, and does not adequately prepare an individual for participation in the political world. Families are nonetheless generally important in determining the *extent* and *direction* of political learning. Attitudes and beliefs learned in
childhood, such as love of country, tend to be the most intensely held and lasting. Families influence
children in three main ways. They provide examples or role models and sometimes even direct
teaching about politics. Children from families that are actively concerned with partisan party politics are likely to be politically active when they grow up. Families are also important in instilling social attitudes and personality traits that will eventually influence how children react to the political
world. Finally, families provide social and economic surroundings, determine the social class of
children as well as their educational values and first language, and, often, even direct what other
socialization agents will affect the child.

The family, therefore, helps to perpetuate traditional values, attitudes and behaviour patterns.
This influence, which is essentially conservative, is not easily manipulated by political leaders.
Families, thus, are generally considered to be beneficial in countries that are trying to maintain the
status quo, but as a hindrance to those trying to alter the political culture or to instigate radical
changes in society. As Table 4.1 shows, however, Canadian families are undergoing fairly dramatic
change that may affect their effectiveness as a socializing agent. They are shrinking in size, are breaking apart more readily and are increasingly headed by a single parent.

Peer groups constitute another primary agent of socialization. Friends, associates, sports teams,
clubs and groups of all sorts comprise this amorphous group that acquires increasing significance as
the child's dependence on the family wanes. The peer group is especially important at about age
13 or 14, and continues to be influential throughout adulthood. Political socialization by peers resembles that by the family. It is haphazard because it is not usually the primary aim of the relationship. Individual relationships are highly personal and emotionally involved. Peer-group
socialization can alter or reinforce the earlier political learning that has taken place in the family
or, in cases where family socialization was weak, provide fundamental political learning.

Peer groups often assume relatively greater importance in complex urban settings that are normally more impersonal and less family oriented than rural societies. Peers use subtle persuasion,
or blatant methods such as ostracism and ridicule, to pressure individuals to conform to group
norms and attitudes. Peer-group and family socialization can be given much credit for the persistence

---

2. Ibid., ch. 5.

TABLE 4.1   TRENDS IN CANADIAN FAMILIES

Divorces (rate per 100 000)	
1967	55
1996	265
Increase	381%
Single-parent families	
1966	371 900
1996	1 137 510
Increase	205%
Births to unmarried women	
1967	30 915 or 8.3% of total live births
1996	97 945 or 26% of total live births
Average family size	
1966	3.9
1996	3.0
Decrease	23%

Sources: *The Globe and Mail*, June 29, 1996, and *The Canada Year Book 1999*, p. 203.

of minority groups in Canada. The Doukhobors are an extreme example of a minority group that has attempted to limit close personal relationships to group members so that traditional values will be reinforced.

EDUCATION AND POLITICAL ORIENTATIONS

The Canadian educational system, pressured from without by American cultural influences and fragmented from within by regional and ethnic interests, strives in an *ad hoc* and diffused way to impart to students an awareness of a common heritage and instill national pride. Lack of centralized control makes this goal difficult, if not impossible, to achieve.

Political socialization in Canada's educational institutions is pressured from the United States in many ways. For example, textbook markets are so much larger and more lucrative south of the border that it is financially advantageous for Canadians to adopt American texts rather than use Canadian-written and -published material. Of particular concern are the availability of Canadian books in the school system and the amount of Canadian content in textbooks, both of which can contribute to a stunted knowledge of Canada and Canadians. Several attempts have been made to regulate this situation in English Canada where the problem is most acute. In Ontario, for example, a primary or secondary school book now must be written by Canadian authors and manufactured in Canada to be approved as a text, and every province has a "Canada first" policy that means that if a Canadian text is available, it must be given priority. Similarly, Canadian immigration regulations include Canadians-first hiring policies, which require that before hiring a non-Canadian, employers must demonstrate that there is no qualified Canadian available. This applies particularly to university professors and heads of cultural institutions.

Yet such policies have had limited impact on building Canadian identity. In particular, Canadians often act as little more than an irascible collection of self-interested groups, provinces, ethnic affiliations and special interests. It has become more politically correct to respond to minority demands than to argue for national standards. Diversity is supported to such a degree that it often undermines pride in Canada. The educational system must share responsibility for the weakness in national pride and cohesiveness that threatens Canadian unity.

The educational system impacts on political culture in many ways. It is a major source of information about politics and how the political system works. It teaches the basic skills that people need to participate and take leadership roles in society. Education, together with occupation and income, is also a principal determinant of social status. It "conveys important political advantages, increasing political interest and awareness, expanding opportunities and developing the political skills necessary for effective participation."[3] Postsecondary education has almost become a necessity for holding high public office. Education is also the primary means by which people achieve upward mobility and escape from poverty. A university education does not guarantee financial success, but it certainly improves the odds. (See Figure 4.1.) In 1997, adult Canadians who had a postsecondary degree or diploma earned 40–45 percent more than those who had not achieved this educational standard.[4]

As well as directing students toward particular roles and class positions in society, educational institutions prepare young people for the political world by teaching them relevant facts, values, predispositions and skills. They are also the main community facility in which numbers of immigrant children learn one or both official languages and acquire basic citizenship training. Recent research indicates that education is significantly associated with both factual and conceptual knowledge,

FIGURE 4.1   EMPLOYMENT AND EDUCATION
(GROWTH OR DECLINE IN EMPLOYMENT BY EDUCATION LEVEL)

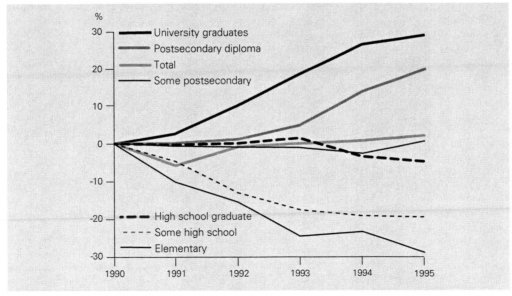

Source: Reproduced from Statistics Canada, *Labour Force Annual Averages, 1909–1994*, plus update for 1995, Catalogue 71-529, 1995.

3. W. Mishler, "Political Participation and Democracy," in M.S. Whittington and Glen Williams, eds., *Canadian Politics in the 1980s*, 2nd ed. (Toronto: Methuen, 1984), p. 183.

4. *Canada Year Book 1999* (Ottawa: Statistics Canada, 1999), p. 318.

especially the latter. Furthermore, it indicates that "education establishes a receptivity to acquire further knowledge long after formal education has terminated."[5]

At 8 percent of gross domestic product (GDP), Canada's expenditure on education is among the highest of the industrialized countries. As a result, Canadians have more education than ever before and are staying in school longer. (See Figure 4.2.) Forty-eight percent of all who were 15 years and over had a university degree or some other postsecondary education. More than one in ten had a university degree. Gender bias in educational institutions has greatly diminished. Women accounted for much of the increase in university graduates from 1971 to 1996.[6]

Despite these clear benefits of education, and the comparatively large amounts of money being spent on it, Canada does poorly in international rankings of scholarly achievement. Canada's education system is failing to prepare a high percentage of the population to earn an adequate living and learn the skills necessary to participate in many aspects of society and politics. In 1990, the reading skills of 16 percent of Canada's adults were too limited to deal with much of the printed material found in everyday life. Twenty-two percent of the adult population could read only simple materials and could not cope with more complex reading contexts.[7] For the functionally illiterate and those with less than a high school diploma, there are few opportunities to enter the work force.

One might think it would be easy to ensure that Canadian students learn the history and literature of their country, understand its culture and environment, and learn to speak, read and write

FIGURE 4.2   EDUCATIONAL ATTAINMENT FOR PERSONS 15 YEARS AND OVER

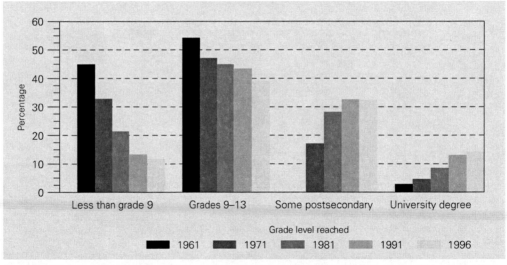

Sources: *1991 Census Highlights: The Daily* (Ottawa: Statistics Canada, May 11, 1993), p. 3; and *Canada Year Book 1999,* p. 173. Not shown on the figure are 25.9 percent who had a postsecondary certificate in 1996.

5. See Ronald D. Lambert et al. "The Sources of Political Knowledge," *CJPS*, vol. 21, no. 2 (June 1988), p. 373.

6. *Canada Year Book,* 1999, pp. 144–177.

7. Statistics Canada, *Adult Literacy in Canada: Results of National Study* (Ottawa: Minister of Industry, Science and Technology, 1991), p. 19. See also Statistics Canada, *Reading the Future: A Portrait of Literacy in Canada* (Ottawa: Human Resources Development Canada, 1996).

8. For a discussion of the relation between education and values in Canada, see Peter C. Emberly and Waller R. Newell, *Bankrupt Education: The Demise of Liberal Education in Canada* (Toronto: University of Toronto Press, 1994).

in two or more languages. That has not proven to be the case.[8] (See "Lack of Civic Knowledge in Canada?" page 115.) There are several reasons why this is difficult in Canada. The fact that education is largely a provincial jurisdiction allows great diversity across the country in curriculum content, standards and administration. The varied historical developments, cultural traditions and geographic, social and economic conditions within the provinces and territories are reflected in 12 unique educational systems that nurture and perpetuate regional political cultures.

In the next section, we briefly survey the decentralized organizational structure of education in Canada. Then we focus more specifically on curriculum and subject content in Canadian schools to illustrate how they strengthen regional and ethnic cultures at the expense of Canadian identity.

Organizational Structure

As an agent of political socialization, the educational system in Canada ideally would reinforce common bonds of national unity while at the same time celebrating the ethnic, linguistic and regional differences that exist. Unfortunately, however, the system is poorly equipped to build a strong Canadian identity. The fact that responsibility for education in Canada is largely in the hands of the provinces and extends downward to the municipal level makes it difficult to establish uniform standards and provide equitable funding across the country. The constitutional division of powers also makes it impossible to ensure that nation-wide interests are put ahead of parochial, provincial interests in terms of curriculum or subject content — or indeed, even considered at all.

CLOSE-UP ON Culture

LACK OF CIVIC KNOWLEDGE IN CANADA?

A survey conducted by the Angus Reid Group in 1997 indicated that a large number of Canadians lack the civic knowledge required to understand and participate in the country's public life. Forty-five percent of respondents failed to answer correctly at least 12 of 20 basic questions on Canadian history, culture, government institutions and laws. In other words, the survey indicated that nearly one in two Canadians would fail the citizenship exam given to immigrants.

The following are examples:

- 95 percent of Canadians knew the title of the national anthem, but only 63 percent knew the first two lines. (Québec residents did the best on this question.)
- Only 8 percent correctly named the Queen as Canada's head of state; 57 percent believed the prime minister fills this role.
- Fewer than one-third were able to name the *Charter of Rights and Freedoms* as the part of the Constitution that protects Canadians' civil rights.
- 36 percent could not place the date of Confederation anywhere in the nineteenth century.

If a Canadian citizen does not know such basics as what Confederation signified in Canadian history, or who the head of state is, or what the *Charter of Rights and Freedoms* is, what does that tell us about socialization in Canada? What does it tell us about politics in Canada? What, if anything, should be done about this situation?

Source: *The Globe and Mail*, October 11, 1997.

During Canada's early colonial years, education was dominated by the Church. Not until the mid-1800s was a public system of education developed in each colony, supplemented in Québec by schools and colleges operated by Roman Catholic orders. In 1867, the Fathers of Confederation awarded education to the provincial sphere of jurisdiction, but also tried to protect English and French minority schools. Section 93 of the *British North America Act* placed education "exclusively" under the control of each province, recognizing the differences that existed at the time of Confederation. The Constitution, however, retained the rights and privileges of Protestant and Roman Catholic minorities in relation to education, and the federal government maintained direct control over the education of persons beyond the jurisdiction of the provinces such as Native peoples.

Today, free and compulsory primary and secondary education is provided to all Canadian children. However, the number of years of actual attendance in school is closely related to factors such as the class, wealth and occupation of the family. Significant inequalities in opportunities for education exist among children for reasons such as family interest, financial need or variation in quality of schools in different municipalities.

Postsecondary education in Canada also began under religious auspices. At Confederation, the few degree-granting institutions in Canada were largely supported and controlled by religious groups for the primary purpose of training clergy. Shortly thereafter, however, English-language institutions began to offer practical and scientific studies under secular control, while the French-language sector continued to emphasize classical studies under clerical control. Demands for university education escalated after the Second World War, coming to a head in the 1960s when baby-boom children graduated from high school in record numbers. Provincial governments increasingly became involved in planning university development. Religious sponsorship and control diminished.

During the 1950s, in an attempt to build a world-class educational system, the federal government inaugurated a system of grants to be distributed to the provinces according to their population size. The provinces in turn distributed the funds to the universities based on full-time enrollment figures. In this manner, the universities, which had operated as private institutions, became heavily dependent on public support.

The fact that the provinces retain the constitutional responsibility for education, while the federal government has borne approximately half of the financial responsibility for postsecondary education, has obviously hindered the development of a cohesive, national educational system. As well, the current system of university finance penalizes provinces for attracting students from outside their borders. Federal financial transfers to the provinces for postsecondary education are based on population, not the number of students. And provinces fund their own universities directly rather than paying the cost of a student's education wherever that student may study in Canada.

Curriculum and Subject Content

Educational curriculum is potentially a major instrument of political socialization. Political instruction can range from general civic education to indoctrination. The former model imparts how a good citizen participates in the political life of his or her country; the latter, undesirable model (known pejoratively as brainwashing) goes well beyond this to teach political values in a restrictive and highly structured manner as directed by the state. Political socialization in Canadian schools is clearly of the former type. Subject material is stressed or ignored to reinforce desirable values and beliefs, and texts can be selected to reinforce biases. However, political instruction is diffused and *ad hoc*.

Across Canada generally, some attempts are made in the educational system to have children understand and relate emotionally to their country from an early age. In Ontario, for example, the Ministry of Education dictates that national symbols are to be regularly brought to the children's attention and the proper reverence for them instilled. As well, an important aim of many of the subjects taught in schools is to impart an awareness of a common heritage and build national pride. The general assumption is that learning the history, geography, literature and language of one's country is important in creating citizens with positive attitudes and beliefs about their state. Consider how effective the teaching of Canadian history and literature is in this regard.

History and Literature

In Canada, curriculum and subject material are not standardized across the country, but are left to provincial jurisdictions. Students in different provinces often learn quite different material and from quite different points of view. This became clear in a study conducted by Marcel Trudel and Geneviève Jain for the Royal Commission on Bilingualism and Biculturalism. Surveying 10 000 Grade 12 students and comparing 14 representative Canadian history textbooks, they found that

English and French texts were very different from each other in organization, themes and objectives.[9] These significant differences corresponded to the wide attitudinal and political cleavages between the French and English. Canadian history courses in the French-language Roman Catholic schools in Québec were preoccupied with the survival of their own society, while the English schools across the country neglected the interests and development of French Canada. The textbooks expounded different myths and different historical memories: the English books stressed economic interpretations whereas the French texts stressed the importance of religion and the survival of the French ethnic group.

The Royal Commission study found that key figures and common experiences in Canadian history were depicted differently as well. For example, the French saw Lord Durham as a great assimilator; the English considered him a great decolonizer. To the French, Riel was a defender of minority rights, but to the English, he was a traitor and murderer. Similarly, the early period of French colonization to 1663 was covered at great length in French texts, but only very briefly in English texts. The periods of the British regime and Confederation were handled so differently that the authors concluded that the two groups did not even seem to be talking about the same country. Books used by francophones attempted to give the students a moral education, while anglophone books attempted to convey a political and social education. Elementary school children in French-language Roman Catholic schools developed strong identification with their own ancestors. At the secondary school level, the interpretations tended to become bitter, resentful and vindictive, with frequent references to resistance.[10]

In the light of the Royal Commission findings, many school textbooks were revised to eliminate blatant biases, as well as other glaring stereotypes, such as the portrayal of Canada's Native peoples as "savages," "heathens" and "fiends."[11] In spite of these changes, differences remain. The Québec nationalist interpretation has become standard in textbooks used in Québec, and is the accepted filter used to analyze political issues. Students continue to learn the nature and glory of the established order through a combination of facts and myths. Many people in Canada's two founding nations have never shared a common national mythology.

Conflicting interpretations of Canadian history are not unique to the English- and French-speaking communities. There are regional variations as well. Contrasting theses have been developed by leading historians from western and central Canada. Donald Creighton, for example, saw Canada as an extension of Ontario. The "Laurentian thesis" that he expounded holds that Canada developed around the extension of the trade routes.[12] Creighton argued that the crucial drive behind Confederation was the commercial development of the St. Lawrence, and that the annexation of the West was an extension of this drive. W.L. Morton, on the other hand, gave a western interpretation when he stated that Creighton's thesis does not take account of regional experience and history, but distorts local history and confirms "the feeling that union with Canada had been carried out against local sentiment and local interest."[13]

---

9. Marcel Trudel and Geneviève Jain, *Canadian History Textbooks: A Comparative Study*, Studies of the Royal Commission on Bilingualism and Biculturalism, no. 5 (Ottawa: Queen's Printer, 1970), ch. 4.

10. Ibid.

11. Garnet McDiarmid and David Pratt, *Teaching Prejudice* (Toronto: Ontario Institute for Studies in Education, 1968). Also David Pratt, "The Social Role of School Textbooks in Canada," in Robert M. Pilke and Elia Zureik, eds., *Socialization and Values in Canadian Society*, vol. 2 (Toronto: Macmillan, 1978), pp. 100–26.

12. Donald G. Creighton, *The Commercial Empire of the St. Lawrence, 1760–1850* (Boston: Houghton Mifflin, 1958).

13. W.L. Morton, "Canadian History and Historians," in A.B. McKillop, ed., *Contexts of Canada's Past: Selected Essays of W.L. Morton* (Toronto: Macmillan, 1980), pp. 33–34.

Morton contended that the study of Canadian history has been limited to the history of the economic and commercial development of Upper and Lower Canada, with little regard for the vigour of regional sentiment. For Morton, the Prairie provinces, unlike British Columbia or the Maritimes, had no option but to join Canada, as the colony of a colony, and have never existed outside that subordinate position. According to Barry Cooper, the result of this emphasis on commercial development and economic exploitation of the West by the "loyalist heartland" has led to a split between political allegiance and local identity. "That split appeared and still appears, as a sense of sectional or regional injustice."[14] Often, political movements or minor political parties such as Social Credit or the United Farmers of Alberta have turned such regional grievances against Ottawa and promoted a western sense of identity.

Divisions within the Canadian political culture are revealed not only in historical interpretations but also in the works of novelists and poets. These works become instruments of political socialization; they mirror and reinforce attitudes about such issues as national unity and regional identity, as the following examples illustrate. Literary critic Northrop Frye wrote that the literature of one's own country can provide the cultivated reader with "an understanding of that country which nothing else can give him."[15] He found in Canadian literature signs of a closely knit, beleaguered society held together by unquestionable morals and authority — what he termed a "garrison mentality." Margaret Atwood expanded this theme, basing her conclusions on a survey of both English and French Canadian literature. The aim of garrison life is survival, and survival, she claimed, is "the central theme for Canada."[16] Literary critic Dennis Duffy further concluded that the strong garrison will of central Canada was reinforced by political strength. The Canadian identity, he argued, has been restricted to the Loyalist heartland and does not extend to the Maritimes or the West.[17] Such literary analyses correspond to historians' emphasis on the importance of central Canada and may, as Cooper speculates, help to explain western political consciousness. If national unity is a symbol expressing "Canadian" identity, and that identity is limited to the Loyalist heartland, then Westerners distrust national unity "because it appears as the manifestation of the garrison will."[18]

The tradition of a "political novel" that celebrates Canadian unity is weak in Canada. Hugh MacLennan's *Two Solitudes* is one of only a very few works of English fiction to explore the French–English dynamic in Canada. MacLennan drew his inspiration from Rainer Maria Rilke's words "Love consists in this, that two solitudes protect and touch and greet each other." As an English Canadian, MacLennan struggled to understand the different historical and cultural realities of the French and English in Canada, and suggested in his novel that hope *did* exist for understanding and tolerance between the two large linguistic groups. He maintained that as long as the fate of a person or nation is still in doubt, the person or nation is alive and real. It is only of the dead that no questions are asked.[19] The issue MacLennan wrote about in 1945 is still relevant today.

Literature and theatre in Québec are flourishing, but they exist in isolation from English-speaking Canada. They are often highly political and supportive of Québec nationalism. For example, in 1993, Marcel Dubé's 1965 play *Les beaux dimanches* was revived. This popular, classic text of

14. Barry Cooper, "Western Political Consciousness," in Stephen Brooks, ed., *Political Thought in Canada* (Toronto: Irwin Publishing, 1984), p. 228.

15. Northrop Frye, *The Bush Garden: Essays on Canadian Imagination* (Toronto: Anansi, 1971), p. 183.

16. Margaret Atwood, *Survival: A Thematic Guide to Canadian Literature* (Toronto: Anansi, 1972), p. 32.

17. Dennis Duffy, *Gardens, Covenants, Exiles: Loyalism in the Literature of Upper Canada/Ontario* (Toronto: University of Toronto Press, 1982), pp. 131–32.

18. Cooper, "Western Political Consciousness," p. 235.

19. Hugh MacLennan, *Two Solitudes* (Toronto: Collins, 1945).

Québec nationalism has long speeches about the historical humiliation of the Québec people and the negative aspects of federalism, told in the context of an appealing story of sexual infidelity and moral aimlessness. Dubé's highly political message is that independence can lead francophone Québeckers out of their "misery."

Today, as the Canadian ethnic tapestry has become increasingly complex, one could perhaps more accurately speak of Canada's three, ten or even more solitudes. Ethnic and regional interpretations of Canadian history are encouraged and often subsidized by the state. They exhibit subtle differences that contribute to or reflect political divisiveness at the expense of national unity.

Education of the country's Indian and Inuit population presents unique problems. Their education is the responsibility of the federal government, and is administered by the Department of Indian Affairs. From its earliest days, the traditional, tacit goal of the government was to provide Native children with the knowledge and skills of mainstream Canadian culture and encourage them to identify with common values. This goal has shifted in recent years to celebrate Native ethnic culture and pride. Some argue that in the former system Native students learned neither Canadian nor ethnic pride, but instead became alienated and disillusioned and that this has contributed to high dropout rates at school and to social and economic problems. As in other facets of educational socialization, the task is to establish an appropriate balance — to celebrate the ethnic differences and contributions that Native peoples make, while at the same time ensuring that they are not isolated, and that they learn to share and help develop the values of a strong and united Canada.

THE MEDIA AND POLITICAL ORIENTATIONS

The mass communications media constitute an increasingly important socializing agent both within and across borders, breaking down the barriers of distance.[20] Media can integrate or fragment the political culture of a country. They have the potential to reach vast audiences and manipulate subject content either to reinforce or to challenge the norms of society. One of the ways they do this is by acting as gatekeepers, selecting which facts, beliefs and perspectives will be covered and how they will be presented. In doing so, they help to shape the values of society and influence the political process. At best, the media offer citizens a broad range of information and informed commentary, and provide a voice for governments and opposition parties alike. At worst, they offer a distorted selection of facts and unbalanced, biased viewpoints.

The media's most significant political role is in setting the agenda for public discussion and debate; that is, in helping determine which issues people think and talk about. The media help legitimize issues and actors, and confer or withhold status on individuals. They conjure up positive or negative views of the country and its institutions. They also build and destroy the public images of political figures by awarding labels that become indelible, and also by selective reporting and commentary. Investigative journalism, in particular, exposes corrosive issues and invites strong reactions.

In Canada, there is little scientific evidence concerning the direct impact of the mass media's agenda-setting on national cohesion. However, it is generally accepted that the extent to which the media provide common images and a cross-regional flow of information, as well as the way in which they present regional and ethno-linguistic conflict, has a significant bearing on national unity.

---

20. Arthur Siegel, *Politics and the Media in Canada*, 2nd ed. (Toronto: McGraw-Hill Ryerson, 1996), especially pp. 82–83.

Because of Canada's federal structure, there is always a danger that the communications system will be either too strongly centralized or too fragmented. Regional and ethnic cultures may be so strong that centrally controlled media that are not sufficiently attuned to such differences may "produce alienation and hostility rather than assimilation to a national culture."[21]

Nation-wide television networks, the Canadian Broadcasting Corporation (CBC) in particular, as well as two English-language newspapers, *The Globe and Mail* and the *National Post,* contribute greatly to developing the national political agenda in Canada. Two other newspapers, *The Toronto Star* and *Le Devoir,* also help set the agenda for national and public affairs, though they are regionally based. The only network other than the CBC to provide national television service from coast to coast is the English-language CTV, which also has a French subsidiary, TVA.

These limited Canadian media sources face many restraints on their attempts to set the agenda for public debate. The obstacles include editorial policy, technological limitations and financial constraints — including the need to attract the large middle class and therefore obtain substantial advertising money. Their relationship with politicians is highly complex. It is particularly intense during elections where every aspect of the campaign involves the media — as shown in Chapter 12.

We turn now to a closer examination of the broadcast media — particularly television and the print media — in order to assess how they affect national unity and what Canadians think about politics. The focus throughout is on four main problems: lack of truly nation-wide communications where all regions contribute significantly to the information flow, American influence, regional divisions and ethnic cleavage. First, however, let us consider briefly the history of communications networks in Canada.

Media Origins and Government Policy

In many ways, Canada represents a triumph of communications. The pattern of the lines of communication is, as Walter Young commented, an "armature on which the figure of Canada as a political community has been shaped."[22] Rivers, lakes, canals and railways were not only avenues of commerce and transportation but also vital means of communication. Communities developed along these lines, and communications links between them were gradually strengthened by technological advances. The network of communications moved steadily outward, from centre to periphery, conquering enormous distances and facilitating political, social and economic movement. The central Canadian elite that directed the development of the media also formulated "national" goals and aspired to preserve establishment values throughout the vast territory. It ensured that its central, national perspective dominated the development of the communications system.

To build a strong national identity, it is important that citizens from various provinces and regions exchange ideas and information among themselves more than with external groups. In this respect, it is unfortunate that Canada shares the North American continent with the most powerful country in the world, a country that not only is English-speaking but also extends along the most densely populated border of almost every Canadian province. North–south communications between the proximate English groups in Canada and the United States flow naturally, while internal communications among French and English regions as well as among the widely separated provinces of English Canada are artificial, and must be protected and nourished.

---

21. Frederick K. Fletcher, *The Newspaper and Public Affairs*, vol. 7, Research Publications of the Royal Commission on Newspapers (Ottawa: Ministry of Supply and Services, 1981), p. 25.

22. Walter D. Young, "The Voices of Democracy: Politics and Communication in Canada," *CJPS*, vol. 14, no. 4 (December 1981), p. 685.

Since the early 1840s, the development of modern communications systems has facilitated the natural north–south links and increased the threat of cultural domination from the south. The history of media development in Canada is to a great extent the record of a struggle by the Canadian government to counter these influences of foreign penetration and bind the country together by better internal communications.

While north–south communications have been easy to establish, east–west links have always been a challenge. All the principal cities of the United States were linked by telegraph by 1846, but the first Canadian line between Toronto and Montréal was not complete until 1847. The most important centres in the Canadas and the Maritime colonies were not linked until 1861.

The 1850s were a great growth period for newspapers. However, from the very beginning, Canadian newspapers found it easier and cheaper to fill their pages with news from the United States than to hire their own reporters. And the competition from established American newspapers was always intense. In the Maritimes in 1865, Canadian newspapers were "a rarity where the foreign and certainly not superior sheets of New York [have] established a regular circulation."[23] Rather than reading news from the provinces, Canadians devoured the shocking and gory events, mainly murders, lynchings and riots, that filled American papers.[24]

Canadian radio services, and later television, were also established in direct response to American infiltration of the Canadian market. Radio began with private initiatives and carried a high percentage of U.S. programs. The CBC was established by the government in 1932 to provide radio services that would carry more Canadian content. CBC radio operated separate English and French stations and also cooperated with affiliated private stations. The same motivation brought CBC television in 1952. In 1977, the CBC began to televise proceedings of the House of Commons on a second channel. Finally, in 1989 it set up a third English-language all-news channel, CBC Newsworld.

The radio and television networks of the CBC, and Radio-Canada, the French-language equivalents, are crucial agents of Canadian culture. While privately owned media exist primarily to make a profit, CBC radio has no commercials and virtually 100 percent Canadian content. CBC television, on the other hand, has been forced to rely more and more on advertising revenue and to compromise high-quality Canadian cultural programming because of lack of sufficient funding.

From newspapers to radio and television channels, through cable and pay television, and, finally, to satellite transmission, the common concern has been how best to protect Canadian cultural sovereignty from massive U.S. media penetration. One Secretary of State for Communications warned that Canada would be "an occupied land, culturally" unless action were taken against the spread of American media, and urged his government to adopt a national cultural policy similar to its National Energy Program.[25] However, steps to achieve such a policy have been slow and uncertain.

Several federal commissions, from the Aird Report in 1929 to the Davey Report on the mass media in 1970, were set up to study and direct the course of broadcasting in Canada. In late 1982, the Applebaum-Hébert Report added a new dimension to discussions of cultural policy in Canada by advocating a federal system of arm's-length funding for all cultural agencies. It was followed in 1986 by the comprehensive report of a federal Task Force on Broadcasting Policy that recommended an industrial and cultural strategy of broadcasting for the next 15 years. These reports set the agenda for discussions of federal cultural policy to the present day.

---

23. *Montreal Gazette*, November 15, 1865; reprinted from the British periodical *Saturday Review*.

24. R. Brunskill, *A Newspaper Content Analysis of Canadian Integration 1845–1895*, Ph.D. dissertation, 1976, ch. 1, p. 55.

25. See *The Toronto Star*, Sunday edition, November 29, 1981. For a useful account of government policy in the cultural industry field, see Stephen Brooks, *Public Policy in Canada: An Introduction* (Toronto: McClelland & Stewart, 1989), ch. 10.

Broadcast Media: Television and Radio

Television is a powerful medium. Canadians spend an average of about 22.8 hours a week watching the box.[26] (See Table 4.2.) There is at least one television set in 97 percent of Canadian households; 84 percent of adults, 87 percent of teens and 90 percent of children watch it every day.[27] Television is primarily an entertainment medium in which impressions and images are more influential than issues. However, it is also the primary source of information for most Canadians, and the chief means of communication between political leaders and the general public. As television has gained ever larger audiences, the relationship between politicians and Canadian citizens has increasingly been filtered by television journalists. Television has placed demands on political leaders, and they in turn have learned ways to maximize their exposure and get the message they want to the public.

TABLE 4.2   PERCENTAGE DISTRIBUTION OF TELEVISION VIEWING TIME

Type of Program	Canadian Programs	Foreign Programs	Total
News and public affairs	17.2	5.6	22.7
Documentary	0.8	0.8	1.6
Instruction			
Academic	0.8	0.4	1.2
Social/recreational	1.6	0.4	1.9
Religion	0.2	0.1	0.3
Sports	5.0	2.4	7.3
Variety and games	4.5	5.0	9.5
Music and dance	0.6	0.5	1.1
Comedy	1.4	15.6	17.0
Drama	4.5	24.7	29.2
Other/unknown	*	8.2	8.2
Total	36.5	63.5	100.0
* Too small to be expressed			

Source: Adapted from Statistics Canada, *1991 Census Highlights: The Daily*, Catalogue 11-001, April 26, 1993.

Consider some of the ways politicians are affected by television. Physical attributes and speaking style that formerly would *not* have been important in a leader's relationship with the public now threaten to damage an individual's chances for political success. Citizens who meet well-known political leaders in person often are surprised at how different the real-life impression is from the television image. Much personal charm is often lost in the electronic transmission, as are intelligence and persuasive arguments. As David Taras notes:

> *Television by nature coarsens and distorts reality. Virtually all mannerisms are exaggerated: imperfect chins look more imperfect, a hand seems to shake more than it actually does, sudden movements give someone a frenetic look.*[28]

26. *Canada Year Book 1999,* p. 282.
27. Lambert et al., "The Sources of Political Knowledge," p. 103.
28. David Taras, *The Newsmakers: The Media's Influence on Canadian Politics* (Scarborough: Nelson, 1990), p. 122.

Politicians have to learn techniques to become more "mediagenic." Speech must be lively rather than slow and deliberate, but not too fast or staccato. They must learn to express a complex idea in 7 or 10 seconds; they have no time for deep or thoughtful arguments.

Considering how influential television is and how it magnifies and distorts political images, it is not surprising that there are major concerns in Canadian politics about how much the government should regulate its content. The primary question driving this issue, however, has been — how real is the danger of assimilation into the American cultural milieu? Selected facts and figures give some indication of the degree of American penetration into our popular culture. Over 80 percent of Canadians have direct access to American television channels. Both of Canada's national broadcasters, the CTV and CBC English networks, show a preponderance of American programs — and surveys show that Canadians overwhelmingly prefer them to Canadian alternatives.[29] Former CBC president A.W. Johnson expressed his concern about U.S. influence this way:

> *The plain truth is that most of our kids know more about the Alamo than they know about Batoche or Chrysler's Farm. They know more about Davey Crockett than they do about Louis Riel.*[30]

Over the years, the federal government has attempted to increase the quantity and quality of Canadian programming in order to counter the threat of American cultural domination. First, as we have seen, CBC radio and television were created to be unifying forces and Canadian content was made part of their mandate. Secondly, the Board of Broadcast Governors and the Canadian Radio-television Commission (now the Canadian Radio-television and Telecommunications Commission [CRTC]) were established to regulate both the CBC and all private broadcasting in Canada. The CRTC was given the goal of safeguarding, enriching and strengthening the cultural, political, social and economic fabric of Canada by regulating the content and standards of Canadian programming.[31] It was given responsibility to set and enforce complicated Canadian-content guidelines for all licensed broadcasters[32] and to determine the percentage of Canadian content and the time frame within which such programming must appear for both television and radio.

The nationalistic recommendations of the CRTC are often highly controversial and politically unpopular. For example, its proposals for tougher Canadian-content rules have often been rejected by Cabinet because they would be strongly opposed by large sections of the public. Ministers argue that stiff regulation of programming and scheduling might mean loss of audience and advertising revenue, and, more recently, that an interventionist approach is obsolete given satellite television and video cassettes.

The extent to which the CBC, under the watchful eye of the CRTC, has been successful in its mission as a public service is open to debate. It does ensure that some of the major people involved in broadcasting in Canada are Canadians. However, the subjects, values and ideas conveyed are often "Americanized" in order to increase their appeal to a broader North American audience and, therefore, make them more profitable. Canadians have shown a predilection for domestic news and

---

29. Ronald R. Manzer, *Canada: A Socio-Political Report* (Toronto: McGraw-Hill Ryerson, 1974), p. 110.

30. A.W. Johnson, *Broadcast Priorities for the 1980s*, CBC Corporate Statement to the CRTC, 1978, p. 3.

31. The CRTC, for example, allows the prime minister special access to the broadcast media. Of course, the prime minister can ask for time on CBC television and radio at any time, but through an instruction from Cabinet, the CRTC can invoke section 18(2) of the *Broadcasting Act* and gain access to all stations. Such an invocation constitutes a directive to all licencees to broadcast any program deemed to be "of urgent importance to Canadians generally."

32. See Stephen Brooks, *Public Policy in Canada,* 3rd ed. (Toronto: Oxford University Press, 1998).

public affairs programs, but even these rely heavily on American sources. This means that U.S. foreign reports tend to displace not only Canadian reports, but even Canadian domestic news. On the other hand, as Table 4.3 shows, many good Canadian TV shows have resulted from public policy.

Since the media helps to set the agenda for public discussion and debate, it is reasonable that a society that depends on another country for its view of the world will absorb some of its norms. Clearly, reliance on American media has a bearing on the fragility of the Canadian national identity.

TABLE 4.3   GOVERNMENT REGULATION OF TELEVISION IN CANADA

Policy	Date	Canadian Programs Appear
CBC radio established	1932	
CBC TV established	1952	
	1957	Front Page Challenge (CBC)
45% Canadian-content (Cancon) rule	1961	
	1963	This Hour Has Seven Days (CBC)
CRTC created to regulate broadcasters and issue licences	1967	
50% Cancon rule	1970	
	1971	The Beachcombers (CBC)
	1973	Definition (CTV)
	1974	King of Kensington (CBC)
Regulations to discourage Canadian advertisers from buying space on U.S. stations	1976	
Canadian networks allowed to substitute their signals for U.S. channels on cable		
	1977	SCTV (City-TV/Global)
CRTC ruling: CTV to show Canadian drama series	1979	The Littlest Hobo (CTV)
Govt. begins subsidy for independent TV through Telefilm Canada	1983	
	1984	Night Heat (CTV)
	1985	Street Legal (CBC)
CRTC ruling: CTV Cancon drama quota set at 2.5 hrs weekly rising to 3.5	1986	
CBC Newsworld established	1989	E.N.G. (CTV)
		Road to Avonlea (CBC)
	1993	This Hour Has 22 Minutes (CBC)
	1994	Due South (CTV)
CRTC ruling: Global to air 3.5 hrs Cancon drama per week, 2 hrs original	1995	
	1997	Traders (Global)
CRTC embarks on complete renewal of TV policy and finance system	1998	

Source: Based on facts from *The Globe and Mail*, July 25, 1998.

Restricting American cultural penetration, however, presents a serious dilemma for Canadians. If Canadians believe in a free press and a free flow of information, then they should leave the borders open to all communications without restriction. Yet doing so would hinder the development of a distinctive Canadian culture and identity. One author described the Canadian solution to the dilemma this way: in Canada, we "follow a classical liberal ideology and let the media directors, advertisers and people choose the media and the media content they wish." This "reinforces U.S. influence and presumably weakens Canadian identity as such."[33]

Financing is another major problem for the CBC in carrying out its mandate concerning Canadian programming. The Corporation has been underfunded since 1953 and this has hampered effective planning in the face of severe competition from a rapidly expanding private television broadcasting system. Despite 1993 Liberal *Red Book* election promises to support the CBC, budget cuts by the Liberal government in 1996–97 were particularly severe, causing staff and programming cuts and closure of some regional stations.

The economic dilemma of all Canadian broadcasters, including the CBC, is that profitability rests largely on the use of imported programs. The United States exports expensively made programs for which costs are amortized in its large domestic market. These products can be purchased by Canadian networks for a fraction of their cost. Private broadcasters try to provide programming with the highest possible appeal at the lowest cost and therefore want to import American shows. This pits them against the CRTC, whose role is to enforce minimum Canadian-content levels.

The CBC has to cope with these economic problems while carrying out its two conflicting mandates. It is required to promote a national identity and culture and, at the same time, to cater to regional, ethnic and other minority interests. Establishing an appropriate balance has proven difficult. As a vocal medium, broadcasting is particularly suited to appeal to awareness of languages and cultures. It does a great deal to develop regional identities but is less successful at reinforcing national values and promoting national unity.

The media in Canada also fail to enhance national unity because they cannot bridge the country's ethnic cleavage. In the early years, rather than providing a powerful unifying link for the whole country, television broadcasting achieved the opposite. In Québec, where the full range of programming was local, the identity that was reinforced was not Canada's but Québec's. Television helped shape and preserve the distinctiveness that promoted Québec nationalism. Montréal sociologist Maurice Pinard commented:

> *The Québec nation was born with television ... I mean by that the Québec nation, as opposed to the French-Canadian people, which is something else altogether.*[34]

Despite the growing availability of English-language television stations, 87.5 percent of francophone viewers watch French-language stations.[35]

Even entertainment shows separate the two communities. In the 1960s and 1970s, French Canadian entertainers such as Pauline Julien and Robert Charlebois were at the forefront of the independence movement. Their role was so prominent that former Parti Québécois leader Jacques

33. Frederick Elkin, "Communications Media and Identity Formation in Canada," in B.D. Singer, ed., *Communications in Canadian Society* (Toronto: Copp Clark, 1975), p. 232.
34. Quoted by Daniel Drolet in "TV Shapes Quebec's Distinctiveness," *The Ottawa Citizen*, February 3, 1991.
35. Rhéal Séguin, "Use of French Rising in Québec," *The Globe and Mail*, June 19, 1991.

Parizeau quipped that the Quiet Revolution was brought about by "three or four ministers, 20 civil servants and 50 chansonniers."[36] Today, many Québec artists like Celine Dion do not publicly endorse the separatist crusade and are building careers in the American market in English, but programming in Québec continues to be distinctively francophone. An example of unique television programming in Québec was the TV series *Les Filles de Caleb*, a 20-part series on Radio-Canada. It was based on Arlette Cousture's novel about the true experiences of her grandmother. The series was the most popular in Québec history: an estimated 3.5 million people — half Québec's entire population — regularly watched the shows. The English-language version was not at all popular in the rest of the country. Director Jean Beaudin commented:

Québeckers like Québec television and Québec movies.[37]

English television programs also tend to restrict their focus to their own language group. They often feature Americans but only rarely francophone Canadians.

Different agendas in the French and English media are often evident in political biases. For example, while English CTV is generally judged to be neutral and the CBC to be establishment-oriented in political leanings, Radio-Canada is considered more partisan and leans to the left and to the Parti Québécois. A good example is the four-part series titled *The History of Nationalism in Québec* broadcast on Radio-Canada in 1992. It was, as Montréal journalist William Johnson commented, really "the nationalist mythology of Québec history." French-speaking Québeckers were presented as oppressed victims persecuted by *les Anglais* for more than 200 years. All the social and economic problems of French Canada were depicted as the fault of *les Anglais*. It was nationalist mythology presented on television as fact.

Separatism has had an impact on even the structure of the CBC. The president of the CBC is a political appointee, often with no previous background in broadcasting. The president presides over the CBC board — which is also appointed by the government. The appointment system reflects the fact that since 1968 prime ministers have been concerned with what they perceive as a separatist threat at Radio-Canada.

Apart from the inability of the national media to provide an integrated service between the French- and English-language communities, other communication issues have generated considerable friction between federal authorities and other ethno-cultural groups. Native audiences, for example, were slow to get services. However, by 1993, all communities of 500 or more had, or were in the process of getting, radio and television services. This progress has assured more community control of northern broadcasting, but decisions about policy and funding are still made in the South. As with northern education policy, efforts are being made to develop and fund programs that are relevant to northern communities and to Native people in particular. But the problem remains how to balance the need to foster national unity while at the same time celebrating differences.

Technological changes will make regulatory control of Canadian content much more difficult in the years ahead. In early 1993, the establishment of DirecTV signalled the first serious threat to Canadian broadcasting from private satellite television operators. The company began offering services in April 1994. It offered Canadian TV viewers 150 channels of entertainment and information

---

36. Peter Maser, "The Muting of the Strident Indépendantistes among the Artistic Community," *The Ottawa Citizen*, June 20, 1992.

37. Ibid.

in the first direct broadcast satellite service backed by a major U.S. company. The CRTC has no legal jurisdiction over what the satellite carries, but the service does, in effect, contribute to the Canadian broadcasting system. For this reason, many nationalists accuse the CRTC of making a mockery of Canadian-content rules. In future, Canadians will be able to order the information and entertainment they want when they want it. They will be able to put together their own newscasts, choosing areas that interest them. Eventually networks, if they exist at all, will be transformed and broadcast executives will lose their power to decide what transmissions individuals receive.[38]

Print Media: Newspapers

The print media, unlike the broadcast media, regulate themselves through press councils and are free of direct regulation by government. They have a more restricted but more attentive public than television has. Only about half of all Canadians read newspapers, but they tend to be among the best educated. Data also show that "the most politically attentive individuals regard newspapers as the single most important source of political information."[39] There is strong evidence supporting the effectiveness of the print media in contributing to political knowledge. Reading newspapers and magazines appears to be more "instructive" on both factual and conceptual knowledge than is viewing television. This is particularly significant in view of the fact that television is growing as the preferred source of political information among Canadians, and that fewer young people are reading newspapers. Newspaper headlines, in particular, influence what the public perceives to be the most important problems facing the country.[40]

The Globe and Mail is read by nearly three-quarters of the country's top decision-makers, and more than 90 percent of media executives read it regularly for ideas and trends. Since *The Globe and Mail* became available on a nation-wide, day-of-issue basis early in the 1980s, it has gained considerable strength as a national newspaper. It is Toronto-based and, although it does carry regional, national and international material, it is still strongly biased toward central Canada and basically views the periphery and the whole country from a central perspective. *The Toronto Star*, Canada's largest independent daily, can be considered national only by virtue of a few widely syndicated articles. The *National Post*, Hollinger's new national newspaper launched in 1998 following its takeover of *The Financial Post*, is also based in Toronto. With regard to the francophone community, *Le Devoir* is comparable to *The Globe and Mail*. Canadian Press (CP) (a cooperative news agency owned and operated by Canadian dailies that provides information to more than 100 media outlets) and a few national magazines must also be included as part of the national scene.[41]

Because of factors such as distance, time and the federal political structure, these national communication networks are supplemented by a wide range of regional daily newspapers that are primarily community-oriented. They, too, depend on centre-oriented agencies such as CP for national and international news, reinforcing the influence of the central establishment on content and values. The steadily improving quality of CP and increased regional coverage by *The Globe and Mail* in particular appear to have contributed to a better cross-regional flow of information, as have the development of major newspaper chains at the expense of independent dailies.

---

38. See Richard Collins, *Culture, Communication and National Identity: The Case of Canadian Television* (Toronto: University of Toronto Press, 1990).
39. Lambert et al., "The Sources of Political Knowledge," pp. 373–74.
40. Fletcher, *The Newspaper and Public Affairs*, p. 17.
41. See Arthur Siegel, *Politics and the Media in Canada*, 2nd ed., ch. 6.

Given the importance of newspapers in setting the national agenda, *ownership* is an important issue and ownership restrictions have been designed to protect Canadian culture. While there are no rules about concentration of media ownership within Canada, newspapers must be Canadian-owned. Today, this is a source of controversy. In 1992, three major chains, Thomson, Southam and Hollinger, dominated the newspaper market in Canada, controlling over 64 percent of all dailies (Thomson 37 percent, Southam 16 percent, Hollinger 11 percent). Ninety dailies out of 108 belonged to the chains. By 1996, only four years later, Black had taken over Southam and controlled 58 newspapers with about 43 percent of Canadian newspaper circulation. (See "Canada's Press Baron, Conrad Black.") Moreover, Rogers, the largest cable operator in Canada, had absorbed Maclean Hunter to create a multimedia giant. This domination by a few owners poses serious questions about lack of competition, less diversity and possible conflict of interest. The Thomson newspapers, for example, are part of an international conglomerate that includes insurance, television, oil, real estate and import companies, among other holdings — as well as *The Globe and Mail*. It is questionable whether running a newspaper is compatible with such interests.

Canada's two major royal commissions into the media — the Davey and Kent commissions in 1970 and 1981 — both recommended that safeguards be introduced to prevent concentration of ownership, but their views were largely ignored. Further concentration of media ownership should be limited,[42] Kent said, because there was a need

> *to preserve the daily newspaper industry; that is, to save newspapers from further absorption into conglomerate business empires within which they are ... valued by their proprietors chiefly for the large cash flow that they can contribute to further empire-building.*[43]

Although it would appear to be in the national interest to maintain diversity of news sources, research has been unable to prove that chain ownership affects newspaper quality, news or editorial coverage. However, the issue points out the need for vigilance and for high-quality, professional journalism. As Kent maintained, journalists always endure conflicting pressures, and when matters become too complex only the most diligent cope by becoming more sophisticated and professional. As the possibilities for manipulation of the press by industry increase, the need for sophisticated, investigative journalism is even greater. But the reality seems to be that jounalism has become less serious — it has become a kind of "info-tainment."

News and Editorials

News presentation and editorial comment have a considerable impact on the political agenda in Canada. We have seen that economics constitutes a powerful factor in American influence on all Canadian media. Its effects are particularly evident in news reporting. The relative cost of "made in

---

42. The Kent Commission was set up after the *Ottawa Journal*, owned by Thomson Newspapers, and the *Winnipeg Tribune*, owned by Southam Inc., shut down on the same day in August 1980. Government legislation to freeze the size of the two largest chains and restrict the size of developing chains to 20 percent of national circulation, among other changes, died at the end of the parliamentary session in late 1983. During the same period, in order to ensure editorial quality and diversity, the government directed the CRTC to restrict cross-ownership between broadcasters and owners of daily newspapers. In December 1983, Southam Inc. and Thomson Newspapers Ltd. were acquitted in the Ontario Supreme Court of criminal charges for conspiracy and merger in the closing of the *Ottawa Journal* and the *Winnipeg Tribune* and undue lessening of newspaper competition in Vancouver.

43. From a comment by Tom Kent on concentration of newspaper ownership. *The Ottawa Citizen*, June 6, 1990.

Canada" news gathering is prohibitive, so that Canadian news relies heavily on U.S. agencies and wire services. This is particularly true in international news, but no Canadian newspaper has nearly the equivalent influence in Canadian foreign policy discussions. Canadian news is also distorted in the amount of coverage accorded to U.S. domestic news. Topics of interest to Americans automatically become of interest to Canadians.

Another primary barrier to developing a "national" political agenda in Canada is that the two founding nations live in separate media worlds that reinforce their linguistic and cultural differences. Newspapers serving anglophone and francophone communities focus on different headlines and stories, and often view even Canadian national events from quite different perspectives. There is a degree of stereotyping and insularity that fosters misunderstandings.

Canadian newspapers reflect community norms and generally support the *status quo*, tending to reinforce the prevailing institutional and cultural patterns of authority and orientation. This "middle of the road" tendency has been explained by three factors. First, since they must compete for advertising revenue, the media attempt to maximize their audience or readership by such methods as packaging their news as entertainment and conforming with existing community values. Second, advertisers are able to wield indirect influence on the content and direction of news and programming. For example, editors

CLOSE-UP ON Culture

CANADA'S PRESS BARON, CONRAD BLACK

As of 1999, Conrad Black owns 57 daily newspapers in Canada — accounting for about 43 percent of the country's newspaper circulation. His 1996 takeover of Southam and purchase of seven Atlantic papers (from Thomson) gave his company, Hollinger Inc., coast-to-coast coverage and made it the third-largest newspaper company in the western world. In 1998, Southam purchased *The Financial Post* (in exchange for four Ontario dailies) in order to integrate it with his new national newspaper the *National Post*, which he launched in 1998.

Appalled by the takeover of Southam and the lack of competition and editorial diversity it could represent, Black's opponents sought a judicial review of the Competition Bureau's approval of the deal. Led by the Council of Canadians, they focused on the shrinking number of outlets for diverse opinions in the media, and decried a growing right-wing bias that they claimed entails diminishing importance for the coverage of labour, health and education issues. Pressures to have the Southam takeover rolled back have not been successful, and may never be. Should they be?

Mr. Black claims that he is only turning flagging newspapers into financial winners, and that he should be allowed to expand even further.

or station managers would hesitate, and probably decline, to run a story that was adverse to the interests of a generous sponsor. Third, as the Special Senate Committee on the Mass Media suggested, many newspapers may be unwilling to challenge the existing power structure in their community because of "lassitude, sloppiness, smugness and too chummy a relationship."[44]

In recent years, there has been a trend toward judgemental journalism. The resulting predominantly negative tone of political coverage may encourage lack of respect for politicians, civil servants, government agencies and Parliament. In 1992, a two-hour television program, "The Betrayal of Democracy" (PBS), examined the role of television and the press in the breakdown of the democratic process and the alienation of the body politic from decision-making. It found that the decay of democracy in America is rooted in the "power relationships surrounding the government itself. Political power has gravitated from the many to the few." The thesis of the television special was that government intentionally excludes citizens from the process of decision-making. "It reduces democracy to a charade in which power is exercised for the benefit of assorted corporate elites ... and the elected officials who rely on them for the funds to remain in office."[45] Television plays a major

---

44. Special Senate Committee on Mass Media, *The Uncertain Mirror*, vol. 1 of the Report of the Special Senate Committee on Mass Media (Ottawa: Information Canada, 1970), p. 87.
45. Quoted by John Haslett Cuff in "Media and Democracy's Decay," *The Globe and Mail*, April 15, 1992.

role in this charade. It limits the amount of air time devoted to political figures to about five seconds per appearance, reducing political discourse to meaningless slogans and simple-minded catch phrases.

These comments apply in Canada as well as the United States. Too often, Canadian journalists treat public affairs as theatre and gossip, stressing personalities rather than social issues, style rather than substance. This may be a reflection of the educational background of journalists (see "Some High-Profile TV and Radio Journalists"); however, it is not entirely their fault. As one study noted,

... the vast majority of viewers/listeners/ readers want all things on their information menu to be black or white, true or false, good or bad — preferably seasoned with a pinch of sensationalism and intimate personal detail of the famous, and served on a platter of conventional belief.[46]

'Having decreed that only violence will successfully attract their attention, the media then denounces violence.'

Reproduced with permission, Paul Gilligan, *The Ottawa Citizen*.

GOVERNMENT INFORMATION AND POLITICAL ORIENTATIONS

The federal government plays a major role in shaping and reinforcing political culture. It informs, educates or propagandizes in order to increase public support and loyalty to the state. It takes on responsibilities for protecting Canadian heritage, even to the point of trying to protect Canada's cultural industries from trade challenges from the United States (see Chapter 15). Governments time their political announcements and broadcasts for peak exposure, advertise their policy positions, televise parliamentary debates and record statements in *Hansard*. They advertise in the various media; public servants answer questions and distribute information; they distribute government booklets on a variety of subjects. As well, government ceremonies are held with pomp and dignity, instilling feelings of respect and a sense of historical continuity.

For a variety of reasons, government communications have increased dramatically in recent years. One justification has been the perceived need to refurbish the image of Parliament and federal institutions; another has been an attempt to promote national unity and combat the centrifugal forces

---

46. Michael J. Trebilcock et al., *The Choice of Governing Instrument* (Ottawa: Minister of Supply and Services, 1982), pp. 16–17.

of separatism and regionalism. Such concerns among political leaders began in the late 1960s when protest movements and vocal separatists started reinforcing the growing cynicism and hostility of Canadians toward the federal government and its work. Since then the federal government has faced several questions. Why does it not reap credit for its programs? Is the problem a breakdown of communications between the government and its citizens?

Early Government Information Services

In 1969, the federal government set up the Task Force on Government Information to address these and other problems of government information. Its report ushered in a controversial era in government information programs. Modern Canadian governments have always advertised to inform the public about such topics as new regulations; in fact, each government department has a budget for such purposes. However, as a result of the 1969 report, a new agency, Information Canada, was set up to provide a direct information service for selling and distributing government pamphlets and providing other information across the country. It included a small "federalism" section, the aim of which was "a defence in depth of Confederation."

Information Canada was immediately viewed as a partisan party propaganda device by both the media and the opposition parties. It was inadequately defended by the government and disbanded in 1976. However, the problem of negative public attitudes toward government remained, and a year after the demise of Information Canada other efforts were instigated to help the government departments advertise their services. The government, in a word, went into the marketing business — to sell itself.

The Issue of Government Advertising

The greatest danger for government information services is that they can be viewed, justifiably or not, as a vehicle for publicizing the programs, policies and views of the governing party — as a partisan political instrument. There are two other concomitant controversies about government advertising. One is the use of advocacy advertising techniques; the other is the financial cost to the taxpayer.

In essence, **advocacy advertising** means selling ideas rather than products or services. Such advertising is used by governments to sustain or change public attitudes concerning the long-term fundamental values that underlie social and political institutions. By ensuring that Canadians are informed without the intermediary interpretation of the press, government representatives tend to view advocacy advertising as a means of building national unity. Government advertisements,

CLOSE-UP ON Culture

SOME HIGH-PROFILE TV AND RADIO JOURNALISTS

CBC
Peter Mansbridge, anchor, *The National*,
Grade 12, Glebe Collegiate Institute, Ottawa

Rex Murphy, essayist/reporter, *The National*; host, *Cross Country Checkup*, CBC Radio
B.A., English Literature, Memorial University of Newfoundland, St. John's; Rhodes Scholar, Oxford

Hana Gartner, former host, *The National Magazine*
B.A., Communications, Loyola College (now Concordia University), Montréal

CTV
Lloyd Robertson, anchor, *National News*,
Grade 13, Stratford Collegiate & Vocational Institute, Stratford, Ontario

Sandie Rinaldo, *National News*,
Honours B.A., Fine Arts, York University, Toronto

Global
Peter Kent, anchor, *Prime Time News*,
Grade 12, Viscount Bennett High School, Calgary

CBC Newsworld
Pamela Wallin, host, *Pamela Wallin Live*,
Honours B.A., Psychology and Political Science, University of Regina; Certificat d'Études Françaises, Collège de Brandol, France

Ian Hanomansing, Vancouver news correspondent,
B.A., Political Science and Sociology, Mount Allison University, Sackville, New Brunswick; LL.B., Dalhousie University, Halifax

Source: Gary Salewicz, "Hey, What Do They Know?" *Elm Street*, October 1996.

therefore, do not contain much specific information but are designed to underscore what the federal government sees as basic national values and to promote understanding of national goals. For instance, ads extolling the virtues of Canada's multicultural society have carried logos such as "Growing Together" and "We have a lot to offer each other."

This type of service becomes controversial when advertisements extoll clearly partisan policies. One of the best examples was the Liberal government advertising concerning the patriation of the Constitution. In October 1980, contracts were awarded (without competition) to three agencies that had had contracts with the Liberal party in the previous election campaign. The advertisements they generated were designed to convince Canadians that the Constitution should be rewritten and patriated despite the differing opinions of provincial premiers and political parties. This aggressive approach, the government declared, was necessary for informing the public on a matter of national interest.

Many commentators felt that this powerful sales effort weakened Parliament and democracy in Canada by undermining the traditional relations between MPs, the electorate and the government. One widely criticized television commercial featured Canada geese as the backdrop for a constitutional message. A federal member complained at the time, "I'll never be able to look at Canada geese or a beaver in quite the same way again. I'll see them as Liberals in disguise."[47] There is little doubt, however, that the advertising campaign contributed to ensuring that the federal message was heard in all provinces. Given the regionalization of the press, which often allows provincial premiers and opponents of the federal government to monopolize news coverage, federal government advertising may well have been necessary for redressing any distortions in the information received by the public.

This scenario was repeated in 1992 by the Mulroney government. Canada's 125th birthday celebrations coincided with the Conservative government's efforts to "sell" the Charlottetown accord to the public. Efforts to make Canadians feel good about themselves and their country were expensive, and "just happened" to appear to be trying to make them feel good about the Conservative party as well. The Department of the Secretary of State was responsible for promoting the birthday celebrations and, as political commentator Hugh Winsor noted,

> ... this relatively minor department is merely a convenient umbrella for the cabinet's propaganda thrust, and the shots are being called in the Federal Provincial Relations Office and Mr. Murray's committee.[48]

"Warm tummy, feel good" advertising filled the media in 1992 as the government spent $21 million on a year-long federal advertising campaign, awarding the most lucrative advertising contracts in Canadian history (without competitive bids) to companies with close political ties to the Mulroney government.[49] The ads reflected the government's twin themes of unity and prosperity. One controversial ad consisted of a song about pride in one's country, sung by a young Mila Mulroney look-alike over a montage of familiar wheat fields, Rockies, fishing harbours and totem poles. The syrupy lyrics had been composed for the Conservative party and, arguably, created a partisan "add-on"

47. Quoted in Frances Phillips, "And Critics Have a Go at Ottawa," *Financial Post*, May 13, 1982.
48. See Hugh Winsor, "Bidding to Quicken Patriotic Heartbeat," *The Globe and Mail*, May 28, 1992.
49. Mark Kennedy and Chris Cobb, "Ad Contracts Given without Bids," *The Ottawa Citizen*, February 6, 1993.

for the Tories.[50] The primary goal was to make viewers more receptive to government advertising when Ottawa tried to sell them a constitutional package later in the year.

When the referendum on the Charlottetown accord was called for October 28, 1992, it, too, was packaged and "sold" by the government with taxpayers' money. The Yes support consisted of the leadership of all three major federal parties and almost all of their provincial counterparts, as well as 191 local or community-based non-partisan organizations, "prominent" Canadians recruited as voluntary "national chairs," and the leadership of the Native, labour, corporate, university, media and cultural elites.[51] But that was not enough. The Yes side also had state-of-the-art technology and polling contracts were handed out freely (largely to Conservative agencies); a bureaucrat from the Federal-Provincial Relations

> ## CLOSE-UP ON Behaviour
>
> ### PROMOTING CANADA
>
> Following the disastrous results of the 1995 Québec referendum, Heritage Minister Sheila Copps declared that "one of the most visible ways to promote our country is with our flag."* Her department set up an elaborate operation to take requests for flags by toll-free lines, facsimile, mail and the Internet. Copps argued that although the flag alone would not save the country, the $23 million investment would heighten awareness of the country. Predictably the Bloc Québécois declared the policy to be sheer propaganda. What do *you* think?
>
> ---
>
> * *The Globe and Mail,* August 30, 1996.

Office (FPRO) remarked confidentially, "there is no budget here. The sky is the limit."[52] The No side, in contrast, had a tiny one-room office, no government funding and no logistical support. With their superior structure, organization and financing, the Yes side dismissed their opponents as malcontents and "enemies of Canada." Instead of an informative campaign that countered the objections of its opponents, the government waged a campaign based on emotion, throwing its resources completely behind one side of the referendum question.

Again, after the very close 1995 Québec referendum, the federal government took several initiatives to counter separatist "myths" about the failure of federalism. It took out full-page newspaper advertisements to counter claims that Québec puts more money into the federation than it gets out. It sent brochures to every Québec household asserting that Prime Minister Jean Chrétien had lived up to his referendum promise to recognize the distinctiveness of Québec. Even the Heritage Minister got into the act with a flag-give-away campaign. (See "Promoting Canada.") The government strategy culminated in the creation of a new federal agency — the Canadian Information Office with a budget of nearly $120 million in 1997 — dedicated to fostering patriotism and promoting the benefits of federalism. It was like 1980 all over again! (See Chapter 7.)

The question of government advertising promises to play a conspicuous role in the years ahead. The federal government has a responsibility to inform Canadians about its policies and programs and yet refrain from using its resources to disseminate partisan political propaganda. The ethnic and regional divisions in Canada's political culture can be alleviated to a degree by ensuring that all citizens are exposed to views that represent the country's interests, not just those of a particular region, province or ethnic group. It is the responsibility of the opposition parties to ensure that the government does not abuse this right, and to date they have shown a marked ability to detect and publicize infractions.

---

50. See Hugh Winsor, "The High Cost of Feeling Better," *The Globe and Mail*, May 26, 1992.

51. Brooke Jeffrey, *Strange Bedfellows, Trying Times* (Toronto: Key Porter, 1993), p. 115.

52. Quoted in Jeffrey, *Strange Bedfellows*, pp. 117–18. Elections Canada revealed that the Yes forces spent 13 times more than the No forces spent.

CLOSE-UP ON
Behaviour

WOMEN AND EDUCATION: A PIONEER OF THE WOMEN'S MOVEMENT

In Britain in 1946, an early feminist, Eleanor Sidgwick, fought for the right of women to have access to university education. She maintained that there are two gifts, one moral and one intellectual, that it is the special privilege of a university to bestow.

The moral gift is "the sense of membership of a worthy community, with a high and noble function in which every member can take part, and at the same time not so vast in extent as to reduce the individual to insignificance." The intellectual gift is the "habit of reasonable self-dependence," which higher education encourages in three ways: it encourages labour, care and precision of thought in arriving at sound conclusions; it teaches a sense of the limits of one's own knowledge and its relation to other areas of learning; and it provides encounters with teachers who think for themselves and advance as well as impart knowledge.

In its time, this was a profoundly subversive argument, as it maintained that intellectual processes were not determined by gender. Today, of course, Canadian women take full advantage of equal access to higher education.

Source: Gillian Sutherland, "The Education of Women in Cambridge," in Richard Mason, ed., *Cambridge Minds* (Cambridge, U.K.: Cambridge University Press, 1994), p. 42.

GENDER, CLASS AND POLITICAL ORIENTATIONS

In the last chapter, we discussed the ethno-linguistic and regional cleavages that divide Canadians into separate groups, creating different "layers" of political culture. There are also other cleavages that cut relatively evenly across all of Canadian society. Some of the most significant of these cleavages are based on class and gender. Each of these cleavages consists of many groups and organizations making unique demands on governments and society. Some act as highly organized units to achieve their ends; others have little or no cohesiveness. Some groups have considerable power and influence; others have very little.

These cleavages are influential in forming the political ideas and orientations of group members. In the next sections, we examine gender and class in Canada, two stratifications that affect how individuals think and behave politically.

Gender Stratification and Inequality

Of the world's more than 5.3 billion people, slightly fewer than half are female. In Canada, women make up slightly more than half the population. In recent decades, women's role in society has undergone massive change, particularly in the industrialized countries of the world.

Throughout history, women have often been treated as inferior to men. Discrimination has been enforced by social customs and laws. As the bearers of children, endowed with less obvious physical strength than men, women have been assigned, and have generally accepted, primary responsibility for children and the family. Until relatively recently, even in developed countries, women have been barred from such societal participation as owning property, holding public office, voting and even higher education. (See "Women and Education: A Pioneer of the Women's Movement.")

Before the mid-1970s there was little hard evidence to back up their claims of relative deprivation, because statistics that were collected tended to ignore the contributions of women to the family and the economy. In 1991, however, the United Nations released the first major statistical portrait and analysis of the situation of women. It continues to monitor and update statistics about the achievement of women around the world in its *Human Development Report*.[53] This report provides the best comparative information to date on the condition of women around the world.

Around the world, both households and governments have spent fewer resources to educate and train girls than boys, reducing the potential social, economic and political contribution of women

---

53. *The World's Women 1970–1990: Trends and Statistics* (New York: United Nations, 1991); and updated yearly, United Nations, *Human Development Report, 1999* (New York: Oxford University Press, 1999).

to society, and leaving women at a disadvantage in making major life decisions. However, the UN study also shows that in much of the world today this is changing so that women are progressing toward equal educational enrollment rates with men. Primary education has been accepted as a fundamental goal by all countries, and enrollment of girls in primary and secondary schools is now comparable to that of boys in most countries. At the university and college level, female enrollment is also increasing. In the developed regions, western Asia, some countries of southern Africa and Latin America and the Caribbean, gender enrollment is now nearly equal. In Canada, women receive over half of all BA degrees, almost half of MA degrees, and 32 percent of PhDs.

Increased education has paid dividends in terms of bringing more of the world's women into political life. Since women are traditionally responsible for the health and well-being of their families, they generally participate extensively in community affairs. Although many have been cut off from men's traditional routes to political leadership, Canadian women are increasingly entering political life through non-governmental organizations, women's movements and associations. They are becoming more active in the politics of their local communities in such areas as discrimination, poverty, health and environmental issues, violence against women and peace movements.

Routes to power in government decision-making are traditionally through political candidacy and the civil service. In most countries, women are more successful in local elections than in national elections. Statistics on women in bureaucratic careers are not generally available, but one pattern is clear: significant numbers of women work at the lower echelons, and their representation dwindles rapidly as pay and status increase. Everywhere there is a need to end occupational segregation and wage discrimination, and to recognize women's unpaid work as economically productive.

The status of the world's women has improved dramatically in the twentieth century, but there is still a long way to go before gender equality will be reached socially and politically. The UN's 1995 *Human Development Report* says that on every continent women work longer hours, earn less money and are more likely to live in poverty than men. It estimates that 70 percent of the world's poor are women.[54] In 1994, more than a quarter of all women 65 and older lived below the poverty line in Canada, compared with 11 percent of men their age.[55]

In 1998, Canada came out best overall in another UN comparative study that sought to determine how women fare regarding a host of issues selected to indicate opportunities available to them.[56] Still, there is no reason for complacency. As in most countries, many women in Canada have fewer job opportunities and lower earnings than men. More live in poverty. Political scientists may debate the underlying causes of gender inequality but there is no doubt about its existence.

Gender Theory

Gender theory explanations about the causes of gender inequality have gained credibility as a subdiscipline in most of the social sciences.[57] The fundamental point on which all feminists agree is that orthodox theories about politics tend to ignore gender and harbour unconscious assumptions about the role of women. Like ethnicity, gender cleavages are generated by prejudice and also by systemic

---

54. United Nations, *Human Development Report, 1995*.
55. Statistics Canada, *A Portrait of Seniors in Canada*, 1997; and *The Globe and Mail*, February 7, 1997.
56. United Nations, *Human Development Report, 1998*.
57. See, for example, Michèle Barrett and Anne Phillips, *Destabilizing Theory: Contemporary Feminist Debates* (Stanford: Stanford University Press, 1992); and Sandra Lipsitz Bem, *The Lenses of Gender* (New Haven: Yale University Press, 1993).

discrimination. The issue is not new. In the nineteenth century, John Stuart Mill argued that the sub-jugation of women is a selfish, egotistical conspiracy by men who want to keep women as a free source of domestic labour.[58] It is, he said, in men's interest to preserve a male-dominated society, so they claim that the subjugation of women is natural, even divinely ordained. Karl Marx and Frederick Engels held that the subjugation of women is based on economic reasons. According to them, it serves the interests of the capitalist class because the female homeworker is unpaid, and this keeps the working class without resources. The traditional family is part of the scheme to ensure the subordination of women, keeping them dependent on their wage-earning husbands.[59]

Early Canadian feminists such as Agnes MacPhail, Canada's first woman elected to Parliament, believed that women's inequality was based on their lack of political and legal rights. Over time those battles were fought and won; women received the right to vote federally in 1918, and gained legal equality rights in the *Charter of Rights and Freedoms* in 1982.

In the nineteenth century, the belief that women inherit physical attributes that determine their personality (such as emotional, intuitive, nurturing and passive traits) was accepted even by the first wave of feminists who won political rights for women. Today, second-wave feminists argue that gender role differences are not inherent but learned. They point out that special learning patterns have discouraged females from participating fully in public life. Gender roles learned in childhood through family, school and other social contacts are carried through to the workplace and other adult social settings. Roles learned in childhood shape the aspirations of children, and this, in turn, helps to provide continuity in society. By the same token, however, clinging to past roles can also make attitudinal change slow and stressful.

The new wave of feminists has targeted society's attitudes toward traditional gender roles and stereotypes and brought new issues into the country's political agenda. They have made specific attempts to change the role socialization of boys and girls. Books that contain traditional stereotypes of adventurous, mischievous boys and docile little girls have been replaced with less restrictive material; toys have become less gender-specific; girls are encouraged to study mathematics and science and aspire to careers other than teacher, nurse or secretary; boys are encouraged to be more sensitive and share household chores. Changes have not been restricted to childhood socialization: gender biases are detected and gender-neutral terms promoted. In short, the issue of gender has become highly politicized.

Canadian Women Today

The role of women has changed dramatically. In 1901, only 13 percent of Canadian women worked outside the home. By 1996, 83 percent did so.[60] Most of that change occurred since the 1950s as improved technology and contraceptives enabled women to make more choices concerning their lives. Women are entering the work force both for economic reasons and in response to the argument that women cannot be dependent and equal at the same time.

In some respects, however, women's role in the workplace has been slow to change. Significant differences still exist between the economic and social conditions of men and women in Canadian society. In 1996, the average female worker earned about $20 902 compared to the average male at $32 248.[61] In some cases, such as for women under age 25 and single women, women now earn

---

58. John Stuart Mill, *On the Subjection of Women* (London: Dent, 1970). First published in 1869.
59. *Women and Communism: Writings of Marx, Engels, Lenin and Stalin* (Westport, Conn.: Greenwood Press, 1973); *and Canada Year Book 1999*, p. 192.
60. Canadian Advisory Council on the Status of Women, *Women and Labour Market Poverty* (Ottawa, 1990), pp. 114–15.
61. *Canada Year Book 1999*, p. 249.

approximately the same as men. However, women are disproportionately represented among the poorest in Canadian society. Single mothers are among the most economically disadvantaged in the country.[62] As well, single persons over age 65 have the lowest incomes of any group over 24 years of age, and women comprise the vast majority of this category.

Although half of the Canadian population is female, women are poorly represented in upper-level political and occupational hierarchies. There have been many firsts for women in recent years — Bertha Wilson was the first woman to serve on the Supreme Court (1982); Jeanne Sauvé was the first female Governor General (1984); Audrey McLaughlin was the first woman to lead a federal political party (1989); in 1993, Kim Campbell became the first female prime minister; and in 1999 Beverley McLachlin became the first female Chief Justice of the Supreme Court. (See Table 4.4.) However, despite these firsts and the fact that no *formal* barrier to their full and equal participation in politics exists, women are still less active than men in politics. They vote and join activities such as political campaigns as frequently as men, but as a group they participate significantly less in more active or demanding jobs. (See Chapter 11.) However, the fact that they are graduating from universities in record numbers has already moved women into traditionally male-dominated areas such as law and commerce, where they are now represented in numbers relatively equal to males. They have done best in medical and health-related fields where 65 percent of managers are now women.[63]

With their increased participation in the work force, women have brought new issues to the government's policy agenda: affirmative action, legal equality rights, equal access to opportunities, pay equity, abortion rights and child care. Issues such as sexual assault have also become more visible, and have confronted and reversed the established view of wives as the property and responsibility of their husbands. Women have argued that the "personal is political" and moved many topics that were previously considered private into the political sphere. A plethora of reforms have taken place. In 1988, for example, the federal government passed an *Employment Equity Act* that called for affirmative action within departments, Crown corporations and federally regulated businesses.[64] Pay equity and sexual harassment policies have also contributed to a more equal workplace for women. There seems to be a growing acceptance among both men and women of the need to address and solve gender-related issues.

Some scholars, however, express a note of caution that is perhaps worth examining. Christopher Lasch, for example, fears that feminism has been "infected" by the spirit of the marketplace. Far from civilizing corporate capitalism, he says, the feminist movement has been corrupted by it and has adopted mercantile habits of thought as its own. He questions that the prospect of upper mobility alone can confer meaning on the lives of women — any more than it can on the lives of men.[65]

The role of women in Canadian government is discussed further in Chapters 8, 9 and 10. The role of women in political parties and elections is discussed in Chapters 11 and 12, while the women's movement is discussed in Chapter 13.

---

62. Statistics Canada, *Perspectives* (Ottawa: Supply and Services, 1993); and *Canada Year Book 1999*, p. 192.

63. Statistics Canada, study quoted in *The Globe and Mail*, January 6, 1997.

64. For a standard overview, see Sandra Burt, "Rethinking Canadian Politics: The Impact of Gender," in Michael S. Whittington and Glen Williams, eds., *Canadian Politics in the 1990s*, 3rd ed. (Scarborough: Nelson, 1994), pp. 176–90. More progressive views about both the composition and even the definition of gender-related issues would include topics such as what constitutes a family and who should receive government benefits.

65. Christopher Lasch, *Women and the Common Life*, Elisabeth Lasch-Quinn, ed. (New York: W.W. Norton, 1996).

TABLE 4.4   IMPORTANT DATES IN ATTAINMENT OF LEGAL AND POLITICAL EQUALITY FOR WOMEN IN CANADA

1916	Manitoba, followed by Saskatchewan and Alberta, gives vote to women in provincial elections
1917	British Columbia and Ontario give vote to women
1917	Women serving in Armed Forces and women with male relatives in uniform are allowed to vote in federal elections
1918	Nova Scotia gives vote to women
1918	Women are given franchise in federal elections
1919	New Brunswick approves women's suffrage
1919	Women gain the right to stand in federal elections
1921	Agnes MacPhail is the first woman elected to Parliament
1922	Prince Edward Island approves women's suffrage
1925	Newfoundland approves women's suffrage
1928	Supreme Court rules women are not "persons" and cannot be appointed to Senate
1929	British Privy Council overturns Supreme Court decision
1931	Cairine Wilson is first woman appointed to the Senate
1940	Québec gives vote to women (the last province to do so)
1947	Married women are restricted from holding federal public service jobs
1955	Restrictions on married women in federal public service jobs are removed
1957	Ellen Fairclough is sworn in as first female federal Cabinet minister
1967	Royal Commission on Status of Women is established
1971	Canada Labour Code is amended to allow women 17 weeks of maternity leave
1973	Supreme Court upholds section of *Indian Act* depriving aboriginal women of their rights
1973	Supreme Court denies Irene Murdoch right to share in family property
1977	*Canadian Human Rights Act* is passed, forbidding discrimination on basis of sex
1981	Canada ratifies UN Convention on the elimination of all forms of discrimination against women
1982	Bertha Wilson becomes first woman appointed to the Supreme Court of Canada
1983	Affirmative action programs are made mandatory in the federal public service
1984	Twenty-eight women are elected to Parliament, six appointed to Cabinet
1984	Jeanne Sauvé becomes Canada's first female Governor General
1985	Section 15 of *Charter of Rights and Freedoms* comes into effect; employment Equity legislation is passed
1989	*Indian Act* is amended to remove discrimination against aboriginal women
1989	Audrey McLaughlin becomes first woman to lead a significant political party (the NDP)
1991	Rita Johnston serves briefly as B.C. premier after Bill Vander Zalm resigns, becoming Canada's first female premier
1993	Catherine Callbeck is first woman elected premier (P.E.I.)
1993	Kim Campbell serves briefly as Canada's first woman prime minister
1997	General election: 60 women are elected to Parliament — the largest number ever
1999	Beverley McLachlin is first woman appointed as Chief Justice of the Supreme Court

Class Stratification and Inequality

Socioeconomic class provides another cleavage in society that helps define political ideas and orientations. Economic inequalities are responsible for profound differences in health, education and quality of life. Upward movement between classes is possible but can be extremely difficult, and the gap between the richest and poorest Canadians is growing.

Defining class is controversial and problematical. **Class** refers to a rank or order in society determined by such characteristics as education, occupation and income. These characteristics provide "objective" indicators that sometimes are different from "subjective" or self-assigned rankings. Depending on which types of indicators are used, different class lines can be detected in the Canadian population.

Class was an important component of Karl Marx's thought. He divided capitalist societies according to economic criteria into the **bourgeoisie** (the economic elite), a small **petite bourgeoisie** (small business people, farmers, self-employed professionals), a **new middle class** (civil servants, teachers, salaried professionals) and the **proletariat** (workers). Marx expected the proletariat eventually to revolt against exploitation by the bourgeoisie, and create a new and egalitarian, classless society. History has not unfolded this way. In Canada, as elsewhere, the "new middle class" has grown, the elite "bourgeoisie" has become increasingly more powerful and internationally based, and, as a group, the "proletariat" is too weak, fragmented and dependent on state subsidies to be able to revolt.

At the beginning of the twenty-first century, class divisions based on wealth and income are evident in Canada. At the top of the economic scale, a tiny elite, or *upper class,* of about 2 to 3 percent of the population holds the top positions in business, industry, professions and the bureaucracy. The extensive holdings of a very few individuals and families in real estate, natural resources, communications and various commercial enterprises, including large corporations, set them apart from other Canadians.[66]

They include some of the wealthiest families in the world — for example, the Irving family (which owns most of New Brunswick); Ken Thomson (whose assets include newspapers, the Hudson's Bay Company, Zellers and Nelson Canada among others); the extended Bronfman family (assets include Seagrams, London Life, Brascan, Noranda, Loblaws and Holt Renfrew to name a few). Many head international firms. Less wealthy, but still with million-dollar-plus incomes, are corporate chief executive officers (CEOs). Between them, these individuals control many of the large corporations operating in Canada, and some sit on the boards of directors of major Canadian banks.

In the 1960s and '70s this wealthy stratum of Canadians was monopolized by Anglo-Saxon Protestants, but this is changing. Several large corporate families in Canada today are Jewish or French Canadian, and those of other ethnic backgrounds are joining this elite group.

The vast majority of Canadians today are part of the huge *middle class* — over 80 percent of the population — that is sandwiched between this tiny economic elite and about 16 percent of the population who are relatively economically deprived. The shape of the economic hierarchy, therefore, is less like a pyramid and more like a bulging onion. Income, occupation and lifestyle subdivide the members of the middle stratum into upper-middle and lower-middle class. The upper-middle tier is generally well educated and financially secure. It does not function as a single unit but has a variety of economic interests and political demands. This group can be further subdivided in various ways, such as between those who are self-employed and those who work for someone else.

---

66. Each year *The Financial Post* lists the wealthiest individuals and corporations in Canada.

The lower-middle class, or working class, is generally considered to consist of those who do manual work as opposed to intellectual work. As a group, this class is less educated and generally earns less money than others in the middle class. Despite the fact that some of them are unionized, changes in the Canadian economy in the 1980s and 1990s have dramatically increased unemployment in this group. The proportion of blue-collar jobs in the work force increased only marginally, while unskilled and labourers' jobs in fishing, mining, agriculture and other primary resources declined sharply. These job losses, combined with inflation and increased taxation, make individuals in this stratum particularly vulnerable to dropping into the lowest strata of economically deprived Canadians.

Within the large, middle economic tier, Canadians of Anglo-Saxon origin appear to have no particular advantage over other groups. Jews, Asians, Dutch and Italians, for example, do equally well or better in terms of average income, percentage of white-collar jobs and percentage with some university education. One ethnic group, however, ranks consistently low in socioeconomic stratification characteristics — Native people, many of whom live in extreme poverty.

The *poor* in Canada are considered to be those who exist below the **poverty line**, a theoretical criterion set by Statistics Canada. They rely on state benefits such as unemployment insurance and welfare to exist. In 1995, about 5.5 million people — or over 18 percent of the population — were living on or below the poverty line.[67] The figure includes those who spend about 55 percent or more of their income on food, shelter and clothing. In dollar terms, Statistics Canada defines this line according to family type and location, for example, as an annual income below $26 049 for a family of four in a city of 100 000 to 5 000 000.[68]

Those economically worst off in Canadian society are most likely to be one-parent families, more than 60 percent of which are headed by females; the young, of whom more than a million are children under 16 years of age (an astounding 18 percent of all Canadian children); the single elderly, who are mostly widows; and Native people. As we have seen, they also tend to be the least educated.

Other income distribution data provide similar conclusions. When the average family income of the top 10 percent of Canadians in 1995 is compared with the average family income of the bottom 10 percent, we find that the top 10 percent earns 22 percent of the total Canadian income, while the bottom 10 percent earns only 2.9 percent. This means that the top group earns 7.6 times more of the national income than the lowest group. Such income disparity is affected by public policy. Government benefits to poor people during the 1970s in Canada slightly reduced this income gap, while neo-conservative policies in the 1980s and 1990s have increased it. As the federal and provincial governments attempt to reduce their social policy commitments and payments to poorer individuals, they are increasing the overall gap between the rich and poor.

This brief overview of class stratification in Canada confirms that Canadians do not have equal chances to prosper. The educational system and social programs currently in place are not adequate to break the cycle of poverty for the least fortunate. The odds of leading a secure, healthy

---

67. *Canada Year Book 1999*, p. 193.

68. Ibid. In Canada, anyone who falls below the poverty line — Statistics Canada's so-called Low Income Cut-off (LICO) — is defined as poor. However, LICO is a relative measure, closely tied to the average income and average consumption patterns of the average Canadian. As such, some claim it tells more about how well off the typical Canadian is than it does about the condition of the truly poor. Furthermore, the line itself is disputed. Christopher Sarlo, for example, in *Poverty in Canada,* noted that half of the households headed by someone 65 years of age or older were considered poor, but almost half of them owned a home, 90 percent mortgage-free. Christopher Sarlo, *Poverty in Canada* (Vancouver: Fraser Institute, 1992).

life decline as one moves down the social scale. Poverty means fewer educational opportunities; higher mortality rates; more physical and mental illness; poorer, more hazardous working conditions; higher crime rates (poverty is the greatest predictor of delinquency); and higher suicide and divorce rates.

The inequalities of opportunity and distribution of wealth in Canada have significant implications for politics. Some writers have concluded that the economic elite is also a dominant political force, that the state and economic elite are linked together and share a "confraternity of power."[69] There is no doubt that the elite exercises considerable influence in the direction of economic development of the country. On the other hand, the economic elite is far from a ruling class. One study, for example, showed that about three-quarters of the state elite has middle-class origins.[70] This indicates that political power in Canada is diffused downward to at least the middle class. As well, the political decision-making process is extremely complex and virtually precludes control by one small group. Governments must maintain popular support, and this puts considerable power in the hands of the majority of the people through voting, membership in political parties, running for election and so on.

Unfortunately, members of the lowest socioeconomic stratum are preoccupied with survival. They express low feelings of personal political power and efficacy, and participate least in the political system. A wide range of federal, provincial and municipal welfare programs exist to help the poor, but these have come under attack in recent years as governments at all levels have attempted to balance their budgets. Pressure on government institutions to expand and make social services more efficient, however, will increase in the twenty-first century as societal problems, such as an aging population, are demographically compounded.[71] The importance of class in voting behaviour is discussed in Chapter 12.

SUMMARY

Many factors condition the political ideas and orientations of Canadians. Informal socializing agents, such as the family and peer groups, and more formal institutions, such as the educational system, the media and even government, help determine the factual knowledge, attitudes and values Canadians have about politics, politicians and government. Other factors, such as gender and socioeconomic class, define the environment in which a person lives, determining life chances and also shaping political attitudes and values.

---

69. The ideological elite is described in John Porter, *The Vertical Mosaic*, p. 460, and later elaborated on by Wallace Clement in *Canadian Corporate Elite* (Toronto: McClelland & Stewart, 1975).

70. Dennis Olsen, "The State Elites," in Leo Panitch, ed., *The Canadian State* (Toronto: University of Toronto Press, 1977).

71. Some argue that welfare policies simply legitimize existing social inequities by preventing the poor from becoming a potent political force. See, for example, Leo Panitch, "The Role and Nature of the Canadian State," in Panitch, *The Canadian State*, p. 8. Also see Allan Moscovitch and Jim Albert, eds., *The "Benevolent" State: The Growth of Welfare in Canada* (Toronto: Garamond Press, 1987).

Political socialization in Canada is a haphazard affair. Early socialization through families and peer groups is casual and informal, with minimal interference by the state. Later socialization, through agents such as education and the media, is often subject to influence by the federal government through public policy. However, state direction is severely limited. Education, for example, is not under the federal jurisdiction, and the mass media, including broadcasting, television and the press, all act independently, to varying degrees. In view of this, governments often attempt to influence the values and beliefs of Canadians more directly through advocacy advertising.

There are many powerful obstacles to building a strong Canadian political culture. Both the media and the education system reflect and reinforce regional, linguistic and ethnic cleavages. French- and English-language media in Canada reinforce the linguistic and cultural isolation of the two official language groups. Educational institutions reinforce provincial, regional and French–English differences. American influence is pervasive. These obstacles to nation-building are part of the constraints of a democratic federal political system and a society that is bilingual and multicultural and located next to a cultural giant. In many ways, the key to Canadian unity lies in cross-regional and cross-cultural interaction.

In liberal democratic societies, basic freedoms ought to be respected. The state cannot assume direct control of the agents of socialization. Few Canadians want totally centralized government socialization in order to instill a stronger national culture. However, over the last three decades the federal government has moved to combat strong divisive forces in the Canadian political culture. It continues to build on the goals of strengthening communications, facilitating access to government and improving the circular flow of information between government institutions and the public. Its methods, though often controversial, are geared to bringing government closer to the people. The nature and effect of new technologies, in particular the Internet and e-mail, are also having a dramatic effect on the relations among individuals and the relations between the people and their government.

The Canadian political culture, initiated and reinforced as it is by the socialization process described in this chapter, contains at least the minimal level of national identity required to legitimize the Constitution and the democratic political process. Canadians expect to live in a liberal society free of government control and indoctrination. They value the assumptions and processes of parliamentary democracy and expect the political system to manage the tensions caused by the various societal cleavages — and to do so democratically.

Social inequalities caused by gender and class tend to be self-perpetuating. Heightened awareness and political activism are required to change patterns of behaviour and redress inequities. Significant change is taking place in the role of women in society. To some extent it has outstripped the amelioration of injustices related to class.

In the next part of the book, we examine how the institutions of the Canadian political system are based upon, and reflect, the essential characteristics of Canadian political culture and social cleavages.

DISCUSSION QUESTIONS

1. Can you detect ways that you have been politically socialized by family, peers, educational institutions and the media? Describe the process and the effect it may have had on you.

2. Can you recall a recent instance of government advertising? In your opinion, was it justified? In what circumstances is it acceptable/unacceptable?

3. In what ways have the social and political orientations of women changed since the Second World War? What major challenges have been met with respect to political equality for women, and what are some problems that still exist?

4. Do all Canadians have equal chances in life? Why or why not?

Selected Bibliography

Education

Economic Council of Canada, *A Lot to Learn* (Ottawa: Supply and Services, 1992).

Emberly, Peter C., *Values, Education and Technology: The Ideology of Dispossession* (Toronto: University of Toronto Press, 1995).

——————, *Zero Tolerance: Hotbutton Politics in Canada's Universities* (Toronto: Penguin, 1996).

—————— and Waller R. Newell, *Bankrupt Education: The Demise of Liberal Education in Canada* (Toronto: University of Toronto Press, 1994).

Horn, Michael, *Academic Freedom in English Canada: A History* (Toronto: University of Toronto Press, 1999).

Media

Collins, Richard, *Culture, Communications and National Identity* (Toronto: University of Toronto Press, 1990).

Desbarats, Peter, *Guide to Canadian News Media* (Toronto: Harcourt Brace Jovanovich, 1990).

Dorland, Michael, ed., *The Cultural Industries in Canada* (Toronto: Lorimer, 1996).

Eaman, Ross, *Channels of Influence* (Toronto: University of Toronto Press, 1994).

Fetherling, Douglas, *The Rise of the Canadian Newspaper* (Toronto: Oxford University Press, 1990).

Hayes, David, *Power and Influence: The Globe and Mail and the News Revolution* (Toronto: Key Porter, 1992).

Holmes, Helen and David Taras, eds., *In the Public Interest: Mass Media and Democracy in Canada* (Toronto: Holt, Rinehart and Winston, 1992).

Lorimer, Rowland and Jean McNulty, *Mass Communication in Canada* (Toronto: McClelland & Stewart, 1991).

Raboy, Marc, *Missed Opportunities: The Story of Canada's Broadcasting Policy* (Montréal and Kingston: McGill-Queen's University Press, 1992).

Siegel, Arthur, *Politics and the Media in Canada*, 2nd ed. (Toronto: McGraw-Hill Ryerson, 1996).

Singer, Benjamin, *Communications in Canadian Society*, 4th ed. (Scarborough: Nelson, 1995).

Taras, David, *The Newsmakers: The Media's Influence on Canadian Politics* (Scarborough: Nelson, 1990).

——————, *Power and Betrayal in the Canadian Media* (Toronto: Broadview Press, 1999).

Task Force on the Canadian Magazine Industry, *A Question of Balance* (Ottawa: Supply and Services, 1994).

Vipond, Mary, *The Mass Media in Canada* (Toronto: Lorimer, 1990).

Women/Gender

Bégin, Monique et al., *Some of Us: Women in Canada in Power and Politics* (Mississauga: Random House, 1991).

Bryson, Valerie, *Feminist Political Theory: An Introduction* (London: Macmillan, 1992).

Burt, Sandra, Lorraine Cade and Lindsay Dorney, *Changing Patterns: Women in Canada* (Toronto: McClelland & Stewart, 1993).

Cairns, A. and C. Williams, eds., *The Politics of Gender, Ethnicity and Language in Canada* (Toronto: University of Toronto Press, 1986).

Evans, Patricia M. and Gerda R. Wekerle, eds., *Women and the Canadian Welfare State* (Toronto: University of Toronto Press, 1997).

Fudge, Judy and Patricia McDermott, *Just Wages: A Feminist Assessment of Pay Equity* (Toronto: University of Toronto Press, 1991).

Gingras, F.-P., ed., *Gender and Politics in Contemporary Canada* (Toronto: Oxford University Press, 1995).

Megyery, K., *Women in Canadian Politics: Toward Equity in Representation* (Toronto: Dundurn Press, 1991).

Razack, Sherene, *Canadian Feminism and the Law: The Women's Legal Education and Action Fund and the Pursuit of Equality* (Toronto: Second Story Press, 1991).

Roach, Ruth et al. *Canadian Women's Issues* (Toronto: Lorimer, 1993).

Shanley, Mary Lyndon and Carol Pateman, eds., *Feminist Interpretations and Political Theory* (University Park, Penn.: Pennsylvania State University Press, 1991).

Wine, Jeri and Janice Ristcock, *Women and Social Change* (Toronto: Lorimer, 1991).

Class

Fleming, James, *Circles of Power: The Most Influential People in Canada* (Toronto: Doubleday, 1991).

Sarlo, Christopher, *Poverty in Canada* (Vancouver: Fraser Institute, 1992).

 # LIST OF WEBLINKS

www.statcan.ca	**Statistics Canada** This Web site offers a variety of information about the social and economic conditions of Canadians.
www.canpress.ca/ canpress	**Canadian Press** This site contains links to various Canadian media resources.

CASE STUDY – CULTURE

FOOTNOTES ON THE FUTURE

In *Boom, Bust and Echo*, economist and demographer David Foot provides students of politics with a compelling expansion of the political culture argument. At one extreme, political culture studies hold that political attitudes are the relatively stable products of a substantial socialization process. However, Foot argues that almost all changes in political attitudes are the result of demographics. What motivates Canadians to act politically? Demographics! Demographics are "all-pervasive": they shape the external environment for "all decision makers"; they determine "what our opportunities are" in terms of tax and social policies. Foot believes demographics tell us all we need to know about Canada's future. Specifically, he argues that political discontent and social unrest will result if the inequalities of opportunity and wealth caused by the baby boom remain unaddressed.

In his study Foot found that Canadian society has five broad age groups: retirees (over 67), 10.7 percent of the population; near retirees (ages 50–66), 15.6 percent; baby boomers (30–49), 32.7 percent; the baby bust generation (20–29), 18 percent; and the echo (children of the boomers), 23 percent. The existence of one group — the boomers — which is much larger than the others has many consequences. Foot traces the housing boom of the 1980s to the boomers' movement through the life cycle. As people age, their needs and wants change. In their thirties the boomers borrowed heavily, buying homes and appliances. When they had all they needed, the boomers stopped spending, with unfortunate but predictable consequences for house builders and appliance manufacturers. A consequence for the following bust generation was the lack of opportunity for employment and advancement: job markets and promotion paths are clogged by the boomers.

Governments borrowed heavily for the boomers, spending on health care, infrastructure and education. Foot argues that the current policy of paying down government debt is wrong. We already know that government revenues will begin to rise in the next decade. Why? Demographics tell us that the echo generation will enter the work force and government revenues from income and consumption taxes will rise. On this basis Foot says we should focus policy on getting people working and providing secure employment. Security of employment is the key factor in consumer confidence.

While Foot maintains that political attitudes may change dramatically in the short run, he argues that politicians and voters must abandon their short-term thinking for sounder policies based on predictable future trends. To address generational inequality, we should institute wealth taxes and maximize the numbers of employed Canadians. Without these changes, high levels of unemployment among younger Canadians will persist and levels of social unrest and intergenerational conflict will increase. Changing political attitudes are the product of generational inequality resulting from the disproportionate numbers of baby boomers.

Questions

1. Many political scientists disagree with Foot. Assess the merits of political culture and demographics as substantial explanations of the formation of attitudes of political discontent.

2. Critics of Foot's work argue that it is unrealistic to expect politicians and voters to abandon short-term considerations and start thinking further ahead. Is this a valid criticism? Is it unreasonable to cast politicians and voters solely as short-term thinkers?

PART

3

Institutions

. . . .

Political institutions reflect the structure and values of society. They establish the process through which public policy is created, implemented, enforced and changed. They also limit the ability of those in government to exercise political power.

Canada's Constitution and its many laws and procedures embody the aspirations of Canadians and guide political activity. The federal constitutional structure also shapes the priorities of contemporary politics. The economic issues of federalism concern how resources are collected and distributed among Canadians in different provinces and regions. The political issues involve, above all, nationalism and regionalism; indeed, in the year 2000, Québec nationalism has assumed such significance that it dwarfs all other political issues, shaking the very foundations of the country.

The formal and political executive — the Governor General, prime minister, ministry and Cabinet — provide leadership (or lack of it) in creating and applying society's laws. Parliament is another vital player in the political process. It gives the executive the power to govern while providing checks on government authority. The bureaucracy, which consists of oft-maligned public servants, forms the permanent administration that carries out the plans of its transient political masters. Together, these core institutions form the nexus of political power in Canada.

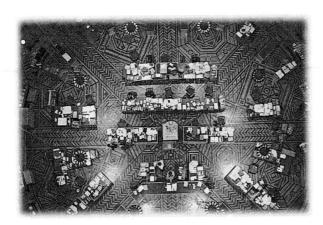

The Constitution Today

• • • • • • •

Legal Foundations, Failed Reforms and the Courts

The establishment of stability and order is a persistent goal of all societies. One way to achieve this end is to create a set of laws and principles that embody the aspirations of the society and, at the same time, provide guidelines for political activity. Although it may take an infinite variety of forms, such a set of rules and procedures is commonly referred to as a constitution. Some societies choose to depend on a constitution in the form of a single, written document that is both a statement of principles and a detailed explication of the relative authority and jurisdiction of the various actors in the political process. In other societies, values and political traditions are so firmly rooted in the political culture that no attempt to codify them is considered necessary. The true test of the significance of a constitution, be it written or unwritten, is the nature of its relationship to the society that produced it. Some constitutions are nothing but a set of lofty platitudes that are rarely observed, while others play an integral role in political affairs.

In this chapter we explore the meaning of the term "constitution," and trace the evolution of the Canadian Constitution since 1867. Of particular interest is the development of law and the problems and difficulties inherent in constitutional amendment and change. The last sections of the chapter deal with courts and judicial interpretations of the *Charter of Rights and Freedoms.*

While matters of fundamental law and legal procedure can be complicated for those unfamiliar with the principles of jurisprudence, this chapter approaches the subject in a non-technical manner, yet considers the political implications of constitutional institutions. The various efforts to patriate the Constitution and develop an amendment procedure acceptable to all the provinces have created enormous controversy in the past half-century. Although the British Parliament passed the 1982 *Canada Act* that brought the Constitution home, the situation is still far from resolved and arguments over the nature of the Canadian Constitution remain a lively political pastime. The defeat of the Meech Lake and Charlottetown accords and the 1995 Québec referendum on autonomy did not end constitutional wrangling, nor did the 1998 Supreme Court ruling.

> *No civilization ... would ever have been possible without a framework of stability, to provide the wherein for the flux of change. Foremost among the stabilizing factors, more enduring than customs, manners and traditions, are the legal systems that regulate our life in the world and our daily affairs with each other.*
>
> **Hannah Arendt**

LAW AND THE CONSTITUTION

Early societies tended to be dominated by individuals who sought to establish traditions and informal rules to govern their people. In more recent times, there has been a tendency for basic rules to be formalized into what is commonly referred to as a "constitution." The origin of this concept can be traced to Greek and Roman times. Further significant constitutional development flourished during the eighteenth and nineteenth centuries, and since then it has become practically universal for political power to be organized by some form of constitution.[1]

In every political system, there is a need to have guidelines for government action — a supreme law or constitution of the state that defines and limits political power. Thus, the fundamental aspect of a **constitution** is that it states the governing principles of a society. In modern times the word is used both empirically and normatively: to depict the organization of government, and to devise restraints on its action.

Constitutionalism means that everyone, including the government, is subject to the rules of the constitution. It depicts the government as the servant of society, not its master. The government may exercise authority and even use coercion, but it must do so according to the rules set out in the constitution and abide by judicial interpretations of its actions.

Though constitutions are products of historical development, they also tend to reflect current conditions. In absorbing contemporary elements, constitutions are able to help shape the future by incorporating the norms of political life. As well, constitutional authorities in most countries insist on the need to incorporate **individual rights** into the supreme law as well as to set the parameters for government action. Therefore, the vast majority of contemporary written constitutions contain a discussion of natural rights and the goals of universal liberty, peace and prosperity. The French *Declaration of the Rights of Man and Citizens* and the American *Constitution,* with its *Bill of Rights,* include statements supporting the principle of the natural rights of *individuals.* Even the most repressive regimes are likely to refer to these objectives in their constitutions.[2]

Many constitutions also acknowledge **collective** or **group rights**. In Canada, such "rights" were accorded to the ethno-religious-linguistic francophone group of Québec and some historical communities along the Eastern Seaboard by the *British North America Act* of 1867. Both "individual" and "group" rights are found in today's *Charter of Rights and Freedoms.* Of course, the fact that such rights are incorporated into a constitution is no guarantee of their actualization. In situations of real or perceived emergency, such claims may carry little weight in even the most liberal of societies.

1. For details, see Robert J. Jackson and Doreen Jackson, *An Introduction to Political Science: Comparative and World Politics* (Toronto: Prentice Hall, 2000).
2. For a discussion of the history of constitutionalism, see Charles M. McIlwain, *Constitutionalism: Ancient and Modern*, 2nd ed. (Ithaca, N.Y.: Cornell University Press, 1947).

The Rule of Law

Above all else, a constitution embodies the rule of law. In addition to setting out a commitment to certain general goals, a constitution is intended to provide a guarantee of impartiality and fairness. The authority of the state is to be exercised rationally and without malice, with all citizens being protected from the abuse of power. The **rule of law** means that a citizen, no matter what his or her transgression, cannot be denied the due process of law. It therefore regularizes the relationship between citizens and their government. No individual or institution is above the law, no one is exempted from it and all are equal before it. No government or administrative official has any power beyond that awarded by law. Whether or not it is formally included, the rule of law is a fundamental principle without which any constitution, written or unwritten, would be meaningless.

Courts are the guardians of the rule of law, and as such should be beyond partisan influence. The principle of the independence of the judiciary is firmly established, with a history of nearly 300 years. It can be traced to the English *Act of Settlement* of 1700 that resulted from the English Revolution of 1688, and provided that judges could be removed only if both Houses of Parliament formally asked the Crown for their removal. Following these British traditions, Canadian judges remain free to deliver decisions against the interests of influential individuals, institutions or governments without fear of recrimination.

In Canada today, judges of the highest courts (the Supreme Court of Canada and the Federal Court) and also the most important provincial trial courts (the Superior Court of Québec, the highest court of the other provinces, as well as the provincial courts of appeal) are removable only by an address to the Governor General by both Houses of Parliament. Such an address would only take place after a formal investigation by the Criminal Judicial Council, including all the chief justices in Canada. No higher-court judge has ever been removed in this fashion. As a further precaution against undue influence on judges, the Canadian Constitution provides that almost all courts are established by the provincial legislatures but that all judges from county courts upwards (except courts of probate in Nova Scotia and New Brunswick) are appointed by the federal government. This tradition of the independence of the judiciary is particularly important in constitutional development because courts interpret the written Constitution and, therefore, define the limits of federal and provincial power as well as apply the *Charter of Rights and Freedoms*.

Aside from the Constitution, the two main sources of law in Canada are **statutory** enactments — legislation passed by the Parliament of Canada and the provincial legislatures — and case law developed by the courts, also known as **common law** or unenacted law. Common law is based upon the rule of precedent, *stare decisis*. That is, the judiciary is bound by previous decisions in deciding current cases. This has resulted in the development of a body of case law that provides guidelines for judges in rendering decisions. As new problems are brought before the courts, judges refer to previous decisions that are deemed relevant, and apply the deciding arguments when making their own judgements. If there is no appropriate precedent, judges rely on common sense and reason. Existing principles are thereby broadened and the body of case law is expanded. Judicial interpretation is, thus, an important source of our law.

The relationship between these two major sources of law is defined by the doctrine of **parliamentary supremacy**, a basic premise of parliamentary democracy, which dictates that all 11 legislatures have the authority, in theory, to repeal or modify any legal principle that applies to their jurisdiction. This power is not absolute, however. While Canada's Constitution grants legislative authority to the 11 legislatures, the legislative competence of each is specifically limited to certain classes of matters. The Supreme Court's ability to declare an act ***ultra vires*** (beyond jurisdiction) on the basis of Canada's federal division of power is an important qualific *trenchment* of individual and group rights in Canada's *Charter of Rights and Freedom* the extent of parliamentary supremacy by placing a body of rights beyond the reach ture. **Entrenchment** means that the provisions are embedded in the Constitution so th tected and can be changed only by formal amendment procedures.

As well as stating fundamental principles, written constitutions describe the government. Some are remarkably complicated documents outlining the entire government of ture and the relative powers and limitations of the various institutions in the political process. There seems to be a general belief that the greater the detail in explicating these relationships, the less the likelihood for the abuse of power. At a minimum, most written constitutions outline the powers and duties of the executive, the legislature, the judiciary and, sometimes, other institutions such as the bureaucracy or the military. However, in modern, complex societies it is not easy to assign one specific function to any one of these bodies since they all perform multifunctional tasks. The courts, for example, adjudicate the law, but, as we have seen, in their accumulated judgements they also legislate.

However restrictive the legal restraints are on the exercise of power, nearly all constitutions contain provisions for enhanced executive power in emergency situations. War, civil unrest or natural disaster may require a government to act in a way that, under normal conditions, would be illegal. The real test of a constitution is whether, after such a crisis, there is a speedy return to compliance with constitutional strictures. The use of the *War Measures Act* to suppress civil rights in Québec in 1970 by the Liberal government of Prime Minister Trudeau was a worrisome example of how constitutions allow governments to handle crises, but the subsequent return to normal procedures after the perceived crisis was a vindication of the viability of Canada's constitutional democracy.

We need not search far to find examples in other countries where constitutional restraints on the exercise of power have been easily subverted by exaggerated crises. Once a group obtains a power base in society, either inside the institutional structure or outside it, the potential always exists to manipulate the provisions of the constitution or even suspend it entirely. As we have said, a written constitution is no guarantee that fundamental principles will be upheld. Unless a constitution is congruent with the prevailing political culture and norms about justice, it stands little chance of having a lasting effect.

We mentioned earlier that some countries possess what are referred to as **unwritten constitutions**. This is not a contradiction in terms; rather, the existence of such a constitution indicates that certain fundamental principles may be so firmly entrenched in the political process of the state that no formal document outlining them is considered necessary. The United Kingdom is perhaps the best-known example of a country with an unwritten constitution. In this case such documents as the *Magna Carta* of 1215, the *Habeas Corpus Act* of 1679 and the *Reform Bill* of 1832 exist, but they do not make up "the" constitution. Despite these and other documents and legal precedents, the real core of Britain's unwritten constitution is the set of values and norms embedded in the political culture: the rights of freedom of speech and assembly and the right of the opposition to participate in the political process, among others. The existence of an unwritten constitution provides certain advantages for a state. It makes it possible, for instance, to adapt more readily to change without the constraints required by a formal constitutional amendment process.

THE ORIGIN AND EVOLUTION OF THE CANADIAN CONSTITUTION

This section examines how the Canadian Constitution evolved from the period before the 1867 *British North America Act* (now renamed the *Constitution Act, 1867*) to the passing of the *Canada Act* in 1982.[3] While many Canadians assume that until 1982 the *BNA Act* was the entire Canadian Constitution, this assertion should be qualified. The Canadian Constitution has always been something of a *hybrid* of the written and unwritten types. Important elements of Canada's unwritten Constitution evolved in Britain for many centuries before Confederation. Common-law precedents and the parliamentary form of government are examples. As British colonists emigrated to Canada they brought with them basic constitutional principles such as the rule of law and the right of parliamentary opposition. The *BNA Act*, with its provision that Canada was to have a form of government "similar in principle to that of the United Kingdom," intended not only that certain institutional arrangements with respect to the formal executive were to be reproduced in Canada, but also that the British parliamentary system, with all its embedded values, was to be transplanted. Important elements of the Canadian Constitution were therefore already implicitly in place when the Fathers of Confederation met at Charlottetown in 1864.

As Ronald I. Cheffins phrased it, "a literal reading of the *Act* itself is not only of little value in understanding the realities of political life, but is in fact dangerously misleading."[4] Even vital procedural matters bearing on the governing of the country go unmentioned in the *BNA Act*; for example, the executive roles of the prime minister and Cabinet are not mentioned specifically. Such constitutional rules that are accepted practice or tradition without being enshrined in the written constitution are called **conventions**. Canada would not be able to govern itself without conventions such as the concept of **responsible government** that requires the government to resign when it is defeated in Parliament over a major issue. Moreover, many issues that preoccupy governments today were not covered in the 1867 document. Over time all levels of government have found ways to expand their responsibilities without increasing their constitutional authority.

The British North America Act

Given these elements of the unwritten Canadian Constitution, what is the significance of the *British North America Act*? Simply put, the Act sets out the basic terms of federalism and sketches the machinery of government based on the British model. The Act was the product of lengthy, complex negotiations between the political leaders over the terms of union. The leaders had differing expectations of what federalism would mean for their regions. They all made efforts to obtain concessions and guarantees that would protect matters of vital local concern. For example, French Canadians sought protection for their culture and language as the price for joining the union, while Nova Scotians were concerned about economic concessions and subsidies. Agreement on the organization and structure of the Senate proved particularly difficult to achieve.

The *BNA Act* is a relatively simple, straightforward document. It lacks the stirring rhetoric of the American Constitution, and whatever commitment it has to the fundamental rights of individuals

---

3. Two copies of the original *BNA Act,* to which Queen Victoria gave Royal Assent on March 29, 1867, can be seen in London, England: one in the Victoria Tower of Westminster Palace and the other in the Public Records Office. Reproductions are in the National Archives of Canada.

4. Ronald I. Cheffins, *The Constitutional Process in Canada* (Toronto: McGraw-Hill, 1969), p. 9.

is merely implied. In some respects the statute is as significant for what it does not say as for what it does say. The *BNA Act* was a document designed to enable the provinces to join in a political union. It was not intended to establish a truly independent state. It provided that the formal authority of Canada was to continue to be vested in the British monarch and that the Act itself could be amended only by the British Parliament.

The established provinces continued to adhere to their colonial constitutions, and the provinces added after Confederation later received their constitutions from the Ottawa government. The heritage from the United Kingdom in English-speaking provinces included the common-law tradition. However, since Confederation did not change existing law, Québec continued to have a system of civil law based on French traditions such as the *Code Napoléon*. According to the *BNA Act*, criminal law was to be a federal responsibility and similar throughout the land. However, general principles such as liberty and the rule of law were considered to be protected by common law and hence were not included.

The *BNA Act* is reasonably detailed with respect to the machinery of formal executive power and on matters concerning the division of authority between the federal and provincial governments. Over time the Act has become less clear-cut on the latter matters as jurisdictional issues have become more complicated.[5] The intent of the authors of the document was to create a strong central government. The federal government was given responsibility for the important topics of trade and commerce, defence and foreign affairs. Jurisdiction over education, welfare and other matters perceived to be of lesser and only local interest in 1867 was left to the provinces. As we see in the next chapter, the responsibilities of the provinces became relatively more important over time and, when legal disputes did ensue between the two levels of government, the British Law Lords often sided with the provinces. At times, therefore, the *BNA Act* has been a very restrictive document and has created an impasse in federal/provincial relations.

We have said that the *BNA Act* did not contain a procedure for amendment except by the passage of a bill in the British Parliament. Over time, this role of the British Parliament was restricted. In 1931, the *Statute of Westminster* established the principle that the British Parliament could not legislate for Canada except at the request of the Canadian government. In 1949, Louis St. Laurent's government secured an amendment to the *BNA Act* that widened the scope of the Canadian Parliament's authority to undertake amendments: it was empowered to amend the Canadian Constitution on its own except when it affected provincial interests, the five-year term of Parliament, and the language and educational rights of minorities. Despite these changes, the *BNA Act* remained an Act of the British Parliament, a fact that raised the ire of Canadian nationalists. It was not until 1982 that the *Canada Act* was passed, severing this link between Canada and the United Kingdom. In total, there had been 18 amendments to the *BNA Act*.

Although the *BNA Act* was the centrepiece of Canada's written Constitution, there were other relevant documents. Besides the various amendments to the *BNA Act* and the *Statute of Westminster*, the Canadian Constitution before 1982 could be said to include the *Royal Proclamation of 1763*, the *Colonial Laws Validity Act* of 1865, the various acts admitting new provinces to the federal union, Letters Patent concerning the office of the Governor General and a whole range of common-law precedents and orders-in-council.

Whether a constitution originates as a single, written document or as a cluster of laws and agreements, there is no doubt that major changes to it occur through judicial interpretation. There

---

5. See Garth Stevenson, *Unfulfilled Union: Canadian Federalism and National Unity*, rev. ed. (Toronto: Gage, 1989).

is always a need for a court or an arbitration process to resolve disputes over jurisdictional authority in every federal system. For most of Canadian history, the court of final appeal was the **Judicial Committee of the Privy Council (JCPC)** — the superior court of the United Kingdom. As we noted, it tended to define federal authority as narrowly and provincial authority as widely as possible. The emergency powers of the federal government, expressed in the clause "Peace, Order and good Government," granted extensive residual power to the federal government, but were interpreted by the JCPC in a way that virtually nullified the apparent centralizing intentions of the authors of the *BNA Act*.[6] The rulings of the JCPC on the law of Canadian federalism were the source of considerable controversy. It was widely felt that the Law Lords were too far removed from the political realities of Canada to render appropriate decisions.[7]

The reign of the JCPC as the court of last appeal ended in 1949. In that year, the **Supreme Court of Canada** gained power as the final arbiter of **constitutional review**. The Supreme Court is the highest court for civil, criminal and constitutional cases. (The Federal Court of Canada, a separate body, oversees matters of law, equity and admiralty.) Until 1982, the Supreme Court was somewhat hampered by the nature of the parliamentary system and the absence of an entrenched bill of rights. It was concerned mainly with jurisdictional disputes, and did not take the activist role for which the American Supreme Court is widely known. In recent years, the provinces have displayed notable reticence to take jurisdictional matters to the Supreme Court because of an alleged pro-centralist bias. Such disputes between the federal and provincial governments are increasingly resolved outside the judicial process through the mechanism of federal/provincial conferences. The development of a new style of federalism has meant that the terms of federalism can be adjusted by methods other than judicial interpretation.

This is not to argue that the Supreme Court is irrelevant on federal issues. On the contrary, there have been very important decisions by the Court on matters such as offshore oil and mineral rights and resource taxation, not to mention its rulings on the federal government's plan of unilateral patriation of the Constitution. Of course, since 1982 the Court has also taken a renewed interest in cases involving civil rights and liberties that can have an influence on federalism. A discussion of the Court's interpretations concerning the *Charter of Rights and Freedoms* is found in the section below on the evolution of the Charter.

The second important determinant of power between federal and provincial governments rests on the financial strength of the two jurisdictions. In a federal state, revenue sources must be divided reasonably between the two levels of government. If not, the federal reality will quickly wither. A key question, therefore, always concerns how taxation funds will be distributed between the provinces and the federal government.

The *BNA Act* conferred on the federal government the ability to raise money by any system of taxation, while at the same time it gave most areas of growing expenditure responsibility to the provinces. From the beginning, provincial authorities were restricted to collecting revenue through direct taxes or the sale of natural resources. (Direct taxes must be paid by the individual or firm assessed, but indirect taxes may be passed along to other persons or institutions.) Thus, it appeared from strict interpretation of the 1867 Act that the provinces could not levy a sales tax (indirect) on commodities that would be passed along to consumers. However, by the ingenious device of making vendors tax collectors for the provincial governments, the rules of the *BNA Act* were evaded

---

6. See Peter J.T. O'Hearn, *Peace, Order and Good Government* (Toronto: Macmillan, 1964).
7. See Alan C. Cairns, "The Judicial Committee and Its Critics," *CJPS*, vol. 4, no. 3 (September 1971), pp. 301–45.

Reproduced with permission, Raeside, *Victoria Times*.

and the provinces were able to employ both types of taxation. Today, even such ploys as this are considered insufficient to alleviate provincial budgetary needs.

In summary, the *British North America Act* was an attempt to graft a federal system of government onto a British heritage of representative and responsible Cabinet government. The Fathers of Confederation, as Professor Janet Ajzenstat has intelligently concluded, went to the bargaining table with quite different philosophical positions on human nature and government.[8] They also had to take into account two dissimilar linguistic groups, a federal system and complex financing regulations. The result is a perplexing division of jurisdictions between the two levels of government, federal and provincial. And, although the Crown, government and Parliament are the central governmental institutions, they are not totally powerful in Canada, as they are in the United Kingdom.

There are, then, three fundamental cornerstones of the Canadian system of government, all of which are enshrined in the Constitution. They are democratic responsible government, the rule of law and federalism. In Chapters 6 and 7 we define and analyze the details of federalism and nationalism, and in Chapter 8 we examine the formal executive, which is bound by principles of responsible government. Here we discuss the Constitution and briefly the basic federal bargain, both of which constitute key elements in Canada's political system. Then we outline the court system and analyze recent constitutional developments.

8. Janet Ajzenstat, *The Political Thought of Lord Durham* (Montreal and Kingston: McGill-Queen's University Press, 1988); and "The Constitutionalism of Etienne Parent and Joseph Howe," in Janet Ajzenstat, ed., *Canadian Constitutionalism: 1791–1991* (Ottawa: Canadian Study of Parliament Group, 1992).

THE FEDERAL CONSTITUTIONAL BARGAIN

have seen that federalism is a key element in the Canadian system of constitutional govern-
nt. The federal dimension was necessitated by the exigencies of the Confederation period and subsequently developed through two forces: judicial interpretation of the constitutional documents
and the evolution of financial relations between the federal and provincial governments.

Today, federalism is central to the way Canadians think about their politics. The winning entry
in a contest for Canadian jokes was a Canadian version of the ancient elephant joke: Of three students, the American wrote his essay on "The President and Elephants," the French student discussed "Sex and the Elephant," while the Canadian's topic was "Elephants: A Federal or Provincial
Responsibility?" In fact, the details of federalism are so significant that the entire Constitution is
printed in Appendix 1 of this book.

The need for a "federal bargain" that would apportion powers between the central and the regional governments was obvious in the nineteenth century. Sir Georges Étienne Cartier and other
French Canadian leaders demanded an element of isolation from central government authority as
part of the bargain. No matter what type of system was adopted, some independence had to be
granted to the local entities. John A. Macdonald, meanwhile, preferred a unitary to a federal form
of government.[9] The federal principle was therefore accepted as a necessary compromise and as a protection for provinces and language groups. Since then, for better or worse, the federal dimension has
pervaded the history and development of Canada.

The 10 provincial constitutions follow the federal pattern. In each of the provinces, the Queen
is represented by a Lieutenant-Governor appointed by governor-in-council on the advice of the
prime minister. The Lieutenant-Governor acts on the advice and with the assistance of his or her ministry or executive council, which is responsible to the legislature, and resigns office under circumstances
similar to those for the federal government. Provincial legislatures are elected for a maximum of
five years and, unlike Parliament, which has two houses, today they are all unicameral.

The three northern territories remain under the constitutional authority of the federal government. Several federal statutes — *Yukon Act, Northwest Territories Act, Government Organization
Act, Federal Interpretation Act,* and the new act providing for the creation of Nunavut — provide their
legal structures, and the Charter also provides a degree of independent legitimacy in sections 3 and
30 by referring to the legislative assemblies of the territories. In real political terms, the first two
territories have fully elected assemblies, responsible executives, called councils, and a form of delegated responsibility for most of the matters under provincial jurisdiction. The commissioners, who
are appointed by the Minister of Indian and Northern Affairs, act as quasi–Lieutenant-Governors
under the authority of the minister. Nunavut, the new territory carved out of the Northwest
Territories, gained official status on April 1, 1999.

As well as being subject to the laws of the federal and provincial governments, Canadians are regulated by local governments. Whether designated as city, town, village or township, these authorities are created by the provinces and territories to provide such services as transportation, public health,
garbage disposal, recreation, firefighting and police work. Local school boards are usually empowered to administer education at the primary and secondary levels.

---

9. P.B. Waite, *The Life and Times of Confederation, 1864–1867* (Toronto: University of Toronto Press,
   1962). See Chapter 6 of this text for further explanation of the terms federal government, unitary
   government and confederation.

The Federal/Provincial Division of Powers

The Fathers of Confederation regarded the American Civil War as an example of what could happen if a central government did not have strong powers and referred to this when they assigned the residual clause to the federal government. **Section 91** of the Constitution states: "It shall be lawful for the Queen, by and with the Advice and Consent of the Senate and the House of Commons, to make Laws for the Peace, Order, and good Government of Canada, in relation to all matters not coming within the Classes of Subjects by this Act assigned exclusively to the Legislatures of the Provinces...." In addition to granting this sweeping authority, **section 91** specified 29 items as belonging exclusively to the federal government, among them trade, commerce, banking, credit, currency, taxation, navigation, citizenship and defence. **Section 92**, on the other hand, delineates 16 specific areas of provincial jurisdiction, including direct taxation, hospitals, prisons, property and civil rights. These latter subjects, although of only limited and local concern in 1867, were later to become much more important than the Fathers could have foreseen in their era of more or less *laissez-faire* government.

Section 93 says that education comes under provincial jurisdiction, but circumscribes that power by special rules setting up denominational schools in Ontario and Québec. **Section 95** establishes **concurrent** or shared federal and provincial powers in regard to agriculture and immigration. The federal Parliament, however, is paramount in these two fields. In other words, if there's a conflict between federal and provincial laws over agriculture or immigration, the federal law prevails in the courts.

Despite these rules, the constitutional status of the provinces appeared insignificant in early Canadian history. The Constitution provided such disproportionate power to the national government that some experts have even referred to the period as one of "**quasi-federalism**"—that is, one whose appearance is federal (i.e., with divided jurisdictions), but whose reality is unitary because no significant power rests in the sub-units. This assertion is based on certain constitutional facts. First, the central government could **disallow** provincial legislation even when the subject matter of the legislation was assigned to the provinces by the *BNA Act* (now the *Constitution Act, 1867*). This rarely used power could be employed in extreme circumstances. For instance, during the Depression years of the 1930s, it was used to stop several acts of William Aberhart's Social Credit government in Alberta. In disallowing Aberhart's proposal to print money, the federal government argued that such an action would destroy the banking system. Although disallowance was employed 112 times after Confederation, it has not been used since 1943. As well, it should be remembered that although the federal government could negate provincial laws, it could not legislate in provincial fields.

The second and third major powers were those of *veto* and *reservation*. At one time, the Lieutenant-Governors may have had the power to employ the royal prerogative to **veto** (block) legislation. Since they did not exercise it, however, it atrophied as a power. On the other hand, the constitutional ability of Lieutenant-Governors to **reserve** provincial legislation for federal approval has been employed quite often: some 70 bills have been reserved since 1867.[10] The most recent case occurred in 1961, when the Lieutenant-Governor of Saskatchewan, Frank Bastedo, without first consulting the federal government, reserved provincial legislation that he believed was of doubtful validity. The federal Department of Justice quickly decided that the bill was within provincial

---

10. R. MacGregor Dawson, *The Government of Canada*, 5th ed., revised by Norman Ward (Toronto: University of Toronto Press, 1970), pp. 213–17.

'o the Lieutenant-Governor gave his assent to the bill. It seems unlikely that such extreme
wielded again in Canada, except perhaps in a circumstance as grave as the secession of
the federal union. Moreover, while the federal government may have the legal au-
any provincial legislation initiating secession, a "technical" solution of this type
satisfactory. If a provincial movement toward secession were clearly supported by a pop-
date, it could not be prevented by legal devices alone.

Problems over the Division of Powers

While the *BNA Act* was a centralist document, it is important to note that the meaning of many
key words has changed over time. Leaving aside for the moment the matter of how judicial interpretation has changed the document, it is clear that certain terms were not defined precisely in the
beginning and others took on new meanings over time. As well, certain matters could not have
been predicted by the Fathers of Confederation. These omissions created a void that both federal and
provincial authorities sought to fill to their own advantage. For example, section 109 gave control
over natural resources to the provinces — but did this control include offshore resources and the taxation of these resources? Section 93 gave power over education to the provinces, but today it is a matter for debate whether education, as a provincial responsibility, encompasses cultural matters,
broadcasting, occupational training and research.

The conflict over division of powers is well illustrated by the case of natural resources. Although
the *BNA Act* assigned the ability to make laws concerning resources to the provinces, it gave the federal government a major voice in the sale of resources by its control of interprovincial and international trade. Thus, the provinces control the oil because it is under the ground, the oil wells are
in the hands of private or public companies, and the Parliament of Canada exercises some authority over oil through taxation and jurisdictional powers. It could be different. Through use of
the **declaratory power** (*BNA Act* s. 92.10(a)), the federal government can assume jurisdiction over
any "work" that is for the benefit of Canada as a whole. For example, in the 1920s Parliament declared that every grain elevator was under federal control but it did not assume ownership. Federal
control over uranium exploration is a more recent example. The provinces have always contested
the use of this declaratory power, but the courts have continually backed the federal authorities' right
to employ it.

Recent technological breakthroughs permitting the exploitation of offshore resources have also
resulted in hot disputes. In 1967, the Supreme Court ruled in an advisory opinion that Ottawa, not
British Columbia, owned the resources off the West Coast. In 1977, the federal government proposed
temporary arrangements with three Maritime provinces that would have given Ottawa 25 percent
and the provinces 75 percent of their offshore resources. Newfoundland never accepted this bargain,
and Nova Scotia quickly backed out after a provincial election. In 1979, the Conservative government
of Joe Clark offered to give complete control of offshore resources to the provinces; however, the return of the Liberals in 1980 left the situation in limbo. Disputants on both sides of the East Coast question finally applied to the courts for settlement: Newfoundland to the provincial Court of Appeal,
Ottawa to the Supreme Court of Canada. After a long-running battle, the courts awarded ownership
of offshore resources along the East Coast to the federal government.

It is clear that the Constitution has been inadequate in clearly demarcating all jurisdictions. As
Garth Stevenson has pointed out, there are now very few areas of policy that are handled by only one
level of government. "The only exclusively federal areas appear to be military defence, veterans' affairs, the post office and monetary policy. The only exclusively provincial areas appear to be municipal

institutions, elementary and secondary education and some areas of law related to property and other non-criminal matters."[11] In all other areas, there is either tacit or explicit agreement by the two major levels of government to engage in activities in the same fields. Sometimes this is harmonious, as for example when the federal government allows the provinces to regulate interprovincial highway transportation. In other areas, such as external trade, employee training, communications, language and culture, the two levels are in constant conflict.

Another aspect of the division of powers that continues to cause controversy concerns joint responsibilities. Section 95 of the Constitution declared joint or **concurrent jurisdiction** — power shared between the Parliament of Canada and the provincial legislatures — in the areas of agriculture and immigration. Moreover, *de facto* concurrent powers have arisen in some other fields because of the federal government's control of the spending power. While the federal government may have little or no jurisdiction over a particular matter such as education, consumer protection or the environment, this does not prohibit Ottawa from spending money in these areas. The provinces have had great difficulty in saying no to such largesse. Moreover, although not mentioned in the Constitution, scientific research, recreational activities, tourism and protection of the environment all are handled as if they are areas of concurrent jurisdiction.

Another issue in Canadian government stems from **asymmetrical federalism** — or the principle that some provinces can be treated constitutionally differently than others. From 1867 onwards there has been a degree of asymmetry in the system. The *British North America Act* gave Québec special constitutional status in the use of the French language, denominational schools and the *Code Civile*. The ferry service between Prince Edward Island and the mainland was specifically subsidized in the *BNA Act*. Today, Québec collects its own income tax, while all the other provinces have theirs collected by Ottawa. Alberta, Ontario and Québec are the only provinces to collect their own corporation taxes. And, to end this list of some of the many asymmetrical situations, eight provinces (but not Ontario and Québec) have contracts with the RCMP to carry out provincial policing duties.

Conflicts over jurisdictional boundaries are to be expected in federal systems. Canada certainly has been no exception to this rule. Successive court decisions by the JCPC of the United Kingdom and, later, the Supreme Court of Canada have cleared up some, but by no means all, questions about jurisdiction in various policy fields. The precise lines of authority remain blurred in many areas. Dissent has arisen mainly over the fact that matters that have grown in significance over the years, such as property and civil rights, are within the provincial sphere, while the "Peace, Order and good Government" clause in section 91 conveys competing authority to the federal government in the same fields in the case of an emergency. With changes in the nature of social and economic policy, this federal power has increasingly conflicted with the specific powers accorded the provinces.

In such disputes, court decisions have varied from restrictive interpretations that left the federal government with very little authority except in the gravest emergencies (e.g., *Local Prohibition*, 1896; *Hodge v. The Queen*, 1883; *Board of Commerce*, 1992; and *Toronto Electric Commissioners v. Snider*, 1925) to granting the federal government such wide scope that the specific powers that appeared to fall exclusively in the provincial field were undermined (e.g., *Canada Temperance Act*, 1878, and *Russell v. the Queen*, 1882). Even such major events as the Great Depression were not

---

11. Garth Stevenson, "Federalism and Intergovernmental Relations," in M.S. Whittington and G. Williams, eds., *Canadian Politics in the 1980's*, 2nd ed. (Toronto: Methuen, 1984), p. 378.

considered significant enough to offset clearly and permanently the arguments that, first, social legislation was under provincial jurisdiction because of the property and civil rights clause and, second, Canada's federal Parliament was restricted to those fields in its specific jurisdiction (*Snider*, 1925). Thus, even in the face of this supreme test of government authority, the federal government could do no more than supply funds to the provinces for fighting the effects of the Depression. It could not act itself. Prime Minister R.B. Bennett's legislation for social insurance, marketing schemes and minimum wages was another piece of legislation struck down by the JCPC in 1937, an action that seriously undermined the federal government's ability to provide any relief in the crisis.[12]

This constitutional position was short-lived. During the Second World War, a surge of nationalism made it possible to circumvent restrictive interpretations of the *BNA Act*. The federal government assumed almost unlimited powers, and the JCPC, apparently sensing the national mood, seemed to shift its position. The result was the 1946 *Canadian Temperance Federation* judgement that declared that laws going beyond local interests could be the concern of the federal authorities. This decision revised the concept of federalism dictated by earlier cases.

An amendment to the *Supreme Court Act* in 1949 gave the power of final arbitration over jurisdictional authority to the Supreme Court. The JCPC's authority was terminated. Since then the federal government has been able to refer either its own legislation or that of a province to the Supreme Court, while a provincial government can refer either its own or federal legislation to the superior court of that province, from which the case may proceed to the Supreme Court on appeal. Since the federal government appoints not only federal judges but also all judges to provincial superior and county courts, it can exercise great power in this field.

The belief that a wholly Canadian court would be somewhat more inclined to take into account Canadian reality and adopt a broader interpretation of federal powers seems to have been borne out by history. Largely since the ascendancy of the Supreme Court of Canada, the federal government has obtained authority over radio, telecommunications and nuclear energy. A classic example of the centralist orientation of the Court is indicated by the 1952 *Johannesson* case, in which the Court upset earlier judgements by proclaiming that since aeronautics was of "national importance" it belonged to the federal authority. James Mallory concluded from this case that the Supreme Court "has begun to develop a more generous interpretation of the federal power than has existed, except in wartime."[13]

In the 1975 *Anti-Inflation* case, the Supreme Court interpreted the federal division of powers in Canada in a similar way. It ruled that the federal government could impose pay restraints on Canadians if a national emergency existed. The Judicial Committee of the British Privy Council had limited the use of the federal government's authority to emergencies such as war, pestilence and famine, but the Canadian Court now added economic factors to the list. It thus greatly broadened the interpretation of the "Peace, Order and good Government" clause. The Court did not approve the federal government's contention that controlling inflation concerned all of Canada, ruling that Parliament could enact legislation in the field of economic regulation only during an emergency. Since the *Anti-Inflation* case, the pro–central government tendency of the Supreme Court has been shown in such cases as *General Motors v. City National Leasing* (1989), which culminated in an extremely robust reading of federal authority in the fields of trade and commerce.[14]

---

12. See Mallory, *Social Credit and Federal Power in Canada*, p. 51.
13. J.R. Mallory, *The Structure of Canadian Government* (Toronto: Macmillan, 1971), p. 354.
14. *General Mills v. City National Leasing* (1989) 1 S.C.R. 641.

RHETORIC AND REALITY OVER CONSTITUTIONAL AMENDMENT

Changing a constitution is an amazingly complex process. The late Senator Eugene Forsey put it forcefully:

> ... let us never forget that, because a constitution is what it is, pervading and shaping every human being in the community, changing it by formal amendment is an immensely serious business. It is not like getting a new hair-do, or growing a beard, or buying new furniture or new clothes, or putting in a new bathroom. It is more like marriage — In the words of the Anglican Prayer Book — 'not by any to be enterprised, nor taken in hand unadvisedly, lightly or wantonly ... but reverently, discretely, advisedly, soberly, and in the fear of God.' What we are dealing with in constitutional change is not paper or things. It is human lives.[15]

In political science terminology, a **rigid constitution** is one that is difficult to amend, whereas a **flexible constitution** can be more easily adapted to changing circumstances. Though arguments may be articulated both for and against the use of either type of amending formula, it is clear that all constitutions must provide *some* means to adapt themselves to new circumstances. (See "Constitution-Speak: Some Jargon You Need to Know.") It is clear that the Canadian Constitution has become more rigid with its patriation in 1982.

Changing the Canadian "federal bargain" struck in 1867 has been extremely difficult.[16] The 1931 *Statute of Westminster* declared that the Parliament of the United Kingdom could no longer legislate for Canada except at the latter's request. At the time of its passage, the British government attempted to persuade Canada to accept a specific amending formula and cut the last tie with the United Kingdom. Unfortunately, Canadian politicians

CLOSE-UP ON ▮nstitutions▮

CONSTITUTION-SPEAK: SOME JARGON YOU NEED TO KNOW

Amending Formula: The rules for changing the Constitution. The debate over the amending process is essentially over whose voices are needed to make a change in the law — the provinces, the regions or the people themselves.

Asymmetry: Different provinces with different powers. Essentially, Québec wants powers that not all other provinces want. Should Canada accommodate differences between the provinces, or would that violate the idea of equality?

Bipolar Federation: A Canadian federation of two units — Québec and the Rest.

Common Market: Five to ten constituent units with a minimal federal government.

Concurrency: Refers to powers that are exercised by both Ottawa and the provinces.

Concurrency with Provincial Paramouncy: Concurrency, but the provinces have the final say if federal and provincial governments disagree.

Confederation of Regions: A loose confederation of four or five regions.

Executive Federalism: Decision-making by the prime minister, the 10 premiers and their governments — pejoratively called bargaining behind closed doors.

Residual Power: Federal government has the ultimate power to deal with matters of national concern to safeguard "Peace, Order and good Government."

Seven and 50: Not a cocktail mix. Stands for seven provinces with more than 50 percent of the national population — the requirement for most constitutional changes. Other important changes require unanimous consent.

Suspensive Veto: Resolution dies if House of Commons votes against proposed constitutional amendment. However, if resolution passes in Commons but Senate votes against it, amendment is merely delayed for six months. Then the Commons votes on it again and, if it passes, the constitutional amendment proceeds without Senate approval.

Triple-E Senate: Equal, elected and effective — an elected Senate that has an equal number of seats for each province and that would be as effective as the House of Commons.

---

15. *Senate Debates*, May 4, 1976, p. 2080.
16. See R.D. Olling and M.W. Westmacott, eds., *The Confederation Debate: The Constitution in Crisis* (Toronto: Kendall-Hunt, 1980); and, by the same authors, *Perspectives on Canadian Federalism* (Scarborough: Prentice Hall, 1988).

could not agree on how the mechanism should work. The British Parliament, therefore, remained responsible for constitutional amendment in Canada. On several occasions after this date, the Constitution was amended in the United Kingdom after a request from Canada. Provincial compliance was obtained, for example, in the 1940 amendment that gave the federal Parliament jurisdiction over unemployment insurance; the 1951 amendment that gave Parliament shared power over old-age pensions; and the 1960 amendment dealing with the retirement of judges. On the other hand, no provincial agreement had to be found (nor was it!) when representation in the Senate was amended in 1915 or when representation in the House of Commons was altered in 1946, 1952 and 1974.

In view of the practices adopted on these occasions, it is clear that a constitutional convention or protocol had developed with regard to the amendment of the *BNA Act*. The British Parliament accepted each of the 18 amendments that emanated from a Joint Address of both houses of the Canadian Parliament. On those amendments that affected the federal balance, the provinces were always consulted and agreed to the proposals. On the other hand, no substantial amendment was ever made at the request of any province or group of provinces, since only communications that arrived by way of the federal Parliament were accepted as legitimate by the British Parliament.

Despite this rigidity on fundamental issues, however, many minor aspects of the Constitution could be changed without the passage of British legislation. From the beginning, for example, the provinces were allowed to amend their own constitutions in all spheres except those concerning the powers of the Lieutenant-Governor. Moreover, with the passage of the *BNA Act* (No. 2) in 1949, the federal Parliament was empowered to amend the Constitution, except with regard to: provincial powers, rights and privileges; the rights of minorities with respect to schools and language protection; the extension of the life of Parliament beyond five years; and the necessity to call at least one session of Parliament per year. These were extensive exceptions, however, as they prevented Ottawa from amending anything that touched on the nature and division of federal/provincial responsibilities, the fundamental cornerstone of the Canadian political system. Moreover, some institutions such as the Senate and the Supreme Court may be considered to be either purely in the federal sphere or to belong to both Ottawa and the provinces. The Senate has a regional basis to its representation and the Supreme Court is the final arbiter of federal/provincial disputes. Such institutions could not be reformed without substantial provincial agreement.

From 1931 until 1981, strenuous efforts were made to cut the remaining ties to Britain. Bringing the Constitution home (or patriation) involved two seemingly insoluble conundrums: how much provincial participation should there be before a decision to patriate the Constitution and what type of amendment process should ensue. Only when Canadian leaders came to an agreement on these two matters would they be able to amend the Constitution without recourse to Britain. The question in Canada had never been *whether* we should have our own constitution, but *what* it should be.

Although efforts to find an acceptable constitutional agreement started in the 1930s, only in the 1960s did coherent discussions take place between the federal government and all of the provinces. Two of the resulting proposals almost succeeded: the Fulton-Favreau formula of 1964 and the Victoria Charter of 1971. The former was significant in Canadian constitutional development because it was the first mechanism that ever received the unanimous support of all 10 provincial premiers.

The 1964 Fulton-Favreau formula proposed drawing up a set of amending mechanisms that would have changed depending on the issue at stake. Parliament would have been able to amend the Constitution subject to approval of the provinces. The rules for this approval would vary issue by issue. Matters such as the powers of the provinces, the use of French and English, and the number of senators, for example, would be amended only if all the provinces agreed with Parliament. Changes in education, on the other hand, could be made with the consent of all the provinces except Newfoundland. Still other portions of the Constitution would only be changed if Parliament could obtain the agreement of two-thirds of the provinces, representing at least 50 percent of the population of Canada. The reality behind this latter proposal was that either Ontario or Québec would have had to concur with all changes in this domain. Furthermore, those aspects of the Constitution directly related to the functions of the federal government could be changed by Parliament acting alone. For a time it appeared that the Fulton-Favreau formula might gain acceptance and thus form the basis of the patriation of the *BNA Act*. However, opposition in Québec prevented its adoption.

In the summer of 1971, another federal/provincial conference came to a tentative agreement on an amending formula.[17] Unlike the Fulton-Favreau formula, the Victoria Charter would not have required the unanimous consent of the provinces for any amendment. Instead, all changes would have required the agreement of Parliament and a majority of the provinces including all provinces with over 25 percent of Canada's population, at least two Atlantic provinces and two western provinces having 50 percent of the population of the West. As with the Fulton-Favreau formula, it seemed for a time that the Victoria Charter might gain acceptance, but it too failed to receive the support of Québec.

In each of these cases, the essential stumbling block to finding an amendment formula was always Québec's desire to be treated as a province unlike the others (*"pas comme les autres"*). To many Québeckers, the idea that federalism refers to a process involving 10 equal provinces and the federal government working as one state is unacceptable. They argue that Canada is a union of two "founding peoples," not 10 equal provinces. This premise is based on the view that the Canadian Constitution is basically a "compact" between two cultural groups or between English and French provinces.[18]

By extension, some Québeckers argue that the Québec state is best able to protect their interests. From this standpoint they develop one of two possible strategies. Some accept the federal system, but want a *special status* for Québec, in which cultural fields such as education and communications are left totally to Québec, and in which the federal government does not intervene in matters such as language policy. In practice, all premiers of Québec since Maurice Duplessis have taken this stand as their minimum position. Even non-separatist premiers Lesage, Johnson and Bourassa all argued that Canada consists of "two nations."[19]

The second strategy advocated by some Québécois is separation from Canada. The rise to power of the Parti Québécois in November 1976 made this strategy a possibility. Lévesque, Parizeau and Bouchard all argued that it was impossible for Québec francophones to protect their language and culture within the federal system and that separate status was essential. The history and detailed development of this option are discussed in Chapter 7; however, a word on the right of constituent provinces to secede from their state may be useful here. As a general rule, such a right does not exist in any of the established federal states — Canada, the United States, Australia, the Federal Republic of Germany or Switzerland. On one occasion, in 1935, the state of Western Australia attempted to secede from Australia and actually passed a referendum to this effect, 136 653 votes to 70 706. The Parliament of the United Kingdom, however, would not allow the case to go forward as British legislation and the proposal died.

---

17. See Simeon, *Federal-Provincial Diplomacy*.

18. See Ramsay Cook, *Provincial Autonomy, Minority Rights and the Compact Theory, 1867–1921*, Study no. 4, Royal Commission on Bilingualism and Biculturalism (Ottawa: Queen's Printer, 1969).

19. See Edward McWhinney, *Canada and the Constitution, 1979–1982* (Toronto: University of Toronto Press, 1982).

Patriation of Canada's Constitution

As we have seen, the long and at times bitter debate over constitutional patriation ended in 1982 with the passage of the *Canada Act* by the British Parliament. While patriation of the Canadian Constitution was primarily symbolic in that it did not represent any changes in federal/provincial jurisdictions or the structure of central government, the inclusion of an entrenched *Charter of Rights and Freedoms* and an amending formula has had profound importance.

The catalyst responsible for what became the final round of the constitutional negotiations leading to patriation was the Québec referendum on sovereignty-association. In May 1980, Premier René Lévesque's Parti Québécois *indépendantiste* government sought authority to negotiate sovereign political status for Québec with continued economic association with Canada.[20] During the provincial referendum campaign, opponents of this proposal — including the federal Liberal party — pledged that Canada would begin a process of "renewal" and constitutional change to address the concerns of Québec citizens if they rejected the referendum. Ultimately, Québec voters rejected Lévesque's plan by a convincing margin, 60 to 40 percent. Patriation of the Constitution was thereby given new momentum, with Prime Minister Pierre Trudeau and the Liberal party exhorting Canadians to "renew" federalism in order to reciprocate Québec's gesture of confidence.

The concept of renewed federalism, while vague, allowed Trudeau to renew his efforts for patriation. The federal government and the provinces conducted a series of meetings culminating in September 1980 in Ottawa. However, government leaders made no progress on the agenda items, which included patriation, an amending formula, the *Charter of Rights and Freedoms*, the principle of equalization, reform of the Senate and the Supreme Court, and redistribution of powers between the two levels of government. Faced with an intransigent group of provincial premiers, Prime Minister Trudeau decided that the federal government would proceed unilaterally.

Trudeau's *unilateral patriation package* proposed an entrenched charter of rights as well as equalization and amendment formulas. Of the 10 provincial governments, however, only New Brunswick and Ontario supported the federal government. The federal government justified its action on the premise that, as the representative of all Canadians, it legitimately spoke for the interests of all Canadians. A special Joint Committee of the Senate and the House of Commons was formed to review the government's resolution. After prolonged debate and more than 70 substantial changes, the government's resolution was adopted. The federal Conservative party opposed the government's unilateral action. The NDP, however, supported the package after it won amendments guaranteeing provincial ownership of natural resources.

The Role of Britain and the Supreme Court

The federal government's decision to act unilaterally moved the site of the political battle from the Canadian to the British Parliament. British MPs became the targets of intensive lobbying efforts. In London, Prime Minister Trudeau and several of his Cabinet ministers attempted to ensure quick passage of the request, suggesting that failure would have serious international repercussions. Dissenting groups and provinces also sent representatives to argue their case.

The 1949 amendment to the *BNA Act* had made it clear that the federal Parliament could amend only those provisions that were already under federal jurisdiction. The procedure for other constitutional changes required a joint address from the House and Senate to the British Parliament. While Britain had always acted automatically on receiving such an address, Britain's role in this

---

20. See Québec's White Paper on sovereignty-association, *Québec-Canada: A New Deal* (Québec: Gouvernement du Québec, 1979).

particular crisis was uncertain. Canada had seldom made requests affecting the division of powers without first obtaining provincial consent, and British parliamentarians were faced with a dilemma, since either accepting or rejecting the Canadian federal government's unilateral request for patriation would leave many Canadians unhappy. Trudeau's remark that British MPs should "hold their noses" and pass the request made their task no easier.

British politicians hoped to escape the dilemma by telling their Canadian counterparts that, given strong provincial opposition, Westminster would be reluctant to pass the request without a ruling by Canada's Supreme Court on the legality of unilateral patriation. Meanwhile, six of the provinces had brought the question of unilateral patriation before the Supreme Court. The Court's ruling, delivered September 28, 1981, offered both sides a measure of support. By a vote of seven to two, the judges ruled that the federal government could "legally" and "unilaterally" submit the constitutional resolution to the British Parliament. However, by a six-to-three vote, the Court ruled that a constitutional convention requiring provincial consent also existed, and that the process embarked upon by Ottawa "offended the federal principle." The Court left vague the extent of provincial consent required by this convention. The Court further noted that conventions are not enforceable by law. Federal justice minister Jean Chrétien agreed, arguing that it is not up to the courts but rather to politicians to decide what political conventions should be.

The patriation package was thus tossed back into the political arena. As a result, another First Ministers Conference was held in November. The federal government was adamant that a patriation package should include a charter of rights and an amending formula similar to that offered at the Victoria Conference in 1971. It proposed that constitutional change should require the consent of Parliament and a majority of legislatures in Canada's four major regions: two in Atlantic Canada, Québec, Ontario and two in the West. The veto power of the two largest provinces would thereby be guaranteed. This formula was opposed by almost all the provinces.

Earlier in 1981, those premiers (including René Lévesque) who were opposed to the federal plans had argued for a patriation package of their own. They had proposed that constitutional change should require the consent of Parliament and seven provinces, representing 50 percent of the population. This proposal would have allowed a province to "opt out" of any amendment that took away existing provincial rights or powers, and would further have entitled any such province to fiscal compensation. Acceptance by Québec of this plan proved to be the basis for later federal efforts to discredit arguments that traditionally Québec had a constitutional veto.

The "Gang of Eight," as the opposing provincial premiers were dubbed, was also against many clauses in the proposed charter of rights. The eight premiers feared that the Charter would give new powers to federally appointed judges and reduce provincial authority. Their other concerns included the prospect of expensive and time-consuming redrafting of provincial legislation to comply with the new charter, the hint of importation of American jurisprudence in the language of the legal rights section and the direct recourse to the courts that the charter would grant to individuals.

Federal/Provincial Constitutional Agreement

Finally, the November 1981 federal/provincial conference ended in agreement between the federal government and nine out of ten of the provinces (Québec was the exception). Several agreements were made to obtain this high degree of consensus. The major compromise was over the inclusion of a **notwithstanding clause** that allowed Parliament or a provincial legislature to override most Charter provisions by declaring that they were doing so when passing legislation. A **"sunset clause"** requiring renewal of this exemption every five years was also included. In the absence of renewal, the Charter's provisions would take precedence.

Those who favoured inclusion of the notwithstanding clause argued that it provided an important democratic check, maintaining the pre-eminence of the legislatures in the event of an "awkward" court ruling. The idea of using "notwithstanding" clauses is of long duration in Canada. It is found in the *Canadian Bill of Rights* passed by the federal Parliament in 1960, as well as in the provincial bills of rights passed by Alberta, Québec, Saskatchewan and Ontario. The federal government has used it only once, during the October Crisis in Québec, in 1970.

Critics of the notwithstanding provision argue that it circumvents the very purpose of an entrenched charter, which is to give the courts the authority to protect fundamental individual freedoms in the event that legislatures and governments fail to do so. According to one constitutional expert, "if legislatures are given the power to cancel ... judicial authority they are most likely to use it when there is a failure of restraint."[21]

Other compromises concerning the Charter were also necessary to obtain provincial agreement to patriation. The case of Native peoples provides a pertinent example. Recognition of their treaty rights was originally excluded from the Charter at the insistence of those provinces that were concerned that Native land claims might reduce provincial control over natural resources. It was only after intense lobbying by Native groups that recognition of these rights for Indian, Inuit and Métis peoples was later restored. In section 25, Native people were guaranteed that the Charter could not be construed "so as to abrogate from any aboriginal, treaty or other rights or freedoms that pertain to the aboriginal peoples of Canada." For greater assurance, section 35 specified that "treaty rights" were defined as "rights that now exist by way of land-claim agreements or may be so acquired."

Another important lobbying effort ensured the restoration of the rights of an overlooked majority group — women. Section 28 of the Charter — which simply stated, "notwithstanding anything in this Charter, the rights and freedoms referred to in it are guaranteed equally to male and female persons" — was excluded by one of the early agreements. In response to this, the Ad Hoc Committee of Canadian Women on the Constitution was formed and in just three weeks it successfully lobbied all 10 provincial premiers to reverse their stand on the issue. Equality of men and women was thus placed outside the reach of the notwithstanding clause.

A further major compromise leading to the success of the November 1981 conference concerned the amending formula. Instead of the federal Liberal proposition, the formula preferred by the provincial "Gang of Eight" was adopted. It called for future jurisdictional amendments to be made by a joint resolution of both the Senate and the House of Commons, as well as by a resolution of the legislative assemblies of at least two-thirds of the provinces, representing at least 50 percent of the population of Canada.[22] In addition, it granted dissenting provinces the right to opt out of all amendments that affected their status and powers.

While federal/provincial agreement on a patriation package removed much of the hesitancy of British politicians to grant the federal government's request for patriation, Indian groups continued to press their opposition in the British courts, arguing that the British Crown was still responsible for them. The British courts rejected this claim, however, finding that while no government should derogate the Indian rights guaranteed in treaties signed with the British and Canadian governments, responsibility for Native groups had long since passed from the Crown in Britain to the Crown in Canada.

---

21. Noel Lyon, *The Globe and Mail*, November 17, 1981.

22. The latest general census would be referred to for such information. While the Senate may delay constitutional change, it does not possess an absolute veto. After 180 days an amendment may be concluded without its agreement.

The British Parliament was finally presented with the revised Canada Bill in mid-February of 1982. The Bill was speedily passed at every stage by large majorities. On March 29, the Queen gave Royal Assent to the *Canada Act*, 115 years to the day after the *BNA Act* had received Royal Assent. In Ottawa, on April 17, 1982, the Queen proclaimed the *Constitution Act, 1982*, completing the patriation process. (See "Canada's Constitutional Highlights.")

THE NEW CANADIAN CONSTITUTION

As part of the final patriation package, there were several changes to the Constitution, none of which affects the main structure of government or significantly alters the division of powers between Parliament and the provincial legislatures. These changes and additions to the Constitution are listed below and in the next section on the Charter.[23]

Change I: There are now five legal formulas for amending the *Constitution Act*. The **first formula** concerns amendments that require **unanimous consent** (section 41). These deal with amendments to the office of the Queen, the Governor General, the Lieutenant-Governors, the right of a province to at least as many seats in the House of Commons as it has in the Senate, the use of the English and French languages (except amendments applying only to a single province), the composition of the Supreme Court of Canada and amendments to the amending formulas themselves. Amendments in these areas must be passed by the Senate and the House of Commons (or by the Commons alone, if the Senate has not approved the proposal within 180 days after the Commons has done so) and by the legislature of every province. This means that every province has a veto over these types of amendments.

The **second formula** concerns amendments under the *general procedure* (section 38). They include amendments that

CLOSE-UP ON Institutions

CANADA'S CONSTITUTIONAL HIGHLIGHTS

1867   *British North America Act* (now the *Constitution Act, 1867*) is enacted

1931   *Statute of Westminster:* Britain can no longer legislate for Canada except at the request of the Canadian government

1949   An amendment to the *BNA Act* widens the scope of the Canadian Parliament's authority to undertake further amendments

1949   Supreme Court of Canada becomes final court of appeal

1961   Diefenbaker Bill of Rights is enacted

1964   Fulton-Favreau formula is rejected by Québec

1971   Victoria Charter is rejected by Québec

1980   Québec referendum on sovereignty-association is defeated

1981   Supreme Court rules Trudeau's constitutional resolution is valid but violates political convention

1981   First ministers make three significant changes to resolution; package is rejected by Québec

1981   Constitutional resolution is passed by Parliament

1982   *Canada Act* passed by British House of Commons and patriated; the *Charter of Rights and Freedoms* and an amendment formula become part of the Canadian Constitution; Québec does not sign

1987   The Meech Lake accord fails

1991   The Spicer Royal Commission reports

1992   The Dobbie-Beaudoin Joint House and Senate Committee report is published followed by constitutional conferences

1992   The Charlottetown accord is approved by federal and provincial leaders

1992   The Charlottetown accord is massively rejected in a referendum

1995   Québec referendum on independence is very narrowly defeated

1996   Parliament passes legislation allowing Québec, Ontario, British Columbia and any two Maritime or Prairie provinces to veto any further constitutional change

1998   Supreme Court answers three questions about Québec separatism

1999   Federal Parliament passes "Clarity Bill" and Québec responds with its own legislation

---

23. These amendments are concisely summarized by Eugene A. Forsey in *How Canadians Govern Themselves* (Ottawa: Minister of Supply and Services, 1982), pp. 12–18; and more fully in James Ross Hurley, *Amending Canada's Constitution* (Ottawa: Supply and Services, 1996).

- take away any rights, powers or privileges of provincial governments or legislatures,
- deal with the proportionate representation of the provinces in the House of Commons,
- deal with the powers of the Senate and the method of selecting senators and their residence qualifications,
- concern the constitutional position of the Supreme Court of Canada (not including its composition, which is covered under the first formula above),
- concern the extension of existing provinces into the territories, and
- concern the *Charter of Rights and Freedoms.*

Amendments in these areas must be passed by the Senate and the House of Commons (or by the Commons alone if the Senate delays more than 180 days), and by the legislatures of two-thirds of the provinces with at least half the total population of all the provinces (excluding the territories). This means that any four less-populous provinces or Ontario and Québec together could veto any amendments in this category, and that either Ontario or Québec would be needed as one of the seven provinces to pass any amendment.

The **third formula** deals with matters that apply to *one or several, but not all, provinces* (section 43). Amendments in these cases must be passed by the Senate and the House of Commons and by the legislature or legislatures of the particular province or provinces concerned. This includes changes in provincial boundaries or changes relating to the use of the English or French language in any province or provinces.

The **fourth formula** concerns *changes in the executive government* of Canada or changes in the Senate and House of Commons that are not covered by the first two formulas. Such amendments can be made by an ordinary act of the Parliament of Canada (section 44). The **fifth formula** concerns amendments that can be made by *individual provincial legislatures alone* (section 45). In the original *BNA Act, 1867* (section 92), with the exception of the office of the Lieutenant-Governor, provinces could amend their own constitutions. Section 92 (1) was repealed and this amendment clause moved to section 45, which places the provinces in a position equivalent to that of the federal government.

Change II: The first three amending formulas *"entrench"* specific parts of the written Constitution. This means that neither Parliament alone nor any provincial legislature has the power to touch them. All changes must be made according to the particular formula that applies. Procedural requirements are also set out (section 39) that establish maximum and minimum times within which constitutional amendments must be passed.

Change III: The provinces obtained *wider powers over their natural resources* than they had had before. Each province now controls the export within Canada of the primary production from its mines, oil wells, gas wells, forests and electric power plants, provided it does not discriminate against other parts of the country in prices or supplies. The federal government can legislate on these matters, however, and, in case of conflict, the federal law will prevail. The provinces can levy indirect taxes on their mines, oil wells, gas wells, forests and electric power plants and primary production from these sources. Such taxes must be the same whether or not the products are exported to other parts of the country.

Change IV: Provisions were included concerning *Native peoples.* First, the Charter is not to be construed so as "to abrogate or derogate from any aboriginal, treaty or other rights or freedoms that pertain to the aboriginal peoples of Canada" (section 25). Second, the existing aboriginal and treaty rights of the Native peoples of Canada were recognized and affirmed (this includes Indian, Inuit and Métis peoples).

Change V: In section 36 (1) on *equalization and regional disparities*, the *Constitution Act* declares that the national government and Parliament and the provincial governments and legislatures "are committed to promoting equal opportunities for the well-being of Canadians, further economic developments to reduce disparities in opportunities, and providing essential public services of reasonable quality to all Canadians." In section 36 (2), the national government and Parliament "are committed to the principle of making equalization payments to ensure that provincial governments have sufficient revenues to provide reasonably comparable levels of public services and reasonably comparable levels of taxation."

Change VI: Official English and French versions of the whole written Constitution are equally authoritative.

Change VII: The new *Constitution Act* includes a *Charter of Rights and Freedoms*. (This important addition is discussed in considerable detail below.)

Change VIII: The Charter shall be interpreted "in a manner consistent with the preservation and enhancement of the multicultural heritage of Canada" (section 27).

The constitutional amendment system that is now in place is quite rigid, so that the chances of further change to the Constitution by amendment are minimal. (See "Constitutional Negotiations — A Unique Canadian Style?") Despite constant efforts and even a national referendum, there have been only seven minor amendments to the Constitution since 1982. In 1984, the Constitution was amended to provide for consultation with the aboriginal peoples of Canada before any amendment is made with respect to their rights. In 1987, an amendment dealt with the entrenchment of the denominational school rights of the Pentecostal Association in Newfoundland. In 1993, the New Brunswick legislature and the federal Parliament used section 43 to make New Brunswick a bilingual province. Fourth, in 1994, an amendment changed the Constitution so that the federal government could be relieved of the obligation of providing steamboat services for Prince Edward Island upon the completion of the bridge joining the island to the mainland. In 1997, fifth and sixth amendments changed the educational rights in Newfoundland and ended the province's constitutionally established church-run school system. After the 1997 general election, the federal Parliament passed a constitutional amendment that changed Québec's religion-based educational system to one based on French and English school boards. The right to amend the Constitution is finally in Canadian hands, but those hands are fairly firmly tied except on very minor issues which concern only one province. For discussion of recent "political" compromises about future amendments see Chapter 7.

CLOSE-UP ON Institutions

CONSTITUTIONAL NEGOTIATIONS — A UNIQUE CANADIAN STYLE?

Section 49 of the 1982 Constitution necessitated that a First Ministers Conference be held within 15 years to review the new amendment provisions — i.e., by April 17, 1997. The issue, put on the agenda by Prime Minister Jean Chrétien at a First Ministers meeting in June 1996, ended in a farce. The premier of Saskatchewan, Roy Romanow, argued that the necessity to meet had already been satisfied during the Charlottetown negotiations in 1992. Premier Lucien Bouchard quickly left the room, saying that he was "under a strict political and legal obligation not to hear anything about the question of section 49 discussion, even about the relevancy of discussing it." A few other premiers joined Bouchard in the washroom. Meanwhile, back in the meeting room, in a couple of minutes the majority of their colleagues agreed that the constitutional necessity to meet had already been met. After the meeting, the First Ministers were not certain whether they needed a legal judgement on the matter.

Source: *The Ottawa Citizen*, June 22, 1996.

THE CHARTER OF RIGHTS AND FREEDOMS

The desirability of an *entrenched Charter of Rights and Freedoms* has been a subject of debate since Confederation. The constitutional entrenchment of rights can be said to have two primary functions, one *symbolic*, the other *substantive*. Symbolically, such a charter is a statement of the ideals valued by a society. While they are not always observed in practice, protection of these principles is a test by which the polity should be judged. A more tangible impact of a charter of rights lies in its restraint of the actions of a government *vis-à-vis* its citizens, preventing authorities from violating the rights of individuals and groups as defined in the charter. It is this restraint that makes the entrenchment of rights contentious.

Why did Canada need a written and entrenched charter of rights when it had existed as a relatively free society for more than one hundred years without such a document? In Britain, civil liberties were, and are, protected by traditions, customs and political culture. Civil liberties are, if you wish, ingrained in the values and beliefs of politicians and the people. Canada, too, relied on the traditional rights provided by British common law and, after 1960, on a statute — the *Canadian Bill of Rights* — which listed the fundamental freedoms that existed in Canada but which was never **entrenched** in the Constitution — i.e., it could be amended by the passage of ordinary legislation. Despite these safeguards many Canadians believed that there was a need for a charter of rights and freedoms that would restrict the actions of governments. Why?

Despite the rule of law and British traditions, Canada's record of ensuring the protection of its citizens' rights is not without blemish. The most celebrated example was the **Québec Padlock Law** of 1937, legislation enacted by the Québec government banning the propagation of "Communism and Bolshevism." The law would have allowed Premier Maurice Duplessis to padlock any premises allegedly used for such purposes and to move arbitrarily against other groups opposed to his regime. In Alberta in 1938, the provincial legislature enacted the **Press Bill**, which allowed the government to force newspapers to reveal the sources of unfavourable comment. A third example occurred in 1953 when Québec restrained the freedom of religion of Jehovah Witnesses by restricting their right to hand out pamphlets without permission.

Although these pieces of legislation were subsequently overturned by the courts, the rationale cited by the judges in their decisions strengthened the argument for the entrenchment of basic rights in the Constitution. The courts based their rulings not on the fact that the legislation represented a violation of fundamental rights, but rather on the contention that provincial governments did not have the right to restrict civil liberties because of the constitutional division of powers. In all these cases the courts declared the actions *ultra vires* — i.e., not within provincial jurisdiction. Under the new 1982 constitutional provisions, however, it is the recognition of rights within the Charter that will be the basis for such court decisions.

Another notable example of a violation of basic rights in Canada's history was the federal government's internment of Japanese Canadians during the Second World War. Under the *War Measures Act* thousands of people were uprooted from their communities and placed in camps for the duration of the war — for "security" reasons. Decades later, in 1970, Prime Minister Trudeau again invoked the *War Measures Act*, this time in response to the terrorist activities of the Front de Libération du Québec (FLQ). This action, which suspended civil liberties and allowed the arbitrary detention of hundreds of suspects, is the most recent major example of government violation of basic human rights in Canada. Both cases indicated that such violations of basic democratic rights could not be prevented without written constitutional guarantees — hence a charter was necessary.

The Charter is a significant improvement on the *Canadian Bill of Rights* because it applies to the federal and provincial governments equally and because, unlike ordinary legislation, it is entrenched in the Constitution, and therefore can be altered *only* through the constitutional amendment process. It consists of a short *preamble* — "Whereas Canada is founded upon principles that recognize the supremacy of God and the rule of law …" — followed by 34 sections. It is the first section that *defines the limits* of Canadians' rights and freedoms, stipulating that they are "subject only to such reasonable limits prescribed by law as can be demonstrably justified in a free and democratic society."

The Charter protects *fundamental freedoms*, including those of conscience and religion, of thought, belief, opinion and expression, and of peaceful assembly and association. The basic democratic rights named in the document include the right of every citizen to vote; a five-year limit on the terms of federal and provincial legislatures, except in time of real or apprehended war, invasion or insurrection; and the requirement for legislatures to meet at least once every 12 months.

The Charter also protects *mobility rights*, i.e., the right of Canadian citizens to enter, remain in and leave Canada, and to move to and work in any province. These rights are limited, however, by recognition of provincial residency requirements as a qualification for the receipt of social services. Affirmative action programs, whose purpose is to ameliorate the conditions of a socially or economically disadvantaged people, are also allowed if the rate of employment in that province falls below the national employment rate.[24]

Legal rights such as the traditional right to life, liberty and security are listed, along with new legal rights provisions. For example, unreasonable search or seizure and arbitrary detention or imprisonment are prohibited. A detained individual is guaranteed the right to be informed promptly of the reasons for detention, to have counsel without delay and to be instructed of that right, as well as to have the validity of the detention determined and to be released if detention is not justified. Individuals charged with an offence have the right to be informed without delay of the specific offence and to be tried within a reasonable time. They have a right against self-incrimination and are to be considered innocent until proven guilty by an impartial and public hearing. Individuals are not to be deprived of bail without just cause, and are permitted trial by jury where the maximum punishment for the offence is imprisonment for five years or more, except in the case of a military offence tried before a military tribunal. They are not to be punished for an action that was not illegal at the time of commission. If acquitted, an individual may not be tried for the same offence again or, if found guilty and punished, may not be tried or punished again. Finally, if the punishment for the offence has changed between the commission of the crime and the time of the sentencing, the individual is subject to the lesser punishment.

Individuals are also protected against cruel and unusual treatment or punishment. Witnesses who testify in any proceedings have the right not to have any incriminating evidence they might give used against them in any other proceedings, except in prosecution for perjury. Evidence obtained in a manner that infringes upon an individual's rights and freedoms shall be excluded, but only if its admission would "bring the administration of justice into disrepute."

The Charter further provides *equality rights* guaranteeing that every individual is equal before and under the law without discrimination, particularly without discrimination based on race, national or ethnic origin, colour, religion, sex, age, or mental or physical disability. However, affirmative action programs aimed at improving the conditions of groups discriminated against are allowed.

The importance of *linguistic rights* is acknowledged in the Charter. English and French are recognized as Canada's official languages and have equal status in all institutions of Parliament and the federal government. Both languages are also recognized in the province of New Brunswick. Thus, in Parliament and New Brunswick's legislature, both languages may be used in debates and other proceedings. Parliamentary statutes and records, as well as proceedings of the courts, are published in both languages. Individuals have the right to communicate with any head or central office of Parliament or government of Canada in either official language, and the same right is extended to other offices where there is significant demand.

---

24. *Canadian Charter of Rights and Freedoms,* section 6 (4).

Under the Charter, all citizens of Canada who received their primary education in Canada in either French or English have the right to have their children educated in the same language if it is the minority language of the province in which they reside. This right, however, applies only "where numbers warrant," i.e., where the number of children warrants the provision of public funds for minority-language instruction. Minority-language education rights are also guaranteed to the children of Canadian citizens whose first language learned and understood is that of the English or French linguistic minority of the province in which they reside, whether or not the parents were able to receive their primary education in that language. This latter guarantee is not applicable to Québec until it is approved by the Québec National Assembly — and to date it has not been.

The Charter includes a variety of other *specific rights*. The rights of the Native peoples are not to be diminished by the Charter's provisions; for example, the provision that guarantees language education rights in French and English may not be interpreted to deprive the Indian people of James Bay of their right to educate their children in Cree. More broadly, the Charter may not be used to deprive anyone of existing rights and freedoms, and its interpretation must recognize Canada's multicultural heritage. The Charter's provisions are to be applied equally to males and females. This absolute guarantee of gender equality was put in the Constitution as section 28 only after considerable lobbying by women's groups.

Despite this impressive list of rights, however, they are not all inviolable. Readers will recall that the new Constitution was patriated only through a series of political compromises. The leaders agreed to *allow restrictions on citizens' rights* in two general ways. First, the Charter begins with an overarching exception when it claims that the rights and freedoms are guaranteed "subject only to such reasonable limits presented by law as can be demonstrably justified in a free and democratic society." This means that the courts are allowed to decide that a piece of federal or provincial legislation that restricts freedoms is still valid according to *their* definition of "reasonable limits." The Supreme Court, for example, has allowed the Ontario legislature to impose film censorship as long as its criteria are prescribed by law.[25] Second, section 33 allows a province or Parliament to enact laws overriding Charter provisions. They can pass legislation *notwithstanding* the Charter on fundamental freedoms, legal and equality rights by means of a notwithstanding clause. They cannot, however, use this device on democratic or mobility rights. A "notwithstanding" procedure becomes inoperative after five years and must be re-passed if it is to remain valid.

We examine some significant Charter cases later in the chapter, following a survey of courts in Canada.

IMPASSE WITH QUÉBEC

Despite the fact that the major proponents of the new Constitution were from Québec — including Prime Minister Trudeau, one-third of his Cabinet and almost all of the 75 MPs from Québec — Québec's political leaders opposed the 1982 constitutional reform with every defence possible except revolution. Premier René Lévesque argued that Québec's cultural security was threatened by the restriction of its exclusive rights in linguistic matters. As will be shown in Chapter 7, the Charter's guarantee of access to English-speaking schools conflicted with Québec's Bill 101, which restricted admission to English schools in that province. He also objected that the measure of bilingualism imposed on Québec was not also imposed on Ontario even though the latter had the largest French-speaking population of any province outside Québec.

---

25. *Ontario Film and Video Appreciation Society v. Ontario Board of Censors* (1984), 45 O.L.R. (2d)80.

Lévesque criticized the Constitution's failure to recognize "in any tangible way" the character and needs of Québec as a distinct national society. The document, he alleged, treated Québec as merely another province of Canada. Finally, he disliked the amending formula's removal of what Québec considered its traditional veto over constitutional changes. While the Constitution gave Québec and the other provinces financial compensation in the important areas of education and culture, Lévesque charged correctly that the amending formula did not guarantee financial compensation for provinces that chose to opt out of other programs set up by constitutional amendment.

The direct attack on the new Constitution did not subside with the death of René Lévesque and the election of Pierre-Marc Johnson as leader of the Parti Québécois in 1984. (See Chapter 7.) But when Robert Bourassa led the Liberals to victory over Johnson in the 1985 election, the tone of Québec–federal relations changed. Bourassa believed that he could strike a deal with the newly elected Conservative prime minister of Canada, Brian Mulroney — and he was right.

The Failed 1987 Constitutional Accord (Meech Lake and Langevin)

The new federal Conservative government, which was elected in 1984, conducted months of bargaining to design amendments that would secure Québec's political assent to the new Constitution. In April 1987, Prime Minister Brian Mulroney and the 10 premiers reached unanimous agreement on a constitutional text that culminated in a draft of the Meech Lake accord. The final text for the proposed constitutional amendment was agreed to after an all-night bargaining session in June in the Langevin Block on Parliament Hill and is known as the Langevin amendment to the Meech Lake accord (we refer to the entire package simply as the Meech Lake accord).

Québec Liberal premier Robert Bourassa had five conditions going into the bargaining session of April 1987 at Meech Lake: a formal voice for Québec in Supreme Court appointments; a say on immigration policy; limits to federal spending powers in areas of provincial jurisdiction; a veto on constitutional amendments affecting the province; and recognition of Québec as a "distinct" society. While it was generally agreed that Québec should be granted "renewed federalism," the nine other premiers also made demands and virtually all were accommodated. Therein lay the crux of the criticism of the accord — that to achieve an agreement the prime minister gave away powers that were necessary to maintain a strong federal government.

Agreement on the Meech Lake accord was billed as a "historic breakthrough." There were seven main areas of change: distinct society, the Supreme Court, spending powers, veto power, immigration, the Senate and the amending formula. However, when the euphoria subsided, serious flaws in the accord made it the subject of national dissension and concern. None of the federal political parties was willing to risk the political consequences of voting against the accord in the House of Commons, although the Liberals submitted eight amendments and the NDP, two. While none of these changes was accepted, John Turner and Ed Broadbent demanded party discipline in voting in favour of the resolution. Parliament passed the Meech Lake accord with little dissent. But as the Meech Lake amendments called for major constitutional revisions, it required the approval of Parliament and all 10 provincial legislatures.

The Meech Lake accord, though hotly discussed in 1987, was not a significant issue in the 1988 general election. It was overshadowed by the issue of free trade. All three major political parties agreed that the benefit of winning Premier Bourassa's support for a revised Constitution was greater than the problems inherent in the ambiguities of the accord. No party wanted to risk the wrath of Québec voters by endangering the agreement, although the Liberal party did present a series of amendments that it promised to implement as soon as the accord became law.

In the final analysis, the Meech Lake accord was defeated because it required unanimity from the provinces, and two (Manitoba and Newfoundland) failed to pass the necessary resolution before the ratification deadline of June 23, 1990. When the proposals did not obtain unanimity, the whole package died and constitutional matters became even more complicated. Canada did not expire with the Meech Lake accord, as the prime minister had threatened. Life went on. However, the Québec independence issue — dormant since the 1980 referendum — was given a new burst of respectability. Predictably, Premier Bourassa announced he would not attend any future federal/provincial conferences, and the Québec National Assembly passed Bill 150, which required a referendum on "sovereignty" to be put to the people of Québec by October 26, 1992.

A New Constitutional Approach

Following the death of the Meech Lake accord, there was an appropriate period of political mourning followed by numerous government-sponsored conferences, symposiums, federal/provincial meetings and even a royal commission. Having insisted that it was Meech or death, Prime Minister Mulroney needed time to resuscitate the corpse. Unfortunately, the federal government ignored the report of the Charest parliamentary committee that had provided detailed proposals to amend the Meech Lake accord but left its substance intact. That sober report had received all-party and unanimous agreement in the House of Commons, but it was left shelved and forgotten.

The prime minister put the next phase of constitutional meetings in the hands of Joe Clark.[26] Under his guidance the federal government called several meetings with nine provinces, two territorial governments and four aboriginal groups. The aboriginal groups themselves then enlisted economic, women's and nationalist umbrella groups to advise them. Québec did not attend. The first of these meetings to draft new constitutional proposals to offer to Québec took place on March 12, 1992. Four months later, on July 7, 1992, an agreement was reached which they inappropriately termed the "Pearson agreement."

The Meech Lake failure had not killed Canada, but it had ended Conservative party unity. When the accord died on June 23, 1990, Mulroney's Minister of the Environment, Lucien Bouchard, left the Cabinet and formed the Bloc Québécois with a band of dissident Québec nationalists who already held seats in the House of Commons. The Québec government, meanwhile, continued to be bound by Bill 150, which called for a provincial referendum on sovereignty by October 27, 1992. The National Assembly set up the Commission on the Political and Constitutional Future of Québec (known as Campeau-Bélanger), whose hearings led to provincial consultations and, eventually, two parliamentary committees: one to examine the costs of sovereignty and the other to examine any offers on renewed federalism that might come from Canada.

Québec's most divisive input into the constitutional debate came on January 28, 1991, from the Liberal party's Allaire Report, *A Quebec Free to Choose*, a document that proposed drastic decentralization of the country. According to the report, Québec would "exercise exclusive discretionary and total authority in most fields of activity," and 22 domains would be in the exclusive power of Québec, including communications, energy, industry and commerce, regional development, and income security. Ottawa was assigned only currency, customs and tariffs, debt management and transfer payments. Decisions of Québec courts on these jurisdictions and other questions would no longer be appealable to the Supreme Court of Canada.

26. For a history of the negotiations and events leading up to the Charlottetown accord, see Robert Jackson and Doreen Jackson, *Politics in Canada*, 3rd ed. (Scarborough: Prentice Hall Canada, 1994), pp. 216–23. For a comparative analysis, see Michael B. Stein, "Improving the Process of Constitutional Reform in Canada," *CJPS*, vol. 30, no. 2 (June 1997), pp. 307–38.

Reproduced with permission, Dennis Pritchard.

The strong decentralizing thrust of the Allaire Report was totally unacceptable to most Canadians because it would have greatly weakened the country. However, it was intended to keep pressure on the federal government and set a strong negotiation position for Québec, and that it accomplished. The Allaire proposals cried out for asymmetry with different status for different provinces or regions within the country depending on their special needs. As mentioned earlier, Canada already has some asymmetry in such areas as agriculture, immigration and the environment. But this did not mean that further asymmetry would be acceptable to the country.

The Pearson Building Proposals

By the spring of 1992, it was time for Mr. Mulroney to begin a countdown. Both the federal government and the provinces were under pressure from the date of Québec's looming referendum. On July 7, 1992, the federal government, the nine provinces, two territorial governments and Native leaders came to a new tentative agreement. In total the proposals would have given greater power to the provinces and weakened federal authority. Québec representatives, of course, had neither attended the meetings nor agreed to the proposals they produced.

Characterized by those present at that decisive meeting in the Lester B. Pearson Building as a "constitutional breakthrough," the proposals would have amended the Constitution in multiple respects. The thrust of the deal can be described simply. Québec would have gotten everything mentioned in the Meech Lake accord, including a veto over future constitutional amendments and recognition as a "distinct society," in return for satisfying Alberta's desire for a "Triple-E" Senate. Aboriginals, too, would have had their wishes granted, with a form of self-government. News commentary tended to concentrate on whether the agreement would "fly" with all the provinces and "sell" in Québec. An "agreement at any price" was necessary to save Canada. It was the "do or die" atmosphere of the Meech accord all over again.

THE FAILED 1992 CHARLOTTETOWN ACCORD

The Pearson Building agreement drew Premier Bourassa out of his bunker in Québec City. After two years of boycotting constitutional discussions, he returned to the bargaining table on August 4, 1992, along with the prime minister, the other premiers, and the leaders of the territories and the aboriginal communities. The result was a complex and controversial constitutional deal known as the Charlottetown accord, agreed to on August 28, 1992. It consisted of an agreement on principles — not a legal text — about what changes should be made to the Constitution, further political accords to be negotiated, and an agreement to put the tentative principles to the Canadian people in a country-wide referendum.

Meech Plus or Minus: The Response to Québec

Essentially, the Meech Lake proposals had consisted of five parts — distinct society, a veto, immigration powers, restrictions on federal spending and appointments to the Supreme Court — each of which responded to an earlier demand by the government of Québec. The same demands were addressed by the Charlottetown accord, but it went much further. It also included proposals to add a definition for *distinct society* to the Constitution in a new clause that would ensure that "Quebec constitutes within Canada a distinct society, which includes a French-speaking majority, a unique culture and a civil law tradition." As well, the proposals affirmed the role of the legislature and government of Québec "to preserve and promote the distinct society of Quebec."

In other areas, such as immigration, the Charlottetown proposals slightly softened the Meech Lake accord. Under Meech, Québec was to obtain a fixed share of immigrants to Canada. Under Charlottetown, Ottawa would only have been committed to negotiate agreements with the provinces, a policy that was already the practice. And, if the federal government spent money in a new Canada-wide shared-cost program in a field of exclusive provincial jurisdiction, as in Meech, a province would have been able to claim compensation if it had a program that was "compatible with the national objectives." On Supreme Court appointments, there was no change from Meech. The current practice of appointing three Supreme Court judges from Québec would have been constitutionalized, only now Ottawa would have been required to select all judges from lists supplied by the provinces.

The main difference between the Meech Lake accord and the Charlottetown proposals was over the constitutional veto. Charlottetown would have given all provinces a veto over future constitutional changes to the country's major political institutions. On the surface this looked as though it met Québec's earlier demands, but in fact it fell far short. The veto would have applied only "after" the Charlottetown changes were made part of the Constitution, in particular those concerning reform of the federal institutions. As in Meech, Québec wanted the veto to ensure that it could prevent a Senate reform of which it did not approve. Québec also wanted a veto over the creation of new provinces, but the Charlottetown accord would have allowed the federal Parliament to create new provinces through a simple bilateral agreement with Ottawa. Moreover, since the proposed changes to the amending formula would have increased the number of matters that required unanimity, every province — not just Québec — would have had an even greater capacity to veto further constitutional proposals. If this change were accepted, it would have been almost impossible to correct any deficiencies in the Constitution at a later time.

Clearly, most of the "offers" that were made to Québec in Meech Lake were included in Charlottetown, but some were "watered down." The deal, therefore, was bound to find opposition *both* inside and outside Québec. It called for major innovation in the way Canada is governed. It included a Canada clause, a new division of powers, new Native self-government clauses, a social and economic union, and institutional changes in the House of Commons and Senate.

The Canada Clause

A "Canada clause" was to be included in the Constitution to express fundamental Canadian values. That clause was extremely important as it would have been justiciable — that is, the courts would have been able to use the Canada clause to guide *all* future interpretations of the *entire* Constitution. As an interpretative provision it would have been binding on the courts in every constitutional case.

Eight "fundamental values" were expressed in the Canada clause. They included values related to democracy, aboriginal rights, the distinct society of Québec, linguistic duality, racial and ethnic equality, individual and collective human rights, the equality of female and male persons, and the equality of the provinces.

On careful scrutiny, the Canada clause proved to be replete with errors in consistency and fairness. It proposed a hierarchy of fundamental Canadian values. While "Canadians and their governments" would have been committed to the development of minority-language communities, only "Canadians" were committed to racial and ethnic equality, individual and collective human rights, the equality of female and male persons and the equality of the provinces. The implication was clear. Governments would have been committed to take action — and presumably to spend money — to defend some groups but not others.

Moreover, some Canadian groups were left out of the Canada clause altogether. Whereas the *Charter of Rights and Freedoms* stipulates equality for people who are physically or mentally disabled, and asserts that individuals should not be discriminated against by age, the proposed Canada clause overlooked these values altogether. Thus, the clause provided a hierarchy in which some groups would be protected by government, other groups would be protected only by Canadians, and still other groups such as the disabled, seniors and children would not be mentioned at all.

Division of Powers

The Charlottetown proposals called for the constitutional decentralization of many federal powers. Job training and culture were to be given to the provinces congruent with their present authority in the field of education. The Charlottetown accord was nuanced on these two topics, however. In job training, the federal government's power would have been narrowed to exclusive jurisdiction for unemployment insurance and involvement in the establishment of national objectives for labour market development. As well, the federal government would have been excluded from a meaningful role in retraining workers for the new global economy. Culture, too, would have been divided artificially between two levels of government. The provinces would have had exclusive jurisdiction over culture "within the provinces," and the federal government would have retained powers over existing national cultural institutions, including the grants and contributions delivered by those institutions. If these proposals had been constitutionalized, the designation of "culture" as an area of exclusive provincial jurisdiction would have led to endless constitutional wrangling in the Supreme Court. As well, the Charlottetown accord called for the federal government to withdraw from several areas including forestry, mining, housing, recreation, tourism, and municipal and urban affairs.

At best, in all of these decentralizing proposals, policies on which Canadians have grown to depend might have remained intact. At worst, some important policies, such as subsidized housing for the needy, might have been discontinued. This rather wide spectrum of possibility proved that the federal government still did not have a handle on viable constitutional change.

Native Self-Government

The demands of Native peoples were not addressed by the Meech Lake proposal and, in the final analysis, this omission contributed to its demise. Native leader and MPP Elijah Harper was the key figure in the Manitoba legislature's rejection of that accord. His dramatic action made him a folk hero and stimulated increased pressure for Native self-government in the next round of constitutional negotiations. As the post-Meech negotiations began, new Native positions were staked out. In one early demand, the leader of the Assembly of First Nations, Ovide Mercredi, asked for all 54 aboriginal languages to have equal status with English and French and for all aboriginal groups to have equal political status with the provinces. In May 1992, Joe Clark announced that all provinces except Québec had accepted the "third level of government" principle for Native peoples. Clark admitted, however, that the details of how such a third level would relate to existing federal and provincial jurisdictions would have to be negotiated politically rather than entrenched in the Constitution.

The Charlottetown proposals went some way toward satisfying aboriginal demands. The Canada clause said that aboriginals "have the right to promote their languages, cultures and traditions and to ensure the integrity of their societies, and that their governments constitute one of three orders of government in Canada." The proposals also included an expanded definition of aboriginal people, a political accord for the Métis and treaty rights to be affirmed in the Constitution. During the first five years of the agreement Native groups would not have been able to employ these clauses in cases before the courts.

Even among staunch supporters of the aboriginal cause, there was considerable controversy over these undefined rights. The most direct attack on the concept of aboriginal rights came from a Québec government report entitled *An Analysis of the Impact of the Constitutional Recognition of the Inherent Right to Self-Government*. It described the proposal as "unquestionably the most profound change to the political structure of Canada since 1867."[27] The report declared that a self-government clause would "threaten Québec's territorial integrity and weaken provincial powers," and without Québec's approval would probably be unconstitutional "because creating a new order of government requires the unanimous consent of all the partners to Confederation." Furthermore, it argued that such an agreement would violate the Charter, which calls for all Canadians to be treated equally under the law. It judged that approval of aboriginal self-government would be exorbitantly expensive, and that territorial disputes and land claims would have a much stronger legal basis.

Elsewhere, the main complaint was that too many small governments might emerge if Native self-government were placed in the Constitution. Worries were also expressed that band and tribal councils would want to negotiate their own laws to govern schools, justice systems, child-welfare agencies and other community organizations. Critics asked if self-government could mean up to 600 tiny governments. If so, would this constitute a new form of segregation? Would the Criminal Code apply to Native peoples? Would educational standards or environmental regulations apply?

Advocates said there was no cause for worry on either theoretical or practical grounds. The Charlottetown deal stated that a law passed by a government of aboriginal peoples "may not be inconsistent with those laws which are essential to the preservation of peace, order and good government in Canada." But this did not eliminate the fear, because the text also specified that "this agreement would not extend the legislative authority of Parliament or the legislatures of the provinces." The practical aspects of Native self-government were clearer. The process would have been extremely drawn out and only about 30 aboriginal governments could have been created in the next half-dozen years. The proposals also circumscribed the power of aboriginal groups to act precipitously

---

27. *The Globe and Mail*, July 23, 1992.

by calling for an orderly transition negotiated "in good faith." Moreover, some provinces may still have been able to opt out of the agreement, and there was no guarantee how much federal or provincial funding would have been available to pay for self-government.

Even among those who favoured self-government for Native peoples, there was a concern that the participants in the negotiations did not fully understand the implications of change for such issues as jurisdictions, lands, resources, human rights, and economic and financial considerations. The Charlottetown accord was replete with such ambiguities and contradictions. Should constitutional amendments of such magnitude be left to the courts to rule on after five years elapse? One wondered if the self-government clause was a "blank cheque," and why it was necessary to make such massive changes in such a short time.

Many aboriginal people knew that their rights can be protected in ways other than constitutional amendment. They have received self-government in negotiated treaties in northern Québec, the Yukon, Nunavut and elsewhere. It is clear that Indians, Inuit and Métis also have rights by virtue of their ancestors' occupancy and use of Canada before European colonization. They can also legitimately claim that *inherent* rights exist in section 35 of the *Constitution Act, 1982,* which states simply that "[t]he existing aboriginal and treaty rights of the aboriginal peoples are hereby recognized and affirmed." For greater clarity and certainty, clause 35(3) affirms that "treaty rights" include "land claims agreements" now and in the future.

Social and Economic Union

If the Charlottetown agreement had been passed, the country would have enjoyed a "social and economic union." The agreement set out objectives for the social union on such topics as providing "a health care system which is comprehensive, universal, portable, publicly administered and accessible," "high quality primary and secondary education to all individuals resident in Canada" and "reasonable access to post-secondary education." Laudable as these goals are, they are merely slogans and platitudes. Even the First Ministers realized this when they concluded in the agreement that citizens could not rely on these statements in the courts. They were — as they agreed — "not justiciable." They might also have pointed out that a non-enforceable social charter is no substitute for real legislative capacity to set national standards.

The Charlottetown agreement committed governments to free trade within Canada. Among other clauses it called for "the free movement of persons, goods, services and capital," "full employment" and a "reasonable standard of living." These clauses (which were to be placed in the Constitution) could not have been taken before the courts. Canadians were asked to trust the rhetoric of political leaders. Even Michael Wilson, the government's trade minister, attacked the Pearson Building proposals as providing too many exceptions — enough to outweigh any good done by the provision of an economic union. The final Charlottetown agreement was even worse than Wilson imagined. It did not *commit* the 11 governments to anything at all on the social and economic union, nor did it allow the courts to make decisions on the basis of the clauses in this section.

Proposed Institutional Changes

The Charlottetown proposals called for a drastic overhaul of the federal institutions. The changes can be summarized briefly as follows:

House of Commons If the Charlottetown proposals had been accepted, the membership of the House of Commons would have been increased to 337. Ontario and Québec would have obtained 18 additional seats, British Columbia four and Alberta two. As well, Québec would have been guaranteed no fewer than 25 percent of the seats in the House of Commons. The issue of female and aboriginal representation would have been left for future consideration.

Senate

1. The Senate was to be elected either by the population of a province or territory or by a legislative assembly.

2. The Senate was initially to total 62 senators. It was to be composed of six senators from each province and one senator from each territory.

3. The Senate would not be able to force the resignation of a government.

4. The Senate would have had some authority over legislation:

   i) It would have been able to delay revenue and expenditure bills for 30 days by a suspensive veto. After that period, the House of Commons would have been able to act on its own. But fundamental policy changes to the tax system (such as the Goods and Services Tax and the National Energy Program) were to be excluded from this section and handled as ordinary legislation.

   ii) It would have had veto power over all legislation on natural resources.

   iii) It would have been able, by a majority vote, to trigger a joint sitting with the House of Commons on all ordinary legislation. The joint sitting would have ultimate authority over this referred legislation.

   iv) On matters that materially affect the French language or culture a double majority of anglophone and francophone senators would have been required.

5. The Senate would have had to ratify the appointment of the Governor of the Bank of Canada and other key federal appointments.

Institutional Complexity

Critics listed 10 ways that these proposed institutional arrangements were inadequate.

1. It would increasingly be regarded as unfair to give Québec 25 percent of the seats in the House of Commons in perpetuity. In 1992, Québec had 25.3 percent of the population. Demographers predicted it would drop below 25 percent by the end of the decade (it did so by 1997) and down to 23.5 percent by the year 2011. By contrast, Ontario, British Columbia and Alberta are all predicted to grow substantially.

2. Equal provincial representation in the Senate would be a source of constant irritation. Ontario, with a population of 10 million, would have been awarded six senators, the same number as Prince Edward Island, which is the size of Nepean, a suburb of Ottawa. The distortion was too great.

3. National standards should be maintained in federal institutions. With these new proposals Canada would have had senatorial elections in some places and nominations in others. It would not have been seen as an improvement to allow the Québec National Assembly rather than federal prime ministers to appoint senators.

4. Since there were to be simultaneous elections for the House and Senate, appointed senators from Québec or elsewhere made no sense. After a general election that swept one party into power in Ottawa, the Québec National Assembly could have appointed senators who did not reflect that change. The electoral results would count everywhere but Québec — or wherever senators were appointed.

5. There would have been too many ways for the Senate to tie up the government and prevent it from acting. Fifty percent of the Senate (representing at minimum only 13.2 percent of the Canadian population) would have been able to block all taxation on natural resources and force all ordinary legislation to a joint sitting with the House of Commons.

6. The Senate's power to send all ordinary legislation, including such major issues as the Goods and Services Tax, to a joint sitting with the House was controversial. Government business might have been disrupted and responsible government diminished.

7. The double majority of anglophone and francophone senators required to pass language and cultural legislation might have proven troublesome. A double majority meant that as few as three Parti Québécois senators (likely there would only be six francophones) would be able to block all the remaining senators from action. And a majority of English senators could have blocked something Québec wanted in this field.

8. The Senate was to have a controlling veto over higher government appointments. The House of Commons, the major democratic institution, would only have been able to scrutinize appointments. Why? Could it have been so that a tiny proportion of the public representing the smallest five provinces could prevent appointments that the government, the majority of the members of the House of Commons and most of the people wanted?

9. If the Senate delayed the legislation of a minority government, the situation would have been destabilizing for responsible government. When there was a divided House, the joint sitting would not have been controlled by MPs. The combination of House and Senate could have blocked legislation and forced the formation of a new government, a new Cabinet coalition or a general election. As well, politicians often block one bill in order to prevent a totally different one from getting through. Senators would have been able to block appointments, taxation on resources, and language and culture bills, and force ordinary legislation to a joint sitting until they got compromises on other matters of which they disapproved.

10. The costs of Parliament would have been much too high given the size of the Canadian population. Taxpayers would have picked up extensive new bills. A House of Commons with 337 seats would have made it more than three-quarters the size of the United States House of Representatives (435) with one-tenth the population. As well, members cost more than senators and elected senators would cost more than appointed senators. The costs of paying for the new Parliament would have been too great.

The proposed Rubik's cube of institutions would work effectively *only* when the following *two conditions* prevailed. First, Canada would need a majority, not a minority, government. On this point one should remember that since the Second World War many governments have been in a minority situation. Second, there would have to be a federalist government in Québec. Without these two conditions in place, the constitutional arrangements would further weaken government and fracture the federal system. If there were a separatist government in Québec, the federal government would be handicapped in dealing with it.

The Charlottetown Senate: A Fatal Attraction?

Prime Minister Mulroney was cornered by the proponents of a Triple-E Senate. His 1984 and 1988 electoral successes and the composition of his Cabinet and caucus were based on a Québec–Alberta alliance. If he opted for what Québec wanted — namely Meech Lake Plus — he would lose support in the West, particularly in Alberta, unless he also appeased Westerners with a form of Triple-E.

For that reason, he accepted the Charlottetown proposals for the Senate — a combination of deals. If the Triple-E Senate could have been devised to strengthen national institutions, it might have been acceptable — but, alas, the politicians wanted to develop a Triple-E Senate that would have strengthened the role of the provincial premiers in the system.

Some supporters of Triple-E point to the example of the United States to illustrate what a good idea it is. But the Canadian and American political systems are very different, and no single feature transferred from one to the other will work the same way in its new surroundings. In particular, the American system has a strong president whose powers can be used to overcome the divisions caused by a deadlock between the House and Senate. This is simply not the case in Canada. We do not have an elected president to promote unity for the country and effectiveness for government. Deadlock and delay would paralyze government in this country if Senate powers were equal to those of the House. How could a do-nothing government solve regional alienation? Even assuming the best, which would be that a U.S.-style senate could work as well in Canada as it does in the United States, there still would be no justification for adopting it. There is no reliable evidence that the United States' political system delivers peace, order or good government any better than the Canadian system already does.

Other Triple-E supporters argue that Australia may be an even better model than the United States for Canada to follow, because it has a relatively similar system of government. This is true. But even here one should be extremely cautious. The reality is that the Australian Triple-E has done little to ameliorate regional tensions and has sometimes made them worse. The problem with simple comparison is that one must look beyond the similar formal legal structure of Australian government to the politics within it. For example, Australian politics is organized by parties, and party discipline in the upper chamber ensures that senators only rarely vote against measures supported by their own party in the lower chamber. In effect, this means that Australian senators are *not* more effective advocates for the regions they represent than are the members of the lower house.

The Australian Senate can also become a house of obstruction. During the mid-1970s, an intractable deadlock between the Senate and the House of Representatives over the budget precipitated dissolution of both houses and a constitutional crisis. The political process has since returned to "normal," but the possibility of another such crisis remains and is worrisome to Australian experts. Under the Charlottetown proposals, such deadlocks would have developed regularly between the House and Senate.

Canada and Australia both have responsible government in which the majority party dominates. Citizens know who to credit or blame for different policies and outcomes, and ideally can support the incumbent party or choose among other competing visions or platforms at election time. In Australia, responsible government is preserved at the expense of regional representation. If the proposed new Canadian Senate had blocked legislation, what would have happened to the idea of responsible government?

How would the government have been held responsible to the people when the proposals it initiated were ultimately turned down by the Senate? Clearly, the two concepts of responsible government and regional representation are in irremediable conflict. If we decide regional representation should dominate, then we would have to jettison responsible government, separate the executive and legislative branches, and adopt the American congressional system and possibly elect a president.

The main problem with the existing Senate is that it lacks legitimacy because it is based on political appointments. The Charlottetown agreement pretended to remedy this. In fact, it would have made it worse. The Senate would have consisted of a hodge-podge of elected and appointed members because the rules could be different for each province. Québec, for example, would have appointed its six senators by a vote in the National Assembly, while elsewhere senators would have been elected directly by the people. In Québec, ordinary citizens would not even have had to be consulted. Such a senate would have no more legitimacy than the current upper house.

THE 1992 CONSTITUTIONAL REFERENDUM

On August 28, 1992, the prime minister, the 10 premiers, first ministers of the two northern territories and leaders of the major aboriginal communities agreed on the constitutional text discussed above. More significantly, they agreed to put the Charlottetown package of proposals to the people in a referendum on October 26, 1992. All three federal party leaders also agreed to the Charlottetown accord and to the referendum. The opponents of the accord appeared weak and disunited. Jacques Parizeau, leader of the Parti Québécois, and Lucien Bouchard, leader of the Bloc Québécois, were opposed. Preston Manning was the most outspoken leader outside of Québec to criticize the referendum proposal, although he was joined by Liberals such as Sharon Carstairs in Manitoba. But the real leader of the No side proved once again to be former prime minister Pierre Elliott Trudeau, who attacked the constitutional deal with fervour and logic.

As the third national referendum in Canadian history (for the constitutional campaign, politics and earlier referendums, see Chapter 12), it proved a divisive, corrosive event. In the final analysis, six provinces decisively voted against the deal and only Newfoundland, Prince Edward Island and New Brunswick voted strongly for it. Ontario very narrowly supported the deal while Yukon voted against and the Northwest Territories voted for the deal. At the national level 72 percent of the Canadian electorate cast their votes and defeated the proposal 54.4 percent to 44.6 percent. The Charlottetown proposal was dead.

The defeat of the Charlottetown accord can be explained as the result of a combination of beliefs — some Québeckers did not believe that the accord gave them enough powers, many English Canadians thought it gave Québec too much, there was a general disillusionment and distrust of political leaders throughout the country, and the deal was too complex and cumbersome for a constitutional amendment. At any rate, the unexpected defeat led federal and provincial politicians to one conclusion — it was time for a moratorium on constitutional discussions. With a federal election due before the end of 1993 and a Québec provincial election in 1994, the leaders turned to "politics as usual."

The Liberal government relegated constitutional reform to the back-burner when it came to power in 1993. Prime Minister Jean Chrétien took the stand that many arrangements between the federal government and the provinces could be dealt with by administrative arrangements outside the Constitution. This, for example, has been the case to some extent with minor changes in the relationship between the federal government and Native peoples. Some First Nations have achieved much of what they had wanted to be included in the Charlottetown accord without a constitutional amendment; others have not. Alas, such doctrines about the administrative devolution of power have not been accepted throughout the country and major problems in federal/provincial relations continue to dominate much debate in Canadian politics, in particular over Québec's future adherence to the Constitution.

In the next two chapters, we examine contested federalism, separatism in Québec, the 1995 provincial referendum, the federal responses to Québec separation, and the coming challenges to Canada.

THE STRUCTURE AND ROLE OF THE COURTS

The Canadian **judiciary** rules in disputes about the Constitution and law. Whether it is **civil law** (regulating disputes between two or more private parties) or **criminal law** (regulating crimes such as theft or murder), the judges deliberate in courts. The basic, unitary structure of the judiciary or court system in Canada is that of a pyramid with a very wide base and a narrow tip with the Supreme

Court of Canada at the apex. Immediately below the Supreme Court of Canada in the judicial pyramid are the provincial superior or supreme courts.

Each province has a superior trial court of general jurisdiction (sometimes called the Superior Court or Supreme Court or the Court of the Queen's Bench) that is charged with administering all laws in force in Canada, whether enacted by Parliament, provincial legislatures or municipalities. Since 1987, they all have an appeal court as well. Some also have county or district courts of both civil and criminal jurisdiction. Article 96 of the Constitution stipulates that appointment to these superior district and county courts is made by the Governor General, in practice by the federal Cabinet. In other words, while each province determines how many judges it will need in these federal courts, Ottawa determines who will be appointed and how they will be paid. All provinces have courts staffed by judges appointed by the province to deal with lesser criminal and other matters. These provincial courts include magistrates' courts, family courts and juvenile courts. The appeal divisions of the provincial supreme or superior courts hear appeals from the lower courts and from certain provincial administrative tribunals.

The Supreme Court of Canada was established in 1875 by the *Dominion Act* as a general court of appeal for Canada. As we saw, however, it was not the final court of appeal; that function was performed in Britain by the JCPC until 1949. Today, nine judges serve on the Supreme Court, three of whom must come from the civil law tradition, meaning for practical purposes from Québec. All are appointed by the **governor-in-council**[28] — the formal executive authority of the Governor General applied upon the advice and consultation of the Cabinet — and do not have to retire until age 75. In 1999, Prime Minister Chrétien appointed Beverley McLachlin to succeed Antonio Lamer as Chief Justice of the Court. (See Table 5.1.) As of 1999 a majority of the judges were appointed by Prime Minister Mulroney.

As it is the highest court in the land, the Supreme Court's decisions are binding on all the courts below. (See Figure 5.1.) The Supreme Court of Canada deals primarily with cases that have already been appealed at least once in the lower courts. In these situations, it is appealed to in order to render "an authoritative settlement of a question of law of importance to the whole nation."[29]

TABLE 5.1 SUPREME COURT JUDGES, 2000

Judge	Year Appointed	Province of Birth	Appointing Prime Minister
Chief Justice Beverley McLachlin	1989	Alberta	Mulroney
Madam Justice Claire L'Heureux-Dubé	1987	Québec	Mulroney
Mr. Justice Charles Gonthier	1989	Québec	Mulroney
Mr. Justice Frank Iacobucci	1991	Ontario	Mulroney
Mr. Justice John Major	1992	Alberta	Mulroney
Mr. Justice Michel Bastarache	1997	New Brunswick	Chrétien
Mr. Justice Ian Binnie	1998	Ontario	Chrétien
Madam Justice Louise Arbour	1999	Ontario	Chrétien
Mr. Justice Louis LeBel	1999	Québec	Chrétien

28. "Governor-in-council" is the formal or legal name under which Cabinet makes decisions. For a complete explanation, see Chapter 8, page 261.

29. Peter H. Russell, "The Jurisdiction of the Supreme Court of Canada: Present Policies and a Programme for Reform," *Osgoode Hall Law Journal* (1969), p. 29.

On rather rare but important occasions, Canada's highest court also deals with questions referred to it directly by the federal government.

Canada's Supreme Court does not accept to hear all appeals. In fact, the significance of its work lies in the fact that it can be highly selective, concentrating its efforts on questions that are of fundamental importance to Canadian society, and then shaping the direction of the law by applying general rules to the specific circumstances at hand. One should remember as well that, as a general court of appeal, the Supreme Court has a right of final say in all areas of law for the country. This combination of selectivity and breadth gives it an extremely powerful role. Since the adoption of the *Charter of Rights and Freedoms*, the Supreme Court has also greatly increased its competence to adjudicate in cases involving civil liberties. It has become the final arbiter of the division of power between governments and the line between the powers of both levels of government and the rights and freedoms of citizens.

Below the Supreme Court of Canada but separate from the provincial courts is the **Federal Court of Canada**, which was established by Parliament in 1971. The Federal Court, which has both a trial and an appeal division, settles claims by or against the federal government on matters relating to maritime law, copyright, patent and trade-mark law, and federal taxation statutes. It also has a supervisory jurisdiction related to decisions of tribunals and inferior bodies established by federal law. There are a few other specialized federal courts, such as the Tax Court of Canada, whose decisions are also subject to review by the Federal Court. Decisions of the Federal Court of Appeal can be appealed to the Supreme Court of Canada when the matter in controversy exceeds a set amount of money. Otherwise, an appeal to the Supreme Court of Canada requires either the volition of the Supreme Court itself or the agreement of the Federal Court of Appeal. If the dispute is interprovincial, or federal/provincial in nature, the route of appeal to the Supreme Court is automatically open.

FIGURE 5.1   THE BASIC CANADIAN COURT SYSTEM

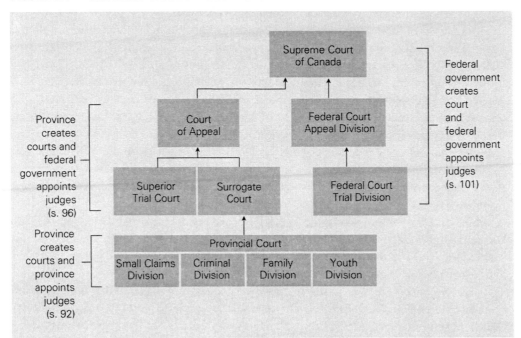

Compared to other countries with a federal system of government, Canada's judicial system is one of the most integrated in the world. A purely federal judicial power is not even mentioned in the Canadian Constitution. Instead, the Constitution provides for an *integrated system* with federally appointed judges to provincial superior and intermediate courts. Canada is the only federation to have this element of judicial integration. As well, Parliament established the Supreme Court of Canada as a "general court of appeal" rather than one that is limited to federal law and constitutional law. Another integrating feature of the judicial system is that Parliament has exclusive jurisdiction in the area of criminal law, even though provincial legislatures have powers to establish courts of criminal jurisdiction. This means that provincially established courts administer federal law.

However, there has been a tendency, particularly in recent years, to move away from this model to a more bifurcated system of dual courts. Evidence for this is found in the proliferation of both provincial and federal courts that are established and staffed by their own respective levels of government. Increasingly, the federal government is relying on judges appointed and paid by the provinces to administer federal laws, and the federal government is showing some tendency to establish federal trial courts for cases involving federal laws. This combination of events illustrates a move in the direction of federalizing Canada's judicial structure. The merits of such a move are highly debatable, in particular because the integrated system has emphasized that the law applies to Canadians equally regardless of their province.

The structure of the judicial system in Canada has evolved slowly since Confederation. Over time, its unitary nature has become slightly more federal, with the proliferation of both provincial and federal courts that are established and staffed by their respective levels of government. But what of the role of the judicial system; has it changed as well?

The answer is a definite yes. The essential judicial function of the courts is that of **adjudication** — the responsibility to provide authoritative settlements in disputes about legal rights and duties. Canadian judges have always exercised legislative powers by making decisions about common and civil law, interpreting statutes and "umpiring" the federal division of powers in the country's written constitution. However, this essential role of the judicial system has adapted and expanded as the social and political environment of the country has changed.

The Fathers of Confederation did not establish the Supreme Court in the Constitution, but left Parliament to propose and establish it through legislation. In the early years of its history, the Supreme Court of Canada was a subordinate, secondary institution. Until 1949, Canadians only had access to the British Judicial Committee of the Privy Council, the Supreme Court of the British Empire. Not until appeal to that body was abolished did the Supreme Court of Canada assume the leadership of the Canadian judicial system. In 1974, its jurisdiction was changed, allowing it basically to control its own agenda. Finally, the patriation of the Constitution, with its *Charter of Rights and Freedoms,* heralded a new and expanded role for all courts in Canada, especially the Supreme Court.

In a 1981 hallmark decision, the Supreme Court judges ruled in the *Patriation Reference* case that the Trudeau government could legally patriate and amend the Constitution unilaterally, but warned that to do so would violate an established "constitutional convention." This ruling on a question of "constitutional convention" was unique in that it reached beyond the law into the realm of politics. It amounted to a legal green light combined with a political red light. Under the circumstances, Mr. Trudeau chose to return to the constitutional bargaining table with the provincial premiers and seek an acceptable compromise before proceeding with patriation.

The *Constitution Act, 1982,* greatly increased the political importance of the Supreme Court of Canada. Under the *Charter of Rights and Freedoms,* the Supreme Court of Canada can overrule legislation and executive acts of government not only on the grounds that they violate the federal division of powers, but also when they are thought to violate the fundamental rights and freedoms of citizens. Increasingly, judges are perceived less as fulfilling an essentially technical and non-political role and more as promoting change in public policy. As Canadians become more conscious of this enhanced judicial power, they will undoubtedly want to scrutinize more closely the impartiality claims of judges.[30]

The appointment procedure may become the object of public debate. Since the Supreme Court was not established by the Constitution, but by federal legislation, there is no mention in the Constitution either of its composition or the method by which judges are appointed. The only mention of the Supreme Court in the *Constitution Act* concerns the amending formula, which requires the agreement of Parliament and all of the provincial legislatures for any change in the composition of the Supreme Court, and the agreement of Parliament and two-thirds of the provinces representing 50 percent of the population for any other constitutional change of the Court. Current reform proposals for the Court, therefore, centre on establishing it in the Constitution so that it will not have to depend on federal legislation for its existence and so that its composition or method of appointment cannot be changed easily.

There is also pressure to reform the process of appointing Supreme Court judges. It has been proposed, for example, that potential government appointees be confirmed by parliamentary hearings or that the prime minister choose his or her nominees from a short-list drawn up by a nominating committee with wide representation.[31]

CHARTER CASES AND THE CONSTITUTION

Charter cases involve extremely difficult questions on issues ranging from Sunday closing of stores to missile-testing to abortion. In 1987, on the fifth anniversary of the Charter, Supreme Court Judge Gerard La Forest commented that he found working with the Charter almost overwhelming at times because of the abstract principles and lack of familiar paths:

> *What is liberty? What should the limits be to it? We all know what we think ourselves. But when it comes to defining liberty, each and every state restriction exists in a proper context. There is no way to escape these problems.... When you are dealing with the Charter, you really don't know what path to choose. This is all new. We are still groping — and I think it's healthy to grope.*[32]

The early court cases were very important for the development of "Charter politics." The first Charter decision of the Supreme Court was *Law Society of Upper Canada v. Skapinker*, in May 1984. It involved the claim that Ontario legislation making Canadian citizenship a condition for practising law violated section 6, the mobility rights section, of the Charter. The Court declared that the Ontario law was not designed to impede movement across provincial borders and therefore did not thwart the mobility guarantee in the Constitution.

---

30. For an excellent summary, see Andrew D. Heard, "The Charter in the Supreme Court of Canada: The Importance of Which Judges Hear an Appeal," *CJPS*, vol. 24, no. 2 (June 1991), pp. 289–307.

31. Jacob S. Ziegel, "Merit Selection and Democratization of Appointments to the Supreme Court of Canada," *Choices: Courts and Legislatures,* vol. 5, no. 2 (June 1999), pp. 3–19.

32. Quoted in Kirk Makin, "Charter's Mandate Gives Judges Role of Wary Surgeons," *The Globe and Mail*, April 14, 1987.

The next four cases concerning Charter claims to be decided — the *Protestant School Boards, Southam, Singh* and *Big M Drug Mart* — were all upheld by the Supreme Court. These decisions went beyond a traditional legalistic approach. The interpretations were based on broad historical and philosophical considerations. In *Southam*, for example, Chief Justice Dickson "traced the right to security from unreasonable searches back to the common law concept of trespass and its application by English judges in the 1700s to make an Englishman's home his castle. He then followed the evolution of this private property interest into a wider concern with personal privacy as a fundamental value of a liberal society."[33]

Many of the Court's other early Charter decisions were more restrained. In *Operation Dismantle*, for example, a coalition of unions and peace groups tried to use the Charter to overturn the decision of the Canadian government to allow testing of American cruise missiles in Canada. They claimed that the agreement increased the likelihood that the country would be involved in a nuclear war, and that this threatened to deprive Canadians of their right to life, liberty and security of the person under section 7 of the Charter.

The Federal Court of Appeal concluded that executive actions and Cabinet decisions could be reviewed by the courts; however, it upheld the government's authority to make decisions on matters of defence and national security. Four of the five judges declared that the coalition had failed to prove that the decision to test the missiles was a break with principles of fundamental justice. The decision of the Supreme Court was that this issue was not a proper question to bring before the courts because "even with the best available evidence, judges could do no more than speculate about the consequences of cruise missile testing."[34] The Court indicated that Charter claims should be rejected when they involve "complex determinations about future behaviour which cannot be satisfactorily assessed through the judicial process."[35] According to one of the most persuasive arguments of the Court, the Charter's guarantees are not, and cannot be, absolute. "We must all die, and many are, at one time or another in their lives, imprisoned or made insecure."[36]

The first cracks in judicial unanimity appeared in the Supreme Court of Canada's decision involving section 8 of the Charter (on search and seizure) — the *Therens* case — in which the judges ruled by seven to two that breathalyzer evidence obtained from someone who had not been advised of their right to counsel could not be used against them in court. Since this event, there have been enough dissenting opinions in other cases that some experts say that it is tentatively possible to assess the judges, or groups of judges, in terms of "liberal," "activist" or "conservative" tendencies. As ideological differences between the judges become more apparent, we can expect the choice of Supreme Court justices to become more politicized, as is the case in the United States. Governments will want to choose judges of their persuasion in order to ensure that their legislative programs survive future court challenges. Obviously, the process of appointing judges will become more controversial.

The majority of Charter cases have arisen through the "legal rights" clause of the Constitution, and these judgements have significantly affected the conduct of police officers and the administration of justice. The *Therens* case, discussed above, threw out improperly obtained breathalyzer evidence. In *Clarkson v. The Queen 1986*, the Court overruled a murder conviction because the

33. Peter H. Russell, *The Judiciary in Canada*, p. 360. For a detailed study of Charter cases and the Constitution, see Michael Mandel, *The Charter of Rights and the Legalization of Politics in Canada* (Toronto: Wall and Thompson, 1989); and Rainer Knopff and F.L. Morton, *Charter Politics* (Scarborough: Nelson, 1992).
34. Russell, *The Judiciary in Canada*, p. 360.
35. Ibid.
36. *Operation Dismantle v. The Queen,* [1985] S.C.R. 651.

accused was too drunk to have understood her right to counsel. In *Manninen 1987*, a robbery conviction was overturned because the accused had not been allowed to telephone his attorney.

Such legal rights issues can become highly political. In *Seaboyer 1991*, the Court ruled that a portion of the "rape shield" law violated the "right to a full answer and defence" when it prevented a person accused of sexual assault from cross-examining his alleged victim about her past sexual activity. Assailed by "feminist" groups, Parliament amended the law to give the trial judge discretion in such cases. This case illustrates once again the political nature of Court judgements and their impact on both interest groups and politicians.

Some of the best-known public policy issues involve Charter decisions by the Supreme Court on fundamental freedoms. The Court threw out the *Lord's Day Act* as an infringement on people who did not accept the Christian Sabbath.[37] On the other hand, the same Court upheld an Ontario act preventing Sunday shopping as long as it was based on a secular rather than religious foundation.[38] Other court cases concerning fundamental freedoms included those on language legislation, pornography, freedom of the press, street prostitution and the right to die.

Equality Rights Cases

The Charter's equality provisions took effect in 1985.[39] Legal equality, including protection from discrimination, is the starting point for any move toward greater equality of opportunity. In the past decade, women's groups have organized effectively to have the courts examine issues such as child care, harassment and violence. Common-law, gay and lesbian rights activists have also made effective cases. The Supreme Court rulings have indicated that while the Constitution explicitly promises equality to every "individual," it is also meant to apply to disadvantaged "groups" such as women and minorities. Critics ask why we prohibit discrimination only on the basis of sex, national or ethnic origin, race, age, colour, religion or disability, when other characteristics such as character and ability are also acquired by chance.

In the first equality case, a white, Oxford-educated male U.S. citizen, Mark Andrews, argued that he had been discriminated against when British Columbia's law society would not let him become a lawyer because he was not a Canadian citizen. He won his case. The Supreme Court argued that equality rights protections in section 15 of the Charter were intended for the disadvantaged. It also ruled that Mark Andrews was a member of a disadvantaged group (non-citizens) and as such was the victim

CLOSE-UP ON Institutions

THE SUPREME COURT AND SEX: PRIVACY AND THE PRESUMPTION OF INNOCENCE

In 1997, Parliament amended the Criminal Code to outline the conditions under which a court could disclose medical, counselling or therapeutic records held by the Crown or a third party relating to a complainant in a sexual assault case. There were many challenges to this law by lawyers for the defence, who argued that unless they had access to these records their clients' right to a fair and full defence would be thwarted.

Two principles clash here: the accused's right to a fair trial and the complainant's right to privacy. In November 1999, the Court ruled by a vote of seven to one that the "rape shield" law was constitutional. This means that judges continue to have the power to block defendants from obtaining such records. The sole dissenting judge, Chief Justice Antonio Lamer, said that the onus should be on the Crown to explain why such disclosure would be unwarranted.

What do you think? Should the law privilege the privacy of the alleged sexual assault victim over the rights of the accused to a fair trial? Or, is this law reasonable given the heinous nature of the crime? Should the courts be allowed to make the final decision in such cases?

---

37. *R. v. Big M Drug Mart Ltd.* (1985), 1 S.C.R. 295.
38. *R. v. Edwards Books and Art Ltd.* (1986), 2 S.C.R. 713.
39. The courts were immediately flooded with serious, but also quite imaginative cases such as one in British Columbia where a chicken owner argued against pet discrimination, saying a local bylaw was unfair because it prohibited fowl within city boundaries. The bylaw was upheld.

of illegal discrimination. The Court went on to say that equality does not mean sameness; sometimes groups need to be treated differently. Based on this same argument, the Court later ruled in a different case that female guards were allowed to see male prisoners while they were using the toilet, but male guards could not do the same with female prisoners.[40]

The Mark Andrews decision proved to be a huge victory for women and minorities. All subsequent decisions in this field stem from this one. The following decisions reflect how the equality section is being interpreted over a decade later.

In May 1995, the Supreme Court announced three significant decisions concerning the "equality rights" section of the Charter. In all three cases the question concerned what constituted discrimination. The first was followed closely by supporters of women's rights; the two others particularly concerned those who supported gay and common-law couples. In essence, the court was being asked to lead social change, or to give official recognition to changes that had taken place.

In the first case, *The Queen v. Suzanne Thibaudeau*, Suzanne Thibaudeau, a divorced woman in Québec, argued that the fact that she (and not her former husband) had to pay tax on support payments for their two children meant that she was being discriminated against. The Court disagreed five to two. It found that there was no discrimination, that the government had already taken this kind of situation into account in taxing divorced parents and that "the tax burden of the couple is reduced and this has the result of increasing the available resources that can be used for the benefit of the children."[41]

The decision created a dilemma for the federal government. If it retained the system, which taxed the recipients of child support, it would face continued agitation from lobbyists claiming it was unfair to women. If it changed the rules to shift the tax to the parent making the support payment, it would anger others. It decided to legislate in favour of the parent who received child support.

The second case, *The Queen v. James Egan and Jack Nesbit*, concerned a homosexual couple from British Columbia. James Egan, a pensioner, applied for a spousal pension for his partner, Jack Nesbit (the law at the time allowed spouses of some pensioners to receive an allowance). Mr. Egan's request was turned down, and he appealed to the Supreme Court on the basis that he had been discriminated against. Again the Court disagreed, even though it unanimously found that homosexuals are covered by the equality provisions of the Charter and cannot be discriminated against on the grounds of sexual orientation. The Court's argument was that Parliament had set up spousal pensions to benefit aged, needy married couples and that marriage is by nature heterosexual. Marriage is "fundamental to the stability and well-being of the family," the Court stated in its decision, so the government was not discriminating in this case, but making political choices. The Constitution stipulates that governments may violate constitutional rights where it is "reasonable" to do so in a free and democratic society.

The judges were badly split in the Egan case (five to four). Two of the dissenting judges even wrote, "This distinction amounts to clear denial of equal benefit of the law." One group of judges, made up of Chief Justice Lamer, Charles Gonthier, Gerard La Forest and John Major, stressed the traditional family structure and opposed extending to gay couples government benefits that were originally designed for the traditional family. Four other judges, namely Beverley McLachlin, Claire L'Heureux-Dubé, Frank Iacobucci and Peter Cory, took a broader view of the contemporary family. They said that legislatures should treat different family structures, including gay couples, roughly the same. The "swing vote" was that of John Sopinka, who agreed that discrimination existed in

---

40. *The Globe and Mail*, April 17, 1995.
41. *The Globe and Mail*, May 26, 1995.

this case but said he was willing to defer to Parliament on the matter. He added that "equating same-sex couples with heterosexual couples ... is still generally regarded as a novel concept."[42]

Lesbian and gay activists saw the Court's recognition of sexual orientation as a basis of discrimination as a *victory* for gay rights, even though this specific case had been lost. The decision had been only one vote away from a win and there was speculation that in future cases John Sopinka might be swayed, or a new judge might change the composition and orientation of the Court. The ruling put pressure on the federal government to move faster on gay rights legislation if it wanted to avoid a spate of lawsuits. In 1996, the federal Parliament amended the human rights legislation to add "sexual orientation" to the Act. The Human Rights Commissioner said, "In terms of what employment benefits will flow from this, that will be decided by the courts as far as I'm concerned."[43]

The third case, *John Miron et al. v. Richard Trudel et al.*, was a clear victory for John Miron and Jocelyn Vallière, a common-law Ontario couple with two children. Mr. Miron had been injured in a car accident as a passenger travelling with an uninsured driver. Miron would have been covered under provincial law by Ms. Vallière's insurance policy, but only if they were married. The Court decided five to four that the provincial policy constituted unjustifiable discrimination by the Ontario government against common-law couples because it required insurance companies to provide benefits to married couples. The ruling went on to argue that common-law couples were a historically disadvantaged group entitled to constitutional protection. This decision meant that federal and provincial governments have had to examine a wide array of laws to ensure that they comply with the ruling.

In the next set of major Charter equality cases, in 1997, the Supreme Court came closer to establishing the importance or effect of equality rights in the Charter. In *Eaton v. Bryant*, the Court ruled that an Ontario school could place a child in a special education class as long as the child did not suffer adverse effects. In *Eldridge v. British Columbia*, the Court drew the same distinction when it ruled that the British Columbia Medical Services Commission violated the Charter when it failed to provide sign-language interpreters, causing a child to suffer adverse effects. And lastly, in *Benner v. Canada*, the Court ruled that the *Citizenship Act* violated equality rights when it made a distinction between males and females in concluding that, before being granted citizenship, a man required a security check if his mother was a Canadian citizen but not if his father was.

The equality case that provoked the most publicity and political controversy involved the *Vriend* decision of April 1998. In that case, the Supreme Court concluded that gays and lesbians should be granted the same protection as others under the Alberta *Individual Rights Protection Act* (IRPA). The decision was remarkable because it was based on a ruling that "a legislative 'omission' bears judicial disapproval on the same basis as the legislature's positive acts."[44] In other words, the Court ruled not on what was *in* the Act but on what had been *omitted* from it. The Court ruled, in effect, that sexual orientation had to be "read into" the IRPA.

On the political front, the Conservative premier of Alberta, Ralph Klein, hinted that he might invoke the notwithstanding clause to overrule the Supreme Court's judgement on this subject, but he backed off when the expected public approval did not emerge. While social conservatives tried to force the premier to nullify the Court ruling on homosexuals, Klein demurred, declaring, "It's like that train. You can't stop it, you have to deal with it."[45] In other words, politicians have to put up with Supreme Court rulings whether they like them or not.

---

42. Ibid.

43. *The Ottawa Citizen*, May 11, 1996.

44. Frederick Vaughan, "Judicial Politics in Canada: Patterns and Trends," *Choices: Courts and Legislatures*, vol. 5, no. 1 (June 1999), p. 15.

45. *Maclean's*, March 29, 1999.

Although equality rights have become a fast-growing area of Charter litigation, it is still too early to determine how far the Supreme Court will use these provisions to expand rights for women, the disabled and others. But there is a "consistent trend towards a liberal judicial philosophy" according to Professor Frederick Vaughan, an astute commentator on judicial trends in Canada. Drawing a line between acceptable and unacceptable forms of discrimination is, according to one Supreme Court justice, one of the most difficult tasks under the Charter: "We are talking about inserting equality into life which is not equal."[46] There are several problems. The Court could require citizens to show that an instance of alleged discrimination is unfair, or it could require governments to justify differing forms of treatment. Prohibitive costs and poor public financing for test cases may make litigants reluctant to challenge governments in court for alleged discrimination. Another issue is deciding how to prove discrimination. Mr. Justice Lamer asked: "What the courts will want is up in the air. Will we need statistical evidence? How will we get at the records we need?"[47] Furthermore, can the courts determine what constitutes equality without Parliament having an opportunity to respond legislatively? In 1988, for example, the Federal Court decided that a section of the *Unemployment Insurance Act* discriminated sexually against natural fathers because it denied them paternity leave benefits. Eventually, the federal government agreed and extended the benefits to fathers. Clearly, this type of ruling affects the balance of power between Parliament and the courts.

The controversy that began with the introduction of the *Charter of Rights and Freedoms* continues. Supporters of both pro- and anti-sides can point to disappointing judgements and unfulfilled expectations. However, a definitive verdict on the value of the Charter will not be clear until much more time has passed.

Unresolved Issues

R.I. Cheffins and P.A. Johnson say that the importance of the Charter for Canada's constitutional future is that it is "centralizing, legalizing and Americanizing."[48] By centralizing, they mean that it provides a common national standard for the protection of civil liberties and engenders national debates that transcend federal/provincial or regional differences. Another commentator has summed up the legalizing and politicizing effect of the Charter this way: it tends "to judicialize politics and to politicize the judiciary."[49]

Clearly, today the nine justices of the Supreme Court of Canada play a very powerful political role. They can overturn legislation that, according to their judgement, conflicts with rights guaranteed in the Charter, and they can have the final say on social policy matters such as union rights and abortion that used to be in the exclusive domain of politicians. This power has been particularly evident in cases concerning legal rights. In January 1988, for example, the Supreme Court declared that the federal abortion law did not conform to the *Canadian Charter of Rights and Freedoms* and struck it down, leaving Canada with no legislation in this field of social policy. In the famous *Morgentaler* case, a majority of the Supreme Court judges ruled that the law restricting access to therapeutic abortions violated the security of the person of the woman and constituted a "profound

46. Mr. Justice Lamer quoted in *The Globe and Mail*, April 14, 1987.

47. Ibid.

48. R.I. Cheffins and P.A. Johnson, *The Revised Canadian Constitution: Politics as Law* (Toronto: McGraw-Hill Ryerson, 1986), pp. 148–49.

49. Peter H. Russell, "The Political Purposes of the Canadian Charter of Rights and Freedoms," *The Canadian Bar Review*, 61, 1983, p. 51.

interference with a woman's body."[50] Despite parliamentary efforts to regain control of abortion policy, the Supreme Court's judgement remains in place with little likelihood of successful legislation. In 1991, the Supreme Court reaffirmed the position that an unborn child (a fetus) is not a person.

Critics of the Charter insist that it inhibits rather than fosters progressive social change. They maintain that by framing the agenda for debate the courts can limit the progression of social reform. The rights protected under the Charter are, they claim, a reflection of middle-class preoccupations; no basic entitlement is included for a decent level of education, housing, nutrition or health care. However, section 36 of the Charter does enshrine the commitment of both federal and provincial governments to provide "essential public services of reasonable quality to all Canadians." And, although it does not protect present social and economic arrangements, the Charter identifies and protects the political and legal rights essential to those who promote social change.

Critics also contend that the Charter confers too much power on lawyers and judges, enabling judges who are not elected to strike down measures enacted by the majority. One supporter, Robert Sharpe, answers these criticisms by pointing out that we cannot equate democracy with "the raw will of the majority.… A true democracy," he states, "is surely one in which the exercise of power by the many is conditional on the respect for the rights of the few."[51] It is unfortunate, but true, that the majority at times overlook minority rights. The Charter assigns the courts the responsibility to ensure that the claims of minorities and those without influence must be considered. Ultimately, of course, elected officials have the final say, because the Charter provides that equality rights are subject to the legislative override provision (the notwithstanding clause) that can be used if legislatures disagree fundamentally with the courts.

Another controversial aspect of Charter cases will be more familiar to Americans than Canadians. Section 24(2) of the Charter declares that a court shall exclude from the proceedings evidence that was obtained in a manner that infringed upon or denied any guaranteed right or freedom. Canadian judges are proving willing to dismiss illegally obtained evidence because it might "bring the administration of justice into disrepute," but these new exclusions are making law enforcement more difficult. Until 1982, illegally obtained evidence was accepted in the courts; today, it is not.

One further area of apprehension concerning the Charter lies in the realm of political culture. Some scholars see the Charter as promoting a shift of values toward those of the United States. They maintain that the traditional, collectivist values that emphasize tradition, order and historical continuity (as discussed in Chapter 3) are becoming more closely aligned with American values that stress individual interests above those of the collectivity. This reflects the emphasis the Charter puts on individual versus group interests. As Cheffins and Johnson put it, the Charter "will bring an essentially counter-revolutionary, non-rationalist communitarian society into direct collision with individual-focused legal rights based upon Charter arguments." Doing so, they maintain, will accelerate the Americanization of Canada.[52]

However, the Charter also has a clearly positive side. Judges have taken the stand that citizens should be allowed to ask courts to declare laws unconstitutional when there is a potential infringement of their rights; they do not have to wait until their rights are actually violated. In response to this, many laws that threatened to deprive individuals of basic rights have been struck down. Supreme

---

50. *R. v. Morgentaler* (1988), 1 S.C.R. 30.
51. Quoted in *The Toronto Star*, April 11, 1987.
52. *The Revised Canadian Constitution*, p. 152.

Court Justice Lamer commented that because of this governments have been more careful since 1982 in drafting laws.[53] This was evident in 1986, when a parliamentary subcommittee presented 85 recommendations for making federal law conform to the Charter. Part of that list, including discrimination against homosexuals in the federal jurisdiction, was acted upon quickly and outlawed.

We conclude that Canadian judicial tradition will continue to influence the conduct of judges when they assess Charter implications, especially in issues of equality. While the opportunity for a more active, interventionist and, some might argue, more creative role for the judiciary now exists, this will not bring about sudden change. There will be a gradual but constant evolution in the power of the Supreme Court. It will take considerable time for precedent-setting cases to be brought before the courts and for judges to determine the nature of their new role. In the meantime, the Charter has become an important Canadian symbol and a significant part of the policy process, a balance to legislative power.

• • • • • • • •

SUMMARY

It is clear that the Canadian Constitution is not a single document that provides clear direction to the political process. As in most democratic countries, it is both a product of the political system and a significant factor in shaping it. The Canadian Constitution can be said to include both written and unwritten dimensions. Among the unwritten elements are the British parliamentary heritage and the democratic norms and values inculcated in the Canadian political culture. The written dimensions of the Canadian Constitution include the well-known *British North America Act* of 1867 (now the *Constitution Act, 1867*) and the *Canada Act* of 1982, as well as a number of other acts and documents. The *Constitution Act* has been altered or expanded numerous times since 1867 by formal amendments and by legal interpretations by the Judicial Committee of the Privy Council and the Supreme Court of Canada.

Since the patriation of the *Constitution Act, 1982,* with its new amending formula and *Charter of Rights and Freedoms,* the role of the courts in the political process has increased considerably. The new Charter is even more comprehensive than the *Bill of Rights* in the United States, and it has strengthened the position of the judicial branch of government in Canada. The Charter ensures that legislators who enact laws must be prepared to justify any inequality of burdens those laws may impose. By doing so, it allows an avenue for minorities and other previously unempowered groups to participate more effectively in the law-making process. This new feature in the Constitution will greatly increase litigation, but should also enhance the democratic quality of government and provide arbitration by a forum that is less vulnerable to the influence of powerful majorities than is the political arena. Court decisions have already begun to alter subtly the make-up of the country by reducing situations where laws vary from province to province.

53. Quoted in *The Globe and Mail,* April 14, 1987.

The 1992 Charlottetown accord was designed to accommodate provincial interest in Confederation. Its defeat has prevented Canada from becoming more decentralized by constitutional means. But challenges to the viability of the state continue unabated. We have patriated the Constitution only to find ourselves mired in constitutional deadlock. The amendment procedures may well prove too rigid to resolve the deficiencies that are already glaringly evident in the country. The constitutional dilemma of how to solve regional aspirations as well as Québec's precise demands while retaining a powerful federal government is probably the most vital political challenge facing Canadians at the turn of the century. The post-1995 politics of the Québec referendum are discussed in Chapter 7.

As Niccolo Machiavelli (1469–1527) warned in *The Prince*, there is nothing more difficult to arrange, more doubtful of success and more dangerous to carry through than initiating changes in a state's constitution. Machiavelli believed that Italian reformers had enemies in all those who profited from the old order and only lukewarm defenders in those who would profit by the new one. Canada faces the same dilemma.

DISCUSSION QUESTIONS

1. What were the two basic obstacles to the 1982 patriation of the Constitution, and what compromises were reached to try to solve them? Why did Québec not agree?

2. What were the main additions to the Constitution when it was patriated in 1982? Why was it patriated without Québec's approval?

3. Describe and evaluate the current formulae for amending the Constitution.

4. How has the *Charter of Rights and Freedoms* affected equality rights in Canada? In the late 1990s?

5. What are the advantages and disadvantages of an integrated court system?

Selected Bibliography

Ajzenstat, Janet, ed., *Canadian Constitutionalism: 1791–1991* (Ottawa: Canadian Study of Parliament Group, 1992).

Bakan, Joel and David Schneiderman, *Social Justice and the Constitution* (Don Mills, Ont.: Oxford University Press, 1992).

Behiels, M., *The Meech Lake Primer: Conflicting Views on the 1987 Constitutional Accord* (Ottawa: University of Ottawa Press, 1989).

Bogdanor, Vernon, *The Monarchy and the Constitution* (Oxford: Clarendon, 1995).

———, and S.E. Finer, *Comparing Constitutions* (Oxford: Clarendon, 1995).

Cairns, A.C., *Charter versus Federalism: The Dilemmas of Constitutional Reform* (Montréal: McGill-Queen's University Press, 1992).

Conklin, William, *Images of a Constitution* (Toronto: University of Toronto Press, 1993).

Cook, Curtis, ed., *Constitutional Predicament* (Montréal: McGill-Queen's University Press, 1994).

Heard, Andrew, *Canadian Constitutional Conventions* (Toronto: Oxford University Press, 1991).

Hogg, Peter, *Constitutional Law of Canada*, 3rd ed. (Toronto: Carswell, 1992).

Jackson, Robert and Doreen Jackson, *Stand Up for Canada: Leadership and the Canadian Crisis* (Scarborough: Prentice Hall, 1992).

Lenihan, Donald, Gordon Robertson and Roger Tassé, *Canada: Reclaiming the Middle Ground* (Montréal: Institute for Research on Public Policy, 1994).

Milne, David, *The Canadian Constitution* (Toronto: Lorimer, 1991).

Monahan, Patrick J., *Meech Lake: The Inside Story* (Toronto: University of Toronto Press, 1991).

Reesor, B., *The Canadian Constitution in Historical Perspective* (Scarborough: Prentice Hall Canada, 1992).

Russell, Peter H., *Constitutional Odyssey* (Toronto: University of Toronto Press, 1991).

Sartori, Giovanni, *Comparative Constitutional Engineering* (New York: New York University Press, 1995).

Watts, Ronald L. and Douglas M. Brown, eds., *Options for a New Canada* (Toronto: University of Toronto Press, 1991).

Weaver, R. Kent, *The Collapse of Canada?* (Washington: Brookings Institution, 1992).

——————, and Bert Rockman, eds., *Do Institutions Matter?* (Washington: Brookings Institution, 1993).

Whitaker, Reg, *A Sovereign Idea* (Montréal: McGill-Queen's University Press, 1992).

The Courts

Gall, Gerald L., *The Canadian Legal System*, 3rd ed. (Toronto: Carswell, 1990).

Knopff, Rainer and F.L. Morton, *Charter Politics* (Scarborough: Nelson, 1992).

Mandel, Michael, *The Charter of Rights and the Legalization of Politics in Canada*, rev. ed. (Toronto: Wall and Thompson, 1994).

Manfredi, Christopher P., *Judicial Power and the Charter: Canada and the Paradox of Liberal Constitutionalism* (Toronto: McClelland & Stewart, 1993).

McCormick, P. and I. Greene, *Judges and Judging* (Toronto: Lorimer, 1990).

Morton, F.L., *Law, Politics and the Judicial Process in Canada*, 2nd ed. (Calgary: University of Calgary Press, 1992).

——————, *Morgentaler v. Borowski: Abortion, the Charter and the Courts* (Toronto: McClelland & Stewart, 1992).

Seidle, F. Leslie, ed., *Equity and Community: The Charter, Interest Advocacy and Representation* (Ottawa: Institute for Research on Public Policy, 1993).

Yates, Richard and Ruth Yates, *Canada's Legal Environment* (Scarborough: Prentice Hall Canada, 1993).

LIST OF WEBLINKS

Canada.justice.gc.ca/ en/dept/pub/trib/ index.html

Canada's Court System This Web page outlines the structure of the Canadian court system.

www.scc-csc.gc.ca

The Supreme Court of Canada This is the Web page of the Canadian Supreme Court.

www.lexum.unmontreal. ca/csc-scc/

Supreme Court Decisions on the Canadian Charter of Rights and Freedoms This site contains Supreme Court decisions based on the *Canadian Charter of Rights and Freedoms*.

6

Contested Federalism

• • • • • • •

The Division of Powers and Financial Resources

In this chapter, we explore the meaning of federalism and its importance for Canadians. One conclusion is obvious. Rather than being a fixed, immutable institutional structure, Canadian federalism has changed dramatically over the years. It is not a simple, static division of powers, but a process whereby the two levels of government adapt and change in order to reduce tensions within the political environment. Although the Canadian federal structure has proven remarkably resilient, during the past three decades powerful pressures have emerged that threaten to overwhelm the system. The ultimate outcome of what is often referred to as the "crisis of Canadian federalism" is by no means certain. Whether these forces will result in a truncated Canada or serve to strengthen the federal system will depend on an array of factors, including leadership, economic prosperity and political circumstances.

Developments in federalism reach into everyone's lives. The threat of Québec separation, the sense of grievance in western provinces, the controversies over language and educational rights for minorities, the disputes over resource control, and many similar troublesome matters — all of these political issues are manifestations of conflicts over the authority and jurisdiction of the federal system. The vast array of social services and programs available to Canadian citizens today is the outgrowth of federal/provincial interaction. While certain programs may be supported by only one level of government, the majority require the financial cooperation of both Ottawa and the provinces. The procedures that lead to the interaction of the federal and provincial governments in these activities reveal much about Canadian politics. On the other hand, the federal system complicates the handling of many issues — for example, economic planning, control of inflation and modern concerns such as job creation, pollution, safety and women's rights.

In Chapter 5, we outlined the constitutional provisions that formally define the relationship between the federal and provincial governments. However, the conduct of politics within Canada's federal structure is also affected by the dynamic social and economic realities of the country. Therefore, more is required to comprehend Canadian federalism than a discussion of the legal division of powers and jurisdictional niceties. We need to understand the complex financial relations among governments as well as the political challenges that threaten to tear the country apart. This chapter focuses on financial relations; the next chapter deals with the political challenges of nationalism and regionalism.

WHAT IS FEDERALISM?

In his influential book on the subject, William Riker contends that the twentieth century is an "age of federalism" and lists numerous federal countries, including the United States, Australia, Germany and Canada.[1] Federalism, he argues, has replaced the empire as a means of governing diverse peoples living on large land masses. This statement is partially correct. Twenty-two of the world's states are federal, including many of the large ones. However, it is also apparent that in 2000 there are more than eight times as many unitary as federal states, and that, even within the systems labelled "federal," the term means quite different things to different people.[2] There is little similarity in the federal aspects of countries such as the United States of America, Australia and Canada compared with Argentina, Brazil, Mexico, Nigeria, the Federated States of Micronesia and the United Arab Emirates. Moreover, some historically federal countries have imploded — the U.S.S.R. has been dismantled, Czechoslovakia has divided and the component parts of the former Yugoslavia have formed several new countries. We shall have to be precise in the use of the term federalism.

Simply put, federalism refers to a division of jurisdiction and authority between at least two levels of government. It is usually characterized by the existence of one central government and two or more regional governments operating simultaneously over the same territory and people. Therefore, **federalism** can be defined as "a political organization in which the activities of government are divided between regional governments and a central government in such a way that each kind of government has some kind of activities on which it makes final decisions."[3]

This definition implies that each level of government has more or less complete authority over specific spheres of activity, while on a few other matters there may be a degree of concurrent jurisdiction. There is certainly no single, ideal way to divide this authority. What is important is that each level has a degree of autonomy. In the federal form, the various levels of government obtain their respective powers from the country's constitution, not from each other. Citizens owe some loyalty to more than one level of government, and both levels may act directly on the citizens.

The history of the concept of federalism has been traced back to the fusion of ancient Israelite tribes. In North America, its first occurrence has been ascribed to the Five Nations of the Iroquois Indians. Its modern meaning, however, is best dated to the eighteenth century. During that period, the United States Constitution provided a system of government that has been emulated ever since. The dual essence of the theory of American federalism was the idea of distribution of government power on a geographical basis, and the philosophy that unity and diversity can co-exist.

1. William H. Riker, *Federalism: Origin, Operation, Significance* (Boston: Little, Brown, 1964), p. 1.
2. Robert J. Jackson and Doreen Jackson, *An Introduction to Political Science: Comparative and World Politics* (Toronto: Prentice Hall Canada, 2000), ch. 1.
3. William H. Riker, "Federalism," in Fred I. Greenstein and Nelson W. Polsby, eds., *Handbook of Political Science,* vol. 5, Government Institutions and Processes (Reading, Mass.: Addison-Wesley, 1975), p. 101.

Concepts of Federalism

One problem has dominated the debate about the meaning of federalism. It concerns those systems that have a federal constitutional structure, but political and social forms that reduce the significance of the bargain between the central and regional governments. An example is Mexico, where the near one-party system links the political forces together in such a way as to produce a state very similar to those that are unitary. On the other hand, some unitary states are highly decentralized, and some, such as Britain, are becoming more decentralized over time. In summary, therefore, federal states may be centralized or decentralized — and so may unitary systems.

William Riker offers a useful continuum by which to measure various federalisms.[4] This continuum ranges from centralized federalism, in which the central government dominates or encroaches on the sub-units, to what may be referred to as decentralized federalism, in which the sub-unit governments dominate. (See Figure 6.1.) For a variety of reasons, most federal states today are of the centralized variety. The requirements of national security, the welfare state and, in general, the growing complexity of society are all factors conducive to a centralization of power at the national level. There are, however, states in which the various regional sub-units retain significant powers. Furthermore, there are countries in which it is possible to discern pendulum swings along the continuum over a period of decades. Although centralized federalism is the more common form today, there is nothing intrinsically superior or inferior about the arrangement.

While considering the continuum of federalism, it is important to note its polar ends: the unitary and confederation forms of government. As its name implies, **unitary government** is characterized by one level of political authority. In this form the central government grants and amends the powers of local or provincial authorities. The archetype of this form may well be France, where virtually all significant final decisions about political life are made in Paris. On the other hand, except in Canada and Switzerland, **confederation** refers to a loose alliance of sovereign states that band together for very narrow reasons. The United States in the period of the Articles of Confederation, 1781–87, is a good example of this form. Admittedly, there may be a fine line between certain decentralized federalisms and confederal states. Perhaps the only way to differentiate between the two types is to ascertain whether the various "regional" units are completely, as opposed to partially, sovereign.

FIGURE 6.1   CONTINUUM OF THE DEGREE OF CENTRALIZATION OF AUTHORITY

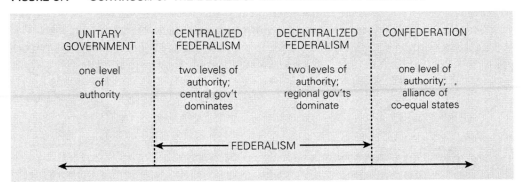

Source: Adapted from concepts proposed by William H. Riker in *Federalism: Origin, Operation, Significance* (Boston: Little, Brown, 1964).

---

4. Riker, *Federalism: Origin, Operation, Significance*, pp. 5–10. See also K.C. Wheare, *Federal Government*, 4th ed. (New York: Oxford University Press, 1963), pp. 31–32.

Many authors dislike the apparent formalism in these legal, political and territorial definitions of federalism. Economists[5] and some political scientists even speak of a "federal society," one in which economic, religious, racial or historical diversities are territorially grouped. W.S. Livingston, for example, believes that certain societies are intrinsically federal because they are pluralist, and that federalism is simply the institutional outcome of the forces that exist in these societies.[6] The inherent difficulty with such definitions is that they concern more than federal unions and could just as well apply to any state composed of more than one ethnic group. Other authors believe that non-territorial federalism can exist. They cite examples such as Estonia in 1925 or Cyprus in 1960. In these instances, legal jurisdiction over cultural and educational affairs was accorded to groups wherever they lived, and was not based on a geographic division of the state.[7]

Evaluations of Federalism and Separatism

Why is federalism adopted? What are its advantages? On these questions there is much disagreement among scholars. Some argue that federalism is synonymous with liberty, that it is a protection for minority rights. Others believe it is chosen essentially to achieve unification without the loss of separate identities by the units. On the other hand, Graham Maddox has argued that many of the so-called altruistic objectives often attributed to federalism are inaccurate and perhaps misleading.[8] Britain, one of the world's most liberal democracies, is a unitary state, while a number of non-democratic countries have, on paper at least, adopted the federal form. Maddox also questions the popular argument that federal governments are "closer to the people."[9] Franz Neumann concludes that federalism may be good, bad or indifferent, depending on other circumstances.[10]

Whatever the ultimate purpose of federalism, it is characteristically adopted because the leaders of the constituent units believe that they have something to gain that they could not achieve if they were to remain autonomous. The two most often-cited motivations underlying federal unions are the desire for military security and the desire for economic or political expansion. A large geographic unit with a degree of coordination of resources provides a more effective defensive unit than a collection of smaller, independent states. And such a unified entity stands a good chance of being able to expand economically and politically. The possibility for self-aggrandizement, rather than lofty idealism, seems to be a more accurate assessment of the motivations for federalism.

While the various sub-units may perceive gains from a federal union, they must also take certain drawbacks into consideration. In order to realize their objectives, the sub-units are obliged to give up some privileges and powers to the central government. Before doing this, they may seek certain guarantees and safeguards so that they may maintain at least a modicum of separate authority. These guarantees are usually in the form of a written constitution clearly dividing political authority and jurisdiction and spelling out certain limitations and restrictions on the new government.

5. See, for example, Wallace Oaks, *Fiscal Federalism* (New York: Harcourt Brace Jovanovich, 1977).
6. See W.S. Livingston, "A Note on the Nature of Federalism," in J. Peter Meekison, ed., *Canadian Federalism: Myth or Reality*, 2nd ed. (Toronto: Methuen, 1971), p. 24.
7. See Karl Aun, "Cultural Autonomy of Ethnic Minorities in Estonia: A Model for Multicultural Society?" paper presented at the Third Conference of Baltic States in Scandinavia, Stockholm, 1975.
8. For a critique of the standard justifications cited for the adoption of federalism, see Graham Maddox, "Federalism: Or Government Frustrated," *Australian Quarterly*, vol. 45, no. 3 (September 1973), pp. 92–100.
9. Ibid., pp. 93–94.
10. Franz Neumann, *The Democratic and the Authoritarian State: Essays in Political and Legal Theory* (Glencoe: Free Press, 1957).

A constitution is, therefore, often referred to as the "umpire" of federalism, serving to protect as well as limit. Whether the constitution is a single, written document or an unwritten collection of statutes and understandings, what is important is that the "federal principle" be enshrined in a way that recognizes the diversity of the country and at the same time provides a check on arbitrary rule by the central government. The component units are usually given equal or disproportionately strong representation at the centre. This is often achieved by having two legislative chambers — one based on population, the other based on a recognition of regionalism. And the importance of constitutions to federal systems is demonstrated by the continuing controversies over how they may be amended or altered.

Many apparently stable federal constitutional systems have endured stresses and strains and, on occasion, even failure. Ronald Watts has found four common conditions of failure: regional divergences of political demands, weak communications, a diminution of the original impetus for union and external influences.[11] All these conditions are present in Canada to some degree; in fact, they are present to some extent in *all* federations — both those that have failed and those that have succeeded. Examples of peaceful secessions include very loose confederations such as Malaysia (Singapore was virtually expelled) and the tenuous arrangements of Syria–Egypt and Senegal–Mali. Three former communist countries (the U.S.S.R., Czechoslovakia and Yugoslavia) fell apart when the glue of communism was removed. The other cases of federal division involved violence. The lesson is clear — rancour and civil war have been the usual means by which federal states have divided.

Thus far, we have described federalism in terms of constitutions that divide the authority of the central and sub-unit governments and balance regional interests. Nonetheless, readers must not take too legalistic an approach and overlook the fact that federalism is fundamentally based on a sociological reality.[12] Were it not for societal diversity, federalism would not be as prevalent in the world as it is today. While federal states may be formed for essentially narrow, pragmatic reasons, this political arrangement is ultimately a recognition that the various sub-units are different and that their special qualities should be preserved and protected. Keeping this in mind, let us now turn to a consideration of how federalism came to be adopted in Canada and how it has evolved over the years.

THE TRAJECTORY OF CANADIAN FEDERALISM

The Origins of Federalism

As noted in Chapter 2, the motivations for the establishment of a federal union in Canada in the 1860s were mixed. Both military security and economic expansion were central themes in the speeches and political programs of the contemporary leaders. Foremost among this handful of politicians was Sir John A. Macdonald, who played the leading role in establishing the federal union in 1867 by placating the objections of the smaller Maritime provinces and holding forth the prospect of a glorious national destiny.[13] By the 1860s, Macdonald, among others, was keenly aware of the need for

---

11. R.L. Watts, "Survival or Disintegration," in Richard Simeon, ed., *Must Canada Fail?* (Montréal: McGill-Queen's University Press, 1977), pp. 42–60.

12. See Michael Stein, "Federal Political Systems and Federal Societies," in Meekison, ed., *Canadian Federalism: Myth or Reality*, pp. 30–42.

13. See Donald Creighton, *John A. Macdonald: The Young Politician* (Toronto: Macmillan, 1952), *John A. Macdonald: The Old Chieftain* (Toronto: Macmillan, 1955), and *The Road to Confederation: The Emergence of Canada 1863–1867* (Toronto: Macmillan, 1964); and Peter Waite, *The Life and Times of Confederation, 1864–1867* (Toronto: University of Toronto Press, 1967).

greater military security. The victory of the northern states in the American Civil War had sent a shiver up the spines of Canadian leaders. British interests in Canada had made no secret of their support for the American Confederacy and, after Appomattox, there was some expectation that Canada might be annexed as part of the spoils of war. Raids by fanatical Fenians across the border into Canada added more urgency to plans for some type of national unification. The British, for their part, were tired of the burden of defending their colonies in North America and were not averse to the prospect of turning over to Canadians the responsibility for their own defence.

At the same time, Macdonald recognized the great potential of the unsettled western territories for the development of a transcontinental nation. The possibility of economic development and expansion was, therefore, another significant motivating factor in establishing federalism. He thought that a political union would not only improve internal trade between the Maritime provinces and Upper and Lower Canada, but also help in the drive to settle the prairies and the far West before the Americans moved into the vacuum.

Each of the British colonies in North America saw certain specific advantages for itself in the new enterprise. The leaders from Upper Canada, a growing and prosperous area, looked forward to further economic expansion and development. Those from Lower Canada, while uneasy about their English Canadian neighbours, were willing to accept a federal union if their language and culture could be protected by law. The sparsely populated Maritime colonies of Nova Scotia and New Brunswick were perhaps the most reluctant, but at the same time they, too, were attracted by economic advantages, namely the building of a transcontinental railway and various subsidies from the future federal government. The Charlottetown and Québec conferences, discussed in Chapter 2, culminated a long process of negotiation resulting in the Dominion of Canada.

The Evolution of Federalism

While the 1867 *BNA Act* authorized the establishment of a type of government in Canada "similar in principle to that of the United Kingdom," the resulting form of government necessarily differed in that jurisdiction and authority were divided between the central government and the provinces. We have seen that the architects of the federal system sought to establish a strong central government, mindful as they were of the threat posed by the movement for states' rights in the American union, which had led to the bloody Civil War of 1861–65. Even a cursory reading of the *BNA Act* confirms the impression that the central government was meant to be predominant. Reversing the American example, it was the federal government in Canada that was to be the beneficiary of the residual "Peace, Order, and good Government" clause. The limited jurisdiction of the provinces was meant to underscore their subordinate position in the federation. While reference is often made to the "Confederation Agreement," it is clear that the authors did not intend Canada to be a confederation in a genuine political sense, but rather a centralized federation.

In a summary article, Howard Cody has traced the evolution of federal/provincial interaction in Canada since 1867.[14] While his argument lacks a rigorous definition of "interaction," his précis does provide an instructive history of federal/provincial relations. Cody identifies at least four eras, and suggests that there have been several pendulum swings between centralization and decentralization. (See Figure 6.2.) While Canada clearly began as a centralized federation, during the latter part of the nineteenth century the relative power of the provinces grew, due to a series of judgements by the Judicial Committee of the Privy Council (JCPC). We have noted that in jurisdictional disputes

---

14. Howard Cody, "The Evolution of Federal-Provincial Relations in Canada: Some Reflections," *American Review of Canadian Studies*, vol. 7, no. 1 (Spring 1977), pp. 55–83.

referred to the JCPC there was a consistent pattern of interpretation favouring provincial rights. Forceful provincial leaders such as Sir Oliver Mowat and Honoré Mercier had the effect of eroding the original dominance of the central government to the point that the *BNA Act* was interpreted by the JCPC as an international treaty rather than as the founding document of a country.[15] This period of decentralized federalism, lasting into the early twentieth century, has been roundly condemned by Garth Stevenson:

> *This peculiar situation, which even the Australians had the foresight largely to avoid, had the effect that for almost a century the most influential concepts of Canadian federalism were largely defined by outsiders, men who had no practical knowledge of Canada, or of federalism, and who were not even required to live in the society that to a large degree was shaped by their opinions.*[16]

FIGURE 6.2   THE EVOLUTION OF CANADIAN FEDERALISM FROM 1867 TO 2000, INDICATING SWINGS OF CENTRALIZATION AND DECENTRALIZATION

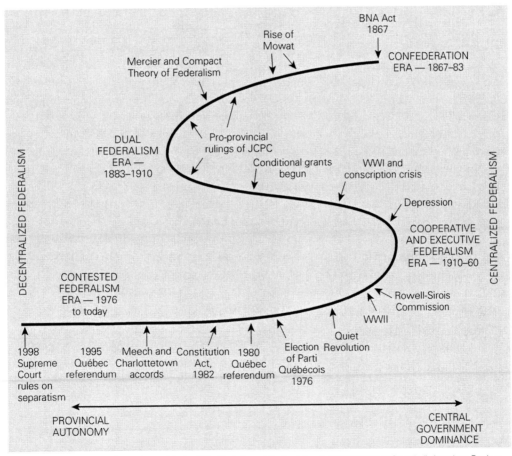

Source: Based on an idea from Howard Cody, "The Evolution of Federal-Provincial Relations in Canada," *American Review of Canadian Studies*, vol. 7, no. 1 (1977), pp. 55–83.

15. See Donald Swainson, ed., *Oliver Mowat's Ontario* (Toronto: Macmillan, 1972), especially Bruce W. Hodgins, "Disagreement at the Commencement: Divergent Ontarian Views of Federalism, 1867–1871," pp. 52–68.
16. Garth Stevenson, *Unfulfilled Union*, rev. ed. (Toronto: Gage, 1982), p. 43.

According to Cody's historical summary, the pendulum began to swing back toward a centralization of authority with the introduction of what became known as "conditional grants." Under the *BNA Act*, the provinces assumed jurisdiction over such matters as education and social welfare, which originally required very little expenditure. As the demand for social services grew in the twentieth century, the provinces found themselves starved for funds. The provisions of the Act made it virtually impossible for them to raise the revenues needed to meet public needs. To help them escape from this impasse, the central government in Ottawa offered the provinces grants "on the condition" that the money be spent in a specified manner. The provinces, for their part, resented this intrusion but had no choice. The Depression further deepened the dependency of the provinces on the federal government. In addition, the necessity for placing Canada on a war footing in 1914 and again in 1939 naturally tended to centralize power in Ottawa. Except perhaps in Québec, where there was considerable opposition to the two world wars, and especially to the policy of conscription, the national government became a focus of patriotism and loyalty for most Canadians.

The dominance of Ottawa can be said to have continued until the late 1950s, when another pendulum shift occurred. New ideas about decentralization had begun to circulate as early as 1937, with the recommendations of the Royal Commission on Dominion-Provincial Relations, perhaps better known as the Rowell-Sirois Commission. This commission was charged with investigating the reasons for the near-bankruptcy of the provinces and recommending ways in which to revitalize the federation. While its suggestions could not be implemented until after the Second World War, the Rowell-Sirois Commission came out strongly against the conditional grants procedure. In addition, it recommended that Ottawa take over such expensive responsibilities as unemployment insurance and pensions, and generally seek to equalize the financial resources of the provinces.

As the provinces began to obtain relief from their heavy financial burdens through new fiscal mechanisms, important changes were also occurring in postwar society. Beginning in the 1960s and increasing in momentum through the decade, Québec underwent the Quiet Revolution, in which traditional French Catholic values and occupational patterns were transformed. A new, confident French Canadian elite, epitomized by the government of Jean Lesage, led the assault on Ottawa's "paternalism."[17] Ottawa countered with an expansion of what were referred to as "conditional grants" or "shared-cost programs," which nonetheless tended to be regarded as distorting provincial spending priorities and therefore still engendered antagonism. In the spirit of Mowat and Mercier, Québec politicians insisted on the right to exercise their independence by "opting out" of certain programs so that they could go their own way. Ottawa had no coherent or effective response with which to meet this challenge. Québec's agitation in the 1960s for "special status" only served to give the other provinces new ideas.

The long-standing sense of grievance in the western provinces against Ottawa also began to erupt during this period. Made confident by their enormous resource revenues, the provinces of Alberta and British Columbia in particular sought greater political clout within the federation to match their recent wealth. While they were not sympathetic to the cultural and linguistic aspirations of the Québécois, the western provinces shared with them a degree of antipathy toward the perceived paternalism of the federal government in Ottawa as well as its perceived favouritism toward central Canada.

17. See Claude Morin, *Quebec versus Ottawa: The Struggle for Self-Government, 1960–72* (Toronto: University of Toronto Press, 1976), pp. 12–28.

FEDERAL/PROVINCIAL MECHANISMS AND CONFLICT RESOLUTION

The constant interplay of relations has brought into being numerous institutions for coordinating policies and resolving disputes between the federal and provincial governments. As we pointed out in the previous chapter, most fields of public policy are managed by both levels of government and many are jointly financed. Both facts necessitate considerable federal/provincial interaction.

In the early days of Confederation, there was not much need for formal federal/provincial consultation, and what meetings did occur were of an *ad hoc* nature, convened to discuss specific problems. However, increased financial power expanded the fields of influence of both levels of government. (See "Federalism and the Provinces.") Commitment to economic policies aimed at full employment, economic growth and trade liberalization, as well as to a wide range of social policies, resulted in a dramatic increase in intergovernmental relations. Effective intergovernmental consultation thus became a basic requirement for the maintenance of Canadian federalism. This development is perhaps best indicated by the widespread establishment of departments or offices whose sole purpose is dealing with federal/provincial issues.

Intergovernmental relations immediately after the Second World War were characterized by constant, reasonably harmonious exchanges of ideas, financial decisions and policies. This period has been labelled one of **cooperative federalism**, albeit with a decided federal predominance. Economic times were good as a result of the postwar boom, and federal/provincial relations were primarily concerned with social programs that did not necessarily involve regional conflict.[18] As a rule, bureaucrats from both levels of government dominated intergovernmental relations, often resolving problems before they reached the political agenda.

The 1960s and 1970s, however, were characterized by less cooperation and more confrontation. Economic downturns and the ascendancy of provincialism (concern for the jurisdictional integrity of the provinces) changed the conduct of relations between levels of government. The term coined to describe this new relationship was **executive federalism**.

The clearest sign of the change from cooperative to executive federalism was the shift of intergovernmental talks from among public servants behind closed doors to among politicians, often in the full glare of publicity. The most public institution in intergovernmental relations today is the **First Ministers Conference**, at which the leaders of the 11 governments meet to hammer out deals, in recent years under the scrutiny of television cameras.

Some of the most important of these meetings lately have been named **Constitutional Conferences**. In recent years, the necessity to hold First Ministers Conferences has even found a place in the Constitution itself. For example, the 1982 constitutional amendment required two substantive meetings of the leaders to deal explicitly with the rights of Canada's aboriginal peoples. And, if the Meech Lake accord had been ratified (see Chapter 5), two annual meetings would have been forced upon the First Ministers thereafter.

Such "constitutionalizing" of these meetings could prove excessive. Compulsory meetings concerning the Constitution would draw the premiers away from dealing with their own provinces and politicize jurisdictional issues on an annual basis. Garth Stevenson is even more critical:

---

18. Timothy B. Woolstencroft, *Organizing Intergovernmental Relations*, Institute Discussion Paper No. 12 (Kingston: Institute of Intergovernmental Relations, 1982), p. 12.

CLOSE-UP ON
Institutions

FEDERALISM AND THE PROVINCES

The devolution of power and authority is a controversial topic at the provincial level as well as the federal level of Canadian politics. At the beginning of the new millennium, both Alberta and Ontario have Conservative governments with right-wing agendas. However, their strategies for deficit reduction differ considerably. Premier Ralph Klein of Alberta has taken the view that most departmental budgets should be downsized in order to reduce the overall size and expense of government. Premier Mike Harris of Ontario has decided that the downsizing of public expenditures should be accompanied by a massive overhaul of the structure of the relations between the provincial and municipal governments. Recall from Chapter 5 that municipalities and education come under provincial jurisdiction under section 92 of the Constitution. For this reason, Mr. Harris was able to transfer responsibilities from Queen's Park to the municipal governments and vice versa. In 1997, among other changes, his government centralized authority over 100 of the 166 school boards and usurped local government responsibility for primary and secondary education. On the other hand, the provincial government has downloaded most responsibility for welfare, social housing, child care, public transit, highways, ambulances and much of health care to regions and municipalities. In the future, these services will be paid for out of local revenues — such as property and commercial taxes.

Should the federal government have intervened to prevent these provincial actions? *Could* they have acted?

[T]he conferences on the economy serve no useful purpose, provide premiers with a platform for irresponsible and partisan criticism of the federal government's policies, and negate the principle that each government is responsible for its own field of jurisdiction.[19]

While Ottawa may have thought that it could placate opposition through such conferences, some have argued that the meetings only provide an instrument for the expression of provincial discontent and resistance.[20] Certainly, the conferences have increasingly become political forums in which each premier appeals not to the other heads of government, but directly to his or her own electorate. Richard Simeon has argued that intergovernmental bargaining has become more like the *diplomatic* relations *between* states than the usual politics *within* a single state.[21] Responsible only to the people who elect them, provincial leaders today are well organized and prepared to take on the federal government through their counter-proposals and independent programs. Moreover, a new practice has developed: the 10 provincial premiers have tended to meet in advance of First Ministers Conferences and approach the final bargaining table as a unified group opposed to the federal government. Ottawa is no longer able to overwhelm its partners in the federation.

There is little question that the era of executive federalism has been one of decentralization characterized by intergovernmental conflict. D.V. Smiley, for example, argues that the rise of intergovernmental specialists has made federal/provincial conflicts more intractable, perhaps to the point of being irreconcilable.[22] Representatives of each level of government, jealous of their position, promote their own narrow interests, thereby impeding compromise.

Yet this argument confuses the process of intergovernmental relations with the causes of conflict. Intergovernmental specialists have also facilitated cooperation and compromise between governments. As Simeon points out, intergovernmental interactions promote consultation between governments and thus contribute to the effectiveness and harmony of intergovernmental cooperation.[23] Intergovernmental specialists are more a consequence of the need for consultation than

19. Stevenson, *Unfulfilled Union*, p. 264.

20. Don Stevenson, "The Role of Intergovernmental Conferences in the Decision-Making Process," in Richard Simeon, ed., *Confrontation and Collaboration — Intergovernmental Relations in Canada Today* (Toronto: Institute of Public Administration of Canada, 1979), p. 94.

21. Richard Simeon, *Federal-Provincial Diplomacy: The Making of Recent Policy in Canada* (Toronto: University of Toronto Press, 1972).

22. D.V. Smiley, "An Outsider's Observations of Federal-Provincial Relations among Consenting Adults," in Simeon, ed., *Confrontation and Collaboration*, pp. 109–11.

23. Simeon, *Federal-Provincial Diplomacy*, passim.

a source of conflict. As well, the concern for jurisdictional integrity has not displaced the ability of government officials to resolve conflicts as, for instance, in the oil-pricing agreements of 1973–74, the Alberta/Ottawa energy agreement of 1979, the constitutional accord of 1982, the Meech Lake accord of 1987 and the Charlottetown agreement of 1992. Intergovernmental interaction provides a means of communications between governments, encouraging an awareness of the views of their respective Cabinets and bureaucracies — a necessary precondition to achieving compromise.

Thus, while federal/provincial relations are often characterized by disagreement, the mechanisms of conflict resolution are important for the functioning of federalism. The ability of the Canadian federation to cope with the fundamental divergences of interest that animate federal/provincial conflict is based largely on the continued effectiveness of these mechanisms.

The constitutional details described in Chapter 5 and this general review of the evolution of federalism reveal the basic patterns of political interaction. Figure 6.2 on page 203 portrays the pendulum swings that we have been describing, and illustrates some developments in federal/provincial interaction. While some specific dates are given, in reality changes of this nature take place very gradually, and we have simply used some specific event or individual as marking a turning point when, in fact, the transformation may have been building for some time.

Despite the imprecision with respect to time in Figure 6.2, it is important that federalism be perceived as something other than a static phenomenon. Of utmost concern today is the fact that the pendulum has been moving toward decentralization with such swiftness that it has threatened to overwhelm the Canadian federal system. While change is to be expected as the normal course of events in any federation, such pressures now threaten Canadian unity with a new intensity. With the first election of the Parti Québécois as the government of Québec in 1976, Canada entered a new period of **contested federalism**.

CONTESTED FEDERALISM AND DECENTRALIZATION

The evolution of Canadian federalism has led to considerable entanglement between federal and provincial programs. Besides the obvious overlap due to concurrent provincial and federal responsibilities in agriculture and immigration, there are departments of health, the environment, natural resources, fisheries and transport at both levels of government. According to Stéphane Dion, Minister of Intergovernmental Affairs, there are 457 bilateral and multilateral programs or agreements between Ottawa and the provinces.[24] The overall result of this evolution in duplication is that 66 percent of federal programs at least partially overlap those of the provinces according to a 1991 study by the Treasury Board Secretariat.

Despite this situation, however, Canada has not been evolving toward a centralized federation as claimed by some critics of Ottawa. Canada remains one of the most decentralized federations in the world. The trend, if any, has been toward *more* decentralization. The provinces have *increased* their power in recent decades. There are numerous examples. In the 1950s, the federal government collected almost three times as much tax revenue as the provinces. Today it collects only slightly more than the provinces. The number of federal employees as a ratio of the country's labour force has actually dropped by almost half since the early 1950s.

---

24. Stéphane Dion, Speech to APEX, April 29, 1996.

Notwithstanding these evident trends, the 1993 federal Liberal government accepted the argument for more decentralization. Pummelled by separatist forces from Québec, neo-conservative decentralizers in some provincial capitals and the Reform party, Jean Chrétien's Liberals began dismantling some federal programs. They withdrew from certain areas of provincial jurisdiction, including labour market training, social housing, mining, forestry and recreation. They reduced the payments for health and social programming and at the same time set up a new fiscal structure for transferring money to the provinces — called the *Canada Health and Social Transfer* (see below).

Yet these manoeuvres do not satisfy the advocates of radical decentralization. The Québec *separatists* want the complete dismantlement of Canada. Québec *federalists* want massive decentralization of practically all federal jurisdictions. Even premiers such as Mike Harris for Ontario and Ralph Klein for Alberta talk about the need to give the provinces more powers. Following the lead of some economists in August 1996, the Conservative Ontario government called for stripping the federal government of control over medicare and the Alberta government advocated provincially determined guidelines to replace "national" standards in health care.

Federation in Canada has reached a new stage at which the balance required between solidarity and autonomy of the union is in danger. Between the "sirens for separation" and the "foghorns for enhanced provincial powers" there are few who stand up for the tremendous benefits of Canada's federal system of government. The regionally fragmented results of the 1997 election exacerbated the problem. (See Chapter 7.)

FINANCING FEDERALISM

Since Confederation, money and ways of obtaining and spending it have been crucial aspects of federal/provincial interaction in Canada. While some conflicts revolve around highly symbolic issues such as nationalism, others are overtly mundane — one of them is the central issue of money.

Four general economic problems lie at the root of federal/provincial financial arguments; all four are interwoven with political sensitivities and historical exigencies.[25] In this section we examine these problems, tracing the conflict they have engendered from 1867 to the current era.

The first and most obvious problem of federal/provincial financial relations is that there has always been a *fundamental incongruence* between jurisdictional responsibilities and sources of revenue at the two levels of government. As noted above, at the birth of the union, the central government acquired the most significant revenue sources and agreed to pay some limited subsidies and annual grants to support the obligations of the provinces. The intention was to create a highly centralized federal system. The Constitution entitled the federal government to raise money "by any mode or system of taxation" (*BNA Act*, 91.3), while the provinces were limited to direct taxation (*BNA Act*, 92.2). As provincial expenditure grew rapidly, the provinces found it necessary to acquire more revenues. This became a constant source of tension and political conflict.

The second problem can be traced to the fact that the provinces have differed widely in their fiscal capacities. In the early years, a relatively prosperous province such as Ontario or even Québec was fortunate in having a strong tax base in the form of a concentration of corporate activities and personal fortunes, and, therefore, had the ability to raise adequate funds to provide social services. Poorer and relatively depressed provinces such as those in the Maritimes were plagued with an

---

25. J.C. Strick, *Canadian Public Finance*, 2nd ed. (Toronto: Holt, Rinehart and Winston, 1978), pp. 100–1.

inability to obtain sufficient tax revenue; increasing the rate of provincial taxation would only lower individual incomes and undermine economic growth. While in every federation some regions are better off than others, in Canada the discrepancies have been extraordinarily sharp. Over time, the ability to obtain high tax revenues has shifted from province to province — for example, from Ontario to Alberta during the period of high energy prices. But the problem of lower revenues persists for the poorer provinces.

The third problem has resulted from the joint occupancy of tax fields. As mentioned above, the *Constitution Act, 1867,* gave the provinces control only over *direct taxation,* while the federal government was granted a blanket authorization to tax in *any* manner. **Direct taxation** refers to individual income tax, corporate income tax and succession duties, among others. The federal government could levy **indirect taxation** through customs and excise duties, but could also institute its own direct taxation in competition with the provinces. Moreover, the provinces eventually managed to obtain the right to collect indirect taxes as well. Thereafter, both the provinces and the federal government began to levy taxes on the same sources. The competition for revenue sources became one of the most contentious aspects of federal/provincial fiscal relations.

The fourth problem relates to the implementation of fiscal policy. In an age of modern economics, with its long-term budgetary manipulation of the economy, the possibility exists that without close cooperation between federal and provincial taxation and spending policies, the overall economy will not be effectively controlled. If, for example, the federal government were seeking to cut taxes to stimulate the economy, while at the same time the provinces were deciding to increase taxation, the impact of the federal initiative would be negated. Without a degree of cooperation there is a significant danger that federal and provincial policies could work at cross-purposes. Today a degree of coordination and consultation between the federal government and the provinces exists, but certainly not all difficulties of this type have been resolved. (See "Québec's Objection to Ottawa's Spending Power.")

Bearing in mind these four problems, we next survey the historical evolution of federal/provincial financial relations in Canada.

A Brief History of Fiscal Federalism

In 1867, the federal government took over existing provincial debts and agreed to pay *per capita* subsidies and annual grants to the provinces to support their activities.[26] However, the provinces did not acquire enough revenue from direct taxation to cover their rapidly escalating

CLOSE-UP ON Institutions

QUÉBEC'S OBJECTION TO OTTAWA'S SPENDING POWER

Institutions

An incident in late 1997 illustrates the ongoing battle between the federal and provincial governments over who should spend taxpayers' money.

Québec insists on protecting education and health as areas of exclusive provincial jurisdiction, as defined in the Constitution. The federal government, however, wants to finance projects it feels are of high priority for the country as a whole. It wants to ensure that all Canadians share funds set aside for items such as research and development, even though they might concern the fields of health and education, which are provincial jurisdictions.

In the February 1997 budget, the federal government announced that it would set up the "Innovation Foundation." This new foundation would give out $8 million to be invested in the research of hospitals, universities and colleges in order to help stem the brain drain of highly qualified researchers to the United States. Québec officials announced that if any universities and hospitals in Québec accepted money from the Innovation Foundation, the Quebec government would simply subtract the same amount of money from what the province would otherwise have given them.

Was Québec's stand legitimate? Was it wise politically?

---

26. Almost from the beginning, however, the provinces were hard pressed for revenue sources. See A. Milton Moore, J. Harvey Perry and Donald I. Beach, *The Financing of Canadian Federation: The First Hundred Years* (Toronto: Canadian Tax Foundation, April 1966), pp. 3–4.

obligations. The federal subsidies promised in 1867 were helpful, but never sufficed to meet the growing need. Federal subsidies continued to decline as a proportion of provincial revenue — from 58 percent in 1874 to 8 percent in 1929. As well, as time went on, economic disparities between the provinces widened.

The First World War period was characterized by strong economic regulation by Ottawa. Increased military expenditures required the imposition of additional taxes to cover the federal debt, which exceeded $2 billion at the end of the war. The federal government also soon took up direct taxation in the form of personal and corporate income taxes to meet its own obligations.[27]

As we have seen, the early twentieth century saw an important development in federal/provincial fiscal relations: the use of *conditional grants* — sometimes called grants-in-aid or shared-cost grants. The federal government was willing to provide funds to the provinces for specific programs on condition that the money was spent in accordance with federal standards. These grants closed the provincial budgetary gap somewhat but did little to redress the fundamental problem of unequal fiscal capacity. The money was typically offered on a "take it or leave it" basis and, while tempting for most provinces, it could be disruptive of budgetary planning and priorities. Perhaps more significantly, the provinces grew increasingly annoyed at the paternalistic way in which the grants were set up and administered.

Before 1930, then, the provinces were already straining under various new obligations. The Great Depression had a devastating impact on their fragile finances. Their tax base was eroded, yet the demand for services, especially in the welfare field, had increased dramatically. Federal conditional grants were stepped up but were not sufficient and led to a certain amount of heavy-handed federal intervention. The 1930s became known as the "decade of the tax jungle." Uncoordinated joint occupancy of tax fields, duplication of administrative bureaucracy and high regressive taxation (sales taxes) all served to exacerbate the effects of the Depression. While other countries were able to launch coordinated assaults on economic stagnation, Canada was caught in a serious bind. The Depression revealed that the division of federal/provincial fiscal jurisdictions was inadequate for the twentieth century; some major restructuring would be necessary if the country were to survive as a coherent federal system.

As noted earlier, the Royal Commission on Dominion-Provincial Relations (the Rowell-Sirois Commission) was established in 1937 to study the issue. Experts were given a sweeping mandate to examine the problems of the federal system and to offer recommendations that would bring about a degree of congruence between obligations and revenue sources. When the Commission presented its recommendations in 1940, it suggested that the federal government assume responsibility for personal and corporate income tax collection, the accumulated debt of the provinces and the support of the unemployed through a social security program.[28] In addition, the Commission recommended a system of national adjustment grants to subsidize the poorer provinces so that the level of social services could be standardized across the country. The latter proposal ran into immediate opposition, especially from wealthier provinces that did not wish to support their poorer compatriots. The outbreak of the Second World War diverted everyone's attention from the issue. Finally, as R.M. Burns concluded, "[p]atriotism accomplished what financial reasoning could not."[29]

27. Strick, *Canadian Public Finance*, p. 102.
28. Moore, Perry and Beach, *The Financing of Canadian Federation*, pp. 11–13.
29. R.M. Burns, "Recent Developments in Federal-Provincial Fiscal Relations in Canada," *National Tax Journal*, vol. 15, no. 3 (September 1962), p. 228.

The wartime period of relative economic prosperity eased the burden of the provinces. Citing the emergency, the federal government usurped the income tax and succession duty fields for itself. In return, the provinces were given compensatory payments. Thus began a complicated series of tax-rental and tax-sharing agreements.[30] The federal government took over, in effect, virtually all provincial sources of revenue from direct taxation in exchange for a payment of "rent." It is clear from this why the federal government in the war years and in the postwar decade was in a position of considerable dominance over the provinces.

By the end of the Second World War, the federal government was spending approximately three-quarters of the money spent by all governments in Canada. It had built up an impressive bureaucratic infrastructure and was intent on implementing its vision of Canada's future. As the war emergency ended, Ottawa began to assume responsibility for the problems of postwar reconstruction. At this time, a new attitude toward the role of government in society also arose. The concept of the balanced budget was replaced by Keynesian economic theory: the federal government committed itself to maintaining a high and stable level of economic growth and employment throughout the country. To do so, it had to adjust federal tax rates and levels of expenditure. It was able to obtain provincial agreement for an extension of the tax-rental arrangement until at least 1952.[31] The pre-eminence of the federal government did not begin to erode until the end of the 1950s, as the various tax-rental agreements between it and the provinces began to engender opposition. Québec, for its part, began to resent both this arrangement and the conditional grants scheme.

As the 1960s approached, the lack of correlation between revenue sources and expenditure responsibilities was accentuated. The welfare state entered the "big money" era. The provinces again began to feel the financial pinch for education and health care, while the federal government was virtually left out of these important jurisdictional areas. Increased provincial responsibilities were matched by the increasing competence and aggressiveness of provincial bureaucrats. The federal government seemed to be losing its grip on the economy as the country experienced a recession and slow economic growth. Sensing weakness, the provinces began to claim more responsibility for their own economies and questioned the feasibility of a national economic policy.

The most obvious indication of provincial self-assertion was in the area of tax-sharing. Tax-sharing was a continuation of the tax-rental program; however, instead of *per capita* grants, the provinces were to get a fixed percentage of three standard taxes: personal income taxes, corporate tax and federal succession duties. Tax-sharing protected provincial autonomy to some extent and was supplemented by an unconditional grant. Despite this apparent liberalization of federal policy, Ontario and Québec objected to the arrangement, and the federal government introduced a tax-abatement system for the two provinces. This meant that the federal government moved out of the tax field to a considerable degree so that the provinces could levy their own taxes. This agreement encouraged agitation by all the provinces for a better deal.

During the 1960s, the abatement system was gradually extended to all provinces. Ottawa thus partially withdrew from the personal and corporate income tax field. Although the federal government continued to collect the tax (and return part of it to the provinces), as long as the provincial tax base remained the same as the federal tax base, the provinces had more room for increasing their taxes. In other words, the provincial portion could vary considerably. In 1966, the tax arrangements were opened up for periodic review, with the provinces asking for even more tax room and more federal money. At that time Ottawa was in no mood to compromise and the arrangement

---

30. See Stevenson, *Unfulfilled Union*, pp. 136–41; and Strick, *Canadian Public Finance*, pp. 106–12.
31. Strick, *Canadian Public Finance*, p. 107.

".. MY NAME IS BOB, AND I'M AN ASYMMETRICAL FEDERALIST.."

Reproduced with permission, Gable, *The Globe and Mail.*

was extended virtually unchanged. By 1972, however, the abatement system was practically at an end. The federal government introduced a guarantee program to prevent provincial loss of revenues resulting from a rationalization of their tax base with that of the federal government.

Today, Ottawa still collects income taxes (at rates set by the provinces) for all the provinces except Québec. With the exception of Ontario, Québec and Alberta, all provinces have tax-collection arrangements with the federal government for corporate income taxes.

Basic Concepts of Fiscal Federalism

Arrangements for the transfer of funds from the federal government to the provinces have evolved over the years from relatively simple grants to complex financial arrangements. To understand these arrangements, it is necessary to understand some basic concepts, including conditional grants, unconditional grants and the spending power.

Conditional Grants, Unconditional Grants and the Spending Power

As we have said, **conditional grants** are funds given by the federal government to provincial governments on the condition that they be spent in a certain way. In Canada, such grants have been considered essential because of the unequal distribution of resources across the country. The first conditional grants in Canada were paid out for agricultural instruction in 1912. Larger-scale grants were offered in 1927 to help the provinces finance old-age pensions. These grants also helped to alleviate the financial problems of the 1930s. After the Second World War, increased spending on health and welfare necessitated another major expansion in the field of conditional grants.

The federal government was able to act in these fields, which are under provincial jurisdiction, because of its spending power. **Spending power** refers to the federal government's blanket authority to spend money for any purpose in any field, even if it has no legal jurisdiction over the area. In most conditional grants programs, Ottawa offered to pay half the costs of a specific program, with the provinces paying the rest. These were shared-cost programs, or so-called "50-cent dollar" programs, in which Ottawa paid 50 percent of costs. They were an attractive proposition for some provinces; they encouraged provincial legislatures to spend their resources on programs chosen by the federal government. Provincial leaders might sometimes have preferred to spend the money on other programs, but there was no way to shift the conditional resources unless Ottawa agreed.

In 1964, as a result of criticism of these programs, the federal government began to allow any province that did not want to be involved in a joint-cost venture to receive an equivalent sum of money, either by way of a federal tax withdrawal or in another form. Only Québec took Ottawa up on this offer, highlighting its claim to "special status" within Confederation. Québec's "different" status was also confirmed by the development of its own hospital and old-age pension schemes.

As the financial health of the provinces improved, it was inevitable that they would seek a revision of these fiscal arrangements. In 1977, led by Québec, and to some extent Alberta and Ontario, the provinces won the struggle to end the restrictive conditional grants system. Ottawa increasingly offered **unconditional grants** — money that the provinces could spend in any way they wished since the money was not designated for any specific policy field. This shift from conditional to unconditional grants can be considered an example of the decentralization of the federal system during the period.

Figure 6.3 highlights the correlation between conditional and unconditional grants, and constitutional centralization and decentralization.

FIGURE 6.3   DEGREE OF CENTRALIZATION AS AFFECTED BY THE FEDERAL/PROVINCIAL FINANCIAL TRANSFERS AND THE DISTRIBUTION OF POWER

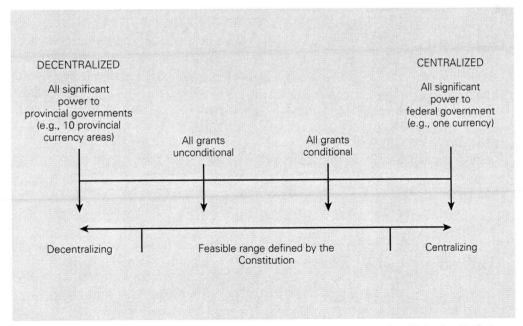

Source: Adapted from Thomas J. Courchene, "The New Fiscal Arrangements and the Economics of Federalism," in *Options*, Proceedings of the Conference on the Future of the Canadian Federation (Toronto: University of Toronto Press, 1977), p. 315.

Key Mechanisms

Over the years, various mechanisms have been put in place to implement conditional and unconditional grants. They include equalization grants and established program funding.

Equalization Grants

We have seen how the differing fiscal capacities of the provinces have posed a continuing problem in federal/provincial relations since Confederation. In 1867, the financial gap between the provinces was already wide; it has been growing ever since. A primary objective of fiscal policy since the Second World War has been to narrow this gap and to provide a degree of economic stability. The main mechanism for accomplishing this has been, and continues to be, the provision of equalization payments to the provinces. **Equalization payments** are unconditional transfer payments to the provinces from the federal government calculated according to the ability of each province to raise revenue. The payments enable less affluent provinces to provide an average level of public services to their residents without resorting to excessive levels of taxation. Since 1957, they have been calculated to bring provinces up to a national average based on a number of provincial revenue sources. The details of equalization programs are renegotiated every five years.

The ultimate objective of equalization policy is to establish a national standard for social services and strengthen federalism by meeting the needs of the less affluent elements in the union. However, the federal government has not been able to convey much sense of urgency to this endeavour. In terms of *per capita* provincial government expenditures, equalization payments have proven successful, but they have not brought the seven "have not" provinces up to the level of the three "have" provinces. The provinces may be relatively equal in terms of providing government services, but interprovincial and interregional disparities remain, despite the presence of equalization payments.

Apart from the equalization program, federal transfers to all but the two poorest provinces are basically paid by taxpayers to the province in which they reside. They do not distribute income across provincial borders. The equalization program is, therefore, vital to achieve "horizontal equity" (the reduction of disparities between provinces in the treatment of persons in similar economic circumstances) as well as "vertical equity" (the reduction of inequalities in real income among individuals). It is not surprising, then, that the concept of equalization was enshrined in the Canadian Constitution of 1982 with the unanimous consent of all governments. Even recent budgets that include proposals to decrease other federal transfers to the provinces continue the commitment of equalization.

Established Program Financing

Conditional grants, like equalization grants, have changed over time. The first significant, comprehensive innovation came in 1977. In that year, the federal program offered the provinces a hybrid **block grant** (a grant of one large sum of money from Ottawa to the provinces to be spent in certain policy fields) earmarked for health and postsecondary education.[32] This block grant program, called **Established Program Financing** (EPF), had both a conditional and an unconditional aspect. The federal monies had to be spent in the general fields of health and education as outlined, but within these broad parameters the provinces were largely free to make their own policy choices.

For the years 1977 to 1982, EPF provided two types of funding for provincial expenditures on health care and postsecondary education — a tax transfer of personal and corporate income tax

---

32. David B. Perry, "The Federal-Provincial Fiscal Arrangement Introduced in 1977," *Canadian Tax Journal*, vol. 25., no. 4 (July/August, 1977), pp. 429–40.

points and a cash transfer.[33] While the federal government interpreted EPF as giving autonomy to the provinces, the legislation also placed some of the most expensive areas of social services squarely in the laps of the provincial governments. From the provinces' point of view, the federal government, which got them into these expensive fields in the first place, simply wished to prepare to disengage itself when costs began to rise.

In spite of the move to block funding in the EPF, the federal government was able to determine how some of the funds were used. In 1984, for example, the federal *Canada Health Act* declared that the health transfer would be reduced for any province that allowed doctors to extra bill or employ user fees.

After the major changes in 1977, the next round of negotiations over the renewal of federal/provincial fiscal arrangements came in 1982. The atmosphere of the negotiations was strained. The federal government sought to correct what it perceived as two fundamental problems.[34] First, there was a growing fiscal imbalance between the federal and provincial governments. While the federal government's deficit was increasing, there was an overall surplus in provincial revenues. Second, the federal government wanted to maintain what it called a proper "political balance." Ottawa argued that its contributions to provincial government services were not sufficiently visible and that this both hindered proper government accountability for taxes and expenditures, and deprived the federal government of recognition for the assistance it did provide. Thus, the federal government sought to cut back the level of transfers to the provinces.

The provinces, on the other hand, generally favoured maintenance of the *status quo*. They argued that the federal deficit was not due to federal transfers to the provinces, but rather to federal policies of indexation, tax expenditures, the subsidization of oil and gas prices, and interest rate policies. The provinces also noted that the overall provincial revenue surplus was the result of the resource wealth of a few provinces and did not reflect the overall fiscal capacity of all the provinces. The Parliamentary Task Force on Federal-Provincial Fiscal Arrangements agreed, stating that

> the mere existence of deficits at one level of government does not indicate the existence of [such] a structural imbalance nor does it mean that such deficits have to be rectified at the expense of another level of government.[35]

The "have not" provinces were especially concerned with the future of the equalization program. The wealthier provinces, for their part, sought to protect the money they already received from the EPF block grants.

Fiscal Arrangements in Flux

In spite of opposition, Ottawa remained determined to reduce its transfers to the provinces. In 1982, after months of inconclusive bargaining, the federal government enacted a new set of fiscal arrangements. The EPF formula was amended so that the provincial entitlement was determined for

---

33. Tax points or tax transfers consist of a reduction in federal taxes and an equivalent increase in provincial taxes.
34. Allan J. MacEachen, Deputy Prime Minister and Minister of Finance, *Federal-Provincial Fiscal Arrangements in the Eighties: A Submission to the Parliamentary Task Force on the Federal-Provincial Fiscal Arrangements* (Ottawa: Supply and Services, April 23, 1981), pp. 8–11.
35. *Fiscal Federalism in Canada*, Report of the Parliamentary Task Force on Federal-Provincial Fiscal Arrangements (Ottawa: Supply and Services, August 1981), p. 33.

a base year with escalation indicators applied for economic and population growth. From this aggregate number, the federal government subtracted the amount of revenue generated by the tax points given to the provinces and then paid out the remainder as a cash grant. In the succeeding years, the federal government reduced the escalation factor and thus limited the total EPF entitlement of the provinces. This action had the effect of transferring an increasing share of the burden of these programs to the provinces. As Allan M. Maslove summarized the situation:

> *Given that the tax points transfer continues to generate more revenue from year to year, the residual cash transfer is diminishing and is projected to approach zero in the not too distant future.*[36]

In 1982, changes were also made in the calculation of equalization payments. The federal government proposed Ontario as the standard for determining eligibility for equalization payments, thereby ensuring the province's continued exclusion from receiving such grants. However, the poorer provinces (and Ontario) objected to having their level of receipts contingent upon Ontario's economic performance, especially in light of that province's economic stagnation during those years. Ottawa therefore dropped the so-called "Ontario standard," replacing it with a formula based on the average revenue of five provinces.

For the 1988–93 period, transfers from the federal to the provincial and territorial governments remained mostly in Established Program Financing, the equalization program and the **Canada Assistance Program (CAP)**, a program by which the federal government finances welfare and other

TABLE 6.1   BASIC FEDERAL/PROVINCIAL FINANCING IN CANADA, 2000

Grants	Unconditional	Conditional	Conditional block	New, larger block (beginning 1996–97)
Programs	Equalization	Canada Assistance Plan (CAP)	Established Program Funding (EPF)	Canada Health and Social Transfer (CHST)
		(Welfare funding)	(Money given in a lump sum for health and education but with some considerations, plus some specific acts)	(Includes funding for education, health and welfare that was covered in CAP and EPF)
Funding Mechanisms	Based on revenue sources	Proportion of actual expenditures	Combination of cash and tax point room — but over time decreasing the cash component	Combination of cash and tax point room — but over time decreasing the cash component

36. Allan M. Maslove, "Reconstructing Federal Fiscalism," in Frances Abele, *How Ottawa Spends, 1992–83* (Ottawa: Carleton University Press, 1992), pp. 57–77.

provincial social services. The CAP was a shared-cost program established in 1966. Under its terms, the federal government paid 50 percent of provincial and municipal programs in welfare, day care, child welfare services and homemakers assistance. The only restriction on federal funding for the CAP was that the provincial social assistance programs had to be based on "need." Programs could vary widely across the country.

The New System during Contested Federalism — Post-1996

In 1995, federal finance minister Paul Martin announced that a major shift in the block funding of provincial transfers would take effect in 1996–97. The Established Program Financing and the Canada Assistance Program would be folded into a new block grant system called the **Canada Health and Social Transfer** (**CHST**). The new CHST was defended by the federal Liberals on the ground that it would simultaneously eliminate federal authority over provincial spending and reduce overall costs. However, at the same time, the federal government maintained that it would continue to apply both its laws in the *Canada Health Act* and the CAP rules concerning residency requirements.

This new federal approach reduced the total federal funds for social programs by some $7 billion. This reduction was approved by those who advocate more decentralization and disapproved by those who fear it will lead to a reduction in national standards in the fields of health, education and welfare. However, as soon as the federal deficit reached zero in 1997, the Finance Minister announced that he would put a floor on CHST transfer reductions. While the premiers applauded the Minister for this decision, they asked for even more money from the federal coffers. Ottawa said that it would find more money if there could be a deal on such topics as internal trade and mobility for all Canadians along with a new agreement on the Canadian social union.

The result was another compromise. The agreement, *A Framework to Improve the Social Union for Canadians*, was accepted by nine premiers and the federal government on February 4, 1999. Only Québec declined to sign it. Under the agreement, Ottawa agreed to collaborate with the provinces over any future Canada-wide initiatives in fields such as health care, postsecondary education and social assistance. Ottawa also agreed to provide one year's notice of any future funding changes, and promised to consult the provinces on any direct payments to individuals. Most important, once Ottawa and any six provinces agree on objectives, new programs in fields such as home-care or pharmacare can be set up by the federal government as long as each province can work out the details of its own program. If a province already has a program in place that meets the objectives of the policy, it will still receive the federal funds. In other words, the federal government has, in effect, allowed provincial constraints on its spending power and in return received provincial acceptance for its willingness to compromise and undertake consultation.

CLOSE-UP ON Institutions

FUNDING FOR COLLEGES AND UNIVERSITIES

Because education is a provincial responsibility, the federal role has simply been to provide transfers to the provinces. At first, payments were earmarked directly for postsecondary education, but later the funds came with no strings attached. That meant Ottawa spent billions on postsecondary education but got little credit and no influence on policy, except through the Canada Student Loans Program.

Today, the CHST does not even specifically mention the words "postsecondary education." But that does not mean the federal government has abandoned the field to the provinces. Ottawa continues to fund university education through the general granting of funds in the CHST, and has also decided to give more money directly to students. Ottawa has also set up a Millennium Scholarship Fund of up to $3 billion, with money going to students on the basis of both merit and need.

Is this use of federal money in postsecondary education justified, or should it be left to the provinces to decide how to allocate funds in this area? What kind of transfer of money to students would you and your fellow students prefer?

This agreement was applauded by Saskatchewan premier Roy Romanow as "80 per cent of the solution to Canadian unity" and by Ontario premier Mike Harris as capping a "tremendous day."[37] But Québec premier Lucien Bouchard would not sign the agreement under which, he claimed, "six provinces and the federal government could trigger a new program, define national objectives, devise a framework for accountability, and then Québec, to get compensation for its part of the program, would have to abide by the national objectives."[38] Premier Bouchard asked that Québec be compensated without having to give any commitment to national objectives. It was classic Canadian federalism.

Finance Minister Paul Martin summarized the government's position as: "Provinces will now be able to design more innovative social programs that respond to the needs of people today rather than to inflexible rules. However, flexibility does not mean a free-for-all."[39] Despite this justification, however, there is little doubt that the Liberal government had decided to loosen its control over provincial financing in order to reduce the pressure on its meagre finances while also placating nationalist tendencies in the province of Québec. (See Figure 6.4.) In light of the massive debt and the continuing separatist challenge in Québec, the Liberal government decided to decentralize the country to the degree possible without amending the Constitution: one major step was to change the method of distributing federal transfers to the provinces.

FIGURE 6.4   BASIC FEDERAL FINANCING FOR "RICHER" AND "POORER" PROVINCES BEFORE 1996 AND TODAY

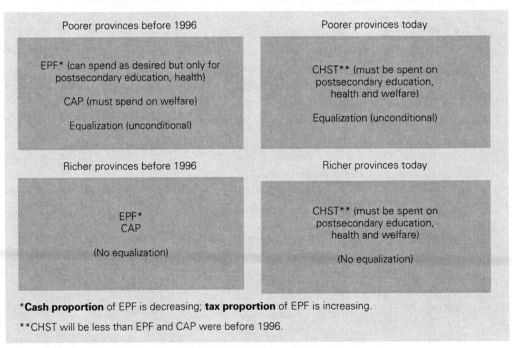

Poorer provinces before 1996

EPF* (can spend as desired but only for postsecondary education, health)

CAP (must spend on welfare)

Equalization (unconditional)

Poorer provinces today

CHST** (must be spent on postsecondary education, health and welfare)

Equalization (unconditional)

Richer provinces before 1996

EPF*
CAP

(No equalization)

Richer provinces today

CHST** (must be spent on postsecondary education, health and welfare)

(No equalization)

*__Cash proportion__ of EPF is decreasing; __tax proportion__ of EPF is increasing.

**CHST will be less than EPF and CAP were before 1996.

37. *Maclean's,* February 15, 1999.
38. Ibid.
39. *The Ottawa Citizen,* February 28, 1995.

SUMMARY

This chapter has explored federalism and some of its challenges in Canada. Rather than being an esoteric topic, federalism shapes many of the issues and controversies in contemporary politics. The chapter began with a general definition of federalism and examined some of the motives and justifications offered for the adoption of the federal form. As stressed, there is nothing intrinsically good or bad about this constitutional arrangement. At a minimum, federalism is simply a means of dividing political authority. In practice, however, federalism assumes a number of other meanings and implications that may lead some to believe that it is synonymous with "the nation."

A review of the history of federalism in Canada reveals pendulum swings of centralization and decentralization. Federal/provincial fiscal relations, for example, have been characterized by the waxing and waning of federal dominance. These shifts were due to individual interpretations of the Constitution as well as to the impact of particular individuals and historical events. The best-known Father of Confederation, Sir John A. Macdonald, thought of federalism as a means of subordinating provincial governments in the political system. His has been called a "quasi-federalist" position. Others have interpreted federalism as an agreement or "compact" between the English and French.

Sometimes, federalism has been described as a clear-cut or "classical" division of powers between the federal and provincial governments. However, over time, the original financial and legislative powers have had to be changed on several occasions. Adjustments to economic reality and societal concerns forced the constitutional system to move from a strict separation of powers to a more "cooperative" system. In recent years, some authors have characterized the federal system as one of federal/provincial "diplomacy" rather than "cooperation" to indicate how the process has evolved and how much the provinces have been asserting their power in the state. The First Ministers Conferences, which bring together the prime minister and the 10 premiers, is the most public manifestation of this form of federalism. Also inseparable from modern concepts of federalism have been the proliferation of ministerial conferences, interprovincial coordinating meetings and the development of entire government departments devoted to federal/provincial relations.

At least five models of federalism have been advanced by Canadian scholars. These models, known by the names quasi-federalism, compact, classical, cooperative and diplomatic federalism, may be used to help explain various aspects of federal/provincial relations. While they are often put forward as if they refer to the evolution of federalism, they more adequately depict which relationships between the federal and provincial governments predominate at any one time. Moreover, there are many other ways to define federalism. In fact, since the election of the Parti Québécois to power in Québec, the concept *contested federalism* better describes Canadian reality than these other somewhat dated terms.

In order to understand Canadian federalism, we must also bear in mind how it is buttressed by social and political forces. The federal dimension provides both advantages and disadvantages to Canada. It decentralizes some decision-making and allows a degree of cultural and linguistic autonomy. But it may give too much weight to either the federal or the provincial governments. In the former case, there can easily be an erosion of provincial prerogatives, as when the federal government is required to aid the provinces in new, but essentially localized, matters. On the other hand, too much provincial control may make it difficult to handle country-wide problems.

Despite a few difficult periods, federalism in Canada has proven remarkably resilient and adaptable. A degree of movement along the centralization/decentralization continuum is to be expected and is not in itself a matter for much concern. However, Québec and, to some extent the western provinces, continue for quite different reasons to seek changes in the present relationship. The possibility that Québec may eventually break away from the federal union is not to be discounted. Neither should feelings of alienation in western or Atlantic Canada be dismissed. The problem, as suggested, is not so much with federalism as it is with the deep cleavages and divisions in our society. There is nothing new in regional pressures. Such challenges go back a long way in Canadian history.

In the search for a creative compromise, politicians will have to enunciate and examine Canada's fundamental problems. Any redefinition of federal arrangements must rest between national and provincial aspirations. Reconciliation must be built on a recognition that Canada has two linguistic groups and several cultures that are often in conflict, as well as heterogeneous socioeconomic regions. The first fact demands constitutional and institutional guarantees; the second, a proper division of the public purse and power. While provincial distinctiveness is the fundamental reason for all federal systems, a sense of positive consensus among the different regional groups is also imperative if unity is to persist.

DISCUSSION QUESTIONS

1. Describe the basic federal/provincial distribution of powers in the Constitution and assess how court interpretations of it have changed from Confederation to today in terms of centralization and decentralization.

2. Should the Canadian political system be decentralized further? Why or why not?

3. What are the key mechanisms for redistributing federal tax dollars to the provinces? How were they changed in 1996?

4. Compare the concept of contested federalism to the Liberal party's policy of "rebalancing" the Constitution introduced before the 1997 general election.

5. Has the Liberal government of Jean Chrétien loosened its control over the "spending power" in order to meet the challenge of a massive federal debt? Or to placate Québec separatists?

Selected Bibliography

Bickerton, James, *Nova Scotia, Ottawa and the Politics of Regional Development* (Toronto: University of Toronto Press, 1990).

Doern, G. Bruce and Mark MacDonald, *Free Trade Federalism: Negotiating the Canadian Agreement on Internal Trade* (Toronto: University of Toronto Press, 1999).

"Fiscal Federalism: Debating Canada's Future," *Policy Options* (December 1993) (articles by several authors).

Gillespie, W. Irwin, *Tax, Borrow and Spend: Financing Federal Spending in Canada* (Ottawa: Carleton University Press, 1991).

Howlett, Michael and David Laycock, *The Puzzles of Power* (Mississauga: Copp Clark Pitman, 1994).

Lazar, Harvey, ed., *Canada: The State of the Federation 1997: Non-Constitutional Renewal* (Kingston: Institute of Intergovernmental Relations, 1998).

Rocher, François and Miriam Smith, eds., *New Trends in Canadian Federalism* (Peterborough: Broadview Press, 1994).

Shugarman, David and Reg Whitaker, eds., *Federalism and Political Community* (Peterborough: Broadview Press, 1989).

Simeon, Richard and Ian Robinson, *State, Society and the Development of Canadian Federalism* (Toronto: University of Toronto Press, 1990).

Stevenson, Garth, *Federalism in Canada* (Markham: McClelland & Stewart, 1990).

Vipond, Robert C., *Liberty and Community: Canadian Federalism and the Failure of the Constitution* (Albany: State University of New York Press, 1991).

Young, Robert, *Confederation in Crisis* (Toronto: Lorimer, 1991).

LIST OF WEBLINKS

collections.ic.gc.ca/ discourspm/anglais/ jam/jam.html

Sir John A. Macdonald This Web site contains information about Canada's first prime minister, who was a key designer of the Canadian political system.

www.pco-bcp.gc.ca/aia

Intergovernmental Affairs Conference Secretariat The Intergovernmental Affairs Conference Secretariat is the branch of government that organizes First Ministers Conferences.

www.fin.gc.ca/ fedprove/ftpe.html

Federal Financial Transfers to the Provinces This Web site identifies the amount of money that the federal government annually transfers to the provinces.

7

Nationalism and Regionalism

• • • • • • •

Québec, the West and the Rest

We have seen that questions about the authority and jurisdictions of the federal and provincial governments often give rise to political conflict in Canada. Some of the most divisive of these problems have been over separatism in Québec and regional alienation in other provinces. This chapter is concerned with the background and contemporary significance of both nationalism and regionalism. In particular, it addresses the issue of the separatist movement in the province of Québec, including the 1995 referendum, the Supreme Court judgement on separatism, and the resultant federal and provincial legislation.

The Canadian federal structure has been remarkably resilient in meeting its various challenges since Confederation in 1867. However, during the past three decades, powerful nationalist pressures have created the most serious challenge to the federal political system that Canada has ever endured, threatening to overwhelm the system. Separatists in Québec view federalism as obsolete and incompatible with the aspirations of their society. Their challenge has created a "crisis of Canadian federalism" that could bring about either a truncated Canada or a strengthened federal system. Of course, the ultimate outcome will depend on many factors, including leadership and political circumstances.

NATIONALISM

Nationalism has appeared in diverse forms in many different states over the centuries. It has been used to justify economic expansionism, protectionism and imperialism. As an ideology it has been employed to espouse the supremacy of particular nations or peoples; it has justified quests for emancipation from colonial rule; and it has been an integrative force in newly independent multiracial or tribal societies in the developing world.[1] It has also been savagely attacked at times. Albert Einstein called nationalism "an infantile sickness ... the measles of the human race."[2]

---

1. On the types of nationalism see Anthony D. Smith, *Nationalism in the Twentieth Century* (Oxford: Martin Robertson, 1979). On the "new" nationalism see Michael Ignatieff, *Blood and Belonging: Journeys into the New Nationalism* (Toronto: Viking, 1993).

2. Attributed to Albert Einstein in Martin Levin, "Nationalism: Disease or Plague," *The Globe and Mail*, June 15, 1995.

In many instances, nationalism has been used to integrate the members of an existing state. But nationalism can also be a divisive force. Territorially concentrated ethnic min were previously the subjects of a larger state sometimes seek increased self-determinati total independence. The breakdown of the former Yugoslavia into multiple republics a sequent violent fragmentation of two of them, Bosnia and Kosovo, is just one example

Not all organized ethnic interest groups should be labelled as nationalistic, howeve nic demands, such as those for minority-language education or ethnically oriented television programs, involve no challenge to the integrity of the existing state and may be quite easily accommodated within its confines. Disputes about nationalism abound, largely because of disagreements over definitions and explanations. Some see nationalism as anti-colonialism, and believe it is fundamentally different in established states than it is in developing countries. Others contend that nationalism can appear only in modern, developed political systems and that it is a product of modernity that arrived with the industrial revolution in Europe. Most authors, however, believe nationalism is closely associated with ethnicity. Some even see it as the political manifestation of ethnicity.[3]

In this book, **nationalism** is defined as the collective action of a politically conscious ethnic group (or nation) in pursuit of increased territorial autonomy or sovereignty. Examples of contemporary nationalist movements may be found in many advanced industrial societies: the Scots and Welsh in the United Kingdom; Bretons and Corsicans in France; Flemings and Walloons in Belgium; and, of course, the Québécois in Canada. In each case, the ethnic minorities have reduced any previous commitment they may have had to the larger state and have acted collectively to develop political parties, nationalist and cultural organizations, and sometimes even terrorist groups, in order to pursue fundamental changes in the territorial boundaries and sovereignty of the state.

Since nationalist groups within a state create divisions that may cause instability and even disintegration, governments, to different degrees, actively foster a strong "national identity" at the state level. There are several components of a strong **national identity**:

- emotional attachment to the geographic territory;

- a common past with heroes and myths;

- special kinship through a common language (bilingual or multilingual countries such as Belgium, Canada and Switzerland are rare; most have one official language);

- a unique culture with shared values and a common literature that generate pride in traditions and customs, and create a sense of familiarity and belonging.

Canada, with two official languages and many cultures, promotes national identity with flags, national-day celebrations, television-content rules, prizes for artistic and sports endeavours, and so on. However, it has not been able to foster a Canadian national identity strong enough to subsume and temper the aspirations of Québec nationalists.

Ethnic nationalist groups in Canada, especially in Québec, have pursued varying degrees of autonomy, up to and including proposing independent statehood. In particular, they have utilized the mechanisms of federalism to challenge the federal *status quo*. But provincial power has also been employed to express regional conflicts that lack an ethnic dimension. Throughout Canadian history, therefore, provincial government power has been used to press *both* ethnic nationalist and regionalist demands on Ottawa.

---

3. There are many interpretations of nationalism. See A.D. Smith, *Theories of Nationalism* (Oxford: Oxford University Press, 1994); A.D. Smith, *Ethnicity and Nationalism* (Leiden, the Netherlands: Brill, 1992); the classic by Hans Kohn, *The Idea of Nationalism: A Study of Its Origins and Background* (New York: Macmillan, 1944); and Liah Greenfeld, *Five Roads to Modernity* (Cambridge, Mass.: Harvard University Press, 1992).

*If every ethnic, religious or linguistic group claimed statehood, there would be no limit to frag-
mentation; and peace, security and well-being for all would become even more difficult to
achieve.*

Boutros Boutros-Ghali, former Secretary-General of the United Nations

Roots of Nationalism: Early French–English Conflicts

After the British conquest of New France in 1760, the Roman Catholic Church encouraged its
French-speaking parishioners to remain socially separate from the English, maintaining an essentially agrarian society. French Canadians generally remained aloof from political affairs, and even
after Confederation the English minority within Québec dominated urban, political and economic
life. By then, the French were a minority in Canada. Most francophones were in Québec, but there
were pockets of French-speaking people in what were to become the Maritimes and the West.

French–English conflicts erupted periodically after Confederation, mainly over linguistic and
education rights. One of the first disputes was in Manitoba. With its large French-speaking community, Manitoba was created in 1870 on the same basis as Québec, with rights to Roman Catholic
schools and bilingual education. By 1885, however, French-speaking Métis in the West were being
swamped by English-speaking settlers. To protest land losses, they rallied around Métis leader Louis
Riel, who had returned from exile in the United States to lead a rebellion against the government.

English Canadians saw Riel as a traitor or a madman and sent troops to quell the disturbance.
Riel was defeated and executed. French Canadians grieved for Riel as a patriot who died in the
struggle to preserve the "Frenchness" of his people. The ethnic groups were thus polarized, and
the stage was set for the restriction of French-language rights in Manitoba. Only five years after
the Riel Rebellion, the government of Manitoba established a completely non-sectarian educational system in which Roman Catholic schools no longer received provincial aid, and French could
no longer be used in the secondary schools.

Two decisions of the British Judicial Committee of the Privy Council (JCPC) upheld the validity
of the Manitoba law, but affirmed the power of the federal government to restore school privileges. This unique situation posed a problem for French Canadians inasmuch as it divided them over
whether to support their ethnic group or their church. To have the anti-French legislation removed,
Québeckers would have had to support a "federal disallowance" of provincial legislation, and French
Québec was against the principle of federal veto power.

The faltering federal Conservative government introduced remedial legislation in 1896, but
under pressure it had to be withdrawn. A bizarre general election ensued in which Manitoba francophones supported the Roman Catholic Church and the federal Conservative party in demanding
federal disallowance of the Manitoba law. Québec francophones, on the other hand, supported the
Liberal party, which argued for provincial autonomy and opposed the federal use of the disallowance power. Ironically, the Liberals were also supported by anti-French, anti-Catholic forces. The
Liberals won in 1896, and thus Québec francophones were instrumental in blocking legislation
that would have protected French Canadian interests in Manitoba.

We have seen that the Confederation arrangement allowed all provinces to legislate in the field
of education. It also gave constitutional protection to both the English and French language in the
federal Parliament and the legislature of Québec. In the other provinces, however, there was no
such protection. The practice until the 1940s was for English-speaking Canadians, wherever they were
in the majority, to deprive French-speaking minorities of public school facilities in their native

language, and to refuse them the use of their language in government institutions. Even within the federal government, where the *BNA Act* had affirmed the right of both groups to communicate in their own languages in debates, records, journals and courts, most government employees were unilingual English.

In 1935, French Canadian nationalist and historian Abbé Lionel Groulx published the following historical summary of French-language and school rights (or lack of rights) outside Québec:

1864	NOVA SCOTIA:	French-speaking Catholic Acadians are forbidden to have French schools
1871	NEW BRUNSWICK:	Catholic schools are closed and teaching of French (and in French) is forbidden in public schools
1877	PRINCE EDWARD ISLAND:	Catholic and French schools are outlawed
1890	MANITOBA:	Separate (Catholic) schools are outlawed and teaching of French (and in French) is forbidden at the secondary level
1892	NORTHWEST TERRITORIES (including what is now Alberta and Saskatchewan):	Teaching in French is outlawed in public schools and Catholic schools are prohibited
1905	ALBERTA AND SASKATCHEWAN:	The regulations of 1892 (Northwest Territories) are confirmed
1915	ONTARIO:	By regulation (Regulation No. 17), French is outlawed in Ontario schools
1916	MANITOBA:	Teaching French is forbidden at all levels
1930	SASKATCHEWAN:	Teaching French is prohibited even outside school hours[4]

Abbé Groulx argued that each of these rulings deprived French Canadians of their basic human rights. This succession of ethnic confrontations formed the history of the loss of French rights outside of Québec. The result was eventual abandonment by francophone Québeckers of French Canadians outside their province, and the gradual assertion of Québec nationalism.

Ethnic division appeared in another guise in the conscription crises of both the First and Second World War. The 1917 federal election was fought on the conscription issue. The governing Conservatives united with English-speaking Liberals to run Union candidates in the election. They won, but they captured only three seats in Québec. The election divided the country along ethnic and linguistic lines; every riding in which French was the majority language voted against the Unionist government and its policy of conscription. Fortunately, the war ended before conscription could be enacted and, therefore, the crisis between English and French subsided.

However, the repercussions for the Conservative party, which was the dominant partner in the Unionist government and had argued strongly for conscription, were severe. The impact was evident in the first postwar election, in 1921. The Conservatives lost *all* their Québec seats to the Liberals. Provincially, as well, the Conservatives were severely defeated. Except for the Diefenbaker sweep in 1958, the Conservative party did not regain the confidence of French Canadians until the Mulroney victory of 1984.

---

4. André Bernard, *What Does Quebec Want?* (Toronto: Lorimer, 1978), p. 27, taken from Abbé Lionel Groulx, *L'enseignement français au Canada* (Montréal: Granger Frères, 1935).

In 1942, during the Second World War, the conscription issue arose again and this time the federal government called a *referendum* to settle it. The campaign was bitter. French-speaking Québec voted against conscription by a huge majority, while English-speaking Canada was overwhelmingly in favour. Overall, 65 percent favoured conscription. (See Chapter 12.) Liberal prime minister Mackenzie King postponed the imposition of conscription, and the delay minimized the crisis because, again, the war ended before the conscripts were sent into battle. However, the apparent helplessness of the French in the face of an English-majority decision on a topic of life or death remained as a humiliating residue and helped to fuel Québec nationalism.

Modern Nationalism in Québec

It was not until the late 1950s and 1960s that fundamental change became apparent in the aspirations of Québec francophones. What began as a "Quiet Revolution" blossomed several decades later as an outright challenge to Canadian federalism and the very existence of the Canadian state.

After Confederation, two strains of nationalism developed in *La belle province.*[5] The first, advanced by Abbé Lionel Groulx, called for a rural vision of Catholic and anti-materialist values, and, on occasion, led to proposals for an inward-looking, corporatist and authoritarian solution to the Québec situation. The second, led by Henri Bourassa, politician and editor of *Le Devoir,* called for a pan-Canadian vision and an equal partnership between English and French Canada. For Bourassa, the Canadian dilemma was to be resolved by building a state that was both bicultural and bilingual.

The inward-looking strain of Québec nationalism was characterized by the Union Nationale governments of Maurice Duplessis, in 1936–39 and 1944–60. The rural-based Union Nationale espoused a philosophy of old-style nationalism buttressed by patronage and intimidation. Until the 1949 Asbestos strike, it was very successful. This strike of 5 000 workers lasted four months and consisted of an alliance between the American-owned asbestos company and the Duplessis government against the workers, who were supported to a large extent by Québec's developing intelligentsia. Québec changed dramatically. The 1950s were characterized by widespread rejection of both clerical influence and Duplessis manipulation. Values in the province changed rapidly from rural to urban and from religious to secular. Industrialization and urbanization helped erode the bases of Union Nationale support.

The new, outward-looking strain of nationalism was typified by the Québec Liberal party, which Jean Lesage led to victory in 1960. In the subsequent Quiet Revolution, Lesage's Liberals reversed the philosophy of previous governments in Québec. Instead of preserving the *patrimoine* (the language, religion and culture of a traditional rural Québec), they defended *la nation* in terms of the economy and social structure of the province. The new government dramatically increased the role of government in society; it secularized the school system, nationalized hydroelectricity and reformed the civil service.

Led by a new middle class, French Canadian nationalism gave way to Québec nationalism. Nationalists were appalled that the use of the French language was on the decline in Canada and that Québec's share of the Canadian population was dropping. The *épanouissement,* or flowering, of Québec-based nationalism was encapsulated in the 1960 political phrase *maîtres chez nous* (masters in our own house). A state-centred nationalism replaced the traditional nationalism.

Québec's new challenges to Canada came in many guises — judicial, social and political. Objections ranged from attacks on specific centralizing mechanisms, such as the constitutional

5. See Léon Dion, *Quebec: The Unfinished Revolution* (Montréal: McGill-Queen's University Press, 1976); and Herbert Guindon, "The Modernization of Québec and the Legitimacy of the Canadian State," in D. Glenday et al., *Modernization and the Canadian State* (Toronto: Macmillan, 1978), pp. 212–46.

power of disallowance, to general claims that the *BNA Act* did not define a true federal system. Some Québec francophones saw the federal union as lacking the free consent of the contracting parties — in other words, it did not provide a basis for the right of self-determination. Others objected to economic injustices.

Québec increased political pressure on the federal government throughout the 1960s. Some French Canadians took up separatism for Québec as their goal, maintaining that only with their own government could they fulfill the aspirations of their community. Their slogan *Vive le Québec libre* gained international credibility following a supportive declaration by visiting French president Charles de Gaulle in 1967. Nationalists focused their criticism on the use of English in the private sector, banks and the federal public service as well as on the economic domination of anglophones.

The Front de la Libération du Québec (FLQ) represented the most extreme separatists. The group initiated terrorist activities, which culminated in the October Crisis of 1970, in which a British diplomat was kidnapped and the Québec Minister of Labour, Pierre Laporte, was kidnapped and murdered. The *War Measures Act* was invoked by the federal government to deal with the events — the first and only time that the Act has been invoked in peacetime. The basic freedoms of many Canadians, mostly French-speaking, were infringed upon. Hundreds of Québeckers were arrested. When the crisis atmosphere faded, it left many Canadians uncertain as to whether the crisis had been sufficiently grave to warrant such large-scale repression.[6]

As Québec nationalism grew in the 1960s and 1970s, Québec intellectuals became increasingly divided. Pierre Elliott Trudeau and his friends Jean Marchand and Gérard Pelletier entered federal politics, where they offered the vision of a bicultural and bilingual federal state, but with no special status for Québec. Later, as Prime Minister of Canada, Trudeau became the major spokesman for Henri Bourassa–style nationalism.

Separatist Parties in Québec

There have been four "successful" nationalist organizations with aspirations for the provincial independence of Québec. The first nationalist party, the Parti Patriote, was elected with a large majority in the early nineteenth century under its very popular leader Louis-Joseph Papineau. In an attempt to win parliamentary control over government expenditures and other concessions, the party instigated an armed rebellion in 1836–37. It was quelled by the troops of the British governor.

The second nationalist party, the Parti Nationale led by Honoré Mercier, was elected in 1886. It was defeated in 1892 because of financial problems, corruption and lack of support for constitutional change. Then, in 1936, the Union Nationale, led by Maurice Duplessis, came into office. This third nationalist party played a traditional nationalist game within the context of Canadian rules.

In the 1960s and 1970s, the separatist challenge grew in Québec. In the 1966 provincial election the Ralliement National (RN) and Le Ralliement pour L'Indépendance Nationale (RIN) gained 10 percent of the vote. Former provincial Cabinet minister René Lévesque left the Liberal party in 1968 and formed the Parti Québécois (PQ). This new separatist party brought together the left-wing RIN, the right-wing RN and other nationalists under a new umbrella organization. Pierre Trudeau, for one, maintained that the Parti Québécois had simply replaced traditional Québec clericalism with the "clericalism of nationalism."[7]

---

6. See Denis Smith, *Bleeding Hearts ... Bleeding Country: Canada and the Québec Crisis* (Edmonton: Hurtig, 1971).

7. For Trudeau's position see Pierre Elliott Trudeau, *Federalism and the French Canadians* (Toronto: Macmillan, 1968), pp. 207–9.

regionalism

/70 Québec election, the Parti Québécois received 24 percent of the popular vote, not ⌐ prevent Liberal leader Robert Bourassa from forming the government. The October ⌐ok place soon after this election. In the next one, in 1973, playing on the fear of separatism ⌐apitalizing on his success with the James Bay Hydro development project, Bourassa won an-⌐ner landslide victory, despite an increase in the PQ vote to 30 percent.

In the face of these defeats the Parti Québécois softened its stance from outright independence to **sovereignty-association** — political independence but with economic association. The purpose of sovereignty-association was to reassure those who were apprehensive about the economic consequences of separation. The party continued to promote its vision of a Québec in which no taxes would be paid to Ottawa and citizens would be subject to no federal law. In the 1976 election, Lévesque ran on an *étapiste* (gradualist) strategy and a platform of "good government." He offered a referendum on the right to negotiate sovereignty-association, and promised a second referendum for Québeckers to ratify the eventual results of the negotiations. This approach worked.[8] Forty-one percent of Québec voters cast their ballots for the Parti Québécois on November 15, 1976, and the PQ became the fourth nationalist party to gain control of the government in Québec.

In preparation for the provincial referendum the Parti Québécois government passed some seductive legislation. It proved moderate in fiscal and monetary policies, and yet nationalized the Asbestos Corporation, to the obvious satisfaction of many nationalists. It also introduced **Bill 101**, the *Charter of the French Language*, in the Québec legislature in April 1977, declaring an intent to make the province unilingual. The Bill imposed French-language requirements on businesses, made French the legal language for statutes and legal documents, required that all commercial signs and billboards be in French, and restricted access to English schools. As language policy is one of the most controversial social policies in Canada and the root of considerable ethnic nationalism in Québec, any discussion of the development of Québec nationalism must include an overview of the language issues.

LANGUAGE ISSUES

There are two official languages in Canada: English and French. Canada's Confederation arrangement was essentially a bargain between the French and English in British North America to create one strong political unit that would protect the rights and assist the advancement of two culturally diverse peoples. On this basis, linguistic duality was embedded in the *British North America Act* of 1867. Linguistic duality has had both positive and negative repercussions for Canadians. For decades, language has evoked divisive social and political tensions between French- and English-speaking Canadians. At the same time, however, the establishment of two official languages has provided one of Canada's most distinctive constitutional traits and, for many, has enriched the experience of being Canadian.

The legal basis for language regulation in Canada is found in three jurisdictions: (a) the Constitution; (b) federal law; and (c) provincial law.

a) The Constitution establishes the framework for rules about language usage and development. In 1867, the *BNA Act* specified that Parliament and the Québec National Assembly were to function in French and English. Much later, in 1982, the *Charter of Rights and Freedoms* enshrined English and French as the two official languages of Canada for matters pertaining to Parliament. Minority-language rights were enshrined in section 23 of the Charter, which stipulates that citizens

---

8. For a summary, see William Coleman, *The Independence Movement in Québec 1945–1980* (Toronto: University of Toronto Press, 1984).

of Canada whose first language is that of the French or English minority of the province in which they reside, or who have received their instruction in one of these languages in Canada, have the right to have their children educated in that language wherever numbers warrant. To amend the minority-language guarantees in the Constitution, all provinces and the federal Parliament must agree.[9]

b) Within the parameters established by the Constitution, the federal government creates language policies within its jurisdiction. In 1963, the federal Liberal government declared Canadian federal institutions to be officially bilingual. This was accomplished in the *Official Languages Act* of 1969. This act was amended and updated in 1988. It has two parts: it regulates bilingualism in federal organizations and federally regulated institutions such as banks and airlines; and it provides a framework for promoting the two official languages. For example, it gives Canadians the right to be served by federal institutions in the official language of their choice where "significant demand" exists, it allows federal employees the right to work in the official language of their choice, and requires an equitable distribution of English and French Canadians in the public service.

c) Provincial assemblies, too, can legislate language policies. However, such language legislation has often been restrictive and controversial. In Québec the provincial government maintains an *Office de la Langue Française,* which enforces the *Charte de la Langue Française.* This Charter makes French the official language of the province and the normal language of communications, business and the workplace generally. The *Charter of Rights and Freedoms* of 1982 expanded the basis for legal challenges by aggrieved minorities on constitutional grounds. Since it came into effect, many cases have been brought to the Supreme Court to challenge provincial governments and force them to accommodate language minorities in their laws and schools.

Because language is such a vital part of French culture, language policy permeates politics in Québec. The widespread fear that French language and culture are in decline in Canada, or may soon be, is used by Québec nationalists to rally support. Québec's fertility rate is lower than that for Canada as a whole, which, as noted, is not adequate to sustain the current population level. Québec, therefore, sees a need to attract, hold and integrate immigrants into the French culture and language. Motivated by these demographic concerns, Québec authorities in the 1960s began to assert and protect the province's distinctive character through language legislation within its jurisdiction.

Despite federal initiatives, Canada's francophone population is increasingly concentrated in Québec. The percentage of Canadians with French as their first language began to drop in 1951. At that time, the French-language group accounted for 29 percent of the total population, compared to only about 23.5 percent by 1996. In 1996, over 85 percent of Canada's French-speaking population lived in Québec (based on single-response mother tongue), a figure that at the present rate of change could reach 95 percent by the next census.

The 1996 census explains the actual situation of the francophone population in Canada.

- The proportion of francophones in Québec has changed little over the century. In 1900, 83 percent of the province's population spoke French; in 1996, 81.5 percent spoke French.

- The English-speaking community in Québec dropped from 24 percent at the time of Confederation to 16 percent in 1970, and then to 8.8 percent in 1996. There are more allophones, people whose first language is neither French nor English, in Québec than anglophones – 9.7 percent. Table 7.1 shows the percentage of English, French and allophones resident in Québec at the time of the last four censuses.

---

9. Governments cannot use the "notwithstanding clause" to exempt the application of these Charter guarantees. See Chapter 5 for a discussion of the notwithstanding clause. In early 1993, Parliament and the New Brunswick legislature passed a constitutional amendment guaranteeing equal status for New Brunswick's French- and English-language communities. See Chapter 5.

TABLE 7.1   PERCENTAGE POPULATION OF QUÉBEC BY FIRST LANGUAGE

	First Language			
	English	**French**	**Allophones**	
	%	%	%	**Total**
1971	13.1	80.7	6.2	100
1981	10.9	82.5	6.6	100
1991	9.2	82.0	8.8	100
1996	8.8	81.5	9.7	100

Source: Statistics Canada

Note: Over the years, the formulae for determining mother tongue had varied based on single and multiple responses, but the data is approximately comparable.

- The English in Québec are learning more French than previously and so are new immigrants to the province. Québec's requirement for immigrant children to go to French schools has increased the assimilation rate of these children into French.

- In most other provinces, however, the proportion of francophones continues to decline because of the high rate of assimilation. About 37 percent of francophones outside Québec speak English at home; fewer than one percent of anglophones speak French at home.

A 1999 study by the Conseil de la Langue Française concluded that the French language has entered a period of slow but steady decline in Canada. Higher Asian immigration and growing numbers of allophones in Québec indicate that Chinese will soon be spoken more than French in English-speaking Canada and French will continue its slow decline in Québec.[10] Since Québec's population is growing more slowly than the national average, its demographic weight within Canada is likely to decline below its 23.5 percent of 1996. Given these trends, Canadians should expect Québec francophones to continue their struggle to preserve the pre-eminence of the French language and culture within their province.

Language Law in Québec

In the 1960s, motivated by such demographic concerns, Québec authorities began to assert and protect the province's distinctive character. (See Table 7.2.) A spiral of restrictive language laws began with an attempt to force immigrants to have their children educated in French. In 1968, the Catholic school board of St. Léonard in suburban Montréal attempted to force allophone children to attend French-language schools, denying English education to the area's largely Italian population. The next year, the provincial Union Nationale government introduced Bill 63, which confirmed the right of parents in Québec to educate their children in the language of their choice.

Nationalists resented Bill 63, so to mollify them the government of Premier Robert Bourassa passed Bill 22 in 1974. It declared French to be the official language of Québec. French was given primacy in the workplace but linguistic dualism was preserved in several areas. The Bill also required children of immigrants to be enrolled in French schools, except for children who could demonstrate a sufficient knowledge of English.

In 1977, the new Parti Québécois government of René Lévesque introduced Bill 101 as the *Charter of the French Language in Québec.* It was much stronger in its promotion of French than

---

10. *The Globe and Mail,* October 28 1999.

TABLE 7.2 LANGUAGE POLICY IN QUÉBEC 1968–99

1968	Catholic school board of St. Léonard attempts to coerce allophone children to attend French-language schools
1969	Québec's Union Nationale government responds: Bill 63 allows parents in Québec to educate children in language of choice
1970	Union Nationale defeated by Robert Bourassa's Liberal party
1974	Bill 22 replaces Bill 63; French is given primacy in the workplace, but linguistic dualism is preserved in several areas; children of immigrants must be enrolled in French schools, except children who demonstrate sufficient knowledge of English
1977	Bill 101, *Charter of the French Language*, declares French the official language of Québec, promotes French much more than Bill 22 and restricts use of English; it further restricts access to English schools and takes measures to make French the language of commerce and business in Québec
1982	*Charter of Rights and Freedoms* is passed with the *Canada Act, 1982*
1982	Bill 62 comes into effect; a new clause is to be appended to each Québec law stating it will operate "notwithstanding" the provision of the federal Constitution
1984	Bill 57 is incorporated into the *Charter of the French Language*, providing guarantees for the survival of English institutions and modifying certain language requirements for businesses
1985	Supreme Court rejects Québec's 1982 argument over Bill 101 and declares sections are incompatible with the *Canadian Charter of Rights and Freedoms*
1987	Québec Court of Appeal rules that banning languages other than French on commercial signs violates freedom of expression as provided by the Québec and Canadian charters of rights
1988	Supreme Court invalidates section 58 of Bill 101 requiring French-only commercial signs in Québec
1988	Premier Robert Bourassa invokes the "notwithstanding" clause from section 33 of the *Canadian Charter of Rights and Freedoms* in order to pass Bill 178
1988	Bill 178 is passed in the National Assembly — continues ban on languages other than French on outdoor signs, and allows English and other languages on indoor signs if French is predominant
1993	Bill 178 is up for renewal (the five-year limit having expired on the use of the notwithstanding clause to override the Supreme Court judgement on the language of signs) but, in June, the National Assembly passes Bill 86, which replaces parts of Bill 101 and all of Bill 178. Since Bill 86 is in line with the Charter and Supreme Court decisions, it does not require the notwithstanding clause. It restores bilingual signs
1996	The Parti Québécois government introduces policy papers indicating they intend to pass more invasive, detailed legislation to increase use of the French language in Québec
1999	A Québec lower court strikes down a section of Québec's language law requiring that French be predominant on commercial signs

Bill 22 had been, and circumscribed the use of English. For example, it restricted access to English schools. Regardless of where a child came from — even from another province within Canada — he or she had to be educated in French unless one of the parents had been educated in an English school *in* Québec. It also took measures to make French the language of commerce and business. Any company with more than 50 employees was instructed to conduct all internal business in French. Furthermore, English, or even bilingual, commercial signs were to be illegal by 1981. And towns, rivers and mountains that bore English names were to be renamed in French.

When the federal government patriated the Constitution in 1982, the Québec government demonstrated its extreme displeasure by passing Bill 62. The action was an attempt to ensure that

Québeckers' fundamental freedoms and legal and equality rights would be subject only to the provincial charter of human rights, not to its new federal counterpart. A new clause was to be appended to each Québec law, stating that it would operate "notwithstanding" the provision of the federal Charter. However, the notwithstanding clause does not apply to language-of-education articles in the Constitution. To bypass this obstacle, Québec relied on section 1 of the Constitution, which states that the federal *Charter of Rights and Freedoms* guarantees the liberties it sets out "subject only to such reasonable limits prescribed by law as can be demonstrably justified in a free and democratic society." The Québec government hoped to prove in court that Bill 101's provisions could be justified on these grounds. However, in 1985 the Supreme Court ruled that the section of Bill 101 limiting eligibility to attend English-language schools to children one of whose parents had received primary education in English in Québec was "incompatible" with the constitutional guarantees set out in the *Canadian Charter of Rights and Freedoms*.

In the mid-1980s, following several court challenges, francophone attitudes toward enforcement of Bill 101 began to soften. The Québec government passed Bill 57 in 1984, incorporating into Bill 101 guarantees for the survival of English institutions, modifying certain requirements for bilingualism and relaxing rules for internal and inter-institutional communications. These special arrangements were meant to encourage businesses to stay in Montréal. On December 22, 1987, the Québec Court of Appeal ruled that the ban on languages other than French on commercial signs violated freedom of expression as protected by the *Charter of Rights and Freedoms*, and also that of Québec. The next year, in December 1988, the Supreme Court ruled on section 58 of Bill 101, finding it violated both the Canadian and Québec guarantees of freedom of expression. The sign law was ruled invalid.[11] Nationalists were enraged and feared a massive unravelling of the Québec language charter.

Almost immediately, Premier Bourassa invoked the notwithstanding clause of the Charter, which allows the federal Parliament or any provincial legislature to pass legislation infringing on individual rights. (An automatic "sunset clause" causes the legislation to lapse after five years unless it is re-passed in the legislature concerned.) In 1988, using the notwithstanding clause to make it constitutionally valid, the National Assembly passed Bill 178, a controversial sign law that expanded on Bill 101. Bill 178 banned languages other than French on *outdoor* signs but allowed languages other than French on *indoor* signs, providing that French was predominant. Predictably, language wars within the province of Québec escalated with ridiculous debates over the size, colour and placement of letters on signs. Self-appointed language "police" reported offenders.[12]

Before December 1993, when the five-year limit on the invocation of the notwithstanding clause concerning Bill 178 was to expire, a new and less controversial law was put in place. The National Assembly passed Bill 86, replacing all of Bill 178 and parts of Bill 101. It changed the sign law so that French was required to appear along with any other languages. Bill 86 was, therefore, in keeping with the spirit of the earlier Supreme Court ruling and did not require the notwithstanding

---

11. The Supreme Court presented two judgements: one was a challenge to section 58 of Bill 101 by five businesses that questioned the rule that commercial sign laws in Québec had to be in French only. The second was the case of Allan Singer dealing with the legality of English-only signs. In the first case, the Supreme Court declared that the sign law was a violation of freedom of expression and stated that a ban on other languages was not needed to defend the French language. In the second case, the Court ruled that the province was entitled to pass a law requiring the predominant display of the French language.

12. In April 1993, the United Nations Human Rights Commission found that Bill 178 contravened the International Covenant on Civil and Political Rights, which Canada has signed. It stated that any limitation on an individual's right to express ideas freely, including advertising, violates the principle of freedom of expression, and argued that francophone rights are not threatened by the ability of others to advertise in a language other than French. *The Globe and Mail*, February 6, 1993.

Chapter 7 Nationalism and Regionalism

clause to be used again. This legislation, passed only a few weeks before Premier Bourassa retired, helped to defuse the volatile language issue in Québec, at least in the short run.

In 1996, the Québec government once more escalated the level of language conflict in Montréal. It produced a general policy paper indicating that it intended to introduce more very detailed and restrictive language laws with increased enforcement measures. The goal was clearly stated that the legislation would reach into all sectors of society in order to increase the "francisization" of Québec. In 1999, however, a Québec lower court judge struck down the section of Québec's language law that required French to be predominant on all commercial signs. This went against the 1988 Supreme Court ruling that restricted the size of English on commercial signs. The Québec government immediately announced it would appeal.

Arguments for and against Bilingualism

Language policy in Canada has become highly politicized. It has sometimes been used as a "social engineering" tool by governments at both federal and provincial levels. Institutional bilingualism has become a magnet for intolerance, often based on misinformation and misunderstanding. A few facts should help dispel some exaggerated myths.

Bilingualism in Canada does not mean that all Canadians must speak both French and English. Rather, it means that Canadians have the right to communicate with their federal government and federally regulated institutions in the official language of their choice and also to have their children educated in that language, wherever numbers warrant. The policy is based on the belief that a highly bilingual government would increase sensitivity, tolerance and respect between the two language communities.

By these criteria, official bilingualism has had mixed results. On the one hand, immersion programs in the schools have produced more bilingual Canadians. The 1996 census indicated that bilingualism had progressed generally across the country since 1961. Seventeen percent of Canadians said they were bilingual.

On the other hand, as we have seen, the assimilation of francophones outside Québec has continued. Although more than 6.4 million Canadians spoke French at home in 1996, up from 6 million in 1986, the increase has not kept pace with overall population growth.

In English-speaking Canada, particularly since Québec's decision to make French preeminent, demands have arisen to end official bilingualism. The desire to revert to unilingualism, however, is often merely a superficial response to separatists (who do not speak for all French Canadians — maybe not even for a majority of those who live in Québec). Often, too, it is based on frustration at seeing certain jobs labelled "bilingual." In fact, very few government jobs require the holder to be bilingual. Across the four western provinces, where the complaints are often strongest, only about 3 percent of government jobs are designated bilingual. Francophones represent just over 2 percent of the population there, so the match is appropriate.

In difficult economic times, it is not surprising to hear claims that official bilingualism is a punitive and expensive failure that deprives anglophones of jobs and impoverishes Canadians as a whole. Such claims are highly exaggerated. In fact, the federal government spends only about one-third of one percent of the total federal budget to provide federal services in both official languages. The cost to the federal government of providing services in both official languages has been calculated at $13 a year for each Canadian, or 3.5 cents a day.[13] This is hardly an outrageous amount

---

13. Office of the Commissioner of Official Languages, *Official Languages: Some Basic Facts* (Ottawa: Supply and Services, 1992), p. 16.

to pay in order to treat fellow Canadians with dignity and respect. The often exaggerated claims about the impact of official language policies on job opportunities for unilingual anglophones create genuine concern that must be addressed and dispelled by governments. The issue of language and culture underlies the political issues that came to a head in two Québec referendums, in 1980 and 1995, and fosters some of the alienation in western Canada.

QUÉBEC REFERENDUMS ON SEPARATION

In 1980 and again in 1995, Québec governments held referendums with the intent to take Québec out of Canada and form an independent country. This history is very complex, as the two events were entwined with other constitutional issues and partisan politics.

The Québec Referendum, 1980

In May 1980, the PQ government led by René Lévesque called a referendum on sovereignty-association. The results were a disaster for Premier Lévesque and the sovereignty forces. The vote required Québec residents to choose between *Oui* — for the Québec government to negotiate sovereignty-association — and *Non* — for it not to negotiate. Even this extremely mild resolution was defeated by almost six out of ten votes. The *Non* forces achieved their large majority in Québec partially because of Prime Minister Trudeau's promise of "renewed federalism."

The threat of independence did not die with this vote. In the 1981 Québec election, the Parti Québécois said it would call another sovereignty referendum. Under the leadership of Lévesque, the PQ won the ensuing election with 47 percent of the vote and 80 of 122 seats in the National Assembly. The Liberals under Claude Ryan, former editor of *Le Devoir*, were crushed. The party replaced Ryan with former premier Robert Bourassa.

Constitutional Patriation, 1982, and Its Aftermath

As discussed in Chapter 5, René Lévesque refused to sign the 1982 constitutional amendment package to patriate the Constitution from the United Kingdom. When the federal government and the other nine provinces went ahead with patriation without Québec's approval, they broke a political impasse, but handed the separatists an emotional weapon. The country, Lévesque said, had separated from Québec. Although Prime Minister Trudeau and a high proportion of the federal Cabinet were from Québec, and public opinion in Québec at the time favoured patriation, the PQ claimed that it alone spoke for the province and announced a boycott of federal/provincial meetings.

After the Conservatives under Brian Mulroney won the 1984 election, Lévesque ended his boycott and began a campaign to delete separation and even the idea of sovereignty-association from the party manifesto. In January 1985, the party convention endorsed his position and the PQ officially became a moderate nationalist party.

Before the next provincial election, Lévesque died, and the party developed major internal splits. Pierre-Marc Johnson became leader and led the party into the 1985 election on a moderate nationalist platform. The party was badly defeated in the election. Bourassa's Liberals won 56 percent of the vote and 98 seats while the PQ was left with 38 percent of the vote and only 24 seats. The non-separatists were back in office, but with a decidedly nationalist leader and agenda.

Repercussions of the Failed Meech Lake and Charlottetown Accords

Immediately upon taking office, Premier Bourassa began to espouse policies that blended federalism and Québec nationalism. In 1985, he successfully demanded that five conditions be included in the Meech Lake constitutional accord (see Chapter 5), and in 1988 he employed the notwithstanding clause of the new Constitution to prevent the use of English signs for business purposes in the province. Meanwhile, in 1988, the PQ replaced Johnson with Jacques Parizeau, an arch-separatist, who rejected the party's moderate stance and revived the *indépendantiste* spirit. Nonetheless, Bourassa's Liberals easily defeated the PQ in the 1989 provincial election.

When the Meech Lake accord failed in May 1990, several Québec members of the Liberal and Conservative federal caucuses, led by Lucien Bouchard (former Minister of Environment in Prime Minister Mulroney's Cabinet), left their parties to form a separatist group in the House of Commons — the Bloc Québécois. As we saw in Chapter 5, the federal government continued its efforts to build a constitutional agreement that would bring Québec "on board." This eventually resulted in a proposal called the Charlottetown accord, which was put before the Canadian people for approval in a referendum in October 1992. But in Québec the proposal was massively rejected, and Québec nationalists resumed their call for separation.

In the general election of October 25, 1993, the Bloc won 54 seats, just enough to become Her Majesty's Loyal Opposition in the House of Commons. The Bloc's next stated goal was to join the Parti Québécois in a campaign to separate Québec from Canada. This became more probable when the PQ under Jacques Parizeau won the 1994 provincial election and promised a referendum on sovereignty by the end of 1995.

Québec leadership was, and remains, divided in its vision for the province. *Separatists* favour outright statehood for Québec; *sovereignists* favour a greater degree of independence for Québec, but do not necessarily define sovereignty as an absolute break from Canada; *devolution sovereignists* favour an extreme decentralization of Canada in which very few powers would be left to the central government; and *federalists* favour the continued existence of Québec within Canada.

The Québec Referendum, 1995

Two elections (the general election of 1993, in which 54 Bloc Québécois members were elected to the House of Commons, and the Québec election of September 1994, which brought the Parti Québécois to power) set the stage for a dramatic separatist offensive. The Québec election gave the Parti Québécois of Jacques Parizeau 44.8 percent of the vote and 77 seats. The Liberals led by Daniel Johnson won 44.2 percent but only 47 seats. The Action Démocratique led by Mario Dumont became the third party with representation in the National Assembly as it won 6.5 percent and one seat.

PQ and Bloc Strategy and Tactics

The PQ had campaigned on the sovereignty issue for the 1994 election, and after the win Parizeau quickly announced that a referendum on sovereignty would be held within a year. The draft bill on sovereignty was unveiled in December and the vote was initially planned for the spring. In the following months, the government set up 16 regional commissions and outlined a detailed strategy to reach grass-roots voters. Its initial proposal was to hold regional consultations and then have the Assembly declare sovereignty. Voters would only be asked to ratify the decision in a referendum. During the lead-up to this strategy, however, poor polling results forced Parizeau to compromise his idea. The separatist program was also set back by the serious illness of Lucien Bouchard, which resulted in the amputation of one of his legs.

Polls indicated that a consistent majority of Québeckers opposed outright separation. But they also showed that support would rise if an association with Canada were adopted as part of the plan. In May 1995, a poll by the Groupe Léger & Léger indicated that such a compromise resolution would win 51.4 percent to 48.6 percent. Professor Maurice Pinard put it like this: "They [Québeckers] are tempted by the option, but afraid of the cost, torn by attraction to independence and fear about the consequence."[14] The focus of the separatists became the undecided Québec voter — dubbed the "Noui" — half *Non*, half *Oui*.

The PQ formed a temporary alliance with the Bloc Québécois and the Parti Action Démocratique. On June 12, 1995, the three party leaders joined to ask Québeckers to support independence for Québec *along with political and economic association with Canada* if the Yes side won the referendum. The deal among the three parties was based on the premise that Québec should first declare independence and then negotiate with Canada for one year over an economic and political association; in other words, after a Yes vote, the Québec National Assembly would proclaim sovereignty and then offer a new set of institutions to Canada. The three-party alliance proposed a "European style" union comprising:

- a parliamentary assembly consisting of Canadian members of Parliament and members of Quebec's National Assembly (25 percent) who would debate issues and write reports but would have no final legislative authority;

- a council composed of an equal number of Canadian and Québec Cabinet ministers who would negotiate agreements between the two sides, each of which would have to agree before a proposal would be put into effect;

- a tribunal (a kind of dispute-settlement mechanism) that would settle economic disputes between the two countries; and

- a secretariat, which would form a kind of super bureaucracy for the two states.

If negotiations succeeded, they said, a treaty would be put in place. It would provide for a customs union, a monetary policy, citizenship, and the mobility of people, capital and services. Deals could be struck on topics such as enhanced trade, common transportation, defence, environmental policies and fiscal policies. If negotiations with Canada failed, Québec would become an independent country anyway, while maintaining the Canadian currency and the Canadian passport.

The thrust of this deal was put into question form for the Québec population to vote on in a referendum on October 30, 1995. The question was highly criticized for being ambiguous and misleading. (See "The Québec Referendum Question, October 30, 1995.") It required those who supported the sovereignist option to vote Yes, and those who did not support it to vote No.

The first two weeks of the campaign went badly for the sovereignists. Polls showed they might only achieve results similar to those of the 1980 referendum; a large majority might vote No. To regain momentum, Parizeau announced that Bouchard would be put in charge of negotiations with Canada after a win in the referendum. "Saint Lucien," as he was dubbed by friends and foes, took over as head of the campaign, and his personal charisma lifted morale and attracted voter support. Bouchard jettisoned PQ economic studies that concluded separation would be very costly and concentrated his campaign on the emotional attraction of sovereignty. He countered what he called the "scare tactics" of the No side by insisting that market forces would push Canada to negotiate with a sovereign Québec. By the end of the campaign the Yes and No forces were virtually tied, with indications that the Yes side might win.

Bouchard's high profile in the campaign brought a new emphasis on perceived historical "humiliations" of French-speaking Canadians, on the definition of French-speaking Québeckers as a "people" and on the need for Québeckers as a people to negotiate "equal to equal" with Canadians, not just as a province like the others. (There was no mention of the fact that Canada had had a

---

14. *The Ottawa Citizen*, December 24, 1994.

prime minister from Québec for 35 of the 50 years since the end of the Second World War, although Québeckers comprise only about 35 percent of the population, or that at the time of the referendum francophones or Québeckers held positions in Ottawa as Governor General, Prime Minister, Minister of Finance, Minister of Foreign Affairs, Chief Justice of the Supreme Court, Clerk of the Privy Council and Chief of Staff of the Prime Minister.) The rhetoric escalated as the campaign neared its conclusion. Prime Minister Jean Chrétien was vilified and ridiculed. Parizeau said, "This man [Chrétien] is sabotaging the economy of Québec, and in the exact way he sabotaged the powers of Québec in 1981. You remember the Night of the Long Knives"[15] (a reference to the all-night negotiations in 1981, when nine premiers and the federal leaders decided on a constitutional deal without out Québec's agreement).

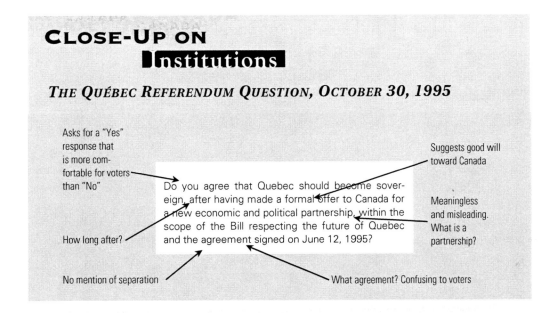

CLOSE-UP ON

Institutions

THE QUÉBEC REFERENDUM QUESTION, OCTOBER 30, 1995

Asks for a "Yes" response that is more comfortable for voters than "No"

Suggests good will toward Canada

Do you agree that Quebec should become sovereign, after having made a formal offer to Canada for a new economic and political partnership, within the scope of the Bill respecting the future of Quebec and the agreement signed on June 12, 1995?

Meaningless and misleading. What is a partnership?

How long after?

No mention of separation

What agreement? Confusing to voters

Federal Strategy and Tactics

In preparation for the referendum campaign, provincial Liberal leader Daniel Johnson appointed Michel Bélanger as president of the organization committee for the No side. Johnson's proclamations were typically qualified. He declared himself to be "first and foremost a Canadian," but later said: "I can conceive, like many, of being a Quebecker without being Canadian; I cannot conceive of being Canadian without being a Quebecker." The federal government appointed Québec minister Lucienne Robillard to speak for the federal Cabinet.

At the beginning, the strategy of the No forces was to wait for the separatists to act. But once the question was set, the opposition became more vocal, mainly attacking the question itself. No matter what the spin doctors tried to call it, they argued, the referendum was about the separation of Québec from Canada. Prime Minister Jean Chrétien put it bluntly the day after the PQ plan was announced: "It's a mirage. It is still a proposition for separation, but they don't have the guts to say they are separatists." Chrétien declared at home and abroad that Québec would never leave Canada. He said separatists have

---

15. United Nations, *Human Development Report 1996* (New York: Oxford University Press, 1996).

Corrigan. Reprinted with permission, Toronto Star Syndicate.

a contempt for democracy ... the way of those who count on tricks and turnarounds.... There is now a very cynical and very transparent attempt to confuse Quebeckers, to mislead them, to suggest that you can separate from Canada and still be Canadian.[16]

He adopted the strategy of lying low and letting the provincial leader direct the No forces. Daniel Johnson waged a campaign based on the economic consequences of separation. His was a cool, unemotional approach that appealed to reason.

Initial polls gave the No forces confidence. After Bouchard took the lead for the separatists, however, the polls started to reverse themselves. Premier Johnson tried to counter the Yes forces with something positive, but on October 21, the prime minister dismissed his appeal for the recognition of Québec as a distinct society. The unity of the No forces was temporarily broken. The dollar plunged. With just over a week to go, Chrétien's strategy changed abruptly. He cancelled other obligations and addressed a federalist rally in Verdun. The next night he addressed the country on television pleading for Canadian unity and suggesting that the federal government would promote acceptance of Québec as a distinct society and a limited veto for Québec. In an unprecedented outpouring of emotion, citizens outside Québec came by the thousands to a massive rally in downtown Montréal, and rallies and vigils were held in every province the weekend before the vote.

Meanwhile, the Cree and the Inuit in northern Québec (whose large territorial claims can be seen in Figure 7.1) held separate referendums. Both voted massively against the sovereignist proposal and leaders expressed a desire to remain in Canada no matter what the outcome of the October 31 referendum.

The Outcome and the Aftermath

In a massive voter turnout of over 93 percent, Québeckers voted narrowly, 50.6 percent to 49.4 percent, to reject the sovereignty proposal. The results showed that the Yes side had made major gains in the vast, mainly francophone regions that stretch from Îles de la Madeleine in the east to Abitibi in the northwest of Québec. Voters produced margins of 50 percent to 70 percent for the Yes side in many areas that had voted No in 1980. (Figure 7.2 shows the growth in support for separatism in Québec in elections and referendums from 1966 to 1995.) All the regions in the province except Montréal, the Eastern Townships and the Outaouais voted to separate. Even Prime Minister Jean Chrétien's riding of St. Maurice voted Yes.

The close finish encouraged Premier Parizeau to adopt a confrontational tone when the results were in. He said that separatists had not really lost the referendum because more than 60 percent of

---

16. *The Globe and Mail*, May 4, 1995.

FIGURE 7.1   MAP SHOWING ABORIGINAL TERRITORIAL CLAIMS IN NORTHERN QUÉBEC

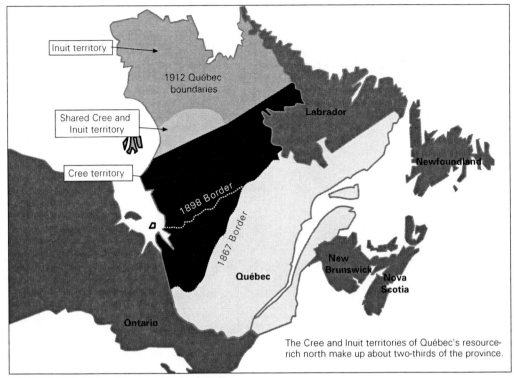

The Cree and Inuit territories of Québec's resource-rich north make up about two-thirds of the province.

Source: Grand Council of the Crees (of Québec).

francophones had voted for independence. "It's true that we were beaten," Parizeau said, "but by whom? Money and ethnic votes." He also spoke of the "temptation for revenge."[17] In doing so he singled out and insulted many people in Québec and in the rest of Canada.

Anglophones and allophones make up about 17 percent of Québec's population, but 80 percent of them live in Montréal and its suburbs. Within metropolitan Montréal, anglophones constitute 15 percent of the population, allophones 17 percent. Together, they form about a third of the population. This numerical strength clearly acted as a powerful counterweight to the francophone vote of the area, which was roughly evenly split. Outside Montréal, with the exception of a handful of ridings along the Ontario boundary and the U.S. border, the anglophone population constitutes less than 2 or 3 percent of the population and the Yes side won easily.

The polarization of the Yes and No votes, therefore, was clearly related to ethnicity, but other forces also seem to have been at play. The division was also typified by urban/rural splits, in which recession-ridden rural areas felt isolated from what they perceived as the political power, economic clout and good life that adhere to big cities such as Montréal.

Leaders for the Yes forces vowed that the issue of Québec separatism was not resolved, and that another referendum would be held in the near future. Within days of the referendum, however, Jacques Parizeau suddenly resigned as premier and was replaced by Lucien Bouchard, who gave up his seat in the House of Commons.

---

17. *The Globe and Mail*, October 31, 1995.

FIGURE 7.2   SUPPORT FOR SEPARATISM IN QUÉBEC, AS EXPRESSED IN KEY PROVINCIAL
ELECTIONS AND REFERENDUMS

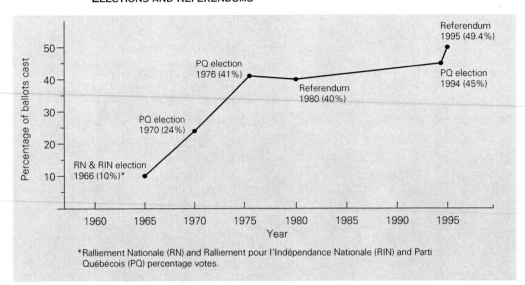

*Ralliement Nationale (RN) and Ralliement pour l'Indépendance Nationale (RIN) and Parti
Québécois (PQ) percentage votes.

Some Unresolved Issues

The campaign raised several issues that could be problematic in the event of a successful referendum
on separation.

- *The dollar.* Could an independent Québec keep using the Canadian dollar? In the long term,
  probably not. There are no examples of large countries that have taken such an option; only
  small, dependent countries use the U.S. dollar. Currency comprises more than "bank notes";
  it is a system of payments, compensation and settlement. Use of the dollar by Québec would
  be difficult because of the "capital flight," the sudden exodus of business and investment,
  that would be set off by separation. Québec would be forced to choose between a credit
  crunch and recession or the establishment of a new currency. The January 1993 example of
  the break-up of the former Czechoslovakia is instructive on this point. At the beginning,
  both new countries tried to share the same currency, but a flight of capital from Slovakia
  after the split forced the Slovaks to create their own, devalued currency.[18]

  There are other questions about the dollar. Would international bankers recognize Québec's
  use of the Canadian dollar? On another level, it verges on the absurd to contemplate an
  independent Québec using as its currency bills and coinage that feature the Queen of
  Canada. Or would Québec be a constitutional monarchy and join the Commonwealth?

- *Passports.* Many contest the idea that a new state of Québec could use the Canadian passport. The Canadian government and Parliament decide who can have a passport. Since the
  document begins with the words "The Secretary of State for External Affairs of Canada
  requests in the name of Her Majesty the Queen ..." even trying to use the passports would be
  a ludicrous situation for independent-minded Québeckers. The question of possible dual
  citizenship remains unresolved. Many Canadians hold passports both from Canada and the
  United States.

---

18. See the article by Stéphane Dion, "The Dynamic of Secessions: Scenarios after a Pro-Separatist Vote in
    a Québec Referendum," *CJPS*, vol. 27, no. 3 (September 1995), pp. 533–51.

- *Debt.* Since the country's debt is in Canada's name, Canada would remain liable for all of it. If Québec separated, Canada could collect only about 77 percent of its former revenue, however. Negotiations about Québec's share of the national debt would therefore be required.

- *Majority vote.* How big a majority would a province need to achieve in order to separate? Is 50 percent plus one large enough? In this scenario, just under half the population of a province would be required to live in a new country for which they did not vote. Moreover, about two and a half million votes would be enough to destroy a country of over 30 million. In 1999, Prime Minister Chrétien declared unequivocally that 50 percent plus one would not be enough. (See Supreme Court judgement in Appendix 2.)

- *Negotiators.* With whom would leaders of a sovereign Québec negotiate? Can a federal leader from Québec negotiate for the rest of Canada in the event of a Québec vote for independence? Prime Minister Chrétien has said he could not negotiate the independence of Québec. In a CTV interview, he said that separation is "completely illegal and unconstitutional." When asked if he could negotiate independence, Chrétien said: "No. It's not in the Constitution," and, "With whom will they negotiate?... Will they honour a negative vote? They did not honour the [1980] vote."

- *Economic repercussions.* What exactly would be the economic repercussions of separation? The majority opinion of economists appears to be that uncertainty and the high debt load would lead to flight of capital. Constitutional lawyer Patrick Monahan concluded: "The economic dislocation in parts of the country would be far greater than that experienced in the Great Depression of the 1930s."[19] Clearly, Canada is extremely vulnerable to foreigners who would sell off Canadian and provincial bonds and treasury bills. A unilateral declaration of independence (UDI) by Québec might provoke an economic and political decline that would last much longer than any final settlement over Québec.

- *Constitutional status of a UDI.* What would come of the fact that Québec separation by a UDI would clearly be unconstitutional? Would other Canadians have the right to contest it? Rather than accept Québec's unilateral declaration, Canadian leaders might, for example, contest its validity in the country and attempt to force the Québec government to back down. Until terms with Canada were worked out, the federal government would have no choice but to contest the Québec action.

- *Use of force.* Would Canadians use force to defend the country against a Québec UDI? Not likely. They would not need to. It would not be the federal government but the new self-declared state of Québec that would have to coerce hundreds of thousands of unwilling citizens into following its laws. It would have to enforce its unconstitutional claims by coercing those Québeckers who did not agree with the Yes side. The new Québec government would have to pass laws, control its citizenship, monitor immigration. It would need a new court system backed up by its own army, police and prison system. States cannot exist without these structures, or they become mere colonies of some other state.

  It would be Québec's show. In fact, without Québec adhering to the Constitution, no federal politicians could respond — unless they were claiming to represent the legitimacy of the Canadian Constitution, in which case the constitutional rules for amending the Constitution would either have to be followed or changed.

---

19. Patrick J. Monahan, "Cooler Heads Shall Prevail: Assessing the Costs and Consequences of Québec Separation," *C.D. Howe Institute Commentary*, no. 65 (January 1995).

- *Other groups' independence.* In the event of a UDI, what would prevent other groups or "nations" within Québec from separating from the new country? Aboriginal claims are strong, and would receive international support. And what about Montréal and the western part of the province near Ottawa, which are certain to vote against separation?

- *Tension and violence.* If a UDI were accepted, this breach of the rule of law could lead to nightmare scenarios of ethnic tension and violence.[20] The Canadian territory would be truncated. The state would, in fact, have to be reinvented, raising the fundamental question of whether Canadians in the remaining provinces would want to continue sharing citizenship under a common constitution. Some provinces might be open to options of separation or joining the United States.

Nationalism and Self-Determination

The issue of Québec independence raises questions about the right of people to self-determination and statehood. International law is instructive but not conclusive on this point. Two principles clash, in fact, as international law seems to recognize both the right to self-determination and the inviolability of borders. Of course, the only thing that actually settles questions of this nature is the political action of states in recognizing a new country or in defending an old country's territory.

The first question is the principle of self-determination. In international law, the right of self-determination extends only to those circumstances in which people are experiencing foreign or alien domination, or are subject to discriminatory regimes. Neither of these situations applies in Québec, where citizens have democratic rights as part of Canada. As Prime Minister Jean Chrétien forcefully put it, "In international law, Québec cannot separate from Canada without Canada's consent."

But recognition of new states has often been accorded even without the parent country's consent. For example, when Canada recognized Ukraine in December 1991, it went against the so-called principle of consent. Canada rushed to recognize Ukraine before there was any consideration of Russian consent. It was a political decision. Canadian leaders did not even wait for other countries in the United Nations to make a declaration. On the other hand, the Canadian government did the opposite in the cases of Slovenia and Croatia. It waited to see what decision other countries would take before recognizing these two new states.

The second question about self-determination concerns borders. If Québec did unilaterally declare independence, what lands could it claim? Using the same logic as employed above, it could only claim the territory and people over whom it could maintain effective control. If two rival governments contest a territory, political, and not legal, justifications are what finally resolve the issue. Borders must be adjusted to conform to the reality of who has the power and legitimacy.

It is extremely unlikely that the federal government would use military power to intervene in a sovereign Québec, but the aboriginal peoples would have the legal justification and power to stay within Canada even if there were a Yes vote in the referendum. The Constitution makes it clear in section 91(24) that "Indians and their lands" come under the federal authority, and section 35(1) protects aboriginal rights and treaties, which were made with Canada and not Québec. Moreover, at a minimum, the federal government would have a moral duty to help those Canadians who did not wish to stay in Québec — including aboriginals and, for example, some Montréalers and Canadians in the western part of Québec.

---

20. For a comparative study of peaceful successions, see Robert A. Young, "How Do Peaceful Successions Happen?" *CJPS*, vol. 27, no. 4 (December 1994), pp. 773–92.

Is the Constitution a "Red Herring"?

Since secession would destroy fundamental institutions in Canada such as the monarchy, Governor General and Lieutenant-Governors, a change of such magnitude would require the most rigid constitutional amendment rule. In other words, any secession would require the unanimous consent of all the provinces of Canada plus a majority of members of both houses of Parliament. Neither federal nor provincial politicians alone have authority to agree to a unilateral declaration of independence, as they are elected only to govern over classes of subjects mentioned in the Constitution, and secession is not one of them.

It is clear, therefore, that a unilateral declaration of independence by Québec would be unconstitutional. The Canadian Constitution provides no rules about the right of a province to secede from Canada. Nowhere in the list of jurisdictional powers does a province have the right to separate from Canada. The courts, therefore, could be called upon by the federal government or by private interests to contest the validity of the referendum and/or any UDI decision. The federal government and the courts have no justification or legal obligation to pay any attention to a UDI. Thus, constitutionally speaking, in the event of a UDI, political legitimacy and power would remain with the federal government.

Claims that by taking part in the 1980 referendum federal forces approved of Québec's ability to secede by a referendum are specious. First, such political rhetoric does not override the Constitution, and second, in 1980 the federal forces only engaged in a referendum about a "mandate to negotiate" separation. No one agreed to the premise that a province could act *unilaterally*. As Prime Minister Chrétien told Radio-Québec: "the Prime Minister has a Constitution to abide by and there is no mechanism in the Constitution that permits the separation of any part of the Canadian territory."

Two arguments are fundamental. Without the guidance of a constitution there would be chaos. Politicians become dictators and the political system becomes authoritarian when there is no legal framework. If Québec were to vote Yes in a future referendum, the federal government would be required to adhere to the Constitution. Prime Minister Chrétien has not said, nor will he say, that Québec has a right to secede; the Constitution does not allow him to make such a statement. Moreover, without adherence to the Constitution there would be no authoritative body to deal with Québec, or no process of law or deliberation about the future of Québec should it decide to separate. Without adherence to the Constitution, whose law would apply to those Québeckers who want to remain Canadians and pay taxes to Ottawa? What courts would determine the status of the Crees and Inuit who did not want to belong to a new Québec?

Those who stress the significance of the Constitution are not naïve. They fully understand that "the will of the people" is important. But how can democracy be actualized? What constitutes a fair and just process? Answers to these questions cannot be determined outside the Constitution. To say that the legal issue is irrelevant is tantamount to saying that a small majority in one province could effectively deprive 30 million citizens of their country. Canada would have to be reinvented.

1995 QUÉBEC REFERENDUM FALLOUT

Federal Strategy

On October 24, six days before the Québec referendum, a desperate Jean Chrétien promised a crowd in Verdun that he was open to change, including constitutional change, and would fight for the concept of a distinct society for Québec. After the referendum, he sought to make a quick and decisive move on his pre-referendum promises. Nationalists had tapped into a sense of historical humiliation, and that needed to be addressed by the federal government. Chrétien therefore examined positive measures to appeal to Québec. The government's response was eventually formulated in two plans, called Plan A and Plan B.

Plan A

Plan A was essentially a reconciliation effort — to sell a majority of Québeckers on the success of Canada and the benefits of staying in the federal union. In a sense, this plan began with the giant No rally in Montréal on October 27, 1995. The steps that followed included:

1) an *overhaul of the Cabinet* in which two star candidates from Québec, Stéphane Dion and Pierre Pettigrew, were approached, found seats where they could win by-elections, and initially given positions in Cabinet as Minister for Intergovernmental Affairs and Minister for International Cooperation respectively.

2) steps to meet the *distinct society* and *veto* promises. Within weeks of the referendum, a "resolution" was passed in the House of Commons recognizing Québec as a distinct society and another one concerning the veto. (See "Parliament's Distinct Society Motion.")

Parliament passed a motion on the distinct society of Québec because the provinces would not allow any "distinct society" concessions to be entrenched in the Constitution. However, discussions between the federal government and the provinces continued a search for compromises, or perhaps words other than distinct society, that would accomplish the same end. There was no solution.

A statutory (but not constitutional) veto was also approved by Parliament in February 1996. It affirmed that any constitutional change approved by Parliament would require consent from Ontario, Québec and British Columbia, as well as two of the four Atlantic provinces and two of the Prairie provinces. In effect, Parliament agreed to bind itself to the demands of the stronger provinces, in particular Québec.[21] (Alberta and British Columbia are required by their own laws to put all constitutional proposals to a provincial referendum.)

3) *decentralization* measures, which were important to show that the government was flexible concerning Québec's desires. The prime minister created a new committee chaired by francophone Marcel Massé to recommend ways far short of wholesale devolution that Ottawa could implement to regain support of francophone Québeckers through the decentralization of some federal programs.

> ## CLOSE-UP ON
> ### Institutions
>
> ### PARLIAMENT'S DISTINCT SOCIETY MOTION
>
> Whereas the people of Québec have expressed the desire for recognition of Québec's distinct society;
>
> 1) the House recognizes that Québec is a distinct society within Canada;
>
> 2) the House recognizes that Québec's distinct society includes its French-speaking majority, unique culture and civil law tradition;
>
> 3) the House undertakes to be guided by this reality;
>
> 4) the House encourages all components of the legislative and executive branches of government to take note of this recognition and be guided in their conduct accordingly.

That committee's report formed the basis of the Throne Speech in February 1996. The speech contained many mini-measures to show that Canada is on the side of fundamental change in the federation. It emphasized devolving powers to the provinces in areas such as forestry, mining, recreation, tourism and social housing. It said the federal government would not use its spending power to encroach further into areas of provincial jurisdiction (such as a national day-care program), and it supported the adoption of measures to strengthen the country's internal economic ties.

In June 1996, a First Ministers Conference was held in Ottawa at which devolution was discussed, particularly with regard to renunciation of the federal government's spending power and withdrawal from job-training programs. An agreement on labour market training was reached in which $2 billion was handed over to the provinces — at least a quarter of which went to Québec. The decentralization of labour market training was significant, as it had been a symbol of federal intransigence in Québec — proof that federalism could not work.

4) a campaign to *extol the virtues of being a Canadian*. Other initiatives were undertaken such as free distribution of flags and the setting up of a Unity Information Office (UIO). These plans were intended to counter the negative image of Canada that the separatists had propagated during the referendum. The UIO claimed that separatist leaders had distorted history and continually used emotive words such as "conquered," "rejected," "hoodwinked" and "betrayed" to describe relations with the rest of Canada.

Plan B

Plan B, dubbed "tough love" by some, was a plan to clarify rational, logical terms for secession — without using harsh federal threats about the risks of partition.

---

21. Andrew Heard and Tim Schwartz, "The Regional Veto Formula and Its Effects on Canada's Constitutional Amendment Process," *CJPS*, vol. 30, no. 2 (June 1997), pp. 339–58.

Reprinted by permission of Zazulak.

The first step in Plan B occurred in April 1996, when the federal government intervened in a court challenge to support the anti-sovereignty campaign waged by Québec lawyer Guy Bertrand. (See "Guy Bertrand's Fight in Québec's Courts.") Specifically, the federal intervention countered Québec's claim that the Constitution and courts would be irrelevant if Québeckers voted for separation. The federal government wanted to clarify that the Constitution would still apply after a Yes vote. But it did not take a position on Mr. Bertrand's basic arguments.

In another move, Prime Minister Chrétien said Québec would never be able to leave Canada unilaterally — even if a majority of Québeckers voted Yes in the next referendum. The law must be respected. The rest of Canada would have to approve the terms of separation through a constitutional amendment.[22]

In September 1996, the federal government sought a ruling on three specific questions from the Supreme Court of Canada, hoping to establish that a unilateral declaration of independence by Québec would be illegal. Despite objections from Québec, the Court ruled unanimously that it could answer the reference questions because there was no constitutional bar to such an advisory role and the questions were justiciable. However, the Court's conclusions in 1998 were woolly and controversial, based more on a broad understanding of Canadian democracy than on a strict reading of the constitutional text and documents. The Court based its interpretation on the "underlying principles"

---

22. *The Ottawa Citizen*, May 15, 1996.

of the Constitution, including principles of federalism, democracy, constitutionalism, the rule of law, and respect for minorities. Clearly aiming for a political compromise, it concluded as follows:

Question 1: *Under the Constitution of Canada, can the National Assembly, legislature or government of Québec effect the secession of Québec from Canada unilaterally?*

Ruling: "The Constitution vouchsafes order and stability, and accordingly secession of a province 'under the Constitution' could not be achieved without principled negotiation with other participants in Confederation within the existing constitutional framework."

And more directly: "The democratic vote, by however strong a majority, would have no legal effect on its own and could not push aside the principles of federalism and the rule of law, the rights of individuals and minorities, or the operation of democracy in the other provinces or in Canada as a whole. Democratic rights under the Constitution cannot be divorced from constitutional obligations."

Clearly, the Court concluded that a regular constitutional amendment would be required in order for separation from Canada to be constitutionally valid. But the Court did not stand with this strong statement alone. It added, "Nor, however, can the reverse proposition be accepted: the continued existence and operation of the constitutional order could not be indifferent to a clear expression of a clear majority of Quebecers that they no longer wish to remain in Canada."

The Court judgement then went on to practically demand that "negotiations" take place if there is a "demonstrated majority support for Quebec secession."

Question 2: *Does international law give the National Assembly, legislature or government of Québec the right to effect the secession of Québec from Canada unilaterally? In this regard, is there a right to self-determination under international law that would give the National Assembly, legislature or government of Québec the right to effect the secession of Québec from Canada unilaterally?*

Ruling: The Court ruled that "[i]n the circumstances, the 'National Assembly, the legislature or the government of Quebec' do not enjoy a right at international law to effect the secession of Quebec from Canada unilaterally."

Question 3: *In the event of a conflict between domestic and international law on the right of the National Assembly, legislature or government of Québec to effect the secession of Québec from Canada unilaterally, which would take precedence in Canada?*

Ruling: In view of the answers to Questions 1 and 2, the Court said that this third question did not need to be answered.

Because this Supreme Court decision may play a major role in the process if there ever is a majority vote for separation in Québec, we include the complete text of answers and summary in Appendix 2.

The immediate political fall-out from the judgement was controversial. The federal Minister of Federal-Provincial Affairs, Stéphane Dion, seized on the *clear question* and *clear majority* clause in the Court response to attack the 1995 referendum. He proffered that any referendum question with the word "partnership" in it would be invalid and that a referendum would need a greater than 50-plus-one majority to be acceptable to the federal government.

On the other hand, separatists latched on to the crucial Supreme Court demand that negotiations would of necessity have to follow a positive vote on separation in Québec. The idea that the federal government and the provinces had to negotiate after a positive provincial referendum certainly encouraged separatists that their demands were legitimate and reasonable.

Of course, one might ask by what constitutional rule the Supreme Court judges came to their decision on this topic. The reason for the decision – to dampen down emotional ire in Québec – is

CLOSE-UP ON
Institutions

GUY BERTRAND'S FIGHT IN QUÉBEC'S COURTS

In August 1995, about two months before the Québec referendum, Québec lawyer Guy Bertrand filed a court action contesting various aspects of the Québec government's proposed separation referendum and requesting an injunction to stop the October 30 referendum. He argued that secession is illegal by virtue of international and Canadian law, and therefore it is illegal to hold such a referendum. He later amended his motion to seek a permanent injunction against any future sovereignty referendums.

In April 1996, the Québec government filed a motion to have the Bertrand action dismissed because, it said, Canadian courts have no jurisdiction when it comes to separation. At this point, the federal government intervened to counter Québec's claim that the Constitution and courts are irrelevant if Québeckers vote for separation.

In August 1996, the Québec Superior Court ruled to reject the motion by the Québec government to throw the Bertrand case out of court. The Court also ruled that a constitutional amendment could be needed for a province to separate legally from Canada. The judge said that in his opinion he did not have the powers to rule on the fundamental issues at stake in Bertrand's application. But he said the application would be heard by a trial judge who would be asked to rule on the legality of Québec's secession. "It is not clearly established whether the process of Québec's accession to sovereignty is sanctioned under international law."* How would *you* judge the case?

---

* Quotations from *The Globe and Mail,* August 31, 1996.

understandable, but the unfortunate part of this decision is that Québec might vote to separate and yet one or all of the provinces or the federal government might object to negotiating with the secessionists. In this case, the separatists could claim that the Court backed their demands for negotiations. In this author's opinion, the Court's judgement in this regard was illegitimate and unconstitutional. Nothing in the Constitution says that those opposed to the separation of Québec are required to negotiate in the face of a positive vote. The judges' hasty and ill-considered decision may one day do more harm than good for the unity of Canada.

In response to the ongoing charge that the federal government was not proactive about Québec separatism, the Chrétien government tabled Bill C-20 in December 1999. This legislation or so-called "clarity bill" sets out the rules by which the government and Parliament of Canada would analyze any future separatist referendum. It concludes that the government will not enter into any negotiations with a province over separation unless the House of Commons determines both that the referendum question is "clear" and that a "clear" expression of will has been obtained by a "clear" majority of the population.

This is bizarre legislation, as few states make such direct provisions about their own destruction. On the other hand, the Liberal government defends the legislation as necessary to spell out precisely how a future referendum in Québec would be handled by the federal government and Parliament. Predictably, this legislation received vitriolic comments from the Bloc Québécois government in Ottawa, and the Parti Québécois government in Québec immediately tabled a competing bill in the National Assembly (Bill 99), claiming that only the Québec people can decide on the legal status of their province and that a 50-percent-plus-one vote will be considered enough for a referendum victory.

Despite the posturing, neither bill is constitutionalized, and both can be changed by any future legislature. The constitutional amendment process remains intact; the secession of a province from Canada would require resolutions to be passed in the federal Parliament and all 10 legislative assemblies. There is no easy way to political change short of this high obstacle. Table 7.3 summarizes some important highlights in Canada/Québec relations 1976–99.

Québec Nationalist Strategy

After the referendum, Québec nationalist leaders began a slow but deliberate strategy to entice a majority of Québeckers to join their cause for Québec autonomy in the future. Lucien Bouchard replaced the less charismatic nationalist Jacques Parizeau as leader of the PQ and premier of Québec.

TABLE 7.3   CANADA/QUÉBEC CONSTITUTIONAL HIGHLIGHTS, 1976–99

1976	Trudeau puts forward constitutional proposals concerning patriation and an amending formula based on the 1971 Victoria Charter; discussions with provinces begin
	November Parti Québécois wins the Québec election; René Lévesque is premier
1978	Trudeau introduces Bill C-60 providing for patriation
1980	Liberals win federal election
	Québec sovereignty referendum fails
1981	PQ win Québec election
	Supreme Court rules that federal unilateral action is legal but not conventional
	Agreement is reached between the federal government and nine provinces; Québec does not sign
1982	Québec Court of Appeal rejects Québec government's claim of veto power over constitutional change
	Constitution is patriated with a revised amending formula and a charter of rights
1984	Trudeau announces intention to resign
	The Conservatives win federal election; Brian Mulroney is prime minister
1985	Québec Liberal party wins provincial election; Robert Bourassa becomes premier
1987	The Meech Lake accord is signed by all First Ministers — must be ratified by the federal Parliament and all provincial legislatures within three years
	Québec is the first province to ratify the accord
1988	The Conservatives win federal election
1989	Clyde Wells becomes premier of Newfoundland
	Meech Lake dies — Newfoundland and Manitoba do not ratify before the deadline
1991	Allaire Report recommends Québec powers increase
	Mulroney unveils a new set of proposals
1992	Ottawa and nine provinces reach consensus about constitutional reform; Québec does not participate
	Bourassa joins discussions
	Charlottetown accord is announced
	Mulroney announces referendum on the accord
	Charlottetown referendum fails 55 percent to 45 percent
1993	Brian Mulroney resigns as prime minister
	The Liberals win the federal election; Jean Chrétien becomes prime minister
	The Parti Québécois win Québec election; Jacques Parizeau is premier
1995	Referendum in Québec on sovereignty fails narrowly; Bouchard replaces Parizeau as premier of Québec
1996	Parliament passes legislation allowing Québec, Ontario, British Columbia and any two Maritime or Prairie provinces to veto any further constitutional change
	Federal government refers three questions about Québec separatism to Supreme Court
1998	Jean Charest becomes leader of Liberal Party of Québec
	Bouchard's Parti Québécois is victorious in provincial election
	Supreme Court rules on questions concerning separation of Québec
1999	Federal Parliament passes "Clarity Bill" and Québec responds with its own legislation

Bouchard convinced a PQ convention to moderate many of its strident positions. He also joined the prime minister's trade mission to Asia in January 1997. These and other moderate stances improved many of the separatist government's tensions with the Québec business community and international investors.

Despite these more temperate positions, Bouchard insists that he will lead Québec out of Canada. However, he continues to delay any hint about the date for a new referendum. Bouchard's narrow November 1998 victory over Jean Charest (the PQ and the Liberals each received 43 percent of the popular vote but maldistribution of the vote gave the PQ 75 seats, the Liberals 48 and the Action Democratique one means that his ability to manoeuvre successfully is limited. Since a Québec election is not required until 2002–3, it is fairly certain that Premier Bouchard will not call a referendum until "the winning conditions" are met – if ever.

Federalist forces in Québec continue to be divided on what strategy to take toward nationalist aspirations. The Liberal party, led by Jean Charest, has adopted a strong devolutionist and pro–distinct society position, which has solidified support in some French quarters while reducing some English and allophone support. The most strident federalists are found in the 35 different groups that hold to the position that parts of Québec will have the right to separate from Québec if Québec ever separates from Canada.

REGIONALISM

In contrast to nationalism, which entails altering existing political structures, **regionalism** refers to territorial tensions "brought about by certain groups that ... demand a change in the political, economic and cultural relations between regions and central powers *within* the existing state."[23] Regionalist discontent is most often expressed in economic terms, especially by representatives of poorer, peripheral regions within a country. Residents of these areas demand a larger share of the affluence enjoyed by others in their society. However, such discontent can also find expression in political terms, particularly, for example, when *nouveau riche* regions object to the central government's power to impose constraints that prevent them from "cashing in" on their new-found prosperity.

In the short term, because regionalism does not directly challenge territorial sovereignty, it appears to present less of a threat to the existing state structure than does nationalism. In the long term, however, persistent indifference to regionalist demands by central authorities may result in a serious loss of legitimacy for the state in certain parts of the country. Moreover, in extreme circumstances it could also provide the basis for the development of a distinct ethnic or national identity seeking separation from the state.

At the very least, regionalist protests add to the flow of demands that must be considered by policy-makers. Because most Canadian political parties, including government parties, to some extent have regional concentrations of support, regionalism has become an important, maybe even the dominant, dimension of political life.

If the greatest modern challenge to federalism is the threat of Québec separatism, the next in significance is undoubtedly the manifestation of alienation in some of the regions. All of the non-central provinces have some grievances against central Canada and its governments in Ottawa,

---

23. Riccardo Petrella, "Nationalist and Regionalist Movements in Western Europe," in C. Foster, ed., *Nations without a State* (New York: Praeger, 1980), p. 10 (emphasis added). See also Janine Brodie, "Regions and Regionalism," in James P. Bickerton and Alain G. Gagnon, eds., *Canadian Politics* (Broadview Press, 1994), pp. 409–25.

Ontario and Québec. The litany includes complaints about official bilingualism, monetary policy, tariff policy, spending decisions, and the treatment of fisheries and resource industries. The Maritimes have always been characterized by a fierce pride and independence, but this has been mitigated by the area's need for federal financial assistance. In the West, alienation combines economic discontent and antipathy toward French Canada in particular with a demand for a stronger role for the West in the federation.

Alienation: Views from the West

As we saw in Chapter 3, alienation is a major component of western Canada's political culture.[24] Throughout the West's history, there has been a strong belief that the resource-rich Prairie provinces were exploited by federal government policies representing central Canadian interests. Perennial disagreements arose over federal freight-rate and tariff policies, which were seen as responsible both for making the West a captive market for higher-priced manufactured goods from central Canada and for increasing the cost of exporting products from the West. Westerners argue that such policies have allowed the East to remain the industrial heartland of Canada while the West carries a disproportionate share of the costs.

Largely because of a "fruitcake" mix of cultures and a relatively small francophone population in the West, political vision on the Prairies is based more on economic development than cultural interests. Recent regionalist sympathies in the West sprang from the period of economic prosperity in the 1970s and early 1980s. The scarcity and high cost of non-renewable energy in the form of oil and gas spurred western economic development. Once one of the weak partners of the federal union, the West began to acquire enormous economic power through its sale of natural resources. As this economic wealth was exploited, migration to the West increased, and the region finally found itself capable of challenging what it considered the intolerable domination of central Canada.

Modern economic issues dividing western and central Canada continue to be interpreted within this context of alienation. Since the 1970s, regional criticism of the political and economic dominance of central Canada has been expressed in a desire for constitutional reform. The western provincial governments, for example, refused to compromise over patriation of the Constitution in 1982 unless the federal government would reduce its power, especially on economic issues. In other words, the jurisdictional issue of whether the provinces or the federal government should control resource development spilled over into the constitutional arena.

Western alienation was evident in the early 1980s in the formation of various groups and political parties dedicated to the separation of the western provinces from Canada. Western separatism was ignited by the re-election of the federal Liberal party in 1980. This election effectively disenfranchised western Canada politically, as the Liberals captured no seats west of Manitoba. Subsequently, the Liberal government initiated two aggressive federal policies: unilateral patriation of the Constitution despite provincial objections; and implementation of the National Energy Program, which many Westerners perceived as an attempt to rob them of their resource wealth.

The two leading separatist groups in that period were the Western Canadian Federation (West-Fed) and the Western Canada Concept (WCC). Frustrated by a lack of political power within the federal government, Westerners felt powerless against "centralist" policies, including bilingualism, metrication and immigration. Yet the popularity of western separatism dissipated as quickly as it had

---

24. On the concept of western alienation see Roger Gibbins, *Prairie Politics and Society* (Toronto: Butterworth, 1980); and Larry Pratt and Garth Stevenson, eds., *Western Separatism* (Edmonton: Hurtig, 1981).

risen. As one observer noted: "The spontaneity of the separatist movement was both the most important reason for its success and its greatest handicap in developing into a solid, permanent political movement."[25] While the movement provided an outlet for the expression of frustration, there was little agreement among the groups, let alone within them, concerning what strategy to follow. Internal dissension assured that minor electoral successes were short-lived.

The acute sentiments of western alienation that characterized the early 1980s declined when high oil prices, which had underpinned provincialism, dropped after Brian Mulroney won the 1984 general election. With Mulroney's victory the western regionalists thought they would obtain strong and effective representation in government. To some extent these expectations were justified: Mulroney's western accord dismantled the National Energy Program and the Trudeau marketing restrictions on the sale of oil and natural gas.

However, the feeling that the political system was stacked against the West lingered and was given voice by Preston Manning, son of the former Social Credit premier of Alberta. In the 1988 general election, Manning headed the newly established Reform party, and conducted a credible campaign for western interests. Its demands for free trade and Senate reform found a ready audience among "small-c" conservative voters. The party named 72 candidates, and while it did not win any seats, it did obtain 15 percent of the votes in Alberta and affected Conservative and NDP results throughout the West.

In the 1993 general election, the Reform party won 51 seats, mainly in Alberta and British Columbia. Given the collapse of the Conservative party, Reform had an opportunity to develop a strong national party and take its place. Instead, Preston Manning chose to accentuate western concerns in the 1997 election. He raised his number of seats to 60 (all from the West) and became leader of the official opposition in the House of Commons.

The Reform party does, however, continue to play on western alienation. It calls for changes to the Senate in order to reduce the power of central Canada, and for populist devices such as referendums, recall and initiatives to reduce the power of the House of Commons. But the centrepiece of Reform policy is the explicit demand for a reduction in taxation and in government expenditures. The party also stands against bilingualism, declaring that attempts by the federal government to "politicize and institutionalize and constitutionalize English–French relations on a national basis and as a raison d'être for the notion itself ... have led again, as they have in the past, not to unity but to crisis."[26] For a discussion of the transition from the Reform Party to the Canadian Reform Conservative Alliance, see Chapter 11.

Many Westerners feel that they put more into the federation than they receive in benefits. If Ottawa is not able to accommodate the ambition of western Canadians, the potential for continued challenges in the West remains — awaiting only a major confrontation with the federal government over the future of Québec within the federation.

25. Denise Harrington, "Who Are the Separatists?" in Pratt and Stevenson, eds., *Western Separatism*, p. 24.

26. Robert J. Jackson and Doreen Jackson, *Stand Up for Canada: Leadership and the Canadian Political Crisis* (Scarborough: Prentice Hall, 1992), p. 198.

SUMMARY

During the past three decades, powerful nationalist pressures in Québec created serious challenges to the federal political system. Two referendums, one in 1980 and another in 1995, asked Québeckers if they wanted to separate from Canada. Canadians outside Québec stood by helplessly, not knowing whether the country would disintegrate. The 1995 referendum was so close that the government found it necessary to clarify what would happen in the event of yet another such occurrence. The Supreme Court issued its 1998 decisions on the constitutionality of secession efforts, and both the federal and Québec legislatures responded with their own policies. Meanwhile, the Federal government also attempted to rebalance the federal financial equilibrium by decentralizing in targeted areas.

It is still not clear whether Canadian federalism will be able to meet the challenge of Québec separatists while still meeting the concerns of other regions. The West in particular, located far from the political centre in Ottawa, has its own unique concerns. Dissatisfaction in the West brought massive political change to Ottawa in the recent general elections, when the electorate abandoned its traditional support for the Conservative and New Democratic parties and voted for a new protest party. In 1997, the result was a new party system with the Reform party strong enough to be the official opposition. The concerns of the two groups, Québec and the West, must be balanced, and in a way that will leave Canada strong and united.

DISCUSSION QUESTIONS

1. Trace the development of nationalism in Québec through past French–English conflicts.
2. Is the French language threatened in Québec? What factors would make this better or worse for citizens of the new country if Québec were an independent country?
3. Why was the result of the 1995 referendum in Québec so close?
4. Do you approve of the federal government strategy toward Québec since the 1995 referendum?
5. Is enough being done to counter regional alienation?

Selected Bibliography

Beheils, M., *Quebec Since 1945: Selected Readings* (Toronto: Copp Clark Pitman, 1987).

Bothwell, Robert, *Canada and Quebec: One Country, Two Histories* (Vancouver: University of British Columbia Press, 1995).

Brubaker, Rogers, *Nationalism Reframed: Nationhood and the National Question in the New Europe* (Cambridge, U.K.: Cambridge University Press, 1996).

Conway, John, *Debts to Pay* (Toronto: Lorimer, 1992).

Côté, Marcel and David Johnson, *If Quebec Goes: The Real Cost of Separation* (Toronto: Stoddart, 1994).

Dodge, William, ed., *Boundaries of Identity: A Quebec Reader* (Toronto: Lester Publishing, 1992).

Drache, Daniel and Roberto Perin, eds., *Negotiating with a Sovereign Quebec* (Toronto: Lorimer, 1992).

Freeman, Alan and Patrick Grady, *Dividing the House: Planning for a Canada without Quebec* (Toronto: Harper Collins, 1994).

Gibbins, Roger and Guy Laforest, eds., *Beyone the Impasse: Toward Reconciliation* (Montréal: Institute for Research on Public Policy, 1998).

Gibson, Gordon, *Plan B: The Future of the Rest of Canada* (Vancouver: Fraser Institute, 1994).

Greenfeld, Liah, *Nationalism: Five Roads to Modernity* (Cambridge, Mass: Harvard University Press, 1992).

Ignatieff, Michael, *Blood and Belonging: Journeys into the New Nationalism* (Toronto: Viking, 1993).

Johnson, William, *A Canadian Myth: Quebec, Between Canada and the Illusion of Utopia* (Montréal: Davies, 1994).

Keating, Michael, *Nations against the State: The New Politics of Nationalism in Quebec, Catalonia and Scotland* (New York: St. Martin's Press, 1996).

Kedourie, Elie, *Nationalism,* 4th ed. (Oxford: Blackwell, 1996).

Lachapelle, Guy, G. Bernier, Daniel Salée and Luc Bernier, *The Quebec Democracy: Structures, Processes and Policies* (Toronto: McGraw-Hill Ryerson, 1993).

Lamont, Lansing, *Breakup: The Coming End of Canada and the Stakes for America* (New York: Norton, 1994).

Lemco, Jonathan, *Turmoil in the Peaceable Kingdom: The Quebec Sovereignty Movement and Its Implications for Canada and the United States* (Toronto: University of Toronto Press, 1994).

Mathews, Georges, *Quiet Resolution* (Toronto: Summerhill Press, 1990).

McRoberts, Ken, *Beyond Quebec: Taking Stock of Canada* (Montréal: McGill-Queen's University Press, 1995).

——————, *Misconceiving Canada: The Struggle for National Unity* (Toronto: Oxford Universtiy Press, 1997).

Monahan, Patrick J., *Cooler Heads Shall Prevail: Assessing the Costs and Consequences of Quebec Separation* (Toronto: C.D. Howe Institute, 1994).

—————— and Michael J. Bryant, *Coming to Terms with Plan B: Ten Principles Governing Secession* (Toronto: C.D. Howe Institute, 1996).

Smith, Anthony D., *National Identity* (Las Vegas: University of Nevada Press, 1991).

Trent, John E., Robert Young and Guy Lachapelle, eds., *Quebec — Canada: What Is the Path Ahead?* (Ottawa: University of Ottawa Press, 1997).

Valaskakis, Kimon and Angeline Fournier, *The Delusion of Sovereignty* (Montréal: Étincelle Éditeur, 1994).

Young, Robert A., *The Secession of Quebec and the Future of Canada* (Montréal: McGill-Queen's University Press, 1995).

LIST OF WEBLINKS

www.visi.com/~homelands/
canada/canada.html

Canadian Secessionist Movements This Web site contains information about various secessionist movements in Canada.

dsp-psd.pwgsc.gc.ca/
InfoSource/Info_1/COL-e.html

Commissioner of Official Languages The Commissioner of Official Languages is responsible for monitoring bilingualism in Canada.

8

The Executive

. . . .

Governor General, Prime Minister and Cabinet

In Canada, there are three separate branches of governmental institutions: the executive, the legislature and the judiciary. This chapter describes and explains the nature of *executive* power, both ceremonial and political. In many respects, this power is comparable to a Shakespearean drama: there is a world of difference between appearance and reality.

The nature of political power and its exercise are exceedingly complex and fascinating phenomena. The analysis of leaders and their policies has always been a favourite pursuit of political scientists and pundits. Perennial debates and studies consider who really exercises power, what the machinery of leadership is and whether power is shifting in some fashion. A factor complicating the analysis is that political power is an abstract commodity, changing in response to the dynamic political and social environment in which a variety of issues, problems and personalities come and go. Political power is, in a manner of speaking, like a complex mathematical equation in which there are a few constant values and many indeterminate ones.

In contemporary states the task of applying the rules of society is concentrated in an **executive**. This broad term is used to depict the institutions, personnel and behaviour of governmental power. Generally, there are two kinds of rules in a society — constitutional laws, or the basic rules of the game, and less fundamental laws, such as policies and resolutions. Both types of rules are implemented by the executive, which, in performing this function, plays a vital role in the political system.

Canada's constitutional heritage from Britain includes a *formal* executive, the Crown and the Governor General, and also a *political* executive concerned primarily with the realities of power in contemporary Canadian politics. We begin this chapter by examining the formal executive, including the heritage of parliamentary government and its effects on executive power. Next, we outline the role of the prime minister and the structure of Cabinet decision-making, including the organization of the 1993 Chrétien government. Studies of conflict of interest and patronage fill out this section. These analyses are followed by an examination of the administrative agencies that support the executive by providing specialized research, advice and assistance in policy formation and implementation. Finally, we conclude by evaluating the ongoing debate about the expanding role of the prime minister and its implications for Canadian politics.

THE FORMAL EXECUTIVE: CROWN, MONARCHY AND GOVERNOR GENERAL

The *Constitution Act, 1867* (formerly the *BNA Act*), sets out in general terms the powers and prerogatives of formal authority in Canada. Section 9 declares that the "Executive Government and Authority of and over Canada ... is vested in the Queen." This principle is fleshed out in the *Letters Patent* and must be understood in the light of the traditional *royal prerogative* (see below).[1] While there is no question that the powers of the formal executive are largely ceremonial, it would be incorrect to dismiss them as trivial and meaningless. There have been situations in which the formal executive has proven a very important element in the political process itself.

Crown and Monarch

Following British tradition, the supreme authority of the Canadian state resides in the sovereign. Government functions are carried out in the name of the *Crown*. In Britain, the Crown has been defined as "the sum total of governmental powers synonymous with the Executive."[2] In Canada, the term **Crown** refers to the composite symbol of the institutions of the state. The Crown may be involved in court proceedings.[3] It also assumes a variety of other duties and responsibilities — for example, government property may be held in the name of the Crown.

The Crown retains some rights from the feudal period, but most of its present authority comes from constitutional and statute law. The few "prerogative powers" can be traced to the period of authoritarian rule in Great Britain when the Crown possessed wide discretionary authority. With the rise of Parliament and the gradual movement toward popular sovereignty, the authority of the Crown eroded to a very few reserve powers. Although Parliament and the political executive still govern in the name of the Crown, there is little question that the monarch is severely limited. Even the ability of the monarch to stay on the throne is no longer a right. In the cases of both James II and Edward VIII in Britain, it was clear that they could not retain their crowns unless the ministers and Parliament were prepared to accept them.

The reigning monarch, currently Queen Elizabeth II, is the personal embodiment of the Crown. The contemporary functions of the monarch are largely ceremonial and non-partisan. The monarch reigns, but does not govern. As British constitutionalist Walter Bagehot put it, the monarch's functions are mainly of the "dignified," not the "efficient," type.[4] By this Bagehot meant that the monarch does not actually govern the country, but rather carries out a myriad of ceremonial responsibilities that generate mass support for government, while the ministers carry out the "efficient" procedures that operate the machinery of government.

Although the monarchy is of necessity personified in an individual, one should separate individual peculiarities and institutional strengths. Individuals come and go, but the Crown is permanent. It provides history, tradition and an institutional framework that can promote political stability as long as the institution is regarded as legitimate by a large majority of the people.

---

1. See Andrew Heard, *Canadian Constitutional Conventions* (Toronto: Oxford University Press, 1991).
2. E.C.S. Wade and A.W. Bradley, *Constitutional Law*, 8th ed. (London: Longman, 1970), pp. 171ff., 678ff.
3. Since the passage of the *Crown Liability Act* of 1952, the Crown can be sued like any other litigant.
4. Walter Bagehot, *The English Constitution* (London: World's Classics, 1928).

Governor General and Lieutenant-Governors

Since the monarch was not based permanently in Canada, a representative known as the Governor General was originally appointed by the British government as dictated by the *Constitution Act, 1867*. As Canada evolved out of colonialism toward autonomy, the nature of this executive link was modified. The Imperial Conference of 1926 sought to make the Governor General a representative of the Crown, *not* of the British government. In 1947, new **Letters Patent** — the instruments that the sovereign makes applicable to each Governor General through his or her commission of appointment — completed the process by allowing the Governor General the power to exercise the powers of the sovereign. However, the monarchical link was never ended. The Queen continues to be Canada's monarch: she makes royal tours to Canada and acts as the symbolic head of the Commonwealth, of which Canada is a member.

As the Queen's representative, the Governor General is appointed by Her Majesty on the recommendation of the Canadian prime minister and the Cabinet. In 1952, the office was further Canadianized by the appointment of Vincent Massey, the first Canadian to hold the position. (See Table 8.1.) It has since become customary to alternate the position between English- and French-speaking Canadians. The appointment of Edward Schreyer in 1979 added a new dimension to this trend, since he was an English-speaking Canadian from neither charter group. The next appointee, in 1984, Jeanne Sauvé, a French Canadian, became the first woman to hold this high office. Governors General have often been selected from outside the partisan political sphere, mainly from the diplomatic or military establishment, but many have been politicians. In 1994, Prime Minister Chrétien appointed the Liberal Senate Speaker, Roméo Leblanc, an Acadian, as Governor General, and in 1999 he chose Adrienne Clarkson, a bilingual journalist who was the first member of a visible minority to be chosen as head of state.

The Governor General, in performing the Queen's "dignified" roles in Canada, provides little practical input into the political process. The tenure of office is usually five years, but the officially recognized term is six years, which has on occasion been extended to seven. In the event of death, incapacity, removal or absence of the Governor General, the Chief Justice of the Supreme Court, Canada's leading judge, acts as the administrator and may carry out all duties of the office.

The functions of the Governor General as head of state provide the official monarchical structure of the Canadian government on an everyday basis. First, many purely ceremonial functions such as conferring Order of Canada awards or reviewing troops are carried out by the appointee. Second, the Governor General also acts as a symbol of the state. After studying loyalty in many political regimes, theorists have found that individuals may be socialized into acceptance of authority through their attachment to august figures such as the Governor General.

TABLE 8.1   CANADIAN-BORN GOVERNORS GENERAL, 1952–2000

Vincent Massey	1952
Georges Vanier	1959
Roland Michener	1967
Jules Léger	1974
Edward Schreyer	1979
Jeanne Sauvé	1984
Ramon Hnatyshyn	1990
Roméo Leblanc	1994
Adrienne Clarkson	1999

Adrienne Clarkson appointed Governor General, September 9, 1999.
Aislin, *The Gazette* (Montréal). Reprinted with permission.

The Governor General is bound to act on almost every piece of advice given by his or her ministers. Nevertheless, certain functions are the Governor General's alone. The most important of these stem from the **prerogative powers** left to the monarch — powers that have not been bypassed by constitutional or statute law. The Letters Patent provide the Governor General with all the powers of the Queen "in respect of summoning, proroguing or dissolving the Parliament of Canada." Clearly, the most significant power is the duty to appoint a prime minister. In order to exercise this prerogative power, the Governor General must have a reasonably free hand to make decisions based on the circumstances and precedents.[5]

On two occasions in the 1890s, the Governor General had to help find someone to be prime minister because the Conservative party had no clear successor to the outgoing leader.[6] In cases where there is a leader of a party who can command a clear majority of the seats in the House of Commons, the Governor General has nothing to do but select the obvious candidate.[7] Today, if there were no obvious leader after a prime minister died in office, for example, the Cabinet and/or caucus would undoubtedly name an interim leader pending a leadership convention, and the Governor General would name this person prime minister.

A major issue remains. If there were no majority for any leader in the House of Commons, the Governor General might have to use his or her discretion in selecting the prime minister. In 28 of the 36 elections since Confederation, one of the two major parties obtained an absolute majority of the seats in the House, so the Governor General was not required to exercise personal discretion. However, when election results are confused or produce no majority, the Governor General could be forced to exercise the prerogative in an independent manner. Such discretionary power would always be subject to controversy, and in every case but one (discussed below) the Governor General has chosen as prime minister the leader of the party that received the *largest* number of seats in the House of Commons — even if he or she did not obtain a *majority* of the seats.

For purposes of discussion, the dissolution of Parliament is too often separated from the appointment of the prime minister. But the two are logically related. It is generally agreed that only a prime minister can ask for and obtain a dissolution of Parliament, although a Governor General once refused such a request. This incident was the famous Byng-King case in 1926. (See "Byng-King and Dissolution.") The precedent is now fairly firm that Governors General should follow the advice of their prime ministers on the dissolution of Parliament. In December 1979, Conservative prime minister

---

5. For a thorough study of the precedents see Andrew Heard, *Canadian Constitutional Precedents* (Toronto: Oxford University Press, 1991).

6. J.T. Saywell, "The Crown and the Politicians," *Canadian Historical Review* (December 1956), pp. 309–37. John A. Macdonald (1891) and John Thompson (1894) both died in office without an obvious successor.

7. Since the 1890s, when Sir John Abbott and Sir Mackenzie Bowell held the prime ministership from the Senate, all prime ministers have held seats in the House of Commons.

Joe Clark, who headed a minority government, was defeated on the budget. Although theoretically the Liberals could have been asked to try to form a government, the Governor General consulted Mr. Clark and dissolved Parliament without discussing the matter with any of the opposition parties.

Can a Governor General dismiss a government? It has always been assumed that this would prove impossible when one party controls a majority in the House. However, the Australian "Canberra case" of November 1975 upset the certainty of this contention. While the Australian constitutional structure differs from that of Canada in many respects (especially in the fact that the upper house is an elected body), it has generally been assumed that the Governors General of both countries were unable to dissolve Parliament. In the Canberra case, however, the Australian Senate had continually held up supply bills from the lower house, creating a financial crisis. The Senate was controlled by the Liberal and Country parties, while the lower house was controlled by the prime minister, Gough Whitlam, and his Labor party. The Governor General wanted to dissolve both houses. Whitlam refused, and the Governor General dismissed him. The Governor General asked the leader of the opposition to form a government on the condition that he would immediately request a dissolution. In the bitter election campaign that followed, the Liberal-Country coalition was elected. In other words, the Governor General's recommendation was electorally upheld.

The effect of this precedent on Canada is difficult to determine, since nothing equivalent has occurred during this century. In view of the changing nature of the Commonwealth and the weakening bonds between the members, constitutional precedents are likely to prove inconsequential. It is fairly safe to say that no Governor General will act in Canada following the manner chosen in Australia, but the matter is not entirely settled.

Perhaps more important than formal constitutional power is the Governor General's opportunity to advise prime ministers. The Governor General meets regularly with the prime minister to discuss general points, personnel or appointments, and on such occasions prime ministers have been known to solicit advice on policy matters. In other words, the Governor General has a degree of access that is denied to most individuals. Sir Wilfrid Laurier confided: "The Canadian Governor General long ago ceased to determine policy, but he is by no means, or need not be, the mere figurehead of the public image. He has the privilege of advising his advisers, and if he is a man of sense and experience, his advice is often taken."[8] Or, as Governor General Adrienne Clarkson put it when she was

CLOSE-UP ON Institutions

BYNG-KING AND DISSOLUTION

Normally, a prime minister who is defeated in the House, or feels he or she may be, can ask to have Parliament dissolved rather than submit his or her resignation. Liberal prime minister Mackenzie King, as head of a minority government, did so in 1926.* The Governor General, Lord Byng, declined King's request for dissolution and an election. Instead, he called on the Conservative leader Arthur Meighen to form a new administration. The Governor General was cognizant of two special factors: the House was in the process of discussing a censure motion against the minority Liberal government, and the Conservatives held the largest number of seats in the House. It was theoretically possible that the Progressive party, which held the balance of power in the House, could have supported a Tory minority government.

As it turned out, however, the Progressives would not give their continued support to the new Conservative government and within three days the government fell. Meighen, in turn, had to ask the Governor General for a dissolution of Parliament.** In the election that ensued, the Liberals charged that the Governor General had favoured the Conservatives and that the British were again interfering in Canada. The electoral victory of the Liberals demonstrated that, although the Governor General may possess some constitutional powers about the dissolution of Parliament, the people are the final arbiters of whether or not the action is appropriate.

* The results of the 1925 election were Conservatives 116, Liberals 99, Progressives 24 and others 6 seats.
** See Eugene A. Forsey, *The Royal Plower of Dissolution of Parliament in the British Commonwealth* (Toronto: Oxford University Press, 1943).

---

8. O.D. Skelton, *Life and Letters of Sir Wilfrid Laurier*, vol. II, David L. Farr, ed. (Ottawa: Carleton University, 1965), p. 86n. Originally published Toronto, 1921.

asked a sensitive question, "If I have a view on that, I will communicate it to the Prime Minister, to whom I have a direct conduit."[9]

The monarch has a representative in each province as well as in Ottawa. A **Lieutenant-Governor** appointed by the governor-in-council on the advice of the prime minister (often chosen from a provincial list) represents the monarch in each province. The Lieutenant-Governor acts on the advice, and with the assistance, of his or her ministry or executive council at the provincial level of government, which is responsible to the legislature, and resigns office under circumstances similar to those for the federal government. It is unclear whether a Lieutenant-Governor can today delay or kill a bill by refusing to sign it. (See discussion of reservation and disallowance in Chapter 5.)

THE POLITICAL EXECUTIVE

Apart from the ceremonial functions of government discussed above, the main task of the executive is providing leadership. The determination of which bodies constitute the executive is complex, as there is no accepted view about how government should be organized. As a result, *executive leadership* may refer to formal roles, to individuals, to types of activities or to the results of such activities. The executive leaders discussed here have been selected on the basis of their formal roles. They include the prime minister, the ministry — including the Cabinet — and their immediate staff.

The central feature of any survey of Canada's political heritage must be the pervasive impact of the British model of parliamentary government. Although other aspects of Canadian life have been strongly influenced by the United States, the parliamentary form of government is firmly entrenched and has proven remarkably resistant to change. The Constitution established a type of government based on the British example, with the exception that there was to be a federal division of legislative powers in recognition of the diversity of the country. Canada was to be governed by a parliamentary system with British historical traditions and procedures, and by a constitutional monarch represented by an appointed Governor General.

Although the Constitution makes it clear that the Governor General is the country's formal executive, his or her powers and prerogatives are in fact severely limited.[10] As we have seen, only in extraordinary situations has a Governor General attempted to interfere directly in the political process. Executive power, although carried out in the name of the Governor General, resides elsewhere in the political structure.

The Constitution also established the Queen's **Privy Council** for Canada. This body was created to assist and advise the Governor General. The members of this largely ceremonial body are nominated by the prime minister and appointed for life. As it includes current and former ministers of the Crown, as well as a few other politically prominent individuals, it cannot function as a decision-making body.[11] In reality, a committee of the Privy Council known as the **Cabinet**, comprising current ministers of the Crown, constitutes the real executive power in Canada. The authority of the prime minister and the ministers rests not on the written Constitution but on convention. As members of the Privy Council, the ministers have the right to the titles Honourable and Privy Councillor for life, while the prime minister is designated as Right Honourable for life.

---

9. *The Globe and Mail,* September 9, 1999.

10. For a thorough discussion, see J.R. Mallory, *The Structure of Canadian Government* (Toronto: Macmillan, 1971).

11. For example, all provincial premiers were made privy councillors in 1967 to celebrate Canada's Centennial.

The term **governor-in-council** refers to the formal executive authority of the Governor General carried out upon the advice and consultation of this committee of the Privy Council, today known as the Cabinet. The decisions rendered by Cabinet on specific matters carrying legal force are referred to as **orders-in-council**. Technically speaking, a Cabinet directive is an agreement arrived at in Council with the Governor General absent. However, the Governor General is obliged by convention to grant formal approval to virtually any Cabinet decision or bill approved by Parliament. Thus, while Canada does have a monarchical form of government embodied in the Governor General and certain legal procedures, the real executive power belongs to the Cabinet. Its power, in turn, comes from maintaining at least a plurality of supporters in the House of Commons.

The foregoing passage described the largely ceremonial role of the formal executive in the parliamentary system. There are other, equally significant features of the monarchical form of government that impinge upon the operations and powers of the political executive in Canada. Perhaps most significant is the fact that, as in the British parliamentary system, the executive and legislative powers are combined. Today, Canadians vote for 301 members of the House of Commons; the prime minister and almost all members of the Cabinet emerge from this body of representatives. Earlier in Canadian history, during the 1890s, Sir John Abbott and Sir Mackenzie Bowell were in the Senate at the time of their appointment as prime minister, but convention now demands that the prime minister be a member of the House of Commons either before or shortly after investiture.

The prime minister and his or her personally selected Cabinet constitute the government; they formulate policy and direct administrative operations as long as they are supported by the House of Commons. When they no longer receive such support, they are replaced or Parliament is dissolved and elections are called. The crucial point is that both the prime minister and the Cabinet ministers are simultaneously members of the legislature and the executive. In contrast, the presidential form of government in the United States provides a clear separation of executive and legislative powers. The American Constitution is based on the premise that a concentration of power is undesirable and that law-making and implementation should be separated by preventing the overlap of key personnel. The presidential/congressional system of checks and balances creates an atmosphere of public political bargaining not found in Canada. In the United States the executive must rely on Congress to authorize funds to implement policy, and the Senate must confirm presidential appointments to Cabinet, the diplomatic service, federal courts, and other boards and commissions.

Also in contrast to the Canadian Constitution, the American chief executive is elected independently by voters, and tenure in office in no way depends on the fate of the legislative program. The executive can frustrate Congress because, for instance, Congress relies on the president to implement its policies, and the executive often controls the information needed to formulate effective policies in Congress. On the other hand, the American legislature can and often does reject executive proposals, an exceedingly rare event in Canada, where a major rejection could cause the government to fall and a new election to take place.

Both houses of the American Congress share fully in legislative activity, and there is often rivalry between them. Unlike their Canadian counterparts, national parties in the United States have little power as organizations over the congressmen or senators they may help to elect. Once in office, American politicians have greater latitude on issues and are much more independent than Canadian MPs, who belong to disciplined, tightly controlled parties. Figure 8.1 illustrates the fusion of power in the Canadian system, where the prime minister is both the leader of the largest party in the legislature and the leader of the administration, and compares it to the American presidential system. Anyone familiar with the parliamentary system and the relatively smooth flow of operations resulting from the fusion of executive and legislative powers may wonder how the American system, with its built-in conflict and rivalry, can possibly work effectively.

FIGURE 8.1   PARLIAMENTARY AND PRESIDENTIAL GOVERNMENT

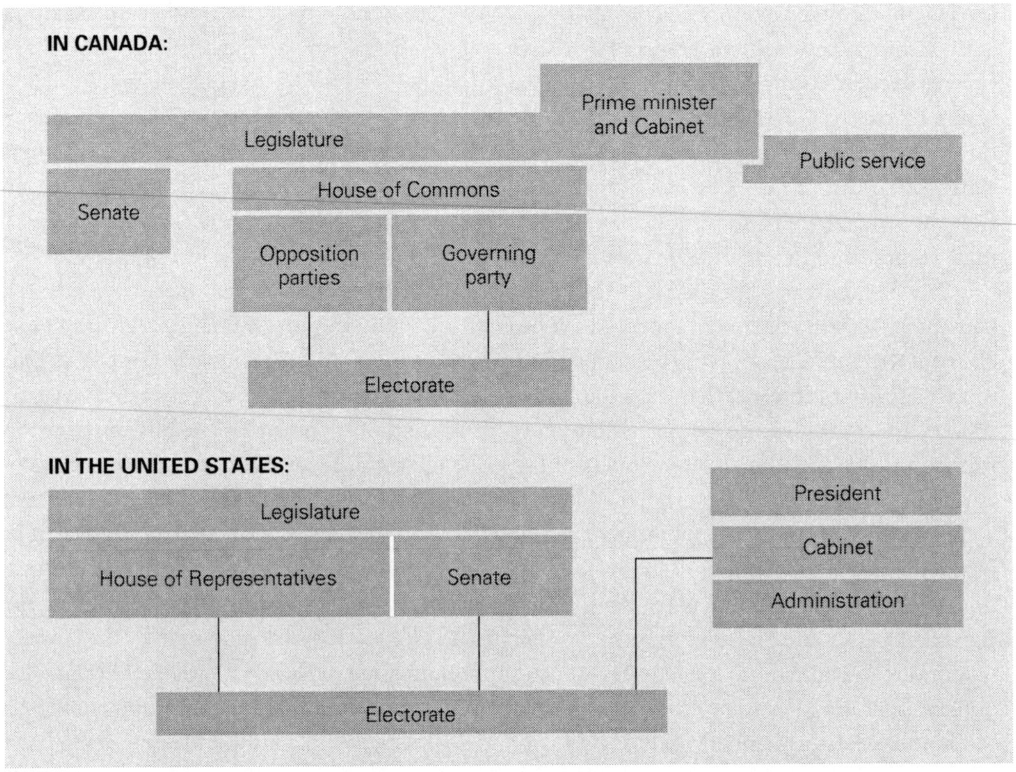

IN CANADA:

Prime minister and Cabinet

Legislature	
House of Commons	Public service

| Senate |

| Opposition parties | Governing party |

| Electorate |

IN THE UNITED STATES:

Legislature

| House of Representatives | Senate |

| President |
| Cabinet |
| Administration |

| Electorate |

Whereas in the United States an individual cannot hold a post in Congress and an executive position at the same time, precisely the opposite is true in Canada. All members of Cabinet, including the prime minister, must be elected to the House of Commons or at least be appointed to the Senate. What is perhaps most important to remember in considering the implications of different types of governmental structures is that the principle of fusion of powers creates, at least theoretically, a form of government that is more coherent and responsive to the will of the people. Assuming it is backed by a parliamentary majority, the Canadian political executive can be assured of legislative support on most of the bills and programs it wishes to enact. It will, of course, be held accountable by the people at the next election, but during the interim it is relatively free to pursue its goals.

THE POWERS OF THE PRIME MINISTER

The prime minister is unquestionably the central figure in Canadian politics. As we have suggested, the pre-eminence of the prime minister and the Cabinet has evolved more from tradition than from any specific part of the Constitution or statute. The basis of the prime minister's power and authority is leadership of the party that commands at least a plurality, and normally a majority, of the seats in the House of Commons. The prime minister is, above all else, an elected member of Parliament who has been chosen national leader of the party at a leadership convention. As leader of the party that has been victorious at the polls, the prime minister can claim that the "right" to govern is based on a popular mandate. The link with the people gives the prime minister enormous legitimacy and authorizes the pursuit of his or her programs and policies under the cloak of popular support until the next election. As leader of the party and the holder of this mandate, the prime minister can command obedience and support from Cabinet ministers and backbenchers alike.

The prime minister and Cabinet together control the making and signing of treaties and the conduct of international relations, including the declaration of war and peace, as these are prerogative powers of the Crown. Another major source of the prime minister's power is control over appointments. The prime minister selects the members of the **ministry** (whether in Cabinet or not) from the membership of the parliamentary caucus. In 1993, Prime Minister Chrétien inaugurated a new ministry system based on that of Britain. Thirty members of the ministry were appointed, but only 22 of them were appointed to the Cabinet as ministers; the other eight were made Secretaries of State to Assist without membership in the Cabinet and with a reduced ministerial salary.

The choice of ministers may be the most difficult task of prime ministers. In fact, once, in signing a visitor's book, Sir John A. Macdonald entered his occupation as "Cabinet-Maker."[12] A number of factors may influence the prime minister's selection of ministers. Most important, there is an obvious advantage in appointing ministers who reflect the regional and ethnic diversity of the country. In this regard, a persistent effort is made to have at least one minister from every province and a significant representative from the largest ethnic and religious groups in the country. This practice is frustrated, of course, when the party does not hold any seats in a particular province or has not attracted any candidates from a specific ethnic or religious group.

Another factor in the selection process is that posts may be used as a reward for favours or services rendered to the prime minister or the party. Conversely, positions may be withheld as a punishment for some misdemeanour. On occasion, a talented but troublesome member or a rival for the party leadership may be included in the ministry in order to silence his or her opposition to the leader. The prime minister may also appoint a particular member on the basis of that person's ability and popular appeal. It is evident that the prime minister must have a certain number of energetic and effective ministers to run the key portfolios of the government, because there could be political repercussions if ministers were perceived as bumbling and incompetent. On the other hand, the prime minister cannot afford to be constantly upstaged and overshadowed by clever ministers.

The prime minister, in consultation with other ministers, is also responsible for appointing parliamentary secretaries. The first two were appointed by order-in-council in 1916, and thereafter their numbers slowly increased until proper legislative recognition was given them with the 1959 *Parliamentary Secretaries Act*. That Act, as amended in 1971, provides for the appointment of the same number of parliamentary secretaries as there are ministers. **Parliamentary secretaries** are appointed by the prime minister to aid ministers in their duties, but have no statutory authority. As one parliamentary secretary put it: "There's no rule; it depends entirely on the minister you are dealing with. Some are given considerable responsibility, others very little. It depends on the understanding between the two people concerned."[13] Usually, parliamentary secretaries have at least the agreement of their minister before being appointed, but even this is not always the case. The prime minister may make an appointment without any consultation whatsoever.

The prime minister, in addition to choosing the members of the executive, also makes a great many other crucial appointments: senators, judges and the senior staff of the public service. Through these selections, the prime minister makes his or her influence felt throughout the governmental

12. Cited in R.M. Punnett, *The Prime Minister in Canadian Government and Politics* (Toronto: Macmillan, 1977), p. 56.
13. Quoted in Claude Majeau, "The Job of a Parliamentary Secretary," *Parliamentary Government*, vol. 4, no. 3 (1983), p. 3.

CLOSE-UP ON
▌Institutions▐

CHRÉTIEN VERSUS BLACK

A small but noisy incident illustrates the prime minister's power over appointments. In June 1999, Prime Minister Chrétien prevented Conrad Black, the media magnate, from acquiring a life peerage in the British House of Lords. While Black had been nominated by William Hague, leader of the British Conservative party, and was subsequently put forward to receive the honour by Tony Blair, Britain's prime minister, the Canadian government asked the British government to deny the appointment. In defence of his action, Chrétien cited the Nickle Resolution, a 1919 House of Commons resolution never passed in the Senate, but mirrored in government policy on honours and custom, that asked the British monarch not to convey titles on Canadian citizens.

The issue in this case is complex because Black had obtained dual citizenship in time to accept the peerage. Black is suing the prime minister, and thus the courts will likely have to settle the matter in more than one case.

In your opinion should Canadians with or without dual citizenship be allowed to hold titles in other countries?

structure. Legally, the prime minister's appointments are mere recommendations of appointment, forwarded to the Governor General for formal approval. However, despite the Governor General's apparent power of discretion, a modern prime minister's appointees are never rejected. In fact, as we have seen, the prime minister chooses the Governor General. In all, there are over 2 100 of these positions for a prime minister to fill. (See "Chrétien versus Black.")

Yet another significant basis of the prime minister's power is the right to advise the Crown to dissolve Parliament. The prime minister alone can determine the timing of an election within the five-year term of Parliament. This power can be used to impose discipline or solidarity on a fractious Cabinet or caucus. Fraught with uncertainty, election campaigns are expensive and risky for most MPs. If the government is clearly defeated on a major bill because of a breakdown of party discipline or loss of confidence of the House of Commons, the prime minister has little choice but to call an election to seek a new mandate. However, this is a rare occurrence. Except in minority situations such as the defeat of Joe Clark's Conservatives in December 1979, the prime minister determines the date of elections. Normally, Parliament is dissolved only when the prime minister believes that the party has a good chance of victory at the polls, although he or she may be constrained by the five-year limit or may misjudge the popular mood. Nonetheless, for the most part, the prime minister's power of dissolution is a potent weapon, helping to maintain the discipline and solidarity of the party and the stability of the Cabinet system.

A final major basis of the prime minister's pre-eminence is his or her power to control the organization of government. Nearly every prime minister has plans for a new organizational structure to streamline or modernize the government. Cabinet structure can be modified, portfolios limited or amalgamated, bureaucratic agencies abolished, Crown corporations created and royal commissions appointed — all on the initiative of the prime minister. However, while the power to make these changes certainly exists, the prime minister must be mindful that unwarranted or unnecessary modifications may generate significant opposition. The prime minister's power to initiate organizational changes extends across the entire government, but there is a tendency to focus on the various executive coordinating agencies that fall directly under his or her jurisdiction. Each prime minister can, therefore, be expected to make some changes in the Prime Minister's Office and the Privy Council Office to reflect his or her own interests or special needs.

The prime minister chairs the Cabinet and is the pivotal figure in the Cabinet committee system. No prime minister, however, could possibly deal with the multifarious matters needing attention and therefore must delegate authority and responsibility to Cabinet members. Before turning to a consideration of the operations of the Cabinet and its methods of arriving at policy decisions, we shall briefly examine the history and approaches of Canada's prime ministers.

PRIME MINISTERS IN PRACTICE

Canada has had 20 prime ministers since 1867, eight Liberal and twelve Conservative. All but Kim Campbell, who was prime minister for a few months in 1993, were male. Joe Clark, at the age of 39, was the youngest in Canadian history. As of Jean Chrétien's election in 1993, the average age of a new prime minister was 56. The selections of Kim Campbell and Jean Chrétien continued the tradition of highly educated party leaders; every appointment since the First World War has gone to a university graduate. With regard to area of residence in adult life, there have been three Maritimers as prime ministers, six Québécois, six Ontarians and five Westerners. (See Table 8.2.) Three provinces — Prince Edward Island, Newfoundland and New Brunswick — have never had a prime minister elected in one of their federal constituencies. Kim Campbell was the second prime minister from British Columbia. John Turner, the first, became a British Columbia member of Parliament only shortly before he lost the 1984 election and was replaced as prime minister.

The regional pattern of electoral support for parties in Canada is illustrated by the fact that all eight Liberal prime ministers have come from Ontario or Québec (John Turner's western credentials notwithstanding), whereas the Conservatives have come from various parts of the country. On the other hand, the Liberals have balanced Canada's religious and ethnic diversity better than the Conservatives in their choice of prime ministers. Of the 20 prime ministers, 7 have been Roman Catholic and 13 Protestant; the Liberals have had 5 Roman Catholics and 3 Protestants. Moreover, since the 1880s, Liberal party leaders have been drawn alternately from English Canada (Blake, 1880; King, 1919; Pearson, 1958; Turner, 1984) and French Canada (Laurier, 1887; St. Laurent, 1948; Trudeau, 1968; Chrétien, 1993).

Until recently, Conservative prime ministers have had much more parliamentary experience than their Liberal counterparts. Until Clark, Mulroney and Campbell, all Conservative prime ministers had 10 years' or more legislative experience at the federal or provincial level before their appointments. Experience in Cabinet before becoming prime minister, however, has been minimal for both parties; all but four had only two years' experience or less. Sir Charles Tupper had the most experience in federal and provincial Cabinets, but he lasted only two months as prime minister. Pierre Trudeau, by contrast, with no provincial experience and only one year of Cabinet experience, survived 11 years in his first period as prime minister and after an electoral defeat was re-elected to a further mandate. Brian Mulroney had no Cabinet experience when he became prime minister in 1984.

The durability of Canadian prime ministers varies enormously. Unlike American presidents, who may serve only two terms, Canadian prime ministers retain power as long as the public and House of Commons support them. Prime ministers in Canada have lasted longer than those in almost all Anglo-American and continental European countries.

The 20 Canadian prime ministers can be divided into three broad groups on the basis of their tenure in office. The shortest careers were those of Meighen, Thompson, Abbott, Bowell, Tupper, Clark, Turner and Campbell, who all served for less than two years (the shortest periods were held by Sir Charles Tupper, 69 days; John Turner, 80 days; and Kim Campbell, 133 days). Seven prime ministers stayed in office for five to eleven years: Borden, St. Laurent, Mackenzie, Bennett, Diefenbaker, Pearson, Mulroney and Chrétien. Four have towered above the rest: King, 22 years; Macdonald, 20 years; Trudeau, 15-and-a-half years; and Laurier, 15 years. Laurier's 15 consecutive years in office were the longest continuous term enjoyed by any prime minister; Trudeau's 15-and-a-half-year term was broken by an electoral loss. These four individuals held the office of prime minister for well over half of Canada's history since Confederation: 72 out of 133 years, as of 2000.

TABLE 8.2   THE PRIME MINISTERS OF CANADA

Prime Minister	Party	Tenure	Birthplace	Adult Residence	Age as PM	Occupation
Sir John A. Macdonald	Lib.-Con.	July 1, 1867–Nov. 5, 1873	Britain	Ontario	52–76	Law
Alexander Mackenzie	Lib.	Nov. 5, 1873–Oct. 9, 1878	Britain	Ontario	51–56	Journalist/Stonemason
Sir John A. Macdonald	Con.	Oct. 9, 1878–June 6, 1891				
Sir John Abbott	Con.	June 15, 1891–Nov. 24, 1892	Québec	Québec	70	Law/Lecturer
Sir John Thompson	Con.	Nov. 25, 1892–Dec. 13, 1894	Nova Scotia	Nova Scotia	48–50	Law/Lecturer
Sir Mackenzie Bowell	Con.	Dec. 13, 1894–Apr. 27, 1896	Britain	Ontario	70–72	Journalist
Sir Charles Tupper	Con.	Apr. 27, 1896–July 8, 1896	Nova Scotia	Nova Scotia	74	Doctor
Sir Wilfrid Laurier	Lib.	July 9, 1896–Oct. 6, 1911	Québec	Québec	54–69	Law
Sir Robert Borden	Con.	Oct. 7, 1911–July 10, 1920	Nova Scotia	Nova Scotia	57–65	Law
Arthur Meighen	Con.	July 10, 1920–Dec. 29, 1921	Ontario	Manitoba	46–52	Law/Business
W.L. Mackenzie King	Lib.	Dec. 29, 1921–June 28, 1926	Ontario	Ontario	47–73	Civil Service
Arthur Meighen	Con.	June 28, 1926–Sept. 25, 1926				
W.L. Mackenzie King	Lib.	Sept. 25, 1926–Aug. 7, 1930				
R.B. Bennett	Con.	Aug. 7, 1930–Oct. 23, 1935	New Brunswick	Alberta	60–65	Law/Business
W.L. Mackenzie King	Lib.	Oct. 23, 1935–Nov. 15, 1948				
Louis St. Laurent	Lib.	Nov. 15, 1948–June 21, 1957	Québec	Québec	66–75	Law
John Diefenbaker	Con.	June 21, 1957–Apr. 22, 1963	Ontario	Saskatchewan	51–67	Law
Lester B. Pearson	Lib.	Apr. 22, 1963–Apr. 20, 1968	Ontario	Ontario	65–70	Civil Service
Pierre Elliott Trudeau	Lib.	Apr. 20, 1968–June 4, 1979	Québec	Québec	48–65	Law/Lecturer
Joseph Clark	Con.	June 4, 1979–Mar. 3, 1980	Alberta	Alberta	39–41	Journalist
Pierre Elliott Trudeau	Lib.	Mar. 3, 1980–June 30, 1984				
John Turner	Lib.	June 30, 1984–Sept. 17, 1984	Britain	Ontario	55	Law
Brian Mulroney	Con.	Sept. 17, 1984–June 25, 1993	Québec	Québec	45–54	Law/Business
Kim Campbell	Con.	June 25, 1993–Nov. 4, 1993	British Columbia	British Columbia	46	Law
Jean Chrétien	Lib.	Nov. 4, 1993–	Québec	Québec	59–	Law

How are prime ministers' terms ended? Few have retired entirely of their own choice; their careers usually were ended by defeat in a general election. Abbott, Borden, King, Pearson, Trudeau and Mulroney retired. Twelve lost their positions through defeat in a general election; one (Mackenzie Bowell) because of a Cabinet revolt, two (Macdonald and King) through defeats in Parliament.

Only Macdonald, King, Meighen and Trudeau managed to stay on as leader and win another general election after their party was defeated in an election. Macdonald and Thompson died in office.

Getting rid of a prime minister, even via the electoral route, is extremely difficult. The statistics show that in about one-third of all elections prime ministers were defeated, whereas in more than two-thirds they were returned to the House of Commons, albeit more than half the time with a reduced majority. Jean Chrétien's 1997 victory followed the usual pattern. Brian Mulroney chose to stand down in June 1993 rather than go into an election with a high level of personal unpopularity. His replacement, Kim Campbell, lost the general election of 1993, but remained as party leader for a short time before being replaced by Jean Charest.

THE MINISTRY AND CABINET

We have said that the prime minister determines which individuals serve as ministers and secretaries of state, and also the extent of their duties. In some parliamentary countries, such as Australia and New Zealand, particular caucuses select the ministers, and the prime minister merely assigns the portfolios. In Canada, however, the prime minister has a free hand, although traditionally most members of the ministry are selected from the House of Commons and, more rarely, the Senate.

In selecting future colleagues for the front bench, the prime minister takes into consideration a number of factors, one of them Cabinet size. Until 1993, all members of the ministry were in Cabinet — there were no ministers outside of it — so with the appointment of each new minister the size of Cabinet grew. Over time, the size of Cabinets gradually increased. By the end of the second Trudeau administration in 1984, the Cabinet included 37 ministers. John Turner's appointments temporarily reduced this number, but the situation was immediately reversed when Brian Mulroney became prime minister. He named the largest number in Canadian history to Cabinet — 40 ministers.

After Brian Mulroney's resignation in 1993, Kim Campbell downsized the Cabinet and restructured the government considerably. She reduced the number of Cabinet ministers to 24. When Jean Chrétien became head of government in November 1993, he left most of Campbell's departmental changes in place (see Chapter 10) but he adopted a new system for central government administration. As we have seen, Chrétien appointed two types of ministers — 22 politicians were appointed to full Cabinet and 8 were made Secretaries of State to Assist. Like full ministers, the latter eight were sworn to the Privy Council and bound by the rules of collective responsibility. But they were only allowed to attend meetings of Cabinet on request and were given a lower salary and less staff than full Cabinet ministers. Going into the year 2000, in Chrétien's second government, there were 27 full ministers, 9 secretaries of state and the prime minister, giving a ministry of 37.

Needless to say, nearly all Cabinet ministers are chosen from the Commons, although in some historical periods a number have been appointed from the Senate, particularly when the governing party lacked elected representatives from a particular region — as the Conservatives did from Québec in 1979 and the Liberals did from the West in 1980–84. In 1997, for example, Senator Alasdair Graham from Nova Scotia was appointed as Government Leader in the Upper House to compensate for the Liberals' lack of representation from that province.

The composition of the ministry and Cabinet also depends on how many seats the government controls in the House of Commons. Most elections have produced **majority governments**, based on the support of only one party in the House of Commons. Only twice have *coalition* Cabinets been formed from more than one party. On other occasions — six times since 1945 — the government had to persist with less than a majority of the members of Parliament. It had to select its Cabinet members carefully to ensure a majority of members would support it. Such **minority governments** have proved quite unstable and have tended to pass less legislation than governments based on single-party, majority control of the House.

Cabinet positions are all doled out to members of the prime minister's own party in Parliament or the Senate. There have been few exceptions. General McNaughton was Defence Minister in 1944–45 without holding a position in either house. After being defeated twice at the polls he gave up the post. On the other hand, Lester Pearson was appointed Secretary of State for External Affairs in 1948, then stood for election in a by-election and won. As noted earlier, the prime minister's choice of ministers is limited by certain considerations, foremost among them regional, ethnic and religious representation. Regional representation is generally, but not necessarily, the most important factor. There is usually a Cabinet member from each province (with the frequent exception of Prince Edward Island) and from the largest cities, with the most populous urban regions receiving extra members.

The correspondence between distribution of Cabinet ministers and provincial population has been relatively constant since Confederation. As a general rule, Ontario has had more members in Cabinet than any other province, with Québec second. However, in recent years this principle has varied somewhat. Trudeau usually had one more Cabinet member from Québec than from Ontario. And on his election in 1984, Mulroney awarded an unusually large number of Cabinet seats to the West. His Cabinet consisted of 13 ministers from the four western provinces and the North, 11 from each of Ontario and Québec and 5 from the Atlantic provinces. Because of his landslide victory in Ontario and slim results from his own province, Jean Chrétien initially chose 12 full ministers from Ontario and only 7 from Québec for his 1997 ministry. (See Table 8.3.)

TABLE 8.3   THE 1993 AND 1997 LIBERAL MINISTRIES BY REGION AND GENDER

A. Region	1993 Ministry Membership	1997 Ministry Membership
Québec	6	9
Ontario	12	13
West	7	9
East	5	5
North	1	1
B. Gender		
Male	24	29
Female	7	8

Ministry includes prime minister, ministers and secretaries of state at initial inauguration and does not include individual ministerial shuffles.

Ethnicity is also significant. According to Malcolm Punnett, 28 percent of the total number of Cabinet ministers serving between 1867 and 1965 were French Canadians, a figure that was remarkably close to the French Canadian percentage of the population.[14] Prime ministers also attempt to appoint a chief lieutenant from the opposite official-language group. The most successful alliance, for example, may have been between Macdonald and Cartier. Jean Chrétien, a francophone,

---

14. Punnett, *The Prime Minister*, passim.

appointed Herb Gray from Ontario as his Deputy Prime Minister. Joe Clark found it necessary to appoint three French-speaking members of the Senate to his Cabinet to balance his weak support in Québec. Brian Mulroney, a Québecker, appointed his first chief lieutenant from Yukon. Other, smaller ethnic groups have usually been under-represented in Cabinet. Protestant and Roman Catholic religions have also been balanced in the Cabinet composition.

Certain posts are distributed according to traditional rules. The post of Minister of Agriculture usually goes to a Westerner, as it did in 1993 when Ralph Goodale from Saskatchewan received the post. When this is difficult, as in the Trudeau Cabinet, a western minister may receive control of the Wheat Board. The Maritimes usually gets the Ministry of Fisheries, but in 1997 David Anderson from British Columbia got this reward. The distribution of seats that the government has obtained throughout the country is also an important factor in determining many assignments. In the case of the Liberals, the Department of Finance has usually been held by an Ontarian, but in the 1980 Trudeau government a French Canadian was appointed to that post to bolster Québec strength in Cabinet. Joe Clark was even more daring — in 1979 he went to Newfoundland for his Finance Minister. Brian Mulroney returned to tradition when he appointed Michael Wilson from Toronto to the position, but Jean Chrétien nominated a bilingual anglophone from Québec, Paul Martin Jr., to this position in both 1993 and 1997.

Nearly all of Canada's minority groups, as well as one majority group — women[15] — have been consistently unrepresented or under-represented in Cabinet. No significant room has been made in Cabinet for Native peoples, for workers and unskilled labourers, or for the poor, all of whose interests have been consistently under-represented. Over-represented are those with higher education and high social status occupations. The most over-represented group is lawyers, who have held approximately half the positions in Cabinet since Confederation; they are an elite, extremely well-educated, financially successful group representing less than one percent of the population. Historically, about one-fifth of Cabinet members have been business people; fewer than one-tenth have been farmers, and fewer still have come from the public sector.

The composition of the 1997 Chrétien ministry followed these principles closely. Every province received one or more ministers, and the membership was reasonably representative of the provinces on a basis proportional to their population with the evident distortion of Québec. Prime Minister Chrétien said he wished he could have nominated more ministers from Québec but only a small number of Liberals had been elected in that province. In 1989, francophones constituted a higher proportion of the Cabinet membership than they did in the country's population as a whole, while in 1997 their proportion was approximately the same as their share of the population.

The new government members in 1997 were highly educated and professionally trained; they still did not form a social or economic cross-section of Canadians. Business and law continued to be the leading employment areas of ministers. There were few farmers and, as usual, labourers and the poor were not represented at all. Women were still in a minority position, but their numbers were continuing to grow — eight ministers and secretaries of state out of a ministry of 36 appointed in the 1997 Liberal administration were female. The Tories had given Canada its first female prime minister, Kim Campbell, and Chrétien countered in 1993 by appointing Sheila Copps as the first female Deputy Prime Minister. In 1997 Herb Gray replaced Sheila Copps.

The 1997 Chrétien Cabinet and its committees reflect government priorities and the 1997 composition of the House of Commons. The prime minister asked Herb Gray to chair the Special

---

15. For a comparative view of this issue see Andrew Reynolds, "Women in the Legislatures and Executives of the World: Knocking at the Highest Glass Ceiling," *World Politics,* vol. 51, no. 4 (July 1999), pp. 547–72.

Committee of Council with responsibilities for the government's overall program in Parliament. This appointment reflected the government's need to control a House that consisted of five official parties and could be very cantankerous. To highlight the government's commitment to the West, despite reduced representation, Anne McLellan from Edmonton, the Minister of Justice, was given the responsibility to chair the Cabinet committee on the Social Union as well as membership in three Cabinet committees. Ralph Goodale from Saskatchewan, the Minister of Natural Resources, was made responsible for the Wheat Board and appointed to head the important Cabinet committee on the Economic Union; and Lucienne Robillard from Quebec was appointed president of the Treasury Board.

Cabinet Conventions

In theory, the Canadian system of government is premised on both *collective* and *individual ministerial responsibility*. Cabinet solidarity, or **collective ministerial responsibility**, allows ministers to be frank in private but requires them to support the government in public. As a group, ministers are supposed to be held accountable to Parliament for their government's actions. In this sense, they may speak about policy only after it has been agreed to in private by their colleagues. The convention of collective responsibility is so pervasive that ministers are expected to support each other even *before* the issue has been discussed in Cabinet. The ministers act collectively in Cabinet to develop policy, approve draft legislation, manage the country's finances and adopt orders-in-council. Cabinet deliberations are held in secret, individual opinions are not publicly voiced, and ministers are not supposed to speak or act except in the name of the entire Cabinet.

The personal responsibility of each minister is referred to as **individual ministerial responsibility**. Ministers receive confidential advice from the public service, make important decisions and are then held accountable for these decisions in Parliament and the country. In other words, in theory at least, there is a trade-off: the public servants forgo public praise in order to avoid public blame, while the ministers accept both credit and criticism.

As we shall see in Chapters 14 and 15, public policy derives from a multitude of sources, but it is the individual minister who puts the final stamp of approval on departmental initiatives. Politicians cannot hope to duplicate the expertise that derives from administration or the information that comes from permanent contact with interest groups. And yet only a minister may carry forward departmental requests to the Cabinet. This iron-clad relationship between minister and department places approval or disapproval upon the appropriate and responsible political official. While ministers may delegate authority to their officials, they remain at the apex for appeals of administrative decisions and must be involved in the initiation and defence of new policies. The complexity of a minister's task can be illustrated by the work of the Minister for Industry, Trade and Commerce. In one year, the department took 4 700 decisions — the minister kept control of only 190 of them, but these constituted well over half the department's expenditures.[16]

In practice, however, it is nearly impossible to adhere to these constitutional doctrines at all times. Where is the line to be drawn between ministerial and departmental responsibility? Ministers do not even know most of the details of decisions that are carried out in their names. They cannot be held responsible for every activity, and, increasingly, ministers have been voicing this problem openly. One even claimed he could not be held accountable for the "shabby research" in his

---

16. Ian Clark, "A 'Back to Basics' Look at the Government Decision-Making Process," unpublished paper, November 4, 1983, p. 13.

department. The main check on ministerial responsibilities, therefore, is not the minister's will or the public servants' activities, but the free and open debate that takes place in Parliament and society about ministers' actions. The minister is judged in the department, in Cabinet, in Parliament, before the media and on the hustings.

The prime minister and Cabinet are assisted in their tasks by the central agencies discussed in the following section. Individual ministers are supported by their departments and by their political appointees. The personnel budget for each minister's office is used to employ an executive assistant, special assistants, a private secretary and other support personnel. At the end of the Mulroney period in 1993, there were hundreds of such political aides in Ottawa, not including those in the Prime Minister's Office. Ministers also second departmental employees to their offices and hire policy and communications advisors under contract. When the Tories came to office in 1984, they operated on the assumption that since all the deputy ministers and other senior officials had been appointed by Liberal governments, they must be partisan. To counteract this, they tried to insulate ministers from the bureaucracy by creating a new layer of political appointee, the Chiefs of Staff, through which all communications between ministers and departments had to flow. Ministers' budgets for other political staff were also augmented.

On his appointment, Prime Minister Jean Chrétien said he would take a fundamentally different approach. He declared his intent to rebuild the relationship between the ministers and the bureaucracy. When he appointed his ministry in 1993, he halved the staff of ministers, reduced their overall budgets and axed the highly paid position of Chief of Staff (except for his own Chief of Staff!). The title **executive assistant** was once again accorded to the senior staff member in each minister's office.

Political aides are part of what Blair Williams has called the "para-political bureaucracy."[17] They are hired by ministers on an individual basis in order to perform largely partisan tasks. They are not subject to the regulations of the public service (and hence are called "exempt staff") and, under provisions of the 1967 *Public Service Employment Act*, they are given high priority for permanent positions in the administration after a period of three years of consecutive political service.

The importance of these staffs varies greatly. Depending on the ministers' views and confidence, they are engaged in any number of personal concerns. Liaison work with the department, constituency, party and Parliament is perhaps the most important. Their partisan work for the ministers is clearly significant. If competent, they strengthen both the minister and the party in power. Their work on policy is very underdeveloped in the Chrétien government because, with few exceptions, they do not have the necessary competence or experience. Their most important policy work is possibly in their "gatekeeping" functions: determining who gets an appointment with the minister and what documents, papers and letters he or she reads.

POLICY-MAKING IN CENTRAL GOVERNMENT

In recent years, prime ministers have made many major alterations in the internal organization of government. In the 1963 Pearson administration, full Cabinet was the major vehicle for Cabinet decision-making: it reviewed almost every decision taken in committee. After Trudeau came to office in 1968, Cabinet and committee meetings were scheduled on a more regular basis and *committees* became much more powerful. The 1979 Clark, 1980 Trudeau and 1984 Mulroney Cabinets decentralized decision-making even further with the introduction of the Policy and Expenditure Management

---

17. Blair Williams, "The Para-Political Bureaucracy in Ottawa," in Harold D. Clarke et al., eds., *Parliament, Policy and Representation* (Toronto: Methuen, 1980), p. 218.

System (PEMS) (see below). Committees were empowered to make final decisions on many policy and financial issues. In 1989, Prime Minister Mulroney completed the process of dismantling PEMS and announced a major structural rearrangement of Cabinet and its committees as well as the process for Cabinet deliberation. He appointed a large Cabinet that year and divided it into 15 committees.

The Priorities and Planning Committee, chaired by the prime minister and consisting mainly of the chairs of Cabinet's other committees, continued to be responsible for setting the government's overall agenda and determining major policies; it prescribed what found its way onto the Cabinet agenda. This committee assumed responsibilities for such activities as preparing the broad policy goals concerning free trade, the Speech from the Throne, the legislative program, macroeconomic policy, constitutional questions and so on. An additional structure was added to ensure coordination: a new Operations Committee, chaired by the deputy prime minister, controlled the flow of policy issues into Priorities and Planning and dealt with political crises. This Operations Committee began to operate informally as early as 1986, and later gained official status, meeting regularly before Priorities and Planning each Monday morning.[18]

Four committees were given broader coordination roles — Legislation and House Planning, Special Committee of Council, Communications, and Security and Intelligence. The Government House Leader chaired Legislation and House Planning. This committee coordinated the flow of legislation, reviewed drafts of bills and supervised all matters pertaining to Parliament. The Special Committee of Council, chaired by the deputy prime minister, met weekly. In 1989, this committee was given the responsibility of controlling regulatory activities and reviewing proposals for the privatization of Crown corporations. Its main order of business, however, was to deal with regulations and routine orders requiring governor-in-council approval. That is, it passed uncontroversial orders-in-council made pursuant to statutory authority that required the government, and not an individual minister, to make a decision.

Orders-in-council are issued by Cabinet to carry out government rule-making and administration. In most cases, they are authorized by provisions contained in statutes. Some orders, however, fall under the royal prerogative. Upon passage, all orders-in-council are published in *The Canada Gazette*. Until recently, their numbers increased yearly. For example, in 1982, 4 379 were passed, ranging from the most trivial to the most urgent. By 1988, however, the number had dropped to 3 223. This was not due to a reduction in Cabinet activities, but rather to a new process in which more than one appointment was made in the same order. Approximately a quarter of the orders consisted of regulations for administering the country; the next greatest number and the most visible, however, were those for appointments. By convention, the prime minister recommends about a hundred deputy head positions on his or her own authority. The other 2 000 full-time order-in-council positions involve the prime minister and/or other ministerial decisions.

Under Mulroney, the Communications Committee of the Cabinet, chaired by the Conservative Leader in the Senate, was responsible for information, publicity and (some would say) the "propaganda" of the government. Security and Intelligence, chaired by the prime minister, met irregularly. It was responsible for protecting the internal security of Canada and its institutions.

The most important change in 1989, however, came in the form of a new Cabinet committee system to control expenditure. Control over policy initiation and expenditure was divided for the first time since 1979; Priorities and Planning retained the power of final decision over expenditure, the Treasury Board enhanced its authority and a new expenditure review committee was set up.

---

18. Control over this committee gave rise to the popular notion that Don Mazankowski was "in charge of everything."

The **Treasury Board** is the only statutory committee of the Privy Council. Chaired by the president of the Treasury Board, it has legal responsibility for the authorization of expenditures and is the committee that allocates resources within the government. It is the only committee that does not position itself into a circle for policy deliberations, but sits like a jury, facing any petitioners and acting as a tribunal. Another Cabinet committee under Mulroney, Expenditure Review, was mandated to see that government expenditures were related to government priorities, including deficit reduction. The committee was often referred to as the "search-and-destroy" committee.

The Mulroney committee system reduced the power of many ministers, constructing a senior and junior ministerial system almost like the British one. Power was centralized in the hands of the prime minister, his Priorities and Planning Committee and the Expenditure Review Committee. Many ministers were reduced almost to the status of eunuchs. Pressures from less powerful ministers to reform this system increased over the life of the government.

As discussed above, in 1993 and 1997 Jean Chrétien changed the governmental system. At the end of 1999, Cabinet membership consisted of only 28 members, including the prime minister, out of a ministry of 37. The new ministry was also given a new committee system. In the second Chrétien government, Cabinet-as-a-whole continues to be the main steering organization. Cabinet is divided into only four committees — Economic Union, Social Union, Special Committee of Council and Treasury Board, each of which can bring forward recommendations to Cabinet. (See Figure 8.2.) Initially, unlike recent prime ministers, Jean Chrétien reverted to the secretive practice of neither publicly naming the members of these committees nor specifying their functions. While *The Canada Gazette* for two decades had named all members of Cabinet committees, the 1993 Liberal government reduced transparency at the very core of democratic government. After much criticism, however, the Chrétien government once again made this information public.

Ministers are expected to bring substantial policies to their Cabinet colleagues for resolution. The formal process for Cabinet approval of a document is illustrated in Figure 8.3. The minister's

FIGURE 8.2   THE MINISTRY AND CABINET IN THE 2000 LIBERAL GOVERNMENT

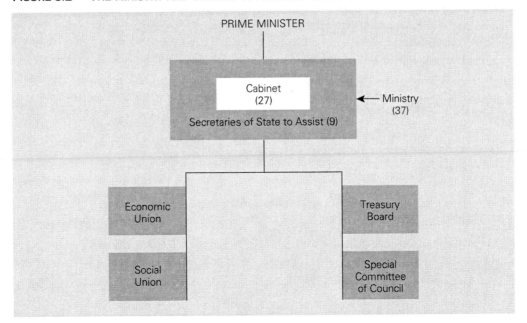

memorandum is forwarded to the Privy Council Office, which distributes it to the Cabinet members. The memorandum is then discussed by the appropriate Cabinet committee and forwarded to Cabinet for final determination. As Figure 8.3 indicates, the Privy Council Office briefs both the chairs of committees and the prime minister. The prime minister is also briefed by the Prime Minister's Office. This series of actions completes the process and Cabinet gives final approval or disapproval in a record of decision. Of course, private conversations about government policies, over the telephone and in person, add immeasurably to the complex pattern of Cabinet business.

The **Memorandum to Cabinet** (MC) is the formal document used by a minister to put his or her views to Cabinet. Each memorandum is numbered and awarded a security classification. The MC consists of an *advocacy* document followed by a detailed *analysis* section. The ministerial recommendation is formulated to convince his or her colleagues of the appropriate course of action, while the analysis is devised as background notes and may be made public under the *Freedom of Information Act*. Ministers may also bring issues orally to the Cabinet table.

All ministers are allowed to place some major policy and legislative proposals on Cabinet's list of priority problems. Cabinet cohesiveness is maintained by encouraging each minister to believe that he or she will succeed in persuading colleagues to accept some of these proposals. If serious Cabinet dissent emerges over a minister's ideas, that minister will be asked to reconsider and resubmit them. Each is made to feel part of a team that values his or her proposals. The participants are united for their own survival — and they know it!

How successful a Cabinet is depends to a large extent on its management of several critical factors, including taxation, expenditures and the legislative program. By controlling these, as well as the machinery of government and senior personnel, the government is able to effect major decisions. Through strategic planning, the government attempts to employ all these resources to accomplish its goals. In theory, the government places all the goals and issues into a hierarchy of interests, but in practice this rarely works. For one thing, long-term policy goals often have to give way to short-term administrative matters. For another, the issues change over time, and the government must be prepared to adjust its targets. Finally, ultimate determination occurs within the ephemeral world of politics, where politicians come and go, change their opinions and are themselves divided over policies. A slight change in personnel can affect the distribution of power that first caused the priority. Nevertheless, the idea of strategic planning comes from the desire to achieve comprehensive, nonurgent policy-making to help counter the piecemeal policies emanating from individual departments. The government is aided in these various tasks by the central coordinating agencies.

FIGURE 8.3   THE FORMAL CABINET POLICY PROCESS, 2000

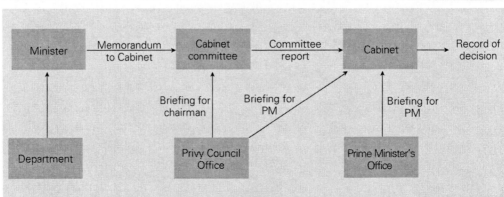

THE CENTRAL COORDINATING AGENCIES

In response to the large scope of the government's role in Canadian society and to the corresponding need for effective policy formation and implementation, new executive agencies have been either created or expanded. Some of these central coordinating agencies have a special responsibility to support the prime minister, Cabinet and ministry. Some have little legal authority, but are organized under the prime minister's prerogative for machinery of government. While their stated purpose is to streamline the governmental process, the executive agencies have recently received considerable public attention and have drawn accusations that Canada is being run by a cabal of "superbureaucrats" who have become powers unto themselves. The closed nature of these agencies makes them a target for criticism. To a considerable extent they also have become recruiting grounds for senior positions throughout the public service.

The centralization of power in the hands of the prime minister as well as in these coordinating agencies appears indisputable. This development has probably been inevitable, given the range of demands for government action in Canada. We shall evaluate the nature of the controversy over this centralization below in the section entitled "Prime Ministerial Government?" (page 285). But first, we will discuss briefly the duties and responsibilities of the four most important executive agencies: the Prime Minister's Office; the Privy Council Office, including the Federal-Provincial Relations Office; the Treasury Board; and the Department of Finance. The first two report directly to the prime minister; the other two have their own ministers.

The Prime Minister's Office

Of the various executive support agencies, the Prime Minister's Office (PMO) is the most overtly political and partisan. The upper echelon of the PMO is composed of personal appointees of the prime minister and sometimes includes those referred to as "Ottawa's best and brightest." It is the largest and most important of the "exempt" staffs, and only very rarely are public servants employed in this central agency. While the PMO lacks the statutory authority of the other executive agencies, its importance is based on the style and personality of the prime minister.

On the advice of ministers and other advisors, the PMO drafts the Speech from the Throne. Perhaps its most crucial task, however, is to act as a monitoring agency tracing political developments and their implications for the prime minister and his or her career. (For an outline of the traditional structure of the PMO, see Figure 8.4.) An official explained the PMO's role as follows:

> *We are just a valve at the junction of the bureaucratic and the political. We add a little of the political ingredient when it appears that it has been overlooked. For instance, if I know that an official in PCO is working on a briefing note to the PM on an issue which I am responsible for, I'll go to him and express the political point of view — I guess we are sort of a Distant Early Warning System for things that are going to cause trouble politically.* [19]

The Prime Minister's Office has grown immensely over the years. Near the end of the Trudeau period (1983–84), the office had a budget of just over $4 million *per annum*, and in the first year of Mulroney's government it spent over $6 million. The importance of the PMO is determined solely

---

19. Cited in Colin Campbell and George J. Szablowski, *The Superbureaucrats: Structure and Behaviour in Central Agencies* (Toronto: Macmillan, 1979), p. 66.

FIGURE 8.4 THE PRIME MINISTER'S OFFICE (BASIC FORM)

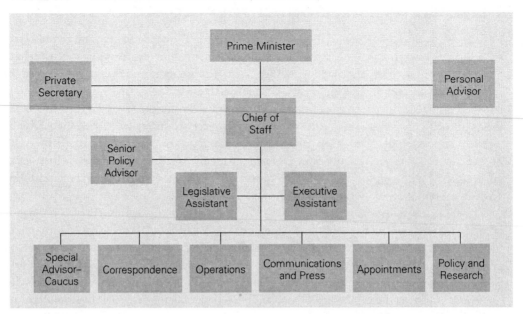

by the prime minister's personality and needs. Yet, as Blair Williams points out, "Today, in its advisory, administrative, and political functions the PMO is the most significant element of the para-political bureaucracy in Ottawa. Indeed ... the PMO might, in many respects, be the most important element of the total governmental policy-making apparatus."[20]

In concert with the Privy Council Office, the PMO provides the prime minister with a range of technical and political advice that may not otherwise be available. The emphasis of the PMO is on the development of practical policy suggestions relevant to the political fortunes of the prime minister and his or her party. In addition, the PMO does much public relations work. It gathers surveys on the popularity of the prime minister and specific policy initiatives, and helps in preparing press conferences and in dealing with the media generally. As a rule, officials in the PMO know and understand the marketing maxim that "It's the sizzle not the steak that sells." Other related responsibilities include answering the prime minister's mail, coordinating the daily appointment schedule and searching for candidates for nomination and awards.

The organization and structure of the PMO remain the prerogative of the prime minister. Throughout Canada's early history, the PMO was a small, relatively insignificant body. However, under Trudeau it achieved unprecedented importance. In 1968, Trudeau appointed Marc Lalonde, who had been with the Pearson administration, to the position of Principal Secretary. In 1984, Brian Mulroney went even further. He increased the staff to approximately 200 employees and put many of his friends in the PMO. He appointed his law school friend, Bernard Roy, as his Chief of Staff. Later, Roy was replaced in turn by Derek Burney, a career public servant; Norman Spector, from the Federal-Provincial Relations Office; Stanley Hartt, an old friend; and the staunchest Tory of them all, Hugh Segal. The extent of the power and influence of this position depends in large measure on the ability of the individual and on the amount of authority the prime minister is willing to delegate. Burney's 1989 appointment as Canada's ambassador to Washington illustrated his importance to

20. Williams, "The Para-Political Bureaucracy," p. 218.

Prime Minister Mulroney. In 1993, Prime Minister Chrétien appointed Jean Pelletier, former mayor of Québec and a defeated Liberal candidate, as his first Chief of Staff, and Eddie Goldenberg, a life-long friend, as Senior Policy Advisor. They are still in office.

The PMO has achieved considerable importance and is likely to continue to be extremely in-fluential in policy-making at the political apex. With a budget of over $6 million and a staff of 68 person-years in the Chrétien period, the PMO is believed to be crucial to the government of the day. The senior staff act as the prime minister's personal advisors and sort out Cabinet and party conflicts; some are closer to Chrétien than his Cabinet colleagues.

The Privy Council Office

The Queen's Privy Council for Canada was established by the *BNA Act* to advise the Governor General. It is a ceremonial body composed mostly of current and former ministers of the Crown. The Cabinet, as we have seen, is a committee of the Privy Council. The main organization supporting the Cabinet and prime minister is the Privy Council Office (PCO). The top position in the PCO is held by the **Clerk**. This position, which has existed since 1867, is mentioned in the Constitution. It was combined with the function of **Secretary to the Cabinet** in 1940.

The PCO performs many of the same functions as the PMO (such as briefing — providing notes and/or giving oral briefings for ministers) but is staffed by career bureaucrats seconded from various government departments. It is responsible for developing and coordinating overall gov-ernment policy. Although the top echelon of PCO staff is appointed by the prime minister on the advice of the Clerk, there is little emphasis on partisan politics — at least, there had been little until Prime Minister Mulroney appointed his friend and political advisor Dalton Camp as the Senior Policy Advisor in the PCO. Under all recent prime ministers, the PCO, like the PMO, has flour-ished in size and scope of responsibility, but it has rarely had political appointees on its staff.

The Privy Council Office possesses an impressive research capability and acts as the "eyes and ears" of the Cabinet in coordinating the numerous governmental departments and agencies. With a staff of about 500 officers and support personnel, the PCO is divided into several principal units. While the structures and powers of these units "ebb and flow" with the styles of different prime ministers, the most influential tend to include Plans, Operations, Senior Personnel, and Security and Intelligence. (See Figure 8.5.) Each of these divisions has its own staff and is responsible for advising the prime minister, the plenary Cabinet and the various Cabinet committees on matters of national policy. To achieve this, the PCO employs a wide range of talent — from clerical staff and legal counsel to technical and scientific experts. It even has a unit to control information requests from the public, called Coordination of Access to Information Requests (CAIR).

The **Clerk of the Privy Council** ranks at the top of Canada's civil service. The role and stature of the Clerk of the Privy Council, like those of the officers of the PMO, depend to a great extent on his or her rapport with the prime minister. Any prime minister would likely consider the Clerk to be a crucial appointment, since this individual is in charge of coordinating Cabinet activities. The Clerk's staff set agendas, take the minutes of Cabinet meetings and convey Cabinet decisions to the bureaucracy. Mel Cappe presently holds the position.

The relationship between Cabinet ministers and officers of the PCO is for the most part cordial and constructive. There is, of course, always the possibility of a rift or tension. Although the staff of the Privy Council may be expert on specific matters of policy, in the end it is the elected ministers, whatever their knowledge or qualifications, who must make the decisions. In principle, the PCO ex-ists to advise and suggest alternatives in an objective and dispassionate manner, since the weight of public responsibility is not on its shoulders.

FIGURE 8.5   BASIC PRIVY COUNCIL OFFICE STRUCTURE UNDER JEAN CHRÉTIEN

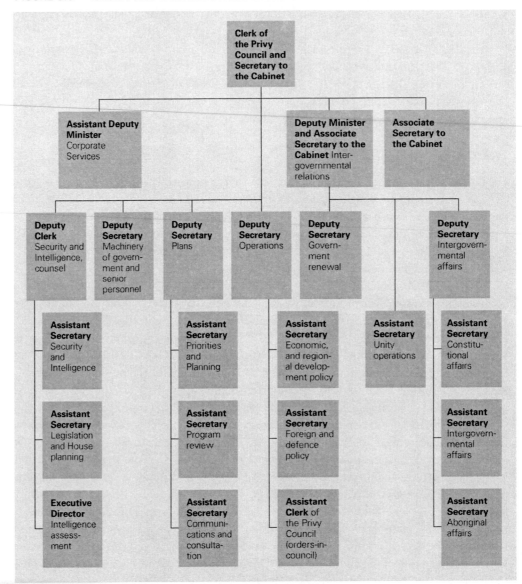

In an article describing developments in the PCO, a former Clerk suggested that it should be non-partisan, politically sensitive and governed by four principles.[21] The first principle is that the PCO should act as a source of policy ideas and should not construe its role as that of an administrative body. Responsibility for implementation and action lies with the various departments headed by the ministers of the Crown. The PCO may play a coordinating role or provide specialized assistance, but should do nothing to undercut the authority of departments charged with specific responsibilities. The second principle is that the units within the PCO should work together and provide mutual

---

21. Gordon Robertson, "The Changing Role of the Privy Council Office," *CPA*, vol. 14, no. 4 (Winter 1971), pp. 487–508.

assistance. The third principle is that the PCO should be maintained as a non-career agency. As indicated earlier, the PCO is for the most part staffed by career bureaucrats on loan from various government departments. The fourth principle is that the PCO should be kept small in size. While it has grown dramatically since the Second World War, the present professional and clerical staff of approximately 300 is probably adequate for meeting its current needs and objectives.

The PCO has a difficult task to perform within the Canadian government. It must be able to offer expert advice to the prime minister on a wide range of problems and policies. Given such expectations, it is not surprising that the PCO is considered one of the most prestigious agencies of the government.

Issues of concern to the federal government and the provinces are periodically negotiated and adjusted through the mechanism of federal/provincial conferences. As we discussed in Chapters 6 and 7, federalism has recently been characterized by a strong challenge to Ottawa's power, particularly from the richer western provinces and Québec. Holding numerous federal/provincial meetings on a wide range of issues, especially constitutional revisions, necessitates intensive planning and preparation on the part of Ottawa. Within the Privy Council Office, a new central agency — the **Federal-Provincial Relations Office (FPRO)** — was established in 1974 and was designated a separate department under the prime minister in 1975. Until 1993 it functioned independently of the PCO while reporting directly to the prime minister. As part of the 1993 restructuring, the FPRO was subsumed once again by the PCO. It now reports to the minister responsible for federal/provincial relations, Stéphane Dion.

The name of the FPRO has recently been changed to **Intergovernmental Affairs Secretariat** to indicate that it is responsible for issues concerning aboriginals and territorial governments as well as the provinces. It continues to conduct research and analysis to help in coordinating Ottawa's interaction with the provinces and in anticipating provincial reactions. In particular, it has a special mandate to monitor events in Québec and prepare scenarios for action *vis-à-vis* its government and the issue of independence. It also has ongoing duties in the areas of aboriginal rights and constitutional planning. Given the continuous and increasing challenges to federalism, it is likely that the responsibilities of this secretariat inside the PCO will continue to increase over the next few years.

The Treasury Board

The third central coordinating agency is the Treasury Board, which, as we have noted, is constitutionally a committee of the Privy Council, i.e., of Cabinet. In 1966, following recommendations of the Glassco Royal Commission on Government Organization, the staff of Treasury Board was removed from the jurisdiction of the Department of Finance and elevated to the legal status of a separate government department. The Treasury Board and its Secretariat are headed by a Cabinet minister, the president of the Treasury Board. The Treasury Board itself includes other Cabinet ministers, one of whom is usually the Minister of Finance. Aided by its Secretariat, the Treasury Board is charged with two broad areas of responsibility: review of government expenditures and personnel management.

Responsibility for the review of expenditures means that the annual budgets of all government departments are screened and approved by this agency. The Treasury Board monitors all requests for money, evaluates them and provides an overall budget in keeping with the priorities and objectives expressed by the prime minister and Cabinet. There is continuous consultation and negotiation between the Treasury Board and representatives of each department, who are usually senior bureaucrats and the minister. Each department attempts to maximize its share of the government's budget, and it is up to the Treasury Board to assess these requests and make its recommendations.

The task of the Treasury Board would be exceedingly difficult, if not chaotic, were it not for improvements in policy-making techniques during the past three decades. The first major reform came in the 1960s with the introduction of the Program, Planning and Budgetary System (PPBS). The second was the 1979 introduction of the Public Expenditure Management System (PEMS), which is discussed in Chapter 9. Despite the government's decision to disband the overall PEMS system in 1989, the financial control procedures remain in place. In recent years, the Board and its secretariat working under the new Expenditure Management System (EMS) have been delegated the responsibility for advising Cabinet on the efficient management of resources. It reviews the **Departmental Business Plans** required under the new expenditure system.

In theory, these procedures force departments to frame their budgetary requirements in terms of government goals and objectives and to do so in the format of a business plan. Whether the Treasury Board has been fully able to meet its heavy responsibility in budgetary control is a matter of contention for various disgruntled department heads and, of course, for the loyal opposition. In fairness, it should be noted that its task is complex. It is continually faced with pressure from both within and without Cabinet. Inevitably, no matter how worthwhile certain programs may be, there is only a finite amount of money to pay for them.

The second major responsibility entrusted to the Treasury Board is management of civil service personnel. In 1967, the Treasury Board replaced the Public Service Commission as the official employer of government personnel; it is thus the responsible party in any collective bargaining negotiations. It exerts control over salaries and job classifications across the civil service, and its purpose is to expand the application of the merit principle. Motivating the Treasury Board above all else is a desire to encourage the effective utilization of human resources.

To assist the six Cabinet members of the Treasury Board there is a highly qualified staff — the **Treasury Board Secretariat (TBS)**. The **Secretary to the Treasury Board** heads the Secretariat and is also Comptroller General of Canada. The **Comptroller General** is responsible for developing financial control mechanisms and enforcing them. Among the TBS staff are some of the brightest and most efficient members of the public service. Its economists, statisticians and efficiency experts conduct much of the preliminary analysis of departmental budgets. The TBS often makes preliminary budgetary adjustments and other decisions that may be challenged by department heads or ministers at the formal meetings of the Board itself. Needless to say, the specialized staff of the TBS can also play an important role in policy-making.

The Department of Finance

The fourth central coordinating agency of the executive is the Department of Finance. While it is a regular government department, by virtue of its subject matter it is one of the most politically sensitive. Created in 1967 out of the financial bodies that predated Confederation, its authority is assigned under the *Financial Administration Act*. The Department of Finance shares some of the general concerns of the Treasury Board, but its chief preoccupation is analyzing taxation policy and the impact of government activity on the economy. That is, the Department is concerned with monitoring Canada's economic prospects and predicting the probable level of tax revenues available to the government. It also engages in long-range economic forecasting and suggests ways to maximize the performance of the economy.

The Department of Finance provides most of the information that reaches the Cabinet on the performance of the economy. It is on the basis of these facts that Cabinet committees weigh and sift various programs and proposals to establish priorities. The Department's predictions and analyses assist other policy-makers in attempting to achieve maximum use of available resources. Public servants employed by the Department of Finance concentrate on analyzing four areas that comprise the Department's statutory authority: taxation policy, economic development and government finance, fiscal policy and economic analysis, and international trade and finance.

Taxation policy is handled by individual units within the Department. Specialists analyze existing tax measures from the perspective of the business community. A personal income tax unit examines proposals relating to personal taxation, deferred income plans such as retirement savings plans, trusts and partnerships. Other tax units attempt to determine the effects of taxation on the distribution of income, on the long-term growth of the economy, and on the behaviour of individuals and corporations. Finally, the Department of Finance maintains an international tax policy unit that negotiates tax treaties with foreign countries and examines the effects of foreign taxation on the Canadian economy.

With respect to the second responsibility, economic development, the Department seeks to devise policies and strategies that encourage the overall growth of the Canadian economy. For instance, policy analysts study plans to foster the development of Canada's natural resources and to promote industrial growth in such diverse fields as communications, transportation, nuclear energy and manufacturing. The Department of Finance is also involved in providing government loans to promote economic development and in negotiating financial guarantees to Crown corporations.

The third responsibility of the Department of Finance is fiscal policy and economic analysis. The Department monitors all indicators of the overall economic conditions of the country and prepares forecasts used in the development of the annual government budget. This involves establishing the annual fiscal framework and maintaining a close link with the Treasury Board Secretariat.

The fourth concern of the Department of Finance is international trade. It investigates and reports on proposals concerning the Canadian customs tariff and its relation to the General Agreement on Tariffs and Trade (GATT) and various bilateral trade agreements such as the Canada–United States Free Trade Agreement and the North American Free Trade Agreement. Recommendations on international trade policy, particularly imports, are formulated. The Department maintains a liaison with international financial organizations and, of course, seeks to promote export development. The international finance section is also concerned with the balance of payments and foreign exchange matters.

The Department of Finance maintains a relatively high profile among government departments. Its minister (currently Paul Martin Jr.) is more than a spokesman for economic decisions made by the Cabinet. While the Minister of Finance must carry out Cabinet's directives, other ministers become involved so late in the budget-planning process that, in effect, the Finance Minister has the dominant voice. It is the minister who presents the government's budget to Parliament and is inevitably the object of criticism or praise by the press and the opposition. Because taxation policy is usually the target of public scorn, however, the finance portfolio has traditionally been considered the graveyard of many a political career.

Conflicts of Interest

One issue that haunts members of the Cabinet as well as other politicians is conflict of interest. A **conflict of interest** is a situation in which a prime minister, minister, member of Parliament or public servant has knowledge of a private, personal economic interest sufficient to influence the exercise of public duties and responsibilities.[22] Even if the conflict is not illegal, it may create doubts or suspicions that the decisions or actions of such individuals are not impartial.

Public attitudes about which situations constitute conflict of interest for ministers have changed considerably over the years; behaviour that was considered normal a few decades ago now engenders cynicism, suspicion and moral condemnation. Until the 1960s, MPs routinely carried on with their private businesses after they became ministers, and conflict-of-interest queries were raised only when their ministerial decisions clearly produced private advantage. In those years, politics was still a part-time, rather poorly paid occupation, and ministers and prime ministers openly and frequently engaged in potentially conflicting activities; they sat on boards of directors, carried on legal practices and accepted private trust funds.

After several mini-scandals in the Pearson government, public tolerance of such practices began to wane. In 1972, Prime Minister Trudeau issued formal guidelines for Cabinet ministers. Like Pearson, he chose to rely on guidelines rather than legislation to handle the problem.[23] A registry of ministers' financial holdings was to be kept, and they could choose one of three options:

1. divest themselves of their financial holdings; or

2. place their financial holdings in a blind trust (which meant, in theory, that ministers should not know what their holdings are and therefore not be able to act on privileged information); or

3. place them in a frozen trust (meaning that ministers could know what their assets were but would not be able to change them).[24]

These guidelines provided rather undefined and ambiguous instructions for ministers about how to arrange their personal affairs to avoid the possibility of conflict of interest. Possible disclosure of conflict situations was considered to be a sufficient deterrent, since it would cause political embarrassment and negative publicity to the extent that a Cabinet minister might feel it necessary to resign in order to protect the government's integrity. However, the guidelines did not provide sufficient sanctions to deter potential conflicts, nor did they establish appropriate mechanisms to determine whether such violations were taking place.

Prime Minister Joe Clark made the guidelines more stringent by extending them to the immediate families of ministers. Blind trusts became mandatory, and for two years after leaving Cabinet ex-ministers could not serve on boards of directors of corporations with which they had dealt as ministers; they could not act on behalf of such people or corporations, or act as lobbyists. For one year they could not accept jobs with companies with which they had dealt, nor could they act as consultants for them. These guidelines were maintained from the Clark government through to the Mulroney government in 1984.

Prime Minister Mulroney abolished the code and introduced new conflict-of-interest guidelines for Cabinet ministers (also guidelines for civil servants) in 1985. Like the earlier version, it stopped short of full, mandatory disclosure in order to strike a balance between protecting the public interest and protecting the private affairs of ministers. The restrictions on business dealings of immediate

22. This is essentially the definition used by Justice William Parker in his 1987 report on the conflicts of interest of former Cabinet minister Sinclair Stevens. See *Commission of Inquiry into the Facts and Allegations of Conflict of Interest Concerning the Honourable Sinclair M. Stevens* (Toronto: The Commission, 1987), p. 294.

23. Pierre Trudeau, Statement on Conflict of Interest, House of Commons, July 18, 1973.

24. See Robert J. Jackson and Michael Atkinson, *Canadian Legislative System* (Toronto: Macmillan, 1980), pp. 209–10.

family members were dropped. It did, however, make it explicit that ministers must not hire their own immediate relatives (or other ministers' relatives) for government jobs.

The ambiguity and lack of enforcement provisions in the new code led to a major conflict-of-interest case when Cabinet minister Sinclair Stevens was faced with a series of conflict allegations in 1986–87. A key charge against Stevens was that his wife obtained a $2.6 million loan from a consultant to a company that had received grants from Stevens' government department. Stevens had ostensibly placed his business holdings in a blind trust; however, the trust was considerably less than "blind" because of his connections with several involved individuals, including his wife (who remained an officer of the company) and his secretary, who could have provided Stevens with information about the affairs of his "blind" trust. The Parker Commission, which investigated the case, concluded that Stevens had violated the conflict code 14 times.

CLOSE-UP ON
Institutions

MORALITY IN PARLIAMENT

Professors Ian Greene and David P. Shugarman believe that the ethics of politicians affect the public: "Leaders who are considered self-interested and untrustworthy create a malaise in government circles that tempts public servants to behave unethically to protect themselves. And these factors combine to erode the public's trust in government as a whole. Conversely, if those at the top are perceived as fair and honest, then these values tend to permeate the entire society."*

Is there empirical evidence to support this contention? Do you agree with the principles stated in this quotation?

* Ian Greene and David P. Shugarman, *Honest Politics* (Toronto: Lorimer, 1997), p. 213.

Concerned that Canadians were indeed losing confidence in the integrity of politicians and politics in general, and also that his government had an extremely poor image in this regard, Mulroney decided that guidelines were no longer sufficient and introduced conflict-of-interest legislation in early 1988. The bill that was put forward attempted to force enough disclosure to keep the government leaders honest, yet not infringe on their private lives so much that highly qualified individuals would be deterred from practising politics. However, Bill C114 died on the Order Paper when the 1988 general election was called. Various other attempts to legislate about conflict of interest have also failed. In the last days of the Mulroney government in 1993, another, more stringent, bill was introduced but it, too, died on the Order Paper when the 34th Parliament was dissolved.

When he came to office in 1993, Liberal prime minister Jean Chrétien took a radically different approach to conflict of interest. Arguing that "integrity in government is not simply a matter of rules and regulations — it is also a matter of personal standards and conduct,"[25] he hired former minister Mitchell Sharp for one dollar a year as a special advisor on integrity of government. In June 1994, the prime minister unveiled yet another "ethics package" about the conflict-of-interest code and lobbying rules. Public officials (ministers, secretaries of state, parliamentary secretaries and senior public servants) were instructed to disclose their assets and outside activities confidentially to a newly appointed "ethics counsellor," Howard Wilson, who was made responsible for both conflict-of-interest and lobbying rules. Problems still exist, however, because the ethics counsellor is not accountable to Parliament, only to the prime minister. This lack of an "independent" counsellor has caused considerable controversy. As well, despite various allegations of wrongdoing and the resignation of two ministers over them (Michel Dupuy and David Collenette), the government has, as yet, not agreed to the idea that "codes of conduct" should be legislated or that regular MPs should even be covered by a code. The Criminal Code, the *Parliament Act* and Standing Orders of the House of Commons continue to apply to any minister or ordinary member involved in fraud, influence peddling or breach of trust.

25. Office of the Prime Minister, Press Release, November 4, 1993, p. 3.

Patronage

A little-studied field closely linked to conflict of interest is the world of political patronage and its near-relative, pork-barrelling. **Patronage**, in the broad sense, concerns the awarding of contracts, employment and other material benefits to individuals or groups on the basis of partisan support rather than according to merit. It means granting jobs and contracts for political reasons. It can include illegal practices such as vote-buying, "treating" (paying for votes with liquor) and other forms of bribery. **Pork-barrelling**, on the other hand, extends favours to whole regions or communities as an inducement for support. Patronage and pork-barrelling usually break no laws but often raise serious questions about ethical conduct.

Some regard patronage and its less attractive cousin as essential parts of politics, providing the oil that makes the system run smoothly and the glue that keeps parties together and the political system stable. For others, patronage and pork-barrelling are immoral activities that impede honest, efficient government services. All would agree that they are enduring features of the Canadian political system. It is in the shadowy world where interest-group behaviour, patronage and pork-barrelling meet, and where secret negotiations lead to connections between influence and favours, that corruption adds its cynical, malodorous quality to Canadian politics.

Patronage has been an important part of the Canadian political culture since the pre-1867 colonial period.[26] The notion that only party supporters have the right to government positions and favours was imported from Britain and has become a distinctive feature of Canadian politics, although it has been modified over time. Patronage traditionally provided an inducement for loyalty and for mobilizing participation. Moreover, the early history of patronage in Canada reflects the struggle to shift control over the distribution of political favours from the monarch and government in Britain to the prime minister and Cabinet in Canada — in effect, to "patriate" the power of patronage.

Four distinct stages have been noted in the development of patronage in Canada.[27] In the colonial years the British governors dispensed patronage, using it to maintain deference and loyalty from the colonists. With the advent of responsible government, the privilege of dispensing patronage shifted to the elected representative. In the second stage, after Confederation, patronage was used first by Sir John A. Macdonald and later by Sir Wilfrid Laurier to help build national parties that would unite a widely scattered population. These prime ministers used material benefits openly and freely to recruit and maintain an active party organization. The third stage of patronage development began about the time of the First World War when Mackenzie King began his long career as prime minister. Patronage and pork-barrelling remained an important part of party management, but during this period the civil service became separate from the party in power, dramatically changing the close relationship that had previously existed between the government and the public sector. The final stage of patronage development began in the 1960s as technological and cultural changes contributed to public intolerance of some of the traditional inducements for loyalty and participation.

Modern prime ministers endeavour to find more acceptable inducements for loyalty and discipline, such as the strength of their personality and popular policies. They use the media — television in particular — to appeal directly to citizens. However strong these direct appeals have become, they have not yet supplanted patronage. It is no surprise that opposition parties seem to have more trouble than governing parties in maintaining internal party cohesion; the government holds all the patronage and pork-barrelling resources in its hands and is often able to secure loyalty from those who expect or receive favours.

---

26. Gordon T. Stewart, *The Origins of Canadian Parties* (Vancouver: University of British Columbia Press, 1986).
27. Jeffrey Simpson, *Spoils of Power* (Toronto: Collins, 1988), p. 6.

Several aspects of patronage have contributed to its sullied reputation. It plays to human weaknesses, encouraging unethical behaviour by individuals, institutions and groups in society. It also has an inflationary aspect: one reward creates a demand for more, and the demand always exceeds supply. The use of patronage to bind together religious, French/English or regional interests is no longer sufficiently broad; it must now extend to women, youth, Natives and those of other ethnic groups.[28]

Recent prime ministers have been plagued with the problem of dispensing patronage without compromising their public position.[29] Joe Clark incurred the wrath of party rank-and-file when he delayed too long in filling patronage positions. He lost his chance to dispense rewards when his minority government was defeated in 1979. John Turner lost the 1984 election when he declared he had "no option" but to honour the "orgy" of appointments demanded by departing Prime Minister Trudeau. Despite the fact that Brian Mulroney had made a major issue out of patronage in his 1984 election campaign, calling the actions of Turner and Trudeau "scandalous," "vulgar" and "unacceptable," he proceeded to fill patronage positions and award government business to party and personal friends. He also saw his own popularity, and that of his party, fall to record lows after patronage binges during his two governments.

In 1993, the new Chrétien government promised to increase integrity in government and decrease patronage appointments. The country waits for the concrete results of these assertions, as almost all of the government appointments by 1997 had gone to well-known Liberals — former Governor General Roméo Leblanc being the most prominent among them.

PRIME MINISTERIAL GOVERNMENT?

Considerable disquiet exists among observers of the Canadian political scene about the role of the prime minister. One basis for this uneasiness is the suggestion that the political executive has overstepped its proper authority; such encroachment is seen as portending grave consequences for responsible government and the parliamentary system. Changes in the rules of House of Commons procedure and the expanding jurisdiction of government have lessened the effectiveness of Parliament in its role of scrutiny and deliberation. The result is that the prime minister exercises a scope of authority analogous to that of the American president.

In an early article discussing this issue, Denis Smith suggested that Parliament had surrendered its important roles of providing a forum for serious public debate and developing public policy.[30] He argued that the establishment of a presidential-style control of government had been evolving for many years. Rather than establishing a trend, recent prime ministers have merely refined and consolidated it. According to Smith, the source of the prime minister's predominance is that the system is devised in such a way that a great deal ultimately depends on him or her. The prime minister appoints ministers and controls their tenure almost entirely. Although Cabinet may include some unusually powerful and prestigious figures, in the end the decisions it reaches depend on the priorities and orientations of the prime minister. Cabinet policy becomes government policy, and backbenchers have little choice but to vote in obedience to the party and prime minister. The recent reforms in House rules permit the government to guide legislation through with a minimum of delay or modification. The opposition parties, lacking adequate research and basic information, may resort to fiery oratory but are rarely able to conduct thorough scrutiny and effective criticism.

28. Ibid., p. 15. Patronage is discussed further in Chapter 11.
29. John Sawatsky, *The Insiders: Government, Business and the Lobbyists* (Toronto: McClelland & Stewart, 1987), chs. 17–19.
30. Denis Smith, "President and Parliament: The Transformation of Parliamentary Government in Canada," in Thomas Hockin, ed., *Apex of Power* (Scarborough: Prentice Hall, 1977), pp. 308–25.

The office of prime minister in Canada today is very strong. Whether the current situation is beneficial for the country and its political process is a matter that will continue to be debated for years to come. Without taking sides in the argument, we can consider what has given rise to this argument about executive leadership. While Canada's total population rose gradually, the demand for services of all kinds rose exponentially. To meet these needs, the government developed large departments and bureaucracies. Faced with a cumbersome and ever-expanding government sector, Prime Ministers Trudeau, Clark and Turner introduced aspects of systematic planning to replace the somewhat haphazard, *ad hoc* policy-making of previous administrations. While pushing for the reform of House procedural rules to streamline the legislative process, the government simultaneously expanded the size and functions of the central coordinating agencies, especially the PMO and PCO.

> *When you're in government ... the choices you make are not between ... strawberries and cream or crème caramel for dessert. You have to sometimes choose between cod liver oil or cough syrup.*
>
> **Ontario premier Bob Rae**

The takeover of exceptional policy-making authority by the prime minister and central executive agencies is resented by ministers, middle and upper echelons of the civil service, and members of Parliament, and distrusted by the press and opposition. Journalistic reports abound of the existence of a coterie of insiders who, being outside the bounds of parliamentary control, are able to manipulate the levers of power in Canada. While the descriptions of flagrant abuse of power may be overstated,[31] the potential for its occurrence has been very real indeed. The power of the prime minister and the executive staff has become enormous and pervasive. Once elected, a prime minister can shape the direction and content of policy, and, except in extraordinary situations, can count on dominating the political process until deciding to call an election.

While our discussion has justifiably focused on the powers and advantages of the prime minister's position, at the same time we must not overlook certain limitations on it. It is our contention that, in fact, Canada does *not* have prime ministerial government. The political resources of the prime minister are undeniably potent and broad. But the power of the prime minister is not exercised in isolation. The prime minister and his or her colleagues must take care to guide the Cabinet and caucus toward policies that avoid hostile reactions from Parliament and the public. As well, the prime minister must secure the loyalty of followers or risk being voted out of office. As summarized in *The Canadian Legislative System*:

> *The Prime Minister's influence stems from an ability to command the maximum possible amount of information about the political environment and to use this resource in persuading political actors to follow his policy initiatives. Administrative secrecy and collective ministerial responsibility permit the executive to acquire requisite political knowledge without revealing conflicts or divisions which may occur within its ranks. However, the ability to conceal the process of decision making at this level in government has sustained the erroneous idea that the executive works in isolation from parliamentary influence and has contributed significantly to the impression that the government acts independently of public opinion.*[32]

31. Walter Stewart, *Shrug: Trudeau in Power* (Toronto: New Press, 1971).
32. Jackson and Atkinson, *Canadian Legislative System*, p. 56.

At certain times, the prime minister can act independently; at others, the prime minister is forced to rely on party colleagues. Malcolm Punnett provides a succinct criticism of the thesis of prime ministerial government. After a detailed examination of the governing style of Canada's prime ministers, he concluded that the argument is not justified "because of the fundamental distinction that exists between the seeming concentration of power in the hands of the prime minister of the day and the realities of his position."[33] The prime minister is constrained in the choice of ministers by the difficulties of holding a Cabinet together, of directing a complex government machine and of securing agreements to proposals from the Cabinet, back bench and often other parties.

There are four basic models of executive government in the political science literature:

1. prime ministerial, in which decisions are taken by the prime minister acting alone;

2. ministerial, in which decisions are taken by individual ministers in their own spheres of interest;

3. Cabinet, in which Cabinet under the direction of the prime minister takes decisions;

4. inner-group, in which decisions are taken by a subgroup of Cabinet along with the prime minister.[34]

In view of the constraints listed above, it is our view that the first model does not apply to Canada. No Canadian prime minister can really act alone and all these models fail to take ministers and bureaucrats into account. Of course, some prime ministers have tried to take more than their share of decision-making responsibility. R.B. Bennett simultaneously held the posts of prime minister, Minister of Finance and External Affairs, and is said to have acted independently of his Cabinet colleagues. A splendid joke was told about him in the 1930s:

> *Visitor to Ottawa: "Who is that man coming toward us?"*
> *Ottawa resident: "Mr. R.B. Bennett, the new Prime Minister."*
> *Visitor to Ottawa: "Why is he talking to himself?"*
> *Ottawa resident: "He is holding a Cabinet meeting."*[35]

However, even Bennett had to avoid coalitions of conflicting interests and often ran into difficulty.

Prime ministers obtain much of their strength from holding their team together. This must be done with conciliation, tact and only rarely with force. Most prime ministers bring particular skills to bear on this responsibility. For example, Pearson was a master chairman-of-the-board type of leader; Mackenzie King was a master electioneer. Mulroney and Chrétien combined both talents. The skills required are so varied that no prime minister can be said to have had all of them. What all prime ministers must demonstrate is the ability to coordinate their colleagues and, hence, policy. The primary ingredient of this ability is anticipation of the actions of all the major actors in the political system. Recent prime ministers have accomplished this by relying on a small coterie of ministers to help them come to compromises and conclusions. Prime Ministers Trudeau and Mulroney both employed a Priorities and Planning Committee of Cabinet to obtain information and enhance consensus. Clark constructed an inner Cabinet to accomplish the same end. On this evidence, the usual prime ministerial pattern could therefore be described as setting up an informal partial Cabinet to help run the government. This is a far cry from the arrangement suggested by those

---

33. Punnett, *The Prime Minister*, p. 157.
34. Ibid., p. 86.
35. Ernest Watkins, *R.B. Bennett: A Biography* (London: Secker and Warburg, 1963), p. 167.

who contend that Canada now has prime ministerial government. Jean Chrétien eliminated these committees and governs with a ministry of 37 members. It remains to be seen whether Chrétien's new process will enhance or reduce prime ministerial power in a House of Commons with only a razor-thin majority.

SUMMARY

This chapter has sought to illuminate the nature of executive power in Canada. While the *Constitution Act, 1867,* established a formal executive in the person of the Governor General, there is no question that real political power is exercised by the prime minister and Cabinet, based on the possession of an electoral mandate. The fusion-of-powers principle, along with other aspects of the British parliamentary tradition such as party discipline and Cabinet solidarity, confers upon the political executive the opportunity to carry out its program knowing that it can count on consistent legislative support except during minority governments. The prime minister has extraordinary powers, such as the authority to make Cabinet appointments, reorganize the government structure and dissolve Parliament at his or her discretion. In order to run the government apparatus efficiently the prime minister must delegate some authority to the members of the ministry and Cabinet. In recent years, the government has evolved an elaborate system of committees and subcommittees, all of which are ultimately responsible to the prime minister. In the last two decades, the various executive co-ordinating agencies have grown greatly in size and authority.

The centralization of power in the hands of the executive and its specialized agencies is a matter for serious attention. While some will find even the appearance of presidential-style government difficult to accept, centralization of power is likely inevitable. It is a political reality, although critics should not overlook the obvious constraints and limitations within which the prime minister must operate. An extraordinary apparatus and structure of power has been built over the years; fortunately for Canada, its prime ministers have thus far been relatively enlightened figures.

DISCUSSION QUESTIONS

1. Where does political power lie in the Canadian system? With the prime minister? With Cabinet? With the Queen or her representative? With Parliament? With the people of Canada?

2. What are the four central coordinating agencies and what are their functions?

3. Are conflict-of-interest rules tough enough and clear enough?

4. Is patronage an essential part of the Canadian political system?

5. Does the prime minister have too much power?

Selected Bibliography

Bakvis, Herman, *Regional Ministers: Power and Influence in the Canadian Cabinet* (Toronto: University of Toronto Press, 1991).

Bliss, Michael, *Right Honourable Men: The Descent of Canadian Politics from Macdonald to Mulroney* (Toronto: HarperCollins, 1994).

Cameron, Stevie, *On the Take: Crime, Corruption and Greed in the Mulroney Years* (Toronto: Macfarlane, Walter and Ross, 1994).

Campbell, Colin and M.J. Wyszomirski, eds., *Executive Leadership in Anglo-American Systems* (Pittsburgh: University of Pittsburgh Press, 1991).

Greene, Ian and David P. Shugarman, *Honest Politics* (Toronto: Lorimer, 1997).

Levine, Allan, *Scrum Wars: The Prime Minister and the Media* (Toronto: Dundurn Press, 1993).

Mancuso, Maureen, R. Price and R. Wagenberg, *Leaders and Leadership in Canada* (Toronto: Oxford University Press, 1994).

Pal, Leslie A. and David Taras, eds., *Prime Ministers and Premiers: Political Leadership and Public Policy in Canada* (Scarborough: Prentice Hall, 1988).

Savoie, Donald J., *Governing from the Centre: The Concentration of Power in Canadian Politics* (Toronto: University of Toronto Press, 1999).

Smith, David E., *The Republican Option in Canada: Past and Present* (Toronto: University of Toronto Press, 1999).

Strom, Kaare, *Minority Government and Majority Rule* (Cambridge: Cambridge University Press, 1990).

Sutherland, Sharon, "Responsible Government and Ministerial Responsibility: Every Reform Is Its Own Problem," *CJPS* (March 1991), vol. 22, no. 1, pp. 91–120.

 # LIST OF WEBLINKS

www.gg.ca/menu_e.html	**Governor General** This is the official Web page of the Governor General of Canada.
pm.gc.ca	**Prime Minister of Canada** This is the official Web page of the Prime Minister of Canada.
www.canada.gc.ca/howgoc/ cab/ministry_e.html	**Cabinet Ministers and Portfolios** This Web site lists the different members of the federal Cabinet and their portfolios.

9

Legislative Politics

· · · · · · · · ·

Symbolism or Power?

In a parliamentary democracy, the federal legislature, or Parliament, should be one of the most important institutions in the political life of the country. However, in Canada a certain degree of dissatisfaction exists among academic and media observers, sections of the general public, and even parliamentarians themselves about the role of Parliament. There is perennial debate on the subject of parliamentary reform. At times, dissatisfaction with Parliament verges on outright cynicism. But the reality is that Canadian democracy could not function without this institution.

In a parliamentary democracy, the political executive receives its power to govern from the legislature. The government needs the approval of Parliament to legitimate its policies and activities, particularly for the expenditure of public funds. In return, the prime minister and Cabinet must hold themselves accountable to Parliament, and may continue to govern only as long as they retain the "confidence" of Parliament or, more correctly in the case of Canada, at least the tacit support of a majority of the House of Commons. Thus, while Parliament gives the executive the authority to govern, it also serves as a check on the absolute or irresponsible use of government power. Prime Minister Chrétien's small majority of MPs makes this crucial in the 36th Parliament.

Parliament, moreover, provides an arena for debate in which the major political issues of the day may be aired — and subsequently relayed to the public by the mass media. As such, it is a public forum for opposition parties to criticize the government of the day and to demonstrate why they, not the governing party, should be returned with a majority of seats at the next general election.

Last, but not least, Parliament serves important functions on behalf of Canadian citizens. In the theory of **parliamentary democracy**, Parliament is the "repository of popular sovereignty": in making laws and ensuring the responsibility of government, Parliament exercises power on behalf of the general public, power vested in it by the electoral process. It is not possible in a country the size of Canada for all citizens to participate directly in the legislative process. Instead, Canada is a **representative democracy** in which, from time to time, we choose certain individuals (members of Parliament) to represent our interests in making national policies. But, on a more practical level, a significant part of the role of parliamentarians is catering to the needs of their constituents. Members of Parliament and their staff spend much of their time taking up the problems of citizens with ministers, public servants or representatives of government agencies. Such personal problems may seem prosaic compared with issues such as Québec separatism and government debt, but they are very important to the people they affect. All Canadians, especially those with no well-organized business lobby or trade union to represent them, need Parliament.

Thus, Parliament is indeed an important institution in Canadian political life. The ongoing debates about parliamentary reform reflect its significance. But it is not always easy to determine whether the importance of Parliament is derived from its *power* to enact legislation, hold the government accountable and control the public purse-strings, or from its perceived *symbolic role* as the repository of popular sovereignty, an arena for political debate and the legitimizer of the actions of government and, perhaps, of the entire policy process.

Like other legislatures, the Parliament of Canada is a multifunctional institution. It plays several roles of importance to the political process and to the Canadian people. Accordingly, its members have a multitude of tasks to perform — as senators and MPs, as members of Cabinet and the opposition, as members of party caucuses and parliamentary committees, and as individual representatives of their constituents. There is a constant tension, visible in many of the reform debates, among the various roles of Parliament and among the tasks that members are expected to carry out.

In this chapter, we examine how these tensions are reconciled through the process of *legislative politics*. We look at several aspects of this reconciliation: how the parliamentary timetable and procedures reflect the competing demands of a government wishing to govern and an opposition seeking to air public issues and criticize the government's method of handling them; how the working subgroups of parliamentarians in committees and party caucuses contribute to the overall work of Parliament; how individual MPs manage the competing demands on their time; how the Senate continues to make a positive contribution; and how adherence to the parliamentary "rules of the game" generally imposes a workable peace on an adversarial system of politics. We commence our examination by defining what a legislature is. Then, in the section that follows, we consider the role of legislatures with particular reference to the concepts of the *power* and *symbolism* of parliaments and to the various meanings that may be attached to the term *legislative politics*.

WHAT IS A LEGISLATURE?

Legislatures are among the most pervasive of political institutions. In 2000, almost all of the more than 192 independent states have some kind of parliamentary chamber; many of these also had legislative assemblies at the subnational level, such as the state legislatures of the United States, the provincial assemblies in Canada and so on. The very ubiquity of the institution makes the definition of a "legislature" and the specification of its functions difficult. It was once common, if not entirely correct, to base such a definition on the characteristics of the American Congress or the British Parliament. However, easy conceptualization has been hindered by the proliferation, particularly in the developing world, of institutions that call themselves "legislatures" or "parliaments" but that possess methods of recruitment, powers and relations to other political structures widely divergent from those of the two traditional models.

Some authors avoid this matter of definition altogether — taking for granted that their readers already know what a legislature is — and plunge directly into their analyses. An alternative strategy to such avoidance and to offering a precise definition is the presentation of a checklist of characteristics that, taken together, are both necessary and sufficient to distinguish legislatures from other political institutions. Thus, Nelson Polsby argues that a

> *... mélange of characteristics — officiality, a claim of legitimacy based on links with the people, multi-memberedness, formal equality, collective decision-making, deliberativeness — typifies and distinguishes legislatures in a wide variety of settings.[1]*

While Polsby's approach is primarily structural, an alternative is the functional perspective that defines legislatures in terms of their tasks or the purpose they serve in the political system. The latter approach shows legislatures performing a multitude of functions — in addition to the apparently tautological "legislative" or "law-making" role — that vary in salience from country to country and even over time within the same political system. The role of the Congress of People's Deputies in the U.S.S.R., for example, was very different from that of the American Congress, and the functions of the British Parliament today have changed considerably since its so-called "Golden Age" over a century ago. Furthermore, the fact that many of the functions attributed to legislatures are also performed by other political institutions merely adds to the terminological confusion.

In a comparative study of legislatures, Michael Mezey offers a personal perception of the concept in which both structural and functional elements are combined:

> *I think of a legislature as a predominantly elected body of people that acts collegially and that has at least the formal but not necessarily the exclusive power to enact laws binding on all members of a specific geopolitical entity.[2]*

This constitutes a valid definition, but there is one major problem with Mezey's conceptualization in the Canadian context. In applying his definition individually to each chamber or "house" of bicameral parliaments, he specifically excludes the Canadian Senate from consideration as a legislature, since its members are appointed rather than "predominantly elected." On the other hand, he does not tell the reader just what a senate is. If it is not a legislature or at least a part of one, what is it? Of course, there would be no problem in the Canadian case if the definition were applied to the whole Parliament of Canada (i.e., the Senate and the House of Commons), since it is "predominantly elected"; but until recently the usage could not be extended to the British Parliament, wherein the membership of the House of Lords, recruited by appointment or by heredity, exceeded that of the popularly elected House of Commons. The application of Mezey's definition may, therefore, be broadened to cover bicameral parliaments if both chambers collectively are considered to constitute the legislature, as long as the lower house (or, in parliamentary systems, the house to which the government is officially responsible) is predominantly elected. With the addition of this proviso, the simplicity and clarity of this conceptualization make it a suitable working definition for this chapter.

THE ROLES OF LEGISLATURES

A frequent source of confusion in the study of parliamentary institutions is the notion that "legislatures must legislate." Given the similarity between the two words and the mythology surrounding the role of legislatures, this assumption is not surprising. But neither should it be encouraged, since

1. Nelson Polsby, "Legislatures," in F. Greenstein and N. Polsby, eds., *Handbook of Political Science*, vol. 5 (Reading, Mass.: Addison-Wesley, 1975), p. 260.
2. Michael L. Mezey, *Comparative Legislatures* (Durham, N.C.: Duke University Press, 1979), p. 6.

it may lead to unfulfilled expectations of what legislatures ought to do and to overly simplistic criticisms of parliamentary institutions. For this reason, one author justifies his usage of "parliament" as a generic term for national legislative assemblies in preference to "legislature" in that the latter is "too restrictively an implied definition of what these bodies do."[3] On the other hand, most legislatures do spend a substantial portion of their time in consideration and passage of legislation. For instance, approximately one-third of all oral debates in the Canadian House of Commons are devoted to discussion of government legislation, as are between one-quarter and one-half of all Commons committee meetings.[4] The essential point is that a distinction must be drawn between the legislative function — the task of initiating, formulating and enacting bills or statutes — and the legislature as an institution. The legislative function is a complex one involving various other actors in the process of devising and drafting bills even before the legislature considers the bills and decides whether they are to become part of the law of the land. As institutions, legislatures are multifunctional, and the passage of legislation is but one of a number of roles they perform.

The delineation of the roles of legislatures has a long history in the study of political institutions, with the result that a bewildering array of functions now appears in the literature. More than a century has passed since the English constitutionalist Walter Bagehot described the major roles of the British House of Commons as *elective, expressive, teaching, informing* and *legislative.*[5] Given the reputation of the British legislature as "the mother of parliaments," it is perhaps not surprising that many subsequent classifications have been based more or less loosely upon Bagehot's classic formulation, although his categories have often been re-labelled with more current terminology or jargon. In fact, after the Second World War, as political scientists increasingly oriented their research to non-western societies, it became apparent that some legislatures had no real power to make laws, to constitute or remove governments, or to articulate the grievances of the population. New functions had to be added to the list to describe the roles of what were little more than "rubber stamp" assemblies; as a result, attention was drawn to the more symbolic functions of parliaments, such as *legitimation* of the regime and *integration* of the political community.

So numerous have the proposed functions of legislatures become that some scholars have turned to a process of consolidation. To take one example, Mezey suggests that, "with only a modest amount of pushing and shoving," all the activities of legislatures and their members "can be grouped into three broad categories: policy-making activities, representational activities, and system-maintenance activities."[6] From this perspective, **policy-making activities** include not only the traditional legislative function (the initiation and passage of legislation), but also all attempts to influence the content of government policy, the publication of political issues through parliamentary debate, and the scrutiny or control of the activities of government and bureaucracy. The **representational activities** of parliamentarians consist largely of expressing the interests and opinions of their respective electorates and dealing with the problems of constituents, particularly with regard to mediating with the bureaucracy on their behalf. Finally, **system-maintenance activities** are the often primarily symbolic functions that contribute to the viability and legitimacy of other parts of the political system or the regime itself. Hence, legislatures often participate in recruiting and

3. David M. Olson, *The Legislative Process: A Comparative Perspective* (New York: Harper & Row, 1980), p. 11.

4. See Thomas A. Hockin, "Adversary Politics and Some Functions of the Canadian House of Commons," in R. Schultz et al., eds., *The Canadian Political Process*, 3rd ed. (Toronto: Holt, Rinehart and Winston, 1979), p. 318.

5. Walter Bagehot, *The English Constitution*, 1st ed., 1867 (London: Fontana/Collins, 1963), pp. 150–54.

6. Mezey, *Comparative Legislatures*, p. 7ff.

socializing future members of the political elite; they aid in regulating and managing conflict and may integrate and build consensus among rival political elites; they frequently elect and thus help to legitimate governments; and, through their participation in the decision-making process, they legitimate public policies.

The relative importance of the various activities of legislatures and their members varies from country to country and, over time, within individual systems. As a consequence of erroneous pre-conceptions of what legislatures *ought* to do, this change in the relative salience of different functions has led some commentators to lament the "decline of legislatures." Here, *decline* refers to a diminishing power of the more established parliaments of western Europe and the original members of the British Commonwealth. Particular attention is given to the dominance of Cabinet and the bureaucracy in the legislative process. Much of the blame for this situation has been placed on the growing volume and increasingly technical nature of legislation in the modern state and the lack of resources available to parliamentarians for coping with this complexity, or on the adverse effect of the emergence of cohesive, disciplined political parties upon the role of individual parliamentarians.

This supposed decline in the powers of parliaments is considered undesirable, especially when parliaments' present roles are compared with the so-called "Golden Age of Parliament" in Britain, which is often held up as the ideal. Admittedly, there was a time when much legislation was either initiated or introduced by private members, when the volume of parliamentary business was sufficiently meagre to allow members to spend long hours in debate and individual displays of grandiose rhetoric, when legislators were virtually independent and formed *ad hoc* majorities according to each issue, and when governments were frequently removed and replaced by parliament without resorting to general elections. But this situation existed only in a few countries and only for a short period during the mid-nineteenth century. It was an era in which state business was minimal and parliaments were well suited "to operate by competition between political parties responsible to a non-democratic electorate."[7] But, although a dominant executive has historically been the norm in Britain, it is in this brief and rather exceptional interlude that many of the myths that currently surround legislatures originate. Not unnaturally, given the time at which the Parliament of Canada was established — on British principles — some idealistic views entered the mythology of Canadian parliamentary democracy.

Although, as we have said, the activities of legislatures have changed over time in response to alterations in the political and socioeconomic environment, it must be pointed out that the decline of some functions has been matched by an enhancement of others. To talk of the "strength" or "weakness" of a legislature is difficult in any case. The concept of power is extremely complex, particularly as it relates to the legislative process. If a given parliament accepts the vast majority of the legislation placed before it by the government, it is not possible to be sure whether this demonstrates the weakness of the legislature *vis-à-vis* the executive or its strength in forcing the government to introduce only those measures that have a high probability of success.

Similarly, *power* and *symbolism* are often posed as dichotomous concepts: either a legislature is powerful or its weakness makes its role primarily symbolic. While this may be partly true in the short term, it may also be argued that, in the long term, only a powerful or effective legislature will have sufficient efficacy to perform a symbolic role in maintaining the legitimacy of the policy process and its outputs. All too often, the power of a legislature is equated with the extent of its involvement in the legislative process, especially with the initiation of legislation or the frequency of rejection

---

7. C.B. Macpherson, *The Real World of Democracy* (Toronto: CBC Publications, 1965), p. 35.

of government policies. But legislatures have multiple functions, and many of their activiti
than law-making reflect their importance in the political system and contribute to the
image and symbolic capabilities. Thus, "power" and "symbolism," rather than constitu
opposites, are parallel concepts that may be applied to the many activities undertaken by legislatu

Legislative Politics

As the title of this chapter suggests, legislative behaviour in an assembly such as the Parliament of
Canada is highly political.[8] But what is meant by the term **legislative politics**? Perhaps the closest analogy we can draw is to the concept of politics as it appears in the popular phrase "office politics" —
that is, the interaction and competition among workers in the same organization for status, influence and power in the life of that institution. Whether in the form of opposition parties seeking to
influence or change the policy of the government, or of the legislature as a whole seeking greater opportunities for effective participation in the decision-making process, or of members of the same party
vying for advancement within the legislative or government hierarchy, there is constant politicking
in the life of a legislature.

Nonetheless, all members of the legislature are bound together by their common participation
in the institution and by codes of ethics and behaviour that are often incomprehensible to the outsider. Political foes on the floor of the House may be friends outside the chamber, while colleagues
from the same party may be fiercely antagonistic. Similarly, members from polar extremes of the political spectrum may join forces in defence of the sovereignty of Parliament in the face of encroachment by the government or some other institution. Meanwhile, through it all may rage a
fierce war of rhetoric between rival parties and competing ideologies.

THE LEGISLATIVE PROCESS IN PARLIAMENT

The *Constitution Act, 1867,* established the Parliament of Canada as a bicameral legislature consisting of an appointed upper house, the Senate, and a popularly elected lower house, the House of
Commons. Indeed, the Constitution also says the Queen is part of the Parliament of Canada. The
monarch plays a formal role in the legislative process through his or her representative, the Governor
General, inasmuch as all bills must receive Royal Assent before becoming part of Canadian law.

In strictly legal terms, the two chambers of the Parliament of Canada have equal legislative
powers in that all bills must be passed in their entirety by both houses in order to receive Royal
Assent, and neither chamber has the power to override the veto or the amendments of the other. In
this regard, the Senate appears to be stronger than its British counterpart, the House of Lords, because the former can defeat legislation, whereas the latter can only exercise a suspensory veto.
However, the Senate rarely employs its amendment powers or vetoes bills; it usually backs down
in the case of dissension between the two chambers. As a result, many commentators view the
Senate as the junior partner in the parliamentary process and often virtually ignore the upper house
in analyzing the Canadian legislature. The fact remains, however, that all bills must be passed by
both chambers before becoming law. The free trade gambit of 1988, when the Liberal-dominated
Senate forced a general election over the issue by refusing to pass the required legislation, is undoubtedly the most important recent example of senatorial power.

---

8. The electoral system and the composition of Parliament after recent elections are discussed in Chapter 11.

The Parliamentary Life Cycle

The Senate and the House of Commons may meet as legislative bodies only during a parliamentary session. **Parliaments** are labelled by consecutive numbers, changing after each general election. For example, the 301 MPs returned in the 1997 election collectively constitute the 36th Parliament. In each Parliament there may be one or more **sessions**, depending upon the wishes of the government of the day and its ability in managing its legislative program, and upon the length of the Parliament — that is, how much time elapses between general elections.

Each parliamentary session begins with the Governor General summoning the MPs and senators to Parliament at the request of the prime minister. Members of both houses come together in the Senate chamber, amid great pomp and ceremony, to hear the Governor General deliver the **Speech from the Throne**, outlining the government's proposed legislative program for the forthcoming session. They then return to their respective chambers to commence business. In the Commons, the debate on the Throne Speech usually occupies the first few days of the session; afterward, the normal timetable of the House comes into effect. A break taken by the House within a session is called an **adjournment**.

Another ceremonial occasion, known as the **prorogation of Parliament**, brings a session to a close. The Governor General again acts upon the advice of the prime minister to prorogue Parliament; therefore, the length of a session is often determined by the government's ability to tidy up the loose ends in its legislative program. Unless there is agreement, any legislation that has not successfully completed all the stages of the process automatically dies when Parliament is prorogued: if the government is still committed to it, the bill must go through the entire process again in the next session. This fact explains the phenomenon of so-called "trial-balloon bills" that governments sometimes introduce close to the end of a session to test parliamentary and public reactions before the bill is redrafted for introduction in the next session.

At one time, each session of Parliament lasted a year or less, but sessions have generally become longer in recent years. Thus, the first session of the 32nd Parliament lasted an unprecedented three years and eight months. Also in the past, MPs and senators used to enjoy a break between sessions, in addition to their vacations from Ottawa when Parliament was adjourned or in recess. Today, prorogation of one session is often followed immediately by the summoning of the next. However, at least once every five years, there must be a proclamation by the Governor General announcing the dissolution of the House of Commons. **Dissolution**, which occurs at the request of a prime minister, brings the Parliament to an end and, in its wake, a general election.[9]

Types of Bills

It is necessary to distinguish between the various types of legislation, since the nature of a bill helps determine its route through Parliament. Parliamentary procedure distinguishes among bills on constitutional and legal grounds on three major levels. (See Figure 9.1.) First, legislation can be divided into **private** and **public bills**. Private bills are those that confer special powers or rights upon specific individuals, groups or corporations, rather than upon society as a whole. They are sometimes utilized to incorporate companies or certain religious and charitable organizations and, until 1964, were required for granting divorces to residents of Québec and Newfoundland. These bills constitute an extremely small proportion of total legislative activity.

---

9. In theory, the Governor General retains some discretionary power in the matter of dissolution; see Chapter 5.

FIGURE 9.1   THE TYPES OF BILLS

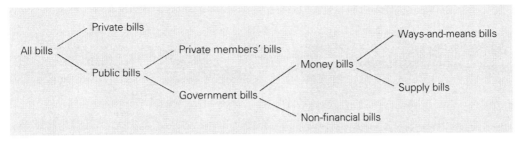

Second, public bills, which seek to change the law concerning the public as a whole, are them-selves divided into two types: **government bills**, those introduced by the Cabinet as government policy; and **private members' bills**, those introduced by individual members of Parliament. In the nineteenth century, when the business of government was relatively limited, private members' bills were an important component of legislative activity. Today, with a restricted number of specific slots in the parliamentary timetable, few even come to a vote, and it is quite unusual for Parliament to pass even one private member's bill during a session.

Finally, government bills are further divided into **financial (money)** and **non-financial bills**. Under the Constitution, money bills, which authorize taxation and appropriations (or expendi-tures), must be introduced first into the House of Commons, and then only by a minister of the Crown, by **Royal Recommendation**. These special provisions relate to the traditional right of Parliament to demand that the Crown hear grievances from the people before **granting supply** — that is, before approving the funds necessary to conduct the Crown's affairs. The consideration of financial measures is therefore intended to be a time when the Cabinet accounts for its manage-ment of the economy and (usually but not always) survives an opposition motion to the effect that the government has failed in its responsibilities. Taxation measures are introduced as **ways-and-means bills** and have become known as "ways and means" of getting the public's money.

Before we leave the subject of the types of legislation, a comment should be made about **dele-gated** or **subordinate legislation**. This type of legislation refers to the power to make decisions — called "regulations" or "statutory instruments" — that have the force of law. Such legislative power is delegated by Parliament under various statutes to the **governor-in-council** (the Cabinet), to min-isters of individual government departments and to a number of agencies and boards. For example, the *Fisheries Act* allows the passage of subordinate legislation on issues such as fishing seasons, num-bers and types of fish that may be caught, and the dates for opening and closing the fishing season. Such subordinate legislation takes the form of "regulations" and in principle is approved by Council (i.e., Cabinet), but is only scrutinized by Parliament *after* it is announced in *The Canada Gazette*.

Today, the Joint Committee on Regulations and Other Statutory Instruments (composed of MPs and senators) may examine a regulation and even recommend that it be rescinded. Unless the government receives a vote of the House of Commons against the Joint Committee's recommen-dation, the regulation is automatically repealed.

The Stages of Legislation

The vast majority of bills passed by the Canadian Parliament are government bills. Although gov-ernment legislation may be introduced first in the Senate (an increasingly rare occurrence), money bills are constitutionally prohibited from this route. Figure 9.2 illustrates the following brief overview of the major stages in the passage of a typical government bill originating in the lower house.

Once the pre-parliamentary processes of policy formulation are over, the minister responsible for the legislation asks the House for leave to introduce the bill. This motion is not debatable. A short description of the aims of the bill may be given. Acceptance of the **First Reading** motion "that this bill be read a first time and be printed" is a matter of course and no vote takes place. It allows the bill to be printed, numbered (with a "C" prefix if it originates in the House of Commons, "S" if in the Senate) and distributed to MPs. Numbers C2 to C200 are reserved for government bills, C201

FIGURE 9.2   HOW A GOVERNMENT BILL BECOMES LAW

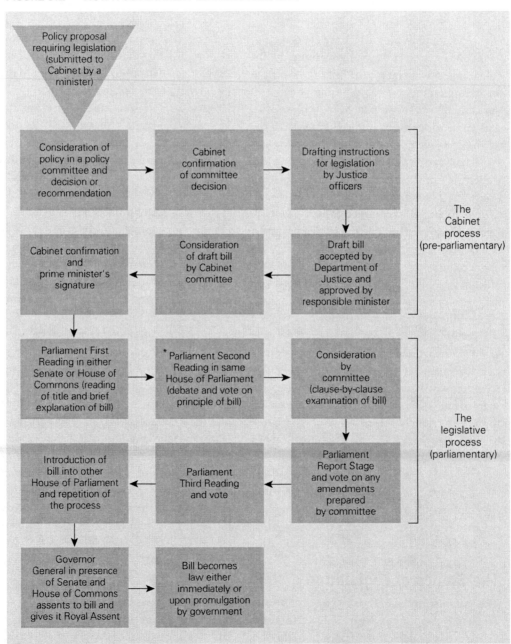

* As of 1994, a bill may be referred to a committee *before* Second Reading.

to C1000 for private members' public bills and C1001 on for private members' private bills. The bill is now on the **Order Paper**, the schedule of pending parliamentary business.

The **Second Reading** motion, usually proposed by the sponsoring minister, permits debate on the principle of the bill; no amendments are accepted by the Speaker. The debate is monopolized by the government and opposition front benches. Normally, the opposition attempts to prove that the legislation is inadequate because it does not address the needs of some "sector" or "regions," while the government defends the overall content and principles of the proposed legislation. As of 1994, as an alternative, bills have been permitted to proceed to the committee stage before Second Reading. This rare procedure was first used for the 1995 *Electoral Boundaries Act*.

After Second Reading, unless otherwise ordered, a bill must be sent directly to a House of Commons committee. This is the **Committee Stage**. (For money bills and certain other legislation upon which the House agrees, the Committee Stage is undertaken by the Committee of the Whole, the whole chamber sitting in committee chaired by the Deputy Speaker.) At this stage, the bill undergoes detailed clause-by-clause consideration. Amendments may be moved by both government and opposition members. The amended bill is then voted on as a whole.

Except in the case of bills examined by the Committee of the Whole, which go straight to **Third Reading**, the recommendations of the appropriate committee are presented to the House at the **Report Stage**. Debate is allowed on both the principle and the details of the bill; amendments proposed by the committee are voted on and further amendments may be introduced. Sometimes the opposition reintroduces amendments defeated in committee or the government seeks to reinstate original clauses altered by the committee. At the conclusion of the debate, a vote is taken on the whole bill, including amendments. Unless unanimously agreed otherwise by the House, Third Reading commences after the Report Stage with the motion "that the bill be now read a third time and passed." Debate is not unknown at this point, but usually takes place only at the insistence of the opposition. A final vote is then taken on the bill.

When the bill has successfully negotiated the various debates, amendments, attempted hoists and divisions (formal votes) in the House of Commons, it has to begin the whole process again in the Senate. However, the upper house usually provides a smoother path than the lower chamber. First and Second Readings are over quickly. It is at the Committee Stage that the major legislative work of the Senate is done. While the upper house rarely uses its powers to amend the substance of a bill, "it does do considerable work 'cleaning up' sloppily drafted bills."[10] The Senate is not allowed to increase taxation or spending. As in the House of Commons, the bill as amended in committee is reported back to the Senate for debate, possible further amendment and acceptance. After the final consideration of the bill by the Senate and the Third Reading vote, it is reported to the House of Commons whether the Senate has rejected, amended or passed the bill.

If the bill is *defeated* by the Senate (which is extremely unusual), it is lost and must pass through the entire process again, from the start. A bill passed by the Commons but *amended* by the Senate returns to the lower house for consideration of the amendments. Since such changes are more often to the wording or to a minor detail of the bill (rather than its substance), they are often accepted by the responsible minister. Once this has happened, or if the bill is passed intact by the Senate, it is ready for **Royal Assent**. In this final stage of the process the Governor General, sitting in the Senate before the assembled members of both houses, puts the final seal of approval on the bill. The bill thereby becomes an Act of Parliament of Canada and is henceforth law unless a requirement for formal government **proclamation** is contained within it.

10. Hockin, "Adversary Politics," p. 174.

THE CANADIAN LEGISLATIVE PROCESS

POLICY ALREADY IN PLACE

WHAT THE FEDERAL GOVERNMENT WANTED

WHAT THE PROVINCES WANTED

LEGISLATION INTRODUCED

AS AMENDED IN COMMITTEE

AS PASSED IN COMMONS

AS AMENDED IN SENATE

AS FUNDED IN ESTIMATES

AS IMPLEMENTED BY BUREAUCRACY

WHAT WAS ACTUALLY NEEDED

Richard Row Illustration, Toronto.

    Money bills follow the same general process as other government legislation, but are unique for four reasons. First, as noted above, they must originate in the House of Commons. Second, ways-and-means bills are not considered in legislative committees in the Commons but by the Committee of the Whole. Third, there are political limitations upon the Senate's ability to amend such bills. Fourth, they tend to have a longer gestation period than other bills, because they are not themselves the only, or even the most important, basis for debate. In the case of tax bills, much debate centres on the budget speech delivered by the Minister of Finance, which outlines the government's economic policy and summarizes the changes that will subsequently appear in tax legislation. With **supply** or **appropriation bills** — those that authorize the spending of public money by government departments and other agencies — the key debates occur during the consideration of departmental estimates by standing committees. Once the estimates are examined, appropriation bills are always passed quickly to give legislative effect to the government's spending proposals.

The entire legislative process is thus complex and variable. The time taken by a bill to pass and its likelihood of success depend upon a number of factors: the importance or controversial nature of the given bill and of other legislation under consideration at the same time; the partisan composition of the two chambers and the presence or absence of a government majority; the willingness of the government to impose, and of Parliament to accept, procedural devices to shorten debate and speed passage of the bill; and last, but not least because Parliament is composed of human beings, the mood of the House at a particular moment. Despite the apparent dominance of governments over the legislative process, the whole procedure looks very much like an obstacle course to the minister introducing a piece of contentious legislation.

Having briefly reviewed the legislative process, we should now focus on the component parts of the legislature. The role of the monarch, through his or her representative, the Governor General, has already been examined in Chapter 8. There remains the analysis of the legislative politics of the two chambers, the House of Commons and the Senate.

THE HOUSE OF COMMONS

It is probably not unreasonable to suggest that, when most Canadians talk about "Parliament," they really mean the "House of Commons." After all, when people vote for a member of Parliament, they are electing a member of the House of Commons, not a senator. And when they write to their MP about some personal or public matter, they expect their constituency representative in the Commons to take action on their behalf. Moreover, media attention is focused mainly on the House of Commons, because it is the chamber to which the government is responsible, and because the more newsworthy and dramatic confrontations in Canadian legislative politics usually occur there.

The job of an MP is multifunctional. In theory at least, members of the Commons are constituency representatives, caucus members, orators, law-makers and watchdogs over the government and bureaucracy. Most of the time, however, members are bound by party discipline and can show little initiative.

In 1997, 241 men and 60 women were elected to Parliament. (For detail on gender representation see Chapter 12.) They acquired a salary and expense allowance equal to about $100 000 of taxed income and an annual overall budget of at least $166 400 for staff. (See Table 9.1.) They usually hire four full-time assistants in their Ottawa offices, and at least one more to manage inquiries at their constituency office. Still, for most members, these resources have barely kept pace with the growth of constituency business in the form of correspondence, telephone calls and personal contacts over recent years. Indeed, a former clerk of the House of Commons has suggested that, while most MPs are adequately staffed for their role as constituency representative, they are not "over-serviced" with respect to either their legislative functions or active participation in the committee system. As Government House Leader Don Boudria put it in 1999: "MPs shouldn't get rich here, but they shouldn't go home broke either."

Some recent reforms and innovations have enhanced the ability of individual MPs to perform their parliamentary tasks more effectively. The new standing committees enable individual members

TABLE 9.1   SALARIES AND BENEFITS FOR PARLIAMENT AND GOVERNMENT, 2000

I Members of Parliament	
Salary	$64 800*
Expense allowance (receipts required)	$21 400
Supplement (for large ridings, etc.)	$21 400–$28 000
Pensions (members pay 10% of annual salary)	75% of average of best six years' service (at the rate of 5% per year with minimum of six years' service)
Staff (divided between office in constituency and House of Commons)	$166 400–$172 200
Travel	64 return trips between Ottawa and constituency
Telephone, mail, equipment and supplies	Paid and basically unlimited
II Senators	
Salary	$64 000
Expense allowance	$10 100
III Officers of Government or Parliament (in addition to the above)	
Prime minister	$74 000
Leader of official opposition, Speaker and all ministers**	$49 400
Parliamentary secretaries	$10 000
Other officials (leaders, deputy speakers, whips)	$7 500–$25 800

* MPs' salaries are now automatically increased by 2 percent annually until the end of the 36th Parliament.
** Except secretaries of state, who have a reduced salary.

to have more input into policy formulation. Reduction of the maximum length of speeches in the House allows more members to take part in debates, and the possibility of a 10-minute rebuttal/debate after each speech has provided more interest and flexibility. But, by and large, effective participation in debate or in the scrutiny of government legislation and estimates is hampered by lack of information, resources and policy expertise. The development of a heightened role for the back-bencher in the legislative process requires more than procedural reform of the House of Commons.

Of course, there are exceptions — members who carve out a particular area of specialization or who adopt some issue as their own. In the 36th Parliament, Liberal Charles Caccia continued to be the dean of commentators on the environment. But for every activist backbencher in Parliament, there are many more who, however diligently they may serve their constituents, play a minimal part in the legislative process. Lack of opportunity is clearly one factor. But it may also be true, as one study alleges, that "private members do not seem to take full advantage of the opportunities available to them" to introduce legislation and initiate criticism of the government.[11]

The attitude of members themselves, and their relations with their constituents, also encourages concentration on representational activities. The electorate is becoming more demanding. With the ever-increasing volume of government legislation and the seemingly omnipresent role of the

---

11. A. Kornberg and W. Mishler, *Influence in Parliament, Canada* (Durham, N.C.: Duke University Press, 1976), p. 311.

government, there is significant pressure from constituents for MPs to act as intermediaries on their behalf in disputes with departments and other central agencies. Such "ombudsman" work usually involves simple, concrete problems readily solved by a telephone call to a department or a brief negotiation with a minister. Policy-making, on the other hand, requires abstract, generalized conceptualization of an issue and a long-term commitment to pursue a particular solution. In terms of results for effort expended, the role of ombudsman is more rewarding than that of a law-maker for the majority of members.

Reproduced with permission, Dennis Pritchard.

Conflict and Compromise

The tone of legislative politics in the House of Commons is profoundly affected by two key factors inherited from the British political tradition: first, an adversarial system of party politics, with a clear dichotomy between government and opposition; second, a code of rules and procedures governing the behaviour of members that counteracts, to some extent, any potential hostility arising from the partisan nature of the House.

The adversarial pattern of relations between government and opposition is clearly reflected in, and perhaps reinforced by, the physical layout of the House. In many legislative chambers, such as the U.S. House of Representatives or the German *Bundestag*, all elected members sit in a semicircle facing the Speaker of the House. However, the seating plan of the Canadian House of Commons follows the British model, forcing government and opposition to face one another across the floor of the House with the government to the Speaker's right and the opposition to the left. The leaders of the two major parties confront each other like old-time gunfighters, each surrounded by his or her immediate lieutenants and backed by the rest of the supporters. The smaller parties also take their place on the opposition side of the House. This face-to-face confrontation, separated only by the open floor of the House, clearly demarcates the government from the opposition and reinforces the sense of political identity and party cohesion on both sides of the Commons.

In the central area of the chamber, between the two main rivals, sit the officials of the House. Most conspicuous among them is the **Speaker,** who, under the Constitution, "shall preside at all meetings of the House of Commons." The Speaker is officially an impartial arbiter elected by the whole House. He or she is not permitted to vote in the House (votes are cast when a "division" is called), except for casting the deciding vote in the event of a tie, when convention dictates that the Speaker support the government of the day.

Until recently, the prime minister nominated the Speaker; however, the position has become increasingly non-partisan. After 1963, the leader of the opposition seconded the prime minister's nomination and, in 1979, Liberal James Jerome became the first Speaker to serve under two different parties when Prime Minister Joe Clark nominated him to continue the role he had fulfilled under the previous Liberal administration. Discussions about how to reform the process for selecting a Speaker were carried on for several years until both the Lefebvre and McGrath parliamentary reform committees recommended that the Speaker be elected by secret ballot. Eventually, the government agreed with this proposal and new Standing Orders to that effect were passed. On September 30, 1986, for the first time, the Speaker was elected by a secret ballot of all members of the House. It took the members 12 hours and 11 ballots to elect John Fraser from among the 39 candidates. In January 1994, Gilbert Parent became the second elected Speaker after six rounds of voting that included a tie on the fifth ballot.

The Speaker is in charge of the administration of the House of Commons. First, this person oversees the staffing of the House with secretaries, clerks and so on. As well, the Speaker shares responsibility with the Board of Internal Economy (a body composed of the Speaker, two members of the Privy Council, the leader of the official opposition and four other members — two from the government caucus and two from the opposition benches) for the economic management of the House, and manages the annual estimates of the cost of running the House of Commons. In the political function of chairing the House, the Speaker is aided by a Deputy Speaker, also elected by fellow MPs at the beginning of each Parliament. The Speaker also is assisted by two chief permanent employees of the Commons, the Clerk of the House and one Administrator. The Clerk is responsible for ensuring that relevant documents are printed and circulated, and advises the Speaker on the day's parliamentary business. In recent years, a senior bureaucrat, called the Administrator, has been added to the House staff to deal with financial and management issues.

The leader of each party in the House designates an MP as manager of party conduct in the House — this MP is known as the party's **House Leader**. The government House Leader is also a member of Cabinet, responsible for obtaining agreement among parties in setting the timetable for the House. The House Leader has the authority to negotiate the timetable and lists of speakers.

In addition to these individuals, there is a professional staff to manage day-to-day activities of the House. The staff includes translators; transcribers, who record verbatim the House of Commons debates in a publication called *Hansard*; secretaries; security personnel; maintenance staff; and staff for the library of Parliament.

In keeping with the Westminster model, the Speaker is simultaneously an ordinary member of the House of Commons and an impartial arbiter removed from the political struggle by the conventions and traditions that bind the office. In the midst of the potential chaos and conflict engendered by the partisan nature of the House, the Speaker is responsible for enforcing the rules designed to permit its orderly functioning. The Speaker must therefore be a skilled parliamentarian, well versed not only in the formal rules contained in the Standing Orders of the House but also in un-written conventions established by past practice.

Certain rules are explicitly designed to reduce the temperature of party politics in the legislature by limiting the direct personal interaction of the members. Verbal confrontations during debate are somewhat constrained by the requirements that no member may speak officially without recognition by the Speaker, to whom all statements must be addressed. Thus, members do not speak to one another directly. Neither may they speak *of* one another directly, inasmuch as individuals are referred to not by name but through more impersonal titles, such as "the prime minister," "the leader of the opposition" or "the honourable member for constituency X."

If all else fails and the debate becomes heated, as it does on occasion, the dignity of individual members and of the House as a whole is protected by the proscription of certain terms deemed to constitute "unparliamentary language."[12] It is not permitted, for example, to use expressions that cast doubt on the legitimacy of a member's birth nor to allege that a speech has been inspired by intoxicating substances. One of the most common infringements of the rule is the suggestion that another member is "lying" to the House. For example, in March 1993, New Democrat MP Dave Barrett was suspended from the Commons for a day after refusing to withdraw an accusation that the government was telling "lies."

The rules of unparliamentary language often have the effect of testing the verbal ingenuity of members in order to convey the sense of a particular epithet without the use of forbidden terms. There may also be other ways of getting one's point across without breaching the rules. Former Conservative MP Gordon Aiken reports the clever and entirely legitimate device employed by one member exasperated by criticism from the other side of the House:

> *"Mr. Speaker," he asked, properly addressing the Chair, "would it be out of order if I called the honourable Member a son-of-a-bitch?" The Speaker nodded his head. "I thought so," said Clancy, resuming his seat.[13]*

Also among the conflict-regulating devices in the House of Commons are the Standing Orders, the procedures and regulations adopted by members for their internal self-government, and the rules of debate. Perhaps most important among the latter is the principle that once recognized by the Speaker, every MP has the right to speak for a certain length of time without interruption, as long as the speech remains relevant to the motion before the House. The Speaker must ensure that members from both sides of the House get a fair hearing, but it is not unknown for the opposition parties to complain that the Speaker is favouring the government side. The rules also protect certain persons (particularly the royal family, the Governor General and the Senate) from explicit attacks in the Commons.[14]

Once a member has the floor, the member's colleagues or opponents are not always capable of containing themselves; thus, some expressions of support and disagreement are, within certain bounds, sanctioned by the Speaker. Outbursts of laughter and cheering or antagonistic remarks are accepted as part of the debate; the euphemistic reporting in *Hansard* of "hear-hear!" or "oh-oh!" may disguise a multitude of sins.

---

12. See the discussion of "Parliamentary Language" and "Parliamentary Behaviour" in R.M. Dawson, *The Government of Canada*, 5th ed., revised by Norman Ward (Toronto: University of Toronto Press, 1970), pp. 110–17.

13. Gordon Aiken, *The Backbencher* (Toronto: McClelland & Stewart, 1974), p. 66.

14. Through precedent established by past Speakers, this protection has been extended to the judiciary, lieutenant-governors and others of "high official station."

All of these formal devices help to maintain peace and reduce conflict emanating from the partisan composition of the House. Other effective mitigating factors are the sense of corporate identity shared by members of the Commons and the extent to which MPs from both sides of the House interact in informal situations outside the chamber, often forging friendships across party lines. In the midst of the rhetoric, the struggle is, after all, "often carried on more in the spirit of a game than a war."[15]

The Business of the House

Once the currents of conflict and compromise within the House of Commons are appreciated, the way in which the House works can perhaps best be understood with reference to the detailed business in the House.[16] Not all parliamentary weeks and days, however, are precisely the same. Daily sittings and endings differ from day to day. Some activities, such as private members' business, occur in different time slots and the whole week's agenda can be disrupted by major events such as the debates on the Speech from the Throne and budget deliberations. The timetable of the House of Commons reflects a compromise among the competing demands of the various groups within it. On the basis of practical usage rather than procedural formality, the business of the House may be arranged into five broad categories: routine business, urgent business, government business, private members' business and opposition business.

The **routine business** of the House usually begins after the daily Question Period and consumes 15 to 20 minutes. The Speaker reads through a list of routine proceedings, not all of which will arise on any particular day: announcements and the raising of questions of privilege; the presentation of reports from inter-parliamentary delegations and committees; the tabling of documents and government papers for the notice of members; statements by ministers regarding government policy; the introduction and First Reading of Commons bills and the First Reading of public bills originating in the Senate; government notices of motions to be introduced later in the Orders of the Day; and other motions, particularly those requesting concurrence in committee reports and those pertaining to special arrangements for the sittings and proceedings of the House.

Next, the Speaker calls upon the Parliamentary Secretary to the Government House Leader to notify the House regarding government responses to **Questions on the Order Paper** (written questions which, after a minimum 48 hours' notice, are usually answered in print in the day's *Debates*) and, on occasion, to reply to requests from members for the tabling of government papers in the House. The Commons is then ready to proceed with what the government regards as the main business, the **Orders of the Day** — the ongoing debate on government legislation.

The **Standing Orders**, or rules of the House, permit any member to move "under S.O. 52 that this House do now adjourn" in order to discuss "a specific and important matter requiring urgent consideration." This motion could, at one time, exhaust considerable time in the House, even when not eventually granted, because members would discuss the matter proposed if leave were given to discuss the urgency of discussing it! Today, the Speaker rules immediately upon the validity of the request and, if he or she rules in the affirmative, gives leave to the member to introduce the adjournment motion later that day. The Standing Order concerned is primarily utilized by the opposition to introduce debate on an issue that is not on the government Order Paper or to criticize the government.

---

15. Dawson, *The Government of Canada*, p. 356.
16. For a succinct summary of procedural rules and timetables, see House of Commons, *Précis of Procedure* (Ottawa: House of Commons, various editions).

The other procedure classified as **urgent business** is the opportunity for MPs to make 60-second statements to the House under Standing Order 31, immediately preceding Question Period. This provision has replaced the old SO 43 that permitted private members to introduce motions relating to a matter of "urgent and pressing necessity" without prior notice. Since the unanimous consent of the House was required for debate to take place, "necessity" was rarely established, and most members using SO 43 were, in fact, primarily concerned with focusing attention on themselves or on some particular issue. The new SO 31 effectively recognizes this fact, as it permits members to make only a very brief statement to the House, allowing them to make a point or gain the desired media exposure without going through the pretense of formulating a motion or of attempting to establish "urgent and pressing necessity." It is an excellent example of sensible and pragmatic innovation in House rules to satisfy the needs of individual members without making a mockery of the formal proceedings of the Commons.

The bulk of the time of plenary sessions of the Commons is consumed by the Orders of the Day, during which the House deals with the public business placed before it. The greater part of this period is devoted to **government business** in the form of the Throne Speech debate, motions dealing with the passage of bills and the referral of legislation, estimates and investigatory tasks to standing and special committees. **Orders** are the prime means by which the House of Commons formulates instructions in response to motions. They serve to guide the Speaker and other members and direct the officers of the House to pursue particular courses of action. Some orders, for example **Standing Orders**, are general and more or less permanent, applying mainly to the procedures of the House. Others are more particular: for example, that a bill must "now be read a second time" or that it must be sent to committee. In the long run, of course, these latter cases result in a change in public policy through new laws. However, some motions result not in orders but in **resolutions**. Herein lies a source of confusion for many observers of Parliament. From time to time, the House makes a resolution on a particular issue on which the government subsequently takes no action. With the exception of *constitutional resolutions*, resolutions are *not binding*; they are simply expressions of the *opinion* of the Commons, as opposed to orders, which are expressions of its *will*. While orders reflect the power of the Commons to impose its will on others, resolutions are primarily symbolic outputs of "Parliament as rhetoric," although they may often be influential in legitimating policies for which the government wants a public expression of support from the House.

Not all of the business conducted during the working week is instigated by the government. **Private members' business** is listed under four categories: requests for tabling papers and documents; private members' bills; private members' motions; and, occasionally, private bills. Since 1986, **private members' motions and bills** have been handled under new procedures. Today, all of them are placed in a lottery or draw. The first 30 items chosen are placed in an "order of precedence," and the Standing Committee on Procedure and House Affairs selects up to five motions and five bills to be voted on automatically. This means that the old system, in which almost every private member's motion or bill was debated and then "talked out," has been replaced by a compulsory vote on at least 10 items after as many as five hours of debate. Under the new rules, therefore, more private members' bills are assured a guaranteed vote. In September 1996, the new system worked satisfactorily, for example, to bring Bill C216, an act to ban negative-option rules in the broadcasting legislation, to a vote.

On certain sitting days during the year, the government motions do not dominate the Orders of the Day. A total of 20 days is officially designated for **opposition business**, when the opposition can lead major debates on government policy. At the start of the session, the House is permitted six days to debate the **Address in Reply** to the Speech from the Throne; since the Throne Speech contains only vaguely worded policy outlines, rules of relevancy are relaxed and debate takes a very general course. A further four days are allocated for the Budget Debate — officially, to discuss the Finance Minister's proposals but effectively, again, to articulate broad criticism of the government's record. As well, after the abolition of the old Committee of Supply in 1968, the opposition parties were compensated by the allocation of 20 **Supply** (or **Opposition**) **Days**, spread unevenly over the three supply periods of the session, on which opposition motions could be debated. Today such debates rarely focus specifically on government expenditures, although that was the original intention. Instead, Opposition Days provide time for individual opposition parties to mount their own attacks on the government, to propose alternative policies and to introduce motions of non-confidence in the government. There are, however, both practical and political limitations on the ability of the opposition parties to effect radical criticism of government activities or produce startlingly different policy proposals.

Far more effective as an instrument for the opposition — primarily because of the amount of media attention devoted to it and because no notice of content is required — is the **Oral Question Period**.[17] This is invariably the high point of the sitting day in the Commons. In theory, it provides an opportunity for any member who can catch the Speaker's eye to ask a question of the prime minister or a member of Cabinet — in fact, the Speaker calls almost all members according to lists supplied by the party whips. Although, technically, questions should be for the purpose of eliciting information and be "concise, factual and free of opinion and argument which might lead to debate,"[18] the Question Period in fact provides a forum for the opposition parties to embarrass the government, criticize its policies and force discussion on issues of the day, frequently based on media stories, leaks by disaffected public servants, and complaints from the public.

As a mechanism for surveillance and accountability of the government, Question Period has many advantages but it is not perfect. Although supplementary questions are permitted by the Speaker, no formal debate is allowed, and ministers can often manoeuvre to avoid the main substance of a question. The time limit of 45 minutes each day is often too short for the number of questions that members wish to raise, yet government backbenchers use up some of the period to ask questions of "minor" constituency interest or to feed "friendly" queries to their own front bench. Finally, the division of the opposition into two or more parties frequently results in a lack of structure or continuity to the proceedings.

To surmount this problem, each party caucus orchestrates its efforts at Question Period in order to provide a more effective attack on specific government ministers. To this end, the opposition parties have a "tactics" meeting each day during parliamentary sessions. At these meetings, they analyze press clippings, determine the order of the questions and practise their political stances. Despite problems, well-directed opposition tactics can make the daily Question Period an important occasion for calling the executive to account for its actions, for effective participation by backbenchers and for the public to see responsible government at work. Considerable effort goes into ensuring that the right "clip" will appear on the television evening news.

Occasionally during Question Period, a member who is dissatisfied with the response from a minister will shout "tonight" across the floor of the chamber. This refers to what is commonly known as "The Late Show," more formally the **Daily Adjournment Debate**, which takes place four days a

---

17. The first oral question was asked within three weeks of the first session of the first Parliament in 1867. For a complete history, see W.F. Dawson, *Procedure in the Canadian House of Commons* (Toronto: University of Toronto Press, 1962); and Francis J. Schiller, "The Evolution of Oral Question Period" (unpublished thesis, Carleton University, September 1992).

18. Ruling given by Speaker of the House Roland Michener, cited in *House of Commons Debates*, February 26, 1959, p. 1393.

week at 6:30 p.m. Unless the House has agreed to sit beyond the normal hour of adjournment for some special purpose, the Speaker proposes on these days "that this House do now adjourn," then recognizes in turn a maximum of three members who have made it known that they wish to speak. Members usually take up unresolved issues from the Oral Question Period; they are permitted to speak for up to seven minutes, addressing their point to a minister or parliamentary secretary.

Under contemporary rules, the House has a four-and-a-half-day working week that may be increased by evening sittings for emergency debates or long series of divisions continuing after the normal hours of adjournment. The House is by no means full most of this time; in fact, it is usually crowded only for Question Period, for important divisions on major items of government legislation and for non-confidence motions. Since October 1977, the public has been able to see empty spaces in the chamber on televised House proceedings, despite occasional attempts by members to arrange themselves around and behind whoever is on camera.

But the average viewer may not be aware that attendance at plenary sessions of the House of Commons is only a part of the total workload of MPs. Apart from their role as members of the House, MPs serve on parliamentary committees, are members of parliamentary parties or caucuses, and have large caseloads of constituency duties to perform. An analysis of procedure and legislative politics in the chamber of the House of Commons is, therefore, only a part of the story of how Parliament works; the next three sections provide a more complete picture by discussing the role of committees, party competition and individual members in the life of the House.

MPs IN GROUPS: THE COMMITTEE SYSTEM

Much of the significant work of members of Parliament takes place not in plenary sessions but in committees. In 1986, the House of Commons adopted a new committee system that was slightly amended in 1991.[19] There are now four basic kinds of committees.

First is the **Committee of the Whole**, in which the entire complement of MPs sits in the chamber in one large committee under the chair of the Deputy Speaker or the Deputy Chair of Committees, and uses committee rules rather than House procedures to govern its activities. At one time, the majority of bills were considered by the Committee of the Whole rather than being sent to smaller, more specialized standing committees, but enormous pressures on the timetable of the House and the workload of MPs have resulted in much more limited use of this procedure. Today, the use of the Committee of the Whole is largely reserved for money bills or, on very rare occasions, to expedite the passage of other legislation.

The second type of committee consists of the relatively permanent House standing committees. (See Table 9.2.) **Standing committees** are set up for the life of a Parliament. Their composition of 7 to 15 members is proportional to party standings in the House. In principle, they elect their own chairs, but the selection is controlled by the government and opposition House Leaders. These committees are empowered by the Standing Orders to study and report on all matters relating to the department or departments that are assigned to them. In particular, they are to report on program

19. The 1991 rules grouped the committees into "envelopes" for administrative reasons — namely to allow the whips to handle substitutions on committees better. See House of Commons, *Standing Orders of the House of Commons* (Ottawa: Supply and Services, November 1988), plus the amendments of April 5, 1989, and April 11, 1991. An assessment of these basic reforms is found in Robert J. Jackson, "Executive Legislative Relations in Canada," in Robert J. Jackson et al., eds., *Contemporary Canadian Politics* (Scarborough: Prentice Hall, 1984), pp. 111–24.

TABLE 9.2   COMMITTEES IN PARLIAMENT, 2000

A.   House Standing Committees
Aboriginal Affairs and Northern Development
Agriculture and Agri-Food
Canadian Heritage
Citizenship and Immigration
Environment and Sustainable Development
Finance
Fisheries and Oceans
Foreign Affairs and International Trade
Health
Human Resources Development
Human Rights and the Status of Disabled Persons
Industry
Justice and Human Rights
National Defence and Veterans Affairs
Natural Resources and Government Operations
Procedure and House Affairs
Public Accounts
Transport
B.   Joint Committees with the Senate
Library of Parliament
Official Languages
Regulations and Other Statutory Instruments

and policy objectives and effectiveness; immediate, medium-term and long-term expenditure plans; the relative success of the department(s); and all other matters of mandate, management, organization and operation. These responsibilities are usually carried out by studying the particular department's annual report and the estimates. Standing committees may also handle the committee stage of legislation, and since the Liberals' election victory in 1993 this has been the standard practice.

The standing committees are empowered to form subcommittees and to "send for persons, papers and records" to aid in their deliberations. Moreover, all individuals appointed by order-in-council are scrutinized by the committees and may be called before their members after their appointments have been published in *The Canada Gazette*. This includes all deputy ministers, heads of Crown corporations, ambassadors and others appointed to high government positions (excluding judges). As of 1994, the Finance Committee has been assigned a new responsibility to participate in pre-budget discussions. It begins to study the government's financial policies in early September and reports before the end of December — before the annual budget is delivered.

The three **joint standing committees** are composed of members of both the House of Commons and the Senate. The Official Languages Committee reviews and reports on official language policies and programs, including the annual report of the Commissioner of Official Languages. The role of the Standing Joint Committee on Regulations and Other Statutory Instruments is much wider. It scrutinizes all delegated legislation by departments, agencies, boards or other authorities. And, last, the Library of Parliament Committee monitors the work of the library and research branches.

The fourth type, the **legislative committees**, may receive bills for examination after Second Reading. The duty of each committee is limited to an examination of its bill, and witnesses are called only on "purely technical" matters. The number of legislative committees depends on the amount of legislation before the House; sometimes there are very few committees, at other times a large number. After the committee reports back to the House on its bill, the committee is dissolved. Members of legislative committees are appointed by the parties, and their numbers, up to 30, are proportionate to party standings in the House. The chairs, however, are *not* appointed from within the committee membership. Instead, at the beginning of each session, the Speaker appoints at least 10 members to chair legislative committees. Together with the chairs of the Committee of the Whole, they constitute the Panel of Chairmen. The Speaker then selects which of them will chair each new legislative committee as bills are presented to the House.

Committee Recruitment, Composition and Staffing

Membership in the standing and legislative committees is allocated by the Committee of Selection, more commonly known as the "Striking Committee." It is composed of seven MPs, including the chief whip of each party and one representative of the Cabinet. The composition of each committee is roughly proportional to the partisan party representation in the Commons as a whole — although a majority government always claims more than 50 percent of the members and the official opposition is usually over-represented compared with minor parties. Individual MPs are appointed to committees on the basis of their chief whip's recommendations, although these often reflect the personal preferences of the member and, in the case of the Conservative and Liberal parties, are usually in accordance with membership in party caucus committees. Recent procedural changes, in addition to reducing the number of MPs on each committee, permit only pre-selected alternate members to substitute for absentees.

The chair and vice-chair of standing committees are elected at the start of each session by the committee members and, since 1968, have almost all been members of the governing party. By convention, however, the opposition provides the chair of the Public Accounts Committee and the vice-chairs of the Standing Committee on Procedure and House Affairs and the Joint Committee on Regulations. Given the preponderance of government members filling these offices, committee chairs are frequently placed in an ambiguous position by the conflicting expectations about their roles: while their responsibility for presiding over committee meetings requires them to be as impartial as the House Speaker, their selection by the government majority results in pressure to serve the interests of the government in pursuance of its policy goals.

Committee deliberations are expedited by the work of several parliamentary organizations. The Staff of the Committees and Private Legislation Branch of the Commons provides procedural and administrative support. Research assistance comes from the Research Branch of the Library and outside consultants. In recent years, standing committees have sometimes been allocated funds by the Board of Internal Economy. This money may be used by the leadership of the committee to retain the services of experts and professional, technical and clerical staff. The significance of this fund should not be exaggerated, however.

Some commentators have insisted that Canadian committees should have the high level of staffing and research resources enjoyed by congressional committees in the United States, but such an increase would be unlikely, in itself, to enhance the influence of committees in the legislative process:

> *Until committees are given an independent capacity to influence public policy, it is unlikely that the addition of even the most competent of research assistants will do more than contribute to the frustrations of MPs and researchers alike.[20]*

As this quotation suggests, there have long been doubts among both politicians and academic observers as to whether the committee system in the House of Commons is effectively fulfilling its major functions. Despite recent innovations many misgivings persist.

The Committee System at Work: An Evaluation

The committee system has been completely restructured in recent years. Committees in the House of Commons now have three principal areas of operation: detailed consideration of legislation after a bill has passed Second Reading in the House; scrutiny of the financial aspects of government and bureaucracy; and investigation of reports, policy proposals and other items.

Consideration of Legislation

The Committee Stage of the legislative process is designed to provide an opportunity for the clause-by-clause examination of the details of each bill by a small group of relatively specialized MPs in legislative committees. Amendments to bills may be proposed in committees and, if accepted, subsequently will be recommended for adoption by the whole House at the Report Stage. Sometimes, the opposition members of a committee try to investigate the general policy behind a bill, especially since they have an opportunity — denied them during debates in the House — to question public servants and other witnesses. However, amendments of principle or major policy differences introduced by the opposition have little hope of adoption in committee, especially if party divisions have been reinforced by heated debate at the Second Reading. Hence, such amendments are usually presented solely for propaganda purposes. Other amendments may be introduced to force the government to explain or defend a particular provision in the bill. Finally, many amendments constitute genuine attempts to improve the bill — either by making substantive changes to its provisions or by altering technical details, wording or the administration of the legislation.

Amendments may be introduced by the government itself to correct problems that have become apparent in committee, or in response to interest-group pressure or to provincial government or departmental concerns. Thus, although some observers have suggested that the number of amendments accepted at this stage may indicate the influence of the committees, the sources of amendments are so many and varied that the measure is at best imprecise.

Once adopted by a committee, the fate of amendments in the House usually depends upon the minister's willingness to accept them at the Report Stage. The government is more likely to agree to amendments when they are supported by influential groups or by provincial governments, are technical rather than substantive in content and relate to bills of minor or relatively nonpartisan nature. Some notable amendments to government legislation have been achieved, but in general the committees do not permit a significant increase in the ability of the opposition parties to influence the executive's legislative program. Usually, a government exerts very tight control over what amendments will be accepted within the committees, and many of the successful amendments originate from the government itself.

20. R.J. Jackson and M.M. Atkinson, *The Canadian Legislative System: Politicians and Policy-Making,* 1st ed. (Toronto: Macmillan, 1980).

Scrutiny of Public Expenditure

The second main function of the committee system is the scrutiny of public expenditure. It is performed through two mechanisms: first, detailed examination of the main estimates (proposals to spend money) of individual departments by the appropriate standing committees each spring;[21] second, investigation of the government's spending practices by the Standing Committee on Public Accounts.

The **estimates** represent the government's projected spending patterns for the forthcoming financial year. They are approved by the Treasury Board and tabled in Parliament each February in the so-called "*Blue Book.*" Before 1968, the main estimates were considered in the Committee of Supply (i.e., the whole House), wherein the supply motion gave the opposition a chance to criticize the government's policies and management of the nation's finances. Since 1968, the supply procedure has been replaced by the introduction of Supply or Opposition Days and the referral of estimates to the newly established standing committees. Today, main estimates should be referred to committees on March 1st and must be reported back by May 31st. If a committee has not reported by that date, the Standing Orders provide that the estimates "shall be deemed to have been reported" anyway.

Theoretically, the opportunity for parliamentary scrutiny of government policy is best afforded by consideration of departmental estimates. Since the government cannot spend money for any purposes not specifically approved by Parliament and since the estimates procedure allows MPs to investigate the aims of public expenditure, the process could permit the committees to scrutinize and influence the direction of government policy. However, this opportunity is by and large not realized to its full potential. Since only ministers of the Crown can propose public spending, no committee can recommend an increase in estimated funding for any program that it considers desirable — committees can only accept, reduce or reject outright the proposed amounts. Thus, in reality, members avoid cutting the estimates and only on the rarest of occasions ever do so. The opportunity to influence financial planning is further limited by infrequent ministerial attendance at committee sessions, and by the considerable information gap that exists between MPs and the departmental officials defending their proposed expenditures.

Then there is the attitude of MPs themselves. To many committee members, the estimates procedure is a boring, routine task, devoid of publicity and offering little political mileage. Hence, many meetings are conducted in the absence of a quorum, and it is not unusual for committees to approve votes at the outset of the meeting — when a quorum is present — and then proceed to question witnesses on the dollars that have just been approved. Those who do participate are most likely to use the estimates process to relay constituents' complaints to departmental bureaucrats or to gain information that may be of use in their constituencies or in embarrassing the government at some future time. Even where there does exist "that rare bird, 'the economy hawk,' who swoops down on the plentiful bait of departmental spending ... saves his attacks for the minor items, like trips and potted plants, that indicate waste and extravagance."[22]

In general, therefore, it is clear that MPs show little commitment to reducing public expenditure or to increasing the efficiency of government departments — however much lip-service they may pay to these aims. Such goals are hampered by the fact that each committee considers the estimates of only one government department at a time, with few opportunities for comparing spending patterns among departments or evaluating the total projected expenditure. One recent change in the

---

21. Supplementary estimates, which detail additional funds required to meet unforeseen circumstances or to compensate for inflation, are tabled later in the financial year.

22. Paul Thomas, "Parliament and the Purse Strings," in H.D. Clarke et al., eds., *Parliament, Policy and Representation* (Toronto: Methuen, 1980), pp. 166–67.

publication style has helped: the estimates are now accompanied by an overall government fiscal plan. But there is still need for a separate committee to review the finances of Crown corporations and for a general estimates committee to undertake a comparative analysis of all departments and provide a more comprehensive view of government expenditure.

Despite its many weaknesses as a mechanism for parliamentary surveillance of government, the current estimates procedure does have some redeeming qualities. Its very existence leads government departments to take extra care in preparing estimates and to eliminate potential excesses before they are spotted by MPs. It also provides an opportunity for members to meet bureaucrats face-to-face and carry out representative functions on behalf of their constituents. As well, committee debate provides an additional forum for the opposition to criticize government policies and program priorities implicit in the projected spending patterns. But, overall, the standing committees, in their estimates function, are incapable of exercising adequate control over government finance or substantially influencing the content of government policy.

The second mechanism for overseeing public expenditure is the post-audit function of the Standing Committee on Public Accounts. This committee is somewhat unusual in that, since 1967, it has always been chaired by a member of the opposition. As well, it receives expert assistance from the **Auditor General**, an independent officer of Parliament. The committee's examination of the annual Public Accounts has often resulted in criticisms of government inefficiency and recommendations for improvements in spending practices.

Investigations

Part of the conventional wisdom concerning committees is that, as small groups, they permit MPs to interact in a manner rather different from their behaviour in the House.[23] In particular, a less formal environment and a relative absence of publicity should permit the development of a less partisan atmosphere and enhance corporate identity in committees. This ought to facilitate an objective criticism of government policies and increase the opportunity for meaningful participation by members. It is in the performance of their investigative function that Canadian standing committees most often live up to that conventional wisdom by displaying non-partisanship, group cohesion and autonomy from party and government control. Possibly the best example of such activities was found in the Standing Committee on Finance in 1987. Combining the new reforms with good leadership and expertise, the committee produced excellent investigations of the government's White Paper on tax reform, the near collapse of the Canadian Commercial Bank, the Green Paper on financial services, credit card rates, and the designation of Vancouver and Montréal as international banking centres.[24]

Investigations may take place at three stages in the policy process. A committee may hear evidence from interested parties and formulate recommendations to help the government establish priorities on an issue for which no policy has yet been formulated. Alternatively, a committee may be utilized to establish reactions to a particular set of policy proposals, usually contained in a government White or Green Paper.[25] Or, a committee may evaluate the strengths and weaknesses of

---

23. On the application of small-group theory to legislative committees, see Malcolm Shaw, "Conclusion," in John Lees and Malcolm Shaw, eds., *Committees in Legislatures* (Durham, N.C.: Duke University Press, 1979), esp. pp. 412–18.

24. See Robert J. O'Brien, "The Financial Committee Carves out a Role," *Parliamentary Government*, vol. 8, no. 1 (1988), pp. 3–10.

25. A **White Paper** is intended to state fairly firm government policy. A **Green Paper** is a government document with suggested policy options. In Canada, this distinction is not held rigidly; on rare occasions the government has even published papers with other colours, thus further distorting the distinction.

existing policies and their administration, especially in an extension of its estimates scrutiny role. Committee reports can elicit considerable partisan controversy — see "To Leak or Not to Leak." In most policy areas, investigatory tasks are referred to the appropriate standing committee, but certain complex or contentious issues sometimes require the establishment of an *ad hoc* or special committee.[26]

Committees: Problems and Reforms

Certain problems experienced by the House of Commons committee system since its inception in the late 1960s have been resolved by the reforms introduced in the 1980s. First, a reduction in the number of members of each committee has permitted individual MPs to become more specialized. Second, smaller committees have operated more efficiently than their larger predecessors and reduced partisan conflict to some extent. Third, the reforms also introduced the practice of drawing up a list of alternate members for each committee. Now, when committee members are unable to attend a meeting, only designated alternates may substitute for them. Previously, any member of the House could substitute in committee hearings, usually to maintain the government's majority when votes were held. Today, alternate members are kept informed of the business before the committee, so they at least know which piece of legislation they are voting on!

An unresolved criticism of the system relates to the lack of autonomy of Commons committees. Committees cannot operate unless their activities are specified in the Standing Orders or unless they receive a reference from the House instructing them to pursue a particular topic. While standing committees do have authority to study the mandate, management and operations of their own departments, the process is effectively controlled by the government through its majority in the committee and the House. Thus, the government may limit the number of referrals to a given committee, or so overburden it with work that there is insufficient time for detailed consideration of any item. In the last resort, the government may create a hand-picked special committee to investigate particularly contentious legislation or issues, or to bypass a committee that is displaying too much independence. However, recent reforms give committees the power to generate their own references for investigations based on the annual reports of Crown corporations and government departments, without referral from the House.

This lack of autonomy is further complicated by the fact that committees do not enjoy an even workload throughout the year. At the beginning of a session, the workload is generally light. The major bills in the government's program usually reach the legislative committees in the spring, just when members of the standing committees are supposed to be carefully scrutinizing the spending proposals

CLOSE-UP ON Institutions

TO LEAK OR NOT TO LEAK

The leaking or disclosing of government and parliamentary papers *before* their publication is an age-old tradition in Canada. It provides much of the excitement of politics, in particular for the press.

In 1999, the House of Commons Speaker, Gilbert Parent, attempted to do something about these leaks. The question of leaking parliamentary committee reports before they were tabled in the House was sent to the Procedure and House Affairs Committee, which concluded that "between September 1997 to the end of December 1998 — at least 19 committee reports out of 50 have been leaked in whole or in part. This represents 38 percent of substantive reports."[*]

The controversial issue reached the level of farce when the report of the committee investigating leaks was itself leaked to the press before it was tabled.

Should Parliament or the government do something to prevent *in camera* discussions or conclusions from being disclosed prior to their being made public? On the other hand, is it a democratic right to leak documents with which one does not agree?

---

*Procedure and House Affairs Committee, February 1999.

---

26. Robert J. Jackson, "The Unreformed Canadian House of Commons," *Les Cahiers de Droit*, vol. 26, no. 1 (March 1985), pp. 161–73.

in the main estimates. The expenditure scrutiny function is therefore undermined, as some of the most experienced members have little time for deliberation. Reports on the estimates are often brief and hastily written and some committees never do report to the House.

Another traditional problem faced by committees has been the fate of their final reports. Prior to 1982, there was no guarantee that a report would ever get a hearing in the House or provoke any government reaction. Under the new House rules, at the request of a committee the government must table a comprehensive response to its report within 150 days. However, it is still too easy for the government to ignore committee proposals and criticisms. The Communications and Culture Committee was simply told that its 1987 report was rejected — all 100 recommendations were to be reconsidered — and that the job of the committee was to recommend policy, not legislation. However, even if, under the new rules, it is not obliged to adopt recommendations put forward by committees, the government does have to explain its reaction to Parliament.

The procedural reforms of the 1990s, which originated in the Lefebvre and McGrath reports, have thus gone some way toward resolving the problems experienced by committees in the House of Commons and alleviating some MPs' deep-seated dissatisfaction with the committee system. But problems do remain. First, in order to function effectively, committees require more professional research staff, expanded budgets for financial autonomy and more generalized references in the Standing Orders to reduce government control over referrals and committee workloads. Second, partisanship continues to dominate committee activities. The House has very few members who are so secure of re-election and independent of party finances that they can ignore the directives of their leader or the party whip. Since only about a quarter of MPs are very active in committees, there are many operational difficulties — overlapping memberships, scheduling conflicts and other practical irritants such as lack of adequate staff and even meeting rooms.

But the area of committee work most in need of reform may well be the expenditure scrutiny function. A paper prepared for the Special Committee on Procedure by MPs Ron Huntington and Claude-André Lachance made specific proposals (not subsequently adopted) for increasing financial accountability, as did the *Final Report* of the Lambert Royal Commission in 1979.[27] We have already mentioned proposals for the establishment of a General Estimates Committee that would develop an overview of total government spending. Perhaps reform needs to go even further — and establish a National Finance Committee, similar to that proposed by the Lambert Commission, that would analyze both revenues and expenditures in order to bridge the gap between standing committees' consideration of individual departmental estimates, the debate in the whole House on the Finance Minister's economic review and taxation proposals in the budget.[28]

MPs in Parties: Government and Opposition

In contrast to the nineteenth century, it is now rare to find independent members in the House of Commons. Today, almost all MPs belong to a political party. This fact has a profound effect on legislative politics in both houses. The government relies on its backbenchers to remain loyal in

---

27. House of Commons Special Committee on Procedure, *Seventh Report* (Ottawa: Queen's Printer, 1982); Royal Commission on Financial Management and Accountability ("Lambert Commission"), *Final Report* (Ottawa: Ministry of Supply and Services, 1979), especially ch. 22.

28. "Lambert Commission," *Final Report*, ch. 21; and Jackson, "The Unreformed Canadian House of Commons," p. 11.

order to secure passage of its legislative proposals and even to stay in office. The opposition parties, as well, rally their troops to present a coherent attack on the government. This process often requires individual members to compromise their short-term interests for the unity of their party.

The role of the independent MP is tenuous indeed. From 1940 to 1993, 31 MPs ran for re-election in the next general election after the parliamentary sittings during which they crossed the floor. Only 12 of these were successful and 3 ran under their original party banner. These figures show that although an MP may think he or she is acting on the constituents' interests when breaking party ranks, the electorate does not reward such behaviour at the polls. This finding is in direct contrast to the idea that the people want MPs to be "free" to vote according to conscience.[29] The election of Independent John Nunziata in 1997 is the one outstanding exception. In the 36th Parliament, a handful of MPs have crossed the floor to join another party caucus. Only the next election results will tell if the electorate is willing to tolerate such "turncoats."

Political parties are the inescapable fact of life in the Canadian Parliament and have a profound effect upon legislative politics in both chambers and their committees. The government relies on cohesion among its backbenchers to keep it in office and to secure the passage of its legislative proposals. Effective opposition likewise depends on the ability of minority party leaders to mobilize their MPs in specific directions. In both cases, individual members often have to compromise their own short-term interests and aims in order that party goals may be achieved.

Intra-Party Relations: Rebels and Whips

Some observers argue that cohesion is imposed upon MPs through party discipline, that backbenchers, especially on the government side, are forced to adhere to the directives laid down by party leaders. Others portray cohesion as the product of a commonality of views, the result of consensus arrived at through regular meetings of the party caucus.

Former Conservative MP Gordon Aiken has asserted that party discipline is imposed equally on both sides of the House to turn opposition backbenchers as well as government supporters into what he calls "trained seals."[30] Certainly, party leaders, especially of the governing party, have a number of sanctions at their disposal to ensure or at least encourage backbenchers to toe the party line. On the negative side, individual members who consistently oppose the party leadership or fail to vote with their colleagues on important issues may be coerced in a number of ways, culminating in the threat of expulsion from the party. Without the official backing of the party, a rebellious MP would have to contest the next election as an independent candidate with little probability of success. More sizable revolts within the governing party may be met by the threat of dissolution of Parliament. Given the high turnover of seats at every general election, this may quell dissent, especially among those backbenchers who represent marginal constituencies. But the dissolution of Parliament on these grounds is a double-edged sword, since it constitutes a public admission of division within the government party and the possible defeat of the prime minister in a general election. Such issues are vital when the government has only a small majority.

Party leaders can resort to specific sanctions to ensure party discipline, i.e., that the party remains united. Individuals may be coerced in a number of ways. They may lose their positions on parliamentary

---

29. See Robert J. Jackson and Paul Conlin, "The Imperative of Party Discipline in the Canadian Political System," in Mark Charlton and Paul Barker, eds., *Contemporary Political Issues*, 2nd ed. (Scarborough: Nelson, 1994).

30. Aiken, *The Backbencher*, passim. For anecdotal description of the life of an MP, there are few studies to match this book. For parallels with Britain see Robert J. Jackson, *Rebels and Whips* (London: Macmillan, 1968).

committees, as several Liberals did when they rebelled against their government's gun control legislation in June 1995. Even Warren Allmand, one of the party's most senior MPs, lost his chairmanship of the Commons Justice Committee for voting against his party on another occasion.

While these negative sanctions are the "sticks" in the enforcement of party discipline, party leaders also have a number of "carrots" available. The prime minister has a large patronage fund that may be used to reward loyal, well-behaved members: promotion to Cabinet minister, parliamentary secretary or committee chair; appointment to the Senate; and numerous positions in public corporations and Crown agencies. Some of these perks are potentially available to the leadership of the major opposition party, but the government has considerably more of them at its disposal.

The discussion of party discipline tends to imply a *conflict approach* to the maintenance of party unity, that there are inherent divisions between leaders and backbenchers that can be overcome only through coercion. On the other hand, it may be argued equally that party cohesion is based primarily on the existence of consensus (rather than conflict) among MPs in each parliamentary party.[31] According to the latter view, party unity may be based on a "value-consensus," a commonality of opinions on major issues shared by members of the same political movement and reinforced by regular meetings of the party caucus. However, while political parties in Canada do not have the organized political tendencies found in some other countries, it should not be forgotten that they are broad "brokerage" coalitions of a variety of regional and other interests. Another view is that unity may be based on the deference of backbenchers toward party leaders — a willingness to accept the decisions of those who derive their legitimacy from selection by national conventions and who, in this era of personality politics, may be perceived as largely responsible for the electoral success of the party. It may also be argued that peer-group pressure from fellow party members serves to reinforce party solidarity.

The **House Leader**, a member appointed by the party leader to manage party conduct in the House of Commons, is assisted by other MPs — a **chief whip** and assistant whips — who help to maintain party cohesion and manage parliamentary activities. The number of whips depends on the size of caucus, but their role is invariable. They keep in close touch with the members, informing them of their duties in the House and in committees. While the whips can make use of some minor rewards and punishments, caucus cohesion is maintained more by party and leader loyalty than by the whips' ability to sanction members. The **party caucus** is a uniquely Canadian institution. Every Wednesday morning while Parliament is in session, all members of the House of Commons (together with any senators who wish to attend) meet in their respective party groups. Caucus meetings are held in private, away from the press and public. In the opposition parties, unlike on the government side, there is relatively little distinction in status between leaders and backbenchers; consequently, all MPs feel equally entitled to their point of view, and debate is often quite heated. However, in both opposition and government caucuses there are very few formal votes and the party leader normally sums up the caucus consensus.

In the governing party, the prevailing attitude is that the primary task of government backbenchers is to support the executive and its legislative program, and since members are often consulted only after policies have already been decided by Cabinet, the major function of the government caucus is to enforce party discipline and ensure Cabinet control of the policy process. Thus, there is "little doubt that the government caucus is of greater utility to the ministry than to the members, and that it is in effect the chief instrument of government control of the House of Commons."[32] However,

31. The consensus view of party cohesion is emphasized by Allan Kornberg, "Caucus and Cohesion in Canadian Parliamentary Politics," APSR, vol. 60, no. 1 (March 1966), pp. 83–92.

32. Mark MacGuigan, "Backbenchers, The New Committee System, and the Caucus," in Paul Fox, ed., *Politics: Canada*, 4th ed. (Toronto: McGraw-Hill Ryerson, 1977), pp. 436–37.

governments have shown time and again that they do *not* act in the face of clear caucus opposition. In 1996, Finance Minister Paul Martin, for example, gave in to caucus demands that he not amend the *Bank Act* to permit banks to sell insurance, and Human Resources Minister Doug Young was forced by caucus to add amendments to an unemployment scheme that would have reduced the amount of money for seasonal workers.

Inter-Party Relations

Although the relationship between government and opposition is basically one of confrontation, both sides of the House have developed behavioural norms to make Parliament work. Opposition members recognize the government's responsibility to carry on the business of governing and sometimes lend their support to that end; simultaneously, they retain the right to criticize government policy. The government, in turn, recognizes the opposition's right to criticize, but denies it the right to obstruct. The debates on the budget and the Throne Speech, and the allocation of Supply Days on which the opposition parties may choose the topics for debate, constitute formal recognition of the right to criticize the government's record in general. The rules of debate, the committee system and the Question Period permit criticism of individual items of policy or administration. Less formally, while the governing party has final control over the timetable of the House, both government and opposition recognize the value of agreements between respective House Leaders or party whips concerning the disposal of parliamentary time in order to foster a spirit of cooperation.

Occasionally, however, cooperation breaks down. This usually takes place when the government, confronted with what it views as obstruction by the opposition, attempts to push through a bill with what the opposition regards as unseemly haste. When this occurs, both sides have various procedural weapons at their disposal. The government may seek to terminate debate by resorting to **closure** (SO 57), an extremely unpopular measure whereby all outstanding discussion and divisions on a particular stage of a bill must be completed within the next sitting day instead of being adjourned from one day to the next, as unfinished business usually is. Closure is a device to which governments turn with the greatest reluctance because of its procedural complexity and political ramifications.[33] As one author has commented, notice of closure "resembles so much a death sentence and a public execution that ministers shrink from using it; and when they do, the opposition, regardless of their true sentiments, feels obliged to lament the end of a thousand years of freedom and democracy."[34] A less drastic alternative to closure as a means of limiting debate lies in a prearranged **allocation of time** to a particular bill or its various stages under SO 78. Here, a balance of power is maintained between government and opposition by rules that become more complex procedurally as they require less inter-party cooperation.

In the 32nd Parliament, for example, the opposition found dramatic weapons to confront an uncooperative government. In March and April 1981, the Progressive Conservatives tied up the business of the House of Commons with a collective "filibuster" — an apparently endless series of "points of order" and "questions of privilege" — in order to prevent further discussion of the resolution on patriation of the Constitution until after it had been ruled upon by the Supreme Court. For two weeks in March 1982, the division bells that call MPs to vote were left ringing on Parliament Hill as the opposition boycotted the House in protest against the Liberals' omnibus bill on energy security. In both cases, the government was forced to compromise its original proposals in order to

---

33. On the origins, procedural details and use of "closure," see Dawson, *Procedure in the Canadian House of Commons*, pp. 121–30.
34. J. B. Stewart, *The Canadian House of Commons: Procedure and Reform* (Montréal: McGill-Queen's University Press, 1977).

get the House back to work. The McGrath reforms ended the future use of a "bell-ringing fili-buster." Now, by Standing Orders, the bells can ring only for 15 minutes, unless it is on a non-debatable motion, in which case 30 minutes is required. The whips may request that a vote be delayed for a day, but during the deferral the bells may not ring and the House continues its normal business.

In the 34th Parliament, the Conservative government's use of closure and time allocation took on a new and harsh quality. From 1913, when closure was first used, until the 1984 election the device was employed only 19 times. During the 33rd Parliament, it was used only twice between 1984 and 1988. But from 1988 until mid-April 1993, it was employed 15 times — almost as many times as in the whole history of closure since 1913. To top it off, time allocation was used 25 times in the 34th Parliament (up to mid-April 1993), much more than in earlier Parliaments. These "gag" rules were nearly always imposed on fairly controversial legislation such as the free trade legislation, the Goods and Service Tax and the *Drug Patent Act*, revealing the partisan nature of their use.

The parliamentary system enhances adversarial politics, as it is the function of the opposition to criticize. But this duty creates a challenge for the main opposition party, which seeks to provide effective criticism but without being perceived as only negative or with no ideas of its own. In the 35th and 36th Parliaments, the Bloc Québécois found it particularly difficult to appear positive while putting forth its own plans for the secession of Québec from Canada.

The parliamentary system also creates a dilemma for the government in that it is its job to get bills passed, and yet it must allow the opposition time to criticize. In any case, the parliamentary rules are so weighted in favour of the government that the Cabinet generally gets it way. Before the opening of the 35th Parliament, Reform MPs predicted that the new Parliament would no longer engage in destructive bickering; instead it would be a model of dignity and decorum. Reform leader Preston Manning vowed there would be none of the old "whimpering and snivelling" from the opposition.[35] Initially, this was the case; the Liberals, Reform and Bloc functioned as three solitudes. Then, fewer than nine weeks into the session, the atmosphere in the House resumed its usual pattern of exchanging insults and accusations. Speaker Gilbert Parent begged MPs to refrain from "going back and forth with insults."[36] It was not long before the Liberals began using time allocation to cut off debate themselves.

In its adversarial relationship with the government, the opposition is disadvantaged by the former's control over the parliamentary timetable and access to departmental information. But the opposition does have sanctions to prevent what it sees as abuse of the parliamentary process. Even the complaint that opposition parties lack the research facilities to compete with the government's monopoly on bureaucratic information has been partly blunted by the provision of public funding for partisan activity by caucus research groups.

Indeed, many of the difficulties encountered by the opposition in formulating effective criticism of government policy have less to do with House of Commons procedures or research facilities than with more fundamental problems that also afflict parliamentary oppositions in other western democracies.[37] One is that the official opposition in Parliament often has trouble being heard above the "hubbub" coming from other political actors. Major interest groups and private research institutes frequently offer articulate and well-publicized criticisms of government policy, and, in a federal context such as Canada, "there is little doubt that the clashes between the provinces and the federal

---

35. *The Globe and Mail*, March 19, 1994.

36. Ibid.

37. For an extended discussion see Andrew J. Milnor and Mark N. Franklin, "Patterns of Opposition Behaviour in Modern Legislatures," in A. Kornberg, ed., *Legislatures in Comparative Perspective* (New York: David McKay, 1973), p. 84; Jackson, "Models of Legislative Reform: Diagnosis and Prescription," *Le Contrôle de l'Administration et la Réforme parlementaire*, Collection Bilans et Perspectives, no. 4 (Ste-Foy, Qué.: École nationale d'administration publique, 1984), p. 4.

government … detract attention from the federal parliamentary opposition on some of the most important issues in Canadian politics."[38]

Sometimes, too, it may be difficult for the opposition parties to offer clear-cut alternatives to government policy. Some issues do not lend themselves to a confrontational style of politics, since they cut across party lines and strain party cohesion on both sides of the House. This is especially true of moral issues such as abortion, AIDS, capital punishment or euthanasia. On other social and economic policy issues, the development of an ideological consensus that supports the mixed-economy and the welfare state tends to preclude the presentation of radical policy alternatives by a "loyal" opposition.

Oppositions have increasingly had to be content with criticizing the specifics of government policy and its administration (rather than developing comprehensive alternatives) and with presenting themselves as an alternative source of leadership and government personnel. In this regard, the opposition parties have been greatly aided by the introduction of television cameras into the House of Commons. Broadcasting Question Period and major debates not only provides a wider audience for their criticisms of the government, but also gives nation-wide exposure to the leaders of the opposition parties and their "teams." Direct communication with the electorate via television may in fact have greatly facilitated the major task of contemporary parliamentary oppositions — that of presenting themselves as viable alternatives. Increasingly, the chief efforts of parliamentary oppositions are directed at explaining to the electorate why the government is making mistakes and why the opposition should be returned to power at the next election.

HOUSE OF COMMONS REFORM: SYMBOLISM OR POWER?

The reform of parliamentary procedure should be an ongoing process. Parliament is in a constant state of evolution, and if its practices are to be effective, they must be adapted when necessary to meet the changing needs of Parliament and reflect the changing conditions of society and the nation.[39]

As this passage from a report by a recent Special Committee on Standing Orders and Procedures illustrates, members of the House of Commons appear to be perfectly aware of the necessity to reform the roles, procedures and customs of the chamber in order to maintain Parliament as a central institution in Canadian society. Yet possibly the most enigmatic feature of parliamentary democracies is that ordinary members know that they possess limitless authority to change the structures of their legislatures but nevertheless persist in ignoring this power.[40]

Periodically, Canadian MPs undertake systematic reforms of the way in which they conduct their activities. After a wave of reforms in the late 1960s, notable among them the establishment of the modern system of committees, more than a decade elapsed until the next round of innovation and experimentation. In the early 1980s, the Lefebvre and McGrath reform committees ushered in major innovations in the election of the Speaker, private members' business, committee structure, scheduling and other items of importance.

---

38. Jackson and Atkinson, *Canadian Legislative System*, p. 119.
39. House of Commons Special Committee on Standing Orders and Procedures, *Third Report* (Ottawa: 1982), p. 5.
40. Jackson, "Models of Legislative Reform," p. 4.

Consequently, a voluminous body of literature exists on proposals for House of Commons reform.[41] It is not our intention to add to it here, although we have drawn attention in the preceding pages to areas in which reform may be desirable, and have made some specific proposals. It may even be justifiably argued that little that is new or innovative can be added to the catalogues of recommendations. What may be more useful is to provide some criteria for evaluating existing and future reform proposals.

First, it should be emphasized that one cannot turn back the clock to the "Golden Age of Parliament" of the mid-nineteenth century. Those who cling to the myth that parliaments were once more important because governments were less so forget all the other changes that have taken place. There has been a remarkable growth of the public sector and state intervention. Constituents today expect more of both their governments and their members of Parliament, and there are more of them to bring problems to each MP. Traditional federal government responsibilities such as economic policy have become increasingly technical in nature, placing additional burdens on parliamentarians. Mass media have created direct channels of communication between government and the general public that have altered the representative, intermediary functions of MPs. Such trends cannot be reversed. Nor, in the absence of substantial realignment in the perceptions of Canadian citizens about the role of government in society, can the scope of federal government activities be significantly reduced. Realistic proposals for reform of the House of Commons must therefore be formulated within this context.

The objectives of parliamentary reform may be grouped under the two broad headings of "power" and "symbolism," the central themes of this chapter. Some reforms are oriented toward increasing the power of Parliament — strengthening the Commons *vis-à-vis* other institutions and increasing its ability to control, criticize and hold government accountable for its actions. Other proposals are primarily symbolic in nature inasmuch as they seek to enhance the image of the House of Commons as a key institution in the democratic process. As we noted earlier, these two categories are not necessarily mutually exclusive, since a parliament that is perceived as weak and ineffective will not be able to sustain, in the long run, the degree of legitimacy necessary to fulfill its symbolic functions. However, the concepts of "power" and "symbolism" do serve as useful organizing devices.

When it comes to a reform measure designed to increase the power of the House of Commons, the probability of success depends upon various implicit norms and constraints that result from the realities of legislative politics in the chamber. First, governments will not accept organizational or procedural changes unless they are assured that changes favourable to the government will also be adopted. Thus, reform packages must be designed to maintain a balance between the competing needs of government and opposition. If, for example, the opposition is to gain increased opportunities for surveillance and criticism of the administration, the government must be guaranteed certain concessions with regard to limiting debate. Political reality dictates that the government will simply deploy its majority in the House to defeat "unbalanced" reform proposals.

We may be sure that governments will continue to deploy their forces cohesively on matters affecting their interests. Proposals that seek to enhance the influence of backbenchers by advocating, for example, that "leaders of both government and opposition parties recognize and adopt in practice a less stringent approach to the question of party discipline and the rules governing confidence,"[42] are

---

41. Among the many comprehensive "reform designs," the reader may wish to consult the discussion in both editions of Jackson and Atkinson, *The Canadian Legislative System*.
42. T. d'Aquino, G.B. Doern and C. Blair, *Parliamentary Democracy in Canada* (Toronto: Methuen, 1983), p. 30.

politically naïve and based on misleading comparisons with the United States, where members of Congress are deemed to be more powerful because they work in a state of partisan anarchy.

As we have already pointed out, the principle of responsible party government in Canada is different from that in the United States, where the president is directly elected and not dependent upon a majority in Congress in order to stay in office. Therefore, pressures in favour of party cohesion are much stronger in Canada — and not only in the government party, since opposition party leaders also rely on support from their MPs to maintain pressure on the government and to present themselves to the electorate as a responsible alternative administration.

Finally, with respect to measures to enhance the power of the House of Commons, it must be emphasized that it is much easier to alter procedures and institutions than to change the attitudes and behaviour of politicians. Many reformers criticize the lack of opportunities for ordinary members to participate in the policy process or to control government spending effectively, without acknowledging that many MPs fail to take advantage of the opportunities that already exist — either because they choose not to, or because pressures of work and competing commitments prevent them from doing so. Thus, members do not take the scrutiny of government estimates very seriously, because much of it is boring, routine work. More committees or more powers for committees will not help; rather, there must be some perceived reward for effective participation, such as exposure to constituents through the televising of committee hearings. If MPs are too overworked to fulfill all expectations of them, giving them more powers will have little effect on their performance.

Reforms designed to increase the power of Parliament *vis-à-vis* other actors such as the government and the bureaucracy may well have a beneficial effect on the symbolic functions of the House of Commons in legitimating the government policies and many other aspects of the political system. But other reforms might also enhance the symbolic role of the House by raising the level of esteem in which it is held by the Canadian public. Thus, although the members of the 36th Parliament and the government they sustain are reasonably representative of Canadian voters across the country, electoral reform might assure the integrative capacity of the House as a representative institution.[43] Increased travel by committees and country-wide consultation would bring Parliament closer to the people. So, too, would more interesting televising of House proceedings — for example, letting cameras do more than merely focus on one talking head at a time, or, following the popular precedent set with the Special Committee on the Constitution, allowing cameras more consistently into committee meetings, where so much of the House's work is done.

As reformers seek to strengthen the House of Commons, all too often the other potential strengths of the House, as a representative institution, as a symbol of societal integration, as a link between government and citizens, are neglected. Changes related to both power and symbolic innovations should be advocated.

THE SENATE

As of 2000, Canada is one of the minority countries in the world with a bicameral legislature — that is, with a second chamber or upper house in addition to the (usually) popularly elected lower house. Second chambers have been adopted or retained for a number of purposes, among them, the representation at the national level of the constituent parts of a federal system and the representation of a particular class (or estate) to act as a conservative restraint upon the potentially unbridled

---

43. See the discussion of the impact of the electoral system on the House of Commons in Chapter 12.

progressivism of the lower house. But the essential case for an upper house has always been that the formulation of legislation and policy issues ought to receive a second consideration, and possibly be rejected, or delayed, by a chamber different from the first in character and composition.[44]

While the notion of the second chamber as a provider of "sober second thought" concerning legislation from the lower house is almost universal, the other functions of upper houses can often be related to their mode of selection. In federal systems, all of which give their subnational territorial units some representation in the national legislature, membership in the upper house is determined in different ways. Sometimes members are directly elected by the public, as in the United States and Australia. Sometimes they are delegates from the state governments or legislatures, as in Germany. Elsewhere, members are appointed as representatives of various economic, occupational or cultural associations, as in the Portuguese Corporative Chamber before 1975. In still other countries (notably Belgium, Italy and Japan), the upper house is popularly elected, but is designed to give rise to a chamber with a political complexion different from that of the lower house. Finally, the predominantly conservative and upper-class tone of the British House of Lords has been modified by the appointment of Life Peers and by the 1999 reforms to eliminate hereditary peers from the upper house altogether.

Recruitment and Formal Roles

The Senate of Canada appears, at first glance, to fit none of these models. It is the only legislative chamber in the western world where members are all appointed. They receive their positions from the Governor General at the behest of the government of the day. Thus, Canadian senators cannot claim to represent directly, or to be delegates of, any electorate, any subordinate level of government or any specific interests within society.

Although Canada is unique in appointing its senators, as in most other countries, there is a regional basis to the system. Since April 1999, the membership of the Senate has been fixed at 105, with 24 each from four main regions — Ontario, Québec, the West (six from each of the four provinces west of Ontario) and the Maritimes (ten each from New Brunswick and Nova Scotia, four from Prince Edward Island) — together with six from Newfoundland and one each from Yukon, Nunavut and the Northwest Territories. There is also provision in the Constitution for the appointment of an additional four or eight senators (drawn equally from the four main regions) to allow for breaking a deadlock within the Senate and the Commons. After the 1988 election, Conservative prime minister Brian Mulroney used this procedure to prevent the Liberal-dominated upper house from blocking the Goods and Service Tax legislation. For the first and only time in Canadian history, eight additional senators were appointed — temporarily increasing the number.

A senator nominally "represents" the province from which he or she was appointed and, unlike a member of the House of Commons, must reside and own property in that province. Thus there is a regional or provincial underpinning to the composition of the Senate, and the Fathers of Confederation did perceive the second chamber as a "federal" institution. According to Sir John A. Macdonald:

> *In order to protect local interests and to prevent sectional jealousies, it was found requisite that the great divisions into which British North America is separated should be represented in the Upper House on the principle of equality.*[45]

44. Robert J. Jackson and Doreen Jackson, *An Introduction to Political Science: Comparative and World Politics* (Toronto: Prentice Hall, 2000), chs. 12 and 13.

45. *Parliamentary Debates on Confederation of the British North American Provinces*, Québec City, 1865 (Ottawa: Supply and Services, 1951), p. 29.

Most federal systems give their constituent states equal representation in the upper house or at least some modified form of representation by population. Although the "great divisions" of Canada are equally represented in the Senate, there are obvious inequities in representation among Canadian provinces, particularly to the detriment of the West.

The unique appointment process means that Canadian senators cannot be held accountable or responsible either to the provinces or to the regions they were originally intended to represent. Instead, the representation of provincial or regional interests in the federal policy-making process has become increasingly institutionalized in the form of federal/provincial conferences and in the regional composition of the Cabinet.

If the Senate does not fill the role of guardian of regional or provincial interests in a federal system, neither does it necessarily seem oriented toward providing a more mature or conservative restraint upon the youthful enthusiasm of the House of Commons. Constitutionally, senators must be at least 30 years of age, but this is considerably younger than almost all new MPs who win election to the lower house. And although the Constitution determined that senators must own property exceeding $4 000 in value — a sum that in the mid-nineteenth century limited potential membership to a fairly narrow and privileged minority — this figure has not been revised since 1867. Thus, the constitutional requirements for membership in the Senate are no longer of great relevance to its composition or perceived role within the legislative process.

Senators were originally appointed for life but, since 1965, newly appointed members have had to retire at age 75. One observer noted, with a touch of black humour, that this formal change has little practical relevance:

> *Senators, on the average, die at the age of 74.... Therefore, the introduction of a compulsory retiring age at 75 would by no means seriously affect the existing situation in the Senate; it would rather formalize a practice already present.*[46]

However, John Macdonald, Canada's oldest serving senator, turned 91 in 1997, after 37 years and service under eight prime ministers. He was appointed in 1960, five years before Parliament made it mandatory for senators to retire at 75.

One potential advantage of the process of appointment is that it can be used to give recognition to economic, ethnic and religious groups that are under-represented in the House of Commons. Thus, members of organized labour have been appointed, as have farmers — though not nearly as many as their numbers in the population would warrant. The Protestant minority in Québec and English-speaking Catholics elsewhere have also tended to be over-represented in the Senate to compensate for their relative lack of seats in the Commons.[47]

As of today, however, very few women have been appointed to the Senate. The first woman senator, Cairine Wilson, was appointed in 1930, after a long constitutional wrangle that was resolved by a decision from the Judicial Committee of the Privy Council that women were equally "persons" under the relevant sections of the *BNA Act* — and therefore were eligible for appointment to the Senate.[48] The fact that only 32 of 105 senators at the end of 1999 were women demonstrates that Senate appointments have not been systematically used as a means of redressing inequities of

---

46. Kunz, *The Modern Senate of Canada*, p. 71.
47. Robert A. Mackay, *The Unreformed Senate of Canada*, rev. ed. (Toronto: McClelland & Stewart, 1963), pp. 148–49.
48. On the question of women in previous Senates and the development of minority group representation in the upper house, see Kunz, *The Modern Senate of Canada*, pp. 46–56.

representation in the House of Commons.[49] Rather, appointments of women as well as leading figures from minority groups have been symbolic, "a token of recognition of their relative importance in the social and political system of the country."[50] Often, such appointments have been motivated by purely partisan interests in an attempt to win electoral support from certain groups.

This last point underlines the true nature of the system used in appointing senators. Although in formal terms "qualified persons" are "summoned" to the Senate by the Governor General, in practice, as with other such appointments, the real power of selection rests with the prime minister. The fact is, therefore, that the primary basis of appointment to the Senate is unashamedly partisan. Senatorships have invariably been regarded as the choicest plums in the patronage basket and they have been used continually as rewards for faithful party service. There have been few more blatant examples of this in recent years than Pierre Trudeau's appointments as he retired and Brian Mulroney's nominations of former ministers, MPs, fundraisers and former employees to the Senate.

It must be acknowledged that the partisan nature of Senate appointments may have some positive value for the political system. It does allow Cabinet ministers and other long-serving party members to be "promoted" to secure, well-paid Senate seats rather than being "relegated" to the back benches. In this way, the prime minister can reshuffle the Cabinet and introduce new blood without appearing to demote colleagues. It also sometimes occurs that a party candidate regarded as potential ministerial material fails to win or retain a seat in the House of Commons. The Senate provides two alternative strategies for a prime minister wishing to include such an individual in the government. One is to elevate to the Senate a member of the caucus who holds a safe seat. This allows a promising candidate to be "parachuted" into that vacant seat at the ensuing election. The other is to appoint the potential minister directly to the Senate and allow him or her to hold the portfolio from that vantage point.

Although this "renewal" function tends to give rise to a Senate composed mainly of semi-retired party faithfuls, the upper house is far from being a geriatric retreat. The number of appointments of relatively young senators has increased in recent years, and some members have played important roles within their national party organizations. Senators are, for example, in an ideal position to direct election campaigns, since they are close to the centres of power in Ottawa but do not have to seek personal re-election. Thus, Senators Michael Kirby (Liberal) and Lowell Murray (PC) served as their respective parties' chief strategists in the 1988 election campaign.

From the foregoing discussion, it may appear that the Senate fulfills only imperfectly many of the formal roles normally ascribed to second chambers. It is not manifestly a representative of provincial rights nor of minority groups; neither is it a straightforward champion of a particular class nor a sanctuary for aging politicians. Therefore, to ascertain the place of the upper house within the Canadian legislative process, we need to consider the actual work done by the Senate and senators' own perceptions of their task.

Organization and Rules

The Senate has two senior officers: the Government House Leader and the Speaker. The **Government House Leader** is appointed by the prime minister to represent and speak for senators in Cabinet and, conversely, to be the voice of the Cabinet in the Senate. Only rarely are there senators in Cabinet other than the Government House Leader. The **Speaker of the Senate**, unlike the elected House Speaker, is appointed by the Governor General on the recommendation of the prime minister for the term

---

49. For details on earlier periods, see Brodie and Vickers, *Canadian Women in Politics: An Overview* (Ottawa: Canadian Research Institute for the Advancement of Women, 1982), p. 42.

of the Parliament. The duties of this position are similar to those of the Speaker of the House of Commons.

Senators earn $64 000 and a tax-free allowance of $10 000. Their other perks include offices, secretarial help, mailing privileges, free telephone service and so on. Although it is rare for a senator to be fired, it is possible for one of several reasons: if the senator fails to attend two consecutive sessions, loses Canadian citizenship, ceases to meet the residence and property qualifications, is adjudged bankrupt or is convicted of a criminal offence. No one can hold a seat in the Senate and the House of Commons at the same time. Like MPs, senators are bound by conflict-of-interest rules, although these are not as stringent as for Cabinet ministers. (See "Formal Conflict-of-Interest Rules for MPs and Senators.")

Many senators hold positions with private companies, are connected to other people who have holdings in corporations, or are with law firms that represent clients who do business with the government. For this reason they have been called the "lobby from within" and have reaped considerable public condemnation for informal conflicts of interest. Liberal senator Michael Kirby, for example, was a member of the Senate banking committee for many years, but he regularly did market research during the same period. This situation is an ongoing problem because there are no appropriate guidelines to regulate senators' behaviour.

Legislative Politics in the Senate

The status of the Senate as an independent and non-partisan counterweight to the Commons has been challenged by many observers. According to this view, senators are partisan appointments; as such, they are vulnerable to external pressures and vested interests. A contrary view is posited by F.A. Kunz. While admitting that "it would be rather naïve to expect a person who is summoned to the Senate at the (average) age of fifty-eight to forget his entire political background,"[51] he argues that strongly held partisan convictions are counterbalanced by the process of socialization into the norms of the upper chamber that a new senator undergoes.

Certainly, the career backgrounds of senators show them to be highly political.[52] However, there is also strong evidence that, once institutionalized into the norms and values of the upper house, senators often forgo overt displays of partisan attachment in favour of other roles. Many perceive themselves as independent statesmen placing their expertise and experience at the service of the country as a whole rather than serving particular party interests. The higher incidence of cross-voting (voting across party lines) in the upper house on important issues of government legislation would suggest that partisanship

CLOSE-UP ON Institutions

FORMAL CONFLICT-OF-INTEREST RULES FOR MPS AND SENATORS

General

- Under the Criminal Code it is illegal for any Cabinet minister, MP or senator to accept or solicit bribes or to accept a benefit for helping someone in a transaction with government (influence peddling).

Senate and MPs

- The Parliament of Canada Act declares that senators and MPs cannot be a party to any contract paid for with federal funds, nor can they sell their services.

- Standing Orders of the House of Commons prevent MPs from voting on any question in which they have a direct financial interest.

- Senate rules declare that senators cannot vote on any question or sit on a committee dealing with a matter in which they have a financial interest not generally held by members of the public.

---

50. Kunz, *The Modern Senate of Canada*, p. 46.

51. Ibid., pp. 113–15.

52. Colin Campbell, *The Canadian Senate: A Lobby from Within* (Toronto: Macmillan, 1978), p. 53 and Appendix II.

is lower in the Senate than in the House of Commons. In 1999, only five senators had no declared loyalties to any of the political parties.

On the whole, the Senate does not reject government legislation. Despite the fact that the Canadian upper house is one of the few second chambers to retain a full set of legislative teeth, it has usually failed to make full use of them. On the few occasions when the upper house has thrown caution to the winds and blocked government initiatives, it has been threatened with dire consequences. Most senators are fully aware of the erosion of powers and, in some cases, even the abolition of second chambers elsewhere. Moreover, the self-perceived role of elders would appear to forbid the obstruction of legislation passed by a House of Commons mandated by popular will. Instead, one of the most important legislative functions performed by the Senate consists of the detailed scrutiny of bills with a view to removing ambiguities of interpretation in the original wording and amending technical items that fall within the particular expertise of individual members.

On occasion, however, the Senate has acted decisively to reject government legislation. As early as 1875, the Senate blocked the construction of an Esquimalt–Nanaimo railway. In 1913, it defeated the Borden Naval Bill and in 1926 it terminated Mackenzie King's old-age pension legislation. More recently, during the tenures of Prime Ministers Mulroney and Chrétien, there were constant clashes between the House and Senate. The Liberal-dominated Senate interfered in or delayed, a borrowing bill and the drug patent bill, and copyright, immigration and income tax legislation. It tried to amend the Meech Lake accord, unemployment insurance payments and the Goods and Services Tax. It succeeded in rejecting an abortion bill when a free vote was called. This was the first senatorial veto in three decades. In the 35th Parliament, the Conservatives initially held a majority of seats in the Senate even though they had only two MPs in the House. With the help of a Liberal senator they stopped the passage of Bill C22, the cancellation of the Pearson Airport development legislation, and delayed many other bills. In the 36th Parliament, the Liberals have a clear majority of senators and government legislation passes smoothly through the system.

The most important instance of the Senate blocking the elected house, was the decision of the Liberal senators, at the request of John Turner, to prevent the passage of free trade legislation. When the trade bill reached second reading, Liberal senators abstained and allowed it to go to the Foreign Affairs Committee. In a deliberate provocation of the Conservative government, the Liberal-dominated committee set up an extensive program of hearings. The government was forced to call an election for November 20, 1988, an election for which the Senate had helped to set the date and the agenda — a partisan act of the highest order.

Despite these occasions of grand obstruction, the senators normally spend their time in leisurely debates or in committee deliberations. Committee work is their most significant contribution. For example, in 1991–92, Senate committees held 301 meetings to discuss legislation, estimates and special studies. In fact, most of the time (62.7 percent) was spent in special committees discussing key social issues and making recommendations for new policy initiatives.

In the 1960s and early 1970s, Senate special committees on such diverse issues as poverty, the mass media, aging and science helped to build social consensus around particular problems and alternative responses. But, like recent House of Commons task forces, these special committees were frequently critical of existing government policy. In fact, they were probably too critical and nonpartisan for their own good, because there has been a tendency in recent years for Government House Leaders in the Senate to allocate investigatory tasks to standing committees, which can be more easily controlled. Reports in the 1980s and 1990s include those on unemployment insurance, the security service, national defence, youth and terrorism.

Prior to the 1984 general election, it appeared that the Senate was developing a new role in the legislative process — that of a supplier of ministers. Ministers in the Senate ensured regional and linguistic balance in the Cabinet to parties denied House of Commons representation from major regions of the country. In 1979, Prime Minister Clark, with only two Conservative MPs elected in Québec, recruited three ministers from the Senate to bolster francophone representation in his Cabinet. Similarly, after the 1980 general election, with no Liberal MPs from the three western provinces, Prime Minister Trudeau included three senators in his government. Although the appointments were criticized by opposition MPs on the grounds that these ministers held no popular mandate, they did provide the Senate with an enhanced opportunity to oversee the work of government and to participate more fully in legislative/executive relations. In the 34th Parliament, with a majority of Conservative MPs elected from all parts of the country, Prime Minister Mulroney had little need of senators to build his Cabinet. However, Senator Lowell Murray played an important role in the Conservative Cabinet, as did Senator Joyce Fairbairn in the 1993 Liberal Cabinet during the 35th Parliament and Alasdair Graham in the 36th Parliament.

CLOSE-UP ON Institutions

FAIRNESS OR SCANDAL IN THE SENATE?

In early 1998, Senator Andrew Thompson became the first member of the upper house to be suspended from his duties. Senator Thompson had missed almost all Senate meetings over the past few years, maintaining that he was very ill and had to stay in Mexico for medical reasons. In the wake of media disclosures that brought negative publicity about the Senate, the Senate formally required him to explain his absences. When he failed to do so, the Senate found Senator Thompson in contempt. It suspended him even though he had never violated any rules of the Senate or the Constitution. He had not missed two consecutive sessions of Parliament and he had always filed medical certificates in his absences.

Was the Senate justified in suspending the Senator when he had not "technically" broken any law or rule?

Senate Reform: Symbolism or Power?

Like the House of Commons, the Senate is the subject of ongoing debate on parliamentary reform. As Henri Bourassa claimed half a century ago, such debate is something that "comes periodically like other forms of epidemics and current fevers."[53] However, in the last two decades, a qualitative shift in the motivation for reform has occurred. With reference again to the central concepts of this chapter, it might be said that the objectives have changed from altering somewhat the power and symbolism of the Senate to radically restructuring the Senate's role in the Constitution. The overall pattern of Senate reform proposals and constitutional change is discussed in Chapters 5, 6 and 7.[54]

In the past, demands for restrictions on the power of the upper house came, not surprisingly, from governments confronted by a "hostile" Senate. Mackenzie King in 1927, Diefenbaker in 1962 and Mulroney in 1988 sought or threatened Senate reform after government legislation had been blocked by an opposition majority in the second chamber. It is also unsurprising that proposals designed to enhance the effective functioning of the upper house have often come from within the Senate itself.

Some critics of the role of the Senate have not contented themselves with proposing minor reforms or even reduced powers. The Progressive party of the 1920s, the CCF and its descendant, the NDP, have all advocated nothing less than abolition of the second chamber, arguing that an unelected body has no place in the legislative process of a democratic society. But total abolition of the upper house is not only constitutionally difficult, it is also politically impractical. When the Constitution of Canada was patriated in 1982, the Senate's powers were left virtually intact with one important

---

53. *House of Commons Debates*, 1926, p. 648.
54. For detailed analysis see Robert J. Jackson and Doreen Jackson, *Stand Up for Canada: Leadership and the Canadian Political Crisis* (Scarborough: Prentice Hall, 1992).

exception: the Senate, acting alone, can now only block legislation on Senate reform for 180 days, after which a constitutional amendment regarding the Senate can be made without its approval.

At one time, both demands for abolition and attempts at reform derived from dissatisfaction with the role and powers of the Senate as the second chamber in the parliamentary system. More recent proposals, from the draft for a new Canadian Constitution through the various constitutional discussions of the late 1970s, the Alberta success in "electing" a senator in 1989,[55] to the provisions in the Meech Lake and Charlottetown accords, were predicated upon the assumption that the upper house could be reshaped into an institution designed to correct perceived deficiencies elsewhere in the political system. As federal/provincial and regional tensions became more acute, reform of the Senate was viewed as a panacea for all manner of perceived ills afflicting Canadian society.

The many reform designs produced a variety of schemes for a more equitable geographical distribution of seats in the upper house, usually to the potential benefit of western Canada.[56] They ranged from allowing some provincial input into the existing appointment system,[57] through joint selection by the federal Parliament and the provincial legislatures in a proposed "House of the Federation," to having an upper house consisting of delegates chosen by and representing provincial governments in a so-called "House of the Provinces" modelled after the German *Bundesrat* (upper house).[58]

The January 1984 report of the Special Joint Committee on Senate Reform recommended that senators be directly elected by the citizens of Canada in order to give it legitimacy.[59] It also proposed amendments to the traditional powers of the Senate. In particular, it suggested that the present absolute veto be replaced by a suspensory veto of up to 120 days by which legislation passed by the House of Commons could be delayed but not rejected outright. Only on legislation of linguistic significance would the absolute veto power be retained. The report argued that, while this may represent a diminution of the formal powers of the upper house, senators might be willing to exercise lesser powers in exchange for playing a more effective role in the legislative process. The proposed direct election of senators for a non-renewable term of nine years would have done little to enhance the accountability of senators. Since, under these proposals, they could not seek re-election, there would be no mechanism by which they could be held responsible by the electorate.

In the 1990s, a western initiative for a new "Triple E" Senate became prominent among the reform proposals. The desire for a Senate that would be *elected, effective* and *equal* for all provinces received the support of the smaller provinces. They favoured the idea of an equal number of senators from each province, regardless of its size or population. In the early deliberations, larger provinces

---

55. In 1989, the province of Alberta held a "senatorial election" when a vacancy opened during the period in which Prime Minister Mulroney said he would appoint senators from provincial "lists." A Reform party candidate, Stan Waters, won the election and Mulroney felt duty bound to appoint him. No other province has followed the precedent.

56. See West Foundation, *Regional Representation: The Canadian Partnership* (Calgary: Canada West Foundation, 1981).

57. The 1969 White Paper and the 1972 Special Committee Report proposed that the provinces would submit short-lists of nominees from which the prime minister would choose one-half of the future appointees.

58. The "*Bundesrat* model," first discussed by academics in the 1960s, was subsequently endorsed by some provincial governments and other public bodies. See, among others, Canadian Bar Association, *Towards a New Canada* (Ottawa: Canadian Bar Association, 1978).

59. Special Joint Committee of the Senate and of the House of Commons on Senate Reform, *Report* (Ottawa: Queen's Printer, 1984). For the detailed views of one of the authors on Senate reform, see Robert J. Jackson, "Remarks to the Special Joint Committee of the Senate and of the House of Commons on Senate Reform," June 23, 1983.

tended to support the idea of a "Double E" Senate, one that would be *elected* and *effective* in its functioning but whose membership would be based on some principle of representation by population.

During the 1987 impasse over constitutional reform, Prime Minister Mulroney gave a political commitment that until there was a comprehensive constitutional change concerning the Senate, he would nominate senators only from lists supplied to him from provincial governments. This commitment was given in order to obtain a consensus over the Meech Lake accord. This practice had no constitutional authority, however, and quickly evaporated after Meech Lake died. Stan Waters from Alberta was the only *elected* senator to be appointed under these rules.

Finally, in 1992, another constitutional package known as the Charlottetown accord was agreed upon by federal and provincial leaders and their assemblies. It proposed a modified Triple-E Senate, with special guarantees for Québec representation in the House of Commons. Under the Charlottetown accord there would have been 62 senators — six from each province and one from each territory. Except in Québec, where they would have been appointed by the National Assembly, the senators would have been elected directly by the people. The details of this proposal and the story of its defeat in the October 1992 referendum are discussed in Chapter 5. Suffice it to say here that the defeat of the Charlottetown accord left Canada with the same method of selecting senators and with the same senatorial powers it had before the accord.

And so the debate continues.[60] While the internal organization and procedures of the Senate have evolved over the last three decades, and one minor adjustment has been made to Senate tenure, the objectives of Senate reform have changed, perhaps rendering the task more difficult. The principle of producing an effective second chamber has largely been abandoned in favour of creating an institution valued more for its symbolic contribution to Canadian unity and maintenance of the federal system than for its role in the legislative process. However, as long as federal/provincial wrangling over the Constitution continues, and until an accepted means of amendment can be found, the Senate will maintain its role as a usually cooperative, sometimes cantankerous, but invariably dignified part of the legislative process. The problem for the Senate is simple — if it does little it is accused of being a "rubber stamp," but if it acts decisively it is reprimanded for blocking "the will of the people." Calls for Senate reform have been made since at least 1893. It is time to reform the Senate *within* the present Constitution.

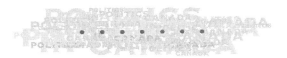

• • • • • • •

SUMMARY

Throughout this chapter we have used the twin concepts of *power* and *symbolism* as reference points in describing the various roles performed by the two chambers of the Canadian Parliament and as an organizing device to evaluate certain proposals or directions for future reform. But we have also stressed that these two concepts are not mutually exclusive. In a relatively open society such as Canada, where the activities of Parliament and its members are subjected to fierce, often critical, scrutiny by the mass media, only a legislative body that is perceived to be powerful can maintain

---

60. See Robert J. Jackson, "Reforming an Unreformed and Unreformable Senate," remarks to the Senate and staff, March 29, 1993, and published by the Senate.

sufficient legitimacy to fulfill its symbolic roles. Reform designs must therefore maintain the delicate balance between power and symbolism if Parliament is to continue to carry out the many functions demanded of it as a key institution linking citizens with their federal government. Proposals that threaten to upset this balance are effectively doomed to failure.

Thus, for example, demands that Parliament be made more powerful, like the American Congress or the German *Bundestag*, must take into account the fact that the Canadian legislature performs different roles. In the United States, members of Congress are perceived to be more influential because they are relatively independent of party ties, but Congress does not have the same importance in sustaining the political executive in office and legitimizing its policies. Hence, any attempt to reduce the level of discipline in the Canadian House of Commons must be accompanied by a careful reconsideration of the concept of government responsibility, which is based currently on the assumption of cohesive party behaviour.

Similarly, the *Bundestag* is perceived to be influential in part because much of its work is carried out by parliamentary committees working in relative isolation from media and public scrutiny; but debates in the legislative chamber itself are often quite stilted and boring affairs, since most issues have already been decided elsewhere. The Canadian House of Commons could grant increased powers and delegate much heavier workloads to committees, but only at the risk of reducing the current importance of plenary sessions to the House both as a forum for debate and as a place where the business of government and opposition is *seen* to be done.

The same delicate balance between power and symbolism must also appear in attempts to reform the upper house. Admittedly, the Senate as currently constituted has rather more formal power than legitimacy in the eyes of most Canadians. But many of the reform designs would tilt the balance too far the other way. The proposed "House of the Federation," for example, would almost certainly have a constantly shifting membership, which would undermine many of the traditional strengths of the upper house. Proposals for a Triple-E Senate are sometimes impractical or naïve.

Some actual and proposed reforms do manage to maintain the balance of power and symbolism. The McGrath reforms increased the influence of backbench members and strengthened the investigative and policy-making roles of the House of Commons while enhancing the representative and symbolic functions of the legislature. It is not always so easy to kill two birds with one stone. However, more comprehensive reform packages can be designed to take into account both the need to strengthen Parliament and the requirement that it continue to serve as the representative and symbolic cornerstone of the governmental process. As society continually evolves in complexity, as the state plays an ever-expanding role in the lives of its citizens, as technological advances provide new links between government and the people, Parliament is struggling to keep up. If Parliament is to maintain its status as the most important institution in Canadian political life, it must evolve too, adjusting both its internal procedures and its external relations with other political actors.

DISCUSSION QUESTIONS

1. What is the value of Parliament? Of mechanisms such as parliamentary Question Period?

2. Is the procedure of passing a bill into law too cumbersome and time-consuming? What measures are used by government and opposition parties to speed up or delay passage of bills?

3. Is strict party discipline a necessary part of the Canadian parliamentary system?

4. Should the Senate be abolished or reformed? Explain. Given Canada's procedures for constitutional amendment, do you think constitutional change is likely to be achieved?

Selected Bibliography

Brooks, Stephen, *Canadian Democracy* (Toronto: McClelland & Stewart, 1992).

Docherty, David C., *Mr. Smith Goes to Ottawa* (Vancouver: University of British Columbia Press, 1997).

Eagles, Munroe, et al., *The Almanac of Canadian Politics* (Peterborough: Broadview, 1991).

Fleming, Robert, *Canadian Legislatures 1992* (Agincourt, Ont.: Global Press, 1992).

Franks, C.E.S., *The Parliament of Canada* (Toronto: University of Toronto Press, 1987).

House of Commons, *Précis of Procedure*, 4th ed. (Ottawa: House of Commons, 1991, revised periodically).

——————, *Standing Orders of the House of Commons* (September 1994).

Jackson, Robert J. and Michael M. Atkinson, *The Canadian Legislative System*, 2nd ed. (Toronto: Macmillan, 1980).

Kunz, F.A., *The Modern Senate of Canada* (Toronto: University of Toronto Press, 1965).

Lijphart, A., ed., *Parliamentary versus Presidential Government* (Oxford: Oxford University Press, 1992).

Mancuso, Maureen et al., *A Question of Ethics: Canadians Speak Out* (Toronto: Oxford University Press, 1998).

Seidle, F. Leslie, ed., *Rethinking Government: Reform or Reinvention?* (Ottawa: Renouf, 1993).

Sproule-Jones, Mark, *Governments at Work* (Toronto: University of Toronto Press, 1993).

Weaver, R. Kent and Bert A. Rockman, eds., *Do Institutions Matter: Government Capabilities in the United States and Abroad* (Washington: The Brookings Institution, 1993).

White, Randall, *Voice of Region: The Long Journey to Senate Reform in Canada* (Toronto: Dundurn Press, 1990).

LIST OF WEBLINKS

www.parl.gc.ca/ 36/main-e.htm

Parliament of Canada This is the official Web page for the Parliament of Canada.

www.cpac.ca

Canadian Parliamentary Affairs Channel CPAC Online provides information about the parliamentary channel and links to other government resources.

www.hansard.ca/links.html

Hansard This is the Web site for the record of the daily debates that take place in the House of Commons.

10

Bureaucracy and Democracy

. . . .

Public Servants, Budgets and Accountability

In this chapter, the primary focus is on the machinery and budgets of the Canadian government and on the major issues relating to the efficient implementation of government policy. However, since it is not easy to separate the administrative process of policy implementation from the political process of policy formulation, it is impossible to ignore the controversies over the role of bureaucracy and the influence of public servants in Canadian politics.

In Canada, as in most democratic societies, there is a distinction between the transient politicians, who come and go, and the permanent administrators who carry out the goals and purposes of their political masters. Constitutionally, the elected executive of the federal government is responsible for formulating policies. The administrative process of implementing those policies is entrusted to permanent state officials employed by the departments, agencies and Crown corporations that constitute the federal bureaucracy.

In the modern state, however, the traditional dichotomy between "politics" and "administration" is not as clear as it once appeared. First, the vastly expanded scope and complexity of contemporary public policy have rendered politicians increasingly dependent upon permanent administrators for information, advice and execution of government policy. Furthermore, as noted in Chapter 9, Parliament has delegated to the bureaucracy substantial decision-making autonomy in many areas of technical policy-making in the fields of regulation and administrative procedure. Fears have consequently been expressed about the increasingly "political" role of the bureaucracy and a perceived lack of bureaucratic accountability in many areas of government policy-making.

At the same time, expansion of the responsibilities and activities of the Canadian government has effected a commensurate growth in the size and scope of public administration. The sheer size and complexity of the bureaucratic leviathan give cause for concern. As well, administrative secrecy, the apparent impenetrability of bureaucratic processes and lack of open accountability have been cited as threats to responsible, democratic government.

WHAT IS BUREAUCRACY?

For centuries, political rulers have relied on permanent officials to carry out the routine tasks of administering government policies. From tax collectors and magistrates of ancient times to modern government departments, public administration is as old and ubiquitous as government itself. *Bureaucracy*, on the other hand, is a relatively new and more limited phenomenon. The term originated as a satirical combination of the French *bureau* (desk) and the Greek *kratein* (to rule), on the analogy of "democracy" and "aristocracy." In popular parlance, it has come to signify depersonalization, inefficiency and inflexibility. But, while anyone who has encountered bureaucratic "red tape" may feel such characterizations are appropriate, these organizations are central to the effective management of modern life.

Similarly, bureaucrats, who carry out the functions of bureaucracies, are regularly condemned as overpaid, under-employed, inefficient and self-serving. Witness this quip by the Honourable Member from Kicking Horse Pass (alias Dave Broadfoot of the Royal Canadian Air Farce):

> *Q: How many civil servants does it take to screw in a light bulb?*
> *A: One, but he's been promoted three levels by the time it's all screwed up.*[1]

Yet Canadians turn to public servants to solve society's toughest problems. Politicians routinely run for office on promises of reducing bureaucracy, then discover that they cannot do without its officials.

The Concept of Bureaucracy

The term **bureaucracy** may be applied to complex organizational forms in a variety of contexts — business corporations, churches, political structures such as party organizations, among others. But the term is most clearly and most often identified in people's minds with the administrative machinery of government. The size of contemporary states and the myriad of governmental responsibilities entailed in the management of modern societies necessitate complex structures that can routinize the administrative decision-making process.

The starting point for most studies of bureaucracy is the "ideal-typical" bureaucratic organization formalized by the German social scientist Max Weber and characterized by

- the specialization of official duties;
- the hierarchical organization of authority;
- operations governed by a consistent application of abstract rules to particular cases;
- impersonal detachment toward subordinates and clients;
- employment based on merit and protection from arbitrary dismissal; and
- maximization of technical and organizational efficiency.[2]

In theory, organizations adopting the characteristics of Weber's model would maximize administrative efficiency and the rationalization of social activity. In reality, however, no bureaucracy

---

1. From the Royal Canadian Air Farce recording *Air Farce Live* (CBC Enterprises, 1983).
2. Summarized by Peter M. Blau, *Bureaucracy in Modern Society* (New York: Random House, 1956), pp. 28–31, passim. See also Max Weber, *The Theory of Social and Economic Organization*, ed. and trans. by A.M. Henderson and Talcott Parsons (Glencoe: Free Press, 1947), pp. 329–41.

conforms exactly to this ideal type; indeed, the concept of ideal type implies a near-perfect standard against which examples in the observable world can be evaluated. Nonetheless, all these characteristics are found to some extent in Canadian federal administrative structures and, as Weber predicted, they have developed partly as a result of "the increasing complexity of civilization," which encourages bureaucratization.[3]

Many characteristics of bureaucracy developed as a consequence of the emergence of democratic forms of government. As the idea of alternation of power between competing parties became accepted under the doctrines of parliamentary democracy and representative government, it became necessary to separate the bureaucracy from the political executive. The bureaucracy has thus been able to maximize rational administration free from political concerns, and individual public servants are protected from arbitrary dismissal on political grounds (e.g., when government changes hands) as long as they maintain partisan neutrality.

The development of liberal democracy also saw demands for the substitution of *merit* for patronage as the primary method of recruitment to government service and promotion within it. Appointments to administrative office were once made on the basis of family and "old school tie" networks or as a reward for political services rendered. Democratization of the public service brought a merit system involving open competition.

Finally, certain characteristics of bureaucracy identified by Weber (decisions made by "the constant application of abstract rules to particular cases" and bureaucrats' "impersonal detachment toward ... clients") enhance administrative efficiency by routinizing the decision-making process. They are also democratic inasmuch as they protect individuals from arbitrary decisions and ensure that all clients are treated equally. Where there may once have been one law for the rich and another for the poor, operations of the ideal-type bureaucracy apply the same rules to all citizens.

Thus, a neutral, professional public service based on the organizational principles of modern bureaucracy has emerged alongside, and partly as a consequence of, the development of liberal democracy. Yet a fundamental contradiction exists in the co-existence of bureaucracy and democracy in a society such as Canada.

Bureaucracy versus Democracy

Bureaucratic and democratic structures are, in part, founded upon different organizing principles: bureaucracy is based primarily on a clearly defined hierarchy of authority established in the interests of efficiency; democracy is based on the principle of fundamental political equality that permits majority rule while respecting minority rights and freedom of dissent. But, as Peter Blau points out, democratic values also demand that social goals be implemented by the most effective means available so that the "will of the majority" may be seen to be done. Effective methods, suggests Blau, are more likely to be governed by the dictates of bureaucracy than by those of democracy.[4] Since bureaucratic efficiency is aided by the routinization of decision-making, the quest for effective implementation may result in uniform standards that reflect the will of the majority but neglect minority interest. In a country such as Canada, where minority ethnic, linguistic and regional interests are particularly sensitive, the result may be the exacerbation of potential conflicts and a loss of legitimacy for both the bureaucracy and the entire policy-making process.

---

3. H.H. Gerth and C. Wright Mills, eds. and trans., *From Max Weber: Essays in Sociology* (New York: Oxford University Press, 1946), p. 212.

4. Blau, *Bureaucracy in Modern Society*, pp. 106–7.

This problem has become particularly acute in the modern era, since many areas of government policy are now so complex that the means of implementing public policies are often as important to their outcomes as the choice of goals. Therefore, it is becoming increasingly difficult to maintain the distinction between administrative and political processes.

We have pointed out that, in Canada, ultimate decision-making power in many fields resides constitutionally with the federal government; the bureaucracy is designated as the neutral, professional administrator of policy. But in practice it is difficult to separate the political and administrative dimensions of government action. While not political *per se*, the bureaucracy does influence the actual formation of public policy in a number of ways.

First, Cabinet ministers who are formally responsible for defining public policies rarely enjoy sufficient tenure to acquire a high degree of expertise in the affairs of their respective ministries. Not only does government occasionally change hands at general elections, but there are also periodic Cabinet shuffles in which ministers are moved from department to department and hence from one policy area to another. Each time this occurs, it takes a while for a minister to come to grips with a new role. Since the average departmental tenure of Canadian Cabinet ministers is very short, it is clear that the average federal minister spends considerable time learning the workings of the department.

In contrast, the permanence of public servants allows them to develop expertise and practical knowledge on which politicians can draw in formulating policies. Consequently, if "knowledge is power,"[5] as Max Weber maintained, then the bureaucracy in a complex, technical society may have great political power. It may screen the data furnished to its political masters, and such filtered information may be fundamental to the direction of government policy.

The relative permanence and access to information enjoyed by bureaucrats may influence the policy process in a number of other ways as well. Bureaucratic tenure permits public servants to develop a more long-term view of policy formulation than is possible for politicians, who must be more responsive to short-term shifts in public opinion. Also, administrative personnel who have close links with "client" interest groups may be in a better position than politicians to identify certain public needs.

Furthermore, the bureaucracy may constitute an "interest group" in its own right.[6] Policy proposals generated within the bureaucracy may influence the government's choice among competing alternatives. Most government departments contain a policy analysis unit that monitors and evaluates the impact of ongoing policies. Here again bureaucrats may be in a better position than politicians to recommend fine-tuning of, or wholesale changes in, existing policies. Finally, even after a political choice has been made by the government, a degree of discretion must be left to public servants with regard to policy implementation.

The bureaucracy, therefore, has numerous opportunities to influence the policy-making process in Canada. But why should the bureaucracy, especially its expanded role in the policy-making process, be viewed as a threat to democracy? Critics propose several arguments.

First, they allege that the bureaucracy is unrepresentative of the general public and therefore is insensitive to the requirements of citizens. Minority groups and interests that are not adequately represented within the bureaucracy may be neglected.

A second, related argument is that the bureaucracy is steered by a narrow and cohesive elite that seeks to impose its own vision of society and the role of the state on the rest of the country. This

---

5. Gerth and Wright Mills, *From Max Weber*, pp. 232–35.
6. See the discussion in Chapter 14 on public policy theory.

argument is sometimes linked to "elite" or "class" theories of politics, which posit that the elitist family and educational backgrounds of bureaucrats render them sympathetic to the interests of friends, relatives and former business colleagues and the upper class.

Third, the growth of the state, the rise in public expenditures, tax increases and escalating budgetary deficits incurred by most western governments are all blamed upon the expansionary tendencies of bureaucracy and the "empire-building" of individual bureaucrats. Supporters of this argument aver that new government programs serve the interests of administrators rather than those of the general public. Furthermore, critics allege that bureaucratic inefficiency wastes economic resources, and demand that measures be initiated to increase financial accountability and bureaucratic efficiency.

Fourth, arguments about the lack of financial accountability are often extended to more general criticisms of the lack of popular, parliamentary or governmental control over the bureaucracy. Politicians may be held accountable by the ballot box: if they have not adequately served the needs of the public, then they may be removed at the next election. However, there are no such mechanisms by which permanent public servants may be held accountable. For this reason, too, critics regard bureaucracy as inimical to the democratic process.

In later sections of this chapter, we examine various aspects of the bureaucracy and the administrative process in Canada in relation to these arguments. But first it should be noted that most critics of bureaucracy tend to view it as an undifferentiated, monolithic monster. Nothing could be further from the truth. The Canadian administrative apparatus is a complex hierarchy of different types of government departments, Crown corporations, agencies and other bodies that serve a wide range of functions. The next section provides a brief guide to the major structures of the administrative apparatus and their respective roles and responsibilities.

ORGANIZATION OF THE FEDERAL BUREAUCRACY

The two formal structures of government with which Canadians most frequently come into direct contact are government departments and Crown corporations (or public enterprises). Few citizens escape encounters — some pleasant, some less so — with institutions such as the Department of National Revenue, which collects taxes and customs duties. Its employees may embarrass us by searching our luggage for contraband at the airport, but it may also provide a welcome tax rebate. Most Canadians deal with Crown corporations every day, for example, by watching CBC television or spending money printed by the Royal Mint.

But departmental officials and public enterprises that interact directly with the public are merely the most visible tip of the administrative iceberg. Three basic organizational forms are found in the Canadian federal bureaucracy: departments, Crown agencies and advisory bodies. Government **departments** are each headed by a Cabinet minister and are largely responsible for the administration of programs serving the public (e.g., Human Resources) or for providing services to the government itself (e.g., Public Works and Government Services). **Crown agencies** include public enterprises (e.g., VIA Rail Canada) and regulatory commissions (e.g., the Atomic Energy Control Board). **Advisory bodies** consist of royal commissions, government and departmental task forces, and a range of advisory councils that collectively provide alternative sources of research and advice for the political executive.

Because of their special role in the policy process, and their often exaggerated elite status, it is possible to classify **central agencies** (introduced in Chapter 8) as a fourth type of bureaucratic organization. With the exception of the Prime Minister's Office (PMO), these agencies are staffed almost exclusively by career public servants appointed under the aegis of the Public Service Commission. They are all formally headed by a Cabinet minister and in all structural and legal respects take the departmental form of organization.

Federal Government Departments

Government departments are administrative units of a government, each of which is headed by a Cabinet minister. They are largely responsible for the administration of a range of programs serving the public. While the minister is politically responsible for the activities of the department and for formulating general policy, the administrative and managerial head of each department or ministry is the **deputy minister** (**DM**) — its senior public servant. Departments, on the whole, obtain their staff from the Public Service Commission and their funding through the standard appropriation acts of Parliament.

The deputy minister is at the apex of a pyramidal structure of authority and organizational agencies. Two or more **assistant deputy ministers** (**ADMs**), heading branches or bureaus, report directly to the DM. Below the ADMs are directorates or branches, each headed by a director-general or director. These directorates are in turn composed of divisions, headed by directors or divisional chiefs; the divisions are further broken down into sections, offices and units. The exact titles of departmental sub-units and their respective senior officials vary from department to department. (See Table 10.1.)

The number of senior officials and the range of sub-units and employees for which they are responsible differ according to the type of department. *Line departments* or *operational departments* generally consist of a large number of sub-units and employ a large staff to deal with the general public. Agriculture and Agri-Food, and Fisheries and Oceans, for instance, each employ several thousand people across the country. *Administrative-coordinative departments,* such as the Department of National Revenue, also tend to be large, complex structures. However, *policy-coordinative departments,* such as Justice and Foreign Affairs and International Trade, tend to be much smaller — in part because they have few, if any, program- or service-delivery functions.

Crown Agencies

The second basic organizational form in the federal bureaucracy is the Crown agency. **Crown agencies** include a wide variety of non-departmental organizations including Crown corporations, regulatory agencies, administrative tribunals and some advisory bodies (discussed separately below). The rationale for distinguishing advisory bodies from Crown agencies is that advisory bodies are primarily involved in formulating policy, while Crown agencies are charged directly with attaining government policy objectives — through administration, public ownership, regulation of the private sector and so on.

Depending upon the definition employed, there are approximately 400 federal Crown agencies. A number of characteristics distinguish Crown agencies from government departments. Agencies are not directly responsible to a minister but usually report to Parliament through a designated minister. The degree of supervision and accountability of Crown agencies varies, but is much smaller than with departments. The personnel of departments are generally recruited by the Public Service Commission, while those of agencies are not. Departments have deputy ministers as administrative heads, while agencies vary widely in the nature of their management. They usually have boards of directors, led by chairs, commissioners or directors.

TABLE 10.1   DEPARTMENTAL AND AGENCY STRUCTURE OF THE PUBLIC SERVICE, 2000

Departments
Agriculture and Agri-Food
Canadian Heritage
Citizenship and Immigration
Environment
Fisheries and Oceans
Foreign Affairs and International Trade
Health
Human Resources Development
Indian Affairs and Northern Development
Industry
Atlantic Canada Opportunities Agency
Federal Office of Regional Development — Québec
Western Economic Diversification
Justice
Labour
National Defence
National Revenue
Natural Resources
Public Works and Government Services
Solicitor-General
Transport
Veterans Affairs
Central Agencies
Finance
Privy Council Office
Treasury Board Secretariat

Crown Corporations

One specific organizational form under the Crown agency rubric in the federal bureaucracy is the Crown corporation. A **Crown corporation** is a semi-autonomous government agency organized in the corporate form to perform a task or group of related tasks in the national interest. The *Financial Administration Act* (FAA) sets out the financial relationship between different types of Crown corporations and the federal government. It classifies Crown corporations according to their main functions and degree of financial autonomy.

The variety of Crown corporations is immense. The Bank of Canada regulates the money supply, the Royal Mint prints money, and the Canada Mortgage and Housing Corporation guarantees housing loans. Transportation Crown corporations include VIA Rail Canada, Canada Ports Corporation and the St. Lawrence Seaway Authority. Economic development is fostered by the Canadian Wheat Board, Export Development Corporation, Farm Credit Corporation and the Federal Development Bank. National integration is aided by the Canada Post Corporation, the Canadian Broadcasting Corporation and the National Film Board.

In recent years, the government has privatized many Crown corporations. Those corporations that could operate in a competitive environment have been the first to go. Among those no longer with the government are the well-known Air Canada, El Dorado Nuclear, Northern Transportation Company, Polymer Corporation, Teleglobe Canada and Petro Canada. (See Chapter 14.)

Regulatory Agencies

Regulation is "the imposition of constraints, backed by government authority, that are intended to modify economic behaviour of individuals in the private sector significantly."[7] A list of the important regulatory agencies includes, for example, the Atomic Energy Control Board, Canadian Labour Relations Board, Canadian Pension Commission, Canadian Radio-television and Telecommunications Commission (CRTC), and many others.

Among other functions, regulatory agencies may be required by government to influence private or corporate behaviour with respect to prices and tariffs, supply, market entry and conditions of service, product content, and methods of production. Furthermore, some agencies have developed quasi-legislative powers that permit them to formulate general rules applicable to all cases under consideration; an example is the "Canadian content" regulations applied by the CRTC. Most agencies also enjoy investigative powers, allowing them to undertake research and pursue inquiries within their field of competence.

Independent regulatory agencies receive their major powers from enabling legislation that also sets out the agency objectives. Commission members are appointed by the governor-in-council, usually for terms of five to ten years. On the whole, the chair and members of the commission are patronage appointments. Most agencies are subject to ministerial directives, but ministers usually are unwilling to infringe upon the traditional arm's-length relationship. Regulatory bodies are required to submit their budgets to the Treasury Board for review (and usually, also, to the Auditor-General), and to present annual reports, through the responsible minister, to Parliament.

Reproduced by permission, John Beutel, cartoonist for Crown Corp/Private Enterprise.

Advisory Bodies

Federal departments and Crown agencies are designed to deal primarily with implementing and administering government policies. **Advisory bodies** are federal organizations whose activities are closely related to the formulation of public policies. They include royal commissions, government and departmental task forces and advisory councils.[8]

---

7. Economic Council of Canada, *Interim Report: Responsible Regulations*, p. xi.
8. "Governmental" task forces should not be confused with the "special committees" of the House of Commons.

Royal commissions and task forces are widely employed by the executive as sources of public policy advice. They are generally set up by the government to investigate an area of critical public concern and to recommend a suitable course of action. Typical issues have included the economy (the Macdonald Royal Commission on the Economic Union and Development Prospects for Canada), cultural policy (the Applebaum-Hébert Federal Cultural Policy Review Committee), Native peoples (the Royal Commission on Aboriginal Issues) and human reproduction (the Royal Commission on Reproductive Technologies).

Such bodies attempt to encourage wide public understanding of serious national problems and at the same time to provide an informed basis for future policy-making by the government. They generally solicit outside views through public hearings, to which individuals, groups and organizations submit briefs. They also initiate programs of directed and commissioned research. Most of the time they have no direct policy impact, although they may contribute to the debate about issues. Government inquiries can be very expensive. The two most expensive in the 1990s have been the Royal Commission on Aboriginal Peoples and the Royal Commission on New Reproductive Technologies.

Semi-Independent Agencies

As well as privatization, governments have tried to introduce other "business efficiency" practices into the government. One organizational device has been to create semi-independent agencies *inside* the public service. Two examples suffice to explain this organizational form. First, listed under ministerial authority, but given considerable independence from that person's control, are operational institutions such as the RCMP, the Canadian Security Intelligence Service (CSIS), Statistics Canada, the Public Service Commission, Elections Canada and the National Archives.

Second, special operating agencies (SOAs) have been set up to promote "arm's-length" relationships between departments and "special units" inside the departments. These SOAs are responsible to the department's deputy minister, but because they operate on a cost-recovery basis, they function independently and almost on a commercial basis. The best-known example is the Passport Office, inside the Department of Foreign Affairs and International Trade, which receives its funds by charging the public directly for passports and visas.

Principles and Linkages: Ministers and Deputy Ministers

An inventory of the main organizational forms within the Canadian federal bureaucracy illustrates the diversity of bureaucratic structures but does not provide a complete picture of the way the bureaucracy operates. One also requires an appreciation of the basic principles on which the bureaucracy is organized as well as of the various linkages that exist, first, among different structures within the bureaucracy and, second, between the bureaucracy and the more overtly political institutions of Cabinet and Parliament.

The chief organizing principle of the bureaucracy is the concept of **departmentalization**, whereby, at least in theory, every administrative function in the federal government is allocated to a single government department. Two reasons may be cited for a clear apportionment of duties among government departments or agencies: it avoids financial waste and administrative confusion; and it helps to clarify lines of accountability for administrative actions, and thus strengthens another principle of bureaucratic organization in Canada — ministerial responsibility and accountability.

The allocation of duties to government departments may be based on one or more of the following criteria: common purpose, clientele, territory or place, expertise, process. Thus, for example, the Department of Veterans Affairs caters to a specific clientele. So, too, in part does the Department of Indian Affairs and Northern Development, although that ministry's traditional responsibility for overseeing the administration of government in Yukon and the Northwest Territories has also been based on the criterion of "place." The Department of Public Works and Government Services is organized according to the use of common facilities — "process" — in acting as a publishing house for much of the federal government.

In many cases, however, these organizational criteria and the activities of individual departments do not correspond. Consequently, different organizational criteria force some departments to pursue internally contradictory goals. In the case of the Department of Indian Affairs and Northern Development cited above, it has been argued that the function of protecting and enhancing the interest and way of life of Native peoples in the North is irreconcilable with the objective of promoting northern resource development.

The processes of policy-making and conflict resolution within and between government departments and agencies are often referred to as **bureaucratic politics**. This term is usually associated with the work of Graham Allison, who argued that the conventional model of foreign policy decision-making, the so-called "rational actor"

CLOSE-UP ON Institutions

DEPARTMENTAL NAMES REFLECT VALUES AND BIASES

The names of federal departments often reflect the values and biases of the government. This is particularly evident in the department dealing with immigration. Since Confederation it has been called:

Canadian Immigration and Quarantine Services — 1867–92

Immigration Branch, Department of the Interior — 1892–1917

Department of Immigration and Colonization — 1917–36

Immigration Branch, Department of Mines and Resources — 1936–50

Department of Citizenship and Immigration — 1950–66

Department of Manpower and Immigration — 1966–77

Canada Employment and Immigration Commission — 1977–93

Immigration divided between Department of Public Security and the Department of Human Resources — 1993

Department of Citizenship and Immigration — 1993 to present

model, did not adequately explain the actions of policy-makers in the 1962 Cuban Missile Crisis. The rational-actor model suggests that government is effectively a unitary, monolithic actor, with a single set of goals or objectives, which selects from a range of alternatives the policy that best serves its perception of the national interest. Allison contended instead that the policy decisions in the Missile Crisis might better be explained by the "bureaucratic politics" model, which assumes that government consists of a variety of individuals, groups and agencies pursuing divergent interests and policy goals, and competing to have their respective values and objectives supported in the final policy outcome.[9] (See Chapter 14.)

Clearly, the Canadian federal bureaucracy is far from being a homogeneous, monolithic entity. The diversity of structural forms found in departments and agencies, the different philosophies of policy-making and administration that develop in each agency, the periodic conflicts that arise between agencies with regard to policy objectives, jurisdictions and modes of implementation — all suggest that the Canadian bureaucracy is relatively pluralistic. On the other hand, Ottawa is not in a state of anarchy. Inter-agency competition and bureaucratic infighting are not always destructive. Disputes between agencies or departments may be constrained by parameters established by Cabinet on the range of possible policy alternatives that may be considered on a particular issue. It might even be argued that bureaucratic politics has its advantages. The greater the degree of competition between agencies, the more information and alternative choices Cabinet has at its disposal in making policy decisions, the greater the extent of political control over the policy-making process.

---

9. Graham T. Allison, *Essence of Decision: Explaining the Cuban Missile Crisis* (Boston: Little, Brown, 1971).

But what control does Cabinet have over the administrative process to ensure that policies, once made, are actually implemented? The second major principle of government organization in Canada — and the primary link between the bureaucracy and the overtly political realm of Cabinet, Parliament and the people — is the doctrine of **ministerial responsibility**. The prime minister appoints members of the Cabinet to assume responsibility for particular ministries or portfolios, and their associated departments, commissions, boards and corporations. Ministers are constitutionally responsible for all of the operations of their departments. Thus, legally, it is ministers who are assigned the powers and duties to be exercised by their departments. Departmental officials, on the other hand, are given scant attention in the law and are responsible exclusively to their ministers, not to Parliament. They are supposed to be non-partisan, objective and anonymous — shielded from the glare of public attention and from the partisan political arena of Parliament by their minister — in order to safeguard their neutrality and ensure their ability to serve faithfully whichever government is in power. In the event of a serious error in the formulation or administration of policy within a department, convention dictates that the minister, rather than officials, be held responsible to Parliament; if the minister cannot account for failures to the satisfaction of Parliament, then convention dictates that the minister should resign.

Experience has shown, however, that there are severe limitations to the actual realization of the doctrine of ministerial responsibility.[10] The individual responsibility of ministers for the operations of their departments is often sacrificed in favour of another principle or responsibility — the **collective responsibility** of the Cabinet to Parliament. Unless political expediency dictates otherwise, as long as a minister retains the confidence and support of the prime minister, that minister is extremely unlikely to be asked to resign. Another problem stems from the fact that ministers cannot be held personally responsible for administrative matters that occurred before their current appointments. Thus, when questions were raised in the House of Commons in the late 1970s about RCMP wrongdoings, the Solicitor General took refuge behind this convention, saying that the events had taken place prior to his appointment; furthermore, the three former Solicitor Generals sitting in the House could not be called to account for the activities of a department for which they were no longer the minister.

Perhaps it is reasonable that ministers not be held responsible to the point of resignation for the administrative errors of public servants. The relative impermanence of Cabinet ministers and their multifunctional roles make it impossible for ministers to involve themselves extensively in the management of their departments. Ministers are expected to direct their attention to policy matters rather than to the details of departmental administration. For this reason, one observer argues, it is "unrealistic to expect a minister to accept personal responsibility for all the acts of his departmental officials. Why should a minister 'carry the can' when he has little or no knowledge of its contents?"[11]

If Cabinet ministers cannot, will not or should not be held responsible to Parliament for the administrative functioning of their departments, then who can? The Lambert Commission proposed that "the minister's responsibility must be shared with the deputy [minister], who should be accountable to Parliament through the Public Accounts Committee as the chief administrative officer

10. Sharon Sutherland, "Responsible Government and Ministerial Responsibility," *CJPS*, vol. 24, no. 1 (March 1991), pp. 91–120, and "The Al-Mashat Affair: Administrative Responsibility in Parliamentary Institutions," *Canadian Public Administration* (Winter 1991), pp. 573–603.

11. Kenneth Kernaghan, "Power, Parliament and Public Servants in Canada: Ministerial Responsibility Re-examined," in H.D. Clarke et al., eds., *Parliament, Policy and Representation* (Toronto: Methuen, 1980), p. 128.

for the day-to-day operations which are, in practical terms, beyond the minister's control."[12] This recommendation is suspect in that it reflects adherence to the distinction between policy matters and administrative tasks, which is at best fuzzy and at worst likely to distort an understanding of the role of the bureaucracy. Moreover, the Commission may well have underestimated the extent to which some ministers seek to participate in the internal administration of their departments, while others seek to deflect criticism to the deputy minister and deny responsibility for policy failures.[13] Although sound reasons exist for re-evaluating the doctrine of ministerial responsibility, there appears to be little point in adding to existing ambiguities surrounding the role of the deputy minister.

If the minister is the key link between the bureaucracy and Cabinet for the purposes of formal political accountability, the role of the **deputy minister** is equally crucial to effective administration and the coordination and direction of policy implementation. Certain financial and managerial responsibilities are laid down by the *Financial Administration Act* and the *Public Service Employment Act*, or are delegated to the DM by the Treasury Board and the Public Service Commission. Otherwise, the DM possesses only that power that the minister chooses to delegate. In fact, the *Interpretation Act* indicates that ministers may delegate any and all of their powers under the law to their deputies, except for the power to make regulations and, of course, their parliamentary duties. Exactly how much a minister chooses to delegate is a personal decision.

The main function of the deputy minister, outside the administrative responsibilities of managing the department, is to act as the minister's chief source of non-partisan advice on public policy. The problem for the DM is how to initiate policy proposals and studies without appearing to undermine the ultimate policy-making responsibility of the minister. In their policy-advisory roles, deputies must strike a delicate balance between political sensitivity and bureaucratic objectivity — especially when they are led by their experience and expertise to disagree with policies put forward by the minister. In such cases, the DM may stress the potential difficulties of implementing the policy.

Deputy ministers are appointed by the governor-in-council on the recommendation of the prime minister. Their office is held "during pleasure," which means that they can be dismissed or transferred at any time without assigned cause and that they are not protected by the provisions of the *Public Service Employment Act*. This insecurity of tenure naturally creates further ambiguity about the role of the deputy minister. Deputies who advise against "damn silly decisions" risk being viewed as obstacles to the government in pursuit of its partisan political objectives and being removed. On the other hand, deputies who are perceived as successful in administering certain government policies may become identified with programs unpopular with the opposition and, therefore, risk losing their jobs when the reins of government change hands. The principle of "rotation in office," whereby deputy ministers and other senior public servants are replaced with each change of government, is not as widely accepted in Canada as in, for example, the United States. The political neutrality and relative permanence of deputy ministers is viewed as both a safeguard against a return to political patronage and partisan bureaucracy and as a source of continuity in administration amid political changes.

The Canadian federal bureaucracy is an extremely complex and diverse organization whose historical development reflects constant tension between the competing demands of democracy and efficiency. The fragmentation of the bureaucracy into many departments and Crown agencies

12. Royal Commission on Financial Management and Accountability, *Final Report* (Ottawa: Minister of Supply and Services, 1979), p. 57.
13. See Paul Thomas, "The Lambert Report: Parliament and Accountability," *CPA*, vol. 22, no. 4 (Winter 1979), esp. pp. 561–62.

in the interests of efficiency somewhat impedes policy coordination. At the same time, the principle of departmentalization underlies the doctrine of ministerial responsibility that, ideally, should enhance the democratic process by providing a line of accountability to Parliament and the people. And between the Cabinet and the great mass of the bureaucracy, the deputy ministers and other senior officials play key pivotal roles. They not only advise their respective ministers on how best to serve the interests of the people and attempt to ensure the efficient management and functioning of their own departments, but also play an important part in the coordination of policy advice and effective policy implementation throughout the bureaucracy as a whole.

THE PUBLIC SERVICE

While "bureaucracy" refers to the structures and principles of organization in the administrative arm of government, the **public service** is the collective term in Canada for the personnel employed in those structures. Like other political institutions described in this book, the public service of Canada has undergone many profound changes since Confederation. It has evolved from a loosely organized, patronage-based service in which most people were recruited on the basis of political connections to a modern professionalized bureaucracy appointed on the principle of merit; from a predominantly anglophone and almost exclusively male preserve to an equal opportunity employer that consciously attempts to reflect Canada's ethnic and linguistic diversity and that has introduced affirmative action programs designed to promote the participation of women, indigenous peoples, visible minorities and disabled persons.

The hierarchical structure fosters a definitive chain of responsibility within the bureaucracy. Within each department a descending order of command is evident, with each employee responsible to a superior. This chain of command, which ultimately begins with a government minister, protects against the arbitrary assumption of power by individuals within the bureaucracy. Bureaucratic "red tape" in the guise of standard forms and triplicate copies is in fact a necessary part of the process of horizontal and vertical communication among employees and departments. Given the immense number of people involved and the diversity of their duties, it is easy to appreciate why the bureaucracy's primary goal of efficiency is sometimes difficult to achieve.

Basic Principles of the Public Service

Since 1867, the federal public service has gone through many major transitions. At Confederation, appointment to the civil service was based exclusively on political patronage. The *Civil Service Act* of 1908 began to replace patronage with the merit principle. The **merit principle** is actually based on two interrelated ideas: first, that all Canadian citizens "should have a reasonable opportunity to be considered for employment in the public service"; and, second, that selection must be based "exclusively on merit, or fitness to do the job."[14] The Act also created the Civil Service Commission (CSC) to enforce the merit principle in the recruitment and promotion of government employees. The 1918 *Civil Service Act* extended the method of appointment by competitive examination to the entire service and re-emphasized the role of the CSC in enforcing implementation of the merit principle. Over the next four decades the CSC had considerable success.

---

14. R.H. Dowdell, "Public Personnel Administration," in Kenneth Kernaghan, ed., *Public Administration in Canada: Selected Readings*, 3rd ed. (Toronto: Methuen, 1977), p. 196.

The *Civil Service Act* of 1961 came about largely as an effort to resolve a power struggle over common areas of responsibility that had built up between the CSC and the Treasury Board. The Act gave the Treasury Board sole responsibility for pay determination and administrative organization. In 1967, two acts were passed that further affected the role of the CSC and permitted it to become a more specialized staffing body. The *Public Service Staff Relations Act* created a collective-bargaining regime in the public service with the power to enter into collective agreements in the name of the government. Responsibility for classification, pay determination and most conditions of employment rested with the Treasury Board. The *Public Service Employment Act* gave the renamed Public Service Commission (PSC) ultimate responsibility for all elements of the staffing process and staff training, especially language training. Today, the PSC reports to Parliament, not to the executive, a status that permits it independence in investigating complaints and hearing appeals against the government. However, its independent status is somewhat compromised by the fact that the three PSC commissioners are appointed for a set term by Cabinet.

According to the **merit principle**, all appointments to, and promotions within, the public service are to be based on ability to do the job, in the interest of creating a qualified and efficient public service. But the role of the Public Service Commission in implementing government directives to promote participation by under-represented groups has threatened to compromise its application of the merit principle. This is not a new issue in public service staffing. Both the 1918 and the 1961 *Civil Service Acts* entrenched absolute preference in hiring for war veterans. Then, following the passage of the *Official Languages Act* of 1969, which required the provision of minority-language services in areas where numbers warranted, the designation of many public service positions as bilingual brought accusations of "reverse discrimination" and "contravention of the merit principle" from unilingual employees and from public service unions.[15]

The *Public Service Employment Act* forbids discrimination in hiring or promotion on the basis of "race, national or ethnic origin, colour, religion, age, sex, marital status, disability, or conviction for an offence for which a pardon has been granted." However, certain groups have remained persistently under-represented in the public service, especially in senior positions. To address this, the PSC in 1983 introduced a service-wide affirmative action program. Affirmative action should not automatically be equated with quota systems or negative discrimination. Much of the affirmative action program is oriented toward education, training and career counselling, rather than toward providing special treatment in hiring or promotion. The PSC insists that the affirmative action program implemented in 1983 does not conflict with merit, which requires that only qualified persons be appointed. The fact that the Commission justifies its programs in such terms reveals its sensitivity to potential criticisms that affirmative action might "unwisely and unnecessarily undermine the merit system of recruitment and promotion and the efficiency of the public service."[16]

In 1989, the government set up *Public Service 2000* in an attempt to reorganize the public service to make it more service-oriented and reduce morale problems caused by fiscal restraint.[17] This new set of proposals to streamline public service practices was incorporated into the *Public Service Reform Act, 1992*, which constituted the first major amendments to staffing legislation in 25 years. Bill C26 provided for more flexible staffing arrangements and mandated the PSC to initiate employment equity programs while retaining the merit principle. (For greater detail, see Chapter 14.)

15. See P.K. Kuruvilla, "Bilingualism in the Canadian Federal Public Service," in Kernaghan, *Public Administration in Canada*.
16. One of the potential criticisms reported but dismissed by P.K. Kuruvilla in "Still Too Few Women," *Policy Options*, vol. 4, no. 3 (May/June 1983), p. 55.
17. Canada, *Public Service 2000* (Ottawa: Supply and Services, 1990).

Profile of the Public Service

The federal government is a major employer in Canada. In 1999, it employed under half a million people. These employees are spread throughout the country and work in the public service, military, corporations, agencies, enterprises and the Royal Canadian Mounted Police. In the discussion of the characteristics of public servants that follows, we refer only to those employed under the auspices of the Public Service Commission or the narrowly defined public service. In 1999, these totalled 186 314 persons, considerably fewer than the 225 056 public servants it employed in 1981. As a result of program review, the public service declined 17.4 percent from 1994 to 1999.[18]

Entrance into the public service is open and carries no restrictions on age, race, sex, religion, colour, national or ethnic origin, marital status or disability. Recruitment is carried out across Canada on the basis of merit. Qualifications are determined through an entrance exam, the results of which determine the applicant's capabilities and job placement. Recruitment programs are sponsored by the Public Service Commission. Since the *Public Service Reform Act, 1992,* the PSC has continued to base its employment practices on merit, but it may initiate employment equity plans to right historical imbalances for designated groups, which include women, aboriginal peoples, persons with disabilities and those from visible minorities.

Competition and appeal procedures ensure that virtually every employee can elevate his or her status. When a position is created or becomes vacant, it is advertised. Depending upon the job, the competition is "open" (available to candidates from both within and outside the public service) or "closed" (available only to those already in the public sector). Once a suitable candidate has been selected, the appeal procedure allows complaints and criticisms against the appointment to be formally voiced and a board is convened to consider the appeal. The PSC prides itself on this procedure, which in combination with the competition process provides an assurance of unbiased hiring and promotion practices.

To some extent, the bureaucracy is expected to be representative of the society it serves. Yet factors such as region, religion, ethnicity, social class, education, language and gender render Canada a highly heterogeneous society, a situation that might hinder egalitarian representation. In what follows, we outline and assess the composition of the public service with reference to some of these factors in order to illuminate the patterns of employment found in the bureaucracy.

Regional and Language Distribution

It is commonly assumed that most federal employees work in Ottawa or, more properly, in the National Capital Region (NCR). However, this is inaccurate, as only about one-third are located in the NCR. Approximately 34 percent of all federal employees are located in the NCR as of 1999. Based on earlier statistics, we can see that Ontario and Québec have 63 percent of all public servants — their approximate share of the total Canadian population. A further 17 percent of public servants are based in the Atlantic provinces; about 24 percent work in the western provinces, Yukon and Northwest Territories, and outside Canada. In relation to regional populations, this means that the Atlantic area has rather more than its fair share of federal employees, while the West is slightly under-represented. By and large, these figures reflect the success of a deliberate attempt by the federal government to decentralize the bureaucracy away from Ontario in general and the NCR in particular. Operational personnel continue to reside mostly outside the NCR, whereas most policy-makers reside in the Ottawa region.

---

18. Unless otherwise acknowledged, figures relating to public service employees are drawn from the annual reports of the Public Service Commission or the Treasury Board Secretariat's 1999 report on public service enlargement.

The early failure to acknowledge the French fact in Canada has been seen by some commentators as the most damning indictment of the recruitment methods of the public service. However, it is important to note the recent importance of "bilingualization" in the public service.

Prior to 1918, at least adequate francophone representation was assured by patronage appointments made by French-speaking Cabinet ministers. But with the rationalization of the bureaucracy on the basis of merit, no procedure evolved to replace the patronage system's assurance of adequate representation based on language. The majority of the public service tended to define "merit" and "efficiency" in accordance with its own cultural and educational values; the result was that "with few francophones in the guiding councils of the public service, its explicit qualifications and implicit assumptions tended to become more unfavourable to francophones."[19]

Thus, while in 1918, 22 percent of government employees were French-speaking, by 1936 only 20 percent were,[20] and, by 1945, the figure was only 12 percent. In 1965, only 5 percent of senior executives appointed by the Public Service Commission were French, while 16.5 percent of political appointees to the bureaucracy were francophone. It was only in the 1960s, after the Glassco Report and the Bilingualism and Biculturalism Report, that there was widespread recognition of the need to increase francophone representation in the federal government. In reaction, a tendency developed to "parachute" French-speakers into top-level political appointments in the bureaucracy.

Many factors combined during these years to reduce levels of francophone recruitment in the federal bureaucracy. The public service became less attractive for French Canadians because no provisions were made to ensure service to French Canadians. Nor were francophones' bilingual skills included in an assessment of their qualifications. Francophones were also hindered by the merit system's examinations and interviews, which reflected the patterns of thought and cultural style of English-speaking Canada. The competitions also emphasized the technical and commercial skills taught in the English educational system, placing French Canadians, with their classical education, at a disadvantage. It is sometimes argued that it is because of this "unsuitable" education that French Canada did not produce the type of administrator who could be used in the public service.

In finally assuming responsibility for language training in the late 1960s, the Public Service Commission found itself at the centre of one of the most significant transformations ever attempted in the bureaucracy. The Commission was directed to aid the government in achieving full and equal participation of anglophones and francophones in the public service while preserving the merit principle in recruitment and promotion.

Progress is slowly being made toward this goal. The percentage of francophone employees in the public service has increased, so that now participation is more comparable to their distribution in the national population: by 1994, their numbers had already increased to 28 percent of all public servants. However, closer examination of the distribution of anglophones and francophones within the public service shows that French-speaking Canadians are still relatively disadvantaged. Francophones are somewhat under-represented in the executive group category of employment, and somewhat over-represented in the administrative support group. Thus, while there is still room for improvement, especially at higher salary levels and ranks, the federal public service is gradually becoming more representative of the official language composition of the Canadian population.

---

19. From the Report of the Royal Commission on Bilingualism and Biculturalism as quoted in Vincent Seymour Wilson, *Staffing in the Canadian Federal Bureaucracy* (Kingston, Ont.: Queen's University, unpublished Ph.D. dissertation, 1970), p. 244.
20. Hodgetts et al., *The Biography of an Institution*, p. 473.

Women and Equity-Designated Groups

If the federal government is to be congratulated for creating a public service more representative of Canada's two main language communities, it has little reason for complacency with regard to its representation of the gender division in Canadian society. Although the federal government is Canada's largest single employer of women, they have long faced both institutional and attitudinal barriers to advancement, which are only slowly being broken down by more sensitive recruitment, training and affirmative action programs.[21]

Discrimination against women in the bureaucracy was officially endorsed in varying degrees until 1967. In direct contradiction of the merit principle, anti-female prejudice was built into the very fabric of civil service legislation and personnel practice.[22] As early as 1908, the CSC admitted that "there are women who have as good executive ability as men, and who might, on the *mere* ground of personal qualifications, fill the higher positions in the service.[23]

In order to "protect the merit principle from itself," deputy heads were instructed to segregate occupational categories into male and female groups, with women being limited to the lowest clerical levels. Since inequality of opportunity thus became a foregone conclusion, and women were not given access to middle-level positions, the issue of equal pay for equal work could not arise. As Kathleen Archibald points out, this occupational sex-typing of jobs was later used as "evidence" to

Reproduced with permission, Dennis Pritchard.

---

21. On institutional and attitudinal barriers to female employees, see the critical review by Kuruvilla, "Still Too Few Women," pp. 54–55.

22. Hodgetts et al., *The Biography of an Institution*, p. 483.

23. Ibid., p. 485 (emphasis in original).

show why women were not capable of filling higher executive positions.[24] In the 1918 *Civil Service Act*, gender was mentioned as a "limiting" factor on an individual's qualifications, and in 1921 formal restrictions were placed on employing married women.

Over the next five decades, the concentration of women in the lower white-collar ranks provided the CSC with a cheap labour supply. During the Second World War, however, it became the patriotic duty of women to fill "male" jobs, so that while in 1938 only 17 percent of public service appointees were female, by 1943 this figure had risen to 65 percent. With the enforcement of the "veterans' preference" in 1946 the proportion of female appointees was halved, and restrictions were once again placed on employing married women.

FIGURE 10.1   HIRING OF WOMEN 1988, 1995, 1997 AND 1998 (PERCENTAGE SHARE)

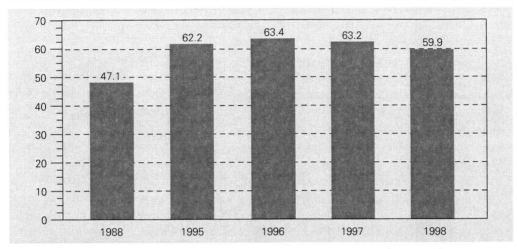

Source: Treasury Board Secretariat, *Annual Report: Employment Equity in the Federal Public Service 1997–98.*

FIGURE 10.2   PROMOTION OF WOMEN 1988, 1995, 1996, 1997 AND 1998 (PERCENTAGE SHARE)

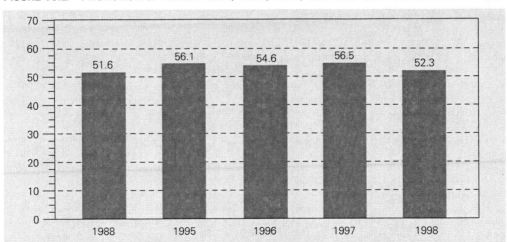

Source: Treasury Board Secretariat, *Annual Report: Employment Equity in the Federal Public Service 1997–98.*

24. Kathleen Archibald, *Sex and the Public Service: A Report to the Public Service Commission of Canada* (Ottawa: Queen's Printer, 1970), pp. 18–23.

In 1955, when one-third of all Canadian working women were married, the CSC finally lifted restrictions on their appointment. The 1950s also witnessed the appointment of the first female Civil Service Commissioner, Ruth Addison. But it was only with the promulgation of the 1967 *Public Service Employment Act* that "sex" was added to "race, national origin, colour and creed" as grounds upon which an individual could not be discriminated against.

The federal administration's position on sex discrimination may be altered legally; but the actual situation of women in the bureaucracy is little improved. While women have constituted an increasingly larger percentage of public servants over time, they are still under-represented in the highest-paid groups in the public service. Effective segregation by occupational category still occurs. In 1995–99, 84.1 percent of the Administrative Support category recruitments were women who tended to be concentrated in traditional job ghettos within administrative support, serving as clerks, secretaries, stenographers and typists. In the executive group category, on the other hand, while their numbers have certainly increased, women are still seriously under-represented in proportion to their total employment in the public service.

There are signs of improvement in the position of women in the public service. As of 1999, women constitute 50.5 percent of all public servants. Nevertheless, current lines of occupational segregation must be broken down if women are to achieve genuine equality of opportunity in the bureaucracy. While the just application of the merit principle might permit women to increase their representation gradually in the long term, in the short term there is a clear need for the public service to commit seriously to continued and expanded affirmative action programs. It appears this has been taking place—see Figures 10.1 and 10.2.

The question of fairness for other historically deprived groups in Canada is a hot topic. Following the *Public Service Reform Act, 1992*, the PSC inaugurated several new programs to improve the recruitment of aboriginal peoples, persons with disabilities and members of minority groups. There has been some improvement. In the executive group — i.e., senior management — the numbers are still small, but at lower levels, there has been more rapid progress. Figures 10.3–10.5 show the hiring and promotion of aboriginal peoples, persons with disabilities, and visible minorities.

FIGURE 10.3   MINORITY-DESIGNATED GROUPS IN THE FEDERAL PUBLIC SERVICE: ABORIGINAL PEOPLES 1988, 1996 AND 1998 (PERCENTAGE SHARE)

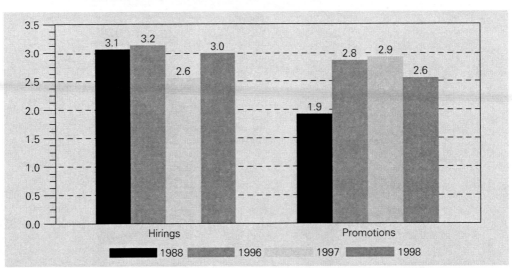

Source: Treasury Board Secretariat, *Annual Report: Employment Equity in the Federal Public Service 1997–98.*

FIGURE 10.4   MINORITY-DESIGNATED GROUPS IN THE FEDERAL PUBLIC SERVICE: PERSONS WITH
DISABILITIES 1988, 1996 AND 1998 (PERCENTAGE SHARE)

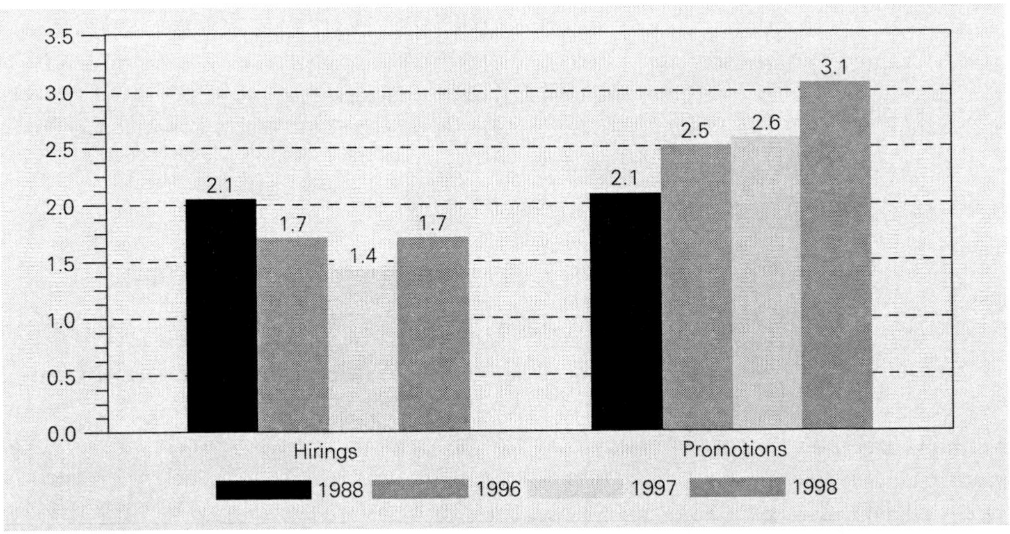

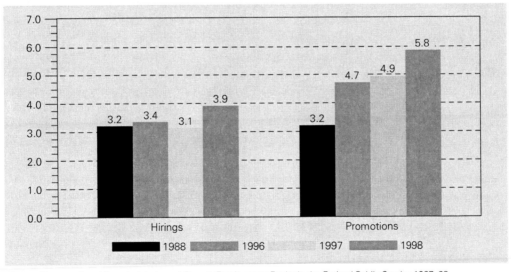

Source: Treasury Board Secretariat, *Annual Report: Employment Equity in the Federal Public Service 1997–98.*

FIGURE 10.5   MINORITY-DESIGNATED GROUPS IN THE FEDERAL PUBLIC SERVICE: VISIBLE
MINORITIES 1988, 1996 AND 1998 (PERCENTAGE SHARE)

Source: Treasury Board Secretariat, *Annual Report: Employment Equity in the Federal Public Service 1997–98.*

In summary, the Canadian public service has, over the last half century, become more representative of the society it serves. There has been an increased sensitivity to the under-representation of francophones, women and other historically disadvantaged groups in the bureaucracy. At the same time, more readily available university education helped to enhance opportunities for the appointment and advancement of individuals from middle- and lower-class backgrounds.

In recent years, the government has made drastic cuts in the public service. Because of the continued high debt of the federal government, the Liberal government announced in its 1995 budget that it would lay off 45 000, or 14 percent, of these public employees by 1998 and began reducing the overall size of the public sector. Some jobs were transferred to the private sector, and early retirement incentives and cash-based payouts were used to eliminate public servant positions. In order to carry out its plan, the government had to pass legislation to rescind the Work Force Adjustment Directive, which guaranteed job security to public servants.

BUREAUCRATS AND BUDGETS: DEFICITS AND DEBTS

If the general public has a single, dominant image of the federal bureaucracy, it is perhaps that of a rather large *drain* down which their hard-earned tax dollars are poured. In one sense, this view is not entirely inaccurate. No government can govern without spending money. But, since most of the money expended by government finds its way back into the Canadian economy, boosting the demand for goods and services, the drain might be as accurately described as a *well* that in many periods of Canadian history has helped to irrigate the economy, providing a stimulus to economic growth.

This having been said, the government is also responsible to Parliament and to the Canadian taxpayer for ensuring that there is not too much seepage from the well. Consequently, a major focus of political and administrative reform over the past quarter-century has been the search for increased efficiency in government spending and greater control over it. During this period, the federal government has gone through several different expenditure/budgetary systems to arrive at the current restraint process. In the sections that follow, we briefly examine the budgetary process, and discuss the efficacy of some of the techniques introduced to monitor public spending.

The Canadian government spends a large amount of taxpayers' money. The federal main estimates (proposed expenditures) for 1999–2000 totalled $156.7 billion.[25] Of this figure, interest payments on the public debt consumed 28 percent, payments to other levels of government 13 percent, and major transfers to individuals (including the unemployed, elderly and veterans) 24 percent. (See Figure 10.6.) The remainder went to pay Crown corporations and operating costs in such fields as justice and legal affairs and industrial, regional, scientific and technological departments.

The Canadian budget, or management of the overall revenue and expenditures on an annual basis, entails two separate processes. This runs contrary to the budgetary practices of some political systems (which are not British parliamentary in origin) and to those of private businesses, where budgets present detailed targets for both spending and revenues.

The budget and its proposals are released only after lengthy preparation. Preliminary discussions are held in the Department of Finance to fix an approximate level of expenditures for the fiscal year and an estimate of revenues expected to be realized from existing tax rates. From these two estimates — expenditure and revenue — emerges a surplus or a deficit. In recent years, the government has always had to borrow money by issuing securities to finance its deficits. The recent accounts show

CLOSE-UP ON Definitions

KEY FINANCIAL TERMS

Deficit: The annual amount by which government spending exceeds revenues.

Debt: The accumulation of annual deficits less surpluses since Confederation.

---

25. Government of Canada, *Budget Plan*, February 16, 1999.

FIGURE 10.6   FEDERAL GOVERNMENT EXPENDITURES BY TYPE OF PAYMENT, 1999–2000
($154 BILLLION)

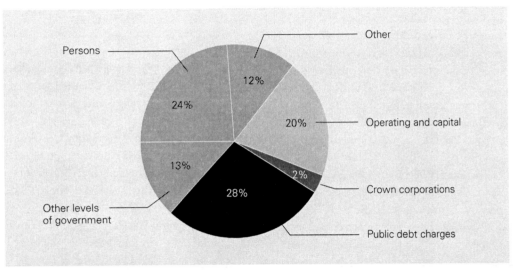

Source: Adapted from *Estimates*, 1999–2000.

that the government raised $156.7 billion in revenue but had $111.2 billion in program expenditures. It therefore had to pay $42.5 billion in debt-servicing charges in 1999–2000.

The Minister of Finance receives an analysis of the economic situation and outlook from departmental officials. These are supplemented by information from the Governor of the Bank of Canada on general economic conditions, conditions in the money markets, monetary policy and the market's capacity to absorb government bonds. Analysis of this information indicates the appropriate budget surplus or deficit and, in the latter event, the size of deficit that can be financed. All of this information contributes to the government's overall fiscal strategy.

In matters of taxation, departmental officials advise the minister of tax loopholes that may be closed, tax reform proposals made by external sources and possible changes to the customs tariff. From these discussions a general pattern of taxation policy emerges. Costs of tax reduction and revenues from tax increases are totalled and compared with the estimates and the desired fiscal stance. The road is then clear to begin drafting the Budget Speech. At this point, the Finance Minister also begins consulting various groups. In 1994, Finance Minister Paul Martin Jr. held pre-budget conferences across the country, and in 1995, the Commons Finance Committee also toured the country and reported to the minister before the budget was delivered. Finance ministers sometimes spring the budget on the Cabinet at the last possible moment before Budget Day. Recently, there has been a strong tendency to undertake more lengthy consultation both outside and inside Cabinet.

The actual address and the debate are regulated by the Standing Orders of the House of Commons. The Budget Speech is often delivered in the evening after the markets have closed. The speech reviews the fiscal plan, the state of the national economy and the financial operations of the government over the past fiscal year, and provides a forecast of spending requirements for the year ahead, taking into account the estimates. At the end of the Budget Speech, the minister tables the ways-and-means motions that become the taxation or excise legislation.

In recent years, there has been considerable debate about the dire state of the federal government's finances. The biggest fear has been that Canada might get into a "debt spiral," with the national debt growing faster than the economy. Minister of Finance Paul Martin forecast a deficit (revenue minus expenditures) of $23 billion for 1996–97. This figure is added to the accumulated net public debt of earlier years to arrive at a predicted total federal debt for the end of 1997 of $602.7 billion, or 74.8 percent of Canada's gross domestic product (GDP). The debt-serving costs for 1996–97 consumed over a third of every tax dollar. These statistics are politically significant because the 1993 Liberal *Red Book* of electoral promises said the Chrétien government would reduce the deficit to 3 percent of GDP by 1997 and they did fulfill that commitment. (See Table 10.2.)

By the time of the 1998 budget, Finance Minister Martin was able to forecast a zero deficit and a decrease in the national debt to $583 billion, or 71 percent of the GDP — the first significant decline in the debt-to-GDP ratio for 25 years. These were all good figures for the Liberals, but not so good that they would scrap the GST. Martin admitted that his party had been wrong to make that promise because the government could not do without the revenue the GST provided. In the most recent budget of February 1999, the Liberal government announced that not only had the deficit been vanquished but that a surplus was likely. The debt as a percentage of the GDP had dropped to 63.7 percent. For details see Table 10.2.

By 2000, the government's cuts in program spending, a declining interest rate and the growing economy provided the expected budgetary surplus. The Liberals continued their 1997 pledge to spend half of any surpluses on debt reduction and half on tax cuts and increases for social policies. Figure 10.7 illustrates the amount of surplus money that theoretically may be available for expenditure in the future. The pressure on the government to cut taxes rather than spend more money is

TABLE 10.2   FEDERAL GOVERNMENT BUDGETS FOR 1998–2000 IN BILLIONS OF DOLLARS

Revenue Outlook (where government money comes from)		
	1998–99	**1999–2000**
Personal income tax	73.7	75.0
Corporate income tax	22.0	20.9
Employment insurance	19.2	18.3
Goods and Services Tax	20.6	21.6
Customs import duties	2.5	2.5
Other excise taxes	8.3	8.2
Other taxes	2.9	2.9
Total taxes	149.1	149.2
Non-tax revenue	7.5	7.5
Total budgeting revenues	156.5	156.7
Total revenues as percent of GDP	17.6	17.2
Expenditure Outlook (where government money goes)		
	1998–99	**1999–2000**
Revenue	156.5	156.7
Program spending	112.1	111.2
Public debt charges	41.4	42.5
Reserves	3.0	3.0
Deficit	0.0	0.0
Non-budgetary transactions	11.5	5.0
Financial requirements (excluding foreign exchange transactions)	11.5	5.0
Net public debt	579.7	579.9
Net public debt as percent of GDP	65.3	63.7

Source: Adapted from discussion and general tables in *Budget* (Ottawa, 1999).

immense. Fiscally conservative Liberals and the Reform party, in particular, are taking the stand that tax reduction is the highest priority for Canadians.

Essentially, governments have four options for cutting a deficit: decreasing expenditures, increasing taxes, reducing interest rates (to reduce payments on the public debt) and increasing economic growth. All governments hope for the last two outcomes, but, alas, ministers have little control in these areas due to Canada's dependence on foreign capital and the country's position in the global economy. The choice, then, is between cutting expenditures and raising taxes. After an extensive program review, the Liberals decided that to meet their deficit target they would reduce expenditures by cutting seven dollars of costs for each dollar of revenue increase. Some of the government's goal was accomplished by reducing the federal public service by more than 45 000 positions over three years, but much of it was simply the result of strong growth in the economy.

FIGURE 10.7   PROJECTED GOVERNMENT SURPLUSES 1998–2015

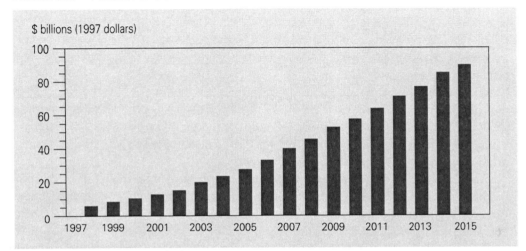

Source: Royal Bank of Canada, as published in *The Globe and Mail*, October 11, 1997.

The Two Budgetary Processes

There are two separate processes in budget deliberations. The first, the **expenditure budget process**, is centred on bringing together the estimated spending requirements of all government departments and agencies for the next fiscal year. It takes place under the watchful eye of the Treasury Board, its secretariat and a Cabinet committee. These estimates are subsequently submitted to Parliament and its committees for scrutiny and approval by means of supply (appropriations) bills (which grant the government permission to spend public funds).

The second process, the **revenue process**, concerns the means by which funds are to be raised — by taxation and other measures. It is largely the responsibility of the Departments of Finance and Revenue. Its parliamentary focal point is the Budget Speech delivered by the Minister of Finance.

Over the years, many different techniques have been attempted for the systematic handling of government budgets. One modern approach, the **Planning, Programming and Budget System (PPBS)**, was a budget system (1963–81) intended to provide a "planned" approach to government. Estimates for various departmental programs were evaluated by the Treasury Board and a new Cabinet committee on Priorities and Planning. Thus, in place of the "bottom-up" approach of the traditional expenditure budget, PPBS was supposed to be a "top-down" system, providing for a more controlled allocation of resources according to the priorities determined by Cabinet.[26]

As it happened, PPBS wasn't much more effective than its predecessors either in restraining the overall growth in government expenditures or in ensuring that funds were allocated according to Cabinet priorities. The ineffectiveness of the system was partly the result of political failures. At no time was the Cabinet able to produce a sufficiently detailed and comprehensive list of government objectives by which departmental programs could be evaluated. The PPBS experiment also suffered from the fact that departments and program managers learned quickly "how to work the system."

Amid growing criticism of the federal government's financial management, PPBS gradually faded into history. In the last months of the 1974–79 Liberal government, work was already underway on a new budget process. The **Policy and Expenditure Management System** (**PEMS**), a new expenditure budget process intended to integrate the processes of policy-making and fiscal and expenditure planning within the Cabinet committee system, came into full operation during the fiscal year 1981–82. The PEMS was designed to integrate the government's decisions on priorities and policies closely with the allocation of resources. With the introduction of the PEMS, the same Cabinet committee would set policy decisions and expenditure limits simultaneously. In addition, the new system would ensure that priorities and expenditure limits were determined before expenditure plans were developed.

The system involved the addition of two new features to the Cabinet system. First, a five-year fiscal plan was added to outline the overall financial constraints on policy choice. Second, specific expenditure limits, called "resource envelopes," were set. A department that wished to spend more money had to delete programs or convince the ministers on the appropriate Cabinet policy committee to reduce allocations elsewhere in that policy sector.

The Treasury Board remained responsible for the preparation of the **Main Estimates** (spending proposals for the upcoming fiscal year). Departmental plans were reviewed in the late fall and in February. The Main Estimates were then tabled in Parliament for the next fiscal year (April 1–March 31). At the departmental level, strategic overviews, multi-year operational plans and budget-year operational plans were made and circulated to the policy committees and central agencies as a basis for decision on departmental requests for policies, programs and funds.

It was the prime minister's Priorities and Planning Committee that determined overall government priorities, established the multi-year fiscal plan and set the size of resource envelopes. In recent years, these funding decisions were made at annual Cabinet retreats where the ministers met to develop the highlights of the government's expenditures, the budget and the Speech from the Throne.

The PEMS could, therefore, be interpreted as an attempt to strengthen collective government control over total government expenditure. This was accomplished in part by the centralization of overall limit-setting and envelope allocation in the Priorities and Planning Committee chaired by the prime minister. At the same time, the decentralization of expenditure decision-making to the sectoral policy committees was designed to enhance individual ministerial responsibility for departmental expenditure management and planning.

In summary, then, given the trying economic circumstances under which it was introduced, the Policy and Expenditure Management System could be labelled a qualified success. Among its

---

26. For a description of the key elements of the PPB system, see A.W. Johnson, "Planning, Programming, and Budgeting in Canada," *Public Administration Review*, vol. 33, no. 1 (January/February 1973), pp. 23–31.

problems was the fact that it was not a single, integrated system. By and large, it did increase both collective and individual ministerial responsibility for public spending.

However, the PEMS was not successful in restraining the escalation of public spending and government deficits. For this reason, the 1988 Conservative government decided to return to the more "politicized" model of earlier years. In 1989, Prime Minister Mulroney disbanded PEMS at the Cabinet level. Control over the relation between policy and expenditure was taken away from sectoral policy committees and given over to a triumvirate of committees — Priorities and Planning, Treasury Board and Expenditure Review. These committees would review the costs of existing programs as well as new ideas coming up from the policy committees of Cabinet. The envelope system had been set up with the assumption of rational policy-making (relating policies to expenditures) and a rising supply of funds. Set on a deficit-cutting strategy, Prime Minister Mulroney believed there would be no purpose to the "envelope system" and so it was dropped. The overall expenditure control within the public service as a whole, however, did not differ greatly from that of the PEMS.

The 1993 Liberal government of Jean Chrétien examined the expenditure system again in an effort to reduce the overall costs of government and to enhance its efficiency. In 1994, the government put in place a program review "to ensure that the government's diminished resources are directed to the highest priority requirements and to those areas where the government is best placed to deliver services."[27] This comprehensive review resulted in several policy changes and an estimated savings of approximately $17 billion over the years 1995–98.

To monitor the new expenditure goals, the Chrétien government set up a new expenditure budget process — the **Expenditure Management System** (**EMS**), still in effect. Departments no longer have access to centralized pools of government funds but instead are forced to fund any new initiatives from within their own departmental budgets. While the system is still based on multi-year planning and is program-centred, the importance of policy has changed. Priorities are driven by the imperatives of budget planning in a time of restraint. The system is now driven by the lack of financial resources. New policies are made only if they can be financed by the *re-allocation* of existing funds at the departmental level.

In line with the language of modern economics, as of April 1997 departments are required to produce **business plans** that link program performance and efficiency to the overall budgetary process. These departmental outlook statements (reports on plans and priorities and departmental performance reports) are circulated to standing committees of the House of Commons for public appraisal. (See Table 10.3.) In 1994, for the first time, the Standing Committee on Finance was involved in the pre-budget consultation process. It now reviews the business plans and the overall revenue and expenditure situation in order to advise the Minister of Finance *before* the budget is delivered.

DEMOCRATIC CONTROL OF THE BUREAUCRACY

Bureaucracy, we have said, is an organizational form ideally suited to providing an efficient means of achieving a given objective. In a parliamentary democracy such as Canada, the selection of policy objectives ought to be the task of the political executive, responsible through Parliament to the people. The bureaucracy's role, in theory, should primarily be to implement the goals chosen by politicians in the most efficient and effective way possible.

27. Government of Canada, *Budget Plan*, February 27, 1995, p. 32.

TABLE 10.3 SUPPLY PROCESS FOR MAIN AND SUPPLEMENTARY ESTIMATES

	Mar.	Apr.	May	June	Sept.	Oct.	Nov.	Dec.	Jan.	Feb.
Parliament (House of Commons and the Senate)	Standing cttees review S.E.; consider S.E. and interim supply bills	Standing cttees review S.E. and report by May 31		Supply bill debate on M.E. June 30; consider M.E. supply bills		Receives public accounts for previous fiscal year — referred to public accounts cttee	Receives first regular S.E. cttees' review of S.E.	Considers supply bill for first regular S.E. December 10		Receives Budget Speech and M.E.
Governor General	Grants Royal Assent to supply bills; signs warrant to release monies			Grants Royal Assent to supply bills; signs warrant to release monies				Grants Royal Assent to supply bills; signs warrant to release monies		
Treasury Board	President tables S.E. and refers them to cttees; introduces S.E. and interim supply bills			President introduces M.E. supply bill			President tables first regular S.E. and refers them to cttees	President introduces S.E. supply bill		President tables M.E. and refers them to cttees
Treasury Board Secretariat	Informs departments that supply has been approved		Prepares supply bill for M.E.	Informs departments that supply has been approved			Preparation of first regular S.E. and supply bill	Informs departments that supply has been approved	Prepares M.E.	Prepares S.E. and supply bills

Legend: M.E. = Main Estimates
S.E. = Supplementary Estimates
Cttees = Committees

Source: Adapted from the Government of Canada, *Fiscal Plan, 1991–92* (Ottawa: Supply and Services, 1992). Reproduced by the authority of the Minister responsible for Statistics Canada, 1993.

However, we have seen that in a complex modern society governed by a highly interventionist state, the distinctions between means and ends or administration and politics are not at all clear. Public servants enjoy relative security in their jobs and have immense organizational resources. These advantages give them considerable influence in the policy-making process. Bureaucrats also have discretionary power in many areas of policy implementation, especially where Parliament has delegated regulatory or administrative decision-making authority to government departments, agencies and tribunals. Given these trends, how do politicians keep the power of unelected bureaucrats in check? There are three important ways: through strengthened parliamentary committees; through the reports of the Auditor General; and by freedom of information legislation.

Parliamentary Committees

Several House of Commons reforms over the last two decades have tried to reduce government dependence on the bureaucracy as a source of information and policy advice. Parliamentary committees have been made more effective, and their reports present a view of government policy that differs from that of the public service. Opposition parties receive research funds to assist them in making more effective policy input or, at least, in developing more informed criticism of existing policy-making and implementation. Increased staff support for individual members of Parliament, while it is still not sufficient, does provide some research potential that enables MPs to question bureaucratic decisions more effectively.

The Auditor General

The role of the **Auditor General** is to provide a critical appraisal of the effectiveness of both public spending and accounting practices — to Parliament and, in particular, to the Public Accounts Committee. The Auditor General is directly responsible to Parliament (not the executive) and the Auditor's reports on government spending trigger major debates in the House of Commons and the press about government policy-making.

Since 1977, the Office of the Auditor General has had the power to carry out "value-for-money" audits — to assess policy and the substance of spending decisions. It "has become concerned not only with whether federal funds are properly accounted for, but with how they are being managed, at what cost, to what end and with what effectiveness."[28] The rising size and costs of the Auditor General's Office prompted one expert to conclude that the Auditor General's Office itself should be subjected to a value-for-money, comprehensive audit.[29]

Parliamentary and administrative reforms in the expenditure budget process have enhanced the potential for democratic control, and the development of multi-year fiscal plans provides a broader, longer-range context for the evaluation of both overall spending plans and individual estimates. Both of these reforms have enhanced the role of the Auditor General.

Freedom of Information

In 1983, the federal government took an important step toward providing more open government when it formally promulgated the *Access to Information Act*. With a number of controversial exceptions, Canadian citizens and permanent residents now have the right to examine records that were previously kept secret by federal government institutions. At stake in many cases is the individual's right to know why certain government decisions were taken, and to determine whether these

---

28. Donald J. Savoie, "Who Is Auditing the Auditor-General?" *The Globe and Mail*, August 25, 1995.
29. Ibid.

decisions were arrived at fairly or whether mistakes were made. If the government refuses to disclose information on request, an appeal can be made first to the Information Commissioner. The commissioner sends an annual report to Parliament, but John Reid, in his first report in 1999, complained that "not once in 16 years has the designated committee held a hearing to consider the annual report."[30] Ultimate recourse, however, is via the Federal Court — an expensive procedure, which also raises the undesirable prospect of having the judicial process replace Parliament as the primary mechanism for ensuring bureaucratic accountability.

The Act is intended to make government more accountable and to reverse whatever public perception exists that public servants scheme to hide blunders or alleged corruption from unsuspecting citizens. Still, some observers are skeptical of the value of the Act in its present form. Donald Rowat has argued that some of the exceptions to access "go against the whole spirit of a freedom of information act by absolutely prohibiting certain types of records from being released, thus turning these exemptions into an extension of the Official Secrets Act."[31] Also disturbing is the long list of subjects for which bureaucrats can make discretionary exemptions, thereby limiting "the accountability of the government to Parliament."[32]

In the final analysis, public confidence in the Act depends on how well the mechanics of releasing information work and on whether information that should be released is actually made public. This, in turn, depends upon the extent to which the Cabinet and the bureaucracy are willing to comply with the spirit as well as the letter of the new law. The issue of freedom of information will undoubtedly remain on the agenda of public debate as the Act continues to be evaluated.

The Ombudsman and Other Proposals

For many years there has been a debate about the establishment of a federal **ombudsman**, an independent officer who would be responsible to Parliament for the investigation of citizens' complaints against the bureaucracy. Although an ombudsman might provide an additional mechanism for overall surveillance of the bureaucracy, it should be noted that Canada already has a number of similar specialized officers, including the Commissioner of Official Languages, the Privacy Commissioner, the Information Commissioner and the Correctional Investigator for Penitentiary Services, who all act as watchdogs over specific aspects of bureaucratic activity.

Other non-parliamentary means of controlling the bureaucracy's role in policy-making have also been proposed. The judicial process, for example, could play a greater role in protecting citizens against arbitrary bureaucratic decisions. But, although there has been an increase in court challenges to bureaucratic decisions since the *Charter of Rights and Freedoms* was implemented, we agree with the conclusion drawn by one opponent of judicial review of the bureaucracy that

> *[i]t would be wrong to abandon democratic processes working through Parliament to check bureaucratic power in favour of a more élitist approach based upon courts, lawyers and tribunals as the primary mechanisms for safeguarding the rights of individuals.*[33]

30. *The Hill Times,* July 26, 1999, p.1.

31. Donald C. Rowat, "The Right of Public Access to Official Documents," in O.P. Dwivedi, ed., *The Administrative State in Canada: Essays in Honour of J.E. Hodgetts* (Toronto: University of Toronto Press, 1982), pp. 185–86.

32. Ibid., p. 187.

33. Paul Thomas, "Courts Can't Be Saviours," *Policy Options*, vol. 5, no. 3 (May/June 1984), p. 27.

Are More Reforms Needed?

The perceived lack of accountability of Crown corporations to Parliament remains a problem. Reports of public enterprises and regulatory agencies are now automatically referred to the appropriate standing committees, but inadequate auditing provisions and difficulties in imposing ministerial responsibility for these semi-autonomous agencies hinder effective parliamentary control.

With this exception, however, the mechanisms for parliamentary control of the bureaucracy are largely in place. The key question is whether MPs have the inclination or the time to devote themselves to ensuring bureaucratic accountability. The Lambert Commission called on parliamentarians to "treat their surveillance role with the same seriousness they accord their political responsibilities"[34] but, in the absence of a structural change and/or widespread change of attitude in the House of Commons, it seems likely that MPs will continue to have little incentive to take full advantage of the opportunities available to them.

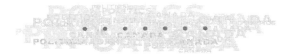

SUMMARY

Many Canadians are extremely suspicious, if not downright cynical, about the federal bureaucracy. In part, as we have argued, this suspicion stems from fear of the unknown or, at least, the inadequately understood. The bureaucracy is not a single monolithic entity whose size and organizational structure automatically present a threat to democratic government. Rather, it is a complex of competing departments, corporations and agencies established to meet the perceived economic, social and political goals of the public. Neither is the bureaucracy an elite group, dominated by a single class or ethnic/linguistic group, and thereby unrepresentative of and unresponsive to the public. Concerted efforts have been made over the last few decades to make the bureaucracy more representative, although there is still substantial room for improvement, especially with regard to increasing opportunities for women and Native people. Nor is there an absence of mechanisms by which control or accountability might be imposed on the bureaucracy by elected institutions. If there is a problem, it may well be described as a lack of political will to make use of these control mechanisms.

Elected politicians in both Cabinet and Parliament feel bound to respond to the immediate demands of constituents and voters in order to secure their re-election. And, since voters and interest groups tend to rush to the defence of threatened programs from which they benefit, reduction of the size of public spending levels is relatively low in the political priorities of Canadians. As long as the bureaucracy continues to serve the needs of most segments of Canadian society, there will not be sufficient impetus for a serious assault on the public service and its programs. Ultimately, as with governments, it may be argued that societies get the bureaucracies they deserve.

---

34. Royal Commission on Financial Management and Accountability, *Final Report* (Ottawa: Minister of Supply and Services, 1979), p. 388.

DISCUSSION QUESTIONS

1. Are politicians the masters of public servants? Should ministers have to take responsibility for mistakes made by public servants?

2. Describe the mechanisms in place to provide democratic control of the bureaucracy.

3. Distinguish between the deficit and the debt and explain the nature of the financial problem Canada faces.

4. What are the four major strategies that can be used for cutting the annual deficit? Why is it such a difficult task for governments? What path would you follow if you were Finance Minister?

Selected Bibliography

Albo, Gregory, David Langille and Leo Panitch, eds., *A Different Kind of State? Popular Power and Democratic Administration* (Don Mills, Ont.: Oxford University Press, 1993).

Blais, A., and S. Dion, eds., *The Budget-Maximizing Bureaucrat: Appraisals and Evidence* (Pittsburgh: University of Pittsburgh Press, 1991).

Brooks, Steven, *Public Policy in Canada: An Introduction,* 3rd ed. (Toronto: Oxford University Press, 1998).

Canada, *Beneath the Veneer: Report of the Task Force on Barriers to Women in the Public Service*, vol. 1 (Ottawa: Supply and Services, 1990).

——————, *Public Service 2000: The Renewal of the Public Service of Canada* (Ottawa: Supply and Services, 1990).

——————, *Public Service 2000: A Report on Progress* (Ottawa: Supply and Services, 1992).

Carleton University, School of Public Administration, *How Ottawa Spends* (Ottawa: Carleton University Press, annual) (edited by different scholars in different years).

Clark, J.D., *Getting the Incentives Right: Toward a Productivity-Oriented Management Framework for the Public Service* (Ottawa: Treasury Board, 1993).

Gillespie, W. Irwin, *Tax, Borrow and Spend: Financing Federal Spending in Canada, 1867–1990* (Ottawa: Carleton University Press, 1991).

Hodgetts, J.E., *Public Management: Emblem of Reform of the Canadian Public Service* (Ottawa: Canadian Centre for Management Development, 1991).

Holland, D., and J.P. McGowan, *Delegated Legislation in Canada* (Toronto: Carswell, 1989).

Huddleston, Mark, *The Public Administration Workbook* (New York: Longman, 1992).

Kernaghan, Kenneth and David Siegel, *Public Administration in Canada: A Text,* 2nd ed. (Scarborough: Nelson, 1991).

——————, and John Langford, *The Responsible Public Servant* (Halifax: Institute of Research on Public Policy, 1990).

McBride, Stephen, *Not Working: State, Unemployment and Neo-Conservatism in Canada* (Toronto: University of Toronto Press, 1992).

Osbaldeston, Gordon F., *Organizing to Govern*, vols. 1 and 2 (Toronto: McGraw-Hill Ryerson, 1992).

Peters, Guy, *The Politics of Bureaucracy* (New York: Longman, 1990).

Plumptre, Timothy, *Beyond the Bottom Line: Management in Government* (Halifax: Institute of Research on Public Policy, 1988).

Savoie, Donald J., *Thatcher, Reagan and Mulroney: In Search of a New Bureaucracy* (Toronto: University of Toronto Press, 1994).

——————, ed., *Innovations and Trends in Management Development* (Toronto: Institute of Public Administration of Canada, 1990).

LIST OF WEBLINKS

**www.Canada.gc.ca/depts/
major/depind_e.html**

Federal Government Departments This Web site lists various federal
government departments and organizations.

www.indigenous.bc.ca

Royal Commission on Aboriginal Peoples The final report of the Royal
Commission is found at the Web site of the Institute of Indigenous
Government.

www.aecb-ccea.gc.ca

Atomic Energy Control Board This is the official Web site for Canada's
nuclear regulatory authority.

www.oag-bvg.gc.ca

Auditor General This is the Web page for Canada's Auditor-General.

CASE STUDY – INSTITUTIONS

QUÉBEC: THE REFERENDUM

The 1995 Québec referendum raises important questions about Canadian federalism, Québec nationalism, and the use of referendums. On October 30, 1995, Québeckers voted by the narrowest of margins to defeat a referendum question which would have propelled them to independence. The federalist "No" side won only 50.6 percent of the votes cast. Clearly, many francophones who had previously rejected separation had changed their minds.

Québec nationalism is not new to Canadian politics: it dates from the early nineteenth century. During the 1960s Quiet Revolution, two modern strains of Québec nationalism emerged. Federalist nationalists like Pierre Trudeau urged Québeckers to be confident, dynamic members of Canadian society, while others advocated the creation of an independent Québec. Defeat in the 1980 referendum and consistent negative opinion polling results convinced separatist leaders that Québeckers would not vote for separation if they thought it would cause economic problems. They therefore introduced the idea of "sovereignty-association," implying both independence from and economic links with Canada.

There is often an ugly face to nationalism and this century has seen considerable nationalist discrimination, hatred and violence. During the 1995 referendum campaign both Lucien Bouchard and Jacques Parizeau contributed to these negative emotions by making statements which divided Québeckers into nationalists and "others" on an ethnic basis. Before resigning as premier, Parizeau blamed the defeat on "money and the ethnic vote," causing Québec's non-francophone population to question how welcome they would be in an independent Québec.

The use and abuse of referendums around the world is well documented. The structure and wording of a referendum question play a major role in determining the results; questions are often calculated to maximize support for one side. In the 1995 referendum the question appeared to ask for support to negotiate a better deal with the rest of Canada. Undoubtedly the vague wording attracted some additional support for the separatists. After the referendum, however, Parizeau revealed that he had planned to go far beyond the question with an immediate unilateral declaration of independence.

Canadian federalism is not static. Relationships between the central government and the provinces have often changed. Many argue that the flexible nature of federal arrangements is a positive sign of Canadian federalism's ability to evolve to meet the challenges of change and diversity. It is now appropriate, however, to describe Canadian federalism as "contested federalism": the arrangements distributing authority and responsibility among the central government and the provinces are hotly disputed with many radical demands to decentralize the federation. Despite demands from Québec and the West, Canadians have been unable to agree on constitutional reform.

Although some Canadians are weary of constitutional debate, they know that there will probably be another referendum in two or three years. The resolution of this issue requires new constitutional ideas. Federalism will continue to be contested by Québec nationalists well into the new millennium.

Questions

1. How significant are economic issues in a debate that seems primarily about nationalism? Can these be resolved within new federal arrangements? Is Québec independence inevitable?

2. The wording of the referendum question was intended to increase support for the separatist side. How was language used to mobilize support for the "Yes" side? Discuss the advantages and deficiencies of referendums as devices for democratic decision-making.

PART
4

Political Behaviour

Political culture and institutions set the parameters of individual and collective action. Part 4, therefore, examines the political behaviour of individuals and groups as they exercise their democratic rights and influence public policy within these established boundaries.

Political parties are important vehicles of mass participation. They possess the organization and leadership to provide the electorate with viable choices about who will govern them. They are nourished by political ideas that evolved over time as part of Canada's cultural inheritance. Liberal, conservative and socialist ideologies contribute to political thought and underpin the many political choices available to Canadians, as do harsh ideas of nationalism, regionalism and neo-conservatism.

Interest groups and social movements also allow collective participation in the political process and seek to influence government. Their relationship with politicians is reciprocal in that each uses the other to further its ends. It is up to Parliament to create rules to regulate these groups.

Finally, elections, and to a limited degree, referendums, provide the ultimate opportunity for political activity. Citizens can choose political candidates and, in principle at least, have a voice in the governance of their society. Electoral rules and norms of political behaviour determine how close that choice comes to achieving the democratic ideal.

11

Political Parties

. . . .

Continuity and Transition

Political parties are a vital part of the Canadian political system. They are agents of representative democracy. With few exceptions, local party organizations select candidates who stand for election as members of Parliament. The prime minister, although formally named by the Governor General, is almost invariably leader of the party that holds the greatest number of elected representatives and is therefore most likely to form a viable government. In short, the party system provides essential organizing and stabilizing functions for government in a large, bureaucratic state.

In spite of their important role, organized political parties are a relatively recent historical phenomenon. As vehicles of mass participation in politics, they became increasingly significant and formalized as the franchise was extended, providing voters with progressively clearer alternatives. In Canada, the Liberal and Conservative parties have assumed an important place in the political culture for over a century, while the New Democratic Party's historical roots go back almost half that length of time. In the 1993 general election, however, two new, regionally based parties — the Reform party and the Bloc Québécois — burst onto the federal scene, cutting into the traditional bases of support of all three established parties and threatening two of them with extinction.

The system still hovers between continuity and change, fragmented by geography and language. The 1997 general election compounded the fragmentation of the two-and-a-half-party pattern. Canada could be characterized as having a multi-party dominant system. While the Liberals form a new majority government, they do so with little representation from the Maritimes or the West. The Reform party — as of the year 2000, the Canadian Reform Conservative Alliance or the "Alliance" — is the official opposition in the House of Commons with no representation east of Manitoba, and the Bloc Québécois holds most of the seats in Québec. The NDP and Conservatives share representation from the Maritimes and are scattered across the country.

When parties are unable to represent the country from sea to sea to sea, the party system fragments and new parties form to promote specifically regional causes, balkanizing the country and providing few voices at the centre to stand up for Canada. This is what happened in 1993 and 1997. The challenges of the debt and separatism in Québec were taken up by regional parties — the Reform party in the West and the Bloc Québécois in Québec — that sapped the support of the traditional parties.

In this chapter, we examine the origins and development of Canadian parties and their organization and structure outside of Parliament. What are their basic functions and how well do they perform them? How representative of the Canadian public are they? How democratic are they in formulating party policy? We also examine the role of the party leader and consider the selection process that thrusts individuals into that prestigious and potentially powerful position. First, however, we examine the definition and role of parties, and survey the wide range of party types and party systems that exist as possible alternatives.

WHAT ARE POLITICAL PARTIES?

Political parties have been defined in a number of ways. Karl Marx, for example, considered them to be a manifestation of class conflict and struggle. Benjamin Disraeli saw them as organized opinion. However, perhaps the most useful definition for our purposes is simply that **political parties** are organizations designed to secure the power of the state for their leaders. The goal of political parties is to gain control of the levers of government and thereby realize their policies or programs. People are motivated to join or support political parties by ideas, issues and ideologies such as liberalism, conservatism, socialism and even separatism. In democratic systems, control of government is achieved by open competition in the electoral process. The voluminous literature on political parties provides general (though not unanimous) agreement that parties constitute a crucial link between society and government.[1]

At a practical level, of course, countries have different rules defining what constitutes an officially recognized political party. In Canada, to be recognized on a ballot at election time and receive other privileges such as tax credits and free advertising broadcast time, a party must field a minimum of 50 candidates. To be officially recognized in the House of Commons, a party must have 12 MPs — although the House may allow exceptions.

Party Functions

Political parties have certain tasks or functions to perform in society; these vary according to the political system in which they operate.[2] It has already been mentioned that political parties add an important element of stability to the political system by legitimizing the individuals and institutions that control political power. In addition, they help to organize the electorate by recruiting candidates, organizing campaigns, encouraging partisan attachments, helping individual voters get their names on polling lists and generally stimulating voter participation. As well, they help to organize the government by providing a degree of policy direction and supplying party leaders as potential prime ministers and Cabinet ministers. The winning party serves to fuse the executive and legislative branches of government in Canada, providing the foundation of Cabinet government.

Within the broad task of organizing the electorate and the government, there are several specific party functions that deserve elaboration.

Recruitment, Nomination and Election of Political Officeholders

It is the task of every political party to enlist suitable candidates for the positions of members of Parliament, government ministers and prime minister, and then get them elected to form a

---

1. Parties are a relatively modern phenomenon, playing a major role in Britain for the first time in the eighteenth century. There has been considerable controversy over their desirability, epitomized in the classic works of M.I. Ostrogorski, *Democracy and the Organization of Political Parties*, 2 vols., trans. by Frederick Clarke (New York: Macmillan, 1902); and Robert Michels, *Political Parties: A Sociological Study of Oligarchical Tendencies of Modern Democracy*, trans. by Eden and Cedar Paul, with introduction by S.M. Lipset (New York: The Free Press, 1966). Modern classics include Leon D. Epstein, *Political Parties in Western Democracies* (New York: Praeger, 1967).

2. See a classic article by Anthony King, "Political Parties in Western Democracies," *Polity*, vol. 2, no. 2 (Winter 1969), pp. 111–41.

government. To achieve this, each party must select and present candidates and mobilize voters by waging a campaign. The winning party forms the government and largely decides who occupies the major policy-making posts, the most powerful tool a party can control. It gains control of numerous patronage appointments throughout the government structure, and is able to reward its own supporters while extending its power and influence. Party leaders, therefore, recruit public appointees such as senators and members of Crown agencies, as well as help to elect representatives to the House of Commons.

Interest Articulation and Aggregation

A vast number of interests are present in modern, complex societies. Parties **articulate** or express those interests in many ways: they educate public opinion by debating important issues, and they provide a legitimate outlet for dissent and pressure for change. The latter is particularly important for accommodating regional or sectional interests. In fact, parties are often referred to as "gatekeepers" in the political system because they allow certain demands to pass directly to decision-makers, while they eliminate or combine others. Political parties also perform the valuable function of bringing together, then reducing and simplifying the morass of interests to manageable sets of policy alternatives. By appealing to the many classes, regions, interests and ethnic groups that make up the country, political parties modify conflict and facilitate decisions. This process, known as **aggregation** of interests, is performed by a variety of structures in society, but political parties may be the most important. Parties constantly monitor the electorate for ideas and conduct opinion polls to help them transform public concerns into vote-winning policies. Effective interest aggregation is important for electoral success in Canada.

Formulation of Public Policy

By winning elections, parties form the government and acquire the ability to formulate and present public policy. The Cabinet, along with senior civil servants who have an important role in drafting policies, leads the policy-making function in the legislative process. Parties provide platforms for election campaigns, but these rarely restrict subsequent policy decisions.

Political Socialization

In stable democracies, political parties normally play a fairly conservative role, reinforcing the established system in order to keep the political process running smoothly. In a parliamentary democracy such as Canada, which lacks a strong, homogeneous political culture, there is a special need for political parties to play a unifying role as "agencies for the creation of national symbols, experiences, memories, heroes, and villains."[3] The failure of Canadian parties to bind regional cleavages by building strong national bases of representation limits their effectiveness.[4] They do, however, inform and educate the public, enlisting a high percentage of Canadians to participate in the electoral process through volunteer work as well as through voting.

Other Functions

Parties sometimes participate in community activities outside the political arena in an attempt to influence constituents indirectly. They also provide a training ground for future political leaders. For those who do not aspire to leadership positions, they give social, psychological and, sometimes, economic benefits and the opportunity to participate in party decisions.

---

3. John Meisel, "Recent Changes in Canadian Parties," in Hugh G. Thorburn, ed., *Party Politics in Canada*, 2nd ed. (Scarborough: Prentice Hall, 1967), p. 34.

4. Alan Cairns was one of the first to argue that the party system "conditioned by the electoral system, exacerbates the very cleavages it is credited with healing." Alan C. Cairns, "The Electoral System and the Party System in Canada, 1921–1965," *CJPS*, vol. 1, no. 1 (March 1968), p. 62.

Classifying Parties and Party Systems

Parties

Political parties can be classified in a great number of ways. One way is to categorize them by their *type of organization*. Another way is to distinguish them according to the *type of appeal* they make to the electorate.

Maurice Duverger formulated a widely used, simple scheme that divides political parties into three categories — mass, cadre or devotee — according to their type of organization.[5] **Mass parties** recruit across class lines to achieve the largest possible membership and then allow that membership a significant role by functioning democratically. Members have significant power over their executive and the parliamentary wing — including the leader, whom they elect — and a meaningful say in policy formulation. The party is financed by membership fees. The theoretical rationale behind mass parties is that a large membership across social class lines helps to counter the power of establishment parties, whose leaders come mainly from the economic, political and social elite of society.

Cadre parties, on the other hand, are highly centralized and recruit only from the politically active elite. They are much less democratic than mass parties, in that the elite runs the party and allows the rest of the party to fall dormant until election time. The parliamentary wing of the party selects the leader, who has no formal accountability. Financing is from a relatively narrow base, usually corporations. Today, such parties are often associated with developing nations but are found throughout the developed world as well. Duverger's third category, **devotee parties**, are those built around a charismatic leader; an example is the Nazi party under Adolf Hitler.

As we examine Canadian parties we will see that the Liberals and Conservatives began and remain as cadre parties, although over time they have taken on some features of the mass party model. The NDP began as a mass party but has shifted toward the cadre model, as has Reform. The Bloc Québécois under Lucien Bouchard had many features of a devotee party. Canada's inability to retain pure mass parties may be explained by Robert Michels' "iron law of oligarchy,"[6] a theory that all large organizations, despite intentions to do otherwise, largely end up in the control of a relatively small group of people at the top. In other words, democracy always gives way to elitism.

A second way to categorize parties is by the *type of appeal* that they make — whether it is ideological or non-ideological.

In classifying parties by their ideological basis, Otto Kirchheimer distinguishes the **catch-all party** from those with high degrees of ideology.[7] He notes that the mass party and the cadre party became relatively unsuccessful at the polls because they had limited electoral bases (the working class for the mass party and the establishment class for the cadre party) but that they tended to expand their appeal when they sought to include the maximum number of social groups. To do this they followed two strategies. First, they abandoned strong ideological prescriptions in favour of softer lines. Second, the parties promised specific rewards to a wide variety of interest groups, from better marketing assistance to farmers and jobs for students to free trade and better conditions for business people. Catch-all parties focus above all on maximizing votes; their platforms become like large vats filled with as many popular ideas and promises as possible. The Republican and Democratic parties in the United States are classic catch-all parties.

---

5. The classic discussion of party organization is found in Maurice Duverger, *Political Parties: Their Organization and Activity in the Modern State* (London: Methuen, 1954).

6. Michels, *Political Parties*.

7. Otto Kirchheimer, "The Transformation of the Western European Party System," in Joseph LaPalombara and M. Wiener, eds., *Political Parties and Political Development* (Princeton, N.J.: Princeton University Press, 1966), pp. 177–200.

In Canada, the Liberal and Conservative parties are clearly in the catch-all category. They attempt to attract as many voters as possible by making the widest appeal possible. Another concept is often used to discuss catch-all parties. **Brokerage parties** seek to maintain cohesion across party divisions and maximize their electoral appeal by adopting middle-of-the-road positions on issues. The two major parties were lodged so firmly in the centre of the political spectrum that they were often portrayed as Tweedledum and Tweedledee. They appealed to the same middle-of-the-road electoral supporters, constantly shifting their principles in search of electoral success. This created a flexible, non-ideological **brokerage party system** because the two main parties act as brokers of ideas, selecting those with the widest appeal and the best chance of attracting electoral support.

George Perlin called the Liberal and Conservative parties modified "brokerage parties" because there were "some basic differences between them, explained partly by a different internal balance in ideological perspectives and partly by their long-term competitive relationship."[8] The Liberals have been considered centre-left and the Progressive Conservatives centre-right, because of a few alleged historical differences such as the Conservative support of free enterprise and the Liberal leadership in social legislation and public ownership. However, they have both displayed remarkable flexibility within this broad range. For example, free trade with the United States historically was a Liberal policy until the Conservatives took it up in 1985.

Advocates of brokerage theory argue that the many cleavages in the country — ethnic, geographic, economic and demographic — have forced parties in Canada to occupy the middle of the road in their attempts to win majorities. Brokerage parties do not appeal to specific socioeconomic groupings, and they are flexible and opportunistic in order to keep the country united. By usurping the middle ground, the Liberals and Conservatives largely restricted radical parties to the sidelines.

History and traditional loyalties, rather than logic or ideology behind party platforms, have been the distinguishing features of Canadian political parties. Divisions such as ethnicity and region have always taken precedence over class.[9] With all five official parties in the 36th Parliament substantially representing different parts of the country, the basic nature of the party system has changed, at least temporarily.

In contrast to the catch-all party, the **ideological party** adheres strictly to an ideology or consistent set of principles. The NDP and Reform fit loosely into this category, although both have had to be more flexible in order to win votes. The Bloc Québécois, too, is close to being an ideological party because its nationalist ideas underpin most of its party platform.

Another category here would be for **single-issue parties** — parties that limit their policy platform to one issue. An example would be an environmental party that runs for office on a strictly environmental platform. In the 1993 and 1997 elections, Québec voted strongly for the Bloc Québécois, an **anti-system party** — a party that does not want to work within the existing political system, but seeks to destroy it and replace it with something else. The Bloc Québécois seeks to dismantle Canada, so it is to the party's advantage to prevent the system of government from working well.

Party Systems

The series of relationships among parties in a political system constitutes the **party system**. Party systems, too, can be classified to assist in making comparisons among states. One way to categorize

8. George Perlin, ed., *Party Democracy in Canada* (Scarborough: Prentice Hall, 1988). See especially articles by Donald Blake, "Division and Cohesion: The Major Parties," pp. 32–53; and Richard Johnston, "The Ideological Structure of Opinion on Policy," pp. 54–70.
9. Richard Johnston et al., *Letting the People Decide* (Montréal: McGill-Queen's University Press, 1992).

them is by the number of active parties. Around the world there are one-party, dominant-party, two-party and multi-party systems.[10]

In the **one-party system**, a single party — which is the only legal party — controls every level of government. Communist and authoritarian regimes such as the former Soviet Union, Cuba, the People's Republic of China and some Marxist-inspired African states are examples.

A **dominant-party system** exists when a single party regularly wins almost every election, though opposition parties are allowed to function freely. An example is in Mexico where the Institutional Revolutionary Party (PRI) has until recently defeated all other parties in congressional and presidential elections.

The **two-party system** is characteristic of much of the English-speaking world. In this system, two major parties dominate; others have only minor political strength. The United States has a classic two-party system. Great Britain, Australia, New Zealand and Canada all have a tradition of two dominant parties that vie for power as well as one or more weaker parties, though Canada shifted away from this model in both the 1993 and 1997 general elections. This model offers the electorate a choice of policies and leaders, and at the same time promotes governmental stability by making it possible for one party to win a majority or near-majority in the legislature.

In the **multi-party system**, popular support is divided among several parties, so that the party in power must generally form coalitions to retain its position. This system, of which present-day Italy, the Third and Fourth French Republics and Weimar Germany are major examples, is often criticized as being unstable. However, there are many examples of multi-party systems with stable governments — notably Switzerland, the Netherlands and Austria. Advocates of this type of system argue that it allows a wide expression of the many interests of a complex society.

More sophisticated classification systems for parties have been devised to distinguish with greater precision among party systems on a worldwide basis. Joseph LaPalombara and Myron Weiner, for example, introduced a *competitive/non-competitive* classification of party systems that has since been expanded by others.[11] (See Table 11.1.)

Competitive systems are classified by the number of parties that compete for and have access to legislative power. In the **dominant one-party** system, a single party regularly wins almost every election, even though opposition parties function freely. In the **two-party** system, two major parties dominate; others have only minor political strength. In the **multi-party** system, popular support is divided among several parties so that the largest party must generally form a coalition with one or more other parties to form a government. As indicated in Table 11.1, multi-party systems can be divided further into **multi-party dominant** in which there are three or more parties, but one of them regularly receives about 40 percent of the vote; or **multi-party loose** in which there are also three or more parties but none of them regularly receives 40 percent of the vote. **Non-competitive systems**, in which one party dominates, are classified by other variables, such as how repressive their governments are. A few have been called **mixed and low competitive** because they include elements of the other two types. In Mexico, for example, opposition parties are allowed, but one party dominates to such an extent that the system is almost non-competitive.

Classification systems are intended for gross comparisons between states. Not all countries fit neatly into any one category, and a country's classification may change over time. Canada is a prime

---

10. Of course, there are more complex definitions and typologies of party systems. See, for example, Giovanni Sartori, *Parties and Party Systems: A Framework for Analysis* (London, U.K.: Cambridge University Press, 1976). Also see R.K. Carty, *Canadian Political Party Systems: A Reader* (Peterborough: Broadview Press, 1992).

11. LaPalombara and Weiner, eds., *Political Parties and Political Development*, pp. 33–41.

TABLE 11.1   PARTY SYSTEMS BASED ON PARTY COMPETITION

Non-Competitive Systems	1. Communist (China)
	2. Authoritarian (Franco's Spain)
Mixed and Low Competitive Systems	1. Low competition (Mexico)
Competitive Systems	1. One-party dominant (Japan until 1993)
	2. Two-party (United States)
	3. Multi-party dominant (three or more parties; one regularly receives about 40% of the vote) (Canada)
	4. Multi-party loose (three or more parties; none regularly receives 40% of the vote) (Italy)

Source: Adapted from Joseph LaPalombara and Myron Weiner, eds., *Political Parties and Political Development* (Princeton, N.J.: Princeton University Press, 1966); and Joseph LaPalombara, *Politics within Nations* (Englewood Cliffs, N.J.: Prentice Hall, 1974), ch. 13.

example. It has a competitive system, but, as we see in more detail in the next section, the nature of the system has changed so that Canada does not clearly belong in any of the above categories.

Until the rise of third parties in 1921, the Canadian party system was developing along the lines of a classic two-party system. Since then, particularly since 1961, third parties have fairly consistently captured about a quarter of the federal vote. (See Figure 11.1.) Until 1993, the Canadian system, therefore, fell somewhere between the two-party and multi-party systems in the classification scheme set out above. Because of this, the arrangement in Canada was often called a "two-and-a-half party" system. With the election of five parties in 1993 and 1997, the party system shifted further toward the multi-party end of the spectrum and became a multi-party dominant system.

THE CANADIAN PARTY SYSTEM: ORIGIN AND DEVELOPMENT

From Origins to Two-Party System

It is difficult to pinpoint the date of origin of political parties in Canada. Until shortly after Confederation, Canadian politics was characterized by factionalism. Party structures as we know them today had not yet formed. Often, candidates did not even commit themselves to a party until they had determined who would win.

Early parties were loosely organized and even less encumbered by ideology than they are today. In their early years, Upper and Lower Canada, Nova Scotia and Prince Edward Island were all governed by oligarchies. The Family Compact, the Château Clique, the Halifax Compact and the landed proprietors in Prince Edward Island controlled the economic and political power in their particular areas. Any opposition that existed was fragmented and factional. The prime requisite for the emergence of parties was, in each case, increased competition for power within the legislature. Nowhere did the factions and interest groups mature into parties until the advent of responsible government. In fact, the formation of parties occurred even after that in the case of Prince Edward Island, where religious rights and land settlement problems cut across party lines. Only when the executive became responsible to the legislature was there a genuine need for political parties to

FIGURE 11.1 PARTIES IN PARLIAMENT: PERCENTAGE OF SEATS WON BY PARTIES IN GENERAL
ELECTIONS, 1945–97

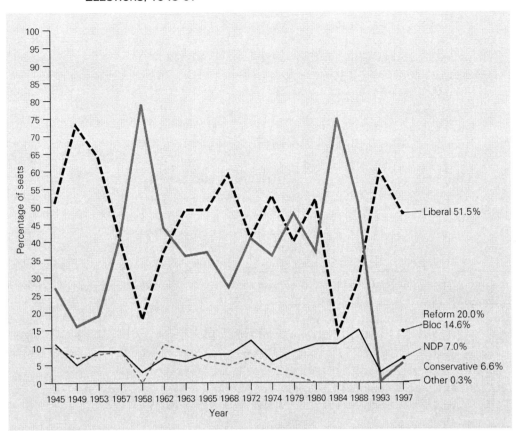

develop. As legislative responsibilities were extended, the franchise expanded, other electoral reforms such as the secret ballot were introduced, the pressure for party cohesion increased and recognizable political parties emerged.[12]

The origin and development of parties were directly influenced by the system of government.
Canadian parties developed within the framework of a democratic parliamentary system and, after
1867, of a federal constitutional arrangement. They were further influenced by internal factors such
as national and industrial development, and external stimuli such as historical precedents and ideological influences from Britain and the United States. Until the 1920s, two major parties, the pre-
cursors of today's Liberals and Progressive Conservatives, were able to aggregate the various interests,
which were not very complex. The economy prospered; regional and rural/urban cleavages were
minimal. The parties focused on parochial constituency issues.

Two-and-a-Half-Party System

In 1921, the first minor parties appeared on the political scene and the focus of party politics shifted
from constituency to region. In 1921, the Progressives suddenly won 23 percent of the vote, largely

---

12. See J.M. Beck, "Nova Scotia, the Party System in Nova Scotia: Tradition and Conservatism," in Martin
Robin, ed., *Canadian Provincial Politics* (Scarborough: Prentice Hall, 1972); and Frank Mackinnon, *The
Government of Prince Edward Island* (Toronto: University of Toronto Press, 1951).

in western Canada. Since 1921, there has been at least one minor party represented in Parliament. From 1961 to 1993, the only significant "third" party was the NDP. On the moderate left of the political spectrum, it has often acted as a social conscience, initiating ideas for social programs that were too extreme for the major parties but that, over time, were taken into the Liberal or Conservative party platforms and eventually implemented in watered-down form. A case in point was the implementation of provincial health-care plans. From more radical left-wing origins, the NDP gradually adopted a moderate-left reform position that, at times, overlaps with centre-left Liberal positions. The middle-of-the-road tendency of all the parties is evident, but the historical relationship between the parties is sufficient to warrant their relative positions on the left-right continuum.[13]

Until 1993, the two major parties together consistently won about 75–80 percent of the vote; the NDP, about 15–20 percent. By helping to broaden the spectrum of political views represented in Parliament, minor or third parties provide a legitimate outlet for political dissent, giving a voice to minority opinion that might otherwise be forced to work outside the system. They are particularly effective at the provincial level, where they often form provincial governments. For example, the CCF-NDP has governed in Saskatchewan, Manitoba, British Columbia and Ontario; Social Credit in Alberta and British Columbia; the Union Nationale and the Parti Québécois in Québec.

In the late 1980s, Canada's modified two-party system began to show signs of shifting toward a multi-party system. By 1994, the Mulroney Conservative government was highly unpopular, the Liberals were not regarded as a satisfactory alternative in Québec and parts of western Canada, and the New Democratic Party remained unable to create a bridge between French- and English-speaking populations. Two new parties, the Reform party and the Bloc Québécois, filled the breach, sapping the support of the established parties in Québec and the West, particularly that of the Conservatives and the NDP. Blessed with militants, money and simple messages, the Bloc and Reform attracted 30 percent of the popular vote in the 1997 general election.

We could also say that, since 1921, the party system has generally had the characteristics of a **one-party dominant** system, where one party receives at least 40 percent of the vote.[14] For the first seven decades of this century, the Liberals dominated. Until 1984, they had fallen below 40 percent of the vote in a federal election only three times: in 1958, 1962 and 1972. The Liberals won 18 of the 25 general elections from 1896 to 1984. Until 1984, therefore, the Liberals, as the government party, monopolized bureaucratic and senatorial appointments and all the other advantages of holding power, including the psychological advantages of being perceived as the government party. During this period, the Conservatives were the main opposition party. From 1984 to 1993, the situation was temporarily reversed and the Conservatives dominated the party system for nine years until their disastrous defeat in 1993.

Multi-Party Dominant System

The 1997 general election dramatically confirmed the new Canadian party system. Five parties were again elected to Parliament, but only one of them, the Liberals, had a significant percentage of the vote and therefore became the dominant party in a multi-party system. Basically, the Reform party

13. On problems encountered in placing Canadian parties on an ideological left-right spectrum, see David Elkins, "The Perceived Structure of the Canadian Party System," *CJPS*, vol. 7, no. 3 (September 1974), pp. 502–24. See also Hugh G. Thorburn, "Interpretations of the Canadian Party System," in Thorburn, ed., *Party Politics in Canada*, 5th ed. (Scarborough: Prentice Hall Canada, 1985), pp. 20–40.

14. See Hugh G. Thorburn, "Interpretations of the Canadian Party System," in Thorburn, ed., *Party Politics in Canada*, 6th ed. (Scarborough: Prentice Hall Canada, 1991); or Reginald Whitaker, *The Government Party: Organizing and Financing the Liberal Party of Canada, 1930–50* (Toronto: University of Toronto Press, 1977).

and the Bloc Québécois represented the West and Québec respectively; and the Conservatives and NDP split the Maritimes with the Liberals and formed small, but significant, official parties in the House of Commons. There were many parties in the House of Commons, but the Liberals were the dominant party.

PROBLEMS IN THE CANADIAN PARTY SYSTEM: FEDERALISM AND REGIONALISM

Federalism

In addition to being competitive, the Canadian party system is both federal and highly regional. While they parallel the federal organization of government, the *provincial* party systems are not necessarily identical to their federal counterparts. Provincially, as federally, the classic two-party system has been found consistently only in the Atlantic provinces, where third parties only rarely win more than 5 percent of the vote. Federal and provincial parties of the same name generally have separate elites, organizations and financial support. Only in the Atlantic provinces are federal/provincial party ties fairly integrated. For this reason, a federal party cannot assume ideological congruence or policy support from its provincial counterparts. The federal Liberal party and the Québec Liberal party, for example, share neither organization nor ideas. The Bloc and the Parti Québécois, on the other hand, share both. Provincial governments generally win support by pugnacious behaviour in taking strong stands for provincial concerns against the federal government. For whatever reason, voters do not necessarily support the same parties federally and provincially. As Garth Stevenson speculates,

> [this] peculiar separation of the party system into federal and provincial layers is per-haps in part a consequence of the intensity of federal-provincial conflict, which makes it difficult for a party affiliated with the federal government to appear as a credible defender of provincial interests.[15]

The federal structure also encourages the establishment of new parties at the provincial level. Some remain unique to one or to a few provinces and never move into the federal system, while others do enter the federal contest but never come close to power. The Parti Québécois, for example, is an important one-province provincial party. In the 1993 and 1997 general elections, it threw its weight behind the new Bloc Québécois as the standard bearer of Québec separatism in the federal Parliament. The English equivalent of the Parti Québécois in Québec, the Equality party, is a minor, provincial-level party also unique to that province. The Social Credit party, on the other hand, has existed at both levels and established roots at the provincial in three provinces. It also flourished briefly federally, but won no federal seats after 1979.

Regionalism

Perhaps the most interesting, but also the most worrisome, feature of the Canadian party system is its strong regional character. In recent years, with the exceptions of 1984 and 1988, general elections increasingly have produced governments with great regional distortions because the parties were

---

15. Garth Stevenson, *Unfulfilled Union: Canadian Federalism and National Unity*, rev. ed. (Toronto: Gage, 1982), p. 182.

unable to build strong national bases. The distortion was apparent in percentage of seats the governing party won in each region and also in the regional composition of the government caucus.

In the 1980 election, for example, the Liberals won 99 percent of the seats in Québec, 55 percent of those in Ontario, 59 percent in the Atlantic region, but just under 3 percent in the West. (See Table 11.2 for an overview of elections from 1867 to 1997.) Translated into parliamentary seats, 74 of the Liberal government's 147 seats came from Québec, 52 from Ontario, 19 from the Atlantic provinces and only 2 from the West (both from Manitoba). This meant that the four western provinces were virtually excluded from the government caucus; they only had about one percent of the membership. They were severely under-represented in virtually all Liberal government caucuses from 1963 to 1997 (today the West has only 10.97 percent of the Liberal caucus). In fact, from 1921 until 1984, the West was mildly or severely under-represented in almost *all* government caucuses.[16] Conversely, Québec was highly over-represented in all Liberal government caucuses during the same period. (See Table 11.3.)

Over the century, the Liberal party increasingly became the party of central Canada, winning 85 percent of its seats there in the 1980 election. In 1984, the Liberals lost their hold on central Canada and did poorly in every other province. In 1988, they increased their support in Ontario, the Maritimes and Manitoba, but did poorly again in Québec. Finally, on return to power in 1993, for the first time in many years the Liberal caucus reflected the regional balance of the country. Ironically, its main opposition was from new regionally based parties, the separatist Bloc Québécois and the western-based Reform party.

The Progressive Conservatives, for their part, had won 50 percent of their seats in 1980 in the western provinces, and only one seat in Québec. In 1984, they won 29 percent in the West and 28 percent in Québec. But their 1984 electoral breakthrough in Québec finally gave Canada a government with a strong national mandate. As Table 11.3 shows, in 1984 and 1988, for the first time since 1958 the percentage regional composition of the Progressive Conservative caucus was extremely close to the percentage regional composition of the House of Commons — just before its devastating defeat in 1993.

These severe regional imbalances in the party system make it difficult for the parties to perform many of their important functions. For decades, selection for political patronage positions was distorted by Liberal party domination of the government, as was recruitment to Cabinet. Interest aggregation and articulation by the parties is also distorted when regions are severely over- or under-represented in governments over several decades. When it happens on a regular basis, as it has in Canada in recent years, it can be expected that regional parties will flourish as a protest against exclusion. Even the socialization function is distorted when there are regional imbalances, because regional cleavages are exacerbated instead of smoothed over. The different political traditions and social and economic cleavages in the regions tend to encourage viewpoints that are parochial and narrow rather than national, and make Canada difficult to govern.

In 1993, the party system fragmented regionally and since then has been dominated by one party — the Liberal party. In 1997 the Liberals won all but two seats in Ontario, but only a handful in Québec, and a few others scattered across the country. In Québec, the party won 26 of 75 seats. Ontario was highly represented in the new Liberal caucus, but Québec, the Maritimes and the West were under-represented. Not only were the Liberals confined to narrow geographical regions — so too were all the other parties. Reform won all 60 of its seats west of Ontario. The Bloc won a majority in Québec. The NDP and Conservatives split the Maritime seats with the Liberals, and the NDP won some seats in the West.

---

16. The only exceptions were during three Progressive Conservative governments, which lasted in total only about six years.

TABLE 11.2   PERCENTAGE OF SEATS IN EACH REGION WON BY GOVERNING PARTY IN CANADIAN GENERAL ELECTIONS, 1867–1997

		% Seats Won by Governing Party in Each Region				
Election	Governing Party	Canada	West	Ontario	Québec	Atlantic
1867	CONSERVATIVE	55.8	–	56.1	69.2	29.4
1872	CONSERVATIVE	51.5	90.0	43.2	58.5	48.6
1874	LIBERAL	64.6	20.0	72.7	50.8	79.1
1878	CONSERVATIVE	66.5	90.0	67.0	69.2	55.8
1882	CONSERVATIVE	66.2	72.7	59.3	73.8	67.4
1887	CONSERVATIVE	57.2	93.3	56.5	50.8	55.8
1891	CONSERVATIVE	57.2	93.3	52.2	46.2	72.1
1896	LIBERAL	54.9	47.1	46.7	75.4	43.6
1900	LIBERAL	62.0	70.6	39.1	87.7	69.2
1904	LIBERAL	65.0	75.0	44.2	83.1	74.3
1908	LIBERAL	60.2	51.4	41.9	81.5	74.3
1911	CONSERVATIVE	60.2	51.4	83.7	41.5	45.7
1917	UNIONIST (CONSERVATIVE)	65.1	96.5	90.2	4.6	67.7
1921	Liberal	49.4	8.8	25.6	100.0	80.6
1925	Liberal	40.4	33.3	13.4	90.8	20.7
1926	Liberal	47.3	34.8	28.0	92.3	31.0
1930	CONSERVATIVE	55.9	44.9	72.0	36.9	79.3
1935	LIBERAL	69.8	48.6	68.3	84.6	96.2
1940	LIBERAL	72.7	59.7	67.1	93.8	73.1
1945	LIBERAL	51.0	26.4	41.5	83.1	69.2
1949	LIBERAL	72.5	59.7	67.5	90.4	73.5
1953	LIBERAL	64.2	37.5	58.8	88.0	81.8
1957	Progressive Conservative	42.3	29.2	71.8	12.0	63.6
1958	PROGRESSIVE CONSERVATIVE	78.5	91.7	78.8	66.7	75.8
1962	Progressive Conservative	43.8	68.1	41.1	18.7	54.5
1963	Liberal	48.7	13.9	61.2	62.7	60.6
1965	Liberal	49.4	12.5	60.0	74.7	45.5
1968	LIBERAL	58.7	40.0	72.7	75.7	21.9
1972	Liberal	41.3	10.0	40.9	75.7	31.2
1974	LIBERAL	53.4	18.6	62.5	81.1	40.6
1979	Progressive Conservative	48.2	73.8	60.0	2.7	56.3
1980	LIBERAL	52.1	2.5	54.7	98.7	59.4
1984	PROGRESSIVE CONSERVATIVE	74.8	76.3	70.5	77.3	78.1
1988	PROGRESSIVE CONSERVATIVE	57.3	53.9	46.5	84.0	37.5
1993	LIBERAL	60.9	32.6	99.0	25.3	96.9
1997	LIBERAL	51.5	18.7	98.1	34.7	34.4

Legend: Upper-case = majority government
          Lower-case = minority government

Note: "West" includes NWT and Yukon.

TABLE 11.3   REGIONAL COMPOSITION OF GOVERNMENT CAUCUS AND HOUSE OF COMMONS, CANADIAN GENERAL ELECTIONS, 1867–1997

Election	Governing Party	% Regional Composition of Government Caucus				% Regional Composition of House of Commons			
		West	Ont.	Qué.	Atl.	West.	Ont.	Qué.	Atl.
1867	CONSERVATIVE	—	45.5	44.6	9.9	—	45.3	35.9	18.8
1872	CONSERVATIVE	8.7	36.9	36.9	17.5	5.0	44.0	32.5	18.5
1874	LIBERAL	1.5	48.1	24.8	25.6	4.9	42.7	31.6	20.9
1878	CONSERVATIVE	6.6	43.1	32.8	17.5	4.9	42.7	31.6	20.9
1882	CONSERVATIVE	5.8	38.8	34.5	20.9	5.2	43.3	31.0	20.5
1887	CONSERVATIVE	11.4	42.3	26.8	19.5	7.0	42.8	30.2	20.0
1891	CONSERVATIVE	11.4	39.0	24.4	25.2	7.0	42.8	30.2	20.0
1896	LIBERAL	6.8	36.8	41.9	14.5	8.0	43.2	30.5	18.3
1900	LIBERAL	9.1	27.3	43.2	20.5	8.0	43.2	30.5	18.3
1904	LIBERAL	15.1	27.3	38.8	18.7	13.1	40.2	30.4	16.4
1908	LIBERAL	13.5	27.1	39.8	19.5	15.8	38.9	29.4	15.8
1911	CONSERVATIVE	13.5	54.1	20.3	12.0	15.8	38.9	29.4	15.8
1917	UNIONIST (CONSERVATIVE)	35.9	48.4	2.0	13.7	24.3	34.9	27.7	13.2
1921	Liberal	4.3	18.1	56.0	21.6	24.3	34.9	27.7	13.2
1925	Liberal	23.2	11.1	59.6	6.1	28.2	33.5	26.5	11.8
1926	Liberal	20.7	19.8	51.7	7.8	28.2	33.5	26.5	11.8
1930	CONSERVATIVE	22.6	43.1	17.5	16.8	28.2	33.5	26.5	11.8
1935	LIBERAL	20.5	32.7	32.2	14.6	29.4	33.5	26.5	10.6
1940	LIBERAL	24.2	30.9	34.2	10.7	29.4	33.5	26.5	10.6
1945	LIBERAL	15.2	27.2	43.2	14.4	29.4	33.5	26.5	10.6
1949	LIBERAL	22.6	29.5	34.7	13.1	27.5	31.7	27.9	13.0
1953	LIBERAL	15.9	29.4	38.8	15.9	27.2	32.1	28.3	12.5
1957	Progressive Conservative	18.8	54.4	8.0	18.8	27.2	32.1	28.3	12.5
1958	PROGRESSIVE CONSERVATIVE	31.7	32.2	24.0	12.0	27.2	32.1	28.3	12.5
1962	Progressive Conservative	42.2	30.2	12.1	15.5	27.2	32.1	28.3	12.5
1963	Liberal	7.8	40.3	36.4	15.5	27.2	32.1	28.3	12.5
1965	Liberal	6.9	38.9	42.7	11.5	27.2	32.1	28.3	12.5
1968	LIBERAL	18.1	41.3	36.1	4.5	26.5	33.3	28.0	12.1
1972	Liberal	6.4	33.0	51.4	9.2	26.5	33.3	28.0	12.1
1974	LIBERAL	9.2	39.0	42.6	9.2	26.5	33.3	28.0	12.1
1979	Progressive Conservative	43.4	41.9	1.5	13.2	28.4	33.7	26.6	11.3
1980	LIBERAL	1.4	35.4	50.3	12.9	28.4	33.7	26.6	11.3
1984	PROGRESSIVE CONSERVATIVE	28.9	31.8	27.5	11.8	28.9	33.7	26.6	11.3
1988	PROGRESSIVE CONSERVATIVE	28.4	27.2	37.3	7.1	30.2	33.6	25.4	10.8
1993	LIBERAL	16.4	55.4	10.7	17.5	30.2	33.6	25.4	10.8
1997	LIBERAL	11.0	65.2	16.8	7.1	30.2	34.2	24.9	10.6

Legend: Upper-case = majority government
Lower-case = minority government

Note: "West" includes NWT and Yukon. Rows may not add up to 100% because of rounding.

IDEOLOGY: THE IDEAS BEHIND CANADIAN POLITICAL PARTIES

Recall that **ideology** is an explicit doctrinal structure that provides a particular diagnosis of the ills of society, and an accompanying "action program" for implementing prescribed solutions for these problems. It is common for ideologies to be associated with particular political parties, structuring their rhetoric and conditioning their policy programs.[17]

Ideological positions are often placed on a left/right spectrum. The concept of left/right stems from politics in France after the Revolution (1789), when the different political factions sat in different locations in a semicircular legislative chamber. The most radical elements, who wanted considerable social change and maximum equality, sat on the far left side of the chamber, while the most conservative elements, who wanted no change and maximum inequality, sat on the right. The moderate, middle-of-the-road groups occupied the centre seats. Over time these groupings became known as the left, centre and right. Gradually, the same labels were applied to groups and ideas outside Parliament, and over time they were adopted in other countries as a shorthand way to identify and explain various groups or ideas in relation to each other.

The most important twentieth-century ideologies are thus often seen as shaded on a spectrum with communism at the extreme left, through social democracy, liberalism and conservatism, which would be relatively central, to Nazism and fascism on the extreme right. (See Figure 11.2.)

It is difficult to apply the left/right ideological spectrum accurately in the real world because ideologies are never manifested in a pure form; rather, they vary considerably over both time and place. One conservative or liberal regime may be considerably further "left" or "right" than another. Ideologies do not always proceed neatly on a continuum when one examines specific issues such as freedom of speech or racial equality. An ideology might be relatively extreme in respect to one issue but not another. The left/right notion does, however, prove useful as a very general method of categorizing political ideas. We can locate Canadian political parties at the centre of the political spectrum running roughly from social democracy to conservatism.

Within Canadian society, the main ideologies are conservative, liberal and socialist. These ideologies have deep historical roots. Liberalism and conservatism originated in Europe in the nineteenth century, as philosophers and thinkers struggled to create logical and consistent patterns of thought about how to restructure the medieval social and political order. Socialism developed later,

FIGURE 11.2 LEFT/RIGHT IDEOLOGICAL SPECTRUM

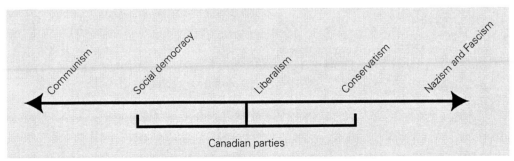

---

17. This section draws heavily on material from Robert J. Jackson and Doreen Jackson, *An Introduction to Political Science: Comparative and World Politics* 3rd ed. (Toronto: Prentice Hall, 2000).

381

but, again, in response to fundamental changes in economics. By the beginning of the twentieth century, the European political and ideological battlefield was a three-way contest as the socialist ideology added socialist, labour and communist parties to those espousing liberalism and conservatism.

Liberalism

Liberalism was the ideology of a rising commercial class that resented the restrictions of the old feudal order on European society. The ideas it generated provided guidance in moral, political and economic spheres. Morally, liberalism affirmed basic values including freedom and dignity. Politically, it espoused basic political rights such as the right of representative government. Economically, it was dedicated to the right to private property, free trade and free-enterprise capitalism.

The historical root of "liberal" is the Latin *liber*, meaning "free" (man). The concept of freedom is at the heart of the liberal ideology. Early proponents of liberalism called for freedom (absence of coercion) in all areas of life: social, political and economic.

John Locke (1632–1704), an English political philosopher, was the most influential of the early thinkers generally referred to as classical liberals. His ideas spread rapidly throughout the western world. Locke argued that all human beings have the right to life, liberty and property, and that they create government to protect and preserve these basic rights. If the government fails in this task, Locke said, the people have the right to overthrow it.[18] He wrote: "Freedom is ... to have a standing rule to live by, common to everyone of that society and made by the legislative power erected in it."[19] Civil liberties, or freedoms such as freedom of expression, freedom of speech, freedom to publish and disseminate one's ideas, have been enshrined in the constitutions of most liberal democracies.

Locke and other classical liberals such as John Stuart Mill and Jean-Jacques Rousseau wanted to organize government to maintain law and order, but not to infringe on human rights. They maintained that the way to accomplish that goal was to force governments to operate under the strict limits of a constitution. Locke believed that legislatures elected by the people should make decisions for society. He based his idea of representative government on the notion that political authority derives from the people. The elected majority, he said, can make the political decisions, but it must respect the natural rights of all citizens.

In one important sense, however, liberalism as it developed in England was quite different from liberalism in France. In England, liberalism was not anti-religious. In France, liberalism was antagonistic to organized religion, and that meant it collided with the Roman Catholic Church. The antipathy of the Church toward liberalism was later exported to Québec where the Church was a very powerful social force for many years and initially prevented liberal ideas from taking root.

Liberalism also had important economic implications for the state. Adam Smith's *The Wealth of Nations* (1793) had greatly influenced the development of western states. It expounded the principle of *laissez-faire*, which essentially means there should be minimum intervention by government in economic affairs. Smith maintained that society, like the physical universe, is governed by natural laws. One such law holds that prices in a free market are determined by supply and demand. Ideally, Smith reasoned, the government would leave the economy entirely to adjust itself through the free market.

Classical liberalism was deemed harsh to the poor and disadvantaged in society because it opposed redistribution of wealth. At the same time, however, it defended the principle of equality

---

18. John Locke, *Two Treatises on Government*, Peter Laslett, ed. (New York: New American Library, 1965).
19. Ibid., Second Treatise, ch. 4.

before the law for all individuals. Economic inequality was unavoidable, classical liberals said, but eventually the free-market system would create wealth and raise living standards for everyone.

Modern-day liberalism has abandoned some of the principles of classical liberalism. The new position is often called reform liberalism because it expanded or "reformed" the classical approach to the concept of freedom. The initial motivation for this new philosophy was to relieve the extensive poverty of the new urban working class in Britain.

Reform liberals departed from the classical roots on three essential issues:

1. The idea that government should be left to the propertied class was replaced by democratic principles of mass participation.

2. The concept of freedom was changed to recognize that the state may have to curb some liberties in order to provide a higher standard of living for the least well-off in society.

3. Reform liberals abandoned *laissez-faire* capitalism to accept the teaching of economist John Maynard Keynes, who argued that reliance on market forces could result in a permanent economic depression, and that this could be avoided by governments adopting appropriate fiscal and monetary measures.

Reform liberals reconciled state action with their notion of individual freedom by arguing that economic intervention was necessary to enable individuals to fulfill their potential and to make the market work effectively. They maintained that government must play a regulatory role in protecting society. The governments of Britain, Canada and the United States all followed this modern liberal reasoning after the Second World War.

Contemporary liberal values include respect for individual rights and freedoms, political equality, limited government, rule of law, minimum conditions of life guaranteed by the state, and modified economic freedom. In other words, modern liberalism favours minimal government intervention in the private lives of citizens, but reasonable government intervention in economic affairs. In recent years, however, this philosophy has come under attack from many quarters. In many respects, there has been a return to pre-Keynesian economics. All five parties in the Canadian House of Commons today espouse a kind of nineteenth-century liberalism in stressing the market's role in the regulation of economic life. None of them, however, has completely departed from all aspects of Keynesianism.

Conservatism

Conservatism as an ideology justified the positions of the aristocracy and Church in the old order of European society. These elements of society resisted the liberal ideology of progressive social change and defended the *status quo*. Their proponents sought to conserve such elements as power, property, status and way of life. This ideology took the term conservative, which comes from the Latin *conservare*, which means to save or preserve.

English scholar Edmund Burke (1729–97) was the first major figure to define and clarify conservatism. He and other early conservatives insisted that society must have a stable order and structure in order for individuals to know their place in the community and live and work within those confines for the good of the whole. Change, they said, must be gradual. Burke believed that being a responsible member of the social whole allowed an individual to achieve greater happiness than could be gained otherwise. Conservatives believed that the social group was more important than individuals and accused liberals of being individualistic and selfish.

Whereas classical liberals were suspicious of state power and wanted to limit it, conservatives believed that state power was necessary in order to achieve social order. Burke, therefore, opposed extending the right to vote, for example, and defended the hereditary aristocracy and established

CLOSE-UP ON
Political Behaviour

THE IDEOLOGICAL SHIFT TO THE RIGHT IN CANADA

In the mid- to late 1990s, Canada witnessed a profound ideological change in its electorate and also in the political parties that represented it. Right-wing populism appeals to those who feel disadvantaged, and by 1995 Canadians had suffered a decline in real incomes for eight of the previous 13 years. Many Canadians blamed big, debt-ridden governments for a growing gap between rich and poor. In protest, they joined forces with an unlikely ally — the corporate elite — to demand cuts in social services and lower taxes. Political parties moved to the right to win public support. The Reform party was the first party to tap into the ideological shift federally, but the Liberal government also moved to the right very quickly following its 1993 victory. The party that once introduced old-age pensions, health care and other social services took up the new mantra of debt reduction.

church. However, Burke also viewed such power as carrying a responsibility to help the weak and less fortunate. In this way, conservatives could argue that their approach was better for the less fortunate of society than that of the liberals, who believed that everyone, including the poor, should be free to look after themselves. Burke and the early conservatives held basically the same economic views as Adam Smith and the classical liberals.

Like liberalism, conservatism adapted and changed. After the Second World War, conservatives gave qualified acceptance to the notion of the welfare state, but they still sought to preserve traditional moral values and a social structure that would provide leadership. European conservatism was never a strong part of American culture because the United States was founded and populated largely by liberals. There was no aristocracy or "old order" to defend. However, in the 1930s those who opposed the welfare state philosophy of modern liberalism adopted the conservative label. American conservatism thus stresses individualism, self-reliance and a dislike for state interference, and views the improvement of the human condition as the inevitable outcome of unfettered interaction among self-interested individuals. European conservatism, on the other hand, ranks order and the good of the community above individual freedom. The Canadian Progressive Conservative party has espoused both the traditional and American versions of conservatism at various times in its history. Essentially, the Reform party adopts the philosophy of American conservatives.

Socialism

Within the first few decades of the nineteenth century, the technological advances of the industrial revolution in Europe created a large, urban working class. Socialists sought to improve the lives of these workers by challenging the liberal idea that governments should not be involved in directing the economy of the country. Socialism championed public ownership, a planned economy and state intervention in the market. Workers required help from the state, but classical liberalism held that the economy should be as free of government control as possible.

In the early years of socialism, there were two versions: the "utopian" version found in Britain and France, and the "scientific" version of Karl Marx in Germany. The scientific socialists, led by Marx, dominated socialist thought by the end of the century. Within this group, however, a doctrinal split emerged. Those who wanted to work within the framework of parliamentary democracy became known as democratic socialists. Those who clung to the Marxist revolutionary prescription came under the label of communist. Both groups sought public control of the means of production and an end to the exploitation of labour under capitalism. But communism went much further, promising equalization of material conditions for everyone.

Even before the breakdown of communism in the Soviet Union there were significant changes to socialist thought. In Britain, nationalization of industry was no longer seen as a key component of their doctrine. Socialist thinker C.A.R. Crosland maintained that the essence of socialism was rather a set of "moral values" summarized as recognizing the need to:

- ameliorate the material poverty and physical squalor produced by capitalism;

- contribute to the social welfare of those in need;

- support equality and the classless society;

- promote fraternity and cooperation; and

- fight the negative effects of capitalism such as mass unemployment.[20]

In 1995, clause 4 of the British Labour party constitution (which called for nationalizing industries) was deleted — marking a major turning point in the development of socialism in political parties and leading to the election of a massive Labour government in 1997. Aspects of the socialist doctrine appear regularly in New Democratic Party ideology.

Nationalism and Populism

Liberal values, based on a belief in a capitalist society, a market economy and the right to private property, dominate in the mass public in Canadian society — however, not to the absolute exclusion of other perspectives. The main parties in the House of Commons from the 1930s until 1993 — the Conservative, Liberal and CCF/NDP parties — reflected the broad ideological differences of conservatism, liberalism and socialism but never strayed very far from the opinions of the broader public. The 1993 general election not only destroyed the familiar party system of the House of Commons but also brought in a Québec nationalist party and a populist party from the West — parties with two new ideologies to compete with the standard ideas of the Canadian party system. (Nationalism and regionalism are discussed in Chapter 7.)

Parties are scrambling to the right to win public support. The Reform party was the first to tap into the ideological shift federally. The Liberal government in Ottawa moved right very quickly after its 1993 electoral victory, as far or further than the Conservatives they replaced. It is following the same ideological path as extreme right-wing Conservative parties in Alberta and Ontario. The New Democratic Party, which normally should be able to appeal to disadvantaged, populist voters, has become almost irrelevant partially because it is too clearly tied to big government and organized labour.

Right-wing populism is an unusual phenomenon in Canada; it appears to be a direct import from the United States. The union of disillusioned voters with the corporate elite is useful for both at the moment, but is not likely to last. The goals of the two groups are almost diametrically opposed. In effect, they are using each other to force governments to downsize. It is unlikely that in the end governments will be able to satisfy both groups. Meanwhile, the right-wing ideological crusade has left almost no voices to speak out for the poorest and most disadvantaged in Canadian society.

ESTABLISHED PARTIES: HISTORY AND IDEAS

Parties are not ossified organizational structures. As political institutions that compete for governmental power, parties are based on ideologies as well as on the interests and opinions of their members. In order to be successful in elections, party leaders understand that they must bring together these ideological foundations with their memberships. Leaders must convince party militants and supporters as well as large segments of the public to support them. In other words, leaders try to balance the philosophical principles and the psychology of their membership while courting large numbers of voters through the techniques of mass communication.

---

20. C.A.R. Crosland, *The Future of Socialism* (New York: Schocken, 1963), p. 67.

The 1993 general election represented a massive shift in public opinion; only a few years earlier pundits were predicting the "death of Liberal Canada." Instead, Canada got a fragmented multi-party dominant system split along regional and linguistic lines, which continued after the 1997 election. In the following section we outline the history and fortunes of the five parties in the 36th Parliament, and also discuss a few minor parties that have had a significant impact over the years.

The Progressive Conservative Party

The oldest party in a country is often the party of established interests, and this is certainly the case in Canada. The privileged elements of Canadian society banded together as early as 1854, when John A. Macdonald gathered a working coalition of various interests under the label Liberal-Conservative. It was an alliance that included eastern commercial interests, conservative French Canadians and Ontario Tories. Their objectives were to bring about Confederation and then work toward a national policy — basically through encouraging national unity and developing the country by promoting a national railway, industry and commerce. Maintenance of the British connection was fundamental to the early Conservatives, as was the establishment of relatively high tariffs.

The Conservative party was traditionally disliked by farmers in the West because of its empathy for big business, and French Canadians were wary of it because of its strong British interest. These latter attitudes were consolidated by both the execution of Riel and the Conscription Crisis of 1917. Conservative support in French-speaking Québec disintegrated, and the Conservative party structure became centralized in Ontario. In the West as well during the pre-war period, there was no strong, single-party tradition, and voters withheld support from the Conservatives. After the First World War, Westerners formed the Progressive party, which allied itself uneasily with the Liberals.

Another misfortune for the Conservatives was that they were in power during the Depression, a situation that assured further unpopularity and erosion of support. Their adversities were compounded by a serious leadership vacuum: neither Arthur Meighen nor R.B. Bennett could make inroads into Québec. Then, in the 1940s, the party wooed Progressive support in the West and chose John Bracken, the Liberal-Progressive premier of Manitoba, as its leader, renaming the party the Progressive Conservatives (PC). George Drew became leader in 1948, but still the party remained in the political wilderness.[21] Not until John Diefenbaker, another Westerner, emerged as leader did Tory fortunes improve. The Conservatives formed a minority government in 1957, followed by a landslide, majority victory the next year.

In 1958, John Diefenbaker's charismatic personality and his appeal to diverse Canadian ethnic, economic, religious and regional groups brought his native Prairies into the fold, along with 50 seats from Québec. The Progressive Conservative party appeared to take over the Liberal stand of moderate reform. However, Diefenbaker's capricious leadership in difficult times ultimately alienated French Canada, the large urban centres, business and industry and the intellectual community. Only the West, his gift to the party, remained loyal. Diefenbaker's electoral defeat in 1963 left the Conservatives floundering and unable to re-enlist the Québec votes they had briefly recaptured; the charismatic leader who had reunited and led the party to victory had lost his magic.

When Diefenbaker failed to resign, Dalton Camp, the party president, engineered his removal at the party convention of 1967. The conflict over "the Chief's" leadership and forced retirement created factions within the party that plagued the Stanfield era that followed.[22] Enough local members

---

21. See W.L. Morton, *The Progressive Party in Canada* (Toronto: University of Toronto Press, 1950).
22. See, for example, Peter Newman, *The Distemper of Our Times: Canadian Politics in Transition, 1963–1968* (Toronto: McClelland & Stewart, 1968).

abandoned active politics to weaken party organization seriously at the local level. The six years of power under Diefenbaker's leadership preceded the Conservatives' second-longest continuous period as the major opposition party. Diefenbaker's successor, Robert Stanfield, with his honest but plodding image, lost his third and final campaign in 1974 by advocating wage and price controls. He was replaced by 36-year-old Joe Clark, member of Parliament for Rocky Mountain, Alberta, in 1976. This move consolidated western support, but by then the PC's other bases of strength had dwindled to the Atlantic provinces and rural and small-town Ontario.

The 1979 election gave the PCs their first hold on power in 16 years, but the prize was snatched just eight months later when their minority government was defeated on a vote on the budget. Joe Clark accepted the results of the vote as a want of confidence in the government and advised the Governor General to dissolve Parliament. The consequence of that combination of events was a severe Conservative defeat in the 1980 election and Clark's own ultimate rejection and defeat as party leader. At the ensuing party policy convention in Winnipeg, Clark submitted to a routine vote of confidence. Although he won 67 percent of the delegate vote, which was technically more than adequate, he asked the executive to call a leadership convention and declared his candidacy. His defeat by Brian Mulroney at that spring convention was a personal humiliation.

Mulroney, who had run unsuccessfully against Clark in the 1976 convention, had no previous experience in public office. He was, however, an extremely astute politician who had diligently paved the way to this leadership position over many years.[23] As a bilingual native of Québec of Irish-French descent, with family connections to the Yugoslavian community, his qualifications were tailor-made to win support from the two major constituencies the Conservatives desperately needed: French Canadians in Québec and ethnic groups, particularly in key Toronto ridings. Mulroney's challenge was to build a significant and durable electoral base in French Canada. In the 1984 general election, and to a lesser extent in 1988, he won relatively evenly across the entire country. In the spring of 1993, however, in the wake of constitutional reform failures, scandals and unpopular policies, the prime minister resigned.

In June 1993, Kim Campbell became leader of the party and prime minister. She led the party into a fall campaign that left the party in ruins. She lost her own seat and ended up with only two MPs, well below the requirement for official party recognition in the House. Two months later, she resigned and Jean Charest became interim leader of the party. The Conservatives temporarily retained their majority in the Senate and this helped to keep the party alive and functioning on Parliament Hill. Charest was elected leader in 1995 and promptly set about rejuvenating the party organization. In the 1997 election campaign he flourished in the TV debates and on the hustings, raising the number of Tory MPs to 20. Shortly after the election, however, Charest deserted the federal Tories and left for Québec City, where he quickly became leader of the Liberal party of Québec. Despite the fact that his party won more votes than Bouchard's Parti Québécois in the ensuing 1998 Québec election, Charest's Liberals won only enough seats to form the opposition.

Meanwhile, the federal Conservative party languished until party members elected former prime minister of Canada Joe Clark as leader. Clark took over the tattered remnants of a once powerful party, a party deeply in debt and in last place among five parties in the House of Commons. As of early 2000, Clark still does not have a seat in the Commons but he is leading an effective rebuilding of the party. He has vigorously objected to the idea of uniting his Conservatives with the Reform party,

---

23. Patrick Martin, Allan Gregg and George Perlin, *Contenders: The Tory Quest for Power* (Scarborough: Prentice Hall, 1983). Also see John Sawatsky, *Mulroney: The Politics of Ambition* (Toronto: Macfarlane Walter & Ross, 1991).

a stance which led to the creation of a new right-of-centre political party — the Canadian Reform Conservative Alliance — in early 2000.

AWE-SOME! thenewcooljoeclark@PCpartyofCanada.net

Aislin, *The Gazette* (Montréal). Reprinted with permission.

The Tory party in Canada is not doctrinaire and has never sought ideological purity. The early Conservative party under Macdonald was dominated by the themes of Canadian nationalism and support for British imperialism with its "innate assumption of moral and racial superiority."[24] Years in the political wilderness and the pressures resulting from expanding American influence in Canada as well as the growing anachronism of British imperialism undermined these Tory traditions. As they entered the 1980s, Conservatives themselves agreed that their party was "hampered by its public image of being pro–big business and anti-labour, anti-ethnic, anti-women and anti-youth, as well as re-actionary on most social issues."[25] This harsh assessment was a formidable burden, and efforts to soften

24. Charles Taylor, *Radical Tories: The Conservative Tradition in Canada* (Toronto: Anansi, 1982), p. 211.

25. Ibid., p. 211.

26. See Robert Stanfield, "Conservative Principles and Philosophy," in Paul Fox, ed., *Politics: Canada*, 6th ed. (Toronto: McGraw-Hill Ryerson, 1987), pp. 260–64.

the image, particularly in accommodating women and youth, culminated in the election, in 1993, of the party's first female leader and Canada's first female prime minister. The party has traditionally been committed to upholding the private enterprise system, but on occasion has let the government intervene in the economy to protect broad collective interests.[26]

The party was traditionally less sensitive to francophone interests than were the Liberals, but that changed after 1984 with a leader from Québec. Historically, the party was wary of American influence; it was also pro-British and supportive of agricultural interests. But, again, this changed dramatically under Mulroney, who led the party to a staunch pro–United States position and brought forth both the *Canada–United States Free Trade Agreement* and the *North American Free Trade Agreement*. Mulroney's electoral success relied heavily on the West and Québec. It was an unlikely union that held together partly because of the desire of both regions for free trade with the United States. In 1993, when those regions deserted the Conservatives, the party was crushed. The great party of Sir John A. Macdonald was forced to reassess its policies and even its very existence.

If the Progressive Conservatives are to become a vital party once more, they will have to inject themselves forcibly back into the national debate. Since the Tories now have official status in the House of Commons with 20 MPs, and an effective leader in Joe Clark, there is no reason why this could not happen. However, the fact that the party came only fifth in the number of seats (even behind the NDP) has limited its opportunities for sustained parliamentary action.

The Liberal Party

The Liberal party was slower than the Conservative to develop as a national force. Its predecessors were the early reformers who generally advocated a radical transformation of society and wanted to solve major inequities through governmental reform. The opposition to Sir John A. Macdonald's first government consisted of Clear Grits from Ontario, the Parti Rouge from Québec and anti-Confederation Nova Scotia MPs. It was generally considered a more egalitarian grouping than the Conservatives. However, there was no real unity among the groups until Wilfrid Laurier became leader in 1887 and transformed them into the national Liberal party. As Canada's first French Canadian prime minister, Laurier firmly entrenched the Liberal party in Québec, with assistance from people such as Honoré Mercier and Israel Tarte. Laurier still holds the record for the longest continuous term in office as prime minister — from 1896 to 1911.

After Laurier, the Liberal party endured a decade of discontent that climaxed in bitter division over the Conscription Crisis in Québec. In 1919, the party elected William Lyon Mackenzie King as party leader. The Liberals won the 1921 election, and King rebuilt the party into a strong organization that dominated Canadian government for most of the next six decades. Mackenzie King set a record for total years in power; he was prime minister for 21 years and 5 months. During his early years in office he astutely tried to accommodate the agrarian protest from the West by forming an alliance with the Progressives, but that initiative collapsed. Louis St. Laurent, who succeeded King (and who was defeated by John Diefenbaker in 1957), his successor Lester Pearson (party leader from 1958 to 1968, prime minister from 1963 to 1968) and Pierre Trudeau (prime minister from 1968 to 1979 and from 1980 to 1984), who followed Pearson, all more or less successfully accommodated Québec discontent but gradually lost the West.

Trudeau's ascent to the leadership in April 1968 was dramatic — a victory by an attractive political neophyte over well-known, experienced Liberal leaders. It spurred a wave of "Trudeaumania"

---

26. See Robert Stanfield, "Conservative Principles and Philosophy," in Paul Fox, ed., *Politics: Canada*, 6th ed. (Toronto: McGraw-Hill Ryerson, 1987), pp. 260–64.

that swept the country and gave his party a large majority in the ensuing election. Throughout the 1960s the Liberal popular vote had increased in the West and, although the 1968 sweep was not as extensive there as in Ontario and Québec, it represented a Liberal high point. Following that election, the party endured an unrelenting decline in support west of Ontario.

Liberal support began to fluctuate. In the wake of accusations of arrogance and insensitivity, the Liberals suffered near-defeat in the 1972 election. However, they won another strong mandate in 1974. Five years later they received another rebuff at the polls. It was not a crushing defeat, just severe enough to allow the Conservatives a tenuous minority hold on power. The Liberals' serious problem in 1979 was the fact that half of their MPs were elected from one province — Québec. That November Trudeau publicly stated his intention to resign as leader, but within weeks the Conservative government was toppled and a new election called. With the Liberals endowed with a new mandate in 1980, Trudeau's stated intent to resign dissolved.[27]

In the spring of 1984, having led his party for over 16 years, Pierre Trudeau resigned. John Turner won the ensuing party leadership convention and called an election within days. The Liberal party won only 28 percent of the popular vote in the 1984 election, the worst result ever for the Liberals in a federal election. Turner stayed on as leader, but his new party caucus was dispirited, fractious and poorly prepared for the realities of opposition status. Issues such as the Meech Lake accord and the Free Trade Agreement with the United States were particularly divisive, and the party went into the 1988 election in debt and divided over both issues and leadership. It lost again but improved its share of the popular vote to 32 percent. Within months Turner resigned and Jean Chrétien was elected party leader to become Canada's twentieth prime minister in November 1993.

The philosophical base of the Liberal party derived originally from British liberalism, but Canadian Liberal leaders have tended to adopt a distinctively pragmatic approach to issues as they arise. Traditional liberal themes such as reform, individual rights, state intervention to enhance the lives of the underprivileged, and national and international conciliation have recurred in various concrete forms in Liberal party platforms and policies. However, as we have noted, practical politics in Canada tend to be ideologically fuzzy and opportunistic. As one observer put it, "certainly there have been sporadic tremors of small 'l' liberalism. But whether unemployment insurance or the National Energy Program, the tremors have usually been in isolation, a reflection of an individual minister rather than concerted Government policies."[28]

After the Second World War, successive Liberal governments gradually expanded their influence in the social and economic spheres. They introduced important social welfare legislation and assumed more responsibility for directing the Canadian economy, particularly by enforcing wage and price controls in 1975. In the late nineteenth century, when the Liberal party was generally in opposition in Ottawa and in government in the provinces, it was a staunch defender of provincial rights. When the Liberals held power in Ottawa, however, they gradually moved into the position of the major opposition party or worse in the provinces, and correspondingly espoused strong centralizing policies. In foreign affairs, Liberal policies have been selectively internationalist. (See Chapter 15.) Internally, bilingualism and a broad commitment to individual and minority rights, both linguistic and legal, were perhaps the most coherently pursued liberal policies under Trudeau, Turner and Chrétien.

When the Liberals came to power in 1993, the need for deficit and debt reduction forced them to abandon policy positions they had supported for generations. In economic policy, trade, human

---

27. Pierre Elliott Trudeau, *Memoirs* (Toronto: McClelland & Stewart, 1993).
28. John Gray, "Who Will Be the Liberals' New Skipper?" *The Globe and Mail*, Toronto, January 6, 1982.

rights, social programs and immigration, the party's "conservative" element began to dominate. As *The Globe and Mail* put it, "the Liberals ... spent much of the term cooking from the previous Tory government's recipe book."[29] Prime Minister Chrétien and his team argued that some Liberal values had to be sacrificed for fiscal responsibility.

By their 1996 party convention, the Liberals smugly awarded themselves a 78 percent grade in keeping their 197 *Red Book* promises. However, there were some glaring omissions and reversals including no child-care program, no scrapping of the GST, no withdrawal from NAFTA and continuing high unemployment. The Liberals had subverted many promises in order to meet their "fiscal responsibilities."

By the 1997 general election the Liberals were able to slightly loosen the national purse strings on the basis that the deficit would be eliminated in 1999. Their efforts won them another term in office with a tiny majority. The only national party in Canada, its prospects for forming the government for some time are high.

Andy Donato/Toronto Sun. Reprinted by permission.

The CCF/NDP

The roots of the NDP are in the Co-operative Commonwealth Federation (CCF), which held its founding convention in 1933. The original CCF was an assortment of Fabian socialists, Marxists, farmers and labourers under the leadership of J.S. Woodsworth. The party had a predominantly western rural backing, and in the ensuing 28 years never attracted more than 16 percent of the popular vote. In 1958,

---

29. *The Globe and Mail*, editorial, October 28, 1996.

the Canadian Labour Congress (CLC) made formal overtures to the party, proposing the need for a broadly based people's movement that would embrace the CCF, the labour movement, farm organizations and professionals. The CCF set up a joint committee with the CLC to create a new party.

In 1961, the CCF was dissolved and the New Democratic Party, with its social democratic platform, was born. The new party retained many CCF leaders, but the participation of organized labour caused difficulties, and tensions between farmers and workers often ran high. The extent to which the party should be influenced by trade unions is still a divisive issue.

Vigorous leadership by Tommy Douglas in the early years, and then by David Lewis and Ed Broadbent, was never enough to overcome the lack of funds and the ideological divisions that kept the New Democratic Party as a third party at the federal level. It has never been able to expand its territorial base to Québec and the Maritimes.[30] In 1988, it achieved its best results ever: 43 seats in the House of Commons and 20.2 percent of the popular vote. Despite this good showing, Broadbent resigned and was replaced as leader by Audrey McLaughlin. In 1993, the party was reduced to nine seats and forced to rethink its purpose and direction. It did not have enough seats to be recognized as an official party in Parliament. It had lost its electoral base in Ontario and the Maritimes, and was again excluded from Québec. It was confined to a handful of MPs scattered throughout the western provinces. In 1995, the party elected Alexa McDonough, formerly of the Nova Scotia legislature, as party leader, and she steered the party closer to the political centre with an economic policy of balanced budgets.

There are several reasons why the NDP failed to become a national winner. As a left-wing party, it has had no strong position or impact on the country's major French/English cleavage. In the early years, it attracted the votes of discontented Westerners. From the 1960s to 1988 the Conservatives encroached on that base, but in the 1988 election the NDP captured 33 of their 43 seats in the West, mostly in British Columbia and Saskatchewan, and it appeared that the party might flourish. However, its traditional protest role was usurped by the Reform party and it was left defending the *status quo*. In 1993, Reform and the Liberals cut NDP seats in its western stronghold to five in Saskatchewan, one in Manitoba and two in B.C. In 1997 McDonough led the party back to a respectable fourth place in number of seats in the House of Commons, largely on her appeal in the Maritimes.

The NDP is considerably stronger at the provincial level than it is federally. In 1999 it held the reigns of government in three provinces — British Columbia, Saskatchewan and Manitoba. Federally, as well, the NDP has played a larger role in Canadian politics than its success at the polls would indicate. During the 1972 minority government, for example, tacit support from the NDP was vital to the Liberals.

In general, the NDP platform is based on democratic socialist goals. The NDP is a fairly ideologically based left-wing party. It advocates policies such as government regulation of the economy, including more government control of private enterprise, higher taxes for big business and industry, increased social welfare and protection from American influence.[31] However, the party leaders have constantly been forced to take on other issues and to compromise the party's strict adherence to social democracy in order to win votes. In 1993, NDP premier Bob Rae's tough measures to reduce the Ontario deficit offended many of the NDP's traditional supporters and caused a rift in the national

---

30. The NDP has never won a seat in Québec in a general election. They did win a by-election seat there in 1990, but afterward were consistently embarrassed by their new Québec MP's independence and nationalist views.

31. For further reading on the NDP, see N.H. Chi and George Perlin, "The New Democratic Party: A Party in Transition," in Thorburn, 4th ed., *Party Politics in Canada*, pp. 177–87; Desmond Morton, *NDP: The Dream of Power* (Toronto: Hakkert, 1974); Alan Whitehorn, "The New Democratic Party in Convention," in George Perlin, ed., *Party Democracy in Canada: The Politics of National Party Conventions* (Scarborough: Prentice Hall, 1988), pp. 272–300; and Janine Brody, "From Waffles to Grits: A Decade in the Life of the New Democratic Party," in Thorburn, *Party Politics in Canada*, 5th ed.

party. In the 1993 general election, the federal NDP lost all of its seats in Ontario. The ruling NDP in British Columbia also cost the federal party support by its pragmatic environmental policies. In 1997 these provincial issues were overridden by the NDP's vigorous defence of new economic and social policies against the more conservative views of the other parties.

NEW PARTIES

The Reform Party

The Reform party, led by Preston Manning, was founded in late 1987. Like other western protest parties, Reform tapped into feelings of economic and political alienation in southern Alberta in particular, and the West in general. Its rallying cry was "the West wants in." (See Chapter 7.) It fielded candidates in the 1988 general election and won no seats but captured 15 percent of the popular vote in Alberta. A few months later it won a by-election in Alberta, electing Deborah Grey its first MP. By April 1991, when opinion polls indicated that it led all parties in the Prairies and some polls even put it ahead of the unpopular ruling Conservatives nation-wide, it decided to send organizers east of Manitoba.[32] In the 1993 general election, it ran candidates in all provinces except Québec.

Reform benefited from widespread cynicism toward politicians in general and a feeling that the traditional parties had atrophied. It appealed particularly to farmers and others who felt outraged and abandoned by the established political parties. The cornerstone of the right-wing Reform policy platform in the 1993 general election was slashing the deficit, which it promised to accomplish in three years. To do this, it vowed to cut programs such as maternity leave and reduce transfer payments for welfare. Job creation was seen primarily as the responsibility of the private sector. It espoused the virtues of thrift and self-reliance, cheaper and less intrusive government. As a populist party it appealed to "plain folks" with "plain talk." Aspects of its platform harked back to the defunct Progressive party and Social Credit. For example, it included support for more democratic input into policies, based on initiative, referendum, recall of MPs, free voting in the Commons and a Triple-E Senate. Economic difficulties and social problems were blamed on scapegoats such as immigrants, bilingualism, multiculturalism, the GST and feminists. The party therefore attracted elements of society that resented immigrants and special status for French-speaking Canadians.

Reform won 52 seats with 19 percent of the popular vote in 1993 — not quite enough to become the official opposition. It displaced the NDP and Conservatives in the West of Canada to become the strongest voice of western interests. However, apart from one seat in Ontario, it had no representation east of Manitoba.

Once in Parliament, Reformers quickly became identified with the elite politicians they had reviled. They were accused by Liberals of pandering to anti-politician sentiments with their concentration on politicians' pay, pensions and perks. By the end of their first session in Parliament, the party had not climbed higher than 14 percent in public opinion polls and the leadership was forced to make many changes in the way the party operated in Parliament.[33]

By the time of their first convention, after the 1993 election Reform had begun changing itself from a protest party into one that could assume power in Ottawa. It continued to oppose the Liberals on policies

---

32. *The Globe and Mail*, editorial, October 7, 1991.

33. Reform adopted a traditional shadow-cabinet system in which individual MPs were given responsibility for questioning and criticizing specific Cabinet ministers. Before that period, Reform's organization had allowed no specialization and many areas of government activity were not adequately monitored. These changes complemented a more aggressive Question Period strategy.

such as transforming the social security system (in preference of an individual savings-based system); but most important, the party did not let up on its demand for a balanced budget (a zero deficit) within three years, while the Liberals only promised to reduce it to 3 percent of the gross domestic product. At the party's first convention, Manning even outlined policies he implied were designed to keep Québec in Canada. The party also diluted some of the ideological purity of its policies in favour of approaches the party's parliamentary wing argued would be more defensible and saleable in mainstream politics.

At its pre-election 1996 convention, the most extremist elements were out-voted as the party attempted to project its image as a more moderate, disciplined party ready to extend its reach to the province of Ontario, the Maritimes, and even Québec. They did, however, affirm that family and marriage involves heterosexuals, not homosexuals; they called for a referendum on abortion and offered their support for the return of capital punishment. They also supported equality for all provinces and "special status" for no one, along with 20 decentralizing proposals for a new confederation "and 20 tough realities about secession."

Reform's policies — especially its tough stance against special rights for Québec — captured considerable attention in the 1997 election campaign, resulting in the election of 60 western MPs. Reform formed the official opposition in Parliament and began to assert itself as a national party. Inside Parliament, the leadership developed a more coherent strategy for Question Period and asserted more discipline on caucus members. After only six years in Ottawa, Manning had suspended or expelled six members of caucus.

Outside Parliament, Manning pushed his United Alternative (UA) idea of uniting individuals from all political parties into a new party to confront the Liberals — including Reformers, Conservatives and even soft nationalists in Québec. In a mail vote, Reform party members voted by 60.5 percent to back the United Alternative. This result led Manning to try to link the Tory and Reform parties together. When this failed he forced the creation of the Canadian Reform Conservative Alliance, which linked dissident Tory groups with Reformers.

It remains to be seen whether the new Alliance party can sustain its appeal and grow into a nationally based party. Of course, it may wither and die like other western, populist movements such as the Progressive party in the 1920s. On the other hand, in the first half of 2000, it has already jolted the Liberal party establishment and dented optimism in the Conservative party.

The Bloc Québécois

The Bloc Québécois was the first separatist party to sit in Parliament. Party leader Lucien Bouchard founded the party from dissidents within Parliament. His own background showed lack of consistent direction. He supported sovereignty-association in 1982, but when the opportunity arose he changed his tune to federalism and accepted Tory patronage to become Canada's Ambassador to France. He came to Ottawa in 1988 as a federal minister and friend of Prime Minister Brian Mulroney. In May 1990, apparently slighted by Mulroney's handling of constitutional negotiations, Bouchard quit Cabinet and the Conservative party. In resigning he cast himself as spokesman for a monolithic, humiliated Québec. He said Canada was not even worth attempting to save:

> *We must stop trying to fit Québec into the mould of a province like the others. Beyond the legal arguments, there is one argument that is unanswerable. Québeckers do not accept this mould. Their very reality shatters it.*[34]

---

34. Quoted in Robert J. Jackson and Doreen Jackson, *Stand Up for Canada: Leadership and the Canadian Political Crisis* (Scarborough: Prentice Hall, 1992), p. 201.

When the Meech Lake accord died in June 1990, Bouchard set up a legislative group in the House of Commons to work for the dismantling of Canada — following essentially the same path as the provincial Parti Québécois under Jacques Parizeau. A handful of MPs followed him to create the Bloc Québécois. Most MPs had defected from the Conservative party, but two were Liberal. They were soon joined by Gilles Duceppe, who was elected in a by-election under the Bloc Québécois banner.

As we noted in Chapter 7, the Bloc Québécois stated its purpose in a draft manifesto as "solely to promote Québec's profound and legitimate interests and aspirations."[35] In the 1993 general election it did not present a comprehensive platform because it did not have, or want to have, any coherent ideas about how to run Canada. Its limited platform placed the Bloc left of centre on the political spectrum, defending progressive social policies but also fiscal conservatism, and reconciling the demands of business and labour under the sovereignty banner. Bouchard advocated free trade to create resources with which to implement social policies. Many of his economic policies mirrored the demands made by Québec business people at the Bélanger-Campeau Commission, which had examined Québec's political options after the failure of the Meech Lake accord. Although polls showed that only a fraction of Québec voters supported the separatist option for Québec, the Bloc appealed to voters to "shake up" the old-line parties. To this end he talked about cutting government waste, job creation and social programs. The party's *raison d'être*, however, was sovereignty. It appealed to uninformed passion — anger, fear and ethnic pride.

The Bloc went into the 1993 general election with 8 seats and came out with 54. It won 14 percent of the popular vote in Canada, but 49 percent in Québec where it ran all of its candidates. It was an impressive win, enough to make it the official opposition party, but was not the landslide it had hoped for. Many of its votes came from disgruntled federalists, indicating that the Bloc would need increased support to win a referendum on sovereignty.

In 1995, when the Québec referendum on separation was narrowly rejected, Québec premier Jacques Parizeau resigned and Bouchard left his position as leader of the Bloc to become provincial leader of the Parti Québécois and premier of Québec. In February 1996, the party establishment elected Michel Gauthier to be the new leader but, a year later, replaced him with Gilles Duceppe in a party-wide postal ballot. Lucien Bouchard remains in charge of the sovereignty agenda. The goal of the Bloc continues to be to bring the issue of Québec separation to the House of Commons, and thereby assist the Québec government of the Parti Québécois to achieve a Yes vote on sovereignty. Gauthier explained the role of the Bloc as "to ensure people in Québec continue to support us" and to "explain to them the advantage of sovereignty."[36]

The 1997 election campaign by the Bloc Québécois was poorly managed by Duceppe (see Chapter 12). The results toppled the BQ from second to third place standing and lost Duceppe his position as leader of the official opposition. Much more significant for the future of the country, the Liberals gained several seats and together with the Conservatives garnered 58 percent of the votes cast in the province. Many sovereignists began to ask — what is the purpose of having a separatist party in office?

Minor and Historical Fringe Parties

There continue to be several minor parties on the fringes of the Canadian party system that never win enough support to gain any influence or credibility. Some are serious, others less so. None has had any lasting significance. In the 1997 election, 10 political parties officially recorded their names with the Chief Electoral Officer and fielded the 50 candidates required to be officially recognized as a

35. Ibid., pp. 201–2.
36. *The Ottawa Citizen*, June 10, 1996.

political party.[37] No candidates from fringe parties won seats in the 1993 election, but some of them showed pockets of strength.

There are several factors involved in the development of minor parties including ethnicity, regionalism, poor economic conditions, charismatic leadership and ideology. Maurice Pinard theorizes that minor parties arise from a period of one-party dominance when voters are dissatisfied with the traditional party and do not like the weak existing alternative party.[38] They prefer instead a new minor party. At best, minor parties provide flexibility in Canadian politics; at worst, they fragment the country, pitting region against region and creating political instability.

One reason fringe parties proliferated in recent years was the rise of powerful single-interest lobbies. Some groups that support issues such as English-first or the environment choose to form new parties rather than work through the traditional parties. Generally, fringe parties do not attempt to develop policies on a cross-section of issues, but field candidates on a limited platform or single issue. Two fringe parties of historical significance federally are Social Credit and the Progressives.

Social Credit

The Social Credit party originated in the West. It was always a regional party, never more than a third party federally and never a serious threat to the party in power. During the Depression and the agricultural failures of the 1930s, a charismatic preacher, William Aberhart, captured the political imagination of Albertans with the unorthodox financial theories of Major C.H. Douglas (which were often labelled "funny money"). Under Aberhart's leadership the Social Credit party advocated the principle of monetary reform, or more explicitly, the right of the provinces to issue money and credit. In 1935, the party flooded the Alberta legislature with members and sent 15 MPs to Ottawa as well. The party's attempts to institute their radical financial reforms in Alberta were declared unconstitutional by the Supreme Court, but Social Credit persisted as a populist conservative party.

At about the time that the Social Credit party appeared in Alberta, Social Credit ideas also took root in Québec. The Québec wing was a failure until the fiery orator Réal Caouette revived it as the Ralliement des Créditistes. In 1961, the Créditistes joined the national Social Credit party, but the two groups were never fully integrated. No Social Credit member has been elected to the federal Parliament from western Canada since 1965, but the Ralliement maintained a small representation for about another decade.[39] It has not won any seats since 1979.

The Progressive Party

Also of historical interest is the Progressive party, which appeared briefly on the national scene in the 1920s. It consisted of a loose coalition of provincial United Farmers, and was based largely in Manitoba, Saskatchewan and Alberta, with some support in Ontario. The party opposed the National Policy tariff that kept the price of central Canada's manufactured goods relatively high and drove up

---

37. See "The 1997 Campaign" in Chapter 12.

38. On third parties see Maurice Pinard, "One Party Dominance and the Rise of Third Parties," *CJPS*, vol. 33, no. 3 (August 1967), pp. 358–73. See also Pinard, *The Rise of a Third Party: A Study in Crisis Politics* (Englewood Cliffs, N.J.: Prentice Hall, 1971); "Third Parties in Canada Revisited: A Rejoinder and Elaboration of the Theory of One-Party Dominance," *CJPS*, vol. 6, no. 3 (September 1973), pp. 439–60; and Graham White, "One Party Dominance and Third Parties: The Pinard Theory Reconsidered," *CJPS*, vol. 6, no. 3 (September 1973), pp. 399–421.

39. The best discussion of the Ralliement is in Michael Stein, *The Dynamics of Right-Wing Protest: A Political Analysis of the Social Credit in Quebec* (Toronto: University of Toronto Press, 1973). See accounts of the Social Credit Movement in Alberta in C.B. Macpherson, *Democracy in Alberta: The Theory and Practise of a Quasi-Party System* (Toronto: University of Toronto Press, 1953); and J.A. Irving, *The Social Credit Movement in Alberta* (Toronto: University of Toronto Press, 1959).

the costs of farming. It also opposed discriminatory freight rates that made it cheaper to ship manufactured goods from central Canada to the West than to ship grain eastward.

The Progressive party made a startling appearance in the 1921 election, sending 65 MPs to Ottawa, 15 more than the Conservatives. However, they refused to form the official opposition and, with no organization, the party quickly disintegrated as a national movement. Four elections later it disappeared from the federal scene; its adherents drifted into other parties. In the early 1940s, John Bracken, former Progressive party leader from Manitoba, became the national leader of the Conservatives and, to take advantage of the potency of the Progressive label in the West, the Conservatives adopted "Progressive" as part of their party's name.

PARTY STRUCTURE AND ORGANIZATION

We have noted that one outstanding feature of the Canadian party system is its federal nature. The Liberals, Conservatives and NDP have party organizations and run candidates at both levels. Reform only runs candidates federally. Parties at the federal and provincial levels may bear the same name but act quite independently, as with the Liberals at the national and provincial levels. At the other extreme, the Bloc Québécois only exists in one province, Québec, and is allied with a provincial party of a different name — the Parti Québécois.

The three traditional parties — Liberal, Conservative and NDP — have relatively similar organizations that are outlined in their constitutions. Each constitution vests final authority in the **party convention** — including both the biennial **policy conventions** and the **leadership conventions** called to select a party leader as necessary. Apart from this, their constitutions reveal little about power and influence; they simply set out the general structure of the party and describe the basic functions of each part of it. As well, the constitutions authorize the appointment of bureaucracies and the establishment of standing committees and commissions with appointed memberships, and guarantee regional and bicultural party representation at the executive level. They also indicate the basic philosophical leanings of the parties.

The traditional parties consist of two wings: the parliamentary wing, composed of the party leader and caucus; and a very large, three-tier extra-parliamentary wing. Both wings are dominated by the party leader (whose role and selection are discussed later in this chapter).

An executive body and a small permanent office stand at the apex of the federal parties; a very wide base of constituency associations is at the foundation. Between elections, virtually all of the structure below the apex dissolves, and communication with the party is through the national organization or the parliamentary wing. This is not true of Britain and other western parliamentary democracies, where the extra-parliamentary party continues to function actively, mobilizing citizens and participating in the dialogue between citizen and state. As well, none of the Canadian parties has a permanent office or professional staff that can compare in size or sophistication with those of British parties. The major parties in Canada have had permanent offices only since the mid-1940s. Until their establishment, the entire extra-parliamentary wing of each party was dormant until an election was called, and then it would arise spontaneously to coordinate the campaign. The extra-parliamentary wing was at one time, therefore, even more cut off from dialogue with the parliamentary wing than it is today.

Figure 11.3, which provides a schematic organization of the Liberal party, shows the Liberal Party National Convention at the heart of the party structure. It elects national officers, establishes party policy and is the party's ultimate decision-making body. The national executive consists of

FIGURE 11.3   SCHEMATIC ORGANIZATION OF THE FEDERAL LIBERAL PARTY 2000:
             PARLIAMENTARY AND EXTRA-PARLIAMENTARY

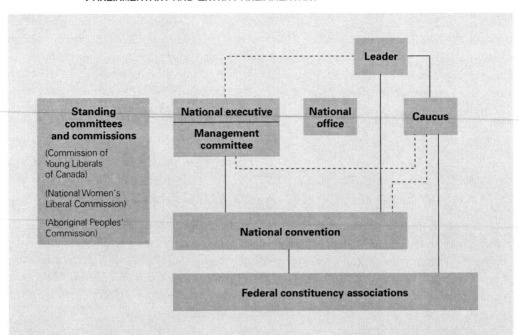

about 50 voting members. Standing committees prepare policy studies in areas including financial
management, constitutional and legal affairs, national platform, national campaign and so on. As well,
three commissions — the Commission of Young Liberals, the National Women's Liberal Commission
and the Aboriginal Peoples' Commission — give these particular groups a voice and formal link
into the party to express their special interests. The federal constituency associations are independent
organizations of local party activists across the country.

Constituency Level

The constituency is the locus of the grass-roots organization of each federal party. Constituency
executives represent the party in the ridings, recruit local volunteers and raise campaign funds. The
constituency level of the party also elects convention delegates and plays a major role in choosing federal candidates. The dedication of members to this basic unit is vital to party fortunes, but it is a relatively weak body within the power structure of the party.

The national office normally sets procedures governing party membership and the selection
of delegates to conventions, but formal decisions fall under the jurisdiction of the provincial party
organizations. Therefore, rules vary from province to province and even within a province. Neither
the Liberals nor the Conservatives have standardized membership qualifications or dues, although
many associations do charge a small fee. Constituency organizations in these two parties issue membership cards easily — indeed, on rare occasions, they have been known to sign up children and
derelicts when the need for votes for certain delegates or candidates was pressing! Before the 1993
election, the Liberals implemented residency requirements for those who vote for candidates, requiring
them to sign up in advance of the vote.

The NDP organization is slightly different, as one would expect of a social democratic party. It has dues and prohibits members from belonging to another party and requires them to pledge support to the constitution and principles of the NDP. An individual who joins the provincial wing of the NDP automatically becomes a member of both the federal and provincial constituency organizations. Fees are shared by the constituency, provincial and federal levels of the party.

In spite of large membership bases, there are few active members in any of the parties at this level, and the constituency associations meet infrequently. Parties do not normally contest municipal elections in Canada and therefore cannot draw on the forum of local government for support. As well, there is little congruence between provincial and federal party constituency boundaries. Another factor that hampers party activity at the local level is that constituency units are often very large and their members widely scattered. If the party is weak electorally in a particular constituency, funds are inevitably scarce, and it becomes difficult to hold activities and attract new members.

National Level

At the upper level of the extra-parliamentary party pyramid is the national organization of each party that unites the provincial associations. The national executive appears in a different form in each party, but it consists essentially of a small elite that conducts party business on behalf of the mass party. It includes a president, vice-president and other officers and several executive committees.

The small permanent office or headquarters maintained by each party contains a handful of bureaucrats and staff who are responsible to the executives from the extra-parliamentary organization and also to the party leader. The national offices of the traditional parties function as links between the provincial organizations and the elected members of Parliament and act as clearing houses for intra-party communications. Despite its permanent position at the apex of the extra-parliamentary party, this body is engaged mainly in service and coordinating functions: it organizes conventions, by-elections and general elections. As Joseph Wearing said of the Liberal National Office, the duties of a national office are chiefly those of keeping the party alive between elections.[40] After their 1993 defeat, the Conservatives had to cut their national and regional offices to mere skeletal services.

The organization of the Reform party reflects its grass-roots, populist philosophy. Constituency associations meet regularly, and have vital organizational, policy-development and election-readiness functions. Elected convention delegates vote into office members of the Executive Council, the governing body of the party.

The organization of the Bloc Québécois reflects its separatist philosophy. It is very closely tied to the provincial Parti Québécois. In 1993, PQ leader Jacques Parizeau campaigned for the Bloc, and long-standing PQ members were elected and assigned key positions in the Bloc shadow cabinet and as House Leader. Close ties were established between the House leaders and the whips of the two parties, and Bloc critics were asked to work closely with their provincial counterparts. Since 1996, Lucien Bouchard has been the PQ leader and close ties between the two parties have continued.

Women in Parties

Women did not have the right to vote federally until 1918 (much later in some provincial elections — Québec was the last to grant the franchise to women, in 1940). Nor did they have a representative of their own gender in the federal Parliament until 1921, the first federal election held after the

---

40. Joseph Wearing, *The L-Shaped Party: The Liberal Party of Canada 1958–1980* (Scarborough: McGraw-Hill Ryerson, 1981), p. 214.

franchise was extended. This first woman MP was Agnes MacPhail, who originally sat as a member of the Progressive party and later joined the CCF.[41]

Until the 1950s political parties, too, were male preserves despite the individual contributions of women such as MacPhail. Women and also youth were gradually acknowledged, but not yet as full partners. In the Liberal party, for example, young people were hived off into affiliated organizations: the Young Liberal Federation and the Canadian University Liberal Federation.[42] Women, who did much of the background work in the ridings, were diverted to the Women's Liberal Federation (WLF). Both groups were effectively barred from any significant part in the national federation.

Gradually, women and youth were integrated into the main organizations. In 1973, the affiliated organizations were replaced by two new ones, the Liberal commission (for women) and the National Youth Commission, which now elect their own executives and "are responsible to caucuses of women or youth delegates respectively at national meetings."[43] These organizations are intended to represent and promote the interests of students, youth and women in the party, and to encourage their participation and party activities. (Later, a third commission was added for aboriginal peoples.)

In time, special organizations designed to encourage women to participate in the parties may be abandoned as women's participation becomes taken for granted. In the meantime, however, to ensure female participation, both the PC and Liberal constitutions guarantee officials of the women's groups positions on the party executive committees and specify that a certain number of voting delegates at the conventions must be women. Partly because of these guaranteed positions, women have achieved higher visibility within party organizations in recent years.

The NDP constitution contains few guarantees with respect to female participation. By 1981, however, the party had an internal affirmative-action program, and two years later approved a requirement for equal representation of men and women on its executive and council. In December 1989, the NDP elected Audrey McLaughlin as its national party leader, making her the first woman ever to lead a national party in Canada. She was succeeded by Alexa McDonough in 1995. Women as electoral candidates and MPs are discussed in Chapters 5, 8, 9 and 12.

PARTY CONVENTIONS

Every two years, each party holds a convention to elect party officials and debate policy resolutions. These resolutions have no formal authority and are not binding on the Liberal or Conservative party leadership but they do constitute important policy guidelines. As well, the debates give delegates the opportunity to air their views and communicate their policy concerns to the political wing; they also attract free publicity. Party leadership conventions are particularly important in marshalling enthusiasm to help heal divided parties, especially after difficult periods in opposition. Conventions also have significant centralizing influence on the Canadian party system.

Party conventions in the three traditional parties are large, widely representative gatherings of several thousand delegates, most of whom have already invested considerable time and energy as

---

41. Agnes MacPhail served as a member of Parliament until she was defeated in 1940 and then moved to provincial politics in her native Ontario. She died in 1954 just before her appointment to the Senate was to be announced.

42. Reginald Whitaker, *The Government Party: Organizing and Financing the Liberal Party of Canada 1930–1958* (Toronto: University of Toronto Press, 1977), pp. 78–79 and 194–95.

43. Wearing, *The L-Shaped Party*, p. 218. For detailed studies of gender and age factors at recent conventions, see Janine Brodie, "The Gender Factor and National Leadership Conventions in Canada"; and George Perlin, Allen Sutherland and Marc Desjardins, "The Impact of Age Cleavage on Convention Politics," in Perlin, *Party Democracy in Canada*, pp. 172–87 and 188–201.

executive officers for the party or as members of women or youth associations. The Liberal and Conservative parties send an equal number of delegates from each constituency to their conventions, joining senators, MPs and defeated candidates. A number of delegates-at-large from the provinces also attend, including people who are prominent in party affairs but are not eligible to become delegates in one of the other categories. Both the Liberals and Conservatives allow *appointed* delegates-at-large and committee members to attend their national conventions, often in the face of vociferous objections that such appointments are elitist and undemocratic.

As a social democratic party, the NDP emphasizes the importance of the individual member. The NDP's national conventions include broad representation from Parliament, constituencies, youth groups and affiliated organizations such as trade unions and farm groups. Unlike the other two parties, the number of delegates from any particular constituency is based on how many members it has. This rewards active associations but does not help the party make inroads into areas where it is weak. Compared to the Liberal and Conservative parties, there are fewer delegates who attend the conventions purely by virtue of their official position. The Reform party, too, emphasizes grassroots participation. At each biennial policy convention it holds a vote to affirm the party leader.

Party conventions clearly are not designed to be representative of Canadian society as a whole, but of that party in society. They are normally more inclusive of the various age, gender, occupational and religious groups than are the party caucuses, but there are glaring deficiencies in comparison to the total population.[44] Delegates are much better educated and economically better off than the general population. Conventions cannot, therefore, be defended as truly representative in any strict sense. Terms such as "democratic" and "representative" are merely part of the rhetoric used by parties and commentators to generate respect and approval for their party conventions.[45]

Party Program Formulation

At the national level, the extra-governmental party takes part in drafting policy resolutions at biennial national conventions. The trend in recent years has been to keep leadership and policy conventions separate because of their complexity. Before a policy convention assembles, party associations are invited to send in suggestions for consideration by the convention. In theory, the resolutions presented to the delegates are debated and passed item by item. However, in fact, the resolutions committee often determines the success of resolutions.

We have pointed out that parties must aggregate, rank and articulate claims of interest in the competition for votes and decide which to present to the electorate as their party platform. Party platforms have contributions from both intra- and extra-parliamentary branches of the parties; they are generally what R.M. Dawson called "conspicuously unsatisfactory documents."[46] Of necessity, items must be vague enough to carry wide appeal — examples are "social reform" or "improved education" — and so end up reading rather like a list of New Year's resolutions. They must also appeal to regional interests such as maritime rights or economic sectors such as wheat exporters. Party platforms are therefore deliberately vague, broadly based documents of compromise that can be used to

44. See J. Lele, G.C. Perlin and H.G. Thorburn, "The National Party Convention," in Thorburn, 5th ed., *Party Politics in Canada*, pp. 89–97. For more detail on the attendance at party conventions, see John Courtney, "Leadership Conventions and the Development of the National Political Community in Canada," in R. Kenneth Carty and W. Peter Ward, eds., *National Politics and Community in Canada* (Vancouver: University of British Columbia Press, 1986).

45. The most recent comprehensive study of party conventions can be found in Perlin, *Party Democracy in Canada*.

46. R.M. Dawson, *The Government of Canada*, 5th ed. (Toronto: University of Toronto Press, 1970), p. 504.

unite the party nationally. As the three traditional parties have vied for the middle ground, their policy resolutions have often overlapped.

Even after the platform is drawn up and approved by the national convention, it is little more than a guide or, as Mackenzie King was fond of stating, a "chart and compass" for the party leader to interpret and follow as deemed opportune when steering the ship of state. The party constitutions give no official status to policy resolutions emanating from the national associations; this situation has been reinforced by successive party leaders.

The issue of extra-parliamentary involvement with policy decisions has been contentious for several decades. Until the late 1950s, party memberships were generally content to provide services at election time. However, by the 1960s both the Liberal and Conservative party federations were demanding to be involved in party affairs on a continuing basis. We have already noted several concrete steps that were taken to make the parties more democratic. Full-time national directors were hired, and national offices were established to operate between elections. Conventions gradually became more regular, and women and youth were brought into the main body of the parties. The philosophical justification for conventions continues to be that their decisions are representative of the party and thus more democratic than those reached by the parliamentary caucus.

One innovation intended to allow wider policy input into the Liberal and Conservative parties was the "Thinkers Conference." These meetings were attended by members of Parliament and of provincial legislatures, academics and other invitees who wished to contribute to policy initiatives. The Liberals held their first one in 1933, but the most notable were held in 1960 by the Liberals at Kingston and in 1967 by the Conservatives at Montmorency Falls. Both these conferences made recognized contributions to party policy and were followed by others. A Liberal meeting in 1969 was to be the first phase in a more ambitious operation intended to stimulate floods of public participation, but the public showed little interest. The Thinkers Conference became unfashionable and has only been revived sporadically, as in 1987, when the opposition Liberal party instigated a series of "Canada Conferences" to encourage wide, grassroots discussion and input into policy formulation. The conferences made a significant contribution to the "40 point" progressive platform that the Liberal party unveiled just before the 1988 election.[47]

The Reform party, more than any of the traditional parties, emphasizes grass-roots input into policy-making. Convention delegates meet with constituency members to discuss policies that will be voted on in convention. Once accepted, policies are recorded in a "Statement of Principles and Policies" and are considered binding on the leadership. However, while the lower echelons of the party regard conventions as a way to dictate future government policy, party officials tend to regard the biennial meetings largely as a media event designed to project a favourable image to Canadians.

A grave shortcoming of the pragmatic policy formulation procedures followed by modern Canadian parties is that parochial concerns often dominate at the expense of a national vision. As Gordon Stewart comments:

> *From the time that modern party formulation began in the 1840's Canada's political culture encouraged only the party leader/prime minister and perhaps one or two lieutenants to take long-term national interests into account.*[48]

---

47. A more modest convention at the beginning of the Chrétien leadership resulted in a volume of essays. See Cleo Mowers, ed., *Towards a New Liberalism: Re-creating Canada and the Liberal Party* (Victoria: Orca, 1991).

48. Gordon T. Stewart, *The Origins of Canadian Politics* (Vancouver: University of British Columbia Press, 1986), p. 100.

This has discouraged creative thinking about long-term policy solutions to problems. Stewart goes so far as to call the parties "political dinosaurs" — with great weight and presence but small brains.

National Party Leadership Selection

Until 1919, leadership selection in Canada followed the British model. Members of the parliamentary caucus and the retiring leader selected the new leader, occasionally with the advice of the Governor General, and then presented him to the party. The Liberal party was the first national political party in Canada to select a leader with the active participation of its extra-parliamentary wing. It happened almost accidentally. The 1919 convention was not intended to be a leadership convention; it was instigated by the prime minister as a policy convention to help reunite his badly divided party. However, Laurier's sudden death, "combined with the peculiar internal conditions of the parliamentary Liberal party, made the convention appear to be a natural way of selecting the next leader of the Liberal party."[49] Mackenzie King became the first party leader selected by a national convention.

The Conservatives chose one more leader — Arthur Meighen — by the caucus method in 1920, but when the party was defeated, and Meighen subsequently resigned in 1926, the party felt compelled to follow the democratic precedent set by the Liberals. In 1927, they elected R.B. Bennett at a national convention. The British leadership selection model whereby party leaders "emerged" after consultations generated by the retiring leader and the party caucus with the parliamentary party was thus abandoned. Open, more American-style conventions were established, gradually becoming more lavish. Liberals subsequently held leadership conventions in 1948, 1958, 1968, 1984 and 1990; the Conservatives in 1938, 1942, 1948, 1956, 1967, 1976, 1983, 1993 and 1994; and the NDP in 1971, 1975, 1989 and 1995. (See Table 11.4 for a list of major-party leaders.)

The appeal of the convention method is that it gives the impression, justified or not, that the party is "open," "democratic" and "representative" in making its decisions. A drawback is that it was not designed for parliamentary government, but rather for a system with separate legislative and executive offices. It has been adapted to Canada's unique federal, parliamentary needs, but not without leaving inevitable contradictions in the Canadian system. For example, leadership candidates must support their party in Parliament at the same time that they appeal for delegate support — something very difficult to do when Cabinet solidarity is at stake. There is often a legacy of bitter feelings that makes it difficult for the new leader to command the full support of the caucus.

As long ago as 1968, Don Smiley pointed out that the nature of the convention was changing, that a new "openness" was being established. He cited five examples. There were many more serious candidates than in early conventions, the major candidates conducted elaborate competitive campaigns across Canada, mass media coverage was extensive, the rank-and-file of the parties were more involved, and token candidates were treated generously.[50] These changes have all been confirmed; to them must be added the beneficial effect of the secret ballot on leadership selection. It would be unthinkable today for outgoing leaders to designate their successors and have the convention duly anoint them, which happened as recently as 1942 for the Conservatives and 1948 for the Liberals. At the same time, as we have noted, conventions are far from representative of Canadian society, and the "establishment" within each party tends to appoint a large number of delegates.

---

49. John C. Courtney, *The Selection of National Party Leaders in Canada* (Hamden, Conn.: Archon Books, 1997), p. 78.

50. D.V. Smiley, "The National Party Leadership Convention in Canada: A Preliminary Analysis," *CJPS*, vol. 1, no. 4 (December 1968), pp. 373–97.

TABLE 11.4   PARTY LEADERS: CONSERVATIVE, LIBERAL, NDP, BLOC QUÉBÉCOIS AND REFORM

Progressive Conservative Party	Liberal Party	New Democratic Party	Bloc Québécois	Reform Party
Sir John A. Macdonald (1854–91)	Alexander Mackenzie (1873–80)	Tommy Douglas (1961–71)	Lucien Bouchard (1991–95)	Preston Manning (1987–)
Sir J.J.C. Abbott (1891–92)	Edward Blake (1880–87)	David Lewis (1971–75)	Michel Gauthier (1996–97)	
Sir John Thompson (1892–94)	Sir Wilfrid Laurier (1887–1919)	Ed Broadbent (1975–89)	Gilles Duceppe (1997–)	
Sir Mackenzie Bowell (1894–96)	Daniel D. McKenzie* (1919)	Audrey McLaughlin (1989–95)		
Sir Charles Tupper (1896–1901)	W.L. Mackenzie King (1919–48)	Alexa McDonough (1995–)		
Sir Robert Borden (1901–20)	Louis St. Laurent (1948–58)			
Arthur Meighen (1920–26)	Lester B. Pearson (1958–68)			
Hugh Guthrie* (1926–27)	Pierre E. Trudeau (1968–84)			
R.B. Bennett (1927–38)	John Turner (1984–90)			
R.J. Manion (1938–40)	Jean Chrétien (1990–)			
R.B. Hanson* (1940–41)				
Arthur Meighen (1941–42)				
John Bracken (1942–48)				
George Drew (1948–56)				
John Diefenbaker (1956–67)				
Robert L. Stanfield (1967–76)				
Joe Clark (1976–83)				
Erik Nielsen* (1983)				
Brian Mulroney (1983–93)				
Kim Campbell (1993)				
Jean Charest (1995–98)				
Joe Clark (1998–)				

* Interim leader

Leadership conventions are similar to policy conventions in terms of basic organization and participation, and their general rules are common to all three parties, although details vary. They are called when a leader resigns or dies, and sometimes even if he or she does not score sufficiently high on a leadership review vote. Rules about when a leadership review will be held differ from party to party. Currently, the Liberal constitution states that a leadership review will be held only during the first national convention after a general election. In practice, Liberal convention delegates have always voted against calling a leadership convention, but the procedure remains a significant reminder that the leader is responsible to the party. In 1992, the Liberals approved a policy of giving all party members a direct say in reviewing the leader's performance after each election, thereby ending the practice of choosing delegates to vote on the leader's performance at a national convention.

In the Conservative party, leadership reviews were first initiated to assess John Diefenbaker's performance in 1967. They later became a regular feature of party conventions.[51] Technically, a Tory leader needs to win only 50 percent of the leadership review vote to continue in office. In 1983, however, Joe Clark resigned as Conservative leader after he failed to secure more than 67 percent of the voting delegates' support. He then submitted himself as a leadership candidate in a final effort to consolidate his party support. The caucus chose a temporary leader from its own membership, and at a subsequent leadership convention the party elected a new leader, Brian Mulroney. The Conservative party amended its review procedure at the 1983 convention to reduce the opportunities for a leadership review vote. Reviews are now held only at the first convention within a year of a federal general election in which the party does not form the government.

The NDP has no leadership review procedure as such, but requires its leader to seek re-election automatically at its biennial national conventions. It opens nominations for the position of leader, but if there is no challenger, no vote is required. In practice, an incumbent has never been defeated. In line with its general philosophy of accountability, the Reform party also asks delegates at every convention whether they want a leadership review. To date that option has always been turned down. The Reform party endorsed Preston Manning's leadership by an 86 percent vote in the automatic leadership review at the end of its 1996 convention.

Leadership conventions take several months to organize once a leader announces the decision to step down. Delegates must be chosen, and the manner in which this is done has important consequences for the leadership candidates. Recent leadership conventions have adopted the festive atmosphere of American conventions, with flamboyant speeches, entertainment and full national television coverage. There are some important differences, however. Balloting at U.S. conventions is by states rather than individuals, and the votes are announced openly, making the event quite ritualistic and predictable. The American primary system and open delegate selection process tend to produce a winner long before the convention. In Canada, the secret ballot (and the not-so-genteel tendency of some delegates to vote differently than they have promised candidates) lends a degree of suspense missing from the American process. Nuisance candidates, although kept to a minimum, are not totally discouraged in either system because of the colour and democratic element they add. In Canada, having several ballots also allows the serious candidates to learn the absolute voting figures and gain time to bargain between ballots while the token candidates are being eliminated. Delegates normally give little public indication of whom they will support if their first-choice candidate is eliminated.

---

51. John Diefenbaker's leadership was in dispute following his defeat in the 1963 general election, and party president Dalton Camp seized the opportunity to argue for the need to "democratize" the party by assessing the leadership. After a bitter struggle, the Camp faction won and a leadership convention was called in 1967.

TABLE 11.5   1990 LIBERAL LEADERSHIP CONVENTION BALLOTING RESULTS

Candidate	First Ballot
Jean Chrétien	2 662
Paul Martin	1 176
Sheila Copps	499
Tom Wappel	267
John Nunziata	64

At the end of each session of balloting, the votes are counted and results announced as a total — there is no potentially divisive breakdown. Victory on the first ballot does not necessarily indicate who will win; Clark won the first ballot in 1983, well ahead of Mulroney, but that lead narrowed in the next two ballots, and was finally reversed on the fourth and final vote. With the withdrawal or elimination of a candidate, coalitions shift and delegates disperse. When the Conservatives elected Joe Clark to lead them again in November 1998, it was under new rules (see "Joe Clark Victorious with PC's Radical New Leadership Selection Process"). Clark won on the second ballot. When Jean Chrétien was elected leader in Calgary in 1990, he won on the first ballot over four other candidates. (See Table 11.5.) In the 1995 NDP leadership convention, Svend Robinson was leading after the first ballot, but withdrew, conceding victory to second-place candidate Alexa McDonough. Preston Manning was elected leader of the Reform party at a 1987 convention after Stan Roberts withdrew his candidacy. Bloc Québécois leader Lucien Bouchard was acclaimed at a party congress in 1991. Five years later, Michel Gauthier became his successor, elected by fewer than 160 people, all from Québec, in one of the fastest, smallest and least publicized gatherings to elect an opposition leader in the postwar era. Gauthier resigned and a new leader, Gilles Duceppe, was elected in March 1997 by the entire party membership, using the format of mailed ballots plus a two-day convention.

Leadership campaign costs have escalated dramatically in recent years. In order to keep costs low, and to discourage candidates from relying on large sums of money from one or two donors who hope for future considerations, the Liberal party constitution now provides for the appointment of a leadership expenses committee whenever a leadership convention is called. The committee is empowered to set a maximum limit for candidates' spending prior to and at the convention, to enforce compliance with that limit, and to ensure complete disclosure of all contributions to leadership campaigns. The Conservative executive placed a $900 000 spending limit per candidate, plus unlimited travel for the 1993 convention. There were, however, few penalties for breaking the rules. Kim Campbell was reported to have spent at least four times the allowed limit.[52]

The 1993 Conservative contest may have been the last of the mega-conventions that began with the 1967 Tory convention in Toronto's Maple Leaf Gardens. The Liberal party decided in 1992 to use a combined direct-vote/convention model when the time comes to replace Jean Chrétien. Under the new process, federal leaders will be elected by a system similar to that used by the Ontario Liberals for the first time in 1992, combining the concept of party members' suffrage with the old system of electing delegates to attend leadership conventions. The hope is to avoid the kind of embarrassing spectacles suffered by the party in 1984 and 1990, when candidates wooed members of specific ethnic groups and used anti-abortion activists to stack meetings and elect slates of delegates. For the next Liberal leadership selection, all party members in each riding will vote for their

52. *The Globe and Mail*, October 30, 1993.

preferred candidate and each riding will then send delegates, proportional to the support garnered by each candidate, to a national convention.[53]

The general criticism that the convention process is too expensive and allows those with the money to walk away with the prize persists. It is unlikely, however, that the parties will forfeit the media exposure the convention method provides, or risk returning to the earlier model of parliamentary selections that were swift and inexpensive but smacked of elitism and anti-democracy.

PARTY LEADERS

Party leaders tend to exhibit similar characteristics, although these vary somewhat depending on the party to which that person belongs. Almost all who enter the fray are university-educated professionals. Since 1989 when Audrey McLaughlin became leader of the NDP, leadership is no longer a strictly male preserve.

In the past, the typical Conservative leader was a Protestant lawyer from one of the Prairie provinces, Ontario or the Maritimes. Today, that person is expected to be bilingual. Brian Mulroney was the party's first elected leader from Québec. Kim Campbell was the Conservatives' first leader from British Columbia, and the first woman to lead the party. The typical Liberal leader has been a lawyer — although this is less likely than for the Conservatives — a Roman Catholic and bilingual. Except for John Turner (who lived in Ontario but ran for office in British Columbia), the Liberals have always chosen their leaders from Ontario or Québec; normally they have alternated between French and English leaders, a tendency that has

CLOSE-UP ON Political Behaviour

JOE CLARK VICTORIOUS WITH PC'S RADICAL NEW LEADERSHIP SELECTION PROCESS

In 1998, the Progressive Conservative party abandoned the convention system of electing its leader and set up a new, direct election procedure. The electoral point system is intended to increase grass-roots support and be more democratic by ensuring the equality of ridings. Each party member casts one vote, but the results are weighted by constituency, so that, for example, if a very large constituency votes 60 percent for Candidate A, that candidate gets 60 percent of the riding's electoral votes. If a very small constituency votes 60 percent for Candidate A, that candidate, too, is awarded with 60 percent of the riding's electoral votes. The percentages of the 301 riding are then totalled to determine each candidate's success. Former prime minister Joe Clark passed the 50 percent hurdle on the second ballot.

Results:

First Ballot (Oct. 24, 1998)	Candidate	Total Percent Votes
	Fortier	4.08
	Orchard	16.33
	Pallister	12.21
	Segal	18.90
	Clark	48.48
Second Ballot (Nov. 14, 1998)	Orchard	22.52
	Clark	77.48

become a matter of principle for many Liberals. This was also a factor in the 1993 Conservative convention. To counter the criticism that he could be the second Québec leader in a row, Charest argued: "As far as the rule of alternation [between a Québécois and non-Québécois leader] is concerned, having had only one leader from Québec in 125 years, we haven't exactly abused the rule."[54]

Prior to the introduction of leadership conventions, leaders of both Liberal and Conservative parties were likely to be experienced career parliamentarians. Since then, previous parliamentary experience has become less significant for party leaders. Brian Mulroney was the first leader of either party to win the position with no legislative experience whatsoever. Not until he won a seat in a by-election several months after the convention was Mulroney sworn in as member of Parliament and, therefore, able to be leader of the official opposition as well as leader of the Progressive

53. Reported in *The Ottawa Citizen*, February 22, 1992.
54. *The Globe and Mail*, March 17, 1993, p. 1.

Conservative party. Reform leader Preston Manning, too, had never been in Parliament when he became leader of the party he had started. Mackenzie King, Pierre Trudeau, Audrey McLaughlin, Alexa McDonough and Michel Gauthier had all been in Parliament less than three years when they were elected leader. In Kim Campbell's case it was four years. Stanfield, Clark, Mulroney, Trudeau, McLaughlin and McDonough were all relatively unknown even by party activists until shortly before the conventions at which they were chosen. John Turner had been out of politics and disassociated from the Liberal government for years, but still remained the darling of the media while he waited in the wings. Lucien Bouchard was first elected to Parliament, as a Conservative, in 1988 — just two years before he became leader of the Bloc Québécois. Michel Gauthier was the first MP to be elected under the Bloc's banner in 1991. It used to appear that a fresh image counted more at a leadership convention than did the experience of a party veteran, although Jean Chrétien was able to counter the epithet "yesterday's man" and turn his many years of parliamentary experience into an asset. Joe Clark's return to the leadership of the Conservative party may confirm the revision of this argument.

The Role of the Leader in the Party

The party leader has a pre-eminent role as decision-maker, figurehead and spokesperson of both the parliamentary and extra-parliamentary branches of a party. The image projected by a leader is extremely important because it provides a simple, differentiating feature between the parties, which otherwise often appear very similar to the electorate. A leader with a poor image can ruin the electoral chances of even the most vital party; this fact encourages enormous preoccupation with image-building and the appearance and personality of the leader, to the detriment of policy issues. The leadership position is a prestigious one carrying considerable powers in the parliamentary system. National party leaders ideally are symbols of unity, figures above sectional interests. The more regionalized the party system becomes, the less this ideal can be met.

The prime minister's position at the apex of government, public service and political party was discussed in Chapter 8. Here it is sufficient to note that the office includes a large support staff and many other perquisites of which political patronage is foremost. Patronage has, since colonial days, been relatively openly entrenched as a legitimate activity. Prime ministers have used patronage to help build and maintain broad bases necessary for national parties.

The prime minister's political patronage powers are second to none. As the top member of the government hierarchy, he or she has Cabinet, government bureaucracy and Senate positions to fill, as well as party appointments. Opposition leaders, whose capacity for largesse is extremely limited, have a much more difficult time keeping a united party.

Much of the prestige of the official leader of the opposition lies in the fact that he or she is a potential prime minister and could inherit the superior status and authority of that coveted position. But because the job is to lead the offensive against the party in power, opposition leaders are often accused of carping and sometimes even unpatriotic behaviour for attacking the government.

We have already noted the extensive authority the leader has over the extra-parliamentary wing of the party, including the power to approve or disapprove the budget for the activities of the party organization. Another power arises from the right to make key appointments on the national executive and to create *ad hoc* committees whose authority may supersede that of the officers elected by the national association. For example, the leader makes appointments to the election campaign committee. Within the parliamentary party the opposition leader appoints a "shadow cabinet," and in many ways enjoys more flexibility than the prime minister does in choosing a Cabinet.

The leader of the official opposition has special status at official functions and in parliamentary ceremonies and even an international standing with foreign governments, but this position is nevertheless very inferior compared to that of the prime minister.[55] Though his or her functions are not governed by statute, the role is officially recognized in the procedures of the House of Commons. Canada first officially recognized the existence of the leader of the opposition in 1905 by granting the occupant of that position a salary equal to that of a Cabinet minister. Surprisingly, Canada was well ahead of Britain in doing so, for it was not until 1937 that the British officially recognized their opposition leader along with their prime minister.[56]

While the prime minister enjoys the many perquisites of government and the official residences at 24 Sussex Drive and Harrington Lake, the opposition leader receives, in addition to a salary and expense allowance as a member of Parliament, other perks such as a car allowance and an official residence — Stornoway in Rockcliffe Park. As for facilities on Parliament Hill, the opposition leader is provided with a large staff and offices in the House of Commons similar to that allocated to the prime minister. In addition, as a member of Parliament, the opposition leader is entitled to a suite of offices and to a constituency office with a full-time staff in Ottawa and in his or her riding.[57] In Parliament, the opposition leader has the right to ask the lead question in Question Period and benefit from the attendant publicity that entails.

The party leader is accountable to the caucus. Without the support of the caucus and the national association, the leader cannot hope for sufficient party unity to achieve electoral victory. The leader's relationship with these two important sectors of the party is complicated because the caucus basically represents federal interests, while the national association tends to be more representative of provincial interests. The task of placating the two is especially difficult for an opposition leader who has general responsibility for the conduct of the members of the caucus but few rewards to offer them. Internecine battles over the leadership during Joe Clark's first tenure contributed to and reinforced the Conservative image of a fragmented party in electoral decline. Similar problems beset John Turner in the Liberal party before the 1988 election.

Nonetheless, the power of the parliamentary caucus is limited *vis-à-vis* the leader because regular meetings are held only a half-day each week and even then no votes are taken. The leader simply interprets the general mood in what he or she determines is the party's best interests. This means, as George Perlin notes, that there is no recognized independent body within the caucus that can challenge the leader.[58] Getting rid of an unpopular leader who is determined to stay on is a difficult matter that requires a vote of non-confidence at a leadership review, as discussed earlier.

The superior status of the party leader in the Canadian system is deeply rooted in parliamentary tradition. The leader is the only party member who can claim broadly based legitimacy. Leaders such as Preston Manning and Lucien Bouchard who founded new parties were quick to legitimate their position by a vote. Chosen by the national convention but also the voice of the parliamentary caucus, the party leader is the most powerful individual in the creation of party policy. The position is, at least theoretically, a symbol of coherence and cohesion for the party.

55. R.M. Punnett, *Front-Bench Opposition* (London: Heinemann, 1973), p. 99.

56. Ghita Ionescu and Isabel de Madariaga, *Opposition: Past and Present of a Political Institution* (London: C.A. Watts and Co. Ltd., 1968), p. 69.

57. Alastair Fraser, "Legislators and their Staffs," in Harold Clarke et al., eds., *Parliament, Policy and Representation* (Toronto: Methuen, 1980), p. 232.

58. George Perlin, *The Tory Syndrome* (Montréal: McGill-Queen's University Press, 1980), p. 26.

PARTY FINANCE

Political parties require funds for three basic purposes. First, they must support expensive election campaigns. Second, they must maintain a small permanent staff between elections. Third, they need money to support research and advisory services for the party leader and elected representatives.

Where do these funds come from and who obtains them? In Chapter 9, we discussed the formula by which party caucuses receive money for research and for leaders' salaries from the House of Commons. To get such funds parties must have a minimum of 12 elected members in Parliament. It is difficult for parties to operate effectively or even stay alive without this funding. The Social Credit party, for example, lost this funding when it dropped to 11 seats in 1974, and it never recovered. The Conservatives and NDP faced a similar prospect with their electoral losses in 1993, but both managed to bounce back enough to achieve official status after the 1997 election.

Besides this internal funding however, parties are actively engaged in seeking funds outside Parliament. In the early years of two-party politics in Canada, both major parties were financed largely from the same corporate contributors. Provincial and federal parties received allotments from central party funds; this highly centralized organization of party finance had an integrative effect that helped counter the centrifugal forces of the federal system. Party leaders played a key role in collecting and distributing campaign funds because there was no special fundraising structure or permanent party organization.

With the advent of minor parties federally and the increased economic and political strength of the provinces regarding the federal government, the centralized nature of party financing began to change. After the Second World War, the concentration on resource and extractive industries, which are under provincial jurisdiction, increased provincial wealth. Large corporations began to seek direct access to provincial governments and to make party contributions at the provincial as well as federal level. Provincial parties in western and central Canada, in particular, were adept at gathering funds. As the provincial governments and provincial parties increased their wealth and power, they were able to compete more and more successfully with their federal counterparts. Gradually, party financing became decentralized; today, it retains little of its earlier integrative role.

The *Election Expenses Act*, which was passed in 1974, had a profound influence on the fundraising patterns of all Canada's parties. The new law was intended to bring party financing into the open and at the same time cap election spending. Until that time, parties were reluctant to admit the extent of their financial dependence on specific sources. There was always a suspicion that those who contributed might have undue influence on the selection of leaders or the determination of party policies. The motivation of donors was suspect even though their reason for contributing might have been as innocent as a desire to do their civic duty.

There were two early political scandals in Canada resulting from parties accepting money from "unsavoury" sources: the Pacific scandal of the 1870s in the Conservative party, and the Beauharnois affair of the 1930s in the Liberal party. The 1960s brought more scandals, particularly the Rivard affair, in which a narcotics smuggler, Lucien Rivard, was linked to the Liberal "old guard" in Québec. These events increased the pressure for full disclosure of sources and amounts of party funds so that parties would be free of the danger of hidden manipulation by contributors. It was hoped that the *Election Expenses Act* would prevent further financial scandals. The resultant changes in campaign spending practices and reimbursements to the parties from public funds are discussed in the following chapter; here we are concerned primarily with party fundraising.

Since the passage of the *Election Expenses Act*, contributors are named publicly if they donate more than $100 to a party or candidate. As of 2001, this will rise to $200 and parties and candidates will have to disclose the addresses as well as the names of donors. Those making contributions up to $500 may claim a tax credit. Each national party must file a detailed expenditure and revenue report within six months of the end of its fiscal year. It also must submit an annual report of contributions received and income tax receipts issued to the Department of National Revenue. The belief behind the 1974 legislation was that it would encourage corporations to contribute relatively equal amounts to the major parties, which rely heavily on corporate contributions. As of 2001, parties will also have to produce more detailed financial reports, including a statement on revenue and trust funds.

The tax credit that individuals receive for contributions is an incentive intended to enable parties to develop broad financial bases as a balance against reliance on corporate funds. Corporations are a major source of campaign funds, and so are trade unions. Funding sources differ greatly from party to party and also from one election to the next. The Liberals, Conservatives and Reform receive virtually no union contributions, but significant funds from corporations, while the NDP receives almost no corporate funding but significant funds from trade unions. (See Figure 11.4.)

FIGURE 11.4   NON-GOVERNMENT FINANCIAL CONTRIBUTIONS TO POLITICAL PARTIES, 1998 ($MILLIONS)

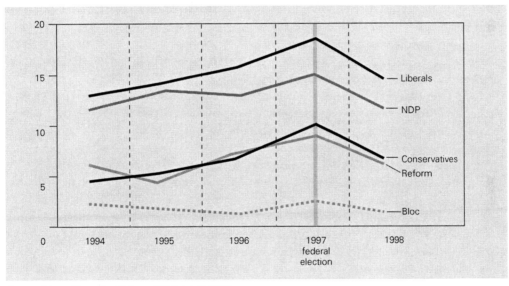

Source: Adapted from *The Globe and Mail*, July 6, 1999.

Besides individuals and corporate donations, parties receive millions of dollars in public subsidies. If they comply with requirements concerning the filing of a tax return for election expenses, and if they spend at least 10 percent of an expense ceiling as determined by Elections Canada, registered parties are reimbursed 22.5 percent of their total national expenditures. They are also refunded for half the costs they incur in the purchase of permitted radio and television advertising time. Individual candidates, too, receive refunds from Elections Canada. Those who garner at least 15 percent of the valid votes cast in their electoral district are refunded their $1 000 deposit and reimbursed by the Receiver-General of Canada for 50 percent of their election expenses.

The *Canada Elections Act* provides detailed rules for the administration of the electoral process, and the raising and spending of campaign funds. There is a ceiling on how much both national parties and candidates can spend. It is set by Elections Canada and monitored by a commission. This limit is determined by a base formula linked to the consumer price index and is adjusted before every election. Spending limits help prevent well-financed interests from dominating the election through lavish spending.

National and local campaigns by the five major parties and by fringe groups in the 1997 general election approached $100 million in officially acknowledged expenditures.[59]

· · · · · · · ·

SUMMARY

The Canadian party system strongly reflects the decentralized nature of the federal system of government within which it operates. Since 1993 and again in 1997, the party system has been fragmented into a multi-party dominant system. The Liberals are the only party with national representation and the ability to form a government, but they are overwhelmingly powerful only in Ontario. The four opposition parties large enough to be official parties are even more regionally based. The Bloc Québécois is restricted to Québec, Reform (now the Alliance) is largely confined to the West and the NDP and Conservatives are primarily from the Maritimes.

At the beginning of the chapter, we outlined the essential functions of all political parties. An examination of the recent history and organization of Canadian parties reveals that the traditional parties have not performed many of those functions well, thereby facilitating the growth of new, regionally based parties at the federal level.

Important party functions include the effective aggregation of demands from society. The Liberal and Conservative parties, which have traditionally supplied the managers and decision-makers of Canadian federal politics, have brought together coalitions of ethnic and regional interests, thereby allowing a means of expression to those interests and providing an integrative force in Canadian society. However, major distortions in regional representation in the two parties have often weakened their ability to be truly national parties. Other parties have arisen to fill the vacuum, but they have been even less successful in aggregating interests across the country. Most have attempted to capture votes by presenting a program based on a single ideology or principle.

Canadian political parties are also limited in their ability to articulate interests. They are effective "gatekeepers," allowing certain demands, and not others, to reach decision-makers. But party programs, expressed as coordinated and consistent politics aimed at achieving specific goals with which the parties are associated, are rare in the Canadian system. Because they have attempted to mediate diverse interests, the the Liberal and Conservative parties in the past could not afford the rigidity of firm policy commitments. Issues are discussed and developed for election campaigns, but, as we shall see in the next chapter, elections are a very poor source of policy communication, with policies often being advanced in a random fashion as *ad hoc* responses to specific problems. Even after winning an election, parties can rarely claim clear policy directives from the electorate, or even that the electorate supports one or all of their policies.

---

59. *Globe and Mail*, April 14, 1997.

Party organizations are designed to achieve electoral victory for their party, and their members are concerned with policy-making mainly as a means to achieve that goal. Between elections they hold policy conventions to agree on policies that are generally designed to win electoral support where they are weak. However, Canadian political parties are not organized very well for policy formulation, and the impact of policy decisions made at conventions on the party leadership is uncertain. Convention policy statements are not binding on the leadership and, although steps are taken to avoid embarrassing contradictions or inconsistencies in party and government policies, such gaffes still happen. The mass party does not have much influence over policy formation; senior party bureaucrats and members of the parliamentary party have more. This is especially true in the government party, because the government caucus, or private meeting of the parliamentary party, has the opportunity to discuss most policy matters before they reach the House of Commons.

By their very nature, political parties are flawed, as Lord Macaulay pointed out in this irreverent analogy:

> *Every political sect ... has its altars and its deified heroes, its relics and its pilgrimages, its canonized martyrs and confessors, and its legendary miracles.*[60]

Political parties even in this electronic age still use all the timeless devices of superstition to win converts and maintain their loyalty: conventions are but pilgrimages; heroes and martyrs provide the spiritual glue of the party; relics are the venerated policies and records that provide the proof of vision and ideas of substance. Along with the manipulation, patronage and distortions, however, parties in Canada allow for the orderly election of representatives and leaders to government and are the means by which thousands of Canadians can actively participate and express themselves in the process. In short, parties are a colourful and important part of the democratic process in Canada, and even with their shortcomings it is difficult to conceive of political representation in this country without them. The next chapter examines the electoral system within which the parties vie for power.

DISCUSSION QUESTIONS

1. How well do Canada's political parties perform their basic functions?
2. Describe the main factors that fragment Canada's party system.
3. What evidence is there to support the view that the Canadian electorate and political parties have shifted strongly to right-wing conservative values?
4. Are political parties sufficiently democratic in terms of policy and leadership selection?

Selected Bibliography

General

Adams, Ian, *Political Ideology Today* (New York: Manchester University Press, 1993).

Bakvis, Herman, ed., *Canadian Political Parties: Leaders, Candidates and Organization*, Royal Commission on Electoral Reform and Party Financing, vol. 13 (Toronto: Dundurn Press, 1991).

---

60. Quoted by Neil A. McDonald in *The Study of Political Parties* (New York: Random House, 1955), p. 20.

Campbell, C. and W. Christian, *Parties, Leaders and Ideologies in Canada* (Toronto: McGraw-Hill, 1996).

Canada, *Reforming Electoral Democracy*, Royal Commission on Electoral Reform and Party Financing, vol. 1, Final Report (Ottawa: Supply and Services, 1991).

Carty, K.R., ed., *Canadian Political Party Systems: A Reader* (Toronto: Broadview, 1992).

Christian, William and Colin Campbell, *Political Parties and Ideologies in Canada*, 4th ed. (Toronto: McGraw-Hill Ryerson, 1995).

Courtney, John, *Do Conventions Matter?* (Kingston/Montréal: McGill-Queen's University Press, 1995).

Day, Allan, *Political Parties of the World*, 4th ed. (New York: Stockton Press, 1995).

Gibbons, Roger and Lolelen Youngman, *Mindscapes: Political Ideologies Towards the 21st Century* (Toronto: McGraw-Hill Ryerson, 1996).

Giddens, Anthony, *Beyond Left and Right: The Future of Radical Politics* (Cambridge, U.K.: Polity Press, 1994).

Katz, Richard S. and Peter Mair, *How Parties Organize: Change and Adaptation in Party Organizations in Western Democracies* (London: Sage, 1994).

Laycock, David, *Populism and Democratic Thought in the Canadian Prairies, 1910–1945* (Toronto: University of Toronto Press, 1990).

Megyery, Kathy, ed., *Women in Canadian Politics: Toward Equity in Representation*, Research Studies of the Royal Commission on Electoral Reform and Party Financing, vol. 6 (Toronto: Dundurn Press, 1991).

Norris, Pippa and Joni Lovenduski, *Political Recruitment* (New York: Cambridge University Press, 1994).

Robin, Martin, *Shades of Right* (Toronto: University of Toronto Press, 1992).

Tanguay, Brian and Alain G. Gagnon, eds., *Canadian Parties in Transition* (Scarborough: Nelson, 1996).

Thorburn, H.G., ed., *Party Politics in Canada*, 6th ed. (Scarborough: Prentice Hall Canada, 1991).

Ware, Alan, *Political Parties and Party Systems* (Oxford: Oxford University Press, 1996).

Conservative Party

Campbell, Kim, *Time and Chance: The Political Memoirs of Canada's First Woman Prime Minister* (Toronto: Doubleday, 1996).

Dobbin, Murray, *The Politics of Kim Campbell* (Toronto: Lorimer, 1993).

Pratte, André, *Charest: His Life and Politics* (trans.) (Toronto: Stoddart, 1998).

Smith, Denis, *Rogue Tory: The Life and Legend of John Diefenbaker* (Toronto: Macfarlane Walter & Ross, 1995).

Liberal Party

Clarkson, Stephen and Christina McCall, *Trudeau and Our Times, Volume I* (Toronto: McClelland & Stewart) 1990.

——————, *Trudeau and Our Times, Volume 2* (Toronto: McClelland & Stewart, 1994).

Greenspon, Edward and Anthony Wilson-Smith, *Double Vision: The Inside Story of the Liberals in Power* (Toronto: Doubleday, 1996).

Trudeau, Pierre Elliott, *Against the Current: Selected Writings 1939–1996*, Gérard Pelletier, ed. (Toronto: McClelland & Stewart, 1996).

Whitaker, Reg, *The Government Party: Organizing and Financing the Liberal Party of Canada 1930–1958* (Toronto: University of Toronto Press, 1977).

——————, "The Government Party," in Ken Carty, ed., *The Canadian Political Party Systems* (Toronto: Broadview, 1992).

CCF/NDP

Archer, Keith, and Alan Whitehorn, *Canadian Trade Unions and the New Democratic Party* (Kingston: Industrial Relations Centre, 1993).

——————, *Political Activists: The NDP in Convention* (Toronto: Oxford University Press, 1997).

Laxer, James, *In Search of a New Left: Canadian Politics after the Neo-Conservative Assault* (Toronto: Viking/Penguin, 1996).

Richards, John, R. Cairns and L. Pratt, *Social Democracy without Illusions* (Toronto: McClelland & Stewart, 1991).

Whitehorn, Alan, *Canadian Socialism: Essays on the CCF-NDP* (Toronto: Oxford University Press, 1997).

Reform Party

Dobbin, Murray, *Preston Manning and the Reform Party* (Toronto: Lorimer, 1993).

Dobbs, Frank, *Preston Manning: The Roots of Reform* (Vancouver: Greystone, 1997).

Flanagan, Tom, *Waiting for the Wave* (Toronto: Stoddart, 1995).

Harrison, Trevor, *Of Passionate Intensity: Right-Wing Populism and the Reform Party of Canada* (Toronto: Toronto University Press, 1995).

Jeffrey, Brook, *Hard Right Turn* (Toronto: HarperCollins, 1999).

Manning, Preston, *The New Canada* (Toronto: Macmillan, 1992).

Sharpe, S., and D. Braid, *Storming Babylon: Preston Manning and the Rise of the Reform Party* (Toronto: Key Porter, 1992).

Other Parties

Bouchard, Lucien, *Un nouveau parti pour l'étape décisive* (St. Laurent, Qué.: Fides, 1993).

Hesketh, Bob, *Major Douglas and Alberta Social Credit* (Toronto: University of Toronto Press, 1997).

LIST OF WEBLINKS

www.psr.keele.ac.uk/thought.htm

Canadian Reform Conservative Alliance – www.canadianalliance.ca

Liberal Party – www.liberal.ca

New Democratic Party – www.ndp.ca

Progressive Conservative Party – www.pcparty.ca

Bloc Québécois – blocquebecois.org

Political Ideologies This Web page provides links to sites describing different types of political thought.

Canadian Political Parties These are the Web pages for some of Canada's major political parties.

12

Elections and Political Behaviour

Voting, Public Opinion and the Media

lections, like parliamentary assemblies, are almost universal. In the past decade, only a handful of the 188 member states of the United Nations have not held a national election to choose either an assembly or a head of state. These include traditional societies in which heredity or family ties determine political office, long-term military dictatorships, and communist or socialist states. The vast majority of countries have held elections at least once during this period, including all liberal democracies. Some countries have fallen by the wayside as far as elections are concerned, especially those where the military has intervened, but other states have restored elections after long periods with no opportunity for citizens to vote.

Although elections are held in a wide variety of political systems, they assume special significance in liberal democracies. There, they afford citizens the opportunity to choose political representatives from competing candidates and, in principle at least, give citizens a voice in the governance of their society. The electoral process aggregates various demands in society into a limited number of choices and assures the representation of diverse opinions in the policy-making arena. As a result, the process accords political leaders legitimacy on which to base their rule and their policies. Elections also have a more direct strategical importance; they decide which parties and leaders achieve political power within the political system.

Electoral outcomes are shaped by many factors. Electoral law defines who has the right to participate in the electoral process — parties, candidates and voters. It may also limit the absolute sum and spending of the financial resources used by candidates. The type of electoral system is also significant. The method by which voter preferences are translated into representation in political institutions affects the outcome and has a long-term impact on the nature of the party system.

Since the electoral process involves an aggregation of the choices made by each voter — first, whether or not to vote; then, which party and/or candidate to vote for — patterns of individual electoral behaviour clearly determine electoral outcomes. The activities of the mass media and the conduct of election campaigns also influence voter choices.

Elections in Canada, as elsewhere, are thus affected by a number of forces. In this chapter, we examine the mechanics of the Canadian electoral process, including the franchise, the means by which candidates are selected, the legal constraints on election spending, the factors that shape individual electoral behaviour, the role of the media, and a brief review of the 1993 election. This is followed by a detailed case study of the 1997 general election. First, however, we consider the topic of elections in comparative terms, examining their role in the overall political process and the various ways by which other countries elect their political representatives.

REPRESENTATION AND ELECTIONS

In large states such as Canada, it is not possible for everyone to be directly involved in the day-to-day policy-making process. In earlier times, when societies consisted mainly of small, more or less autonomous communities, direct democracy was possible; all citizens in a community could participate personally in collective deliberation and decision-making about how they would be governed. To some, this represented the ideal form of democracy. Today, town meetings in some small New England communities and the *Landesgemeinde* in certain Swiss communes are legacies of a time when collective self-government was a simpler process. These are exceptions. As societies grew larger and more complex, direct democracy was replaced by **representative democracy**, wherein certain individuals are selected to represent the interests of their fellow citizens in the policy-making process. In most societies, the means by which such representatives are chosen is the electoral process. For the most part, democratic government now means government by representatives of the people, chosen by their peers in elections. However, there are occasions when citizens can participate more directly in policy-making.

Referendums

The major exception to the general rule of indirect representation in modern democracies is the *referendum*. A **referendum**, sometimes known as a **plebiscite** (there is no clear universally accepted distinction between the two, although in Canada a plebiscite is taken to mean a *non-binding* referendum), is a means by which a policy question can be submitted directly to the electorate for decision rather than being decided exclusively by elected representatives. A referendum may consist of a single, direct question or statement requiring a simple *yes* or *no* vote of the public, or a selection of one alternative from several policy options.

Referendums may be used in various ways. Some are merely *consultative*, providing a kind of official public opinion poll on an issue in order to guide politicians. Others are *binding* in that they force the government to follow the majority decision in the referendum. Still others are essentially *instruments of ratification*, the final seal of approval on a course of action adopted by a law-making institution; this is the case, for example, when proposed constitutional amendments must be ratified by the electorate.

Not all referendums are designed to permit the electorate a voice in how their country is governed. Especially in non-democratic systems, referendums may be used to give the illusion of popular participation without any meaningful choice. Such referendums may be useful in lending an air of legitimacy to decisions already made by the ruling elite. Not surprisingly, the results often provide almost unanimous support for the government's policies.[1]

---

1. David Butler and Austin Ranney, eds., *Referendums around the World* (Washington, D.C.: American Enterprise Institute for Public Policy Research, 1994).

Where referendums do allow a meaningful choice, however, they can be said to enhance the democratic process. Proponents of referendums argue that they represent a form of direct democracy. Voters are given an opportunity to have a much more immediate influence on public decisions than is possible through the election of representatives. Advocates also point out that widespread consultation increases the legitimacy of political decisions. This legitimizing function of referendums is particularly important when it comes to fundamental changes in the political system such as, for example, the ratification of significant constitutional amendments.

Notwithstanding these apparent advantages, referendums are not widely used in most liberal democracies, although there are exceptions such as Switzerland and Australia. Critics argue that it detracts from the sovereignty of Parliament; bypassing Parliament by appealing directly to the voters downgrades the importance of the sovereign law-making body. Others argue that it is unreasonable to ask relatively uninformed citizens to make decisions, especially on technical or legal matters, about which they have neither the time nor the expertise to evaluate complex issues. Furthermore, it is not feasible to consult citizens on every issue that might be regarded as fundamental.

Another basic criticism of referendums concerns their inflexibility — they usually require a straight yes/no decision that may oversimplify complex political problems and make subsequent compromise difficult. As well, there is always the danger that unscrupulous politicians could use the referendum, as Hitler did, to appeal to populist sentiments and gain support for extremist and non-democratic measures. Finally, it is argued that referendums, especially if used frequently, pose a threat to minorities. In a country as diverse as Canada, the final and uncompromising nature of a referendum is potentially divisive. Majority rule, while a central component of democracy, must be tempered by the protection of minorities, lest it turn into a "tyranny of the majority."

Therefore, most countries tend to use referendums with extreme caution and only in specific circumstances. The most frequent use, perhaps, is associated with the process of constitutional amendment to ratify changes. Referendums are also widely employed to decide questions of national importance such as sovereignty, secession or autonomy. (See Table 12.1.) Another common use of referendums is in allowing citizens to decide what might be called "moral" issues over which political parties are internally divided. Thus, a number of countries have held national or local referendums on such matters as prohibition, licensing laws and drinking hours, divorce, abortion and

TABLE 12.1   SELECTED SECESSION REFERENDUMS ABROAD

Date	Country and Question
1905	Norway voted to separate from Sweden by 99.95%. Question: "Do you agree with the dissolution of the Union or not?"
1944	Iceland voted to end the union with Denmark by 98.65%. Question: "The Althing resolves to declare that the Danish-Iceland Act of 1918 is terminated."
1990	Lithuania voted to be an independent state by 93.2%. Question: "Are you for the independent and democratic Republic of Lithuania?"
1991	Estonia voted to be independent by 79.6%. Question: "Do you want the restoration of the state sovereignty and independence of the Republic of Estonia?"
1991	Latvia voted to be independent by 74.9%. Question: "Do you support the democratic and independent statehood of Latvia."

nuclear energy. On such sensitive issues politicians often appear happy to allow parliamentary sovereignty to be bypassed and let the citizens decide for themselves!

Referendums in Canada

Federal politicians in Canada have shared a mistrust of referendums with their counterparts elsewhere. Only three referendums have been held at the national level in Canada, all of them consultative.

The first was held in 1898, when the federal government was contemplating prohibition of alcohol. Although a small majority voted in favour of prohibition (51 percent), there was a very low turnout (44 percent) and Prime Minister Wilfrid Laurier did not believe that support was strong enough to go ahead. It should be noted that the proposal was massively rejected in Laurier's home province of Québec, a fact that undoubtedly influenced his decision not to proceed.

The second national referendum was called during the Conscription Crisis of 1942. Prime Minister Mackenzie King proceeded with conscription only after a referendum that asked whether the federal government could overturn its previous pledge not to institute a draft. The referendum was supported by 65 percent of the voters. Québec, however, voted heavily against conscription (71 percent), exacerbating relations between English and French Canadians. King delayed the implementation of conscription so long that the conscripts were never used in battle.

The third national referendum was on the Charlottetown constitutional accord in 1992. The result was a 54.4 percent popular vote against the accord and 44.6 percent for it. Because of the significance of this event for contemporary politics the 1992 referendum is discussed in detail below.

Referendums have also been used by other levels of government in Canada. At the provincial level, Newfoundland held a referendum on the question of joining Confederation — in fact, it held two.[2] In the first, in June 1948, Newfoundlanders were given three choices as to their future status. Responsible self-government was supported by 45 percent of the voters, joining Canada by 41 percent, and remaining under the control of a board of commissioners appointed by the British government by 14 percent. Six weeks later, with the choice narrowed to self-government or Confederation, 52 percent voted to join Canada. Newfoundland held another constitutional referendum in 1995 on the issue of reforming the education system. The reforms won 55 percent approval.

The only other province to hold referendums relating to the question of sovereignty was Québec. In May 1980, the Parti Québécois government held a referendum asking the voters of the province for "a mandate to negotiate sovereignty-association" with the rest of Canada. Sixty percent of the voters voted *Non*, and the *status quo* was maintained. In 1995, it held yet another referendum on independence. This time the results were so close that barely one percent of voters provided the margin of *Non* votes that kept Québec in Canada. (See Chapter 7.) The threat of a future referendum on this question continues to plague Canadian and Québec politics.

Referendums have been used for other questions. Practically every province has had at least one vote on alcohol regulations, and many municipalities have asked their residents to choose between "wet" and "dry" — in other words, to decide whether or not they wanted liquor outlets in their area. In addition, some municipalities have held votes on other issues, sometimes even on matters outside their jurisdiction, such as votes to be "nuclear-free" zones. In fact, during the discussions on constitutional patriation in 1982, Prime Minister Pierre Trudeau suggested that a referendum might be used as a means of ratifying amendments on which the federal and provincial

---

2. See Henry B. Mayo, "Newfoundland's Entry into the Dominion," *CJPS*, vol. 15, no. 4 (November 1949), pp. 505–22.

governments were unable to agree, although no such provision was included in the amending formula in the new Constitution. Finally, politicians from both Alberta and British Columbia have promised referendums before they will accept any future constitutional amendments.

The 1992 Referendum

In Chapter 5, we outlined the constitutional issues surrounding the Charlottetown accord. In their effort to achieve a political consensus Prime Minister Brian Mulroney and the 10 premiers met in Charlottetown. They gave final agreement to the accord and unanimously decided to hold a national referendum to legitimate the proposal. In the House of Commons, the three party leaders, Brian Mulroney, Audrey McLaughlin and Jean Chrétien, all agreed to defend the accord. They were joined by provincial, territorial and aboriginal leaders as well as business, labour, and other elites and organizations.

For a time it appeared that the accord would obtain a majority in every province. However, eventually three major opposition groups developed. In Québec, the Bloc Québécois and the Parti Québécois argued that Charlottetown was weaker than Meech Lake and did not give enough powers to Québec. In the West, the Reform party, led by Preston Manning, campaigned against the accord on the basis that it gave too much to Québec and did not assure sufficient protection for the interests of the less populous provinces. Across the country, No committees sprang up at the grass-roots level. The most important of these, "Canada for all Canadians," argued that the document was incomplete, incoherent and took away rights already accorded to Canadians under the *Charter of Rights and Freedoms*. Their message was buttressed by former prime minister Trudeau in a well-publicized speech that galvanized Canadians who had been unaware of the significance of the proposed constitutional change. In the final analysis, aboriginal people, too, were divided on the provisions in the accord.

The Yes forces, massively funded by corporations and governments, launched a highly professional campaign based on the election machinery of all three parties and their experts. They campaigned essentially on the basis that a Yes vote was a vote for Canada and national unity, obscuring the facts that there was no legal text to the agreement and that it would entail massive reorganization of Canadian government. Their appeal was directed essentially to the emotions of Canadians.

Rag-tag groupings of No forces battered the details of the deal, maintaining that approximately one-third of the Canadian Constitution was being amended in one vote. There was little organization to their attacks, but their lack of cohesion allowed different groups to focus on specific sectors of the country and on particular issues in the agreement.

The proponents of Charlottetown had a difficult task to perform. In order for the referendum to be passed, it had to receive a majority vote in each and every province as well as in the country as a whole. This requirement was due to the fact that the amendments proposed in Charlottetown required the unanimous approval of the legislatures of every province. Morally, no provincial legislative assembly could approve the Charlottetown resolution if its electorate voted no. This led the No forces to attempt to stop the referendum in at least one province.

In the final analysis, the emotional rhetoric and massive advertising of the Yes forces worked to their disadvantage. Opinion polls showed that many voters used the vote to vent their anger and frustration against the prime minister, premiers, politicians and governments in general. Only in the Maritimes was there a solid Yes vote for the accord. Québec and all of the western provinces voted strongly No. As Table 12.2 shows, in Ontario the Yes forces won — but only by a whisker.

The result was a national humiliation for Prime Minister Mulroney, the 10 premiers and politicians generally. When the numbers were announced, Canada's leading politicians reversed their dire predictions and said that Canada was not in danger. In fact, they shelved the constitutional issue in favour of pressing economic issues.

However, the defeat of Charlottetown did not end the need to accommodate a wide range of interests, from Québec nationalism to aboriginal self-government. What it did do was end the career of Prime Minister Brian Mulroney, and set the stage for the massive defeat of the Progressive Conservative party in the 1993 general election and also for the 1995 sovereignty referendum in Québec.

FUNCTIONS OF ELECTIONS

At the most basic level, the primary function of elections is to provide a mechanism for selecting the individuals who will occupy seats in representative institutions. Hence, in Canada, the federal electoral process is the means by which voters in various constituencies throughout the country choose which men and women will represent their interests in the House of Commons.

But in liberal democratic societies such as Canada, elections fulfill an even more important function: they provide for the orderly succession of government, by the peaceful transfer of authority to new rulers. Elections held at regular intervals provide citizens with opportunities to review the record of the government, to assess its mandate and to replace it with an alternative administration. In certain countries, such as the United States, the political executive (the president) is elected, reconfirmed or replaced by the people directly through the electoral process. In Canada and other parliamentary democracies, however, the election of constituency representatives to the House of Commons assumes additional significance in that the government arises out of the majority within the legislature and is subsequently responsible to the legislature for the exercise of executive power until the next election.

Once a government has been elected, directly or indirectly, it may claim a mandate from the voters to rule on their behalf. Thus, the electoral process helps to legitimate the government of the day and also the policies that it has been elected to carry out. Furthermore, elections also legitimate the entire system of government. To the extent that Canadians, for example, turn out in relatively large numbers at the polls (on average, around three-quarters of the electorate have voted in federal general elections in this century), they are expressing confidence in the system by their very participation.

TABLE 12.2   1992 CHARLOTTETOWN CONSTITUTIONAL REFERENDUM RESULTS BY PROVINCE

Province	% Yes	% No
Newfoundland	62.9	36.5
Prince Edward Island	73.6	25.9
Nova Scotia	48.5	51.1
New Brunswick	61.3	38.0
Québec	42.4	55.4
Ontario	49.8	49.6
Manitoba	37.8	61.6
Saskatchewan	44.5	55.2
Alberta	39.7	60.1
British Columbia	31.7	68.0
Northwest Territories	60.6	38.7
Yukon	43.4	56.1

It is this function of legitimation of the political system that makes elections so common around the world, not just in liberal democracies, but also in communist regimes and other forms of government where no real element of choice is put before the voters. Elections in all countries provide an opportunity for citizens to participate in the political process and to express their support for the system. But they serve an additional role in many countries, since in non-competitive state-controlled systems, *international* acceptance counts for at least as much as national legitimation.

In **competitive elections** — those involving more than one party with a chance of forming a government — political parties are forced to aggregate interests in their search for a political majority. Through campaign literature, speeches and personal contacts, candidates attempt to "educate" voters and persuade them to vote the "right" way. But even where there may be only a single slate of candidates, as in the former Soviet Union, the campaigns provide "an immediate and solemn occasion for the transmission of orders, explanations and cues from the government to the population."[3]

Finally, in competitive systems at least, elections provide a forum for airing views not heard in everyday political debate. Widespread media coverage, all-candidates meetings and the distribution of political literature all allow minor parties, interest groups, independent politicians and the occasional "odd-ball" an opportunity to air their ideas and opinions. To the extent that some people vote for minor parties and independent candidates, elections may be viewed as a kind of safety valve that allows voters to express dissatisfaction with the major parties and support ideas not generally represented in the federal political arena.[4]

TYPES OF ELECTORAL SYSTEMS

There is a tendency to believe that one's own electoral system is the best way of choosing a government. But history reminds us that there are many perceptions of what is best; different electoral systems may be viewed as institutional expressions of these competing values. According to one observer of electoral practices around the world, there are four primary objectives of elections, which may be regarded as the principles upon which different electoral systems are based:

1. A legislature reflecting the main trends of opinion within the electorate.

2. A government according to the wishes of the majority of the electorate.

3. The election of representatives whose personal qualities best fit them for the function of government.

4. Strong and stable government.[5]

Some electoral systems place a high premium on the concept of "representation," inasmuch as they are designed to ensure that all significant shades of public opinion are represented in parliament. Others appear to be concerned more with providing majority governments that are commonly assumed to be stronger and more stable than minority or coalition governments.

To illustrate these points, we outline next the major types of electoral systems and their effects on party competition and government outcomes. In essence, two factors are determined by electoral systems: how many candidates are elected in each geographical district (usually known as

---

3. Guy Hermet, "State Controlled Elections: A Framework," in G. Hermet et al., ed., *Elections without Choice* (London: Macmillan, 1978), pp. 13–14.

4. Andrew J. Milnor, *Elections and Political Stability* (Boston: Little, Brown, 1969).

5. Enid Lakeman, *How Democracies Vote: A Study of Electoral Systems*, 4th rev. ed. (London: Faber and Faber, 1974), p. 28.

"constituencies" or "ridings"); and how votes are translated into parliamentary seats. Using these criteria, we can identify four basic varieties of electoral systems: single-member plurality, single-member majoritarian, multi-member proportional representation and mixed systems.

Single-Member Plurality

The single-member **plurality** system is used primarily in the "Anglo-American" democracies of the United Kingdom, the United States, New Zealand and Canada. Under this system, one member or representative is elected from each constituency. Each elector has one vote, which is cast by indicating (usually with an "X") one's favourite candidate. The translation of votes into seats is based on the achievement of a plurality — that is, the candidate with the most votes wins. It is important to note that the victorious candidate is not required to gain an absolute majority of votes, but merely to receive more votes than anyone else. For this reason, the system is sometimes known by other labels, such as the "simple majority" or "relative majority" (as opposed to "absolute majority") system.

In Canada, all members of the House of Commons are now elected by plurality voting in single-member constituencies. But it is also theoretically possible to conduct elections under the plurality formula in districts that return more than one member. In such systems, the rules are essentially the same, except that the voter has as many votes as there are seats to be filled in the geographical territory. Thus, in a two-member constituency, each voter marks two names, and the two candidates with the most votes are the winners. As recently as the 1965 general election, there were federal constituencies in Canada that returned two members to the House of Commons.[6] Even today, the 32 members of the provincial legislature of Prince Edward Island are elected in 16 two-member ridings, and many municipal councils and school boards are still elected "at large" or in multi-member districts using the plurality formula. However, most contemporary national elections that use the plurality formula, including those in Canada, employ single-member constituencies.

Single-Member Majoritarian

In plurality systems, the candidate who receives the most votes is the winner whether or not he or she has an absolute majority of all votes cast. Other electoral systems based on single-member constituencies are designed to ensure the certainty of the winning candidate's receiving an absolute majority of votes cast in the constituency. These "majoritarian" formulas are essentially of two types: the alternative vote (AV) and the second ballot.

Under the **alternative vote** system, for example, in elections to the federal House of Representatives in Australia, voters rank candidates in order of preference. They place "1" beside their favourite candidate, "2" beside their second choice and so on. When the votes are counted, each ballot is assigned to the candidate it ranks first. If a candidate has an absolute majority of votes, that candidate is declared elected. Otherwise, the candidate with the least votes is excluded and his or her supporters' ballots are transferred to the remaining candidates according to the second preferences. This process of excluding candidates and transferring votes continues until one candidate has an absolute majority over all other remaining contenders.

Another variation on the single-member constituency format is the **second ballot** system, used on occasion in France. There, electors initially opt for a single candidate, but if no one obtains an absolute majority on this first vote, a run-off election is held, usually a week or two later. On this second ballot, candidates who failed to get a specified proportion of the votes the first time around

---

6. See T.H. Qualter, *The Election Process in Canada* (Toronto: McGraw-Hill, 1970), pp. 118–23, for a discussion of single-member and multi-member constituencies in Canadian elections.

are excluded; usually, only the two leading candidates reappear and, therefore, the elected representative normally can claim the support of a majority of voters in the constituency.

The second-ballot system has never been used in Canada, but the alternative vote has, but not at the federal level. In the provincial elections of 1952 and 1953, the entire legislature of British Columbia was elected by the AV system, although plurality voting was subsequently reintroduced. In Alberta from 1926 to 1959, rural members of the legislative assemblies (MLAs) were returned from single-member ridings using AV, while those from Calgary and Edmonton were elected by the multi-member proportional representation (PR) system described below. Similarly, rural MLAs in Manitoba were elected by AV from 1927 to 1936, while members from Winnipeg were again elected under a PR formula.

Multi-Member Proportional Representation

Multi-member proportional representation systems provide an opportunity to elect two or more members from each constituency. They are designed to ensure that parties, or groups of voters, are represented more fairly than is often the case under single-member plurality or majoritarian formulas. In other words, PR formulas attempt to ensure that parties receive representation in parliament in proportion to their respective shares of the popular vote. PR systems are essentially of two types: party list systems and the single transferable vote (STV) formula.

Party list systems of PR are used extensively in Europe. In its simplest form, the **party list** system allows electors in a multi-member constituency to vote for a party or a slate of candidates, rather than for one or more individuals. Seats are allocated to each party roughly in proportion to its share of the popular vote. Assume, for example, that a constituency sends 10 members to the parliament and that 100 000 people turn out to vote. Theoretically, if Party A receives 50 000 votes, Party B 30 000 and Party C 20 000, the resulting seat distribution is five, three and two respectively — i.e., each party receives exactly the same percentage of seats as votes. In real life, the percentages of voters are rarely distributed so conveniently, and a number of different procedures exists to allocate seats. But the general effect is that parties receive representation approximately proportional to their popular support.

In party list systems, seats are usually awarded to individual candidates on the basis of their position on the party's slate. Before the election, each party publishes a list of candidates in order of rank and, under normal circumstances, if Party A receives five seats in our hypothetical constituency, the top five names on the party list are declared elected. In some countries, however, the electoral rules permit voters to express preferences for one or more individuals within the party list and, therefore, to effect a change in the rank ordering of candidates. The basic principle of all party list systems is that seats are awarded in the first instance to political parties according to their relative shares of the popular vote; the actual representatives who will occupy those seats are essentially a secondary concern. This is in direct contrast to single-member constituency systems, where the election of individual members is the immediate objective, and the relative strengths of the parties in Parliament is the product of the individual constituency races.

The second variety of proportional representation places greater emphasis on individual candidates than does the party list system. The **single transferable vote** formula is used in the Republic of Ireland and also in Australia for electing the Senate. Representatives are elected from multi-member constituencies, but electors vote for individual candidates rather than for a party list.

In the STV, as in the alternative vote system, voters rank candidates in order of preference, and ballot papers are initially assigned to the first-choice candidate. To be elected, a candidate must obtain a specified number of votes or "quota." Candidates who receive first-preference votes in excess of the quota are declared elected and their "surplus" votes (those in excess of the quota) are transferred to the remaining candidates according to subsequent preferences. If no candidate receives a quota on the first count, or if seats remain to be filled after all surpluses have been distributed, the least popular candidate is excluded and his or her votes are transferred. This process continues until all seats have been allocated. Although the STV system need not be used with proportional representation of political parties in mind, its effect in countries such as the Irish Republic is very similar to electoral outcomes under other PR formulas.

Unlike the party list form of PR, the STV system has been used in Canada, although again not at the federal level. Members of the Alberta legislature from Calgary and Edmonton were elected by this system from 1926 to 1959, as were Winnipeg's representatives in the Manitoba provincial assembly from 1920 to 1953. STV was also used for municipal elections in Winnipeg until 1972.

Mixed Systems

Mixed systems or **additional member** systems (AMS) represent a combination of plurality and PR formulas. A certain percentage of the seats are filled by plurality voting in single-member constituencies, while the remainder are awarded to parties according to their popular support in order to achieve an approximately proportional representation in the legislature.

Such a system is used in Germany for electing both the federal *Bundestag* (analogous to Canada's House of Commons) and the *Land* (provincial) legislatures. Under the German system, each elector has two votes, one for a constituency candidate and one for a party list. The "first" votes, those for candidates in single-member constituencies, determine half the seats in the *Bundestag*. The "second" votes, cast for a party list, determine the share of total seats each party will obtain. Parties are awarded additional seats if the number of representatives directly elected in the constituencies is less than their overall proportional entitlement based on their shares of the "second" votes.

While the German system represents an equal mix of the plurality and PR party list systems, the AMS places greater emphasis on the plurality formula. Here, the majority of seats in the legislature are still elected in single-member constituencies, but a small reserve of seats are allocated to parties according to their share of the popular vote in order to alleviate some of the disproportional effects of the plurality system. Variations on the AMS have been proposed by several contributors to the debate on electoral reform in Canada.

THE EFFECTS OF ELECTORAL SYSTEMS

There is a large body of literature on the effects of different electoral systems on the politics of their respective countries. Many of these works are highly polemical since they are contributions to debates on electoral reform, either defending the existing system or propounding the adoption of an alternative method. In the following discussion, therefore, we outline what might be called the "conventional wisdom" on the effects of different electoral systems, keeping in view three main criteria: their impact on representation at the constituency level; the representation of political parties and effects on the party system; and the type of governmental outcome that each system typically produces. These effects are summarized in Table 12.3.

One of the advantages claimed for single-member formulas (plurality or majoritarian) is that they maintain the traditional link between the individual MP and the constituents. There is no

TABLE 12.3   TYPES OF ELECTORAL SYSTEMS AND THEIR EFFECTS

Electoral System (Examples)	Constituency Representation	Representation of Parties	Governmental Outcome
Single-member plurality (U.K., U.S., Canada)	– Maintains traditional link between MP and constituents – MPs often elected on a minority of total votes – Discourages multiplication of parties — tendency toward two-party system	– Distortion of votes/seats ratio – Minor parties disadvantaged unless support is regionally concentrated	– Tends to "over-represent" largest party – Usually single-party majority government – Some alternation of government between two dominant parties
Single-member majoritarian (a) Alternative vote (AV) (Australia, House of Reps.)	– Both maintain traditional link between MP and constituents	– Distortion of votes/seats ratio	– Tends to "over-represent" largest party (parties)
(b) Second ballot (France, historically)	– Representatives party majority usually elected by a majority – Tendency toward multi-party system	– "Wasted vote" thesis does not apply; therefore, small parties survive even if unsuccessful	– Usually single-majority government or stable coalition
Proportional representation (PR) (a) Party list (Netherlands, Switzerland)	– Individual representatives usually owe election more to party than to voters	– Approximate congruence between vote shares and seat allocations	– Coalition governments — may be stable (Sweden) or unstable (Italy, historically)
(b) Single transferable vote (STV) (Rep. of Ireland, Australia, Senate)	– Representatives forced to compete for "first preference" votes	– Minor parties usually gain "fair" representation – Easy entry for new parties – Tendency toward multi-party systems	– Alternation of government sometimes
Mixed plurality/PR (Germany)	– Maintains traditional link between MP and constituents – Minor parties usually gain "fair" represen-tation, unless measures are adopted (as in Germany) to prevent representation of "splinter" groups	– Approximate congruence between vote shares and seat allocations	– Reasonably stable coalition government

ambiguity about who is designated to represent the voters and, since the representatives owe their election to the voters rather than to their positions on a party list, it is in their personal interests to represent their constituents if they wish to be re-elected. Furthermore, the representatives' task is made easier because, even in relatively large and populous countries, division into a large number of single-member districts limits the size of both the area and the electorate of each constituency. These generalizations apply equally to representatives elected in single-member constituencies under a mixed or AMS formula.

In party list systems of PR, on the other hand, MPs owe their election (especially their position on the party list) more to their party than to their constituents. Furthermore, constituencies may be too large for individual representatives to maintain contact with all constituents, making it difficult to establish representative responsibility. Thus, members may focus on maintaining their popularity within the party, and hence their standing on the party list, rather than on representing the interests of their constituents. This is less true with the STV system of PR, especially as it operates in Ireland. There, since each candidate attempts to gain as many first-preference votes as possible, members do have to pay considerable attention to constituency interests.

What effect do electoral systems have on political representation and party competition within a society? Proportional representation systems are by definition designed to achieve a more or less proportional allocation of seats to parties according to their respective shares of the popular vote. However, the degree of congruence between the percentage of votes and the number of seats won by each party tends to vary from country to country. A key factor here is the number of members returned by each constituency. The Netherlands elects its legislative chamber, the *Tweede Kamer*, by treating the whole country as if it were a single constituency, and achieves an almost perfect correspondence between votes and seats for each party. However, where constituencies are smaller, returning, say, three or four members each, it is more difficult to achieve congruence when allocating seats according to popular votes; there is the likelihood that some parties will be persistently over- or under-represented in each constituency, and thus overall in the legislature.

If we take the argument concerning constituency size to its logical conclusion, it follows that the proportional allocation of seats according to shares of the popular vote is least likely to occur in systems where electoral districts return only one member each — i.e., in single-member plurality and majoritarian systems. This can easily be illustrated by the 1979, 1980 and 1984 general elections in Canada, all of which were conducted under single-member plurality voting rules. (See Table 12.4.) In 1979, the Progressive Conservatives gained more seats than the Liberals and thus formed the

TABLE 12.4   CANADIAN GENERAL ELECTION RESULTS 1979, 1980, 1984

	Shares of Votes and Seats by Party								
	1979			1980			1984		
	% Votes	% Seats	No. of Seats	% Votes	% Seats	No. of Seats	% Votes	% Seats	No. of Seats
LIB	40	40	(114)	44	52	(147)	28	14	(40)
PC	36	48	(136)	33	37	(103)	50	75	(211)
NDP	18	9	(26)	20	11	(32)	19	11	(30)
SC	5	2	(6)	2	0	(0)	0	0	(0)
Other	2	0	(0)	1	0	(0)	3	0	(1)

Note: Percentages may not add up to 100% because of rounding.

government, although they received a smaller share of the popular vote, 36 percent to the Liberals' 40 percent. This outcome was rather exceptional, and the normal pattern reasserted itself in 1980, with the Liberals getting the most votes and the most seats. In 1984, the Conservatives returned with a massive majority of both votes and seats.

Table 12.4 demonstrates some of the negative characteristics typically associated with the plurality system: a tendency to favour the two largest parties, with an additional "bonus" of seats for the largest party; and, conversely, a tendency to under-represent third or minor parties, especially those whose support is spread fairly evenly but thinly across the country.

In 1993, the Liberals won 177 seats (60 percent) with only 41 percent of the vote. The Conservatives were reduced to two seats even though they had won 16 percent of the vote — more than the Bloc Québécois, which won only 14 percent of the vote but got 54 seats. (See Table 12.5.) Because its votes were concentrated in Québec, the Bloc also gained more seats than Reform, which got 52 seats for 19 percent of the vote. In this electoral system it does not matter how well you do in second place — the system loves only winners. In 1993 it took about 31 320 votes to elect a Liberal, but more than one million to elect a Conservative! In 1997, the Conservative and Reform parties both won 19 percent of the vote, but Reform got 60 seats, the Conservatives only 20. The Bloc got 44 seats with 11 percent of the vote.

According to Maurice Duverger, there are two reasons why a single-member plurality system tends to reward the party that comes first with more seats than it deserves, and the second and following parties with fewer seats. First, an arithmetical consequence rewards the party that gets the largest share of the vote with more seats. The exception to this general rule occurs when a minor party has its support strongly concentrated in a particular region, as happened in 1993 and 1997 with the Bloc Québécois in Québec, or in some earlier elections with the Social Credit and Créditiste parties in Alberta and Québec. Second, voters who might otherwise support a minor party tend to refrain from voting for it for fear of "wasting" their votes — casting votes that have no effect on the election of individual representatives or on the formation of a government. Thus, Duverger suggested that the association between the plurality electoral formula and the two-party system is close to being a "true sociological law."[7] (For seats won by region by each party, see Table 12.6.)

As a consequence of the tendency to under-represent minor parties, the plurality system is often said to favour the development or maintenance of a two-party system of electoral competition.

TABLE 12.5   FIRST PAST THE POST: HOW VOTES TRANSLATED INTO SEATS, 1993 AND 1997

	PC		Liberals		NDP		Reform		Bloc	
	1993	1997	1993	1997	1993	1997	1993	1997	1993	1997
No. of seats	2	20	177	155	9	21	52	60	54	44
% of total seats*	0.7	6.6	60	51	3.1	6.9	17.6	19.9	18.3	14.6
% of votes*	16	19	41	38	7	11	19	19	14	11

*Total seats and % of votes exclude one independent elected in 1993.

Source: Based on data from Elections Canada.

---

7. Maurice Duverger, *Political Parties: Their Organization and Activity in the Modern State* (London: Methuen, 1954), p. 217. For a test of Duverger's hypothesis regarding the plurality formula, see Douglas Rae, *The Political Consequences of Electoral Laws* (New Haven: Yale University Press, 1971), pp. 93ff.

TABLE 12.6   SEATS WON IN GENERAL ELECTIONS BY REGION, 1945–97

	1945	1949	1953	1956	1958	1962	1963	1965	1968	1972	1974	1979	1980	1984	1988	1993	1997
Atlantic																	
LIB	19	25	27	12	8	14	20	15	7	10	13	12	19	7	20	31	11
PC	6	7	5	21	25	18	13	18	25	22	17	18	13	25	12	1	13
SC	–	–	–	–	–	–	–	–	–	–	–	–	–	–	–	–	–
CCF/NDP	–	1	1	–	–	1	–	–	–	–	1	2	–	–	–	–	8
Reform	–	–	–	–	–	–	–	–	–	–	–	–	–	–	–	–	–
Bloc	–	–	–	–	–	–	–	–	–	–	–	–	–	–	–	–	–
Other	1	1	–	–	–	–	–	–	–	–	–	1	–	–	–	–	–
Total	27	34	33	33	33	33	33	33	32	32	32	32	32	32	32	32	32
Québec																	
LIB	54	66	66	63	25	35	47	56	56	56	60	67	74	17	12	19	26
PC	1	2	4	9	50	14	8	8	4	2	3	2	1	58	63	1	5
SC	–	–	–	–	–	26	20	–	–	15	11	6	–	–	–	–	–
CRED	–	–	–	–	–	–	–	9	14	–	–	–	–	–	–	–	–
CCF/NDP	–	–	–	–	–	–	–	–	–	–	–	–	–	–	–	–	–
Reform	–	–	–	–	–	–	–	–	–	–	–	–	–	–	–	–	–
Bloc	–	–	–	–	–	–	–	–	–	–	–	–	–	–	–	54	44
Other	9	5	5	3	–	–	–	2	–	1	–	–	–	–	–	1	–
Total	64	73	75	75	75	75	75	75	74	74	74	75	75	75	75	75	75
Ontario																	
LIB	34	56	50	20	14	43	52	51	64	36	55	32	52	14	43	98	101
PC	48	25	33	61	67	35	27	25	17	40	25	57	38	67	46	–	1
SC	–	–	–	–	–	–	–	–	–	–	–	–	–	–	–	–	–
CCF/NDP	–	1	1	3	3	6	6	9	6	11	8	6	5	13	10	–	–
Reform	–	–	–	–	–	–	–	–	–	–	–	–	–	–	–	1	–
Bloc	–	–	–	–	–	–	–	–	–	–	–	–	–	–	–	–	–
Other	–	1	1	1	1	1	–	–	1	1	–	–	–	1	–	–	1
Total	82	83	85	85	85	85	85	85	88	88	88	95	95	95	99	99	103
West																	
LIB	19	43	27	10	1	7	10	9	2	7	13	3	2	2	8	29	17
PC	11	7	9	21	66	49	47	46	26	43	50	59	51	61	48**	–	1
SC	13	10	15	19	–	4	4	5	–	–	–	–	–	–	–	–	–
CCF/NDP	27	10	21	22	5	12	11	12	16	20	7	18	27	17	33	9	13
Reform	–	–	–	–	–	–	–	–	–	–	–	–	–	–	–	51	60
Bloc	–	–	–	–	–	–	–	–	–	–	–	–	–	–	–	–	–
Other	–	–	–	–	–	–	–	–	–	–	–	–	–	–	–	–	–
Total	71	71	72	72	72	72	72	72	70	70	70	80	80	80	89	89	91

*including the Northwest Territories and Yukon.
**48 Conservatives were elected, but one died before being sworn in, leaving the official party standing as 47 from the West, with one vacant.

Source: Adapted from various editions of the *Canadian Parliamentary Guide* and Elections Canada.

Like the plurality system, the alternative vote and second-ballot formulas both tend to result in severely disproportional allocations of seats, often in favour of the largest parties.[8] But they do not tend to "squeeze out" minor parties to the same extent as the plurality formula. Voters do not have to worry about wasting their votes, as the majoritarian formulas effectively give them a "second bite at the cherry." Electors can give their first preferences (under the AV) or their "first ballots" (under the second-ballot system) secure in the knowledge that, if their favourite candidate is unsuccessful, subsequent preferences or the "second ballot" will be used to choose between the major protagonists in the constituency.

Under PR formulas where all parties, including minor ones, receive seats more or less in proportion to their shares of the popular vote, there is also a tendency toward multiple political parties. Some countries attempt to counteract this tendency by imposing a threshold — a certain proportion of votes that small parties must exceed before they are allotted any seats. Germany, for example, makes things more difficult for new or splinter parties by requiring that they must gain at least 5 percent of the popular vote or win seats in three single-member constituencies.

Lastly, the electoral system has an impact on the formation of governments. Because the plurality formula favours the development of a two-party system (or at least of two dominant parties) and because the largest single party in any election receives a "bonus" of seats, elections conducted by single-member plurality voting are more likely to result in the creation of relatively stable single-party governments. Frequently, these governments enjoy majority support in Parliament, although minority governments may sometimes occur.

A further characteristic of the plurality system is that relatively small swings in votes between parties often result in large numbers of seats changing hands. Perhaps the most outstanding example in Canada occurred in the 1935 general election, when the Liberals swept back into power. Although their share of the popular vote increased by less than one percent, their number of seats nearly doubled, from 91 to 173. Such amplification of small voting shifts across the country into large-scale changes in seat allocation causes the plurality system to tend to encourage alternation in government between the two dominant parties.

Most of the typical characteristics ascribed here to the plurality system are also true of the majoritarian AV and second-ballot formulas. The major exception is that coalition governments are more frequent under the latter two than under the plurality system. Australia is ruled today by a coalition of the Liberal and Country parties, and French governments have often had to rely on support from more than one party in the National Assembly during the Fifth Republic.

Since PR systems do not give significant bonuses of seats to any party, and since they are usually associated with multi-party systems, it often happens that no single party is in a position to form a majority government. In such cases, coalition or minority governments often result. Sometimes such governments can be highly unstable, as in Italy, which had more than one new government annually between the Second World War and 1996. Elsewhere, however, PR formulas may be associated with stable coalitions, as in Austria, Holland or Switzerland.

Because PR formulas do not exaggerate vote swings to the extent that single-member systems do, alternation of government between major parties or blocs of parties is less frequent in the former. Changes of administration usually result from changes in the alliance strategies of parties in and around the governing coalition, rather than from mass changes in voter allegiance at elections.

---

8. In particular, both the alternative vote and the second ballot tend to "over-represent" parties that can reach agreements or alliances with other parties regarding the destination of second preferences or second ballots. Thus, centrist or moderate parties are often "over-represented" compared with extremist parties of either the right or left, since the latter often cannot persuade supporters of other parties to transfer allegiance to them in the latter stages of voting.

Electoral systems do not completely determine the nature of party systems, nor the type of government, majority or minority, single-party or coalition, in any country. Governmental outcomes are largely a function of the balance of party forces; the party system, in turn, is largely shaped by a country's political culture and social structure and by the electoral behaviour of its citizens. However, the electoral system — which translates votes into seats — is a powerful intermediary force, modifying the competition among parties, distorting or faithfully reproducing the electoral preferences of the voters. Since elections provide the chief mechanism of political participation for most people, the means of translating individual votes into political representation is naturally an important factor in a country's political system.

ELECTIONS IN CANADA

The Franchise and the Ridings

At Confederation the electoral rules were unjust. The federal **franchise** — the right to vote — was based on provincial laws and was restricted to male property owners. There was flagrant discrimination in favour of the upper classes and the ruling Conservative party.

The property qualification was doubly discriminatory because of plural voting; that is, citizens were allowed to vote in each area in which property was owned. Instead of having a single election day, voting was staggered, so the government could control the timing of elections in each region. Elections were held first in those areas where the government was most popular, moving to areas of lesser support only later. The government benefited from this arrangement, since areas in which government support was not as prevalent were encouraged to fall into line, supporting the likely "winner" in order to gain favours from the future government.

In 1885, balloting was brought under federal jurisdiction. Former restrictions remained, however, and a new one, the disenfranchisement of Asians, was added. The two world wars also affected the development of the franchise. In 1917, Canadians of central European descent lost their vote. On the other hand, women, if they were relatives of soldiers, were given the right to vote for the first time, along with Native Indians serving in the Armed Forces, in the expectation that they would support the Union government's call for conscription. The following year all women were granted equal voting rights. Canadians of Asian descent were not granted normal voting privileges until 1948, and the Inuit, disenfranchised in 1934, did not have that right restored until 1950. Religious conscientious objectors, mainly Mennonites, who had been disenfranchised as early as 1920, did not receive voting rights until 1955. Reservation Indians received voter status in 1960.

In the light of the *Charter of Rights and Freedoms*, which states that every citizen of Canada has the right to vote, the Chief Electoral Officer recommended in 1983 that Parliament reconsider the status of the approximately 80 000 Canadians who continued to be denied that right. Resulting amendments to the *Canada Elections Act* in 1993 removed disqualifications for several groups, including judges, persons who are "restrained of their liberty of movement or deprived of the management of their property by reason of mental disease" and inmates serving sentences of less than two years in a correctional institution.

New mechanisms were also established to allow Canadian citizens to vote if they are absent from Canada for less than five consecutive years and intend to return to reside in Canada, or if they are temporarily outside of the country or their electoral district. Very few persons are still specifically prohibited from voting. They include the Chief Electoral Officer, the Assistant Electoral Officer,

FIGURE 12.1 FORMULA FOR CALCULATING REPRESENTATION IN THE HOUSE OF COMMONS

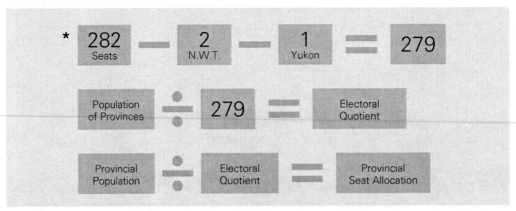

*The calculation starts with the 282 seats that the House of Commons had in 1985.
Source: Representation in the Federal Parliament (Ottawa: Chief Electoral Officer of Canada, 1993), p. 5.

returning officers in each riding, inmates of penal institutions serving a sentence of more than two years and individuals disqualified by law for corrupt or illegal practices.

Constituency Boundaries

Under federal election law, independent, three-member commissions in each province redraw constituency boundaries once every 10 years in order to ensure that each riding has roughly the same number of voters. (See "How Much Is Your Vote Worth?") The rules for carrying out this readjustment of electoral district boundaries are laid out in the *Electoral Boundaries Readjustment Act* (EBRA). Since the 1940s, there have been three fundamental changes to the representation formula and one major change in the boundary readjustment process.[9] In 1985, the *Representation Act* simplified the formula for calculating representation. First, the number of seats for each province is determined. (See Figure 12.1.) Second, seats are added because of the constitutional rule (the "senatorial clause") that guarantees that no province shall have fewer members in the House of Commons than it has in the Senate; and the "grandfather clause" that guarantees that no province shall have fewer seats than it had in 1976 during the 33rd Parliament. Lastly, the seats for NWT and Yukon are added. In 1997 this formula determined that the House of Commons would consist of 301 MPs.

Readjustments following the 1991 census were delayed because of constitutional deliberations and were not in place for the 1993 general election. However, redistribution went ahead for the 1997 election. The 1991 census figures increased the size of the House of Commons to 301 and increased the number of seats for Ontario by four and British Columbia by two for the 1997 election. The redistribution altered the boundaries of all but 31 ridings.

By-elections

By-elections are held to fill vacancies of legislative seats that occur between general elections. The timing of federal by-elections is at the discretion of the prime minister, who, within six months of the date the Speaker issues the notification warrant acknowledging the vacancy, may name any date.

9. R. Kenneth Carty, "The Electoral Boundary Revolution in Canada," *The American Review of Canadian Studies*, vol. 15, no. 3 (1985), pp. 273–87.

By-elections may be held soon after a vacancy appears, a year or more later or not at all if the writs for a general election are issued before the by-election takes place.

While much fanfare and attention accompanies most by-elections, their significance is limited as a predictor of party fortunes in general elections. By-elections tend to be idiosyncratic because of a variety of factors, including the small number of seats contested at any given time (and therefore the lack of regional representativeness), their inability to alter the government's status, changing political conditions between the time of by-elections and the general election and the absence of national campaigns by the political parties.[10] The lack of congruence between by-election and general election results is demonstrated by the Conservative failure to win a majority government in 1979, although the federal Liberal government had lost 13 of 15 by-elections the previous year.

Nevertheless, by-elections are an important part of the democratic process, providing an outlet for voters to air their frustrations and send the government a message. They also are important in maintaining representation. It is in the performance of this latter function that Canada's election laws are lacking. Outrageous delays have sometimes occurred between the time seats became vacant and the calling of subsequent by-elections. In 1975, for example, Trudeau left St. John's West with no representative for 13 months and 10 days.[11] The prime minister and his or her advisors are not anxious to call a by-election if they believe the result will be perceived as unfavourable. This hesitancy is reinforced by the tendency of governments to lose by-elections. However, most reformers agree that political considerations should not obstruct the basic right of citizens to representation in Parliament for very long.

Usually, a by-election is called because an MP dies or resigns, but occasionally an MP will be asked to resign in order to allow the opportunity for another individual to win a seat. Prime Minister Chrétien arranged by-elections in 1995 and 1996 to bring strong French-speaking candidates from Québec into his Cabinet. To bring in Lucienne Robillard to help in the Québec referendum, for example, he called a by-election in St. Henri–Westmount in Montréal. Liberal David Berger, who had held that seat for 16 years, accepted a position in the Prime Minister's Office.

If the leader of a winning party is defeated in his or her own constituency, an apparently safe seat is quickly found. When Brian Mulroney became PC leader in 1983, he had not yet been elected to the House, and the member from Central Nova in Nova Scotia resigned to let him contest and win that seat in a by-election.

CLOSE-UP ON Political Behaviour

HOW MUCH IS YOUR VOTE WORTH?

One person, one vote is a basic democratic principle upheld in Canada. However, all votes are not equal. There are huge discrepancies in riding populations, and thus some votes count more than others; small provinces get more seats in Parliament than their population warrants; rural areas elect more representatives than their numbers indicate they should.

Provincial guarantees in the Constitution distort the principle of representation by population. In 1915, the Maritimes won a constitutionalized "Senate floor" rule: no province can have fewer members of Parliament than it does senators. Based on today's population Prince Edward Island should have only two MPs, but it gets four; New Brunswick should have nine, not ten.

The *Representation Act* of 1985 provided more exceptions. No province can have fewer seats in the House of Commons than it had in 1976. That means that Saskatchewan would otherwise have 10 MPs, not 14 as it does now, and Manitoba would have 11 MPs, not 14.

Besides this, constituency populations vary widely. The rule is that constituency populations should not be more than 25 percent larger or smaller than the ideal average — although there can be exceptions. Labrador, for example, with just over 30 000 people, elects one member. So does St. John's West in Newfoundland, with just over 101 000 people. Rural ridings generally have fewer voters than urban ones, so their votes are worth more. Suburban votes are often worth least because of their heavily populated areas.

Should Canada adhere more strictly to "rep for pop"?

---

10. See Barry J. Kay, "By-elections as Indicators of Canadian Voting," *CJPS*, vol. 14, no. 1 (March 1981), pp. 37–52.

11. This has been the longest vacancy to date.

Electoral Procedure

According to the Constitution, the prime minister must ask the Governor General to dissolve Parliament and call an election at least once every five years. The opposition parties may defeat the government and force the prime minister to call an election at an earlier date, as they did, for example, in 1974 and 1979. Technically, however, they have no part to play in the choice of election date. The prime minister's decision is usually taken some time in the fourth year, at the most favourable opportunity for the governing party.[12] The election is always held on a Monday, except if the Monday in question is a statutory holiday, in which case it is held on the next day. The Cabinet (officially the governor-in-council) formally instructs the Chief Electoral Officer, an independent official responsible to the House of Commons, to set the election machinery in motion. The Chief Electoral Officer issues the writs of election to the returning officers in all constituencies or ridings, who in turn supervise the collation of voters lists, appoint deputy returning officers for each polling subdivision and receive nominations of candidates.

The government assumes responsibility for enrolling the voters. In the seventh week before an election, an army of canvassers, in couples representing the two leading parties in each constituency (except in rural areas, where one enumerator suffices), has traditionally visited every residence to register the names of eligible voters.[13] There followed a period where voters missed or wrongly included in the blitz could apply to the courts of revision. Finally, 17 days before election day, the voting lists were closed. From the issuing of the writ to the closing of the polls, the 1993 election campaign lasted 48 days.[14]

New electoral rules passed by Parliament in late 1996 and 1997 were in effect for the 1997 election. The election campaign was considerably shorter — reduced to the new minimum of 36 days from 47. Redistribution was finally approved, so that there were six new Commons seats — up to 301 from 295. And, for the first time, ballot counting took place at almost the same time from coast to coast, regardless of time zones. Results were not announced until the polls closed in Ontario and Québec, so that results from the East were not known before polls closed in the West.

Another change, concerning enumeration, also took effect after the 1997 election. In April 1997, Chief Electoral Officer Jean-Pierre Kingsley conducted the last federal enumeration following the old rules. In the future, that 1997 voters list will form the nucleus of a permanent voters list. Since the 1997 election, this permanent, computerized list is being constantly updated from provincial motor-vehicle licence bureaus, vital-statistics registries, citizenship registries and National Revenue records. When the next elections are called, electors on the voters list will be notified, and any errors or omissions can be rectified. (See "Summary of the New Electoral Rules.")

Voting procedure is carefully controlled. Each returning officer designates the locations of the polling stations in his or her constituency, such as church halls or schools. On election day, the balloting is overseen at each polling station by deputy returning officers and their polling clerks, and two scrutineers are allowed for each candidate. The voter identifies himself or herself to the polling clerk, who has a list of eligible voters for that polling station and gives the voter an official, bilingual ballot that lists in alphabetical order the official candidates and their party affiliations. Candidates not representing a registered party are listed as independents, unless they request the returning officer to show no designation.

---

12. Five of the 13 elections since 1958 were held well into the government's fifth year. The 1962 and 1972 elections resulted in the party in power being reduced to a minority, and the 1979, 1984 and 1993 elections brought government defeats.

13. As of 1993, enumeration by mail or fax is possible.

14. In 1993, no enumeration was conducted outside of Québec because it had been carried out for the Charlottetown referendum and the lists were reused.

Voters mark their ballot in a private booth, and (in 1993 for the first time) may place their own ballots in the ballot box.[15] When the polling booth closes, the deputy returning officer, with the polling clerk and scrutineers, counts the ballots, seals them in the box and delivers them to the returning officer. An unofficial result is made public shortly after balloting is closed. The official count by the returning officer is not made until later, in some cases not for several days when the vote from overseas is in. A recount is automatically requested by the returning officer if the difference between the first and second candidates is less than one one-thousandth of the ballots cast. In the very rare event of a tie vote, the returning officer casts the deciding ballot.

Electoral Irregularities

We have noted that Canadians did not benefit from a universal franchise until relatively recently. **Gerrymandering** — deliberate manipulation of boundaries by a governing party for their own benefit — and maldistribution were not brought under control until 1964 with the *Electoral Boundaries Commission Act*. While different patterns of boundaries clearly produce different electoral outcomes, mischievously redrawn boundaries are not necessarily illegal acts. In 1986, for example, when the electoral commission began drawing the new electoral boundaries, the Conservative party was accused of coordinating efforts to influence the redistribution in the party's favour.[16] Tories were coached on how to make cases at public hearings for certain boundaries based on "community of interest or community of identity" such as school districts and transportation routes. They did not, of course, reveal that most of their proposals were also strategically advantageous for themselves. The Liberals and NDP had little influence in the boundary changes at that time, largely because they were both preoccupied with internal party matters. When the boundaries were settled and Elections Canada transposed the 1984 votes into the new ridings, it showed the Tories would have won 17 extra seats using the new boundaries. This was not "gerrymandering" as such, but a legal use of influence. However, there are other ways in which elections in this country have been, and in some cases, remain, less than just.

In the past, fraudulent election irregularities have included multiple voting (ballot stuffing), impersonating, bribing, intimidating, and either excluding real names from (false enumeration) or adding fictitious names to (padding) voters lists. None of these actions is an accepted part of the national political culture today, and, if discovered, would damage the popularity and credibility of the candidate involved. Two examples of false enumeration occurred in Toronto in 1957 and 1962, when blocks of names were left off the voters lists. Padding also occurred in Toronto in the 1988 municipal election. Among eligible voters listed were "residents" of gas stations as well as deceased persons. In all of these instances, court cases led to prosecutions. Most irregularities that occur now are at the municipal or

CLOSE-UP ON Political Behaviour

SUMMARY OF THE NEW ELECTORAL RULES

In late 1996, Parliament passed into law three significant changes for electoral procedure. By early 1997, it also agreed to change some electoral boundaries and expand the House of Commons. The changes were as follows:

- Election campaigns will last a minimum of 36 days (down from 47).

- Redistribution added six new Commons seats (four for Ontario and two for British Columbia) for a new total of 301 MPs (from 295).

- Ballot-counting now takes place at almost the same time from coast to coast so that results from the East are not announced before polls close in the West.

- For the next general election after 1997, there will be a permanent voters list.

---

15. Previously this was done by the deputy returning officer, who first verified that it was a valid ballot. Also, for the first time the sale of alcohol was no longer prohibited on polling day.

16. *Maclean's*, October 10, 1988, p. 18.

provincial level rather than the federal level. Gifts of money or liquor to voters, for example, have been an accepted part of the Maritime political culture, although the practice is much less common than even a generation ago. In any case, the secret ballot renders such favours almost meaningless today.

One of the most unusual situations in Canadian electoral history occurred in the riding of York North in the 1988 federal election. The Conservative candidate was declared the winner on election night. Three days later, a recount awarded the seat to the Liberals. A judicial recount gave the seat back to the Conservatives before yet another recount returned it to the Liberals, who kept the seat. The exchange was accompanied by charges of double voting, illegal voting and the exclusion of thousands of eligible votes.[17]

The Candidates

Virtually any elector can become a candidate.[18] All that is necessary is to file nomination papers with the signatures of 100 other electors and deposit $1 000 with a returning officer.[19] The deposit is intended to discourage nuisance candidates, but still allow participation by interested citizens. Local party organizations usually pay the deposit fee for their candidates. It is refundable as follows: 50 percent if the candidate submits the required election expenses return and unused official receipts within the prescribed time limit, and 50 percent if the candidate obtains 15 percent of the ballots cast in the electoral district. Candidates may withdraw until three hours after the close of nominations (which is the 21st day before polling day under the 1997 rules). A prospective candidate need not have the backing of a political party or even reside in the constituency he or she would like to represent. However, it is extremely difficult for a candidate without party endorsement to be elected in Canada. In 1997, only one candidate (former Liberal John Nunziata) was elected as an independent.

As we saw in the preceding chapter, near the time of parliamentary dissolution party organizations spring to life and rush to legitimate their candidates through the nomination process. The procedure varies from one constituency to the next. Local party organizations generally take the initiative in candidate recruitment, and, although automatic renomination of candidates sometimes occurs, locally controlled delegate conventions are usually held. Local organizations use this opportunity to recruit new members and raise money. The openness of the procedure has some problems. In 1984 and 1988, for example, many Tories complained that certain ridings had been "captured" by anti-abortionists, and in 1988 some Liberal constituencies were "seized by the mobilization of one ethnic group" that was asked to make almost no commitment to the party.[20]

Since 1970, by virtue of the *Canada Elections Act*, all party leaders have had a veto over the choice of party candidates. However, only in exceptional cases does the national party headquarters or the party leader interfere with local nominations because such interference tends to generate criticism and divisive quarrels. Local party associations for the most part retain the main responsibility for candidate recruitment; however, a requirement for candidates to be endorsed by the party leader or a designated representative allows the leader to reject candidates in order to protect "national" party interests. For example, in the lead-up to the 1997 election, the National Council of the Reform party advised Preston Manning to refuse to sign certain nomination papers. It also

---

17. *The Globe and Mail*, January 12, 1989.
18. Persons convicted of certain crimes, mental patients and those holding certain public offices or appointments are excluded.
19. The number of signatures and the deposit were revised upward to these amounts in the 1993 amendments to the *Canada Elections Act*.
20. *The Globe and Mail*, editorial, November 23, 1992.

stripped several Ontarians of membership because of their extreme views, thereby preventing them from seeking nominations as Reform candidates in 1993.[21]

In February 1992, the Liberal convention gave party leader Jean Chrétien a unique new power: the leader can now appoint candidates directly without having to go through the local riding associations. In 1993, Chrétien used the power in a handful of ridings to "parachute" in "star" candidates. He used the rule again in 1997 to ensure more female candidates. Well before the general election was called, Chrétien appointed women candidates in specific ridings in order to ensure his commitment that one-quarter of all Liberal candidates would be female.[22]

The Campaigns

With the announcement of an election, the national headquarters of the largest parties become nerve centres of nation-wide campaigns. Their functions include coordinating the meetings and tours of party leaders, issuing literature, arranging broadcasts, employing public relations firms, issuing news releases and collecting public opinion data. All major parties have two foci during an election campaign: the national campaign, the aim of which is electing the party; and 301 separate constituency campaigns, which aim to elect individual candidates.

In all parties, the leader's role in the campaign is paramount. The personal charisma and flamboyant campaign style exhibited by Diefenbaker in 1958, Trudeau in 1968 and Mulroney in 1984 are credited with the large majorities won by their parties. When leaders are popular, they and their families are paraded before party gatherings from coast to coast in an effort to have some of their charisma rub off onto the local candidates.

The candidates, meanwhile, are busy making themselves as visible as possible in their constituencies. Speeches, door-to-door canvassing, coffee parties and media appearances fill each day. A campaign manager makes efficient use of the candidate's time and organizes financing and other details. Party advisors include a large percentage of media people: communications strategists, advertising personnel, public relations experts and public opinion pollsters. It is their job to plan strategy, obtain maximum media coverage for their candidate, communicate the party's promises and build images. The basic duties of phoning constituents, distributing literature, and organizing babysitting and rides to and from the polling booths on election day all fall to volunteers.

A candidate plans campaign strategy with two goals in mind: retaining traditional party supporters and attracting as many undecided and opponent votes as possible. To achieve these aims, analysis and targeting of the various voting groups in the constituency are essential. Their importance to the candidate depends on their size, turnout on election day and party commitment. What percentage of time should a particular candidate spend wooing the farm or trade-union vote? What issues should be emphasized or avoided?

At the party level, the same knowledge is essential to plan a competent overall campaign strategy. Here, too, the growing complexity of campaigns necessitates professional help. In what geographical areas does a party have a great chance of winning? Where is there little chance? What issues should be stressed? How should financial and other resources be allocated?

---

21. *The Globe and Mail*, August 4, 1993.
22. The other parties took different approaches to finding women candidates in 1997. The NDP acted on its affirmative action ruling that requires ridings to have a woman or minority candidate before a nomination vote can be held. PC and Reform parties relied on search committees and riding associations to identify strong candidates, including women.

Public Opinion Surveys

The first psephologist, R.B. McCallum, remarked after completing his study of the 1945 general election in Britain that election studies should cease, or they would take all the mystery out of voting.[23] His ironical advice, of course, went unheeded, and survey research now plays a large role in both pre- and post-election analyses in most western countries.

A great fund of election data is available in Canada. Major opinion surveys have been conducted by academics in most elections since 1965.[24] Recent elections have also witnessed a proliferation of pre-election polls, which are commonly used to predict election outcomes and probe specific issues. Perhaps the most widely known survey organizations are Canadian Gallup, Decima Research, Reid, Environics, Pollinara, Ekos and Léger and Léger, which publish their results in various newspapers. The media compete by offering their own polls. Both major television networks, the CBC and CTV, conduct national surveys. Local television and broadcasting stations often do their own polls at the town or city level. Besides these sources, there exist many other private surveys, done for various groups by either Canadian or American firms. Large numbers of polls are also commissioned for the private use of political parties.

Canada's immense size and uneven population distribution cause pollsters two major problems. First, it is expensive to sample an adequate number of Canadians to represent the whole population. Second, regions often differ dramatically in their opinions, and often are at variance with the national pattern. Whereas in a geographically smaller country like Britain it is usually possible to measure the swing of votes for or against the government as a uniform movement across the country, it is sometimes impossible in Canada. This situation is caused by strong regional differences, but it is compounded by the fact that some parties that are important in certain regions are often non-existent in others. These and other factors make Canadian election forecasters reluctant to predict the distribution of seats in Parliament from national opinion trends.

From 1993 until 1998, publishing opinion polls was banned from midnight the Friday before polling day until the close of all polling stations. (See "Polling Restrictions: Are They Justified?") The essential problem with polls is that they are often presented as factual data that require no explanation. In fact, they are a mere collection of attitudinal information on a given day from a random sample of the population used to assess attitudes of the population as a whole. There is always a margin of error and the statistics require proper interpretation. On the other hand, proponents of polls argue that they provide valuable aid for parties and governments in reading public opinion. Journalists and political scientists defend the public's right to have the same information that the politicians have. Moreover, the results of polls have proven remarkably accurate. In 1997, for example, the last Ekos poll indicated the Liberals would win a majority government with 38 percent of the popular vote — exactly what they won.

Attention to the following items could serve as a check on the quality of a poll:

■ Examine the wording of the question to be sure it is clear. Also, check the order of the questions to see if it could affect responses. For example, leading questions are sometimes asked just before a question on voting intentions.

■ Check the polling time. When was it taken? Over what length of time? A poll represents a snapshot of attitudes at a given time, not on the day it is published. The specific day, or even the time of day it was taken, can affect results.

23. R.B. McCallum and A. Readman, *The British General Election of 1974* (Oxford: Macmillan, 1974).
24. See, for example, Richard Johnston, André Blais, Henry E. Brady and Jean Crête, *Letting the People Decide: Dynamics of a Canadian Election* (Montréal: McGill-Queen's University Press, 1992).

- Note the percentage of "undecideds"; high numbers can render the results meaningless.

- Note the size of the sample and the sample-error factor; the sample error depends on the sample size. In extrapolating from a few thousand to many million there will always be a statistical error. In reputable election polls the margin is usually between plus or minus three percentage points. In Canada, a representative sample of 1 500 people, for example, is generally considered to be an accurate reflection of the national opinion within plus or minus 2.5 percentage points, 95 percent of the time.

- Watch for the percentage of "soft" voters who are only weakly decided and could easily change their positions.

- Consider the name and reputation of the polling firm and especially who paid for the survey.

Media and Voters

The relationship between politicians and journalists is reciprocal: each wants something of the other and affects the other's conduct. During an election campaign, party strategists structure their daily campaign itineraries around the demands of television and, to a lesser extent, radio. For example, the timing and presentations of policy pronouncements can ensure inclusion on network evening newscasts. Policy statements delivered early in the day allow reporters enough time to meet their deadlines. Television crews are provided the best vantage points at campaign rallies and other "media events." Appropriate photogenic backgrounds are arranged to highlight the theme of policy pronouncements, and "advance crews" are sent ahead to campaign stops to ensure a proper expression of support for their candidate.

The mass media play a crucial role in helping voters choose among parties at election time. There is, however, a growing concern about how well they perform this role. Many observers resent the excessive concentration placed on style rather than on substance and complain that Canadian election coverage is analogous to a horse race or a game. Emphasis tends to be placed on polls, campaign strategies and party prospects in individual ridings, in an attempt to determine which party is "winning." Serious analysis of party pronouncements or investigation into areas of voter concern are for the most part ignored. Thus, the voter is provided little information on which to base a decision. Penetrating the motives of the party campaigns, and thereby focusing on the campaign style of each party, is done at the expense of analyzing campaign issues.

Emphasis on style also results in a "leader fixation," since campaigns are based around leaders' tours. Polls conducted throughout the campaign also focus on leadership in an attempt to predict the outcome of the election and to explain it in terms of leader appeal. The polls are presented as measures to gauge how the leaders' campaigns are faring. In this sense, media coverage misrepresents the political system, narrows the focus of public debate and denigrates political leaders and institutions.

CLOSE-UP ON Political Behaviour

POLLING RESTRICTIONS: ARE THEY JUSTIFIED?

In 1993, Parliament amended the *Canada Elections Act* to read: "No person shall broadcast, publish or disseminate the results of an opinion survey respecting how electors will vote at an election or respecting an election issue that would permit the identification of a political party or candidate from midnight the Friday before polling day until the close of all polling stations."

It did this on the grounds that polls might be wrong or might unduly influence citizens before they vote. But is this sufficient reason to suspend Canadians' rights to freedom of thought, belief, opinion and expression, including freedom of the press and other means of communication?

Southam Inc. and Thomson Newspapers Co. Ltd. challenged the law in court. In 1996, the Ontario Court of Appeal supported the eve-of-the-election ban on public opinion polls, even though it concluded "there is no empirical evidence as to the extent of the influence of opinion polls upon the voter, nor can it be said with certainty that the impact of the opinion polls is undue." In May 1998, by a vote of 5–3, the Supreme Court struck down both the lower court ruling and the law.

Opinion polls may now be published without restriction before an election.

Is the Supreme Court ruling justified, or would a law be desirable?

A study of the 1984 election showed that there was "less reporting of the leaders' statements and more assessments of their performances." Almost 60 percent of news reports on *The National* (CBC) and in *The Globe and Mail* concerning the party leaders made an explicit assessment of the leader or his performance.[25] In 1993 and 1997, the media spotlight was almost entirely on the party leaders, rather than on the "team" seeking election.

We noted earlier that the media are highly political instruments. Television is the most powerful medium of all because of the vast number of voters who can be reached. Until 1993, television and radio coverage tended to be partisan toward the three established parties. The bias against minor parties was evident in newspapers as well, where editors propagandized in editorials and influenced the contents of the headlines and news pages. Minor parties were thus at a severe disadvantage. However, in 1993, the Bloc Québécois and Reform parties captured considerable media attention because of their strong regional support. A contributing factor was that they already had membership in Parliament, and therefore were eligible to be represented in the nationally televised leadership debates. This proved true again in 1997, not only for these parties, but also for the Conservatives and the NDP.

The media time allotted for parties during election campaigns is strictly governed by law. According to the *Election Expenses Act*, all broadcasters are required to sell up to a maximum of six-and-one-half hours of prime-time spots to registered political parties at a most-favoured advertising rate. The number of hours is divided among the parties according to a formula revised in August 1993. The formula is based on the number of Commons seats held, the number of candidates each party ran in the previous election and the percentage of the popular vote each party won. Often, only a fraction of the time is actually used because it is so expensive.

Free time is allocated on the same basis as paid advertising; naturally, all of it is used. These time regulations were designed to provide registered political parties with a reasonable opportunity to present themselves directly to the public and help equalize access to the airwaves. However, it is important to note that, while this law establishes some equity for the largest federal parties represented in Parliament, it also reinforces the bias against minor and new parties and independent candidates. Political advertising is also regulated. None is allowed during the first four weeks of the campaign, nor on the last two days before the election nor on polling day itself. The object is to prevent a last-minute "ad blitz."[26] A 1993 amendment to the *Canada Elections Act* placed a $1 000 limit on advertising expenses incurred by non-party organizations for the purpose of promoting or opposing a particular registered party or candidate. The restriction, supported by the three major parties, was intended to prevent individuals or groups from dominating political discourse during the election campaign. However, an Alberta trial judge ruled in 1993 that the changes in the *Elections Act* that limited spending in election campaigns violated freedom of expression under the Charter. The federal government launched an appeal, but Canada's Chief Electoral Officer lifted restrictions on the right of citizens and lobby groups to buy political advertising during the 1993 campaign. The federal government did not file an appeal to the Supreme Court, so the law no longer exists.[27]

Elections have become big business, with the establishment of public relations firms whose primary purpose is to build the leaders' images and direct political campaigns. Typically, public relations experts determine the voters' key prejudices by means of public opinion polls, then tailor

25. Frederick K. Fletcher, "The Media and the 1984 Landslide," in H.R. Penniman, ed., *Canada at the Polls, 1984* (Durham, N.C.: Duke University Press, 1988), p. 169.

26. See the 1997 election case study below, pp. 455–57.

27. *The Globe and Mail*, August 20, 1993, and October 9, 1996.

the campaign to avoid unpopular subjects that might alienate large voting blocs. They devise catchy slogans such as "The Just Society" or "The Politics of Inclusion" that fix a name and personality in the voters' minds in connection with a positive proposal.

Perhaps the most important aspect of the *Election Expenses Act* is that it recognizes parties as legal entities, thereby rendering them publicly accountable. They can therefore benefit from the Act but also be prosecuted for infractions of it.[28] The Act controls election spending by limiting the campaign costs of both parties and candidates to a base formula linked to the consumer price index and adjusted before every election. It also encourages the parties to develop broader financial bases by granting generous tax credits, primarily for small donations, as a balance against reliance on corporate funds. A further provision to reduce the reliance of candidates on large contributors is the refunding of deposits and partial reimbursement of election expenses for candidates; as we have noted, a candidate who obtains 15 percent of the valid votes cast in his or her electoral district is refunded the $1 000 deposit and partially reimbursed by the Receiver General of Canada for election expenses. As well, provided that they comply with the requirements concerning the filing of a return of election expenses,[29] registered parties are reimbursed for one-half the costs incurred in the purchase of permitted radio and television advertising time. More important, recognized national parties can also get taxpayers to subsidize 22.5 percent of their campaign costs if they spend just 10 percent of the expense limit set by Elections Canada.[30]

Parties make extensive media preparations before the election is called (money spent then is not deducted from the party's spending limits); later, in the midst of a campaign, more commercials may be produced quickly as pollsters target issues of most concern to voters. While there may be something degrading about politicians being packaged and sold like soap flakes, advertising does have positive aspects. Despite evident media distortions, the simplification of issues and the personalization of the political campaigns arouse wide interest, and therefore probably increase awareness and participation in the democratic political process. (See "Advertising Agencies and Electoral Campaigns.")

Election Financing

The rising costs of financing general election campaigns raise questions about the degree and fairness of political competitiveness. Does the expense hinder or exclude individuals, groups and parties from active involvement in the election process? The 1974 enactment of the *Election Expenses Act*, discussed in the previous chapter, represented an important attempt to address such questions. Many ideas in the Act originated with the Task Force on Election Expenses and it received its main thrust from Privy Council Office president Allan MacEachen and his aides from 1970 to 1974. According to its provisions, which were embodied in a series of amendments to the *Canada Elections Act*, the *Broadcasting Act* and the *Income Tax Act*, federal candidates, for the first time, were required to give a detailed accounting of money received and spent. They were also compelled to observe spending limits, and candidates who received 15 percent of the votes were eligible for subsidies from the national treasury.

---

28. A "registered" political party is defined as a political party that was either (a) represented in the House of Commons on the day before the dissolution of Parliament, immediately preceding the general election, or (b) had officially nominated candidates in at least 50 electoral districts in Canada, 30 days before polling day at the general election.

29. Only "registered" political parties can take advantage of these income tax credits. However, a contribution during a federal election made directly to a candidate allows the contributor to claim a tax credit whether or not the candidate represents a registered political party.

30. In addition to campaign reimbursements for national and riding campaigns, the cost of the election includes staff salaries, compiling the voters list, computerization, mail-in ballots, printing ballots and running polling stations — for an estimated grand total of about $100 million in 1997.

CLOSE-UP ON Political Behaviour

ADVERTISING AGENCIES AND ELECTORAL CAMPAIGNS

The Liberal and Conservative parties first used advertising agencies to plan their campaigns in the 1940s. In 1948, the Walsh Advertising Agency, in *A Formula for Liberal Victory*, wrote,"we stripped away all the mysticism of political campaigns and 'sold' Liberalism as we would sell any other product or service ... by modern merchandising methods."* Of course, the opposite effect can occur if the slogan is badly chosen. The 1972 Liberal slogan "The Land Is Strong" drew this widely repeated comment in rural areas: "What makes my land strong is horse shit."

---

* R. Whitaker, "The Liberal Party Enters the Age of the Ad Man: Advertising Agencies and the National Liberal Party 1943–58," unpublished paper.

F. Leslie Seidle and K.Z. Paltiel ascribe the motivating forces behind the adoption of the *Election Expenses Act* partly to financial difficulties encountered by political parties: between 1957 and 1965 Canada experienced a rapid succession of five elections, which taxed the fundraising capabilities of the major parties.[31] Compounding this problem was the increasing cost of elections, arising mainly from the accelerated use of television advertising. Another motivation was the party financing scandals that aroused the ire of the public. Continued concerns about party fundraising activities and the influence of the Watergate scandal in the United States encouraged politicians to take steps to prevent further mistrust on the part of the public.

All campaign expenses and the amount and sources of party contributions must be disclosed. We stated earlier that the *Election Expenses Act* requires parties to provide audited financial statements in order to expose fundraising practices and election expenses to public scrutiny. Six months after the end of the party's fiscal year, an audited return containing a detailed statement of the party's contributions and operating expenses must be sent to the Chief Electoral Officer. Contributors of $200 or more during the fiscal year must be named. Candidates are also required to file detailed, audited returns after each general or by-election. These are public documents and are thus available for scrutiny. In order to prevent outside interference in elections, a 1993 amendment to the *Canada Elections Act* prohibited contributions to a candidate from sources outside the country.[32] Apart from this, there are no limits placed on the amount that individuals or organizations may donate to a political party.

ELECTORAL BEHAVIOUR

Studies of electoral behaviour attempt to describe how and explain why people vote as they do and what impact political events, personalities, issues and other factors have on their decisions.

Voters and Non-Voters

As we have noted, virtually every Canadian 18 years of age and over has the right to vote. However, certain citizens are more apt to exercise their franchise than others. There are several standard factors involved in whether a person votes or not. First, some individuals are more gregarious and therefore are more likely to have a psychological predisposition to participate actively in the electoral process. As well, the poor and the uneducated are much less apt to vote than are individuals in the higher income levels with a college education. The wealthy are more apt to vote because they feel

---

31. F. Leslie Seidle and K.Z. Paltiel, "Party Finance, the Election Expenses Act and Campaign Spending in 1979 and 1980," in H.R. Penniman, ed., *Canada at the Polls, 1979 and 1980*, pp. 229–30.

32. Specifically, contributions are prohibited from: an individual who is not a Canadian citizen or permanent resident in Canada; an association that does not carry on activities in Canada; a union that is not entitled to bargain collectively in Canada; and a foreign state or political party.

they have more at stake in an election outcome, and more highly educated people are more interested and better informed than others. The abstention rate also reflects feelings of efficacy. In general, lower-class workers have a low feeling of efficacy; that is, they don't feel their vote matters, while corporation presidents, at the other extreme, tend to believe that they can further their interests by electing the right candidate. Voter turnout in Canada is highest in the middle-aged range; the youngest and the oldest tend to abstain most. Men cast their vote more often than women.[33] Incidental factors such as issues and campaigns may also affect non-voting and so, too, may the level of civic responsibility instilled in some voters through socialization.

Although meaningful generalizations about political participation are difficult to make with precision, it would appear that while socioeconomic factors are significant in motivating participation, there is little substantial variation based on ethnicity or regionalism. Interestingly, no significant difference between ethnic groups in terms of their overall index of electoral activity has been found at the federal level. Moreover, levels of participation in the various regions have also been discovered to be roughly similar across the country. A stereotypical Canadian voter, then, is a middle-aged, white-collar worker with at least some postsecondary education. The counterpart, the typical non-voter, would be a young person with little formal education and a blue-collar job. These are, of course, crude generalizations, but they are supported by studies that show that political participation is basically a middle-class affair.

Electoral Choice

Many factors influence how and why Canadians vote. These can be grouped loosely, as indicated in Figure 12.2, into long-term and short-term factors. Long-term factors contribute to an individual's basic *identification* with a political party. They include socioeconomic indicators such as class, religion, gender and ethnicity, urban/rural distinctions and so on. Short-term factors arise from the *specifics* of an election campaign, including issues, leaders, candidates, debates, polls and media coverage. It is possible to visualize voting behaviour as a funnel that has flowing into it long-term factors that endure over time and then short-term factors that have an impact just before the vote emerges at the mouth of the funnel.

FIGURE 12.2 FUNNEL OF INFLUENCE IN VOTING BEHAVIOUR

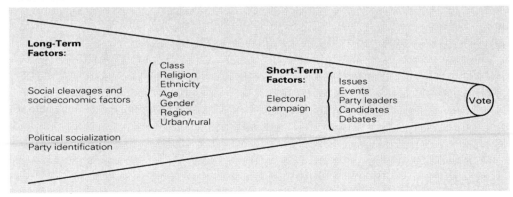

---

33. See B.J. Kay, R.D. Lambert, S.D. Brown and J.E. Curtis, "Gender and Political Activity in Canada," *CJPS*, vol. 20, no. 4 (1987), pp. 851–63; and Peter Wearing and Joseph Wearing, "Does Gender Make a Difference in Voting Behaviour?" in Joseph Wearing, *The Ballot and Its Message: Voting in Canada* (Toronto: Copp Clark Pitman, 1991).

Long-term factors begin early in an individual's life, as attitudes toward politics and political parties are acquired through socialization and social group factors. These factors have a bearing on one's political ideas (see Chapter 4), party identification and voting intentions to varying degrees. Long before an election campaign starts, an individual may have acquired a degree of party identification. The *configuration* and *intensity* of social divisions are important factors in whether or not those divisions affect electoral behaviour. As Martin Harrop and William Miller state:

> *Where cleavages such as class and religion run deep and reinforce each other, so as to give sharply-etched sub-cultures, voting choice merely reflects communal loyalties. But where divisions are cross-cutting or simply less intense, voting becomes a genuinely political act, shaped but not dominated by an elector's social identity.*[34]

During the campaign, short-term factors influence the voter, confirming or changing the effect of long-term factors. Two short-term factors in particular are significant: leadership and issues. Changing technology, campaign strategies and media, especially performance on television, have increased the impact of short-term factors on voting in recent years at the expense of long-term factors including regionalism, religion, urban/rural environment, ethnicity, gender and age.[35] Today, short-term factors can cause significant fluctuation in public opinion.

Long-Term Factors in Election Outcomes

Region

People in specific areas of the country have traditionally supported one party over others, and shifted their allegiance only periodically, and in unusual circumstances. However, as a long-term factor, region has shown wide variations. Québec, for example, voted massively Liberal before the turn of the century, from the days of Laurier until 1984. However, aberrations in this pattern did occur, first with the severe defeat of the Liberals by the Conservatives under Diefenbaker in 1958 and again by the Conservatives, led by Brian Mulroney in 1984 and 1988. In 1993 and 1997, it was the Bloc Québécois that routed the Liberals in Québec.

The Prairie provinces and British Columbia voted heavily Conservative in federal elections from about 1957 to 1993, when they switched their support — largely to the new, populist Reform party. British Columbia, Saskatchewan and Manitoba also have a history of periodic support for the NDP. The Prairie provinces have a tradition of supporting protest parties. In 1997, the West as a whole gave 60 seats out of 91 to the Reform party. The region gave rise to the Progressives, the CCF, the NDP and the Reform party (now the Alliance party). While usually voting Liberal, Québec has also nurtured the Créditistes and today nurtures the Bloc Québécois.

Regional voting patterns have not been consistent, even in the Maritimes. Newfoundland voted strongly Liberal from 1949 to 1968 (while Joey Smallwood led the Liberal party in the province); but that support gradually diminished until 1993 when Newfoundlanders once more gave the Liberals all of their seats. In 1993 the Liberals won 31 of the 32 seats in the Maritimes, but this was reduced to 11 in 1997.

---

34. Martin Harrop and William L. Miller, *Elections and Voters: A Comparative Introduction* (London: Macmillan, 1987), p. 211.

35. For a more extensive review of the debates about the role of class, region and religion in Canadian voting, and of the concept of party identification, see Elisabeth Gidengil, "Canada Votes: A Quarter Century of Canadian National Election Studies," *CJPS*, vol. 25, no. 2 (June 1992), pp. 219–48.

Large urban areas have been even less consistent in their support for the two major parties. The largest metropolitan centres, Vancouver, Winnipeg, Toronto and Montreal, voted massively Liberal in the 1960s (with a few NDP constituencies in Toronto, Winnipeg and Vancouver). In the 1970s, the Conservatives gained strength in these areas, particularly in the West.

While Liberals have attracted a disproportionate number of urban voters, the Conservatives and Reform have traditionally received a higher degree of rural support. In 1993 and 1997 the Liberals dominated in urban areas, winning most city ridings across the country. However, these associations may not be statistically meaningful. In Canada, the impact of community size on voting is likely to be associated with several other cleavages and voting influences, and so it is impossible to separate its impact from other variables. In any case, the Liberals have shown the greatest ability to attract a variety of voters by cutting across urban/rural lines.

Ethnicity

The major ethnic distinction in Canadian voting behaviour is between French- and English-speaking Canadians. French Canadians have traditionally awarded a high level of support to the Liberals, while English-speaking Canadians have been more evenly divided in their support for the Liberals and the Conservatives. The Progressive Conservatives have attracted "disproportionate support" from Canadians of British descent, those from the Protestant monarchies of northern Europe and those of eastern European origin. Post–Second World War immigrant voters have been more attracted to the Liberals. The ability of the Liberal party to bridge the two founding ethnic groups and at the same time appeal to immigrant voters has been the principal reason for its dominance of Canadian politics during most of the twentieth century.

The 1984 and 1988 elections shattered many of the traditional ethnic patterns of voter support for the Tories as Québec and the West voted massively for Brian Mulroney and the Conservative party. With the rise of the Bloc Québécois in the 1990s, the pattern shifted again with the Tories and Liberals routed from francophone areas. In the 1997 election Liberals and Tories received support mainly where the composition of the ridings was not largely francophone.

Class

In many countries social class is an important determinant of voting behaviour, although it has not proven to be a significant determinant in Canada. However, debate about the importance of class as an indicator of voting preferences continues.[36] Historically, only a proportion of working-class voters support the NDP, the Liberal party tending to attract support from all classes. Although it may be argued that the results of some opinion polls have shown a degree of class awareness in Canada, there is no evidence to indicate that it has had a significant impact on electoral choice. As class orientations are spread relatively evenly across the country, their political impact is effectively nullified by the single-member plurality electoral system. Canada's electoral system and its homogenizing effect, therefore, work against the emergence of class-based politics.

36. Ronald D. Lambert et al., "Social Class and Voting," in James Curtis et al., eds., *Social Inequality in Canada* (Scarborough: Prentice Hall, 1988); and Keith Archer, *Political Choice and Electoral Consequences* (Montréal: McGill-Queen's University Press, 1990). More recently, see Ronald Lambert and James Curtis, "Perceived Party Choice and Class Voting," *CJPS*, vol. 26, no 2 (June 1993), pp. 273–86; and Reza Nakhaie and Robert Arnold, "Class Position, Class Ideology and Class Voting: Mobilization of Support in the New Democratic Party in the Canadian Election of 1984," *Canadian Review of Sociology and Anthropology*, vol. 33 (1996), 181–212.

On the other hand, the question of the ideological content of Canadian electoral behaviour remains unresolved. In his study of identification with federal political parties, Michael Stevenson found "a slight bias toward more upper-class identification with the Progressive Conservative Party and more lower-class identification with the Liberal Party."[37] Analysis of the 1988 election results confirmed this voting pattern because of the free trade issue. The Conservative party was strongly supported by higher-income business groups while the Liberals and New Democrats tended to receive their support from lower-income groups.[38] The impact of region in the 1993 and 1997 elections may have nullified even this slight trace of class voting.

Religion

Religion has consistently correlated with voting behaviour in Canada. Roman Catholics show a strong tendency to vote Liberal, regardless of their ethnicity, region or class. This held true even during the free trade campaign of 1988 when Protestants still tended to be Conservatives, Catholics tended to be Liberals and the NDP had no religiously differentiated base. Canadians of "other" or "no" religion were the least partisan politically.[39] Political scientist Richard Johnston has argued that Catholics are distributed unevenly across the country, and that this allows them to control the electoral agenda where their numbers are relatively large. "Where Catholics are numerous, class or union/non-union differences are suppressed ... where Catholics are few, class differences, at least in NDP voting, can flourish."[40]

No simple logic is adequate to explain the impact of religious affiliation on voting preference. Religion is often confounded with linguistic and regional patterns. Results of the 1984, 1988, 1993 and 1997 elections show that the Liberal hold on their French, Catholic base has been greatly weakened in Québec. The answer is perhaps intertwined with the historical evolution of Canada and its party system. An anti-Catholic sentiment on the part of some Tories during the nineteenth century may have alienated English Canadian Catholics. As well, French Canadians are overwhelmingly Catholic and, until 1984, tended to vote strongly Liberal.

Urban/Rural Environment

Despite its relatively small population and its enormous land mass, Canada has a remarkably large urban population. For our purposes, "urban" is defined as habitation in a town or city of at least 5 000 people. As we noted in Chapter 1, the Canadian population is overwhelmingly concentrated in urban regions in the provinces of Ontario, Québec and British Columbia. The Conservatives have traditionally received a significant degree of rural support, while the Liberals tend to attract a disproportionate number of urban voters. Support for the New Democratic Party also tends to be urban. Reform has a strong rural appeal. In most of the twentieth century, the Liberal party, while receiving considerable urban support, has been best able to attract a variety of voters by cutting across urban/rural lines.

---

37. H. Michael Stevenson, "Ideology and Unstable Party Identification in Canada: Limited Rationality in a Brokerage Party System," *CJPS*, vol. 20, no. 4 (December 1987), pp. 813–50.

38. Johnston et al., *Letting the People Decide*, ch. 3.

39. See Laurence LeDuc, "The Flexible Canadian Electorate," in H.R. Penniman, *Canada at the Polls, 1984*, pp. 37–54; Richard Johnston, "The Reproduction of the Religious Cleavage in Canadian Elections," *CJPS*, vol. 25, no. 1 (March 1985), pp. 99–113, and the rejoinder by William P. Irving in the same volume, pp. 115–17.

40. Richard Johnston, "The Geography of Class and Religion in Canadian Elections," in Joseph Wearing, *The Ballot and Its Message*, p. 128.

The impact of community size on voting is likely to be associated with several other cleavages and voting influences. In order to establish its independent effect, a researcher would have to control for the various historical influences and factors in the political demography of the constituencies being examined.

Short-Term Factors in Election Outcomes

A useful guide to voting behaviour in any single election is to think of the factors that influence voters as a triangle with leaders, issues and party identification each constituting one of its angles. The degree of party identification indicates the percentage of votes that could theoretically change hands, while leaders and issues influence voters in the short term, confirming or losing party support.

Issues, along with other factors such as party leadership, candidates, leadership debates and specific events, play an important part in influencing the individual voter's decision. Voters in Canada shift their attention to new problems in each election.

For an issue to have an impact on the outcome of an election it must meet three conditions. First, it must be salient to voters; that is, voters must have an opinion on it and they must consider it relatively important. Second, the issue must be linked with partisan controversy. It will have little impact on election outcomes if all the parties are perceived to have the same position on it. Third, opinion must be strongly skewed in a single direction and not simply reflect the usual degree of attachment to the various political parties.

The perception that issues are an important factor in a voter's choice leads strategists to rely heavily on public opinion surveys. Party planners identify those groups that contain possible supporters and strive to mobilize their support through appeals and policies tailored to a winning electoral coalition. The measure of success, of course, is the election result. Although free trade, for example, played a major role in determining voter choice in the 1988 election, it was relatively insignificant in 1993 and not even mentioned in 1997.

Modern political leaders tend to embody the party image. This is largely due to television coverage. Leaders put a personal stamp on their parties. John Turner, Pierre Trudeau and Jean Chrétien had very different personal images that adhered to the Liberal party.

Although Canada has a parliamentary system, the leader plays a central role in determining voter choices. Leadership was an important issue early in the 1988 campaign, and again in the final week. Inevitably, complex political issues are personalized; personality is often easier for the electorate and the media to evaluate. John Turner's leadership ability was undermined by his poor performance in 1984, and he never fully recovered from that negative perception. His strong performance in the run-up to the 1988 election and the television debate in particular helped him considerably, but negative Conservative ads in the last week of the campaign reinforced the previous image of him as an indecisive, weak leader. In the 1993 campaign, Jean Chrétien trailed PC leader Kim Campbell in popularity by a wide margin at the start of the campaign, but passed her by the last week. Campbell's stumbles and indiscretions caused harmful public rifts in the party. In 1997, Jean Charest's personal appeal was credited for a revival of Conservative fortunes.

It is evident that a number of factors influence voting. The contradictory perceptions and influences weighing on voters' minds as they enter the polling booths are indeed difficult to disentangle. We have identified a number of the leading factors in an attempt to understand electoral choice. There is undoubtedly a degree of interaction and reinforcement among the factors that makes the precise independent effect of each difficult to determine. Each campaign is unique in the extent to which leaders and issues are influential.

Party Identification and Historical Analysis of Electoral Outcomes

One of the most controversial topics in the field of electoral studies is the role of **party identification**, the degree to which citizens identify with a particular party. It is thought by some that parental party identification is transmitted to children through the socialization process and that the resulting attachment has a long-term effect on voting behaviour, filtering the effects of short-term factors such as party leaders or campaign issues. While in the preceding analysis we discussed "group" phenomena such as region, class, religion and ethnic identity, the question of party identification directs us to the level of the individual voter. How important is this factor in influencing voting behaviour?

Studies of electoral behaviour indicate that party identification is widespread in Canada but is relatively low in intensity.[41] In 1988, only 35 percent of the electorate did not identify themselves with a party. This was similar to percentages of non-identifiers in the previous four elections.[42] Non-partisans are particularly susceptible to issues, leaders and other short-term factors in the election campaign. Transient and newly eligible voters generally seem to favour the incumbent government.[43] The impact of specific issues and the image of the leader are credited with many recent defections from party loyalty. While there continues to be a small, stable core of loyalists, a significant proportion shifts from one party affiliation to another.

In Canada, volatility in party identification is tending to increase over time, and this suggests the increasing possibility of large pendulum swings of political support. Michael Stevenson has found that unstable partisanship is at least partially related to ideology. His research indicates that in the 1977–88 period, "the largest bloc of unstable partisans was closest ideologically to the more left-wing stable New Democratic Party partisans, and shifted only between the New Democratic and Liberal Parties." He also found that the smaller bloc of unstable partisans, which moved to the Conservative party, "was ideologically closest to its more right-wing stable partisans."[44]

Another broad approach has been to use long-term aggregate data analysis to produce explanations of electoral success in Canada. A study by André Blais and Richard Nadeau concludes that two factors — a leader from Québec and a recent history of government job creation — have been key elements in every general election since 1953.[45] They conclude that every increase of one percent in the unemployment rate "reduces the incumbent government's share of the vote by around two percentage points." Conversely, every increase in employment rate increases their chances. Second, Blais and Nadeau also found that when a major party selects a leader from Québec, it "gets a five-to-six point boost in its share of the vote." In fact, every time there has been a party leader from Québec [from a major party] that leader has received a plurality of votes in the country. If the leaders of both major parties are from Québec, the advantage is cancelled out. Certainly, these findings should provide "fodder" for arguments about the need to reform Canada's party and electoral systems. They are also instructive in understanding the Liberal vote in 1997. Chrétien was from Québec, and there had been no increase in the unemployment rate during his tenure.

---

41. See Lawrence LeDuc, "The Flexible Canadian Electorate," pp. 40–41
42. This is close to the non-partisan rates in the United States. Party identification percentages for the main parties in 1988 were Conservative 29, Liberal 24, NDP 11. Johnston et al., *Letting the People Decide*, pp. 82–84.
43. Alan Frizzell, Jon Pammett and Anthony Westell, *The Canadian General Election of 1988* (Ottawa: Carleton University Press, 1989).
44. Stevenson, "Ideology and Unstable Party Identification in Canada," p. 815.
45. Richard Nadeau and André Blais, "Explaining Election Outcomes in Canada: Economy and Politics," *CJPS*, vol. 26, no. 4 (December 1993), pp. 775–90.

GENERAL ELECTION RESULTS, 1867–1997

Since Confederation, Canada has held 36 general elections. Either the Liberals or Conservatives have won each time.[46] As we saw in Figure 11.1, with the exception of the Liberal victory of 1874, the Conservative party dominated federal politics from 1867 until nearly the turn of the century (1896). The Liberal party was ascendant until 1984, holding power for most of the twentieth century. (See Table 12.7.) The most important element in the Liberals' success during these earlier years was the capture and maintenance of Québec. Today, it is Liberal control of Ontario that makes it the predominant party in the country.

CASE STUDY OF THE 1997 GENERAL ELECTION

Background: The 1993 General Election

When Prime Minister Mulroney stepped down as prime minister in the spring of 1993, the coalition he had built to give the Conservatives their 1984 and 1988 victories was in tatters.[47] He had taken Québec separatists into his party and government and they were deserting to the Bloc; Reformers were eating into his support in the West. There were several overlapping crises in the country: a leadership vacuum, widespread cynicism and distrust of politicians and government, a growing philosophy of difference that pitted groups of Canadians against each other, shattered aspirations for constitutional change and a record economic debt and high unemployment. Alienation and regionalism were rampant. The combination of problems called for a new kind of politics. The new Conservative leader, Kim Campbell, took advantage of the opportunity to appeal for a new "politics of inclusiveness." The circumstances also gave ideal conditions for protest parties such as the Reform party and the Bloc Québécois to flourish.

The Conservative government was in the last year of its mandate when Mulroney resigned his party leadership. In many ways the election campaign began when Kim Campbell was sworn in as party leader on June 25, 1993. The new leader spent the summer on the barbecue circuit building her image. Mulroney left ample funds for the campaign and an election strategy, including a throne speech and an electoral platform. Campbell discarded both. Caught in the dilemma of having to disassociate herself from the unpopular former government of which she had been a prominent member, she replaced experienced strategists and fundraisers associated with her predecessor and cut ties with many senior ministers.

When Prime Minister Campbell called the election on September 8, she was still riding a wave of personal popularity, and the party was running close to the Liberals in terms of percentage of support. The polls began to plummet almost immediately. The Conservatives ran one of the most disastrous political campaigns in modern Canadian history. Campbell lost public respect through a series of blunders. Her problems began with an announcement that she would cut a few of the proposed EH-101 helicopters in order to save some money. She was immediately tagged as indecisive.

---

46. See Elisabeth Gidengil, "Canada Votes: A Quarter Century of Canadian National Election Studies."
47. For more background on the 1984 and 1988 elections see the 1990 and 1994 editions of this book.

TABLE 12.7   GENERAL ELECTION RESULTS, 1878–1997

Election Year	Gov't Formed	Total Seats	Con Seats	Con % Votes	Lib Seats	Lib % Votes	CCF/ NDP Seats	CCF/ NDP % Votes	Ref Seats	Ref % Votes	Bloc Seats	Bloc % Votes	Oth Seats	Oth % Votes
1878	Con	206	140	53	65	45	–	–	–	–	–	–	1	2
1882	Con	211	138	53	73	47	–	–	–	–	–	–	–	–
1887	Con	215	128	51	87	49	–	–	–	–	–	–	–	–
1891	Con	215	122	52	91	46	–	–	–	–	–	–	2	2
1896	Lib	213	88	46	118	45	–	–	–	–	–	–	7	9
1900	Lib	213	81	47	132	52	–	–	–	–	–	–	–	1
1904	Lib	214	75	47	139	52	–	–	–	–	–	–	–	1
1908	Lib	221	85	47	135	51	–	–	–	–	–	–	1	2
1911	Con	221	134	51	87	48	–	–	–	–	–	–	–	1
1917	Con[1]	235	153	57	82	40	–	–	–	–	–	–	–	3
1921	Lib	235	50	30	116	41	–	–	–	–	–	–	69[2]	29
1925	Lib	245	116	46	99	40	–	–	–	–	–	–	30[3]	14
1926	Lib	245	91	45	128	46	–	–	–	–	–	–	26[4]	9
1930	Con	245	137	49	91	45	–	–	–	–	–	–	17[5]	6
1935	Lib	245	40	30	173	45	7	9	–	–	–	–	25	16
1940	Lib	245	40	31	181	51	8	8	–	–	–	–	16	10
1945	Lib	245	67	27	125	41	28	16	–	–	–	–	24	16
1949	Lib	262	41	30	190	49	13	13	–	–	–	–	18	8
1953	Lib	265	51	31	170	49	23	11	–	–	–	–	21	9
1957	Con	265	112	39	105	41	25	11	–	–	–	–	23	9
1958	Con	265	208	54	48	34	8	9	–	–	–	–	1	3
1962	Con	265	116	37	100	37	19	14	–	–	–	–	31	12
1963	Lib	265	95	33	129	42	17	13	–	–	–	–	24	12
1965	Lib	265	97	32	131	40	21	18	–	–	–	–	16	10
1968	Lib	264	72	31	155	45	22	17	–	–	–	–	15	7
1972	Lib	264	107	35	109	38	31	18	–	–	–	–	16	9
1974	Lib	264	95	35	141	43	16	15	–	–	–	–	12	6
1979	Con	282	136	36	114	40	26	18	–	–	–	–	6	7
1980	Lib	282	103	33	147	44	32	20	–	–	–	–	0	3
1984	Con	282	211	50	40	28	30	19	–	–	–	–	1	–
1988	Con	295	169[6]	43	83	32	43	20	–	–	–	–	–	4
1993	Lib	295	2	16	177	41	9	7	52	19	54	13	1	4
1997	Lib	301	20	19	155	38	21	11	60	19	44	11	1	2

[1] Wartime coalition

[2] Includes 65 Progressives

[3] Includes 24 Progressives

[4] Includes 20 Progressives

[5] Includes 12 Progressives

[6] 169 Conservatives were elected on November 21, 1988, but one died before being officially sworn in, leaving the seat technically vacant.

As a leader, Campbell was seen to be outspoken, inexperienced, naïve and overconfident. She began the campaign by saying that unemployment would continue to be high to the end of the century; she could not explain her deficit projections; she blamed her problems on "bad government bookkeeping"; and she said that the election was the "worst possible time" to debate social programs, indicating that she had a secret agenda. She was advised by Allen Gregg, pollster for the Conservatives, to concentrate on personality over policies. When it became obvious that she needed policies, a "*Blue Book*" outlining them was hastily prepared, but it did not stand up to scrutiny. Campbell's team was disorganized — it was still hiring key players during the campaign, and communications were poor — and workers complained they weren't sure who was in charge. In Québec, the Campbell and Jean Charest forces did not mesh and by the end of the campaign squabbled openly. Donors fled, and the Conservative campaign that had begun with so much promise ended over $7 million in debt.

The Liberals under Jean Chrétien's leadership, by contrast, ran a near flawless campaign. They were tagged by their opponents as a "tax-and-spend," patronage-hungry, Québec-focused party led by "yesterday's man." In reply they picked a simple message — the theme of "jobs, jobs, jobs" — and stuck to it. They played to their leader's strength — his experience, which contrasted favourably with that of his inexperienced opponents. John Rae, who directed the campaign, made the decision to bring out the party's "*Red Book*" of policies early in the campaign.[48] The heart of the policy

Early perceptions about what might emerge from the 1993 general election—the proportions were quite wrong, but the number of "slices" was correct.

Reprinted with permission, Alan King, *The Ottawa Citizen*.

---

48. Liberal Party of Canada, *Creating Opportunity: The Liberal Plan for Canada* (Ottawa: Liberal Party of Canada, 1993).

CLOSE-UP ON
Political Behaviour

ARE ELECTION PROMISES MEANINGFUL? THE LIBERALS AND THE GST

In the 1993 general election, one of the Liberals' campaign promises was to replace the unpopular Goods and Services Tax, which had been brought in under Brian Mulroney. Sheila Copps is on record as saying:

"I've already said personally and very directly that if the GST is not abolished, I'll resign. I don't know how clear you can get. I think you've got to be accountable for the things that you're going to do and you have to deliver on it."*

Later, in 1996, when the government said it would only try to make the tax simpler and more efficient, starting with harmonizing it with provincial sales tax in three Atlantic provinces, Copps was called to account for her very specific promise to resign. Her initial response was not to resign because:

"The fact is that, when you're on the campaign trail, you get excited and sometimes you shoot from the lip."**

In the end, she resigned, ran in a by-election, and won back her seat and her position as deputy prime minister and Minister of Canadian Heritage. GST was not an issue in the 1997 election.

Should Ms. Copps have resigned? Should she have been re-elected?

---

* Quoted in *The Globe and Mail*, April 29, 1996.
** Ibid.

book was a two-year program of spending on infrastructure to create thousands of new jobs annually, replace the GST, cancel the $5.8 billion helicopter program and make other defence cuts, and reduce the deficit to 3 percent of gross domestic product by the end of their term in office. The Liberals, who had already held power for 65 of the last 100 years, swept to a majority government, making Jean Chrétien the twentieth prime minister.

The Liberal share of the popular vote was 41 percent with representation from all provinces and the Northwest Territories. They won 31 of 32 Atlantic seats and 98 of 99 in Ontario. And, they had their best results in the West for many elections: no federal Liberal had been elected in Alberta since 1968 — now they had four. They had an embarrassment of riches in terms of talent and background, a mix of experienced MPs and former ministers and new talent, a wide range of ethnic representation and an ability to field ministers from every region. (See Table 12.8.)

The Conservative party was dealt a stunning blow, winning only two seats in Parliament with 16 percent of the popular vote. It was a dramatic repudiation of the party and its record. Leader Kim Campbell lost her seat after only four months as Canada's first female prime minister. With just four years of experience as a party member, with no party roots or debts to call in, she became an unpaid, interim, caretaker leader. Within two months, she retired and was replaced as leader by Jean Charest. The election left the party in financial ruin, and, having no official status in the House, the party found it extremely difficult to recover.

The NDP, with nine seats, faced its worst electoral defeat in history. Its predecessor, the CCF, had been reduced to eight seats in 1958, but shortly afterward it was replaced by a new party.

The Reform party had entered into its second national election with only one seat, which it had won in a by-election. It emerged from the campaign with greatly increased credibility and almost enough seats to be the official opposition. It won 52 seats altogether. In its western base, it won 51 seats: 22 in Alberta, 24 in British Columbia, 4 in Saskatchewan and 1 in Manitoba. Outside western Canada, it won only 1 seat in Ontario, although it finished in second place in 56 Ontario ridings.

The Bloc Québécois went into its first election with eight MPs and ended up with the second-highest number of seats in the House of Commons and a healthy majority in Québec. It won 54 seats and 14 percent of the popular vote, 49 percent in Québec where it ran all of its candidates.

The 1993 federal election was a watershed for the country — what one expert called "the domestic equivalent of the 1989 fall of the Berlin Wall in Europe."[49] It created a fundamental realignment of parties from which the Liberals profited. Capturing 41 percent of the vote, they obtained 177 seats in the House of Commons, regained power and formed a majority government. It was the only

---

49. Patrick J. Monahan, Osgoode Hall Law School, *The Globe and Mail*, October 11, 1993.

Election Promises
Reprinted with permission, D. Jackson.

party that could claim national status. The opposition in Parliament was fragmented and regionalized. Canada appeared to be undergoing a fundamental change from a two or two-and-a-half-party system toward one that is multi-party dominant. (For types of party systems, see Chapter 11.)[50]

TABLE 12.8   1993 GENERAL ELECTION SEATS BY PROVINCE

Party	Total	Nfld.	PEI	NS	NB	Qué.	Ont.	Man.	Sask.	Alta.	BC	Y	NWT
Lib	177	7	4	11	9	19	98	12	5	4	6	–	2
Bloc	54	–	–	–	–	54	–	–	–	–	–	–	–
Reform	52	–	–	–	–	–	1	1	4	22	24	–	–
NDP	9	–	–	–	–	–	–	1	5	–	2	1	–
PC	2	–	–	–	1	1	–	–	–	–	–	–	–
Ind	1	–	–	–	–	1	–	–	–	–	–	–	–
Total	295	7	4	11	10	75	99	14	14	26	32	1	2

Source: Elections Canada.

50. For analysis of the 1993 general election see the 1994 edition of this book, and Alan Frizzel, Jon Pammett and Anthony Westell, *The Canadian General Election of 1993* (Ottawa: Carleton University, 1994).

The 1997 Campaign

The 1997 election was called only 43 months into the Liberal party's mandate — the earliest a majority government had gone to the polls since Laurier had called an election (and then he was defeated!) in 1911. From the beginning there was little doubt the Liberals would win — the only question was by how much. Jockeying for position was restricted to those who might win the coveted official opposition status in the House of Commons.

In spite of 6.5 billion dollars worth of traditional pre-election pork-barrelling, the incumbent Liberals still got off to a shaky start. Many voters resented a majority government calling such an early election. The timing was particularly bad for Manitobans, who were undergoing one of the worst floods in the province's history. It also did not help when Reform leader Preston Manning ceremoniously leaked the Liberal platform, *Red Book II*, several days before its formal launch.

Overall, the Liberal campaign was tightly scripted and lacklustre. Jean Chrétien emphasized the success of the Liberal deficit reduction program, stressing that the federal government was on the brink of posting a budgetary surplus. In mid-campaign he even set a timetable for the end of the federal deficit — within two years. With this announcement, the Liberals captured the middle ground on fiscal matters, placing themselves between the NDP's call for increased spending and higher taxes on the rich on one hand and the Reform and Tory proposals for lower taxes and reduced spending on the other. Their other policy promises to the electorate consisted of a range of relatively small offerings, with little said about the continued high unemployment rates. Throughout the campaign the Liberals stressed their Plans A and B on national unity. Fortunately for the Liberals, their lack of commitment over employment was more or less ignored after the national unity issue came to the fore early in the campaign.

By the final days of the campaign, polls indicated that the Liberals had tumbled to their lowest level of support since the 1993 election. With the possibility of a minority government imminent, Chrétien hastily warned the country that it could be stuck with a gridlocked Parliament.

The Reform party, meanwhile, ran a much more aggressive campaign that reflected the rather desperate position of Preston Manning. He needed to prove that Reform was more than just a western protest party, which required a breakthrough in Ontario. The party ran only a few token candidates in Québec and the Maritimes where it had little or no prospects. The Liberal party's fiscally prudent course had undercut much of Reform's economic policy differences with the government. The highlight of Reform's "Fresh Start" program was a call for tax cuts and a promise to pour billions dollars of federal money into unconditional health-care transfers to the provinces.

Before the mid-point of the campaign, in a desperate attempt to consolidate support in the West where it could tap into an anti-Québec sentiment, Manning began to focus dramatically on the national-unity issue. Although this strategy was effective in the West, in the rest of Canada it reinforced the party's reputation for extremism and intolerance. Manning presented an essentially anti-historical attitude to Québec and stressed that his party was fundamentally opposed to recognizing that francophones in Québec constitute a "distinct" society within Canada.

The Conservative party had fewer expectations than Reform. Initially, Jean Charest set a minimal goal of 12 seats in the House of Commons, but raised his sights during the campaign. The party had few star candidates and relied almost exclusively on Charest's energy and charisma to stage its come-back. Charest presented himself as a leading national conciliator between French and English and stressed that the country needed a nation-wide opposition, a position only the PCs could fill. They soared in the polls following the two televised leaders' debates.

Conservatives were not always clear about where to target their strategy. They aimed their "Plan for the 21st Century" at Reform supporters and the hard-right conservatives who had elected

Premier Mike Harris in Ontario. Their initial strategy was to move their platform to the right and dislodge Reform, and then to concentrate on soft Liberals in Ontario and soft nationalists in Québec, where pollsters indicated the main opening in the political spectrum was to be found.

The Conservative wish-list included promises to cut taxes, reduce government debt, slash government spending and other policies aimed at the West, including getting rid of gun control. It was enough to win Charest an endorsement from Alberta premier Ralph Klein, but not from Mike Harris in Ontario. Some Conservatives also worried that this agenda would hurt social democratic voters in Québec, who would find the Conservative platform too right-wing.

The NDP modestly admitted from the outset that it would not be running to form the government. It staked out its grounds to the left of the other parties. The platform amounted to an uncosted wish-list, as the party contended it would spend to create more jobs. Leader Alexa McDonough emphasized the role of the NDP as the party with a social conscience: "As New Democrats we never made government, but we always made a difference."[51]

In many ways, the focus of the 1997 electoral campaign was in Québec where Liberals, Conservatives and the Bloc engaged in a powerful struggle for votes. From the beginning the Bloc was on the defensive. By May 10, for the first time since the 1993 election campaign, the number of decided voters saying they would vote Liberal exceeded the number opting for the Bloc.[52]

The Bloc Québécois campaign got off to a disastrous start. Its support plunged in the wake of campaign blunders and voter dissatisfaction with Québec premier Lucien Bouchard's spending cuts. As well, new Bloc leader Gilles Duceppe lacked Bouchard's charisma and electoral savvy.

In week two of the campaign former premier Jacques Parizeau became the shocking focus of the campaign with media reports that he had developed a covert strategy to get the National Assembly to approve a UDI (unilateral declaration of independence) within 10 days of a "Yes" vote in the 1995 referendum. It was evident that either Bouchard and Duceppe knew that Parizeau planned the UDI and were lying, or they were duped. Parizeau denied having any such plan but the controversy cast doubt on the trustworthiness of separatist leaders. By week three, Bloc organizers were frantic over the sharp drop in support among francophone voters throughout Québec. A surge in support for the PCs turned the federal election in Québec into a three-way race. Morale hit bottom when the president of the Québec Federation of Labour publicly questioned the need for the party, asking if the Bloc was really of any use to Québec.[53] Although provincial leaders normally stay out of federal campaigns, both Bouchard and Parizeau gave impassioned speeches that may have salvaged the Bloc's campaign.

Media, Polls and Party Advertising in the Campaign

The 1997 election demonstrated once again the key role of the media and opinion polls in modern Canadian elections. Operating alongside the traditional media, there was a remarkable flood of new electronic information as innovative Web sites on the Internet proliferated.

On the basis that campaign events have little impact unless they are noticed by the media, campaign strategists, as usual, tried to harness the media and employ it for their own purposes. Since paid ads and free-time broadcasts are strictly regulated, party strategists focused on the "earned media" of news broadcasts. As usual, the media, in turn, focused public attention on leaders' personalities with much less emphasis on local candidates and extremely little discussion of policy issues.

51. *The Globe and Mail,* March 13, 1997.
52. *The Globe and Mail,* May 10, 1997.
53. CBC Radio Canada, May 23, 1997.

Did the media act as a conduit or as a filter in this election? Did they convey or distort reality? In an Ekos poll, 44 percent of those asked were satisfied with the overall quality of the media coverage of the campaigns. Overall, both the print and electronic media were seen as having done a competent job of presenting the issues. About 39 percent thought that media coverage had been superficial and 34 percent thought it had been "biased."[54] Many newspapers endorsed specific parties and candidates during the campaign. For example, *The Globe and Mail* editorially endorsed Charest; the *Ottawa Citizen* endorsed Chrétien and the Liberals, but called for a smaller majority. Others, like Montreal's ethnic press, which called for "anybody but the Bloc," attempted to narrow the options for voters.

As has become customary, there were two televised leadership debates, one in each official language.[55] As demonstrated by the 1988 free trade controversy, a party leader who gives a strong performance in these debates can make significant gains in public opinion, even if gains following debates traditionally disperse fairly quickly. It normally takes a few days for a consensus to form about who won, so following the debate teams of party "spin-doctors" cast their leaders' performances in the best possible light. The media tend to focus on who won or lost and whether there was a "defining moment" rather than on policy issues. This was particularly valid in 1997.

In this case, Jean Charest was quickly declared the winner of both debates by most prominent journalists. Comment on the French debate, however, was confused by the untimely cancellation of the debate when the moderator fainted just as the divisive issue of national unity was to be discussed. The final portion of the debate had to be held a week later, which gave Jean Chrétien plenty of time to rehearse his lines on the corrosive question.

Following the debates, a large surge in support materialized for Jean Charest in Québec. Even at this point, however, there were doubts that the Tories would be able to translate their popularity into votes. Polls showed that 61 percent of Canadians watched at least one of the national debates (68 percent of Québeckers). This made the debates the salient single vehicle for communicating political ideas in the campaign. However, polls also indicated that 73.6 percent who followed the French-language debate said it would not influence their vote.[56]

Opinion polls provided prospective voters with a clear expression of public opinion until they were banned at midnight the Friday before the vote.[57] They regularly confirmed that the Liberals held a comfortable lead, sufficient to form another majority government.[58] Not until the final week of the campaign did the polls indicate that the Liberal majority could be in jeopardy.

In Québec, voter intentions were not so clear or steady. In the third week, there was a 10 percent jump in Conservative support in Québec, which was largely attributed to French-speaking federalist women aged 22–24 switching their vote from the Liberals to the Conservatives. Pollsters made it clear, however, that the Conservative support was not firm. By May 25, polls showed very

54. Ekos press release, May 26, 1997.

55. The National Action Committee on the Status of Women hosted another televised election debate on women's issues on May 26, 1997. Alexa McDonough was the only party leader to attend. The first televised debate in a Canadian election was in 1968, after the format was created in the 1960 U.S. presidential campaign debate between John F. Kennedy and Richard Nixon. They did not become an automatic and central feature of Canadian election campaigns until 1984 when Brian Mulroney and John Turner were the leading contenders.

56. Leger and Leger poll, *The Globe and Mail*, May 19, 1997.

57. The Supreme Court refused to suspend a law forbidding the publication of opinion-poll results in the 72 hours before an election. *The Globe and Mail*, May 8, 1997.

58. Two Internet companies said they would continue publishing opinion polls on their Web sites up to election day, defying a ban on reporting polls in the final 72 hours of the campaign. Former polls were published on several Internet sites.

similar levels of support for the Bloc, Liberals and Conservatives in Québec, although the Bloc still led among francophones (that is, in most ridings off Montreal Island).

Negative or critical ads played a role in the campaign. Reform's were first out, and the most controversial. One painted all party leaders from Québec in the same light as separatists. The ad featured a large red circle with a slash through images of Chrétien, Charest, Duceppe and Bouchard, implying that the Reform party stood for all Canadians, not just for Québeckers.

As usual, election advertising was unique in Québec. There, party agencies used different images and focused a bit more on national unity than elsewhere. Liberal Québec ads also gave more prominence to Liberal ministers, while ads in the rest of Canada tended to focus on Mr. Chrétien at 24 Sussex Drive. The Bloc, of course, limited its ads to Québec, emphasizing how wonderful Québec is and how important it is for the Bloc to defend the province's interests in Ottawa.

Issues in the Campaign

Citizens surveyed by Angus Reid polls just before the election confirmed results found elsewhere that the most important issues were jobs, national unity, health care, the deficit/debt, taxes, the economy in general and education, in that order.[59] In fact, however, national unity quickly became the dominant issue in the political campaign nationally, while other issues had various degrees of significance in different regions.

In all, the election was strongly personality-driven, with media attention focused almost exclusively on the party leaders. There was virtually no debate of many important issues, including foreign policy, education, health care and environmental issues. Even those issues that had dogged the Liberals over their last mandate were largely ignored, including the cancellation of the Pearson Airport privatization contract, the Airbus affair involving former prime minister Brian Mulroney, public integrity and good management, cultural protection policies, aboriginal issues, the premature closing of the Somalia inquiry, and even the GST.

The Economy

The Liberals wanted their handling of the economy to be the predominate issue of the election, and in the early days of the campaign it was. The deficit had gone down faster than even the Minister of Finance predicted, and to a degree the election became a contest over how to distribute the "spoils." The Liberals' position was that they would be able to balance the budget as early as 1999, and then split the ensuing surpluses between tax and debt relief and enhanced social programming such as a national drug plan. As promised, for every billion dollars of fiscal dividend, "one half will go to a combination of reducing taxes and reducing the national debt and one half will address social and economic needs through program expenditures."[60]

Although polls consistently showed that jobs were high on the agenda for the electorate, employment was much less of an issue than in 1993. The NDP tried almost daily to bring pressure to bear on the topic, but, except perhaps for the Maritimes, it did not happen. Chrétien's Liberals continued to utter the right-wing mantra that it is up to the private sector to create jobs, not the government.

National Unity

National unity surfaced as a campaign issue on May 9 with the news that Québec premier Jacques Parizeau planned to declare his province independent unilaterally after a "Yes" vote. This revelation virtually dominated debate until the end of the campaign. As it became evident that Reform was not

---

59. Angus Reid news release, May 29, 1997.
60. *The Globe and Mail*, April 30, 1997.

making any headway with voters, Manning reversed his original commitment to play down the national unity issue and in the final third of the campaign accused both Liberals and Conservatives of being weak, old-fashioned accommodators of Québec. His strategy was to use voter disagreements on "distinct society" to head off Conservative gains that were drawing headlines.

By the third week of the campaign, Manning declared that Jean Chrétien and Jean Charest were as dangerous to national unity as Québec separatists because they wouldn't prepare for another referendum, and implied that Québec-born politicians could no longer be considered capable of representing the whole of Canada.[61] This, along with a national unity message of equal treatment for all provinces and special status for none, was well received in the West.

The Liberals meanwhile reaffirmed their recognition of distinct society for Québec and their intentions to push forward Plan B (see Chapter 7). Intergovernnmental Affairs Minister Stéphane Dion said the Liberals could not negotiate Québec's secession unless Ottawa had a say in the wording of the referendum question, the conduct of the campaign and the size of the winning majority.[62] Chrétien said that a 50 percent plus one referendum victory would not constitute a sufficient majority for separation — not even if the federal government had a say in the referendum question. Preston Manning, on the other hand, declared that "Yes means yes" and Jean Charest said he would respect the result of a referendum, but wanted to ensure that there would not be one.

The Outcome

Canadians were relatively complacent about the 1997 election campaign. In the end, only about 67 percent of eligible voters (about 13 million Canadians) cast their ballots — the lowest turnout for an election for three-quarters of a century. Regionally, Québec voters had the best showing at 71 percent and the Prairie provinces the lowest with about 62 percent. Justifications for the low turnout include the "cross-pressures" that come from multiple parties and a general dissatisfaction with politics and politicians.

The Liberals won a razor-thin second majority with 155 seats, but like the four opposition parties their representation is now basically limited to a specific region of the country.[63] The regionalization of their support means that about two-thirds of the Liberal caucus is from Ontario. Reform replaced the Bloc in second place and therefore won recognition as the official opposition in the

TABLE 12.9   1997 GENERAL ELECTION SEATS BY PROVINCE

Party	Total	Nfld.	PEI	NS	NB	Qué.	Ont.	Man.	Sask.	Alta.	BC	Y	NWT
Lib	155	4	4	0	3	26	101	6	1	2	6	–	2
Reform	60	–	–	–	–	–	–	3	8	24	25	–	–
Bloc	44	–	–	–	–	44	–	–	–	–	–	–	–
NDP	21	–	–	6	2	–	–	4	5	–	3	1	–
PC	20	3	–	5	5	5	1	1	–	–	–	–	–
Ind	1	–	–	–	–	–	1	–	–	–	–	–	–
Total	301	7	4	11	10	75	103	14	14	26	34	1	2

Source: Elections Canada and CBC. For detailed official results consult Elections Canada at www.elections.ca

61. *The Ottawa Citizen*, May 25, 1997.
62. *The Globe and Mail*, May 13, 1997.
63. Party standings in the House at the time the election was called were Lib 174, BQ 50, Reform 50, NDP 9, PC 2, Ind. 6 and Vacant 4.

TABLE 12.10   PERCENTAGE VOTES IN 1993 AND 1997 GENERAL ELECTIONS BY PARTY

Party	1993	1997
Lib	41.3	38.3
Ref	18.7	19.4
Bloc	13.5	10.7
NDP	6.9	11.1
PC	16.0	18.9
Other	3.6	1.7

Source: Elections Canada and CBC. For detailed official results consult Elections Canada at www.elections.ca

House of Commons. Among the ten registered parties that contested the election Canadians supported five — the Liberals, Bloc, Reform, Conservatives and NDP — in sufficient force for them to obtain formal recognition in the House. See Tables 12.9 and 12.10.

The chastened but victorious Liberals emerged with their base of support highly concentrated in Ontario where they captured 101 of the 103 seats. They also gained several ridings in Québec, raising their total to 26 and giving them the extra seats there they needed to form a majority government. Québec gave the Liberals 18 fewer seats than the Bloc, based on only a slightly smaller percentage of the vote. However, they were shut out of all but about one-quarter of the seats outside Ontario. In the Maritimes they lost 20 of the seats they had won in 1993 and they did not win a single seat in Nova Scotia. The Liberals did a bit better in the West than the East, losing only 12 of their seats and ending up with 17 of the 91 seats west of Ontario.

The loss of their substantial majority and the further regionalization of their support qualified the fact that for the second time in 40 years a Liberal government had achieved a majority in back-to-back elections (Louis St. Laurent was the last Liberal to win such a majority, in 1953). The Liberal victory also disguised a 3 percent drop in share of the popular vote and the defeat of two prominent Cabinet ministers — Doug Young and David Dingwall from the Maritimes.

The Reform party, which won solid victories in Alberta, British Columbia and to a lesser degree Saskatchewan, replaced the Bloc as the official opposition in the House. The Conservatives and NDP returned to official party status. The Conservatives won a plurality of seats in Atlantic Canada and a handful in Québec while the NDP won a scattering of seats in Manitoba, Saskatchewan and British Columbia and eight in the Atlantic region — the first time any NDP MPs have been elected from Atlantic Canada in nearly 20 years. Support for the Bloc declined by about 11 percent, and it lost 10 seats from its 1993 election total, thereby losing its official opposition status. It did, however, hold 44 of Québec's 75 federal seats, well over half the seats in the province.

When nominations closed for the general election, a total of 1 672 candidates were registered to stand.[64] As usual, most candidates had party affiliations, but 45 ran as independents, and 31 had no political affiliation. When the election was over on June 2, 301 people were elected to the 36th Parliament. Eighty percent (241) were men, and 20 percent (60) were women. Women are still in a small minority, but the trend continues the steady gains made since 1980.[65] (See Figure 12.3.) The

---

64. Of this total, 408 (24.4%) were women, 64 fewer than in 1993. Altogether, 22.4 percent fewer people sought office this time than in 1993.

65. A study of 179 parliaments by the Inter-Parliamentary Union says women hold only 11.7 percent of all seats in the world. Canada places 21st in terms of percentage of women MPs elected. Reported in *The Globe and Mail*, February 14, 1997.

FIGURE 12.3   WOMEN IN THE HOUSE OF COMMONS, 1921–97

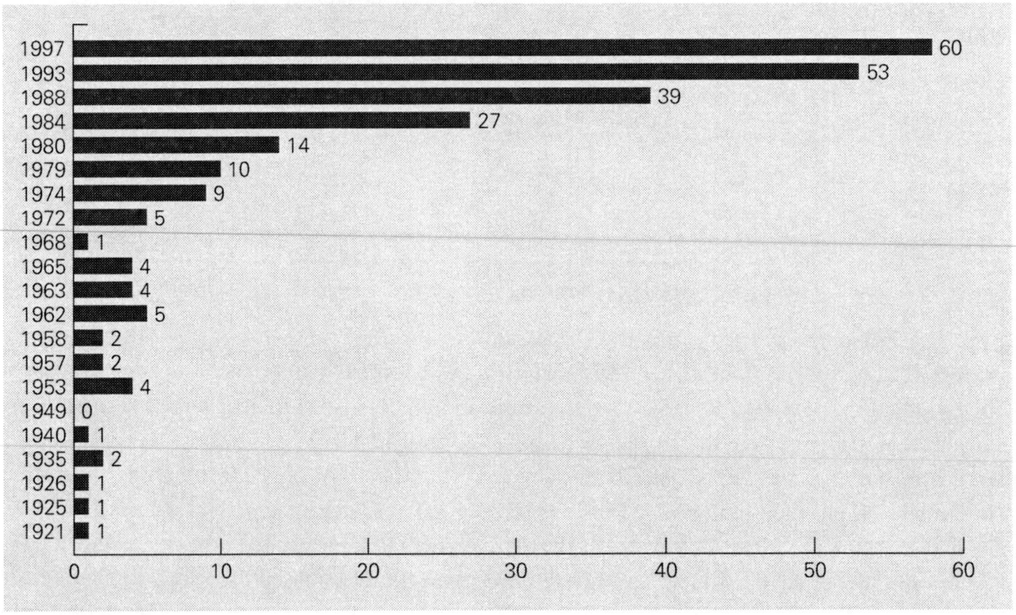

Year	Number
1997	60
1993	53
1988	39
1984	27
1980	14
1979	10
1974	9
1972	5
1968	1
1965	4
1963	4
1962	5
1958	2
1957	2
1953	4
1949	0
1940	1
1935	2
1926	1
1925	1
1921	1

Source: Robert Cross, *The Ottawa Citizen.*

education and age variables continued to be important — nearly 70 percent (209) had some university education and 77 percent (232) were in their forties or fifties. Independent John Nunziata, a former Liberal, was also elected in Toronto.

Analysis

The 1997 election dramatically increased the regionalization of federal politics. The Liberals lost much of their support in the Atlantic provinces and the West. Parliament has become more bitterly balkanized with deep regional divisions over national unity and the economy. The new federal Cabinet is hobbled by the lopsided geography of the victory, which is solidly anchored again in Ontario, with some gains in Québec.[66]

The message from the electorate seemed essentially to be that Atlantic Canada wants more attention to job creation; the West wants Ottawa to stop framing its constitutional goals in only Québec terms and to continue to pursue a fiscally prudent economic course; and Québeckers continue to want some kind of special status. Only Ontario is genuinely satisfied with the course the Liberals are taking.

In Québec, the Liberal vote — about 36 percent — was mostly concentrated in the anglophone and allophone ridings of Montréal. The Liberal gains were mainly due to three-way splits caused by the resurgent Conservatives. The Tories won 22 percent of the vote. They took federalist votes from the Liberals and also some of the anti-Liberal vote away from the Bloc.

For the Liberals, who are now barely a national party, what specifically went wrong? In part, the Liberals were the only party trying to run a national campaign rather than targeting their messages to specific geographical audiences. The Liberals also ran a lacklustre campaign, and many blamed

66. Elisabeth Gidengil et al., "Making Sense of Regional Voting in the 1997 Canadian Federal Election," *CJPS,* vol. 32, no. 2 (June 1999), pp. 247–72.

Chrétien's mediocre leadership as their large lead turned into a fight for survival. They noted that he even had difficulty articulating why he had called the election early and then why people should vote Liberal. Indeed, to some extent Chrétien emerged from the campaign more survivor than victor.

The Liberal party platform was unfocused, partly because of attempts to compromise between the two wings of the party. The right wing wanted a fiscally prudent course; the left wing wanted more social spending and a major jobs initiative. The platform essentially adhered to the fiscally prudent budget prescription, allowing a historic breakthrough for the NDP in Atlantic Canada and enabling the Tories to beat the Liberals in several ridings. The key Liberal message of fiscal management did not carry nearly the appeal in the West that the Liberals had hoped. Their spending spree before the election may also have hurt them, along with some imprudent *Red Book* promises.

Reform proved a formidable opponent in the West, where it also ran a strong campaign. The party conducted its campaign much as a "home team." It had the advantage of not having to appeal to Canadians in all provinces, and it hit all the right notes in British Columbia and Alberta by playing on persistent feelings of alienation and resentment.

In Québec, the Bloc was the only clear loser in the election, but those losses were much less than the federalists had hoped. The party retained about 39 percent of the popular vote in spite of a disastrous campaign. If the result of the federal election is an indication, the number of Québeckers who believe strongly in sovereignty has declined at least from 49.4 percent of the Yes vote in the 1995 referendum to 38.3 percent of the Québec vote.

For Reform and the Conservatives, what went wrong? The two parties split the vote on the right; their combined vote was about the same as the Liberals' vote. Reform was unable to win seats east of Manitoba because of its tough stand on Québec. The Tories were unable to move West because they courted Québec soft-nationalists. Neither is a very credible government-in-waiting. As long as Québec sovereignty remains the central issue, the right will be divided; and as long as the right is divided, it cannot win in Ontario and therefore cannot aspire to power. Although Charest's popularity and personality were key in the Conservative come-back, the party was relatively weak in organization and deeply in debt. Reform's status will be greatly enhanced as the official opposition in the House, and this factor will weaken the Conservatives further.

The Liberal shift to economic conservatism — free trade and deficit-cutting — robbed both the Conservatives and Reform of key issues. The Liberals also successfully split the difference between the two approaches to Québec. Liberals took a harder line toward secession than Conservatives but a more conciliatory line than the Reform party. They stood for a country that transcends language and cultural differences, a one-nation Canada.

Polls released during the election give some idea of the mood and intentions of the voting public. There was a large section of the voting population without firm commitment to a party in this election. Almost half (48 percent) of voters surveyed in a *Globe and Mail*/Environics Poll released May 17 would have considered changing their vote in some circumstances to have a stronger opposition in the House of Commons. There was therefore a large potential for change before election day. There was a danger for the Liberals that some of their supporters, convinced their party would win the election, would vote for another party, thereby threatening the Liberal majority. As it turned out, these worries were exaggerated.

Many Liberals are apprehensive about the prospect of Jean Chrétien leading the federalist forces into another separatist referendum after their mediocre performances in Québec in the 1993 election, the 1995 referendum and the 1997 election. Others are more positive. With the Reform party as official opposition, the Liberals might appear more as the defenders of Québec, and this could strengthen their hand there. As well, the improving economic circumstances and a slim majority may force the neo-conservatives in the Liberal cabinet to shift to a more progressive position.

As Warren Allmand, former Liberal MP, said: "My own view is that you get a better government if you've got a government with a slim majority.... When you've got a tough opposition, and it looks like the NDP, Tories, Bloc and Reform will all be there, the government will have to be on its toes — there will be less arrogance and better government."[67]

The election results have given Canada a multi-party confusion with one dominant party. The 36th Parliament is polarized and fractious. The Liberals have had to adjust to the new parliamentary reality by adopting tactics to accommodate to the five-party situation. Clearly, regional interests are well represented in the new House. It is not so clear that *Canada's* interests are.

• • • • • • • •

SUMMARY

Elections have an important role in Canadian politics. By providing a stable means of transferring government office between contesting political parties as well as an opportunity for voters to express their acceptance of or displeasure with the decisions of the government, elections legitimate the exercise of political power. Furthermore, the mobilization of voters' interest in electoral contests confers legitimacy on the political regime itself, as well as on the individual office-holders.

Through the party organizations based upon them, elections are vital in reconciling diverse interests within society. They provide a national forum for discussion and allow issues to be raised and compromises to be arrived at, leading thereby to a measure of consensus. However, there are grounds to question the performance of this role in Canada. The results of Canadian general elections often appear to be more divisive than consensual, pitting region against region and eroding the legitimacy of the "national" government. This concern has motivated calls for electoral reform. Yet elections continue to generate support for Canada's political system. In the long run, it may even be that the viability of elections themselves may be more significant than the actual partisan results.

The crown Jean Chrétien inherited in 1993 was somewhat tarnished in 1997.

Reproduced with permission, Alan King, *The Ottawa Citizen*.

---

67. Montréal *Gazette*, June 3, 1997.

Elections also have an impact on government decision-making. By determining which party forms the government, elections influence the choices made by policy-makers. They establish the broad policy parameters of political parties and the government. Issues perceived as important during the campaign must usually be addressed by the government; otherwise, the government risks defeat in the next general election. Defeated parties may also adjust their behaviour and policy positions both to prevent repetition of their mistakes and to broaden their support. To this extent, therefore, elections help politicians by providing reference points for guiding their actions.

In summary, the main importance of elections in Canada stems from the legitimacy they confer on government and its actions. Because of the democratic and consistent nature of elections, most voters perceive that the government is representative of their interests. Although few would express unqualified support of government, most Canadians are committed to Canada's basic electoral structures and their results.

The 1993 general election dramatically realigned Canada's party system. For the first time, a separatist party moved into the heart of the federal Parliament as official opposition. In 1997 regional fragmentation deepened with five parties elected to the House of Commons, each basically representing a different part of the country. For now, Canada has become a fragile democracy with a multi-party dominant system inside a contested federal regime.

DISCUSSION QUESTIONS

1. In what respects could Canadian elections be more democratic? Be sure to consider the method of determining who wins, the technique for counting votes, who runs for office, who is allowed to vote, who finances political parties and how electoral boundaries are drawn.

2. Do you think that Canada should hold more referendums to allow more citizen input into decision-making? Why or why not?

3. What factors contributed to Canada ending up with a fragmented party system following the 1993 general election? What exacerbated the increased regionalization in 1997?

4. Do politicians use the media, or do the media use politicians? Are voters manipulated in the process?

Selected Bibliography

Archer, Keith, *Political Choices and Electoral Consequences* (Kingston/Montréal: McGill-Queen's University Press, 1990).

Bakvis, H., *Voter Turnout in Canada* (Toronto: Dundurn Press, 1991).

Bell, David V.J. and Frederick K. Fletcher, eds., *Reaching the Voter: Constituency Campaigning in Canada*, Royal Commission on Electoral Reform and Party Financing, vol. 20 (Toronto: Dundurn Press, 1991).

Boyer, J. Patrick, *The People's Mandate: Referendums and a More Democratic Canada* (Toronto: Dundurn, 1992).

Brennan, Geoffrey and Loren E. Lomasky, *Democracy and Decision: The Pure Theory of Electoral Preference* (Cambridge, U.K.: Cambridge University Press, 1993).

Brook, Tom, *Getting Elected in Canada* (Stratford: Mercury Press, 1991).

Butler, David and Austin Ranney, eds., *Referendums around the World* (Washington, D.C.: American Enterprise Institute for Public Policy Research, 1994).

Canada, *Reforming Electoral Democracy: Final Report*, Royal Commission on Electoral Reform and Party Financing, vol. 1 (Ottawa: Supply and Services, 1992).

Clarke, Harold D. et al., *Absent Mandate: Interpreting Change in Canadian Elections*, 2nd ed. (Toronto: Gage, 1991).

Courtney, John C., Peter MacKinnon and David E. Smith, eds., *Drawing Boundaries: Legislatures, Courts and Electoral Values* (Saskatoon: Fifth House Publishers, 1992).

Elections Canada, *Annual Reports of the Chief Electoral Officer* (various years).

Ewing, K.D., *Money, Politics and Law: A Study of Electoral Campaign Finance Reform in Canada* (Don Mills, Ont.: Oxford University Press, 1992).

Frizzell, Alan, Jon Pammett and Anthony Westell, *The Canadian General Election of 1993* (Ottawa: Carleton University Press, 1994).

Ginsberg, Benjamin, *Do Elections Matter?* (New York: M.E. Sharpe, 1991).

Government of Canada, *A History of the Vote in Canada* (Ottawa: Public Works, 1997).

Johnston, J. Paul and Harvey Pasis, *Representation and Electoral Systems* (Scarborough: Prentice Hall, 1990).

Johnston, Richard et al., *Letting the People Decide* (Montréal: McGill-Queen's University Press, 1992).

Laschinger, John and Geoffrey Stevens, *Leaders and Lesser Mortals* (Toronto: Key Porter, 1992).

Lijphart, Arend, *Electoral Systems and Party Systems* (New York: Oxford University Press, 1994).

Seidle, Leslie F., *Issues in Party and Election Finance in Canada*, Royal Commission on Electoral Reform and Party Financing, vol. 5 (Toronto: Dundurn Press, 1991).

Small, David, ed., *Equality and Efficacy of the Vote: Canadian Electoral Boundary Reform*, Royal Commission on Electoral Reform and Party Financing, vol. 11 (Toronto: Dundurn Press, 1991).

Wearing, Joseph, *The Ballot and Its Message: Voting in Canada* (Toronto: Copp Clark Pitman, 1991).

LIST OF WEBLINKS

www.elections.ca

Elections Canada Elections Canada organizes and monitors national elections in Canada.

www.cbc.ca

Canadian Broadcasting Corporation The CBC and other news providers play an important role in conveying information during election campaigns.

www.Angusreid.com/ welcome2.htm

Public opinion polls The following sites link to two of the major political polling companies in Canada, the Angus Reid Group and Pollara.

www.pollara.ca/ new/POLLARA_NET.html

13

Interest Groups and Political Movements

. . . .

Influencing Public Policy

Canadians organize in numerous and novel ways to influence the government's decision-making process. Some work through political parties; some prefer to act individually, petitioning agencies or MPs; others hire lobbyists to act for them; still others join groups in order to participate in and enjoy the benefits of collective action. There are organizations to represent business, labour, loyalists, separatists, nature lovers and economic developers. Practically everyone belongs to some organization or other. Large or small, these groups are active in pressing their needs, principles and demands on other Canadians. When such groups act in the political arena without becoming full-fledged political parties they are usually called *interest groups* or, more pejoratively, *pressure groups*.

Sometimes broad collective identities form that are neither organized interest groups nor political parties. They, too, seek social change, but they are based on ideas and altruism rather than organizational form. These are *movements*. Movements may subsume interest groups, and both interest groups and movements may transform themselves into political parties. Movements are tied to ideologies that seek broad social change — such as nationalism, the women's movement, the environmental movement, and gay or other minority-rights movements. Interest groups are more particularistic and tend to reside inside specific countries.

Groups are an important element in the political life of all modern societies, but their form and importance vary from one country to the next. In Japan, for example, the *chingodan*, a group of rural petitioners, often bearing gifts of fruit, traditionally visits Tokyo when the national budget is being prepared in order to present its arguments to government officials and politicians. In some communist countries, on the other hand, where citizens have few legal rights to organize associations, unauthorized interest groups attempt to influence the government by means of dramatic events such as strikes intended to attract international publicity, such as has happened at China's Tiananmen Square. These examples illustrate that the structure and behaviour of interest groups and movements are closely related to the political system in which they operate.

In Canada, interest groups organize legally to petition and cajole the government. They operate in and help to mould the federal political system. Interest groups are, however, regulated by the laws of the land. In the year 2000, Bill C-2 limited their spending during elections to $50 000 and to no more than $3 000 supporting or opposing a particular candidate. Nevertheless, interest groups are ubiquitous, representing interests as varied as business (Canadian Manufacturers Association), labour (Canadian Labour Congress), agriculture (Canadian Federation of Agriculture), professionals (Canadian Medical Association), consumers (Consumers' Association of Canada), women (National Action Committee on the Status of Women), religious groups (Canadian Council of Churches and the Canadian Jewish Congress), ethnic groups (Canadian Polish Council and Ukrainian National Association) and even public interests such as a clean environment (Greenpeace or Energy Probe) and foreign affairs and development issues (Tools for Peace). Canadians are familiar with organizations such as the Brewers' Association of Canada, which attempts to prevent the import of inexpensive foreign beer, and the Canadian Federation of Students, which demands lower fees for university students.

Thousands of individuals work in Ottawa representing these multifarious interests. Some organizations are powerful; others are practically insignificant. Some interest groups employ experts such as professional lobbyists, public relations firms or highly paid lawyers to promote their interests. Others occasionally send their local officials or chief executive officers to argue their cases. Still others attempt to attract public attention through the media. What they all have in common is the desire to influence government policy, legislation, regulation or expenditures.

Much of the public is dismayed by the power of these interest groups and their shadowy connections with patronage and pork-barrel activities by the government. Citizens' groups complain about big business; business people admonish the special pleading of narrowly formed organizations. Many skeptics complain that interest groups are associated with unethical means such as bribery or blackmail. Some even harbour the suspicion that they are evil because they conflict with the basic attributes of democracy. Political scientists, on the other hand, usually counter that such groups are inevitable and important for the political process.

This chapter is concerned initially with descriptions and explanations of interest groups and their activities (especially lobbying), and then turns to discuss political movements — in particular, the women's movement as a case study of movements in action.

WHAT ARE INTEREST GROUPS?

There are many sociological meanings to the word "group." But, in this volume, "interest groups" are distinguished from others by their orientation to the political system. We are not interested in groups with no relation to the political system or with no organizational element. Thus, an **interest group** is here defined as an "organized association which engages in activity relative to governmental decisions."[1]

This is a very wide definition that includes many types of groups, from those that are relatively transient and issue-oriented to others that are institutionalized, with many general as well as specific interests. The common denominator is, as the definition states, that they are non-publicly accountable organizations that attempt to further their common interest by affecting public policy.

Paul Pross identifies four prime characteristics of interest groups.[2] First, they have a formal structure of organization that gives them continuity. Organization is essential to allow them to determine their objectives and strategies for action. Second, interest groups are able to articulate and aggregate

1. Robert H. Salisbury, "Interest Groups," in Fred I. Greenstein and Nelson W. Polsby, eds., *Handbook of Political Science*, vol. 4 (Reading, Mass.: Addison-Wesley, 1975), p. 175.
2. A. Paul Pross, "Pressure Groups: Adaptive Instruments of Political Communication," in Pross, ed., *Pressure Group Behaviour in Canadian Politics* (Toronto: McGraw-Hill Ryerson, 1975).

interests. Third, they attempt to act within the political system to influence policy outputs. Fourth, they try to influence power rather than exercise the responsibility of government themselves.

Mobs are not interest groups because they lack organizational structure. Political parties, too, are excluded, although the first three of these criteria apply equally to them. However, parties have different goals than interest groups; they seek political power by having their candidates elected to government office, whereas interest groups try to influence political parties and government officials toward certain policies rather than enact these policies themselves. Interest groups can, and often do, try to win the support of all parties. The similarities between parties and interest groups have led to different opinions about how the two are related. Some analysts, for example, believe that a rise in interest group power has been at least partially responsible for the decline in the role of political parties. In countries where traditionally there are two dominant political parties, the distinction between parties and interest groups is fairly evident. Today, in Canada many small parties compete, so that minority parties often represent the very narrow interests of one group or geographical area and then the distinction becomes less clear. The Bloc Québécois is a political party, but it represents the interest of only one group — Québec nationalists.

Interest Groups, Policy Communities and Networks

The study of interest groups by political scientists grew out of a sociological revolt against the narrow confines of formal institutional analysis. Politics came to be viewed as something associated with, but much larger than, "government."

Of seminal importance to a theory of politics that centred on the interaction of social groups was the work of A.F. Bentley. His *Process of Government*, first published in 1908, cited the "group" as the basic unit of all political life.[3] Rejecting the concept of the state as "no factor in our investigation" and the idea of sovereignty as a "piteous, threadbare joke," Bentley put the case for identifying the group as the fundamental point of departure for the study of politics:

> *All phenomena of government are phenomena of groups pressing one another, forming one another, and pushing out new groups and group representatives (the organs or agencies of government) to mediate the adjustments. It is only as we isolate these group activities, determine their representative values, and get the whole process stated in terms of them, that we approach a satisfactory knowledge of government.[4]*

While Bentley displayed a disinclination to indulge in precise definitional rigour, even a cursory review of monographic group studies from the 1930s onward serves to illustrate the power of his influence. These works were in fundamental agreement with Ambrose Bierce's definition of politics as "a strife of interest masquerading as a contest of principles."[5] Earl Latham's research on the evolution of American anti-trust legislation, for example, began with the assertion that organized groups, as "structures of power," are the vehicles through which social values cherished by individuals are realized, and concluded that one of the ways in which politics can be properly understood is as "the struggle of groups to write in their favor the rules by which the community is governed."[6]

---

3. Arthur F. Bentley, *The Process of Government, A Study of Social Pressures*, edited by Peter H. Odegard (Cambridge, Mass.: Harvard University Press, 1967).

4. Ibid., p. 269.

5. Ambrose Bierce, *The Devil's Dictionary* (New York: Dover, 1958), p. 101.

6. Earl Latham, *The Group Basis of Politics: A Study in Basing-Point Legislation* (Ithaca, N.Y.: Cornell University Press, 1952), pp. 1, 12, 209.

The work of greatest theoretical importance to the contemporary study of interest groups, however, is unquestionably David Truman's monumental work on interests and public opinion, *The Governmental Process*.[7] For Truman, the fundamental justification for emphasizing groups as basic social units lay in "the uniformities of behaviour produced through them." Uniformity of behaviour, he pointed out, does not deny the existence of individual will; on the contrary, the nature and frequency of interaction between individuals determine the existence or nonexistence of a group.

If a motorist stops along a highway to ask directions of a farmer, the two are interacting, but they can hardly be said to constitute a group except in the most casual sense. If, however, the motorist belongs to an automobile club the staff of which he and the other members more or less regularly resort to for route information, then staff and members can be designated as a group.[8]

Truman's primary concern was the functioning of groups in the political process. He arrived at an unusually broad definition of interest group as

> *any group that, on the basis of one or more shared attitudes, makes certain claims upon other groups in society for the establishment, maintenance, or enhancement of forms of behaviour that are implied by the shared attitudes.*[9]

At the same time, he inveighed against the popular inclination to credit interest groups with inherently sinister intentions — an inclination typified by the use of terms such as "vested interest," "special interest" and "pressure group." Indeed, the concept of interest group as found in Bentley, Truman and their theoretical disciples can be said to be an indispensable component of later pluralist theories. To pluralist scholars, interest groups represent highly functional cogs in the variegated machinery of the participatory democratic process. As aggregators and articulators of the needs of their constituent membership, interest groups serve to place issues on the political agenda of society, pre-digest the disparate views of individual members and formulate coherent demands for insertion into the legislative process. (See Chapter 14.)

Yet no matter how political scientists have come to evaluate the role of interest groups in contemporary politics, most have found it necessary to begin with a definition of "interest group" that is more discriminating than the one offered by Truman. We accept the definition of **interest group** as an "organized association which engages in activity relative to government decisions."[10] **Lobbying**, on the other hand, is activity aimed at securing favourable policy decisions or the appointment of specific government personnel. It is the narrow political activity of an interest group thus defined.

Political science has identified several contributions of interest groups to liberal democratic politics. Interest groups are a major source of mediation between the government and the individual, articulating aggregated opinions and protecting the individual from undue control by the state. They provide a mechanism for political representation that supplements the electoral process, assisting the political system by marshalling support for issues and providing ideas for public policy. Interest groups allow the political process to be more responsive than the electoral process to social and economic differences in society.[11] Such groups also feed the government valuable information, both

7. David B. Truman, *The Governmental Process: Political Interests and Public Opinion* (New York: Alfred A. Knopf, 1951).
8. Ibid., p. 24.
9. Ibid., p. 33.
10. This is the definition offered by Robert H. Salisbury in Greenstein and Polsby, *Handbook of Political Science*.
11. Adapted from a list by Amitai Etzioni, "Making Interest Groups Work for the Public," *Public Opinion*, vol. 5, no. 4 (August/September 1982), pp. 53–55.

facts and opinion, that can be used to help formulate policies and test policy proposals. This circular process of communication provides a valuable link between citizens and public policy by helping to keep the government in touch with shifts of opinion in society.

Groups also supplement government agencies: bureaucrats delegate administrative responsibilities to certain groups. For example, the Canadian Medical Association actually regulates its own professional activity. This largely unpaid service can be an enormous assistance to the government bureaucracy — and to the pockets of doctors! As well, professional groups indirectly help the civil service to disseminate information by publishing explanations of government policy in their journals.[12]

Finally, interest groups have valuable internal functions. Membership in a group may provide benefits won through communication with government such as tax incentives or other legislation. Of course, not only the membership at large benefits from the organization; there are also career advancements for those who hold leadership positions within subgroups.

Interest groups in liberal democracies, including Canada, thrive within **pluralist systems** — that is, systems that allow a plurality of interests to be pursued by a wide variety of associations. In this book and elsewhere, this state–interest group interaction is studied bearing in mind concepts such as *policy community* and *policy network* that attempt to convey the complex interaction between state agencies and interest groups. Interest groups often band together formally or informally. A **policy community** or **policy network** includes all of the actors or potential actors, whether inside or outside government, who share a common policy focus and help shape policy outcomes over time.[13] The word "community" implies a closer, more permanent arrangement than a "network," which may be looser or at least more tenuous. Many interest groups are narrow and would be part of only one policy community or network. Others, such as the Canadian Manufacturers Association, are very broad and are part of many policy communities or networks.

The broad idea is that policy is affected by a loose and informal relationship among a large number of specific actors who are concerned about the policy field. This concept is of great interest, as it directs our attention away from pure institutional analysis and toward more amorphous and informal pressures in the policy process. For example, environmental experts in the private sector spend a lot of time with their equivalents in government departments, and the same is basically true in all policy fields.

But the term "policy communities" is also woolly, as it does little to direct scholars to the source of policy or its implementation. That many people are involved in making policy is a given in open and democratic societies. Moreover, the party variable is almost totally omitted in this framework, and that omission would be ridiculous in Canada. While the party is not the only actor in the policy process, the prime minister and Cabinet members (who owe their positions to the success of their party) certainly are powerful actors in the process.[14]

INTEREST GROUPS IN CANADA

The number and variety of interest groups in Canada is immense. The *Associations Canada* directory lists several thousand organizations. In Ottawa alone there are well over 300 trade and professional

---

12. See Evert Lindquist "Public Managers and Policy Communities: Learning to Meet New Challenges," *Canadian Public Administration*, vol. 35 (Summer 1992), pp. 127–59.

13. William D. Coleman and Grace Skogstad, "Policy Communities and Policy Networks: A Structural Approach," in Coleman and Skogstad, eds., *Policy Communities and Public Policy in Canada* (Toronto: Copp Clark Pitman, 1990), p. 25.

14. See Robert J. Jackson and Doreen Jackson, *An Introduction to Political Science: Comparative and World Politics,* 3rd ed. (Toronto: Prentice Hall, 2000), ch. 13.

organizations. It has been estimated that these groups, representing only the tip of a giant iceberg, employ several thousand staff to improve "public relations" with the government.

Few individual corporations can afford to have full-time employees in Ottawa. Instead, their interests are "protected" by their public relations departments and chief executive officers. According to one survey, 27 percent of chief executive officers who had participated in the study had been before a parliamentary committee at least once; 33 percent had direct regular contact with the government; 29 percent were on a government board or in an advisory group; and 42 percent had made a personal representation to the government.[15]

Classifying Interest Groups

Two typologies of interest groups have had lasting acceptance in Canadian political science. F.C. Engelmann and M.A. Schwartz divide interest groups into economic and non-economic categories, then subdivide the first into agriculture, labour and business groups.[16] The non-economic category is further subdivided into nine subtypes. Such distinctions, based on the primary basis of affiliation for their members, help to explain the basic differences in origin, activities and goals of the groups. This typology has often been used by others, for example by Elizabeth Riddell-Dixon to discuss the impact of groups on Canadian foreign policy.[17]

The economic/non-economic distinction, however, does not convey any information about the activities or relative importance of the various groups. There is a wide disparity in their powers. They range from relatively transient issue-oriented groups to others that are well established and assert a strong influence on political and economic life. They differ in terms of structure, resources, tactics and goals, and while these differences seem to affect the success or failure of groups in reaching their goals, there is very little certainty to this contention.

Pross has addressed this problem in the most satisfactory categorization of Canadian interest groups to date.[18] His typology is designed to relate the groups to one another and to the policy system at large. Groups are classified as institutionalized, issue-oriented, fledgling or mature; each is then categorized according to its objectives, organizational features and levels of communication with government. Of course, the distinction between the categories is not clear-cut, and any one group may not conform exactly to this pattern.

Institutionalized groups are relatively well structured and enduring. In Pross's definition, they have five main characteristics: organizational continuity and cohesion; exclusive knowledge of the appropriate sectors of government and their clients; stable membership; operational objectives that are clear and concrete; and organizational imperatives on which the credibility of the organization is based that generally are more important than any particular objective or specific policy. At the opposite extreme of institutionalized interest groups are **issue-oriented** groups. Their organizational continuity and cohesion are weak, their knowledge of government poor and their membership

15. James Gillies, *Why Business Fails* (Montréal: Institute for Research on Public Policy, 1981). On business and politics more generally, see Robert J. Jackson, "Politics and Business: Partners and Antagonists," in Rinus Van Schendelen and Robert J. Jackson, eds., *The Politicization of Business in Western Europe* (London: Croom Helm, 1986).

16. F.C. Engelmann and M.A. Schwartz, *Political Parties and the Canadian Social Structure*, 2nd ed. (Scarborough: Prentice Hall Canada, 1975).

17. Elizabeth Riddell-Dixon, *The Domestic Mosaic: Domestic Groups and Canadian Foreign Policy* (Toronto: Canadian Institute of International Affairs, 1985).

18. Pross, "Pressure Groups," pp. 9–18. See also, by the same author, *Group Policy and Public Policy*, 2nd ed. (Toronto: Oxford University Press, 1992).

fluid. They also have trouble formulating and adhering to long-range objectives, and maintain a low regard for their own organizational mechanisms. What issue-oriented groups lack in size and organization they make up for in flexibility; they can be excellent vehicles for generating immediate public action on specific issues. They are little constrained by fear of disturbing their relationship with government officials. Good examples were some of the early environmental groups and peace organizations in Canada that have been very active publicly but normally short-lived. The **fledgling** and **mature** groups fall between these two extremes.

Canadian Groups: A Catalogue

To familiarize readers with the main groups and lobbyists in the political area, we summarize here the activities of some of the largest and most active of them. It is not an exhaustive list but does indicate the multiplicity of groups in Canada. Because of the federal political structure of the country, most of the major interest groups have federated organizations. Interests in the economic sphere, for example, are regulated by both federal and provincial governments; as a result, groups representing the various agriculture, labour and business interests may require federated organizations with bureaucracies in Ottawa and the provincial capitals. It should be noted that while the majority of interest groups are privately funded, a number of them are financed by government.

Business

Business groups are especially active in political persuasion. At least 660 nationally relevant business associations have existed since Confederation, not including 125 farmers' associations.[19] The economic viability of the businesses they represent often directly depends on government policies and contracts. Large organizations such as the Canadian Manufacturers Association and the Canadian Trucking Association retain offices in the national capital, while others send public relations officers on regular or irregular visits to Ottawa.

The largest business association in Canada is the Canadian Chamber of Commerce, which represents some 500 local chambers and boards of trade. Although its headquarters is in Montréal, its president is frequently in Ottawa representing the business community that funds it. Another large organization that aims at influencing government policy in such fields as corporate regulation and taxation is the Canadian Manufacturers Association. It represents about 80 percent of Canadian manufacturing and is funded by this corporate membership. Yet another powerful organization, the Business Council on National Issues (BCNI), represents the executives of 150 of the largest firms in the country. BCNI, for example, spent millions of dollars to support the Free Trade Agreement with the United States.

Business interests in domestic affairs are also defended and promoted by associations representing particular sectors. These include the Canadian Industries Association, which represents manufacturing companies, and the Canadian Nuclear Association, which represents companies and organizations interested in the development of nuclear energy. The interests of manufacturing groups can often be recognized by their names: examples are the Automobile Industries Association, the Canadian Chemical Producers Association, the Mining Association of Canada, and even the Confectionery Manufacturers' Association. The petroleum industry is represented by the huge Canadian Petroleum Association, which has member companies involved in the exploration and production of oil and gas, as well as by the far smaller Independent Petroleum Association.

---

19. William D. Coleman, *Business and Politics: A Study of Collective Action* (Kingston/Montréal: McGill-Queen's University Press, 1988), p. 14.

The various financial interests are also well organized. The Canadian Life and Health Insurance Association represents all companies in the insurance business. The Canadian Bankers' Association represents all banks. Small business is centralized as an interest group by the Canadian Federation of Independent Business, which consists of private enterprises.

Business groups also try to influence government foreign policies. Probably the most significant of these groups is the Canadian Business and Industry International Advisory Committee. The CBIIAC is an umbrella organization that includes the Canadian Chamber of Commerce, the Canadian Manufacturers Association, the Canadian Export Association, the Canadian Import Association and other organizations concerned with trade policy. Of course, this means there can be incongruities in the CBIIAC. The Canadian Import Association wants reduction of tariffs and non-tariff barriers, while the Canadian Export Association, representing 500 corporations, wants to increase access to foreign markets and obtain government assistance and tax concessions.

Agriculture and Fisheries

The Fisheries Council of Canada is the largest organization representing fishing interests. It comprises provincial associations of companies in fishing and fish processing.

Agriculture has two major organizations. The largest, the Canadian Federation of Agriculture (CFA), enrolls about two-thirds of the country's farmers. It is composed of provincial federations of agriculture and many commodity organizations such as the Canadian Pork Council. The CFA makes representations to the federal government, but is somewhat less willing to engage in direct confrontation with the government than is the smaller National Farmers' Union.[20]

Labour

Labour can be a powerful force in Canadian politics. Approximately one out of every three paid workers outside agriculture is a member of a labour union. The major umbrella organization is the Canadian Labour Congress (CLC). It consists of affiliated trade unions. The CLC is a federation with 12 regional offices and 120 local councils. Representation is geographically dispersed: the Ottawa office deals with issues at the national or international levels, and the regional and local branches focus on issues under provincial jurisdiction. Unlike most interest groups, the Canadian Labour Congress supports one political party — the NDP.

A second major worker association, the Canadian Federation of Labour, comprises 10 building trade unions. It differs from the CLC in emphasizing cooperation with the government and in being nonpartisan; it does not uniquely support the NDP. Québec has its own major labour organization, the Confederation of National Trade Unions, which represents members in a number of Québec labour unions.

Workers are also affiliated with their particular sector of the economy or trade; examples are the Québec Woodworkers Federation and the United Automobile Workers of America. Government employees are represented by organizations such as the Canadian Union of Public Employees (CUPE) and the Canadian Union of Postal Workers (CUPW).

Other Economic Groups

Another prominent category of economic interest groups comprises those representing consumers. The Consumers' Association of Canada represents the interests of consumers to government. This function often brings it in conflict with both business and labour.

---

20. See Riddell-Dixon, *The Domestic Mosaic*, p. 25.

Reproduced with permission, Dennis Pritchard.

In a separate category are professional workers. The Canadian Bar Association, the Canadian Association of Broadcasters and the Canadian Council of Professional Engineers, among others, attempt to secure government policies conducive to their professional interest. Perhaps the best-known group in this category is the powerful Canadian Medical Association; other prominent organizations in the health field are the Canadian Dental Association and the Canadian Nurses Association.

Non-economic Groups

This category is possibly the largest; it is certainly the most diffuse. As indicated earlier, such groups may be transitory or permanent. Religious interests are fostered by the Canadian Council of Churches, the Canadian Conference of Catholic Bishops and the Christian Movement for Peace. Ethnic representation is made by groups such as the Canadian Jewish Congress, the Arab Palestine Association, the Ukrainian National Association and the Canadian Polish Congress. Women are represented by the National Action Committee on the Status of Women, which represents some 600 women's organizations, as well as REAL Women and the YWCA.

Weaker and more transitory than the above-named are public interest groups. Issue-oriented groups can develop anywhere and at any time a corrosive issue arises. Motivated by a mixture of principle and ideology, these groups usually see themselves as representing the unrepresented or underrepresented. Usually they depend on favourable media coverage. Of course, all groups believe they represent the "public interest," but these particular groups specialize in this approach rather than in one based on occupation, nationality, religion, gender or ethnicity. They include such vocal advocates of environmental causes as Friends of the Earth, Greenpeace, Energy Probe, and such peace organizations as Amnesty International and Operation Dismantle. Also well recognized as interest groups of this type are the Non-Smokers' Rights Association and the National Poverty Organization.

Since the introduction of the *Charter of Rights and Freedoms* in 1982, interests associated with language, gender and ethnicity have increasingly pursued legal challenges based on the Constitution in order to have legislation that they consider offensive declared unconstitutional. Women's organizations, for example, have used the courts to launch attacks on specific public policies.

Ingredients for Interest Group Success

Perhaps the most fundamental ingredient for the political success of an interest group is that its values, goals and tactics are compatible with the country's political culture and therefore are perceived as legitimate. Without public support a group has very little chance of receiving government recognition. Groups that use the tactic of violent demonstration rather than negotiation meet rigid resistance in the Canadian system, as do those that approve goals foreign to the Canadian political culture such as, say, state control of family planning.

Another ingredient for success is an appealing issue — one that will gather very broad public sympathy and increase the size of the group, or at least increase its support. Good leadership is also important; a strong, vocal and prestigious leader brings valuable publicity and direction. A high-status general membership further increases the chance of success, since distinguished, influential people bring contacts and other resources, and have easier personal access to bureaucrats and politicians. A permanent organizational structure is important because it helps the group act cohesively. Internal divisions weaken the group. Sections of society that have common interests but are unorganized, such as homemakers or pensioners, usually have little long-term impact on public policy.

Similarly, large budgets naturally assist in achieving and maintaining access to policy-makers. Prosperity does not guarantee success, but it certainly increases its possibility. The fact that a large number of interest groups can claim tax deductions or other tax advantages because of their organizational status makes them more powerful than less-organized groups that fight for a cause.

Flexibility is another important factor in achieving success, since it is often necessary to compromise one part of a demand to achieve another. As one lobbyist said: "We are often forced to ask ourselves should we shoot for the moon or try to give suggestions politicians might accept. It is an important calculation in our work." Successful groups often join at least temporarily with other groups to bolster one another's claims. Interest groups must also be flexible enough to make use of all the access points available to them. They therefore need to know where to plug into the policy-making system. An important condition of success consists of knowing where and at what state access to policy-makers can be achieved.

Many groups that otherwise would not be able to function receive financial support from government agencies. Most prominent women's organizations in Canada, for example, receive funding from the government — although support has been reduced considerably since 1991. At its height, the National Action Committee on the Status of Women (NAC) received about 80 percent of its funding from Ottawa. To receive funding, the interest group must have goals that are compatible with the funding program, and its internal procedures must receive government approval. NAC therefore (unlike BCNI and other groups) receives money to lobby on a variety of economic and social issues. Receiving that money, at least initially, has been key to the group's success.[21]

Attempts to measure the success of lobbying activities statistically have had only limited utility. Observations of the frequency and nature of the contact between interest groups, legislators and bureaucrats have often led to disappointing assessments that border on truisms. It is true but regrettable that interest group politicking is a well-practised but little understood art. Part of the problem is definitional. David Truman's definition of an interest group, for example, does not specify a political content to "interest,"[22] while, at the other extreme, the state of Texas has designated as a political lobbyist anyone who comes in contact, however casual, with a legislative representative. Political lobbying is a poorly studied phenomenon generally, and has been the victim of misunderstanding on a number of levels.

LOBBYING IN CANADA

The term "lobby" comes from the corridor in the British House of Commons where constituents may meet their MPs to cajole or pressure them about policy or legislation. Interest groups live in the

21. See Leslie A. Pal, *Interests of the State: The Politics of Language, Multiculturalism and Feminism in Canada* (Kingston/Montréal: McGill-Queen's University Press, 1993).

22. See Truman, *The Governmental Process*, p. 33.

"half-light" of politics.[23] For all too many Canadians, that "half-light" gives rise to suspicion of donations to parties or campaigns that may allow access, influence and treatment not available to others. While nothing is more proper in a democratic process than for individuals to attempt to influence their government, social taboos construe such activity as embarrassing and imprudent.

Yet, for all the prudery, Ottawa and the provincial capitals *are* full of lobbyists. It is worth noting that while business people, for example, display contempt for the dirty world of politics, they exhibit remarkable ability to hold their noses and socialize when something is to be gained for their organization. These relationships are both accommodating and antagonistic. Government regulates business yet also subsidizes and protects it.

Lobbyists are paid to influence the government. Their organizations break down roughly into two groups: those focused primarily on general government policy, such as the Business Council on National Issues; and those with a more specific focus, typified by the Pharmaceutical Manufacturers Association or the Mining Association of Canada. Trade and umbrella groups send scores of lawyers before regulatory tribunals to secure the modification of regulations, while voluntary groups press their causes with MPs, Cabinet ministers and bureaucrats. One organization, the Canadian Federation of Independent Business, actually convinced the government to create the Ministry of State for Small Business. Yet the entire scene remains obscure and a substantial portion of Ottawa's lobbyists describe their occupation simply as "public relations."

Given the complexity of government, lobbying is essential. As noted, lobbyists provide valuable assistance to government and Parliament in that they assemble and provide facts that are necessary for informed decisions. Governments periodically call lobbyists together for advice or research. And they hire lobbyists of their own, as the Canadian government did to represent Canadian interests in the acid-rain issue in the United States. Lobbyists are useful to governments because their information enables bureaucrats and politicians to develop policies that garner votes. As one former senior government official put it, "being able to develop a policy that will gain votes is worth more than a contribution to the party.... Whatever the contribution, you could blow it away if you lose votes."[24]

Since it is so widely practised and performs a valuable function, why then does lobbying have such an insalubrious reputation? Obviously, the concern is not about the provision of facts but lobbying's close relation to influence peddling in which money is exchanged for favours. Influence peddling comes under the Criminal Code and carries a five-year prison term.

While many interest groups lobby on their own behalf, others hire professionals to carry out this function. Since the enactment of the *Lobbyists Registration Act*, the members and organizations of this profession have become well known through publications such as the *Lobby Digest* and *Lobby Monitor*. A list of the leading lobby firms would include Executive Consultants, Government Consultants International, Public Affairs International, William H. Neville and Associates, the Capitol Hill Group, S.A. Murray Consulting, Government Policy Consultants and Fred Doucet Consulting International. But these are not the only professional hired guns in the lobbying business. Most law firms in Canada's capitals also lobby — although they prefer to be called consultants or lawyers. Many single individuals, too, such as former MPs, senators and "bagmen" of parties are paid by organizations to work on their behalf.

---

23. Pross, "Pressure Groups," p. 1.

24. Quoted in Margot Gibb-Clark, "Lobbying: No Respect but It Gets Things Done," *The Globe and Mail*, December 14, 1987.

Legislation to Control Lobbying

To make lobbying more open and fair, Parliament has considered establishing rules to regulate it. In 1985, when the Mulroney Conservative government finished its first year in office plagued with scandals and shrouded in perceptions of patronage and favouritism, the incentive for regulations gained impetus. To improve his government's image, Mulroney promised a new code of conduct. Hearings of the Commons Standing Committee on Elections, Privileges and Procedure ensued. Not surprisingly, the lobbying profession generally was against any form of registration.

By January 1987, the parliamentary committee released a unanimous report recommending that registration should be required of paid lobbyists, listing the name of the lobbyist, the client and the issue. Five months later, Bill C82, the *Lobbyists Registration Act*, was tabled. It was a weak bill that did not include many of the more stringent recommendations of the Standing Committee. It did not attempt to regulate lobbyists, but simply required registration. Lobby groups were relatively satisfied with such weak measures and, in September 1988, the bill was given Royal Assent, to be proclaimed in June 1989, when the infrastructure for implementing the bill was in place.

The Act divides lobbyists into two tiers — "professional lobbyists" and "paid lobbyists" — and sets out different requirements for each.

Tier I includes "an individual who, for pay, provides certain types of lobbying services on behalf of a client." These *professional* lobbyists must (1) file a new registration for every lobbyist-client relationship; and (2) include in every registration their own name, the name and address of their firm, the name of client, the name of corporate owners or subsidiaries of the client, the general area of concern of the lobbying effort and the class of undertaking that the lobbying was intended to influence.

Tier II includes those "whose job involves a 'significant' amount of government lobbying for his or her employer" — lobbyists employed by corporations, umbrella associations and public interest groups. These lobbyists are required to register within two months of initiating the lobbying activity and once a year thereafter. They need only give their name and the name and address of the corporation that employs them. Neither group has to provide any financial information. The penalties for noncompliance are a maximum fee of $100 000 and/or a two-year prison sentence.

Incorporated into the new Act was a provision to review the legislation three years after it came into effect. The review took place in 1993 and it was evident that reformers wanted major changes while others, particularly lobbyists, desired to leave the law intact. On the positive side, the new Act confirmed the legitimacy of lobbying the government in Canada and set up a registry of lobbyists. However, by late 1994 only 3 000 were formally registered.

In 1993, the Liberal party campaigned on reforming the lobbying business and, shortly after assuming power, the new government introduced legislation to make lobbying more transparent. Lobbyists immediately formed their *own* lobbying organization, the Government Relations Institute, to ensure that they would not be adversely affected. In particular, they wanted the fees paid to them to remain tax deductible to their clients.

Bill 43, which made some relatively minor amendments to the *Lobbyist Registration Act*, was passed in June 1995. As amended, the Act continues to divide lobbyists into two tiers — "professional" or "consultant" lobbyists, and "in-house corporate and organization lobbyists."

As of June 1995, the functions of the registrar (who monitors the Registry of Lobbyists) are subsumed in the duties of the ethics counsellor. This new office is to submit an annual report to Parliament about the workings of the *Lobbyist Registration Act* and to work with interested parties to develop a code of conduct for lobbyists. The job of Ethics Counsellor is to enforce the code after it has been approved by a parliamentary committee. The penalties for noncompliance are a maximum fine of $100 000 and/or a two-year prison sentence. In spite of these new regulations, several problems remain:

- Only paid lobbyists have to register — others have *no obligation* to file or disclose information. This provides a gigantic loophole for the use of contingency fees. Essentially, lobbyists who do not receive payment until *after* contacting the officeholder or bureaucrat can avoid disclosing information, because they have not been paid.

- The *definition* of Tier II lobbyists is particularly weak. It only includes someone who devotes a "significant" part of his or her duties to lobbying. A lobbyist who does not want to register can simply maintain that lobbying is not a "significant" part of his or her duties.

- Not enough information is required, especially of Tier II lobbyists. Spending *disclosure* might relieve the negative image of lobbyists. As well, the subject categories given are too vague and can be used to mislead rivals or critics.

- Interest groups do not have to file any *information* about their objectives.

- *Enforcement* is inadequate. The registrar has no power to verify the information submitted by the lobbyists. The RCMP, which enforces the Act, will launch an investigation only when a complaint is raised against an individual. The Criminal Code's statute of limitations on summary offences limits the ability of the RCMP to obtain prosecutions under the Act to a period of six months. By the time a complaint is made it may be too late to punish the perpetrator.

- *Noncompliance* is a problem. Many lobbyists are reportedly refusing to register at all and are getting away with it. A bureaucrat or individual being lobbied is not required to ensure that the lobbyist is registered.

- There is a strong argument that *all* lobbyists should have the same requirements. The two-tier system creates a hierarchy of lobbyists, inferring that some individuals have the potential to be more subversive to the policy process than others.

Furthermore, one of the main factors behind public cynicism about interest groups is that governments spend more money because of lobbying. As we have seen, governments make direct payments to some groups. They also allow corporations to treat lobbying as a business expense, and certain types of interest groups are allowed to register as charities and receive tax credits for charitable donations. It can be argued that a more open system would eliminate the source of public discontent. Reformers maintain, therefore, that it is in the public interest that the lobbying registration procedure provide *access* and *transparency*. Public access should be equitable, not selective or privileged, and the public should have the opportunity to know who is attempting to influence the government. Instead, the current legislation provides what one expert calls "little more than a registry of the more professionally minded lobbyists."[25] The public is given the impression that lobbying in Ottawa is controlled, when it is not.[26]

The debate continues. One can expect that in the future minor amendments will be made to the *Lobbyists Registration Act*, but there will not likely be fundamental changes in the system.

---

25. A. Paul Pross and Iain Steward, "Lobbying, the Voluntary Sector and the Public Purse," in Susan D. Phillips, ed., *How Ottawa Spends 1993–94* (Ottawa: Carleton University Press, 1993) p. 121.

26. The number of lobbyists is monitored by the Lobbyists Registration Branch. The numbers are updated regularly — see strategis.ic.gc.ca/lobbyist/

Common Tactics and Strategies

The lobbying strategy chosen by an interest group depends largely on the type of group it is, its resources and the type of issues involved. Some groups concentrate on the pre-parliamentary stages of government, while others prefer buttonholing MPs. In all cases, the strategies used must include more than an attempt to influence legislators and bureaucrats. Public opinion must be aroused, too. No amount of persuasion of the government will be effective unless public opinion is in agreement with a lobby, or at least not hostile to its demands.

Many lobbyists establish friendly relationships with legislators, bureaucrats and media or other group contacts, in order to present their cases in informal, friendly ways. Robert Presthus' research showed that about 75 percent of MPs of all parties had frequent or occasional contact with interest groups.[27] This contact generally concerned interests that the MPs already supported, and was aimed at convincing them to influence their colleagues. Lobbyists also disseminate literature, present briefs, provide research results, promote letter-writing campaigns, support groups at committee hearings and entertain. At the same time, they must keep close track of what is happening in Parliament, so that they and the group they represent will know when and where to take appropriate action.

In his classic study of the Canadian Medical Association (CMA), Bernard Blishen shows the multiple ways in which a pressure group promotes its interests. Positive relations with the press and personal contacts are considered important to the CMA. Both formal and informal contacts between the profession and government are pursued. This is facilitated by the fact that many senior officials of the federal and provincial government health departments, as well as Ministers of Health, have been physicians. In addition to these contacts, "institutional patterns" between the CMA and the government are well established. For example, close contacts are fostered between the profession and the public service by the medical care payment plans in the area of health insurance. A final significant tactic used by this group is referred to as the "tie-in-endorsement," which refers to the effort to "tie members in" with related groups such as other health professionals, hospital associations, insurance industries and other health programs in an effort to protect similar interests and policies. In all its activities, group members make every effort to act in unison, in the knowledge that their influence depends to a large degree on the cohesion of the Association.[28]

Lobbying MPs is probably *least effective* when the policy concerned is already before Parliament in the form of proposed legislation. Policies are made before they reach Parliament, and by the time they are set in a bill it is difficult for any group to alter them. At this stage, legislation is more apt to be blocked or delayed than changed. The *most effective* form of lobbying is probably to target key bureaucrats and ministers while policy is in the gestation stage.

Occasionally, interest groups use the judicial process to pursue their goals. It is possible for group leaders to initiate suits directly on behalf of their group. Or they may support in the courts an individual who seeks to achieve the same goals as their own. For example, a stay-at-home mother might obtain the support of a women's organization before the courts because the interest group considers that her case provides the best opportunity to have the law interpreted in favour of the women's movement. Or parents who take court action against a provincial government because their child is not allowed to attend the school of their choice might be supported by a group whose

27. Robert Presthus, "Interest Groups and Parliament Activities, Interaction, Legitimacy and Influence," *CJPS*, vol. 4, no. 4 (December 1971), p. 460.

28. Bernard R. Blishen, *Doctors and Doctrines: The Ideology of Medical Care in Canada* (Toronto: University of Toronto Press, 1969), p. 101.

own cause is thereby represented. Since the introduction of the *Charter of Rights and Freedoms* in 1982, interest groups have increasingly sponsored legal challenges in order to get the courts to clarify or change laws concerning rights and freedoms in these regards.

We have pointed out that public relations campaigns are expensive, and, as a result, groups with large memberships, extensive financial resources and influential connections often have major advantages. Direct advertising or program sponsorship is often too expensive for many groups. However, there are other avenues. Poorer interest groups often create newsworthy events so that information about their group and their activities will be publicized without charge. Some groups employ other tactics to obtain free media coverage. For example, they may stage employee strikes against management in order to force the government to listen to their demands through the media. Picketers affect not only management but also public opinion.

Nonviolent demonstrations are yet another means of seeking publicity. The tactic has become increasingly popular since the nonviolent U.S. civil rights movement in the 1950s and 1960s. It is especially popular with minority and low-income groups. But neither nonviolent nor violent protest fits within the norms of mutual accommodation between interest groups and policy-makers in Canada. Such a tactic presents an ultimatum that precludes negotiation of individual group claims; on the whole, groups that use this strategy are likely to be ignored, discredited or placated with purely symbolic action. Lobbyists who act harshly are often ostracized from government circles.

Many of the tactics and strategies described here were used by tobacco manufacturers and health groups in one of the most sophisticated lobbying campaigns in modern Canadian history. It began in 1987–88 over the government's bill (Bill C51) to ban tobacco advertising and promotion. Both sides used unique lobbying and public relations techniques. On one side, the tobacco manufacturers engaged an influential, well-connected lobbyist, William Neville, to stop Bill C51. On the other side, health groups banded together to support the bill and counter every tactic Neville and his clients mounted. In the summer of 1987, the tobacco manufacturers took out full-page advertisements in newspapers, and Neville conducted a sophisticated direct-mail campaign to mobilize all those who profit from tobacco, and enlist the support of those who benefit from tobacco company sponsorship. The anti-tobacco campaign retaliated by publishing full-page ads in 24 newspapers attacking the direct-mail campaign. And the Canadian Medical Association asked "two physicians in every riding to get in touch with their MP directly and asked all 59 000 physicians in the country to write MPs in support of the bill."[29]

The tobacco industry organized a press conference; the health groups held one, too. The industry provided tobacco retailers with an information kit that included a computer-generated letter of protest to the store owner's MP, then made three follow-up phone calls to encourage the merchants to sign and mail the letters. The Canadian Cancer Society responded with 35 000 black-edged postcards to MPs (one for each tobacco-related death forecast for each MP's riding).

MP Ronald Stewart spoke out against Bill C51, and the coalition of health groups promptly sent out letters to every household in Stewart's riding, pointing out that he was involved in the wholesale tobacco distribution business. One of the coalition's members commented: "We're trying to be sophisticated enough to use our relatively modest resources to blow the industry's multi-million-dollar campaign out of the water." Neville, on the other hand, claimed that he was merely trying to inform those who would be affected by the legislation.[30]

---

29. Graham Fraser, "Lobby Fight on Tobacco Legislation Smolders On," *The Globe and Mail*, December 16, 1987.

30. Ibid.

Besides the sophisticated lobbying techniques employed by the two sides in this affair, this contest was unusual in that the tobacco industry did not try to lobby individual MPs to kill the bill, but only to reduce its priority on the legislative agenda. They knew that delay can kill a bill as effectively as a defeat. The bill had broad public support, confirmed health benefits, and the support of a minister and a majority of MPs, but effective lobbying delayed its passage for a considerable time. Bill C51 did not receive Royal Assent until June 1988, and only took effect in January 1989, with rules for advertising and labelling to be phased in over a five-year period. Even then, the tobacco lobby did not give up, but appealed to the Supreme Court of Canada.

In September 1995, the Supreme Court ruled in favour of the tobacco lobby. It found that the 1988 *Tobacco Products Control Act* was unconstitutional because Ottawa's nearly total advertising ban violated the industry's right to free speech. Bold, unattributed health warnings, such as "smoking can kill you," were deemed unconstitutional, so that companies could put their logos and trademarks back on promotional items. The decision meant that tobacco companies were free to resume all forms of advertising. The Court justified the decision by saying that the government had failed to prove that a total ban on advertising was appropriate.

The Court did preserve Parliament's right to legislate in the matter; however, it said that the federal government must pass a new law if it wants to continue to restrict tobacco advertising. In late 1996, the government tabled another bill on smoking. Bill C71 was designed to give Ottawa sweeping powers to regulate the content of tobacco products and to severely limit advertising — including where and in what form tobacco company logos can appear on advertisements for arts and sporting events. It, too, was challenged by tobacco companies and their allies. (See "The Ongoing Debate on Cigarette Advertising.")

Access Points: Pre-Parliamentary and Parliamentary

A lobbyist once commented that "our political system is great if the government is doing what you like — otherwise there are never enough access points."[31] To be successful, groups must be flexible enough to approach all parts of the legislative process and adapt their tactics to all of the available access points. "We throw out our line everywhere" is the usual approach of successful lobbyists.

We have seen that access is available to the policy process through individual MPs by way of the committee system or caucus and, of course, the Cabinet. But, of course, interest groups also operate outside Parliament. Since the bureaucracy is concerned with policy at its earliest formation, it is often the most important focus of lobbying. Such activity at the pre-parliamentary stage has been known to provoke complaints that interest groups bypass ministers and other elected representatives.

In both arenas, the interaction between pressure group leaders and politicians or bureaucrats is characterized by a spirit of cooperation that has been termed an "ethos of mutual accommodation." In order for the system to work, all parties must receive some benefits and value from the interaction. This ethos is evident in the following remark by an interest group leader: "We are concerned to always give full and accurate information to bureaucrats because if we don't create a confidence and they depend on advice which is biased toward us — they have a long memory and will hold it against us later."[32]

It is important for interest groups to use the access points provided within the political system and establish a framework for mutual consultation. Once a pattern is established, it indicates that the

---

31. Based on personal interviews by the authors.
32. Ibid.

group has obtained recognition as *the* representative for its particular interests. The interaction is a symbol of the compatibility of its goals and tactics with both Canadian political culture and the goals of the government.

If we trace the course of a bill through the pre-parliamentary stages to the parliamentary stages, the relative importance of the various access points becomes clearer. The interaction process can be very complex, and most of it takes place on an informal, confidential basis. The bureaucracy and Cabinet are significant access points in the pre-parliamentary stages of a bill. Many political analysts believe that the bureaucracy is the most widely used arena for successful pressure group activity. There is a close relationship between civil servants and pressure groups because civil servants are required to research and evaluate policy proposals for Cabinet, to give advice on the public acceptability of these policies and even to help educate and inform the public about them.

The availability of access points to a group varies according to many factors, particularly the group's position within a specified policy community or network. The federal Cabinet and a lead agency or department are at the core of a policy community in the federal jurisdiction. Around the decision-making core are "concentric rings" of other institutions and policy actors such as MPs, departments, provincial governments, groups and individuals. The closer they are to the core, the more influential interest groups are. The most influential interest groups tend to have direct, institutionalized access to the policy core — they might be called a policy network.

Successful access to the policy-making process necessitates knowledge of the institutional and procedural structures of government and the legislative system — such as, for instance, how a bill originates and what affects its passage. The early stages of a bill are particularly important for interest groups because, as we noted in an earlier chapter, Parliament passes laws but rarely originates them. Legislation and expenditures are generally approved by the executive as a package. By the time a particular package reaches Parliament, the government has publicly committed itself to the policies therein, and little can be done to change the details of single bills or estimates without destroying the delicate compromises on which the "deal" has been constructed.

CLOSE-UP ON Political Behaviour

THE ONGOING DEBATE ON CIGARETTE ADVERTISING

There were powerful interests on both sides of the anti-smoking Bill C71 which was tabled in the House of Commons in late 1996. The medical community in particular deplored the fact that smoking-related diseases kill about 45 000 Canadians a year. But the rights to smoke and to advertise cigarette products were passionately defended by the tobacco industry and its allies. Over the years, tobacco companies enlisted community support by sponsoring sports teams and events such as car races, and arts events such as the Vancouver International Film Festival. Many of these groups had come to depend on tobacco sponsorship and could not find alternative funding. In this particular case, several threatened to leave Canada, raising cries especially in Québec.

When Bill C71 reached committee stage in the House, lawyers and lobbyists for the tobacco industry once again claimed that banning advertisements was an infringement of the *Charter of Rights and Freedoms* and was nothing short of trying to re-impose the ban already struck down by the Supreme Court. Critics claimed that in order to justify its new restrictions and its infringement on one of the highest Charter values, the government wanted to prove that these measures would reduce the incidence of smoking among young people. In response to such pressure, in March 1997 the government introduced changes that would delay the implementation of provisions of Bill C71. The critics continued their pressure.

Health Minister David Dingwall characterized the approach of the tobacco lobby — which included several senators and former high-ranking Liberal and Conservative aids — as "tough, vicious and personal." He said, "We are not going to be hijacked by an industry who has its friends writing articles that this is a breach of civil liberties [and] the freedom of expression."

Which side are you on in this ongoing debate? Should lobbyists for particular interest groups be able to delay, amend and even block government proposed legislation?

Sources: *Maclean's*, November 18, 1996, p. 18, and *The Globe and Mail*, December 10, 1996.

Another opportunity for pressure exists again during the drafting and amendment of a bill, but this is a difficult stage at which to have much influence. One lobbyist stated his preferences this way: "After a bill is printed it is almost impossible to have a great effect. We prefer the white paper process so that the minister is not married to his bill." Professional lobbyists are particularly critical about the lack of influence in the closed atmosphere around taxation legislation: "Too few people get involved in the final projects.... We prefer the American system where there is a greater airing of views on each bill."[33]

Since responsibility for initiation and control of legislation is in the hands of the government, the Cabinet is a natural target for interest group activity. In the pre-parliamentary stages of a bill, the minister who prepares a new policy is responsible for gathering information from interest groups. At the same time, government secrecy requires that the groups not be informed about the government's intentions regarding decisions or policy details. This relationship can be exceedingly complex or simple. Sometimes the relationships between ministers and interest groups are extremely close; for example, when Mitchell Sharp and C.M. Drury entered the Cabinet, they were both members of the Canadian Manufacturers Association.

An interest group leader's approach to a Cabinet minister can be illustrated by an incident in 1977. A Toronto lobbyist asked an acquaintance who was a friend of Cabinet minister A.C. Abbott to tell the minister over lunch that he wanted to be sure that an insurance company would have the opportunity to present a brief at the committee stage of a certain bill (*Borrowers and Depositors Protection Act*, 1977). Abbott assured him that his clients would be heard, and they were.[34] Some interest group relations with Cabinet are more formalized. Every year, specific national groups are invited to present annual briefs to the whole Cabinet. This recognition is greatly valued. Apart from publicity and prestige, it gives these groups an opportunity to air their views directly to ministers.

Paul Pross has argued convincingly that interest groups have contributed to the enhancement of Parliament's role in the policy process. Approaches by interest groups to MPs have increased because they have "found it useful to exploit the legitimacy and publicizing capacities of parliament."[35] Interest groups seek access to individual MPs more for their long-term political influence than because the groups need immediate assistance. Because legislation is approved and passed, rather than initiated, in the House of Commons, unless an MP has special information or interest (or is strategically located in a minority government situation) he or she can be of little direct help. Also, interest group leaders complain that "it is almost impossible to get backbenchers involved in the technical details of bills" and that "there has to be public appeal in order to get backbenchers involved." On the other hand, it is always possible that a friendly member may bring an issue to the attention of a Cabinet minister, become a Cabinet minister or, together with fellow backbenchers, force desired change in Cabinet decisions. In addition, since opposition MPs may, after the next election, gain key positions in the government, they cannot be ignored. As a rule, however, opposition MPs receive most interest group attention during minority governments, when their vote is more significant.

An MP may take up the cause of an interest group for various reasons. It could be politically expedient to do so. Or the group might provide information for a well-informed question or speech in the House, which would earn the MP credit and recognition within party caucus.

---

33. Ibid.

34. Based on personal interview by the authors. Grace Skogstad examines the activities of interest groups in parliamentary committees in "Interest Groups, Representation and Conflict Management in the Standing Committees of the House of Commons," *CJPS*, vol. 18, no. 4 (December 1985), pp. 739–72.

35. A. Paul Pross, "Parliamentary Influence and the Diffusion of Power," *CJPS*, vol. 17, no. 2 (June 1985), p. 263.

Caucus gives individual MPs an opportunity to express their views. On the government side, the outline of bills that are about to be introduced in the House is presented first to the caucus. Caucus committee meetings follow in which the MPs have an opportunity to express the interest of groups that have approached them. Caucus continues to debate bills even after they have been introduced in the House, and, on occasion, can even prevent the moving of Second Reading. If Cabinet and interest groups' opinions diverge, it is usual for interest groups to attempt to form a coalition of anti-government forces. It has been noted:

> *Generally cabinet opinion prevails when the caucus, the provinces, or the relevant interest groups can be attracted to cabinet's side. Cabinet has the least chance of imposing its views where all three of these elements resist its direction.*[36]

The committee system is yet another attractive access point for interest groups because the very purpose of committees is to gather information. In fact, some scholars have found that committees are the most frequent site of interest group impact on legislators. It is not uncommon for interest groups, both in Ottawa and the provincial capitals, to have their own representatives on legislative committees. The Royal Canadian Legion, for example, is usually well represented on the committee for Veterans Affairs.

Some interest groups prefer Senate committees over House committees as a lobbying forum. Senate committees tend to handle testimony from corporations less politically than do House of Commons committees. Business people, for example, find dealing with House committees unsatisfactory because the deliberations are unsystematic and partisan.

When legislation is before a House committee, all interests are invited to present briefs. As we have already noted, even after bills are before the House a great many devices exist for slowing down their progress. Passage of legislation is at best a very lengthy process, often taking several years, thereby giving interest groups extensive opportunities to lobby and conduct public relations campaigns. And, in many circumstances, delaying a bill may be just as effective as killing it.

Although organized groups normally prefer to transmit their demands directly through the bureaucracy or legislative system, political parties constitute a further possibility for access to decision-making. Interest groups attempt to influence party policy resolutions because political parties supply the government leaders; party decisions therefore may become government policy decisions. However, fearing that such an attachment will close their routes of access to other parties, many groups declare nonpartisanship. The Canadian Manufacturers Association is a classic example of a group that has achieved success by avoiding identification with a single party. On the other hand, some interests, particularly labour associations, not only openly identify themselves with specific political parties, but also affiliate with them, providing both financial and political support. For example, the Canadian Labour Congress first openly identified with, then directly associated with, the CCF/NDP. In 1943, it endorsed the CCF as the political arm of labour in Canada, and in 1961 the joint CLC-CCF Committee founded the NDP.

Primary Interest Group Targets

As a whole, Cabinet is closely involved in the policy-making process and is the target for intense lobbying. It is not, however, a monolithic block of power, but rather the sum of its ministerial parts.

36. Robert J. Jackson and Michael Atkinson, *The Canadian Legislative System*, 2nd ed. (Toronto: Macmillan, 1980), p. 40.

While the whole Cabinet is involved in major issues because of the principle of collective responsibility, its committee system forms the nexus of many significant decisions. Moreover, for the lobbyist, access to the committee system involves contact with the relevant minister, often via the ministerial bureaucracy or exempt staff.

Reinforcing the myth of Cabinet monopoly is the handy commonplace that, while the members of the House of Commons pass legislation, very few of them initiate it. At face value, this statement is true; however, on close examination of the workings of the House, it is revealed as an unscholarly distortion. To be sure, lobbyists do spend less time approaching MPs than their American counterparts do Congress representatives. Nevertheless, members of Parliament are now more significant in terms of briefings, committee hearings and new task forces than ever before. Proof of this assertion can be found in a survey that showed that some 75 percent of the chief executive officers of Canadian business corporations or their representatives have frequent contact with members of Parliament.[37]

Since MPs have a small staff, lobby groups become a major source of information. In a period of a week, a total of 200 briefs, magazine articles and letters were forwarded to one MP from groups eager to inform him of their points of view and perhaps win support. Thus, backbenchers often become a barometer of the political climate:

> ... *special interest groups can give an MP a reading of the political pros and cons of a particular proposal. This is very important to the MPs who are often more concerned about public attitudes on legislation than are members of the bureaucracy or the Cabinet. Moreover, MPs usually have more time to see lobbyists than do Cabinet ministers or senior bureaucrats.*[38]

Consequently, interest groups or their representative public relations firms often distribute responsibility for all the legislators among members of their organizations in order to provide a consistent and geographically based influence. For organizations that can afford such a broad and sustained effort, this strategy represents a calculated investment in the future. As we said earlier, Cabinet ministers are, to a large degree, recruited from the ranks of the government back bench, and neither they nor opposition backbenchers can be allowed to feel isolated or ignored.

Yet, even in the short term, the skillful lobbying of backbenchers can have considerable impact on the legislative output of the government. The primary forum for backbench influence is caucus. When a substantial coalition of backbenchers with the support of one or more concerned interest groups opposes the Cabinet's position, the likelihood that the government's proposals will be reviewed increases. Further leverage is often available via a three-way alliance between lobbyists, backbenchers and disgruntled provincial governments.

Canadian interest groups also focus directly on the federal bureaucracy. Business groups tend to approach lower- and middle-level bureaucrats "on the premise that policy becomes more set and less easy to change the higher up it moves and that the lower level bureaucrats rely on business for information."[39] Hence there exists a reciprocity of dependency. Effective lobbying of the public service presupposes, of course, a fairly sophisticated understanding of the bureaucratic process

---

37. Robert J. Jackson, "Lobbying and the Political Process," paper prepared for the Social Science Federation of Canada, October 22, 1982, p. 12.

38. J. Gillies and J. Pigott, "Participation in the Legislative Process," *CPA*, vol. 25, no. 2 (Summer 1982), p. 256.

39. Riddell-Dixon, *The Domestic Mosaic*, p. 7.

and sufficient knowledge about the best timing and point of contact. In the perception of one former lobbyist, the campaign to influence legislative outputs cannot begin too early "because you don't even see the tip of the iceberg until there's a hell of a lot of ice down there."[40]

The effectiveness of focusing on public servants at the pre-parliamentary stage of the process is augmented at later stages. Legislation is often returned to departments for further consideration; thus, the entire process is reopened to groups that seek to block or stall disadvantageous proposals. The complexities of the legislative system and the rough landscape of Canadian politics give some indication of why it is often considered easier to block or slow down proposals than to initiate them.

The increased salience of bureaucracy is general to all advanced industrial societies. There is, however, a tendency to overstress the political significance of the bureaucratic process. This is especially true of journalists, for whom the use of the word "mandarin" in reference to senior civil servants carries an aura of omnipotence. Observations abound to the effect that "any lobbyist who is worth either the handsome retainer or the comfortable salary that goes with the title will tell you that the real levers of power in Ottawa lie within the bureaucracy."[41] Those wasting their time with MPs and Cabinet ministers, so the reasoning goes, are simply not in the know.

The habit of using language such as "the real levers of power" stems from an inadequate appreciation of the concept of political "power." (See Chapter 1.) In this journalistic interpretation, the competition for access to government decision-makers is seen as a zero-sum game. Power is viewed as a kind of football in the lobbyists' free-for-all; if one group has it, other groups do not.

The fact is that while certain interests single out specific components of the legislative system for special attention, no successful group fosters illusions about "power" having a single address. Flexibility and concern to touch all the bases are the hallmarks of the most seasoned practitioners of the art of lobbying. When business groups suspect, for example, that their efforts at the mid-level of bureaucracy are too late or simply insufficient, they send their chief executive officers to engage in discussions with members of Cabinet — an activity that is frequently coordinated by large umbrella organizations.

All groups appreciate the importance of monitoring developments in Ottawa very closely and making regular contact with government officials. Despite this common characteristic, no two groups are identical in goals or resources, organization or methods. The National Farmers' Union (NFU) does not hesitate to employ confrontational tactics when they are deemed necessary. The larger Canadian Federation of Agriculture (CFA) makes representations to the federal government on matters of macro- and micro-agricultural policy, paying special attention to the development of export markets. While the NFU has placed greater emphasis on the economic viability of the family farm and the dignity of the Canadian farmer, it does have a community of interest with the CFA in promoting trade policies that will increase exports and protect domestic producers generally.[42]

The broad membership of the Canadian Business and Industry International Advisory Committee dictates concern with a very wide range of issues. Traditionally, it worked closely with the Department of Industry Canada but departmental reorganization now requires it to give greater attention to the Department of Foreign Affairs and International Trade. Other groups feature more exclusive membership and a concomitantly narrower focus, stressing a specific geographic area or a particular sector of the economy.

---

40. Quoted in John Gray, "Insiders Go to Mandarins before Minister," *The Globe and Mail*, Toronto, October 25, 1980.

41. Gray, "Insiders Go to Mandarins before Minister."

42. Riddell-Dixon, *The Domestic Mosaic*, p. 24.

Depending on their styles and resources, certain groups consistently stress one link of the legislative process over others. While the financial capacity of certain lobbies may enable them to wage a long-term campaign at every level, one should be careful of the assumption that wealthy lobbies are necessarily the most influential. An aide to the Minister of Energy, Mines and Resources described the tactics of oil interests as "unbelievably bad."[43] Their attempts at dramatizing first Canada's oil wealth and later its relative poverty contributed to a substantial erosion of their credibility in government circles. Moreover, even enormous financial resources may not be enough to offset salient political factors.

Regionalism has a considerable impact, especially when federalism affords interest groups differing areas of opportunity. David Kwavnick has noted how competition between the Canadian Labour Congress and the Québec-based Confederation of National Trade Unions demonstrates that "rival groups representing the same interest, but having access to different levels of government in a federal system, will attempt to shift power to the level of government to which they enjoy access."[44]

All these groups recognize the multifaceted nature of the legislative process and exert a long-term, systematic yet flexible effort at as many points of access as possible. Lobbyists are aware that political power is not some finite substance that necessarily ebbs in the legislature as it flows in the bureaucracy. They know that government structures are not held together by nuts and bolts; a search for the "real lever of power" is for bare-handed amateurs. Government, like a growing onion, continues to change size; the political process features so many different but similar layers that it is impossible to distinguish which of them really counts. Successful lobbyists have learned that they *all* count — in fact, each layer has meaning only because of its relation to the others.

The relative utility of any one facet of the legislative system to lobbyists can and does change over time. This is true in regard to backbench MPs, who are now considered more suitable targets for lobbying than in the past. Here again, zero-sum assumptions about the exercise of influence and political authority have tended to cloud an understanding of the subtle relations between administrative and legislative branches of government. Rare indeed is the contemporary political science text that does not make much ado about the increasing importance of specialized, bureaucratized expertise to government in the contemporary welfare state. Students of politics seem to regard knowledge held by the bureaucrat to be knowledge lost to the politician; elected representatives are held to be overshadowed by civil service technocrats. However, few elected representatives would claim to have been the artless victims of manipulative bureaucrats or lobbyists. To paraphrase Senator Duff

CLOSE-UP ON Political Behaviour

USING THE SYSTEM

A high official attached to a certain foreign embassy in Ottawa thought that an issue concerning a certain aspect of his country's relation with Canada should have an airing in the House of Commons. This official contacted an opposition member and armed him with a particularly contentious question with which to confront the government. The member asked the question in the House. When the Minister of Foreign Affairs asked his staff to brief him on the substance of the matter so that he could respond, they of course sought information from a foreign embassy — information they duly received from the very man who had originally formulated the question and inserted it into the system. The foreign diplomat had, in fact, both set the question and determined the answer.* Yet politicians are neither unaware of such manoeuvring nor unappreciative of the perceptions and ideas that filter through this way.

* Anecdote based on personal interviews.

---

43. James Rusk, "Powers in the Oil Lobby Cull Clout from the Flag," *The Globe and Mail*, October 27, 1980.

44. David Kwavnick, "Interest Group Demands and the Federal Political System: Two Canadian Case Studies," in Pross, *Pressure Group Behaviour*, p. 77.

Roblin, former Conservative premier of Manitoba, "I've never had an original idea in my life, but I know one when I see it!" MPs can, of course, be manipulated unwittingly. (See "Using the System.")

When substantive legislation is the target of interest group activity, a sustained campaign is important. It is perhaps in endurance that well-financed lobbies have great advantages. A controversial drug bill was tabled in the House of Commons in 1962, yet by the time all concerned interests had aired their views and conducted their public relations blitzes, two governments had been in power, and the bill did not become law until 1968.[45] The legislation, which was designed to reduce the retail cost of pharmaceuticals by encouraging druggists to substitute generic alternatives for more expensive brand-name products, was not acceptable to foreign-based multinationals. It allowed Canadian pharmaceutical manufacturers to be granted licences to produce the drugs of foreign companies domestically after just four years of patent protection. One hysterical voice on their side went so far as to claim that the principle of private property in Canada was being subverted by "godless consumerism." Years of counteroffensive followed until the law was changed again in 1987 and 1993, this time in favour of the multinationals.[46]

Lobbying in Canada: Casting the Net Wide

By now it should be apparent that the relatively unregulated practice of lobbying in Canada is an art of enormous complexity. Far from operating in a "restricted" environment, interest groups have the advantage of multiple access points to the legislative process. It is also obvious that scenarios that speak of the "virtual monopoly" of Cabinet clash with those that view federal bureaucrats as "the" unseen power brokers in Ottawa. Both are misrepresentations of a complicated reality.

The relationship of lobbyists, bureaucrats and politicians in Canada is not one of zero-sum games or of sinister cabals in the corridors of power. The interaction of interest groups with the political system is at all points permeated by an ethos of mutual accommodation. Each party involved in the process recognizes that all other parties have an investment in the outcome of the legislative process and hence a legitimate share in the formulation of public policy. The spirit of accommodation thrives where no party is seen to dominate all of the time and when each party receives sufficient satisfaction to justify further participation.

This process of *elite accommodation* tends to include interest groups, particularly business, with the Cabinet and the bureaucracy. To some extent, labour is left out of the process. In many industrialized democracies a social partnership or consensus known as **corporatism** exists instead of Canadian-style accommodation. In the corporatist model, a formal or institutionalized process of consultation between the state, business and labour shapes economic policy for society as a whole. Normally, such a process cannot take place in Canada because no single business or labour association can claim to represent all the significant interests in their respective communities and even the largest associations are accorded no functional representation in government policy-making.

In Canada, a successful and fruitful relationship with government actors begins with a group's recognition of the complexity of the contemporary democratic state and the opportunities that such complexity offers. A concern to leave no point of contact or influence untried, to cast one's net in as wide an arc as possible, is the cardinal rule of interest group politics. This means that while certain

---

45. Donald Coxe, "A License to Loot: How Ottawa Promotes Drug Piracy and Drives Away R & D," *Canadian Business*, March 1982, p. 142.
46. "Critics Say Ottawa Drug Changes Will Add Millions to Consumer Cost," *The Globe and Mail*, May 28, 1983. This case is discussed in John Sawatsky, *The Insiders: Government, Business and the Lobbyists* (Toronto: McClelland & Stewart, 1987), pp. 315–17. In February 1993, Bill C91 became law. It eliminates compulsory licensing, extending full patent protection of 20 years to all new, innovative drugs.

Alan King, *The Ottawa Citizen*, December 18, 1994. Reprinted by permission.

components such as Cabinet and the bureaucracy may be more significant than others, no facet of the process can be dismissed as unimportant.

The Canadian Senate, for example, is popularly considered to be the inconsequential artifact of a British political heritage. We have remarked that this contention is incorrect from the point of view of the lobbyist. Indeed, one author has called the Senate "a lobby from within," by which he meant that most senators already represented lobbying interests before they were appointed to the upper house.[47] Formally, the Senate is responsible for detailed amendments to legislation from the House of Commons, a task for which it possesses a committee system capable of analyzing the impact that details of legislation have on the business community.

Often the key to lobbying success is a sense of timing. Clause-by-clause consideration of bills, for example, almost always takes place in one of the several committees of the House of Commons after the Second Reading. MPs representing all parties are members of these committees. And, while the government side of each committee is "whipped" to ensure the bill's passage, lobbyists have a good chance to secure amendments at this time, either by serving as witnesses or prompting backbench initiatives.

Finally, it should be stressed that interest group activities do not occur in a social vacuum. Casting a wide net can also involve the careful nurturing of broad public support or opposition to certain policies by interest groups. The size of the social constituency sought will, of course, depend on the nature and substance of the issue. The past record and perceived social "legitimacy" of an interest group affects its ability to harness social support.

---

47. Colin Campbell, *The Canadian Senate: A Lobby from Within* (Toronto: Macmillan, 1978).

In recent years another kind of group that aims to influence governments and change social policy has become influential within many countries and also internationally. We turn next to a brief study of such movements and an examination of the women's movement in particular.

WHAT ARE SOCIAL AND POLITICAL MOVEMENTS?

Return for a moment to the four prime characteristics of interest groups. They (1) have an organization; (2) articulate and aggregate interests; (3) act within the political system to influence policy; and (4) seek to influence government rather than exercise government responsibility themselves.

Social and political movements are also political phenomena that share some of these interest group characteristics. **Social and political movements** are rather fluid expressions of interests or collective identities with a broad, utopian appeal that often flows across state boundaries. They generally have no well-developed formal organization. Rather, they loosely subsume a variety of interest groups that may have different aspirations and agendas, although they share the same broad philosophy. Peace movements, environmental movements, nationalist movements and those supporting gay, disabled or animal rights are examples of broad, unstructured movements that offer a particular vision of how people should live. Social and political movements may include coalitions of many associations and interest groups that support the same general cause. The Canadian environmental movement, for example, is estimated to comprise at least 1 800 different organizations.[48] Such movements bring new issues and problems to public attention outside of the channels of political parties. Most are broadly based and inclusive, emphasizing citizen participation. They maintain that citizens should be equal to enjoy the goods and services of society and to participate in the political decision-making process. Susan Phillips says social movements

> ... have accentuated a decline in the public's acquiescence and deference to elites and experts, and accelerated an increase in the public's interest in creating opportunities for direct participation and improving mechanisms for holding public officials accountable for policy decisions.[49]

Movements may remain in a loose form as innovators or they may harden into organized cohesive pressure groups or even become new political parties.[50]

Some movements have a long history. Nationalist movements, for example, have roots extending back to the seventeenth century. Nationalist and ethnic movements espouse the belief that a group of people represents a "natural" community and should be united under one political system. They stress local identities and loyalties based on ethnicity, language, culture and so on, which may or may not correspond to state boundaries. Sometimes nationalist movements create a political party, or

48. Jeremy Wilson, "Green Lobbies: Pressure Groups and Environmental Policy," in Robert Boardman, ed., *Canadian Environmental Policy: Ecosystems, Politics and Process* (Toronto: Oxford University Press, 1992).

49. Susan D. Phillips, "A More Democratic Canada...?" in Susan D. Phillips, *How Canada Spends* (Ottawa: Carleton University Press, 1993).

50. See Claude Galipeau, "Political Parties, Interest Groups and New Social Movements: Toward New Representation?" in Alain Gagnon and Brian Tanguay, eds., *Political Parties in Transition* (Scarborough: Nelson, 1989).

parties, as in Québec with the Parti Québécois and Bloc Québécois. The same kind of transformation took place in a loose farmers' movement in Alberta at the beginning of the century. In the early 1900s, farmers organized pressure groups to fight for their interests in Ottawa. Discouraged with their results in the early 1920s, they entered the political forum as the Progressive party. In spite of considerable electoral success, they soon withdrew their party status and returned to pressure group activity. What began as a farmers' movement hardened into a pressure group, then a political party and finally reverted back to pressure group activity.

As well as movements with deep historical roots, there are a multitude of modern movements related to what has been called "the new politics." These concern issues such as environmentalism, feminism and other group rights that began to emerge in western democracies in the 1960s and 1970s.

The environmental movement appeared in western societies as people became concerned with the deteriorating quality of the environment and the depletion of world resources. Broadly speaking, environmentalists regard economic growth as less important than the protection of "quality of life." They support pollution controls even though these may mean greater expense, hamper industrial development, and limit or decrease material affluence. A great many interest groups come under the umbrella of the environmentalist movement, such as those seeking government regulations on acid rain, reforestation, preservation of threatened animal species and so on. In some countries, the environmental movement has established political parties. In many European countries, these parties regularly receive up to 5 percent of the vote at general elections. In Germany, they are part of the government coalition. In Canada, the environmental movement includes the Canadian Environmental Network, which contains about 200 groups as well as small Green parties in several provinces and at the federal level. The federal Green party is extremely weak, undoubtedly because established parties also have taken up ecological issues.

Ron Inglehart has offered a theory to explain the proliferation of these new movements. He suggests that western democracies have undergone social, economic and cultural changes that have contributed to a growing politicization of their citizens. At the same time, political behaviour is moving beyond the constraints of traditional organizations like parties. He says that elite-directed participation is giving way to *ad hoc* groups concerned with specific issues and policy changes. There are growing numbers of people with high political skills but without close party ties.[51] Because of this, he predicts more movements and parties will appear. The established parties, he says, came into being in an era dominated by social class conflict and economic issues, and tend to remain polarized on this basis. But, in recent years, a new axis of polarization has arisen based on cultural and quality-of-life issues. He goes on to say that parties today

> *. . . do not adequately reflect the most burning contemporary issues, and those who have grown up in the postwar era have relatively little motivation to identify with one of the established parties.*[52]

Whether or not Inglehart's explanation for the rise of new movements is valid, there has been a proliferation of new organizations around issues such as the environment. The word "movement"

51. Ron Inglehart, *Culture Shift in Advanced Industrial Society* (Princeton, N.J.; Princeton University Press, 1990), pp. 363–68. For a commentary on Inglehart's ideas see Thomas M. Trump, "Value Formation and Postmaterialism: Inglehart's Theory of Value Change Reconsidered," *Comparative Political Studies*, vol. 24, no. 3 (October 1991), pp. 365–90.
52. Inglehart, *Culture Shift in Advanced Industrial Society,* p. 363.

has been used to capture these new interests because it implies broad, mass appeal and the notion that there is inevitability for the success of these causes. Recognizing the emotional appeal of movements, parties everywhere have adjusted their platforms to accommodate their demands. In Canada today, the Bloc Québécois espouses nationalist rhetoric and all three traditional federal parties have adopted policy positions that give credence to the philosophies of environmentalism, feminism and so on. To explore these relations among movements, interest groups and parties and the general appeal of political movements, we assess the women's movement in Canada.

The Women's Movement: A Case Study

The women's movement is one of the most active and widespread movements reaching across state borders today. It has manifested itself on and off since the nineteenth century, seeking rights for women to vote and to hold political positions and appointments for paid employment. The women involved share no doctrine *per se* and, in fact, are often in bitter disagreement about how to achieve their goals. The fundamental point of all feminists, however, is that orthodox theories about politics tend to ignore gender and harbour unconscious assumptions about the role of women.

Since the 1960s, the movement generally has focused on women's liberation, denouncing traditions of male supremacy in the family and in other political and social structures that assign women an inferior position in society. In short, the various strands of the movement seek for women the same social and political rights enjoyed by men, and share a theoretical assumption that historically men have exploited women using gender differences to establish a division of labour. Women's role in society was thereby limited to child-rearing and domestic chores.

To achieve their ends, women's movements have built solid organizational and leadership structures within many countries and also at the international level.[53] At this broad level, the women's movement has no unified ideology, but a neo-Marxist framework has provided much of its ideological basis. Capitalism and its social and political superstructures are often identified as the forces behind the oppression of women. It is argued that since men control the means of production, they have used their position to institutionalize norms and values that keep women in an inferior position.[54] To this end, they identify and expose perceived cultural stereotyping, socialization and distortions of history that have been and continue to be used to ensure male dominance.

To date, the women's movement has generally sought to influence the policies of existing political parties rather than institute their own, although there are women's political parties in a few countries such as Colombia and Iceland. Since the rise of the modern women's movement, female politicians have become increasingly prominent. Sirimavo Bandarana-Ike of Sri Lanka was the world's first elected woman prime minister (1960–65, 1970–77). She was followed by, among others, Indira Gandhi in India (1966–77; 1980–84), Golda Meir in Israel (1969–70), Benazir Bhutto in Pakistan (1988–90) and Kim Campbell in Canada (1993). Although female politicians are particularly evident in Scandinavia, in most national legislatures their numbers are disproportionately low compared to their share of the population.

---

53. See Mary Fainsod Katzenstein and Carol McClurg Mueller, eds., *The Women's Movement of the United States and Western Europe* (Philadelphia: Temple University, 1987), pp. 64–88.

54. See Robert J. Jackson and Doreen Jackson, *An Introduction to Political Science: Comparative and World Politics*, 3rd ed. (Toronto: Prentice Hall, 2000).

In Canada today, many groups advance women's causes.[55] Interestingly, about 100 women form a core that is active across most of these groups. The 1970 Royal Commission on the Status of Women provided the impetus to make gender an important factor in Canadian social and political life. The National Action Committee on the Status of Women (NAC) was established in 1972 to pressure for implementation of the recommendations of the Royal Commission. Initially, as we have seen, about 80 percent of its funding came from the government. NAC has become an umbrella lobbying group for about 580 local and national member groups representing about three million women.

Susan Phillips' study of 33 national Canadian women's organizations shows that the diverse groups "form an expansive, but loosely coupled, network, that is bound by a collective identity of 'liberalized' feminism."[56] In its attempt to speak for women, NAC addresses a broad range of issues. In the 1980s, they included free trade, abortion, the GST, child care and the Meech Lake accord. Since the early 1990s, the government's financial difficulties has meant a diminishing commitment to the priorities of women. NAC interpreted the reduction of its funds as an attempt to "silence" the women's movement. However, NAC continues to be active, especially in rights-related questions. It has continually fought to ensure that (1) equality rights are inviolable; (2) equality rights are clearly articulated in terms relevant to the needs of women; and (3) that affirmative action should be more clearly and positively entrenched in the Charter. Canadian women do not, however, speak with one voice. REAL Women (Realistic, Equal, Active for Life), formed in 1974, opposes feminist demands, and various anti-abortion groups also attack feminist viewpoints.

The women's movement in Canada has raised the awareness of women's position in society, changed attitudes and introduced many issues into the policy agendas of political parties. It has not tried to create a party itself, but has stayed outside of traditional political and interest group organization. Lynn McDonald, former president of NAC, commented: "We have decided that at no time will we support one party.... Our members come from all political parties and we have to work with whomever is in government."[57] In keeping with this philosophy, women's groups have extensive ties and interests outside of the women's movement — though not primarily with class-based organizations. According to the policy network mapped by Phillips, 29 of 33 national organizations were connected through NAC. REAL women, the Catholic Women's League and two professional associations were the exceptions.[58]

The women's movement can be credited with improvements in legislation concerning women as well as with attitudinal changes concerning participation.[59] Details of women's other achievements in Canadian society are discussed in the chapters on political culture, the Constitution, Parliament, political parties, elections and the public service.

55. For the history of the women's movement, see M. Janine Brodie and Jill McCalla Vickers, *Canadian Women in Politics: An Overview* (Ottawa: Canadian Research Institute for the Advancement of Women, 1982). See also Susan D. Phillips, "Meaning and Structure in Social Movements: Mapping the Network of Canadian Women's Organizations," *CJPS*, vol. 24, no. 4 (December 1991), pp. 755–82; Pal, *Interests of State: The Politics of Language, Multiculturalism and Feminism in Canada*; and Sandra Burt, "The Women's Movement: Working to Transform Public Life," in James P. Bickerton and Alain G. Gagnon, eds., *Canadian Politics* (Broadview Press, 1994), pp. 209–23.

56. Phillips, "Meaning and Structure in Social Movements," p. 757.

57. *The Ottawa Citizen*, May 16, 1979.

58. Phillips, "Meaning and Structure in Social Movements," p. 774.

59. See Anne Phillips, *Engendering Democracy* (London: Polity Press, 1991).

SUMMARY

Lobbying in Canada is a well-practised but poorly studied art. Simplistic interpretations of the relationship between government and interest groups stem from a lack of appreciation of the complexity and evolution of the Canadian legislative process and the policy network. It is quite likely that if a government were to establish more rigorous rules for lobbying and draw back the veil of obscurity and suspicion, social scientists would be able to bring greater sophistication to their study of the phenomenon. Above all, tired clichés, conspiracy scenarios, and zero-sum characterizations of power and influence should be abandoned. The multifaceted and changing relationship between public and private actors must be acknowledged in future studies of interest groups in Canada. Sensitive description must precede analysis. Accurate diagnosis must precede prescription.

How well do interest groups serve the average Canadian? We have seen that interest groups are a widely accepted part of the political culture. The interaction between groups and the political system is characterized by an ethos of accommodation or cooperation in which the interaction is deemed mutually worthwhile. Sometimes, terms such as policy community or network are a reasonable depiction of political life. The fact that interest groups are accepted within the political culture means that there is a legitimate channel for complaints and frustrations, an opportunity for citizens to articulate viewpoints and defend them, so that citizens do not have to resort to extralegal behaviour to be heard. Once they are part of such a legitimized group, the members are committed to acting within the system. Interest groups in this sense act as a safety valve for individual frustrations by allowing the possibility of joining with others to influence legislation. They thus provide a crucial and culturally acceptable link between citizen and public policy.

Interest groups widen the range of interests that are taken into account in the legislative process. On the premise that more information can help achieve fairer laws, this is good — but what assurance is there that the most worthy groups are heard? Deserving groups might be ignored because of lack of funds or prestige, or competition from more powerful groups. And where is the fine line between information and propaganda in the expert advice offered to lawmakers? Groups can be expected, even within the realm of mutual accommodation, to give selective information, making their own cases as strong as possible and not making the cases for their competitors. We know, too, that interest groups are elite-dominated. People with higher status participate more, and groups tend to be dominated by the most active and vocal members. And what of unorganized interests? Who is to press the urgent claims of pensioners, children or stay-at-home mothers? To be fair, the system must be responsive to those who do not have the resources to sustain mass organization.

Representation in the Canadian political system is sought through the electoral process. It is clear that interest groups constitute another legitimate form of political representation. Yet these representatives seek influence on their own initiative and are responsible only to themselves. Some seek the good of the whole, but never to the detriment of their own interests. Interest group supporters say that extra representation through interest groups is good because the constituency form of representation cannot meet all the demands of groups in the political system, and that the modern welfare state makes interest group representation a necessary adjunct to government activity.

However, should interest groups play such an important role in making public policy? Could the representation allowed to interest groups erode political responsibility in a representative democracy? This problem within the system is aggravated when one political party dominates the government for a long period of time and relationships become well ingrained. Then we find more highly placed and experienced bureaucrats leaving the public service to sell their knowledge and contacts to interest groups through private consulting services. If interest groups are to exist as representative bodies complementary to the elected representatives, steps should be taken to eliminate some of these injustices.

In recent years, another influence on policy-making in western societies has become widespread. Movements have become a powerful force in changing societal attitudes and influencing governments. They are amorphous currents of interest that flow easily across borders because of their broad and inclusive philosophies. They often subsume existing interest groups and stimulate new ones; sometimes they stay as movements and sometimes they solidify as political parties. When political parties fragment and represent narrow, regional interests or groups, movements often help to unify people by embracing national and even international issues or points of view.

Discussion Questions

1. Distinguish between interest groups and parties, and between interest groups and policy networks.

2. Is lobbying something that should be encouraged?

3. Is the "women's movement" a lobby group? Why or why not?

4. Should the government give more money to the National Action Committee on the Status of Women? To REAL women? To environmental groups such as Pollution Probe or Greenpeace?

Selected Bibliography

Interest Groups

Brooks, Stephen and Andrew Strich, *Business and Government in Canada* (Scarborough: Prentice Hall Canada, 1991).

Coleman, William and Grace Skogstad, *Policy Communities and Public Policy in Canada* (Mississauga: Copp Clark Pitman, 1990).

Cunningham, Rod, *Smoke and Mirrors: The Canadian Tobacco War* (Ottawa: IDRC, 1996).

Gifford, C.G., *Canada's Fighting Seniors* (Toronto: Lorimer, 1991).

Pross, Paul, "Pressure Groups: Talking Chameleons," in M.S. Whittington and G. Williams, eds., *Canadian Politics in the 1990s* (Scarborough: Nelson, 1994).

Richardson, Jeremy, *Pressure Groups* (Oxford: Oxford University Press, 1993).

Seidle, Leslie, *Interest Groups and Elections in Canada* (Toronto: Dundurn Press, 1991).

——————, *Equity and Community: The Charter, Interest Advocacy and Representation* (Montréal: Institute for Research on Public Policy, 1993).

Stanbury, William, *Business-Government Relations in Canada*, 2nd ed. (Scarborough: Nelson, 1993).

Movements

Agnew, Vijay, *Resisting Discrimination: Women from Asia, Africa and the Caribbean and the Women's Movement in Canada* (Toronto: University of Toronto Press, 1996).

Boardman, Robert, ed., *Canadian Environmental Policy: Ecosystems, Politics and Process* (Toronto: Oxford University Press, 1992).

Brodie, J., *Politics on the Margin: Restructuring and the Canadian Women's Movement* (Halifax: Fernwood, 1995).

Davies, Miranda, *Women and Violence* (London: Zed Books, 1994).

Randall, Vicky and Joni Lovenduski, *Contemporary Feminist Politics* (Oxford: Oxford University Press, 1993).

Tarrow, Sidney, *Power in Movement: Social Movements, Collective Action and Politics* (Cambridge, U.K.: Cambridge University Press, 1994).

Vickers, Jill, Christine Appelle and Pauline Rankin, *Politics as If Women Mattered* (Toronto: University of Toronto Press, 1993).

 # LIST OF WEBLINKS

www.chamber.ca   **Canadian Chamber of Commerce** The Canadian Chamber of Commerce is the largest business association in Canada.

www.web.net/~cec   **Canadian Ethnocultural Council** The Canadian Ethnocultural Council is an organization set up to represent ethno-cultural interests in Canada.

green.ca   **Green Party of Canada** The Green party is a political party with close ties to the environmental movement in Canada.

CASE STUDY – POLITICAL BEHAVIOUR

CONSERVATIVES: WHAT KIND OF FUTURE?

An important function of a political party is to elect a government. To succeed in Canada a party must build a coalition, assembling support from the diverse provincial, regional and other interests across the country. Under its first leader, Sir John A. Macdonald, the Conservative party forged coalitions that recognized diversity and the regional character of this vast country. Conservative success continued in the nineteenth century and throughout much of the twentieth. However, successful coalition-building is difficult since the country is so large and arrangements encourage the development of regional parties.

Following a disastrous campaign in 1993, only two Progressive Conservatives were elected to the House of Commons. Unable to qualify for Official Party Status, the party faced extinction. Its new leader, Jean Charest, undertook formidable challenges; he had to rebuild the party while fending off the Reform party and also opponents within his own party who demanded the Conservatives move to the right. The 1997 election allowed the party to regain its official status with 20 seats, but the challenges continue as the party has the lowest number of MPs of any party and is saddled with enormous financial problems.

Canadian Conservatives embody two strains. One, influenced by U.S. conservatism, proclaims the American ideology of individualism, self-reliance, and a dislike for state interference. In the 1990s many of these conservatives abandoned the PCs for the right-wing populism of the Reform party. The other conservatism (derived from England's Edmund Burke) has a strong sense of social responsibility and traditional beliefs in the use of state power.

Canadian conservatism, like other ideologies, has adapted and changed over time. As the Canadian political spectrum moved to the right in recent years, so did Canadian political parties. To strengthen his party Jean Charest had to build on his 1997 electoral achievements by holding the Youth Wing and the Red Tories together and bringing in new coalition partners from Québec, Ontario and the West. However, Mr. Charest deserted the party to become leader of the Québec Liberal party. In 1999, former prime minister Joe Clark returned to lead the PCs.

The Conservative party has considerable support, but it is dispersed thinly throughout the country. It won 16 percent of the total popular vote in 1993. In 1997, it advanced by only two percentage points. To win in Canada's first-past-the-post electoral system, that support must be deepened, and that means recouping losses that have been made to the Reform party. Conservatives have made strides toward this goal of returning the Conservatives to their historic place as one of Canada's two national parties, but that achievement is far from assured.

Questions

1. Compare and contrast the two forms of conservative ideology found in Canadian conservatism. Which of the beliefs in American conservatism is most difficult to reconcile with those derived from English conservatism?

2. Discuss the obstacles faced by Charest as a coalition-builder in the Canadian politics of the late 1990s. Given the poor results in the 1997 election, is there a future for the Progressive Conservative party? For Joe Clark?

Public Policy

Culture, institutions and behaviour come together in the policy-making process.

A society's political culture shapes the demands made on policy-makers, providing opportunities and imposing constraints on the range of possible responses.

Institutional structure also influences the process of policy-making. Room for policy-makers to move is limited by the federal nature of Canada's political system, by aspects of the Constitution, by the dictates of governmental responsibility and accountability to Parliament, as well as by non-institutional factors and, of course, by the availability of finances.

Political behaviour, manifested in politics, parties, interest groups and the electoral arena, constitutes the means by which citizens express their demands to policy-makers. The electoral process requires governments to respond to public opinion, but may also influence the substance and timing of key policy initiatives.

Public policy has both domestic and foreign aspects. To a substantial degree, public policy determines the well-being of a country's citizens as well as their security and influence in the larger world of states.

Policy-making therefore takes place within constraints determined by Canadian culture, institutions and behaviour, and it occurs within a process of international politics and institutions increasingly shaped by the forces of globalization.

14

Public Policy and Government Expenditure

· · · · · · ·

Choice and Restraint

In earlier chapters, we examined the role of government in Canada and noted the increase in intervention by governments at all levels in most western industrialized states since the Second World War. State action is more complex than it was formerly and therefore more difficult to understand. The current popularity of the study of public policy stems from the realization that governments have come to play an ever more important role in the social and economic life of the country.

Thus, when governments increase or decrease public spending, or raise taxes or abolish a Crown corporation, we want to know why they have chosen a particular course of action and what has influenced and shaped their decisions. Sometimes governments fail to act on a particular issue. This, too, is of vital interest to students of public policy. The study of non-decisions, or situations in which the government fails to act on public demands, helps one understand some of the constraints within which policy-makers operate. The options open to policy-makers are limited by the availability of resources in the physical and economic environments, and also by the cultural, institutional and behavioural patterns examined in earlier chapters.

In the policy process, these elements — culture, institutions and behaviour — all come together. In this chapter, we demonstrate the nature and extent of theoretical linkages between culture, institutions, behaviour and public policy. Pluralism, Marxism, public choice and state-centred approaches to the understanding of public policy are explained in light of these four concepts. We then consider questions about the relations between public policy and public expenditure. Lastly, we turn to a discussion of public policy during economic restraint in the Mulroney and Chrétien governments. Our first task, however, is to define what we mean by the term "public policy."

WHAT IS PUBLIC POLICY?

One of the most common problems in any field of study is securing agreement on the definition and scope of its subject matter. This has certainly been the case in public policy analysis. The word "public" here merely points out that the policy in question is initiated and carried out by "public authorities" — those involving the state or government, or the "public" sector — as opposed to policies of "private" institutions such as chartered banks, private-sector corporations or other social organizations. The primary distinguishing feature of "public" policy, therefore, is that it is ultimately backed by the force of law and the coercive sanctions of the state.

The second half of the concept, the word "policy," has proven more difficult to delineate. As one author complained, "no term in social science has suffered more ambiguity and abuse."[1] This ambiguity stems largely from the many contexts in which the term is employed. "Policy" is applied to phenomena ranging from narrow individual decisions, such as building an airport in a particular location, to broad philosophical precepts such as a vague commitment to a "just society." However, the concept "policy" may more usefully be employed as involving a series of more or less related activities, rather than a single decision, since grandiose objectives such as "balancing the budget" involve changes in a wide range of public policies.

Between these two extremes, "policy" is used somewhat indiscriminately in at least three contexts: to describe the *intentions* of politicians, the *actions* of government, or the *impact* of government. These three usages reflect different dimensions of public policy. A policy, whether public or private, is first and foremost a program or course of action pursued in response to a particular problem or issue. But it is also, in most cases, linked to particular goals or objectives (the "intentions" of politicians). Furthermore, the study of public policy is concerned with the effects of policies on society ("the impact of government"), whether such results are the intended or unintended consequences of pursuing a certain course of action.

There is one further dimension of policy that is not revealed by any of the above interpretations of the term. On occasion, a government or some other actor may decide *not* to take action on a given problem. In this case, "policy" takes the form of inaction or non-intervention rather than a positive series of activities. This aspect of policy is well illustrated by Thomas Dye's much-quoted definition of public policy as "whatever governments choose to do or not to do."[2] **Public policy** is, therefore, the broad framework within which decisions are taken and action (or inaction) is pursued by governments in relation to some issue or problem. The study of public policy is "the study of *how, why* and to *what effect* different governments pursue particular *courses of action and inaction.*"[3]

This definition raises a further dimension of public policy analysis. How can we divide the total activities of government into more manageable chunks for the purpose of analyzing public policy? A number of classifications of types of public policy may be proposed.

The most obvious division is the traditional separation of foreign policy from domestic public policy. **Foreign policy** shapes Canada's place in the international political system and determines Canada's relations with other states and international organizations such as the United Nations and NATO. **Domestic public policy**, on the other hand, is directed toward the internal economic, social and political environment.

---

1. Eliot J. Feldman, "Review Article: Comparative Public Policy: Field or Method?" *Comparative Politics*, vol. 10, no. 2 (January 1979), p. 288.
2. Thomas R. Dye, *Understanding Public Policy*, 3rd ed. (Englewood Cliffs, N.J.: Prentice Hall, 1978), p. 3.
3. Arnold J. Heidenheimer et al., *Comparative Public Policy*, 2nd ed. (New York: St. Martin's Press, 1983), p. 4 (emphasis in original).

As the world becomes more interdependent, it is increasingly difficult to maintain a sharp distinction between domestic and foreign policy. This is especially the case for a country such as Canada whose economy is closely integrated with that of a much larger and more powerful neighbour. But, despite the gray areas created by growing interdependencies, there remains a sufficiently clear distinction between domestic and foreign policy, and the respective policy-making processes, to justify the division of these two types of government activity. Therefore, we shall conform to conventional usage by restricting our discussion of public policy to the domestic activities of government, and examine foreign policy separately in Chapter 15.

As the umbrella term "foreign policy" covers a number of government activities — ranging from functional areas such as defence, foreign aid and trade policy to policies toward specific regions or countries — so, too, may the domestic activities of government be divided into different policy areas. Again, we find that a much-used dichotomy — social policy and economic policy — serves as a basic organizing device, but may also be less meaningful when applied to specific activities and programs of government.

"Social policy" is the more easily defined. In general terms, **social policy** encompasses activities oriented toward the education, health and welfare of the population. The term "economic policy," on the other hand, may be applied to two different levels of government activity. From a macro perspective, **economic policy** refers to the overall management and stabilization of the country's economic environment; that is, to government attempts to control the money supply and interest rates, manage government spending and taxation, and foster balanced economic growth, without incurring the "twin evils" of rampant inflation and mass unemployment. Social policy cannot be divorced from economic policy in this broad sense, because public spending on social programs is manipulated to increase or deflate aggregate demand in the economy. Social expenditure is thus one of the tools available to governments in implementing macroeconomic policy. On another level, **economic policy** is a generic term for a number of sectoral policy frameworks to develop or conserve national resources, promote industrial growth, reduce regional disparities, or provide communications and transportation systems. In this sense, "economic policy" and "social policy" are more easily distinguished. Even so, some overlaps persist. For a general guide to the overall major policy concerns of Canadian governments, see "A Typology of Selected Domestic Policy Activities."

PUBLIC POLICY AND THEORIES OF POLICY-MAKING

The models and approaches used to study public policy may be distinguished from one another by their portrayal of the major actors in the policy process, their assumptions regarding the nature of society and politics, the role of government/state relations, and their evaluation of the interests served by public policy outputs. Each model or approach directs our attention to different features of public policy — they are like different lenses through which policy may be observed. They are "as indispensable to political analysis as a map or compass is to a traveller crossing unknown terrain."[4]

There is no universally accepted theory of public policy. Consequently, we outline some of the more frequently used approaches and note some of their respective strengths and weaknesses. To organize our discussion, we have divided the contending theories into two categories: **micro-level** models, which focus mainly on the making of individual policy decisions, and **macro-level** approaches,

---

4. Stephen Brooks, *Public Policy in Canada* (Toronto: McClelland & Stewart, 1989), p. 41.

CLOSE-UP ON
Public Policy

A TYPOLOGY OF SELECTED DOMESTIC POLICY ACTIVITIES

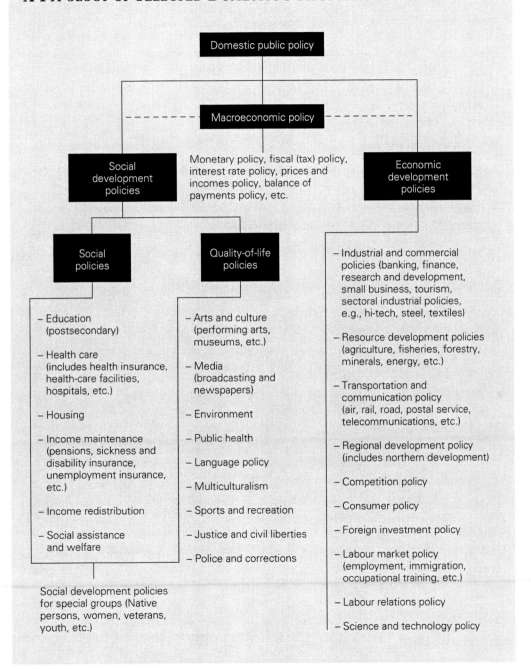

which are more concerned with accounting for broader patterns of public policy as part of the relationship between the state and society.

Micro-Level Approaches to Public Policy Analysis

Micro-level theories of decision-making are intended to explain how individual decisions are taken within a broad framework of public policy. By and large, they concentrate on the study of the selection of the best available means of achieving the goals of governmental action. They assume that governmental priorities and objectives have already been established via the political process, and tend to focus instead on the choice of means to attain those goals via the administrative process.

Over the years, the relative merits of different theories of decision-making have been debated. The most widely known controversy centres on the confrontation between advocates of the *rationalist* and *incrementalist* approaches to decision-making.[5]

The Rational-Comprehensive Model

The **rational-comprehensive** model can best be described by the elements or stages in the decision-making process. According to this idea, decision-making follows this sequence:

1. The rational decision-maker is presented with a problem that can be distinguished from other problems, or at least compared meaningfully with them.

2. The values, goals and objectives that guide the decision-maker are reviewed and ranked in order of priority.

3. A list of alternative means of achieving these goals is compiled.

4. The consequences (costs and benefits) that would ensue from each alternative are estimated.

5. Each alternative, and its likely consequences, is then compared with all other alternatives.

6. Finally, the rational decision-maker selects the course of action, and its consequences, that offers maximum attainment of the values, goals or objectives identified in Step 2.[6]

According to the advocates of this model, the end product of the process will be a "rational" decision — that is, one that selects the most effective and efficient means of achieving a given end. Ideally, the rational-comprehensive process may be the way that some decisions *ought* to be made; but does it describe accurately the way in which all, or even most, decisions are made?

Critics maintain that the rationalist model is wrong on both counts — it neither describes reality nor represents an ideal to be emulated.[7] First, it is argued that, in a complex industrial society, very few of the issues confronting governments can be singled out easily for this kind of comprehensive analysis. Second, such a process makes totally unreasonable demands on decision-makers with regard to the information needed and the time and resources necessary to evaluate the costs and benefits of all possible alternative courses of action. Thus, the model is claimed to be impractical, as the costs of undertaking a search for the most efficient means of implementation may well be greater than the savings realized by deploying it. Third, it is argued that the rational-comprehensive approach

---

5. See, especially, Charles E. Lindblom, "The Science of 'Muddling Through,'" *PAR*, vol. 19, no. 2 (Spring 1959), pp. 79–88; the critique by Yehezkel Dror, "Muddling Through — 'Science' or Inertia?"; and Lindblom's response, "Contexts for Change and Strategy: A Reply," both in *PAR*, vol. 24, no. 3 (September 1964), pp. 153–57 and 157–58.

6. Adapted from James E. Anderson, *Public Policy-Making* (New York: Holt, Rinehart and Winston, 1984), pp. 9–10.

7. See, among others, Lindblom, "The Science of 'Muddling Through.'"

is actually a normative or prescriptive model. It does not describe how decisions are actually made; rather, it *prescribes* how some people think policies and decisions *ought* to be made.

The Incrementalist Model

Charles Lindblom has advocated an alternative to the rational-comprehensive model that, he argues, is more descriptive of the way decision-makers actually proceed. This alternative approach has been variously labelled "disjointed incrementalism," "policy-making by successive limited comparisons," "the science of muddling through" or, in its simplest form, "incrementalism."[8]

The **incrementalist** model assumes that most problems facing decision-makers are complex and interrelated, and that decision-makers operate in a climate of uncertainty and limited resources. In contrast to the rational-comprehensive approach, the point of departure for incremental decision-making is not some ideal goal to be attained in the most efficient manner, but the policies and programs already in place in a given issue area. From that basis, only a limited number of policy alternatives are considered, and only a few foreseeable consequences are evaluated for each alternative. Incrementalism, therefore, results in alterations at the margins of existing policies.

The incrementalist model claims to resolve the problem of inadequate information and uncertainty, since marginal adjustments to policies and programs can easily be reversed or altered. Thus, incrementalism may be the more "rational" way to proceed, because it avoids making serious, lasting errors. Moreover, successive limited comparisons consume less time and other resources than the exhaustive search process of the rational-comprehensive model. Finally, since there is rarely agreement on the values and objectives of government intervention, an incremental approach to decision-making offers endless opportunities for redefining goals and adjusting both the means (programs, activities) and ends (values, priorities) of public policy-making.

The incrementalist approach, too, is criticized on a number of grounds. Many criticisms are subjective in nature, arguing that, whether or not the model is empirically valid, it is just not the way that decisions *should* be made. Given the preoccupation of advocates of rationalism with "improving" the decision-making process in the interests of technical efficiency, it is perhaps not surprising that they are appalled by the prospect of decision-makers "muddling through" on most issues. Yehezkel Dror has labelled Lindblom's model an inherently "conservative" recipe for maintaining the *status quo* since it provides an "ideological reinforcement of the pro-inertia and anti-innovation forces prevalent in all human organizations, administrative and policy-making."[9]

A much more important problem, in our view, is the fact that although the incrementalist model is supposed to provide a general description of how policy decisions are made by making marginal adjustments to the policies and programs already in place, it quite clearly cannot account for occasional radical departures from existing patterns of activity or inactivity. Thus, it cannot explain the entry of governments into new areas of policy intervention, nor can it account for drastic alterations to, or innovations in, existing policy.

Resolving the Rationalist versus Incrementalist Puzzle

The central problem in the rationalist/incrementalist debate is that the two sides have different conceptions of the term "model" and its functions. In political science, as in everyday language, "model" is sometimes used to refer to a normative ideal that all should seek to emulate, as in "that person is

---

8. Lindblom, "The Science of 'Muddling Through'"; David Braybrooke and Charles Lindblom, *A Strategy of Decision* (New York: Free Press, 1963), especially ch. 5; and Lindblom, "Still Muddling, Not Yet Through," *PAR*, vol. 39, no. 6 (November/December 1979), pp. 517–26.
9. Dror, "Muddling Through — 'Science' or Inertia?" p. 155.

a model citizen." But "model" is more rigorously used in the sense of a simplified version of reality designed to show how various components fit together and work, as in a "working model" of a car or steam engine. The rational-comprehensive model is of the former type, since it assumes that general agreement can be reached on long-term values and goals, and prescribes how decisions ought to be made in the interests of technical efficiency. It is, therefore, a prescriptive model to which decision-makers and policy analysts may aspire, but is strictly impractical for routine decision-making. Incrementalism, on the other hand, is a simplified "working model" that purports to explain and describe how decision-makers actually proceed. To a great extent, therefore, the two sides are advocating totally different things, and the debate between incrementalists and rationalists is based on differing conceptions of the roles and purposes of decision-making models.[10]

As a theoretical approach to aid our understanding of how decisions are made within the broader framework of public policy, the rational-comprehensive model is faulty in many respects. Incrementalism, on the other hand, is a more descriptive model that may accurately portray the tendency of governmental decision-makers to "muddle through" from day to day on many issues. But it also has limitations, inasmuch as it cannot account for key decisions such as government involvement in a new issue area, where no clear policy programs existed previously. Neither of these contending models, nor any attempt to develop a middle ground between them, has yet provided a generally accepted theory of decision-making for the study of public policy.

Decision-making is only a part of the overall process of public policy activity. Therefore, to the extent that any model can tell us *how* policy decisions are made, it still would not be able to provide guidance as to *why* governments pursue particular directions in public policy, nor *to what effect*. That requires a broader perspective on the role of the state and its relationship with society than decision-making theories can provide.

Macro-Level Approaches to Public Policy Analysis

Macro-level approaches focus on the wide relationship between state and society and, therefore, on the broad patterns of public policy, rather than on the details of how individual policy decisions are made within the government. In the pages that follow, we outline four of these approaches: *pluralism, public choice theory, neo-Marxism* and *state-centred*, together with some of their respective strengths and weaknesses, as frameworks for analyzing Canadian public policy. These theories tend to differ from one another with respect both to the relative emphasis they place on economic, social and political factors, and to their views of the interests served by the government in its policy activities.

Pluralism

The **pluralist** approach to the study of public policy emphasizes the role of political actors and organized interests in the policy process, especially parties and interest groups. Pluralists treat economic factors and cultural and ideological differences as sources of political conflict. They see shifting groups all seeking to have their members' preferences translated into public policy. These groups may be based on ethnicity, language, religion, gender, region, province, ideology or other interests. For pluralists, politics is the process by which individuals and groups seek to promote their interests through organization, political mobilization and alliance-building in order to influence the policy outputs of government. Political parties are seen as broad coalitions of interests, seeking legislative majorities in the electoral arena. Government is viewed as a neutral arbiter that referees

---

10. Smith and May, "The Artificial Debate," pp. 121–23.

the group struggle, adjudicates among competing group demands, and implements and enforces public policies in the national interest or, at least, according to the wishes of the majority on each issue.

Thus, pluralists regard public policies as the outcomes of competition between groups and parties. The essence of the pluralist approach is the assumption that power is widely dispersed in society. Since, in its *extreme* forms, pluralism does not admit to the existence of structural inequalities within society, all individuals and groups are seen as having approximately equal access to the policy-making process. Therefore, they all have potentially equal influence on public policy outputs as long as they organize themselves and play by the "rules of the game" — that is, as long as they abide by the underlying consensus on political values and procedures. The tendency for coalitions and alliances of groups to change composition from one issue to another means that there are no permanent winners and losers in the group struggle. Power, defined in simple terms as "the ability to get things done," therefore shifts from coalition to coalition according to the issue at stake and is never the exclusive preserve of any one group or elite.[11]

The more advanced schools of pluralism assert the importance of the competition between elites within an overall consensus from the mass public. In his famous volume *Capitalism, Socialism and Democracy*, Joseph Schumpeter showed how elitist decision-making could be reconciled with democracy. He compared the competition between elites for democratic votes with the operation of an economic market.[12] Later, Robert Dahl invented the term *polyarchy* to depict how minority rule could take place within a consensus on democratic values.[13]

Critics argue that some interest groups never get a fair hearing because obstacles prevent them from placing certain issues on the agenda of political debate. For example, it may be argued that the federalist organization of Canadian political life is more conducive to the expression of linguistic and regional issues than to the expression of issues based on economic class. Since many class-based issues such as labour legislation and welfare policies fall under provincial jurisdiction, it is more difficult to mobilize these interests across provincial boundaries. Thus, they are partially "organized out" of federal politics, while cultural and regional issues are "organized in."[14]

In any case, it is harder for the poor and the working class to become politically organized than for the rich or for business interests. The latter groups have more political and economic resources, and their relatively small numbers facilitate mobilization. Consequently, "the flaw in the pluralist heaven is that the heavenly chorus sings with a strong upper-class accent. Probably about 90 percent of the people cannot get into the pressure (group) system."[15]

The idea that some issues are "organized out" of politics by the "mobilization of bias" inherent in all political systems is taken a step further in the concept of *non-decision-making*. Peter Bachrach and Morton Baratz condemned the pluralists for emphasizing one aspect of power — "the ability to get things done" — to the exclusion of "the ability to stop things getting done" — the power of non-decision.[16] They argued that elite groups within or outside government take advantage of the

---

11. The classic pluralist statement of the diffusion of political power is found in Robert A. Dahl, *Who Governs?* (New Haven: Yale University Press, 1961).

12. Joseph A. Schumpeter, *Capitalism, Socialism and Democracy* (New York: Harper, 1943).

13. Robert Dahl, *A Preface to Democratic Theory* (Chicago: University of Chicago Press, 1956).

14. For a comprehensive critique of this position, see Charles Lindblom, *Politics and Markets* (New York: Basic Books, 1977); and Brooks, *Public Policy in Canada*, ch. 2.

15. E.E. Schattschneider, *The Semisovereign People: A Realist's View of Democracy in America* (Hinsdale: Dryden Press, 1975), pp. 34–35.

16. Peter Bachrach and Morton S. Baratz, "The Two Faces of Power," *APSR*, vol. 56, no. 4 (December 1962), pp. 947–52.

"mobilization of bias," a set of predominant values, beliefs, rituals and institutional procedures that operate systematically and consistently to the benefit of certain persons and groups at the expense of others in order to prevent some issues from ever reaching the agenda of political debate.[17]

Obviously, non-decisions present serious methodological problems since by their very nature they cannot readily be identified, especially where issues have been successfully suppressed or excluded from the political agenda. However, this critical approach does serve to sensitize one to the facts that some interests and issues are more easily organized than others and that various groups do not have equal political resources or enjoy equal access to the policy-making process. It is a serious criticism of the simpler forms of pluralism.

To be sure, interest groups do organize in attempts to influence policy-makers, and it is necessary to examine their effects when studying public policy, especially in a liberal democracy such as Canada where governments must maintain a degree of responsiveness to pressures from society. But, for a variety of reasons, some groups have *greater* influence on policy-making than others. The next three macro-level approaches attempt to explain why this is the case.

Public Choice Theory

Public choice analysis can be defined as "the economic study of non-market decision-making or simply the application of economics to political science."[18] The basic premise of this theory, borrowed directly from classical liberal economics, is that each individual is essentially a self-interested, rational, utility-maximizing actor. Individual wants are constrained by a world characterized by scarcity and populated by other individuals who want the same things. Thus, when people engage in collective non-market decision-making in the political arena (making "public" choices), they behave in exactly the same way that many economists believe they do when making market-oriented choices in the economic sphere — that is, they act in a rational and calculating fashion to maximize their own interests. Voters, for example, will support the party that offers programs most likely to maximize their individual well-being. Interest groups will lobby for their particular concerns. And, when politicians and bureaucrats formulate policies, they do so not according to some vague notion of "the public interest" but largely to satisfy their own narrow individual interests.

Individuals do not have equal opportunities to realize their respective interests in the public choice model, however. The average voter, for example, is fairly peripheral to the public choice view of the policy process. Voters are important only when they have the periodic opportunity to choose, through elections, which politicians will have most influence in government. Otherwise, except when they participate in an effective special interest group, ordinary citizens are little more than consumers of public policies.

According to public choice theorists, the central actors in the policy-making process are powerful interest groups, bureaucrats and politicians (especially the leaders of the governing party).[19] But this is not just pluralism in disguise. First, in the public choice approach, the primary unit of political action is the individual, not the group. Although individuals may join forces in pursuit of their interests, they do so only when collective action promises greater rewards than acting alone and when the benefits of collective action outweigh the costs of group participation. When the benefits

---

17. Peter Bachrach and Morton S. Baratz, *Power and Poverty: Theory and Practice* (New York: Oxford University Press, 1970), p. 43ff.

18. Dennis C. Mueller, *Public Choice* (Cambridge, U.K.: Cambridge University Press, 1979), p. 1.

19. Some public choice writers also include the media as a fourth influential actor in the policy process, because the media help to structure the agenda of political debate.

of group action are uncertain, or when they might possibly be derived without paying the costs of group membership, it is often more rational for the individual not to participate in collective action.

Second, some groups have more difficulty organizing and mobilizing support than others. Small, relatively homogeneous groups with much to win or lose from public policy changes, such as specific business interests, are more easily mobilized and enjoy proportionately greater resources than larger, disparate groups such as consumers or environmentalists. Thus, unlike the extreme pluralists, who consider that all groups have equal access to and potentially equal influence on the policy-making process, public choice analysts argue that "there is no reason to believe that the pressure exerted on decision-makers by special interest groups ... is in any sense balanced or fair or offsetting."[20]

The third major departure from pluralism is that public choice views government not as a neutral arbiter refereeing the group struggle in the public interest, but rather as a complex process of interaction and bargaining among bureaucrats and politicians seeking to maximize their own individual self-interests. Thus, for example, it is assumed that politicians will support policies that benefit marginal voters in order to maximize the likelihood of their election or re-election to office. Bureaucrats, on the other hand, push for policies that will expand their departmental budgets, increase the number of programs or staff under their responsibility or enhance their opportunities for promotion and influence.[21]

Although it draws upon the long-established tradition of classical economic theory, public choice as an approach to politics and public policy analysis is still a relatively underdeveloped art. Its assumptions about "rationality" have been savagely attacked by many students of politics. While its application has produced some interesting insights into the policy-making process — especially in its recognition that politicians and bureaucrats are not mere servants of external pressures, but rather have their own interests and objectives — its focus remains rather restrictive. Despite its ambitions toward formulating a more general theory of the political process, public choice theory is, at best, only a partial aid for understanding how and why public policies are developed.

Neo-Marxist Analysis

An alternative political economy approach to public policy is **neo-Marxist analysis.** Neo-Marxism is a generic label for various contemporary theories and propositions that seek to develop a systematic conceptualization of politics and the role of the state in capitalist society based upon assumptions originally formulated by Karl Marx concerning the relationships among economic, social and political structures. There are, at present, a number of strands of neo-Marxist theory; the following brief overview attempts to simplify some fairly complex concepts and arguments.

The essence of Marxist theory is that, at all stages of historical development, social and political relations are determined largely by the economic basis of society. The relations between classes are necessarily antagonistic and are based on the mode of production that exists at any given time. In the present era (the capitalist mode of production), two main social classes are differentiated by their respective economic roles: the capitalist class, or bourgeoisie, which owns and controls the means of production (factories, financial capital and so on), and the working class, or proletariat, which sells its labour to the capitalists. According to Marx's economic theory, the dynamics of capitalism require that capitalists extract "surplus value" from labour — that they effectively exploit the

---

20. Michael J. Trebilcock et al., *The Choice of Governing Instrument: A Study Prepared for the Economic Council of Canada* (Ottawa: Supply and Services, 1982), p. 10.

21. See Mark Sproule-Jones, "Institutions, Constitutions and Public Policies," in Michael M. Atkinson and Marsha A. Chandler, *The Politics of Canadian Public Policy* (Toronto: University of Toronto Press, 1983), p. 127.

working class — because this is the chief mechanism whereby capitalists make profits for further investment and accumulation of capital. This exploitative economic relationship between capital and labour forms the basis for unequal, conflictual class relations in social and political life.

According to Marxists, the primary function of the state in capitalist society is to serve the interests of capitalism by creating and maintaining conditions favourable to profitable capital accumulation. However, in order to reduce conflict between classes and forestall the possibility of revolution by the exploited working class, the liberal democratic state must also create and maintain conditions of social harmony by providing policies that legitimize the capitalist society. Marxists believe that one of the factors in state survival is the dominant ideology of capitalist countries. This includes beliefs about private property, the possibility of upward socioeconomic mobility and the economic market, all of which buttress the role of the state and make it difficult for the vast majority of individuals to understand that they are being exploited.

Most public policies, in the neo-Marxist view, may be categorized roughly according to their intentions or effects as serving either the *accumulation* or *legitimation* functions of the capitalist state. Examples of accumulation-oriented policies in the Canadian context include the provision of industrial infrastructure (e.g., transportation networks, public utilities such as hydro), subsidies or tax expenditures for private-sector businesses, and fiscal and monetary policies aimed at creating a healthy climate for investment. Legitimation policies would include most social welfare programs, occupational health and safety regulations, environmental pollution controls and language and cultural policies. Some programs or policies, however, may serve both accumulation and legitimation roles; hence these two functions are not necessarily mutually exclusive. For example, the introduction of free, mass education may enhance the legitimacy of the state in the short term but, by providing a better-trained, more skilled labour force, it may also aid capital accumulation.[22]

The key question in neo-Marxist analysis, of course, is why the state pursues particular public policies and courses of action. The **instrumentalist** view of the state suggests that it serves the interests of the capitalist class because of the strong links (common class backgrounds, family ties and old school networks) that exist between political and bureaucratic elites and the business community.[23] The **structuralist** view argues that the capitalist class is itself internally divided into a number of competing elements or *factions* (finance capital, manufacturing capital, resource capital, etc.). Hence, the state must be *relatively autonomous* or independent so that it can serve the long-term interests of capitalism rather than the short-term profit-maximizing interests of individual capitalists.[24] Therefore, the state often pursues policies such as social welfare programs that respond to working-class demands even if these policies are opposed by much of the capitalist class.

If one accepts the premises on which their arguments are based, neo-Marxist analyses can be seen to account for broad patterns in public policy in different societies and for the expanding economic and social activities of the state over time. For example, since Marxist economics predicts that the rate of return on capital investment tends to fall as capitalism progresses, it becomes increasingly necessary for governments to underwrite some of the costs of production (e.g., by subsidizing research and development expenditures). Neo-Marxist analysis is also explicitly oriented toward matters of inequality and distribution of power in Canadian society. In addition, more than any other approach

22. For further discussion of the functions of the Canadian state, see Leo Panitch, "The Role and Nature of the Canadian State," in Leo Panitch, ed., *The Canadian State: Political Economy and Political Power* (Toronto: University of Toronto Press, 1977), pp. 3–27.

23. See, for example, Ralph Miliband, *The State in Capitalist Society* (London: Weidenfeld and Nicolson, 1969).

24. The state is only "relatively" autonomous because its activities are constrained by the underlying social and economic (class) relations in society. See Nicos Poulantzas, *Political Power and Social Classes* (London: New Left Books, 1973).

considered here, it addresses issues of external constraints on Canadian policy-making, especially in an era of extensive foreign ownership, multinational corporations and the interdependence of capitalist economies. But, despite numerous attempts to get inside the policy process and to develop a neo-Marxist approach to public policy analysis, neo-Marxism remains unclear on exactly how the state makes specific policy choices or decisions at particular moments in time.

State-Centred Analysis

A state-centred approach blossomed in the study of comparative politics and, to a lesser degree, in the examination of Canadian public policy in the 1980s and 1990s.[25] Its advocates object to the notion that social forces determine what state authorities do. Instead, they view the state as able to act independently of the demands of society. The state is visualized as "autonomous," independent of the public's interests, as expressed in the pluralist or public choice models, and certainly not derivative of class interests, as found in neo-Marxist thought.

According to the rawest form of this type of explanation of public policy, government officials can act in any way they determine is best for the country — irrespective of demands from society. In other words, the argument is state-centred and not society-centred. Although some attention is paid to the role of elected politicians, much of the research based on this approach focuses on bureaucratic politics: how unelected officials (public servants, judges, police and military) initiate and implement public policy.

This state-centred approach is based on the assumption that those individuals with the greatest knowledge determine to a great extent the policy outputs of a society. Apparently, the modern world requires legislation and policy that is based on expertise not possessed by the mass public, interest groups or transient politicians. Since the bureaucracy is the only permanent repository of the knowledge required to carry out modern government, it is able to use this information to manipulate societal forces. Bureaucrats derive their power from the institutions that empower them, and the perceptions and actions of these officials are in turn shaped by the very institutions that they serve.

This approach has been attacked as being based on untenable assumptions. First, the knowledge required to govern the country is not "scientific." Those who determine the direction of public policy are those who possess and convince others to accept a guiding philosophy for the direction of governmental action. After the politicians determine the priorities — which is more a question of philosophy or personal choice than scientific knowledge — the public servants are left with the administration of this choice, which is much less significant than the choice of policy orientation. Second, many members of the senior bureaucracy in Canada are as transient as some leading politicians. Deputy ministers may be dismissed, and often are, while some Cabinet members remain in the government much longer than a decade.

Third, despite the state-centred assumption that political parties do not present policy alternatives — often the case in Canada — it is not always true. The 1988 election provided a clear-cut choice between those parties that favoured a free trade deal with the United States and those that did not. Moreover, referendums, such as the one on the Charlottetown accord, allow the public direct decision-making power. In that particular vote, the people chose a course of action diametrically opposed to that put forward by almost every political leader and bureaucrat in the country. Fourth, the

---

25. The classic literature includes James G. March and Johan P. Olsen, "The New Institutionalism: Organizational Factors in Political Life," *APSR*, vol. 78, no. 3 (September 1984), pp. 734–49; and Peter B. Evans, Dietrich Rueschemeyer and Theda Skocpol, eds., *Bringing the State Back In* (Cambridge, U.K.: Cambridge University Press, 1985). For a critique, see Gabriel A. Almond, *A Discipline Divided: Schools and Sects in Political Science* (Newbury Park: Sage, 1990).

bureaucracy cannot act in isolation. Even if the politician's role is discounted, the bureaucrats need the help of interest groups. Specific sectors of the public service ally themselves with societal interests to forge "policy communities."[26] This effort to save the hypothesis that the state drives public policy by adding pluralist assumptions to the model merely highlights the weaknesses in the theory.

The extent to which the state-centred approach provides a new paradigm for analysis is hotly contested. Some theorists call it a pernicious fad that caricatures pluralism and neo-Marxism without itself being able to sustain its argument without adding ideas from earlier approaches.[27]

The Approaches Compared

It has been argued that a comprehensive approach to the study of public policy must involve at least three levels of analysis. For example, according to Richard Simeon, although the policy process itself has "some independent effect on policy outcomes," it also reflects and is shaped by a broader framework that imposes constraints on the alternative policies considered by policy-makers and on their freedom of action.[28] This broader framework consists of two sets of factors. Furthest removed from the policy process are the resources and constraints that flow from the social and economic environments. But the effects of these influences are profoundly shaped by a number of important intervening factors, including the system of power relations, the dominant values and ideas of society and the structure of political institutions. The combination of these three levels of analysis "suggests a sort of funnel of causality." In this model of policy analysis, all three groups of factors are considered relevant, but the relative importance of factors in determining actual policy outputs increases as the "funnel" narrows from left to right. (See Figure 14.1.)

We have noted that no single approach to policy analysis has gained overall acceptance. One reason is that the various approaches tend to focus on particular aspects of the policy process — on different parts of the "funnel." For example, micro-level models such as incrementalism and rationalism and, to a lesser extent, the public choice macro-level approach are more concerned with the process of policy-making *inside* government than with the wider relationship *between* government and its socioeconomic environment or broader questions of the distribution of power, ideas and institutions.

The neo-Marxist and pluralist approaches bring together more elements from the "funnel." Neo-Marxists explicitly address the influence of the economic and social environments, linking the role of the state to changes in the social structure and the economy. In addition, inequalities in power, income and resources between social classes, and the role of ideology and values are central themes in neo-Marxist analysis. However, as we have already noted, this approach has not yet come to terms with the influence of independent actors within the policy-making process in determining public policy outcomes such as those found in the state-centred approaches.

The pluralist approach implicitly takes into account the socioeconomic environment, since the growing complexity of industrial society gives rise to more and more issues and interests for which groups may be mobilized. Pluralists emphasize the interaction of interest groups with the policy-making process; they also stress the mediating effects of institutions such as the electoral process. However, the traditional pluralist view has often been criticized for its failure to recognize inequalities of power and influence and for its emphasis on government as a reactive agent — as a neutral arbiter that responds only to the balance of group pressures. Today, many authors in the pluralist

26. William Coleman and Grace Skogstad, eds., *Policy Communities and Public Policy in Canada* (Mississauga: Copp Clark Pitman, 1991).

27. See Gabriel A. Almond, "The Return to the State," *APSR*, vol. 82, no. 3 (September 1988), pp. 853–74.

28. Richard Simeon, "Studying Public Policy," *CJPS*, vol. 9, no. 4 (December 1976), p. 556.

FIGURE 14.1   POLICY "FUNNEL OF CAUSALITY"

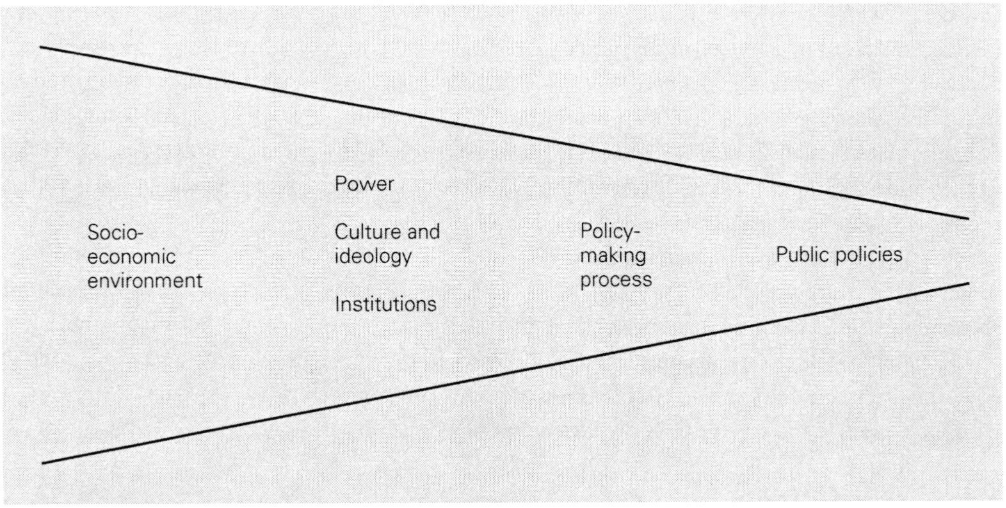

Source: Graphic adaptation of ideas discussed in Richard Simeon, "Studying Public Policy," *CJPS*, vol. 9, no. 4 (December 1976), esp. p. 556.

tradition allow that the modern state possesses its own dynamic in the policy process.[29] But, while the granting of "autonomy" to the state or government frees it from being a mere cipher of group demands, the argument fails to develop a comprehensive analysis of how, why and to what effect the state takes advantage of its newly discovered freedom.

A further problem that has served to inhibit the emergence of a generally accepted approach to public policy analysis lies in the ideological and political rhetoric associated with some of the theories sketched out above. Too often, theoretical models of public policy are used for support rather than illumination. This problem is particularly acute in the case of the two so-called political economy approaches — public choice and neo-Marxism.

The public choice argument that politicians and bureaucrats pursue their own interests in formulating public policies rather than some vague notion of the public interest is attractive to those who think that government has grown too large and that public expenditures have risen out of control. By providing a theoretical rationale for allegations of bureaucratic empire-building and for the supposed self-serving actions of politicians, public choice lends additional weight to the arguments of neo-conservatives who wish to lower tax rates, reduce the size of the bureaucracy and social programs and generally "get government off the backs of the private sector."

While public choice theory may reinforce the negative views that many people hold toward bureaucrats and politicians, the assumptions of neo-Marxism tend to challenge the way most North American citizens think about politics. Indeed, it provides a critical, alternative way of looking at the role of the state in Canada and makes one question assumptions about the way government operates. However, neo-Marxist analysis often is also difficult to disentangle from ideological rhetoric. Many critics believe that it is impossible to use neo-Marxist concepts as an approach to analysis without also adhering to the ideology of Marxism, with its prescription for the revolutionary

---

29. Eric A. Nordlinger, *On the Autonomy of the Democratic State* (Cambridge, Mass.: Harvard University Press, 1981). Michael Laslovich has applied this idea to Canadian transportation policy; see his "Changing the Crow Rate: State-Societal Interaction" (unpublished Ph.D. thesis, Carleton University, 1987).

overthrow of capitalist society. Others simply refuse to accept the premises of class division and conflict on which neo-Marxist theories of the state are based. In either case, strong opposition is further reinforced by the determinist and hyper-theoretical nature of much neo-Marxist writing.

Rather than promoting research that will enhance understanding of the policy process and the role of the state or government in formulating and implementing public policies, both public choice and neo-Marxist analysis may be reduced to facile sloganeering. By attributing every perceived evil of the modern state to the self-interest of bureaucrats or to the inequities of capitalism, political economy is sometimes reduced to *polemical* economy.

For a variety of reasons, therefore, it is extremely unlikely that any of the approaches outlined in this section will emerge as a universally accepted theory of public policy-making. But these models do represent the dominant frameworks of analysis found in the current literature on public policy. Each approach has its strengths and weaknesses in explaining how, why and to what effect governments choose to act on certain issues. Students of Canadian politics should be conversant with these models and be able to apply them to policy decisions and policy frameworks.

POLICY INSTRUMENTS AND PROCESSES

Public policy-making and decision-making are not restricted to setting governmental objectives and priorities; they also entail selecting means by which these ends are to be achieved. **Policy instruments** relate to the methods used by governments to attain their policy goals. This section illustrates the range of instruments that governments have at their disposal when attempting to put policy proposals into effect.

Exhortation and Symbolic Outputs

Exhortation (or, as it is sometimes called, "suasion") consists of a variety of attempts by policy-makers to induce individuals and groups to comply *voluntarily* with government objectives. Whatever the examples cited — from television chats by the prime minister urging economic restraint through government-sponsored advertising extolling the benefits of the Charlottetown accord — exhortation is widely used by governments trying to change patterns of private behaviour. (See Figure 14.2.)

Exhortation is often used in pursuit of specific objectives when the government is unable to resort to other policy instruments such as taxation or regulation. **Symbolic policy outputs**, on the other hand, are mainly ways of demonstrating government concern over an issue; they are often used when no clear policy response has yet been formulated, but the government must be seen to be "doing something" about the perceived problem. Examples of symbolic policies include ministerial speeches and resolutions on pressing issues, or the establishment of special committees or royal commissions on matters of public concern. Sometimes these symbolic acts are accompanied or quickly followed by more substantive policy responses, such as the allocation of new public funds to deal with a problem area. But they may also be used as a form of "non-decision-making," to defuse or deflect public opinion and to delay action on an issue of perceived importance. Too much smoke and mirrors, however, may eventually alienate rather than placate the electorate.

Expenditure Instruments

To a certain extent, all government actions involve public expenditure — for example, even advocacy advertising must be paid for, as must the administrative costs of royal commissions. As a distinct category of policy instruments, however, **public expenditures** refer to those funds that are

FIGURE 14.2 INSTRUMENTS OF GOVERNING

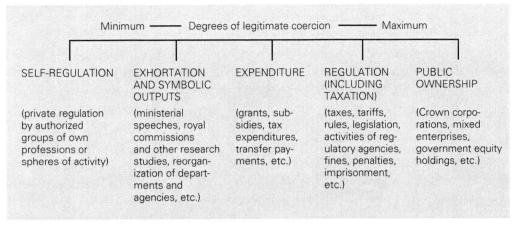

Source: Adapted from G. Bruce Doern and Richard W. Phidd, *Canadian Public Policy: Ideas, Structure, Process* (Toronto: Methuen, 1983), Figure 5.1, p.111, and Figure 5.3, p. 134.

explicitly directed toward achieving government objectives. The most obvious is the provision of direct transfers to individuals — old-age pensions, child allowances, unemployment insurance — in order to redistribute income. As well, the federal government also makes fiscal transfers to provinces, to ease regional disparities and contribute to the funding of social programs such as health care and postsecondary education. These transfer expenditures (directly to individuals or via transfers to provinces) account for more than half of federal government spending.

But expenditure instruments may also be used in other policy areas. In recent years, the federal government has employed a broad array of subsidies, grants, loans and loan guarantees to aid new enterprises, to bail out troubled firms, to promote small business and so on. Furthermore, the government's own capital expenditures not only attain immediate objectives such as the modernization of port and rail facilities, but may also serve indirectly to approach other goals, for instance, by the awarding of contracts to firms from economically depressed areas. The present Liberal government, despite its reluctance to talk about its handouts to industry, has given many gifts to businesses — tax concessions to oil-sand producers in northern Alberta, compensation packages to fisheries on both coasts, an $87 million loan to Québec-based Bombardier Inc. and a bail-out to Canadian Airlines.

Also of interest to policy analysts is a less visible subcategory of expenditure instruments, known as "tax expenditures." **Tax expenditures** are the revenues foregone by the government by providing tax deductions or tax credits to individuals and corporations. Some deductions for individual taxpayers are intended to encourage personal spending on "socially desirable" purposes such as charitable donations and Registered Retirement Savings Plans (RRSPs), while others, including medical expense deductions and child tax credits for low-income families, are part of the social safety net of the welfare state. In the corporate tax sector, too, there are two major categories of tax expenditures: those that give preferential treatment to certain kinds of income (e.g., small business tax credits) and those that reward certain objectives of corporate spending (e.g., investment tax credits and allowances for research and development expenditures).

Since tax expenditures are revenues forgone by the government rather than funds collected and subsequently disbursed, they are less easily quantified than ordinary expenditures, which must be accounted for in the expenditure-budgetary process. Some studies estimate that the volume of tax expenditures has grown rapidly in recent years. At the same time, there has been concern that tax

POLITICAL PLOY # 3726

DO IT DURING THE PLAYOFFS!...

Reproduced with permission, Dennis Pritchard.

expenditures favour upper-income earners and profitable corporations, thereby counter-acting redistributive effects else-where in the expenditure and tax processes.

Regulation

Regulation can be viewed *politically* as rules of behaviour backed up directly by the legitimate sanctions of the state. From this broad perspective, the concept of **regulation** comprises all rules of conduct imposed by government on individual and corporate citizens. It encompasses statutory legislation (including, for example, the Criminal Code), the tax system, as well as the activities of semi-autonomous regulatory agencies that lay down codes of conduct within their respective spheres of operation. In this broad sense, in addition to regulatory agencies, the actors in the regulatory process include Parliament and Cabinet, which formulate regulations, and bureaucratic departments, the police and the court system, which administer and enforce them. However, much of the emphasis in the public policy literature on regulation is about the more limited area of regulation of private *economic* activity. From this narrower perspective, regulation is sometimes seen as a policy instrument aimed at forcing private economic actors to adopt behaviour that they would not normally choose in the absence of regulation, that is, in a completely *laissez-faire*, free-market economy. The study of economic regulation, therefore, focuses on "public intervention by way of non-market controls in a mixed but primarily market-oriented economy."[30]

Governments impose non-market controls on private economic behaviour in many areas. Direct economic regulation includes government action to control prices and rates of return (e.g., telephone rates), entry to the market (e.g., broadcasting licences for television and radio stations), market exit (e.g., ensuring that railways or public utilities serve remote communities) and output (e.g., supply management by agricultural marketing boards). In addition, governments may also regulate economic behaviour in pursuit of social objectives such as "health, safety and fairness."[31]

In summary, then, governments use regulation as a policy instrument for one of three purposes: to remedy market failures, to serve as an instrument of redistribution, and to meet social and cultural objectives.[32] However, to the extent that some of these objectives might be met by other policy instruments, there may be a political rationale for the choice of regulation to achieve policy goals, in addition to economic, social and cultural objectives. Regulation may be managed directly by government departments, as in the case of most forms of social regulation; it may be delegated to semi-autonomous agencies such as the Canadian Radio-television and Telecommunications

---

30. Richard J. Schultz, *Federalism and the Regulatory Process* (Montréal: Institute for Research on Public Policy, 1977), p. 8.

31. Economic Council of Canada, *Responsible Regulation*, pp. 43–45.

32. Ibid., pp. 45–52; and Schultz, *Federalism and the Regulatory Process*, pp. 9–12.

Commission, the Canadian Transport Commission and the National Energy Board; or powers of self-regulation may be granted to professional associations such as medical and bar associations.

Regulatory regimes are comparatively inexpensive. In an era of widespread criticism of growing federal spending and budgetary deficits, regulation is therefore an attractive option for governments seeking an instrument to realize policy goals. The major cost of regulation, it is argued, is that of compliance, borne not by government, but by businesses, shareholders and consumers in the private sector. Consequently, there has been growing support in Canada for "deregulation," for lessening the constraints on private behaviour in certain sectors of the economy — evidenced, for example, by the abandonment of regulated oil and gas pricing. At the same time, however, it is apparent that many powerful vested interests support the continuation of regulatory regimes.

Public Ownership

Public ownership or **public enterprise** — the direct provision of goods and services by corporations owned partly or wholly by the government — has a long history in Canada at both the federal and provincial levels. Indeed, some observers have labelled Canada a "public enterprise culture."[33] Among major federal enterprises, the most enduring has been the Canadian National Railways, which was finally privatized in 1995. It was established soon after the First World War, but it was predated by provincially owned enterprises such as Ontario Hydro and publicly owned telephone systems in the Prairies. From these early beginnings, public ownership has expanded to other transportation, energy and communications facilities, as well as resource development, manufacturing, finance and a number of other sectors of the economy. Today, several federal public corporations such as the Canada Post Corporation and the Canadian Wheat Board can be found among Canada's largest business enterprises.

The realm of public ownership partly overlaps that of Crown corporations (discussed in detail in Chapter 10) but the two are not identical. Federal agencies classified as Crown corporations may be mechanisms for policy implementation or advisory bodies that contribute to the formation of public policy. On the other side of the coin, public ownership need not entail 100 percent government ownership and control. Apart from wholly owned Crown corporations and their subsidiaries, governments may turn to mixed (public-private) enterprises or to equity-holding (share-holding) in a private company in their attempts to realize certain policy goals.

As these examples illustrate, the objectives of public ownership as a policy instrument are many and varied. Some early public enterprises, such as state-owned railways and Trans-Canada Airlines (later Air Canada), were established to develop essential economic infrastructure in situations where "the private sector was unwilling or unable to take the initiative."[34] These transportation facilities also played a part in national integration; a similar motive lay behind the creation of the Canadian Radio Broadcasting Commission (now the CBC) in 1932. Other public enterprises have been founded to provide financial infrastructure for the Canadian economy. Thus, the Canadian Business Development Bank and the Export Development Corporation were designed to "fill gaps in the financial system and to assist interests whose financial needs were only partially met by established (private) leaders."[35] As well, public ownership has been used to develop enterprises involving high cost or commercial

33. Herschel Hardin, *A Nation Unaware: The Canadian Economic Culture* (Vancouver: J.J. Douglas Ltd., 1974).

34. John W. Langford, "Crown Corporations as Instruments of Policy," in G. Bruce Doern and Peter Aucoin, eds., *Public Policy in Canada* (Toronto: Macmillan, 1971), p. 248.

35. Allan Tupper and G. Bruce Doern, "Understanding Public Corporations in Canada," *Canadian Business Review*, vol. 9, no. 3 (Autumn 1982), p. 34.

risks that were deemed to be in the long-term public interest. For example, federal government involvement in Atomic Energy of Canada is intended to foster new technologies.[36]

In many of these cases, public enterprises complemented, rather than competed with, the interests of the private sector. In recent years, however, more controversial examples of government ownership have brought the public sector into conflict with private enterprise over market shares and investment resources. Opposition to public ownership crystallized around two major issues: first, the growing concern about a perceived lack of accountability of Crown corporations; second, the losses suffered in recent years by some corporations. These issues have lent extra ammunition to arguments that resources devoted to public enterprise might be more profitably and efficiently allocated in the private sector. Critics of public ownership have adopted as a solution to both problems the "privatization" of a number of Crown corporations.

Between 1984 and 1993, the federal Conservative government privatized many Crown corporations, in particular those that functioned as private enterprises. Arguing that the private sector operates more efficiently than the public sector, and that the government had to reduce the deficit, the Tories sold off such illustrious Crown corporations as Air Canada, CN Hotels, CN Route, Canadair, de Havilland Aircraft, Eldorado Nuclear, Fisheries Products International, Northern Transportation Commission, Petro-Canada and Teleglobe Canada. As well, Canada Post Corporation was changed from a government department to a Crown corporation so that it could function like a private enterprise. However, the federal government kept some enterprises intact and the provinces retained their public enterprises such as Ontario Hydro and Hydro-Québec.

Public ownership continues to be under fire from neo-conservatives, who view any government intervention as an infringement upon the supremacy of the free-market economy. Thus, while it is improbable that privatization will be carried as far as it has been in some countries, it seems certain that public ownership will be much less prominent within the federal government's arsenal of public policy instruments during the twenty-first century and that the present "privatization" projects will continue.

Policy Instruments and the Policy Process

There are several academic approaches to explain how and why particular policy instruments are chosen by governments. One is based on a continuum of governing instruments. Some scholars hypothesize that "politicians have a strong tendency to respond to policy issues by moving successively from the *least coercive* governing instrument to the *most coercive.*"[37] Applied to the continuum (as shown in Figure 14.2), this idea suggests that governments tend to respond first with symbolic outputs such as the establishment of a royal commission and with attempts to secure voluntary compliance through exhortation. Later, however, they may shift to expenditure instruments and, if these incentives are insufficient to ensure compliance with policy objectives, they may subsequently deploy more coercive measures such as regulation or even public ownership. Thus, Allan Tupper and G. Bruce Doern suggest that in the majority of cases they studied "the direct ownership instrument was selected *after* extensive use of other instruments including regulation, spending and taxation."[38]

However, when adopting new instruments as they move along the continuum, policy-makers rarely discontinue the use of less coercive means. Instruments, differentiated from each other by

---

36. Marsha Gordon, *Government in Business* (Montréal: C. D. Howe Institute, 1981), ch. 6.

37. G. Bruce Doern and V. Seymour Wilson, eds., *Issues in Canadian Public Policy* (Toronto: Macmillan, 1974), p. 339 (emphasis in original).

38. Tupper and Doern, "Public Corporations and Public Policy in Canada," p. 19 (emphasis in original).

the degrees of coercion attributed to them, are therefore additive or complementary in nature, rather than constituting alternatives. Thus, when public enterprises are established, rather than re-placing other measures, "public ownership is more frequently *added* to an array of existing instru-ments that have been tried and found wanting, or at least are *believed* to be found wanting."[39]

At first glance, this hypothesis of instrument choice appears plausible, although both it and the continuum from which it is derived are based on some assumptions that may not be accept-able to all public policy analysts. It does have the advantage that it can be tested empirically. However, applications of the hypothesis to different fields of public policy have yielded mixed results. While the study of some policy areas such as energy policy supports the contention that governments progress along the continuum in developing policy responses (leaving regulation and especially public ownership as a last resort), examination of sectors such as broadcasting policy indicates that public ownership was among the first instruments deployed by the federal government.

A full explanation for the selection of policy instruments by governments has to take into account a multiplicity of economic, legal, political and external constraints on governmental freedom of choice. For example, within the Canadian federal system, governments are precluded from using the full range of instruments in some policy areas by the constitutional division of powers among ju-risdictions. Thus, the federal government is effectively limited to exhortation and spending in many fields of Canadian social policy. Economic constraints in a period of growing criticism of the expansion of public expenditures and budgetary deficits make both regulation and relatively hidden tax in-centives more attractive than large, visible spending programs. International agreements such as the General Agreement on Tariffs and Trade (GATT) militate against raising tariffs (a form of tax-ation or regulation) and force governments to resort to alternative methods (non-tariff barriers) to control the volume of imports flowing into the country. Even the nature of the policy-making process itself may have an effect. While routine, day-to-day or year-to-year policy-making may tend toward the kind of incrementalist instrument selection hypothesized above, one study of policy-making in crisis management situations shows that, after initial symbolic responses, gov-ernments are most likely to resort to highly coercive instruments, including emergency regulations and the deployment of armed forces. Only after the crisis is over will they return to legislation and public spending in order to pre-empt the occurrence of further crises.[40]

Clearly, we need to learn more about the dynamics of public policy-making in order to reach a more complete explanation of the choice of policy instruments by governments. But while the concept of a continuum of governing instruments has weaknesses, it has proven to be a useful heuristic device in promoting research and in sensitizing policy analysts to the multiplicity of means of policy implementation that governments have at their disposal.

THE GROWTH AND SIZE OF THE CANADIAN STATE

The proportion of total national income spent by the various levels of government has increased greatly over the years. However, the rate has by no means been constant; there have been distinct periods of growth and decline. Moreover, the overall growth disguises substantial shifts in the relative importance of different levels of government. Seventy-five years ago, local and municipal

---

39. Ibid.
40. Robert J. Jackson, "Crisis Management and Policy-Making," in Richard Rose, ed., *The Dynamics of Public Policy* (Beverly Hills, Ca.: Sage Publications, 1976), p. 214.

FIGURE 14.3 FEDERAL FINANCIAL SURPLUS (+) / REQUIREMENTS (-), PUBLIC ACCOUNTS BASIS

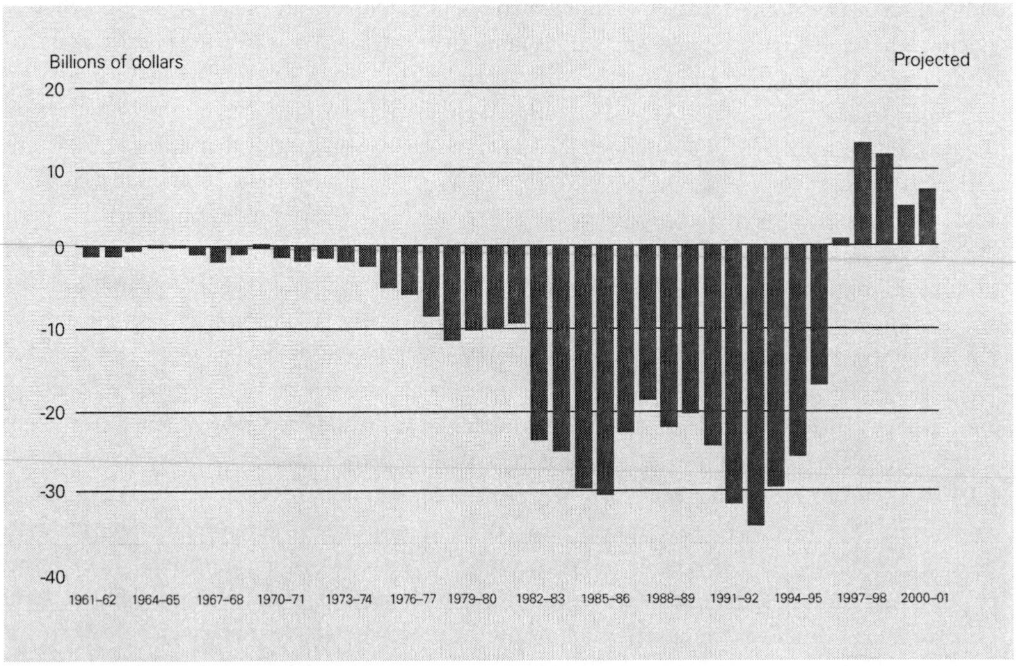

Source: *The Budget Chart Book 1999.*

governments were the biggest spenders, since they were primarily responsible for financing education and limited social welfare functions. During the Great Depression, local and provincial governments were unable to cope with demands on their budgets, so the federal government began to spend more; it continued to do so to meet the costs of the war effort. Since the mid-1960s, the largest increase in expenditure has occurred at the provincial level. However, it is also true that until recently federal spending in dollar terms has risen substantially.

In 1996–97, the federal government spent about $159 billion, compared with only $13 billion in 1971. Of course, government expenditure has to be paid for out of revenues. Like expenditures, the revenues of all levels of government have had to increase over the last half century. In 1996–97, the federal government raised about $135 billion, leaving a federal deficit of approximately $24 billion. By the end of 1997, the national debt was projected to be about $603 billion. Of course, it is important to relate the size of the Canadian deficit/debt to the size and strength of the economy — in 1996–97 the GDP was calculated at $806 billion, making the debt equal to 75 percent of the GDP. For a comparison of Canada with other G-7 countries, see Figure 14.5. The financial problems are not limited to the federal government; provincial deficits, too, escalated in the early 1990s before being brought under control. (See Figure 14.6.)

Not all state activity is measurable in terms of public expenditure. While many public policies do require the outlay of money, others need very little — particularly those that seek to regulate or control the behaviour of either individual or corporate members of society. Thus, as the state has become more involved in its citizens' lives, the volume of legislation, statutes and regulations has increased. This aspect of the growth of the Canadian state was aptly summarized by former Conservative justice minister Senator Jacques Flynn in a speech to the Canadian Bar Association:

FIGURE 14.4 FEDERAL PROGRAM SPENDING, PUBLIC ACCOUNTS BASIS

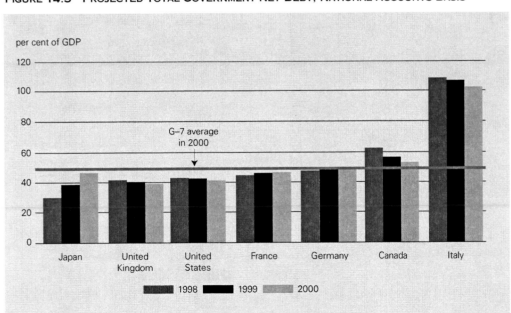

Sources: *The Budget Chart Book 1999.*

FIGURE 14.5 PROJECTED TOTAL GOVERNMENT NET DEBT, NATIONAL ACCOUNTS BASIS

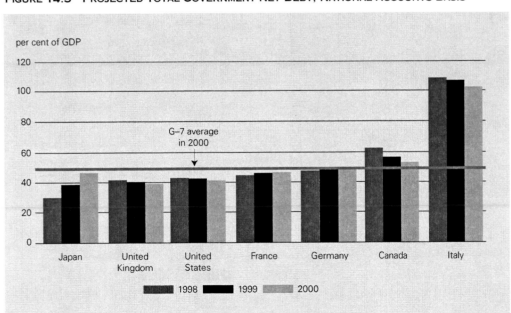

Source: *The Budget Chart Book 1999.*

> *We recently published a consolidation of federal regulations — 15,563 pages of them. Add to that 10,000 pages of Revised Statutes (Canada's Statutes were last revised and consolidated in 1970) and 8,000 to 10,000 pages of Statutes since the revision, plus hundreds of thousands of pages of provincial laws and regulations to say nothing of municipal by-laws, orders and regulations. Now you begin to realize that we've come a long way from 10 clauses on a slab of stone.*[41]

Finally, as the state has increasingly intervened in social and economic life, so the actual machinery of government has become more complex. The number of federal government departments and branches quadrupled between 1870 and 1990. There are approximately 400 federal government Crown corporations and agencies, of which almost half were created after 1970. Similarly, the number of people employed by the federal state has also grown to about half a million. As in the case of public expenditure, however, the "real" growth in terms of the percentage of total employment in the public sector has been relatively much smaller.[42]

In 1960, for example, federal government employment constituted 5.2 percent of the total labour force; in 1994 the public sector employed 19.1 percent of the total labour force, higher than in the United States, the same as in Britain, and lower than in France, Germany, Italy and Sweden.

FIGURE 14.6 FEDERAL AND PROVINCIAL-TERRITORIAL SURPLUS (+) / DEFICIT (–), PUBLIC ACCOUNTS BASIS

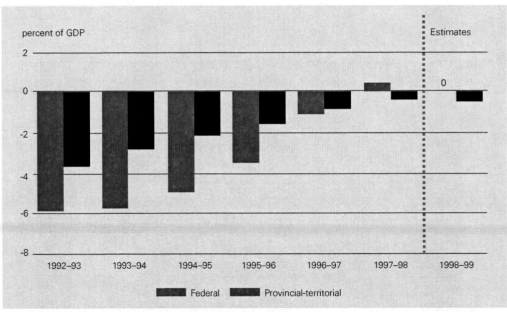

Source: *The Budget Chart Book 1999.*

41. Quoted by Donald John Purich, "Too Many Laws? There May Not Be Enough!" *The Chronicle-Herald*, Halifax, February 2, 1980.
42. Richard M. Bird et al., *The Growth of Public Employment in Canada* (Scarborough: Butterworths, for the Institute for Research on Public Policy, 1979), p. 43.

Whichever indicators we choose, it is unarguable that in Canada the state has grown over the last century — or even the last 20 years — although when measured in real terms this expansion is by no means as large as some critics of government intervention would suggest. Still, the question remains: How do we account for the growth of the state?

Explanations for the Growth and Size of the State

Why did the government, or the public sector, grow in Canada? So many authors have attempted to explain the growth of the state in Canada that, according to Richard Bird,

> ... *the problem is not that there are no explanations of the growth of government in Canada since the war: it is rather that there are too many explanations, each one of which probably contains both some truth and some misleading elements.*[43]

In the following discussion, we focus on the more pertinent among this plethora of explanations. We begin with historical and theoretical arguments.

Most of the major federal programs that comprise the modern Canadian welfare state were initiated or consolidated in the quarter-century after the Second World War, including hospital and medical insurance, the Canada and Québec pension plans, the Canada Assistance Plan and federal participation in other shared-cost programs such as postsecondary education. These were added to such wartime initiatives as unemployment insurance and family allowances to create a comprehensive package of social and welfare programs.

The expansion of state activities can be attributed to a number of factors. First, the period was marked by the emergence of Keynesian economics as the dominant paradigm of macroeconomic management in western industrial societies. The Keynesian model legitimized large-scale government intervention as a means of manipulating the level of aggregate demand to control the kind of extreme cyclical fluctuations in the economy that had given rise to the Great Depression of the 1930s. It should be noted, however, that Keynesian economics was never fully implemented in Canada, since, even though successive federal governments intervened to boost aggregate demand as an incentive to economic growth, they rarely followed Keynes' prescriptions of expenditure cutbacks and tax hikes to deflate the economy in times of expansion and inflation.

Second, the period from 1945 to 1970 was, by and large, an era of rapid and sustained economic growth fuelled by postwar reconstruction, the injection of foreign investment and the spread of mass affluence. This economic growth led to an expansion of government revenues through increasing tax returns and enhanced the fiscal capacity of the state to intervene. It also enabled the government to involve itself in major redistributive programs, since there were sufficient resources to distribute to the less privileged without depriving more affluent and politically influential groups of a share of the ever-expanding national pie.

From a pluralist perspective, therefore, the government as neutral arbiter was able to satisfy the demands of more societal groups, including an increasingly influential labour movement that had organized behind the trade unions and the growing electoral force of the CCF/NDP. In the public choice and state-centred views, however, the growth of the state could be attributed to the competitive bidding practices of party politicians anxious to gain governmental power and to the

---

43. Richard M. Bird, *Financing Canadian Government: A Quantitative Overview* (Toronto: Canadian Tax Foundation, 1979), p. 82 (emphasis in original).

expansionist tendencies of bureaucrats seeking to enlarge their spheres of influence in the policy process.

The neo-Marxist approach would interpret the growth of the state in different terms again. The need to promote accumulation of private capital after the war required the state to intervene on behalf of capital through incentives to investment, by boosting aggregate demand (e.g., universal child allowances) and by helping to underwrite the costs of reproducing the labour force (e.g., health and education policies). At the same time, the growing power of organized labour led the state to introduce programs that helped to legitimate its capital accumulation role and disguise the exploitative nature of capitalism. As capitalism becomes increasingly monopolistic and as the rate of profit falls (a central tenet of Marxist economics), the state will intervene more and more to maintain both capital accumulation and legitimation until it reaches "fiscal crisis," a situation in which government revenues can no longer satisfy the simultaneous demands of the dual role of the state.[44] Thus, for some left-wing analysts, the current language of restraint and the social policy cutbacks undertaken by neo-conservative governments in Canada are natural consequences of fiscal crisis and the fundamental contradiction between the state's accumulation and legitimation functions.

There are many other less theoretical approaches to the growth of the state. Some are essentially apolitical in that they view the expansion of the role of government as a product of exogenous (externally determined) forces. For example, the growth and changing age structure of the population may call for increased state activity. More expenditure and more government personnel are needed to provide services to a larger number of people, and the fact that more people are living longer necessitates more pensions and health care for the aged. Alternatively, the vast technological development undergone by Canadian society in the last century may have increased the scope for government intervention. For example, the coming of the motor vehicle alone has given rise to a great variety of government activity: road building and maintenance, traffic laws, seat-belt legislation, driver and vehicle licensing, exhaust emission controls, vehicle safety regulations and much more.

But the growth of the state was not the *direct* consequence of demographic change or technological innovation; these are background factors that create increased potential for state intervention. The current extent of state activity *is* the result of an extensive series of political decisions — to increase public expenditure on a particular item, to move into a new functional area, to create another regulatory agency — each one taken by politicians acting in the context of the political process. Therefore, although the number of people over 65 already exceeded 5 percent of the population in 1901, it was another quarter-century before government pensions were introduced for some people over the age of 70, and 50 years before pensions were granted to those over 65.

Many attempts to explain the growth of the state focus on the bureaucratic forces that underlie its activities. It is sometimes argued that bureaucrats judge their personal success by the growth rate of the budgets, number of employees and volume of programs administered by their departments. A more benevolent view might ascribe the growth to genuine concern for the target population or to a response to political pressures. The dominant modes and structures of policy-making in state bureaucracies may also play a part, especially with respect to the growth of public spending. Incremental decision-making has predominated in the budgetary process over much of the past century. While attempts have been made to reform the budgetary process in recent years, it has proven difficult to counterbalance the tendency toward continued expansion of public expenditure. While the federal deficit was eliminated before the turn of the millennium, the national debt level will continue at very high levels for much of the twenty-first century.

---

44. James O'Connor, *The Fiscal Crisis of the State* (New York: St. Martin's Press, 1973), passim.

The role of political ideas or ideologies is sometimes overlooked in explorations of the decisions underlying the growth of the state. However, it may be argued that an interventionist role for the state has traditionally been considered legitimate in the Canadian political culture. Canadians do not share the anti-statist liberalism and the free enterprise ethic to the same extent as the general public in the United States. In the nineteenth century, the Canadian versions of "Toryism" and nationalism motivated state intervention in the interests of private enterprise and national economic development through the National Policy. From the Second World War to the mid-1970s, the acceptance of Keynesian economics and the embracing of a "welfare state ideology" served to legitimate an interventionist role for the state.

Historically, why have political parties competed to expand government services and public expenditure rather than to reduce state intervention and cut tax rates? One answer lies in the public expectations of the role of the state in Canada, although, as Bird points out, "the popular postwar ideology that government can — and should — solve most problems is now, however, increasingly being questioned in the face of the strong evidence that it cannot." An alternative suggestion is that support for tax cuts is much more diffuse than opposition to reductions in services — that reductions are more directly felt and are more likely to be translated into votes against the party proposing such measures. This may especially be the case in Canada where approximately 40 percent of the electorate is employed in some way by government and is therefore opposed to any significant reduction in the role of the state.

With so many alternatives to choose from, it is perhaps not surprising that no universally accepted explanation of the growth of the Canadian state has emerged. One point upon which most analysts agree is that, while demographic, technological and economic factors provide the contextual background to the growth of the state, the key to a comprehensive and satisfactory explanation lies more in the political field than in other processes.

GOVERNMENT RESTRAINT, DOWNSIZING AND RENEWAL

In the past decade, there has been a concerted attack on the size and complexity of modern government in most liberal democracies. Bureaucrats are portrayed as being motivated mainly by their desire to increase their budgets, staffs and importance. Conservatives, in particular, think that the problems of bureaucracy can be solved by reducing its power. They demand that government administration to be made smaller, more decentralized, less expensive and more flexible in responding to public demands. The election platforms for the Conservative, Liberal, Reform and even New Democrat parties in recent years have been a set of proposals to weaken Ottawa bureaucracy.

Such political demands have often been accompanied by ever grander schemes for reform. The "new public management" or "managerialism" schools in social science call for the introduction of business management practices into government.[45] One example would be the claim that "pay for performance" or merit pay should be advanced further in the public sector. This idea is often accompanied by the philosophy that "customer orientation" should be the reigning principle for public servants. The approach has become so shrill that it is more like an ideology than a theory of public administration.

---

45. A. Massey, *Managing the Public Sector* (Aldershot: Edward Elgar, 1993); C. Campbell, *Political Leadership in an Age of Constraint* (Pittsburgh: University of Pittsburgh Press, 1992); and J. Dilulio, *Deregulating the Public Service: Can Government be Improved?* (Washington, D.C.: The Brookings Institute, 1994).

Another approach has been to call for the "privatization" of government, either by selling off government enterprises or by "contracting out" services to the private sector. The idea is based on the premise that self-interested decisions in the marketplace will be made more efficiently than those made by tenured civil servants in the bureaucracy. Probably the clearest example of this philosophy in recent years has been the decision to privatize many Crown corporations such as Air Canada, Petro Canada and so on (discussed in Chapter 10).

Lastly, a case has been made against the centralization of bureaucracies in capital cities. The claim is that better (read "more efficient") decisions would be made if they were made closer to the people that they affect. In other words, decentralization is supposed to enhance decision-making and prevent the waste that is prevalent in large, centralized administrations.

The dangerous philosophy inherent in such policies is clear. When the marketplace is used to enforce efficiency, it may be to the advantage of the most conservative forces in society. "New public management" is essentially a belief that the more politicians can be kept out of public administration the better off the country will be. When governments reduce their size, privatize their functions and decentralize, they lose a substantial measure of democratic control. How will democratic responsiveness be enhanced by these new managerial techniques of government? Nevertheless, optimists continue to be led by the ideas put forth by David Osborne and Ted Gaebler in their best-selling popular book, *Reinventing Government,* in which they argue that "the entrepreneurial spirit" can transform public administration.[46]

One major consequence of modern economics has been the advent of what American economist Lester Thurow has labelled "the zero-sum society."[47] In earlier times, governments could redistribute resources to the underprivileged without eroding at least the money income, if not the relative position, of more affluent groups. The growing national pie permitted "positive-sum" politics. However, once the pie stopped growing, redistribution to some groups could be undertaken only at the expense of others. In the zero-sum society, then, distributional conflicts become more polarized, since somebody must "lose" for someone else to "win." Thus, new or expanded social programs must be financed from savings obtained from reducing other programs.

Public Policy and Bureaucracy in an Age of Restraint: Mulroney and Chrétien

In the last two decades of the millennium, "restraint" became a watchword of federal policy-making, as successive governments attempted to cope with inflation, recession, declining tax revenues, growing deficits and the task of reviving a faltering Canadian economy. Government "restraint" became the policy of choice during the 1984 and 1988 Conservative governments and also of the Liberals in 1993 and the early years of the 1997 government.

One consequence of the restraint philosophy has been the efforts of the Mulroney and Chrétien governments to "reform" public policy and the public service along the lines of "managerialism" or "new public management theory." This business-oriented philosophy can be summarized as an effort to *privatize* public policy services whenever possible and to *deregulate* the economy to the maximum possible. At the bureaucratic level, this philosophy has resulted in cutbacks and layoffs in

---

46. David Osborne and Ted Gaebler, *Reinventing Government* (New York: Plume, 1993). Their ideas were foreshadowed by Tom Peters and Robert Waterman in their best-selling book about management in business, *In Search of Excellence* (New York: Harper and Row, 1982).

47. Lester C. Thurow, *The Zero-Sum Society: Distribution and the Possibilities for Economic Change* (New York: Basic Books, 1980).

the public service in an effort to reduce the overall costs of government. The 1984 Nielsen Task Force (ministerial task force on program review) may be cited as the first of the studies and programs intended to make the federal government more like a business. But it was not the last.

Public Service 2000 and Public Service Renewal

The result of the Nielsen Task Force was essentially negative. The bureaucracy fought the changes at every stage, and the actual effects on public administration were minimal. Therefore, the 1988 Mulroney government attempted another strategy. In line with "managerialism ideas" an effort was made to change the basic attitudes or culture of the bureaucracy. Public Service 2000 consisted of a comprehensive philosophy to make the bureaucracy more service-oriented (i.e., provide better services to the clients of government), more flexible (respond to the public's wishes) and more decentralized (i.e., make the managers manage rather than follow orders or rely on the central agencies of government for direction). The concrete results of Public Service 2000 were quite different from the rhetoric. Public service morale plummeted and many senior bureaucrats retired or were fired.

After the short and disastrous effect of Kim Campbell's tenure on the public service, another comprehensive review of all government programs was undertaken by the 1993 Chrétien government. The prime minister appointed Marcel Massé, as the minister responsible for **Public Service Renewal**, to begin "reinventing" government. Despite the rhetoric about the "tests" of good government that enveloped these reports, the ultimate objective was to reduce government expenditures by eliminating programs and laying off 45 000 public servants. In order to alleviate other public pressures about government expenditure, Chrétien also reduced the size of ministerial staffs. For example, under Mulroney the number of political staffers in the Department of International Trade was 78. Chrétien reduced this to 20 person-years.

The impact of Public Service 2000 and Public Service Renewal has been in line with managerialism and the new philosophy of neo-conservative governments. A smaller bureaucracy, carrying out fewer tasks, has been created by program cutbacks, public service reductions, privatization and deregulation. The Canadian government under both Conservatives and Liberals has adopted almost without question the philosophy of "the less government the better."

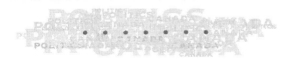

SUMMARY

The primary objectives of this chapter have been to introduce some of the central concepts in policy-making and the most commonly used approaches to public policy analysis, and to illustrate some of the constraints within which federal policy-makers have to operate. Whichever perspective one takes on the role of the state in Canadian society, it is clear that certain fundamental realities of Canadian political life have a major influence on federal policy-making, and that their net effect is to militate against comprehensive decision-making in favour of a general tendency toward incremental policy-making or the fine art of "muddling through."

First, Canada is a liberal democracy in which political parties must compete for electoral support and governments must remain responsive to the promptings of key interest groups, both as lobbyists and as potential organizers of public opinion and votes. The need to win, and especially to maintain, electoral support from societal groups usually requires that governments refrain from making major policy changes that might alienate significant portions of the electorate.

Second, Canada has a federal system of government in which the constitutional division of powers imposes both legal and political constraints upon federal policy-makers. The legal constraints limit the instruments available to the federal government in pursuit of its objectives in many policy areas, while the values and goals of provincial governments and the policies these governments implement often contradict and reduce the effectiveness of federal policy outputs. The need to secure federal/provincial cooperation in many policy areas again dictates that policy-making must move in small, incrementalist steps rather than in giant strides.

Third, Canada is not a political system in isolation. Changes in the world economic and political environments create a climate of uncertainty for policy-makers of all states. But the political and economic influence of the United States and of U.S.-based multinational corporations in particular imposes extra demands and constraints on policy-makers in Canada; federal policy-makers must constantly adjust their priorities and instruments of policy implementation in response to events south of the 49th parallel.

None of this is intended to argue against policy-makers attempting to make better policy decisions. All Canadians would like to think that their federal government makes the most rational policy choices available to it, subject to the constraints under which it is working. However, the requirements of a democratic political process, a federal institutional structure and the constraints imposed by the domestic and international economies usually combine with short-term political expediency to ensure that policy-makers follow the path of least resistance by "muddling through." Canadians should, perhaps, demand of their governments that, if they are going to "muddle through," they at least do so in a more "rational" way.

DISCUSSION QUESTIONS

1. Why are broad concepts such as "public policy" used in the analysis of Canadian government?
2. Which macro-level approaches to public policy analysis do you favour? Why?
3. Explain the growth and size of the Canadian state. Why has it stopped growing in recent years?
4. Given the options the government has for financial restraint, is it targeting the most effective areas for cuts?
5. Discuss the impact of "managerialism" in the public service.

Selected Bibliography

Atkinson, Michael, ed., *Governing Canada* (Toronto: Harcourt Brace, 1993).

Brodie, M. Janine, *Women and Canadian Public Policy* (Toronto: Harcourt Brace, 1996).

Brooks, Steven, *Public Policy in Canada: An Introduction,* 3rd ed. (Toronto: Oxford University Press, 1998).

———— and Andrew Strich, *Business and Government in Canada* (Scarborough: Prentice Hall Canada, 1991).

Carleton University, School of Public Administration, *How Ottawa Spends* (Ottawa: Carleton University Press, annual). Edited by various scholars in different years.

Clark, J.D., *Getting the Incentives Right: Toward a Productivity-Oriented Management Framework for the Public Service* (Ottawa: Treasury Board, 1993).

Coleman, William and Grace Skogstad, *Policy Communities and Public Policy in Canada* (Mississauga: Copp Clark Pitman, 1990).

Dilulio, J., *Deregulating the Public Service* (Washington, D.C.: The Brookings Institution, 1994).

Gillespie, W. Irwin, *Tax, Borrow and Spend: Financing Federal Spending in Canada, 1867–1990* (Ottawa: Carleton University Press, 1991).

Kuttner, Robert, *Everything for Sale: The Virtues and Limits of Markets* (New York: Alfred A. Knopf, 1997).

Massey, Andrew, *Managing the Public Sector* (Aldershot: Edward Algar, 1993).

McQuaig, Linda, *Shooting the Hippo: Death by Deficit and Other Canadian Myths* (Toronto: Viking, 1995).

Osborne, David and Ted Gaebler, *Reinventing Government* (New York: Addison Wesley, 1992).

Parsons, Wayne, *Public Policy: An Introduction to the Theory and Practice of Policy Analysis* (Aldershot: Edward Elgar, 1995).

Pierson, Paul, *Dismantling the Welfare State* (Cambridge, U.K.: Cambridge University Press, 1994).

Reich, Robert, *The Work of Nations* (New York: Simon and Schuster, 1991).

Savoie, Donald, *The Politics of Public Spending in Canada* (Toronto: University of Toronto Press, 1990).

Sproule-Jones, Mark, *Governments at Work: Canadian Parliamentary Federalism and Its Public Policy Effects* (Toronto: University of Toronto Press, 1993).

Strick, John C., *The Public Sector in Canada: Programs, Finance and Policy* (Toronto: Thompson, 1999).

Tuohy, Carolyn J., *Policy and Politics in Canada: Institutionalized Ambivalence* (Philadelphia: Temple University Press, 1992).

Weaver, R. Kent and Bert A. Rockman, eds., *Do Institutions Matter?* (Washington, D.C.: The Brookings Institution, 1993).

 # LIST OF WEBLINKS

www.psc-cfp.gc.ca	**Canadian Public Service Commission** This is the Web site for the Public Service Commission, which is responsible for overseeing and organizing the Canadian Public Service.
www.crtc.gc.ca	**Canadian Radio-television and Telecommunications Commission** This is the Web site for the CRTC, which regulates broadcasting and communications in Canada.
www.mailposte.ca	**Canada Post Corporation** This is the official Web site of this national service, which was recently changed from a government department to a Crown corporation.
www.ccra-adrc.gc.ca	**Canadian Department of Revenue** This is the Web page for the Canadian Department of Revenue.

15

Canada in the Global Economy

· · · · · · · ·

Foreign, Trade and Defence Policy

anada is far from self-sufficient with regard to either economic prosperity or national security. Increasingly, the well-being and security of Canadian citizens depend on how they collectively respond to the constraints and opportunities that flow from the international environment. The world has entered an era of rapid technological change and increasing economic interdependence, and the study of Canadian government can no longer legitimately be undertaken without an understanding of international affairs.

Canadian students of international affairs have always had considerable difficulty depicting Canada's place in the international power hierarchy.[1] Some scholars simply assume the self-description of Canada as an influential "middle power." This notion was endorsed by the Canadian government after the end of the Second World War when it rallied with other like-minded states to contest the positions of the "great" powers to dominate the future United Nations. After that period, officials and scholars alike began to use the phrase somewhat indiscriminately.

Those in the intellectual left in Canada have never accepted the term middle power. Arguing that Canada is dominated by U.S. economic interests, they believe Canada depends on its southern neighbour for security as well as prosperity. For some, Canada merely went from being a colony of Britain to a colony of the United States. While this argument has its merits, it is nevertheless true that Canada has opposed American policies and not always acted as a satellite — Canada's opposition to the American embargo of Cuba is an obvious case in point.

A third group of academics asserts that Canada is not as insignificant as either a satellite of the United States or a middle power. These individuals claim more grandly that Canada is a "foremost" or "major" or "principal" power. Many justifications have been advanced for this ranking: "surveys" that show this is how Canadians regard their country; the fact that it is a member of the prestigious economic club, the G-7; and assertions that the end of the Cold War reduced the

---

1. Kim Richard Nossal, *The Politics of Canadian Foreign Policy*, 3rd. ed. (Scarborough: Prentice Hall Canada, 1997).

bipolarity of the world and allowed countries such as Canada to ascend to new power positions in the diffuse arrangements.

We cannot resolve this debate in this volume. In any case, whether Canadians consider Canada to be a major, middle or dependent power is almost irrelevant. What matters is what other countries *think* about Canada's importance and political resources in the global competition.

Determining Canada's relative economic performance in terms of gross domestic product (GDP) is, of course, much easier than measuring overall power and influence. By this narrow economic measure, Canada certainly hovers in the top group. In 2000, for example, Canada had one of the largest economies in the world. In the global perspective, Canadians are economically very well off. They have a high standard of living that furnishes them with goods, from mobile telephones to fax machines, items that citizens of other countries consider extreme luxuries. As the former diplomat John Holmes put it, Canada is regarded as "filthy rich."[2]

Official relationships outside Canadian borders are conducted in two ways. One involves maintaining active multilateral relations, particularly through international institutions. The other is through selective bilateral relations; in 1997, Canada had 129 missions and 33 satellite offices abroad. Canada's foreign policy generally aims to build strong relationships with countries that are most important to Canada's economic development and offer long-term markets for Canadian exports. The parameters of these relationships are determined to a significant degree by defence arrangements with the United States and western Europe.

In this chapter, we examine the concept of foreign policy. Then we turn to an examination of the sources of foreign policy in Canada and a discussion of the four main components of Canadian foreign policy: trade policy, activity in international organizations, bilateral relations and defence policy. The last among these focuses on our role in defence organizations and peacekeeping.

WHAT IS FOREIGN POLICY?

The study of **international relations** refers to the broad network of relations among states and includes the activities of their citizens and non-state institutions as well. The global system, therefore, is the result of the behaviour of states and also non-governmental actors. The **foreign policy** of countries, on the other hand, is much more narrow. It depicts state or government behaviour that has external ramifications.[3] It includes the diplomatic and military relations among states, as well as their cultural, economic, technological and, increasingly, ecological interests.

There are basic similarities and dissimilarities between domestic and international affairs. Both consist of the struggle for advantage among organized groups with different interests and values. In neither situation can all the interests and values at stake be satisfied; therefore, disputes and conflicts often erupt. In domestic politics, the result of such conflict may extend to violence or revolution. In international politics, the result may be warfare among states.

The main distinction between the two types of politics is that the international system has no world government to mitigate disputes and determine "who gets what, when and how." The world's states exist in a kind of anarchy without a higher form of government to guide them. They compete in a world of insecurity and danger. Of course, states sometimes cooperate for their own interests and

---

2. John Holmes, cited in Peyton V. Lyon and Brian Tomlin, *Canada as an International Actor* (Toronto: Macmillan, 1979), p. 70.
3. Robert J. Jackson and Doreen Jackson, *An Introduction to Political Science: Comparative and World Politics*, 3rd ed. (Toronto: Prentice Hall, 2000), ch. 21.

in that sense they develop "law-like" customs and practices that shape their behaviour. On the whole, then, external behaviour of states is characterized by legal and political anarchy as well as by customs or proper behaviour.

Politics among states takes many forms ranging from diplomacy to war. Routine relations are carried out by negotiations between diplomats and other officials who assert the claims of their states in "bilateral" (between two of them) and "multilateral" (among several of them) frameworks.[4] Diplomacy may result in agreement or conflict among states. Treaties and protocols may be negotiated and signed. If agreement cannot be reached among states, other approaches to the disputes may be sought, ranging from public complaints, to propaganda, subversion and even outright war.

Unlike domestic politics, which takes place within a set of more or less developed laws and which is ultimately related to the authority of government and sovereignty of the territory, international politics possesses no international government that can impose its laws on people everywhere. States may join international organizations for mutual benefit, but few accept a higher set of decision-makers or laws than those provided by their own domestic authorities.

Making foreign policy is considerably different than making domestic policy. The state is able to achieve domestic objectives because it has authority over its internal environment. A government has no legal authority outside its borders; as a result, foreign policy decisions must be set within the context of the opportunities and constraints of the international system. In concrete terms, foreign policy-making in Canada differs from domestic policy-making because the former sometimes amounts to little more than striking an image. Only rarely is legislation necessary; often Parliament and even the bureaucratic elite have little more than spectator status, as the prime minister and the Ministers of Foreign Affairs, International Trade and National Defence determine initiatives.

SOURCES OF CANADIAN FOREIGN POLICY

The traditional view of the relationship between politicians and civil servants depicts elected politicians as responsible for the determination of the policy that bureaucrats administer. Politicians make decisions; bureaucrats merely implement them. However, as we have shown in Chapter 14, the government bureaucracy has always been involved in policy-making. This situation is especially evident in the formulation of foreign policy, an area where Canada's political leadership depends heavily on bureaucratic expertise and advice concerning the conduct of its international affairs. Nonetheless, the prime minister and the Ministers of Foreign Affairs and National Defence remain at the apex of decision-making.

Prime Minister and Cabinet

At the level of political leadership, responsibility for foreign policy falls primarily on the prime minister and the Minister of Foreign Affairs. In fact, until 1946 the prime minister personally retained the Foreign Affairs portfolio. It is only recently that foreign policy has begun to involve the participation of other Cabinet members, as a result of efforts to strengthen the collective involvement of Cabinet in decision-making.[5] Today, the insistence that the bureaucracy and ministers provide

4. For an overview on this subject, see Sir Harold Nicholson, *Diplomacy*, 4th ed. (New York: Oxford University Press, 1988).
5. Nossal, *The Politics of Canadian Foreign Policy*.

Cabinet with alternatives rather than allow single-option recommendations and attempts to establish national priorities at the Cabinet level have helped to open the foreign-policy process to other departments and ministers. Still, the prime minister remains the central political actor, able to provide leadership and place his or her concerns high on the government's political agenda. Prime Minister Mulroney's implementation of a free trade arrangement with the

Reprinted with permission, Gable, *The Globe and Mail.*

United States in 1988 and the signing of the *North American Free Trade Agreement* with Mexico and the United States in 1992 are dramatic examples of the strong role the prime minister plays in foreign affairs.

When he became prime minister, Jean Chrétien did not even bother setting up a specific Cabinet committee to look after foreign affairs; responsibility for high policy went directly to Cabinet. Chrétien also attempted to distinguish himself from Mulroney in some policy fields. He cancelled the refit of an Airbus 310 for ministerial travels, talked about making the foreign policy-making process more democratic and began the "Team Canada" trade trips around the world.

The role of the Minister of Foreign Affairs is also extremely important. This minister is not only the chief spokesman on international affairs and the top administrator for the Department of Foreign Affairs and International Trade, but often also the second most powerful person in the Cabinet. Louis St. Laurent and Lester Pearson both became prime minister after being Secretary of State; Allan MacEachen held the dual position of Secretary of State and deputy prime minister for several years. Joe Clark became Secretary of State after being ejected as leader of the Conservative party and Prime Minister of Canada, and André Ouellet took on the office after being the Liberal party co-campaign manager during the 1993 election. The present foreign minister, Lloyd Axworthy, is the most powerful western voice in Cabinet and a potential leadership aspirant.

Department of Foreign Affairs and International Trade

The Department of Foreign Affairs and International Trade (DFAIT) is at the centre of the bureaucratic complex responsible for Canada's external relations. The term "external" was originally used rather than "foreign" because many of the relationships Canada had with other countries involved other members of the British Empire and therefore were not regarded as "foreign" in the strict sense. The 1909 Act of Parliament that established the Department charged it with the conduct of all official communications between the Government of Canada and the governments of other countries in connection with the external affairs of Canada. These responsibilities have grown substantially over time. Today, the Department performs three interrelated functions: the provision and integration of advice on foreign and international trade; the coordination and integration of Canada's foreign relations; and the implementation of foreign operations.

As the repository of policy advice, the Department conducts research and analysis, contributes to domestic policy formulation and provides leadership in establishing policies in the international sphere. The coordination and integration of foreign policy involves providing a framework for the full range of governmental activities overseas, monitoring and influencing other departments' and the provincial governments' international activities, and bringing coherence to a patchwork of priorities and programs. Foreign operations include representation of Canada's interests to other countries, analysis of information regarding developments abroad, negotiation, management and supervision of programs overseas.

While DFAIT retains primary responsibility for the conduct of Canada's foreign policy, other governmental and non-governmental bodies have become increasingly salient in the foreign policy-making process. What were once considered purely domestic matters have increasingly taken on an international dimension. The foreign policy process has become more diffuse within government and also more open, in that non-governmental groups increasingly are involved. Domestically, interest groups, private citizens, business people, as well as regional interests and their provincial government representatives seek to influence foreign policy decisions. Internationally, a new layer of non-governmental organizations is active, including multinational firms pursuing commercial relations

FIGURE 15.1   DEPARTMENT OF FOREIGN AFFAIRS AND INTERNATIONAL TRADE

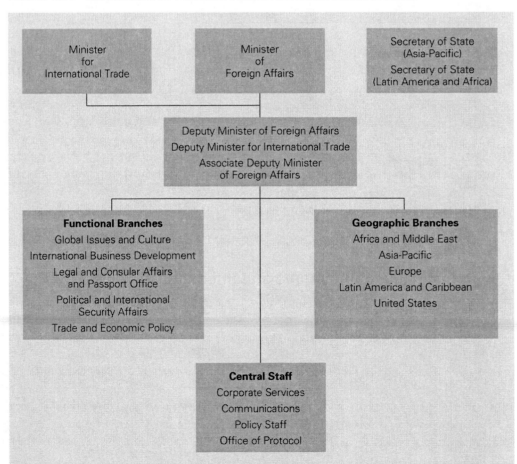

Source: Treasury Board of Canada Secretariat, *Estimates, 1996–97, Foreign Affairs and International Trade* (Ottawa: Supply and Services, 1996), p. 6. Reproduced with the permission of the Minister of Public Works and Government Services Canada, 1997.

and private groups advocating protection of human rights. Consequently, traditional foreign policy-makers have had to accept increasing levels of participation by other actors in international affairs.

Changes in federal intra-governmental structures have also eroded DFAIT's dominance in conducting Canada's foreign relations. The prime minister's support agencies — the Prime Minister's Office and the Privy Council Office — have become more influential in foreign policy decisions. New or revamped departments have also eroded the former predominance of DFAIT, to the point of duplicating some of the Department's functions. Many contemporary issues require expertise that Foreign Affairs does not possess: acid rain, energy policy and nuclear and grain exports, to name a few. The participation of such diverse departments and government bodies as Environment, Natural Resources, the National Energy Board, Atomic Energy of Canada, the Department of Agriculture and the Canadian Wheat Board is therefore essential.

Provincial governments and their agencies, as well as Crown corporations, have become important actors in the foreign policy process. While Québec's international activities tend to receive the most publicity, nearly all the provinces are active on the international scene. Western provinces concern themselves with such matters as resource exports and tariffs, while Atlantic Canada has interests in fisheries, the law of the sea and offshore resources — all issues with important foreign policy implications. In addition, the provinces are all concerned with federal government policies that affect international trade.

As a response to the diffusion of the contemporary foreign policy-making process, attempts have been made to coordinate the various departments, groups and policies involved. In 1962, the Glassco Commission, in its review of the Department of External Affairs, recommended structural changes and suggested periodic reviews and reforms of the Department's internal structure. Further studies resulted in a 1970 federal White Paper, *Foreign Policy for Canadians,* that led to the establishment of the Interdepartmental Committee on External Relations. In March 1980, the federal government announced further consolidation of responsibilities. Foreign service officers from the Department of Industry, Trade and Commerce and the Canadian Employment and Immigration Commission were integrated into the Department of External Affairs, along with foreign service officers from Employment and Immigration at the operational level and the field staff from the Canadian International Development Agency (CIDA). The stated purposes of the consolidation were: to improve the economy and efficiency of foreign operations without affecting the policy and program development roles of the departments involved; to create a more cohesive and coherent foreign service; to strengthen the role of heads of posts; and to improve the career prospects and experiences of foreign service personnel.

The Department of External Affairs was restructured further in January 1982. Its aims were expanded to enhance Canada's ability to pursue international markets and give greater priority to economic matters in the development of foreign policy, or, in the words of Undersecretary of External Affairs Marcel Massé, "to give greater weight to economic factors in the design of foreign policy, to ensure the conduct of foreign relations serves Canadian trade objectives, to improve the service offered exporters in an increasingly competitive international marketplace and to ensure policy and program coherence in the conduct of Canada's range of relations with the outside world."[6] The functions of trade policy and promotion of the Department of Industry, Trade and Commerce were therefore transferred to External Affairs, completing the consolidation on economic matters. Then, in 1992, another shuffle took place and the primary responsibility for immigration was returned to the Department of Employment and Immigration.

---

6. Marcel Massé, "Department of External Affairs: Changes to Organizational Structure," memo no. USS-241 (Department of External Affairs, July 8, 1983), p. 1.

Since 1994, the prominence of economic objectives is reflected in a two-minister team at DFAIT. (See Figure 15.1.) The Minister of Foreign Affairs is responsible for the management of the Department, integrating its various parts as well as relating it to the rest of the government. He or she is supported by the Minister for International Trade. They, in turn, are backed up by two Secretaries of State to Assist — one for the Asia-Pacific region and one for Africa and Latin America. These ministers are charged with providing a link between the concerns of government outside and within Canada. Concern for coordination is also evident at the senior bureaucratic level of the Department (refer again to Figure 15.1). At the head of the Department are two deputy ministers — one for foreign affairs and one for international trade.

The Liberal government has shifted the Department's priorities further toward concern for Canadian national interests — trade and Canadian culture. As described in the 1995 foreign policy statement, *Canada in the World*, the objectives of the Department are:

- the promotion of prosperity and employment
- the protection of our security with a stable global framework
- the projection of Canadian values and culture in the world.

As well, the Liberal government has gone a long way to adopt the principles of the parliamentary committee that Jean Chrétien created in 1994. As the authors of the report of the Special Joint Committee Reviewing Canadian Foreign Policy put it:

> *Foreign policy must operate with an effective domestic base, and that domestic base must rest on the effective projection of key elements of the national life. In this sense, foreign policy is domestic policy.*[7]

Moreover, the Liberal party has broadened the concept of *security* to include emerging issues such as environmental degradation, population growth, criminal activity and health pandemics.

DFAIT is now expected to be responsible for the delivery of almost all government programs abroad, through a single, unified foreign service. All positions are filled by career civil servants on the basis of open competitive examination. There are exceptions. For example, the Canadian ambassadors in Paris and Washington and the High Commissioner in London are often political appointees. Normally, officials change their postings every two or three years, with occasional intervals in Ottawa.

Parliament and Political Parties

In western liberal democracies, legislatures and political parties provide an important link between citizens and their government. In Canada, Parliament provides a forum for public debate, while parties mobilize public opinion, coordinate political activity and function as intermediate instruments of political activity for those not elected to office. Therefore, in the realm of foreign policy formulation, Parliament and political parties provide channels through which diverse pressures from the domestic community are brought to bear on the policy process.

For example, Question Period in the House of Commons provides MPs the opportunity to raise foreign policy issues. The House of Commons Standing Committee on External Affairs, the

---

7. Canada's Special Joint Committee, *Canada's Foreign Policy: Principles and Priorities for the Future* (Ottawa, 1994), p. 6.

Standing Committee on National Defence and the Senate Committee on Foreign Affairs have conducted major reviews of various aspects of Canadian foreign and defence policy in addition to performing their routine function of examining the budgetary estimates of the foreign policy establishment. Special parliamentary task forces and subcommittees have been formed to report on important issues such as Canadian–American relations and peacekeeping.

However, the role of Parliament and political parties in making foreign policy is constrained by the powers of the government. Control over foreign policy is firmly in the hands of the executive. While Cabinet takes into consideration the anticipated reaction of Parliament in its policy deliberations, only a few cases exist in which formal parliamentary debate can be said to have had a decisive impact on government behaviour in the foreign policy field.[8] Because of the nature of diplomacy, governments have almost exclusive control over information in this area. Requirements of discretion over matters involving national security and relations with foreign countries therefore limit the impact of outside groups and individuals on the foreign policy process; the government's ability to assume policy and make treaties with foreign countries without ratification by Parliament constrains the impact of government backbenchers, opposition parties and societal groups.

Non-Governmental Actors: Interest Groups, the Media and Public Opinion

Other means of expression of international policy interests include representations from private interest groups, the media and popular opinion as measured by polling. How much influence each has varies from issue to issue.[9] Some interest groups possess sufficient expertise or political clout to be asked by government to participate in the process. For example, representatives of domestic interest groups are included among the advisors to Canadian delegations attending international conferences. Most groups, however, must gain access to politicians and bureaucrats through meetings, presentation of position briefs, the media and/or mobilization of their constituents. The number of interest groups concerned with foreign policy has grown substantially over the years. New issues such as nuclear radiation and waste, acid rain, survival of whales and seals, the over-fishing of cod and turbot, and the disruption of Arctic communities by resource development have joined traditional foreign policy issues, including global security and nuclear proliferation.

The media's impact on the foreign policy process is indirect. According to a prominent observer, the press "has little effect upon the substance of foreign policy per se, but … it exerts a very significant impact upon the day-to-day activities of the men who make it."[10] By providing coverage of external events and taking editorial positions, the media disseminate information and opinion, and, at times, prescribe solutions, thereby articulating public and elite foreign policy concerns.

---

8. Important exceptions include the Suez Crisis of October 1956, in which the Liberal government supported American-sponsored efforts to force British, French and Israeli forces to withdraw from captured Egyptian territory; the issue of equipping Canadian fighter planes and missile system with nuclear warheads during Diefenbaker's prime ministership; and the TransCanada Pipeline debate. See Dewitt and Kirton, *Canada as a Principal Power*, pp. 171–77; Lawrence Martin, *The Presidents and the Prime Ministers* (Toronto: Doubleday, 1982), ch. 12; and William Kilbourn, *Pipeline: TransCanada and the Great Debate — A History of Business and Politics* (Toronto: Clarke, Irwin, 1970).

9. On the impact of interest groups and the media on foreign policy, see Special Issue, "Domestic Causes of Canada's Foreign Policy," *International Journal*, vol. 39, no. 1 (Winter 1983–84); Elizabeth Riddell-Dixon, *The Domestic Mosaic: Domestic Groups and Canadian Foreign Policy* (Toronto: Canadian Institute of International Affairs, 1985).

10. Denis Stairs, "The Press and Foreign Policy in Canada," *International Journal*, vol. 31, no. 2 (Spring 1976), p. 238.

Professional diplomats' feelings toward the proper role of public opinion in foreign policy-making are critical or ambivalent; many believe that it is not an appropriate guide for the conduct of foreign policy. Because of the constraints diplomats face in the international arena, as well as the complexity of the issues, the impact of public opinion may at times be detrimental:

> From the professional's traditional perspective the international working environment is … a world of nuance and subtlety and craft, and certainly no place for the amateur. But nuance, subtlety, and craft are not the most obvious characteristics of the constituent public, or of their opinions. Public reactions to foreign policy issues, especially but not solely in political-security contexts, are often one sided, ill informed, transient, fickle, and given, at their worst, to emotional excess.[11]

While public opinion may not have an immediate impact on the determination of policy, it has the capacity to set limits on what policy-makers can do "politically." Policy-makers must take account of latent opinions and anticipate the public's reactions to various policy alternatives. Thus, decision-makers follow election campaigns and public opinion polls not as a source of policy ideas but rather as an indicator of the public's potential response to various policy options. Some elections convey a sense of what the public wants: in 1988 the free trade issue was crucial, whereas in 1997 there was no debate whatsoever on foreign policy.[12]

Provinces and Foreign Policy

Provincial governments have a keen interest in the conduct of Canadian foreign policy and over the years have attempted to increase their international visibility, often by opening foreign offices.[13] Such offices are important to provinces that depend heavily on external trade. Provincial governments sponsor trade and cultural missions, receive visiting foreign dignitaries, participate in ongoing multilateral conferences and become involved in joint federal/provincial programs.

Fields over which provinces have concurrent or exclusive jurisdiction have become increasingly important in the international arena, and this necessitates the inclusion of provincial concerns in the formation of Canada's foreign policy. Within the context of growing provincial power in Canadian federalism, provincial interests are important to the extent that "the range and frequency of provincial international activity is now sufficient to complicate the design and conduct of Canadian foreign policy, indeed, to frustrate central control over foreign policy in some areas."[14]

Increased international activity on the part of provincial governments has not been without periods of confrontation and conflict. This is not surprising, given that matters of national interest in a country as large and disparate as Canada are in question. The federal government, presiding over a varied populace, is sometimes faced with incompatible demands.

Federal/provincial conflict in this field is exacerbated by the absence of a clear delineation of constitutional authority regarding treaties and international relations. Section 132 of the *Constitution*

11. Ibid., p. 142.
12. Ibid., pp. 133–34.
13. For further discussion, see Ronald G. Atkey, "The Role of Provinces in International Affairs," *International Journal*, vol. 26, no. 1 (Winter 1970–71), pp. 249–73; and Dewitt and Kirton, *Canada as a Principal Power*, pp. 186–92.
14. P.R. Johannson, "Provincial International Activities," *International Journal*, vol. 33, no. 2 (Spring 1978), pp. 357–78.

Act, 1867, for example, refers only to the implementation of treaties affecting the British Empire. Moreover, the range of powers vested in the provinces necessitates at least some measure of involvement in foreign policy. Consequently, there has been, and to some extent continues to be, both legal and political debate over the proper role of the provinces in foreign affairs.

Some argue for the independent international competence of the provinces, believing that the Constitution's silence on foreign relations implies that the provinces have a legal right to negotiate and sign treaties on provincial subjects. Support for this position is based on a number of factors. First, the provinces were judicially conceded the exclusive right to *implement* treaties in the 1936 *Labour Conventions* case. Since treaty-making and treaty implementation are virtually inseparable, it is argued that if provincial governments can legally implement provisions of treaties, they should also be able to negotiate them.

Second, international law, specifically the 1966 *International Law Commission* of the United Nations, adds support to the concept of provincial international competence. According to article 3(2): "State members of a federal union may possess a capacity to conclude treaties if such capacity is admitted by the federal constitution and within the limits laid down."[15] The silence of the Constitution is again assumed to be supportive of the provincial case.

Third, the experiences of other federal states where component units have been allowed to make treaties are noted as precedents. For example, treaty-making powers exist in the sub-units in Switzerland and the Federal Republic of Germany.

Fourth, efforts of various Québec governments to obtain recognition of their special linguistic and cultural status are claimed to have provided precedents strengthening the position of the provinces. For example, in 1964 Québec concluded an educational exchange agreement with France without the participation of or prior consultation with Ottawa. In November 1965, Canada and France signed a cultural agreement and arranged an exchange of letters recognizing possible *ententes* providing for educational and cultural exchanges between France and the provinces of Canada. However, that same month, Québec and France concluded an *entente* on cultural cooperation without reference to the Ottawa/France agreement. Although the federal government gave its consent to both the 1964 and 1965 exchanges, the agreements were initiated by Québec alone and implemented by Québec officials. Such actions are said to be creating a *de facto* provincial competence in international affairs.

Advocates of exclusive federal competence in all international matters view the situation differently.[16] The prerogative of treaty-making power for Canada, it is argued, was vested exclusively in the Queen in 1867, as stated in section 9 of the *BNA Act.* Through a process of evolution from 1871 to 1939, direct power over foreign affairs devolved to Canada to be exercised by the government in the name of the Governor General. At no time during this period did the provinces acquire treaty-making power. Rather, as evidenced by the new Letters Patent issued to the Governor General by the Crown in 1947 and the *Seals Act* of 1939, the federal government was given all powers previously exercised by the British Crown.

Several Supreme Court judgements also support the federalist position. For example, before the 1936 *Labour Conventions* case was appealed to Britain's Judicial Committee of the Privy Council

---

15. Ibid., p. 262.

16. For a discussion of the exclusive federal competence view, see the federal government's White Paper, Canada, Department of External Affairs, *Federalism and International Relations* (Ottawa: Queen's Printer, February, 1968); and its supplement, *Federalism and International Conferences on Education* (Ottawa: Queen's Printer, 1968). As well, see Ontario Advisory Committee on Confederation, *The Confederation Challenge: Background Papers and Reports*, vols. 1 and 2 (Toronto: 1967, 1970).

(JCPC), it drew comments from several Supreme Court justices, including Chief Justice Duff, that the authority to enter into international agreements resided exclusively in the federal government even on matters of provincial legislative competence. However, since the case concerned the power to implement and not negotiate treaties, the JCPC did not consider this issue relevant.

Finally, support for the exclusivity of federal treaty-making power is derived from the international law of recognition. Advocates of this position argue that, during Canada's evolution to independence, only the federal government, not the provincial governments, was recognized as having responsibility for foreign affairs.

Thus, both sides have recourse to legal precedents that make it difficult if not impossible to arrive at a legal solution by unilateral action. The dispute has necessitated a more functional approach that recognizes the concerns of both levels of government; it is this approach that has been adopted by the federal government. Reacting to the demands of Québec, the federal government issued what it perceived to be the proper international role for the provinces:

- The provinces have no treaty-making powers, but they do have the right to enter into private commercial contracts with foreign governments, as well as to make bureaucratic agreements of a non-binding nature with foreign governments.

- The provinces may open offices in foreign countries in pursuit of their legitimate needs and interests in that country, so long as the office only engages in arrangements of a non-binding nature.

- The provinces claim the right to be involved in the formulation stages of treaty-making activities when the subject matter of the treaty falls within provincial legislative competence.

- The provinces may be included in Canadian delegations attending international gatherings and play a role in formulating and enunciating the Canadian position, when the subject matter falls within provincial legislative competence.[17]

While the federal government's purpose was to prevent provincial government initiatives when possible, jurisdictional realities necessitated a framework that would accommodate provincial interests to some extent. Ottawa's policy of primacy in foreign affairs has therefore been tempered by accommodation.

It is evident, then, that foreign policy-making in Canada is becoming ever more diffuse. While the Department of Foreign Affairs remains the most important bureaucratic component, other departments have become more prominent. The increased activity of non-governmental actors continued the trend. The response of the federal government has been to initiate bureaucratic reorganization and to continue to seek accommodation of regional interests as expressed by provincial governments in an attempt to provide a coherent and effective foreign policy.

Québec Foreign Policy

The province of Québec shares with the other provinces many of the same international interests and objectives. However, because of its sovereignist aspirations, it also has its own unique agenda. Québec nationalism is discussed in Chapter 7, but it is important to note here the impact of the nationalist agenda on Québec's relations with foreign countries and the consequent strain often placed on Ottawa–Québec relations.

17. Johannson, "Provincial International Activities," pp. 361–62.

With the advent of the Quiet Revolution in 1960, the Québec government assumed the role of protector of Québécois culture, language and ethnicity. Initially, the emphasis was on developing special relations with the international francophone community in order to bolster the new Québécois interests in science, commerce and management. This generally manifested itself in the form of delegations to international conferences on francophone education, culture and training. As Kim Nossal notes, however, once the Parti Québécois came to power in Québec in 1976, what had begun as "an external expression of functional provincial interests" became "an issue of symbolic national interest for the Québec government."[18] Québec began to challenge the federal government's monopoly over the conduct of Canada's foreign relations. At the same time, the nationalist goal began to shift from seeking special provisions within Canada to bringing about the separation of Québec from Canada and international recognition of Québec's sovereign status. France provided international support and encouragement for this project.

In 1980, when the Québec government held the first referendum on sovereignty-association, Québec's political leaders sought to impress the world that it would be a responsible member of the international community. The White Paper released by the Lévesque government before the 1980 referendum included a full foreign policy program for an independent Québec. Again, in 1995, the PQ government released a pre-referendum plan stressing that an independent Québec would continue traditions of peacekeeping and multilateral involvement. To win international acceptance, the government stressed that it would work jointly with Canada in these endeavours.

Québec's goal of becoming a sovereign state has created confrontation within Canada and perplexed foreign governments. The primacy of the Canadian government in external relations is universally recognized. However, protocol, particularly in France and the United States, has often been awkward as Québec sought and sometimes received treatment that created implications for domestic politics in Québec and also for Canada–France and Canada–U.S. relations.

During the 1995 referendum, French president Jacques Chirac promised that France would recognize Québec after a Yes vote. This was a break from the more qualified approach of "non-interference but non-indifference" that had held since the 1980 referendum had failed. On the other hand, the United States increased the tempo of its standard line — that the United States prefers a United Canada, but it is up to Canadians to make their own decisions. Two weeks before the 1995 referendum, U.S. Secretary of State Warren Christopher noted that no one should assume that agreements such as the North American Free Trade Agreement (NAFTA) would remain unchanged if Québec became independent. A few days later, President Bill Clinton said that "a strong and united Canada has been a wonderful partner for the United States, and an incredibly important and constructive citizen throughout the entire world" — a "great model for the rest of the world and I hope that can continue."[19]

Over the past three decades, the federal government has made several changes in the content and process of foreign policy to meet Québec's challenges. For example, the countries of la Francophonie have been singled out for increased development assistance, cooperation with Québec at summits of la Francophonie has been highlighted, and French-language services in Canadian missions abroad have increased.

---

18. Nossal, *The Politics of Canadian Foreign Policy*, p. 317.
19. Ibid., p. 325.

CANADIAN TRADE POLICY

Canada has a mid-size economy whose prosperity depends heavily on exports of goods and services and foreign investment in its currency, stocks and bonds. Foreign trade is vital to Canadian economic interests. Canada has a low ratio of population to land and resources and is by necessity one of the largest trading states in the world. The domestic market of 30 million is too small to sustain all the flourishing industries, so well over one-third of GDP depends on exports. Most of these exports come from primary industries based on natural resources, of which Canada has an abundance.

Canada has three main kinds of natural resources. The first is agricultural land, which climatic and soil conditions make amenable to cultivating crops and raising livestock. It is limited to the southernmost part of the country and is steadily being encroached upon by industrial development and urban sprawl. The second category is non-renewable resources, such as mineral deposits. Canada is a leading exporter of minerals — crude petroleum, natural gas, iron ore, nickel and copper. The third type of natural resources consists of renewable resources, of which wood, fish, fur and grains are, or have been, particularly important to Canada's economic growth.

This present-day pattern of the Canadian economy essentially was laid out in the colonial period. Basically, Canada exports primary goods and imports secondary or manufactured goods. Most Canadians live and work in urban, industrialized areas, but agricultural products, lumber and mineral resources provide the bulk of our exports and pay for imported manufactured goods. In 1998, we exported $322 billion worth of goods and services and imported $303 billion.

Canadian trade is conducted on a bilateral basis, and requires careful day-to-day management of issues that arise between Canada and its main trading partners. However, the fact that the contractual framework for most of Canada's bilateral trade is provided by international treaties illustrates the important multilateral dimension of economic relations.

Canada and Global Economics

At the end of the Second World War, the leading economic countries met at Bretton Woods in the United States to reorganize the war-torn economies of the trading world. They decided to fix (peg) the exchange rate of the American dollar to the gold standard and other currencies to the dollar. The currencies could be "unpegged" only within stipulated regulations. Eventually, the rules unravelled due to pressures on the American dollar and the entire exchange system became unregulated. Since then, currencies have floated freely and states have had little authority to regulate the world economy.

As for international trade, the U.S., Britain and Canada were the principal proponents of a new order that resulted in 1947 in the *General Agreement on Tariffs and Trade* (GATT), an agreement that sought to establish a trading order based on reciprocity, nondiscrimination and multilateralism. It covered over 80 percent of world trade and included most major industrialized countries. The **GATT** is both a treaty and an institution. As a treaty, it sets out a code of rules for the conduct of trade; as an institution, it oversees the application of the trade rules and provides a forum in which countries can discuss trade problems and negotiate reductions in trade barriers.

The main benefit for Canada of the GATT was that it provided a contractual basis for Canada–U.S. trade relations while facilitating the expansion of trade relations with other countries. As a signatory of the GATT, Canada could negotiate basic resource needs with its powerful southern neighbour more easily. World trade grew steadily after the GATT was founded and then slowed in the 1970s, with the Organization of Petroleum Exporting Countries (OPEC) showing most rapid growth during that decade. In 1981, for the first time since the GATT was established, there was no real growth in world trade. After that, the world economy demonstrated three significant characteristics: slow international market growth, financial instability and increased international competitiveness. Financial markets were volatile, with developing countries building up enormous debt loads that threaten to disrupt the international economic system.

In its efforts to improve the world economy and reduce protectionism, the GATT held several rounds of negotiations to amend the trading rules. The last of these discussions among 109 states began in 1986 in Uruguay, and thus was named the **Uruguay Round.** This round lasted seven years and was completed only in 1994. It made major breakthroughs in solving difficulties facing the international trading community. The participants agreed to transform the GATT secretariat into a somewhat more powerful **World Trade Organization** and to reduce tariffs on a long list of goods. Tariffs on industrial goods, for example, which have already been reduced to a current average of about 5 percent in developed countries, are to be reduced by another 38 percent. Technical agreements were also concluded on issues in the service sector, including banking, insurance, telecommunications, broadcasting and so forth, and on intellectual copyright for subjects such as patents and licences.

As the global economy grows, so, too, does the importance of international economic organizations such as the **International Monetary Fund** (IMF) and the **World Bank**. Both organizations were set up at the end of the Second World War.[20]

The purposes of the IMF are to foster stability in money markets, to encourage cooperation among states on monetary matters, to aid in the establishment of a payment system and to promote international trade. Currently, 179 states are members of this organization, which lends funds to member states and provides technical assistance to their economies. The importance of each state in the IMF is based on its voting strength as determined by its financial contributions to the fund. The United States holds about 18 percent of the votes.

The World Bank lends money to countries or states that commercial banks or other lenders will not support, and generally tries to reduce poverty among its members. A total of 177 countries belong to the World Bank. It makes decisions in a manner similar to that of the IMF. It tends to support problem projects and has large holdings with several developing countries.

Canada also belongs to many other multilateral organizations concerned with the global economy and development. The best known and most prestigious of them are the G-7 economic summits, annual gatherings of the seven largest industrialized democracies — United States, Japan, Germany, Britain, France, Italy and Canada — and the Commission of the European Community. The summits, which began in 1975 at Rambouillet in France, have taken on a semi-permanent character, although there is no permanent secretariat. They have become huge media events, but they provide the opportunity for leaders to discuss trade issues and international economic topics.

The meetings are particularly important to Canada for several reasons. First of all, the economic summits provide recognition of status; political leaders want to be part of this elite group. Canada joined the group largely due to American and Japanese sponsorship. But more important, Canada has a major stake in the economic relationships among the "Big Seven." Of the seven, Canada is the most affected by the economic policies of the United States. Still, many observers believe that the summits are meaningless exercises. A balanced view is that they are significant, but their importance is easy to exaggerate.

Canada has an important role to play in these and other international institutions. It is the seventh-largest exporting country in the world and the eighth-largest importer. More than 40 percent of the goods and services produced are sold in foreign markets. In particular, manufactured goods,

---

20. See Robert J. Jackson and Doreen Jackson, *A Comparative Introduction to Political Science* (Upper Saddle River, N.J.: Prentice Hall, 1997), p. 439.

motor vehicles and parts, metals, minerals, pulp and paper, lumber and sawmill products, natural gas and wheat sell extremely well. However, as usual, Canada consumes more *services* (such as tourism, freight and government procurement) from other countries than it sells, and pays out more interest to investors abroad than it earns on foreign investments. In fact, about 80 percent of the deficit in non-merchandise trade goes to pay interest to foreigners — in return for money that is used by Canadians to finance spending and investments.

Canada has also been affected by world trends. The rise of multinational corporations has combined with more open trade rules to develop what many observers call *globalization*. The impact on the Canadian economy has been dramatic. For example, in the past two decades almost every province's economy has come to depend more on exports to other countries than on exports to other Canadian provinces. Goods and services are not the only things that flow more easily around the world — so, too, does money. In fact,

> *[i]t has been estimated that the total annual value of trade in financial assets in world markets increased from $5 trillion in 1980 to $35 trillion in 1992, or twice the combined GDPs of all the member countries of the Organization for Economic Cooperation and Development.*[21]

There has been an emergence of a *global economy* in terms not just of trade but of all the elements of wealth creation — finance, investment, production, distribution and marketing — which are increasingly being organized regionally and globally. The changing structure of the world economy has seriously affected the Canadian economy and trade patterns in other ways. There has been a pronounced shift in industrial power toward Japan, Europe and the so-called newly industrialized countries (NICs). Major oil-exporting countries have retained their vastly increased purchasing power. New technologies are developing rapidly and forcing industries in developed countries such as Canada to adapt to increasingly competitive conditions or be left behind as standard technologies are taken over by developing countries with low labour costs.

INTERNATIONAL AND MULTILATERAL ORGANIZATION

For historical and political reasons, Canadian foreign policy has always been directed predominantly toward Europe (especially Britain) and the United States. Political relations, defence and economic policies therefore have all developed certain basic continuities. Long-standing defence ties, considered in detail later in this chapter, are with the U.S. and western Europe through the North Atlantic Treaty Organization (NATO) and North American Aerospace Defence Command (NORAD). Multilateral relations are primarily conducted through the United Nations and its related agencies. Bilateral political and economic relations are strongest with the U.S., the Commonwealth, western Europe and the French-language community. But Asia, especially Japan, has recently become even more important to Canada than Europe in purely economic relations.

Canada and the United Nations

Canada played a central role in creating the United Nations and in directing its evolution as an international organization. Sponsorship of the United Nations by the Canadian government

---

21. Canada, *Canada Year Book 1996* (Ottawa: Supply and Services, 1996), p. 292.

demonstrated the radical change from the pre-war policy of isolationism to postwar international-ism as a means of avoiding war. Both Louis St. Laurent, who became Secretary of State for External Affairs in 1946, and Lester Pearson, who followed in that position, were avowed internationalists. Pearson wrote in his memoirs, "everything I learned during the war confirmed and strengthened my view as a Canadian that our foreign policy must not be timid or fearful of commitments but ac-tivist in accepting international responsibility."[22] The United Nations seemed the natural medium for bringing states together to promote peace.

Initially, the UN had 57 charter members and in the 1950s Canada was a major participant. But the club was too restrictive. In 1955, Paul Martin, chairman of the Canadian UN delegation, per-suaded the UN Security Council to agree to a package deal for accepting new members. New members flooded in, and today Canada is no longer a principal player, but is merely one of 188 countries in an institution no longer dominated by western democratic powers. As president of the UN General Assembly, Lester Pearson was responsible for introducing one of its most important innovations: the peacekeeping force. The UN Charter provided for a standing army, but one was never created.

However, no other organization has arisen to replace the UN as a forum for the discussion of world problems. Canada has been involved at the UN in several significant issue areas during recent years, including the law of the sea, the north–south dialogue between rich and poor nations, human rights, chemical warfare and abolition of land mines. Canada is also a strong supporter of the UN's many specialized multilateral agencies — the World Health Organization, the International Labor Organiza-tion and the International Monetary Fund, among others — that have earned considerable respect throughout the world. Another agency, the International Civil Aviation Organization, has its headquarters in Montréal. These agencies are all working to improve the quality of life, particularly in the large number of new states represented at the UN.

The rather tarnished contemporary image of the UN may be a result of exaggerated expectations of what it can accomplish. John Holmes summarized the situation in this way: "When people worry whether the UN has lived up to the ideals of the Charter, in some ways it's the wrong question. Rather than see whether it has been able to carry out a mandate carved in stone it may be better to ask whether it has been able to grow and fit in with changing circumstances.... To a great extent it has."[23] Holmes was correct. (See discussion of Canadian peace-keeping, page 557.)

The Commonwealth

At Confederation, Canada was part of the British Empire, exercising autonomy in domestic policy but dependent on Britain in foreign affairs. The First World War was the

CLOSE-UP ON ▮Public▮Policy▮

ETHICAL FOREIGN POLICY?

Soon after his appointment as Minister of Foreign Affairs, Lloyd Axworthy began to speak about the need for a more ethical dimension in Canada's foreign policy. While not deny-ing the need for realistic self-interest in making foreign pol-icy, he stressed the role of morality in this process. To involve the public more in the foreign policy process, Axworthy set up a series of National Forums on Canada's International Relations and an Advisory Committee to the Minister. The government sought new policies concerning child soldiers, land mines and the International Criminal Court (ICC). Denying that only states should determine foreign policy, Axworthy declared that the UN Commission on Human Rights should "develop standards that apply globally, and ... monitor their implementation without the bias inherent in any purely national review."*

Do you share Mr. Axworthy's concern about "human security," or do you think Canadian foreign policy should be based mostly on Canada's national interests? Are the two objectives compatible?

* Lloyd Axworthy, Speech to the 54th Session of the UN Commission on Human Rights, 1998.

---

22. Lester B. Pearson, *Mike: The Memoirs of Lester Pearson, vol. I: 1897–1948* (Toronto: University of Toronto Press, 1972), p. 283.
23. John Holmes, quoted in *The Toronto Star*, November 20, 1982.

catalyst for Canada attaining complete autonomy and the Empire transforming into the Commonwealth. The transition was achieved at a succession of imperial conferences in the 1920s that culminated with the Balfour Declaration in 1926. The dominions within the British Empire were equal, autonomous communities "united by a common allegiance to the Crown, and freely associated as members of the British Commonwealth of Nations."[24] This sentiment was enshrined in the 1931 *Statute of Westminster,* which formally laid the old Empire to rest. The Commonwealth at that time consisted of Britain, Australia, Canada, Newfoundland, the Irish Free State, the Union of South Africa and New Zealand. Now, almost seven decades later, it numbers 54 member states and embraces more than a billion people and about a quarter of the Earth's surface. Louis St. Laurent and Lester Pearson played important roles in the evolution of this new Commonwealth. Pearson particularly was a key figure in negotiating an acceptable formula for admission of new republics — a development that changed the essentially anglocentric focus of the Commonwealth association. Canada has consistently encouraged the strengthening of the association as a vehicle for practical cooperation among member states.

Commonwealth heads of government meet regularly every two years and sponsor various fields of technical cooperation, scholarships and the Commonwealth Games. There are no binding rules of membership, and decisions are made by consensus rather than vote. Perhaps the most valuable feature of Commonwealth meetings, however, is simply the opportunity for heads of state and government to meet relatively informally and discuss vital common issues such as human rights and intra-Commonwealth aid. For instance, at the meeting in Lusaka in 1979, in an atmosphere of civil war, the issue was how to end Rhodesia's illegal white supremacist regime. The Commonwealth meeting provided a forum for negotiations, and its result was an independent Zimbabwe. Canada also played an important role in Commonwealth activities over apartheid in South Africa. Canadian leaders worked assiduously to keep racial cleavages from dividing the organization over the quarrels that led to South Africa's departure until its eventual return in June 1995 with Nelson Mandela as the newly elected president. The 1991 meeting in Harare, Zimbabwe, was used by Canada mainly to highlight issues of human rights, democratic development and equality for women, but there was little instrumental effect from all the talk. Since then, meetings in Limassol, Cyprus; Aukland, New Zealand; and Edinburgh, U.K., have stressed economic and trade issues. In recognition of democracy, the 1999 conference took place in Durban, South Africa.

La Francophonie

In recent years, the French-language community has built its own organization similar to the British Commonwealth. Under Lester Pearson's leadership and especially under Pierre Trudeau, the Canadian government encouraged strengthening Canada's ties with francophone countries, mainly through multilateral programs and organizations such as the Agency for Cultural and Technical Cooperation. The Agency's programs centre on three main areas: development, education, and scientific and technical cooperation. The issue of Québec's participation as distinct from Canada's has occasionally caused overt hostility between the respective governments when the federal government interpreted Québec's actions as a challenge to its primacy in foreign policy. However, since 1971 Québec has had "participating government" status in the Agency, a privilege that also was extended to New Brunswick in 1977. Finally, in Paris in 1986, *la Francophonie,* with a membership of 41 countries, was born. Canadian representation was fleshed out with members from Québec and New Brunswick using a controversial formula that implied an enhanced role for the provinces in foreign affairs. In 1996, Jean Chrétien appointed a minister responsible for la Francophonie.

---

24. G.P. de T. Glazebrook, *A History of Canadian External Relations* (Toronto: McClelland & Stewart, 1966), pp. 90–91.

The organization has met with limited success. In 1995 at Cotonou, Benin, Prime Minister Jean Chrétien tried to encourage la Francophonie to get "more active in political debate."[25] In fact, as usual, the conference could not come to any firm action because the members were split over what policy to adopt on a number of issues.

The 1999 meeting in New Brunswick was particularly contentious. Opponents of the conference complained that the leaders of Burundi, Burkina Faso, Congo and Rwanda should not have been invited because of their poor records on human rights. Prime Minister Chrétien worked around the criticism by allowing the leaders into the country but proclaiming, "Let us work to ensure that the legacy we leave to future generations is a Francophonie made up of countries where democratic values are embraced." As well, journalists in English and French Canada used the occasion for unusually vitriolic comments about the leaders from the four countries in question. *The Globe and Mail* ran a cartoon showing a uniformed African dictator seated on a pile of skulls. A well-dressed Frenchman was shown sipping champagne and saying, "Still, his accent is flawless!" The French New Brunswick paper *L'Acadie Nouvelle,* on the other hand, proclaimed Moncton to be the "centre of the universe Francophone."

Canada and the OAS

Canada was late to join the Organization of American States (OAS), the main institution that unites the states of the western hemisphere. It was formed in 1948 from the Pan-American Union at a time when Canada was primarily concerned with seeking security through NATO and the UN, and hence did not seriously consider joining the organization. The issue of Canadian membership first became significant in the early 1960s. Proponents argued that Canada should become a member of the hemisphere and thereby establish prestige in the region and increase trade opportunities. Opponents warned that if Canada did join the OAS the country soon would become embroiled in disputes between the United States and Latin America. The latter view was accepted by the government and the issue was not seriously raised again as a foreign policy option until the 1980s.[26] During this period, Canada maintained a limited "permanent observer" status at the OAS.

Over time, arguments for joining the OAS became stronger. Advocates believed that membership would give Canada a stronger voice in planning development strategies for Latin America, as well as allow Canada to make a contribution in the field of human rights. As countries such as Mexico and Venezuela have become stronger, the fear that Canada would be caught in disputes between the United States and Latin America has diminished. Canada finally ratified its full membership in the OAS in January 1990. One of the most important results has been increased cooperation between Canada and other OAS members to stabilize democracy throughout South America.

CANADA'S RELATIONS WITH THE UNITED STATES

U.S. president John F. Kennedy said that "geography made us neighbours, history made us friends and economics made us partners." There is no more important external relationship for Canada than that with the United States. But the long history of cooperation in NATO and NORAD belies the fact

---

25. *The Globe and Mail*, December 24, 1995.

26. Robert J. Jackson, "Canadian Foreign Policy in the Western Hemisphere," in Viron P. Vaky, ed., *Governance in the Western Hemisphere* (New York: Praeger, 1984), pp. 119–34.

that much of Canada's history, including Confederation itself, was inspired by efforts to be independent of the United States and protected from American domination.

Approximately $503 billion in trade crossed the border in 1998 — by a large margin, the world's leading two-way trade relationship. The U.S. accounted for over 83 percent of Canadian exports and 77 percent of imports, making it our most important trading partner. On the other hand, Canada took only a small percentage of total American exports and provided even less of its imports. Even at these significantly lower percentages of total trade, Canada is the most important trading partner of the United States. Leading Canadian exports to the U.S. include passenger autos and chassis, communications and electronic equipment, aerospace components, natural gas, forest products, and crude petroleum and petrochemicals. In turn, Canada imports motor vehicles and parts, electronic computers, crude petroleum and aircraft. Both import and export trade with the U.S. have grown dramatically in recent years. (See the next section on free trade.)

Relations with the United States clearly are critical to Canada's economic well-being. The high degree of dependence is not, however, mutual. Although both geography and history provided the backdrop for an early special relationship between Canada and the United States, the relationship has inevitably been one-sided. This fact was perhaps best illustrated in symbolic terms by the relative urgency assigned to initial political visitations at the highest level. The first Canadian prime ministerial visit to Washington was in 1871; the first presidential visit to Ottawa did not occur until over seven decades later, in 1943. The relationship between these unequal neighbours over the years has been friendly, but, on the part of Canadians, necessarily guarded, as the attitudes of American leaders were perceived to fluctuate from the extremes of annexation to complete indifference. Ulysses S. Grant, for example, aspired to absorb Canada in time for his 1872 election bid — in fact, he wanted the British to cede Canada in exchange for damage caused by a British ship![27]

Because the Canadian economy is so closely entwined with that of the United States, a priority in foreign policy must be soothing bilateral irritants. There are significant differences that affect every aspect of the relationship. The governments differ in structure and functions, and these subtle differences are not always understood or appreciated. In the early 1980s, for example, a bilateral fishing agreement was scuppered after long negotiations when the U.S. Senate refused to give its assent. This ratification procedure, which is foreign to the Canadian political system, brought howls of outrage. In Canada, ratification is part of the powers of the executive and there is no constitutional requirement for the government to seek parliamentary approval. This incident was not unusual. In fact, according to Christian Wiktor, there have been more than 200 treaties negotiated by American administrators with various countries over the past 200 years that were never ratified by the Senate, 18 of them concerning Canada directly.[28]

There are other important differences. The two governments have disparate approaches to the roles of government in the economy. In Canada, both federal and provincial governments take an active role in the marketplace to a degree unknown and unacceptable in the United States.

Perhaps the most obvious difference, however, is that Canada's population is only one-tenth that of the U.S. We discussed in Chapters 2 and 4 some of the inevitable repercussions of such a disparity; basically, it makes Canada vulnerable to pressures from the United States in the fields of culture, economy and defence. A few facts serve to indicate the economic issue: in 1991, Canada's net international investment position was negative. The amount Canadians owed non-residents over what they owed residents was $269.9 billion; 30 percent of the leading 65 000 corporations

27. Martin, *The Presidents and the Prime Ministers,* p. 12.
28. *The Globe and Mail,* May 7, 1981.

were foreign-controlled; and, of the largest 500 companies in Canada, 38 percent were foreign-controlled and 28 percent fully foreign-owned.[29]

These underlying economic and cultural differences between the two countries surface periodically as policy conflicts between Ottawa and Washington. This was particularly evident in the late 1970s and early 1980s, a time of growing tension between the two countries, both of which were caught in a deep economic recession. The poor economic climate exacerbated cleavages when each country acted to protect and strengthen its home industries. Disputes arose in such areas as fisheries, trucking regulations and advertising rights.[30] Most conflict, however, centred around the Liberal government's Foreign Investment Review Agency (FIRA), set up to monitor and restrict foreign investment, and the National Energy Program (NEP), designed to increase Canadian ownership of natural resources. Both impinged on foreign interests, especially those of the United States. The conflict continued until the 1984 Conservative government got rid of the NEP and undermined FIRA, turning it into Investment Canada.

Measures such as the NEP and FIRA were adopted by the Canadian government to regulate escalating foreign ownership, which was seen as depriving Canadians of the ability to control and benefit from the country's industries, particularly resource industries. Canada's prosperity is linked to the rest of the world through not only trade, but also the importation of foreign capital. We have seen that the level of foreign investment is particularly high. As one expert put it, "Canada cannot be compared with capital-rich economies such as the American and British. The combination of a small population and huge natural resources necessitate, even in the best of economic times, reliance on external financing to satisfy our economic expansions."[31] Individual Canadians save at double the rate of Americans, but the country does not come close to satisfying its own capital requirements. In recent years, much foreign investment has not been "new" American capital but has come from within Canada itself. Foreign subsidiaries simply retain earnings and depreciation reserves and put them back into the economy as investments.

Most foreign capital comes in the form of direct investment, not interest or portfolio investment. This means that rather than involving bank loans or bonds, which can be paid off, investment in the Canadian economy brings a high degree of control and ownership by foreigners, especially in the manufacturing and resource sectors. Such branch plants allow the importation of American technology and market access as well as American values. They are subject not only to market forces and Canadian government regulation but also to American interests.

There can be little doubt that foreign investment improves Canada's standard of living and has helped to transform Canada into an industrialized country. However, there is equally little doubt that it has greatly increased the dependence of Canada's economy on that of the United States.

FREE TRADE: FTA AND NAFTA

One of the most controversial trade issues concerns free trade, a recurring theme in Canada's relationship with the United States. The issue originated, and caused heated debate, as far back as the 1870s. In the early years of statehood, Sir John A. Macdonald won the hearts of Canadians with his

---

29. Statistics Canada, *Canada's Investment Position 1988–91* (Ottawa: Supply and Services, 1992), pp. 42–43. See charts and details in Mel Hurtig, *The Betrayal of Canada*, 2nd ed. (Toronto: Stoddart, 1992), ch. 11.

30. For an interesting view of Canada–U.S. tensions, see Stephen Clarkson, *Canada and the Reagan Challenge* (Toronto: Lorimer, 1982).

31. James R. Niniger, President, The Conference Board of Canada, quoted in *The Ottawa Citizen*, May 14, 1984.

National Policy of high tariffs to protect fledgling Canadian industries. Much later, in 1911, Sir Wilfrid Laurier failed to win re-election partly because he wanted to eliminate tariffs on less than one-quarter of cross-border trade. He could not compete with the opposition slogan of "No truck or trade with the Yankees." More recently, many tariff cuts were made following GATT agreements. Some Canadian tariffs remained high — for example, those on petrochemicals and textiles. Other selected markets were protected by indirect means such as quotas, marketing boards, government "standards and specifications," and health and safety regulations.

In the early 1980s, the controversy was over whether to move toward full free trade across the border or, as the Liberal government recommended in 1983, to build **sectoral free trade** in selected items, among them steel, agricultural equipment, urban mass transit equipment and "informatics" such as computer communications services. This type of policy had been implemented in the 1965 Auto Pact and had proved extremely successful in increasing the flow of Canadian automobiles and parts across the U.S. border. Advocates of further sectoral free trade argued that it would raise productivity, lower inflation and create jobs, unlike protectionism, which, it was argued, hinders an increase in trade.

However, the sectoral free trade position was dropped when the Conservatives came to office in 1984. Their position was buttressed by the 1985 report of the Royal Commission on the Economic Union and Development Prospects for Canada (the Donald Macdonald Commission), which argued strongly in favour of **general free trade**.[32] Opponents of this new policy argued that free trade would destroy many Canadian companies (especially in textiles and footwear) and inevitably lead to the formation of common institutions that would be dominated by the U.S., therefore eroding Canada's political sovereignty.

In the course of his first mandate, Prime Minister Mulroney reversed his earlier position *against* free trade and entered into negotiations for a comprehensive, general trade agreement with the United States. The reasons for this shift are not completely known, but he received strong political support from Québec and the western provinces for doing so. At the time, many Canadian business people were worried about a growing demand for protectionism in Washington due to the massive U.S. trade deficit. Two major trade disputes came to the fore while Canada–U.S. free trade negotiations were taking place. In 1986, the United States introduced a countervailing duty against softwood lumber imported from Canada, a source of trade worth about $4 billion annually to Canadian companies. Canada negotiated with the U.S. to apply its own 15 percent export tax rather than submit to the countervailing duty. Later the same year, the United States imposed a five-year tariff on Canadian red cedar shakes and shingles, and Canada was forced to retaliate.[33]

On September 26, 1985, Canada formally requested that the United States enter negotiations for a comprehensive free trade agreement. Two years later, the deal was concluded; the legal text was released and signed by President Ronald Reagan and Prime Minister Brian Mulroney on January 2, 1988. In the meantime, Federal Liberal leader John Turner called on the Liberal-controlled Senate to block the agreement. The 1988 election ensued with the free trade deal as the primary election issue. (See Chapter 12.) When the Tories won the election, they allowed the agreement to come into force on January 1, 1989.

---

32. *Report of the Royal Commission on the Economic Union and Development Prospects for Canada*, vol. 1 (Ottawa: Minister of Supply and Services, 1985).

33. For a summary of these disputes, see Leyton-Brown, "Canada-U.S. Trade Disputes and the Free Trade Deal," in Maureen Molot and Brian W. Tomlin, eds., *Canada among Nations 1987: A World of Conflict* (Toronto: Lorimer, 1988).

Reproduced with permission, Raeside, *Victoria Times*.

The *Canada–United States Free Trade Agreement* was intended to enhance market access and reduce trade conflicts between the two countries. The agreement provided a set of **dispute resolution mechanisms** and the goal of gradual elimination of all tariffs between the two countries. Special and technical agreements were made in the fields of services, investment, finances, energy, agriculture, automobiles, cultural industries and even alcoholic beverages. However, free trade as such was never completed. Each country reserved the right to continue to impose trade retaliation, such as countervailing duties, anti-dumping and other trade remedies. Each country also reserved the right to change its trade legislation even after the agreement came into force but any new laws would only apply to the partner country if it was so specified in the legislation.

Canadian opposition to this deal was widespread and centred on three issues. First, it was argued that the deal did not obtain *secure* access to the American market for Canadian products since American trade remedies continued to apply. Second, the agreement was attacked as giving away too much in investment, financial services, agriculture, energy and service sectors and getting too little in return. An important issue also centred around the definition of what constituted a trade "subsidy"; opponents of the deal argued that Canadian social programs — such as unemployment insurance and provincial health insurance — could fall into such a category. And, last, the deal was attacked by some provincial leaders for eroding provincial powers and by some federal politicians for reducing the ability of Canadian governments to act freely in the economy and hence reduce Canadian sovereignty.

Although the 1988 election settled the basic question about the free trade deal,[34] questions about the impact of the trade agreement on Canadian interests and indeed on Canadian sovereignty remained.[35] Almost before the ink was dry on the free trade agreement, the Canadian government began negotiations with Mexico and the United States for a *North American Free Trade Agreement* (NAFTA).[36] This agreement called for a three-country deal that incorporated the *Canada–United States Free Trade Agreement* and expanded it to include clauses on intellectual property, medical services and more explicit rules about national treatment. In May 1993, Parliament approved the legislation, allowing the government the right to implement the agreement if side deals on labour and the environment were worked out among Canada, Mexico and the United States.

TABLE 15.1   THE NAFTA EQUATION

	U.S.	Canada	Mexico
Population (millions)	267	30	93
Human Develoment Index 1998, rank	4th	1st	49th
Per capita GDP (1995)	26 997	21 916	6 769
Trade (as % of GDP 1993–95)	24	71	48
Net foreign direct investment (as % of GNP 1993–94)	–0.6	–0.2	2.9
Living standard (per 1 000 inhabitants)			
Telephones lines (1995)	626	590	96
Personal computers (1995)	328	193	26.1
Television sets (1995)	776	647	192
Doctors (1993)	2.3	2.2	1
Infant mortality (per 1 000 births 1996)	5	6	27
Adult literacy (1995)	99	99	89.6
Life expectancy at birth (1995)	76.4	79.1	72.1

Sources: Adapted from various OECD Surveys and *Human Development Report, 1998* (New York: United Nations, 1998). Figures in U.S. dollars.

34. It should be noted, however, that more Canadians voted *against* the Conservatives, who espoused free trade, than voted for them. See election figures in Chapter 10.

35. The arguments in favour of the free trade deal have been carefully summarized in John Crispo, ed., *Free Trade: The Real Story* (Toronto: Gage, 1988). A delightful summary of the opposition arguments is found in Marjorie M. Bowker, *On Guard for Thee* (Hull: Voyageur, 1988). For a longer view, see Robert Bothwell, *Canada and the United States* (Toronto: University of Toronto Press, 1992).

36. Much more opposition comes from outsiders than from political parties — see Maude Barlow and Bruce Campbell, *Take Back the Nation* (Toronto: Key Porter, 1991); and Mel Hurtig, *Betrayal of Canada*, 2nd ed. (Toronto: Stoddart, 1992).

In the November 1993 general election, the Liberals under Jean Chrétien promised to reopen some of the most controversial parts of the agreement for renegotiation. On January 1, 1994, the agreement was made law, despite the fact that the new Liberal government had not achieved any of its goals. The agreement linked Canada to a market of 383 million people and a combined economy of $7 trillion. For basic information on the three countries and the NAFTA, see Tables 15.1 and 15.2.

NAFTA was discussed in the 1993 general election (see Chapter 12) but did not prove nearly as significant an issue as free trade in the 1988 election because the Liberals did not directly oppose the deal. All five major parties seemed to agree that as captive neighbours on this continent, the only reasonable policy for the three states to adopt is one that fosters a mutually satisfactory relationship. In the coming years, the advent of free trade with Mexico and the United States may well transform the nature of politics in Canada.

The free trade debate continues. In 1994, at the Summit of the Americas, negotiations to extend NAFTA to Chile and the intention to create a hemispheric free trade zone by the year 2005 were announced. The same year, Canada signed the Asian-Pacific Economic Cooperation (APEC) agreement, which proposes the establishment of a Pacific free trade and investment zone for developed economies by 2010 and for developing economies by 2020.

Another controversy continues to fester. In 1995 member states of the OECD began secret negotiations on a Multilateral Agreement on Investment (MAI). While this agreement has never been concluded (and may never be), it set off a storm of criticism, especially from the left in Canada, because it would have secured a "binding" international investors' agreement that would have enhanced the rights of corporations to invest in any country and would have severely limited the ability of any government to prevent or regulate the activity.[37]

TABLE 15.2   NAFTA FRAMEWORK

Facts about the North American Free Trade Agreement	
Tariffs:	Eliminated over a 15-year period. Levies on half of the more than 9 000 products phased out immediately, 65 percent of them within five years.
Agriculture:	Some tariffs on all farm products phased out but producers given 15 years to adjust to duty-free status on sensitive products.
Automobiles:	To qualify for duty-free treatment, the North American content of cars (then 50 percent) must reach 62.5 percent within eight years.
Financial services:	Mexico allows U.S. and Canadian banks, brokerage firms and insurance companies free access after a six-year transition period during which bans on foreign ownership are phased out.
Textiles:	Mexico avoids high duties on shipments to the U.S. and Canada as long as the clothing is made from yarns and fabrics from North America.
Trucking:	Mexico allows foreigners to invest in its trucking firms, and U.S., Mexican and Canadian trucking companies allowed to do business on cross-border routes previously prohibited.

37. For the opposition viewpoint see Tony Clarke, *Silent Coup* (Ottawa: Canadian Centre for Policy Alternatives, 1997).

CANADA'S RELATIONS WITH OTHER AREAS

Canada and Western Europe

Canada's historical and cultural ties with western Europe have always been close, and Canadian governments have counted on this region of the world to counterbalance American influence. In the 1970s in particular, fears were rife that Canada was too dependent on American markets. It was at this time that Prime Minister Pierre Trudeau initiated his so-called Third Option, whose purpose was to increase trade with western Europe and Japan in order to diminish reliance on the United States. As an extension of that philosophy, Trudeau achieved a weak contractual link with the European Community, known as the Framework Agreement. However, little but platitudes came from this agreement, and trade with the United States continued to increase while that with Europe stagnated.

The Canadian–British link, the strongest tie Canada had in western Europe, became weaker after Britain entered the European Common Market in 1973. The Canadian share of the British market decreased, and the trade balance eventually tilted in Britain's favour, largely because of North Sea oil exports to Canada. Despite this, in 1995, Britain remained Canada's third-largest trading partner and educational and travel links continued to be very strong.

The 15 countries that make up the European Union (EU) constitute the world's largest trading entity. The EU is one of Canada's largest markets for agricultural products and several resource-based products, including forest products and fish. In 1995, the EU imported only about 6 percent of Canada's total merchandise exports. Since this figure represented an even smaller percentage of total EU imports, however, the relationship is much more important to Canada than to the EU.

EU members generally desire access to Canada's pulp, oil, uranium and other mineral resources, and in return would like to offer Canadians manufactured goods. The Canadian government is justifiably reluctant to accept these nineteenth-century conditions of trade. On the other hand, access to European Union markets is also difficult for Canadians to achieve, and despite traditional political ties the trade relationship is unlikely to improve much.

In 1990, Canada and the EU signed the Transatlantic Declaration, which brought the two together on good terms but did very little for economic interests. In 1996, the two signed a Joint Action Plan (JAP), which is very broad in scope but does not include a free trade agreement as envisaged at the beginning of the negotiations. Its main components call for a trade *study* to identify tariff and non-tariff barriers to more trade between Canada and the EU.

Canada and the Pacific Rim

While Canadian trade with western Europe stagnated in recent years, it increased rapidly in the Pacific Rim. In 1983, for the first time, Canada traded more with Asia than with western Europe. It is increasingly evident that trans-Pacific trade is another opportunity for a counterbalance in the American-dominated Canadian economy; it may eventually be Canada's new third option.

Countries of the Pacific Rim — Japan, Korea, Taiwan and Singapore — in particular are challenging world markets with outstanding management, technological and production techniques. While Japan's economy has slowed, those of the "Asian tigers" continue to grow strongly. Since 1973, Japan has been Canada's second-largest national trading partner. In 1995, two-way trade reached over $20 billion. Despite its recent sluggish economy, Japan remains Canada's fastest growing export market among our major trading partners. Canadian–Japanese trade relations are those of a resource-rich supplier and a resource-poor industrial nation: almost all of Japan's exports to Canada are fully manufactured, while most of Canada's exports are either raw materials or semi-processed products. China too is looming as an important trade partner for Canada. Of special importance is how China integrated Hong Kong after its hand-over on July 1, 1997. As of early 2000, Canada–China relations continue to be satisfactory, but the arrival of illegal "boat people" on the shores of British Columbia has complicated the situation.

Canada, Developing Countries and the Rest of the World

Under the World Trade Organization, the developing countries of the world enjoy various types of differential and preferential treatment in the effort to nurture their nascent agricultural and manufacturing industries. Canadian trade with developing areas is relatively modest, although it has grown slightly in recent years. Most developing countries have economic situations similar to Canada's and thus compete in many of the same areas. They generally export tropical foodstuffs and raw materials. The more industrialized among them, including Brazil, Venezuela, Mexico, China, Korea and Saudi Arabia, also produce labour-intensive standard technology goods and were considered by the Canadian government to be the best targets for expanded exports in the 1980s.[38] On the whole, developing countries continue to be more important trade partners for Japan, the U.S. and the EU than for Canada, because Canada competes with these developing countries to sell raw materials. Another serious problem inhibiting trade with developing countries is their enormous debt burden.

Since Canada has no coherent foreign policy that embraces the entire hemisphere, Canadian relations with countries in South and Central America and the Caribbean consist mainly of bilateral trade, political, economic and humanitarian interests.[39] A high percentage of Canadian exports in the area are processed or manufactured goods. Canadian imports from the area were about twice the volume of the exports. They consisted primarily of petroleum products, particularly from Venezuela and Mexico, and tropical food products, as well as some manufactured products from Brazil and Mexico. Although trade is paramount, Canada is also an active investor in the region. Canadian banks have been active in Latin America and the Caribbean since the nineteenth century.

Economic and commercial matters are the most concrete evidence of Canadian relations south of the United States, but political and humanitarian issues, too, concern Canadian governments. Despite protests from the United States, Canada maintained political relations with Cuba after the 1959 revolution. Today, Canada continues trade and political relations with Cuba even in the face of a U.S. embargo. The Canadian government has disagreed with the ideological commitment and some of the policies and activities of the Cuban government, but, unlike some American administrations, it does not condemn Cuba and communism as the only sources of conflict in Central America and the Caribbean. In 1996, Jesse Helms, a chairman of the United States Senate Foreign Relations Committee, likened Lloyd Axworthy, Canada's Minister of Foreign Affairs, to Neville Chamberlain and his appeasement of Hitler for Canada's opposition to U.S. embargoes against Cuba.

Canada's best relations in the area south of Mexico are with Brazil and Venezuela. Both have been given priority ratings by the Canadian government. Their large markets and relatively stable political systems provide the foundation for increased, successful ties.

---

38. *A Review of Canadian Trade Policy*, p. 224.

39. These are considered in detail in Robert J. Jackson, "Canadian Foreign Policy and the Western Hemisphere." For a historical summary, see D.R. Murray, "The Bilateral Road: Canada and Latin America in the 1980s," *International Journal*, vol. 37, no. 1 (Winter 1981–82), pp. 108–31.

Canada naturally has links with many other countries and areas which, although important in other ways, are not very significant in an economic sense. Relations with Australia and New Zealand are long-standing and close because of the early Commonwealth connection. These countries are a small but important part of Canada's global trade relationship. Mention must also be made of Russia, the republics of the former U.S.S.R. and other eastern European countries. These states account for only a tiny percentage of Canada's total trade, but Russia is a major grain importer and therefore economically important to Canada.

CANADIAN DEFENCE POLICY

The objectives of defence and security policy are intertwined with foreign policy objectives and, more specifically, with deterring war. Over time, Canadian objectives in this field have varied according to changes in the international strategic environment and the political configuration of the country. But at all times there have been commitments to preserving the independence of Canada, its borders, institutions and values, to pursuing the peaceful settlement of disputes and to preventing hostilities and warfare.

Such aspirations are accepted by almost all Canadians. However, the policies and programs required to fulfill these goals are constantly in dispute. Should Canada continue to be a part of a collective security arrangement such as NATO or, like Sweden, be more independent? Should Canada be part of the nuclear bomb club or keep nuclear devices off native soil? Even if there were agreement on such general policies, an analyst would still need to know what programs would be required to execute them. For example, should more government funds be spent on arms than on social programs? Should Canadians be deployed overseas in potential combat zones? Should Canadians participate in international peacekeeping missions? How should military personnel be kept accountable when they are on missions such as those in Bosnia, Haiti, Somalia and Kosovo.

These are deep and difficult questions that touch on the basic values of the country. Given that Canadians are essentially a "non-militaristic" people, what visible security policies have been developed? Furthermore, what set of policies could be designed to protect Canadian citizens and to defend the second-largest land mass and the longest coastline in the world?

The ingredients of Canada's policy have remained essentially the same since the end of the Second World War. Canada has sought security in collective agreements — it has not been neutral. As set out in the *Departmental Outlook* of the Department of National Defence, Canada's security policy is "to protect Canada, contribute to world peace and protect Canadian interests abroad."[40] To carry out these objectives, the military must be capable of:

- *defending Canada* — protecting Canada's national territory and areas of jurisdiction; helping civil authorities protect and sustain national interests; and assisting in national emergencies;

- *defending North America* — protecting the Canadian approaches to the continent in partnership with the United States, particularly through NORAD; promoting Arctic security; and pursuing opportunities for defence cooperation with the U.S. in other areas; and,

- *contributing to international security* — participating in a full range of multilateral operations through the United Nations, NATO, other regional organizations and coalitions of like-

---

40. National Defence, *1996 Departmental Outlook,* p. 1.

minded countries; supporting humanitarian relief efforts and restoration of conflict-devastated areas; and participating in arms control and other confidence-building measures.[41]

Canadian Security Policy

The basic pattern of the international environment today is one of sharply decreased east–west differences and an increase in local and regional conflicts throughout the world, particularly in the developing world but also in middle and eastern Europe. Explanations for the continuation of hostile acts throughout the globe are beyond the scope of this book, but they include economic, cultural, religious and ideological frustrations and aggression.[42]

In 1998, there were 27 major armed conflicts going on around the world, almost all of them inside the boundaries of extant states.[43] The annual number of conflicts and wars has been relatively stable for a decade. In the face of such intractable conflicts, it could be said that Canada's defence forces are insignificant. However, given the size of Canada's population and the few direct conflicts in which Canada is engaged, the military commitment is reasonable. In 1999–2000, approximately $10.6 billion was forecast for the defence envelope.

Despite these facts, the focus of Canadian defence policy has changed dramatically in recent years. With astonishing speed the Cold War, which had defined world politics since 1949, ended. The two superpowers no longer threaten to collide and Americans (and Canadians) have no reason to intervene overseas to combat Soviet expansionism. Canada's strategic importance has also declined with the end of the Cold War. Canada has not pulled out of NATO, but all bases and troops have been removed from Europe and government budgets earmarked for NATO are continually reduced.

Canada's position between Russia and the United States is no longer as important as it used to be. For example, while NORAD remains operative, the North Warning System has been downsized and many CF-18 interceptors have been mothballed. Its tasks have also shifted to new emerging issues — in 1991, NORAD was given responsibility for counter-narcotic monitoring and surveillance.

Organization of National Defence

The Department of National Defence (DND) was created by the *National Defence Act* in 1922. Led by the Minister of National Defence, the DND is involved in both the formulation and implementation of Canadian defence policy. Foreign affairs and defence policies are inextricably interrelated, and therefore they concern both the Minister of Foreign Affairs and the Minister of National Defence. The Defence Minister specifically and the Cabinet generally are accountable to Parliament for national defence matters.

The responsibilities of the Minister of National Defence include the control and management of the Department itself, the Canadian Armed Forces and all matters relating to works and establishments concerned with Canada's defence. The Minister is also responsible for Defence Construction Canada, a Crown corporation that functions as a contracting and construction supervisory agency for major construction and maintenance projects of the DND. It ensures that adequate standards of supervision and inspection are maintained throughout the life of construction contracts.

The deputy minister of the DND is the senior civilian advisor to the Minister. The deputy minister ensures that governmental policy direction is reflected in the administration of the DND and in

---

41. Ibid.
42. See Jackson and Jackson, *A Comparative Introduction to Political Science,* chs. 20 and 21.
43. See *SIPRI Yearbook* (Oxford: Oxford University Press, 1999).

military plans and operations. The senior military advisor to the Minister is the Chief of the Defence Staff (CDS), who is responsible for the conduct of military operations and for the preparedness of the Canadian Forces to meet commitments assigned by the government. (See Figure 15.2.)

The Canadian Forces

The Canadian Forces are the military element of the Canadian government and are part of the Department of National Defence.[44] In 1994, the total military personnel in the Canadian Forces was 72 000 — but the numbers have been shrinking each year, and by 1998–99, a reduction of 20 percent resulted in a force of only 60 000 regulars and 30 000 primary reservists. The number of generals dropped from 72 to 65 in the same period. Since 1968, the Canadian Forces have had a unified structure to carry out their tasks. They perform a number of roles, including surveillance of Canadian territory and coastlines to protect Canadian sovereignty, defence of North America in cooperation with American forces, fulfillment of NATO commitments and performance of international peacekeeping roles. The military also provides assistance to other federal government departments, civil authorities and civilian organizations — for example, air and ground transportation for royal visits, meetings of foreign government officials, sporting events, emergency and disaster relief, and a search and rescue program. Finally, the forces provide training for allied military personnel in Canada and aid in the form of military training to developing countries.

Defence expenditures are not, however, without their critics. The charges of left-wing opponents are often based on the belief that there is a so-called military-industrial complex that controls the government, especially in the United States. The basic argument is that there is collusion between

FIGURE 15.2 ORGANIZATION OF NATIONAL DEFENCE HEADQUARTERS

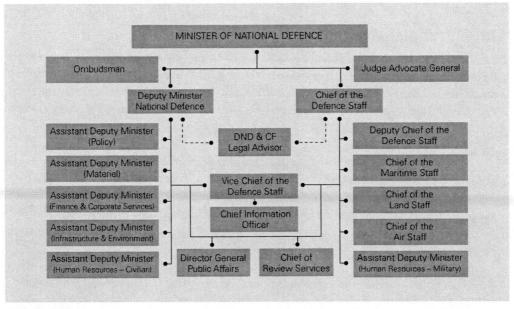

Source: www.dnd.ca

44. Formally the Governor General of Canada, as the sovereign's representative, is Commander-in-Chief of the Canadian Forces.

FIGURE 15.3   DEFENCE EXPENDITURE (IN MILLIONS)

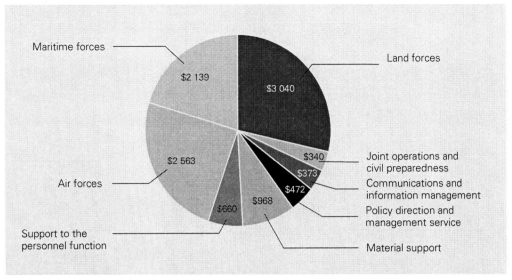

Source: Composed from Department of National Defence, *Estimates*, Part 3 (1996–97).

powerful industrialists and military planners to keep international tension high in order to sell expensive weapons to the government. This assertion is usually coupled with a belief that such expenditures would be better used in other fields such as health, education and social welfare. Its exponents believe that the costs of Canadian defence could be reduced by a radical shift toward neutralism in international affairs. The issue is raised here not to resolve it but to point to the fundamental debate over whether government funds should be spent on the military or other policies. This issue has been compounded because of scandals in the department. (See "Department of National Defence and Somalia.")

What does Canada do with these expenditures on defence? Figure 15.3 shows that almost three-quarters of the funds are for the combined maritime, land and air forces.

Canadian military expenditures basically cover protection of Canada's territory, a special partnership with the U.S. in NORAD and membership in NATO. Although Canada is involved in strategic nuclear planning, the country's chief role in NATO has until recently involved stationing Canadian land and air forces in Europe as part of the forward defence strategy. In 1994, Canada closed these bases and brought all troops home from Europe. Canada's commitment to NATO is lower than its allies would prefer. Canada remains the second-lowest contributor with regard to concrete support for defence measures.[45]

Peacekeeping

In keeping with the fundamentally "non-militaristic" nature of Canadian security policy, the government's most visible activity has been in the field of international peacekeeping. In 2000, the largest overseas forces were with the troops in the former Yugoslavia (in Kosovo and Bosnia) and East Timor. Earlier operations of Canadian troops as part of UNPROFOR in Bosnia-Herzegovina and OP SHARP GUARD in the Adriatic to help enforce UN sanctions and resolutions have been closed

---

45. For a discussion of this issue, see Robert J. Jackson, ed., *Europe in Transition* (New York: Praeger, 1993).

TABLE 15.3   CANADIAN PEACEKEEPING OPERATIONS, 2000

Locaton	Mission		Theatre Personnel
East Timor	International Force for East-Timor (INTERFET) OP TOUCAN		639
Guatamala	United Nations Verification Mission in Guatemala (MINUGUA) – OP QUARTZ		1
Haiti	United Nations Civilian Police Mission in Haiti (MIPONUH) – OP COMPLIMENT		5
Croatia	United Nations Mission of Observers in Prevlaka (UNMOP)		1
Bosnia-Herzegovina	United Nations Mine Action Centre in Bosnia-Herzegovina (UNMACBH) – OP NOBLE		2
Bosnia-Herzegovina	NATO Stabilization Force (SFOR)	OP JOINT FORCE (including OP PALLADIUM, the Multinational Staff and NATO posts)	1 362
		NATO Airborne Early Warning Force (NAEWF)	8
KOSOVO	OP KINETIC		1 445
	OP ECHO		106
	OP QUADRANT		5
Middle East Sanctions	OP AUGMENTATION		239
Cyprus	United Nations Peacekeeping Force in Cyprus (UNFICYP) – OP SNOWGOOSEOP ECHO		2
Golan Heights	United Nations Disengagement Observer Force (UNDOF) – OP DANACA		189
Iraq-Kuwait	United Nations Iraq-Kuwait Observation Mission (UNIKOM) – OP RECORD		5
United Nations Special Commission	UNSCOM – Iraq OP FORUM		0
	UNSCOM – New York OP FORUM		2
Middle East	United States Air Force Airborne Warning and Control Systems (AWACS) – Monitor Iraq no-fly zone		3
Israel and Egypt	Multinational Force and Observers (MFO) – OP CALUMET		28
Middle East	United Nations Truce Supervision Organization (UNTSO)		11
Cambodia	United Nations Development Program – Cambodian Mine Action Centre (CMAC)		7
Multinational Staff	(AFOR) – OP ALLIED HARBOUR		9
Central Africa Republic	United Nations Verification Mission in Central Africa Republic (MINURCA) – OP PRUDENCE		52
Mine Action Centre	OP MODULE		3
CARE Canada	OP CONNECTION		0
Korea	(UNCMAC)		0
Field Study Team	OP CONTACT		0
Democratic Republic of Congo	OP CROCODILE		1
	TOTAL		4 125

Source: www.dnd.ca/menu/operations

down. Even earlier, in 1993, Canada had brought home its battalion from patrolling the Nicosia area as part of the UN contingent there to prevent hostilities between Greek and Turkish Cypriots. At the time of writing, Canada continues to retain troops in scattered places such as Croatia, Haiti, Golan Heights, Persian Gulf, Central Africa Republic, Cambodia, Sinai, Iraq and Kuwait. (See Table 15.3.) In total, 4 125 personnel serve in UN and other missions in 1990–2000. On the whole, Canadian participation in peacekeeping represents an important contribution to global and Canadian security, and enhances Canada's international reputation.

· · · · · · ·

SUMMARY

Canada's role in world affairs continues to develop so that among the world's states it is one of the most powerful both economically and politically. This relative position makes it mandatory that Canada participate fully in international organizations such as the United Nations and its specialized agencies. Canada's international importance has also increased because of economic and security requirements.

The importance of international relations to Canada is also illustrated by its defence policies. While Canada

CLOSE-UP ON Public Policy

DEPARTMENT OF NATIONAL DEFENCE AND SOMALIA

The Department of National Defence has been under severe organizational stress over the last half decade. Budgets have been slashed and the number of troops cut. But none of these managerial policies has affected activities and morale as much as the Somalia tragedy.

Canada's glowing image as a peacekeeper was severely tarnished after an incident that occurred in Somalia in 1993. Members of the Canadian Airborne Regiment in Belet Huen tortured and killed a young Somali, Shidane Arone, who had been caught entering the Canadian compound. Several members of the Canadian Forces were charged, and in 1995 the regiment was disbanded. The Minister of National Defence initiated a civilian-led public inquiry. Following revelations that documents relating to the scandal had been destroyed, several officers resigned, including, eventually, General Jean Boyle, Chief of the Defence Staff.

Before the affair was over, David Collenette also resigned as Minister of Defence (although for other reasons). He was replaced by Doug Young, who immediately declared there would be another shake-up in the defence establishment. Young forced the commission of inquiry to terminate its investigation by the spring of 1997, well before it had intended to do so. Later, he announced there would be somewhat more independence for military police in future investigations and less reliance on the standard chain of command.

contributes to the security of the West by membership in NATO and NORAD, its overall military budget is small compared to that of most countries. Because of an essentially non-militaristic position Canada is acceptable to many countries as an intermediary in troubled areas. The most concrete example is the Canadian contribution to peacekeeping.

The international strategic environment, however, is changing. Most conflicts take place outside the western European theatre and, except as peacekeepers, Canada has had little role to play in the ethnic superpower and religious conflicts of the Middle East and the Balkans. In the remainder of the world, essentially south of the Tropic of Cancer, Canada plays a modest, usually rhetorical, role. Canadian efforts to help end apartheid in South Africa and to bring a political solution to other troubled areas have sometimes landed on fertile ground. In sum, then, the Canadian contribution to world politics outside North America, Europe and a few countries with old Commonwealth ties is marginal and largely symbolic, except at the important humanitarian and peacekeeping levels.

Decision-making in domestic and international policy spheres has been quite dissimilar. However, the foreign policy process has been changing due to widespread concern for international peace, changing definitions of security and a growing awareness of the importance of globalization and trade to the Canadian economy. Canada's role in international trade organizations such as the World

Trade Organization and NAFTA are crucial. Many new actors are now involved in foreign policy-making. The historically important roles of the prime minister and the Ministers of Foreign Affairs and National Defence remain but the relative significance of other ministers and departments has grown, as have interest group activities.

As Canada evolved into a full-fledged state, it gradually adopted an internationalist posture and dropped its older style of isolationism. Issues of peace, world trade and humanitarian concerns actively interest many Canadians, and political leaders have forced the government toward a foreign policy that is in tune with Canada's domestic concerns and issues. Today, the realization that globalization is prevalent and that no country can be totally self-sufficient is an accepted maxim of international and Canadian politics.

DISCUSSION QUESTIONS

1. Do you agree with the contention that in Canada "foreign policy is domestic policy"? Why or why not?
2. Do you agree with the idea that Canadian foreign policy should be a projection of Canadian national interests? Especially, our economic concerns?
3. Does Canada have good relations with other countries? With the right countries?
4. Does Canada spend too much money on defence policy?
5. Can the reputation of the Department of National Defence be restored? How?

Selected Bibliography

Blanchard, James, *Behind the Embassy Door: Canada, Clinton and Quebec.* (Toronto: McClelland & Stewart, 1998).

Bothwell, Robert, *Canada and the United States* (Toronto: University of Toronto Press, 1992).

Brzezinski, Zbigniew, *Out of Control: Global Turmoil on the Eve of the 21st Century* (New York: Scribners, 1993).

Clarke, Tony and Maud Barlow, *MAI and the Threat to Canadian Sovereignty* (Toronto: Stoddart, 1997).

Cooper, Andrew F., *Canadian Foreign Policy: Old Habits and New Directions* (Scarborough: Prentice Hall, 1997).

Dewitt, David B. and David Leyton-Brown, eds., *Canada's International Security Policy* (Scarborough: Prentice Hall Canada, 1995).

Doern, G. Bruce and Brian W. Tomlin, *Faith and Fear* (Toronto: Stoddart, 1991).

Granatstein, J.L. and Robert Bothwell, *Pirouette: Pierre Trudeau and Canadian Foreign Policy* (Toronto: University of Toronto Press, 1990).

Hampson, Fen Osler and Christopher J. Maule, *Canada among Nations 1993: Global Jeopardy* (Ottawa: Carleton University Press, 1993).

Head, Ivan L., *On a Hinge of History: The Mutual Vulnerability of South and North* (Toronto: University of Toronto Press, 1991).

Head, Ivan and Pierre Trudeau, *The Canadian Way: Shaping Canada's Foreign Policy, 1968–84* (Toronto: McClelland & Stewart, 1995).

Himes, Mel, *Canadian Foreign Policy Handbook* (Montréal: Jewel Publications, 1996).

Jackson, Robert J., ed., *Europe in Transition* (New York: Praeger, 1993).

Keating, Tom, *Canada and World Order* (Toronto: McClelland & Stewart, 1993).

Kennedy, Paul, *Preparing for the Twenty-First Century* (New York: HarperCollins, 1993).

Miall, Hugh, *The Peacemakers* (London: Macmillan, 1992).

Moynihan, Daniel Patrick, *Ethnicity in International Politics* (New York: Oxford University Press, 1992).

Rosenau, James N., *Turbulence in World Politics* (New York: Harvester Wheatsheaf, 1990).

Rothgeb, John, *Defining Power: Influence and Force in the Contemporary International System* (New York: St. Martin's Press, 1993).

LIST OF WEBLINKS

www.dfait-maeci.gc.ca	**Canada's Department of Foreign Affairs and International Trade** This is the Web page for the Department of Foreign Affairs and International Trade.
www.un.org	**The United Nations** This is the United Nations' Web page.
www.oas.org	**The Organization of American States** This is the Web page for the Organization of American States; it includes links to other resources in the Americas.

BUDGET '96: WHAT'S IN IT FOR YOU?

Public policy is often defined as being "whatever government decides to do or not to do." Arguably the most important single statement of federal government policy is the annual Budget: it is a statement of priorities. It lists and justifies the resources the government allocates to (or withholds from) a vast array of programs. It determines the amount of taxes you pay.

The 1996 Budget of Finance Minister Paul Martin followed the "neo-conservative" track laid down in his 1995 budget. He did not introduce significant new taxation; he confirmed the consolidation and reduction of transfers to provincial governments; he refused to fund new job creation programs. His budgets (and those of the Mulroney governments) reflect three policy arguments. First, the pre-condition for economic recovery is reduced government spending, with balanced budgets achieved by cuts to social programs and reduced transfers to the provinces. Second, a private sector—unhindered by new taxation and regulation—will expand, creating wealth and providing jobs. Third, private sector managerialism is superior to public administration and should be copied by the government to improve the delivery of public goods such as health care.

Critics of neo-conservatism disagree. First, they say that the vast majority of Canadians want to retain the security provided by social programs. Second, they charge that a lower-taxed, less regulated "new economy" private sector has not produced "jobs, jobs, jobs"; moreover, the wealth which has been created has been funnelled into the pockets of an elite few in Canadian society. Third, as a comparison of health care in Canada and the United States shows, there are few benefits to be gained from copying private-sector managerialism in all parts of the public sector.

Questions

1. The policy-making process is assumed to be more or less rational: many voters expect governments to use resources to achieve stated policy goals. Using Richard Simeon's "funnel of causality," construct a defence of the Budget as a "reasonably rational exercise in policy-making" given the constraints under which the Finance Minister operated.

2. It is sometimes said that in the 1993 election Canadians voted against neo-conservatism when they cast their ballots for the Liberal party and Chrétien's promise of "jobs, jobs, jobs." Despite unemployment levels consistently above 9 percent, Martin insisted he would "stay the course," maintaining that his budget "responds to what people want." Can you account for this apparent contradiction? What explanation is suggested by public choice theory? By neo-Marxism? By state-centred theory? By pluralists? By the Reform (Alliance) party?

A
CONSOLIDATION
OF THE
CONSTITUTION
ACTS
1867 TO 1982

CONSTITUTION ACT, 1867

(THE BRITISH NORTH AMERICA ACT, 1867)

[Note: The present short title was substituted for the original short title (in italics) by the *Constitution Act, 1982* (No. 44 *infra*).]

30 & 31 Victoria, c. 3 (U.K.)

An Act for the Union of Canada, Nova Scotia, and New Brunswick, and the Government thereof; and for Purposes connected therewith

[29th March 1867]

Whereas the Provinces of Canada, Nova Scotia, and New Brunswick have expressed their Desire to be federally united into One Dominion under the Crown of the United Kingdom of Great Britain and Ireland, with a Constitution similar in Principle to that of the United Kingdom:

And whereas such a Union would conduce to the Welfare of the Provinces and promote the Interests of the British Empire:

And whereas on the Establishment of the Union by Authority of Parliament it is expedient, not only that the Constitution of the Legislative Authority in the Dominion be provided for, but also that the Nature of the Executive Government therein be declared:

And whereas it is expedient that Provision be made for the eventual Admission into the Union of other Parts of British North America:

Be it therefore enacted and declared by the Queen's most Excellent Majesty, by and with the Advice and Consent of the Lords Spiritual and Temporal, and Commons, in this present Parliament assembled, and by the Authority of the same, as follows:

[Note: The enacting clause was repealed by the *Statute Law Revision Act, 1893* (No. 17 *infra*).]

I. PRELIMINARY

Short Title

1. *This Act may be cited as The British North America Act, 1867.*

Short title

1. This Act may be cited as the *Constitution Act, 1867.*

[Note: Section 1 (in italics) was repealed and the new section substituted by the *Constitution Act, 1982* (No. 44 *infra*).]

Application of Provisions referring to the Queen

2. *The Provisions of this Act referring to Her Majesty the Queen extend also to the Heirs and Successors of Her Majesty, Kings and Queens of the United Kingdom of Great Britain and Ireland.*

[Note: Repealed by the *Statute Law Revision Act, 1893* (No. 17 *infra*).]

II. UNION

DECLARATION OF UNION

Declaration of Union

3. It shall be lawful for the Queen, by and with the Advice of Her Majesty's Most Honourable Privy Council, to declare by Proclamation that, on and after a Day therein appointed, not being more than Six Months after the passing of this Act, the Provinces of Canada, Nova Scotia, and New Brunswick shall form and be One Dominion under the Name of Canada; and on and after that Day those Three Provinces shall form and be One Dominion under that Name accordingly.

[Note: The first day of July, 1867 was fixed by proclamation dated May 22, 1867.]

4. *The subsequent Provisions of this Act shall, unless it is otherwise expressed or implied, commence and have effect on and after the Union, that is to say, on and after the Day appointed for the Union taking effect in the Queen's Proclamation; and in the same Provisions,* unless it is otherwise expressed or implied, the Name Canada shall be taken to mean Canada as constituted under this Act.

Construction of subsequent Provisions of Act

[Note: The words in italics were repealed by the *Statute Law Revision Act, 1893* (No. 17 *infra*).]

5. Canada shall be divided into Four Provinces, named Ontario, Quebec, Nova Scotia, and New Brunswick.

Four Provinces

[Note: Canada now consists of ten provinces (Ontario, Quebec, Nova Scotia, New Brunswick, Manitoba, British Columbia, Prince Edward Island, Alberta, Saskatchewan and Newfoundland) and two territories (the Yukon Territory and the Northwest Territories). See the note to section 146.]

6. The Parts of the Province of Canada (as it exists at the passing of this Act) which formerly constituted respectively the Provinces of Upper Canada and Lower Canada shall be deemed to be severed, and shall form Two separate Provinces. The Part which formerly constituted the Province of Upper Canada shall constitute the Province of Ontario; and the Part which formerly constituted the Province of Lower Canada shall constitute the Province of Quebec.

Provinces of Ontario and Quebec

7. The Provinces of Nova Scotia and New Brunswick shall have the same Limits as at the passing of this Act.

Provinces of Nova Scotia and New Brunswick

8. In the general Census of the Population of Canada which is hereby required to be taken in the Year One thousand eight hundred and seventy-one, and in every Tenth Year thereafter, the respective Populations of the Four Provinces shall be distinguished.

Decennial Census

III. EXECUTIVE POWER

9. The Executive Government and Authority of and over Canada is hereby declared to continue and be vested in the Queen.

Declaration of Executive Power in the Queen

10. The Provisions of this Act referring to the Governor General extend and apply to the Governor General for the Time being of Canada, or other the Chief Executive Officer or Administrator for the Time being carrying on the Government of Canada on behalf and in the Name of the Queen, by whatever Title he is designated.

Application of Provisions referring to Governor General

11. There shall be a Council to aid and advise in the Government of Canada, to be styled the Queen's Privy Council for Canada; and the Persons who are to be Members of that Council shall be from Time to Time chosen and summoned by the Governor General and sworn in as Privy Councillors, and Members thereof may be from Time to Time removed by the Governor General.

Constitution of Privy Council for Canada

12. All Powers, Authorities, and Functions which under any Act of the Parliament of Great Britain, or of the Parliament of the United Kingdom of Great Britain and Ireland, or of the Legislature of Upper Canada, Lower Canada, Canada, Nova Scotia, or New Brunswick, are at the

All Powers under Acts to be exercised by Governor General with Advice of Privy Council, or alone

Union vested in or exerciseable by the respective Governors or Lieutenant Governors of those Provinces, with the Advice, or with the Advice of Consent, of the respective Executive Councils thereof, or in conjunction with those Councils, or with any Number of Members thereof, or by those Governors or Lieutenant Governors individually, shall, as far as the same continue in existence and capable of being exercised after the Union in relation to the Government of Canada, be vested in and exerciseable by the Governor General, with the Advice or with the Advice and Consent of or in conjunction with the Queen's Privy Council for Canada, or any Members thereof, or by the Governor General individually, as the Case requires, subject nevertheless (except with respect to such as Exist under Acts of the Parliament of Great Britain or of the Parliament of the United Kingdom of Great Britain and Ireland) to be abolished or altered by the Parliament of Canada.

[Note: See the note to section 129.]

Application of Provisions referring to Governor General in Council

13. The Provisions of this Act referring to the Governor General in Council shall be construed as referring to the Governor General acting by and with the Advice of the Queen's Privy Council for Canada.

Power to Her Majesty to authorize Governor General to appoint Deputies

14. It shall be lawful for the Queen, if Her Majesty thinks fit, to authorize the Governor General from Time to Time to appoint any Person or any Persons jointly or severally to be his Deputy or Deputies within any Part or Parts of Canada, and in that Capacity to exercise during the Pleasure of the Governor General such of the Powers, Authorities, and Functions of the Governor General as the Governor General deems it necessary or expedient to assign to him or them, subject to any Limitations or Directions expressed or given by the Queen; but the Appointment of such a Deputy or Deputies shall not affect the Exercise by the Governor General himself of any Power, Authority, or Function.

Command of Armed Forces to continue to be vested in the Queen

15. The Command-in-Chief of the Land and Naval Militia, and of all Naval and Military Forces, of and in Canada, is hereby declared to continue and be vested in the Queen.

Seat of Government of Canada

16. Until the Queen otherwise directs, the Seat of Government of Canada shall be Ottawa.

IV. LEGISLATIVE POWER

Constitution of Parliament of Canada

17. There shall be One Parliament for Canada, consisting of the Queen, an Upper House styled the Senate, and the House of Commons.

Privileges, etc., of Houses

18. *The Privileges, Immunities, and Powers to be held, enjoyed, and exercised by the Senate and by the House of Commons and by the Members thereof respectively shall be such as are from Time to Time defined by Act of the Parliament of Canada, but so that the same shall never exceed those at the passing of this Act held, enjoyed, and exercised by the Commons House of Parliament of the United Kingdom of Great Britain and Ireland and by the Members thereof.*

18. The privileges, immunities and powers to be held, enjoyed, and exercised by the Senate and by the House of Commons, and by the members thereof respectively, shall be such as are from time to time defined by Act of the Parliament of Canada, but so that any Act of the Parliament of Canada defining such privileges, immunities, and power shall not confer any privileges, immunities, or powers exceeding those at the passing of such Act held, enjoyed, and exercised by the Commons House of Parliament of the United Kingdom of Great Britain and Ireland, and by the members thereof.

[Note: Section 18 (in italics) was repealed and the new section substituted by the *Parliament of Canada Act, 1875* (No. 13 *infra*).]

19. The Parliament of Canada shall be called together not later than Six Months after the Union.

First Session of the Parliament of Canada

[Note: The first session of the first Parliament began on November 6, 1867.]

20. *There shall be a Session of the Parliament of Canada once at least in every Year, so that Twelve Months shall not intervene between the last Sitting of the Parliament in one Session and its first sitting in the next Session.*

Yearly Session of the Parliament of Canada

[Note: Repealed by the *Constitution Act, 1982* (No. 44 *infra*). See also section 5 of that Act, which provides that there shall be a sitting of the Parliament at least once every twelve months.]

The Senate

21. The Senate shall, subject to the Provisions of this Act, consist of *Seventy-two* Members, who shall be styled Senators.

Number of Senators

[Note: The Senate now consists of 104 Members, as amended by the *Constitution Act, 1915* (No. 23 *infra*) and modified by the *Newfoundland Act* (No. 32 *infra*) and as again amended by the *Constitution Act (No. 2), 1975*, (No. 42 *infra*).]

22. In relation to the Constitution of the Senate Canada shall be deemed to consist of *Three* Divisions:

Representation of Provinces in Senate

1. Ontario;
2. Quebec;
3. *The Maritime Provinces, Nova Scotia and New Brunswick;*

which *Three* Divisions shall (subject to the Provisions of this Act) be equally represented in the Senate as follows: Ontario by Twenty-four Senators; Quebec by Twenty-four Senators; and the Maritime Provinces by Twenty-four Senators, *Twelve* thereof representing Nova Scotia, and *Twelve* thereof representing New Brunswick.

In the case of Quebec each of the Twenty-four Senators representing that Province shall be appointed for One of the Twenty-four Electoral Divisions of Lower Canada specified in Schedule A. to Chapter One of the Consolidated Statutes of Canada.

[Note: Prince Edward Island, on admission into the Union in 1873, became part of the third division with a representation in the Senate of four members, the representation of Nova Scotia and New Brunswick being reduced from twelve to ten members each. See section 147.

A fourth division represented in the Senate by twenty-four senators and comprising the Western Provinces of Manitoba, British Columbia, Alberta and Saskatchewan, each represented by six senators, was added by the *Constitution Act, 1915* (No. 23 *infra*).

Newfoundland is represented in the Senate by six members. See the *Constitution Act, 1915* (No. 23 *infra*) and the *Newfoundland Act* No. 32 *infra*).

The Yukon Territory and the Northwest Territories are represented in the Senate by one member each. See the *Constitution Act (No. 2), 1975* (No. 42 *infra*).]

Qualifications of
Senator

23. The Qualifications of a Senator shall be as follows:

1. He shall be of the full age of Thirty Years:

2. He shall be either a natural-born Subject of the Queen, or a Subject of the Queen naturalized by an Act of the Parliament of Great Britain, or of the Parliament of the United Kingdom of Great Britain and Ireland, or of the Legislature of One of the Provinces of Upper Canada, Lower Canada, Canada, Nova Scotia, or New Brunswick, before the Union, or of the Parliament of Canada after the Union:

3. He shall be legally or equitably seised as of Freehold for his own Use and Benefit of Lands or Tenements held in Free and Common Socage, or seised or possessed for his own Use and Benefit of Lands or Tenements held in Franc-alleu or in Roture, within the Province for which he is appointed, of the Value of Four thousand Dollars, over and above all Rents, Dues, Debts, Charges, Mortgages, and Incumbrances due or payable out of or charged on or affecting the same:

4. His Real and Personal Property shall be together worth Four thousand Dollars over and above his Debts and Liabilities:

5. He shall be resident in the Province for which he is appointed:

6. In the Case of Quebec he shall have his Real Property Qualification in the Electoral Division for which he is appointed, or shall be resident in that Division.

[Note: For the purposes of the *Constitution Act (No. 2), 1975* (No. 42 *infra*), the term "Province" in section 23 has the same meaning as is assigned to the "province" by section 35 of the *Interpretation Act* (Canada).]

Summons of
Senator

24. The Governor General shall from Time to Time, in the Queen's Name, by Instrument under the Great Seal of Canada, summon qualified Persons to the Senate; and, subject to the Provisions of this Act, every Person so summoned shall become and be a Member of the Senate and a Senator.

*Summons of First
Body of Senators*

25. *Such Persons shall be first summoned to the Senate as the Queen by Warrant under Her Majesty's Royal Sign Manual thinks fit to approve, and their Names shall be inserted in the Queen's Proclamation of Union.*

[Note: Repealed by the *Statute Law Revision Act, 1893* (No. 17 *infra*).]

Addition of
Senators in certain
Cases

26. If at any Time on the Recommendation of the Governor General the Queen thinks fit to direct that *Three or Six* Members be added to the Senate, the Governor General may by Summons to *Three or Six* qualified Persons (as the Case may be), representing equally the *Three* Divisions of Canada, add to the Senate accordingly.

[Note: The number of members who may be added to the Senate was increased from three or six to four or eight, representing equally the four divisions of Canada. See the *Constitution Act, 1915* (No. 23 *infra*).]

Reduction of
Senate to normal
number

27. In case of such Addition being at any Time made, the Governor General shall not summon any Person to the Senate, except on a further like Direction by the Queen on the like Recommendation, until each of the *Three* Divisions of Canada is represented by Twenty-four Senators and no more.

[Note: Superseded by the *Constitution Act, 1915*, paragraph 1(1)(iv), No. 23 *infra*). This paragraph reads as follows:

"In case of such addition being at any time made the Governor General of Canada shall not summon any person to the Senate except upon a further like direction by His Majesty the King on the like recommendation to represent one of the four Divisions until such Division is represented by twenty-four senators and no more:"]

28. The Number of Senators shall not at any Time exceed *Seventy-eight.*

[Note: The maximum number of senators is now 112, as amended by the *Constitution Act, 1915 (No. 23* infra) and the *Constitution Act (No. 2), 1975* (No. 42 *infra).*]

Maximum Number of Senator

29. *A Senator shall, subject to the Provisions of this Act, hold his Place in the Senate for Life.*

Tenure of Place in Senate

29. (1) Subject to subsection (2), a Senator shall, subject to the provisions of this Act, hold his place in the Senate for life.

Tenure of place in Senate

(2) A senator who is summoned to the Senate after the coming into force of this subsection shall, subject to this act, hold his place in the Senate until he attains the age of seventy-five years.

[Note: Section 29 (in italics) was repealed and the new section substituted by the *Constitution Act, 1965* (No. 39 *infra).*]

Retirement upon attaining age of seventy-five years

30. A Senator may by Writing under his Hand addressed to the Governor General resign his Place in the Senate, and thereupon the same shall be vacant.

Resignation of Place in Senate

31. The Place of a Senator shall become vacant in any of the following Cases:

Disqualification of Senators

1. If for Two consecutive Sessions of the Parliament he fails to give his Attendance in the Senate:

2. If he takes an Oath or makes a Declaration or Acknowledgement of Allegiance, Obedience, or Adherence to a Foreign Power, or does an Act whereby he becomes a Subject or Citizen, or entitled to the Rights or Privileges of a Subject or Citizen, of a Foreign Power:

3. If he is adjudged Bankrupt or Insolvent, or applies for the Benefit of any Law relating to Insolvent Debtors, or becomes a public Defaulter:

4. If he is attainted of Treason or convicted of Felony or of any infamous Crime:

5. If he ceases to be qualified in respect of Property or of Residence; provided, that a Senator shall not be deemed to have ceased to be qualified in respect of Residence by reason only of his residing at the Seat of the Government of Canada while holding an Office under that Government requiring his Presence there.

32. When a Vacancy happens in the Senate by Resignation, Death, or otherwise, the Governor General shall by Summons to a fit and qualified Person fill the Vacancy.

Summons on Vacancy in Senate

33. If any Question arises respecting the Qualification of a Senator or a Vacancy in the Senate the same shall be heard and determined by the Senate.

Questions as to Qualifications and Vacancies in Senate

34. The Governor General may from Time to Time, by Instrument under the Great Seal of Canada, appoint a Senator to be Speaker of the Senate, and may remove him and appoint another in his Stead.

Appointment of Speaker of Senate

[Note: See also the *Canadian Speaker (Appointment of Deputy) Act, 1895* (No. 18 *infra*) and the provisions concerning the Speaker of the Senate in the *Parliament of Canada Act* (Canada).]

Quorum of Senate

35. Until the Parliament of Canada otherwise provides, the Presence of at least Fifteen Senators, including the Speaker, shall be necessary to constitute a Meeting of the Senate for the Exercise of its Powers.

Voting in Senate

36. Questions arising in the Senate shall be decided by a Majority of Voices, and the Speaker shall in all Cases have a Vote, and when the Voices are equal the Decision shall be deemed to be in the Negative.

The House of Commons

Constitution of House of Commons in Canada

37. The House of Commons shall, subject to the Provisions of this Act, consist of *One hundred and eighty-one* Members, of whom *Eighty-two* shall be elected for Ontario, *Sixty-five* for Quebec, *Nineteen* for Nova Scotia, and *Fifteen* for New Brunswick.

[Note: On October 31, 1987, the House of Commons consisted of 282 members: 95 for Ontario, 75 for Quebec, 11 for Nova Scotia, 10 for New Brunswick, 14 for Manitoba, 28 for British Columbia, 4 for Prince Edward Island, 21 for Alberta, 14 for Saskatchewan, 7 for Newfoundland, 1 for the Yukon Territory and 2 for the Northwest Territories.

These figures result from the application of section 51 as re-enacted by the *Constitution Act, 1974* (No. 40 *infra*) and amended by the *Constitution Act (No. 1), 1975* (No. 41 *infra*), and of the *Electoral Boundaries Readjustment Act* (Canada).]

Summoning of House of Commons

38. The Governor General shall from Time to Time, in the Queen's Name, by Instrument under the Great Seal of Canada, summon and call together the House of Commons.

39. A Senator shall not be capable of being elected or of sitting or voting as a Member of the House of Commons.

Senators not to sit in House of Commons

Electoral Districts of the Four Provinces

40. Until the Parliament of Canada otherwise provides, Ontario, Quebec, Nova Scotia, and New Brunswick shall, for the Purposes of the Election of Members to serve in the House of Commons, be divided into Electoral Districts as follows:

1. ONTARIO

Ontario shall be divided into the Counties, Ridings of Counties, Cities, Parts of Cities, and Towns enumerated in the First Schedule to this Act, each whereof shall be an Electoral District, each such District as numbered in that Schedule being entitled to return One Member.

2. QUEBEC

Quebec shall be divided into Sixty-five Electoral Districts, composed of the Sixty-five Electoral Divisions into which Lower Canada is at the passing of this Act divided under Chapter Two of the Consolidated Statutes of Canada, Chapter Seventy-five of the Consolidated Statutes for Lower Canada, and the Act of the Province of Canada of the Twenty-third Year of the Queen, Chapter One, or any other Act amending the same in force at the Union, so that each such Electoral Division shall be for the Purposes of this Act an Electoral District entitled to return One Member.

3. Nova Scotia

Each of the Eighteen Counties of Nova Scotia shall be an Electoral District. The County of Halifax shall be entitled to return Two Members, and each of the other Counties One Member.

4. New Brunswick

Each of the Fourteen Counties into which New Brunswick is divided, including the City and County of St. John, shall be an Electoral District. The City of St. John shall also be a separate Electoral District. Each of those Fifteen Electoral Districts shall be entitled to return One Member.

[Note: The federal electoral districts of the 10 provinces and the Northwest Territories are now set out in the schedule to Proclamations issued from time to time pursuant to the *Electoral Boundaries Readjustment Act* (Canada), as amended for particular districts by other Acts of Parliament.

The electoral district of the Yukon Territory is set out in section 30 of the *Electoral Boundaries Readjustment Act* (Canada).]

41. Until the Parliament of Canada otherwise provides, all Laws in force in the several Provinces at the Union relative to the following Matters or any of them, namely,—the Qualifications and Disqualifications of Persons to be elected or to sit or vote as Members of the House of Assembly or Legislative Assembly in the several Provinces, the Voters at Elections of such Members, the Oaths to be taken by Voters, the Returning Officers, their Powers and Duties, the Proceedings at Elections, the Periods during which Elections may be continued, the Trial of controverted Elections, and Proceedings incident thereto, the vacating of Seats of Members, and the Execution of new Writs in case of Seats vacated otherwise than by Dissolution,—shall respectively apply to Elections of Members to serve in the House of Commons for the same several Provinces.

Continuance of existing Election Laws until Parliament of Canada otherwise provides

Provided that, until the Parliament of Canada otherwise provides, at any Election for a Member of the House of Commons for the District of Algoma, in addition to Persons qualified by the Law of the Province of Canada to vote, every Male British Subject, aged Twenty-one Years or upwards, being a Householder, shall have a Vote.

[Note: The principal provisions concerning elections are now found in the *Parliament of Canada Act, Canada Elections Act* and *Dominion Controverted Elections Act* (all three enacted by Canada). The right to vote and hold office is provided for in section 3 of the *Constitution Act, 1982* (No. 44 *infra*).]

42. *For the First Election of Members to serve in the House of Commons the Governor General shall cause Writs to be issued by such Person, in such Form, and addressed to such Returning Officers as he thinks fit.*

Writs for first Election

The Person issuing Writs under this Section shall have the like Powers as are possessed at the Union by the Officers charged with the issuing of Writs for the Election of Members to serve in the respective House of Assembly or Legislative Assembly of the Province of Canada, Nova Scotia, or New Brunswick; and the Returning Officers to whom Writs are directed under this Section shall have the like Powers as are possessed at the Union by the Officers charged with the returning of Writs for the Election of Members to serve in the same respective House of Assembly or Legislative Assembly.

[Note: Repealed by the *Statute Law Revision Act, 1893* (No. 17 *infra*).]

As to Casual
Vacancies

43. *In case a Vacancy in the Representation in the House of Commons of any Electoral District happens before the Meeting of the Parliament, or after the Meeting of the Parliament before Provision is made by the Parliament in this Behalf, the Provisions of the last foregoing Section of this Act shall extend and apply to the issuing and returning of a Writ in respect of such Vacant District.*

[Note: Repealed by the *Statute Law Revision Act, 1893* (No. 17 *infra*).]

As to Election of
Speaker of House
of Commons

44. The House of Commons on its first assembling after a General Election shall proceed with all practicable Speed to elect One of its Members to be Speaker.

As to filling up
Vacancy in Office
of Speaker

45. In case of a Vacancy happening in the Office of Speaker by Death, Resignation, or otherwise, the House of Commons shall with all practicable Speed proceed to elect another of its Members to be Speaker.

Speaker to preside

46. The Speaker shall preside at all Meetings of the House of Commons.

Provision in case of
Absence of Speaker

47. Until the Parliament of Canada otherwise provides, in case of the Absence for any Reason of the Speaker from the Chair of the House of Commons for a Period of Forty-eight consecutive Hours, the House may elect another of its Members to act as Speaker, and the Member so elected shall during the Continuance of such Absence of the Speaker have and execute all the Powers, Privileges, and Duties of Speaker.

[Note: See also the provisions concerning the Speaker of the House of Commons in the *Parliament of Canada Act* (Canada).]

Quorum of House
of Commons

48. The Presence of at least Twenty Members of the House of Commons shall be necessary to constitute a Meeting of the House for the Exercise of its Powers, and for that Purpose the Speaker shall be reckoned as a Member.

Voting in House of
Commons

49. Questions arising in the House of Commons shall be decided by a Majority of Voices other than that of the Speaker, and when the Voices are equal, but not otherwise, the Speaker shall have a Vote.

Duration of House
of Commons

50. Every House of Commons shall continue for Five Years from the Day of the Return of the Writs for choosing the House (subject to be sooner dissolved by the Governor General), and no longer.

[Note: See for an extension of this term the *British North America Act, 1916* (No. 24 *infra*). See also section 4 of the *Constitution Act, 1982* (No. 44 *infra*).]

Decennial
Readjustment of
Representation

51. *On the Completion of the Census in the Year One thousand eight hundred and seventy-one, and of each subsequent decennial Census, the Representation of the Four Provinces shall be readjusted by such Authority, in such Manner, and from such Time, as the Parliament of Canada from Time to Time provides, subject and according to the following Rules:*

1. Quebec shall have the fixed Number of Sixty-five Members:

2. There shall be assigned to each of the other Provinces such a Number of Members as will bear the same Proportion to the Number of its Population (ascertained at such Census) as the Number Sixty-five bears to the Number of the Population of Quebec (so ascertained):

3. In the Computation of the Number of Members for a Province a fractional Part not exceeding One Half of the whole Number requisite for entitling the Province to a Member shall be disregarded; but a fractional

Part exceeding One Half of that Number shall be equivalent to the whole Number:

4. On any such Re-adjustment the Number of Members for a Province shall not be reduced unless the Proportion which the Number of the Population of the Province bore to the Number of the aggregate Population of Canada at the then last preceding Re-adjustment of the Number of Members for the Province is ascertained at the then latest Census to be diminished by One Twentieth Part or upwards:

5. Such Re-adjustment shall not take effect until the Termination of the then existing Parliament.

51. (1) The number of members of the House of Commons and the representation of the provinces therein shall, on the coming into force of this subsection and thereafter on the completion of each decennial census, be readjusted by such authority, in such manner, and from such time as the Parliament of Canada from time to time provides, subject and according to the following rules:

Readjustment of representation in Commons

1. There shall be assigned to each of the provinces a number of members equal to the number obtained by dividing the total population of the provinces by two hundred and seventy-nine and by dividing the population of each province by the quotient so obtained, counting any remainder in excess of 0.50 as one after the said process of division.

Rules

2. If the total number of members that would be assigned to a province by the application of rule 1 is less than the total number assigned to that province on the date of coming into force of this subsection, there shall be added to the number of members so assigned such number of members as will result in the province having the same number of members as were assigned on that date.

(2) The Yukon Territory as bounded and described in the schedule to chapter Y-2 of the Revised Statutes of Canada, 1970, shall be entitled to one member, and the Northwest Territories as bounded and described in section 2 of chapter N-22 of the Revised Statutes of Canada, 1970, shall be entitled to two members.

Yukon Territory and Northwest Territories

[Note: The original section 51 (in italics) was repealed and a new section 51 substituted by the *British North America Act, 1946* (No. 30 *infra*).

The section enacted in 1946 was repealed and a new section 51 substituted by the *British North America Act, 1952* (No. 36 *infra*).

Subsection (1) of the section 51 enacted in 1952 was repealed and a new subsection 51(1) substituted by the *Constitution Act, 1974* (No. 40 *infra*). The subsection 51(1) enacted in 1974 was repealed and the present subsection 51(1) substituted by the *Constitution Act, 1985 (Representation)* (No. 47 *infra*).

Subsection (2) of the section 51 enacted in 1952 was repealed and the present subsection 51(2) substituted by the *Constitution Act (No. 1), 1975* (No. 41 *infra*).

The words from "of the census" to "seventy-one and" and the word "subsequent" of the original section had previously been repealed by the *Statute Law Revision Act, 1893* (No. 17 *infra*).]

51A. Notwithstanding anything in this Act a province shall always be entitled to a number of members in the House of Commons not less than the number of senators representing such province.

Constitution of House of Commons

[Note: Added by the *Constitution Act, 1915* (No. 23 *infra*).]

52. The Number of Members of the House of Commons may be from Time to Time increased by the Parliament of Canada, provided the pro-

Increase of Number of House of Commons

portionate Representation of the Provinces prescribed by this Act is not thereby disturbed.

Money Votes; Royal Assent

Appropriation and Tax Bills

53. Bills for appropriating any Part of the Public Revenue, or for imposing any Tax or Impost, shall originate in the House of Commons.

Recommendation of Money Votes

54. It shall not be lawful for the House of Commons to adopt or pass any Vote, Resolution, Address, or Bill for the Appropriation of any Part of the Public Revenue, or of any Tax or Impost, to any Purpose that has not been first recommended to that House by Message of the Governor General in the Session in which such Vote, Resolution, Address, or Bill is proposed.

Royal Assent to Bills, etc.

55. Where a Bill passed by the Houses of the Parliament is presented to the Governor General for the Queen's Assent, he shall declare, according to his Discretion, but subject to the Provisions of this Act and to Her Majesty's Instructions, either that he assents thereto in the Queen's Name, or that he withholds the Queen's Assent, or that he reserves the Bill for the Signification of the Queen's Pleasure.

Disallowance by Order in Council of Act assented to by Governor General

56. Where the Governor General assents to a Bill in the Queen's Name, he shall by the first convenient Opportunity send an authentic Copy of the Act to One of Her Majesty's Principal Secretaries of State, and if the Queen in Council within Two Years after Receipt thereof by the Secretary of State thinks fit to disallow the Act, such Disallowance (with a Certificate of the Secretary of State of the Day on which the Act was received by him) being signified by the Governor General, by Speech or Message to each of the Houses of the Parliament or by Proclamation, shall annul the Act from and after the Day of such Signification.

Signification of Queen's Pleasure on Bill reserved

57. A Bill reserved for the Signification of the Queen's Pleasure shall not have any Force unless and until, within Two Years from the Day on which it was presented to the Governor General for the Queen's Assent, the Governor General signifies, by Speech or Message to each of the Houses of the Parliament or by Proclamation, that it has received the Assent of the Queen in Council.

An Entry of every such Speech, Message, or Proclamation shall be made in the Journal of each House, and a Duplicate thereof duly attested shall be delivered to the proper Officer to be kept among the Records of Canada.

V. PROVINCIAL CONSTITUTIONS

Executive Power

Appointment of Lieutenant Governors of Provinces

58. For each Province there shall be an Officer, styled the Lieutenant Governor, appointed by the Governor General in Council by Instrument under the Great Seal of Canada.

Tenure of office of Lieutenant Governor

59. A Lieutenant Governor shall hold Office during the Pleasure of the Governor General; but any Lieutenant Governor appointed after the Commencement of the First Session of the Parliament of Canada shall not be removeable within Five Years from his Appointment, except for

Cause assigned, which shall be communicated to him in Writing within One Month after the Order for his Removal is made, and shall be communicated by Message to the Senate and to the House of Commons within One Week thereafter if the Parliament is then sitting, and if not then within One Week after the Commencement of the next Session of the Parliament.

60. The Salaries of the Lieutenant Governors shall be fixed and provided by the Parliament of Canada.

[Note: See the *Salaries Act* (Canada).]

Salaries of Lieutenant Governors

61. Every Lieutenant Governor shall, before assuming the Duties of his Office, make and subscribe before the Governor General or some Person authorized by him Oaths of Allegiance and Office similar to those taken by the Governor General.

Oaths, etc., of Lieutenant Governor

62. The Provisions of this Act referring to the Lieutenant Governor extend and apply to the Lieutenant Governor for the Time being of each Province, or other the Chief Executive Officer or Administrator for the Time being carrying on the Government of the Province, by whatever Title he is designated.

Application of Provisions referring to Lieutenant Governor

63. The Executive Council of Ontario and of Quebec shall be composed of such Persons as the Lieutenant Governor from Time to Time thinks fit, and in the first instance of the following Officers, namely,—the Attorney General, the Secretary and Registrar of the Province, the Treasurer of the Province, the Commissioner of Crown Lands, and the Commissioner of Agriculture and Public Works, within Quebec the Speaker of the Legislative Council and the Solicitor General.

[Note: See the *Executive Council Act* (Ontario) and the *Executive Power Act* (Quebec).]

Appointment of Executive Officers for Ontario and Quebec

64. The Constitution of the Executive Authority in each of the Provinces of Nova Scotia and New Brunswick shall, subject to the Provisions of this Act, continue as it exists at the Union until altered under the Authority of this Act.

[Note: The instruments admitting British Columbia, Prince Edward Island and Newfoundland contain similar provisions and the *Manitoba Act, 1897, Alberta Act* and *Saskatchewan Act* establish the executive authorities in the three provinces concerned. See the note to section 146.]

Executive Government of Nova Scotia and New Brunswick

65. All Powers, Authorities, and Functions which under any Act of the Parliament of Great Britain, or of the Parliament of the United Kingdom of Great Britain and Ireland, or of the Legislature of Upper Canada, Lower Canada, or Canada, were or are before or at the Union vested in or exerciseable by the respective Governors or Lieutenant Governors of those Provinces, with the Advice or with the Advice and Consent of the respective Executive Councils thereof, or in conjunction with those Councils, or with any Number of Members thereof, or by those Governors or Lieutenant Governors individually, shall, as far as the same are capable of being exercised after the Union in relation to the Government of Ontario and Quebec respectively, be vested in and shall or may be exercised by the Lieutenant Governor of Ontario and Quebec respectively, with the Advice or with the Advice and Consent of or in conjunction with the respective Executive Councils, or any Members thereof, or by the

Powers to be exercised by Lieutenant Governor of Ontario or Quebec with Advice, or alone

Lieutenant Governor individually, as the Case requires, subject never-theless (except with respect to such as exist under Acts of the Parliament of Great Britain, or of the Parliament of the United Kingdom of Great Britain and Ireland,) to be abolished or altered by the respective Legislatures of Ontario and Quebec.

[Note: See the note to section 129.]

Application of provisions referring to Lieutenant Governor in Council

66. The Provisions of this Act referring to the Lieutenant Governor in Council shall be construed as referring to the Lieutenant Governor of the Province acting by and with the Advice of the Executive Council thereof.

Administration in Absence, etc., of Lieutenant Governor

67. The Governor General in Council may from Time to Time appoint an Administrator to execute the Office and Functions of Lieutenant Governor during his Absence, Illness, or other Inability.

Seats of Provincial Governments

68. Unless and until the Executive Government of any Province otherwise directs with respect to that Province, the Seats of Government of the Provinces shall be as follows, namely,—of Ontario, the City of Toronto; of Quebec, the City of Quebec; of Nova Scotia, the City of Halifax; and of New Brunswick, the City of Fredericton.

Legislative Power

1. ONTARIO

Legislature for Ontario

69. There shall be a Legislature for Ontario consisting of the Lieutenant Governor and of One House, styled the Legislative Assembly of Ontario.

Electoral districts

70. The Legislative Assembly of Ontario shall be composed of Eighty-two Members, to be elected to represent the Eighty-two Electoral Districts set forth in the First Schedule to this Act.

[Note: See the *Representation Act* (Ontario).]

2. QUEBEC

Legislature for Quebec

71. There shall be a Legislature for Quebec consisting of the Lieutenant Governor and of Two Houses, styled the Legislative Council of Quebec and the Legislative Assembly of Quebec.

[Note: The Legislative Council was abolished by the *Act respecting the Legislative Council of Quebec*, Statutes of Quebec, 1968, c. 9. Sections 72 to 79 following are therefore spent.]

Constitution of Legislative Council

72. The Legislative Council of Quebec shall be composed of Twenty-four Members, to be appointed by the Lieutenant Governor, in the Queen's Name, by Instrument under the Great Seal of Quebec, one being appointed to represent each of the Twenty-four Electoral Divisions of Lower Canada in this Act referred to, and each holding Office for the Term of his Life, unless the Legislature of Quebec otherwise provides under the Provisions of this Act.

Qualification of Legislative Councillors

73. The Qualifications of the Legislative Councillors of Quebec shall be the same as those of the Senators for Quebec.

74. The Place of a Legislative Councillor of Quebec shall become vacant in the Cases, *mutatis mutandis*, in which the Place of Senator becomes vacant.

Resignation, Disqualification, etc.

75. When a Vacancy happens in the Legislative Council of Quebec by Resignation, Death, or otherwise, the Lieutenant Governor, in the Queen's Name, by Instrument under the Great Seal of Quebec, shall appoint a fit and qualified Person to fill the Vacancy.

Vacancies

76. If any Question arises respecting the Qualification of a Legislative Councillor of Quebec, or a Vacancy in the Legislative Council of Quebec, the same shall be heard and determined by the Legislative Council.

Questions as to Vacancies, etc.

77. The Lieutenant Governor may from Time to Time, by Instrument under the Great Seal of Quebec, appoint a Member of the Legislative Council of Quebec to be Speaker thereof, and may remove him and appoint another in his Stead.

Speaker of Legislative Council

78. Until the Legislature of Quebec otherwise provides, the Presence of at least Ten Members of the Legislative Council, including the Speaker, shall be necessary to constitute a Meeting for the Exercise of its Powers.

Quorum of Legislative Council

79. Questions arising in the Legislative Council of Quebec shall be decided by a Majority of Voices, and the Speaker shall in all Cases have a Vote, and when the Voices are equal the Decision shall be deemed to be in the Negative.

Voting in Legislative Council

80. The Legislative Assembly of Quebec shall be composed of Sixty-five Members, to be elected to represent the Sixty-five Electoral Divisions or Districts of Lower Canada in this Act referred to, subject to Alteration thereof by the Legislature of Quebec: Provided that it shall not be lawful to present to the Lieutenant Governor of Quebec for Assent any Bill for altering the Limits of any of the Electoral Divisions or Districts mentioned in the Second Schedule to this Act, unless the Second and Third Readings of such Bill have been passed in the Legislative Assembly with the Concurrence of the Majority of the Members representing all those Electoral Divisions or Districts, and the Assent shall not be given to such Bill unless an Address has been presented by the Legislative Assembly to the Lieutenant Governor stating that it has been so passed.

Constitution of Legislative Assembly of Quebec

[Note: Declared to be of no effect by the *Act respecting electoral districts*, Statutes of Quebec, 1970, c. 7.]

3. Ontario and Quebec

81. *The Legislatures of Ontario and Quebec respectively shall be called together not later than Six Months after the Union.*
[Note: Repealed by the *Statute Law Revision Act, 1893* (No. 17 *infra*).]

First Session of Legislatures

82. The Lieutenant Governor of Ontario and of Quebec shall from Time to Time, in the Queen's Name, by Instrument under the Great Seal of the Province, summon and call together the Legislative Assembly of the Province.

Summoning of Legislative Assemblies

83. Until the Legislature of Ontario or of Quebec otherwise provides, a Person accepting or holding in Ontario or in Quebec any Office, Commission, or Employment, permanent or temporary, at the Nomination of the Lieutenant Governor, to which an annual Salary, or any Fee,

Restriction on election of Holders of offices

Allowance, Emolument, or Profit of any Kind or Amount whatever from the Province is attached, shall not be eligible as a Member of the Legislative Assembly of the respective Province, nor shall he sit or vote as such; but nothing in this Section shall make ineligible any Person being a Member of the Executive Council of the respective Province, or holding any of the following Offices, that is to say, the Offices of Attorney General, Secretary and Registrar of the Province, Treasurer of the Province, Commissioner of Crown Lands, and Commissioner of Agriculture and Public Works, and in Quebec Solicitor General, or shall disqualify him to sit or vote in the House for which he is elected, provided he is elected while holding such Office.

[Note: See also the *Legislative Assembly Act* (Ontario) and the *National Assembly Act* (Quebec).]

Continuance of existing Election Laws

84. Until the Legislatures of Ontario and Quebec respectively otherwise provide, all Laws which at the Union are in force in those Provinces respectively, relative to the following Matters, or any of them, namely,— the Qualifications and Disqualifications of Persons to be elected or to sit or vote as Members of the Assembly of Canada, the Qualifications or Disqualifications of Voters, the Oaths to be taken by Voters, the Returning Officers, their Powers and Duties, the Proceedings at Elections, the Periods during which such Elections may be continued, and the Trial of controverted Elections and the Proceedings incident thereto, the vacating of the Seats of Members and the issuing and execution of new Writs in case of Seats vacated otherwise than by Dissolution,—shall respectively apply to Elections of Members to serve in the respective Legislative Assemblies of Ontario and Quebec.

Provided that, until the Legislature of Ontario otherwise provides, at any Election for a Member of the Legislative Assembly of Ontario for the District of Algoma, in addition to Persons qualified by the Law of the Province of Canada to vote, every Male British Subject, aged Twenty-one Years or upwards, being a Householder, shall have a Vote.

[Note: See also the *Election Act* and *Legislative Assembly Act* (Ontario) and the *Elections Act* and *National Assembly Act* (Quebec).]

Duration of Legislative Assemblies

85. Every Legislative Assembly of Ontario and every Legislative Assembly of Quebec shall continue for Four Years from the Day of the Return of the Writs for choosing the same (subject nevertheless to either the Legislative Assembly of Ontario or the Legislative Assembly of Quebec being sooner dissolved by the Lieutenant Governor of the Province), and no longer.

[Note: Now five years in both provinces: see the *Legislative Assembly Act* (Ontario) and the *National Assembly Act* (Quebec). See also section 4 of the *Constitution Act, 1982* (No. 44 *infra*).]

Yearly Session of Legislature

86. There shall be a Session of the Legislature of Ontario and of that of Quebec once at least in every Year, so that Twelve Months shall not intervene between the last sitting of the Legislature in each Province in one Session and its first Sitting in the next Session.

[Note: See section 5 of the *Constitution Act, 1982* (No. 44 *infra*).]

Speaker, Quorum, etc.

87. The following Provisions of this Act respecting the House of Commons of Canada shall extend and apply to the Legislative Assemblies of Ontario and Quebec, that is to say,—the Provisions relating to the

Election of a Speaker originally and on Vacancies, the Duties of the Speaker, the Absence of the Speaker, the Quorum, and the Mode of voting, as if those Provisions were here re-enacted and made applicable in Terms to each such Legislative Assembly.

4. NOVA SCOTIA AND NEW BRUNSWICK

88. The Constitution of the Legislature of each of the Provinces of Nova Scotia and New Brunswick shall, subject to the Provisions of this Act, continue as it exists at the Union until altered under the Authority of this Act; *and the House of Assembly of New Brunswick existing at the passing of this Act shall, unless sooner dissolved, continue for the Period for which it was elected.*

[Note: The words in italics were repealed by the *Statute Law Revision Act, 1893* (No. 17 *infra*). The note to section 64 also applies to the Legislatures of the provinces mentioned therein. See also sections 3 to 5 of the *Constitution Act, 1982* (No. 44 *infra*) and sub-item 2(2) of the Schedule to that Act.]

Constitutions of Legislatures of Nova Scotia *and New Brunswick*

5. ONTARIO, QUEBEC, AND NOVA SCOTIA

89. *Each of the Lieutenant Governors of Ontario, Quebec and Nova Scotia shall cause Writs to be issued for the First Election of Members of the Legislative Assembly thereof in such Form and by such Person as he thinks fit, and at such Time and addressed to such Returning Officer as the Governor General directs, and so that the First Election of Member of Assembly for any Electoral District or any Subdivision thereof shall be held at the same Time and at the same Places as the Election for a Member to serve in the House of Commons of Canada for that Electoral District.*

[Note: Repealed by the *Statute Law Revision Act, 1893* (No. 17 *infra*).]

First Elections

6. THE FOUR PROVINCES

90. The following Provisions of this Act respecting the Parliament of Canada, namely,—the Provisions relating to Appropriation and Tax Bills, the Recommendation of Money Votes, the Assent to Bills, the Disallowance of Acts, and the Signification of Pleasure on Bills reserved,—shall extend and apply to the Legislatures of the several Provinces as if those Provisions were here re-enacted and made applicable in Terms to the respective Provinces and the Legislatures thereof, with the Substitution of the Lieutenant Governor of the Province for the Governor General, of the Governor General for the Queen and for a Secretary of State, of One Year for Two Years, and of the Province for Canada.

Application to Legislatures of Provisions respecting Money Votes, etc.

VI. DISTRIBUTION OF LEGISLATIVE POWERS

Powers of the Parliament

91. It shall be lawful for the Queen, by and with the Advice and Consent of the Senate and House of Commons, to make Laws for the Peace, Order, and good Government of Canada, in relation to all Matters not coming within the Classes of Subjects by this Act assigned exclusively to the Legislatures of the Provinces; and for greater Certainty, but not so as to restrict the Generality of the foregoing Terms of this Section, it

Legislative Authority of Parliament of Canada

is hereby declared that (notwithstanding anything in this Act) the exclusive Legislative Authority of the Parliament of Canada extends to all Matters coming within the Classes of Subjects next hereinafter enumerated; that is to say,—

Amendment as to legislative authority of Parliament of Canada

1. *The amendment from time to time of the Constitution of Canada, except as regards matters coming within the classes of subjects by this Act assigned exclusively to the Legislatures of the provinces, or as regards rights or privileges by this or any other Constitutional Act granted or secured to the Legislature or the Government of a province, or to any class of persons with respect to schools or as regards the use of the English or the French language or as regards the requirements that there shall be a session of the Parliament of Canada at least once each year, and that no House of Commons shall continue for more than five years from the day of the return of the Writs for choosing the House: Provided, however, that a House of Commons may in time of real or apprehended war, invasion or insurrection be continued by the Parliament of Canada if such continuation is not opposed by the votes of more than one-third of the members of such House.*

[Note: Class 1 was added by the *British North America Act (No. 2), 1949* (No. 33 *infra*) and repealed by the *Constitution Act, 1982* (No. 44 *infra*).]

1A.   The Public Debt and Property.

[Note: Re-numbered 1A by the *British North America Act (No. 2), 1949* No. 33 *infra*).]

2. The Regulation of Trade and Commerce.

2A.   Unemployment insurance.

[Note: Added by the *Constitution Act, 1940* (No. 28 *infra*).]

3. The raising of Money by any Mode or System of Taxation.

4. The borrowing of Money on the Public Credit.

5. Postal Service.

6. The Census and Statistics.

7. Militia, Military and Naval Service, and Defence.

8. The fixing of and providing for the Salaries and Allowances of Civil and other Officers of the Government of Canada.

9. Beacons, Buoys, Lighthouses, and Sable Island.

10. Navigation and Shipping.

11. Quarantine and the Establishment and Maintenance of Marine Hospitals.

12. Sea Coast and Inland Fisheries.

13. Ferries between a Province and any British or Foreign Country or between Two Provinces.

14. Currency and Coinage.

15. Banking, Incorporation of Banks, and the Issue of Paper Money.

16. Savings Banks.

17. Weights and Measures.

18. Bills of Exchange and Promissory Notes.

19. Interest.

20. Legal Tender.

21. Bankruptcy and Insolvency.

22. Patents of Invention and Discovery.

23. Copyrights.

24. Indians, and Lands reserved for the Indians.

25. Naturalization and Aliens.

26. Marriage and Divorce.

27. The Criminal Law, except the Constitution of Courts of Criminal Jurisdiction, but including the Procedure in Criminal Matters.

28. The Establishment, Maintenance, and Management of Penitentiaries.

29. Such Classes of Subjects as are expressly excepted in the Enumeration of the Classes of Subjects by this Act assigned exclusively to the Legislatures of the Provinces.

And any Matter coming within any of the Classes of Subjects enumerated in this Section shall not be deemed to come within the Class of Matters of a local or private Nature comprised in the Enumeration of the Classes of Subjects by this Act assigned exclusively to the Legislatures of the Provinces.

[Note: Legislative authority has also been conferred by the *Rupert's Land Act, 1868* (No. 6 *infra*), *Constitution Act, 1871* (No. 11 *infra*), *Constitution Act, 1886* (No. 15 *infra*), *Statute of Westminster, 1931* (No. 27 *infra*) and section 44 of the *Constitution Act, 1982* (No. 44 *infra*), and see also sections 38 and 41 to 43 of the latter Act.]

Exclusive Powers of Provincial Legislatures

92. In each Province the Legislature may exclusively make Laws in relation to Matters coming within the Classes of Subjects next hereinafter enumerated; that is to say,—

Subjects of exclusive Provincial Legislation

1. The Amendment from Time to Time, notwithstanding anything in this Act, of the Constitution of the Province, except as regards the Office of Lieutenant Governor.

[Note: Class 1 was repealed by the *Constitution Act, 1982* (No. 44 *infra*). The subject is now provided for in section 45 of that Act, and see also sections 38 and 41 to 43 of the same Act.]

2. Direct Taxation with-in the Province in order to the raising of a Revenue for Provincial Purposes.

3. The borrowing of Money on the sole Credit of the Province.

4. The Establishment and Tenure of Provincial Offices and the Appointment and Payment of Provincial Officers.

5. The Management and Sale of the Public Lands belonging to the Province and of the Timber and Wood thereon.

6. The Establishment, Maintenance, and Management of Public and Reformatory Prisons in and for the Province.

7. The Establishment, Maintenance, and Management of Hospitals, Asylums, Charities, and Eleemosynary Institutions in and for the Province, other than Marine Hospitals.

8. Municipal Institutions in the Province.

9. Shop, Saloon, Tavern, Auctioneer, and other Licences in order to the raising of a Revenue for Provincial, Local, or Municipal Purposes.

10. Local Works and Undertakings other than such as are of the following Classes:—

a. Lines of Steam or other Ships, Railways, Canals, Telegraphs, and other Works and Undertakings connecting the Province with any other or others of the Provinces, or extending beyond the Limits of the Province:

b. Lines of Steam Ships between the Province and any British or Foreign Country:

c. Such Works as, although wholly situate within the Province, are before or after their Execution declared by the Parliament of Canada to be for the general Advantage of Canada or for the Advantage of Two or more of the Provinces.

11. The Incorporation of Companies with Provincial Objects.

12. The Solemnization of Marriage in the Province.

13. Property and Civil Rights in the Province.

14. The Administration of Justice in the Province, including the Constitution, Maintenance, and Organization of Provincial Courts, both of Civil and of Criminal Jurisdiction, and including Procedure in Civil Matters in those Courts.

15. The Imposition of Punishment by Fine, Penalty, or Imprisonment for enforcing any Law of the Province made in relation to any Matter coming within any of the Classes of Subjects enumerated in this Section.

16. Generally all Matters of a merely local or private Nature in the Province.

Non-Renewable Natural Resources, Forestry Resources and Electrical Energy

Laws respecting non-renewable natural resources, forestry resources and electrical energy

92A. (1) In each pro-vince, the legislature may exclusively make laws in relation to

(a) exploration for non-renewable natural resources in the province;

(b) development, conservation and management of non-renewable natural resources and forestry resources in the province, including laws in relation to the rate of primary production therefrom; and

(c) development, conservation and management of sites and facilities in the province for the generation and production of electrical energy.

Export from provinces of resources

(2) In each province, the legislature may make laws in relation to the export from the province to another part of Canada of the primary production from non-renewable natural resources and forestry resources in the province and the production from facilities in the province for the generation of electrical energy, but such laws may not authorize or provide for discrimination in prices or in supplies exported to another part of Canada.

Authority of Parliament

(3) Nothing in subsection (2) derogates from the authority of Parliament to enact laws in relation to the matters referred to in that subsection and, where such a law of Parliament and a law of a province conflict, the law of Parliament prevails to the extent of the conflict.

Taxation of resources

(4) In each province, the legislature may make laws in relation to the raising of money by any mode or system of taxation in respect of

(a) Non-renewable natural resources and forestry resources in the province and the primary production therefrom, and

(b) sites and facilities in the province for the generation of electrical energy and the production therefrom,

whether or not such production is exported in whole or in part from the province, but such laws may not authorize or provide for taxation that differentiates between production exported to another part of Canada and production not exported from the province.

(5) The expression "primary production" has the meaning assigned by the Sixth Schedule.

"Primary production"

(6) Nothing in subsections (1) to (5) derogates from any powers or rights that a legislature or government of a province had immediately before the coming into force of this section.

Existing powers or rights

[Note: Added by section 50 of the *Constitution Act, 1982* (No. 44 *infra*).]

Education

93. In and for each Province the Legislature may exclusively make Laws in relation to Education, subject and according to the following Provisions:—

Legislation respecting Education

(1) Nothing in any such Law shall prejudicially affect any Right or Privilege with respect to Denominational Schools which any Class of Persons have by Law in the Province at the Union:

(2) All the Powers, Privileges, and Duties at the Union by Law conferred and imposed in Upper Canada on the Separate Schools and School Trustees of the Queen's Roman Catholic Subjects shall be and the same are hereby extended to the Dissentient Schools of the Queen's Protestant and Roman Catholic Subjects in Quebec:

(3) Where in any Province a System of Separate or Dissentient Schools exists by Law at the Union or is thereafter established by the Legislature of the Province, an Appeal shall lie to the Governor General in Council from any Act or Decision of any Provincial Authority affecting any Right or Privilege of the Protestant or Roman Catholic Minority of the Queen's Subjects in relation to Education:

(4) In case any such Provincial Law as from Time to Time seems to the Governor General in Council requisite for the due Execution of the Provisions of this Section is not made, or in case any Decision of the Governor General in Council on any Appeal under this Section is not duly executed by the proper Provincial Authority in that Behalf, then and in every such Case, and as far only as the Circumstances of each Case require, the Parliament of Canada may make remedial Laws for the due Execution of the Provisions of this Section and of any Decision of the Governor General in Council under this Section.

[Note: Altered for Manitoba by section 22 of the *Manitoba Act, 1870* (No. 8 *infra*) confirmed by the *Constitution Act, 1871* No. 11 *infra*); for Alberta, by section 17 of the *Alberta Act* (No. 20 *infra*); for Saskatchewan, by section 17 of the *Saskatchewan Act* (No. 21 *infra*); and for Newfoundland, by Term 17 of the Terms of Union of Newfoundland with Canada, confirmed by the *Newfoundland Act* (No. 32 *infra*). See also sections 23, 29 and 59 of the *Constitution Act, 1982* (No. 44 *infra*).]

Uniformity of Laws in Ontario, Nova Scotia, and New Brunswick

94. Notwithstanding anything in this Act, the Parliament of Canada may make Provision for the Uniformity of all or any of the Laws relative

Legislation for Uniformity of Laws in Three Provinces

to Property and Civil Rights in Ontario, Nova Scotia, and New Brunswick, and of the Procedure of all or any of the Courts in those Three Provinces, and from and after the passing of any Act in that Behalf the Power of the Parliament of Canada to make Laws in relation to any Matter comprised in any such Act shall, notwithstanding anything in this Act, be unrestricted; but any Act of the Parliament of Canada making Provision for such Uniformity shall not have effect in any Province unless and until it is adopted and enacted as Law by the Legislature thereof.

Legislation respecting old age pensions and supplementary benefits

94A. The Parliament of Canada may make laws in relation to old age pensions and supplementary benefits, including survivors' and disability benefits irrespective of age, but no such law shall affect the operation of any law present or future of a provincial legislature in relation to any such matter.

[Note: Substituted by the *Constitution Act, 1964* (No. 38 *infra*) for the section 94A that was originally added by the *British North America Act, 1951* (No. 35 *infra*).]

Agriculture and Immigration

Concurrent Powers of Legislation respecting Agriculture, etc.

95. In each Province the Legislature may make Laws in relation to Agriculture in the Province, and to Immigration into the Province; and it is hereby declared that the Parliament of Canada may from Time to Time make Laws in relation to Agriculture in all or any of the Provinces, and to Immigration into all or any of the Provinces; and any Law of the Legislature of a Province relative to Agriculture or to Immigration shall have effect in and for the Province as long and as far only as it is not repugnant to any Act of the Parliament of Canada.

VII. JUDICATURE

Appointment of Judges

96. The Governor General shall appoint the Judges of the Superior, District, and County Courts in each Province, except those of the Courts of Probate in Nova Scotia and New Brunswick.

Selections of Judges in Ontario, etc.

97. Until the Laws relative to Property and Civil Rights in Ontario, Nova Scotia, and New Brunswick, and the Procedure of the Courts in those Provinces, are made uniform, the Judges of the Courts of those Provinces appointed by the Governor General shall be selected from the respective Bars of those Provinces.

Selection of Judges in Quebec

98. The Judges of the Courts of Quebec shall be selected from the Bar of that Province.

Tenure of Office of Judges of Superior Courts

99. *The Judges of the Superior Courts shall hold Office during good Behaviour, but shall be removable by the Governor General on Address of the Senate and House of Commons.*

Tenure of office of judges

99. (1) Subject to subsection (2) of this section, the judges of the superior courts shall hold office during good behaviour, but shall be removable by the Governor General on address of the Senate and House of Commons.

(2) A judge of a superior court, whether appointed before or after the coming into force of this section, shall cease to hold office upon attaining the age of seventy-five years, or upon the coming into force of this section if at that time he has already attained that age.

[Note: Section 99 (in italics) was repealed and the new section substituted by the *Constitution Act, 1960* (No. 37 *infra*).]

100. The Salaries, Allowances, and Pensions of the Judges of the Superior, District, and County Courts (except the Courts of Probate in Nova Scotia and New Brunswick), and of the Admiralty Courts in Cases where the Judges thereof are for the Time being paid by Salary, shall be fixed and provided by the Parliament of Canada.

Salaries, etc., of Judges

[Note: See the *Judges Act* (Canada).]

101. The Parliament of Canada may, notwithstanding anything in this Act, from Time to Time provide for the Constitution, Maintenance, and Organization of a General Court of Appeal for Canada, and for the Establishment of any additional Courts for the better Administration of the Laws of Canada.

General Court of Appeal, etc.

[Note: See the *Supreme Court Act, Federal Court Act* and *Tax Court of Canada Act* (Canada).]

VIII. REVENUES; DEBTS; ASSETS; TAXATION

102. All Duties and Revenues over which the respective Legislatures of Canada, Nova Scotia, and New Brunswick before and at the Union had and have Power of Appropriation, except such Portions thereof as are by this Act reserved to the respective Legislatures of the Provinces, or are raised by them in accordance with the special Powers conferred on them by this Act, shall form One Consolidated Revenue Fund, to be appropriated for the Public Service of Canada in the Manner and subject to the Charges in this Act provided.

Creation of Consolidated Revenue Fund

103. The Consolidated Revenue Fund of Canada shall be permanently charged with the Costs, Charges, and Expenses incident to the Collection, Management, and Receipt thereof, and the same shall form the First Charge thereon, subject to be reviewed and audited in such Manner as shall be ordered by the Governor General in Council until the Parliament otherwise provides.

Expenses of Collection, etc.

104. The annual Interest of the Public Debts of the several Provinces of Canada, Nova Scotia, and New Brunswick at the Union shall form the Second Charge on the Consolidated Revenue Fund of Canada.

Interest of Provincial Public Debts

105. Unless altered by the Parliament of Canada, the Salary of the Governor General shall be Ten thousand Pounds Sterling Money of the United Kingdom of Great Britain and Ireland, payable out of the Consolidated Revenue Fund of Canada, and the same shall form the Third Charge thereon.

Salary of Governor General

[Note: See the *Governor General's Act* (Canada).]

106. Subject to the several Payments by this Act charged on the Consolidated Revenue Fund of Canada, the same shall be appropriated by the Parliament of Canada for the Public Service.

Appropriation from Time to Time

107. All Stocks, Cash, Banker's Balances, and Securities for Money belonging to each Province at the Time of the Union, except as in this Act mentioned, shall be the Property of Canada, and shall be taken in Reduction of the Amount of the respective Debts of the Provinces at the Union.

Transfer of Stocks, etc.

Transfer of
Property in
Schedule

108. The Public Works and Property of each Province, enumerated in the Third Schedule to this Act, shall be the Property of Canada.

Property in Lands,
Mines, etc.

109. All Lands, Mines, Minerals, and Royalties belonging to the several Provinces of Canada, Nova Scotia, and New Brunswick at the Union, and all Sums then due or payable for such Lands, Mines, Minerals, or Royalties, shall belong to the several Provinces of Ontario, Quebec, Nova Scotia, and New Brunswick in which the same are situate or arise, subject to any Trusts existing in respect thereof, and to any Interest other than that of the Province in the same.

[Note: The Provinces of Manitoba, British Columbia, Alberta and Saskatchewan were placed in the same position as the original provinces by the *Constitution Act, 1930* (No. 26 *infra*).

Newfoundland was also placed in the same position by the *Newfoundland Act* (No. 32 *infra*).

With respect to Prince Edward Island, see the Schedule to the *Prince Edward Island Terms of Union* (No. 12 *infra*).]

Assets connected
with Provincial
Debts

110. All Assets connected with such Portions of the Public Debt of each Province as are assumed by that Province shall belong to that Province.

Canada to be liable
for Provincial
Debts

111. Canada shall be liable for the Debts and Liabilities of each province existing at the Union.

Debts of Ontario
and Quebec

112. Ontario and Quebec conjointly shall be liable to Canada for the Amount (if any) by which the Debt of the Province of Canada exceeds at the Union Sixty-two million five hundred thousand Dollars, and shall be charged with Interest at the Rate of Five per Centum per Annum thereon.

Assets of Ontario
and Quebec

113. The Assets enumerated in the Fourth Schedule to this Act belonging at the Union to the Province of Canada shall be the Property of Ontario and Quebec conjointly.

Debt of Nova Scotia

114. Nova Scotia shall be liable to Canada for the Amount (if any) by which its Public Debt exceeds at the Union Eight million Dollars, and shall be charged with Interest at the Rate of Five per Centum per Annum thereon.

[Note: As to sections 114, 115 and 116, see the *Provincial Subsidies Act* (Canada).]

Debt of New
Brunswick

115. New Brunswick shall be liable to Canada for the Amount (if any) by which its Public Debt exceeds at the Union Seven million Dollars, and shall be charged with Interest at the Rate of Five per Centum per Annum thereon.

Payment of interest to Nova Scotia
and New
Brunswick

116. In case the Public Debts of Nova Scotia and New Brunswick do not at the Union amount to Eight million and Seven million Dollars respectively, they shall respectively receive by half-yearly Payments in advance from the Government of Canada Interest at Five per Centum per Annum on the Difference between the actual Amounts of their respective Debts and such stipulated Amounts.

Provincial Public
Property

117. The several Provinces shall retain all their respective Public Property not otherwise disposed of in this Act, subject to the Right of Canada to assume any Lands or Public Property required for Fortifications or for the Defence of the Country.

118. *The following Sums shall be paid yearly by Canada to the several Provinces for the Support of their Governments and Legislatures:*   Grants to Provinces

	Dollars
Ontario	Eighty thousand.
Quebec	Seventy thousand.
Nova Scotia	Sixty thousand.
New Brunswick	Fifty thousand

Two hundred and sixty thousand;

and an annual Grant in aid of each Province shall be made, equal to Eighty Cents per Head of the Population as ascertained by the Census of One thousand eight hundred and sixty-one, and in the Case of Nova Scotia and New Brunswick, by each subsequent Decennial Census until the Population of each of those two Provinces amounts to Four hundred thousand Souls, at which Rate such Grant shall thereafter remain. Such Grants shall be in full Settlement of all future Demands on Canada, and shall be paid half-yearly in advance to each Province; but the Government of Canada shall deduct from such Grants, as against any Province, all Sums chargeable as Interest on the Public Debt of that Province in excess of the several Amounts stipulated in this Act.

[Note: Repealed by the *Statute Law Revision Act, 1950* (No. 34 *infra*). The section had been previously superseded by the *Constitution Act, 1907* (No. 22 *infra*). See the *Provincial Subsidies Act* and the *Federal-Provincial Fiscal Arrangements and Federal Post-Secondary Education and Health Contributions Act* (Canada).]

119. New Brunswick shall receive by half-yearly Payments in advance from Canada for the Period of Ten Years from the Union an additional Allowance of Sixty-three thousand Dollars per Annum; but as long as the Public Debt of that Province remains under Seven million Dollars, a Deduction equal to the Interest at Five per Centum per Annum on such Deficiency shall be made from that Allowance of Sixty-three thousand Dollars.   Further Grant to New Brunswick

120. All Payments to be made under this Act, or in discharge of Liabilities created under any Act of the Provinces of Canada, Nova Scotia, and New Brunswick respectively, and assumed by Canada, shall, until the Parliament of Canada otherwise directs, be made in such Form and Manner as may from Time to Time be ordered by the Governor General in Council.   Form of Payments

121. All Articles of the Growth, Produce, or Manufacture of any one of the Provinces shall, from and after the Union, be admitted free into each of the other Provinces.   Canadian manufactures, etc.

122. The Customs and Excise Laws of each Province shall, subject to the Provisions of this Act, continue in force until altered by the Parliament of Canada.   Continuance of Customs and Excise Laws

[Note: See the current federal customs and excise legislation.]

123. Where Customs Duties are, at the Union, leviable on any Goods, Wares, or Merchandises in any Two Provinces, those Goods, Wares, and Merchandises may, from and after the Union, be imported from one of those Provinces into the other of them on Proof of Payment of the Customs Duty leviable thereon in the Province of Exportation, and on Payment of   Exportation and Importation as between Two Provinces such further Amount (if any) of Customs Duty as is leviable thereon in the Province of Importation.

Lumber Dues in New Brunswick

124. Nothing in this Act shall affect the Right of New Brunswick to levy the Lumber Dues provided in Chapter Fifteen of Title Three of the Revised Statutes of New Brunswick, or in any Act amending that Act before or after the Union, and not increasing the Amount of such Dues; but the Lumber of any of the Provinces other than New Brunswick shall not be subject to such Dues.

Exemption of Public Lands, etc.

125. No Lands or Property belonging to Canada or any Province shall be liable to Taxation.

Provincial Consolidated Revenue Fund

126. Such Portions of the Duties and Revenues over which the respective Legislatures of Canada, Nova Scotia, and New Brunswick had before the Union Power of Appropriation as are by this Act reserved to the respective Governments or Legislatures of the Provinces, and all Duties and Revenues raised by them in accordance with the special Powers conferred upon them by this Act, shall in each Province form One Consolidated Revenue Fund to be appropriated for the Public Service of the Province.

IX. MISCELLANEOUS PROVISIONS

General

As to Legislative Councillors of Provinces becoming senators

127. *If any Person being at the passing of this Act a Member of the Legislative Council of Canada, Nova Scotia, or New Brunswick, to whom a Place in the Senate is offered, does not within Thirty Days thereafter, by Writing under his Hand addressed to the Governor General of the Province of Canada or to the Lieutenant Governor of Nova Scotia or New Brunswick (as the Case may be), accept the same, he shall be deemed to have declined the same; and any Person who, being at the passing of this Act a Member of the Legislative Council of Nova Scotia or New Brunswick, accepts a Place in the Senate, shall thereby vacate his Seat in such Legislative Council.*

[Note: Repealed by the *Statute Law Revision Act, 1893* (No. 17 *infra*).]

Oath of Allegiance, etc.

128. Every Member of the Senate or House of Commons of Canada shall before taking his Seat therein take and subscribe before the Governor General or some Person authorized by him, and every Member of a Legislative Council or Legislative Assembly of any Province shall before taking his Seat therein take and subscribe before the Lieutenant Governor of the Province or some Person authorized by him, the Oath of Allegiance contained in the Fifth Schedule to this Act; and every Member of the Senate of Canada and every Member of the Legislative Council of Quebec shall also, before taking his Seat therein, take and subscribe before the Governor General, or some Person authorized by him, the Declaration of Qualification contained in the same Schedule.

Continuance of existing Laws, Courts, Officers, etc.

129. Except as otherwise provided by this Act, all Laws in force in Canada, Nova Scotia, or New Brunswick at the Union, and all Courts of Civil and Criminal Jurisdiction, and all legal Commissions, Powers, and Authorities, and all Officers, Judicial, Administrative, and Ministerial, existing therein at the Union, shall continue in Ontario, Quebec, Nova

Scotia, and New Brunswick respectively, as if the Union had not been made; subject nevertheless (except with respect to such as are enacted by or exist under Acts of the Parliament of Great Britain or of the Parliament of the United Kingdom of Great Britain and Ireland,) to be repealed, abolished, or altered by the Parliament of Canada, or by the Legislature of the respective Province, according to the Authority of the Parliament or of that Legislature under this Act.

[Note: The restriction against altering or repealing laws enacted by or existing under statutes of the United Kingdom was removed by the *Statute of Westminster, 1931* (No. 27 *infra*), except in respect of certain constitutional documents. See also Part V of the *Constitution Act, 1982* (No. 44 *infra*).]

130. Until the Parliament of Canada otherwise provides, all Officers of the several Provinces having Duties to discharge in relation to Matters other than those coming within the Classes of Subjects by this Act assigned exclusively to the Legislatures of the Provinces shall be Officers of Canada, and shall continue to discharge the Duties of their respective Offices under the same Liabilities, Responsibilities, and Penalties as if the Union had not been made.

Transfer of Officers to Canada

131. Until the Parliament of Canada otherwise provides, the Governor General in Council may from Time to Time appoint such Officers as the Governor General in Council deems necessary or proper for the effectual Execution of this Act.

Appointment of new Officers

132. The Parliament and Government of Canada shall have all Powers necessary or proper for performing the Obligations of Canada or of any Province thereof, as Part of the British Empire, towards Foreign Countries, arising under Treaties between the Empire and such Foreign Countries.

Treaty Obligations

133. Either the English or the French Language may be used by any Person in the Debates of the Houses of the Parliament of Canada and of the Houses of the Legislature of Quebec; and both those Languages shall be used in the respective Records and Journals of those Houses; and either of those Languages may be used by any Person or in any Pleading or Process in or issuing from any Court of Canada established under this Act, and in or from all or any of the Courts of Quebec.

Use of English and French Languages

The Acts of the Parliament of Canada and of the Legislature of Quebec shall be printed and published in both those Languages.

[Note: See also section 23 of the *Manitoba Act, 1870* (No. 8 *infra*) and sections 17 to 23 of the *Constitution Act, 1982* (No. 44 *infra*).]

Ontario and Quebec

134. Until the Legislature of Ontario or of Quebec otherwise provides, the Lieutenant Governors of Ontario and Quebec may each appoint under the Great Seal of the Province the following Officers, to hold Office during Pleasure, that is to say,—the Attorney General, the Secretary and Registrar of the Province, the Treasurer of the Province, the Commissioner of Crown Lands, and the Commissioner of Agriculture and Public Works, and in the Case of Quebec the Solicitor General, and may, by Order of the Lieutenant Governor in Council, from Time to Time prescribe the Duties of those Officers, and of the several Departments over which they shall preside or to which they shall belong, and of the Officers and Clerks

Appointment of Executive Officers for Ontario and Quebec

thereof, and may also appoint other and additional Officers to hold Office during Pleasure, and may from Time to Time prescribe the Duties of those Officers, and of the several Departments over which they shall preside or to which they shall belong, and of the Officers and Clerks thereof.

[Note: See the *Executive Council Act* (Ontario) and the *Executive Power Act* (Quebec).]

Powers, Duties, etc. of Executive Officers

135. Until the Legislature of Ontario or Quebec otherwise provides, all Rights, Powers, Duties, Functions, Responsibilities, or authorities at the passing of this Act vested in or imposed on the Attorney General, Solicitor General, Secretary and Registrar of the Province of Canada, Minister of Finance, Commissioner of Crown Lands, Commissioner of Public Works, and Minister of Agriculture and Receiver General, by any Law, Statute, or Ordinance of Upper Canada, Lower Canada, or Canada, and not repugnant to this Act, shall be vested in or imposed on any Officer to be appointed by the Lieutenant Governor for the Discharge of the same or any of them; and the Commissioner of Agriculture and Public Works shall perform the Duties and Functions of the Office of Minister of Agriculture at the passing of this Act imposed by the Law of the Province of Canada, as well as those of the Commissioner of Public Works.

Great Seals

136. Until altered by the Lieutenant Governor in Council, the Great Seals of Ontario and Quebec respectively shall be the same, or of the same Design, as those used in the Provinces of Upper Canada and Lower Canada respectively before their Union as the Province of Canada.

Construction of temporary Acts

137. The Words "and from thence to the End of the then next ensuing Session of the Legislature," or Words to the same Effect, used in any temporary Act of the Province of Canada not expired before the Union, shall be construed to extend and apply to the next Session of the Parliament of Canada if the Subject Matter of the Act is within the Powers of the same as defined by this Act, or to the next Sessions of the Legislatures of Ontario and Quebec respectively if the Subject Matter of the Act is within the Powers of the same as defined by this Act.

As to Errors in Names

138. From and after the Union the Use of the Words "Upper Canada" instead of "Ontario," or "Lower Canada" instead of "Quebec," in any Deed, Writ, Process, Pleading, Document, Matter, or Thing, shall not invalidate the same.

As to Issue of Proclamations after Union

139. Any Proclamation under the Great Seal of the Province of Canada issued before the Union to take effect at a Time which is subsequent to the Union, whether relating to that Province, or to Upper Canada, or to Lower Canada, and the several Matters and Things therein proclaimed, shall be and continue of like Force and Effect as if the Union had not been made.

As to issue of Proclamations before Union, to commence after Union

140. Any Proclamation which is authorized by any Act of the Legislature of the Province of Canada to be issued under the Great Seal of the Province of Canada, whether relating to that Province, or to Upper Canada, or to Lower Canada, and which is not issued before the Union, may be issued by the Lieutenant Governor of Ontario or of Quebec, as its Subject Matter requires, under the Great Seal thereof; and from and after the Issue of such Proclamation the same and the several Matters and Things therein proclaimed shall be and continue of the like force and Effect in Ontario or Quebec as if the Union had not been made.

141. The Penitentiary of the Province of Canada shall, until the Parliament of Canada otherwise provides, be and continue the Penitentiary of Ontario and of Quebec.

[Note: See the *Penitentiary Act* (Canada).]

Penitentiary

142. The Division and Adjustment of the Debts, Credits, Liabilities, Properties, and Assets of Upper Canada and Lower Canada shall be referred to the Arbitrament of Three Arbitrators, One chosen by the government of Ontario, One by the Government of Quebec, and One by the Government of Canada; and the Selection of the Arbitrators shall not be made until the Parliament of Canada and the Legislatures of Ontario and Quebec have met; and the Arbitrator chosen by the Government of Canada shall not be a Resident either in Ontario or in Quebec.

Arbitration respecting Debts, etc.

143. The Governor General in Council may from Time to Time order that such and so many of the Records, Books, and Documents of the Province of Canada as he thinks fit shall be appropriated and delivered either to Ontario or to Quebec, and the same shall thenceforth be the Property of that Province; and any Copy thereof or Extract therefrom, duly certified by the Officer having charge of the Original thereof, shall be admitted as Evidence.

Division of Records

144. The Lieutenant Governor of Quebec may from Time to Time, by Proclamation under the Great Seal of the Province, to take effect from a Day to be appointed therein, constitute Townships in those Parts of the Province of Quebec in which Townships are not then already constituted, and fix the Metes and Bounds thereof.

Constitution of Townships in Quebec

X. INTERCOLONIAL RAILWAY

145. *Inasmuch as the Provinces of Canada, Nova Scotia, and New Brunswick have joined in a Declaration that the Construction of the Intercolonial Railway is essential to the Consolidation of the Union of British North America, and to the Assent thereto of Nova Scotia and New Brunswick, and have consequently agreed that Provision should be made for its immediate Construction by the Government of Canada: Therefore, in order to give effect to that Agreement, it shall be the Duty of the Government and Parliament of Canada to provide for the Commencement, within Six Months after the Union, of a Railway connecting the River St. Lawrence with the City of Halifax in Nova Scotia, and for the Construction thereof without Intermission, and the Completion thereof with all practicable speed.*

[Note: Repealed by the *Statute Law Revision Act, 1893* (No. 17 *infra*).]

Duty of Government and Parliament of Canada to make Railway herein described

XI. ADMISSION OF OTHER COLONIES

146. It shall be lawful for the Queen, by and with the Advice of Her Majesty's Most Honourable Privy Council, on Addresses from the Houses of the Parliament of Canada, and from the Houses of the respective Legislatures of the Colonies or Provinces of Newfoundland, Prince Edward Island, and British Columbia, to admit those Colonies or Provinces, or any of them, into the Union, and on Address from the

Power to admit Newfoundland, etc., into the Union

Houses of the Parliament of Canada to admit Rupert's Land and the North-western Territory, or either of them, into the Union, on such Terms and Conditions in each Case as are in the Addresses expressed and as the Queen thinks fit to approve, subject to the Provisions of this Act; and the Provisions of any Order in Council in that Behalf shall have effect as if they had been enacted by the Parliament of the United Kingdom of Great Britain and Ireland.

[Note: Rupert's Land and the North-Western Territory (subsequently designated the Northwest Territories) became part of Canada, pursuant to this section and the *Rupert's Land Act, 1868* (No. 6 *infra*), by the *Rupert's Land and North-Western Territory Order* (June 23, 1870) (No. 9 *infra*).

The Province of Manitoba was established by the *Manitoba Act, 1870* (No. 8 *infra*). This Act was confirmed by the *Constitution Act, 1871* (No. 11 *infra*).

British Columbia was admitted into the Union pursuant to this section by the *British Columbia Terms of Union* (May 16, 1871) (No. 10 *infra*).

Prince Edward Island was admitted into the Union pursuant to this section by the *Prince Edward Island Terms of Union* (June 26, 1873 (No. 12 *infra*).

The Provinces of Alberta and Saskatchewan were established, pursuant to the *Constitution Act, 1871* (No. 11 *infra*), by the *Alberta Act* (July 20, 1905) (No. 20 *infra*) and the *Saskatchewan Act* (July 20, 1905) (No. 21 *infra*) respectively.

Newfoundland was admitted as a province by the *Newfoundland Act* (March 23, 1949) (No. 32 *infra*), which confirmed the Agreement containing the Terms of Union between Canada and Newfoundland.

The Yukon Territory was created out of the Northwest Territories in 1898 by *The Yukon Territory Act* (No. 19 *infra*).

147. In case of the Admission of Newfoundland and Prince Edward Island, or either of them, each shall be entitled to a Representation in the Senate of Canada of Four Members, and (notwithstanding anything in this Act) in case of the Admission of Newfoundland the normal Number of Senators shall be Seventy-six and their maximum Number shall be Eighty-two; but Prince Edward Island when admitted shall be deemed to be comprised in the third of the Three Divisions into which Canada is, in relation to the Constitution of the Senate, divided by this Act, and accordingly, after the Admission of Prince Edward Island, whether Newfoundland is admitted or not, the Representation of Nova Scotia and New Brunswick in the Senate shall, as Vacancies occur, be reduced from Twelve and Ten Members respectively, and the Representation of each of those Provinces shall not be increased at any Time beyond Ten, except under the Provisions of this Act for the Appointment of Three or Six additional Senators under the Direction of the Queen.

As to Representation of Newfoundland and Prince Edward Island in Senate

[Note: See the notes to sections 21, 22, 26, 27 and 28.]

CANADA ACT, 1982

including the

CONSTITUTION ACT, 1982

1982, c. 11 (U.K.)
[29th March 1982]

[Note: The English version of the *Canada Act 1982* is contained in the body of the Act; its French version is found in Schedule A. Schedule B contains the English and French versions of the *Constitution Act, 1982*.]

An Act to give effect to a request by the Senate and House of Commons of Canada

Whereas Canada has requested and consented to the enactment of an Act of the Parliament of the United Kingdom to give effect to the provisions hereinafter set forth and the Senate and the House of Commons of Canada in Parliament assembled have submitted an address to Her Majesty requesting that Her Majesty may graciously be pleased to cause a Bill to be laid before the Parliament of the United Kingdom for that purpose.

Be it therefore enacted by the Queen's Most Excellent Majesty, by and with the advice and consent of the Lords Spiritual and Temporal, and Commons, in this present Parliament assembled, and by the authority of the same, as follows:

1. The *Constitution Act, 1982* set out in Schedule B to this Act is hereby enacted for and shall have the force of law in Canada and shall come into force as provided in that Act.

Constitution Act, 1982 enacted

2. No Act of the Parliament of the United Kingdom passed after the *Constitution Act, 1982* comes into force shall extend to Canada as part of its law.

Termination of power to legislate for Canada

3. So far as it is not contained in Schedule B, the French version of this Act is set out in Schedule A to this Act and has the same authority in Canada as the English version thereof.

French version

4. This Act may be cited as the *Canada Act, 1982*.

Short title

SCHEDULE B

CONSTITUTION ACT, 1982

PART I

CANADIAN CHARTER OF RIGHTS AND FREEDOMS

Whereas Canada is founded upon principles that recognize the supremacy of God and the rule of law:

Guarantee of Rights and Freedoms

Rights and freedoms in Canada

1. The *Canadian Charter of Rights and Freedoms* guarantees the rights and freedoms set out in it subject only to such reasonable limits prescribed by law as can be demonstrably justified in a free and democratic society.

Fundamental Freedoms

Fundamental freedoms

2. Everyone has the following fundamental freedoms:

(a) freedom of conscience and religion;
(b) freedom of thought, belief, opinion and expression, including freedom of the press and other media of communication;
(c) freedom of peaceful assembly; and
(d) freedom of association.

Democratic Rights

Democratic rights of citizens

3. Every citizen of Canada has the right to vote in an election of members of the House of Commons or of a legislative assembly and to be qualified for membership therein.

Maximum duration of legislative bodies

4. (1) No House of Commons and no legislative assembly shall continue for longer than five years from the date fixed for the return of the writs at a general election of its members.

Continuation in special circumstances

(2) In time of real or apprehended war, invasion or insurrection, a House of Commons may be continued by Parliament and a legislative assembly may be continued by the legislature beyond five years if such continuation is not opposed by the votes of more than one-third of the members of the House of Commons or the legislative assembly, as the case may be.

Annual sitting of legislative bodies

5. There shall be a sitting of Parliament and of each legislature at least once every twelve months.

Mobility Rights

Mobility of citizens

6. (1) Every citizen of Canada has the right to enter, remain in and leave Canada.

Rights to move and gain livelihood

(2) Every citizen of Canada and every person who has the status of a permanent resident of Canada has the right
(a) to move to and take up residence in any province; and
(b) to pursue the gaining of a livelihood in any province.

Limitation

(3) The rights specified in subsection (2) are subject to

(a) any laws or practices of general application in force in a province other than those that discriminate among persons primarily on the basis of province of present or previous residence; and

(b) any laws providing for reasonable residency requirements as a qualification for the receipt of publicly provided social services.

(4) Subsections (2) and (3) do not preclude any law, program or activity that has as its object the amelioration in a province of conditions of individuals in that province who are socially or economically disadvantaged if the rate of employment in that provide is below the rate of employment in Canada.

Affi
pro

Legal Rights

7. Everyone has the right to life, liberty and security of the person and the right not to be deprived thereof except in accordance with the principles of fundamental justice.

Life, liberty and
security of person

8. Everyone has the right to be secure against unreasonable search or seizure.

Search or seizure

9. Everyone has the right not to be arbitrarily detained or imprisoned.

Detention or imprisonment

10. Everyone has the right on arrest or detention

Arrest or detention

(a) to be informed promptly of the reasons therefor;

(b) to retain and instruct counsel without delay and to be informed of that right; and

(c) to have the validity of the detention determined by way of *habeas corpus* and to be released if the detention is not lawful.

11. Any person charged with an offence has the right

Proceedings in
criminal and penal
matters

(a) to be informed without unreasonable delay of the specific offence;

(b) to be tried within a reasonable time;

(c) not to be compelled to be a witness in proceedings against that person in respect of the offence;

(d) to be presumed innocent until proven guilty according to law in a fair and public hearing by an independent and impartial tribunal;

(e) not to be denied reasonable bail without just cause;

(f) except in the case of an offence under military law tried before a military tribunal, to the benefit of trial by jury where the maximum punishment for the offence is imprisonment for five years or a more severe punishment;

(g) not to be found guilty on account of any act or omission unless, at the time of the act or omission, it constituted an offence under Canadian or international law or was criminal according to the general principles of law recognized by the community of nations;

(h) if finally acquitted of the offence, not to be tried for it again and, if finally found guilty and punished for the offence, not to be tried or punished for it again; and

(i) if found guilty of the offence and if the punishment for the offence has been varied between the time of commission and the time of sentencing, to the benefit of the lesser punishment.

12. Everyone has the right not to be subjected to any cruel and unusual treatment or punishment.

Treatment or
punishment

Self-crimination

13. A witness who testifies in any proceedings has the right not to have any incriminating evidence so given used to incriminate that witness in any other proceedings, except in a prosecution for perjury or for the giving of contradictory evidence.

Interpreter

14. A party or witness in any proceedings who does not understand or speak the language in which the proceedings are conducted or who is deaf has the right to the assistance of an interpreter.

Equality Rights

Equality before and under law and equal protection and benefit of law

15. (1) Every individual is equal before and under the law and has the right to the equal protection and equal benefit of the law without discrimination and, in particular, without discrimination based on race, national or ethnic origin, colour, religion, sex, age or mental or physical disability.

Affirmative action programs

(2) Subsection (1) does not preclude any law, program or activity that has as its object the amelioration of conditions of disadvantaged individuals or groups including those that are disadvantaged because of race, national or ethnic origin, colour, religion, sex, age or mental or physical disability.

[Note: This section became effective on April 17, 1985. See subsection 32(2) and the note thereto.]

Official Languages of Canada

Official languages of Canada

16. (1) English and French are the official languages of Canada and have equality of status and equal rights and privileges as to their use in all institutions of the Parliament and government of Canada.

Official languages of New Brunswick

(2) English and French are the official languages of New Brunswick and have equality of status and equal rights and privileges as to their use in all institutions of the legislature and government of New Brunswick.

Advancement of status and use

(3) Nothing in this Charter limits the authority of Parliament or a legislature to advance the equality of status or use of English and French.

Proceedings of Parliament

17. (1) Everyone has the right to use English or French in any debates and other proceedings of Parliament.

Proceedings of New Brunswick legislature

(2) Everyone has the right to use English or French in any debates and other proceedings of the legislature of New Brunswick.

Parliamentary statutes and records

18. (1) The statutes, records and journals of Parliament shall be printed and published in English and French and both language versions are equally authoritative.

New Brunswick statutes and records

(2) The statutes, records and journals of the legislature of New Brunswick shall be printed and published in English and French and both language versions are equally authoritative.

Proceedings in courts established by Parliament

19. (1) Either English or French may be used by any person in, or in any pleading in or process issuing from, any court established by Parliament.

Proceedings in New Brunswick courts

(2) Either English or French may be used by any person in, or in any pleading in or process issuing from, any court of New Brunswick.

20. (1) Any member of the public in Canada has the right to communicate with, and to receive available services from, any head or central office of an institution of the Parliament or government of Canada in English or French, and has the same right with respect to any other office of any such institution where

> (a) there is a significant demand for communications with and services from that office in such language; or
>
> (b) due to the nature of the office, it is reasonable that communications with and services from that office be available in both English and French.

Communications by public with federal institutions

(2) Any member of the public in New Brunswick has the right to communicate with, and to receive available services from, any office of an institution of the legislature or government of New Brunswick in English or French.

Communications by public with New Brunswick institutions

21. Nothing in sections 16 to 20 abrogates or derogates from any right, privilege or obligation with respect to the English and French languages, or either of them, that exists or is continued by virtue of any other provision of the Constitution of Canada.

Continuation of existing constitutional provisions

22. Nothing in sections 16 to 20 abrogates or derogates from any legal or customary right or privilege acquired or enjoyed either before or after the coming into force of this Charter with respect to any language that is not English or French.

Rights and privileges preserved

Minority Language Educational Rights

23. (1) Citizens of Canada

> (a) whose first language learned and still understood is that of the English or French linguistic minority population of the province in which they reside, or
>
> (b) who have received their primary school instruction in Canada in English or French and reside in a province where the language in which they received that instruction is the language of the English or French linguistic minority population of the province,

have the right to have their children receive primary and secondary school instruction in that language in that province.

[Note: See also section 59 and the note thereto.]

Language of instruction

(2) Citizens of Canada of whom any child has received or is receiving primary or secondary school instruction in English or French in Canada, have the right to have all their children receive primary and secondary school instruction in the same language.

Continuity of language instruction

(3) The right of citizens of Canada under subsections (1) and (2) to have their children receive primary and secondary school instruction in the language of the English or French linguistic minority population of a province.

> (a) applies wherever in the province the number of children of citizens who have such a right is sufficient to warrant the provision to them out of public funds of minority language instruction; and
>
> (b) includes, where the number of those children so warrants, the right to have them receive that instruction in minority language educational facilities provided out of public funds.

Application where numbers warrant

Enforcement

Enforcement of guaranteed rights and freedoms

24. (1) Anyone whose rights or freedoms, as guaranteed by this Charter, have been infringed or denied may apply to a court of competent jurisdiction to obtain such remedy as the court considers appropriate and just in the circumstances.

Exclusion of evidence bringing administration of justice into disrepute

(2) Where, in proceedings under subsection (1), a court concludes that evidence was obtained in a manner that infringed or denied any rights or freedoms guaranteed by this Charter, the evidence shall be excluded if it is established that, having regard to all the circumstances, the admission of it in the proceedings would bring the administration of justice into disrepute.

General

Aboriginal rights and freedoms not affected by Charter

25. The guarantee in this Charter of certain rights and freedoms shall not be construed so as to abrogate or derogate from any aboriginal, treaty or other rights or freedoms that pertain to the aboriginal peoples of Canada including

(a) any rights or freedoms that have been recognized by the Royal Proclamation of October 7, 1763; and

(b) any rights or freedoms that may be acquired by the aboriginal peoples of Canada by way of land claims settlement.

(b) any rights or freedoms that now exist by way of land claims agreements or may be so acquired.

[Note: Paragraph 25*(b)* (in italics) was repealed and the new paragraph substituted by the *Constitution Amendment Proclamation, 1983* (No. 46 *infra*).]

Other rights and freedoms not affected by Charter

26. The guarantee in this Charter of certain rights and freedoms shall not be construed as denying the existence of any other rights or freedoms that exist in Canada.

Multicultural heritage

27. This Charter shall be interpreted in a manner consistent with the preservation and enhancement of the multicultural heritage of Canadians.

Rights guaranteed equally to both sexes

28. Notwithstanding anything in this Charter, the rights and freedoms referred to in it are guaranteed equally to male and female persons.

Rights respecting certain schools preserved

29. Nothing in this Charter abrogates or derogates from any rights or privileges guaranteed by or under the Constitution of Canada in respect of denominational, separate or dissentient schools.

Application to territories and territorial authorities

30. A reference in this Charter to a province or to the legislative assembly or legislature of a province shall be deemed to include a reference to the Yukon Territory and the Northwest Territories, or to the appropriate legislative authority thereof, as the case may be.

Legislative powers not extended

31. Nothing in this Charter extends the legislative powers of any body or authority.

Application of Charter

Application of Charter

32. (1) This Charter applies

(a) to the Parliament and government of Canada in respect of all matters within the authority of Parliament including all matters relating to the Yukon Territory and Northwest Territories; and

(b) to the legislature and government of each province in respect of all matters within the authority of the legislature of each province.

Exception

(2) Notwithstanding subsection (1), section 15 shall not have effect until three years after this section comes into force.

[Note: This section came into force on April 17, 1982. See the proclamation of that date (No. 45 *infra*).]

33. (1) Parliament or the legislature of a province may expressly declare in an Act of Parliament or of the legislature, as the case may be, that the Act or a provision thereof shall operate notwithstanding a provision included in section 2 or sections 7 to 15 of this Charter.

Exception where express declaration

(2) An Act or a provision of an Act in respect of which a declaration made under this section is in effect shall have such operation as it would have but for the provision of this Charter referred to in the declaration.

Operation of exception

(3) A declaration made under subsection (1) shall cease to have effect five years after it comes into force or on such earlier date as may be specified in the declaration.

Five year limitation

(4) Parliament or the legislature of a province may re-enact a declaration made under subsection (1).

Re-enactment

(5) Subsection (3) applies in respect of a re-enactment made under subsection (4).

Five year limitation

Citation

34. This Part may be cited as the *Canadian Charter of Rights and Freedoms.*

Citation

PART II

RIGHTS OF THE ABORIGINAL PEOPLES OF CANADA

35. (1) The existing aboriginal and treaty rights of the aboriginal peoples of Canada are hereby recognized and affirmed.

Recognition of existing aboriginal and treaty rights

(2) In this Act, "aboriginal peoples of Canada" includes the Indian, Inuit and Métis peoples of Canada.

Definition of "aboriginal peoples of Canada"

(3) For greater certainty, in subsection (1) "treaty rights" includes rights that now exist by way of land claims agreement or may be so acquired.

Land claims agreements

(4) Notwithstanding any other provision of this Act, the aboriginal and treaty rights referred to in subsection (1) are guaranteed equally to male and female persons.

Aboriginal and treaty rights are guaranteed equally to both sexes

[Note: Subsections 35(3) and (4) were added by the *Constitution Amendment Proclamation, 1983* (No. 46 *infra*).]

35.1 The government of Canada and the provincial governments are committed to the principle that, before any amendment is made to Class 24 of section 91 of the *"Constitution Act, 1867",* to section 25 of this Act or to this Part,

Commitment to participation in constitutional conference

(a) a constitutional conference that includes in its agenda an item relating to the proposed amendment, composed of the Prime Minister

of Canada and the first ministers of the provinces, will be convened by the Prime Minister of Canada; and

(b) the Prime Minister of Canada will invite representative of the aboriginal peoples of Canada to participate in the discussions on that item.

[Note: Added by the *Constitution Amendment Proclamation, 1983* (No. 46 *infra*).]

PART III

EQUALIZATION AND REGIONAL DISPARITIES

Commitment to promote equal opportunities

36. (1) Without altering the legislative authority of Parliament or of the provincial legislatures, or the rights of any of them with respect to the exercise of their legislative authority, Parliament and the legislatures, together with the government of Canada and the provincial governments, are committed to

(a) promoting equal opportunities for the well-being of Canadians;

(b) furthering economic development to reduce disparity in opportunities; and

(c) providing essential public services of reasonable quality to all Canadians.

Commitment respecting public services

(2) Parliament and the government of Canada are committed to the principle of making equalization payments to ensure that provincial governments have sufficient revenues to provide reasonably comparable levels of public services at reasonably comparable levels of taxation.

PART IV

CONSTITUTIONAL CONFERENCE

Constitutional conference

37. *(1) A constitutional conference composed of the Prime Minister of Canada and the first ministers of the provinces shall be convened by the Prime Minister of Canada within one year after this Part comes into force.*

Participation of aboriginal peoples

(2) The conference convened under subsection (1) shall have included in its agenda an item respecting constitutional matters that directly affect the aboriginal peoples of Canada, including the identification and definition of the rights of those peoples to be included in the Constitution of Canada, and the Prime Minister of Canada shall invite representatives of those peoples to participate in the discussions on that item.

Participation of territories

(3) The Prime Minister of Canada shall invite elected representatives of the governments of the Yukon Territory and the Northwest Territories to participate in the discussions on any item on the agenda of the conference convened under subsection (1) that, in the opinion of the Prime Minister, directly affects the Yukon Territory and the Northwest Territories.

[Note: Part IV was repealed effective April 17, 1983 by section 54 of this Act.]

PART IV.1

CONSTITUTIONAL CONFERENCES

Constitutional conferences

37.1 *(1) In addition to the conference convened in March 1983, at least two constitutional conferences composed of the Prime Minister of*

Canada and the first ministers of the provinces shall be convened by the Prime Minister of Canada, the first within three years after April 17, 1982 and the second within five years after that date.

(2) Each conference convened under subsection (1) shall have included in its agenda constitutional matters that directly affect the aboriginal peoples of Canada, and the Prime Minister of Canada shall invite representatives of those peoples to participate in the discussion on those matters.

Participation of aboriginal peoples

(3) The Prime Minister of Canada shall invite elected representatives of the governments of the Yukon Territory and the Northwest Territories to participate in the discussions on any item on the agenda of a conference convened under subsection (1) that, in the opinion of the Prime Minister, directly affects the Yukon Territory and the Northwest Territories.

Participation of territories

(4) Nothing in this section shall be construed so as to derogate from subsection 35(1).

Subsection 35(1) not affected

[Note: Part IV.1 was added by the *Constitution Amendment Proclamation, 1983* (No. 46 *infra*). By the same proclamation, it was repealed effective April 18, 1987. See section 54.1 of this Act.]

PART V

PROCEDURE FOR AMENDING CONSTITUTION OF CANADA

38. (1) An amendment to the Constitution of Canada may be made by proclamation issued by the Governor General under the Great Seal of Canada where so authorized by

General procedure for amending Constitution of Canada

(a) resolutions of the Senate and House of Commons; and

(b) resolutions of the legislative assemblies of at least two-thirds of the provinces that have, in the aggregate, according to the then latest general census, at least fifty per cent of the population of all the provinces.

(2) An amendment made under subsection (1) that derogates from the legislative power, the proprietary rights or any other rights or privileges of the legislature or government of a province shall require a resolution supported by a majority of the members of each of the Senate, the House of Commons and the legislative assemblies required under subsection (1).

Majority of members

(3) An amendment referred to in subsection (2) shall not have effect in a province the legislative assembly of which has expressed its dissent thereto by resolution supported by a majority of its members prior to the issue of the proclamation to which the amendment relates unless that legislative assembly, subsequently, by resolution supported by a majority of its members, revokes its dissent and authorizes the amendment.

Expression of dissent

(4) A resolution of dissent made for the purposes of subsection (3) may be revoked at any time before or after the issue of the proclamation to which it relates.

Revocation of dissent

39. (1) A proclamation shall not be issued under subsection 38(1) before the expiration of one year from the adoption of the resolution initiating the amendment procedure thereunder, unless the legislative assembly of each province has previously adopted a resolution of assent or dissent.

Restriction on proclamation

Idem

(2) A proclamation shall not be issued under subsection 38(1) after the expiration of three years from the adoption of the resolution initiating the amendment procedure thereunder.

Compensation

40. Where an amendment is made under subsection 38(1) that transfers provincial legislative powers relating to education or other cultural matters from provincial legislatures to Parliament, Canada shall provide reasonable compensation to any province to which the amendment does not apply.

Amendment by unanimous consent

41. An amendment to the Constitution of Canada in relation to the following matters may be made by proclamation issued by the Governor General under the Great Seal of Canada only where authorized by resolutions of the Senate and House of Commons and of the legislative assembly of each province:

(a) the office of the Queen, the Governor General and the Lieutenant Governor of a province;

(b) the right of a province to a number of members in the House of Commons not less than the number of Senators by which the province is entitled to be represented at the time this Part comes into force;

(c) subject to section 43, the use of the English or the French language;

(d) the composition of the Supreme Court of Canada; and

(e) an amendment to this Part.

Amendment by general procedure

42. (1) An amendment to the Constitution of Canada in relation to the following matters may be made only in accordance with subsection 38(1):

(a) the principle of proportionate representation of the provinces in the House of Commons prescribed by the Constitution of Canada;

(b) the powers of the Senate and the method of selecting Senators;

(c) the number of members by which a province is entitled to be represented in the Senate and the residence qualifications of Senators;

(d) subject to paragraph 41(d), the Supreme Court of Canada;

(e) the extension of existing provinces into the territories; and

(f) notwithstanding any other law or practice, the establishment of new provinces.

Exception

(2) Subsections 38(2) to (4) do not apply in respect of amendments in relation to matters referred to in subsection (1).

Amendment of provisions relating to some but not all provinces

43. An amendment to the Constitution of Canada in relation to any provision that applies to one or more, but not all, provinces, including

(a) any alteration to boundaries between provinces, and

(b) any amendment to any provision that relates to the use of the English or the French language within a province,

may be made by proclamation issued by the Governor General under the Great Seal of Canada only where so authorized by resolutions of the Senate and House of Commons and of the legislative assembly of each province to which the amendment applies.

Amendments by Parliament

44. Subject to sections 41 and 42, Parliament may exclusively make laws amending the Constitution of Canada in relation to the executive government of Canada or the Senate and House of Commons.

Amendments by provincial legislatures

45. Subject to section 41, the legislature of each province may exclusively make laws amending the constitution of the province.

46. (1) The procedures for amendment under sections 38, 41, 42 and 43 may be initiated either by the Senate or the House of Commons or by the legislative assembly of a province.

Initiation of amendment procedures

(2) A resolution of assent made for the purposes of this Part may be revoked at any time before the issue of a proclamation authorized by it.

Revocation of authorization

47. (1) An amendment to the Constitution of Canada made by proclamation under section 38, 41, 42 or 43 may be made without a resolution of the Senate authorizing the issue of the proclamation if, within one hundred and eighty days after the adoption by the House of Commons of a resolution authorizing its issue, the Senate has not adopted such a resolution and if, at any time after the expiration of that period, the House of Commons again adopts the resolution.

Amendments without Senate resolution

(2) Any period when Parliament is prorogued or dissolved shall not be counted in computing the one hundred and eighty day period referred to in subsection (1).

Computation of period

48. The Queen's Privy Council for Canada shall advise the Governor General to issue a proclamation under this Part forthwith on the adoption of the resolutions required for an amendment made by proclamation under this Part.

Advice to issue proclamation

49. A constitutional conference composed of the Prime Minister of Canada and the first ministers of the provinces shall be convened by the Prime Minister of Canada within fifteen years after this Part comes into force to review the provisions of this Part.

Constitutional conference

PART VI

AMENDMENT TO THE CONSTITUTION ACT, 1867

50. The *Constitution Act, 1867* (formerly named the *British North America Act, 1867*) is amended by adding thereto, immediately after section 92 thereof, the following heading and section:

Amendment to Constitution Act, 1867

"Non-Renewable Natural Resources, Forestry Resources and Electrical Energy

92A. (1) In each province, the legislature may exclusively make laws in relation to
  (a) exploration for non-renewable natural resources in the province;
  (b) development, conservation and management of non-renewable natural resources and forestry resources in the province, including laws in relation to the rate of primary production therefrom; and
  (c) development, conservation and management of sites and facilities in the province for the generation and production of electrical energy.

Laws respecting non-renewable natural resources, forestry resources and electrical energy

(2) In each province, the legislature may make laws in relation to the export from the province to another part of Canada of the primary production from non-renewable natural resources and forestry resources in the province and the production from facilities in the province for the generation of electrical energy, but such laws may not authorize or provide for discrimination in prices or in supplies exported to another part of Canada.

Export from provinces of resources

Authority of
Parliament

(3) Nothing in subsection (2) derogates from the authority of Parliament to enact laws in relation to the matters referred to in that subsection and, where such a law of Parliament and a law of a province conflict, the law of Parliament prevails to the extent of the conflict.

Taxation of re-
sources

(4) In each province, the legislature may make laws in relation to the raising of money by any mode or system of taxation in respect of
  (a) non-renewable natural resources and forestry resources in the province and the primary production therefrom, and
  (b) sites and facilities in the province for the generation of electrical energy and the production therefrom,
whether or not such production is exported in whole or in part from the province, but such laws may not authorize or provide for taxation that differentiates between production exported to another part of Canada and production not exported from the province.

"Primary produc-
tion"

(5) The expression "primary production" has the meaning assigned by the Sixth Schedule.

Existing powers or
rights

(6) Nothing in subsections (1) to (5) derogates from any powers or rights that a legislature or government of a province had immediately before the coming into force of this section."

Idem

51. The said Act is further amended by adding thereto the following Schedule:

"THE SIXTH SCHEDULE

*Primary Production from Non-Renewable Natural Resources and
Forestry Resources*

1. For the purposes of Section 92A of this Act,
  (a) production from a non-renewable natural resource is primary production therefrom if
    (i) it is in the form in which it exists upon its recovery or severance from its natural state, or
    (ii) it is a product resulting from processing or refining the resource, and is not a manufactured product or a product resulting from refining crude oil, refining upgraded heavy crude oil, refining gases or liquids derived from coal or refining a synthetic equivalent of crude oil; and
  (b) production from a forestry resource is primary production therefrom if it consists of sawlogs, poles, lumber, wood chips, sawdust or any other primary wood product, or wood pulp, and is not a product manufactured from wood."

PART VII

GENERAL

Primacy of
Constitution of
Canada

52. (1) The Constitution of Canada is the supreme law of Canada, and any law that is inconsistent with the provisions of the Constitution is, to the extent of the inconsistency, of no force or effect.

Constitution of
Canada

(2) The Constitution of Canada includes
  (a) the *Canada Act 1982*, including this Act;

(b) the Acts and orders referred to in the schedule; and

(c) any amendment to any Act or order referred to in paragraph *(a)* or *(b)*.

(3) Amendments to the Constitution of Canada shall be made only in accordance with the authority contained in the Constitution of Canada.

Amendments to Constitution of Canada

53. (1) The enactments referred to in Column I of the schedule are hereby repealed or amended to the extent indicated in Column II thereof and, unless repealed, shall continue as law in Canada under the names set out in Column III thereof.

Repeals and new names

(2) Every enactment, except the *Canada Act 1982*, that refers to an enactment referred to in the schedule by the name in Column I thereof is hereby amended by substituting for that name the corresponding name in Column III thereof, and any British North America Act not referred to in the schedule may be cited as the *Constitution Act* followed by the year and number, if any, of its enactment.

Consequential amendments

54. Part IV is repealed on the day that is one year after this Part comes into force and this section may be repealed and this Act renumbered, consequentially upon the repeal of Part IV and this section, by proclamation issued by the Governor General under the Great Seal of Canada.

[Note: On October 31, 1987, no proclamation had been issued under this section.]

Repeal and consequential amendments

54.1 *Part iv.1 and this section are repealed on April 18, 1987.*

[Note: Added by the *Constitution Amendment Proclamation, 1983* (No. 46 *infra*).]

Repeal of Part iv.1 and this section

55. A French version of the portions of the Constitution of Canada referred to in the schedule shall be prepared by the Minister of Justice of Canada as expeditiously as possible and, when any portion thereof sufficient to warrant action being taken has been so prepared, it shall be put forward for enactment by proclamation issued by the Governor General under the Great Seal of Canada pursuant to the procedure then applicable to an amendment of the same provisions of the Constitution of Canada.

[Note: On October 31, 1987, no proclamation had been issued under this section.]

French version of Constitution of Canada

56. Where any portion of the Constitution of Canada has been or is enacted in English and French or where a French version of any portion of the Constitution is enacted pursuant to section 55, the English and French versions of that portion of the Constitution are equally authoritative.

English and French versions of certain constitutional texts

57. The English and French versions of this Act are equally authoritative.

English and French versions of this Act

58. Subject to section 59, this Act shall come into force on a day to be fixed by proclamation issued by the Queen or the Governor General under the Great Seal of Canada.

[Note: The *Constitution Act, 1982* was, subject to section 59 thereof, proclaimed in force on April 17, 1982 (No. 45 *infra*).]

Commencement

59. (1) Paragraph 23(1) (a) shall come into force in respect of Quebec on a day to be fixed by proclamation issued by the Queen or the Governor General under the Great Seal of Canada.

Commencement of paragraph 23(1)(a) in respect of Quebec

(2) A proclamation under subsection (1) shall be issued only where authorized by the legislative assembly or government of Quebec.

Authorization of
Quebec

(3) This section may be repealed on the day paragraph 23(1)(a) comes into force in respect of Quebec and this Act amended and renumbered, consequentially upon the repeal of this section, by proclamation issued by the Queen or the Governor General under the Great Seal of Canada.

Repeal of this section

[Note: On October 31, 1987, no proclamation had been issued under this section.]

60. This Act may be cited as the *Constitution Act, 1982*, and the Constitution Acts 1867 to 1975 (No. 2) and this Act may be cited together as the *Constitution Acts, 1867 to 1982*.

Short title and citations

61. A reference to the "*Constitution Acts, 1867 to 1982*" shall be deemed to include a reference to the "*Constitution Amendment Proclamation, 1983.*"

References

[Note: Added by the *Constitution Amendment Proclamation, 1983* (No. 46 *infra*). See also section 3 of the *Constitution Act, 1985 (Representation)* (No. 47 *infra*).]

REFERENCE RE SECESSION OF QUEBEC

IN THE MATTER OF Section 53 of the *Supreme Court Act*, R.S.C., 1985, c. S-26;

AND IN THE MATTER OF a Reference by the Governor in Council concerning certain questions relating to the secession of Quebec from Canada, as set out in Order in Council P.C. 1996-1497, dated the 30th day of September, 1996

Indexed as: Reference re Secession of Quebec

File No.: 25506.

1998: February 16, 17, 18, 19; 1998: August 20.

Present: Lamer C.J. and L'Heureux-Dubé, Gonthier, Cory, McLachlin, Iacobucci, Major, Bastarache and Binnee JJ.

* * * * *

Pursuant to s. 53 of the *Supreme Court Act*, the Governor in Council referred the following questions to this Court:

1. Under the Constitution of Canada, can the National Assembly, legislature or government of Quebec effect the secession of Quebec from Canada unilaterally?

2. Does international law give the National Assembly, legislature or government of Quebec the right to effect the secession of Quebec from Canada unilaterally? In this regard, is there a right to self-determination under international law that would give the National Assembly, legislature or government of Quebec the right to effect the secession of Quebec from Canada unilaterally?

3. In the event of a conflict between domestic and international law on the right of the National Assembly, legislature or government of Quebec to effect the secession of Quebec from Canada unilaterally, which would take precedence in Canada?

Issues regarding the Court's reference jurisdiction were raised by the *amicus curiae*. He argued that s. 53 of the *Supreme Court Act* was unconstitutional; that, even if the Court's reference jurisdiction was constitutionally valid, the questions submitted were outside the scope of s. 53; and, finally, that these questions were not justiciable.

Held: Section 53 of the *Supreme Court Act* is constitutional and the Court should answer the reference questions.

(1) *Supreme Court's Reference Jurisdiction*

Section 101 of the *Constitution Act, 1867* gives Parliament the authority to grant this Court the reference jurisdiction provided for in s. 53 of the *Supreme Court Act*. The words "general court of appeal" in s. 101 denote the status of the Court within the national court structure and should not be taken as a restrictive definition of the Court's functions. While, in most instances, this Court acts as the exclusive ultimate appellate court in the country, an appellate court can receive, on an exceptional basis, original jurisdiction not incompatible with its appellate jurisdiction. Even if there were any conflict between this Court's reference jurisdiction and the original jurisdiction of the provincial superior courts, any such conflict must be resolved in favour of Parliament's exercise of its plenary power to establish a "general court of appeal". A "general court of appeal" may also properly undertake other legal functions, such as the rendering of advisory opinions. There is no constitutional bar to this Court's receipt of jurisdiction to undertake an advisory role.

The reference questions are within the scope of s. 53 of the *Supreme Court Act*. Question 1 is directed, at least in part, to the interpretation of the *Constitution Acts*, which are referred to in s. 53(1)(*a*). Both Questions 1 and 2 fall within s. 53(1)(*d*), since they relate to the powers of the legislature or government of a Canadian province. Finally, all three questions are "important questions of law or fact concerning any matter" and thus come within s. 53(2). In answering Question 2, the Court is not exceeding its jurisdiction by purporting to act as an international tribunal. The Court is providing an advisory opinion to the Governor in Council in its capacity as a national court on legal questions touching and concerning the future of the Canadian federation. Further, Question 2 is not beyond the competence of this Court, as a domestic court, because it requires the Court to look at international law rather than domestic law. More importantly, Question 2 does not ask an abstract question of "pure" international law but seeks to determine the legal rights and obligations of the legislature or government of Quebec, institutions that exist as part of the Canadian legal order. International law must be addressed since it has been invoked as a consideration in the context of this Reference.

The reference questions are justiciable and should be answered. They do not ask the Court to usurp any democratic decision that the people of Quebec may be called upon to make. The questions, as interpreted by the Court, are strictly limited to aspects of the legal framework in which that democratic decision is to be taken. Since the reference questions may clearly be interpreted as directed to legal issues, the Court is in a position to answer them. The Court cannot exercise its discretion to refuse to answer the questions on a pragmatic basis. The questions raise issues of fundamental public importance and they are not too imprecise or ambiguous to permit a proper legal answer. Nor has the Court been provided with insufficient information regarding the present context in which the questions arise. Finally, the Court may deal on a reference with issues that might otherwise be considered not yet "ripe" for decision.

(2) *Question 1*

The Constitution is more than a written text. It embraces the entire global system of rules and principles which govern the exercise of constitutional authority. A superficial reading of selected provisions of the written constitutional enactment, without more, may be misleading. It is necessary to make a more profound investigation of the underlying principles animating the whole of the Constitution, including the principles of federalism, democracy, constitutionalism and the rule of law, and respect for minorities. Those principles must inform our overall appreciation of the constitutional rights and obligations that would come into play in the event that a clear majority of Quebecers votes on a clear question in favour of secession.

The Court in this Reference is required to consider whether Quebec has a right to unilateral secession. Arguments in support of the existence of such a right were primarily based on the principle of democracy. Democracy, however, means more than simple majority rule. Constitutional jurisprudence shows that democracy exists in the larger context of other constitutional values. Since Confederation, the people of the provinces and territories have created close ties of interdependence (economic, social, political and cultural) based on shared values that include federalism, democracy, constitutionalism and the rule of law, and respect for minorities. A democratic decision of Quebecers in favour of secession would put those relationships at risk. The Constitution vouchsafes order and stability, and accordingly secession of a province "under the Constitution" could not be achieved unilaterally, that is, without principled negotiation with other participants in Confederation within the existing constitutional framework.

Our democratic institutions necessarily accommodate a continuous process of discussion and evolution, which is reflected in the constitutional right of each participant in the federation to initiate constitutional change. This right implies a reciprocal duty on the other participants to engage in discussions to address any legitimate initiative to change the constitutional order. A clear majority vote in Quebec on a clear question in favour of secession would confer democratic legitimacy on the secession initiative which all of the other participants in Confederation would have to recognize.

Quebec could not, despite a clear referendum result, purport to invoke a right of self-determination to dictate the terms of a proposed secession to the other parties to the federation. The democratic vote, by however strong a majority, would have no legal effect on its own and could not push aside the principles of federalism and the rule of law, the rights of individuals and minorities, or the operation of democracy in the other provinces or in Canada as a whole. Democratic rights under the Constitution cannot be divorced from constitutional obligations. Nor, however, can the reverse proposition be accepted: the continued existence and operation of the Canadian constitutional order could not be indifferent to a clear expression of a clear majority of Quebecers that they no longer wish to remain in Canada. The other provinces and the federal government would have no basis to deny the right of the government of Quebec to pursue secession should a clear majority of the people of Quebec choose that goal, so long as in doing so, Quebec respects the rights of others. The negotiations that followed such a vote would address the potential act of secession as well as its possible terms should in fact secession proceed. There would be no conclusions predetermined by law on any issue. Negotiations would need to address the interests of the other provinces, the federal government and Quebec and indeed the rights of all Canadians both within and outside Quebec, and specifically the rights of minorities.

The negotiation process would require the reconciliation of various rights and obligations by negotiation between two legitimate majorities, namely, the majority of the population of Quebec, and that of Canada as a whole. A political majority at either level that does not act in accordance with the underlying constitutional principles puts at risk the legitimacy of its exercise of its rights, and the ultimate acceptance of the result by the international community.

The task of the Court has been to clarify the legal framework within which political decisions are to be taken "under the Constitution" and not to usurp the prerogatives of the political forces that operate within that framework. The obligations identified by the Court are binding obligations under the Constitution. However, it will be for the political actors to determine what constitutes "a clear majority on a clear question" in the circumstances under which a future referendum vote may be taken. Equally, in the event of demonstrated majority support for Quebec secession, the content and process of the negotiations will be for the political actors to settle. The reconciliation of the various legitimate constitutional interests is necessarily committed to the political rather than the judicial realm precisely because that reconciliation can only be achieved through the give and take of political negotiations. To the extent issues addressed in the course of negotiation are political, the courts, appreciating their proper role in the constitutional scheme, would have no supervisory role.

(3) *Question 2*

The Court was also required to consider whether a right to unilateral secession exists under international law. Some supporting an affirmative answer did so on the basis of the recognized right to self-determination that belongs to all "peoples". Although much of the Quebec population certainly shares many of the characteristics of a people, it is not necessary to decide the "people" issue because, whatever may be the correct determination of this issue in the context of Quebec, a right to secession only arises under the principle of self-determination of people at international law where "a people" is governed as part of a colonial empire; where "a people" is subject to alien subjugation, domination or exploitation; and possibly where "a people" is denied any meaningful exercise of its right to self-determination within the state of which it forms a part. In other circumstances, peoples are expected to achieve self-determination within the framework of their existing state. A state whose government represents the whole of the people or peoples resident within its territory, on a basis of equality and without discrimination, and respects the principles of self-determination in its internal arrangements, is entitled to maintain its territorial integrity under international law and to have that territorial integrity recognized by other states. Quebec does not meet the threshold of a colonial people or an oppressed people, nor can it be suggested that Quebecers have been denied meaningful access to government to pursue their political, economic, cultural and social development. In the circumstances, the "National Assembly, the legislature or the government of Quebec" do not enjoy a right at international law to effect the secession of Quebec from Canada unilaterally.

Although there is no right, under the Constitution or at international law, to unilateral secession, the possibility of an unconstitutional declaration of secession leading to a *de facto* secession is not ruled out. The ultimate success of such a secession would be dependent on recognition by the international community, which is likely to consider the legality and legitimacy of secession having regard to, amongst other facts, the conduct of Quebec and Canada, in determining whether to grant or withhold recognition. Even if granted, such recognition would not, however, provide any retroactive justification for the act of secession, either under the Constitution of Canada or at international law.

(4) *Question 3*

In view of the answers to Questions 1 and 2, there is no conflict between domestic and international law to be addressed in the context of this Reference.

* * * * *

IV. Summary of Conclusions

148   As stated at the outset, this Reference has required us to consider momentous questions that go to the heart of our system of constitutional government. We have emphasized that the Constitution is more than a written text. It embraces the entire global system of rules and principles which govern the exercise of constitutional authority. A superficial reading of selected provisions of the written constitutional enactment, without more, may be misleading. It is necessary to make a more profound investigation of the underlying principles that animate the whole of our Constitution, including the principles of federalism, democracy, constitutionalism and the rule of law, and respect for minorities. Those principles must inform our overall appreciation of the constitutional rights and obligations that would come into play in the event a clear majority of Quebecers votes on a clear question in favour of secession.

149   The Reference requires us to consider whether Quebec has a right to unilateral secession. Those who support the existence of such a right found their case primarily on the principle of democracy. Democracy, however, means more than simple majority rule. As reflected in our constitutional jurisprudence, democracy exists in the larger context of other constitutional values such as those already mentioned. In the 131 years since Confederation, the people of the provinces and territories have created close ties of interdependence (economically, socially, politically and culturally) based on shared values that include federalism, democracy, constitutionalism and the rule of law, and respect for minorities. A democratic decision of Quebecers in favour of secession would put those relationships at risk.

The Constitution vouchsafes order and stability, and accordingly secession of a province "under the Constitution" could not be achieved unilaterally, that is, without principled negotiation with other participants in Confederation within the existing constitutional framework.

150   The Constitution is not a straitjacket. Even a brief review of our constitutional history demonstrates periods of momentous and dramatic change. Our democratic institutions necessarily accommodate a continuous process of discussion and evolution, which is reflected in the constitutional right of each participant in the federation to initiate constitutional change. This right implies a reciprocal duty on the other participants to engage in discussions to address any legitimate initiative to change the constitutional order. While it is true that some attempts at constitutional amendment in recent years have faltered, a clear majority vote in Quebec on a clear question in favour of secession would confer democratic legitimacy on the secession initiative which all of the other participants in Confederation would have to recognize.

151   Quebec could not, despite a clear referendum result, purport to invoke a right of self-determination to dictate the terms of a proposed secession to the other parties to the federation. The democratic vote, by however strong a majority, would have no legal effect on its own and could not push aside the principles of federalism and the rule of law, the rights of individuals and minorities, or the operation of democracy in the other provinces or in Canada as a whole. Democratic rights under the Constitution cannot be divorced from constitutional obligations. Nor, however, can the reverse proposition be accepted. The continued existence and operation of the Canadian constitutional order could not be indifferent to a clear expression of a clear majority of Quebecers that they no longer wish to remain in Canada. The other provinces and the federal government would have no basis to deny the right of the government of Quebec to pursue secession, should a clear majority of the people of Quebec choose that goal, so long as in doing so, Quebec respects the rights of others. The negotiations that followed such a vote would address the potential act of secession as well as its possible terms should in fact secession proceed. There would be no conclusions predetermined by law on any issue. Negotiations would need to address the interests of the other provinces, the federal government, Quebec and indeed the rights of all Canadians both within and outside Quebec, and specifically the rights of minorities. No one suggests that it would be an easy set of negotiations.

152   The negotiation process would require the reconciliation of various rights and obligations by negotiation between two legitimate majorities, namely, the majority of the population of Quebec, and that of Canada as a whole. A political majority at either level that does not act in accordance with the underlying constitutional principles we have mentioned puts at risk the legitimacy of its exercise of its rights, and the ultimate acceptance of the result by the international community.

153   The task of the Court has been to clarify the legal framework within which political decisions are to be taken "under the Constitution", not to usurp the prerogatives of the political forces that operate within that framework. The obligations we have identified are binding obligations under the Constitution of Canada. However, it will be for the political actors to determine what constitutes "a clear majority on a clear question" in the circumstances under which a future referendum vote may be taken. Equally, in the event of demonstrated majority support for Quebec secession, the content and process of the negotiations will be for the political actors to settle. The reconciliation of the various legitimate constitutional interests is necessarily committed to the political rather than the judicial realm precisely because that reconciliation can only be achieved through the give and take of political negotiations. To the extent issues addressed in the course of negotiation are political, the courts, appreciating their proper role in the constitutional scheme, would have no supervisory role.

154   We have also considered whether a positive legal entitlement to secession exists under international law in the factual circumstances contemplated by Question 1, i.e., a clear democratic expression of support on a clear question for Quebec secession. Some of those who supported an affirmative answer to this question did so on the basis of the recognized right to self-determination that belongs to all "peoples". Although much of the Quebec population certainly shares many of the characteristics of a people, it is not necessary to decide the "people" issue because, whatever may be the correct determination of this issue in the context of Quebec, a right to secession only arises under the principle of self-determination of peoples at international law where "a people" is governed as part of a colonial empire; where "a people" is subject to alien subjugation, domination or exploitation; and possible where "a people" is denied any meaningful exercise of its right to self-determination within the state of which it forms a part. In other circumstances, peoples are expected to achieve self-determination within the framework of their existing state. A state whose government represents the whole of the people or peoples resident within its territory, on a basis of equality and without discrimination, and respects the principles of self-determination in its internal arrangements, is entitled to maintain its territorial integrity under international law and to have that territorial integrity recognized by other states. Quebec does not meet the threshold of a colonial people or an oppressed people, nor can it be suggested that Quebecers have been denied meaningful access to government to pursue their political, economic, cultural and social development. In the circumstances, the National Assembly, the legislature or the government of Quebec do not enjoy a right at international law to effect the secession of Quebec from Canada unilaterally.

155   Although there is no right, under the Constitution or at international law, to unilateral secession, that is secession without negotiation on the basis just discussed, this does not rule out the possibility of an unconstitutional declaration of secession leading to a *de facto* secession. The ultimate success of such a secession would be dependent on recognition by the international community, which is likely to consider the legality and legitimacy of secession having regard to, amongst other facts, the conduct of Quebec and Canada, in determining whether to grant or withhold recognition. Such recognition, even if granted, would not, however, provide any retroactive justification for the act of secession, either under the Constitution of Canada or at international law.

GLOSSARY

A

adjournment (recess) — a break period taken by the House of Commons within a session.

adjudication — the responsibility of the courts to provide authoritative settlements in disputes about legal rights and duties.

advisory bodies — federal organizations whose activities are closely related to the formulation of public policies. They include royal commissions, government and departmental task forces and advisory councils.

amendment formula — the procedure required to change a constitution.

assistant deputy minister (ADM) — one of two or more individuals who heads a branch or bureau and reports directly to the deputy minister.

attitudes — orientations toward political objects that are more differentiated and fleeting than basic values, but which may be more immediate determinants of political behaviour.

Auditor General — the official who appraises the effectiveness of public spending and accounting practices and reports directly to Parliament and the Public Accounts Committee.

authoritarian political system — a system of government that imposes one dominant interest, that of the political elite, on all others.

authority — the government's power to make binding decisions and issue obligatory commands. **Traditional authority** arises from custom and history and is most frequently gained through inheritance, such as that enjoyed by royal dynasties. **Charismatic authority** derives from popular admiration of the personal "heroic" qualities of the individual in whom authority is vested, such as a prophet or warlord. **Rational–legal** or **bureaucratic** authority is vested in the offices held by those in power and in the mechanism that placed them there.

autocratic political system — a system that imposes one dominating interest on all others.

B

backbenchers — members of Parliament on the government side who are not ministers, or on the opposition side who are not designated party critics.

bicameral legislature — a legislature composed of two houses.

bilingualism — the right of Canadians to communicate with the federal government in the official language of their choice, and to have their children educated in that language, wherever numbers warrant, as outlined in the *Official Languages Act*.

block grant — a grant of one large sum of money from the federal government to the provinces to be spent in certain policy fields.

brokerage theory — the theory that the two oldest parties in Canada have no central ideological interests but rather act as brokers of ideas, selecting those that have the widest appeal and the best likelihood of attracting electoral support.

budget — a document primarily concerned with setting out where the revenue will come from to carry out the government's program.

budget debate — the four-day (not necessarily consecutive) debate that follows the presentation of the budget.

bureaucracy — a form of hierarchical organization intended to facilitate arbitrary decision-making.

by-election — an election held in a constituency to fill a legislative seat that has become vacant between general elections.

C

Cabinet — the body of advisors (selected from the ministry and appointed by the prime minister) which acts in the name of the Privy Council.

Canada Assistance Program (CAP) — a program of the federal government that helps finance welfare and other provincial social services.

Canada Health and Social Transfer (CHST) — a new system of block grants formed by adding together the funds for the Established Program Financing and the Canada Assistance Programs.

Glossary

Canadian Bill of Rights — a piece of legislation passed in 1960 that listed fundamental freedoms but was never entrenched in the *Constitution*.

Chief Electoral Officer (CEO) — a permanent public employee appointed by the Cabinet under the authority of the *Canadian Election Act* to head Elections Canada.

citizen — an individual who is a formal member of a state, and therefore eligible to enjoy specified rights and privileges.

civil law — the rules that regulate relations between or among private individuals and corporations, mainly concerned with property and civil rights and based on provincial authority.

class — a rank or order in society determined by such characteristics as education, occupation and income.

cleavages — major and persistent differences among groups that are politically relevant.

Clerk of the House — the official responsible for ensuring that relevant documents are printed and circulated and advising the Speaker of the House of Commons on the parliamentary business of the day.

closure — a measure to terminate debate in the House of Commons.

coalition government — a government formed from more than one party.

code — a single body of law that provides a relatively complete set of rules in one or more fields of law.

collective ministerial responsibility — the duty that holds ministers as a group accountable to Parliament for their government's actions.

collective or **group rights** — privileges or duties owed to certain groups by the state.

Committee of the Whole — a committee made up of all members of Parliament chaired by the Deputy Speaker or the Deputy Chair of Committees.

common law — the rules developed by the courts and based on the principle of *stare decisis*. Sometimes referred to as **case law**.

compact theory of Confederation — the notion of "two founding nations," which is used to provide some French Canadians with a collective claim to equality rather than minority status within Canada.

competitive party system — a party system with two or more parties that compete for legislative power. In the **dominant one-party** system, a single party wins most elections and opposition parties function freely. In the **two-party** system, two parties dominate; others have minor political strength. In a **multi-party system**, popular support is divided among several parties and the largest party forms a coalition to form a government. If there are three or more parties, it is a **multi-party dominant** system if one party receives 40 percent of the vote; if none regularly receives 40 percent of the vote, it is a **multi-party loose** system. A **mixed and low competitive** system includes elements of both competitive and non-competitive types.

concurrent power — power shared between the Parliament of Canada and the provincial legislatures.

conditional grant — funds given by the federal government to provincial governments on the condition that they be spent in a certain way. Sometimes called **grant-in-aid** or **shared-cost grant**.

confederation — a form of political organization that loosely unites strong provincial units under a weak central government.

conflict of interest — a situation in which a prime minister, minister or public servant has sufficient knowledge of a private economic interest to influence or appear to influence his or her exercise of public duties and responsibilities.

constituency (riding) — a geographical area that provides the locus of the grass-roots organization of political parties.

constitution — the body of supreme law that defines and limits political power and states the governing principles of a society.

constitutional law — a body of fundamental rules in a constitution, written and unwritten, that condition the making of other laws.

constitutionalism — the principle that everyone, including government, is subject to the rules of the constitution.

convention — a custom or practice that, while not necessarily a legal necessity, is nevertheless based on accepted reasons and practices.

criminal law — the rules that regulate offences against the state, which come under federal authority in Canada.

Crown — the composite symbol of the institutions of the state. The Crown assumes a variety of duties and responsibilities; for example, it may be involved in court proceedings.

Crown agencies — a wide variety of non-departmental organizations including Crown corporations, regulatory agencies, administrative tribunals and some advisory bodies.

Crown corporation — a semi-autonomous agency of government organized under the corporate form to perform a task or group of related tasks in the national interest.

customary law — the rules that result from the evolution of norms that affect the way individuals and groups are expected to act toward one another.

D

debt — the accumulation of deficits over years.

declaratory power — the power that allows the federal government to assume jurisdiction over any "work" considered to be for the benefit of Canada as a whole (e.g., uranium exploration).

deficit — the amount by which government spending exceeds revenues in one year.

democratic political system — a system of government that reconciles competing interests by competitive elections.

deputy minister (DM) — a senior public servant who is the administrative and managerial head of a department or ministry.

direct taxation — taxes collected directly by the government, such as individual income tax, corporate income tax and succession duties.

disallowance — the power of the federal government to void provincial legislation, even in areas of legislation assigned to the provinces.

dissolution — the end of a particular Parliament, which occurs at the request of a prime minister who seeks a new mandate or whose government has been defeated in the House of Commons.

E

Elections Canada — a special government agency that administers elections and is responsible solely to the House of Commons.

electoral system — the means by which votes cast for candidates are translated into legislative seats.

entrenchment — the embodiment of provisions in a constitution so that they are protected and can be changed only by formal amendment procedures.

equalization payments — unconditional transfer payments to the provinces from the federal government calculated according to the ability of each province to raise revenue.

Established Program Financing (EPF) — a block grant program of the federal government that is essentially conditional in nature.

ethnic origin — the ethnic or cultural group(s) to which an individual's ancestors belonged; it pertains to the ancestral roots or origins of the population, and not to place of birth, citizenship or nationality.

ethnicity — primarily a subjective term used to describe groups of people who share customs, language, dialect and/or cultural heritage, and sometimes distinct physical or racial characteristics.

executive — a broad term that refers to the institutions, personnel and behaviour of governmental power. In modern times, executives are the organizational centre of political systems.

expenditure budget process — the process of determining the estimated spending requirements of all government departments and agencies for the next fiscal year.

Expenditure Management System (EMS) — a process of budgeting set up by the Chrétien government to monitor new expenditure goals.

extra-parliamentary wing — a wing of traditional parties composed of the national executive, standing committees and permanent national office, as well as provincial associations and local constituency organizations.

F

Federal Court of Canada — the court established by Parliament in 1971 to settle claims by or against the federal government on matters relating to maritime law, copyright, patent and trade-mark law, and federal taxation statutes, and to supervise the decisions of tribunals and inferior bodies established by federal law.

federalism — a form of political organization in which the activities of government are divided between regional governments and a central government so that each level of government has activities on which it makes final decisions.

financial bills — money bills that authorize taxation and expenditures that must first be introduced into the House of Commons by a minister of the Crown, using a Royal Recommendation.

flexible constitution — a constitution that can be amended easily and adapted to changing circumstances.

franchise — the right to vote.

G

gerrymandering — deliberate manipulation of electoral boundaries by a governing party for its own benefit.

government — the authoritative structures of the political system.

government bills — bills introduced by the Cabinet as government policy.

government department — an administrative unit of government that is headed by a Cabinet minister and largely responsible for the administration of a range of programs serving the public.

Governor General — the representative of the monarch in Canada, appointed by the monarch on the recommendation of the Canadian prime minister and Cabinet.

governor-in-council — the formal executive authority of the Governor General applied upon the advice of the Cabinet.

gross domestic product (GDP) — the market value of all final goods and services produced in a specific period.

H

House Leader — a member of Parliament designated by the leader of each party in the House of Commons to manage party conduct in the House.

I

ideology — an explicit doctrinal structure that provides a particular diagnosis of the ills of society, plus an accompanying "action program" for implementing prescribed solutions for them.

indirect taxation — taxes that are collected by persons or institutions and passed along to the government, such as sales tax.

individual ministerial responsibility — the duty that holds ministers as individuals accountable to Parliament and the public for their decisions.

individual rights — privileges or duties owed to individuals by the state.

institution — a social structure organized to achieve goals for society, such as constitutions, parliaments, bureaucracies and executives.

interest group — an organized association that engages in activity related to governmental decisions.

J

joint standing committees — committees composed of members of both the House of Commons and the Senate.

Judicial Committee of the Privy Council (JCPC) — the superior court of the United Kingdom, which was the court of final appeal in Canada until 1949 when Canada's Supreme Court was established.

L

law — a body of rules originating with government and backed up by the threat of state coercion.

Leader of Her Majesty's Loyal Opposition — the leader of the party with the second largest number of seats in the House of Commons.

legality — the constitutional or legal propriety of undertaking certain activities.

legislative committees — committees set up to receive bills for examination after passing second reading.

legislative (statute) law — the rules created by legislation passed by Parliament or the provincial legislatures to supplement customary or common law.

legislature — the branch of government that makes or amends laws.

legitimacy — the principle that citizens accept that a government should, or has the right to, make decisions for them.

Letters Patent — the prerogative instruments defining the office of the Governor General bestowed by the monarch.

Lieutenant-Governor — the monarch's representative in each province, appointed by the governor-in-council on the advice of the prime minister.

lobbying — activity aimed at influencing policy decisions or appointments. **Lobbyists** are individuals paid to lobby on behalf of an interest group.

M

majority government — a government based on the support of only one party in the House of Commons.

member of Parliament (MP) — a person elected to the legislature who represents a constituency and is usually (but not necessarily) a member of a political party.

Memorandum to Cabinet — formal document used by a minister to put his or her views to Cabinet.

ministry — the group of elected officials appointed by the prime minister to serve as ministers of the Crown or secretaries of state to assist.

minority government — a government in which the governing party has less than a majority of the members of Parliament.

monarch — the personal embodiment of the Crown — currently Queen Elizabeth II.

money bills — government bills for raising or spending money.

multiculturalism — the concept that ethnic customs and cultures should be valued, preserved and shared within the context of citizenship and economic and political integration.

N

nation — a politically conscious and mobilized group of people, often with a sense of territory, which may aspire to greater autonomy or even statehood.

nation-state — the conceptual marriage between the cultural principle of "nation" and the territorial and governmental principles inherent in the idea of "state."

national identity — a sense of belonging to a particular community, often (but not necessarily) reinforced by a common language, culture, customs, heritage or the shared experience of living under the same government.

National Policy — a policy of the Conservative party under John A. Macdonald intended to develop a comprehensive railway system, open up western Canada by means of immigration, settlement and agriculture on the prairies, and encourage national economic development by protecting Canadian industries by means of an external tariff.

nationalism — the collective action of a politically conscious ethnic group (or nation) in pursuit of increased territorial autonomy or sovereignty.

neo-Marxist analysis — a systematic conceptualization of politics, economics and the state, based on a theory originally formulated by Karl Marx.

non-competitive party system — a party system with two or more parties that is dominated by one party that forms a repressive government.

notwithstanding clause — a clause in the Constitution that allows Parliament or a provincial legislature to override most Charter provisions by a simple declaration to that effect when passing legislation.

O

ombudsman — an independent officer responsible to Parliament for the investigation of citizens' complaints against the bureaucracy.

one-party dominant system — a multi-party system of government dominated by one party.

Opposition Days (Supply Days) — days on which opposition motions can be debated in the House of Commons (there are 20 opposition days per session).

orders-in-council — decisions rendered by Cabinet under the auspices of the Privy Council that carry legal force.

Orders of the Day — the prime means by which the House of Commons formulates instructions in response to motions and deals with the public business placed before it.

P

parliamentary democracy — a system of government in which the political executive receives its power to govern from the legislature and requires approval of Parliament to legitimate its policies and activities; in return, the prime minister and Cabinet are held accountable to Parliament.

parliamentary privilege — a House rule that enables members of Parliament to express themselves freely and without intimidation.

parliamentary secretaries — civil servants who aid ministers in their duties but have no statutory authority.

parliamentary supremacy — the basic premise of parliamentary democracy that states that all legislatures have the theoretical authority subject to the Constitution to repeal or modify any principle set out in common law.

parliamentary wing — one wing of traditional parties, composed of the party leader and caucus.

party caucus — a group comprising all members of the House of Commons (and any senators who wish to attend) of a particular party in Parliament that meets every Wednesday when Parliament is in session.

party leader — the individual chosen by party members to fulfill the pre-eminent role as decision-maker, figurehead and spokesperson in both the parliamentary and extra-parliamentary branches of the party. The party leader with the majority support in the House of Commons is the prime minister.

party system — the series of relationships among parties in a political system.

patriation — the act of bringing a constitutional document to its home country.

patronage — the awarding of contracts, employment and other benefits to individuals or groups on the basis of partisan support rather than on merit.

pluralism — the idea that power is widely dispersed and many groups compete for it.

pluralist theory — a theory that contends that power in democracies is not held by a single ruling class but is reasonably diffused in society, so that public policy reflects the conflict, cooperation and compromise of mainly independent interest groups.

policies — broadly based patterns of government action.

Policy and Expenditure Management System (PEMS) — a budgeting process that integrates fiscal, expenditure and policy-making planning within the Cabinet committee system.

political culture — the broad patterns of values, beliefs and attitudes in a society toward political objects.

political customs — the conventional and accepted practices that are part of the political system.

political elite — a relatively small number of people who dominate the political process.

political parties — organizations designed to secure the power of the state for their leaders.

politics — all activity that involves binding decisions about who gets what, when and how, and that brings together contending interests and differences for the supposed advantage of society.

pork-barrelling — the extension of favours by a political party or politician to whole regions or communities as an inducement for support.

power — the ability to influence and/or coerce others to accept certain objectives or behave in a particular manner.

prerogative authority — the powers of a monarch (or his or her representatives) that have not been by-passed by constitutional or state law.

Press Gallery — a formal organization in Ottawa to which journalists are assigned by their employers to cover the activities of the legislature and government.

Prime Minister's Office (PMO) — a group of individuals appointed by the prime minister to provide advice and monitor political developments and that has no statutory authority over other executive agencies.

private bills — bills that seek to change the law concerning specific individuals, groups or corporations.

private members' bills — bills sponsored by individual members of Parliament.

Privy Council — a largely ceremonial body composed of current and former ministers of the Crown and other individuals nominated by the prime minister and appointed for life to advise the Governor General. The **Privy Council Office (PCO)** is the main public service organization responsible for developing and co-ordinating government policy.

procedural rights — privilege of citizens to have access to certain processes (such as a fair trial) that provide protection from arbitrary action by governments.

proclamation — the act of proclaiming, publishing or declaring a statute that thereby becomes law.

proportional representation (PR) — an electoral system in which parties receive representation in Parliament relative to their respective shares of the popular vote.

prorogation — the closing of a session of Parliament, formally done by the Governor General upon the advice of the prime minister.

public bills — bills that seek to change the law concerning the public as a whole, which can be classified as **government bills** and **private members' bills.**

public choice analysis — a theory of politics based on classical economics that assumes that individuals act in a rational and calculating fashion to maximize their own interests.

public opinion — the sum of individual opinions on a given topic.

public opinion polls — studies of the aggregate of individuals' opinions on specific topics.

public policy — the broad framework within which decisions are taken by governments in relation to some issue or problem.

public servants (bureaucrats) — tenured state officials involved in advising government ministers and implementing policies.

public service — the collective term in Canada for the personnel employed in the administrative arm of government.

Q

Question Period — a 45-minute period held in the House of Commons five days a week during which opposition parties can elicit information from the government, criticize its policies and force discussion on selected issues.

Questions on the Order Paper — written questions presented in the House of Commons that are usually answered in print.

R

recall — the procedure by which a public official may be removed from office by popular vote.

referendum — a means by which a policy question can be submitted directly to the electorate rather than being decided exclusively by elected representatives.

regionalism — territorial tensions caused by groups that demand a change in the political, economic and cultural relations between regions and central powers.

regulation — the imposition of constraints, backed by government authority, intended to modify economic behaviour of individuals.

representative democracy — a political system in which elected officials make decisions with the force of law because they have achieved legitimacy as a result of free elections.

reservation — the constitutional ability of Lieutenant-Governors to reserve provincial legislation for federal approval.

residual clause — a clause in the Constitution that allows the federal government to intervene in any matter not specifically assigned to the provinces.

responsible government — the concept that the prime minister and Cabinet are accountable to Parliament and may govern only so long as they retain the "confidence" of the majority of the House of Commons.

revenue process — the means by which funds are raised.

rights — legal entitlements owed to individuals or groups, as duties by others, or by the government.

rigid constitution — a constitution that is difficult to amend.

royal assent — the final seal of approval granted by the monarch or the monarch's representative that a bill must obtain before it becomes law.

royal commission — a group or individual appointed by the Crown on behalf of the government to investigate an area of public concern and to recommend a suitable course of action.

rule of law — a guarantee that the state's actions will be governed by law, fairly and without malice, and that no individual is above the law or exempt from it.

S

section 91 — a section of the Constitution that specifies the areas belonging exclusively to the federal government.

section 92 — a section of the Constitution that specifies 16 areas of provincial jurisdiction, including direct taxation, hospitals, prisons, property and civil rights.

self-determination — a shared belief that people have the right to establish their collective identity in the form of a sovereign state.

session — working period when Parliament is open for business.

shared-cost programs — so-called "50-cent dollar" programs in which the federal government pays 50 percent of costs.

single-member plurality system (first-past-the-post system) — a political system by which the candidate who receives the most votes (a plurality) wins that constituency.

sovereign state — a state that wields power and maintains order within its territorial boundaries, and that is usually recognizable by its internal and external powers (e.g., tax its citizens, conduct external relations).

sovereignty-association — the policy of Québec's political independence while maintaining an economic association with the federal government of Canada.

Speaker of the House of Commons — the official who acts as impartial arbiter in the House and is elected by the whole House.

Speaker of the Senate — the official who acts as impartial arbiter in the Senate and is appointed by the Governor General on the recommendation of the prime minister.

Speech from the Throne — the speech that outlines the government's proposed legislative program for the forthcoming session and is delivered by the Governor General.

spending power — the federal government's blanket authority to spend money for any purpose in any field, even where it has no legal jurisdiction.

standing committees — committees that are relatively permanent for the life of a Parliament.

Standing Orders — the permanent rules of the House of Commons.

stare decisis — the principle of following precedents set down in earlier court cases.

state — a form of political organization in which governmental institutions are capable of maintaining order and implementing rules or laws (through coercion if necessary) over a given population and within a given territory.

state-centred analysis — a theory based on the idea that the state is often able to act independently of the demands of society.

statute law — see **legislative law.**

substantive rights — fundamental rights as defined in a constitution.

supply bills (appropriation bills) — bills that authorize the spending of money by the government.

Supreme Court of Canada — Canada's highest court for civil, criminal and constitutional cases.

T

task force — a group appointed to gather information and public opinion concerning proposed government policy.

time allocation — a time limit on debate in the House of Commons.

Treasury Board Secretariat (TBS) — an administrative unit of government with a highly qualified staff which assists the six Cabinet members of the Treasury Board.

"Triple E" Senate — a proposal that the Senate be elected, effective and equal in its representation of all provinces.

U

ultra vires — an act that is beyond a legislature's jurisdiction on the basis of Canada's federal division of powers.

unconditional grants — funds granted to the provinces by the federal government to be spent as determined by the provinces and not designated for any specific policy field.

unitary government — a form of government characterized by one level of political authority that grants and amends the powers of local or provincial authorities.

unwritten constitution — a constitution that consists mainly of custom, convention, or statutes and is not written down in one comprehensive document.

V

values — shared beliefs that provide standards of judgement about what is right, important and desirable in society.

veto — the power to block legislation or to block a constitutional amendment.

W

ways-and-means bills — taxation measures introduced as bills in the House of Commons.

ways-and-means committee — a committee of the whole that considers the resolutions containing the proposals of the Minister of Finance.

whips — members of Parliament assigned by their party leader to help maintain party cohesion.

writ — a document commanding that an election be held and giving the date of the election, the date by which nominations must be received, and the date by which results must be finalized.

written constitution — the fundamental law set down in one or more documents.

INDEX

A

Abbott, A.C., 404, 482
Abbott, Sir John, 261, 265, 266
Aberhart, William, 157, 396
Absolutism, 15
Acadians, 33
Acts of Parliament
    Access to Information Act (1983), 361–62
    Act of Union (1840), 36, 52
        Canada East, 36–37
        Canada West, 36–37
        ethnic and religious antagonisms, 36–37
    BNA Act. See British North America Act
    Canada Act, 1982, 148, 154, 164, 167
    Canada Elections Act, 411, 436, 440, 442
    Canada Health Act, 215, 217
    Canadian Human Rights Act, 138
    Citizenship Act, 191
    Civil Service Act, 1918, 346, 347, 351; 1961, 347
    Colonial Laws Validity Act, 153
    Constitution Act, 1867, 256, 295
    Constitution Act, 1982, 54, 167–69, 536–37
        changes in, 167–69
    Constitutional Act, 1791, 36
    Constitutional Act, 1869 (BNA Act), 157
    Dominion Act, 1875, 184
    Drug Patent Act, 320
    Election Expenses Act, 410, 440
    Employment Equity Act, 137
    Federal Interpretation Act, 156
    Financial Administration Act, 280
    Fisheries Act, 297
    Freedom of Information Act, 274
    Government Organization Act, 156
    Indian Act, 94, 138
    Individual Rights Protection Act, 191
    Lobbyists Registration Act, 475, 476
    Multiculturalism Act, 88
    Northwest Territories Act, 156
    Official Languages Act (1969), 229, 347
    Parliamentary Secretaries Act, 263
    Public Service Employment Act, 271, 347, 352
    Public Service Reform Act, 1992, 347, 348, 352
    Public Service Staff Relations Act, 347
    Québec Act, 1774, 35

    Representation Act (1985), 433
    Supreme Court Act, 160
    Tobacco Products Control Act (1988), 480, 488
    Unemployment Insurance Act, 192
    War Measures Act, 17, 151, 170, 227
    Yukon Act, 156
Adams, Henry, 9
Addison, Ruth, 352
Ad Hoc Committee of Canadian Women on the
    Constitution, 166
Aesop, 23
Aiken, Gordon, 305, 317
Air Canada, 515, 516, 524
Ajzenstat, Janet, 155
Allaire Report, 174–75
Allison, Graham, 343
Allmand, Warren, 318, 462
Almond, Gabriel, 12, 65, 66
American Revolution, 34, 35, 47
Amnesty International, 473
Anderson, David, 69
Andrews, Mark, 89–90
Angus Reid poll, 75
Anti-Americanism, 34
Arab Palestine Association, 473
Arbour, Louise, 184
Archibald, Kathleen, 350–51
Arendt, Hannah, 149
Aristotle, 23–24, 26, 27
Asbestos Corp.,
    nationalization of, 228
Ashley, William, 11
Asian-Pacific Economic Cooperation Agreement, 551
Assembly of First Nations, 178
Atlantic provinces
    social and economic profile, 99–100
    and UN Human Development Index, 100
Atomic Energy of Canada, 57, 516
Atwood, Margaret, 118
Auditor General, 314, 361
Autocracy, 24
Automobile Industries Association, 471
Axworthy, Lloyd, 531, 543, 553

B

Bachrach, Peter, 505–6
Bagehot, Walter, 106, 256, 293
Balfour, Earl of, 106
Bandarana-Ike, Sirimavo, 491
Bank of Canada, 57
Baratz, Morton, 505–6
Barratt, Dave, 305
Bastarache, Michel, 184
Bastedo, Frank, 157–58
Beaudin, Jean, 126
Bélanger, Michel, 237
Bell, David, 70
Bennett, R.B., 160, 265, 266, 287, 386, 403, 404
Bentley, A.F., 467, 468
Berger, David, 433
Bertrand, Guy, 246, 248
Bhutto, Benazir, 491
Bierce, Ambrose, 467
Bilingualism, 172, 229, 233–34
    criticism of, 233–34
    definition, 233
    immersion programs, 233
    institutional, 233
    official, 233
    Royal Commission on Bilingualism and
    Biculturalism, 83, 88, 90–91, 116–17
Bills. See also Legislation;
    Bill C-20 ("Clarity Bill"), 248, 249
    Bill C-51 (banning tobacco advertising), 479–81
    Bill C-114 (on conflict of interest), 283
    Bill 99 (Québec bill on right to define own
    status), 248
    Borden's Naval Bill, 328
    granting supply, 297
    language bills, 230–33
    process of becoming law, 297–301
    Royal Recommendation, 297
    Québec language legislation
        Bill 22, 230–31
        Bill 57, 231–32
        Bill 62, 231
        Bill 63, 231
        Bill 86, 231–32
        Bill 101, 172, 228, 230–32
        Bill 178, 231–32
        section 58 of Bill 101, 231
    types of, 296–97
        government bills, 297–98
        money bills, 297, 300
        non-financial bills, 297, 301

        private bills, 297
        private members' bills, 297, 299
        public bills, 297
        supply (appropriation) bills, 301
        ways-and-means bills, 297
Binnie, Ian, 184
Bird, Richard, 521, 523
Black, Conrad, 128, 129, 264
Blais, André, 448
Blake, Edward, 404
Blau, Peter, 336
Blishen, Bernard, 478
Bloc Québécois, 174, 235, 394–95. See individual party
    leaders
    party leaders, 404
Bombardier Inc., 513
Borden, Sir Robert, 73, 266, 404
Bouchard, Lucien, 2, 82, 404, 408, 409
        Bloc Québécois, 174, 371, 406
        and Charlottetown accord, 183
        complex political career of, 394–95
        and 1995 Québec referendum on sovereignty,
        235–36, 238, 366
        at 1996 First Ministers Conference, 169
        1998 election victory, 250
        policy of moderation, 250
        as PQ leader, 239, 248, 249, 399
        rejection of 1999 social union agreement, 218
        separatist policy of, 163
        and unilateral declaration of independence, 455
Boudria, Don, 301
Bourassa, Henri, 226, 329
Bourassa, Robert, 234, 249
        advocate of "two nations," 163
        and Charlottetown accord, 176
        language legislation, 232–33
        and Meech Lake accord, 173–75
        1970 Québec election, 228
Bourinot, George, 11
Boutros-Ghali, Boutros, 224
Bowell, Mackenzie, 261, 266, 404
Bracken, John, 86, 397, 404
Brady, Alexander, 11
Brewers Association of Canada, 466
British Columbia, social and political profile, 102
British Commonwealth, 543–44
British North America Act, 31, 39, 74, 152–55, 162
        amendment procedure, 53–54, 153
        Colonial Laws Validity Act of 1865, 153
        compared to American Constitution, 152
        division of powers under, 153, 203–4

and education, 115
executive power, 153
and nationalism, 160
patriation of, 163
Royal Assent, 38
special status for Québec, 159
Broadbent, Ed, 173, 392, 404
Broadfoot, Dave, 335
Bronfman family, 139
Brown, George, 37
Budget, 354–57, 562
    Budget Speech, 355–56, 357
    Budget Debate, 308
    debt, 7–8, 354–56, 519
    deficit, 354–56, 520
    expenditure by type, 355
    federal government budget for 2000, 356
    revenue outlook, 1998–2000, 356
    projected surpluses for 1998–2015, 357
Budgetary process, 7, 358–59
    business plans, 359
    expenditure budget process, 357
    Expenditure Management System, 359
    five-year fiscal plan, 358
    incremental decision making, 522
    Main Estimates, 358
    Planning, Programming and Budget System, 357–58
    Policy and Expenditure Management System, 271–72, 358
    pre-budget supply process for main and supplementary estimates, 359, 360
    revenue process, 357
Bureaucracy, government, 334–63. See also Auditor General; Ombudsman; Parliamentary committees; Public service
    appointments to administrative office, 336
    bureaucratic tenure, 337
    characteristics of, 336
    critics of, 337–38
    definitions of, 335
    democratic control of, 359–63
    vs. democracy, 336–38
    "empire-building" tendencies of, 338
    freedom of information, 361–62
    organization of federal bureaucracy, 338–46
        advisory bodies, 338, 341–42
        Crown agencies, 338, 339
        Crown corporations, 340–41
        departments, 338–39, 342–46
            administrative-coordinative, 339

            assistant deputy ministers, 339
            changing names of, 343
            deputy ministers, 339, 345–46
            duties of, 342
            goals of, 342–43
            line or operational, 339
            policy-coordinative, 339
        regulatory agencies, 341
        royal commissions, 342 (see also Royal commissions)
        semi-independent agencies, 342
Bureaucratic politics, 343
Burke, Edmund, 383–84
Burnet, Jean, 92
Burney, Derek, 276
Burns, R.M., 210
Business Council on National Issues, 471, 475
Byng, Lord, 258, 259

C

Cabinet, 262–64, 267–74. See also Ministry and Cabinet
    and committees, 271–73
    conventions of, 270–71
    Chiefs of Staff, 271
    collective/individual ministerial responsibility, 270
    executive assistant, 271
    Memorandum to Cabinet, 274
    ministry and, 267–70
    policy-making, 271–74
Cabinet members
    budgets of, 271
    ethnicity of 268–69
    political aides, 271
    religion of, 269
    representativeness of electorate, 268
    responsibilities of, 270–71
Cabot, John, 33
Caccia, Charles, 302
Cairns, Alan, 370
Callbeck, Catherine, 138
Camp, Dalton, 277, 386
Campbell, Alex, 102–3
Campbell, Colin, 69–70
Campbell, Kim, 137–38, 265, 266, 267, 269, 404, 407, 408, 491
    effect of, on public service, 525
    1993 federal election, 387, 447, 449, 451, 452
Canada. See also Government; International relations
    Confederation, 37–39
    constitutional monarchy, 22, 26, 74

Index

contemporary political life, 32
defence policy, 554–58
    Canadian Forces, 556–57
    defence expenditures, 559
    Department of National Defence, 555–56
    National Defence Headquarters, 556
    peacekeeping, 557–58
        Somalia, 557
    security policy, 555
as a democracy, 22–26
democratic rights in, 71
demographic trends (fertility rates, immigration, internal migration, life expectancy, mortality rates), 44–45
early history, 32–39, 52–53
early settlers/immigration, 42–44
economic relations with U.S., 5, 47, 541
economy, 4–6, 7–9, 56–57, 72, 529
external sovereignty, 53–54
family income, 101
federal/provincial relations, 57
foreign policy, 499–500, 528–39
    bureaucracy, 530
    and the Commonwealth, 543–44
    on Cuba, 554
    definition, 529
    Department of Foreign Affairs and International Trade, 530–34
    ethical dimensions of, 543
    federal competence in, 537–38
    federal/provincial conflict, 536–37
    la Francophonie, 544–45
    influence of interest groups, media, and the public, 535–36
    Minister of Foreign Affairs, 530–31
    multilateral organizations, 542–43
    Parliament and political parties, 534–35
    process of making, 530–39
    and the provinces, 536–38
    and Québec, 538–39
    relations with the European Union, 552
    relations with other countries, 553–54
    relations with the Pacific Rim, 552–53
    relations with the U.S., 545–47
    role of prime minister and Cabinet, 530–31
    Supreme Court jurisdictional rulings, 537
    and the United Nations, 542–43
founding nations, 34–37
global context, 528–29, 541–42
influence of American Revolution, 34
internal conflicts, 48–49, 57
international context, 528–29
key issues of unity and economic prosperity, 6–9
language issues, 228–34
law enforcement, 55
myths about, 64
National Policy, 55–57
national symbols (flag, anthem), 47
nation-building, 45–52
as a parliamentary democracy, 32
political challenges in, 5–6
political culture, 66–107
    studies of, in Canada, 65–66
political system, basis of, 31
population, 3
    aging of, 46
    distribution, 44–45, 100, 101
    growth, 42–43
poverty, 58–59
railways, importance of, 39, 55–56
religious division in, 42
role and size of government, 56–58
social and economic profile, 4–5
social welfare policies, 58–59
state-building, 52–58
territorial expansion, 39–41
trade policy, 6, 56, 540–42
    general free trade, 548
    free trade, 547–51
    global economy, 540–42
    sectoral free trade, 548
United Kingdom, dependence on, 32
United States, 54
    in contrast to, 47, 71–72
    cultural assimilation by, 47–48
    economic influence of, 54
    and environmental policy, 54
    limits on policy-making, 54
Canada Assistance Plan, 216–17, 521
The Canada Gazette, 272, 273, 310
Canada Pension Plan, 521
Canada Post Corporation, 516
Canadair, 16
Canada–United States Free Trade Agreement, 106, 548–51
    Canadian opposition to, 549
    dispute resolution mechanisms, 549
Canadian Airlines, 513
Canadian Association of Broadcasters, 473
Canadian Bankers Association, 472
Canadian Bar Association, 473
Canadian Bill of Rights, 86, 87, 166, 170, 172

Canadian Business and Industry International Advisory Committee, 472, 485

Canadian Business Development Bank, 515

Canadian Cancer Society, 479

Canadian Chamber of Commerce, 471

Canadian Charter of Rights and Freedoms, 70–71, 106, 149, 151, 169–72. See also Supreme Court of Canada–Charter challenges

    aboriginal rights, 86, 166, 172

    entrenched rights, 169–72

    legal challenges under, 187–94, 473, 479

    limits of, 170–71

    linguistic rights, 171–72

    notwithstanding clause, 165, 166, 172, 232, 235

        sunset clause, 165, 233

    preamble to, 170

    restrictions of citizens' rights, 172

    specific rights, 172

    and women, 166

    unresolved issues, 192–94

Canadian Chemical Producers Association, 471

Canadian Conference of Catholic Bishops, 473

Canadian Council of Churches, 466, 473

Canadian Council of Professional Engineers, 473

Canadian Dental Association, 473

Canadian Environmental Network, 490

Canadian Export Association, 472

Canadian Federation of Independent Business, 472

Canadian Federation of Agriculture, 466, 472, 485

Canadian Federation of Labour, 472

Canadian Federation of Students, 466

Canadian Import Association, 472

Canadian Industries Association, 471

Canadian Jewish Congress, 466, 473

Canadian Labour Congress, 466, 472, 483

Canadian Life and Health Insurance Association, 472

Canadian Manufacturers Association, 466, 471, 483

Canadian Medical Association, 466, 473, 478, 479

Canadian National Railways, 57, 515

Canadian Nuclear Association, 471

Canadian Nurses Association, 473

Canadian Polish Congress, 466

Canadian Pork Council, 472

Canadian Radio Broadcasting Commission, 57, 515. See also CBC

Canadian Reform Conservative Alliance, 368, 394

Canadians

    vs. Americans, 71–72, 79, 85–86

    attitudes, 71–72

    ethnic origins of, 85

    issues of importance to, 75–76

    level of public respect for national institutions, 77

    myths about, 64

    political participation of, 72, 79

    self-perceptions, 64

    values of, 69–79

Canadian state

    growth of, 517–23

        factors affecting, 521–23

        neo-Marxist approach, 522

        pluralist perspective, 521

        state-centred perspective, 521–22

        technological development, 522

    intervention of, in social and economic life, 520

    public expectations of, 523

Canadian Temperance Federation judgement, 160

Canadian Trucking Association, 471

Canadian Union of Postal Workers, 472

Canadian Union of Public Employees, 472

Caouette, Réal, 396

Capitol Hill Group, 475

Cappe, Mel, 277

Carleton, Guy, 35

Carstairs, Sharon, 183

Cartier, Georges Etienne, 81, 156, 268

Cartier, Jacques, 33

Catholic Women's League, 492

CBC (Canadian Broadcasting Corporation), 438, 515, 552

CCF (Co-operative Commonwealth Federation), 58, 329, 391–92, 483. See also NDP

Central coordinating agencies, 275–85. See also Conflict of interest; Department of Finance; Patronage; Prime Minister's Office; Privy Council Office; Treasury Board

Chamberlain, Neville, 553

Charest, Jean, 174, 267, 387, 399, 404, 407, 454, 459–60

Charlebois, Robert, 125

Charlottetown accord, 7, 48, 176–83

    Canada clause, 177

    compared to Meech, 176

    and constitutional veto, 176

    creation of new provinces, 176

    criticisms of, 180–81

    defeat of, 183, 195

    distinct society clause, 176

    on division of powers, 177

    Native self-government, 178–79

    proposed institutional changes, 179–80

    referendum on, 133, 183, 235

    social and economic union, 179

    Triple-E Senate, 181–82, 331

Charlottetown Conference (1864), 37

Cheffins, R.I., 152, 192

Index

Chief Electoral Officer, 442

Chingodan, 465

Chirac, Jacques, 539

Chrétien, Jean, 2, 249, 255, 257, 265, 266, 287, 328, 390–91, 404

    appointment of judges, 184

    by-elections, 433

    Cabinet restructuring, 273

    "Clarity Bill," 248

    conflict of interest, 283

    and Conrad Black, 264

    and constitutional negotiations, 169

    and constitutional reform, 183

    decentralizing trends, 208

    deficit commitments of, 356

    election as Liberal leader in 1990, 406

    and Expenditure Management System, 359

    foreign affairs, 531, 534

    la Francophonie, 544–45

    and government bureaucracy, 271

    ministry of, 269, 288

    and NAFTA, 551

    and Native self-government, 97

    1993 federal election, 267, 447

    1997 federal election, 267–68, 454–57, 461, 462

    1995 Québec referendum, 133, 236–38, 420

    and patriation of Constitution, 165

    and patronage, 285

    and PCO, 278

    and PMO, 277

    power to appoint candidates, 437

    public policy under, 524–25

    stance on future Québec referendums, 241–44, 246

    "Yesterday's Man," 408

Christian Movement for Peace, 473

Christian, William, 69–70

Christopher, Warren, 539

Churchill, Winston, 25

Cicero, 31

Citizen, 16

    relationship to state, 16

Citizen's Forum on Canada's Future, 76

Clark, Joe, 264

    Cabinet of, 287, 329

    conflict-of-interest guidelines, 282

    policy-making, 286

    as PC leader, 406, 407, 408, 409

    post Meech constitutional meetings, 174, 178

    as prime minister (1979–80), 158, 258–59, 265, 266, 269, 271, 387, 404

    resignation of, 405

    as Secretary of State, 531

    Speaker nominated by, 304

Clarkson, Adrienne, 257, 259

Class stratification, 139–41

    bourgeoisie, 139

    class consciousness, 71

    economic hierarchy, 139–41

    and Native people, 140

    poverty and, 139–41

    proletariat, 139

    social policy and, 140–41

    upper/middle/lower class, 139–40

Clinton, Bill, 539

Clokie, H.M., 11

CN Hotels, 516

CN Route, 516

Code Napoléon, 153

Cody, Howard, 202, 204

Collenette, David, 283

Colony, definition of, 33–34

Columbus, Christopher, 33

Committee system, House of Commons, 271–73, 309–16. See also Policy-making -committees

    Board of Internal Economy, 316

    Committee of the Whole, 309, 311

    consideration of legislation function, 312

        amendments, 312

        Report Stage, 312

    "envelopes," 309, 359

    expenditure scrutiny function, 313–14, 316

        attitude of MPs, 313

        Blue Book, 313

        Committee of Supply, 313

        estimates, 313–14, 355

        post-audit function, 314

        Standing Committee on Public Accounts, 313–14

    investigative function, 319

        Standing Committee on Finance, 314

    joint standing committees, 310–11

    leaks, issue of, 315

    legislative committees, 311

    parliamentary committees in 2000, 310

    problems and reforms, 315–16

        lack of autonomy, 315

        Lefebvre and McGrath reports, 316

        procedural reforms, 316

        uneven workload, 315

        lack of attention given reports, 316

    Public Accounts Committee, 311

recruitment, composition and staffing, 311–12
  Committee of Selection ("Striking Committee"), 311
  Staff of Committees and Private Legislation Branch of the Commons, 311
  standing committees, 309–16
    Standing Committee on Procedure and Organization, 311
    subcommittees, 310
Confectionery Manufacturers' Association, 471
Confederation, 37–39
  Charlottetown Conference, 37
  Dominion of Canada, 38–39
  Fathers of Confederation, 47, 81, 155
  problems solved by, 38–39
  Québec Conference, 37
  72 resolutions, 37
  Westminster Palace Conference, 38
Confederation of National Trade Unions, 470, 486
Conflict of interest, 281–83, 327
  Bill C-114, 283
  blind trust, 282–83
  and Criminal Code, 283
  "ethics counsellor," 283
  "ethics package," 283
  formal guidelines for Cabinet ministers, 282
  frozen trust, 282
  and Parliament Act, 283
  public attitudes toward, 282
  and Standing Orders of the House of Commons, 283
Conscription, issue of, 48, 82, 204, 225, 226, 386
  referendum on, 226
Conservatism. See Ideology–conservatism
Constitution. See also Canadian Charter of Rights and Freedoms
  amendments to/amending formula, 7, 161–63, 166, 169
    suspensive veto, 161
  asymmetry, 161
  bipolar federation, 161
  Canada Act, 54, 164
  collective/individual rights, 149
  as a compact, 163
  Constitution Act, 1982, 54, 167–69, 536–37
  constitutional highlights, 167
  conventions, 152
  cornerstrones of, 155
  definitions of, 149
  entrenchment in, 151
  executive federalism, 161

  federal/provincial constitutional agreement (1981), 165–68
  flexibility/rigidity of, 161
  and foreign policy, 537
  Fulton-Favreau formula, 162–63
  group rights under, 41
  jargon relating to, 161
  and the law, 149–51, 155
  and Meech Lake, 173–74
  patriation of, 2, 17, 74, 132, 163–67
    Britain's role in, 164–65
    Canada Act, 1982, 54, 164
    Gang of Eight, 165–66
    opposition to, 164, 165
    patriation package, 166–72
    Royal Assent to, 167
    ruling by Supreme Court, 165
    unilateral patriation package, 164
    veto power, 165
  proclamation of, 59
  as a red herring in Québec, 243–44
  written and unwritten, 148, 151
Constitutional bargain, 156–60
  division of powers, 156–57
    problems over, 158–60
  protection of language rights, 156
  protection of provinces, 156
  Québec isolationism, 156
Constitutional Conferences, 202, 205–6
  on Native rights, 205
  on Meech Lake accord, 205
Constitutionalism, 149
Consumers' Association of Canada, 466, 472
Cooper, Barry, 118
Copps, Sheila, 135, 269, 406, 452
Corry, J.A., 11
Cory, Peter, 190
Courts. See also Canadian Charter of Rights and Freedoms; Supreme Court of Canada
  adjudication function, 186
  appeals system, 185
  appointment of judges, 153, 186
  basic court system, 185
  and Charter of Rights and Freedoms, 150, 187–94
  criminal and civil law, 183
  Federal Court of Canada, 185, 192
    Unemployment Insurance Act, 192
  as guardians of the rule of law, 150
  interpretation of federal powers, 160
  Judicial Committee of the Privy Council, 154, 202–3, 224

removal of judges, 162
retirement of judges, 162
structure and role of, 183–87
Cousture, Arlette, 126
Creighton, Donald, 117
Crick, Bernard, 24
Criminal Code, 178, 189, 475, 477
Crosland, C.A.R., 384–85
Crown, 256. See also Government–formal executive
Crown corporations, 57, 272, 515–16, 524
CTV, 123, 438

D

Dahl, Robert, 27, 505
Dawson, MacGregor, 11
Dawson, R.M., 401
Debt, 6, 7–8, 354, 354–56, 518, 519
   national, 522
   net, in G-7 countries, 518, 519
   as percentage of GDP, 8, 356
   servicing costs, 7, 356
de Champlain, Samuel, 33
Decima Research 438
Defence policy. See Canada–defence policy
Deficit, 7, 215, 217, 354, 354–57, 518, 520
   federal, 522
   options for cutting 357
   zero deficit, 7, 356
de Gaulle, Charles, 227
de Haviland Aircraft, 516
Democracy, 22–27
   Aristotle, 23, 24, 26, 27
   in Canada, 22–23, 25–26, 70–71
   concept of, 24, 70
   constitutional democracy, 25–26
   critics of, 27
   crossnational comparisons, 26
   elite theories, 27
   pluralist theories, 27
   pure models, 25
   representative democracy, 25, 71, 290, 417
   ties to monarchy, 26
   values of, 25, 71
Democratic rights, 70–71
Demography, 145. See also Canada–demographic trends
Department of Finance, 280–81, 357. See also Budget;
   Budgetary process; Taxation
   Budget Speech, 355–56
   estimates, 355
   Financial Administration Act, 280
   fiscal policy and economic analysis, 281

   fiscal strategy, 354–55
   level of expenditures, 354
   taxation policy, 281
Department of Foreign Affairs and International Trade,
   342, 531–34
   and CIDA, 533
   functions of, 531
   hierarchy of, 539
   objectives of, 534
   restructuring of, 533–34
Department of Indian and Northern Affairs, 95, 97, 119
Dickson, Brian, 188
Diefenbaker, John, 225, 265, 386–87, 389, 404, 405, 437,
   444
Dingwall, David, 481
Dion, Léon, 81, 226
Dion, Stephane, 207, 244, 279
Disraeli, Benjamin, 369
Distant Early Warning Line, 49
Doern, G. Bruce, 516
Douglas, Major C.H., 396
Douglas, Tommy, 392, 404
Doukhobors, 49, 112
Drew, George, 386, 404
Dror, Yehezkel, 503
Drury, C.M., 486
Dubé, Marcel, 118–19
Duceppe, Gilles, 395, 404, 406, 455
Duffy, Dennis, 118
Dumont, Mario, 235
Dunn, Martin, 93
Duplessis, Maurice, 163, 170, 226, 227
Dupuy, Michel, 283
Durham, Lord, 36, 52, 117
Duverger, Maurice, 371, 428
Dye, Thomas, 499

E

Easton, David, 9
Education system, 112–19
   and American influence, 112
   "Canada first" policy, 112
   and class, 140
   church-sponsored, 115–16
   curriculum, 116
   differences in teaching of history and literature,
      116–19
   and employment, 113
   evolution of, 115
   expenditure on, as percentage of GDP, 114
   gender bias in, 114

history of French school rights outside Québec, 224–25
and national unity, 113
of Native peoples, 119
organizational structure, 115–16
political socialization, 112
postsecondary system, 116
    federal funding for, 217
and poverty, 113
provincial jurisdiction, 115–16
Egan, James, 190
Einstein, Albert, 222
Ekos, 438
Eldorado Nuclear, 516
Elections, 416–17, 421–62
    by-elections, 432–33
    candidates, 436–37
    constituency boundaries, 432
    Elections Expenses Act, 440, 441
    electoral behaviour, 442–48
        factors determining choice, 443
        voters and non-voters, 442–43
    electoral irregularities, 435–36
        gerrymandering, 435
    electoral procedure, 434–35
    electoral systems, 422–25
        alternative vote, 423
        effects of different systems, 425–28, 430–31
        mixed/additional member, 425
        multi-member proportional, 424–25
        second ballot, 423–24
        single-member majoritarian, 423–24
        single-member plurality, 423
    factors affecting outcome, 416, 444–47
    financing, 441–42
    franchise and ridings, 431–32
    functions of, 421–22
    governing party regional representation, 1867–1997, 379–80
    limits on election spending, 441
    media and voters, 439–41, 455–57
    1867–1997 election results, 449, 450
    1979, 1980, 1984 general election results, 427
    1993 general election, 385, 428, 449, 451–53, 463
    1997 general election, 428, 454–62
        analysis of, 460–62
        the campaign, 454–57
        issues, 457–60
        media, 455–56
        outcome, 458–60
    party advertising, 440–41, 457

party identification, 448
public opinion surveys, 438–39
seats won by region in general elections, 1945–97, 429
value of the vote, 433
Elkins, David, 90–91, 105
Energy Probe, 466, 473
Engelmann, F.C., 470
Engels, Frederick, 136
Empire Loyalists, 36, 42, 47, 81
English Canada. See also Canada; Canadians; French Canadians
    as a cultural fruitcake, 85–86
    and educational curriculum, 117–19
    English-French cleavages, 80–85
    idea of nation, 81
    linguistic differences, 66
    outside influences, 81
    political participation, 79
Environics, 438
Erasmus, Georges, 94
Established Programs Financing, 214, 215, 216–17
Estimates, 313–14, 355, 357. See also Budgetary process
    Main Estimates, 358
Ethnicity, 17, 18, 80, 90
    and Canadian unity, 90–91
    efficacy of federal system regarding, 90
    and political culture, 90–92
    and voting behaviour, 445
Ethnic minorities, 19–20, 102, 223
    adoption of provincial norms, 91
    in English-speaking Canada, 91
    liberal views toward, 88
    as percentage of Canada's population, 101
    in Québec, 18, 88, 91
Ethnic nationalism, 18–20, 223
Ethnic origins, 80
European Union, 15, 22, 552
Executive, 255–88. See also Formal executive; Cabinet; Governor General; Political executive; Prime minister
Executive Consultants, 475
Export Development Corporation, 515

F

Fairbairn, Joyce, 329
Fairclough, Ellen, 138
Family, as a socializing agent, 111
Family Compact, 36
Fathers of Confederation, 28, 81, 158, 186
Federalism, 198–204
    asymmetrical, 159

centralized/decentralized, 199, 213
concepts of, 199–200
conditions of failure, 201
Confederation, 199
Constitutional Conferences, 202, 205–6
Constitution as umpire of, 201
Constitution's importance for, 201
contested, 2, 207–8, 219
cooperative, 205
definition, 198
devolution of power, 206
evolution of, 202–4
  American Civil War, 202
  BNA Act, 202
  Charlottetown and Québec conferences, 202
  Confederation Agreement, 202
  states' rights movement (U.S.), 202
  threat of Fenian raids, 202
executive, 161, 205–6, 334
federal bargain, 156, 161
federal principle, 201
federal/provincial relations, 202–7 (see also Québec)
  conflict resolution mechanisms, 206–7
  economic problems, 208–9
  financing, 208–18
  Rowell-Sirois Commission, 204, 210
  western discontent, 204
fiscal federalism, 208–18
  basic concepts, 212–13
    conditional grants, 204, 210, 212
    spending power, 209, 213
    unconditional grants, 213
  block grant funding, 214–15
  Canada Health and Social Transfer, 217
  direct/indirect taxation, 209
  federal spending power, 159, 209, 213
  history of, 209–12
  implementation of fiscal policy, 209
  key mechanisms, 214
    equalization payments, 214
    Established Program Financing, 214–15, 217
  social union agreement, 1999, 217
  tax-sharing, 211–12
  transfers to provinces, 213, 214–17
motivation behind, 200
origins of, 201–2
sub-units, 200–5
unitary vs. federal government, 26, 156, 198, 199
Federalists, 2, 6

Federal/provincial division of powers, 7, 157–60
  asymmetrical federalism, 159
  boundaries, 159
  under the Constitution, 157–59
  disallowance of provincial legislation, 157
  federal areas, 158
  Fulton-Favreau formula, 162–63
  powers of Lieutenant-Governors, 157–58, 162
  problems over, 158–60
    concurrent jurisdiction, 159
    declaratory power, 158
    natural resources, 158
  provincial areas, 157–58
  quasi-federalism, 157
  Victoria Charter of 1971, 162, 163
Federal-Provincial Relations Office (FPRO), 133, 279
Feudal fiefdom, 15
Financial Post, 127
First Ministers Conferences, 169, 205–6, 219, 245
Fisheries Act, 297
Fisheries Council of Canada, 472
Fisheries Products International, 516
Flynn, Jacques, 518–19
Foot, David, 46, 145
Foreign affairs. See Canada–foreign policy; International relations
Formal executive, 255–60
  Crown, 256
  Governor General, 257–60
    advise prime ministers, 259
    appointment of, 257
    Byng-King case, 258–59
    dissolution of Parliament, 258–59
    functions and powers of, 257–58
    Letters Patent, 153, 257, 258
    prerogative powers, 257–58
    symbolism of, 257
  Lieutenant-Governor, 260
    appointment of, 260
  monarch, 256, 260
Forsey, Eugene, 82, 161
Francophonie, 5, 544–45
  New Brunswick meeting, 545
Fraser, John, 304
Fred Doucet Consulting International, 475
French Canadians
  and assimilation, 35, 81
  and Catholic Church, 81, 83
  civil law, 35, 81
  colonists, 35, 81
  cultural heritage, 35

as a cultural nation, 81, 82–83
and educational curriculum, 117–19
and ethnic groups, 91
feudal catholicism, 68
French-English cleavages, 49, 80–85
historical crises, 82
idea of nation, 81
isolationism, 156
linguistic differences, 66
minority status, 81, 82
nationalist attitudes/movements, 83–85
participation in politics, 79
Québec Act of 1774, 35
Quiet Revolution, 83, 88, 126
relevance of English monarchy to, 74
seigneurial system, 35
and separatist movements, 82 (see also October
    Crisis; Parti Québécois; Québec)
support for federalism, 84
support for sovereignty-association, 84
la survivance, 82
French-English conflict, 48–49, 224–26
French Revolution, 81
Friends of the Earth, 473
Front de la Libération du Québec (FLQ), 227. See also
    October Crisis
Frye, Northrop, 118

G

Gaelber, Ted, 524
Galt, Alexander, 37
Gandhi, Indira, 491
Gartner, Hana, 131
Gauthier, Michel, 395, 404, 406, 408
Genco, Stephen, 12
Gender issues, 134–38. See also Women
General Agreement on Tariffs and Trade, 281, 540–41
    Uruguay Round, 541
Gibbins, Roger, 69
Gidengil, Elisabeth, 76, 449, 460
Globalization, 9, 542
Goldenberg, Eddie, 277
Gonthier, Charles, 184, 190
Goodale, Ralph, 269, 270
Goods and Services Tax, 320, 324, 328, 391, 452
Government. See also Cabinet; Executive; Federalism;
    Formal executive; House of Commons; Prime minister
    advocacy advertising, 131–33
    American system, 261–62, 323
    backbenchers, 316, 318, 320
    bureaucratic politics, 343

collective responsibility, 344
and Commonwealth, 5
cornerstones of, 155
definition, 10
executive, models of, 287
forms of, 26
information services. See Information services
intra-party relations, 317–19
    caucus, 318
    chief whip, 318
    House Leader, 318
    party discipline, 317–18
    party unity, 318
    patronage, 318–19
    value-consensus
local, 156
majority government, 267
ministerial responsibility, 344
minority government, 268
nature of Canada's, 3
and opposition parties, 316–21 (see also Question
    Period)
    adversarial nature of relationship between,
        319–20
    alternatives to government policy, 321
    media coverage, 321
    role as policy critics, 320
parliamentary vs. presidential government, 261–62
prime ministerial government, 285–88 (see also
    Prime minister)
programs, 521 (see also individual programs)
regulating private sector, function of, 21
representative, 52
responsible, 52, 152
restraint/down-sizing, 8, 523–25
    Mulroney and Chrétien eras, 524–25
    managerialism, 524–25
spending, 8–9, 517–23
test of good government, 5
unitary vs. federal form, 26, 156, 198, 199
and United Nations, 5
Government Consultants International, 475
Government Policy Consultants, 475
Governor General, 74, 150, 153, 257–60, 264, 295, 296, 324
Governor-in-council, 184, 297
    functions of, 297, 345
Graham, Alasdair, 267, 329
Grant, George, 68
Grant, Ulysses, 546
Gray, Herb, 269
Green Paper, on financial services, 314

Greenpeace, 466, 473
Gregg, Allen, 451
Grey, Deborah, 393
Gross domestic product, 4, 5, 8, 57, 529
    debt as percentage of, 8
    education expenditures as percentage of, 114
    government expenditures and, 71
    and visible minorities, 90
Gross national product, 57
Groulx, Abbé Lionel, 225, 226
Group of Seven nations (G-7), 31, 528, 541
Guthrie, Hugh, 404

H

Habeas Corpus Act (1679), 151
Hanomansing, Ian, 131
Hanson, R.B., 404
Harper, Elijah, 178
Harris, Mike, 8, 206, 208, 218, 455
Harrop, Martin, 444
Hartt, Stanley, 276
Hartz, Louis, 67–68, 81
Helms, Jesse, 553
Herz, John, 20
Hitler, Adolf, 371, 418, 553
Hollinger Inc., 128
Holmes, John, 529, 543
Homosexuality
    gay rights, 189, 190–91
    spousal benefits, 190–91
Horowitz, Gad, 68, 69
House of Commons, 295, 301–9. See also Government;
    Question Period
    adversarial system of party politics, 303
    attendance, 309
    attitude of MPs, 302–3
    backbenchers' role, 302, 322
    business of the House, 306–9
        daily adjournment debate, 308–9
        government business, 307
        opposition business, 307–8
            Supply or Opposition Days, 308
        Oral Question Period, 308
        Orders, 307
        Orders of the Day, 306
        private members' motions and bills, 307
        Questions on the Order Paper, 306
        resolutions, 307
        routine business, 306
        Standing Orders, 305, 306–7, 315
        urgent business, 307

code of rules and procedures, 303
conflict/regulating devices, 305–6
debate, 319
    allocation of time, 319
    closure, 319
    filibuster, 319
Hansard, 130, 304
House Leaders, 304
members. See Members of Parliament
parliamentary reform, 321–23
    criteria for evaluation, 322
    effect of media, 322
    enhance influence of backbenchers, 322
    Lefebvre and mcGrath reform committees,
    316, 321
    objectives of, 322
    Special Committee on Standing Orders and
        Procedures, 321
physical layout of the House, 303
Speaker, 303–5
    duties of, 304–5
    election of, 304
    Westminster model, 304
unparliamentary language, 305
women in, 460
working week, 309
Hudson's Bay Company, 39, 55
Huntington, Ron, 316
Hydro-Québec, 516

I

Iaobucci, Frank, 184, 190
Ideology, 67–71, 381–85. See also Political parties;
    individual parties
    conservatism, 67–69, 70, 383–84
    definition, 67, 381
    liberalism, 67–69, 70, 382–83, 390
    populism, 385
    shift to right in Canada, 384
    socialism, 67, 68, 384–85
        Canadian, 69, 70
Immigrants, 69–70
    cultural ghetto, 92
    English-speaking, 35, 43, 68
    Loyalists, 68, 69
    to New France, 70
    as percentage of population, 44
Immigration, 35, 86–92
    Canada/Québec Accord, 86
    countries of origin, 87

cultural baggage, 68
discrimination, 43, 88
early, 35
impact of Canadian Bill of Rights on, 87
infrastructures to accommodate, 88–89
by metro area, 86
patterns and policy, 86–87
peak years, 88
by province, 89
and state-building, 56
ten-year plan, 87
trends in, 43–44
Imperial Conferences, 53
Independent Petroleum Assoiciation, 471
Influence-peddling, 283, 475
Information services
appeals to Information Commissioner, 362
Canadian Information Office, 133
Coordination of Access to Information Requests, 277
early services, 131
impact on political culture, 130–31
Information Canada, 131
Information Commissioner's report, 362
Unity Information Office, 245
Inglehart, Ron, 490
Innis, Harold, 11
Institutions, 13
declining confidence in, 76
as epiphenomena, 13
study of behaviour and, 14
overload thesis, 22
Intellectual left, 528
Interest groups, 466–74. See also Lobbying
in Canada, 469–74
agriculture and fisheries, 472
business, 471–72
other economic groups, 472–73
labour, 472
non-economic groups, 472–73
classifying, 470–71
fledgling, 471
institutionalized, 470
issue-oriented, 470
mature, 471
definition, 466–67
effect of, on policy, 467–69
function of, in society, 468
ingredients for success, 473–74
and policy communities and networks, 469
within pluralist system, 469
study of, 467–69

International Monetary Fund, 541
International relations, 44, 529–69. See also Canada—defence policy; Canada–foreign policy
bilateral/multilateral, 530
Canada-U.S. relations, 545–47
defence policy, 554–59
Department of Foreign Affairs and International Trade, 531–34
developing countries, 553–54
vs. domestic politics, 529–30
European Union, 552
globalization, 542
influence of interest groups, media and public opinion, 535–36
international/multilateral organizations, 542–45
Commonwealth, 543–44
la Francophonie, 544
OAS, 545
UN, 542–43
Pacific Rim countries, 552–53
peacekeeping role, 557–58
province's role in, 536–38
and Québec, 538–39
trade policy, 540–42, 547–51
Inuit. See Native peoples–Inuit
International Monetary Fund, 541
Irving family, 139

J

Jain, Geneviève, 117
Jay's Treaty, 34
Jerome, James, 304
Johnson, A.W., 123
Johnson, Daniel, 163, 235, 237–38
Johnson, P.A., 192, 193
Johnson, Pierre-Marc, 173, 234
Johnson, William, 126
Johnston, Richard, 372, 446
Johnston, Rita, 138
Judicial Committee of the Privy Council, 154, 224
Judicial system. See Courts
Julien, Pauline, 125

K

Kennedy, John F., 545
Kent, Peter, 131
Kent, Tom, 128
Kent Commission, 128
Keynsian economics, 521, 523

King, William Lyon Mackenzie, 265, 266–67, 389, 402, 403, 404, 408
    and Byng-King affair, 258, 259
    and conscription, 226, 419
    and patronage, 284
    political skills of, 287
    and Senate reform, 329
King Charles II, 39
King Edward VIII, 256
King James II, 256
Kingsley, Jean-Pierre, 434
Kirby, Michael, 326, 327
Kirchheimer, Otto, 371
Klein, Ralph, 8, 191, 206,208, 455
Kunz, F.A., 327

L

Labour, organized, 472, 483, 487, 521–22
Labrador, 41
Lachance, Claude-André, 316
La Forest, Gerald, 187, 190
Lalonde, Marc, 276
Lambert Royal Commission, 316
Lamer, Antonio, 184, 190, 192, 194
Language. See also Bilingualism
    and BNA Act, 225, 228
    and the Constitution, 228–29
    constitutional protection of, 224
    decline of use of French language, 230
    federal policies, 228–29
    first language in Québec, 230
    francophone population in Canada, profile of, 229–30
    history of French outside Québec, 225
    issues, 228–34
    legal basis for language legislation, 228–29
    minority-language rights, 228
    Official Languages Act (1969), 229
    provincial legislation, 229
    Québec legislation, 230–33 (see also Bills–Québec language legislation)
    unilingualism, 233
    use of English in private sector in Québec, 227
Lasswell, Harold, 9
LaPalombara, Joseph, 13, 16, 373
Laporte, Pierre, 227
Lasch, Christopher, 137
Latham, Earl, 467
Laurier, Sir Wilfrid, 259, 265, 266, 389, 403, 404, 444, 548
Lavallée, Calixa, 73
Law. See also Courts; Supreme Court of Canada

    and the Constitution, 149–51
    common/case law, 150
        stare decisis, 150
    parliamentary supremacy, 150–51
    precedent, 150
    rule of, 71, 150–51, 157
    statutory, 150–52
    ultra vires, 151
Leacock, Stephen, 11
Leblanc, Roméo, 257, 285
Lefebvre and McGrath parliamentary reform committees, 304, 316
Leger and Leger, 438
Legislation. See also Acts of Parliament; Bills
    Committee Stage, 299, 312
    if defeated by Senate, 299
    delegated or subordinate, 297
    First Reading, 298–99
    legislative process, 297–301
        domination of Cabinet and bureaucracy, 294
    Order Paper, 299
    proclamation, 299
    Report Stage, 299, 312
    Royal Assent, 295, 299
    Second Reading, 299, 312, 488
    Senate process, 299
    stages of, 297–301
    tax legislation
    Third Reading, 299
    time frame, 301
Legislative politics, 295
Legislatures. See also House of Commons; Senate
    bicameral legislature, 295
    comparative study of, 292
    policy-making activities of, 293
    representational activities of, 293
    role of British House of Commons, 293
    roles and functions of, 292–95
    system-maintenance activities of, 293
Lesage, Jean, 83, 163, 204, 226
Letters Patent, 153, 257, 258
Lévesque, René, 163, 164, 165, 172–73, 227–28, 230, 234, 249, 539
Lewis, David, 392, 404
Liberal party, 389–91. See also individual party leaders
    party leaders, 404
    Red Book (1993), 87, 125, 356, 391, 451–52; (1997) 454
    response to Royal Commission on Aboriginal Peoples, 98
Lieutenant-Governor, 156, 260

Lindblom, Charles, 503

Lipset, Seymour Martin, 69, 71

Livingston, W.S., 200

Lobbying, definition of, 468

Lobbying in Canada, 474–89. See also Interest groups
    access points/targets, 480–83
        backbenchers, 484
        Cabinet, 482, 484
        committees, 483, 484
        federal bureaucracy (public service), 481, 484–85
        pre-parliamentary stage, 480
    corporatism, 487
    Ethics Counsellor, 476
    legislation to control
        Bill 43, 476–77
        Lobbyists Registration Act, 475, 476
    lobbyists, a catalogue of, 471–73, 475
    relationship between lobbyists and politicians/
        bureaucrats, 487–88
    Senate and, 488
    tactics and strategies, 478–80
    tobacco manufacturers, lobbying campaign to stop
        Bill C71, 479–80, 481

Locke, John, 68, 70, 382

Lower, A.R.M., 54

Lower Canada, 36. See Québec

M

Macdonald, Sir John A., 37, 156, 201–2, 219, 263, 265–66, 267, 268, 388
    early political activity of, 386
    and National Policy, 55–56, 547–48
    opposition to, 389
    and patronage, 284
    and Senate, 324

Macdonald, John (senator), 325

MacEachen, Allan, 441, 531

Machiavelli, Niccolo, 10, 195

Mackay, R.A., 11

Mackenzie, Alexander, 266, 404

Mackenzie, William Lyon, 36

Maclean Hunter, 128

MacLennan, Hugh, 118

MacPhail, Agnes, 136, 138, 400

Maddox, Graham, 200

Magda Carta of 1215, 151

Main Estimates. See Estimates

Maillet, Antonine, 83

Major, John, 184, 190

Mallory, James, 160

Mandela, Nelson, 544

Manion, R.J., 404

Manitoba
    French-language rights, 224
    and Métis, 224
    non-sectarian education system, 224

Manitoba Schools Question, 82, 224

Manning, Preston, 183, 252, 320, 393–94, 404, 405, 408, 409, 410, 420, 436, 458

Mansbridge, Peter, 131

Marchand, Jean, 227

Martin, Paul, Jr., 8, 217–18, 269, 281, 319, 355–56, 406

Martin, Paul, Sr., 543

Marx, Karl, 12, 136, 139, 369, 384, 507

Maslove, Allan M., 216

Massé, Marcel, 245, 525

Massey, Vincent, 74, 257

McCallum, R.B., 438

McDonald, Lynn, 492

McDonough, Alexa, 392, 404, 406, 408

McKenzie, Daniel D., 404

McLachlin, Beverley, 137, 138, 184, 190

McLaughlin, Audrey, 137, 138, 392, 400, 404, 407, 408, 423

McLellan, Anne, 270

McNaughton, General, 268

McRae, Kenneth, 47, 68–69, 81

Media, 119–30.
    Aird Report, 121
    American cultural domination of Canadian, 120, 123–25, 128–29
    Applebaum-Hébert Report, 121
    broadcast media, 121–27
        Canadian Broadcasting Corporation (CBC), 120–21, 123–26, 131
            Newsworld, 121, 131
        Canadian Radio-television and
            Telecommunications Commission, 123, 127 514–15
            Canadian content, 121, 123–24, 125, 127,
        CTV (English), 126
        DirecTV, 126
        economic dilemma of, 125
        government regulation of TV, 1932–98, 124
        Global, 124, 131
        Public Broadcasting System (PBS), 129
        Radio-Canada, 126
            perceived as separatist threat, 126
        satellite services, 126
        Task Force on Broadcasting Policy, 121
    Davey Report, 121
    east-west link, 120–21

and elections, 439–41
education of journalists, 130, 131
and English-French relations, 121
friction between government and different
    language/ethnic groups, 126
government policy, 120–21
history of media in Canada, 121
north-south communications, 120–21
limitations on, 120
and political orientations, 119–30
political role of, 119
print media, 121
    Canadian Press (CP), 127
    le Devoir, 120, 127
    The Financial Post, 129
    The Globe and Mail, 120, 127
    National Post, 120, 127, 129
    news and editorials, 128–29
        American influence on, 128–29
        reflection of community norms, 130
    The Toronto Star, 120, 127
    public vs. private, 121, 125
    promotion of national identity, 125
    in Québec, 125–26
    role in breakdown of democratic process, 129
    role in setting or affecting political agenda, 119,
    125
Meech Lake accord, 7, 48, 82, 173
    Bourassa's five conditions, 173, 234–35
    failure of, 173–74, 234–35
    Langevin amendment, 173
    seven areas of change, 173,
Meighen, Arthur, 265, 266, 267, 386, 403, 404
Meir, Golda, 491
Members of Parliament (MPs), 301–3
    independent, 316–17
    as party members, 316–17
    role as constituency representative, 301–3
    salaries and expenses, 301
    "turncoats," 317
    workload, 309
Mercier, Honoré, 203, 204, 227, 389
Mercredi, Ovide, 178
Métis. See Native peoples–Métis
Mezey, Michael, 292
Michels, Robert, 27, 371
Mill, John Stewart, 136, 382
Miller, William L., 444
Mining Association of Canada, 471, 475
Ministry and Cabinet, 267–74. See also Cabinet
    as affected by number of seats in House, 267–68

basis for appointment to, 267–68
composition of, 267, 269
ethnicity, 268–69
in Liberal government, 2000, 273
1993 and 1997 Liberal ministries, 268
occupations of members, 269
as representative of Canada's regions, 269
size of, 267
women in, 269
Minority rights. See Canadian Charter of Rights and
    Freedoms
Miron, John, 191
Monahan, Patrick, 241
Monarch. See Formal executive–monarch
Morgentaler case, 192–93
Morton, W.L., 74, 117
Mosca, Gaetano, 27
Movements, 465, 489–90
    in Canada, 490–91
    environmental, 490
    in Europe, 490
    nationalist, 20, 489–90
    rise of new, 490
    social and political, 489–92
    women, 491–92
Mowat, Oliver, 203, 204
Mulroney, Brian, 249, 266, 376, 389, 394, 404, 405, 406,
    407, 408, 433, 437
    appointments by, 269
    Charlottetown accord referendum, 76, 132, 183,
        420–21
    conflict-of-interest guidelines, 282–83
    disbandment of PEMS, 359
    and elections, 444, 445
    free trade agreements, 531, 548
    government advertising, 132
    government of, 57
    Meech Lake accord, 173–74
    1984 election victory, 225, 234, 252
    patronage, 285, 326
    Pearson Building constitutional proposals, 175
    PMO, 275–77
    policy-making in government of, 271–73
    political aides, 271
    resignation of, 267, 449
    skills of, 287, 387
    Triple-E Senate, 181–82
    Senate, 324, 328–29, 331
Mulroney, Mila, 132
Multiculturalism, 71, 87–89, 91–92
    Minister of State for, 88

Multiculturalism and Citizenship Canada, 88
Multiculturalism Directorate, 90
	Race Relations Unit, 90
	policy of, 87–89
	tensions as a result of, 88
Multilateral Agreement on Investment (MAI), 551
Murdoch, Irene, 138
Murphy, Rex, 131
Murray, Lowell, 326

N

Nadeau, Richard, 448
NAFTA (North American Free Trade Agreement), 47, 106, 281, 389, 550–51
Nation, 17–18. See also Canadian state; State
	compact between English and French, 81
	cultural nation, 81
	definition, 17–18
	objective criteria, 17
	vs. state, 18
National Action Committee on the Status of Women, 9, 466, 473, 474, 492
National Farmers Union, 472, 485
National Poverty Organization, 473
National Energy Program, 121, 251, 390, 547
National identity, 17–18, 223
	components of, 223
Nationalism, 18–20, 222–28
	definition, 20, 223
	disputes about, 223
	as a divisive force, 19, 223
	ethnic demands, 20
	ethnic minorities and, 223
	in modern Québec, 226–38
	movements, 20
	vs. regionalism, 20
	roots of, 224–26
		English-French conflict, 224–25
	state-centred, 226
	territorial tensions, 20
National Policy, 55–56, 57, 547–48
Nation-building, 18, 46–52
	and contemporary politics, 51–52
Native Canadians, 51, 92–98. See also Department of Indian and Northern Affairs; Nunavut
	aboriginal rights, 93–94
	assimilation of, 35, 51, 93
	and Charlottetown accord, 178–79
	and Charter of Rights and Freedoms, 166, 172
	and constitutional amendment, 169
	and constitutional meetings, 174

dependency on federal government, 93
developments of significance in aboriginal affairs, 99
and discrimination, 49, 89
education and, 96, 119, 172
and ethnic division, 80, 92
and the franchise, 49
fur trade, 34–35
land claims, 51, 96–97
	Nisga'a claim, 96
	in Québec, 96–97
Indian Act, 92–93, 94
Indians
	benefits from federal government, 92
	definition, 92
	non-status Indian, 49, 92–93
	status Indian, 49, 92–93
	urbanization, 92, 95
Inuit, 40, 93
	Dene Nation, 50
	geographical isolation, 49
	poverty and, 49
	right to vote, 49
	relinquishing of land claim, 39
	Tapirisat of Canada, 50
Métis, 49, 93
nation-building process and, 49, 51
past treatment, 94–95
population, 35, 42, 92–93
poverty, 49, 94–95, 140
pre-history of, 32
and Québec separation, 97
relations with British Crown, 34–35
relative deprivation of, 94–95
relations with federal and provincial governments, 51
representation in public service, 352
reserves, 35
Royal Proclamation of 1763, 35
self-government, 40, 51, 96, 97–98, 175, 178–79
settlements at time of European contact, 33
statistics on social deprivation, 94–95
traditional leadership, 94
traditional lifestyle, 93–94
treaty negotiations, 35
two-row wampum, 94
undefined in Constitution Act, 94
under-representation in government, 269
NATO (North Atlantic Treaty Organization), 5, 22, 31, 542, 556, 557

NDP (New Democratic Party), 391–93, 483. See individual party leaders
    party leaders, 404
Neo-Marxist analysis, 507–9
    instrumentalist view, 508
    structuralist view, 508
Nesbit, Jack, 190
Neumann, Franz, 200
Neville, William, 479
Nevitte, Neil, 69, 72, 79
New Brunswick, language rights, 171
Newfoundland, 419
    and education, 169
    and Labrador, 41
New France, immigrants to, 70
Nielsen, Erik, 404
Nielsen Task Force (on program review), 525
Non-Smokers' Rights Association, 473
NORAD (North American Aerospace Defence Command), 542, 557
Northern Transportation Commission, 516
North-West Mounted Police, 55
Northwest Territories, 102
Nunavut, 40–41, 102, 156
    government, 40, 49
    political boundaries, 102
    population, 102
    self-government, 102
Nunziata, John, 317, 406, 436, 460

O

October Crisis 1970, 17, 48, 166, 227, 228
OECD (Organization for Economic Cooperation and Development), 551
Ombudsman, 362
Ontario
    social and economic profile, 101
Ontario Hydro, 516
Operation Dismantle, 473
Oregon Treaty, 34
Organization for Economic Cooperation and Development, 31
Organization of American States, 545
Osborne, David, 524
Ouellet, André, 531

P

Pacific Rim, 552–53
Paltiel, K.Z., 442
Papineau, Louis-Joseph, 36, 227
Parent, Gilbert, 304, 315, 320

Pareto, Vilfredo, 27
Parizeau, Jacques, 2, 163, 248, 249
    and BQ 1993 campaign, 399
    Charlottetown accord referendum, 183
    comment on Quiet Revolution, 125–26
    election to PQ leadership, 235
    1995 Québec referendum on sovereignty, 235–37
    reaction to 1995 referendum loss, 7, 238–39
    unilateral declaration of independence, 455
Parliament. See also House of Commons; Legislatures
    bicameral parliaments, 292
    dissolution of, 317
    Golden Age of, 294, 322
    morality/ethics in 283
    overview of Canada's, 295
    parliamentary life cycle, 296
        prorogation of Parliament, 296
        sessions, 296
        Speech from the Throne, 296
    power of, 291
    salaries and benefits for officers and members, 302
    symbolic role of, 291, 293
Parliamentary committees, 310, 361. See also Committees; Policy-making–committees
Parliamentary democracy, 290
Parti Action Démocratique, 236
Parti Nationale, 227
Parti Québécois, 49, 163, 173, 207, 227–28, 235–36
Patronage, 284–85, 336
    development of, in Canada, 284
    pork-barrelling, 285, 466
Peacekeeping, 557–58
Pearson, Lester B., 266, 268, 271, 282, 287, 389, 404, 531, 543, 544
Pearson Building proposals, 175–76, 179
Peer groups, 111
Pelletier, Gérard, 227
Pelletier, Jean, 277
Perlin, George, 372, 409
Petro-Canada, 57, 516, 524
Pettigrew, Pierre, 244
Pharmaceutical Manufacturers Association, 475
Phillips, Susan, 492
Pinard, Maurice, 84, 125, 235–36, 235–36, 396
Plato, 25
Policy-making, 271–74, 303. See also Public policy
    committees, 271–74
        Cabinet-as-a-whole
        Communication, 272
        Economic Union, 273

Expenditure Review, 272–73
Legislation and House Planning, 272
Operations, 272
Priorities and Planning, 272, 287
Security and Intelligence, 272
Social Union, 273
Special Committee of Council, 272
formal process for Cabinet approval, 273–74
Memorandum to Cabinet, 274
orders-in-council, 272
Policy and Expenditure Management System, 271–72, 358
Treasury Board, 272–73
Political culture, 65–106. See also Political orientations
definition, 65
divisions within, 117–19, 134
effect of new technologies, 142
general culture of a society, 65
ideology and, 67–70
national cultures, 66
political attitudes, 75–78
political participation, 78–79
and political system, 65
roots of Canadian, 67–70
study of, 66–70
symbols of, 65, 72–74
three strands of, 66
ethnic and linguistic cleavages, 66, 80–98
regionalism, 66, 98–106
values and attitudes, 65–66, 67–79
Political executive, 260–62
accountability, 261
British model, 260–61
Cabinet, 260
in contrast to American system, 261–62
and Governor General, 261
governor-in-council, 261
history of, 261
prime minister, 260–61
Political orientations, 110–42
acquiring of, 110–33
political socialization, 110–11
authority figures, 110
class and, 134, 139–41
divisions within Canada, 118–19
education, 112–19
civic knowledge, 115
link with employment, 113
reinforcing regional cleavages, 116–19
subject to American influence, 112
factors determining, 109

families and peer groups, 111–12
gender and, 134–38
government information and, 130–33
and the media, 119–30
and political symbols, 110
Political parties. See also individual parties
Canadian system, 374–80
origins of, 374–75
inherent problems with, 377–78
federalism, 377
regionalism, 377–78
definitions, 368–69
established federal parties in Canada, 85–93
CCF/NDP, 391–93
Liberal party, 389–91
Progressive Conservative party, 386–89
functions of, 369–70
minor and historical federal parties in Canada
Progressives, 396–97
Ralliement des Créditistes, 396
Social Credit, 396
new federal parties in Canada, 393–95
Bloc Québécois, 394–95
Canadian Reform Conservative Alliance, 394
Reform party, 393–94
party finance, 410–12
contributions, 411
election expenses, 410–12
party leaders, 404, 407–9
party representation in the Commons, 375
structure and organization, 397–400
constituency level, 398–99
national level, 399
party conventions, 397, 400–7
leadership conventions, 397, 403, 405–7
policy conventions, 397
policy formulation, 401–3
systems of parties (competitive/non-competitive systems, dominant one-party, dominant-party, multi-party, multi-party dominant, one-party, two-party, two-and-a-half-party), 372–77
types of parties (anti-system, brokerage, cadre, catch-all, devotee, ideological, mass, single-issue), 371–72
Political power
division of, 153–55
executive, 153
and BNA Act, 153
legal restraints on, 151
parliamentary supremacy, 150–51
residual, 159

Index

Political science
   approaches to, 10–15
      concept of power, 10
      functionalism, 11
      general theory of the polity, 11
      legal/formal description, 11
      political economy, 12
         neo-Marxism, 12
         public choice, 12
         public policy, 12
      structural functionalism, 11
      systems analysis, 11
   pluralism, 12
   state-centred, 12
   the study of Canadian politics, 13–15
      diachronic approach, 15
      synchronic approach, 15
Political socialization, 110–42. See also Political culture;
   Political orientation
Political symbols, 72–74
   coat of arms, 73
   flag, 73
   Governor General, 74
   historical heroes, 74
   monarch, 74
   national anthem, 73
   official name, 72
Polls/polling. See Public Opinion Surveys/Polls
Polsby, Nelson, 291–92
Popper, Karl R., 14
Porter, John, 42
Poverty
   and class, 140–41
   and education, 113
   and Native peoples, 94–95
   and political participation, 79
   and women, 137
Poverty line, 140
Prairie provinces, 101–2
Press Bill, 170
Pressure groups. See Interest groups
Presthus, Robert, 478
Prime minister, 285–88, 262–67.
   abuse of power, 286
   appointment of ministry, 263
   appointment of parliamentary secretaries, 263
   basis of authority, 262–64
   dissolving Parliament, 264
   list of Canada's prime ministers, 266
   organization of government, 264
   policy-making authority of, 286–87

powers of, 262–64, 285–87
   in practice, 265–67
      gender, 265
      language spoken, 265
      previous experience, 265
      regional pattern of support, 265
      religious and ethnic diversity, 265
      tenure in office, 266–67
Prime Minister's Office, 275–77
   budget of, 275
   influence in policy-making, 276–77
   role of, 275
   structure of, 276
Privatization, 272, 516, 524. See also Public policy–public
   ownership
Privy Council Office, 277–79
   Clerk of the, 277
   Federal-Provincial Relations Office (FPRO), 279
   functions and powers of, 277–79
   Intergovernmental Affairs Secretariat, 279
   Secretary to the Cabinet, 277
   size of, 279
   as a source of policy ideas, 279
   structure under Chrétien, 278
Program Planning and Budgeting System, 280
Progressive party, 329, 396–97
Progressive Conservative party, 386–89, 496. See individ-
   ual party leaders
   party leaders, 404
Pross, Paul, 466, 470, 482
Provinces. See also individual provinces/regions
   constitutions, 156, 162
   and foreign policy, 536–69
      federal/provincial conflict over, 536–37
   legislatures, 156, 162
Public Affairs International, 475
Public Expenditure Management System, 280
Public opinion surveys/polls, 65–66, 438–39, 455–57
   most widely known polling organizations, 438
   on Québec separation, 84–85
Public policy, 14–15. See also Policy-making
   definition, 499
   domestic policy, 499–500, 501
   economic policy, 500
   foreign policy, 499–500, 528–39 (see also
      Canada–foreign policy; International relations)
   policy instruments, 512–17
      exhortation, 512
      and policy process, 516–17
      public expenditure, 512–14
      public ownership, 515–16

regulation, 514–15

symbolic policy outputs, 512

social policy, 500

theories of, 500–512

comparison of approaches, 510–12

macro-level approaches, 500, 504–10

neo-Marxist analysis, 507–9

pluralism, 504–6

public choice theory, 506–7

state-centred analysis, 509–10

micro-level approaches, 500, 502–4

incrementalist model, 503

rational-comprehensive model, 502–3

rationalist vs. incrementalist, 503–4

Public service, 346–54

acts governing, 346–48

basic principles of, 346–47

bilingualization of, 349

and budgets, 354–59

competition for positions, 352

cutbacks in, 354, 523–25

definition, 346

employment equity programs, 347–48

francophone representation in, 349

merit principle, 346, 350, 352

profile of, 348

Public Service Renewal, 525

Public Service 2000, 347, 525

regional distribution, 348–49

veterans' preference, 351

women and equity-designated groups, 350–54

Punnett, Malcolm 268, 287

Q

Québec. See also Lower Canada; Bills–Québec language legislation

aboriginal territorial claims, 239

Allaire Report, 174–75

Asbestos strike, 226

Campeau-Bélanger Commission, 174

Canada/Québec constitutional highlights, 1976–96, 249

Charte de la Langue FranÁaise, 229

Conseil de la Langue FranÁaise, 1999 study of, 230

as a distinct society, 173, 176, 245

division of, 36

economic and social profile, 100

English-speaking minority, 229–30

fertility rate, 229

foreign policy, 538–39

francophone population, 229–30

French-English conflicts, 224–26

Labrador and, 41

language issues, 228–34

language law, 230–33

language legislation, 229–33

language policy, 231

language statistics, 229–30

linguistic and education rights, 224

Meech Lake and Charlottetown failures as factors in politics of, 234–45

nationalism/self-determination, 7, 226–28, 242

nationalist/separatist parties

Parti Patriote, 227

Parti Québécois, 227

Ralliement National (RN), 227

Ralliement pour l'indépendance nationale (RIN), 227

Union Nationale, 227

Office de la Langue FranÁaise, 229

Oka Indian reserve, 19

patriation and the Constitution, 164, 165, 172–73, 234

Quiet Revolution, 126, 204, 226, 366, 539

referendum on sovereignty-association (1980), 164, 234

referendum on sovereignty (1995), 6–7, 235–42, 366

fall-out, 244–48

the question, 237

strategy, 235–38

unresolved issues, 240–42

separatism, support for, 240

separatist movement, 174, 227–28 (see also Bouchard; Léveque; Bloc Québécois; Parti Québécois)

social and economic profile, 100

sovereignty-association, 164, 228, 234

sovereignty bill (Bill 150), 174

special powers for, 85

special status, 163

unilateral declaration of independence (UDI), 243–44, 246–48, 455

Québec Conference, 1864, 37

Quebec Padlock Law, 170

Québec Woodworkers Federation, 472

Queen Elizabeth II, 26, 74, 256

Queen Victoria, 37

Question Period, 308, 319, 534

R

Racial discrimination, 89–90
    in Canadian government, 90
    Japanese Canadians, 89
    Race Relations Unit/Multiculturalism Directorate, 90
    systemic discrimination, 89–90
Rae, Bob, 392
Rainer, Maria Rilke, 118
Reagan, Ronald, 548
REAL Women, 473, 492
Referendums, 417–24. See also Conscription; Charlottetown accord–referendum on; Québec–referendums
    in Canada, 419–20
    outside Canada, 418
    definition, 417
    functions of, 417–18
    vs. plebiscites, 417
Reform Bill (1832), 151
Regionalism, 50–51, 66, 98–106, 250–52. See also Québec
    alienation, 103–4, 251–52
    core-periphery relationships, 50
    definitions, 20, 99, 250
    discontent, 20, 104–5, 250–52
    disparities between regions, 98, 104
    and federal system, 50–51
    objection to patriation, 251
    and political culture, 98–105
    positive aspects of, 104–5
    profiles
        Atlantic provinces, 99–100
        British Columbia, 102
        Northland, 102
        Ontario, 101
        Prairie provinces, 101–2
        Québec, 100
    regional cleavages, 104–5
    regional cultures, 104–5
    regional vs. national loyalty, 105
    western demands, 105, 252
    western separatist groups
        Western Canadian Federation (WestFed), 251
        Western Canada Concept, 251
    western views, 251–52
Riddell-Dixon, Elizabeth, 470
Riel, Louis, 48, 55, 123, 224, 386
Riker, William, 13, 199
Rinaldo, Sandie, 131
Rivard, Lucien, 410

Roberts, Stan, 406
Robertson, Lloyd, 131
Robillard, Lucienne, 237, 433
Robinson, Svend, 406
Roblin, Duff, 486–87
Rogers Inc., 128
Romanow, Roy, 169, 218
Rousseau, Jean-Jacques, 382
Rowat, Donald, 362
Roy, Bernard, 276
Royal Canadian Legion, 483
Royal Canadian Mounted Police, 55, 477
Royal commissions
    on Aboriginal Peoples, 97–98, 99
    on Bilingualism and Biculturalism, 83, 88, 90–91, 116–17
    on Dominion-Provincial Relations (Rowell-Sirois), 204, 210
    on Financial Management and Accountability (Lambert Commission), 316
    on the mass media (Davey Commission), 128
    on Newspapers (Kent Commission), 128
    Senate special committees in 1960s and 1970s, 328
    on the Status of Women, 138, 492
Royal Proclamation of 1763, 35, 153
Rush-Bagot Treaty, 34
Russell, Peter, 192
Ryan, Claude, 234

S

Samuel, John T., 90
S.A. Murray Consulting, 475
Sauvé, Jeanne, 137, 138, 257
Schreyer, Edward, 257
Schumpeter, Joseph, 27, 505
Schwartz, M.A., 470
Scott, F.R., 74–75
Segal, Hugh, 76
Seidle, F. Leslie, 442
Senate, 295, 323–32
    Australian Senate, 182
    bicameral legislation, 323–24
    Bundesrat model, 330
    Charlottetown accord proposals for, 180–82
    compared to the British House of Lords, 295
    delaying tactics of, re free trade legislation, 328
    functions of, 324
    legislative politics and, 324, 327–29
    members, 324–26
        appointment of, 324–25

accountability, 325
as regional representatives, 162, 324, 325
inequities in regional representation, 325
patronage, 326
suspension of, 329
women, 325
workload, 328
organization and rules, 326, 27
conflict-of-interest rules, 327
senior officers, 326
salaries and perks, 327
political limitations of, 300
Senate reform, 329–31
absolute veto, 330
direct election of senators, 330
limits on ability to block legislation, 330
modified Triple-E Senate, 330–31, 332
Special Joint Committee on Senate Reform, 330
suspensory veto, 330
special committees, 328, 483
Triple-E Senate, 161, 175, 181–82
Separatism. See Bloc Québécois; Bouchard; Lévesque;
Québec
Sharp, Mitchell, 283, 482
Sidgwick, Eleanor, 134
Simeon, Richard, 50, 104, 206, 510
Smallwood, Joey, 444
Smiley, D.V., 206, 403
Smith, Adam, 382
Smith, Denis, 285
Social Credit party, 118, 396
social union agreement, 1999 (A Framework to Improve
the Social Union for Canadians), 217
Solicitor General, 344
Sopinka, John, 190
Southam Inc., 128, 129, 439
Sovereignty (national), 16–17
Sovereignty-association, 228, 419. See also Québec–
sovereignty-association
Speaker of the House, 303–5
Spector, Norman, 276
Spending power of federal government, 159, 209, 213
St. Laurent, Louis, 265, 266, 389, 404, 459, 531, 543, 544
Stairs, Denis, 535
Standing Committee on Finance, 314
Stanfield, Robert, 387, 404, 408
State, 15–22. See also Canadian state
aristocracy, 23
Aristotelian classification, 23–24
autocratic system, 24
Canada as a, 15

and citizens, 15–16
definitions, 15
democratic system, 24
development of modern, 20–22
functions of state institutions, 57
Greek city-states, 23
growth of, 56–57
legitimacy of, 16–17
powers of, 16
sources of authority, 16
sovereignty, 16
state-building in Canada, 52–59
Statute of Westminster, 53, 54, 153, 161, 544
Stevens, Sinclair, 283
Stevenson, Garth, 158–59, 203, 205–6, 377
Stevenson, Michael, 446, 448
Stewart, Gordon, 70, 402
Stewart, Ronald, 479
Strom, Harry, 103
Supreme Court of Canada
Anti-Inflation case, 160
and appeals, 185
appointment of judges, 153, 184, 187
Charter and Constitution cases, 154, 186–94
civil liberties cases, 185
effect of Constitution Act, 1982, upon, 186–87
establishment of, 184
federal/provincial jurisdictional disputes, 154
final arbiter of constitutional review, 154, 160,
162, 185
General Motors vs. City National Leasing, 160
interpretation of federal powers, 160
Johannesson case, 160
judges in year 2000, 184
legal and equality rights cases, 188–92
patriation of Constitution, 17, 165, 186
Patriation Reference case, 186
power of, 186, 187
role of, 184
ruling on Bill 101, 232
ruling on law restricting therapeutic abortions, 192
ruling on Québec right to unilateral declaration of
independence, 246–48
ruling on Tobacco Products Control Act, 480
ruling on "rape shield" issue, 189
Supreme Court Act, 160
Therens case (breathalyzer issue), 188
vs. U.S. Supreme Court, 154
Sydenham, Lord, 52

Index

T

Taras, David, 122
Tariff policy, 22
Tarte, Israel, 389
Taxation, 154, 159, 208–12. See also Goods and Services
    Tax; Department of Finance
    corporation taxes, 159, 211
    direct, 154, 209
    federal/provincial agreements on, 211–12
        abatement system, 211
        tax-rental program, 211
        tax-sharing, 211–12
    indirect taxation, 209
    in federal state, 154
    legislation, 300–1
    personal income tax, 211, 281
    policy, 281
        international tax policy, 281
    provincial sales tax, 154–55
    tax expenditures, 513–14
    ways-and-means bills, 297
Tax Court of Canada, 185
Teleglobe Canada, 516
Telesat Canada, 57
Tepperman, Lorne, 70
Thibaudeau, Suzanne, 190
Thompson, Andrew, 329
Thompson, Sir John, 265, 266, 404
Thompson Newspapers Ltd., 128, 439
Thomson, Ken, 139
Throne Speech, 272, 296, 307, 319
    Address in Reply, 307
Thurow, Lester, 524
Tools for Peace, 466
Trade policy. See Canada–trade policy; Canada-U.S. Free
    Trade Agreement; NAFTA
Treasury Board, 272–73, 279–80
    Comptroller General, 280
    Departmental Business Plans, 280
    management of civil service personnel, 280
    responsibilities of, 279–80
    Secretary to, 280
    staff of, 279–80
    Secretariat, 280
Treaty of Ghent, 34
Treaty of London, 34
Treaty of Paris, 33, 34, 42
Treaty of Utrecht, 33
Treaty of Versailles, 35
Trudeau, Pierre, 249, 266, 267, 366, 389, 404, 408, 447
    bilingualism, 92, 390

    by-elections, 433
    Cabinet and committees, 271, 287, 329
    conflict-of-interest guidelines, 282
    and francophone countries, 544
    National Energy Program, 252
    1980 Québec referendum, 234
    1982 constitutional reform, 172
    1992 constitutional referendum, 183, 420
    and patriation of Constitution, 54, 164–65, 167,
        186, 234, 419
    and patronage, 285, 326
    personal charisma of, 437
    PMO, 276
    policies of, 390
    policy-making, 286
    politics of, 227
    resignation of, 390
    Senate appointments, 326
    and the Third Option, 552
    War Measures Act, 151, 170
Trudel, Marcel, 116–17
Truman, David, 468
Tupper, Allan, 516
Tupper, Sir Charles, 37, 38, 265, 266, 404
Turner, John, 265, 266, 390, 404, 407, 408
    efforts to use Senate to block free trade
        legislation, 328, 548
    leadership ability, 447
    policy-making, 286
    and Meech Lake accord, 173
    and patronage, 285

U

Ukrainian National Association, 473
United Automobile Workers of America, 472
United Farmers of Alberta, 118
United Nations, 22, 31, 134
    admittance to, 16
    Human Development Index, 4, 100
    Human Development Report, 4, 134, 135
    recognized states, 15
Upper Canada, 36, 52. See also Ontario

V

Valliëre, Jocelyn, 191
Vander Zalm, Bill, 138
Vaughan, Frederick, 192
Verba, Sidney, 65, 66
Victoria Charter, 162, 163

Visible minorities, 89–92, 353. See also Ethnic groups;
    Ethnicity; Native peoples; Multiculturalism

W

Wallin, Pamela, 131
Wappel, Tom, 406
War of 1812, 34, 47
Waters, Stan, 330, 331
Watts, Ronald, 201
Wearing, Joseph, 399
Weber, 16, 335–36, 337
Webster-Ashburton Treaty, 34
Weiner, Myron, 373
Welfare state, 21–22, 58–59
Wells, Clyde, 249
White Paper
        on PQ foreign policy, 539
        on tax reform, 314
        on Senate reform, 330
Whitlam, Gough, 259
Wiktor, Christian, 546
William H. Neville and Associates, 475
Williams, Blair, 271, 276
Wilson, Bertha, 137–38
Wilson, Cairine, 138, 325
Wilson, Howard, 283
Wilson, Michael, 179, 269
Winnipeg General Strike (1919), 55
Woodsworth, J.S., 391

Women
    and Charter, 136, 166, 174
    education, 114, 134–35
    Employment Equity Act, 137
    equality-rights and Charter cases, 189–91
    evolving roles of, 135–38
    feminism and feminist issues, 135–37, 189–91
    gender discrimination, 135–36
    gender theory, 135–36
    in House of Commons, 460
    important dates in women's history, 138
    involvement in politics, 79, 135, 137, 138, 257,
        399–400, 459–60
    and poverty, 135
    right to vote, 136
    in Senate, 325
    stereotypes, 136
    unequal status of, 109, 134–36, 140
    women's movement, 135–37, 491–91
    in the workplace, 135, 136–37
World Bank, 541
World Health Organization, 543
World Trade Organization, 541

Y

Yeats, W.B., 23
Young, Doug, 319
Young, Walter, 120
Yukon, 102
YWCA, 477